The Complete Learning Disabilities Directory

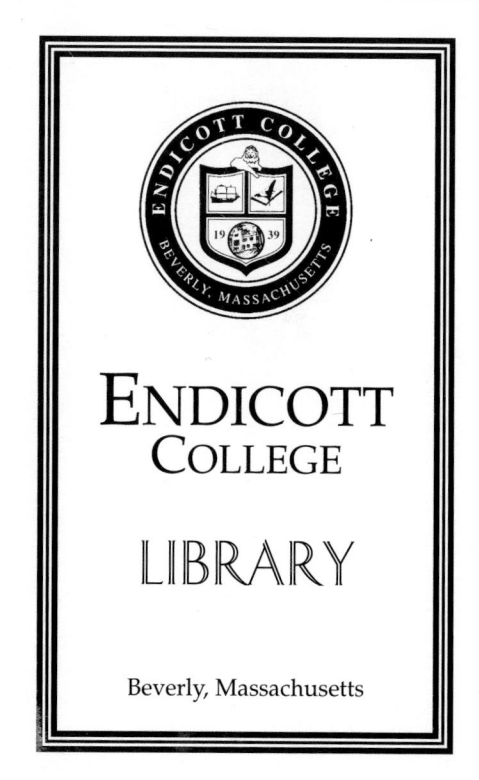

2004/05
Eleventh Edition

The Complete
Learning
Disabilities
Directory

Associations • Products • Resources • Magazines
Books • Services • Conferences • Web Sites

A SEDGWICK PRESS Book

Grey House
Publishing

PUBLISHER: Leslie Mackenzie
EDITORIAL DIRECTOR: Laura Mars-Proietti

PRODUCTION MANAGER: Karen Stevens
ASST. PRODUCTION MANAGER: Cecilia Acerbo
PRODUCTION ASSISTANTS: Stephanie Capozzi, Pamela Degnan, Elizabeth Corteville,
                          Debra Giordano, Alison Import, Sharon Moskiewicz
MARKETING DIRECTOR: Jessica Moody

A Sedgwick Press Book
Grey House Publishing, Inc.
185 Millerton Road
Millerton, NY 12546
518.789.8700
FAX 518.789.0545
www.greyhouse.com
e-mail: books @greyhouse.com

First edition published 1993
Eleventh edition published 2004
Printed in the USA
The complete learning disabilities directory. -- 1994-

    v. ; 27.5 cm.
    Annual
    Continues: Complete directory for people with learning disabilities
    Includes index.

1. Learning disabled--Education--United States--Directories. 2. Learning disabilities--United States--Bibliography. 3. Education, Special--United States--Bibliography. 4. Education, Special--United States--Directory. 5. Learning Disorders--rehabilitation--United States--Bibliography. 6. Learning Disorders--rehabilitation--United States--Directory. 7. Rehabilitation Centers--United States--Bibliography. 8. Rehabilitation Centers--United States—Directory.

LC4704.6 .C66
371.9025
ISBN 1-59237-049-7   softcover

Table of Contents

Preface

The National Center for Learning Disabilities is pleased to recognize this latest edition of *The Complete Learning Disabilities Directory*. With opportunities to access information both via print and online, it continues to be a valuable resource to parents, professionals and individuals with LD.

So much in the field of learning disabilities has changed since the first edition of this guide was published over a decade ago. Public awareness of the needs of students with LD has increased dramatically, and efforts to provide special education students with access to the general education curriculum has had a dramatic impact upon schools and their models of instruction and support. Our understanding of the science underlying different sub-types of learning disabilities has grown, and with new knowledge about effective instructional practices, opportunities for students with learning disabilities have never been better.

And that's where *The Complete Learning Disabilities Directory* can make a difference. By listing organizations and material resources in over 100 categories, it offers thousands of easy-to-access entries for individuals who are searching for information about LD that will help them make informed decisions about school, work, and leisure activities. It serves as a catalog of organizations, products, and Web sites that covers the landscape in terms of variety and need, and provides multiple points of entry to help find the best set of resources for individuals with LD of all ages.

Some keys to success for individuals with learning disabilities? A solid understanding of one's learning disability, a readiness to self-advocate for specific types of help and appropriate accommodations, a willingness to be creative and flexible in searching for and negotiating access to services and supports, an organized and thoughtful system for anticipating problems and seeking solutions (including building and cultivating a community of support), and the optimism and courage to persist and overcome the inevitable challenges that arise for individuals with LD throughout their lives. This Directory can be helpful in addressing all of these needs.

For more than 25 years, NCLD too has been addressing these challenges by promoting public awareness and understanding of learning disabilities, conducting educational programs, and offering services that advance research-based knowledge, and providing national leadership in shaping public policy. We are pleased to be listed in this Directory and encourage readers to also visit our Web site at www.LD.org for access to our LDInfoZone, featured newsletters, policy updates, and lots more, including a free, online early literacy screening tool (www.GetReadytoRead.org).

Thank you Grey House Publishing for once again, providing the public with this guide.

Dr. Sheldon H. Horowitz
Director of Professional Services
National Center for Learning Disabilities

Introduction

Welcome to the eleventh edition of *The Complete Learning Disabilities Directory* (*LDD*). Published since 1992, *LDD* continues to be a comprehensive and sought after resource for professionals, families and individuals in the learning disabilities community. This edition in particular is further distinguished by recognition by the **National Center for Learning Disabilities** (see Preface), and a major overhaul effort that included expanded sections and a brand new Glossary of Terms.

Although listings in all chapters were researched, updated and enhanced, we intently focused on several that our users say are most important to them. These include Classroom Resources, Camps & Summer Programs, and Publishers. The Adult Literacy chapter was changed to Literacy & Learning Skills, with listings for all ages. State resources are more comprehensive, especially those relating to Learning Centers and Vocational & Transitional Skills.

The Table of Contents is your guide to this database in print form. *The Complete Learning Disabilities Directory* includes more than 6,300 listings, organized into 21 major chapters and more than 100 sub chapters to quickly pinpoint the exact type of reference you are looking for. Access to the listings in *LDD* is made even easier by its three indexes: Entry Name Index; Geographic Index; and Subject Index.

LDD includes a large variety of resources, including Associations, National and State Programs, Publications, Audio, Video, Web Sites, Products, Conferences, Schools, Learning and Testing Centers, Summer Programs. Listings provide valuable contact information, including fax numbers, web sites, and key executives. Users will find brief descriptions and other pieces of valuable data, such as founding year, designed-for age, and size of LD population.

The Complete Learning Disabilities Directory provides comprehensive and far-reaching coverage not only for individuals with LD, but for parents, teachers, professionals and friends. Users will find answers to legal and advocacy questions, as well as especially designed computer software.

New to *LDD* this year is a Glossary of Terms that includes hundreds of useful terms and abbreviations, from AAD (adaptive assistive devises) to YTP (youth transition program), to eliminate guesswork and increase your knowledge as you search for listings specific to your needs.

The Complete Learning Disabilities Directory, 2004/05, makes it possible, in this age of information overload, to have one resource with important LD information readily available at every school and library across the country, not just at state or district level special education resource centers. Now, every special education teacher, student, or parent can have at their fingertips a wealth of information on the critical resources that are available to help individuals achieve in school and in their community.

This data is also available as **The Complete Learning Disabilities Directory – Online Database**. Using powerful search and retrieval software, this interactive Online Database quickly accesses the information in the print version, searchable by dozens of criteria.

As always, we welcome your comments and suggestions.

User Guide

Descriptive listings in *The Complete Learning Disabilities Directory (LDD)* are organized into 21 chapters and 84 subchapters. You will find the following types of listings throughout the book:

- National Agencies & Associations
- State Agencies & Associations
- Camps & Summer Programs
- Exchange Programs
- Classroom & Computer Resources
- Print & Electronic Media
- Schools & Learning Centers
- Testing & Training Resources
- Conferences & Workshops

Below is a sample listing illustrating the kind of information that is or might be included in an entry. Each numbered item of information is described in the paragraphs on the following page.

---

1 ▶ 1234

2 ▶ **Association for Children and Youth with Disabilities**

3 ▶ **1704 L Street NW**

Washington, DC 20036

4 ▶ **075-785-0000**

5 ▶ **FAX: 075-785-0001**

6 ▶ **800-075-0002**

7 ▶ **TDY: 075-785-0002**

8 ▶ **info@AGC.com**

9 ▶ **www.AGC.com**

10 ▶ Peter Rancho, Director
Nancy Williams, Information Specialist
Tanya Fitzgerald, Marketing Director
William Alexander, Editor

11 ▶ Advocacy organization that ensures children and youth with learning disabilities receive the best possible education. Services include speaking with an informed specialist, free publications, database searches, and referrals to other organizations.

12 ▶ *$6.99*

13 ▶ *204 pages*

14 ▶ *Paperback*

15 ▶ *1996*

User Key

1 → **Record Number**: Entries are listed alphabetically within each category and numbered sequentially. The entry numbers, rather than page numbers, are used in the indexes to refer to listings.

2 → **Organization Name**: Formal name of organization. Where organization names are completely capitalized, the listing will appear at the beginning of the alphabetized section. In the case of publications, the title of the publication will appear first, followed by the publisher.

3 → **Address**: Location or permanent address of the organization.

4 → **Phone Number**: The listed phone number is usually for the main office of the organization, but may also be for sales, marketing, or public relations as provided by the organization.

5 → **Fax Number**: This is listed when provided by the organization.

6 → **Toll-Free Number**: This is listed when provided by the organization.

7 → **TDY**: This is listed when provided by the organization. It refers to Telephone Device for the Deaf.

8 → **E-Mail**: This is listed when provided by the organization and is generally the main office e-mail.

9 → **Web Site**: This is listed when provided by the organization and is also referred to as an URL address. These web sites are accessed through the Internet by typing http:// before the URL address.

10 → **Key Personnel**: Name and title of key executives within the organization.

11 → **Organization Description**: This paragraph contains a brief description of the organization and their services.

The following apply if the listing is a publication:

12 → **Price:** The cost of each issue or subscription, often with frequency information. If the listing is a school or program, you will see information on age group served and enrollment size.

13 → **Number of Pages**: Total number of pages for publication.

14 → **Paperback:** The available format of the publication: paperback; hardcover; spiral bound.

15 → **Year:** Date of publication.

Legal

1   ADA Clearinghouse and Resource Center

National Center for State Courts
300 Newport Avenue
Williamsburg, VA   23185

800-616-6165
FAX 757-564-2002
http://www.ncsc.online.org

Disseminates information on ADA compliance to state and local court systems. Will develop a diagnostic checklist and strategies for compliance specifically relevant to the state and local courts.

2   ADA Information Line

US Department of Justice
PO Box 66738
Washington, DC   20035   202-514-0301
800-514-0301

Answers questions about Title II (public services) and Title III (public accommodations) of the Americans with Disabilities Act (ADA). Provides materials and technical assistance on the provisions of the ADA.

3   ADA Technical Assistance Programs

US Department of Justice
950 Pennsylvania Avenue NW
Washington, DC   20530   800-949-4232
http://www.usdoj.gov/crt/ada/taprog.htm

Federally funded regional resource centers that provide information and referral, technical assistance, public awareness, and training on all aspects of the Americans with Disabilities Act (ADA).

4   American Bar Association Center on Children and the Law: Information Line

740 15th Street NW
Washington, DC   20005   202-662-1000
800-285-2221
FAX 202-662-1032
http://www.abanet.org
e-mail: service@abanet.org

Provides information on legal issues and referrals to local Bar Associations.

5   Community Alliance for Special Education

1600 Howard Street
San Francisco, CA   94103   415-431-2285
FAX 415-431-2289
e-mail: none

Laura Gonzalez, Intake Worker

Provides special education advocacy, representation at individual education program (IEP) meetings and due process proceedings, free technical assistance consultations and training throughout the San Francisco Bay area.

6   Disability Rights Education & Defense Fund (DREDF)

2212 6th Street
Berkeley, CA   94710   510-644-2555
800-466-4232
FAX 510-841-8645
TDY:800-466-4232
http://www.dredf.org
e-mail: dredf@dredf.org

Susan Henderson, Administration Director
Mary Lou Breslin, Co-Founder

A nonprofit organization dedicated to advancing the civil rights of individuals with disabilities through legislation, litigation, informal and formal advocacy, and education and training of lawyers, advocates and clients with respect to disability issues. DREDF operates a Department of Justice funded national ADA information hotline for Titles II and III of the ADA. DREDF also provides training, advocacy, technical assistance and referrals for parents of disabled children.

7   ED Law Center

PO Box 81-7327
Hollywood, FL   33081   954-966-4489
FAX 954-966-8561
http://www.edlaw.net

Provides information on special education law and offers listing of attorneys.

8   Equal Employment Opportunity Commission

1801 L Street NW
Washington, DC   20507

800-669-4000
FAX 202-663-4639
TDY:800-669-6820
http://www.eeoc.gov

Federal agency that provides assistance with discrimination complaints about employment.

9   Home School Legal Defense Association

PO Box 3000
Purcellville, VA   20134   540-338-5600
FAX 540-338-2733
http://www.hslda.org

Betty Statnick, Special Needs Coordinator

A membership organization that offers legal assistance for homeschooling issues.

10   Legal Services for Children

1254 Market Street
San Francisco, CA   94102   415-863-3762
FAX 415-863-7708
http://www.lsc-sf.org

Shannan Beth Wilber, Executive Director

Founded in 1975. Nonprofit law firm for children and youth. Legal Services for Children provides free legal and social services to children and youth under 18 years old in the San Francisco Bay area.

11 National Association for Community Mediation

1527 New Hampshire Avenue NW
Washington, DC 20036   202-667-9700
                               FAX 202-667-8629
                               http://www.nafcm.org
                               e-mail: nafcm@nafcm.org
Joanne Hartman, Associate Director

Supports the maintenance and growth of community-based mediation programs and processes; acts as a resource for mediation information; locates a center to help individuals and groups resolve disputes.

12 National Association of Protection and Advocacy Systems (NAPAS)

900 2nd Street NE
Washington, DC 20002   202-408-9514
                               FAX 202-408-9520
                               TDY:202-408-9521
        http://www.protectionandadvocacy.com
                               e-mail: info@napas.org
Curtis Decker, Executive Director

NAPAS, the voluntary national membership association of protection and advocacy systems and client assistance programs, assumes leadership in promoting and strengthening the role and performance of its members in providing quality-based advocacy services. NAPAS has a vision of a society where people with disabilities exercise self-determination and choice and have equal opportunity and full participation.

13 National Center for Youth Law

405 14th Street
Oakland, CA 94612   510-835-8098
                               FAX 510-835-8099
                               http://www.youthlaw.org
                               e-mail: info@youthlaw.org
John F O'Toole, Director

Uses the law to protect children from harms caused by poverty, and to improve the lives of children living in poverty. Works to protect abused and neglected children through work with advocates, foster parents and others striving to reform state child welfare systems. Expands access to health care for children and youth through the state and federal levels to see that children get the health insurance and health care services to which they are entitled.

14 National Council of Juvenile and Family Court Judges (NCJFCJ)

1041 N Virginia Street, 3rd Floor
Reno, NV 89507   775-784-6012
                               FAX 775-784-6628
                               http://www.ncjfcj.org
                               e-mail: admin@ncjfcj.unr.edu
David Gamble, Director

Founded in 1937 by a group of judges dedicated to improving the effectiveness of the nation's juvenile courts, the National Council of Juvenile and Family Court Judges (NCJFCJ) strives to increase awareness and sensitivity to children's issues. The National Council focuses on providing meaningful assistance to the judges, court administrators and related professionals in whose care the concerns of children and their families have been entrusted.

15 Public Interest Law Center of Philadelphia

125 S 9th Street
Philadelphia, PA 19107   215-627-7100
                               FAX 215-627-3183
                               TDY:215-627-7300
                               e-mail: pubint@aol.com
Stephen Gold, Contact
Michael Churchhill, Executive Director

A public interest law firm with a disabilities project specializing in class action by individuals and organizations.

National Programs

16 ABLE DATA

8630 Fenton Street
Silver Spring, MD 20910
                               800-227-0216
                               FAX 301-608-8958
                               http://www.abledata.com
                               e-mail: abledata@macroint.com
Sponsored by the National Institute on Disability and Rehabilitation Research (NIDRR) of the US Department of Education; provides information on more than 27,000 assistive technology products, including detailed descriptions of each product, price and company information.

17 ADA Information Hotline

Great Lakes Disability & Business Technical Center
374 Congress Street
Boston, MA 02210   617-695-1225
                               800-949-4232
                               FAX 617-482-8099
                               http://www.adaptenv.org
                     e-mail: info@adaptiveEsvironments.org
Charlie Savatier, Contact

Provides technical assistance, information services and outreach regarding the Americans with Disabilities Act.

18 AVKO Dyslexia Research Foundation

3084 W Willard Road
Clio, MI 48420   810-686-9283
                               866-285-6612
                               FAX 810-686-1101
                               http://www.avko.org
                               e-mail: DonMcCabe@avko.org
Don McCabe, Research Director

AVKO is a nonprofit, tax exempt membership organization founded in 1974. The AVKO Dyslexia Research Foundation has been founded to help determine what dyslexia is, why traditional methods of teaching and writing fail and help most dyslexics learn to read and write.

19 Alliance for Technology Access
1304 Southpoint Boulevard
Petaluma, CA 94954   707-778-3011
                             800-455-7970
                         FAX 707-765-2080
                         TDY:707-778-3015
                    http://www.ataccess.org
                  e-mail: atainfo@ataccess.org
Mary Lester, Executive Director

A national organization dedicated to providing access to technology for people with disabilities through its coalition of 39 community-based resource centers in 28 states and in the Virgin Islands. Each center provides information, awareness, and training for professionals and provides guided problem solving and technical assistance for individuals with disabilities and family members.

20 American Academy of Pediatrics National Headquarters
141 NW Point Boulevard
Elk Grove Village, IL   60007   847-434-4000
                                   800-433-9016
                               FAX 847-434-8000
                            http://www.aap.org
Maureen DeRosa, Director Marketing/Publications

An organization of 55,000 pediatricians that publishes professional and patient education materials. Brochures include Learning Disabilities and Children, Guidelines for Parents, Understanding the ADHD Child and Learning Disabilities and Young Adults.

21 American Art Therapy Association
1202 Allanson Road
Mundelein, IL   60060   847-949-6064
                               888-290-0878
                           FAX 847-566-4580
                       http://www.arttherapy.org
                     e-mail: info@arttherapy.org
Ed Stygar, Executive Director

An organization of professionals dedicated to the belief that the creative process involved in the making of art is healing and life enhancing. Its mission is to serve its members and the general public by providing standards of professional competence, and developing and promoting knowledge in, and of, the field of art therapy.

22 American Association for Adult and Continuing Education
4380 Forbes Boulevard
Lanham, MD   20706   301-918-1913
                          FAX 301-918-1846
                        http://www.aaace.org
                     e-mail: aaace10@aol.com
Stephen J Steurer PhD, Managing Director
Cle Anderson, Executive Administrator

Mission is to provide leadership for the field of adult and continuing education: by expanding opportunities for adult growth and development; unifying adult educators; fostering the development and dissemination of theory, research, information and best practices; promoting identity and standards for the profession; and advocating relevant public policy and social change initiatives.

23 American Association for the Advancement of Science (AAAS)
1200 New York Avenue NW
Washington, DC   20005   202-326-6400
                            FAX 202-789-0455
                          http://www.aaas.org
                    e-mail: webmaster@aaas.org
Jill Perla, Senior Manager Operations
Melissa Risenthan, Program Associate

According to AAAS's constitution, its mission is to: further the work of scientists; facilitate cooperation among them; foster scientific freedom and responsibility; improve the effectiveness of science in the promotion of human welfare; advance education in science and increase the public's understanding and appreciation of the promise of scientific methods in human progress.

24 American Association of Collegiate Registrars and Admissions Officers
One Dupont Circle NW
Washington, DC   20036   202-293-9161
                            FAX 202-872-8857
                         http://www.aacrao.com
                     e-mail: info@aacrao.org
Dan Gardner, Information Specialist
Lisa Rosenberg, Senior Education Consultant

The mission is to provide professional development, guidelines and voluntary standards to be used by higher education officials regarding the best practices in records management, admissions, enrollment management, administrative information technology and student services.

25 American Association of Health Plans
601 Pennsylvania Avenue NW
Washington, DC   20004   202-778-3200
                            FAX 202-331-7487
                          http://www.aahp.org
                    e-mail: webmaster@aahp.org

National trade association representing more than 1,000 health maintenance organizations, preferred provider organizations, point-of-service plans, and other similar health plans that care for more than 140 million Americans.

26 American Camping Association
5000 State Road 67 N
Martinsville, IN   46151   765-342-8456
                              FAX 765-342-2065
                         http://www.acacamps.org
Peg Smith, Executive Director

Provides support, education and information on best practices and accreditation programs for camp programs throughout the US. Offers an online bookstore with outdoor education, youth development, adventure resources and a web site with an interactive, searchable database of camps.

27 American Coaching Association

PO Box 353
Lafayette Hill, PA   19444   610-825-4505
                                    FAX 610-825-4505
                                    http://www.americoach.com

Links people who want coaching with people who do coaching; coaches help individuals to set goals, accept limitations and acknowledge strengths, develop social skills and create strategies that enable them to be more effective in managing their day-to-day lives.

28 American College Testing Program

ACT Universal Testing
PO Box 168
Iowa City, IA   52243   319-337-1000
                               FAX 319-339-3021
                               http://www.act.org
Sandy Schlote, Testing Coordinator
Ed Colby, Public Relations

Helps individuals and organizations make informed decisions about education and work. We provide information for life's transitions.

29 American Council of the Blind (ACB)

1155 15th Street NW
Washington, DC   20005   202-467-5081
                                800-424-8666
                                FAX 202-467-5085
                                http://www.acb.org
                                e-mail: info@acb.org
Melanie Bronson, Acting Executive Director

A national membership organization established to promote the independence, dignity and well-being of blind and visually-impaired people. Members are blind, visually-impaired or fully sighted people from all walks of life. People who are blind and visually-impaired comprise the vast majority of members and are responsible for governing, administering and setting organizational policy. Formed in 1961, ACB is one of the largest US organizations of blind people.

30 American Counseling Association

5999 Stevenson Avenue
Alexandria, VA   22304   703-823-9800
                                800-347-6647
                                FAX 800-473-2329
                                TDY:703-823-6862
                                http://www.counseling.org
                                e-mail: aca@counseling.org
David Kaplan, President

The mission is to enhance the quality of life in society by promoting the development of professional counselors, advancing the counseling profession, and using the profession and practice of counseling to promote respect for human dignity and diversity.

31 American Dance Therapy Association (ADTA)

2000 Century Plaza, Suite 108
Columbia, MD   21044   410-997-4040
                              FAX 410-997-4048
                              http://www.adta.org
                              e-mail: info@adta.org

Tina Erfer, Eastern Region
Stacey M Hurst, Central Regioin
Nancy Goldov, Western Region

ADTA stimulates communication among dance/movement therapists and members of allied professions through publication of the ADTA Newsletter, the American Journal of Dance Therapy, monographs, bibliographies and conference proceedings.

32 American Occupational Therapy Association

4720 Montgomery Lane
Bethesda, MD   20824   301-652-2682
                              800-377-8555
                              FAX 301-652-7711
                              TDY:800-377-8555
                              http://www.aota.org
                              e-mail: praota@aota.org
Jodi Greenblatt, Public Relations Department

Advances the quality, availability, use, and support of occupational therapy through standard setting, advocacy, education, and research on behalf of its members and the public.

33 American Printing House for the Blind

1839 Frankfort Avenue
Louisville, KY   40206   502-895-2405
                                800-223-1839
                                FAX 502-899-2274
                                http://www.aph.org
                                e-mail: cs@aph.org
Tuck Tinsley III, President
Fred Gissoni, Customer Support
Tony Grantz, Business Development Manager

To promote the independence of blind and visually-impaired persons by providing special media, tools, and materials needed for education and life.

34 American Psychological Association

750 1st Street NE
Washington, DC   20002   202-336-5500
                                800-374-2721
                                FAX 202-336-5500
                                http://www.apa.org
Diane F Halpern, PhD, President of the Board

Works to advance psychology as a science, a profession, and a means of promoting human welfare.

35 American Public Human Services Association (APHSA)

810 1st Street NE
Washington, DC   20002   202-682-0100
                                FAX 202-289-6555
                                http://www.aphsa.org
                                e-mail: jfriedman@aphsa.org
Jerry Friedman, Executive Director
Elaine Ryan, Director Government Affairs

The association's mission is to develop, promote, and implement public human service policies that improve the health and well-being of families, children, and adults. APHSA is also an umbrella for several component groups.

36 American Red Cross
2025 E Street NW
Washington, DC   20006   202-639-3520
                                          800-797-8022
                                          FAX 202-942-2024
                                          http://www.redcross.org
                                          e-mail: info@usa.redcross.org
Marsha J Evans, President/CEO

A humanitarian organization led by volunteers, guided by its Congressional Charter and the fundamental principles of the International Red Cross Movement, will provide relief to victims of disasters and help people prevent, prepare for, and respond to emergencies.

37 American Rehabilitation Counseling Association (ARCA)
5999 Stevenson Avenue
Alexandria, VA   22304   703-823-9800
                                          800-347-6647
                                          FAX 703-823-0252
                                          http://www.nchhrtm.okstate.edu/arca/
Susan Bruyere, President

In its pursuit of its mission, ARCA exercises leadership in developing the profession and science of rehabilitation counseling and advocates for the maintenance of standards in rehabilitation counseling, practice and education.

38 American Speech-Language-Hearing Association
10801 Rockville Pike
Rockville, MD   20852   301-897-5700
                                          800-638-8255
                                          FAX 301-571-0457
                                          http://www.asha.org.asha
                                          e-mail: actioncenter@asha.org
Eileen Pietrarton, Executive Director
Lawrence H Higdon, President of the Board

A certifying body of 98,000 professionals providing speech, language and hearing services to the public. It is an accrediting agency for college and university graduate school programs in speech-language pathology and audiology.

39 Assistive Technology Industry Association
401 N Michigan Avenue
Chicago, IL   60611   312-321-5172
                                          877-687-2842
                                          FAX 312-673-6659
                                          http://www.atia.org
                                          e-mail: nfo@atia.org
Sharon Spencer, Director
M David Dikter, Executive Director

A nonprofit membership organization of organizations manufacturing or selling technology-based devices for people with disabilities, or providing services associated with or required by people with disabilities.

40 Association of Educational Therapists
1804 W Burbank Boulevard
Burbank, CA   91506   818-843-1181
                                          800-286-4267
                                          FAX 818-843-7423
                                          http://aetcaetonline.org
                                          e-mail: aetla@aol.com

A national professional organization dedicated to establishing ethical professional standards, defining the roles and responsibilities of the educational therapist, providing opportunities for professional growth, and to studying techniques and technologies, philosophies and research related to the practice of educational therapy.

41 Association on Higher Education and Disability
100 Morrissey Boulevard
Waltham, MA   02454   781-788-0003
                                          FAX 781-788-0033
                                          http://www.AHEAD.org
                                          e-mail: AHEAD@ahead.org
Stephan Smith, Executive Director

An international, muiticultural organization of professionals committed to full participation in higher education for persons with disabilities. The Association is a vital resource, promoting excellence through education, communication and training.

42 Association on Higher Education and Disability (AHEAD)
University of Massachusetts-Boston
100 Morrissey Boulevard
Boston, MA   02125   617-287-3880
                                          FAX 617-287-3882
                                          http://www.ahead.org
                                          e-mail: ahead@postbox.acs.ohio-state.edu

An organization of professionals committed to full participation in higher education for persons with disabilities; provides information resources and training on issues related to disabilities.

43 Attention Deficit Disorder Association
PO Box 543
Pottstown, PA   19464   484-945-2101
                                          FAX 610-970-7520
                                          http://www.add.org
                                          e-mail: mail@add.org
Michele Novotni PhD, President
Robert Tudisco, VP
David Giwerc, VP

A national nonprofit organization that provides information, resources and networking to adults with AD/HD.

44 Autism Research Institute
4182 Adams Avenue
San Diego, CA   92116   619-281-7165
                                          FAX 619-563-6840
                                          http://www.autism.com
Bernard Rimland, Director
Mallie Odle, Director's Assistant

A nonprofit organization established in 1967 devoted to conducting research and to disseminating the results of research on the causes of autism and on methods of preventing, diagnosing and treating autism and other severe behavioral disorders of childhood.

45   Autism Society of America

7910 Woodmont Avenue
Bethesda, MD   20814   301-657-0881
                                         800-328-8476
                                    FAX 301-657-0869
                        http://www.autism-society.org
                        e-mail: info@autism-society.org

The mission is to promote lifelong access and opportunities for persons within the autism spectrum and their families, and to help them to be fully included, participating members of their communities through advocacy, public awareness, education and research related to autism.

46   Autism Treatment Center of America

2080 S Undermountain Road
Sheffield, MA   01257   413-229-2100
                                         800-714-2779
                                    FAX 413-229-3202
                            http://www.son-rise.org
                        e-mail: correspondence@option.org
Barry Kaufman, Co-Founder
Bryn Hogan, Director

Provides innovative training programs for parents and professionals caring for children challenged by Autism, Autism Spectrum Disorders, Pervasive Developmental Disorder (PDD) and other developmental difficulties. The Son-Rise Program teaches a specific yet comprehensive system of treatment and education designed to help families and caregivers enable their children to dramatically improve in all areas of learning.

47   Birth Defect Research for Children (BDRC)

930 Woodcock Road
Orlando, FL   32803   407-895-0802
                                         800-313-2232
                                    FAX 407-895-0824
                            http://www.birthdefects.org
                        e-mail: abcd@birthdefects.org
Betty Mekdeci, Executive Director

Nonprofit organization that provides parents and expectant parents with information about birth defects and support services for their children. BDRC has a parent matching program that links families who have children with similar birth defects.

48   Boy Scouts of America

Scouting for the Handicapped Services
1325 W Walnut Hill Lane
Irving, TX   75015   972-580-2000
                                    FAX 972-580-2502
                            http://www.scouting.org
Joe Glascock, Chief Scout Executive

Provides an educational program for boys and young adults to build character, to train in the responsibilities of participating citizenship, and to develop personal fitness.

49   Brain Injury Association

8201 Greensboro Drive
McLean, VA   22102   703-761-0750
                                         800-444-6443
                                    FAX 703-236-6001
                            http://www.biausa.org
Ian Elliot, President

Mission is to create a better future through brain injury prevention, research, education and advocacy.

50   Career College Association (CCA)

10 G Street NE
Washington, DC   20002   202-336-6700
                                    FAX 202-336-6828
                            http://www.career.org
                        e-mail: cca@career.org
Nick Glakas, President

Represents more than 1,000 private for profit post secondary schools, institutes, colleges and universities.

51   Center for Applied Special Technology (CAST)

39 Cross Street
Peabody, MA   01960   978-531-8555
                                    FAX 978-531-0192
                            http://www.cast.org
                        e-mail: cast@cast.org

An educational, not-for-profit organization that uses technology to expand opportunities for all people, including those with disabilities; develops learning models, approaches and tools that are usable by a wide range of learners.

52   Clearinghouse on Disability Information

Office of Special Education and Rehabilitative Svc
US Department of Education
Washington, DC   20202   202-205-8241
                        http://www.ed.gov/offices/osers/index.html

53   Closing the Gap

Computer Technology in Special Education & Rehab.
520 Main Street
Henderson, MN   56044   507-248-3294
                                    FAX 507-248-3810
                            http://www.closingthegap.com
                        e-mail: info@closingthegap.com

Provides information on the use of computer-related technology by and for persons with disabilities.

54   Commission on Accreditation of Rehabilitation Facilities (CARF)

4891 E Grant Road
Tucson, AZ   85712   520-325-1044
                                         888-281-6531
                                    FAX 520-318-1129
                            http://www.carf.org
Brian Boon PhD, President/CEO

Promotes the quality, value and optimal outcomes of services through a consultative accreditation process that centers on enhancing the lives of the persons served.

55   Communication Aids: Manufacturers Association

205 W Randolph
Chicago, IL   60606
                                         800-441-2262
                                    FAX 312-229-5445
                            http://www.aacproducts.org
                        e-mail: cama@northshore.net
James Neils, President

A nonprofit organization of the world's leading manufacturers of augmentative and alternative communication software and hardware.

56 Computer Learning Foundation
47 Northgate Boulevard
Sacramento, CA   95834   916-595-4766
                               FAX 916-565-0220
                      http://www.computerlearning.org
                      e-mail: clf@computerlearning.org
Sally Bowman Alden, Executive Director

An international nonprofit educational foundation, dedicated to improving the quality of education and preparation of youth for the workplace through the use of technology. To accomplish its mission, the foundation provides numerous projects and materials to help parents and educators use technology effectively with children.

57 Council for Educational Diagnostic Services
Council for Exceptional Children
1110 N Glebe Road
Arlington, VA   22201   703-620-3660
                               800-224-6830
                               FAX 703-264-9494
                      http://www.cec.sped.org
                      e-mail: cathym@cec.sped.org

The mission of the Council for Educational Diagnostic Services is: to promote the most appropriate education of children and youth through appraisal, diagnosis, educational intervention, implementation, and continuous evaluation of a prescribed educational program.

58 Council for Exceptional Children (CEC)
1110 N Glebe Road
Arlington, VA   22201   703-620-3660
                               800-224-6830
                               FAX 703-264-9494
                      http://www.cec.sped.org
                      e-mail: cec@cec.sped.org
Drew Albritten, Executive Director

CEC is a non-profit association. Accomplishes its mission which is carried out in support of special education professionals and others working on behalf of individuals with exceptionalities, by advocating for appropriate governmental policies, by setting professional standards and by providing continuing professional development.

59 Council for Learning Disabilities
PO Box 4014
Leesburg, VA   20177   571-258-1010
                               FAX 571-258-1011
                      http://www.cldinternational.org
Diane Pedrotty Bryant, President

An international organization that promotes effective teaching and research. CLD is composed of professionals who represent diverse disciplines and who are committed to enhancing the education and life span development of individuals with learning disabilities.

60 Council on Rehabilitation Education
1835 Rohlwing Road
Rolling Meadows, IL   60008   847-394-1785
                                     FAX 847-394-2108
                      http://www.core-rehab.org
                      e-mail: dclink@wans.net
Donald C Linkowski, Executive Director

Seeks to provide effective delivery of rehabilitation services to individuals with disabilities by stimulating and fostering continuing review and improvement of master's degree level rehabilitation counselor education programs.

61 Disability International Foundation
PO Box 1781
Longview, WA   98632   360-577-0243
                               FAX 360-636-1680
                      http://www.teleport.com/-dif/
                      e-mail: dif@teleport.com
Dr Robert E Arnsdorf, MD, Director

A nonprofit, educational foundation providing global awareness, consultation, networking, publications, and training in fostering progress for the inclusion of people with disabilities children, youth and adults.

62 Distance Education and Training Council (DETC)
1601 18th Street NW
Washington, DC   20009   202-234-5100
                                 FAX 202-332-1386
                      http://www.detc.org
                      e-mail: detc@detc.org
Michael P Lambert, Executive Director

Nonprofit educational association located in Washington, DC. DETC serves as a clearinghouse of information about the distance study/correspondence field and sponsors a nationally recognized accrediting agency called the Accrediting Commission of the Distance Education and Training Council.

63 Division for Culturally and Linguistically Diverse Learners
Council for Exceptional Children
1110 N Glebe Road
Arlington, VA   22201   703-620-3660
                               888-232-7733
                               FAX 703-620-2521
                      http://www.cec.sped.org
Nancy D Safer, Executive Director
Bruce A Ramirez, Deputy Executive Director
Gwendolyn Webb-Johnson, Division President

Dedicated to advancing and improving educational opportunities for culturally and linguistically diverse learners with disabilites and/or who are gifted, their families and the professionals who serve them.

64 Division for Early Childhood
Council for Exceptional Children
1110 N Glebe Road
Arlington, VA   22201   703-620-3660
                               888-232-7733
                               FAX 703-264-9494
                      http://www.cec.sped.org
                      e-mail: cathym@cec.sped.org

Organization designed for individuals who work with, or on behalf of children with special needs, birth through eight, and their families. Members include early childhood intervention professionals as well as parents of children who have disabilities, are gifted, or are at risk of future developmental problems. Members receive two quarterly publications as well as discounts on other DEC publications and the annual conference.

65 **Division for Learning Disabilities**

Council for Exceptional Children
1110 N Glebe Road
Arlington, VA   22201   703-620-3660
                                         800-224-6830
                                  FAX 703-264-9494
                             http://www.cec.sped.org
                          e-mail: cathym@cec.sped.org

Promotes improved services, research and legislation
for individuals with learning disabilities. Members include teachers, teacher educators, administrators, policy makers, researchers, parents and related service
providers. Members receive a quarterly journal and
three newsletters per year.

66 **Division for Research**

Council for Exceptional Children
1110 N Glebe Road
Arlington, VA   22201   703-620-3660
                                         888-232-7733
                                  FAX 703-264-9494
                             http://www.cec.sped.org
                          e-mail: cathym@cec.sped.org

Devoted to the advancement of research related to the
education of individuals with disabilities and/or who
are gifted. Members include university, public and
private school teachers, researchers, administrators,
psychologists, speech/language clinicians, parents of
children with special learning needs and other related
professionals and service personnel. Members receive
quarterly journal and newsletter three times a year.

67 **Division on Career Development**

Council for Exceptional Children
1110 N Glebe Road
Arlington, VA   22201   703-620-3660
                                         888-232-7733
                                  FAX 703-264-9494
                             http://www.cec.sped.org
                          e-mail: cathym@cec.sped.org

Focuses on the career development of individuals
with disabilities and/or who are gifted and their transition from school to adult life. Members include professionals and others interested in career development
and transition for individuals with any exception at
any age. Members receive a journal twice yearly and
newsletter three times per year.

68 **Division on Visual Impairments**

Council for Exceptional Children
1110 N Glebe Road
Arlington, VA   22201   703-620-3660
                                         888-232-7733
                                  FAX 703-264-9494
                             http://www.cec.sped.org
                          e-mail: cathym@cec.sped.org

Advances the education of children and youth who
have visual impairments that impede their educational
progress. Members include teachers, teacher educators, other practitioners and administrators. Members
receive quarterly newsletter.

69 **Dyslexia Research Institute**

5746 Centerville Road
Tallahassee, FL   32309   850-893-2216
                                  FAX 850-893-2440
                             http://dyslexia-add.org
                          e-mail: dri@dyslexia-add.org
Patrica K Hardman PhD, Director
Robyn A Rennick MS, Assistant Director

Addresses academic, social and self-concept issues
for dyslexic and ADD children and adults. College
prep courses, study skills, advocacy, diagnostic testing, seminars, teacher training, day school, tutoring
and an adult literacy and life skills programs are available using an accredited MSLE approach.

70 **Easter Seals**

230 W Monroe Street
Chicago, IL   60606   312-726-6200
                                         800-221-6827
                                  FAX 312-726-1494
                                  TDY:312-726-4258
                             http://www.easter-seals.org
                          e-mail: info@easter-seals.org
Samuel H Howard, Chairman
James E Williams Jr, President/CEO

Easter Seals' mission is to create solutions that
change lives for children and adults with disabilities,
their families, and their communities. We work to
identify the needs of people with disabilities and to
provide appropriate developmental and rehabilitation
services. Our Easter Seals operate 450 sites that provide services to children and adults with disabilities
and their families. All sites provide different services.
Call to inquire about Easter Seals in your community.

71 **Educational Advisory Group**

2222 E Lake Avenue E
Seattle, WA   98102   206-323-1838
                                  FAX 206-267-1325
                             http://www.eduadvisory.com
Yvonne Jones, Associate
Paul Auchterlonie, Associate

Specializes in matching children with the learning environments that are best for them and works with families to help them identify concerns and establish
priorities about their child's education.

72 **Educational Equity Concepts**

100 5th Avenue
New York, NY   10011   212-243-1110
                                  FAX 212-627-0407
                             http://www.edequity.org
                          e-mail: information@edequity.org
Ellen Rubin, Coordinator Disability Programs

A national nonprofit organization that promotes bias
free learning through innovative programs and materials. Founded in 1982, our mission is to decrease discrimination based on gender, race/ethnicity,
disability, and level of family income.

73 Educational Testing Service: SAT Services for Students with Disabilities

College Board SAT Program
PO Box 6200
Princeton, NJ   08541   609-771-7137
                                       FAX 609-771-7944
                             http://www.collegeboard.org
                         e-mail: ssd@info.collegeboard.org

Offers testing accommodations to attempt to minimize the effect of disabilities on test performance. The SAT Program tests eligible students with documented visual, physical, hearing, or learning disabilities who require testing accommodations for SAT.

74 Families and Advocates Partnership for Education FAPE

PACER Center
8161 Normandale Blvd.
Minneapolis, MN   55437
                                        888-248-0822
Paula Goldberg, Director

The FAPE project is a strong partnership that aims to improve the educational outcomes for children with disabilities. FAPE links families, advocates, and self-advocates to communicate the new focus of the Individuals with Disabilities Education Act (IDEA). The project represents the needs of six million children with disabilities.

75 Federation for Children with Special Needs

1135 Tremont Street
Boston, MA   02120   617-236-7210
                                       800-331-0688
                                     FAX 617-572-2094
                                     TDY:617-236-7210
                                    http://www.fcsn.org
                             e-mail: fcsninfo@fcsn.org
Richard Robison, Executive Director

The mission of the Federation is to provide information, support and assistance to parents of children with disabilities, their professional partners and their communities. Major services are information and referral and parent and professional training.

76 GT/LD Network

PO Box 30239
Bethesda, MD   20824   301-986-1422
                               http://www.gtldnetwork.org
                             e-mail: gldnews@hotmail.com
Greg Rosenthal

Targeted toward parents, students, families and professionals with services such as a telephone hotline, monthly meeting on a specific topic or recent research, a kid panel that speaks to groups, bibliography, library and advocacy.

77 General Educational Development Testing Service

American Council on Education
1 Dupont Circle NW
Washington, DC   20036   202-939-9490
                                       800-626-9433
                                     FAX 202-833-4760
                                    http://www.acenet.edu
                             e-mail: ged@ace.nche.edu
Joan Auchtner, Executive Director

78 HEATH Resource Center

George Washington University
2121 K St. NW
Washington, DC   20036   202-973-0903
                                       800-544-3284
                                     FAX 202-973-0908
                                    http://www.heath.gwu.edu
                             e-mail: askheath@heath.gwu.edu
Lynda West, Principal Investigator
Joel Gomez, Co-Principal Investigator
Pamela Ekpone, Director

Higher Education and Adult Training for People with Handicaps (HEATH) is a national clearinghouse that provides free information on postsecondary education and related issues for individuals with learning disabilities

79 HEATH Resource Center: The George Washington University

2121 K Street NW
Washington, DC   20037   202-973-0904
                                       800-544-3284
                                     FAX 202-973-0908
                                    http://www.heath.gwu.edu
                             e-mail: askheath@heath.gwu.edu
Dr. Pamela Ekpone, Director

Support from the US Department of Education enables the center to serve as an information exchange about educational services, policies, procedures, adaptations, and opportunities at American campuses, vocational-technical schools, and other postsecondary training entities.

80 Independent Living Research Utilization Program

2323 S Shepherd Drive
Houston, TX   77019   713-520-0232
                                     FAX 713-520-5785
                                    http://www.ilru.org
                             e-mail: ilru@ilru.org
Linda CoVan, Director

National center for information, training, research, and technical assistance in independent living. Its goal is to expand the body of knowledge in independent living and to improve utilization of results of research programs and demonstration projects in this field. It is a program of The Institute for Rehabilitation and Research, a nationally recognized medical rehabilitation facility for persons with disabilities.

81 Institute for Educational Leadership

1001 Connecticut Avenue NW
Washington, DC   20036   202-822-8405
                                     FAX 202-872-4050
                                    http://www.iel.org
                             e-mail: iel@iel.org
Elizabeth L Hale, President
Louise A Clarke, Chief Administrator
Bert Berkley, Chairman of the Board

Mission is to improve education and the lives of children and their families through positive and visionary change. Everyday, we face that challenge by bringing together diverse constituencies and empowering leaders with knowledge and applicable ideas.

82   Institutes for the Achievement of Human Potential

8801 Stenton Avenue
Wyndmoore, PA   19038   215-233-2050
                                            800-736-4663
                                         FAX 215-233-9312
                                         http://www.iahp.org/
                                    e-mail: institutes@iahp.org
Glenn Doman, Founder

Nonprofit educational organization that serves children by introducing parents to the field of child brain development. Parents learn how to enhance significantly the development of their children physically, intellectually and socially in a joyous and sensible way. The goal of the institute is to raise significantly the intellectual, physical, and social abilities of all children. Accepts brain injured children, however severely hurt, and helps them advance.

83   International Dyslexia Association: National Headquarters

8600 Lasalle Road, Chester Building
Baltimore, MD   21286   410-296-0232
                                            800-223-3123
                                         FAX 410-321-5069
                                        http://www.interdys.org
                                  e-mail: MBIDA4@hotmail.com
Cathy Rosemond, President

Nonprofit, scientific and educational organization dedicated to the study and treatment of dyslexia. Focus is educating parents, teachers and professionals in the field of dyslexia in effective teaching methodologies. Programs and services include: information and referral; public awareness; medical and educational research; governmental affairs; conferences and publications.

84   International Reading Association

800 Barksdale Road
Newark, DE   19714   302-731-1600
                                            800-628-8508
                                         FAX 302-731-1057
                                        http://www.reading.org
                                   e-mail: pubinfo@reading.org
Janet Butler, Public Information Associate

A professional association with more then 80,000 members in nearly 100 counties dedicated to promoting higher achievement levels in literacy, reading and communication worldwide.

85   Landmark Outreach Program

Landmark School
429 Hale Street
Prides Crossing, MA   01965   978-236-3010
                                         FAX 978-927-7268
                                     http://www.landmarkschool.org
                              e-mail: outreach@landmarkschool.org
Dan Ahearn, Program Director
Kathryn Frye, Administrative Assistant

Provides consultation and training to public and private schools, professional organizations, parent groups, and businesses on topics related to individuals with learning disabilities. Services are individually designed to meet the client's specific needs and can range from a two-hour workshop to a year-long training project. Options include consulting services, training workshops, summer training program, seminars and parent workshops.

86   Learning Disabilities Association of America (LDA)

4156 Library Road
Pittsburgh, PA   15234   412-341-1515
                                            888-300-6710
                                         FAX 412-344-0224
                                      http://www.ldaamerica.org
                                  e-mail: info@ldaamerica.org
Jane Browning, Executive Director
Marianne Toombs, President
Suzanne Fornaro, VP

Formed on behalf of children with learning disabilities in 1964, LDA is the only national organization devoted to defining and finding solutions for the broad spectrum of learning disabilities. LDA has 50 state affiliates with more than 350 local chapters. Membership totals over 50,000, including parents, professionals from many sectors and concerned citizens. Makes available publications, rental films, a newsletter and journal. Holds an annual international conference.

Free fact sheet

87   Learning Resource Network

1130 Hostetler
Manhattan, KS   66502   785-539-5376
                                            800-678-5376
                                         FAX 785-539-7766
                                        http://www.lern.org
                                    e-mail: rebel@lern.org
William Draves, Director

This network for educators provides resources to adult education and adult basic education service providers.

88   MATRIX: A Parent Network and Resource Center

555 Northgate Drive
San Rafael, CA   94903   415-884-3535
                                            800-578-2592
                                         FAX 415-884-3555
                                         TDY:415-884-3554
                                     http://www.matrixparents.org
                                  e-mail: info@matrixparents.org
Nora Thompson, Executive Director

A place where parents can turn to when they discover that their child has a special need or disability and a place for parents to find emotional support and information from parents who have been there.

89 Menninger Clinic: Center for Learning Disabilities

2801 Gessner
Houston, TX   77280   713-275-5000
                                800-351-9058
                            FAX 713-275-5107
                        http://www.menninger.edu
                        e-mail: info@menninger.edu
Ian Aitken, President/CEO

The mission of Menninger is to be a national resource providing psychiatric care and treatment of the highest standard, searching for new knowledge and better understanding of mental illness and human behavior, teaching what we know and what we learn, and applying this knowledge in useful ways to promote individual growth and better mental health.

90 Moving Forward

1186 East Avenue
Napa, CA   94559   510-337-2460
                            FAX 510-934-9022
            http://www.iser.com/movingforward-CA.html
                        e-mail: aia1@aol.com

An association offering information, referrals, resources, counseling, newspapers and more for persons with disabilities.

91 Nat'l Association for the Education of African American Children with Learning Disabilities

PO Box 09521
Columbus, OH   43209   614-237-6021
                            FAX 614-238-0929

The NAEAACLD has the latest information on educating African American Children with learning disabilities and links to many other resources.

92 National Admission, Review, Dismissal: Individualized Education Plan Advocates

PO Box 16111
Sugar Land, TX   77496   281-265-1506
                            FAX 253-295-9954
                        http://www.narda.org
                e-mail: louisadvo@mylinuxisp.com
Louis H Geigerman, President

National ARD Advocates is dedicated to obtaining the appropriate educational services for children with special needs.

93 National Adult Education Professional Development Consortium

444 N Capitol Street NW
Washington, DC   20001   202-624-5250
                            FAX 202-624-1497
                        http://www.naepdc.org
                        e-mail: dc1@naepdc.org
Patricia Bennett MD, Chairman
Dr Lennox McLendon, Executive Director

The Consortium, incorporated in 1990 by state adult education directors, provides professional development, policy analysis, and dissemination of information important to state staff in adult education.

94 National Adult Literacy & Learning Disabilities Center

Academy for Educational Development
1825 Connecticut Avenue NW
Washington, DC   20009   202-884-8000
                                800-953-2553
                            FAX 202-884-8400
                        http://www.aed.org
                        e-mail: admindc@aed.org
Denise Glyn Borders, Senior VP/Director
Edward W Russell, Chairman

A nonprofit organization established by the National Institute for Literacy, which provides information regarding learning disabilities and trends impacting the provision of literacy services.

95 National Association for Adults with Special Learning Needs

PO Box 716
Bryn Mawr, PA   19010   610-525-8336
                                800-869-8336
                            FAX 610-446-6129
                        http://www.ldonline.org
                e-mail: 75250.1273@compuserv.com

A nonprofit organization designed to organize, establish, and promote an effective national and international coalition of professionals, advocates, and consumers of lifelong learning for the purpose of educating adults with special learning needs.

96 National Association for Gifted Children

1707 L Street NW
Washington, DC   20036   202-785-4268
                            FAX 202-785-4248
                        http://www.nagc.org
                        e-mail: nacg@nagc.org
F Richard Olenchak, President

An organization of parents, educators, other professionals and community leaders who unite to address the unique needs of children and youth with demonstrated gifts and talents as well as those children who may be able to develop their talent potential with appropriate educational experiences. We support and develop policies and practices that encourage and respond to the diverse expressions of gifts and talents in children and youth from all cultures.

97 National Association for the Education of Young Children (NAEYC)

1509 16th Street NW
Washington, DC   20036   202-232-8777
                                800-424-2460
                            FAX 202-328-1846
                        http://www.naeyc.org
                        e-mail: naeyc@naeyc.org
Jane Weichel, President

NAEYC exists for the purpose of leading and consolidating the efforts of individuals and groups working to achieve health development and constructive education for all young children. Primary attention is devoted to assuring the provision of high quality early childhood programs for young children.

98   National Association of Developmental Disabilities Councils (NADDC)

1234 Massachusetts Avenue NW
Washington, DC   20005   202-347-1234
                              FAX 202-347-4023
                              http://www.naddc.org
                              e-mail: info@naddc.org
Karen Flippo, Executive Director
Pat Seybold, President

A national organization for Developmental Disabilities Councils that advocate and work for change on behalf of people with developmental and other disabilities, and their families. NADDC promotes national policy to enhance the quality of life for all people with developmental disabilities.

99   National Association of Private Special Education Centers

1522 K Street NW
Washington, DC   20005   202-408-3338
                              FAX 202-408-3340
                              http://www.napsec.com
                              e-mail: napsec@aol.com
Sherry L Kolbe, Executive Director/CEO
Alison Figi, Communications Coordinator
Dr. Mike Rice, President

A nonprofit association whose mission is to ensure access for individuals to private special education as a vital component of the continuum of appropriate placement and services in American education. The association consists solely of private special education schools that serve both privately and publicly placed children with disabilities.

100   National Business and Disability Council

201 IU Willets Road
Albertson, NY   11507   516-465-1515
                              FAX 516-465-3730
                              http://www.businessdisability.com
Lynn Broder, Contact

A leading resource for employers seeking to integrate people with disabilities into the workplace and companies seeking to reach them in the consumer marketplace. As a non-profit we are providing educational, vocational, rehabilitation and research opportunities for persons with disabilities through the Henry Viscardi School, the Edwin W Martin, Jr. Career and Employment Institute, the Research and Training Institute and the Mary Jean and Frank P Smeal Learning Center.

101   National Camp Association

610 5th Avenue
New York, NY   10185   212-645-0653
                              800-966-2267
                              FAX 845-354-5501
                              http://www.summercamp.org
                              e-mail: info@summercamp.org
Jeffrey Solomon, Executive Director

Dedicated to helping parents find the right sleep-away camp for their children.

102   National Center for ESL Literacy Education (NCLE)

4646 40th Street NW
Washington, DC   20016   202-362-0700
                              FAX 202-363-7204
                              http://www.cal.org/ncle
                              e-mail: ncle@cal.org
Joy Kreeft Peyton, Director
Miriam Burt, Associate Director

A national organization focusing on literacy education for adults and out-of-school youth learning English as a second language. NCLE publishes many documents on its website.

103   National Center for Family Literacy

325 W Main Street
Louisville, KY   40202   502-584-1133
                              877-famlit-1
                              FAX 502-584-0172
                              http://www.famlit.org
                              e-mail: ncfl@famlit.org
Sharon Darling, President

Provides leadership for family literacy development nationwide; promote policies at the national and state level to support family literacy; designs, develops and demonstrates new family literacy practices that address the needs of families in a changing social, economic and political landscape; deliver high quality, dynamic, research-based training, staff development and technical assistance; conducts research to expand the knowledge base of family literacy.

104   National Center for Learning Disabilities (NCLD)

381 Park Avenue S
New York, NY   10016   212-545-7510
                              888-575-7373
                              FAX 212-545-9665
                              http://www.ld.org
                              e-mail: help@ncld.org
James Wendorf, Executive Director

The National Center for Learning Disabilities' (NCLD) mission is to increase opportunities for all individuals with learning disabilities to achieve their potential. NCLD accomplishes its mission by increasing public awareness and understanding of learning disabilities, conducting educational programs and services that promote research-based knowledge, and providing national leadership in shaping public policy. We provide solutions that help people with LD participate fully in society.

105   National Center of Higher Education for Learning Problems (HELP)

Myers Hall
520 18th Street
Huntington, WV   25755   304-696-6313
                              FAX 304-696-3231
                              e-mail: painter@marshall.edu
Barbara P Guyer, Director HELP Program
Debbie Painter MA, Coordinator Diagnostics

The HELP program offers a full battery of comprehensive psychoeducational tests to determine if an individual has learning and/or attention deficits. The team of professionals can identify specific problems for all ages, such as school age children, college students, medical students, and professionals.

106 National Clearinghouse for Professions in Special Education

Council for Exceptional Children
1110 N Glebe Road
Arlington, VA   22201

800-641-7824
FAX 703-264-1637
http://www.specialedcareers.org/
e-mail: ncpse@cec.sped.org

Lynn Boyer, Director
Rebecca Presgrares, Administrative Specialist

Committed to enhancing the nation's capacity to recruit, prepare, and retain well qualified diverse educators and related services professionals for children with disabilities.

107 National Council on Disability

1331 F Street NW
Washington, DC   20006

202-272-2004
FAX 202-272-2022
http://www.ncd.gov
e-mail: mquigley@ncd.gov

Lex Frieden, Chairman
Ethel D Briggs, Executive Director

An independent federal agency comprised of 15 members appointed by the President and confirmed by the Senate.

108 National Council on Independent Living Programs

1916 Wilson Boulevard
Arlington, VA   22201

703-525-3406
FAX 703-525-3409
http://www.ncil.org
e-mail: ncil@ncil.org

Anne-Marie Hughey, Executive Director

A membership organization that advances the independent living philosophy and advocates for the human rights of, and services for, people with disabilities to further their full integration and participation in society.

109 National Council on Rehabilitation Education

Emporia State University
1200 Commercial Street
Emporia, KS   66801

620-341-1200
FAX 620-341-5073
http://www.rehabeducators.org

Margaret Glen, President
Vilia M Tarvydes PhD CRC, Board President

An organization which has as its purpose promoting the improvement of rehabilitation services available to people with disabilities through quality education and rehabilitation research.

110 National Data Bank for Disabled Student Services

University of Maryland
Shoemaker Building
College Park, MD   20742

301-314-7682
FAX 301-405-0813
http://www.umd.edu/dss

Susan McMenamin, Coord Disability Support Service

Provides colleges the means for accessing statistics related to services, staff, budget and other components of disabled student services programs across the country.

111 National Dissemination Center for Children with Disabilities

PO Box 1492
Washington, DC   20013

202-884-8200
800-695-0285
FAX 202-884-8441
TDY:202-884-8200
http://www.nichcy.org
e-mail: nichcy@aed.org

Susan Ripley, Director Information Specialist

An information and referral clearinghouse that provides free information on disabilities and disability related issues. Services include speaking with an information specialist, receiving free publications, database searches and referrals to other organizations. Also provides a state resource sheet which identifies resources in each state including state agencies, disability organizations and parent groups.

112 National Early Childhood Technical Assistance Center

Univ of N Carolina at Chapel Hill
Chapel Hill, NC   27599

919-962-2001
FAX 919-966-7463
TDY:919-843-3269
http://www.nectas.unc.edu
e-mail: nectas@unc.edu

Pascal Trohanis, Director
Judi Shaver, Coordinator

Assists states and other designated governing jurisdictions as they develop multidisciplinary, coordinated and comprehensive services for young children with special needs and their families

113 National Education Association (NEA)

1201 16th Street NW
Washington, DC   20036

202-833-4000
FAX 202-822-7974
http://www.nea.org

Rug Weaver, President

NEA is a volunteer-based organization supported by a network of staff at the local, state and national level. At the local level, NEA affiliates are active in a wide variety of activities, everything from conducting professional workshops on discipline and other issues that affect faculty and school support staff to bargaining contracts for school district employees. At the state level, NEA affiliate activities are equally wide-ranging.

114 National Federation of the Blind

1800 Johnson Street
Baltimore, MD   21230

410-659-9314
FAX 410-685-5653
http://www.nfb.org
e-mail: nfb@nfb.org

Dr Betsy Zaborowski, Executive Director
Mrs Patricia Maurer, Directpr Community Relations

The purpose of the National Federation of the Blind is two-fold: to help blind persons achieve self-confidence and self-respect and to act as a vehicle for collective self expression for the blind. Provides public education about blindness, information and referral services, scholarships, literature and publications about blindness, aids and appliances and other adaptive equipment for the blind, advocacy services and protection of civil rights and job opportunities for the blind.

115   National Institute of Art and Disabilities

551 23rd Street
Richmond, CA   94804   510-620-0290
                                      FAX 510-620-0326
                                  http://www.niadart.org
                               e-mail: admin@niadart.org
Pat Coleman, Executive Director
Elias Katz, President

Mission is to provide an art program for people with developmental disabilities which promotes creative expression, independence, dignity and community integration.

116   National Jewish Council for Disabilities Summer Program

YACHAD East Coast Adventure
11 Broadway
New York, NY   10004   212-613-8369
                                      FAX 212-613-0796
                                   http://www.njcd.org
                                e-mail: yadbyad@ou.org
Nechama Braun, Administrator

117   National Lekotek Center

3204 W Armitage Avenue
Chicago, IL   60647   773-276-5164
                                          800-366-7529
                                      FAX 773-276-8644
                                  http://www.lekotek.org
                              e-mail: lekotek@lekotek.org
Helen Hilken McCarthy, Executive Director

The mission of the National Lekotek Center is driven by the philosophy that children learn best when play is a family-centered activity that includes all children, regardless of their abilities or disabilities, in family and community activities. We offer play-centered services to children with disabilities and supportive services to their families. We also offer computer play, parent support and national resources for families and professionals.

118   National Organization for Rare Disorders (NORD)

Nord Literature
55 Kenosia Avenue
Danbury, CT   06813   203-744-0100
                                          800-999-6673
                                      FAX 203-798-2291
                                      TDY:203-797-9590
                              http://www.rarediseases.org
                           e-mail: orphan@rarediseases.org
James Broatch, Chairman

Information clearing house on rare disorders.

119   National Organization on Disability (NOD)

910 16th Street NW
Washington, DC   20006   202-293-5960
                                      FAX 202-293-7999
                                      TDY:202-293-5968
                                   http://www.nod.org
                                e-mail: ability@nod.org
Alan A Reich, Founder
Michael R Deland, Chairman

Promotes the full and equal participation of America's 54 million men, women and children with disabilities in all aspects of life. Funded entirely by private sector contributions, NOD is the only national disability network organization concerned with all disabilities, all age groups and all disability issues.

120   National Rehabilitation Association

633 S Washington Street
Alexandria, VA   22314   703-836-0850
                                          888-258-4295
                                      FAX 703-836-0848
                                      TDY:708-836-0849
                              http://www.nationalrehab.org
                           e-mail: info@nationalrehab.org
Annemarie Hohman, Executive Director

A member organization whose mission is providing opportunities through knowledge and diversity for professionals in the field of rehabilitation of people with disabilities.

121   National Rehabilitation Information Center

4200 Forbes Boulevard
Lanham, MD   20706   301-459-5900
                                          800-346-2742
                                      FAX 301-459-4263
                                   http://www.naric.com
                         e-mail: naricinfo@heitechservices.com
Mark X Odum

A library and information center on all aspects of disability and rehabilitation.

122   PACER Center

8661 Normandale Boulevard
Minneapolis, MN   55437   952-838-9000
                                          800-537-2237
                                      FAX 952-838-0199
                                   http://www.pacer.org
                                e-mail: pacer@pacer.org
Paula F Goldberg, Executive Director

The mission of PACER Center is to expand opportunities and enhance the quality of life of children and young adults with disabilities and their families, based on the concept of parents helping parents.

123   Parent Educational Advocacy Training Center (PEATC)

6320 Augusta Drive
Springfield, VA   22150   703-923-0010
                                          800-869-6782
                                      FAX 703-923-0030
                                      TDY:703-923-0010
                                   http://www.peatc.org
                              e-mail: partners@peatc.org
Cherie Takemoto, Executive Director

Assists the families of children with disabilities through education, information and training. PEATC builds parent-professional partnerships to promote success in school and community life through information and assistance to families in understanding and negotiating the education and service systems for their children with disabilities.

124   Parents Helping Parents: Family Resource for Children with Special Needs

3041 Olcott Street
Santa Clara, CA   95054   408-727-5775
                                  FAX 408-727-0182
                                  http://www.php.com
                                  e-mail: general@php.com

Dr Michael Amalyon
Margueritte Garretty

Helping children with special needs receive the resources, love, hope, respect, health care, education and other services they need to achieve their full potential by providing them with strong families and dedicated professionals to serve them.

125   Pioneers Division

Council for Exceptional Children
1110 N Glebe Road
Arlington, VA   22201   703-620-3660
                                  888-232-7733
                                  FAX 703-264-9494
                                  http://www.cec.sped.org
                                  e-mail: cathym@cec.sped.org

Promotes activities and programs to increase awareness of the educational needs of children with disabilities and/or who are gifted, and the services available to them. Supports CEC's programs and activities. Membership is only open to CEC life members, retired life members and members of twenty years' standing. Members receive newsletter three times yearly.

126   Promote Real Independence for Disabled & Elderly Foundation

391 Long Hill Road
Groton, CT   06340   560-445-7320
                                  800-332-9122
                                  FAX 860-445-1448
                                  http://www.sewtiqueonline.com
                                  e-mail: dresspride@aol.com
Evelyn S Kennedy, Executive Director

Rehabilitation assistance utilizing fashion and grooming along with home management and independence in dressing. Speakers and resources are available for outreach services.

127   RFB&D Learning Through Listening

Anne T MacDonald Center
20 Roszel Road
Princeton, NJ   08540   609-452-0606
                                  800-221-4792
                                  FAX 609-987-8116
                                  http://www.rfbd.org
                                  e-mail: custserv@rfbd.org
William Scribner, President/CEO

The nation's educational library for people with print disabilities. We provide educational materials in recorded and computerized formats from kindergarten through postgraduate level.

128   Reach for Learning

1221 Marin Avenue
Albany, CA   94706   510-524-6455
                                  FAX 510-524-5154
Corinne Gustafson, Director

Educational center providing diagnosis, instruction, consultation for children, youth, adults with learning disabilities or under achievement.

129   Rehabilitation Engineering and Assistive Technology Society of North America (RESNA)

1700 N Moore Street
Arlington, VA   22209   703-524-6686

Dedicated to improving the potential of people with disabilities to achieve their goals through the use of technology; maintains listing of State Assistive Technology Programs. Services include an annual conference and publications.

130   Rehabilitation International

25 E 21st Street
New York, NY   10010   212-420-1500
                                  FAX 212-505-0871
                                  http://www.rehab-international.org
                                  e-mail: rehabintl@rehab-international.org
Mr Lex Frieden, President

A federation of national and international organizations and agencies working for the prevention of disability, the rehabilitation of people with disabilities and the equalization of opportunities within society on behalf of persons with disabilities and their families throughout the world.

131   Rural Clearinghouse for Lifelong Education & Development

Kansas State University
101 College Court Building
Manhattan, KS   66506   913-532-5560
                                  FAX 913-532-5637
                                  e-mail: abyers@ksuksu.edu
Jacqueline Spears, Director

A national effort to improve rural access to continuing education.

132   Rural Education and Small Schools

Appalachia Educational Laboratory
1031 Quarrier Street
Charleston, WV   25301   304-347-0400
                                  800-624-9120
                                  FAX 304-347-0487
                                  TDY:304-347-0448
                                  http://www.ael.org
Sara Aikin, Senior Executive Assistant
Terry Eidell, Interim Direcotr

Economic, cultural, social or other factors related to educational programs and practices for rural residents.

133 Sertoma International/Sertoma Foundation

1912 E Meyer Boulevard
Kansas City, MO 64132   816-333-8300
                                FAX 816-333-4320
                          http://www.sertoma.org
                     e-mail: infosertoma@sertoma.org
Steven Murphy, Executive Director

Activities focus on helping people with speech and hearing problems, but also have programs in the areas of youth, national heritage, drug awareness and community services.

134 Son-Rise Program

Autism Treatment Center of America
2080 S Undermountain Road
Sheffield, MA 01257   413-229-2100
                                800-714-2779
                          FAX 413-229-8931
                          http://www.son-rise.org
                   e-mail: information@son-rise.org
Sean Fitzgerald, Assistant Director Program
Barry Kauffman, Co-Founder
Bryn Hogan, Director

Since 1983, the Autism Treatment Center of America has provided innovative training programs for parents and professionals caring for children challenged by autism, autism spectrum disorders, pervasive developmental disorder (PDD) and other developmental difficulties. The Son-Rise Program teaches a specific yet comprehensive system of treatment and education designed to help families and caregivers enable their children to dramatically improve in all areas of learning.

135 Stuttering Foundation of America

3100 Walnut Grove Road
Memphis, TN 38111   901-452-7343
                                800-992-9392
                          FAX 901-452-3931
                      http://www.stutteringhelp.org
                 e-mail: stutter@stutteringhelp.org
Jane Fraser, President

Provides information to parents of children, adults, and teens who may have a stuttering problem.

136 Teacher Education Division (TED)

Council for Exceptional Children
1110 N Glebe Road
Arlington, VA 22201   703-620-3660
                                888-232-7733
                          FAX 703-264-9494
                          http://www.tedcec.org
                   e-mail: cathym@cec.sped.org

TED promotes the preparation and continuing professional development of effective professionals in special education and related service fields. Members receive Teacher Education and Special Education quarterly and the TED Lines newsletter three times a year.

137 Team of Advocates for Special Kids

100 W Cerritos Avenue
Anaheim, CA 92805   714-533-8275
                          FAX 714-533-2533
                          http://www.taskca.org
                     e-mail: tasca@yahoo.com
Marta Anchondo, Executive Director

A parent training and information center serving families of children with disabilities. Provides support, legal rights information, phone advocacy, workshops and referral services. Conducts assistive technology assessments for ages 12 months through adulthood and workshops on adapted toys, adaptive hardware and specialized software. Newsletter with legal updates, technology and disability information.

138 Technology and Media Division

Council for Exceptional Children
1110 N Glebe Road
Arlington, VA 22201   703-620-3660
                                888-232-7733
                          FAX 703-264-9494
                          http://www.cec.sped.org
                   e-mail: cathym@cec.sped.org

Promotes the availability and effective use of technology and media for individuals with disabilities and/or who are gifted. Members include special education teachers, speech and language therapists, rehabilitation therapists, counselors, researchers, teacher educators and others. Members receive two quarterly newsletters.

139 Thinking and Learning Connection

239 Whitclem Court
Palo Alto, CA 94306   650-493-3497
                          FAX 650-494-3499
Lynne D Stietzel, Co-Director
Eric R Stietzel, Co-Director

A group of independent associates committed to teaching students to learn new paths of knowledge and understanding. Our primary focus is working with dyslexic and dyscalculia. Individualized educational programs utilize extensive multisensory approaches to teach reading, spelling, handwriting, composition, comprehension, and mathematics. The students are actively involved in learning processes that integrate visual, auditory, and tactile techniques.

140 Very Special Arts (VSA)

1300 Connecticut Avenue NW
Washington, DC 20036   202-737-0645
                                800-933-8721
                          FAX 202-737-0725
                          http://www.vsarts.org
                     e-mail: info@vsarts.org
Soula Antoniou, President

Founded in 1974 by Jean Kennedy Smith as an affiliate of the John F. Kennedy Center for the Performing Arts, and led by president Doris Dixon, VSA is an international organization that creates learning opportunities through the arts for people with disabilities. The organization offers arts-based programs in creative writing, dance, drama, music and the visual arts implemented primarily through our vast network in 39 states and 70 international affiliates.

141 Washington PAVE: Specialized Training of Military Parents

6316 S 12th Street
Tacoma, WA 98465   253-565-2266
                                800-572-7368
                          FAX 253-566-8052
                    http://www.washingtonpave.org
              e-mail: wapave9@washingtonpave.com
Joanne Butts, Executive Director

STOMP, a parent directed project exists to empower military parents, individuals with disabilities, and service providers with knowledge, skills and resources so that they might access services to create a collaborative environment for a family and professional partnerships without regard to geographic location.

142 World Institute on Disability (WID)

510 16th Street
Oakland, CA   94612   510-763-4100
                                   FAX 510-763-4109
                                   http://www.wid.org
                                   e-mail: webpoobah@wid.org

A nonprofit public policy center dedicated to promoting independence and full societal inclusion of people with disabilities. Since its founding in 1983 by Ed Roberts, WID has earned a reputation for high quality research and public education on a wide range of issues. Newsletter is published on a regular basis.

143 Young Adult Institute (YAI): National Institute for People with Disabilities

460 W 34th Street
New York, NY   10001   212-273-6100
                                    FAX 212-629-4113
                                    TDY:212-290-2787
                                    http://www.yai.org
                                    e-mail: staff@yai.org

Joel M Levy DSW, CEO
Philip H Levy PhD, President/COO
Abbe Wittenberg, Professional Information

Award-winning network of not-for-profit health and human service agencies for people with developmental and learning disabilities. YAI has received national acclaim for its television series, On Our Own, and its Emmy nominated training videos and manuals. YAI conferences on MR/DD have been co-sponsored by prestigious organizations such as the United Nations and the President's Committee on Mental Retardation.

Alabama

144 Division of Rehabilitation Services and Childrens Rehabilitation Services

3800 E Highway 34
Pierre, SD   57501   605-773-3195
                                    FAX 605-773-5483
                                    http://www.state.sd.us/dhs/drs
Grady Kickul, Executive Director

Our mission is to assist individuals with disabilities to obtain employment, economic self-sufficiency, personal idependence and full inclusion in society.

145 Learning Disabilities Association of Alabama

PO Box 11588
Montgomery, AL   36111   334-277-9151
                                    FAX 334-284-9357
                                    http://www.ldaal.org
                                    e-mail: alabama@ldaal.org

Mattie Ray, President
Linda Graham, First VP

Educational, support and advocacy group for individuals with learning disabilities and Attention Deficit Disorder.

146 UAB Sparks Center for Developmental and Learning Disorders

University of Alabama at Birmingham
1720 7th Avenue S
Birmingham, AL   35233   205-934-5471
                                    800-UAB-CIRC
                                    FAX 205-975-2380
                                    e-mail: sparksinfo@civmail.circ.uab.edu
Dr Michael J Friedlander, Executive Director

The Sparks Clinics provide an extensive range of interdisciplinary offerings including comprehensive diagnosis, evaluation and treatment of the needs of children and adults with mental retardation and developmental disabilities. Each of the clinics consults with clients in a context that considers the unique needs of individuals and their family members. Additionally, the Sparks Clinics complex is a major site for clinical research.

Alaska

147 Center for Human Development (CHD) University Affiliated Program

University of Alaska
2210 ARCA Drive
Anchorage, AK   99508   907-272-8270
                                    800-243-2199
                                    FAX 907-274-4802
                                    http://www.alaskachd
                                    e-mail: info@alaskachd.orgdu
Karen M Ward PhD, Director
Beverly Tallman, Associate Director

Provides training, research, and support for people with developmental disabilities. The CHD is an interdisciplinary unit within the University of Alaska Anchorage, under the College of Health, Education, and Social Welfare. Faculty and staff represent a variety of disiplines. The center has a variety of projects which provide paid work experience for student assistants.

148 Learning Disabilities Association of Alaska (LDAALaska)

PO Box 243172
Anchorage, AK   99524   907-563-LDAA
                                    http://www.ldaalaska.org
                                    e-mail: info@ldaalaska.org

Colleen Deal, Contact

A nonprofit organization whose members are individuals with learning disabilities, their families, and the professionals who work with them.

Arizona

149 Arizona Center for Disability Law

100 N Stone Avenue
Tucson, AZ   85701   520-327-9547
                                    800-922-1447
                                    FAX 502-884-0992
                                    http://www.acdl.com
                                    e-mail: center@acdl.com
Leslie Cohen, Executive Director

Advocates for the legal rights of persons with disabilities to be free from abuse, neglect and discrimination.

150 Institute for Human Development: Northern Arizona University

PO Box 5630
Flagstaff, AZ 86011 928-523-4791
FAX 928-523-9127
http://www.nau.edu.ihd
e-mail: richard.carroll@nau.edu
Richard W Carroll PhD, Director

Training, research and support for people with development disabilities.

151 Parent Information Network

Arizona Department of Education
1535 W Jefferson Street
Phoenix, AZ 85007 602-542-4361
800-352-4558
FAX 602-542-5440
http://www.ade.az.gov
e-mail: rkeniso@ade.az.gov
Rita Kenison, Parent Network/Child Find Coord.

Provides free training and information to parents on federal and state laws and regulations for special education, parental rights and responsibilities, parent involvement, advocacy, behavior, standards and disability related resources. Provides a clearinghouse of information targeted to parents of children with disabilities. Also assists schools in promoting positive parent/professional/ regional partnerships.

Arkansas

152 Center for Applied Studies in Education Learning (CASE)

University of Arkansas at Little Rock
1120 Marshall Street
Little Rock, AR 72202 501-569-3422
FAX 501-569-8503
http://www.ualr.edu/coedept/CASE
e-mail: rhbradley@ualr/edu
R H Bradley, Professor

Improves the quality of education and human services in Arkansas and globally through a number of inter-related activities: conducting research on the effectiveness of programs and practices in education and human services; providing technical assistance in statistics, research design, measurement methodologies, data management, and program evaluation to students, faculty, and external groups and agencies; providing formal and informal consultation, technical assistance and instruction.

153 Disability Rights Center

1100 N University Avenue
Little Rock, AR 72207 501-296-1775
800-482-1174
FAX 501-296-1779
http://www.arkdisabilityrights.org
e-mail: panda@arkdisabilityrights.org
Nan Ellen East, Executive Director

Protection and advocacy system for Arkansas.

154 Learning Disabilities Association of Arkansas (LDAA)

7509 Cantrell Road
Little Rock, AR 72207 501-666-8777
FAX 501-666-4070
http://www.ldaarkansas.org
e-mail: ldaa@sbcglobal.net
Dana Jackson, Executive Director

A nonprofit, volunteer organization of parents and professionals. It is devoted to defining and finding solutions to the broad spectrum of learning problems. LDAA is a state affiliate to ACLD

California

155 Bay Area Adult Dyslexic Support Group

239 Whitelem
Palo Alto, CA 94306 650-493-3497
FAX 650-494-3499

Lynne Stietzel, Contact

A support group for any adults with learning differences interested in sharing or listening.

156 Berkeley Planning Associates

4440 Grand Avenue
Oakland, CA 94610 510-465-7884
FAX 510-465-7885
TDY:510-465-4493
http://www.bpacal.com
e-mail: info@bpacal.com
Frances Laskey, Human Resources Director

Conducts social policy research and program evaluations in various topic areas, including disability policy. Although the research typically does not focus on specific disabilities, the reports or other deliverables deriving from the projects may include specific information relating to particular disabilities, and are available for purchase.

157 California Association of Special Education & Services

CASES Executive Office
1722 J Street
Sacramento, CA 95814 916-447-7061
FAX 916-447-1320
http://www.capses.com
e-mail: info@capses.com
Barbara Browning, Executive Director

The purposes are to serve as a liaison between the public and private sectors and to lend support for a continuum of programs and objectives which improve the delivery of services provided to the exceptional individual.

158 Client Assistance Program (CAP)California Division of Persons with Disabilities

PO Box 944222
Sacramento, CA   94244   916-263-7367
                                800-952-5544
                            FAX 916-263-7464
        http://www.dor.ca.gov/public/contacts
                e-mail: capinfo@dor.ca.gov
Sheila Conlon Mentkowski, Director

The CAP is mandated by the Federal Rehabilitation Act. CAP provides free services to consumers and applicants of projects, programs, and facilities funded under the Rehabilitation Act. CAP services involve the analysis of issues a consumer/applicant may have and provision of advocacy services regarding Rehabilitation Act funded services.

159 Dyslexia Awareness and Resource Center

928 Carpinteria Street
Santa Barbara, CA   93103   805-963-7339
                             FAX 805-963-6581
           http://www.dyslexiacenter.com
           e-mail: info@dyslexiacenter.com
Leslie V Esposito CFRE, Executive Director
Joan T Esposito, Founder/Director Programs

The mission of the Center is to inform, educate and raise awareness of parents, students, adult dyslexics, professionals, educators, law enforcement agencies, employers and mental and health professionals about dyslexia, attention disorders and other learning disabilities and the characteristics that often accompany them. The Center accomplishes its mission by providing comprehensive information, workshops, and advocacy information and programs free of charge.

160 International Dyslexia Association: Inland Empire Branch

PO Box 6701
San Bernardino, CA   92412   909-686-9837
                             FAX 909-686-9835
              http://www.dyslexia-ca.org
Regina G Richards, President

An international 501(c)(3) nonprofit, scientific and educational organization dedicated to the study and treatment of dyslexia. Provides educational and support resources for individuals with dyslexia.

161 International Dyslexia Association: Los Angeles Branch

4383 Tujunga Avenue
Studio City, CA   91604   818-506-8866
                             FAX 818-506-1111
               http://www.interdys.org
               e-mail: dyslexiala@aol.com
Wynne Good, Contact

The Los Angeles County Branch of The International Dyslexia Association believes that all individuals have the right to realize their potential, that individual learning abilities can be strengthened, and that language and reading skills can be achieved.

162 International Dyslexia Association: Northern California Branch

PO Box 78008
San Francisco, CA   94107   650-328-7667
                                800-ABC-D123
                             FAX 415-753-0701
              http://www.dyslexia-ncbida.org
Francis Dickson, President

Founded to increase public awareness of dyslexia in Northern California and Northern Nevada.

163 International Dyslexia Association: San Diego Branch

2515 Camino Del Rio Drive
San Diego, CA   92138   619-295-3722
                             FAX 760-723-7168
                http://www.dyslexiasd.org
                  e-mail: pph@tfb.com
Jose Cruz, President

An international 501(c)(3) nonprofit, scientific and educational organization dedicated to the study and treatment of dyslexia. All branches hold at least one public meeting, workshop or conference per year.

164 Learning Disabilities Association of California

PO Box 601067
Sacramento, CA   95860   916-725-7881
                                866-532-6322
                             FAX 916-725-8786
               http://www.volunteerinfo.org
                 e-mail: lda@June.com

Support and advocacy for children and adults with learning disabilities.

165 Lutheran Braille Workers: Sight Saving Division

13471 California Street
Yucaipa, CA   92399   909-795-8970
                             FAX 909-795-8970
                 http://www.lbwinc.org
                 e-mail: lbw@lbwinc.org
Loyd Coppenger, Executive Director

Provides the message of Salvation to the blind and visually impaired throughout the world.

166 Recording for the Blind & Dyslexic: Los Angeles

5022 Hollywood Boulevard
Los Angeles, CA   90027   323-664-5525
                                800-499-5525
                             FAX 323-664-1881
                 http://www.rfbdla.org
            e-mail: los_angeles@rfbdla.org
Carol Smith, Executive Director
Stacey Eubank, Outreach Director

A national, nonprofit organization providing recorded textbooks, library services and other educational materials to students who cannot read standard print because of a visual, physical or learning disability. $50.00 registration fee and a $25.00 annual renewal fee. No fee for students whose schools are members.

167 Recording for the Blind & Dyslexic: Northern California Unit

488 W Charleston Road
Palo Alto, CA 94306 650-493-3717
800-221-4792
FAX 650-493-5513
http://www.rfbd.org
John Stevenson, Executive Director
Valley Brown, Outreach Director

A national network of thirty three studios with headquarters in Princeton, NJ. The sole purpose is to provide educational materials in recorded and computerized formats at every academic level. The materials are for all people unable to read standard print because of a visual, perceptual (dyslexia), or other physical disability.

168 Recording for the Blind & Dyslexic: Santa Barbara Chapter

3970 La Colina Road
Santa Barbara, CA 93110 805-687-6393
FAX 805-682-8197
http://www.rfbd.org
e-mail: jkarpenko@rfbd.org
Julie Karpenko, Interim Executive Director

The Santa Barbara Unit was founded in 1976. Over 300 volunteers produce textbooks on tape for students at local schools and around the country.

169 Recording for the Blind and Dyslexic: Inland Empire-Orange County Unit

1844 W 11th Street
Upland, CA 91786 909-949-4316
FAX 909-981-8457
http://www.rfbd.org
e-mail: mdavis@rfbd.org
Maureen Ahearn, Production Director
Mike Davis, Executive Director
Maggie Tupman, Educational Outreach Director

Volunteers record texts on audio cassettes and computer disks for the visually, physically and perceptually disabled.

Colorado

170 International Dyslexia Association: RockyMountain Branch

PO Box 3598
Boulder, CO 80307 303-721-9425
e-mail: ida_rmb@yahoo.com
Shelia R Phillips, President

An international 501(c)(3) nonprofit, scientific and educational organization dedicated to the study and treatment of dyslexia. All branches hold at least one public meeting, workshop or conference per year.

171 Learning Disabilities Association of Colorado

4596 E Iliff Avenue
Denver, CO 80222 303-894-0992
FAX 303-830-1645
http://www.ldanatl.org
e-mail: info@ldacolorado.com
Tim Carroll, Public Relations

A non-profit volunteer organization dedicated to advocacy and education of learning disabled children and adults.

172 Rocky Mountain Disability and Business Technical Assistance Center

3630 Sinton Road
Colorado Springs, CO 80907 719-444-0268
800-949-4232
FAX 719-444-0269
TDY:719-444-0268
http://www.adainformation.org
e-mail: mdbtac@mtc-inc.com
Patrick Going, Project Director

Provides information, training and technical assistance to employers, people with disabilities and other entities with responsibilities and rights under the ADA of 1990.

Connecticut

173 Connecticut Association for Children and Adults with LD

CACLD
25 Van Zant Street
East Norwalk, CT 06855 203-838-5010
FAX 203-866-6108
http://www.CACLD.org
e-mail: CACLD@opt.online.net
Beryl Kaufman, Executive Director

Helping children and adults with learning disabilities and attention disorders.

174 Connecticut Association of Private Special Education Facilities (CAPSEF)

330 Main Street
Hartford, CT 06106 860-525-1318
FAX 860-541-6484
http://www.capsef.org
e-mail: abrunetti@tcors.com
Alan J Deckman
Allyson J Deckman

Provides a basis for unity and action to serve the common interests among all private education facilities, including cost reporting, the state approval process and the private special education community.

175 Connecticut Capitol Region Educational Council

111 Charter Oak Avenue
Hartford, CT 06106 860-247-2732
877-850-2832
FAX 860-246-3304
http://www.crec.org
e-mail: info@ctec.org
Dr. Bruce Douglas, Executive Director

CREC is a nonprofit, regional educational service center serving 35 greater Hartford public school districts. It was founded in 1966 by local school districts working together to solve common problems. Today, CREC administers more than 100 programs and services spanning the entire educational spectrum with the same goal in mind. We work with local boards of education of the capitol region to improve the quality of public education for all learners.

176   Learning Disabilities Association of Connecticut

999 Asylum Avenue
Hartford, CT   06105   860-560-1711
                                 FAX 860-560-1750
                            http://www.ldact/org
                            e-mail: ldact@idact.org
Terry Assidy, Executive Director

Helps families and individuals in Connecticut who are affected by learning disabilities. Assists both children and adults in securing appropriate education and employment opportunities.

177   Parent-to-Parent Network of Connecticut

Family Center Dept. of CT Children's Med. Center
282 Washington
Hartford, CT   06105   860-545-9021
                                 FAX 860-545-9201
                            http://www.ccmckids.org
                            e-mail: mcole@ccmckids.org
Laura Glomb, Network Director

A group of trained parent volunteers who help other parents who are seeking professional information and emotional support. Parent volunteers attend a series of training workshops designed to prepare them to provide support and information to other parents.

178   Recording for the Blind & Dyslexic: Connecticut Chapter

209 Orange Street
New Haven, CT   06510   203-624-4334
                                 FAX 203-865-0203
                            http://www.rfbd.org
                            e-mail: connecticut@rfbd.org
Anne Fortunato, Studio Director

Provides textbooks on tape and computer disks to individuals who cannot read standard print because of a visual, perceptual or physical disability. Books span the entire educational spectrum from kindergarten through post graduate work and professional support. Master Tape Library contains almost 80,000 books on tape including a wide variety of science and technology books.

179   Special Education Resource Center of Connecticut

25 Industrial Park Road
Middletown, CT   06457   860-632-1485
                                 FAX 860-632-8870
                            http://www.ctserc.org
                            e-mail: info@ctserc.org
Marianne Koerner

Serves as a centralized resource for professionals, families, and community members on early intervention, special education and pupil services for individuals with special needs.

District of Columbia

180   Georgetown University Medical Center Child Development Center

3307 M Street NW
Washington, DC   20007   202-687-8635
                                 FAX 202-687-8899
                            http://www.gucdc.georgetown.edu
                            e-mail: info@georgetown.edu
Phyllis R Magrab, Director

Seeks to improve the quality of life for all children and youth, especially those with special needs and their families. Founded on an interdisciplinary approach to service, training programs, research, community outreach, and public policy.

181   Learning Disabilities Association: District of Columbia

PO Box 6350
Washington, DC   20015   202-624-8581
                                 FAX 202-667-9140

A nonprofit organization whose members are individuals with learning disabilities, their families, and the professionals who work with them.

182   Recording for the Blind & Dyslexic of Metropolitan Washington

5225 Wisconsin Avenue NW
Washington, DC   20015   202-244-8990
                                 FAX 202-244-1346
                            http://www.rfbd.org
                            e-mail: washingtondc@rfbd.org
Betsy Paull O'Connell, Executive Director
Toni Thomas, Outreach Director
Elizabeth Ratigan, Chairman

Provides unlimited numbers of recorded textbooks to students with documented learning disability. Serves students in the District of Columbia, Montgomery and Prince Georges counties Maryland, and Northern Virginia.

183   University Legal Services: Client Assistance Program

300 I Street NE
Washington, DC   20002   202-547-0198
                                 FAX 202-547-2662
                                 TDY:202-547-2657
                            http://www.dcpanda.org
Joe Cooney, Executive Director

Provides legal assistance to students and consumers.

Florida

184 Florida Advocacy Center for Persons with Disabilities

2671 W Executive Center Circle
Tallahassee, FL 32301   850-488-9071
                                800-342-0823
                            FAX 850-488-8640
                            TDY:800-346-4127
                http://www.advocacycenter.org
                e-mail: advocacyn@aol.com
Elizabeth Hollifield, Chairman

The Advocacy Center for Persons with Disabilities is a nonprofit organization providing protection and advocacy services in the State of Florida. Our mission is to advance the dignity, equality, self-determination and expressed choices of individuals with disabilities.

185 Florida Bureau of Instructional Support & Community Services

325 W Gaines Street
Tallahassee, FL 32399   850-488-1570
                            FAX 850-921-8246
                      http://www.fldoe.org
Michele Polland, Interim Bureau Chief

The bureau has a broad range of responsibilities in the outgoing examination of state and federal laws, rules and regulations affecting public education and coordinating among other agencies, the delivery of services to public school students in Florida.

186 Florida Protection & Advocacy Agency for Persons with Disabilities

2671 Executive Center Circle W
Tallahassee, FL 32301   850-488-9071
                                800-342-0823
                            FAX 850-488-8640
Marcia Beach, Executive Director

Offers help for people with disabilities.

187 International Dyslexia Association: Florida Branch

10770 SW 84 Street
Miami, FL 33173   305-252-3474
                            FAX 305-274-0337
                      http://www.interdys.org
e-mail: ear228@aol.com (identity IDA as your sub-
                                          ject)
Carole R Reprensek, President

An international 501(c)(3) nonprofit, scientific and educational organization dedicated to the study and treatment of dyslexia. All branches hold at least one public meeting, workshop or conference per year.

188 Learning Disabilities Association of Florida

331 E Henry Street
Punta Gorda, FL 33950   941-637-8957
                      http://www.lda-fl.org
                e-mail: ldaf00@sunline.net
Gail Kurz, Executive Board Member

189 Learning Disabilities Association of Florida

331 E Henry Street
Punta Gorda, FL 33950   941-637-8957
                            FAX 941-637-0617
                      http://www.lda-fl.org
                e-mail: ldaf00@sunline.net
Cheryl Kron, Executive Secretary

The Learning Disabilities Association of Florida is a nonprofit volunteer organization of parents, professionals and LD adults.

190 Mailman Center for Child Development: University of Miami Department of Pediatrics

University of Miami School of Medicine
PO Box 01820
Miami, FL 33101   305-243-5790
                            FAX 305-326-7594
            http://http://pediatrics.med.miami.edu
                e-mail: reuben@miami.edu
Ruben Garcia, Director

The mission is to enhance the lives of individuals with developmental disabilities and their families by supporting personal and family relationships and facilitating independence, productivity, integration and inclusion.

Georgia

191 International Dyslexia Association: Georgia Branch

1951 Greystone Road NW
Atlanta, GA 30318   404-256-1232
                                800-223-3123
                            FAX 404-351-7652
                      http://www.idaga.org
e-mail: info@midaga.org   rdavis@schenk.org
Rosalie Davis, President

An international nonprofit, scientific and educational organization dedicated to the study and treatment of dyslexia. All branches hold at least one public meeting, workshop or conference per year.

192 Recording for the Blind & Dyslexic: Georgia Chapter

120 Florida Avenue
Athens, GA 30605   706-549-1313
                            FAX 706-227-6161
                      http://www.rfbd.org
Lenore Martin, Executive Director

Offers recordings of educational books on audio cassette and computer disk.

Hawaii

193 Aloha Special Technology Access Center

710 Green Street
Honolulu, HI 96813   808-523-5547
                            FAX 808-536-3765
                e-mail: astachi@yahoo.com
Ruth Akiona, Program Coordinator

A private, nonprofit group of volunteers, parents of disabled children, adults with disabilities and professionals in the field of health and education. The aim of the center is to increase the awareness and use of computers by disabled people through a program of educational activities and events. This technology empowers people through communication, access to information and markets, and entry to new job opportunities.

194   Assistive Technology Resource Centers of Hawaii

414 Kuwili Street
Honolulu, HI   96817   808-532-7110
                                         800-645-3007
                                    FAX 808-532-7120
                                    TDY:808-532-7110
                                    http://www.atrc.org
                                    e-mail: atrc@atrc.org
Barbara Fischlowitz-Leong, Executive Director

A non-profit organization that is dedicated to linking individuals with technology so all people can participate in every aspect of community life. Empowers individuals to maintain dignity and control in their lives by promoting technology through advocacy, training. information, and education

195   International Dyslexia Association: Hawaii Branch

PO Box 61610
Honolulu, HI   96839   808-538-7007
                                    FAX 808-566-6837
                                    http://www.interdys.org
                                    e-mail: info@HIBIDA.org
Sally Lambert, Co-President
Sue Voit, Co-President

An international 501(c)(3) nonprofit, scientific and educational organization dedicated to the study and treatment of dyslexia. All branches hold at least one public meeting, workshop or conference per year.

196   Learning Disabilities Association of Hawaii (LDAH)

200 N Vineyard Boulevard
Honolulu, HI   96817   808-536-9684
                                         800-533-9684
                                    FAX 808-5376780
                            http://www.idanatl.org/Hawaii
                                    e-mail: ldah@ldaHawaii.org
Jennifer Schember-Lang, Executive Director

A nonprofit agency founded in 1968 by parents of children with learning disabilities. LDAH serves families of children with learning disabilities and other special needs that interfere with learning by providing educational advocacy training and support in order to remove barriers and promote awareness and full educational opportunity.

Idaho

197   Comprehensive Advocacy of Idaho

4477 Emerald Street
Boise, ID   83706   208-336-5353
                                         800-632-5125
                                    FAX 208-336-5396
                                    TDY:208-336-5353
                            http://users.moscow.com/co-80
                            e-mail: coadinc@cableone.net
Linda Flesner, Administrative Assistant
Jim Baugh, Executive Director

Private, nonprofit legal services organization designated by the Governor as the Protection and Advocacy System for the state of Idaho. Operates federally funded grant programs to protect the legal rights of persons with disabilities.

198   Idaho High Reachers Employment and Training

High Reachers-ARC
140 E 2nd Street
Mountain Home, ID   83647   208-587-5804
                                         800-559-5804
                                    TDY:208-343-2950
Lisa Cahill

Illinois

199   Child Care Association of Illinois

300 E Monroe
Springfield, IL   62701   217-528-4409
                                    FAX 217-528-6498
                                    http://www.cca-il.org
                                    e-mail: ILCCAMB@aol.com
Margaret M Berglind, President/Executive Director

A voluntary, nonprofit organization dedicated to improving the delivery of social services to the abused, neglected, and troubled children, youth and families of Illinois.

200   Illinois Catholic Guild for the Blind

180 N Michigan Avenue
Chicago, IL   60601   312-236-8569
                                    FAX 312-236-8128
                            http://www.guildfortheblind.org
                            e-mail: info@guildfortheblind.org
Kathy Firak, Operations Manager

Support and information for families and individuals with visual disabilities.

201 Illinois Protection & Advocacy Agency:Equip for Equality

11 E Adams Street
Chicago, IL 60603   312-341-0022
800-537-2632
FAX 312-341-0295
TDY:312-341-0022
http://www.equipforequality.org
e-mail: hn6177@handsnet.org
Peter Grosz, Relations Manager

Equip for Equality is a not-for-profit Federally-funded organization that advocates for disability rights in the state of Illinois.

202 International Dyslexia Association: Illinois/Missouri Branch

751 Roosevelt Road, Building 7
Glen Ellyn, IL 60137   630-469-6900
FAX 630-469-6810
http://www.interdys.org
e-mail: ilbranch@ameritech.net
Carolyn Swallow PhD, Executive Director
Gail Oliphant

Formed to increase public awareness of dyslexia in Illinois and Eastern Missouri. We have been serving individuals with dyslexia, their families, and professionals for 25 years. One of our primary objectives is to increase early intervention efforts.

203 Jewish Children's Bureau of Chicago

216 W Jackson Boulevard
Chicago, IL 60606   312-444-2090
FAX 312-855-3754
http://www.jcbchicago.org
Provides Jewish children and their families a range of services which preserve, strengthen and protect the emotional well-being of children.

204 Learning Disabilities Association of Illinois

10101 S Roberts Road
Palos Hills, IL 60465   708-430-7532
FAX 708-430-7592
http://www.idanatl.org/illinois
e-mail: ldaofil@ameritech.net
Sharon Schussler, Administrative Assistant

A nonprofit organization dedicated to the advancement of the education and general welfare of children and youth of normal or potentially normal intelligence who have learning disabilities of a perceptual, conceptual or coordinative nature or related problems.

205 Recording for the Blind & Dyslexic: Chicago Loop Studio & Administrative Offices

18 S Michigan Avenue
Chicago, IL 60603   312-236-8715
FAX 312-236-8719
e-mail: sbryant@rfbd.org
Sara Bryant, Studio Director

Offers information on recordings of books on audio cassette and computer disk.

206 Recording for the Blind & Dyslexic: Lois C Klein Studio

9612C W 143rd Street
Orland Park, IL 60462   312-349-9356
http://www.rfbd.org
e-mail: selhenicky@rfbd.org
Sandy Elhenicky, Studio Director

Offers information on recordings of books on audio cassette and computer disk.

207 Recording for the Blind & Dyslexic: Naperville Chapter

1266 E Chicago Avenue
Naperville, IL 60540   630-420-0722
FAX 630-420-8975
http://www.rfbd.org
e-mail: nleone@rfbd.org
Nina Leone, Production Director

One of 21 units of a national nonprofit organization that provides educational materials in recorded and computerized formats for people who cannot effectively read standard print due to a visual, perceptual or other physical disability.

Indiana

---

208 Bridgepointe Goodwill & Easter Seals

1329 Applegate Lane
Clarksville, IN 47131   812-283-7908
FAX 812-283-6248
e-mail: trichards@bridgepointe.org
C Marshall, Director

Helps children and adults with disabilities expand their independence.

209 Indiania Vocation Rehabilitation Services Goodwill Industries

1452 Vaxter Avenue
Clarksville, IN 47129   812-288-8261
FAX 812-282-7048
Edwin Haines, Interim Area Supervisor

Purpose is to assist the community by providing services which allow individuals to maximize their potential and to participate in work, family and the community. To do this we will provide rehabilitation, education and training.

210 International Dyslexia Association: Indiana Branch

1100 W 42nd Street
Indianapolis, IN 46208   317-926-1450
FAX 317-927-9285
http://www.interdys.org
e-mail: inbofida@hotmail.com
Yvonne Gill, President

An international nonprofit, scientific and educational organization dedicated to the study and treatment of dyslexia. All branches hold at least one public meeting, workshop or conference per year.

211 Learning Disabilities Association of Indiana (LDA-IN)
PO Box 20584
Indianapolis, IN 46220   574-272-3058
                                800-284-2519
                                FAX 317-255-5087
                                http://www.lda-in.org
                                e-mail: ldain@ldain.org
Barbara Uhrig, Director

LDA-IN is the state chapter of the Learning Disabilities Association of America. LDA-IN is an all volunteer group that provides information and support. Membership brings national and state newsletters and reduced conference fees. Dues ($25.00 per year) permit LDA to fund projects and provide free and inexpensive literature to anyone who requests information. Fall state conference is held in Indianapolis.

212 Southwestern Indiana Easter Seal
Rehabilitation Center
3701 Bellemeade Avenue
Evansville, IN 47714   812-479-1411
                                FAX 812-437-2634
                                e-mail: info@evansvillerehab.com
Ray Rasior, President

Helps children and adults with disabilities expand their independence.

Iowa

213 International Dyslexia Association: Iowa Branch
2215 Westdale Drive SW
Cedar Rapids, IA 52404   319-551-2851
                                FAX 319-365-1038
                                http://www.interdys.org
                                e-mail: sue_ida_ia@yahoo.com
Pat McGuire, President

An international nonprofit, scientific and educational organization dedicated to the study and treatment of dyslexia. All branches hold at least one public meeting, workshop or conference per year.

214 Iowa Center for Disabilities and Development
100 Hawkins Drive
Iowa City, IA 52242   319-353-6135
                                877-686-0031
                                FAX 319-356-8284
                                TDY:877-686-0032
                                http://www.medicine.uiowa.edu
                                e-mail: disability-resources@uiowa.edu
Dennis Harper PhD, Director

Center for people with disabilities or special needs.

215 Iowa Program for Assistive Technology
Center for Disabilities and Development
100 Hawkins Drive
Iowa City, IA 52242   319-356-0550
                                800-331-3027
                                FAX 515-242-4809
                                http://www.uiowa.edu/infotech/
                                e-mail: jane-gay@uiowa.edu
Jane Gay, Director
Amy Mikelson, Outreach Coordinator
Alicia Audry, Secretary

Provides free information and referral about available assistive technology, used equipment referral service, and bimonthly newsletter. Makes referral for free legal advocacy relating to access to AT devices and services.

216 Learning Disabilities Association of Iowa
1930 Waterloo Road
Cedar Falls, IA 50613   515-280-8558
                                FAX 515-282-9117
Connie Sullivan, President

A nonprofit organization whose members are individuals with learning disabilities, their families, and the professionals who work with them.

Kansas

217 International Dyslexia Society: Kansas Western Missouri Branch
2812 SW Osborn Road
Topeka, KS 66614   816-838-7323
                                http://www.hcity.com/kwmida
                                e-mail: ks_wmo_ida@hotmail.com
C Wilson Anderson, President

Focuses efforts on Kansas and Western Missouri. By hosting events and establishing a presence, the leaders have begun to work with parents, schools and teachers to help children with dyslexia. Maintains a list of individuals who have specialized training and who are available for remediation of reading, writing and spelling problems. Provides information for parents and teachers, an annual spring conference, quarterly newsletter dealing with local issues, and teacher training.

218 Kansas Advocacy & Protective Services
3745 SW Wanamaker Road
Topeka, KS 66610   785-273-9661
                                877-776-1541
                                FAX 785-273-9414
                                http://www.ksadv.org
                                e-mail: info@ksadv.org
Tim Voth, Intake Coordinator

Works in partnership with persons with disabilities to protect, advocate for, and advance their human, legal and service rights.

219   Learning Disabilities Association of Kansas

PO Box 4424
Topeka, KS   66604   785-273-4505
                                         FAX 785-228-9527
                                         http://ldakansas.org
                                         e-mail: marciasu@aol.com
Andrea Blair, Manhattan President

Information and referral service to parents of the learning disabled child and to adults with learning disabilities.

Kentucky

220   Learning Disabilities Association of Kentucky

2210 Goldsmith Lane
Louisville, KY   40218   502-473-1256
                                            877-587-1256
                                         FAX 502-473-4695
                                         http://www.ldaofky.org
                                         e-mail: ldaofky@aol.com
Catherine Senn, Executive Director

Embraces the challenge to educate the general public on the characteristics of learning disabilities such as attention deficit disorder, dyslexia and more.

221   Recording for the Blind & Dyslexic: Kentucky Chapter

240 Haldeman Avenue
Louisville, KY   40206   502-895-9068
                                         FAX 502-897-1145
                                         http://www.rfbd.org
                                         e-mail: mseay@rfbd.org
Margie Seay, Outreach Director

Offers information on recordings of books on audio cassette and computer disk.

Maine

222   Learning Disabilities Association of Maine (LDA)

PO Box 67
Oakland, ME   04963   207-465-7700
                                         FAX 207-465-4844
                                         http://www.ldame.org
                                         e-mail: ldame@ldame.org
Cathy Lashin-Otisfield, President
Brenda Bennett, Executive Director

LDA of Maine is a statewide, nonprofit, volunteer organization including individuals with learning disabilities, their families, and professionals. The organization is dedicated to enhancing the quality of life for all individuals with learning disabilities and their families, to alleviating the restricting effects of learning disabilities, and to supporting endeavors to determine the causes of learning disabilities.

223   Maine Parent Federation

PO Box 2067
Augusta, ME   04338   207-623-2144
                                            800-870-7746
                                         FAX 207-582-3638
                                         http://www.mpf.org
                                         e-mail: parentconnnect@mpf.org

Parent Training and Information Program views parents as full partners in the educational process and a significant source of support and assistance to each other. Funded by the Division of Personnel Preparation, Office of Special Education Programs, these programs provide training and information to parents to enable them to participate more effectively with professionals in meeting the educational needs of disabled children.

Maryland

224   International Dyslexia Association: Maryland Branch

PO Box 792
Brooklandville, MD   21022   410-825-2881
                                         e-mail: MBIDA4@hotmail.com
Cathy Rommel, President

225   Learning Disabilities Association of Maryland

PO Box 792
Brooklandville, MD   21022   410-825-2881
                                         e-mail: MBIDA4@hotmail.com
Cathy Rommel, President

Nonprofit, volunteer association dedicated to enhancing the quality of life for all individuals with learning disabilities and their families.

226   Maryland Association of University Centers on Disabilities

1010 Wayne Avenue
Silver Spring, MD   20910   301-588-8252
                                         FAX 301-588-2842
                                         http://www.aucd.org
                                         e-mail: gjesien@aucd.org
George Jesien PhD, Executive Director
David Johnson PhD, Board President

Helps member agencies to enhance quality of life for people with developmental disabilities through disciplinary training and technical assistance with information and research.

Massachusetts

227   Learning Disabilities Association of Massachusetts (LDAM)

PO Box 142
Weston, MA   02493   781-891-5009
                                         FAX 781-647-5141
                                         http://www.ldam.org

Teresa Citro, Executive Director
David Bradburn, President

Works to enhance the lives of individuals with learning disabilities, with emphasis on the underserved. To identify and support unrecognized strengths/capabilities of persons with learning disabilities. Strive to increase awareness and understanding of LD through multilingual media productions/publications that serve populations across cultures. Educational enrichment programs are designed to serve individuals with learning disabilities, their families and the professionals in their lives.

228 Massachusetts Association of 766 Approved Private Schools (MAAPS)

591 N Avenue
Wakefield, MA 01880   781-245-1220
                             FAX 781-245-5294
                       http://www.spedschools.com
                  e-mail: maaps@spedschools.com
James V Major, Executive Director

Nonprofit association of Chapter 766 approved private schools dedicated to providing educational programs and services to students with special needs throughout Massachusetts. Concerned that children with special needs have appropriate, quality education and that they and their families know the rights, policies, procedures and options that make the education process a productive reality for special needs children.

229 Massachusetts Shriver Center: University Affiliated Program

200 Trapelo Road
Waltham, MA 02254   781-642-0223
                           FAX 781-894-9968
William McIlvane, Director
Charles Hamad, Associate Director
Laura Massei, Administrator

The Center promotes the understanding of neurological, cognitive and behavioral development associated with disabilities, emphasizing mental retardation. We conduct basic and applied research to determine the biological and environmental factors that influence typical and atypical development and provide training and service programs that directly benefit people with developmental disabilities and their families.

230 New England ADA & Accessible IT Center

Adaptive Environments
374 Congress Street
Boston, MA 02210   617-695-1225
                           800-949-4232
                       FAX 617-482-8099
                       TDY:617-695-1225
            http://www.adaptiveenvironments.org
          e-mail: info@adaptiveenvironments.org
Valerie Fletcher, Executive Director
Andy Washburn, Information Specialist

Adaptive Environments promotes design that works for everyone across the spectrum of ability and age and enhances human experience.

231 Recording for the Blind & Dyslexic: Boston

58 Charles Street
Cambridge, MA 02141   617-577-1111
                           FAX 617-577-1113
                    e-mail: ajones@rfod.org
Christina Raimo, Executive Director
Kelly Hill, Outreach Coordinator
Amy Deangelis, Director Educational Outreach

A nonprofit volunteer organization and educational library serving people who cannot effectively read standard print because of visual impairment, dyslexia or other physical disability. We strive to create opportunities for individual success by providing accessible educational material. Comprehensive source of recorded textbooks and other educational printed matter. One-time registration fee of $50.00 plus a $25.00 annual fee. School memberships are available.

232 Recording for the Blind & Dyslexic: Berkshire/Lenox/Williamstown

55 Pittsfield/Lenox Rd, Lenox 01240
Williamstown, MA 01267   413-637-0889
                               413-458-3641
                       http://berkshire@rfbd.org
Alan Alibozek, Studio Director

The Berkshire United Way operates recording studios in both Lenox and Williamstown. The studios offer information on recordings of books on audio cassette and computer disk, and provides outreach to: four western counties of Massachusetts; Albany, Columbia, Rensselaer, Saratoga, Schenectady and Washington counties in New York; Bennington County in Vermont; Litchfield County in Connecticut.

Michigan

233 International Dyslexia Association: Michigan Branch

4050 Waverly Place
Ann Arbor, MI 48105   734-663-9884
                       http://www.idamib.org
                e-mail: postmaster@idamib.org
Jim Grant, President

An international 501(c)(3) nonprofit, scientific and educational organization dedicated to the study and treatment of dyslexia. All branches hold at least one public meeting, workshop or conference per year.

234 Learning Disabilities Association of Michigan (LDA)

200 Museum Drive
Lansing, MI 48933   517-485-8160
                            888-597-7809
                        FAX 517-485-8462
              http://www.ldaofmichigan.org
          e-mail: info@ldaofmichigan.org or
                            ldami@aol.com

Ed Schlitt, President

A nonprofit, volunteer association that is dedicated to enhancing the quality of life for all individuals with learning disabilities and their families through advocacy, education, training, services and support of research. Our goal is to see LD understood and addressed and the individuals with learning disabilities will thrive and participate fully in society.

1,200 Members

235 Michigan Citizens Alliance to Uphold Special Education (CAUSE)

6412 Centurion Drive
Lansing, MI 48917   517-886-9167
                        800-221-0105
                        FAX 517-886-9366
                        http://www.causeonline.org
                        e-mail: info@causeonline.org
Patricia Keller, Executive Director

Provides a collaborative forum where consumers and providers can actively support an individualized, Free and Appropriate Education (FAPE) that enables all students to maximize their options in the world community. Our priority is the protection of the rights of students with disabilities. We are a Parent Training Information Center providing free information, referrals, support, advocacy and workshops for parents/professionals working with children who have special needs.

236 Recording for the Blind & Dyslexic Learning Through Listening: Michigan Unit

5600 Rochester Road
Troy, MI 48098   248-879-0101
                     FAX 248-879-9927
                     http://www.rfbd.org
                     e-mail: creeb@rfbd.org
Carla Reeb, Executive Director
Don Haffner, Studio Director

Recording for the Blind & Dyslexic is the nation's educational library serving people who cannot effectively read standard print because of visual impairment, dyslexia or other physical disability. We provide textbooks, educational and professional materials in an audio format. The Michigan Unit's outreach volunteers offer students and their parents training sessions at the studio by appointment.

Minnesota

237 International Dyslexia Association: Upper Midwest Branch

5021 Vernon Avenue
Minneapolis, MN 55436   651-450-7589
                            e-mail: umbida@hotmail.com
Trish Vickman, President

An international 501(c)(3) nonprofit, scientific and educational organization dedicated to the study and treatment of dyslexia. All branches hold at least one public meeting, workshop or conference per year in Minnesota, North Dakota and South Dakota.

238 Minnesota Access Services

Minneapolis Public Schools Community Education
1006 W Lake Street
Minneapolis, MN 55408   612-668-4326
                            FAX 612-627-3101
Manny Boeser, Contact

Provides outreach and integration services for adults with disabilities.

239 Minnesota Disability Law Center

430 1st Avenue N
Minneapolis, MN 55401   612-332-1441
                            800-292-4150
                            FAX 612-334-5755
                            http://www.mndlc.org
Luther Granquist, Attorney
Pamela Hoopes, Director

Mission is to protect, promote and expand the rights of people with disabilities and mental illness.

Mississippi

240 International Dyslexia Association: Mississippi

PO Box 2485
Laurel, MS 39442   601-428-0857
                       FAX 601-362-9180
Judy Robinson, President

An international 501(c)(3) nonprofit, scientific and educational organization dedicated to the study and treatment of dyslexia. All branches hold at least one public meeting, workshop or conference per year.

241 Learning Disabilities Association of Mississippi

4080 Old Canton Road
Jackson, MS 39216   601-362-1667
                        FAX 601-362-9180
                        http://http://www.ldams.org
                        e-mail: ldams@bellsouth.net
Camille Yates, President

A nonprofit organization whose members are individuals with learning disabilities, their families, and the professionals who work with them. Dedicated to enhancing the quality of life of all individuals with LD and their families; alleviating the restricting effects of LD; supporting endeavaors to determine the cause of LD.

Montana

242 Montana Advocacy Program (MAP): Helena

400 N Park, 2nd Floor
Helena, MT 59624   406-449-2344
                       800-245-4743
                       FAX 406-449-2418
                       http://www.mtadu.org
        e-mail: advocate@mtadv.org or bernie@mtadv.org
Bernadette Franks-Ongoy, Executive Director
Liesl Beck, Advocacy Specialist
Karin Billings, Advocacy Specialist

A nonprofit corporation administering eight protection and advocacy programs and one private program that advocate the rights of Montanans with disabilities. MAP staff include professional advocates and attorneys. Mission is to protect and advocate the human, legal and civil rights of Montanans with mental and physical disabilities while advancing dignity, equality and self-determination.

243 Montana Advocacy Program (MAP): MissoulaOffice

1280 S 3rd West, Suite 4
Missoula, MT   59801
406-541-4357
800-245-4743
FAX 406-541-4360
http://www.mtadu.org
e-mail: advocate@mtadv.org or bernie@mtadv.org
Bernadette Franks-Ongoy, Executive Director
Liesl Beck, Advocacy Specialist
Karin Billings, Advocacy Specialist

A nonprofit corporation administering eight protection and advocacy programs and one private program that advocate the rights of Montanans with disabilities. MAP staff include professional advocates and attorneys. Mission is to protect and advocate the human, legal and civil rights of Montanans with mental and physical disabilities while advancing dignity, equality and self-determination.

244 Montana Parents, Let's Unite for Kids (PLUK)

516 N 32nd Street
Billings, MT   59101
406-255-0540
800-222-7585
FAX 406-255-0523
http://www.pluk.org/
e-mail: plukinfo@pluk.org
Dennis Moore, Executive Director

PLUK is a private, nonprofit organization formed by parents of children with disabilities and chronic illnesses. Its purpose is to provide information, support, training and assistance to aid parents with their children at home, in school and as adults. We keep current on best practices in education, medicine, law, human services, rehabilitation, and technology to insure families with disabilites have access to high quality services.

Nebraska

245 International Dyslexia Association of Nebraska

2830 Kipling Circle
Lincoln, NE   68516
402-434-6434
FAX 410-321-5069
http://www.interdys.org
e-mail: gcarlson@lps.org
Gwelda Carlson, President

An international 501(c)(3) nonprofit, scientific and educational organization dedicated to the study and treatment of dyslexia. All branches hold at least one public meeting, workshop or conference per year.

246 Learning Disabilities Association of Nebraska

1941 S 42nd Street
Omaha, NE   68105
402-348-1567
FAX 402-934-1479
http://www;ldonline.com
e-mail: LDAofNE@aol.com
Sharon Bloechle, Administration Director

Support groups for parents and teachers, information for school and community regarding ADHD and LD children/adults, book and video library, educational seminars and conferences, parent panel for discussion, summer camp (ages 8-15) and verified LD/ADHD students. Monthly newsletter.

Nevada

247 Nevada Economic Opportunity Board: Community Action Partnership

PO Box 270880
Las Vegas, NV   89127
702-647-1510
FAX 702-647-6639
http://www.eobcc.org
Marcia Walker, Executive Director

Located in one of the fastest growing and most diverse communities in the United States, the Economic Opportunity Board of Clark County is a highly innovative Community Action Agency. Our mission is to eliminate poverty by providing programs, resources, services, and advocacy for self-sufficiency and economic empowerment.

New Hampshire

248 Easter Seals New Hampshire

555 Auburn Street
Manchester, NH   03103
603-623-8863
800-870-8728
FAX 603-625-1148
Gloria Fulmer, Executive Director

Easter Seals New Hampshire is one of the most comprehensive affiliates in the nation, assisting more than 18,000 children and adults with disabilities through a network of more than a dozen service sites around the state and in Vermont. Each center provides top-quality, family-focused and innovative services tailored to meet the specific needs of the particular community it serves.

249 Learning Disabilities Association of New Hampshire

35 Marty Drive
Merrimack, NH   03054
603-424-6667
e-mail: hhlda@aol.com
Jan Carlton, Adult Issues

Resources for people with learning disabilities.

250 New Hampshire Disabilities Rights Center (DRC)

18 Low Avenue
Concord, NH   03302
603-228-0432
800-834-1721
http://www.drcnh.org
e-mail: advocacy@drcnh.or
Richard Cohen, Esq, Executive Director
Ronald Lospennato, Esq, Legal Director

New Hampshire's protective and advocacy system for individuals with a disability, a development disability, and mental illness. Information about your rights; referral to someone who can help you; legal advice about your situation; legal representation. Fully accessible office. DRC is independent from state service providers and dedicated to equal enjoyment of civil and legal rights for people with disability. We are authorized by federal statute to pursue legal and administrative remedies.

251 New Hampshire Easter Seals Early Intervention Program

25 Nashua Road
Londonderry, NH 03053   603-432-1945
FAX 603-749-0981
http://www.eastersealsnh.org
Gloria Fulmer, Contact

Helps people with learning disabilities cope.

252 New Hampshire-ATEC Services

67 Communications Drive
Laconia, NH 03246   603-528-3060
800-932-5837
FAX 603-524-0702
http://www.nhassistivetechnology.org
e-mail: lorraineh@atechservices.org
Lorraine Halton, MA, Clinical Director
Therese Willkomm, PhD, ATP, Executive Director
Donna Furlong, BS, Administrative Assistant

ATECH's mission is to enable comunity participation and achievement of personal goals through the provision of education, information, and assistive technology services for persons with disability. Technical Division: Leo Benoit, Concord 603-226-2900; Sales/Marketing: Paul Luff, Concord 800-427-3338

253 Parent to Parent of New Hampshire

12 Flynn Street
Lebanon, NH 03766   603-448-6393
800-698-LINK
http://www.parenttoparentnh.org
e-mail: p2p@nhsupport.net

If you are a parent of a child with special challenges and you would like to speak to a parent whose child has similar needs - someone who will understand, Parent to Parent is a network of families willing to share experiences. Should you call a Supporting Parent will contact you by phone or visit within 24 hours. All information will be kept confidential and there is no cost for the service.

New Jersey

254 American Self-Help Clearinghouse of New Jersey

Saint Clare's Health Services
100 E Hanover Avenue
Cedar Knolls, NJ 07927   973-326-6789
800-367-6274
FAX 973-326-9467
TDY:973-625-9053
http://www.njgroups.org
e-mail: mkerin@saintclaires.org

Puts callers in touch with any of several hundred national and international self-help groups covering a wide range of illnesses, disabilities, addictions, bereavement and stressful life situations.

255 Family Support Center of New Jersey

Lions Head Office Park
Brick, NJ 08723   723-262-8020
800-372-6510
FAX 732-262-4373
TDY:800-852-7899
http://www.familysupportnj.com
e-mail: fsnj@familysupport.com
Veronica Trathen, Director
Natalie Trump, Resources Coordinator

A clearinghouse offering up-to-date information on all types of disabilities as well as national, state and local support programs and services. We offer free services including telephone helpline, resource data base, private respite care networks, lending library, OPTIONS manual, cash subsidy program, speakers bureau, assistive technology.

256 International Dyslexia Association of New Jersey

PO Box 32
Long Valley, NJ 07853   908-879-1179
FAX 908-876-3621
http://www.interdys.org
e-mail: NJIDA@msn.com
Georgette C Dickman, MA, LDT/C, Presidesnt
Mary Jo Rieg, Branch Office Administrator

An international nonprofit, scientific and educational organization dedicated to the study of dyslexia. We offer tutoring and testing referrals, as well as support teacher education and hold outreach programs. Teacher Scholarships are offered to our Annual Fall Conferences, Wilson Reading Overviews and Project Read programs. Newsletter published bi-annually.

257 New Jersey Family Resource Associates

35 Haddon Avenue
Shrewsbury, NJ 07702   732-747-5310
FAX 732-747-1896
http://www.familyresourceassociates.org
e-mail: frabook@aol.com
Nancy Phalanucorn, Executive Director

Private, nonprofit agency servicing children with disabilities and their families. Sibling support services are provided via newsletters and sibling groups. Also recreational technology resources and family support programs. State funded infant program services for children aged birth to 3.

258 New Jersey Protection and Advocacy (NJP&A)

210 S Broad Street
Trenton, NJ 08608   609-292-9742
800-922-7233
FAX 609-777-0187
TDY:800-852-7899
http://www.njpanda.org
e-mail: advoc@njpanda.org
Sarah W Miyvhrll, Executive Director

NJP&A is a private nonprofit consumer driven organization established to advocate for and protect the civil, human, and legal rights of citizens of New Jersey with disabilities.

259 New Jersey Special Parent Assistance and Resources for Kids for Life & Education (SPARKLE)

201-289-0169
http://www.geocities.com/sparkleofucp
e-mail: sparkleofucp@yahoo.com
Michelle Evan, Co-Founder

SPARKLE is a network of support for parents of special needs children of all disabilities by providing social and recreational activities for the entire family, local friendship circles, respite resources and creating a network for parents in a friendly environment to help one another. SPARKLE provides information and referrals regarding resources, education/workshops, advocacy and awareness.

New Mexico

260 International Dyslexia Association of New Mexico

PO Box 25891
Albuquerque, NM 87125   505-255-8234
FAX 505-262-8547
http://www.interdys.org
e-mail: swlda@southwestlda.com
Linda Curry, President

Committed to the training of teachers and other professionals in appropriate instructional methods for individuals with dyslexia. Provides a 24-hour hotline with information and assistance for dyslexia related problems. There are eight regional offices: Gallup 772-2844, Farmington 326-1525, Taos 776-8279, Las Cruces, 525-8076, Hobbs 393-6269, Silver City 535-2399, El Paso 915-921-6835, Santa Fe 995 0801. Offers support with tutor/diagnostic referrals, conferences/events and college scholarships.

261 Learning Disabilities Association of New Mexico: Las Cruces

PO Box 20001/3SPE
Las Cruces, NM 88003   505-646-5971
FAX 505-867-3398
http://http://education.nmsu.edu/projects/NMLDA
e-mail: epoel@nmsu.edu
Dr Elissa Wolfe Poel, President
Pam Gough, Vice-President

A nonprofit organization of volunteers including individuals with learning disabilities. Dedicated to identifying causes and promoting prevention of learning disabilities and enhancing the quality of life for individuals with LD by encouraging effective identification and intervention, fostering research, protecting rights under the law. LDA seeks to accomplish this through awareness, advocacy, empowerment, education, service and collaboarative efforts.

262 Learning Disabilities Association of New Mexico: Albuquerque

6301 Menaul Boulevard NE
Albuquerque, NM 87110   505-851-2545
http://www.vivanewmexico.com/nm/nmldal
Patricia Davies Useem, President

New York

263 Advocates for Children of New York

151 W 30th Street
New York, NY 10001   212-947-9779
FAX 212-947-9790
http://www.advocatesforchildren.org
e-mail: info@advocatesforchildren.org

Works on behalf of children from infancy to the age of 21 who are at greatest risk for school-based discrimination and academic failure.

264 Attention Deficit Disorder of Westchester County

10 W Hyatt Avenue
Mount Kisco, NY 10549   914-241-0682
FAX 914-241-0684

Helps and guides people on how to cope with ADD.

265 Developmental Disability Center of New York

St. Lukes-Roosevelt Hospital
New York, NY 10019   212-523-6230
FAX 212-523-6241
http://none
Dr. Steven Wolf, Director

Working in neurology. Offers pre-school program.

266 International Dyslexia Association of Suffolk County

728 Route 25A
Northport, NY 11768   631-423-7834
FAX 631-261-7834
http://www.interdys.org/3-suff.stm
e-mail: ckent@optonline.net
Carol Kent, President

Our objectives are to increase awareness of dyslexia in the community; provide support for parents and teachers; promote teacher training. We offer a telephone message system for information requests; sponsor an annual conference and four topic workshops as well as a summer Orton-Gillingham course. We have a network of local school officials, parents, attorneys and other professionals to help parents navigate the channels of the school system.

267 International Dyslexia Association: Buffalo Branch

c/o Gow School
South Wales, NY 14139   716-687-2030
http://www.interdys.org
e-mail: bufida@gow.org
Kathy Rose, President

Strives to be a resource for information and services that address the full scope of dyslexia in a way that builds cooperation, partnership and understanding among professional communities and dyslexic individuals so that everyone is valued and has the opportunity to be productive and fulfilled in life. Newsletter and teacher training scholarships.

268 International Dyslexia Association: New York

71 W 23rd Street
New York, NY 10010   212-691-1930
                         FAX 212-633-1620
http://www.interdys.org/3-ny.stm
e-mail: info@nybida.org
Pat Rudick, President
Linda Selvin, Executive Director

This is a nonprofit organization whose mission is to provide continuing education in appropriate diagnostic remedial approaches and to support the rights of people with dyslexia in order that they may lead fulfilling lives. To this end, the NYB-IDA disseminates information, publishes a quarterly newsletter, and provides information and referral services, teacher training, conferences, adult support groups, and workshops for parents. Annual teen conference.

269 International Dyslexia Association: Troy, New York Branch

Capital District Regional Group
1046 Madison Avenue
Troy, NY 12180   518-272-4064
e-mail: ldteams@taconic.net

An international, nonprofit, scientific and educational organization dedicated to the study of dyslexia.

270 Learning Disabilites Association of Central New York

722 West Manlium Street
East Syracuse, NY 13057   313-432-0665
                              800-253-2269
                         FAX 315-431-0606
http://www.ldacny.org
e-mail: LDACNY@LDACYN.org
Agnes Gavin, Executive Director

We provide many services at no cost to clients including educational consultations about LD/ADD to assist parents; adult services including consultations with a coordinator for education, employment, housing and finances; adult recreation with an emphasis on social skills and outings; referral services including tutors, psychologists, counselors, evaluations. We have a library, an A/V resource center and employment services.

271 Learning Disabilites Association: New York Capital Region

2995 Curry Road Extension
Schenectady, NY 12303   518-356-6410
                         FAX 518-356-3603
                         TDY:518-356-6331
http://www.wildwood.edu
e-mail: LDACNY@LDACYN.org
Ms Linda A Mensching-Quinn, Executive Director
Ms Marie Gunner, Director Family Support Services

Sponsors Wildwood Programs for children and adults with LD, autism and other neurological disabilities. Programs include: Wildwood School—Preschool through Young Adult; Camp Wildwood; Wildwood Recreational Services, such as Saturday recreation, Thursday evening teen community center, and nights and weekend adult recreation; Wildwood Family Services and Service Coordination; Wildwood Residential Services; Employment/Vocational Services; and Captain's Choice small business employment opportunity.

272 Learning Disabilities Association of Kenmore/Fredonia, New York

2555 Elmwood Avenue
Kenmore, NY 14217   716-874-7200
                         FAX 716-874-7205
http://www.members@aol.com/ldaofwny/home/html
e-mail: LDAofWNY@aol.com
Mike Helman, President

To create conditions under which persons with learning disabilities, neurological impairments, and developmental disabilities are given opportunities to make choices and develop and achieve independence. The association also addresses each individual's health, future, participation in the community, and personal relationships. LDA Southern Fredonia Tier branch can be reached at 716-679-1601.

273 Learning Disabilities Association of NewYork City

27 W 20th Street
New York, NY 10011   212-645-6730
                         FAX 212-924-8896
http://www.learningdisabilitynyc.org
e-mail: ldanyc@verizon.net
Stephen Baldwin, Executive Director

The Learning Disabilities Association of New York City is a non profit, citywide organization affiliated with the Learning Disabilities Association of New York State and the Learning Disabilities Association of America. The Association is dedicated to facilitating access to needed services for individuals with learning disabilities and to providing support for those individuals and their families. All services are provided at no cost to consumers.

274 Learning Disabilities Association: Albany

90 S Swan Street
Albany, NY 12210   518-436-4633
                         FAX 518-432-5902
e-mail: lda@associationresources.org

A nonprofit organization whose members are individuals with learning disabilities, their families, and the professionals who work with them.

275 Learning Disabilities of the Genesee Valley

339 East Avenue
Rochester, NY 14604   585-263-3323
http://www.ldagvi.org
e-mail: info@ldagvi.org

James Buchholz, President
Timothy McNamara, VP
Margaret Mecredy, Secretary

Providing ongoing parent/student support services including after school and saturday programs, summer recreation, GED/Adult Education, library, movies, sports events, concerts, miniature golf, bowling and employment services. We offer comprehensive Service Coordination to develop, implement and maintain an Individualized Service Plan (ISP) that covers the spectrum of a person's life and functions as a daily guide.

276   National Center for Learning Disabilities (NCLD)

381 Park Avenue S
New York, NY   10016   212-545-7510
                                     888-575-7373
                        FAX 212-545-9665
                        http://www.ld.org
                        e-mail: help@ncld.org
Sheldon Horowitz EdD, Director Professional Services

Provides national leadership in support of children and adults with learning disabilities by offering information and an online resource locator, developing and supporting innovative educational programs, such as Get Ready to Read! (including an early literacy screening tool), providing leadership in guiding policy in Washington, and promoting awareness of learning disabilities.

277   New York Easter Seal Society

230 Washington Avenue
Albany, NY   12206
                                     800-727-8785
                        FAX 518-456-5094
                 http://www.ny.easter-seals.org
James Berry, Director

Although it was created to help polio victims, the New York Easter Seal society now helps children and adults disabled from any cause to live independently if living in New York State.

278   Resources for Children with Special Needs in New York

116 E 16th Street
New York, NY   10003   212-677-4650
                        FAX 212-254-4070
                 http://www.resourcesnyc.org
                 e-mail: info@resourcesnyc.org
Karen Thoreson Schlesinger, Executive Director
Helene F Crane, Associate Director

An independent, nonprofit organization that provides information and referral, case management and support, individual and systemic advocacy, parent and professional training and library services to New York City parents and caregivers of children with disabilities and special needs and to professionals who work with them. Our publications include: Camps 2004; After School and more; The Comprehensive Directory; and Schools for Children with Autism Spectrum Disorders.

279   Strong Center for Developmental Disabilities

Golisano Children's Hospital at Strong
601 Elmwood Avenue
Rochester, NY   14642   585-275-0355
                        FAX 585-275-3366
            http://www.urmc.rochester.edu/gchas/div/scdd
                 e-mail: scdd@cc.urmc.rochester.edu
Philip W Davidson PhD, Chief

Strong is a University Center of Excellence for Developmental Disabilaity, Education, Research, Service and a federally designated interdisciplinary division of the Department of Pediatrics involving faculty, students, departments, schools of the University of Rochester and area institutions of higher learning. Interdisciplinary diagnoses and treatment are provided to children and adults with developmental disabilities and their families from the western New York region.

280   Westchester Institute for Human Development

Westchester Medical Center
Cedarwood Hall
Valhalla, NY   10595   914-493-8202
                        FAX 914-493-1973
                 http://www.nymc.edu/wyhd
                 e-mail: WIHD@nymc.edu
Ansley Bacon, Director
David O'Hara, Associate Director

Enhances the quality of life of individuals with or at risk for disabilities, and their families. We believe that all people have the right to live independently, enjoy self-determination, contribute to society, and participate fully in the mainstream of daily life. Our work is based on a vision of a society that includes individuals with disabilities as full participants, valued citizens and friends.

North Carolina

281   All Kinds of Minds of North Carolina

1450 NC Highway 54 W
Chapel Hill, NC   27517   919-933-8082
                        FAX 919-843-9955
                 http://www.allkindsofminds.org
Robert Evans, Presidesnt
Mel Levine, MD, Co-Chair
Charles R Schwab, Co-Chair

Helps students measurably improve their success in school and in life by providing programs that integrate educational, scientific expertise. Our goal is to make the Institute's programs and services broadly accessible to parents, teachers, clinicians and students who struggle with differences in learning, and to change the educational environment supporting these children.

282   Learning Disabilities Association of North Carolina (LDANC)

PO Box 68084
Raleigh, NC   27613   919-493-5362
                        FAX 919-489-0788
                 http://www.Idanc.org
                 e-mail: idanc@mindspring.com
Pat Lillie, Director

For 29 years, LDANC has been committed to improving the lives of, and serving as a voice for, all persons in the state with learning disabilities and or attention disorders. Branches: Asheville: 828-250-5317; Charlotte: 704-542-0470; Dare County: vgrist@mindspring.com; Guilford County: 336-855-5900; Orange County: bmblack@email.unc.edu; Eastern Carolina: 252-321-1111; Wake County: 919-616-8766; Winston-Salem: 336-722-6810.

North Dakota

283 **Learning Disabilities Association of North Dakota**
409 3rd Avenue NW
Mandan, ND 58554   701-222-1490
                              FAX 701-222-1490

Jane Greer, President

A nonprofit organization whose members are individuals with learning disabilities, their families, and the professionals who work with them.

Ohio

284 **Easter Seals: Youngstown, Ohio**
299 Edwards Street
Youngstown, OH 44502   330-743-1168
                           FAX 330-743-1616
                           TDY:330-743-1168
              http://www.mtc.easter-seals.org
Karen J Sklenar CHE, President/CEO
Bill Addington, Conatct

Occupational, physical and speech therapy available.

285 **Learning Disabilities Association of Central Ohio**
PO Box 835
Worthington, OH 43085
                              614-436-9266
                           FAX 614-436-7450

Elliot Resnick, President

Oklahoma

286 **Learning Disabilities Association of Oklahoma**
PO Box 2315
Stillwater, OK 74076
                              800-532-6365
                           FAX 405-377-4745
                       http://www.ldao.com
                    e-mail: lado@fullnet.net

Susan Parker, President

287 **University Affiliated Program of Oklahoma (UAP)**
College of Medicine
PO Box 26901
Oklahoma City, OK 73190   405-271-4500
                                800-627-6827
                           FAX 405-271-1459
                           TDY:405-271-1464
                         http://www.ouhsc.edu
            e-mail: firstname-lastname@ouhsc.edu
Valerie Williams, Director

The UAP is a federally designated organization dedicated to promoting the independence, productivity and inclusion of people with disabilities in the life of the community. The core value of the UAP is to build an accepting, respectful and accessible environment for all.

Oregon

288 **Eugene Easter Seal Service Center**
3575 Donald Street
Eugene, OR 97405   541-344-2247
                                800-224-5289
                           FAX 541-687-0803
Helps individuals with disabilities and special needs, and their families, live better lives.

289 **International Dyslexia Association: Oregon Branch (ORBIDA)**
PO Box 3677
Portland, OR 97208   503-228-4455
                                800-530-2234
                           FAX 503-228-3152
              http://www.aracnet.com/~orbida
                  e-mail: orbida@aracnet.com
Gary Wright, President

An international 501(c)(3) nonprofit, scientific and educational organization dedicated to the study and treatment of dyslexia. All branches hold at least one public meeting, workshop or conference per year.

290 **International Dyslexia Society: Oregon Branch**
PO Box 3677
Portland, OR 97208   503-228-4455
                           FAX 503-228-3152

Elizabeth Barton, President

An international nonprofit, scientific and educational organization dedicated to the study of dyslexia.

291 **Learning Disabilities Association of Oregon: Portland**
1734 NE 55th Avenue
Portland, OR 97213   503-731-4793
                           FAX 503-731-3466
     http://www.Idana.org/Oregon/LDAwebpage1.html
            e-mail: mudjekeewis@hotmail.com
Vicki Williams, Secretary

Works to promote the welfare of children and adults with learning disabilities. LDA of Oregon, affiliated with the national Learning Disabilities Association of America, is a nonprofit organization that serves as a resource, referral, and information center for adults with learning disabilities, parents of children with learning disabilities, and professionals working in the field of learning disabilities.

292 **Learning Disabilities Association of Oregon: Beaverton**

PO Box 1221
Beaverton, OR 97008   503-641-3768
FAX 503-641-3769
http://www.ldanetl.org/
e-mail: Oregon@LDAwebpage1.html
Donna Newton, President

A nonprofit organization whose members are individuals with learning disabilities, their families, and the professionals who work with them.

293 **Oregon Disabilities Commission**

1257 Ferry Street SE
Salem, OR 97310   503-378-3142
800-358-3117
FAX 503-378-3599
http://www.oda.state.or.us/
Janine DeLaunay, Executive Director
Danielle Knight, Office Assistant

State ADA coordinator and building code advisor offers resources and advice to the governor and state legislative on disability issues.

294 **University of Oregon for Excellence in Developmental Disabilities**

Center on Human Development College of Education
5252 University of Education
Eugene, OR 97403   541-346-3591
FAX 541-346-2594
http://www.uoregon.edu/~uocedd/
Jane Squires, Associate Director

To improve quality of life for persons with developmental disabilities and their families within community settings.

Pennsylvania

295 **Adult Basic Educational Development Programs in Pennsylvania**

Philadelphia Library for the Blind
919 Walnut Street
Philadelphia, PA 19107   215-683-3213
FAX 215-683-3211
Jill Gross, Director

Adult basic education, GED classes and GED testing for the disabled.

296 **Easter Seal Society of Beaver County**

997 Route 228
Mars, PA 16046   724-776-9400
FAX 724-776-4830

Helps children and adults with disabilities expand their independence.

297 **Easter Seal Society of Western Pennsylvania: Fayette Division**

141 Oakland Avenue
Uniontown, PA 15401   724-437-4047
FAX 724-437-5485
Alice G Young, Division Director

Speech, language, learning disabilities and hearing evaluations and therapy for all ages. PA licensed preschool on the premises. Open five days per week; 12 months. Call for an appointment or information on the programs provided.

298 **Huntingdon County PRIDE**

307 10th Street
Huntingdon, PA 16652   814-643-5724
FAX 814-643-6085
e-mail: pride@huntingdon.net
Sandra Bair, Executive Director

Speech evaluation and therapy, occupational therapy, advocacy, equipment, self-determination, specific assistance, home modification consulting, summer recreation, therapeutic horseback riding and swimming, social/recreation, information and referral.

299 **Learning Disabilities Association of Pennsylvania (LDA)**

Toomey Building
Uwchland, PA 19480   610-458-8193
http://www.ldanet.org/Pennsylvania/Index.html
Anna Mary McHugh, President

LDA of Pennsylvania is a nonprofit organization of dedicated individuals whose mission is to promote quality education and to support the general welfare of children and adults with learning disabilities.

300 **Pennsylcania Center for Disability Law and Policy**

1617 JFK Boulevard
Philadelphia, PA 19103   215-557-7112
800-742-8877
FAX 215-557-7602
http://www.equalemployment.org/
e-mail: info@equalemployment.org
Stephen Pennington Esquire, Director
Jamie Ray Esquire, Managing Attorney

CDLP provides advocacy and legal representation to persons with disabilities in employment, disability rights and education areas.

301 **Philadelphia Dyslexia Association**

PO Box 251
Bryn Mawr, PA 19010   610-527-1548
FAX 610-527-5011
http://www.gpbida.org
e-mail: dyslexia@gpbida.org
Marianne Cook, President

A nonprofit, scientific and educational organization dedicated to the study of dyslexia.

South Carolina

302 **International Dyslexia Association: South Carolina Branch**

213 Hominy Hills Drive
Six Mile, SC 29682 803-772-8065
FAX 803-772-8065

Felicia Robbins, President

An international 501(c)(3) nonprofit, scientific and educational organization dedicated to the study and treatment of dyslexia. All branches hold at least one public meeting, workshop or conference per year.

303 **Literacy Volunteers of America: Laurence County**

221 W Laurens Street
Laurens, SC 29360 864-984-0466
FAX 864-984-2920
e-mail: lclc@backroads.net

JoAn Boehm

Laurence County Literacy Council promotes literacy for people of all ages in Laurence County.

304 **South Carolina Center for Disability Resourses: Department of Pediatrics**

University of South Carolina School of Medicine
8301 Farrow Road
Columbia, SC 29203 803-935-5231
FAX 803-935-5059
http://www.cdd.sc.edu

Richard A Ferrante, Director

Committed to promoting the independence, productivity, and inclusion of persons with a wide range of disabilities.

South Dakota

305 **Learning Disabilities Association of South Dakota**

PO Box 9760
Rapid City, SD 57709 605-388-9291
888-388-5553
http://www.geocities.com/athens/ithaca/8835
e-mail: dthom@rapidnet.com
Dee Thompson, Executive Director

The Association conducts workshops and conferences, assists local communities, collaborates with other organizations with similar missions and concerns, and provides 1-on-1 assistance to individuals and families. Most visible among its efforts is the Association's statewide annual conference.

306 **South Dakota Center for Disabilities**

1400 W 22nd Street
Sioux Falls, SD 57105 605-357-1439
800-658-3080
FAX 605-357-1438
http://www.usd.edu/cd
Judy Struck, Executive Director

Center focuses on academic training, community education and technical assistance, information dissemination, research and evaluation, and services and support.

Tennessee

307 **International Dyslexia Association: Tennessee Branch**

PO Box 22014
Knoxville, TN 37933 865-769-0770
877-836-6432
FAX 615-353-6412
http://www.interdys.org/3-tn.stm
Susan M Smartt PhD

The Tennessee Branch of the International Dyslexia Association was formed to increase awareness about dyslexia in the state of Tennessee. TNBIDA supports efforts to provide individuals with dyslexia-appropriate instruction and to identify individuals at-risk for dyslexia before they enter first grade. IDA and TNBIDA believe that multisensory sequential structured language teaching is one of the best approaches currently available.

308 **International Dyslexia Society: Tennessee West/Middle Tennessee Branch**

6525 Brownlee Drive
Nashville, TN 37205
877-836-6432
FAX 615-353-6412
http://www.tn-interdys.org
Susan Smartt, President

An international nonprofit, scientific and educational organization dedicated to the study of dyslexia.

309 **Recording for the Blind & Dyslexic: Tennessee Chapter**

205 Badger Road
Oak Ridge, TN 37830 865-482-3496
FAX 865-483-9934
http://www.rfbd.org
e-mail: kperry@rfbd.org
Brian Jenkins, Executive Director
Karen Perry, Outreach Director

Part of the national, nonprofit organization which records educational and career-related materials for print impaired students and professionals. The special focus is educational books. Blind and other print impaired students at every level, from elementary through graduate school, depend on RFBD tapes for the texts they need.

Texas

310 **Easter Seals of Central Texas**
919 W 28 1/2 Street
Austin, TX 78705   512-478-2581
                                    FAX 512-476-1638
            http://www.eastersealstx.com/index2.html
Sharon Miller, President/CEO
Pam Brooks, Outpatient Rehabilitation Dir.

Easter Seals - Central Texas creates solutions and
changes lives of children and adults with disabilities.

311 **Easter Seals of Greater Dallas**
4443 N Josey Lane
Carrollton, TX 75010   972-394-8900
                                    FAX 972-394-6266
            http://www.easterseals.com
            e-mail: info@easterseals.com
To help children and adults with disabilities and special needs achieve their highest level of independence
and self-esteem, regardless of ability to pay.

312 **Learning Disabilities Association of Texas**
1011 W 31st Street
Austin, TX 78705   512-458-8234
                                     800-604-7500
                                    FAX 512-458-3826
            http://www.ldattx.com
            e-mail: ldatexas@cs.com
Ann Robinson, State Coordinator

Support, information and referral services for persons
with learning disabilities, their families and the professionals who serve them.

313 **Learning Disabilities Association: El Paso Council**
8929 Viscount Boulevard
El Paso, TX 79925   915-591-8080
                                    FAX 915-591-8150
Lina Monroy, Executive Director

Support, information and referral services for persons
with learning disabilities, their families and the professionals who serve them.

314 **North Texas Rehabilitation Center**
1005 Midwestern Parkway
Wichita Falls, TX 76302   940-322-0771
                                    FAX 940-766-4943
            http://www.ntrehab.org
Kathy Mickus, Child Achievement Supervisor

A rehabilitation center for people with disabilities.
Physical therapy, occupational therapy, speech language therapy, and academic services available.

Utah

315 **Learning Disabilities Association of Utah**
PO Box 520232
Salt Lake City, UT 84152   801-363-6320
                                    FAX 801-363-6332
            http://www.ldau.org
            e-mail: LDAU@madmac.com
Bonnie Hussey, Executive Secretary

A nonprofit association that promises the independence, dignity and well-being of persons through programs, resource materials and services for individuals
and professionals.

Vermont

316 **Learning Disabilities Association of Vermont**
PO Box 1041
Manchester Center, VT 05255   802-362-3127
                                    FAX 802-362-3128
Christina Thurston, President

A nonprofit organization whose members are individuals with learning disabilities, their families, and the
professionals who work with them.

317 **Vermont Protection and Advocacy**
141 Main Street
Montpelier, VT 05602   802-229-1355
                                     800-834-7890
                                    FAX 802-229-1359
            http://www.vtpa.org
            e-mail: info@vtpa.org
Christopher Holliday, Supervising Attorney

Mission is to defend and advance the rights of people
who have been labeled mentally ill.

Virginia

318 **Learning Disabilities Association of Virginia**
3115 17th Street N
Arlington, VA 22201   703-243-2614
                                    FAX 703-243-0894
            http://www.ldanatl.org/Virginia
            e-mail: info@ldavirginia.org
A nonprofit organization whose members are individuals with learning disabilities, their families, and the
professionals who work with them.

Washington

319 Learning Disabilities Association of Washington

7819 159th Place NE
Redmond, WA 98052   425-882-0820
                            800-536-2343
                      FAX 425-861-4642
                      http://www.ldawa.org
                      e-mail: dsiegel@ldawa.org
Phil Mortenson, President

Promotes and provides services and support to improve the quality of life for individuals and families affected by learning and attentional disabilities.

320 Washington Parent Training Project: PAVE

6316 S 12th Street
Tacoma, WA 98465   253-565-2266
                           800-572-7368
                      FAX 253-566-8052
                      TDY:253-569-2266
                      http://www.washingtonpave.org
                      e-mail: wapave9@washingtonpave.com
Joanne Butts, Executive Director

PAVE helps parents understand their child's school program and to become their child's best advocate. The parent resource coordinators on staff, all of whom are parents of children with disabilities, help other parents learn about the rights of children with special learning needs.

321 Washington Protection & Advocacy Agency

1401 E Jefferson
Seattle, WA 98122   206-324-1521
                            800-562-2702
                      FAX 425-776-0601
Mark Stroh, Executive Director

West Virginia

322 Learning Disabilities Association of West Virginia

850 Somerset Drive
Charleston, WV 25302   304-344-0252
                          FAX 304-344-0252
Jane Crist, President

A nonprofit organization whose members are individuals with learning disabilities, their families, and the professionals who work with them.

Wisconsin

323 Easter Seals of Southeast Wisconsin

3090 N 53rd Street
Milwaukee, WI 53210   414-449-4444
                         FAX 414-449-4447
                      e-mail: agency@wi-se.easter-seals.org
Timothy Bionds, Executive Director
Michelle Gardner, VP Programs

Two child development centers in southeast Wisconsin offer an integrated environment for children ages 6 weeks-12 years. Birth-Three Early Intervention Services provide speech, physical, and occupational therapies. After School Recreation Program provides recreational activities for ages 12-21 with a range of disabilities. The Adult Recreation program offers classes and recreation opportunities to adults with disabilities. Call for additiional programs.

324 International Dyslexia Association: Wisconsin Branch

1614 Laurel Crest
Madison, WI 53705   608-238-4343
                      FAX 608-238-6093
                      e-mail: bbliss@chorus.net
Barbara Blissz, CEO Assoc Orton-Gillingham Tutor
Nira Scherz-Busch

Clearinghouse for information on dyslexia. Offers information on testing and tutoring throughout the state. Has lists of Wisconsin residents who have been trained to tutor using the Orton-Gillingham method. Also trains teachers and parents to use this method. There is a Dane County Dyslexia Support Group meeting 3rd Tuesday of every month.

National Programs

325   Attention Deficit Disorder Association

PO Box 543
Pottstown, PA   19464   484-945-2101
                                     FAX 610-970-7520
                                     http://www.add.org
                                     e-mail: mail@add.org
Michele Novotni PhD, President
Robert Tudisco, VP
David Giwerc, VP

A national nonprofit organization that provides information, resources and networking to adults with AD/HD.

326   Attention Deficit Disorder Warehouse

300 NW 70th Avenue
Plantation, FL   33317   954-792-8100
                                     800-233-9273
                                     FAX 954-792-8545
                                     http://www.addwarehouse.com
                                     e-mail: sales@addwarehouse.com

Comprehensive collection of ADHD-related books, videos, training programs, games, professional texts and assessment products. Because of its tremendous depth, and the quality of the products we carry, our catalog is a recommended source of help in practically every book written on ADHD, and is provided to patients by hundreds of health professionals across the country.

327   Attention Deficit Information Network

58 Prince Street
Needham, MA   02492   781-455-9895
                                     http://www.addinfonetwork.com
                                     e-mail: adin@gis.net

A nonprofit volunteer organization that offers support and information to families of children and adults with ADD, and to professionals.

328   Children and Adults with Attention Deficit Hyperactivity Disorder (CHADD)

8181 Professional Place
Landover, MD   20785   301-306-7070
                                     800-233-4050
                                     FAX 301-306-7090
                                     http://www.chadd.org
                                     e-mail: national@chadd.org
Mary Durheim, President

CHADD is a national nonprofit organization providing education, advocacy and support for individuals with AD/HD.

329   Dyslexia Research Institute

5746 Centerville Road
Tallahassee, FL   32309   850-893-2216
                                     FAX 850-893-2440
                                     http://www.dyslexia-add.org
                                     e-mail: dri@dyslexia-add.org
Patrica K Hardman PhD, Director
Robyn A Rennick MS, Assistant Director

Addresses academic, social and self-concept issues for dyslexic and ADD children and adults. College prep courses, study skills, advocacy, diagnostic testing, seminars, teacher training, day school, tutoring and an adult literacy and life skills program is available using an accredited MSLE approach.

330   Learning Disabilities Association of America

4156 Library Road
Pittsburgh, PA   15234   412-341-1515
                                     888-3—6710
                                     FAX 412-344-0224
                                     http://www.ldaamerica.org
                                     e-mail: info@ldaamerica.org
Jane Browning, Executive Director
Marianne Toombs, President
Suzanne Fornaro, VP

An information and referral center for parents and professionals dealing with Attention Deficit Disorders, and other learning disabilities. Free materials and referral service to nearest chapter.

331   School Based Assessment of Attention Deficit Disorders

Nat'l Clearinghouse of Rehab. Training Materials
206 W 6th Street
Stillwater, OK   74078   405-744-2000
                                     800-223-5219
                                     FAX 405-744-2001
                                     TDY:405-744-2002
                                     http://www.nchrtm.okstate.edu
                                     e-mail: ahlerti@okstate.edu

To promote the exchange of information and enhance the outcome of the public rehabilitation program by collecting, archiving and disseminating the rehabilitation training materials developed by Rehabilitation Services Administration Grantees.

Publications

332   ADD Challenge: A Practical Guide for Teachers

Research Press
PO Box 9177
Champaign, IL   61826   217-352-3273
                                     800-519-2707
                                     FAX 217-352-1221
                                     http://www.researchpress.com
                                     e-mail: rp@researchpress.com
Ann Wendell, President

Provides educators with practical information about the needs and treatment of children and adolescents with ADD. The book addresses the defining characteristics of ADD, common treatment approaches, myths about ADD, matching intervention to student, use of behavior-rating scales and checklists evaluating interventions, regular verses, special class placement, helps students regulate their own behavior and more. Case examples are used throughout. *$17.95*

196 pages
ISBN 0-878223-45-2

333 ADD and Adults: Strategies for Success

CHADD
8181 Professional Place
Landover, MD 20785   301-306-7070
                                 800-233-4050
                                 FAX 301-306-7090
                                 http://www.chadd.org
                                 e-mail: national@chadd.org
Mary Durheim, President

A series of articles written by many of the nation's leading experts. Includes important topics/issues such as: Diagnosing ADD in Adults; Coaching, Anger Management Training, Succeeding in the Workplace with ADD; Adults with ADD and the Military; Using Strategies and Services for Success in College; Interpersonal and Social Problems in Adults with ADD, and much more. *$19.00*

118 pages

334 ADD and Creativity: Tapping Your Inner Muse

Taylor Publishing
1550 W Mockingbird Lane
Dallas, TX 75235   214-637-2800
                                 800-677-2800
                                 FAX 214-819-8580

Lynn Weiss, PhD, Author

Raises and answers questions about the dynamic between the two components and shows how they can be a wonderful gift but also a painful liability if not properly handled. Real-life stories and inspirational affirmations throughout.

Paperback
ISBN 0-878339-60-4

335 ADD and Romance: Finding Fulfillment in Love, Sex and Relationships

Taylor Publishing
1550 W Mockingbird Lane
Dallas, TX 75235   214-637-2800
                                 800-677-2800
                                 FAX 214-819-8580
Jonathan Scott Halverstadt, Author

A look at how attention deficit disorder can damage romantic relationships when partners do not take time, or do not know how to address this problem. This book provides the tools needed to build and sustain a more satisfying relationship.

240 pages   Paperback
ISBN 0-878332-09-0

336 ADD and Success

Taylor Publishing
1550 W Mockingbird Lane
Dallas, TX 75235   214-637-2800
                                 800-677-2800
                                 FAX 214-819-8580
Lynn Weiss, PhD, Author

Presents the stories of 13 individuals and their experiences and challenges of living with adult attention disorder and achieving success.

224 pages   Paperback
ISBN 0-878339-94-9

337 ADD in Adults

Taylor Publishing
1550 W Mockingbird Lane
Dallas, TX 75235   214-637-2800
                                 800-677-2800
                                 FAX 214-819-8580
Lynn Weiss, PhD, Author

Updated version of this best-selling book on the topic of ADD helps others to understand and live with the issues related to ADD.

Paperback
ISBN 0-878339-79-5

338 ADD: Helping Your Child

Warner Books
1271 Avenue of the Americas
New York, NY 10020   212-484-2900
                                 FAX 212-484-3860
                                 http://www.twbookmark.com
Warren Umansky, Author
Barbara S Smalley, Author

This guide to an organic condition that affects between three and ten percent of grade-school children is designed to help parents obtain accurate diagnosis, improve their child's self-esteem, develop classroom strategies, and become informed about medicine. *$10.99*

244 pages   Paperback
ISBN 0-446670-13-8

339 ADHD

Learning Disabilities Association of America
4156 Library Road
Pittsburgh, PA 15234   412-341-1515
                                 FAX 412-344-0224
                                 http://www.ldanatl.org
                                 e-mail: info@ldaamerica.org
Larry B Silver, MD, Author

A booklet for parents offering information on Attention Deficit-Hyperactivity Disorders and learning disabilities. *$3.95*

340 ADHD Challenge Newsletter

PO Box 2277
West Newbury, MA 01960
                                 800-233-2322
                                 FAX 800-233-2322
Jean C Harrison, Executive Director

National newsletter on ADD/ADHD that presents interviews with nationally-known scientists, as well as physicians, psychologists, social workers, educators, and other practitioners in the field of ADHD. *$35.00*

12 pages   Bimonthly

341 ADHD Report

Guilford Publications
72 Spring Street
New York, NY 10012   212-431-9800
800-365-7006
FAX 212-966-6708
http://www.guilford.com
e-mail: info@guilford.com

Presents the most up-to-date information on the evaluation, diagnosis and management of ADHD in children, adolescents and adults. This important newsletter is an invaluable resource for all professionals interested in ADHD. *$77.00*

Bimonthly
ISSN 1065-8025

342 Attention Deficit Disorder in Adults Workbook

Taylor Publishing
1550 W Mockingbird Lane
Dallas, TX 75235   214-637-2800
800-677-2800
FAX 214-819-8580
http://www.taylorpub.com/index1.html
Lynn Weiss, Author

Dr. Lynn Weiss's best-selling Attention Deficit Disorder In Adults has sold over 125,000 copies since its publication in 1991. This updated volume still contains all the original information — how to tell if you have ADD, ways to master distraction, ADD's impact on the family, and more—plus the newest treatments available. *$17.99*

192 pages Paperback
ISBN 0-878338-50-0

343 Attention Deficit Disorder: A Concise Source of Information for Parents

Temeron Books
PO Box 896
Bellingham, WA 98227   360-738-4016
FAX 360-738-4016
http://www.temerondetselig.com
e-mail: temeron@telusplanet.net
H Moghadam, MD and Joel Fagan, MD, Author

The authors travel from a brief historical review of ADD, through a description of symptoms and consequences, to a discussion of treatment. *$15.95*

128 pages Paperback
ISBN 1-550590-82-0

344 Attention Deficit Disorder: A Different Perception

Underwood-Miller
708 Westover Drive
Lancaster, PA 17601   717-285-2255
FAX 717-285-2255
Thomas Hartmann, Author

Attention Deficit Disorder is a disease that stigmatizes millions of Americans and causes many of them to fail—first in school, then later in adult life. It has been estimated that 90% of the prison population has ADD. This book takes a unique look at the disorder, suggesting that it is not really a disease, but rather an evolutionary adaptation to life in a hunting society. *$9.95*

180 pages Paperback
ISBN 0-887331-56-4

345 Attention Deficit Disorders: Assessment & Teaching

Brooks/Cole Publishing Company
511 Forest Lodge Road
Pacific Grove, CA 93950   831-373-0728
FAX 831-375-6414
Janet W Lerner, et al., Author

Paperback $18.95
ISBN 0-534250-44-0

346 Attention Deficit Hyperactivity Disorder: Handbook for Diagnosis & Treatment

Western Psychological Services
12031 Wilshire Boulevard
Los Angeles, CA 90025   310-478-2061
800-648-8857
FAX 310-478-7838
http://www.wpspublish.com/
Russell A Barkley, PhD, Author

This second edition helps clinicians diagnose and treat Attention Deficit Hyperactivity Disorder. Written by an internationally recognized authority in the field, it covers the history of ADHD, its primary symptoms, associated conditions, developmental course and outcome, and family context. A workbook companion manual is also available.

700 pages Hardcover

347 Attention Deficit-Hyperactivity Disorder: Is It a Learning Disability?

Georgetown University, School of Medicine
37th and O Street NW
Washington, DC 20007   202-687-0100
FAX 202-662-9444
Larry Silver, Author

Offers information on learning disabilities and related disorders.

348 Attention-Deficit Hyperactivity Disorder

72 Spring Street
New York, NY 10012   800-365-7006
FAX 212-966-6708
http://www.guilford.com
e-mail: info@guilford.com
Russell A Barkley, Author

Provides a comprehensive analysis of ADHD. *$55.00*

747 pages

349   CHADD Educators Manual

CHADD
8181 Professional Place
Landover, MD 20785   301-306-7070
                                             800-233-4050
                                         FAX 301-306-7090
                                         http://www.chadd.org
                                      e-mail: national@chadd.org
Mary Fowler, Author
Mary Durheim, President

An in-depth look at Attention Deficit Disorders from an educational perspective. *$10.00*

350   Children with ADD: A Shared Responsibility

Council for Exceptional Children
1110 N Glebe Road
Arlington, VA 22201   703-620-3660
                                             888-232-7733
                                         FAX 703-264-9494
                                      http://www.cec.sped.org/

This book represents a consensus of what professionals and parents believe ADD is all about and how children with ADD may best be served. Reviews the evaluation process under IDEA and 504 and presents effective classroom strategies.

35 pages
ISBN 0-865862-33-8

351   Cognitive-Behavioral Therapy with ADHD Children: Child, Family & School

Western Psychological Services
12031 Wilshire Boulevard
Los Angeles, CA 90025   310-478-2061
                                             800-648-8857
                                         FAX 310-478-7838
                                      http://www.wpspublish.com/
Lauren Braswell, Michael L Bloomquist, Author

Presents a model for treating Attention-Deficit Hyperactivity Disorder and associated disruptive behavior disorders that is uniquely sensitive to environmental and developmental factors. It applies cognitive-behavioral techniques in settings where problems actually occur — at home and at school — thus encouraging a truly effective therapeutic partnership that involves not only the child, but also the school and family. *$52.00*

391 pages

352   Coping: Attention Deficit Disorder: A Guide for Parents and Teachers

Temeron Books
PO Box 896
Bellingham, WA 98227
                                         FAX 360-738-4016
                                      http://www.temerondetselig.com
                                      e-mail: temeron@telusplanet.net
Mary Ellen Beugin, Author

The author investigates medical and behavioral interventions that can be tried with ADD children and gives suggestions on coping with these children at home and at school. *$15.95*

173 pages Paperback
ISBN 1-550590-13-8

353   Driven to Distraction: Attention Deficit Disorder from Childhood Through Adulthood

200 Glebe Road
Arlington, VA 22201   703-524-7600
                                             800-950-6264
                                         FAX 703-524-9094
                                         TDY:703-516-7227
                                         http://www.nami.org
Edward M Hallowell, Author
John Ratey, Author

Through vivid stories of the experience of their patients, Drs. Hallowell and Ratey show the varied forms ADD takes — from the hyperactive search for high stimulation to the floating inattention of daydreaming — and the transforming impact of precise diagnosis and treatment.

ISBN 0-684801-28-0

354   Dyslexia Research and Resource Guide

Books on Special Children
PO Box 305
Congers, NY 10920   413-256-8164
                                         FAX 413-256-8896
                                      http://www.boscbooks.com/
                                      e-mail: irene@boscbooks.com
CS Spafford, Author

A definitive book on dyslexia, which is defined as a reading disorder whereby an individual fails to attain reading skills. Book has resources, teaching ideas and strategies for people with LD. Other forms of LD discussed, such as memory disorders, math disabilities, ADHD, aphasia, etc. *$47.00*

340 pages hardcover
ISBN 0-205159-07-9

355   Fact Sheet-Attention Deficit Hyperactivity Disorder

Learning Disabilities Association of America
4156 Library Road
Pittsburgh, PA 15234   412-341-1515
                                         FAX 412-344-0224
                                         http://www.ldanatl.org
Marianne Toombs, President
Suzanne Fornaro, VP
Connie Parr, VP

A pamphlet offering factual information on ADHD. *$10.00*

356   Focus Magazine

Attention Deficit Disorder Association
PO Box 543
Pottstown, PA 19464   484-945-2101
                                         FAX 610-970-7520
                                         http://www.add.org
                                      e-mail: mail@add.org
Michele Novotni PhD, President
Robert Tudisco, VP
David Giwerc, VP

The National Attention Deficit Disorder Association is an organization focused on the needs of adults and young adults with ADD/ADHD, and their children and families. We seek to serve individuals with ADD, as well as those who love, live with, teach, counsel and treat them.

357 Focus Your Energy: Succeeding in Business with ADD

Pocket Books
1230 Avenue of The Americas
New York, NY   10024
212-698-7000
FAX 212-698-7007

Thom Hartmann, Author

Focus Your Energy will help you to understand and overcome the symptoms of ADD that may be holding you back, and take advantage of the traits that mark you for success. *$10.00*

Paperback
ISBN 0-671516-89-2

358 Getting a Grip on ADD: A Kid's Guide to Understanding & Coping with ADD

Educational Media Corporation
6021 Wish Avenue
Encino, CA   91316
818-708-0962
FAX 818-345-2980
http://www.educationalmedia.com

Kim T Frank, Author
Susan J Smith, Author

Help your elementary and middle school students cope more effectively with Attention Deficit Disorders. *$9.95*

64 pages   Paperback
ISBN 0-932796-60-3

359 Helping Your Child with Attention-Deficit Hyperactivity Disorder

Learning Disabilities Association of America
4156 Library Road
Pittsburgh, PA   15234
412-341-1515
FAX 412-344-0224
http://www.ldanatl.org
e-mail: ldanatl@usaor.net

Marianne Toombs, President
Suzanne Fornaro, VP
Connie Parr, VP

A parents's guide to identifying, understanding and helping your child with ADD. *$12.95*

360 Helping Your Hyperactive-Attention Deficit Child

Prima Publishing
3000 Lava Ridge Court
Roseville, CA   95661
916-787-7000
800-632-8676
FAX 916-787-7001
http://www.primapub.com

John F Taylor, Author

For parents on how to help your child with ADD. *$19.95*

ISBN 1-559584-23-8

361 How to Own and Operate an Attention Deficit Disorder

Learning Disabilities Association of America
4156 Library Road
Pittsburgh, PA   15234
412-341-1515
FAX 412-344-0224
http://www.ldanatl.org
e-mail: ldanatl@usaor.net

Marianne Toombs, President
Suzanne Fornaro, VP
Connie Parr, VP

Clear, informative and sensitive introduction to ADHD. Packed with practical things to do at home and school, the author offers her insight as a professional and mother of a son with ADHD. *$10.45*

43 pages

362 How to Teach ADD-ADHD Children

Council for Exceptional Children
1110 N Glebe Road
Arlington, VA   22201
703-620-3660
888-232-7733
FAX 703-264-9494
http://www.cec.sped.org

Practical techniques, strategies, and interventions for helping children with attention problems and hyperactivity. *$27.95*

245 pages
ISBN 0-876264-13-6

363 Hyperactive Child Book

St. Martin's Press
175 5th Avenue
New York, NY   10010
212-674-5151
800-321-9299
FAX 212-420-9314
http://www.stmartins.com

Patricia Kennedy, Author
Leif Terdal, Author
Lydia Fusetti, Author

Treating, educating and living with an ADHD child. *$12.95*

ISBN 0-312112-86-6

364 Hyperactive Child, Adolescent and Adult

Oxford University Press
198 Madison Avenue
New York, NY   10016
212-726-6000
800-451-7556
FAX 212-726-6440
http://www.aup-usa.org

Paul H Wender MD, Author

How does one know if a youngster is hyperactive? How do you know if you are hyperactive yourself? The answers may lie in this easy-to-read and comprehensive volume written by one of the leading researchers in the field. *$9.95*

172 pages

365 **Hyperactivity, Attention Deficits and School Failure: Better Ways**

Learning Disabilities Association of America
4156 Library Road
Pittsburgh, PA 15234   412-341-1515
                              FAX 412-344-0224
                              http://www.ldanatl.org
                              e-mail: ldanatl@usaor.net

$6.00

366 **International Reading Association Newspaper: Reading Today**

800 Barksdale Road
Newark, DE 19714   302-731-1600
                         FAX 302-731-1057
                         http://www.reading.org
                         e-mail: jbutler@reading.org
Janet Butler, Public Information Associate

The International Reading Association is a professional membership organization dedicated to promoting high levels of literacy for all by improving the quality of reading instruction, disseminating research and information about reading, and encouraging the lifetime reading habit. Our members include classroom teachers, reading specialists, consultants, administrators, supervisors, university faculty, researchers, psychologists, librarians, media specialistss and parents.

367 **LD Child and the ADHD Child**

John F Blair, Publisher
1406 Plaza Drive
Winston-Salem, NC 27103   336-768-1374
                                 800-222-9796
                                 FAX 336-768-9194
                                 http://www.blairpub.com
                                 e-mail: blairpub@blairpub.com
Suzanne H Stevens, Author
Ed Southern, Sales Director

The author recommends other options that can be explored to treat LD and ADHD children without drugs. *$12.95*

261 pages   Paperback
ISBN 0-895871-42-4

368 **LDA Alabama Newsletter**

Learning Disabilities Association Alabama
PO Box 11588
Montgomery, AL 36111   334-277-9151
                              FAX 334-284-9357
                              http://www.ldaal.org
                              e-mail: alabama@ldaal.org
Debbie Gibson, President

Educational, support, and advocacy group for individuals with learning disabilities and ADD.

369 **LDA Georgia Newsletter**

Learning Disabilities Association Georgia
130 W Wieuca Road
Atlanta, GA 30342   404-303-7774
                          FAX 404-303-7161
                          http://www.ldag.org
                          e-mail: services@ldag.org
Christopher Lee, Executive Diredtor
Franches Rolster, President

Information and helpful articles on learning disabilities. Mailed free four times a year to members. *$40.00*

Quarterly

370 **LDA Illinois Newsletter**

Learning Disabilities Association Illinois
10101 S Roberts Road
Palos Hills, IL 60465   708-430-7532
                               FAX 708-430-7592
                               http://www.idanatl.org/illinois
Sharon Schussler, Administrative Assistant

A nonprofit organization dedicated to the advancement of the education and general welfare of children and youth of normal or potentially normal intelligence who have perceptual, conceptual, coordinative or related learning disabilities.

371 **Maybe You Know My Kid: A Parent's Guide to Identifying ADHD**

Birch Lane Press
120 Enterprise Avenue S
Secaucus, NJ 07094   201-866-0186
                            800-447-2665
                            FAX 201-866-1886
Mary Fowler, Author

A guide for parents of children diagnosed with ADD discusses the recent changes in the education of these children and offers practical guidelines for improving educational performance. *$13.25*

222 pages

372 **Natural Therapies for Attention Deficit Hyperactivity Disorder**

Comprehensive Psychiatric Resources
831 Beacon Street
Newton Centre, MA 02459   617-332-1336
                                 FAX 617-332-9936
                                 http://www.natualadd.com
                                 e-mail: cprinc2@aol.com

A full day workshop professionally recorded on six audiotapes featuring Dr. James M. Greenblatt, M.D., neuropsychiatrist. Dr. Greenblatt explores updated research on nutrition and ADD, food additives, food allergies, fatty acids and more, provides practical treatment strategies and helps you make informed choices between effective and worthless therapies.

373 **Parent's Guide to Attention Deficit Disorders**

Dell Publishing
1540 Broadway
New York, NY 10036   212-354-6500
                            212-302-7985
                            FAX 212-782-9523
Lisa J Bain, Author

In this first book in a new series with the renowned Children's Hospital of Philadelphia, doctors at the hospital discuss the conditions known as ADD and offer means of diagnosing them, up-to-date medical and behavioral therapies, and a listing of organizations specializing in their treatment.

374 Parenting Attention Deficit Disordered Teens

Connecticut Assoc. for Children and Adults with LD
25 Van Zant Street
East Norwalk, CT   06855   203-838-5010
FAX 203-866-6108
http://www.CACLD.org
e-mail: cacld@optonline.net
Patricia C Land, Author
Marie Armstrong, Information Specialist

Small pamphlet with amazingly detailed outline of the various problems of adolescents with ADHD. *$3.25*

14 pages $2.50 shipping

375 Parents' Hyperactivity Handbook: Helping the Fidgety Child

Plenum Publishers
233 Spring Street
New York, NY   10013   212-620-8000
FAX 212-463-0742
http://www.wkap.nl/
e-mail: info@plenum.com
DM Paltin, Author

305 pages $27.50
ISBN 0-306444-65-8

376 Putting on the Brakes

APA
750 1st Street NE
Washington, DC   20002   800-374-2721
FAX 202-336-5502
http://www.apa.org/books
Patricia O Quinn, Author
Judith M Stern, Author

This is one of the most popular books written on attention deficit-hyperactivity disorder and a most useful resource for kids with ADHD. The authors describe the symptoms and theories of ADHD in warm, kid-friendly terms and discuss family support, medication, and tips on getting organized.

377 Rethinking Attention Deficit Disorders

Brookline Books
PO Box 97
Newton, MA   02464   617-868-0360
800-666-2665
FAX 617-558-8011
http://www.brooklinebooks.com
e-mail: brooklinebks@delphi.com
Milt Budoff, President

Groundbreaking analysis of ADHD. *$27.95*

ISBN 1-571290-37-0

378 Shelley, the Hyperactive Turtle

Woodbine House
6510 Bells Mill Road
Bethesda, MD   20817   301-897-3570
800-843-7323
FAX 301-897-5838
http://www.woodbinehouse.com
e-mail: info@woodbinehouse.com
Deborah M Moss
Carol Schwartz, Ilustrator

Shelley the turtle has a very hard time sitting still, even for short periods of time. During a visit to the doctor, Shelley learns that he is hyperactive, and that he can take medicine every day to control his wiggly feeling. *$ 12.95*

20 pages   Hardcover
ISBN 0-933149-31-X

379 Special Parent, Special Child: Parents of Children with Disabilities

Books on Special Children
PO Box 305
Congers, NY   10920   845-638-1236
FAX 845-638-0847
http://www.boscbooks.com/
e-mail: irene@boscbooks.com
T Sullivan, Author

Parents share the depths of their feelings, despair and disappointments. Author asks his mother about his blindness, then speaks with parents of six children with disabilities: blind; deaf; Cerebral Palsy; leukemia; ADD; and Down Sydrome. Discusses initial reaction upon learning their child had a disability, family repercussions, advocacy and other special insights. *$24.95*

239 pages   hardcover
ISBN 0-874777-82-8

380 Teach and Reach Students with Attention Deficit Disorders

MultiGrowth Resources
12345 Jones Road
Houston, TX   77070   218-890-5334
FAX 281-894-8611
e-mail: multigrowthresources@compuserve.com
Nancy L Eisenberg, Author
Pamela H Esser, Author

Handbook and resource guide for parents and educators of students with ADHD. *$23.95*

200 pages
ISBN 0-963084-71-2

381 Understanding and Teaching Children With Autism

Books on Special Children
PO Box 305
Congers, NY   10920   845-638-1236
FAX 845-638-0847
http://www.boscbooks.com/
e-mail: irene@boscbooks.com
R Jordan, Author

The triad of impairment: social, language and communication and thought behavior aspects of development discussed. Difficulties in interacting, transfer of learning and bizarre behaviors are part of syndrome. Many LD are associated with autism. *$57.00*

> *175 pages   hardcover*
> *ISBN 0-471958-88-3*

382   Why Can't Johnny Concentrate: Coping With Attention Deficit Problems

Bantam Doubleday Dell
1540 Broadway
New York, NY   10036   212-782-9000
                              800-323-9872
                              FAX 212-302-7985
                              http://www.bantum.com

R Moss, Author
H Dunlap, Author

How to cope with ADD problems.

383   Why Can't My Child Behave?

Pear Tree Press
PO Box 30146
Alexandria, VA   22310
                              800-321-3287
                              FAX 703-768-3619
                              http://www.childbehave.com

Jane Hersey, Author

This book shows how foods and food additives can trigger learning and behavior problems in sensitive people. It provides practical guidance on using a simple diet to uncover the causes of ADD and ADHD. *$22.00*

> *400 pages*
> *ISSN 0965-1105*

384   You Mean I'm Not Lazy, Stupid or Crazy?

Scribner
1230 Avenue of Americas
New York, NY   10020   212-698-7000
                              800-622-6611
                              FAX 212-698-7007

Peggy Ramundo, Author
Kate Kelly, Author

This new book is the first written by ADD adults for other ADD adults. A comprehensive guide, it provides accurate information, practical how-to's, and moral support. Among other issues, readers will get information on: unique differences in ADD adults; the impact on their lives; up-to-date research findings; treatment options available for adults; and much more. *$24.95*

> *444 pages*
> *ISBN 1-882522-00-1*

Web Sites

385   www.add.org
Attention Deficit Disorder Association

The National Attention Deficit Disorder Association is an organization focused on the needs of adults and young adults with ADD/ADHD, and their children and families. We seek to serve individuals with ADD, as well as those who love, live with, teach, counsel and treat them.

386   www.addhelpline.org
ADD Helpline for Help with ADD

A site dedicated to providing information and support to all parents, regardless of their choice of treatment, belief or approach toward ADD/ADHD.

387   www.additudemag.com
Attitude Magazine

ADDitude: The Happy Healthy Lifestyle Magazine for People with ADD offers articles, information and support.

388   www.addvance.com
ADDvance Online Newsletter

A resource for girls and women with ADD. Site has books, tapes, support groups, chat and links.

389   www.addwarehouse.com
ADD Warehouse

The world's largest collection of ADHD-related books, videos, training programs, games, professional texts and assessment products.

390   www.adhdnews.com/ssi.htm

Guidance in applying for Social Security disability benefits on behalf of a child who has ADHD.

391   www.cec.sped.org
Council for Exceptional Children

Dedicated to improving educational outcomes for individuals with exceptionalities, students with disabilities, and/or the gifted.

392   www.chadd.org
National Resource Center on AD/HD

CHADD works to improve the lives of people affected by AD/HD.

393 **www.childdevelopmentinfo.com**
Child Development Institute

Online information on child development, child psychology, parenting, learning, health and safety as well as childhood disorders such as attention deficit disorder, dyslexia and autism. Provides comprehensive resources and practical suggestions for parents.

394 **www.dyslexia.com**
Davis Dyslexia Association

Links to internet resources for learning. Includes dyslexia, Autism and Asperger's Syndrome, ADD/ADHD and other learning disabilities.

395 **www.my.webmd.com**
Web MD Health

Medical website with information which includes learning disabilities, ADD/ADHD, etc.

396 **www.ncgiadd.org**
National Center for Gender Issues and AD/HD

Offers knowledge and understanding of girls and women with ADHD to improve their lives.

397 **www.nichcy.org**
Nat'l Dissemination Ctr for Children Disabilities

Provides information on disabilties in children and youth and programs and services.

398 **www.oneaddplace.com**
One A D D Place

A virtual neighborhood of information and resources relating to ADD, ADHD and learning disorders.

399 **www.therapistfinder.net**

Locate psychologists, psychiatrists, social workers, family counselors, and more specializing in all disorders.

Publications

400 Directory of Summer Camps for Children with Learning Disabilities

Learning Disabilities Association of America
4156 Library Road
Pittsburgh, PA   15234   412-341-1515
                          FAX 412-344-0224
                          http://www.ldanatl.org
                          e-mail: ldanatl@usaor.net

Offers a full range of listings for the learning disabled.
$4.00

401 Guide to ACA Accredited Camps

American Camping Association
5000 State Road 67 N
Martinsville, IN   46151   765-342-8456
                          800-428-2267
                          FAX 765-349-6357
                          http://www.acacamps.org
                          e-mail: bookstore@acacamps.org
Melody Snider, Bookstore Director

A national listing of accredited camping programs.
Listed by activity, special clientele, camp name, and
specific disabilities. *$14.95*

285 pages   Annually
ISBN 0-876031-66-1

402 Guide to Summer Camps and Summer Schools

Porter Sargent Publishers
11 Beacon Street
Boston, MA   02108   617-523-1670
                          800-342-7470
                          FAX 617-523-1021
                          http://www.portersargent.com
                          e-mail: info@portersargent.com
Dan McKeever, Senior Editor
John Yonce, General Manager
Leslie Weston, Production Manager

Covers a broad spectrum of recreational and educational summer opportunities in the US and abroad.
Current facts from 1300 camps and schools, as well as
programs for those with special needs and disabilities.
$27.00

640 pages   Biannual/Paper
ISBN 0-875581-45-5

403 Learning Disabilities: Guide for Directors of Specialized Camps

Learning Disabilities Association of America
4156 Library Road
Pittsburgh, PA   15234   412-341-1515
                          FAX 412-344-0224
                          http://www.ldanatl.org
                          e-mail: ldanatl@usaor.net

$6.50

404 Learning Disabled: Camp Directors Guide on Integration

Learning Disabilities Association of America
4156 Library Road
Pittsburgh, PA   15234   412-341-1515
                          FAX 412-344-0224
                          http://www.ldanatl.org
                          e-mail: ldanatl@usaor.net

$6.50

Alabama

405 Camp ASCCA

PO Box 21
Jacksons Gap, AL   36861   256-825-9226
                          800-843-2267
                          FAX 256-825-8332
                          http://www.campascca.org
                          e-mail: info@campascca.org
Tom Collier, Camp Director
John Stevenson, Administrator

Helps children and adults with disabilities achieve
equality, dignity and maximum independence. This is
to be accomplished through a safe and quality program of camping, recreation and education in a
year-round barrier-free environment. Founded 1976.

406 Easter Seals Gulf Coast

2448 Gordon Smith Drive
Mobile, AL   36617   251-471-1581
                          800-411-0068
                          FAX 251-476-4303
                          e-mail: esmob@zebra.net
Frank Harkins, CEO

Camperships camping and recreation services offered.

Arizona

407 Easter Seals Arizona

903 N Second Street
Phoenix, AZ   85004   602-252-6061
                          800-626-6061
                          FAX 602-252-6065
                          e-mail: brian@azseals.org
Brian Patchett, VP Programs

The following are camping and recreation services offered: Adventure, camp respite for children,
camperships, canoeing, day camping for children,
recreational services for children and water skiing.

408 Easter Seals Tucson

5740 E 22nd Street
Tucson, AZ   85711   520-745-5222
                          FAX 520-745-9030
Donna Lucas, Coordinator

The following are camping and recreation services offered: Camp respite for children.

Arkansas

409 Easter Seals Adult Services Center

11801 Fairview Road
Little Rock, AR 72212   501-221-8400
                               877-533-3600
                          FAX 501-221-8842
              e-mail: mail@easter-seals.org
Sharon Moone-Jochums, President/CEO

Day camping for children. Founded 1976.

California

410 Easter Seals Bay Area: San Jose

730 Empey Way
San Jose, CA 95128   408-295-0228
                          FAX 408-275-9858
                 e-mail: polson@esba.org
Peter Olson, Director Health & Wellness

Recreational services for adults.

411 Easter Seals Bay Area: Tri-Valley Campus

7425 Larkdale Avenue
Dublin, CA 94568   925-828-8857
                          FAX 925-828-5245
              e-mail: kcarnahan@esba.org
Kara Carnahan, Service Supervisor

Recreational services for adults.

412 Easter Seals Central California

9010 Soquel Drive
Aptos, CA 95003   831-684-2166
                          FAX 831-685-6055
              e-mail: dalvarez@es-cc.org
Donna Alvarez, VP Finance & Program Services

The following are camping and recreational services offered: Recreational services for adults, residential camping programs and therapeutic horseback riding.

413 Easter Seals Central California: Camp Harmon

16403 Highway 9
Boulder Creek, CA 95006   831-684-2380
                          FAX 831-685-6055
              e-mail: jennifer@es-cc.org
Jennifer Johnson, Camping Services Coordinator

The following are camping and recreational services offered: Easter Seals own and operated camps and residential camping programs.

414 Easter Seals Eureka

3289 Edgewood Road
Eureka, CA 95502   707-445-8841
                               800-675-7325
                          FAX 707-445-3106
Eddie Morgan, Program Manager

The following are camping and recreational services offered: Camperships, computer program, day camping for children, recreational services for adults and recreational services for children.

415 Easter Seals Monterey

PO Box 1796
Monterey, CA 93942   831-684-2166
                 e-mail: dalvarez@es-cc.org
Donna Alvarez, VP Finance & Program Services

Recreational services for adults.

416 Easter Seals Northern California

20 Pimentel Court
Novato, CA 94949   415-382-7450
                          FAX 415-382-6052
      e-mail: jreinhardt@ca-no.easter-seals.org
Jackie Reinhardt, President/CEO

The following are camping and recreational services offered: Before/After school program (Ages 6 through 18), camp respite for adults, camperships, recreational services for adults and recreational services for children.

417 Easter Seals Northern California: RohnertPark

5440 State Farm Drive
Rohnert Park, CA 94928   707-584-1443
                               800-234-7325
                          FAX 707-584-3438
      e-mail: skreuzer@ca-no.easter-seals.org
Susanne Kreuzer, VP Program Services

The folllowing are camping and recreational services offered: Camp respite for adults, camperships, day camping for children, recreational services for children and residential camping programs.

418 Easter Seals Superior California

3205 Hurley Way
Sacramento, CA 95864   916-485-6711
                               888-877-3257
                          FAX 916-485-6711
      e-mail: info@easterseals-superiorca.org
Gary Kasai, President/CEO

Camping and recreational services offered are: Swim programs.

419 Easter Seals Superior California: Stockton

102 W Bianchi Road
Stockton, CA 95207   209-473-0441
                          FAX 209-473-4128
      e-mail: info@easterseals-superiorca.org
Gary Kasai, President/CEO

Camping and recreational services offered are: Swim programs.

420 Easter Seals Tri-Counties California

10730 Henderson Road
Ventura, CA 93004   805-647-1141
                          FAX 805-647-1148
              e-mail: eastertc@pacbell.net
Jamie Polis

Camping and recreational services offered are: Camperships and swim programs.

421   Los Angeles School of Gymnastics Day Camp

8450 Higuera Street
Culver City, CA   90232   310-204-1980
                                       888-849-6627
                                  FAX 310-204-6864
                                  http://lagymnastics.com
                                  e-mail: info@lagymnastics.com
Alla Svirsky, Executive Director

Runs summer and winter camps for boys and girls. Founded 1975.

Colorado

422   Easter Seals Camp Rocky Mountain Village

PO Box 115
Empire, CO   80438   303-569-2333
                                   FAX 303-569-3857
                                   e-mail: campinfo@cess.org
Roman Krafczyk, Camp Director

Camping and recreational services are: Adventure, camp respite for adults, camp respite for children, camperships, conference rental, family retreats, recreational services for adults, recreational services for children, residential camping programs, swim programs and therapeutic horseback riding.

423   Easter Seals Colorado

5755 W Alameda Avenue
Lakewood, CO   80226   303-233-1666
                                   FAX 303-233-1028

Lynn Robinson, CEO

Camping and recreational services offered are: Swim programs.

424   Easter Seals Southern Colorado

225 S Academy Boulevard
Colorado Springs, CO   80910   719-574-9002
                                   FAX 719-574-1330
                            e-mail: pwaldera@#easter-sealssc.org
Paula Waldera-Hundt

Camping and recreational services offered: Camp respite for adults, camp respite for children and camperships.

425   Learning Camp

PO Box 1146
Vail, CO   81658   970-524-2706
                                   FAX 970-524-4178
                             http://www.learningcamp.com
                             e-mail: info@learningcamp.com
Ann Cathcart, Founder/Director
Tom Macht, Director

Summer camp that focuses on helping children with learning disabilities, such as dyslexia, ADD, ADHD and other learning challenges.

426   Synthesis Summer Camp Program Foothills Unitarian Church

1815 Yorktown Avenue
Denver, CO   80222   303-759-0307
                                   FAX 303-759-2841

Edwin A Miller, Co-Director
Johanna Small, Co-Director
Ryan Acuna, Co-Director

A summer day camp for children with ADD/ADHD.

Connecticut

427   CREC Summer School

River Street School
11 Charter Oak Avenue
Hartford, CT   06106   860-298-9079
                                   FAX 860-246-3304
                                   http://www.crec.org
                                   e-mail: pfernandez@rss.crec.org
Paula Fernandez, Case Worker

Offers an educationally oriented program with recreational opportunities, strong behavior management and highly structured groupings.

428   Camp Hemlocks Easter Seals

Smith Street
Hebron, CT   06248   800-244-2756
                                        800-244-2756
                                   FAX 508-751-6444
                             http://www.eastersealsma.org
                             e-mail: rozf@eastersealsma.org
Offers an environment that allows campers with disabilities optimal independence.

429   Camp Horizons

PO Box 323
South Windham, CT   06266   860-456-1032
                                   FAX 860-456-4721
                             http://www.camphorizons.org
                             e-mail: staffpage@camphorizons.org
Chris McNaboe, Executive Director
Janice Chamberlain, Associate Director
Lauren Perrotti, Director

To provide high quality residential, recreational, support and work programs for people who are developmentally disabled or who have other challenging social and emotional needs.

430   Camp Lark

Litchfield County Association for Retarded Citizen
84 Main Street
Torrington, CT   06790   860-482-9364
                                   FAX 860-489-2492
Katherine Marchand-Beyer, Director Community Services

Program offers arts and crafts, swimming, field sports, archery, outdoor education, music, drama and adventure courses. Once a week overnights are offered and the program runs in conjunction with the Torrington YMCA camp, Northwest YMCA, Camp Torymca. Additional staff supports are available when needed.

431 Camp Tepee

204 Stanley Road
Monroe, CT   06468   203-261-2566
                                 FAX 203-261-3146
Dawn Dalryntle, Executive Director

Each summer, over 1,700 campers experience exciting thrills and make memories that last a lifetime. We are a fully modernized facility located on 47 beautiful acres nestled in the Stephney section of Monroe, CT. We pride ourselves on providing a safe and nurturing environment in which children of all ages conquer new challenges, make new friends, and share in the unique and wonderful experience that is day camp.

432 Cyber Launch Pad

Learning Incentive
139 N Main Street
West Hartford, CT   06107   860-236-5807
                                 FAX 860-233-9945
                                 http://www.tli.com
                                 e-mail: tli@tli.com
Dr. Aileen Stan-Spence, Director

Half days camp where children and their parents learn to use Cyberslate which is learning keyboarding, word processing, programming and remedial sessions in reading, writing and arithmetic for learning disabled children.

433 Eagle Hill Southport School

214 Main Street
Southport, CT   06490   203-254-2044
                                 FAX 203-255-4052
                        http://www.eaglehillsouthport.org
                        e-mail: info@eaglehillsouthport.org
Lea Sylvertro, Administrative Assistant

The summer program at Eagle Hill is designed to help students 6 to 13 years old maintain their academic progress.

434 Eagle Hill Summer Program

45 Glenville Road
Greenwich, CT   06831   203-622-9240
                                 FAX 203-622-0914
                        http://www.eaglehillschool.org
Sharon Pearlman, Director
Abby Hanrahan, Director

Designed for children experiencing academic difficulty. Open to boys and girls ages 5-11.

435 East Hartford Special Education Camp

East Hartford Park and Recreation Department
50 Chapman Place
East Hartford, CT   06108   860-528-1458
                                 FAX 860-282-8239
Roger Moss, Director

For East Hartford residents only. A day camp offering swimming, sports, arts and crafts, projects, music and field trips.

436 Easter Seals Camp Hemlocks

85 Jones Street
Hebron, CT   06248   860-228-9496
                                   800-832-4409
                                 FAX 860-228-2091
                        e-mail: johnq@eastersealsofct.org
Mark Kline, Director Camping & Recreation

Camping and recreational services offered are: Camp respite for adults, camp respite for children, camperships, computer program, conference rental, family retreats, recreational services for adults, recreational services for children, residential camping programs and swim programs.

437 Haddam-Killingworth Recreation Department

95 Little City Road
Higganum, CT   06441   860-345-8334
                                 FAX 860-345-8252
                http://www.haddam.org/town_departments
                                 e-mail: hkrec@snet.net
Frank Sparks, Director
Robyne Brennan, Assistant Director

Programs offered include arts and crafts, games, sports workshops, field trips, movies, special events and a carnival.

438 Kiwanis Easter Seal Day Camp

Easter Seal Rehabilitation Center
Munson Road
Wolcott, CT   06716   203-879-2343
Alice Hubbell
Ronnie Genova

Programs offered include swimming, athletics, camping, hiking, outdoor education, music activities, arts and crafts and special day activities.

439 Marvelwood Summer

Marvelwood School
PO Box 3001
Kent, CT   06757   860-927-0047
                                   800-440-9107
                                 FAX 860-927-0021
                http://www.themarvelwoodschool.com
                        e-mail: marvelwood.school@snet.net
W Bradley Gottschalk, Director Admissions
Katherine Almquist, Director Summer Admissions

A coeducational boarding and day school enrolling 150 students in grades 9-12. Provides an environment in which young people of varying abilities and learning needs can prepare for success in college and in life. In a nurturing, structured community, students who have not thrived academically in traditional settings are guided and motivated to reach and exceed their personal potential.

440 Middletown Summer Day Programs

Middletown Parks and Recreation Department
319 Butternut Street
Middletown, CT 06457   860-343-6620
                             FAX 860-344-3319

Wesley Downing, Director

These camps offer a variety of recreational and social activities. Each camp will be integrated with at least 12% population of children with disabilities. Campers must be Middletown residents.

441 Milford Recreation Department Camp Happiness

70 W River Street
Milford, CT 06460   203-783-3280
                             FAX 203-783-3284
      http://www.ci.milford.ct.us/parkrec.html
         e-mail: cschneider@ci.milford.ct.us
Marelene Sanchez, Director Summer Camp

A camp specifically designed for learning disabled children from the Milford area.

442 Norwalk Public Schools: Special Education Summer Programs

125 E Avenue
Norwalk, CT 06851   203-854-4133
                             FAX 203-854-4125

Offers pre-school/elementary students developmental and remedial academics.

443 Shriver Summer Developmental Program

Nathan Hale School
5 Taylor Road
Enfield, CT 06082   860-763-8899
                             FAX 860-763-8897

Maria Bonney

Academic/recreational program including instructional swimming for the learning disabled.

444 Timber Trails Camps

Connecticut Valley Girl Scout Council
340 Washington Street
Hartford, CT 06106   860-522-0163
                             FAX 860-548-0325
             http://www.girlscouts-ct.org
             e-mail: info@girlscouts-ct.org
Shannon Nolan, Camps Director

All girls age 6 to 17 who can function in a group in a mainstream environment are welcome, including those with chronic illnesses, learning disabilities, and physcial or emotional needs.

445 Wilderness Challenge

Wheeler Clinic
91 NW Drive
Plainville, CT 06062   860-747-6801
                             800-793-3588
                         FAX 860-793-3520
             http://www.wheelerclinic.org
         e-mail: alarouche@wheelerclinic.org
Dr. David Berkowitz, Executive Director

A three-week program offering therapeutic outdoor education programs which include a variety of non-competitive group games and activities.

446 YMCA: Valley-Shore

Spencer Plains Road
Westbrook, CT 06498   860-399-9622
                             FAX 860-399-8349
                http://www.vsymca.org
Bryan McFarland, Camp Director

Day camps which include music, arts and crafts, swimming, hiking, sports, games, nature study, archery and overnight camp outs.

Delaware

447 Cedars Academy

PO Box 103
Bridgeville, DE 19933   302-337-3200
                             FAX 302-337-8496
             http://www.cedarsacademy.com
Mary Pauer, Headmaster

A seven week program which encourages positive feelings of self worth and increased interpersonal skills. Activities include camping, sailing and art.

District of Columbia

448 Summer Camps for Children who are Deaf or Hard of Hearing

National Deaf Education Network and Clearinghouse
Gallaudet University
Washington, DC 20002   202-651-5000
                             FAX 202-651-5704
             http://www.pr.gallaudet.edu
         e-mail: public.relations@gallaudet.edu

To serve as a comprehensive, multipurpose facility of higher education for deaf and hard of hearing.

Florida

449 3D Learner Program

3121 NW 108th Drive
Coral Springs, FL   33065   954-341-2578
                              FAX 954-796-3883
                        http://www.3dlearner.com
                   e-mail: succes@3dlearner.com
Mark Halpert, Co-Director
Mira Halpert MEd, Co-Director

3D Learner Program, a one-week program for struggling students who learn best when they see and experience information. We have had students from all over the US. We address attention, self-esteem and reading with a natural and effective method. Our students make immediate gains and often see significant gains with 3 months.

450 ALERT-US

Coalition for Independent Living
6800 Forest Hill Boulevard
West Palm Beach, FL   33413   561-966-4288
                                   800-683-7337
                              FAX 561-641-6619
                           http://www.cilo.org
To promote the independence for peole with disabilties.

451 Easter Seals Florida: Central Florida

31600 Camp Challenge Road
Sorrento, FL   32776   321-383-4711
                                   800-377-3257
                              FAX 321-383-0744
               e-mail: mguinta@fl.easter-seals.org
Melissa Guinta, Director Camping & Recreation

Camping and recreational services offered are: Camp respite for adults, camperships, conference rental and residential camping programs.

452 Easter Seals Volusia and Flagler Counties

1219 Dunn Avenue
Daytona Beach, FL   32120   386-255-4568
                                   877-255-4568
                              FAX 386-258-7677
               e-mail: info@fl-vf.easter-seals.org
Lynn Sinnott, President

Camping and recreational services are: Day camping for children.

453 Eckerd Family Youth Alternatives

100 N Starcrest Drive
Clearwater, FL   33765   727-461-2990
                              FAX 727-442-5911
Karen Waddell, CEO

Designed to combine the wilderness living experience with the reality treatment perspective, the psychology perspective and behavior modification techniques. Founded 1968

454 YMCA: Lakeland

3620 Cleveland Heights Boulevard
Lakeland, FL   33803   863-644-3528
                              FAX 863-644-2517
Alice Colins, CEO

Camp runs June through July, and is coed, ages 12-16.

Georgia

455 Easter Seals Southern Georgia

1906 Palmyra Road
Albany, GA   31701   229-439-7061
                                   800-365-4583
                              FAX 229-435-6278
              e-mail: benglish@swga-easterseals.org
Beth English, Executive Director

Camping and recreational services offered are: Camp respite for adults, camp respite for children, day camping for children and therapeutic horseback riding.

456 Squirrel Hollow

5665 Milam Road
Fairburn, GA   30123   770-774-8001
                              FAX 770-774-8005
                  http://www.thebedfordschool.org
Betsy E Box, Director

The five week camp meets on campus of Atlanta Christian College and includes a camping trip in the north Georgia mountains.

Hawaii

457 Easter Seals Hawaii: Oahu Service Center

710 Green Street
Honolulu, HI   96813   808-536-1015
                              FAX 808-536-3765
              e-mail: brian@eastersealshawaii.org
Brian Lawton, Youth Services Program Manager

Camping and recreational services offered are: Residential camping programs.

Illinois

458 Camp Algonquin

1889 Cary Road
Algonquin, IL   60102   847-658-8212
                              FAX 847-658-8431
                  http://www.campalgonquin.org
                  e-mail: info@campalgonquin.org
Jim Roth, Executive Director

To inspire, educate and strengthen individuals, families and groups toward growth, achievement, positive community and environmental stewardship through education, experiential and recreational opportunities.

459   Camp Little Giant: Touch of Nature Environmental Center

Southern Illinois University
1208 Touch of Nature Road
Carbondale, IL   62901   618-453-1121
FAX 618-453-1188
http://www.tonec.siu.edu
e-mail: tonec@tonec.siu.edu
Randy Osborn, Program Coordinator
Chilang Lanless, Registar

A residential camp program designed to meet the recreational needs of adults and children with disabilities.

460   Easter Seals Camping and Recreation List

National Easter Seals Society
230 W Monroe Street
Chicago, IL   60606   312-726-6200
800-221-6827
FAX 312-726-1494
http://www.easter-seals.org
e-mail: info@easter-seals.org
Jim Williams, CEO

Various programs with the united purpose of giving disabled children a fun and safe camping or recreational experience. Call for information on activities in your state.

461   Easter Seals Central Illinois

2715 N 27th Street
Decatur, IL   62526   217-429-1052
FAX 217-423-7605
e-mail: info@easterseals-ci.org
Janet Kelsheimer, Executive Director

The following are Camping and Recreational services offered: Recreational services for adults and recreational services for children.

462   Easter Seals Jayne Shover Center

799 S McLean Boulevard
Elgin, IL   60123   847-742-3264
FAX 847-742-9436
e-mail: admin@il-js.easter-seals.org
Gwen Upshaw, Client Financial Services Mgr.

The following are Camping and Recreational services offered: Recreational services for adult and recreational services for children.

463   Easter Seals Joliet

212 Barney Drive
Joliet, IL   60435   815-773-9362
FAX 815-773-9365
e-mail: dcondotti@il-wg.easter-seals.org
Debra Condotti, President

The following are camping and recreational services offered: Camperships.

464   Easter Seals Missouri

602 E 3rd Street
Alton, IL   62002   618-462-7325
FAX 618-462-8170
e-mail: mail@mo-easter-seals.org
Craig Byrd, CEO

The following are camping and recreational services offered: Camperships.

465   Easter Seals UCP: Peoria

20 Timber Pointe Lane
Hudson, IL   61748   309-365-8021
FAX 309-365-8934
e-mail: kpodeszw@easterseals-ucp.org
Kurt Podeszwa, Director Camping/Outdoor Prog.

The following are Camping and Recreational services offered: Recreational services for adults and recreational services for children.

466   Western Du Page Special Recreation Association

116 N Schmale Road
Carol Stream, IL   60188   630-681-0962
FAX 630-681-1262
TDY:630-681-0962
http://www.wdsra.com
e-mail: info@wdsra.com
Jane Hodgkinson, Executive Director
Peg Wilson, Superintendent Recreation

Offers year-round recreational services and programs to special residents of its nine member communities.

Indiana

467   Camp Brosend: Brosend Ministries

7599 Brosend Road
Newburgh, IN   47630   812-853-3466
FAX 812-853-5585
http://www.campbrosend.org
e-mail: campmail@campbrosend.org
Kevin Heil, Director

Campers enjoy a wide variety of program activities while building confidence.

468   Easter Seals ARC of Northeast Indiana

2542 Thompson Avenue
Fort Wayne, IN   46807   260-456-4534
800-234-7811
FAX 260-745-5200
e-mail: shinkle@easarc.org
Steve Hinkle, CEO

The following are camping and recreational services offered: Recreational services for adults and camp respite for adults.

469   Easter Seals Wayne & Union Counties

5632 US Highway 40 E
Centerville, IN   47330   765-855-2482
FAX 765-855-2482
e-mail: easterseals@juno.com
Patricia Powers, Program Director

The following are camping and recreational services offered: Camperships and recreational services for children.

470 Englishton Park Academic Remediation & Training

PO Box 228
Lexington, IN   47138   812-889-2046
http://www.englishtonpark.org
e-mail: tbarnet@venus.net
Thomas Barnett, Co-Director
Lisa Barnett, Co-Director

To improve academic skills, change attitudes toward learning, modify behavior interferring with learning in the classroom. Founded 1968

471 Worthmore Academy

Center for Learning Disabilities
5220 E Fall Creek Parkway N Drive
Indianapolis, IN   46220   317-253-5367
FAX 317-253-5824
http://www.iser.com/worthmore-IN.html
e-mail: worthmor@indy.net
Brenda J Jackson, Director
Sandy Foster, Assistant Director

A place where children with learning differences may come and receive individualized instruction to help remediate their learning differences. Goal is to help each child return to a traditional academic setting within one to two years.

Iowa

472 Easter Seals Camp Sunnyside

401 NE 66th Avenue
Des Moines, IA   50313   515-274-1529
FAX 515-274-6434
e-mail: info@eastersealsia.org
Marcia Tope, Coordinator Intake/QA
Angela Chandler, Program Coordinator

The following are Camping and Recreational services offered: Adventure, camp respite for children, day camping for children, easter seals own and operated camps and residential camping programs.

Kentucky

473 Bethel Mennonite Camp

2773 Bethel Church Road
Clayhole, KY   41317   606-666-4911
FAX 606-666-4911
http://www.bethelcamp.org
e-mail: grow@bethelcamp.org
Roger Voth, Director

A camp with an emphasis on bible study. Founded 1957

474 Camp Kysoc

Kentucky EasterSeal Society
1902 Easterday Road
Carrollton, KY   41008   502-732-5333
FAX 502-732-0783
e-mail: fun@kysoc.org
Sally Price, Executive Director

Traditional outdoor camp program.

475 Easter Seals Camp KYSOC

1902 Easterday Road
Carrolton, KY   40504   502-732-5333
FAX 502-732-0783
e-mail: fun@kysoc.org
Sallie Price, Director

The following are camping and recreational services offered: Camp respite for adults, camp respite for children, camperships, canoeing, day camping for children and family retreats.

476 Easter Seals Kentucky

2050 Versailles Road
Lexington, KY   40504   859-254-5701
800-888-5377
FAX 859-367-7155
e-mail: kgg@cardinalhill.org
Kerry Gillihan, President/CEO

The following are camping and recreational services offered: Daycamping for children.

477 Easter Seals of Northern Kentucky

31 Spiral Drive
Florence, KY   41042   859-491-1171
FAX 859-491-8132
e-mail: clw@cardinalhill-northernky.org
Cynthia Lawhorn-Williams, Executive Director

The following are camping and recreational services offered: Daycamping for children.

Louisiana

478 Easter Seals Louisiana

305 Baronne Street
New Orleans, LA   70112   504-523-7325
800-695-7325
FAX 504-523-3465
e-mail: essla@aol.com
Mark Stafford, Contact

The following are camping and recreational services offered: Camperships.

479 Med-Camps of Louisiana

102 Thomas Road
West Monroe, LA   71291   318-329-8405
FAX 318-329-8407
http://www.medcamps.com
Larry McDonald, Director

Regardless of special needs this camp offers participants a sense of well being, belonging, accomplishment and self worth.

Maine

480 Camp Waban

Waban's Projects
5 Dunaway Drive
Sanford, ME 04073   207-324-7955
FAX 207-324-6050
http://www.waban.org
e-mail: waban@gwi.net
Jan Fraser, Executive Director

This program provides campers from a wide geograhic area a chance to enjoy the outdoors in a theraputic recreational setting.

Maryland

481 Camp Fairlee Manor

22242 Bay Shore Road
Chestertown, MD 21620   410-778-0566
FAX 410-778-0567
http://www.fairleemanor.org
e-mail: fairlee@dmv.com
Bill Morgan, Camping Director

Dedicated to providing social, recreational and educational activities for participants while helping them achieve greater independence.

482 Jemicy Community Outreach

11 Celadon Road
Owings Mills, MD 21117   410-356-7656
http://www.jemicyschool.org/camps.html
e-mail: info@jemicyschool.org
Dave Lasalle, Director

Two special camps for dyslexic children that blends fun camp activities which includes swimming and nature experiences.

483 Kamp A-Kom-plish

9035 Ironsides Road
Nanjemoy, MD 20662   301-870-3226
FAX 301-870-2620
http://www.kampakomplish.org
e-mail: kampakomplish@melwood.com
Heidi Aldous, Director

A sleep-away camp for for children and teens aged 8 to 16 years old. Located on 108 acres there are air-conditioned cabins, fishing, boating and trails for hiking. Founded 1968

Massachusetts

484 Camp Half Moon for Boys & Girls

PO Box 188
Great Barrington, MA 01230   413-528-0940
FAX 413-528-0941
http://www.camphalfmoon.com
e-mail: info@camphalfmoon.com
Ed Mann, Director/Owner
Til Mann, Director/Owner
Gretchen Mann, Director/Owner

The philosophy is based on six principles: structure, social values, sound learning skills, spirit, guidance and individuality. Half Moon provides a safe orderly environment that stresses skill improvement rather than high competition.

485 Camp Holiday

Everett Recreation Center
90 Chelsea Street
Everett, MA 02149   617-394-2390
FAX 617-394-2358
Flora Formosi, Program Director

A five week program for Everett residents that includes arts and crafts, physical fitness and more.

486 Camp Joy

Boston Centers for Youth & Families
1483 Tremont Street
Roxbury, MA 02120   617-635-4920
FAX 617-635-5074
e-mail: michaeltriant@ci.boston.ma.us
Michael Triant, Program Manager
Kevin Stanton, Dir. After/Out School Services

A therapeutic recreational program for special needs children and adults. Currently serving over 700 participants with a professionally qualified staff of 290 at 15 sites throughout the city. Serves the physically and cognitively challenged, multi-handicapped, behaviorally involved, legally blind/visually impaired, deaf/hearing impaired, learning disabled, and pre-school special needs children.

487 Camp Lapham

731 S Road
Ashby, MA 01431   781-834-2700
FAX 781-834-2701
http://www.crossroads4kids.org/lapham.html
e-mail: office@crossroads4kids.org
Ian Moorhouse, Director

Designed to meet the needs of children who thrive in a small, structured environment. The program emphasis includes anger and behavior management, along with strong self-image building all in a fun, noncompetitive camp atmosphere. With a maximum of 50 children enrolled per session and a low camper to counselor ratio of 1 to 4, the campers experience success in a more family-like atmosphere which enables each child to focus on personal goals and nonviolent methods of interaction.

488 Camp Polywog

Malden YMCA
83 Pleasant Street
Malden, MA   02148   781-324-7680
                                        FAX 781-324-7856
Susan Hogan, Program Director

Offers a gym, swimming, city tours and more. Structured recreation that teaches.

489 Camp Ramah

35 Highland Circle
Needham, MA   02494   781-449-7090
                                        FAX 781-449-6331
                             http://www.campramahne.org
                        e-mail: billym@campramahne.org
Billy Mencow, Director
Brooke Gadasi, Registration

Young people have fun while developing skills, strong friendships and a Jewish conciousness that lasts a lifetime through a variety of experiences such as sports, nature, music, study, Shabbat and Judaica.

490 Camp Six Acres

475 Winthrop Street
Medford, MA   02155   781-391-2220
                                        FAX 781-393-4864
Roz Abukasis, Program Director
Mary Hoarty

Two week camp for mild to moderately mentally impaired children. Transportation is provided free of charge.

491 Carroll School Summer Camp

25 Baker Bridge Road
Lincoln, MA   01773   781-259-8342
                                        FAX 781-259-8361
                             http://www.carrollschool.org
                        e-mail: info@carrollschool.org
Sharon Lloyd Clark, Head School

Summer at Carroll is designed to offer academic intervention and remediation to children diagnosed with primary language learning difficulties, such as dyslexia. Small group teaching, individualized instruction and attention to the needs of goals of the students are what Carroll prides themselves on.

492 Crossroads for Kids

119 Myrtle Street
Duxbury, MA   02332   781-834-2700
                                             888-543-7284
                                        FAX 781-834-2701
                             http://www.crossroads4kids.org
                        e-mail: office@crossroads4kids.org
Jeffery Rumph, Executive Director

The daily programs provide a good balance between active and quiet, sport, cultural, group and individual activities. We place campers into smaller, age appropriate groups so they receive the extra support, care and encouragement they need to feel at home here at camp.

493 Easter Seals Massachusetts

484 Main Street
Worcester, MA   01608   508-751-6345
                                               800-244-2756
                                          FAX 508-831-9768
                        e-mail: maryd@eastersealsma.org
Mary D'Antonino, Disability Resource Manager

The following are camping and recreational services offered: Camp respite for adults, camp respite for children, canoeing, computer camp, computer program, day camping for children, residential camping programs, sailing, swim programs, therapeutic horseback riding and water skiing.

494 Kolburne SchoolSummer Program

343 NM Southfield Road
New Marlborough, MA   01230   413-229-8787
                                        FAX 413-229-4165
                             http://www.kolburne.net
Jeane Weinstein, Executive Director
Christopher Ezzo, Chief Administrator

A family operated residential treatment center located in the Berkshire Hills of Massachusetts. Through integrated treatment services, effective behavioral management, recreational programming, and positive staff relationships, our students develop the emotional stability, interpersonal skills and academic/vocational background necessary to return home with success.

495 Landmark Summer Adventure Ropes Program

Landmark School
429 Hale Street
Prides Crossing, MA   01965   978-236-3010
                                        FAX 978-927-7268
                             http://www.landmarkschool.org
                        e-mail: jtruslow@landmarkschool.org
Robert Broudo, Headmaster
Carolyn Orsini, Director of Admission

The adventure ropes program offers students 10 years and older an opportunity to spend part of their summer experience in an outdoor adventure-based program. Students spend half the day on the ropes understanding group dynamics and developing self esteem. They spend the next half of the day in a one-to-one language tutorial, a math class, and a language arts class.

496 Landmark Summer Marine Science Program

Landmark School
429 Hale Street
Prides Crossing, MA   01965   978-236-3010
                                        FAX 978-927-7268
                             http://www.landmarkschool.org
                        e-mail: jtruslow@landmarkschool.org
Robert Broudo, Headmasterdmission
Carolyn Orsini, Director of Admission

A program offered to students who are interested in the natural and physical world. Students spend half the day exploring local coastal ecosystems, working on research teams and collecting data. The other half of the day is spent in academic or preparatory classes in which students develop their language skills through a one on one tutorial and language arts and math classes.

497 Landmark Summer Seamanship Program

Landmark School
429 Hale Street
Prides Crossing, MA   01965   978-236-3010
FAX 978-927-7268
http://www.landmarkschool.org
e-mail: jtruslow@landmarkschool.org
Robert Broudo, Headmaster
Carolyn Orsini, Director of Admission

Students attend academic classes for half of the school day and learn seamanship and sailing skills during the other half.

498 Patriots' Trail Girl Scout Council SummerCamp

985 Berkeley Street
Boston, MA   02116   617-350-8335
FAX 617-482-9045
http://www.ptgirlscouts.org/camp.htm
e-mail: SummerCamp@ptgirlscouts.org
Canoeing, swimming, windsurfing, life-saving, sailing, biking and trips.

499 Ramah in New England

39 Bennett Street
Palmer, MA   01069   413-283-9771
FAX 781-449-6331
http://www.campramahne.org
Billy Mencow, Director
Joel Stavsky, Business Manager

Offers a special program to meet the social and religious needs of developmentally challenged Jewish adolescents. The program provides the youth with a full experience in boating, swimming, sports, and the arts.

500 Valleyhead

79 Reservoir Road
Lenox, MA   01240   413-637-3635
FAX 413-637-3501
http://www.valleyhead.org
e-mail: cmacbeth@valleyhead.org
Christine Macbeth ACSW LICSW, Executive Director

A residential school for girls nestled in the scenic Berkshire Hills of Lenox, Massachusetts. We provide a home and education for girls ages 12-22 with emotional needs. Most of our girls come from abusive and traumatic backgrounds.

Michigan

501 Adventure Learning Center at Eagle Village

5044 175th Avenue
Hersey, MI   49639   231-832-1424
800-748-0061
FAX 231-832-1468
http://www.eaglevillage.org
e-mail: alc@eaglevillage.org
Jeremy Shafer, Summer Camp Director

Offers a variety of fun camp experiences for any child, including those with emotional and/or behavioral impairments. Challenging activities make the camps rewarding experiences.

502 Easter Seals Genesee County

1420 W Third Avenue
Flint, MI   48504   810-238-0475
FAX 810-238-9270
e-mail: efauster@eastersealsgenco.com
Elliott Fauster, Executive Director

The following are camping and recreational services offered: Recreational services for adults, recreational services for children, residential camping programs and therapeutic horseback riding.

503 Easter Seals Michigan

4065 Saladin Drive SE
Grand Rapids, MI   49546   616-942-2081
FAX 616-942-5932
David Lankford, Information & Referral

The following are camping and recreational services offered: Camperships.

504 Easter Seals Michigan: Saginaw

804 S Hamilton
Saginaw, MI   48602   989-797-0880
800-757-3257
FAX 989-797-0888
e-mail: esofmi@aol.com
Julie Dorcey, Regional Director

The following are camping and recreational services offered: Camperships.

505 Easter Seals Michigan: Traverse City

109 S Union
Traverse City, MI   49684   231-941-1271
FAX 231-941-1990
e-mail: essofmich@aol.com
Liz Hughes, Director

The following are camping and recreational services offered: Swim programs.

506 Fowler Center Summer Camp

2315 Harmon Lake Road
Mayville, MI   48744   989-673-2050
FAX 989-673-6355
John Fowler, Chairman/Founder

The Fowler Center is an outdoor recreation and education facility that provides programs with paraticular emphasis on people with developmental and physical disabilities.

Minnesota

507 Camp Buckskin

PO Box 389
Ely, MN   55731   218-365-2121
http://www.campbuckskin.com
e-mail: buckskin@spacestar.net
Tom Bauer, Director

Buckskin operates a therapeutic summer program for youth with ADD/ADHD and related difficulties. We have two 32-day sessions which utilize a combination of traditional camp activities and academics (reading, writing, environmental education) to allow multiple successes which develop self-confidence and improves self-esteem. High staff to camper ratio provides individualized instruction. The program is supportive, yet provides adequate structure to improve social skills and peer relations.

508 Camp Chi Rho

9 Rustic Lodge W
Minneapolis, MN   55409   612-827-7123
FAX 612-825-8824
http://www.chirhocenter.org
e-mail: sjchirho@aol.com
Sandra Rader, Camp Director
James W Greenlee, Executive Director

A year round ecumenical retreat and conference center available for rental.

509 Camp Confidence

1620 Mary Fawcett Memorial Drive
Brainerd, MN   56401   218-828-2344
FAX 218-828-2618
http://www.campconfidence.com
e-mail: info@campconfidence.com
Jeff Olsen, Executive Director

A year-round center for persons with developmental disabilities specializing in recreation and outdoor education. Aimed at promoting self confidence and self esteem and the necessary skills to become full, contributing members of society.

510 Camp Friendship

Friendship Ventures
10509 108th Street NW
Annandale, MN   55302
800-450-8376
FAX 952-852-0123
http://www.friendshipventures.org
e-mail: fv@friendshipventures.org
Georgann Rumsey, President

A summer resident camp that is open to anyone five or older who has developmental and/or physical disabilities.

511 Winnebago

19708 Camp Winnebago Road
Caledonia, MN   55921   507-724-2351
FAX 507-724-3786
Cathy Greeley, Director

Nebraska

512 Camp Easter Seals

7171 Mercy Road
Omaha, NE   68106   402-345-2200
FAX 402-345-2500
http://www.ne.easter-seals.org
e-mail: smasten@ne.easter-seals.org
Sara Masten, Camp Director

Residential camp for people with disabilities. Encourages independence, social development and self confidence.

513 Camp KitakiYMCA

6000 Cornhusker Highway
Lincoln, NE   68507   402-434-9225
FAX 402-434-9226
http://www.ymcalincoln.org
e-mail: campkitaki@ymcalincoln.org
Chris Klingenberg, Camp Director

A Christian camp for children with ADD and other disabilities. Archery, climbing, horseback riding, fishing and aquatic activities are some of the activities.

514 Easter Seals Nebraska

7171 Mercy Road
Omaha, NE   68106   402-345-2200
800-650-9880
FAX 402-345-2500
e-mail: sfratt@ne.easter-seals.org
Sheryl Fratt, Camp Recreation & Respite Dir.

The following are camping and recreational services offered: Camp respite for adults, camp respite for children, camperships, recreational services for children and residential camping programs.

New Hampshire

515 Camp Calumet Lutheran

Ossipee Lake Road
Ossipee, NH   03890   603-539-3223
FAX 603-539-3385
http://www.calumet.org/contact.htm
e-mail: boomchickaboom@calumet.org
Donald G Johnson, Executive Director

Families and adults, young and not so young come to this beautiful site for fellowship, relaxation and a Christian community atmosphere.

516 Camp Runels

270 Gage Hill Road
Pelham, NH   03076   603-635-1662
                                    FAX 603-635-2366
Karen Martin, Program Director

General camping, aquatics, arts, drama, hiking, sailing and more.

517 Easter Seals Camp Carpenter

555 Auburn Street
Manchester, NH   03103   603-623-8863
                                    800-870-8728
                                    FAX 603-625-1148
Doug Gordon, Director

Promote and assure maximum independence and quality of life for people with disabilities and their families.

518 Easter Seals New Hempshire

1 Mammoth Road
Manchester, NH   03104   603-621-3601
                                    FAX 603-364-0230
                          e-mail: dgordon@eseals.org
Doug Gordon, Camp Director

The following are camping and recreational services offered: Camp respite for adults, camperships, day camping for children, recreational services for children and residential camping programs.

New Jersey

519 Alpine Scout Camp

Route 9W
Alpine, NJ   07620   201-768-1910
                                    FAX 201-784-1663
Tony Cardiello, Director

Offers short term camping for scouts.

520 Camp Merry HeartEaster Seals

21 O'Brien Road
Hackettstown, NJ   07840   908-852-3896
                                    FAX 908-852-9263
          e-mail: campmerryheart@mendhamrotary.org
Alex Humanick, Director Camping

A coed camp for people with disabilities.

521 Camp Tikvah

Jewish Community Center on the Palisades
411 E Clinton Avenue
Tenafly, NJ   07670   201-569-7900
                                    FAX 201-569-7448
            http://www.jcconthepalisades.org
Shmuel Abramson, Coordinator

Camp Tikvah is designed to meet the special needs of children and adolescents who have been classified with mild neurological and/or perceptual impairment.

522 Easter Seals Camp Merry Heart

21 O'Brien Road
Hackettstown, NJ   07840   908-852-3896
                                    FAX 908-852-9263
              e-mail: ahumanick@nj.easter-seals.org
Alex Humanick, Director

The following are camping and recreational services offered: Camp respite for adults, camperships, canoeing, day camping for children, recreational services for adults and residential camping programs.

523 Elks Camp Moore

PO Box 375
Pompton Lakes, NJ   07083   973-835-1542
                                    FAX 973-835-4125
                          e-mail: GCarr1426@aol.com
Jennifer Salmon, Director

Serving children with asthma, behavior disorders and learning disabilities. Activities include hiking, water sports and arts and crafts.

524 Harbor Hills Day Camp

75 Doby Road
Mt Freedom, NJ   07970   973-895-3200
                                    FAX 973-895-7239
                                    http://www.hhdc.com
                          e-mail: info@hhdc.com
Robyn Tanny, Executive Director

A seven-week, co-ed day camp for children ages 5-15 with special needs. Provides a nurturing and supportive summer. The camp is oriented towards youngsters with learning disabilities and/or attention deficit disorders. It may also be appropriate for children with other types of learning challenges.

525 Round Lake Camp

21 Plymouth Street
Fairfield, NJ   07004   973-575-3333
                                    FAX 973-575-4188
                    http://www.roundlakecamp.org/
                          e-mail: rlc@njycamps.org
Eugene Bell, Contact

A camp for children who have been identified with ADD, and/or mild social disorders.

New Mexico

526 Easter Seals New Mexico

2819 Richmond Drive NE
Albuquerque, NM   87107   505-888-3811
                                    800-279-5261
                                    FAX 505-888-0490
                          e-mail: esnm1@aol.com
Marlis Hadley, President/CEO

The following are camping and recreational services offered: Residential camping programs.

New York

527 Camp Agape Pioneer Retreat Center

9324 Lake Shore Road
Angola, NY 14006   716-549-1420
                          FAX 716-549-6018
                    http://www.pioneercamp.org
                    e-mail: pioneercamp@wzrd.com
Linda Gage, Executive Director

Offers a variety of activities for growing in faith and in service towards one another. Children, teens, adults and seniors are welcome all summer.

528 Camp DunnabeckKildonan School

425 Morse Hill Road
Amenia, NY 12501   845-373-8111
                          FAX 845-373-9793
                    http://www.kildonan.org
Bonnie Wilson, Director of Admissions

Specializes in helping intelligent children with specific reading, writing and spelling disabilities. Provides Orton-Gillingham tutoring with camp activities, including swimming, sailing, waterskiing, horseback riding, ceramics, tennis and woodworking.

529 Camp HASC

Old Route 17
Parksville, NY 12768   914-292-6821
                          FAX 718-851-6100
                    e-mail: chayam.hasc@verizon.net
Chaya R Miller, Director

Provides over 300 mentally and physcially handicapped children and adults with the opportunity to enjoy a seven week sleep away camp experience.

530 Camp Huntington

56 Bruceville Road
High Falls, NY 12440   845-687-7840
                          FAX 845-687-7211
                    http://www.kidscamps.com
                    e-mail: camphtgtn@aol.com
For boys and girls with learning disabilities and developmental disabilities, ADD and PDD.

531 Camp Kehilla

Sid Jacobson Jewish Community Center
300 Forest Drive
East Hills, NY 11548   516-484-1545
                          FAX 516-484-7354
                    e-mail: susee210@aol.com
Ashley Fields, Director

A summer day camp for high functioning children and teens with minimal learning disabilities, speech and language delays and ADHD.

532 Camp Northwood

132 State Route 365
Remsen, NY 13438   315-831-3621
                          FAX 315-831-5867
                    http://www.nwood.com
                    e-mail: campinfo@nwood.com
Gordon W Felt, Director/Owner
Donna Felt, Director/Owner

Oriented toward a population of socially immature, isolated, nonaggresive children ranging in age from 8-18 that experience difficulties in social and academic settings due to a variety of types of learning challenges.

533 Camp Pa-Qua-Tuck

PO Box 677
Center Moriches, NY 11934   631-878-1070
                          FAX 631-878-2596
          http://www.camppaquatuck.org/contact.html
                    e-mail: camppaquatuck@webtv.net
Garrett Nagle PhD, Executive Director

Handicapped children experience the joys of boating, fishing, campfires and more. In a supportive, enriching environment they are encouraged to reach beyond the limits of their handicaps and join with their fellow campers in activities designed to enhance their lives.

534 Camp Sunshine-Camp Elan

Mosholu-Montefiore Community Center
3450 Dekalb Avenue
Bronx, NY 10467   718-882-4000
                          FAX 718-882-6369
                    e-mail: daycamp@mmcc.org
Mike Halpern, Director

Serves children who are intellectually limited, emotionally impaired and/or demonstrate special learning disabilities.

535 Coda's Day Camp

Community Opportunity Development Agency
564 Thomas S Boyland Street
Brooklyn, NY 11212   718-345-4779
Dr. Emil D DeLoache, Director

536 Cross Island YMCA Day Camp

23810 Hillside Avenue
Bellerose, NY 11426   718-479-0505
                          FAX 718-465-1665
                    e-mail: mwright@mcanyc.org
Michele Wright, Director

Day camp offers opportunity to improve self esteem through age appropriate, structured activities and trips.

537 Easter Seals Albany

230 Washington Avenue Extension
Albany, NY 12203   518-456-4880
                          800-727-8785
                          FAX 518-456-5094
                    e-mail: info@ny.easter-seals.org
Jeremy Kohomban, Senior VP

The following are camping and recreational services offered: Camp respite for children, camperships, day camping for children and recreational services for children.

538 **Easter Seals East Rochester**
349 W Commercial Street
East Rochester, NY 14445 585-264-9550
FAX 585-264-9547
e-mail: info@ny.easter-seals.org
Jeremy Kohomban, Senior VP

The following are camping and recreational services offered: Recreational services for children.

539 **GAP Summer Program**
Syosset/Woodbury Community Park
977 Hicksville Road
Massapequa, NY 11758 516-797-7900
FAX 516-797-4145
Mary Ryan, Director

A program for children with mental and learning disabilities.

540 **Gow Summer Programs**
Emery Road
South Wales, NY 14139 716-655-2900
FAX 716-652-3457
http://www.gow.org
e-mail: summer@gow.org
Brett Marcoux, Director

For boys and girls who have experienced past academic difficulties and have learning differences but possess the potential for success.

541 **Harlem Branch YWCA Summer Day Camp**
YWCA
154 W 127th Street
New York, NY 10027 212-283-8543
FAX 212-491-3178
Patricia Fraser, Director

Camp size 50 per session, coed.

542 **Jimmy Vejar Day Camp**
United Cerebral Palsy of Westchester
PO Box 555
Purchase, NY 10577 914-937-3800
FAX 914-937-0967
http://www.ucpw.org
e-mail: elatainer@ucpw.org
Evan Latanier, Director

Camp for people with disabilities.

543 **Kamp Kiwanis**
NY District Kiwanis Foundation
9020 Kiwanis Road
Taberg, NY 13471 315-336-4568
FAX 315-336-3845
http://www.kiwanis-ny.org/kamp
e-mail: kampkiwanis@mybizz.net
Christopher W Henske, Director

Serves youths with many forms of disabilities to include ADD, autism, and learning disabilities.

544 **MAC Mainstreaming at Camp**
Frost Valley YMCA
460 W 34th Street
New York, NY 10001 212-273-6658
FAX 212-273-6161
http://www.frostvalley.org
Susan Pasette, Director

MAC is designed to serve children with developmental disabilities and to promote inclusion into the broader camp community.

545 **Maplebrook School's Summer Program**
5142 Route 22
Amenia, NY 12501 845-373-9511
FAX 845-373-7029
http://www.maplebrookschool.org
e-mail: mbsechs@aol.com
Jennifer L Scully, Director Admissions

Academic instruction is given in the morning hours of each weekday and afternoon hours are filled with culturally enriching classes in drama, dance and art.

546 **New Country Day Camp**
Educational Alliance
197 E Broadway
New York, NY 10002 212-780-2300
FAX 212-979-1225
http://www.edalliance.org
Robin Bernstein, Executive Director

Clients must be toilet trained. A special program for teens and young adults emphasizes independent living skills and prevocational training.

547 **Old Forge Center**
PO Box 1159
Old Forge, NY 13420 315-369-2740
800-351-5327
FAX 315-369-2807
Laurie Pasquence, Director Admissions

The summer enrichment program provides academic support to students with learning disabilities.

548 **Parkside School**
48 W 74th Street
New York, NY 10023 212-721-8888
FAX 212-721-1547
A. Miller, Director

A New York State chartered, not-for-profit school established in 1986 for children with language-based learning problems in the New York City area. An educational setting that promotes active participation in learning.

549   Queens REACH Camp Smile

Flushing Meadows Corona Park
Flushing, NY   11368   718-699-4213
                              FAX 718-699-4243
                              http://www.nyc.gov/parks
Adrian Benepe, Commissioner

550   Samuel Field/Bay Terrace YM & YWHA Special Services

58-20 Little Neck Parkway
Little Neck, NY   11362   718-225-6750
                                 FAX 718-423-8276
                          http://www.samuelfieldy.org
                          e-mail: samfieldy@aol.com
Steven Goodman, VP

Committed to providing the residents of northeast Queens and western Nassau with an outstanding array of high quality and diverse services, innovative programming and a wide variety of community events and celebrations.

551   School Vacation Camps: Youth with Development Disabilities

YWCA of White Plains-Central Westchester
515 N Street
White Plains, NY   10605   914-949-6227
                                  FAX 914-949-8903
Camp for people with developmental disabilities.

552   Shield Summer Play Program

Shield Institute
14461 Roosevelt Avenue
Flushing, NY   11354   718-886-1534
                              FAX 718-961-7669
                              http://www.shield.org
                     e-mail: webmaster@shield.org
Helen Berman, Director

553   Summit Travel Program

Summit Travel
11045 71st Road
Forest Hills, NY   11375   718-268-0020
                                  800-323-9908
                                  FAX 718-268-0671
Dr. Gil Skyer, Director

Represents the logical extension of the camping program for young adults who have outgrown the traditional camping experience, but still require opportunities for structured and supervised social experiences as well as recreational opportunities of a more adult nature. This program offers 1,2,3 and 6 week programs of domestic and/or foreign travel.

554   Trailblazers Camp JCC of Northern Westchester

600 Bear Ridge Road
Pleasantville, NY   10570   914-741-0333
                                   FAX 914-741-6150
                              http://www.rosenthaly.org
Tom Naviglis, Camp Director

Located on 19 acres of scenic woodland. Offers a swim program, softball, arts and crafts, music, drama and Jewish culture for children with special needs.

555   YAI/Rockland County Association for the Learning Disabled (YAI/RCALD)

2 Crosfield Avenue
West Nyack, NY   10994   845-358-5700
                                FAX 845-358-6119
Joel Levy, Chief Executive Officer
Erin DeWard, Coordinator

YAI/RCALD conducts a wide variety of programs, supervised by experienced and professional staff, designed to build life skills, promote self-esteem, provide information exchange and offer other support services for individuals with learning and other developmental disabilities. The programs include, vocational evaluation and placements, recreational, residential, camping, service coordination and support groups.

North Carolina

556   Camp Timberwolf

PO Box 457
Hendersonville, NC   28793   828-697-9379
                          http://www.camptimberwolf.com
                     e-mail: timberwolf@camptimberwolf.com
Tony Coburn, Director
Hal Mahan, Director

An camping program specifically designed for boys and girls with ADD, ADHD, LD, OCD and similar behavioral challanges.

557   SOAR Camp

2319 Rosemount Road
Balsam, NC   28707   828-456-3435
                            FAX 828-456-3449
                            http://www.soarnc.org
Jonathan Jones, Executive Director
John Wilson, Director

Features success-oriented, high-adventure programs for learning disabled and ADD preteens, teens and adults. Emphasis is placed on developing self-confidence, social skills, problem-solving techniques, a willingness to attempt new challenges and the motivation that comes through successful goal orientation.

558 Talisman Summer Camp

601 Camp Elliot Road
Hendersonville, NC 28711
828-669-8639
888-972-7736
FAX 828-669-2521

Includes three programs for children with learning disabilities, high functioning Autism and Asperger's Snydrome.

559 Wilderness Experience

Ashe County 4-H
134 Government Circle
Jefferson, NC 28640
336-219-2650
FAX 336-229-2682
e-mail: gsantucc@ashe.ces.ncsu.edu
Dave Mueller, Director

Ohio

560 Camp Cheerful: Achievement Center for Children

15000 Cheerful Lane
Strongsville, OH 44136
440-238-6200
FAX 440-238-1858
Gregory McGrath, Director

A residential camp for children who are high functioninig autistic, and Asbergers Syndrome

561 Camp Happiness at Corde Campus

Catholic Charities Disability Services
7911 Detroit Avenue
Cleveland, OH 44102
216-334-2963
FAX 216-334-2905
Molly Worthington, Camp Director

To provide educational, social and recreational services to children and adults with developmental disabilities during the summer months.

562 Camp Happiness at St. Augustine

Catholic Charities Disability Services
7911 Detroit Avenue
Cleveland, OH 44102
216-334-2963
FAX 216-334-2905
Molly Worthington, Camp Director

To provide educational, social and recreational services to children and adults with developmental disabilities during the summer months.

563 Camp Happiness at St. Joseph Center

Catholic Charities Disability Services
7911 Detroit Avenue
Cleveland, OH 44102
216-334-2963
FAX 216-334-2905
Molly Worthington, Camp Director

To provide educational, social and recreational services to children and adults with developmental disabilities during the summer months.

564 Camp Nuhop

404 Hillcrest Drive
Ashland, OH 44805
419-289-2227
419-938-7151
FAX 419-289-2227
http://www.campnuhop.org
e-mail: campnuhop@zoominternet.net
Jerry Dunlap, Director
Terrie Dunlap, Director
Fred Boll, Director

A residential camp for all children with learning disabilities, attention deficit disorders and behavior disorders.

565 Camp SuccessMarburn Academy

1860 Walden Drive
Columbus, OH 43229
614-433-0822
FAX 614-433-0812
http://www.marburnacademy.org
Barbara Davidson, Director

A four program academic day camp for children with LD and dyslexia.

566 Camp-I-Can

The Children's Home of Cincinnati
5050 Madison Road
Cincinnati, OH 45227
513-272-2800
FAX 513-272-2807
http://www.thechildrenshomecinti.org
Stephen L Black, President

A summer day camp that enhances creativity and promotes positive social skills.

567 Easter Seals Broadview Heights

1929 A E Royalton Road
Broadview Heights, OH 44147
440-838-0990
888-325-8532
FAX 440-838-8440
e-mail: spowers@eastersealsneo.org
Susan Powers, Director Rehabilitation Services

The following are camping and recreational services offered: Camperships and day camping for children.

568 Easter Seals Central and Southeast Ohio

565 Children's Drive W
Columbus, OH 43205
614-228-5523
FAX 614-228-8249
e-mail: tshiverd@easterseals-cseohio.org
Tracey Shiverdecker, Contact

The following are camping and recreational services offered: Aquatics.

569 Easter Seals Cincinnati

231 Clark Road
Cincinnati, OH   45215   513-821-9890
                                FAX 513-821-9895
        e-mail: twatson@oh-sw.easter-seals.org
Tammy Watson, CEO

The following are camping and recreational services offered: Adventure.

570 Easter Seals Lorain

1909 N Ridge Road
Lorain, OH   44055   440-277-7337
                           888-723-5602
                    FAX 440-277-7339
        e-mail: eastersealsnwohio.org
Linda Zander, Contact

The following are camping and recreational services offered: Camperships and day camping for children.

571 Easter Seals Marietta

609 Putnam Street
Marietta, OH   45750   740-374-8876
                              FAX 740-374-4501
Melanie Alloway, Office Manager

The following are camping and recreational services offered: Camp respite for children and therapeutic horseback riding.

572 Easter Seals Northeast Ohio

3085 W Market Street
Akron, OH   44333   330-836-9741
                           FAX 330-836-4967
        e-mail: susan@eastersealsneo.org
Susan Powers, Director Rehabilitation Services

The following are camping and recreational services offered: Swim programs.

573 Easter Seals Youngstown

299 Edwards Street
Youngstown, OH   44502   330-743-1168
                                FAX 330-743-1616
        e-mail: jwalston@mtc.easter-seals.org
Janet Walston, Manager Pediatric Services

The following are camping and recreational services offered: Recreationsl/Day care for Ages 6-12.

574 Pilgrim Hills Camp

33833 Township Road 20
Brinkhaven, OH   43006   740-599-6314
                                800-282-0740
                         FAX 740-599-9790
        e-mail: campregistrar@ocucc.org
Cynthia Speller, Camp Director

Many camp programs for all children including learning disabled.

575 Recreation Unlimited Farm and Fun

7700 Piper Road
Ashley, OH   43003   740-548-7006
                            FAX 740-747-2640
        http://www.recreationunlimited.org
        e-mail: info@recreationunlimited.org
Paul Huplin, Director

Is a not-for-profit organization providing programs in sports, recreation and education for individuals with physical and developmental disabilities on an accessible 165-acre campus in a safe, fun and challenging environment.

Oklahoma

576 Camp Arrowhead YMCA

500 N Broadway
Oklahoma City, OK   73102   405-733-9622
                                   FAX 405-733-9626
Tammy Bratcher, Camp Director

A camp that puts Christian principles into practice through programs that build healthy spirit, mind and body.

577 Camp Fire USA

706 S Boston
Tulsa, OK   74119   918-592-2267
                           FAX 918-592-3473
        e-mail: vproctor@Tulsacampfire.org
Denny Winters, Camp Director

A coed overnight non-competitive camp building self esteem.

578 Easter Seals Oklahoma

701 NE 13th Street
Oklahoma City, OK   73104   405-239-2525
                                   FAX 405-239-2278
        e-mail: esok1@coxinet.net
Patricia T Filer, President

The following are camping and recreational services offered: Camperships.

Oregon

579 Easter Seals Central Pennsylvania

501 Valley View Boulevard
Altoona, PA   16602   814-944-5014
                             888-463-3093
                      FAX 814-944-6500
        e-mail: jhanlin@eastersealscentralpa.org
Jeanne Hanlin, CEO

The following are camping and recreational services offered: Day camping for children, recreational services for children and therapeutic horseback riding.

580 Easter Seals Medford

33 N Central Avenue
Medford, OR   97501   541-842-2199
                            FAX 541-842-4048
e-mail: medford@or.easter-seals.org
Diane Mathews, Program Coordinator

The following are camping and recreational services offered: Day camping for children, recreational services for adults and recreational services for children.

581 Easter Seals Oregon

5757 SW Macadam Avenue
Portland, OR   97239   503-228-5108
                              800-556-6020
                         FAX 503-228-1352
e-mail: info@or.easter-seals.org

The following are camping and recreational services offered: Residential camping programs.

582 Mobility International USA

PO Box 10767
Eugene, OR   97440   541-343-1284
                           FAX 541-343-6812
http://www.miusa.org
e-mail: info@miusa.org

Susan Sygall, Director

A nonprofit organization founded in 1981 to empower people with disabilities around the world through international exchange promoting cross-cultural understanding and providing leadership and disability rights training to people with disabilities. We also provide consultation, publications, resources and technical assistance promoting the full participation of people with disabilities in international exchange opportunities and at all levels of the international development process.

583 Upward Bound Camp for Special Needs

PO Box C
Stayton, OR   97383   503-897-2447
                            FAX 503-897-4116
http://www.upwardboundcamp.org
e-mail: ubc@open.org

Jerry Pierce, Co Director
Laura Pierce, Co Director

Christian-based camp for people with developmental disabilities age 12 and up. Activities include fishing, hiking, swimming, arts and crafts, archery, Bible study, nature explorations, campfires, games, basketball, volleyball, horseshoes and badminton. Founded 1978

Pennsylvania

584 Camp Hebron

957 Camp Hebron Road
Halifax, PA   17032   717-896-3441
                             800-864-7747
                        FAX 717-896-3391
http://www.camphebron.org
e-mail: hebron@camphebron.org
Lanny Millette, Executive Director
Mike Ford, Program Director

A place where people connect with God, nature and each other. This is accomplished through the creation of a Christ-centered sanctuary where people find renewal and growth through recreation, teaching and fellowship in God's creation.

585 Camp Joy

3325 Swamp Creek Road
Schwenksville, PA   19473   610-754-6878
                                  FAX 610-754-7880
http://www.campjoy.com
e-mail: campjoy@fast.net
Angus Murray, Director

Sleeover and day camp for kids and adults with developmental disabilities: mental retardation, autism, brain injury and neurological disorders.

586 Easter Seals Bethlehem

2200 Industrial Drive
Bethlehem, PA   18017   610-866-8092
                              FAX 610-866-3450
e-mail: barbaracc@easterseals-easternpa.org
Barbara Carlson, VP Program

The following are camping and recreational services offered: Recreational services for children and day camp for children.

587 Easter Seals Downingtown

797 E Lancaster Avenue
Downingtown, PA   19335   610-873-3990
                                FAX 610-873-3992
e-mail: dkeiths@easterseals-sepa.org
Donna Keiths, Division Director

The following are camping and recreational services offered: Day camping for children, recreational services for children.

588 Easter Seals Eastern Pennsylvania

1040 Liggett Avenue
Reading, PA   19611   610-775-1431
                            FAX 610-796-1954
Mark Ruggiero, VP Berks/Schuylkill Division

The following are camping and recreational services offered: Camperships, day camping for children and recreational services for children.

589 Easter Seals Franklin

200 12th Street
Franklin, PA   16323   814-437-3071
                             FAX 814-433-2226
e-mail: dgriffith@pa-ws.easter-seals.org
Donna Griffith, Division Director

The following are camping and recreational services offered: Day camping for children, recreational services for children.

590 Easter Seals Kulpsville

1161 Forty Foot Road
Kulpsville, PA   19443   215-368-7000
                               FAX 216-368-1199
e-mail: bstrasser@easterseals-sepa.org
Carl Webster, Executive Director

The following are camping and recreational services offered: Day camping for children, recreational services for children.

591   Easter Seals Levittown

2400 Trenton Road
Levittown, PA   19056   215-945-7200
                                 FAX 215-945-4073
          e-mail: lremick@easterseals-sepa.org
Lois Remick, Division Director

The following are camping and recreational services offered: Day camping for children, recreational services for children.

592   Easter Seals Media

468 N Middletown Road
Media, PA   19063   610-565-2353
                                 FAX 610-565-5256
          e-mail: jwright@easterseals-sepa.org
Jan Wright, Division Director

The following are camping and recreational services offered: Day camping for children, recreational services for children.

593   Easter Seals South Central Pennsylvania

2201 S Queen Street
York, PA   17402   717-741-3891
                                 FAX 717-741-5359
Matt Ernst, Director Therapeutic Recreation

The following are camping and recreational services offered: Adventure, day camping for children, recreational services for adults, recreational services for children, sports camp, swim programs, therapeutic horseback riding, water skiing and snow skiing.

594   Easter Seals of Southeastern Pennsylvania

3975 Conshohocken Avenue
Philadelphia, PA   19131   215-879-1001
                                 FAX 215-879-8424
          e-mail: jpodgajny@easterseals-sepa.org
John Podgajny, Division Director

The following are camping and recreational services offered: Day camping for children, recreational services for adults and recreational services for children.

595   Summit Camp Program

Summit Camp Program New York Office
18 E 41st Street
New York, NY   10017   212-689-3880
                                    800-323-9908
               http://www.summitcamp.com
               e-mail: summitcamp@aol.com
Mayer Stiskin, Director
Ninette Stiskin, Director

Summit camp in Honsdales Pennsylvania serves boys and girls diagnosed with Attention Deficit Disorders, Asperger Snydrome and learning disabilities.

596   Wesley Woods

RR 1
Grand Valley, PA   16420   814-436-7802
                                    800-295-0420
                                 FAX 814-436-7669
               http://www.wesleywoods.com
               e-mail: wesleywoods@tbscc.com
Herb West, Director

The mission is to meet spiritual needs of children, youth, and adults in a Christian camp and retreat setting.

South Carolina

597   Easter Seals Greenville

1122 Rutherford Road
Greenville, SC   29609   864-232-4185
                                 FAX 864-232-8161
               e-mail: eastersgvl@aol.com
Tom Hovland, Director

The following are camping and recreational services offered: Residential camping program.

598   Easter Seals Pierre

1351 N Harrison Avenue
Pierre, SD   57501   605-224-5879
                                 FAX 605-224-1033
          e-mail: administrator@sd.easter-seals.org
Patricia Miller, CEO

The following are camping and recreational services offered: Day camping for children.

599   Easter Seals South Carolina

614 S Hazard Street
Georgetown, SC   29442   843-546-2212
                                 FAX 843-545-5251
               e-mail: eastergt@ftc.net
Lisa Hutto, Affiliate Director

The following are camping and recreational services offered: Therapeutic horseback riding.

Tennessee

600   Camp Discovery Tennessee Jaycees Foundation

400 Camp Discovery Lane
Gainesboro, TN   38562   615-293-4497
                                 FAX 423-265-7879
               http://www.camp-discovery.org
               e-mail: hickman_sped@yahoo.com
Dawn Hickman, Director
John Garner, President/Jaycees Foundation

Provides summer camp for people with special needs.

601 Easter Seals Camp

6300 Benders Ferry Road
Mt. Juliet, TN   37122   615-444-2829
                                       FAX 615-444-8576
                     e-mail: escamp@bellsouth.net
Tam Adams, Director Camping

The following are camping and recreational services
offered: Camp respite for adults, camp respite for children, camperships and residential camping programs.

602 River's Way Outdoor Adventure Center

889 Stoney Hollow Road
Bluff City, TN   37618   423-538-0405
                                       FAX 423-538-8183
                     http://www.riversway.org
                     e-mail: tom@riversway.org
Tom Hanlon, Executive Director
Jamie Scott, Director

Providing opportunities for youth of all abilities to
work, learn and have fun together in educational and
outdoor adventure settings. Founded 1993

Texas

603 ADD/ADHD Summer Camp

River Oaks Academy
10600 Richmond Avenue
Houston, TX   77042   713-783-7200
                                       FAX 713-783-7286
                     http://www.riveracademy.com
Dr. Sandra Phares, Director

A specialized summer camp for children and adolescents with ADHD or conduct disorder.

604 Austin Wilderness Counseling Services

1300 W Lynn Street
Austin, TX   78703   512-472-2927
                                       FAX 512-472-2913
Nelda Beard

Day camps and wilderness trips for children and adolescents who can benefit from structured activities led
by trained counselors.

605 Easter Seals Central Texas

919 W 28 1/2 Street
Austin, TX   78705   512-478-2581
                                       FAX 512-476-1638
                     e-mail: smiller@eastersealstx.com
Sharon Miller, President/CEO

The following are camping and recreational services
offered: Day camping for children.

606 El Paso LDA Vacation Adventure

8929 Viscount Boulevard
El Paso, TX   79925   915-591-8080
                                       FAX 915-591-8150
Barbara Lino, Director
Lina Monroy, Executive Director

Summer developmental learning program for children currently placed in Special Education or section
504 programs.

607 Girl Scout Camp La Jita

10443 Gulfdale Street
San Antonio, TX   78216   210-349-2404
                                       FAX 210-349-2666
                     http://www.sagirlscouts.org
Kathy Grantham, Executive Director

Mainstream camp open to children with disabilities.

608 Rocking L Guest Ranch

240 Van Zandt County Road #3837
Wills Point, TX   75169   903-560-0246
                                       FAX 972-495-1131
                     http://www.rockinglguestranch.net
                     e-mail: bradlarsen@rockinglranch.com
Brad Larsen, Owner
Alicia Larsen, Owner

Campers benefit mentally, physically and socially
from the camp experience. Additional activities include canoeing, fishing, volleyball, basketball and
swimming.

609 Star Ranch: Summer Program

HC 7 Box 39C
Ingram, TX   78025   830-367-4868
                                       FAX 830-367-2814
                     http://www.starranch.org
                     e-mail: pbrouse@starranch.org
Cody Schrank, Program Coordinator
Paul Brouse, Program Director
Rand Southard, Executive Director

A camp that teaches Christian values and is geared
specifically to deal with children that have severe
learning disabilities.

**610 Vacation Adventure Summer Developmental
Program**

8929 Viscount
El Paso, TX   79925   915-591-8080
                                       FAX 915-591-8150
Barbara Lino

A summer program for learning disabled children specifically ADD.

Utah

611   **Camp Easter Seals East**

20500 Easter Seal Drive
Milford, VA   22514   804-746-1007
      FAX 804-746-9214
e-mail: info@va.easter-seals.org
Ginger Ellis, Director Program Administration

The following are camping and recreational services offered: Family retreats.

612   **Camp Easter Seals West**

Route 2
New Castle, VA   24127   540-864-5750
      FAX 540-864-6797
e-mail: dduerk@va.easter-seals.org
Deborah Duerk, Director

The following are camping and recreational services offered: Adventure, camperships, canoeing, conference rental, family retreats, residential camping programs, climbing wall, creative arts, finishing marksmanship, nature study, occupational therapy, swimming, sports camp, speech therapy and therapeutic horseback riding.

613   **Easter Seals Utah**

638 E Wilmington Avenue
Salt Lake City, UT   84106   801-486-3778
      800-388-1991
      FAX 801-486-3123
e-mail: rstarley@uw.org
Richard Starley, President

The following are camping and recreational services offered: Camp respite for children and day camping for children.

614   **Reid Ranch**

3310 S 2700 E
Salt Lake City, UT   84109   801-468-3274
      800-468-3274
      FAX 801-463-0388
http://www.reidranch.com
e-mail: greid@reidranch.com
Gardner Reid, Owner

Provides students, ages 8-18, with an opportunity to receive small group and tutorial instruction in reading and language skills development. The program operates three weeks during the summer.

Vermont

615   **Easter Seals Vermont**

641 Comstock Road
Berlin, VT   05602   802-223-4744
      FAX 802-229-0848
e-mail: mjohnso@eseals.org
Mark Johnson, VP

The following are camping and recreational services offered: Camp respite for children, camperships.

616   **Silver Towers Camp**

1116 US Route 5
East Dummerston, VT   05346
      800-385-8524
      FAX 802-254-7661
http://www.silvertowers.com
e-mail: enc550@sover.net
Earl Cavanagh

A one-week residential camp for exceptional people six years old and up to enjoy varied opportunities for personal enrichment and development of social skills, including swimming, arts and crafts, sing alongs, music, dancing and bowling

Virginia

617   **Fairfax County Community and Recreation**

12011 Government Center Pkwy.
Fairfax, VA   22035   703-324-5532
      FAX 703-222-9788
http://www.fairfaxcounty.gov\rec
Therapeutic recreation services summer activities for children with disabilities to include LD and ADHA.

618   **Sensational Explorers Day Camp**

PO Box 10693
Burke, VA   22009   703-764-3495
Nancy Malina

A camp for high functioning children with sensory integration needs. The camp is run by sensory integration clinicians.

619   **Summer Adventure Program**

Trinity College
125 Michigan Avenue NE
Washington, DC   20017   202-244-8089
e-mail: lciotassoc@aol.com
Shiraz Kashani

A six week day camp to enhance sensory motor development. Activities include tactile activity, gross and fine motor skills, swimming instruction, music, language and visualization skills.

620   **Summer Intensive Fluency Therapy**

4208 Evergreen Lane
Annandale, VA   22003   703-941-8903
      877-586-4152
http://www.afccafet.com
Offers programs for stuttering and dyslexia.

Washington

621 Camp Easter Seals West

17809 S Vaughn Road
Vaughn, WA 98394   253-884-2722
FAX 253-884-0200
http://www.seals.org
e-mail: eastersealare@seals.org
Mary McIntyre, Office Manager
Mike Mooney, Summer Camp Director
Lori Hall, Respite Coordinator

The camp offers six day sessions geared to the age, level of ability and needs of the camper. Includes a wide range of activities including horseback riding, dancing and waterfront activities.

622 Camp Killoqua Camp Fire USA

Snohomish County Council
4312 Rucker Avenue
Everett, WA 98203   425-258-5437
FAX 452-252-2267
http://www.campfireusasnohomish.org
e-mail: info@campfireusasnohomish.org
Megan McArthur, Contact

Provides a unique outdoor experience for youth and adults offering a full range of options and opportunities.

623 Camp Sweyolakan

524 N Mullan Road
Spokane, WA 99206   509-747-6191
800-386-2324
FAX 509-747-4913
http://www.campfireiec.org
e-mail: campfireiec@msn.com
Peggy Clark, Camp Director
Judy Lippman, Special Programs

Both resident and day camp on 300 wooded acres is open to all boys, girls, adults, those with special needs and families.

624 Easter Seals Spokane

W 606 Sharp
Spokane, WA 99201   509-326-8292
FAX 509-326-2261
e-mail: gperkins@wa.easter-seals.org
Ginette Perkins, Program Manager

The following are camping and recreational services offered: Recreational services for children and residential camping programs.

625 Easter Seals Washington

17809 S Vaughn Road KPN
Vaughn, WA 98394   253-884-2722
FAX 253-884-0200
e-mail: camp@seals.org
Mary McIntyre, Office Manager

The following are camping and recreational services offered: Camp respite for adults, camp respite for children, camperships, computer program, conference rental, family retreats, residential camping programs and swim programs.

West Virginia

626 Easter Seals West Virginia

1305 National Road
Wheeling, WV 26003   304-242-1390
800-677-1390
FAX 304-243-5880
e-mail: ateaster@stargate.net
Martha Hon, President/CEO

The following are camping and recreational services offered: Day camping for children, sports camp and therapeutic horseback riding.

627 Mountain Milestones

Stepping Stones
15 Cottage Street
Morgantown, WV 26501   304-296-0150
800-982-8799
FAX 304-296-0194
http://www.steppingstonecenter.net
e-mail: abilitywv@hotmail.com
Missy Weimer, Director
Jerry Jones, President
Adam Bullian, Recreation Coordinator

People with disabilities of all ages can take part in a variety of recreation programs that include adventures, team sports, special events and camps.

Wisconsin

628 Bike Farm Summer Camp

2780 230th Street
Cushing, WI 54006   715-648-5773
FAX 715-648-6800
http://www.bikefarm.org
e-mail: sclark@bikefarm.org
Stephen J Clark, Director
Carl Gaede, Supervisor

Residential and day camp that provides an opportunity through activities to create, support and grow.

629 Easter Seals Camp Wawbeek

101 Nob Hill Road
Madison, WI 53713   608-277-8288
800-422-2324
FAX 608-277-8333
e-mail: wawbeek@wi-easterseals.org
Chris Hollar, Director

The following are camping and recreational services offered: Adventure, camperships, canoeing, conference rental, day camping for children, family retreats, residential camping programs and swim programs.

630 Easter Seals Madison

101 Nob Hill Road
Madison, WI 53713   608-277-8288
800-422-2324
FAX 608-277-8333
e-mail: tpaprock@wi-easterseals.org
Ken Saville, VP Program Development

The following are camping and recreational services offered: Vacation get-away program.

631   **Easter Seals Menomonee Falls**

N79W14845 Homestead Drive
Menomonee Falls, WI   53051   262-253-5550
                                     FAX 262-253-6503
Julie Hagenstein, CDC Director

The following are camping and recreational services offered: Before/After school program for Ages 6 through 18, recreational services for adults and recreational services for children.

632   **Easter Seals Southeastern Wisconsin**

3090 N 53rd Street
Milwaukee, WI   53210   414-449-4444
                               FAX 414-449-4447
            e-mail: agency@easterseals-sewi.org
Tim Biondo, CEO

The following are camping and recreational services offered: Before/After school program for Ages 6 through 18.

633   **Timbertop Nature Adventure Camp**

Stevens Point Area YMCA
1000 Division Street
Stevens Point, WI   54481   715-342-2980
                                   FAX 715-342-2987
                  http://www.spymca.org
              e-mail: pmatthai@spymca.org
Audrey Schmeeckle, Operations Director
Jackie Clussman, Special Needs Director

For youth identified by their school districts as needing extra help for a learning disability. Combines traditional camp activities focused on dealing with learning disabilities in a structured daily setting. Special attention is paid to peer relations, building self-confidence and learning new skills.

634   **Wisconsin Elk/Easter Seals Respite Camp**

101 Nob Hill Road
Madison, WI   53713   608-277-8288
                             800-422-2342
                             FAX 608-277-8333
            e-mail: respite1@wi-easterseals.org
Kelly Housman, Director

The following are camping and recreational services offered: Camp respite for adults, camp respite for children, canoeing, family retreats, residential camping programs and swim programs.

Language Arts

635 100% Concepts: Intermediate

LinguiSystems
3100 4th Avenue
East Moline, IL 61244

800-776-4332
FAX 309-755-2377
TDY:800-933-8331
http://www.linguisystems.com
e-mail: service@linguisystems.com
LinguiSystems Staff, Author
Linda Bowers, Owner
Rosemary Huisingh, Owner

Concepts learning doesn't stop in the early grades. Your older students with language disorders need to understand the terms they hear in the classroom. These terrific activities will help. Teach higher level concepts, including location and direction, quality or condition, comparison, time and occurrence, and relationship. *$37.95*

174 pages   Ages 10-14

636 100% Concepts: Primary

LinguiSystems
3100 4th Avenue
East Moline, IL 61244

800-776-4332
FAX 309-755-2377
TDY:800-933-8331
http://www.linguisystems.com
e-mail: service@linguisystems.com
LinguiSystems Staff, Author
Linda Bowers, Owner
Rosemary Huisingh, Owner

Concepts are the building blocks of language. This approach gives students practice with familiar concepts in different formats for strong language comprehension skills. You'll teach tons of concepts, including following directions, grouping, association, math, and time. *$37.95*

157 pages   Ages 5-9

637 100% Grammar

LinguiSystems
3100 4th Avenue
East Moline, IL 61244

800-776-4332
FAX 309-755-2377
TDY:800-933-8331
http://www.linguisystems.com
e-mail: service@linguisystems.com
Mike LoGiudice, Carolyn LoGiudice, Author
Linda Bowers, Owner
Rosemary Huisingh, Owner

Make the link between grammar and communication skills with this incredible resource. You'll get relevant, fun activities to develop clear, accurate, excellent communication skills. Covers all the essential grammar areas including nouns, pronouns, complements, verbals, clauses, and fine points. *$37.95*

174 pages   Ages 9-14

638 100% Grammar LITE

LinguiSystems
3100 4th Avenue
East Moline, IL 61244

800-776-4332
FAX 309-755-2377
TDY:800-933-8331
http://www.linguisystems.com
e-mail: service@linguisystems.com
Mike LoGiudice, Carolyn LoGiudice, Author
Linda Bowers, Owner
Rosemary Huisingh, Owner

Teach one grammar concept at a time. Compared to 100% Grammar, this resource is lighter in the amount of content per page and contextual demands of the practice items. The fun art and light approach will appeal to your hardest-to-teach students. The book is divided into two sections covering parts of speech and sentence structures. *$37.95*

178 pages   Ages 9-14

639 100% Vocabulary: Intermediate

LinguiSystems
3100 4th Avenue
East Moline, IL 61244

800-776-4332
FAX 309-755-2377
TDY:800-933-8331
http://www.linguisystems.com
e-mail: service@linguisystems.com
Vicki Rothstein, Rhoda Zacker, Author
Linda Bowers, Owner
Rosemary Huisingh, Owner

Teach vocabulary through an organized, systematic approach that works. These challenging semantic exercises teach word flexibility and verbal reasoning skills. You'll teach strategies for understanding word relationships with activities for classification, absurdities, comparisons, exclusion and more. *$37.95*

188 pages   Ages 9-14

640 100% Vocabulary: Primary

LinguiSystems
3100 4th Avenue
East Moline, IL 61244

800-776-4332
FAX 309-755-2377
TDY:800-933-8331
http://www.linguisystems.com
e-mail: service@linguisystems.com
Vicki Rothstein, Rhoda Zacker, Author
Linda Bowers, Owner
Rosemary Huisingh, Owner

Help younger students begin to understand complex word relationships with these outstanding exercises. Students work through a hierarchy of task complexity based on how we think about words. Students will recognize answers with yes/no or true/false, choose answers from alternatives, and infer answers when information isn't directly stated. *$37.95*

187 pages   Ages 6-9

641 **125 Vocabulary Builders**

LinguiSystems
3100 4th Avenue
East Moline, IL   61244

800-776-4332
FAX 309-755-2377
TDY:800-933-8331
http://www.linguisystems.com
e-mail: service@linguisystems.com
LinguiSystems Staff, Author
Linda Bowers, Owner
Rosemary Huisingh, Owner

This resource goes beyond teaching words by teaching students how to recognize, learn, and integrate new words into their daily vocabulary. Gives students strategies for connecting new vocabulary words to each other, to curriculum and to their prior experience. Your students will learn and remember sets of words because they're used in meaningful ways. *$35.95*

158 pages   Ages 10-15

642 **A to Zap!**

Sunburst Technology
400 Columbus Avenue
Valhalla, NY   10595

914-747-3310
800-321-7511
FAX 914-747-4109
http://www.sunburst.com
e-mail: support@sunburst.com

A whimsical world of magical talking alphabet blocks and energetic playful characters this program provides young children with exciting opportunities to explore new concepts through open-ended activities and games. Mac/Win CD-ROM

643 **Ablenet**

1081 10th Avenue SE
Minneapolis, MN   55414

612-379-0956
800-322-0956
FAX 612-379-9143
http://www.ablenetinc.com
e-mail: customerservice@ablenetinc.com
Cheryl Volkman, Chief Developmental Officer

Simple assistive technology for teaching children with disabilities including communication aids, switches, environmental control, mounting systems, literacy and teacher resources, kits and more.

644 **American Heritage Children's Dictionary**

Sunburst Technology
400 Columbus Avenue
Valhalla, NY   10595

914-747-3310
800-321-7511
FAX 914-747-4109
http://www.sunburst.com
e-mail: support@sunburst.com

This multimedia dictionary uses sound, color illustrations and animations to demonstrate the spelling, definition and pronunciation of 13,000 words. Three additional word games enhance the students' language usage and vocabulary levels. Available formats in MAC CD-ROM, Win CD-ROM. *$99.95*

645 **Analogies 1, 2 & 3**

Educators Publishing Service
31 Smith Place
Cambridge, MA   02139

617-547-6706
800-435-7728
FAX 888-440-2665
http://www.epsbooks.com
e-mail: eps@epsbooks.com
Arthur Liebman, Author
Nick Gaehde, President

Studying analogies helps students to sharpen reasoning ability, develop critical thinking, understand relationships between words and ideas, learn new vocabulary, and prepare for the SAT's and for standardized tests.

646 **Artic Shuffle**

LinguiSystems
3100 4th Avenue
East Moline, IL   61244

800-776-4332
FAX 309-755-2377
TDY:800-933-8331
http://www.linguisystems.com
e-mail: service@linguisystems.com
Tobie Nan Kaufman, Author
Linda Bowers, Owner
Rosemary Huisingh, Owner

Your students can play Go Fish, Crazy Eights, or Concentration while they practice their target sounds. Use them for vocabulary drills or naming practice. *$89.95*

Ages 5-Adult

647 **Artic-Pic**

The Speech Bin
1965 25th Avenue
Vero Beach, FL   32960

772-770-0007
FAX 772-770-0006
http://www.speechbin.com
e-mail: info@speechbin.com

You're just going to love this topsy-turvy upside-down book! Artic-Pic is a clever book that gives you delightful interactive practice materials for those troublesome r and s sounds. You get twenty story poems for each phoneme, each with Artic-Pic answer choices featuring the target sound in varying co-articulatory contexts. Item number 1513. *$19.95*

648 **ArticBURST Articulation Practice for S, R, Ch, and Sh**

LinguiSystems
3100 4th Avenue
East Moline, IL   61244

800-776-4332
FAX 309-755-2377
TDY:800-933-8331
http://www.linguisystems.com
e-mail: service@linguisystems.com
LinguiSystems Staff, Author
Linda Bowers, Owner
Rosemary Huisingh, Owner

Here's a fun quick thinking game for your older students and clients who continue to need articulation therapy. You'll get a set of cards for each of the toughest sounds. Players have to think of a word with their target sound in these four areas: rhyming, compounds, antonyms, and synonyms. *$37.95*

Ages 10-Adult

649 Articulation 3-Vowels: Software

The Speech Bin
1965 25th Avenue
Vero Beach, FL   32960   570-770-0007
                                         800-477-3324
                                    FAX 888-329-2246
                          http://www.speechbin.com
                          e-mail: info@speechbin.com

This terrific articulation software is a speech-language pathologist's dream come true! It gives you 572 full-color photo stimuli featuring those troublesome r-controlled vowels and r clusters in 76 categories. *$99.00*

650 Autism & PPD: Concept Development

LinguiSystems
3100 4th Avenue
East Moline, IL   61244
                                         800-776-4332
                                    FAX 309-755-2377
                                    TDY:800-933-8331
                         http://www.linguisystems.com
                        e-mail: service@linguisystems.com
Pam Britton Reese, Nena Challenner, Author
Linda Bowers, Owner
Rosemary Huisingh, Owner

This great program teaches a variety of concepts grouped by themes. The simple, realistic artwork provides the visual clues so many students need. As students work through each concept-building program, they'll also develop important language skills such as naming, attributes, categorizing, and giving descriptions. *$155.70*

Ages 3-8

651 Autism & PPD: Pictured Stories and Language Activities

LinguiSystems
3100 4th Avenue
East Moline, IL   61244
                                         800-776-4332
                                    FAX 309-755-2377
                                    TDY:800-933-8331
                         http://www.linguisystems.com
                        e-mail: service@linguisystems.com
Patricia Snair Koski, Author
Linda Bowers, Owner
Rosemary Huisingh, Owner

These sequential picture stories focus on simple, easy-to-follow elements. The repetition, structure, and routine make this a great program for students with autism, PPD, or delayed language development. It's a field tested program that works. *$149.75*

Ages 3-8

652 Basic Signing Vocabulary Cards

Harris Communications
15155 Technology Drive
Eden Prairie, MN   55344   952-906-1180
                                         800-825-6758
                                    FAX 952-906-1099
                                    TDY:952-906-1180
                           http://www.harriscomm.com
                          e-mail: mail@harriscomm.com
Bill Williams, National Sales Manager

Designed to build signed English vocabulary at a beginners level. Two sets. *$6.95*

100 cards/set

653 Basic Words for Children: Software

The Speech Bin
1965 25th Avenue
Vero Beach, FL   32960   772-770-0007
                                         800-477-3324
                                    FAX 772-770-0006
                          http://www.speechbin.com
                          e-mail: info@speechbin.com

This exciting software uses beautiful full color photos and action videos to teach 100 basic words essential for the young child's vocabulary. Item number L197: English, Item number L174: Spanish. *$99.00*

654 Blonigen Fluency Program

The Speech Bin
1965 25th Avenue
Vero Beach, FL   32960   570-770-0007
                                    FAX 561-770-0006
                          http://www.speechbin.com
                          e-mail: info@speechbin.com
Julie Blonigen, Author

The Blonigen Fluency Program is a systematic approach to teaching the stuttering modification technique of prolongation to treat stuttering in 7-17 year olds. It features easy-to-follow step-by-step directions and exercises to identify and alter disfluency patterns and gain control over the moment of stuttering. *$24.95*

Ages 7-17

655 Bubbleland Word Discovery

Sunburst Technology
400 Columbus Avenue
Valhalla, NY   10595   914-747-3310
                                         800-321-7511
                                    FAX 914-747-4109
                            http://www.sunburst.com
                          e-mail: support@sunburst.com

Build and sharpen language arts skills with this multimedia dictionary. Students explore ten familiar locations that include a pet shop, zoo, toy store, hospital, playground, beach and airport where they engage in 40 activities that build word recognition, pronunciation and spelling skills.

656   Carolina Picture Vocabulary Test

Pro-Ed
8700 Shoal Creek Boulevard
Austin, TX   78757   512-451-3246
                            800-897-3202
                        FAX 800-397-7633
                    http://www.proedinc.com
Thomas Layton and David Holmes, Author

A norm-referenced, validated, receptive sign vocabulary test for deaf and hearing-impaired children. *$133.00*

657   Central Auditory Processing Kit

LinguiSystems
3100 4th Avenue
East Moline, IL   61244
                            800-776-4332
                        FAX 309-755-2377
                        TDY:800-933-8331
                    http://www.linguisystems.com
                e-mail: service@linguisystems.com
Mary Ann Mokhemar, Author
Linda Bowers, Owner
Rosemary Huisingh, Owner

This unique, comprehensive program addresses auditory processing skills with a direct focus on academics including decoding, following directions, and more. Three books cover a wide range of skills including auditory memory, discrimination, closure, synthesis, figure ground, cohesion, and compensatory strategies. *$89.95*

180 pages   Ages 6-13

658   Complete Oral-Motor Program for Articulation: Book Only

LinguiSystems
3100 4th Avenue
East Moline, IL   61244
                            800-776-4332
                        FAX 309-755-2377
                        TDY:800-933-8331
                    http://www.linguisystems.com
                e-mail: service@linguisystems.com
Harriet Pehde, Ann Geller, Bonnie Lechner, Author
Linda Bowers, Owner
Rosemary Huisingh, Owner

Manual guides you through oral-motor lessons with clear instructions for exercise. Students will increase oral-motor awareness, strength and tone. There's even a specific sound remediation program for S, Z, Sh, Ch, J, and R. *$39.95*

159 pages   Ages 3-12

659   Complete Oral-Motor Program for Articulation

LinguiSystems
3100 4th Avenue
East Moline, IL   61244
                            800-776-4332
                        FAX 309-755-2377
                        TDY:800-933-8331
                    http://www.linguisystems.com
                e-mail: service@linguisystems.com
Harriet Pehde, Ann Geller, Bonnie Lechner, Author
Linda Bowers, Owner
Rosemary Huisingh, Owner

These authors have pooled their years of experience to create this big, best selling kit. You'll get everything you need to help students increase awareness, strength and tone of oral musculature, associate oral-motor function to speech sound musculature, associate oral-motor function to speech sound production, and improve overall articulation skills. *$119.95*

159 pages   Ages 3-12

660   Complete Oral-Motor Program for Articulation: Refill Kit

LinguiSystems
3100 4th Avenue
East Moline, IL   61244
                            800-776-4332
                        FAX 309-755-2377
                        TDY:800-933-8331
                    http://www.linguisystems.com
                e-mail: service@linguisystems.com
Harriet Pehde, Ann Geller, Bonnie Lechner, Author
Linda Bowers, Owner
Rosemary Huisingh, Owner

Refill kit for Complete Oral-Motor Program for Articulation. *$54.95*

Ages 3-12

661   Create-A-Story

The Speech Bin
1965 25th Avenue
Vero Beach, FL   32960   772-770-0007
                            FAX 772-770-0006
                        http://www.speechbin.com
                        e-mail: info@speechbin.com

Here's a powerful language learning game that simplifies the creative process of storytelling and writing for 5-99-year-olds. It fosters their imaginations, organizes their thoughts, and boosts their confidence as they build a narrative. The game can be played by 1-6 players as groups or individuals. Item number C151. *$44.95*

662 Curious George Pre-K ABCs

Sunburst Technology
400 Columbus Avenue
Valhalla, NY 10595

914-747-3310
800-321-7511
FAX 914-747-4109
http://www.sunburst.com
e-mail: support@sunburst.com

Children go on a lively adventure with Curious George visiting six multi level activities that provide an animated introduction to letters and their sounds. Students discover letter names and shapes, initial letter sounds, letter pronunciations, the order of the alphabet and new vocabulary words during the fun exursions with Curious George. Mac/Win CD-ROM

663 Curriculum Vocabulary Game

LinguiSystems
3100 4th Avenue
East Moline, IL 61244

800-776-4332
FAX 309-755-2377
TDY:800-933-8331
http://www.linguisystems.com
e-mail: service@linguisystems.com
Paul Johnson, Stephen Johnson, Author
Linda Bowers, Owner
Rosemary Huisingh, Owner

The organized lessons teach the classroom vocabulary your students need to know. Each lesson is curricular, flexible, and comprehensive. You'll tap all the learning styles in your case-load. Activities work through a hierarchy from introducing the concepts, to hands-on activities, to writing and take home practice. *$44.95*

Ages 9-13

664 Daily Starters: Quote of the Day

LinguiSystems
3100 4th Avenue
East Moline, IL 61244

800-776-4332
FAX 309-755-2377
TDY:800-933-8331
http://www.linguisystems.com
e-mail: service@linguisystems.com
Dave Wisniewski, Author
Linda Bowers, Owner
Rosemary Huisingh, Owner

Get your students off to a focused start in therapy or in the classroom. These quick activities help older students integrate several language arts skills at once including writing, thinking, grammar, punctuation, vocabulary, and more. *$21.95*

142 pages Ages 12-18

665 Dyslexia: An Introduction to the Orton-Gillingham Approach

Educators Publishing Service
31 Smith Place
Cambridge, MA 02139

617-547-6706
800-225-5750
FAX 888-440-2665
http://www.epsbooks.com
e-mail: eps@epsbooks.com
Nick Gaehde, President

This ten-lesson, online course provides an introduction to the Orton-Gillingham approach to teaching students with dyslexia. Topics include: the nature of the individual with dyslexia; principles of the Orton-Gillingham approach; multisensory instruction and the brain; and the phonology, structure, and history of the English language.

666 ESPA Success in Language Arts Literacy

Harcourt Achieve
6277 Sea Harbor Drive
Orlando, FL 32887

800-531-5015
FAX 800-699-9459
http://www.steckvaughn.com
e-mail: info@steckvaughn.com
Steck-Vaughn Staff, Author
Tim McEwen, President/CEO
Jeff Johnson, Dir Marketing Communications
Chris Lehmann, Team Coordinator

Prepares students for one of their most important early assessments. Especially in the early years, children learn at their own pace. Make sure your students aren't exposed to an early disappointment by providing a thorough preparation for the ESPA.

667 Early Communication Skills

Therapro
225 Arlington Street
Framingham, MA 01702

508-872-9494
800-257-5376
FAX 508-875-2062
http://www.theraproducts.com
e-mail: info@theraproducts.com
Libby Kumin PhD, Author
Karen Conrad, President

Provides professional expertise in understandable terms. Parents and professionals learn how their skills are evaulated by professionals, and what activities they can practice with a child immediately to encouarge a childs's communication skill development. *$19.95*

368 pages Ages Birth-K

668 Early Listening Skills

Therapro
225 Arlington Street
Framingham, MA 01702

508-872-9494
800-257-5376
FAX 508-875-2062
http://www.theraproducts.com
e-mail: info@theraproducts.com
Diana Williams, Author
Karen Conrad, President

Two hundred activities designed to be photocopied for classroom or home. Includes materials on auditory detection, discrimination, recognition, sequencing and memory. Describes listening projects and topics for the curriculum. Activity sheets for parents are included. A practical, comprehensive and effective manual for professionals working with preschool children or the older child with special needs. *$55.00*

669 Earobics Step 2: Home Version

The Speech Bin
1965 25th Avenue
Vero Beach, FL   39260   772-770-0007
                               FAX 772-770-0006
                               http://www.speechbin.com
                               e-mail: info@speechbin.com

Step 2 teaches critical language comprehension skills and trains the critical auditory skills children need for success in learning. It offers hundreds of levels of play, appealing graphics, and entertaining music to train the critical auditory skills young children need for success in learning. Item number C483. *$59.00*

670 Earobics Step 2: Specialist/Clinician Version

The Speech Bin
1965 25th Avenue
Vero Beach, FL   32960   772-770-0007
                               FAX 772-770-0006
                               http://www.speechbin.com
                               e-mail: info@speechbin.com

Earobics features: tasks and level counter with real time display; adaptive training technology for individualized programs; and reporting to track and evaluate each individual's progress. Step 2 teaches critical language comprehension skills and trains the critical auditory skills children need for success in learning. Item number C484. *$299.00*

671 Easy Does It for Fluency: Intermediate

LinguiSystems
3100 4th Avenue
East Moline, IL   61244
                               800-776-4332
                               FAX 309-755-2377
                               TDY:800-933-8331
                               http://www.linguisystems.com
                               e-mail: service@linguisystems.com
Barbara Roseman, Karin Johnson, Author
Linda Bowers, Owner
Rosemary Huisingh, Owner

This program addresses the motor, linguistic, and psychosocial components of stuttering as students work toward fluent speech. This updated and revised version of an old favorite will help your students become fluent. *$49.95*

165 pages   Ages 6-11

672 Easy Does It for Fluency: Preschool/Primary

LinguiSystems
3100 4th Avenue
East Moline, IL   61244
                               800-776-4332
                               FAX 309-755-2377
                               TDY:800-933-8331
                               http://www.linguisystems.com
                               e-mail: service@linguisystems.com
Barbara Roseman, Karin Johnson, Author
Linda Bowers, Owner
Rosemary Huisingh, Owner

This systematic program of fluency shaping uses slow, easy speech for the youngest stutterers. The therapy manual contains step-by-step activities with goals and objectives. There are also sample lesson plans for individualizing therapy, strategies and materials to involve care givers. *$49.95*

117 pages   Ages 2-6

673 Elementary Spelling Ace ES-90

Franklin Electronic Publishers
1 Franklin Plaza
Burlington, NJ   08016   609-386-2500
                               800-525-9673
                               FAX 609-387-1787
                               http://www.franklin.com
                               e-mail: info@frankling.com
John Applegate, Director
Bettie Albertson, Executive Assistant

Designed for elementary children, provides them with spelling correction for over 80,000 words. Accompanied by Webster's Elementary Dictionary. *$34.95*

674 Every Child a Reader

Sunburst Technology
400 Columbus Avenue
Valhalla, NY   10595   914-747-3310
                               800-321-7511
                               FAX 914-747-4109
                               http://www.sunburst.com
                               e-mail: support@sunburst.com

Traditional reading strategies in a rich literary context. Designed to promote independent reading and develop oral and written language expression.

675 Explode the Code: Wall Chart

Educators Publishing Service
31 Smith Place
Cambridge, MA   02139   617-547-6706
                               800-225-5750
                               FAX 888-440-2665
                               http://www.epsbooks.com
                               e-mail: eps@epsbooks.com
Nancy M Hall, Rena Price, Author
Nick Gaehde, President

Learning sounds is exciting with the new Explode The Code alphabet chart! Each letter is represented by a colorful character from the series and is stored inside a felt pocket embroidered with the letter's name.

676 Expressive Language Kit

LinguiSystems
3100 4th Avenue
East Moline, IL   61244
                               800-776-4332
                               FAX 309-755-2377
                               TDY:800-933-8331
                               http://www.linguisystems.com
                               e-mail: service@linguisystems.com
Linda Bowers, Rosemary Huisingh, Carolyn
LoGiudice, Author
Linda Bowers, Owner
Rosemary Huisingh, Owner

It's our biggest language therapy kit ever. The focus is on strengthening expressive language skills so your students will become effective communicators. A combination of colorful photographs, picture cards, and activity sheets work together to create an outstanding expressive language program. A comprehension therapy manual is included to help you direct this incredibly wide variety of language activities. *$149.95*

250 pages   Ages 5-11

677 **Famous African Americans**

Harcourt Achieve
6277 Sea Harbor Drive
Orlando, FL   32887

800-531-5015
FAX 800-699-9459
http://www.steckvaughn.com
e-mail: info@steckvaughn.com

Booth, Author
Tim McEwen, President/CEO
Jeff Johnson, Dir Marketing Communications
Chris Lehmann, Team Coordinator

Introduce students to dozens of African-American achievers while improving language and thinking skills. High interest, three-page lessons highlight a defining moment in each individual's life and provide activities to build and apply skills in a curriculum context. Subjects are drawn from such diverse fields as science, government, education, sports, fine arts, and the military.

678 **Figurative Language**

Harcourt Achieve
6277 Sea Harbor Drive
Orlando, FL   32887

800-531-5015
FAX 800-699-9459
http://www.steckvaughn.com
e-mail: info@steckvaughn.com

Steck-Vaughn Staff, Author
Tim McEwen, President/CEO
Jeff Johnson, Dir Marketing Communications
Chris Lehmann, Team Coordinator

A delightful series that promotes critical thinking and vocabulary development through the use of literal and figurative language.

679 **First Phonics**

Sunburst Technology
400 Columbus Avenue
Valhalla, NY   10595

914-747-3310
800-321-7511
FAX 914-747-4109
http://www.sunburst.com
e-mail: support@sunburst.com

Targets the phonics skills that all children need to develop, sounding out the first letter of a word. This program offers four different engaging activities that you can customize to match each child's specific need.

680 **Fluharty Preschool Speech & Language Screening Test 2**

The Speech Bin
1965 25th Avenue
Vero Beach, FL   32960

772-770-0007
800-477-3324
FAX 888-329-2246
http://www.speechbin.com
e-mail: info@speechbin.com

Nancy Buono Fluharty, Author

Carefully normed on 705 children, the Fluharty yields standard scores, percentiles, and age equivalents. The form features space for speech-language pathologist to note phonological processess, voice quality, and fluency; a Teacher Questionnaire is also provided. Item number P882. *$153.00*

681 **Focus on Listening**

Harcourt Achieve
6277 Sea Harbor Drive
Orlando, FL   32887

800-531-5015
FAX 800-699-9459
http://www.steckvaughn.com
e-mail: info@steckvaughn.com

Cimchowski, Author
Tim McEwen, President/CEO
Jeff Johnson, Dir Marketing Communications
Chris Lehmann, Team Coordinator

A one-of-a-kind solution for students who need to improve their listening skills, students who are tested for their listening ability, or students who need practice with comprehending oral instructions. This program uses audio cassettes and teacher read material to practice listening comprehension of narrative, informational, persuasive, and workplace language.

682 **Follow Me! 2**

LinguiSystems
3100 4th Avenue
East Moline, IL   61244

800-776-4332
FAX 309-775-2377
TDY:800-933-8331
http://www.linguisystems.com
e-mail: service@linguisystems.com

Grace Frank, Author
Linda Bowers, Owner
Rosemary Huisingh, Owner

These activities are relevant to classroom listening demands. The directions relate specifically to an accompanying worksheet. It's a pick-up-and-use-now resource to teach the vocabulary of language arts, math, social studies and more. *$34.95*

201 pages   Ages 7-11

683 **Fun with Language: Book 1**

Therapro
225 Arlington Street
Framingham, MA   01702

508-872-9494
800-257-5376
FAX 508-875-2062
http://www.theraproducts.com
e-mail: info@theraproducts.com

Kathleen Yardley, Author
Karen Conrad, President

A wonderful reproducible workbook of thinking and language skill exercises for children ages 4-8. Perfect when you need something on a moment's notice. Over 100 beautifully illustrated exercises in the following categories: Spatial Relationships; Opposites; Categorizing; Following Directions; Temporal Concepts; Syntax & Morphology; Same and Different; Plurals; Memory; Reasoning; Storytelling; and Describing. Targets both receptive and expressive language as well as problem- solving skills. *$55.00*

684 GEPA Success in Language Arts Literacy and Mathematics

Harcourt Achieve
6277 Sea Harbor Drive
Orlando, FL   32887

800-531-5015
FAX 800-699-9459
http://www.steckvaughn.com
e-mail: info@steckvaughn.com

Steck-Vaughn Staff, Author
Tim McEwen, President/CEO
Jeff Johnson, Dir Marketing Communications
Chris Lehmann, Team Coordinator

With these workbooks, you can ensure that your students are becoming more proficient users of language and math as well as more skilled test takers. Your students will gain valuable practice answering the types of questions found on the GEPA, such as open-ended and enhanced multiple choice items.

685 Get the Story! City News: Country News CD-ROM

Iarcourt Achieve
6277 Sea Harbor Drive
Orlando, FL   32887

800-531-5015
FAX 800-699-9459
http://www.steckvaughn.com
e-mail: info@steckvaughn.com

Tim McEwen, President/CEO
Jeff Johnson, Dir Marketing Communications
Chris Lehmann, Team Coordinator

Develop investigation and communication skills in the context of publishing a newspaper. Students take on the roles of editors, reporters, and photographers to get the scoop on events in a big city, in a small town, and on a farm. Tasks include gathering information through interviews and clips files.

686 Goldman-Fristoe Test of Articulation: 2nd Edition

The Speech Bin
1965 25th Avenue
Vero Beach, FL   32960   772-770-0007
FAX 772-770-0006
http://www.speechbin.com
e-mail: info@speechbin.com

The Goldman-Fristoe has been revised! This 2000 edition of your perennial articulation testing favorite systematically measures a child's production of 39 consonant sounds and blends. Its age range is expanded to 2-21 years, and age-based standard scores have separate gender norms. Item number A195. *$209.99*

687 HELP 1

LinguiSystems
3100 4th Avenue
East Moline, IL   61244

800-776-4332
FAX 309-775-2375
TDY:800-933-8331
http://www.linguisystems.com
e-mail: service@linguisystems.com

Andrea Lazzari, Patricia Peters, Author
Linda Bowers, Owner
Rosemary Huisingh, Owner

Get the books clinicians have relied on for years as their number one therapy resource. Written by two speech-language pathologists who know language remediation, this series has set the industry standard for practical, pick-up-and-use-now language therapy activities. HELP 1 includes activities for auditory discrimination, question comprehension, auditory association, and auditory memory. *$39.95*

163 pages   Ages 6-Adult

688 HELP 2

LinguiSystems
3100 4th Avenue
East Moline, IL   61244

800-776-4332
FAX 309-755-2377
TDY:800-933-8331
http://www.linguisystems.com
e-mail: service@linguisystems.com

Andrea Lazzari, Patricia Peters, Author
Linda Bowers, Owner
Rosemary Huisingh, Owner

Get the books clinicians have relied on for years as their number one therapy resource. Written by two speech-language pathologists who know language remediation, this series has set the industry standard for practical, pick-up-and-use-now language therapy activities. HELP 2 includes activities for word-finding, categorization, answering different question forms and grammar practice. *$39.95*

175 pages   Ages 6-Adult

689 HELP 3

LinguiSystems
3100 4th Avenue
East Moline, IL   61244

800-776-4332
FAX 309-755-2377
TDY:800-933-8331
http://www.linguisystems.com
e-mail: service@linguisystems.com

Andrea Lazzari, Patricia Peters, Author
Linda Bowers, Owner
Rosemary Huisingh, Owner

Get the books clinicians have relied on for years as their number one therapy resource. Written by two speech-language pathologists who know language remediation, this series has set the industry standard for practical, pick-up-and-use-now language therapy activities. HELP 3 includes activities for basic concepts, paraphrasing, thinking and problem-solving, and social language skills. *$39.95*

194 pages   Ages 6-Adult

690 HELP 4

LinguiSystems
3100 4th Avenue
East Moline, IL   61244

800-776-4332
FAX 309-755-2377
TDY:800-933-8331
http://www.linguisystems.com
e-mail: service@linguisystems.com

Andrea Lazzari, Patricia Peters, Author
Linda Bowers, Owner
Rosemary Huisingh, Owner

Get the books clinicians have relied on for years as their number one therapy resource. Written by two speech-language pathologists who know language remediation, this series has set the industry standard for practical, pick-up-and-use-now language therapy activities. HELP 4 includes activities for defining and describing activities, written language exercises, linguistic concepts, and the language of humor and riddles. *$39.95*

190 pages   Ages 6-Adult

691   HELP 5

LinguiSystems
3100 4th Avenue
East Moline, IL   61244

800-776-4332
FAX 309-755-2377
TDY:800-933-8331
http://www.linguisystems.com
e-mail: service@linguisystems.com

Andrea Lazzari, Patricia Peters, Author
Linda Bowers, Owner
Rosemary Huisingh, Owner

Get the books clinicians have relied on for years as their number one therapy resource. Written by two speech-language pathologists who know language remediation, this series has set the industry standard for practical, pick-up-and-use-now lanuage therapy activities. HELP 5 includes activities for processing information and messages; comparing and contrasting words; understanding math language and concepts; and communicating needs, feelings, and opinions. *$39.95*

190 pages   Ages 6-Adult

692   HELP for Articulation

LinguiSystems
3100 4th Avenue
East Moline, IL   61244

800-776-4332
FAX 309-755-2377
TDY:800-933-8331
http://www.linguisystems.com
e-mail: service@linguisystems.com

Andrea Lazzari, Author
Linda Bowers, Owner
Rosemary Huisingh, Owner

This pick-up-and-use resource gives you a great variety of target sounds and activities. The hierarchy of tasks ensures mastery along the way and keeps your articulation therapy organized. Best of all, it's designed to span ages 6 through adult so you'll have articulation practice for your entire caseload. *$39.95*

195 pages   Ages 6-Adult

693   HELP for Auditory Processing

LinguiSystems
3100 4th Avenue
East Moline, IL   61244

800-776-4332
FAX 309-755-2377
TDY:800-933-8331
http://www.linguisystems.com
e-mail: service@linguisystems.com

Andrea Lazzari, Patricia Peters, Author
Linda Bowers, Owner
Rosemary Huisingh, Owner

Functional communication improves when auditory processing skills are strong. Work on skills necessary to receive, interpret, and internalize language. Work through a hierarchy of auditory processing strategies with exercises for processing information in word classes, following a variety of directions, listening for sounds in words, and more. *$39.95*

190 pages   Ages 6-Adult

694   HELP for Grammar

LinguiSystems
3100 4th Avenue
East Moline, IL   61244

800-776-4332
FAX 309-755-2377
TDY:800-933-8331
http://www.linguisystems.com
e-mail: service@linguisystems.com

Andrea Lazzari, Author
Linda Bowers, Owner
Rosemary Huisingh, Owner

Get in-depth grammar practice arranged in developmental order so skill builds upon skill. Get grammar training and practice with oral and written language exercises including identifying and matching grammar types, categorizing grammar types, applying grammar skills in context, and more. *$39.95*

191 pages   Ages 8-Adult

695   HELP for Vocabulary

LinguiSystems
3100 4th Avenue
East Moline, IL   61244

800-776-4332
FAX 309-755-2377
TDY:800-933-8331
http://www.linguisystems.com
e-mail: service@linguisystems.com

Andrea Lazzari, Author
Linda Bowers, Owner
Rosemary Huisingh, Owner

Your students will expand word knowledge and learn to apply vocabulary skills in context with these great exercises. The hierarchy of tasks lets you see where breakdowns occur. Each page is a complete lesson with an IEP goal and ready-to-use exercise. *$39.95*

180 pages   Ages 8-Adult

696   HELP for Word Finding

LinguiSystems
3100 4th Avenue
East Moline, IL   61244

800-776-4332
FAX 309-755-2377
TDY:800-933-8331
http://www.linguisystems.com
e-mail: service@linguisystems.com

Andera Lazzari, Patricia Peters, Author
Linda Bowers, Owner
Rosemary Huisingh, Owner

Expand the speed, quality, and variety of word recall strategies within practical, everyday context. Stimulus items progress in difficulty within each task to cover a broad age range as well as range of ability. Clients practice word-finding strategies with exercises for automatic associations, words grouped in themes, and more. *$39.95*

179 pages   Ages 6-Adult

697   HSPA Success in Language Art Literacy

Harcourt Achieve
6277 Sea Harbor Drive
Orlando, FL   32887

800-531-5015
FAX 800-699-9459
http://www.steckvaughn.com
e-mail: info@steckvaughn.com
Steck-Vaughn Staff, Author
Tim McEwen, President/CEO
Jeff Johnson, Dir Marketing Communications
Chris Lehmann, Team Coordinator

These workbooks ensure your students are enchancing their language arts skills, while learning and practicing the skills they need for improved test performance.

698   HearFones

The Speech Bin
1965 25th Avenue
Vero Beach, FL   32960
772-770-0007
FAX 772-770-0006
http://www.speechbin.com
e-mail: info@speechbin.com

his unique nonelectronic self-contained headset is made of composite and plastic materials, and it's easy to clean. It lets users hear themselves more directly and clearly so they can analyze their own speech sound production and voice quality. Item number N261. *$29.00*

699   I Can Say R

The Speech Bin
1965 25th Avenue
Vero Beach, FL   32960
772-770-0007
FAX 772-770-0006
http://www.speechbin.com
e-mail: info@speechbin.com

Helping children overcome problems saying R sounds is one of the most perplexing dilemmas speech and language pathologists face in their caseloads. Here's a terrific book packed with innovative practice materials to make that task easier. Item number 1477. *$26.95*

700   Idiom's Delight

Academic Therapy Publications
20 Commercial Boulevard
Novato, CA   94949
415-883-3314
800-422-7249
FAX 888-287-9975
http://www.academictherapy.com
e-mail: sales@academictherapy.com
John Arena, Author
Jim Arena, Production
Anna Arena, Publisher

Offers 75 idioms and accompanying reproducible activities. Delightful illustrations portraying humorous literal interpretations of idioms are sprinkled throughout the book to enhance enjoyment. *$14.00*

64 pages
ISBN 0-878798-89-7

701   Island Reading Journey

Sunburst Technology
400 Columbus Avenue
Valhalla, NY   10595
914-747-3310
800-321-7511
FAX 914-747-4109
http://www.sunburst.com
e-mail: support@sunburst.com

Enhance your reading program with meaningful summary and extension activities for 100 intermediate level books. Students read for meaning while they engage in activities that test for comprehension, build writing skills with reader response and essay questions, develop usage skills with cloze activities and improve vocabulary/word attack skills.

702   Just for Kids: Apraxia

LinguiSystems
3100 4th Avenue
East Moline, IL   61244
800-776-4332
FAX 309-755-2377
TDY:800-933-8331
http://www.linguisystems.com
e-mail: service@linguisystems.com
Martha Drake, Author
Linda Bowers, Owner
Rosemary Huisingh, Owner

Work through a sequence of skills to help your young students achieve intelligibility. Sessions are organized using the alphabet as a theme. Each phase gives you all the materials you need including goals, for moving to the nest phase, family letter for take-home practice, supplemental word lists, oral-mouth posture pictures, and ABC flash cards. *$39.95*

157 pages   Ages 4-8

703   Just for Kids: Articulation Stories

linguiSystems
3100 4th Avenue
East Moline, IL   61244
800-776-4332
FAX 309-755-2377
TDY:800-933-8331
http://www.linguisystems.com
e-mail: service@linguisystems.com
Jennifer Preschern, Author
Linda Bowers, Owner
Rosemary Huisingh, Owner

Work through target sounds at the word, carrier sentence, sentence, and conversation levels. For each target sound, you'll get a wonderful organized lesson with child-centered vocabulary, appealing pictures, fun stories and interactive activities. *$39.95*

175 pages   Ages 4-9

704 Just for Kids: Grammar

LinguiSystems
3100 4th Avenue
East Moline, IL   61244

800-776-4332
FAX 309-755-2377
TDY:800-933-8331
http://www.linguisystems.com
e-mail: service@linguisystems.com

Janet Lanza, Lynn Flahive, Author
Linda Bowers, Owner
Rosemary Huisingh, Owner

This kid friendly approach to grammar teaches the parts of speech your students need to know. The practice centers around natural, meaningful activities. Each chapter includes a pre-and post-test, picture cards, sequence story, rebus story, and family letter. *$39.95*

186 pages   Ages 4-9

705 Just for Kids: Phonological Processing

LinguiSystems
3100 4th Avenue
East Moline, IL   61244

800-776-4332
FAX 309-755-2377
TDY:800-933-8331
http://www.linguisystems.com
e-mail: service@linguisystems.com

Lynn Flahive, Janet Lanza, Author
Linda Bowers, Owner
Rosemary Huisingh, Owner

Teach phonological processing skills through fun, themed activities. You'll love each comprehensive, pick-up-and-use-now lesson! This terrific program gives you 22 theme-related lessons that target common phonological processes. *$ 39.95*

188 pages   Ages 4-9

706 Just for Me! Game

LinguiSystems
3100 4th Avenue
East Moline, IL   61244

800-776-4332
FAX 309-755-2377
TDY:800-933-8331
http://www.linguisystems.com
e-mail: service@linguisystems.com

Margaret Warner, Author
Linda Bowers, Owner
Rosemary Huisingh, Owner

Follow-up on the early language skills from all five Just for Me! books with this fun new game. It's a hands-on approach as youngsters mix up specially designed puzzle pieces to make funny faces. Each piece gives you five questions. That's 360 questions in all! Each puzzle piece covers an early language skill and corresponds to one part of the face. *$37.95*

Ages 4-7

707 Just for Me! Grammar

LinguiSystems
3100 4th Avenue
East Moline, IL   61244

800-776-4332
FAX 309-755-2377
TDY:800-933-8331
http://www.linguisystems.com
e-mail: service@linguisystems.com

Margaret Warner, Author
Linda Bowers, Owner
Rosemary Huisingh, Owner

Teach oral grammar to your youngest students. Through a variety of engaging activities, your students will become familiar with basic parts of speech, correct word order, and simple grammar concepts. These activities provide a solid foundation for later formal grammar training in the classroom. *$24.95*

150 pages   Ages 3-6

708 Just for Me! Vocabulary

LinguiSystems
3100 4th Avenue
East Moline, IL   61244

800-776-4332
FAX 309-755-2377
TDY:800-933-8331
http://www.linguisystems.com
e-mail: service@linguisystems.com

Margaret Warner, Author
Linda Bowers, Owner
Rosemary Huisingh, Owner

Your youngest students will love these fun cut-and-create activities for vocabulary. Each unit starts with poem introducing the key vocabulary words for the unit. *$24.95*

148 pages   Ages 3-6

709 Kaufman Speech Praxis Test

The Speech Bin
1965 25th Avenue
Vero Beach, FL   32960

772-770-0007
FAX 772-770-0006
http://www.speechbin.com
e-mail: info@speechbin.com

This standardized test utlizes a hierarchy of simple to complex motor-speech movements, from oral movement and simple phonemic/syllable to complex phonemic/syllable level. The complete kit contains manual, guide, and 25 test booklets. Item number W325. *$150.00*

710 Keys to Excellence in Integrated Language Arts

Harcourt Achieve
6277 Sea Harbor Drive
Orlando, FL   32887

800-531-5015
FAX 800-699-9459
http://www.steckvaughn.com
e-mail: info@steckvaughn.com

Steck-Vaughn Staff, Author
Tim McEwen, President/CEO
Jeff Johnson, Dir Marketing Communications
Chris Lehmann, Team Coordinator

Extensive instruction and assessment for improved test scores. Instruction and preparation for integrated language arts assessments. Boosts skills and scores.

711 LILAC

The Speech Bin
1965 25th Avenue
Vero Beach, FL 32960   772-770-0007
                          FAX 772-770-0006
                  http://www.speechbin.com
                  e-mail: info@speechbin.com

LILAC uses direct and naturalistic teaching in a creative approach that links spoken language learning to reading and writing. Activities to develop semantic, syntactic, expressive, and receptive language skills are presented sequentially from three-to five-year-old developmental levels. Item number 1428. *$27.95*

712 Language Activity Resource Kit: LARK

The Speech Bin
1965 25th Avenue
Vero Beach, FL 32960   772-770-0007
                          FAX 772-770-0006
                  http://www.speechbin.com
                  e-mail: info@speechbin.com

It's portable, stimulating, and easy-to-use with your adults who have aphasia and related disorders; you'll find many uses for it in your practice. The LARK includes a manual and 30 common objects familiar to adults represented in a variety of ways. Item number Q894. *$135.00*

713 Language Arts Handbook

Harcourt Achieve
6277 Sea Harbor Drive
Orlando, FL 32887
                               800-531-5015
                          FAX 800-699-9459
                  http://www.steckvaughn.com
                  e-mail: info@steckvaughn.com
Steck-Vaughn Staff, Author
Tim McEwen, President/CEO
Jeff Johnson, Dir Marketing Communications
Chris Lehmann, Team Coordinator

This comprehensive, all in one handbook of reproducibles provides activities on every aspect of language arts skills. Each book's grade appropriate content and organization are easy to follow and thorough in scope.

714 Language Exercises

Harcourt Achieve
6277 Sea Harbor Drive
Orlando, FL 32887
                               800-531-5015
                          FAX 800-699-9459
                  http://www.steckvaughn.com
                  e-mail: info@steckvaughn.com
Jones, Author
Tim McEwen, President/CEO
Jeff Johnson, Dir Marketing Communications
Chris Lehmann, Team Coordinator

Provides focused practice in six complex areas of language. Each book consists of six units addressing key skill areas such as vocabulary, sentences, grammar usage, capitalization and punctuation, composition, readiness and study skills.

715 Language Handbooks

Harcourt Achieve
6277 Sea Harbor Drive
Orlando, FL 32887
                               800-531-5015
                          FAX 800-699-9459
                  http://www.steckvaughn.com
                  e-mail: info@steckvaughn.com
Steck-Vaughn Staff, Author
Tim McEwen, President/CEO
Jeff Johnson, Dir Marketing Communications
Chris Lehmann, Team Coordinator

Language reference, modeling, and practice combined. These comprehensive reference and practice resources cover grammar usage, mechanics, and writing at appropriate levels for grades 1-6.

716 Language Practice

Harcourt Achieve
6277 Sea Harbor Drive
Orlando, FL 32887
                               800-531-5015
                          FAX 800-699-9459
                  http://www.steckvaughn.com
                  e-mail: info@steckvaughn.com
Moeller, Author
Tim McEwen, President/CEO
Jeff Johnson, Dir Marketing Communications
Chris Lehmann, Team Coordinator

Focuses students attention on the six most complex areas of language or only on the ones that need work. Now teachers can fine tune language skills with consistent, grade appropriate instruction with exercises covering vocabulary, sentences, grammar usage, capitalization and punctuation, composition, readiness and study skills.

717 Language Processing Kit

LinguiSystems
3100 4th Avenue
East Moline, IL 61244
                               800-776-4332
                          FAX 309-755-2377
                          TDY:800-933-8331
                  http://www.linguisystems.com
                  e-mail: service@linguisystems.com
Gail Richard, Mary Anne Hanner, Author
Linda Bowers, Owner
Rosemary Huisingh, Owner

You'll get a variety of activities in developmental progression for improving processing skills. It's your comprehensive follow-up to the Language Processing Test-Revised. You'll also get an outline of compensatory cueing and prompting strategies with helpful tips on how to teach them. *$124.95*

143 pages   Ages 5-11

718 Language Rehabilitation
Pro-Ed
8700 Shoal Creek Boulevard
Austin, TX   78757   512-451-3246
                                      800-897-3202
                                   FAX 800-397-7633
                            http://www.proedinc.com
James Martinoff, Rosemary Martinoff, Author

Offers practical exercises for developing language in older children or rebuilding language in aphasic adults. *$99.00*

719 LanguageBURST: A Language and Vocabulary Game
LinguiSystems
3100 4th Avenue
East Moline, IL   61244
                                      800-776-4332
                                   FAX 309-755-2377
                                   TDY:800-933-8331
                        http://www.linguisystems.com
                       e-mail: service@linguisystems.com
Lauri Whiskeyman, Author
Linda Bowers, Owner
Rosemary Huisingh, Owner

Expand your student's language and vocabulary skills with this quick-thinking game. Many of the items are based on the curriculum for grades 3-8 so your therapy is classroom-relevant. Students think quickly as they practice skills in four key language areas: fill-in-the-blank; categories; comparing and contrasting; and attributes. *$37.95*

Ages 9-15

720 Learning 100 Language Clues Vocabulary and Spelling
Harcourt Achieve
6277 Sea Harbor Drive
Orlando, FL   32887
                                      800-531-5015
                                   FAX 800-699-9459
                        http://www.steckvaughn.com
                       e-mail: info@steckvaughn.com
Steck-Vaughn Staff, Author
Tim McEwen, President/CEO
Jeff Johnson, Dir Marketing Communications
Chris Lehmann, Team Coordinator

Help your learners build vocabulary and spelling skills through a variety of exercises, including word attack, usage, dictionary, context clues, spelling, and cloze exercises. Use this print-based program alone or in conjunction with Language Clues Software to build vocabulary by providing instruction, practice, and reinforcement through the application of 19 essential skills.

721 Learning 100 Thinking Strategies Series
Harcourt Achieve
6277 Sea Harbor Drive
Orlando, FL   32887
                                      800-531-5015
                                   FAX 800-699-9459
                        http://www.steckvaughn.com
                       e-mail: info@steckvaughn.com
Steck-Vaughn Staff, Author
Tim McEwen, President/CEO
Jeff Johnson, Dir Marketing Communications
Chris Lehmann, Team Coordinator

Make your students better listeners and readers. Criterion referenced tests help you evaluate comprehension skills. Audio cassettes and written instructions help learners develop essential thinking processes and communication skills.

722 Letter Sounds
Sunburst Technology
400 Columbus Avenue
Valhalla, NY   10595   914-747-3310
                                      800-321-7511
                                   FAX 914-747-4109
                            http://www.sunburst.com
                       e-mail: service@sunburst.com
Students develop phonemic awareness skills as they make the connection between consonant letters and their sounds.

723 Linamood Program (LIPS Clinical Version):Phoneme Sequencing Program
LinguiSystems
3100 4th Avenue
East Moline, IL   61244
                                      800-776-4332
                                   FAX 309-755-2377
                                   TDY:800-933-8331
                        http://www.linguisystems.com
                       e-mail: service@linguisystems.com
Patricia Lindamood, Phyllis Lindamood, Author
Linda Bowers, Owner
Rosemary Huisingh, Owner

Help your students develop phoneme awareness for competence in reading, spelling, and speech. This multisensory program meets the needs of the many children and adults who don't develop phonemic awareness through traditional methods. *$247.00*

Birth-Adult

724 Listening Kit
LinguiSystems
3100 4th Avenue
East Moline, IL   61244
                                      800-776-4332
                                   FAX 309-755-2377
                                   TDY:80-933-8331
                        http://www.linguisystems.com
                       e-mail: service@linguisystems.com
Susan Simms, Mark Barrett, Rosemay Huisingh, Author
Linda Bowers, Owner
Rosemary Huisingh, Owner

This listening curriculum combines thinking, reasoning, and language skills for improved listening and attending. It's an unbeatable combination. The Listening Book organizes listening skills into the areas of paying attention, listening with an open mind and reasoning. *$119.95*

185 pages   Ages 5-11

725   Listening and Speaking for Job and Personal Use

AGS Publishing
4201 Woodland Road
Circle Pines, MN   55014   651-287-7220
                                         800-328-2560
                                  FAX 800-471-8457
                           http://www.agsnet.com
                        e-mail: agsmail@agsnet.com
L Ann Masters, Author
Karen Dahlen, Associate Director
Matt Keller, Marketing Manger

With an interest level of High School through Adult, and a reading level of Grade 5-6, this series has modules in Listening Skills and Speaking Skills. Self-paced texts have applications-oriented exercises.

726   Listening for Articulation All Year 'Round

IinguiSystems
3100 4th Avenue
East Moline, IL   61244
                                         800-776-4332
                                  FAX 309-755-2377
                                  TDY:800-933-8331
                           http://www.linguisystems.com
                        e-mail: service@linguisystems.com
Brenda Brumbaugh, Nan Thompson-Trenta, Author
Linda Bowers, Owner
Rosemary Huisingh, Owner

Get your young students on their way to intelligible speech with this book devoted to early-developing sounds. Pictures and activities can be used for phonology or articulation therapy. The program includes practice with minimal pairs, tips for establishing production, a variety of stimulus pictures, and activity sheets organized by phoneme. *$39.95*

208 pages   Ages 5-10

727   Listening for Language All Year 'Round

LinguiSystems
3100 4th Avenue
East Moline, IL   61244
                                         800-776-4332
                                  FAX 309-755-2377
                                  TDY:800-933-8331
                           http://www.linguisystems.com
                        e-mail: service@linguisystems.com
Brenda Brumbaugh, Nan Thompson-Trenta, Author
Linda Bowers, Owner
Rosemary Huisingh, Owner

Reinforce word relationships while you teach these important language concepts: synonyms, antonyms, classification, comparisons, multiple meanings, and idioms. Special notebook activities give structured writing practice. *$39.95*

196 pages   Ages 7-11

728   Listening for Vocabulary All Year 'Round

LinguiSystems
3100 4th Avenue
East Moline, IL   61244
                                         800-776-4332
                                  FAX 309-755-2377
                                  TDY:800-933-8331
                           http://www.linguisystems.com
                        e-mail: service@linguisystems.com
Brenda Brumbaugh, Nan Thompson-Trenta, Author
Linda Bowers, Owner
Rosemary Huisingh, Owner

Save time and energy with these ready-to-use listening and vocabulary lessons that match the themes of your school year. This book includes language stories, hands-on listening activities, home lessons, and terrific artworks! *$ 39.95*

196 pages   Ages 5-8

729   Look! Listen! & Learn Language!: Software

The Speech Bin
1965 25th Avenue
Vero Beach, FL   32960   772-770-0007
                                  FAX 772-770-0006
                           http://www.speechbin.com
                        e-mail: info@speechbin.com

Interactive activities for children with autism, PDD, Down syndrome, language delay, or apraxia include: hello; Match Same to Same; Quack; Let's talk About It; visual scanning/attention and match ups! Item number L177. *$99.00*

730   M-SS-NG L-NKS

Sunburst Technology
400 Columbus Avenue
Valhalla, NY   10595   914-747-3310
                                  800-321-7511
                           FAX 914-747-4109
                        http://www.sunburst.com
                     e-mail: service@sunburst.com

This award-winning program is an engrossing language puzzle. A passage appears with letters or words missing. Students complete it based on their knowledge of word structure, spelling, grammar, meaning in context, and literary style.

731   MCLA: Measure of Cognitive-Linguistic Abilities

The Speech Bin
1965 25th Avenue
Vero Beach, FL   32960   772-770-0007
                                  FAX 772-770-0006
                           http://www.speechbin.com
                        e-mail: info@speechbin.com

The MCLA includes the Family Questionnaire, Information Processing Checklist, Communication Functioning Interview and these valuable subtests: functional reading, paragraph comprehension, story recall and oral mechanism screening. The MCLA is normed for individuals 16 to 55+ years. Item number 1450. *$89.00*

732 Many Voices of Paws

The Speech Bin
1965 25th Avenue
Vero Beach, FL   32960   772-770-0007
                                    FAX 772-770-0006
                              http://www.speechbin.com
                              e-mail: info@speechbin.com

Julie Reville, Author
Jan J Binney, Editor-in-Chief

The Many Voices of Paws shows young stuttering
children how to modify their speaking rates and vocal
behaviors in a way that's easy for them to understand.
Beautifully illustrated, the story about Paws, the cat,
combines pretending, talking, and playful interaction
and helps children accept their disfluencies in a positive way. Item number 1568. *$19.95*

  64 pages
  ISBN 0-937857-11-4

733 Max's Attic: Long & Short Vowels

Sunburst Technology
400 Columbus Avenue
Valhalla, NY   10595   914-747-3310
                                          800-321-7511
                                    FAX 914-747-4109
                               http://www.sunburst.com
                              e-mail: service@sunburst.com

Filled to the rafters with phonics fun, this animated
program builds your students' vowel recognition
skills.

734 Maxwell's Manor: A Social Language Game

LinguiSystems
3100 4th Avenue
East Moline, IL   61244
                                          800-776-4332
                                    FAX 309-755-2377
                                    TDY:800-933-8331
                           http://www.linguisystems.com
                        e-mail: service@linguisystems.com

Carolyn LoGiudice, Nancy McConnell, Author
Linda Bowers, Owner
Rosemary Huisingh, Owner

This fun game will teach your students the social skills
they need to get along with others, be more accepted
by their peers, and be successful in the classroom.
Maxwell, the loveable dog, leads the way as your students practice positive social language skills. *$44.95*

  Ages 4-9

735 Middle School Language Arts

Harcourt Achieve
6277 Sea Harbor Drive
Orlando, FL   32887
                                          800-531-5015
                                    FAX 800-699-9459
                             http://www.steckvaughn.com
                             e-mail: info@steckvaughn.com

Steck-Vaughn Staff, Author
Tim McEwen, President/CEO
Jeff Johnson, Dir Marketing Communications
Chris Lehmann, Team Coordinator

This skill-specific series reinforces and enhances the
middle school language arts curriculum. It provides
teachers and parents with a tool to focus on the skills
that students need to review and reinforce. The lessons provide step-by-step instructions and follow-up
activities to enable students to work independently.

736 Mike Mulligan & His Steam Shovel

Sunburst Technology
400 Columbus Avenue
Valhalla, NY   10595   914-747-3310
                                          800-321-7511
                                    FAX 914-747-4109
                               http://www.sunburst.com
                              e-mail: service@sunburst.com

This CD-ROM version of the Caldecott classic lets
students experience interactive book reading and participate in four skills-based extension activities that
promote memory, matching, sequencing, listening,
pattern recognition and map reading skills.

737 Mouth Madness

The Speech Bin
1965 25th Avenue
Vero Beach, FL   32960   772-770-0007
                                    FAX 772-770-0006
                              http://www.speechbin.com
                              e-mail: info@speechbin.com

This unique manual uses oral imitation, motor planning, and breath control activities to improve the articulation and feeding skills of preschool and primary
children. Games, manipulative tasks, silly sentences,
rhymes, and funny faces target higher organizational
levels of motor planning. Item number C758. *$51.95*

738 My First Phonics Book

The Speech Bin
1965 25th Avenue
Vero Beach, FL   32960   772-770-0007
                                    FAX 772-770-0006
                              http://www.speechbin.com
                              e-mail: info@speechbin.com

Shows that words are made of sounds, then helps to
recognize the letter symbols for the sounds. It's organized in easy-to-locate alphabetical order of sounds,
with one page for each of the 42 sounds of English.
Item number H585. *$ 16.95*

**739 Myrtle's Beach: A Phonological Awareness and
Articulation Game**

LinguiSystems
3100 4th Avenue
East Moline, IL   61244
                                          800-776-4332
                                    FAX 309-755-2377
                                    TDY:800-933-8331
                           http://www.linguisystems.com
                        e-mail: service@linguisystems.com

LinguiSystems Staff, Author
Linda Bowers, Owner
Rosemary Huisingh, Owner

Myrtle's Beach is a fun place to practice phonological awareness, articulation, and language skills. The flexible format allows you to meet the varied needs of all the students in your speech and language groups. *$44.95*

Ages 4-9

740   No-Glamour Grammar

LinguiSystems
3100 4th Avenue
East Moline, IL   61244

800-776-4332
FAX 309-755-2377
TDY:800-933-8331
http://www.linguisystems.com
e-mail: service@linguisystems.com

Suzanna Mayer Watt, Author
Linda Bowers, Owner
Rosemary Huisingh, Owner

This best-selling grammar book teaches all the basic grammar skills your students need. The no-frills approach is great for students with language or learning disorders. You'll teach one skill at a time with tons of practice pages. The units progress in difficulty as students master each grammar skill. *$41.95*

415 pages   Ages 8-12

741   No-Glamour Grammar 2

LinguiSystems
3100 4th Avenue
East Moline, IL   61244

800-776-4332
FAX 309-755-2377
TDY:800-933-8331
http://www.linguisystems.com
e-mail: service@linguisystems.com

Diane Hyde, Author
Linda Bowers, Owner
Rosemary Huisingh, Owner

Get more grammar skill practice with a variety of activity sheets. From nouns to verbs, adjectives to adverbs, your students will apply their knowledge to these challenging, fun activity pages. *$41.95*

320 pages   Ages 8-12

742   No-Glamour Vocabulary

LinguiSystems
3100 4th Avenue
East Moline, IL   61244

800-776-4332
FAX 309-755-2377
TDY:800-933-8331
http://www.linguisystems.com
e-mail: service@linguisystems.com

Diane Hyde, Author
Linda Bowers, Owner
Rosemary Huisingh, Owner

With one vocabulary skill to a page, students can focus on the semantic areas that give them the most trouble. These vocabulary worksheets target absurdities, multiple meanings, associations, definitions, synonyms, antonyms, and more. *$41.95*

278 pages   Ages 7-12

743   Oral-Motor Activities for School-Aged Children

LinguiSystems
3100 4th Avenue
East Moline, IL   61244

800-776-4332
FAX 309-755-2377
TDY:800-933-8331
http://www.linguisystems.com
e-mail: service@linguisystems.com

Elizabeth Mackie, Author
Linda Bowers, Owner
Rosemary Huisingh, Owner

Multisensory, oral-motor approach to treating articulation disorders. Great for older students with developmental delays or any student who needs to improve oral-motor function for better speech production. *$39.95*

171 pages   Ages 7-12

744   Oral-Motor Activities for Young Children

LinguiSystems
3100 4th Avenue
East Moline, IL   61244

800-776-4332
FAX 309-755-2377
TDY:800-933-8331
http://www.linguisystems.com
e-mail: service@linguisystems.com

Elizabeth Mackie, Author
Linda Bowers, Owner
Rosemary Huisingh, Owner

Whether your are new to oral-motor skills training or an experienced oral-motor skills clinician, these activities get results. *$39.95*

119 pages   Ages 3-8

745   PLAID

The Speech Bin
1965 25th Avenue
Vero Beach, FL   32960

772-770-0007
FAX 772-770-0006
http://www.speechbin.com
e-mail: info@speechbin.com

PLAID is a top-notch clinical tool that gives you practical practice materials featuring twenty different phonemes — just what you need for your apraxic and aphasic adults — all in one resource. Item number 1424. *$29.95*

746   Pair-It Books: Early Emergent Stage 1

Harcourt Achieve
6277 Sea Harbor Drive
Orlando, FL   32887

800-531-5015
FAX 800-699-9459
http://www.steckvaughn.com
e-mail: info@steckvaughn.com

Steck-Vaughn Staff, Author
Tim McEwen, President/CEO
Jeff Johnson, Dir Marketing Communications
Chris Lehmann, Team Coordinator

Includes 30 eight-page books with simple concepts, predictable and repetitive text patterns, and a strong matching of art or photos to support the text.

Classroom Resources/Language Arts

747 Pair-It Books: Early Emergent Stage 1 in Spanish

Harcourt Achieve
6277 Sea Harbor Drive
Orlando, FL 32887

800-531-5015
FAX 800-699-9459
http://www.steckvaughn.com
e-mail: info@steckvaughn.com

Steck-Vaughn Staff, Author
Tim McEwen, President/CEO
Jeff Johnson, Dir Marketing Communications
Chris Lehmann, Team Coordinator

Includes 30 eight-page books with simple concepts, predictable and repetitive text patterns, and a strong matching of art or photos to support the text. Six big books encourage shared reading and strategy instruction. Students can read these texts with ease and view themselves as successful readers.

748 Pair-It Books: Early Emergent Stage 2

Harcourt Achieve
6277 Sea Harbor Drive
Orlando, FL 32887

800-531-5015
FAX 800-699-9459
http://www.steckvaughn.com
e-mail: info@steckvaughn.com

Steck-Vaughn Staff, Author
Tim McEwen, President/CEO
Jeff Johnson, Dir Marketing Communications
Chris Lehmann, Team Coordinator

A series of 20 books, each containing 16 pages, that gradually become more difficult and reflect more complex text structures such as dialogue, content vocabulary and question and answer formats. All stories are available on audio cassette, and four are available in big book format.

749 Pair-It Books: Early Emergent Stage 2 in Spanish

Harcourt Achieve
6277 Sea Harbor Drive
Orlando, FL 32887

800-531-5015
FAX 800-699-9459
http://www.steckvaughn.com
e-mail: info@steckvaughn.com

Steck-Vaughn Staff, Author
Tim McEwen, President/CEO
Jeff Johnson, Dir Marketing Communications
Chris Lehmann, Team Coordinator

A series of 20 books, each containing 16 pages, that encourage native Spanish speakers with early reading success in their first language. Simple concepts, predictable language, and well chosen art support students efforts.

750 Pair-It Books: Early Fluency Stage 3

Harcourt Achieve
6277 Sea Harbor Drive
Orlando, FL 32887

800-531-5015
FAX 800-699-9459
http://www.steckvaughn.com
e-mail: info@steckvaughn.com

Steck-Vaughn Staff, Author
Tim McEwen, President/CEO
Jeff Johnson, Dir Marketing Communications
Chris Lehmann, Team Coordinator

A series of 30 books, each containing either 16 or 24 pages, and six big books that introduce tables, folktales, tall tales and plays that invite readers to respond in writing.

751 Pair-It Books: Early Skills

Harcourt Achieve
6277 Sea Harbor Drive
Orlando, FL 21887

800-531-5015
FAX 800-699-9459
http://www.steckvaughn.com
e-mail: info@steckvaughn.com

Steck-Vaughn Staff, Author
Tim McEwen, President/CEO
Jeff Johnson, Dir Marketing Communications
Chris Lehmann, Team Coordinator

Give students an early start on academic achievement with grade appropriate, cross-curricular excercises. Easy-to-understand lessons with helpful graphics are ideal for independent or small group learning.

752 Pair-It Books: Fluency Stage 4

Harcourt Achieve
6277 Sea Harbor Drive
Orlando, FL 32887

800-531-5015
FAX 800-699-9459
http://www.steckvaughn.com
e-mail: info@steckvaughn.com

Steck-Vaughn Staff, Author
Tim McEwen, President/CEO
Jeff Johnson, Dir Marketing Communications
Chris Lehmann, Team Coordinator

A series of 20 books, each containing 24 or 32 pages, and four big books. Readers encounter diaries, journals, biographies, and mysteries and explore written responses in a variety of formats. Students emerge as confident readers and writers of both narrative and informational texts.

753 Pair-It Books: Proficiency Stage 5

Harcourt Achieve
6277 Sea Harbor Drive
Orlando, FL 32887

800-531-5015
FAX 800-699-9459
http://www.steckvaughn.com
e-mail: info@steckvaughn.com

Steck-Vaughn Staff, Author
Tim McEwen, President/CEO
Jeff Johnson, Dir Marketing Communications
Chris Lehmann, Team Coordinator

A series of 30 books, each containing 32 or 40 pages, that take readers from fluency to proficiency, presenting a wide variety of genres and text structures. Offers helpful strategies and activities for improving phonics skills, vocabulary, and reading and language skills, as well as take-home letters in Spanish and English.

754 Pair-It Books: Transition Stage 2-3

Harcout Achieve
6277 Sea Harbor Drive
Orlando, FL 32887

800-531-5015
FAX 800-699-9459
http://www.steckvaughn.com
e-mail: info@steckvaughn.com

Tim McEwen, President/CEO
Jeff Johnson, Dir Marketing Communications
Chris Lehmann, Team Coordinator

A series of 20 books, each containing 16 pages, that provide readers with a gradual transition into early fluency. All stories are available on audio cassette, and four are avaiable in big book format.

755 Patterns Across the Curriculum

Harcourt Achieve
6277 Sea Harbor Drive
Orlando, FL 32887

800-531-5015
FAX 800-699-9459
http://www.steckvaughn.com
e-mail: info@steckvaughn.com

Steck-Vaughn Staff, Author
Tim McEwen, President/CEO
Jeff Johnson, Dir Marketing Communications
Chris Lehmann, Team Coordinator

Develop students awareness and understanding of patterns in the real world. Exercises allow students to identify, complete, extend, and create patterns. Developed across math, language, social studies, and science. This flexible organization allows teachers to utilize content specific activities in coordination with other classroom assignments, providing additional richness in learning.

756 Patty's Cake: A Describing Game

LinguiSystems
3100 4th Avenue
East Moline, IL 61244

800-776-4332
FAX 309-755-2377
TDY:800-933-8331
http://www.linguisystems.com
e-mail: service@linguisystems.com

Julie Cole, Author
Linda Bowers, Owner
Rosemary Huisingh, Owner

Teach describing skills with Patty's Cake. Two levels of play in this fun game give you flexibility to meet individual students learning needs. Players describe age-appropriate picture vocabulary cards by naming attributes such as category, function, shape, color, or location. Your students will improve their skills in listening, memory, word retrieval, categorizing, naming attributes, formulating sentences, and giving descriptions. *$44.95*

Ages 4-9

757 PhonicsMart CD-ROM

Harcourt Achieve
6277 Sea Harbor Drive
Orlando, FL 32887

800-531-5015
FAX 800-699-9459
http://www.steckvaughn.com
e-mail: info@steckvaughn.com

Steck-Vaughn Staff, Author
Tim McEwen, President/CEO
Jeff Johnson, Dir Marketing Communications
Chris Lehmann, Team Coordinator

Five interactive games offer practice and reinforcement in 19 phonics skills at a variety of learning levels! Over 700 key words are vocalized, and each is accompanied by sound effects, colorful illustrations, animation, or video clips!

758 Phonological Awareness Kit

LinguiSystems
3100 4th Avenue
East Moline, IL 61244

800-776-4332
FAX 309-755-2377
TDY:800-933-8331
http://www.linguisystems.com
e-mail: service@linguisystems.com

Carolyn Robertson, Wanda Salter, Author
Linda Bowers, Owner
Rosemary Huisingh, Owner

Help your students learn to use phonological information to process oral and written language with this fantastic kit. Written by an SLP and special educator, this best-seller links sound awareness, oral language, and early reading and writing skills. The kit uses a multisensory approach to ensure success for all learning styles. *$69.95*

115 pages   Ages 5-8

759 Phonological Awareness Kit: Intermediate

LinguiSystems
3100 4th Avenue
East Moline, IL 61244

800-776-4332
FAX 309-755-2377
TDY:800-933-8331
http://www.linguisystems.com
e-mail: service@linguisystems.com

Carolyn Robertson, Wanda Salter, Author
Linda Bowers, Owner
Rosemary Huisingh, Owner

Now there's hope for your older students who have struggled with reading through their early school years. Give them strategies to crack the reading code with this comprehensive program. Great for students with deficits in auditory processing, decoding, and written language. *$69.95*

116 pages   Ages 9-14

760 Phonological Awareness Test: Computerized Scoring

LinguiSystems
3100 4th Avenue
East Moline, IL   61244   309-755-2377
                                 800-776-4332
                                 FAX 800-577-4555
                                 TDY:800-933-8331
                        http://www.linguisystems.com
                        e-mail: service@linguisystems.com
Carolyn Robertson, Wanda Salter, Author
Linda Bowers, Owner
Rosemary Huisingh, Owner

Designed to save time, this optional CD-ROM software allows you to accurately, conveniently, and quickly score The Phonological Awareness Test. Just plug in the raw scores and the program does everything else. You'll be able to print out all the scores you need to include in a student's assessment report. *$69.95*

Ages 5-9

761 Phonology: Software

The Speech Bin
1965 25th Avenue
Vero Beach, FL   32960   772-770-0007
                                FAX 772-770-0006
                        http://www.speechbin.com
                        e-mail: info@speechbin.com

This unique software gives you six entertaining games to treat children's phonological disorders. The program uses target patterns in a pattern cycling approach to phonological processes. Item number L183. *$99.00*

762 Plunk's Pond: A Riddles Game for Language

LinguiSystems
3100 4th Avenue
East Moline, IL   61244
                                 800-776-4332
                                 FAX 309-755-2377
                                 TDY:800-933-8331
                        http://www.linguisystems.com
                        e-mail: service@linguisystems.com
LinguiSystems Staff, Author
Linda Bowers, Owner
Rosemary Huisingh, Owner

Encourage divergent thinking, sharpen listening skills, and improve vocabulary with this fun riddle game. With a picture on one side and three clues on the other, these cards are great for all kinds of therapy games. Target attributes such as function, color, category, and more. *$44.95*

Ages 4-9

763 Poetry in Three Dimensions: Reading, Writing and Critical Thinking Skills through Poetry

Educators Publishing Service
31 Smith Place
Cambridge, MA   02139   617-547-6706
                                800-225-5750
                                FAX 888-440-2665
                        http://www.epsbooks.com
                        e-mail: eps@epsbooks.com
Carol Clark, Alison Draper, Author
Nick Gaehde, President

Help your students improve their reading comprehension and writing through the study of poetry in this collection of multicultural poems. With poems and questions on facing pages, students are encouraged to annotate the text of the poem and to go back to the text to respond to the questions.

764 Polar Express

Sunburst Technology
400 Columbus Avenue
Valhalla, NY   10595   914-747-3310
                              800-321-7511
                              FAX 914-747-4109
                        http://www.sunburst.com
                        e-mail: service@sunburst.com

Share the magic and enchantment of the holiday season with this CD-ROM version of Chris Van Allsburg's Caldecott-winning picture book.

765 Preschool Motor Speech Evaluation & Intervention

The Speech Bin
1965 25th Avenue
Vero Beach, FL   32960   772-770-0007
                                800-477-3324
                                FAX 800-329-2246
                        http://www.speechbin.com
                        e-mail: info@speechbin.com

This comprehensive criterion-based assessment tool differentiates motor-based speech disorders from those of phonology and determines if speech difficulties of children 18 months to six years old are characteristic of: oral nonverbal apraxia; dysarthria; developmental verbal dyspraxia; hypersensitivity; differences in tone and hyposensitivity. Item number J322. *$59.00*

766 Progress with Puppets: Speech and Language Activities for Children

Therapro
225 Arlington Street
Framingham, MA   01702   508-872-9494
                                800-257-5376
                                FAX 508-875-2062
                        http://www.theraproducts.com
                        e-mail: info@theraproducts.com
Joanne Hanson MS CCC-SLP, Author
Karen Conrad, President

A much needed book of activities to use during therapy with puppets. Great ideas for working on chewing and feeding, language stimulation, articulation training, fluency and more. Suggestions offered for use with the Puppets that Swallow. *$29.95*

767 Promoting Communication in Infants & Children

The Speech Bin
1965 25th Avenue
Vero Beach, FL   32960   772-770-0007
                               FAX 772-770-0006
                               http://www.speechbin.com
                               e-mail: info@speechbin.com

Gives you down-to-earth information, activities, and step-by-step suggestions for stimulating children's speech and language skills. Topics are conveniently organized, concisely presented, and written in easy-to-understand language. Item number 1512. *$14.95*

768 Python Path Phonics Word Families

Sunburst Technology
400 Columbus Avenue
Valhalla, NY   10595   914-747-3310
                             800-321-7511
                             FAX 914-747-4109
                             http://www.sunburst.com
                             e-mail: service@sunburst.com

Your students improve their word-building skills by playing three fun strategy games that involve linking one-or two-letter consonant beginnings to basic word endings.

769 RULES

The Speech Bin
1965 25th Avenue
Vero Beach, FL   32960   772-770-0007
                               FAX 772-770-0006
                               http://www.speechbin.com
                               e-mail: info@speechbin.com

Faced with young children whose speech is unintelligible? RULES is the perfect program for these preschool and elementary children. It remediates the processes: cluster reduction;, final consonant deletion, stopping; and prevocalic voicing. Item number 1557. *$43.95*

770 Receptive One-Word Picture Vocabulary Test (ROWPVT-2000)

The Speech Bin
1965 25th Avenue
Vero Beach, FL   32960   772-770-0007
                               FAX 772-770-0006
                               http://www.speechbin.com
                               e-mail: info@speechbin.com

This administered, untimed measure assesses the vocabulary comprehension of 0-2 through 11-18 years. New full-color test pictures are easy to recognize; many new test items have been added. It is ideal for children unable or reluctant to speak because only a gestural response is required. Item number A305. *$140.00*

771 Remediation of Articulation Disorders (RAD)

The Speech Bin
1965 25th Avenue
Vero Beach, FL   32960   772-770-0007
                               FAX 772-770-0006
                               http://www.speechbin.com
                               e-mail: info@speechbin.com

RAD treats articulation and speech intelligibility as important parameters of language. It gives you thematic pictures and worksheets to facilitate the development of critical sounds. Each picture also has a problem-solving element that provides rich opportunities for discussion and narratives. Item number 1420. *$19.95*

772 Retell Stories

The Speech Bin
1965 25th Avenue
Vero Beach, FL   32960   772-770-0007
                               FAX 772-770-0006
                               http://www.speechbin.com
                               e-mail: info@speechbin.com

You'll use them for pre-/post-testing, treatment sessions, and home practice. This approach emphasizes systematic training of error phonemes in a semantically potent core vocabulary of the child's own words. It enables children to use whole words intelligibly as powerful tools for real-life communication. Item number 1441. *$17.95*

773 Ridgewood Grammar

Educators Publishing Service
31 Smith Place
Cambridge, MA   02139   617-547-6706
                               800-225-5750
                               FAX 888-440-2665
                               http://www.epsbooks.com
                               e-mail: eps@epsbooks.com
Terri Wiss, Nancy Bison, Author
Nick Gaehde, President

Grammar is an important part of any student's education. This new series, from the school district that developed the popular Ridgewood Analogies books, teaches 3rd, 4th, and 5th graders about the parts of speech and their use in sentences.

774 Rocky's Mountain: A Word-finding Game

LinguiSystems
3100 4th Avenue
East Moline, IL   61244
                               800-776-4332
                               FAX 309-755-2377
                               TDY:800-933-8331
                               http://www.linguisystems.com
                               e-mail: service@linguisystems.com
Gina Williamson, Susan Shields, Author
Linda Bowers, Owner
Rosemary Huisingh, Owner

Tackle stubborn word-finding problems with this fun game! Game cards are organized by four word-finding strategies so you can pick the strategy that best meets your students' needs. Teach these strategies for word-finding: visual imagery; word association; sound/letter cueing; and categories. *$44.95*

Ages 4-9

Classroom Resources/Language Arts

775 Room 14

LinguiSystems
3100 4th Avenue
East Moline, IL   61244

800-776-4332
FAX 309-755-2377
TDY:800-933-8331
http://www.linguisystems.com
e-mail: service@linguisystems.com

Carolyn Wilson, Author
Linda Bowers, Owner
Rosemary Huisingh, Owner

Build social skills by offering a variety of teaching approaches to meet the language and learning needs of your students. Through stories, comprehension activities, and organized lessons, students learn to: make and keep friends. fit in at school, handle feelings, and be responsible for their actions. *$59.95*

198 pages   Ages 6-10

776 SLP's IDEA Companion

LinguiSystems
3100 4th Avenue
East Moline, IL   61244

800-776-4332
FAX 309-755-2375
TDY:800-933-8331
http://www.linguisystems.com
e-mail: service@linguisystems.com

Shaila Lucas, Author
Linda Bowers, Owner
Rosemary Huisingh, Owner

Set goals and objectives that match the guidelines outlined in the Individuals with Disabilities Education Act. You'll be able to link your therapy goals to the classroom curriculum, determine appropriate benchmarks for students, and determine levels of performance using the baseline measures provided in the book. *$39.95*

162 pages   Ages 5-18

777 SPARC Artic Junior

LinguiSystems
3100 4th Avenue
East Moline, IL   61244

800-776-4332
FAX 309-755-2377
TDY:800-933-8331
http://www.linguisystems.com
e-mail: service@linguisystems.com

Beverly Plass, Author
Linda Bowers, Owner
Rosemary Huisingh, Owner

Reach intelligibility goals faster with these take-home exercises. The practice words have been carefully selected to control the phonetic context. It's a programmed, research-based approach that will get results. Activities are divided by primary and secondary phonological processes. *$39.95*

211 pages   Ages 3-7

778 SPARC Artic Scenes

LinguiSystems
3100 4th Avenue
East Moline, IL   61244

800-776-4332
FAX 309-755-2377
TDY:800-933-8331
http://www.linguisystems.com
e-mail: service@linguisystems.com

Susan Rose Simms, Author
Linda Bowers, Owner
Rosemary Huisingh, Owner

Each picture scene is loaded with target sounds to get the most speech practice in your limited therapy time. You'll take care of your entire caseload with these articulation and language activities. Activities include vocabulary lists, story starts, thinking questions, categorizing and multiple meanings. *$39.95*

207 pages   Ages 4-10

779 SPARC for Grammar

LinguiSystems
3100 4th Avenue
East Moline, IL   61244

800-776-4332
FAX 309-755-2377
TDY:800-933-8331
http://www.linguisystems.com
e-mail: service@linguisystems.com

Susan Thomsen, Kathy Donnelly, Author
Linda Bowers, Owner
Rosemary Huisingh, Owner

Teach grammar in meaningful contexts! The lessons provide a wealth of opportunities for your students to hear, repeat, answer questions and tell stories using targeted language structures. *$39.95*

165 pages   Ages 4-10

780 SPARC for Phonology

LinguiSystems
3100 4th Avenue
East Moline, IL   61244

800-776-4332
FAX 309-755-2377
TDY:800-933-8331
http://www.linguisystems.com
e-mail: service@linguisystems.com

Susan Thomsen, Kathy Donnelly, Author
Linda Bowers, Owner
Rosemary Huisingh, Owner

This excellent resource includes 80 pages of 16 pictures each... that's 1280 pictures in all! Each picture page has corresponding 20-word auditory bombardment list. These great lessons cover syllable reduction, consonant deletion, cluster reduction, gliding, vowelization, fronting, backing, stopping, stridency deletion, affrication, deaffrication, voicing and devoicing. *$39.95*

165 pages   Ages 4-10

781 SPARC for Vocabulary

LinguiSystems
3100 4th Avenue
East Moline, IL   61244

800-776-4332
FAX 309-755-2377
TDY:800-933-8331
http://www.linguisystems.com
e-mail: service@linguisystems.com

Susan Thomsen, Kathy Donnelly, Author
Linda Bowers, Owner
Rosemary Huisingh, Owner

Teach vocabulary skills through themes! Rapid-naming skills will improve as vocabulary knowledge increases. This invaluable picture resource gets your students learning and thinking about new words. *$39.95*

165 pages   Ages 4-10

782 Scissors, Glue, and Artic, Too!

LinguiSystems
3100 4th Avenue
East Moline, IL   61244

800-776-4332
FAX 309-755-2377
TDY:800-933-8331
http://www.linguisystems.com
e-mail: service@linguisystems.com

Susan Rose Simms, Author
Linda Bowers, Owner
Rosemary Huisingh, Owner

Hands-on projects that beg to be talked about are perfect for young students in articulation therapy. This wonderfully illustrated manual is filled with puzzles, books, animals, and more that come to life in the hands of students. *$39.95*

189 pages   Ages 4-9

783 Scissors, Glue, and Grammar, Too!

LinguiSystems
3100 4th Avenue
East Moline, IL   61244

800-776-4332
FAX 309-755-2377
TDY:800-933-8331
http://www.linguisystems.com
e-mail: service@linguisystems.com

Susan Boegler, Debbie Abruzzini, Author
Linda Bowers, Owner
Rosemary Huisingh, Owner

Even your youngest students can learn correct grammar and syntax skills. This interactive approach is the perfect resource. These cut-and-paste activities are so much fun, your students won't realize they're learning regular and irregular verbs, comparatives and superlatives, wh- questions, and more! *$39.95*

174 pages   Ages 4-9

784 Scissors, Glue, and Phonological Processes, Too!

LinguiSystems
3100 4th Avenue
East Moline, IL   61244

800-776-4332
FAX 309-755-2377
TDY:800-933-8331
http://www.linguisystems.com
e-mail: service@linguisystems.com

Gayle H Daly, Author
Linda Bowers, Owner
Rosemary Huisingh, Owner

Eliminate error patterns with minimal pair contrasts at the word and phrase level. Watch your young students cut and paste their way to better speech with these engaging, interactive activities. *$39.95*

174 pages   Ages 4-9

785 Scissors, Glue, and Vocabulary, Too!

LinguiSystems
3100 4th Avenue
East Moline, IL   61244

800-776-4332
FAX 309-755-2377
TDY:800-933-8331
http://www.linguisystems.com
e-mail: service@linguisystems.com

Barb Truman, Patti Halfman, Lauri Whiskeyman,
Author
Linda Bowers, Owner
Rosemary Huisingh, Owner

These cut-and-paste activities keep young students motivated. The rich vocabulary content gets them using new words in new ways. You'll not only teach vocabulary skills but listening and following directions too. Each lesson gives you a list of key vocabulary, scripted directions, a family letter, and several enrichment activites. *$39.95*

187 pages   Ages 4-9

786 Sequential Spelling 1-7 with Student Response Book

AVKO Dyslexia Research Foundation
3084 W Willard Road
Clio, MI   48420

810-686-9283
FAX 810-686-1101
http://www.avko.org
e-mail: avkoemail@aol.com

Don McCabe, Author
Don McCabe, Research Director

Sequential Spelling uses immediate student self-correction. It builds from easier words of a word family such as all and then builds on them to teach; all, tall, stall, install, call, fall, ball, and their inflected forms such as: stalls, stalled, stalling, installing, installment. *$79.95*

72 pages
ISBN 1-664003-00-0

Classroom Resources/Language Arts

787 Sign Language Classroom Resource

Harris Communications
15155 Technology Drive
Eden Prairie, MN 55344   952-906-1180
                                        800-825-6758
                              FAX 952-906-1099
                              TDY:952-906-1198
                    http://www.harriscomm.com
Traci Jacobson, Author

Learn basic signs quickly and easily. Contains pictures of 100 essential signs. Each picture is presented on an 8.5x11 page and may be copied for bulletin boards or classroom walls. Also includes smaller versions of the pictures to distribute to individual students and family members. *$32.00*

143 pages   Paperback

788 Silly Sentences

The Speech Bin
1965 25th Avenue
Vero Beach, FL 32960   772-770-0007
                             FAX 772-770-0006
                    http://www.speechbin.com
                    e-mail: info@speechbin.com

Children love to have fun. Silly Sentences lets them have fun while they play these engaging card games to learn: subject verb agreement, speech sound articulation; S+ V+ O sentences, questioning and answering; humor and absurdities and present progressive verbs. Item number P506. *$41.00*

789 Soaring Scores CTB: TerraNova Reading and Language Arts

Harcourt Achieve
6277 Sea Harbor Drive
Orlando, FL 32887
                                        800-531-5015
                             FAX 800-699-9459
                    http://www.steckvaughn.com
                    e-mail: info@steckvaughn.com
Steck-Vaughn Staff, Author
Tim McEwen, President/CEO
Jeff Johnson, Dir Marketing Communications
Chris Lehmann, Team Coordinator

Through a combination of targeted instructional practice and test-taking tips, these workbooks help students build better skills and improve CTB-TerraNova test scores. Initial lessons address reading comprehension and language arts. The authentic practice test mirrors the CTB's format and content.

790 Soaring Scores in Integrated Language Arts

Harcourt Achieve
6277 Sea Harbor Drive
Orlando, FL 32887
                                        800-531-5015
                             FAX 800-699-9459
                    http://www.steckvaughn.com
                    e-mail: info@steckvaughn.com
Steck-Vaughn Staff, Author
Tim McEwen, President/CEO
Jeff Johnson, Dir Marketing Commuications
Chris Lehmann, Team Coordinator

Help your students develop the right skills and strategies for success on integrated arts assessments. Soaring Scores presents three sets of two lengthy, thematically linked literature selections. Students develop higher-order thinking skills as they respond to open-ended questions about the selections.

791 Soaring Scores on the CMT in Language Arts& on the CAPT in Reading and Writing Across Disciplines

Harcourt Achieve
6277 Sea Harbor Drive
Orlando, FL 32887
                                        800-531-5015
                             FAX 800-699-9459
                    http://www.steckvaughn.com
                    e-mail: info@steckvaughn.com
Steck-Vaughn Staff, Author
Tim McEwen, President/CEO
Jeff Johnson, Dir Marketing Communications
Chris Lehmann, Team Coordinator

Make every minute count when you are preparing for the CMT or CAPT. Fine tune your language arts test preparation with the program developed specifically for the Connecticut's assessments. Questions are correlated to Connecticut's content standards for reading and responding, producing text, applying English language conventions, and exploring and responding to texts.

792 Soaring Scores on the NYS English Language Arts Assessment

Harcourt Achieve
6277 Sea Harbor Drive
Orlando, FL 32887
                                        800-531-5015
                             FAX 800-699-9459
                    http://www.steckvaughn.com
                    e-mail: info@steckvaughn.com
Steck-Vaughn Staff, Author
Tim McEwen, President/CEO
Jeff Johnson, Dir Marketing Communications
Chris Lehmann, Team Coordinator

With these workbooks, students receive instructional practice for approaching the assessment's reading, listening and writing questions.

793 Soaring on the MCAS in English Language Arts

Harcourt Achieve
6277 Sea Harbor Drive
Orlando, FL 32887
                                        800-531-5015
                             FAX 800-699-9459
                    http://www.steckvaughn.com
                    e-mail: info@steckvaughn.com
Steck-Vaughn Staff, Author
Tim McEwen, President/CEO
Jeff Johnson, Dir Marketing Communications
Chris Lehmann, Team Coordinator

Instructional practice in the first section builds skills for the MCAS language, literacy, and composition questions. A practice test models the MCAS precisely in design and length.

794 Sound Connections

The Speech Bin
1965 25th Avenue
Vero Beach, FL   32960   772-770-0007
                                    FAX 772-770-0006
                              http://www.speechbin.com
                              e-mail: info@speechbin.com

This program teaches the critical connections between the sounds kids hear and speaking, reading, and writing. Dozens of activities and worksheets, 19 phoneme-based stories, and 100s of pictures. Item number 1487. *$41.95*

795 Sounds Abound

LinguiSystems
3100 4th Avenue
East Moline, IL   61244

                                        800-776-4332
                                  FAX 309-755-2377
                                  TDY:800-933-8331
                          http://www.linguisystems.com
                          e-mail: service@linguisystems.com
Hugh Catts, Tina Olsen, Author
Linda Bowers, Owner
Rosemary Huisingh, Owner

Delayed speech and language skills DO impact reading skills. Give your young students an edge with Sounds Abound. They'll connect letters with sounds as they meet their speech and language goals. This best-selling manual is loaded with activities for speech sound awareness, rhyming skills, beginning and ending sounds, segmenting and blending sounds, and putting sounds together with letters. *$37.95*

190 pages   Ages 4-9

796 Sounds Abound Game

LinguiSystems
3100 4th Avenue
East Moline, IL   61244

                                        800-776-4332
                                  FAX 309-755-2377
                                  TDY:800-933-8331
                          http://www.linguisystems.com
                          e-mail: service@linguisystems.com
Hugh Catts, Tina Olsen, Author
Linda Bowers, Owner
Rosemary Huisingh, Owner

Teach critical features about sounds in words for better language skills. Your students will love this fun game because it's easy to play. This game targets the sounds students use the most: f; s; p; t; and m. These essential sounds are critical for early literacy success. *$39.95*

Ages 4-9

797 Sounds Abound Multisensory Phonological Awareness

LinguiSystems
3100 4th Avenue
East Moline, IL   61244

                                        800-776-4332
                                  FAX 309-755-2377
                                  TDY:800-933-8331
                          http://www.linguisystems.com
                          e-mail: service@linguisystems.com
Jill Teachworth, Author
Linda Bowers, Owner
Rosemary Huisingh, Owner

The multisensory approach in this phonological program reinforces knowledge and retention of sound-symbol correspondence. Students will learn through their best modality as they look, listen, feel, play, and even sing the sounds. *$37.95*

201 pages   Ages 4-7

798 Source for Apraxia Therapy

LinguiSystems
3100 4th Avenue
East Moline, IL   61244

                                        800-776-4332
                                  FAX 309-755-2377
                                  TDY:800-933-8331
                          http://www.linguisystems.com
                          e-mail: service@linguisystems.com
Kathryn J Tomlin, Author
Linda Bowers, Owner
Rosemary Huisingh, Owner

This resource combines a visual-auditory-kinesthetic approach to help your clients improve intelligibility. Three sections target phoneme production, articulation, fluency, and phrasing, and paralinguistic drills. You'll know just where to start therapy for clients with mild, moderate, or severe apraxia. *$41.95*

195 pages   Adults

799 Source for Bilingual Students with Language Disorders

LinguiSystems
3100 4th Avenue
East Moline, IL   61244

                                        800-776-4332
                                  FAX 309-755-2377
                                  TDY:800-933-8331
                          http://www.linguisystems.com
                          e-mail: service@linguisystems.com
Celeste Roseberry-McKibbin, Author
Linda Bowers, Owner
Rosemary Huisingh, Owner

Focus on teaching vocabulary and phonolgical awareness skills, the most important skills your bilingual students need for overall English proficiency and literacy. This resource gives you activities and materials based on a hierarchy of second language acquisition, *$41.95*

250 pages   Ages 5-18

Classroom Resources/Language Arts

800 Source for Processing Disorders

LinguiSystems
3100 4th Avenue
East Moline, IL   61244

800-776-4332
FAX 309-755-2377
TDY:800-933-8331
http://www.linguisystems.com
e-mail: service@linguisystems.com

Gail J Richard, Author
Linda Bowers, Owner
Rosemary Huisingh, Owner

This great resource helps you differentiate between language processing disorders and auditory processing disorders. Chapters cover: the neurology of processing and learning; the central auditory processing model; the language processing model; and a lot more! *$41.95*

181 pages   Ages 5-Adult

801 Source for Stuttering and Cluttering

LinguiSystems
3100 4th Avenue
East Moline, IL   61244

800-776-4332
FAX 309-755-2377
TDY:800-933-8331
http://www.linguisystems.com
e-mail: service@linguisystems.com

David A Daly, Author
Linda Bowers, Owner
Rosemary Huisingh, Owner

Author David Daly, a former stutterer and respected speech pathologist, puts his clinical expertise and personal passion into this comprehensive program. Your clients will become fluent, confident speakers with this excellent, field-tested resource. *$44.95*

210 pages   Ages 13-Adult

802 Source for Syndromes

LinguiSystems
3100 4th Avenue
East Moline, IL   61244

800-776-4332
FAX 309-755-2377
TDY:800-933-8331
http://www.linguisystems.com
e-mail: service@linguisystems.com

Gail J Richard, Debra Reichert Hoge, Author
Linda Bowers, Owner
Rosemary Huisingh, Owner

Do you often wish someone would just tell you what to do with a specific youngster on your caseload? The Source for Syndromes can do just that. Learn about the speech-language characteristics for each sydrome with a focus on communication issues. This resource covers pertinent information for such sydromes such as Angelman, Asperger's, Autism, Rett's Tourette's, Williams, and more. *$41.95*

147 pages   Ages Birth-18

803 Spectral Speech Analysis: Software

The Speech Bin
1965 25th Avenue
Vero Beach, FL   32960

772-770-0007
FAX 772-770-0006
http://www.speechbin.com
e-mail: info@speechbin.com

This exciting new software uses visual feedback as an effective speech treatment tool. Speech-language pathologists can record speech and corresponding visual displays for clients who then try to match either auditory or visual targets. These built-in visual patterns can be displayed as either sophisticated spectrograms or real-time waveforms. Item number P227 — windows only. *$159.95*

804 Speech & Language & Voice & More

The Speech Bin
1965 25th Avenue
Vero Beach, FL   32960

772-770-0007
FAX 772-770-0006
http://www.speechbin.com
e-mail: info@speechbin.com

Contains eighty-eight practically perfect reproducible games and activities ideal for your K-5 clients. It gives you: manipulable activities to keep active leaners learning; tasks to match a multitude of interests and abilities; and vocal hygiene worksheets targeted to reduce vocal abuse. Item number 1496. *$19.95*

805 Speech Sports

The Speech Bin
1965 25th Avenue
Vero Beach, FL   32960

772-770-0007
FAX 772-770-0006
http://www.speechbin.com
e-mail: info@speechbin.com

Speech Sports makes every child in your caseload a shining sports star. Reproducible gameboards and language activities feature 19 different sports from boating to skating, bowling to running, basketball to soccer. Item number 1590. *$24.95*

806 Speech Viewer III

The The Speech Bin
1965 25th Avenue
Vero Beach, FL   32960

772-770-0007
FAX 772-770-0006
http://www.speechbin.com
e-mail: info@speechbin.com

SpeechViewer III creates entertaining interactive displays that let them do just that! It has all the Visual Voice Tools and so much more! Begin with simple sound awareness and advance to complex speech tasks, increasing phoneme awareness and improving speech sound production. Users enjoy constant and objective real time visual feedback from graphical speech displayed. Item number E280 — windows only. *$899.00*

807 Speech-Language Delights

The Speech Bin
1965 25th Avenue
Vero Beach, FL 32960 772-770-0007
FAX 772-770-0006
http://www.speechbin.com
e-mail: info@speechbin.com

Cook up lots of fun with Speech-Language Delights! Delectably delicious speech and language activities and games provide rich opportunities and hands-on activities with food-related themes to enrich K-8 kids. Item number 1541. *$ 29.95*

808 SpeechCrafts

The Speech Bin
1965 25th Avenue
Vero Beach, FL 32960 772-770-0007
FAX 772-770-0006
http://www.speechbin.com
e-mail: info@speechbin.com

Children love to create decorative and useful objects. They also love the surprise of using common and ordinary objects in unexpected ways. Best of all, children learn best when engaged in tangible, concrete, hands-on projects that are designed to enhance learning. Activities develop skills in: sequencing; language; basic concepts; vocabulary; articulation and following directions. Item number 1490. *$23.95*

809 Spelling: A Thematic Content-Area Approach Reproducibles

Harcourt Achieve
6277 Sea Harbor Drive
Orlando, FL 32887
800-531-5015
FAX 800-699-9459
http://www.steckvaughn.com
e-mail: info@steckvaughn.com
Kelley, Author
Tim McEwen, President/CEO
Jeff Johnson, Dir Marketing Communications
Chris Lehmann, Team Coordinator

Help students master the words they will use most frequently in the classroom. Organized lessons incorporate word analysis of letter patterns, correlations to appropriate literature, writing exercises, and application and extension activities.

810 Stepping Up to Fluency

The Speech Bin
1965 25th Avenue
Vero Beach, FL 32960 772-770-0007
FAX 772-770-0006
http://www.speechbin.com
e-mail: info@speechbin.com

Stepping Up to Fluency gives you a systematic program to help your clients from five years old to adults understand their disfluencies and gain control of their speech in 25-35 sessions. It presents high-interest strategies and materials in two levels, K-3 and grade 4 to adult. Item number 1360. *$34.95*

811 Stories and More: Time and Place

Riverdeep
500 Redwood Boulevard
Novato, CA 94947 415-763-4700
800-362-2890
FAX 415-763-4385
http://www.edmark.com
e-mail: info@riverdeep.net
Barry O'Callaghan, Chairman/CEO
Simon Calver, COO
John Rim, VP CFO

Combines three well-loved stories - The House on Maple Street, Roxaboxen, and Galimoto with engaging activities that strengthen students' reading comprehension.

812 Straight Speech

The Speech Bin
1965 25th Avenue
Vero Beach, FL 32960 772-770-0007
FAX 772-770-0006
http://www.speechbin.com
e-mail: info@speechbin.com
Jane Folk, Author
Jan J Binney, Editor-in-Chief

Lateral lisps can be one of the most preplexing articulation problems you encounter. Straight Speech gives you an effective, easy-to-implement program for lateral lisps. Developed by an experienced speech-language specialist, Straight Speech is a practical, step-by-step program tailored to meet this long-standing need. Item number 1525. *$22.95*

80 pages
ISBN 0-937857-32-7

813 Stuttering: Helping the Disfluent Preschool Child

The Speech Bin
1965 25th Avenue
Vero Beach, FL 32960 772-770-0007
FAX 772-770-0006
http://www.speechbin.com
e-mail: info@speechbin.com

Written in the warm encouraging style for which this author is known, Stuttering: Helping the Disfluent Preschool Child is the perfect tool for parents and teachers of young stuttering children. It uses a Speech Thermometer to show them ways to turn talking into an area of strength. Item number 1489. *$13.95*

814 Sunken Treasure Adventure: Beginning Blends

Sunburst Technology
400 Columbus Avenue
Valhalla, NY 10595 914-747-3310
800-321-7511
FAX 914-747-4109
http://www.sunburst.com
e-mail: service@sunburst.com

Focus on beginning blends sounds and concepts with three high-spirited games that invite students to use two letter consonant blends as they build words.

815 TARGET

The Speech Bin
1965 25th Avenue
Vero Beach, FL 32960
772-770-0007
FAX 772-770-0006
http://www.speechbin.com
e-mail: info@speechbin.com

TARGET is the kind of resource aphasia clinicians beg for — a practical resource that answers not only the what and how questions of treatment but also the why. It describes dozens of treatment methods and gives you practical exercises and activities to implement each technique. Item number 1434. *$49.95*

816 TOLD-P3: Test of Language Development Primary

The Speech Bin
1965 25th Avenue
Vero Beach, FL 32960
772-770-0007
FAX 772-770-0006
http://www.speechbin.com
e-mail: info@speechbin.com

This revised test of 4-8 year olds' language gives unbiased test items that reflect the most modern language theories, Two new subtests — Phonemic Analysis and Relational Vocabulary, full-color contemporary photos young children like and norms include minority and disability groups. Item number P501. *$246.00*

817 TOPS Kit-Adolescent: Tasks of Problem Solving

LinguiSystems
3100 4th Avenue
East Moline, IL 61244
800-776-4332
FAX 309-755-2377
TDY:800-933-8331
http://www.linguisystems.com
e-mail: service@linguisystems.com
Linda Bowers, Rosemary Huisingh, Mark Barrett, Author
Linda Bowers, Owner
Rosemary Huisingh, Owner

Teach your teens how to use their language skills to think, think, think. We combine literacy, thinking, writing, humor, and language arts practice to cover these thinking skills: using content to make references; analyzing information; taking another's point of view; and more. It's a literacy- based approach that gets dramatic results! *$59.95*

192 pages   Ages 12-18

818 TOPS Kit-Elementary: Tasks of Problem Solving

LinguiSystems
3100 4th Avenue
East Moline, IL 61244
800-776-4332
FAX 309-755-2377
TDY:800-933-8331
http://www.linguisystems.com
e-mail: service@linguisystems.com
Linda Bowers, Rosemary Huisingh, Mark Barrett, Author
Linda Bowers, Owner
Rosemary Huisingh, Owner

Reveal thinking and language skills your students didn't know they had with this remarkable kit. TOPS Kit-Elementary combines thinking and expressive language skills to develop better communications. *$119.95*

209 pages   Ages 6-12

819 Take Home: Oral-Motor Exercises

LinguiSystems
3100 4th Avenue
East Moline, IL 61244
800-776-4332
FAX 309-755-2377
TDY:800-933-8331
http://www.linguisystems.com
e-mail: service@linguisystems.com
Lisa Loncar-Belding, Author
Linda Bowers, Owner
Rosemary Huisingh, Owner

Stop writing your own take-home letters and exercises for carryover! These homework pages work on the earliest developing vowel and consonant sounds. Created for use with deaf and hearing-impaired students, this resource is great for all of your oral-motor and articulation cases. *$31.95*

129 pages   Ages 2-6

820 Take Home: Phonological Awareness

LinguiSystems
3100 4th Avenue
East Moline, IL 61244
800-776-4332
FAX 309-755-2377
TDY:800-933-8331
http://www.linguisystems.com
e-mail: service@linguisystems.com
Carolyn Robertson, Wanda Salter, Author
Linda Bowers, Owner
Rosemary Huisingh, Owner

These activities are easy for parents and caregivers to follow. Activities are organized at the word, syllable, phoneme, and grapheme level. You'll target these skills: rhyming; blending; isolation; segmentation; deletion; substitution; and phoneme-grapheme correspondence. *$31.95*

144 pages   Ages 5-8

821 Take Home: Preschool Language Development

LinguiSystems
3100 4th Avenue
East Moline, IL 61244
800-776-4332
FAX 309-755-2377
TDY:800-933-8331
http://www.linguisystems.com
e-mail: service@linguisystems.com
Martha Drake, Author
Linda Bowers, Owner
Rosemary Huisingh, Owner

Home follow-up is essential for your little ones with speech and language delays. Get everything you need for a comprehensive take-home program with this time saver! Each take-home lesson is easy to follow. *$31.95*

191 pages   Ages 1-5

822   Talk About Fun

The Speech Bin
1965 25th Avenue
Vero Beach, FL   32960   772-770-0007
                                FAX 772-770-0006
                       http://www.speechbin.com
                       e-mail: info@speechbin.com

Talk About Fun takes advantage of children's natural
love of play and making things to achieve your
speech-language goals. Target phonemes featured include p-b-m, t-d-n, f, k-g, s, sh-ch-j, i, and consonant
blends. Carryover projects, sequence stories, and letters to parents are an added bonus. Item number 1485.
$29.95

823   Talkable Tales

The Speech Bin
1965 25th Avenue
Vero Beach, FL   32960   772-770-0007
                                FAX 772-770-0006
                       http://www.speechbin.com
                       e-mail: info@speechbin.com

Talkable Tales gives you a wealth of stories to build
speech and language skills. Comprehension and challenge questions accompany each story. Stories are a
uniform length so you may use them with groups
working on multiple sounds. Each has ten key words
containing the target sound. Item number 1540.
$25.95

824   Talking Time

The Speech Bin
1965 25th Avenue
Vero Beach, FL   32960   772-770-0007
                                FAX 772-770-0006
                       http://www.speechbin.com
                       e-mail: info@speechbin.com

Jeanette Stickel, Author
Jan J Binney, Editor-in-Chief

Talking times gives you sequenced activities to foster
language and cognitive programs by parents, family
members, and caregivers. Talking Time also includes
guidelines for language development and directions
and rationale for use. Item number 1589. *$17.95*

>   *64 pages*
>   *ISBN 0-937857-24-6*

825   Teaching Phonics: Staff Development Book

Harcourt Achieve
6277 Sea Harbor Drive
Orlando, FL   32887
                                800-531-5015
                                FAX 800-699-9459
                       http://www.steckvaughn.com
                       e-mail: info@steckvaughn.com

Steck-Vaughn Staff, Author
Tim McEwen, President/CEO
Jeff Johnson, Dir Marketing Communications
Chris Lehmann, Team Coordinator

Fine-tune your instructional approach with fresh insights from phonics experts. This resource offers informative articles and timely tips for teaching phonics
in the integrated language arts classroom.

**826   Test for Auditory Comprehension of Language:
TACL-3**

The Speech Bin
1965 25th Avenue
Vero Beach, FL   32960   772-770-0007
                                800-477-3324
                                FAX 888-329-2246
                       http://www.speechbin.com
                       e-mail: info@speechbin.com
Elizabeth Carrow-Woolfolk, Author

The newly revised TACL-3 evaluates the 0-3 to 9-11
year-old's understanding of spoken language in three
subtests: Vocabulary, Grammatical Morphemes and
Elaborated Phrases and Sentences. Each test item is a
word or sentence read aloud by the examiner; the child
responds by pointing to one of three pictures. Item
number P792. *$261.00*

**827   Test of Early Language Development 3rd Edition:
TELD-3**

The Speech Bin
1965 25th Avenue
Vero Beach, FL   32960   772-770-0007
                                FAX 772-770-0006
                       http://www.speechbin.com
                       e-mail: info@speechbin.com

TELD-3 for children 0-2 through 7-11 quickly and
easily measures receptive and expressive language
and yields an overall Spoken Language Score. Stimulus pictures are colorful and contemporary. Standardized on 2,217 children, this test has little or no bias.
Item number P576. *$272.00*

**828   Test of Language Development: Intermediate
(TOLD-I:3)**

The Speech Bin
1965 25th Avenue
Vero Beach, FL   32960   772-770-0007
                                FAX 772-770-0006
                       http://www.speechbin.com
                       e-mail: info@speechbin.com

This well-normed test is one popular measure of language development; it's an ideal choice for
speech-language pathologists' use in schools. The
complete kit includes an examiner's manual, picture
stimulus book, and 25 test forms. Item number P574.
$179.00

829   That's LIFE! Life Skills

LinguiSystems
3100 4th Avenue
East Moline, IL   61244
                                800-776-4332
                                FAX 309-755-2377
                                TDY:800-933-8331
                       http://www.linguisystems.com
                       e-mail: service@linguisystems.com
Patricia Smith, Author
Linda Bowers, Owner
Rosemary Huisingh, Owner

Students get hands-on language experience in everyday events. Units are organized by consumer affairs,
government, health concerns, money matters, going
places, and homemaking. Tasks include identifying
vocabulary, making inferences, predicting, and more.
$37.95

>   *192 pages   Ages 12-18*

830 Therapy Guide for Language & Speech Disorders: Volume 1

The Speech Bin
1965 25th Avenue
Vero Beach, FL   32960   772-770-0007
                               FAX 772-770-0006
                        http://www.speechbin.com
                        e-mail: info@speechbin.com

This structured language rehabilitation program contains 429 color-coded pages containing exercises for listening, reading comprehension, speech and language, gestures, writing, and number skills. A word communication notebook and worksheets suitable for carryover are included. Item number V368. *$47.95*

831 Therapy Guide for Language and Speech Disorders: Volume 2

The Speech Bin
1965 25th Avenue
Vero Beach, FL   32960   772-770-0007
                               FAX 772-770-0006
                        http://www.speechbin.com
                        e-mail: info@speechbin.com

 Volume 2 answers your need for materials at a higher level. This large print workbook covers oral language comprehension, word retrieval, sentence formulation, general knowledge, thought organization, definitions, number skills, and daily needs. Item number V370. *$38.95*

832 Thought Organization Workbook

Therapro
225 Arlington Street
Framingham, MA   01702   508-872-9494
                                800-257-5376
                               FAX 508-875-2062
                        http://www.theraproducts.com
                        e-mail: info@theraproducts.com
Therapro Staff, Author
Karen Conrad, President

Completing letter and word puzzles, composing sentences and organizing shapes, numbers, events and language. *$10.50*

833 Tic-Tac-Artic and Match

LinguiSystems
3100 4th Avenue
East Moline, IL   61244
                                800-776-4332
                               FAX 309-755-2377
                               TDY:800-933-8331
                        http://www.linguisystems.com
                        e-mail: service@linguisystems.com
Carol A Vaccariello, Author
Linda Bowers, Owner
Rosemary Huisingh, Owner

Tic-Tac-Artic and Match gives you five games on every page and tons of practice per session. Each page has 16 pictures for one target phoneme. To play Tic-Tac-Artic, use the special game template to create four different tic-tac-toe style games. *$34.95*

157 pages   Ages 4-12

834 Visual Voice Tools

The Speech Bin
1965 25th Avenue
Vero Beach, FL   32960   772-770-0007
                               FAX 772-770-0006
                        http://www.speechbin.com
                        e-mail: info@speechbin.com

Seven visual voice tools help your clients develop vocal control through engaging visual and auditory feedback. The tools include: Sound Presence; Loudness Range; Voice Presence; Voice Timing; Voice Onset; Pitch Range and Pitch Control. Item number E278. *$199.95*

835 Vocabulary Connections

Harcourt Achieve
6277 Sea Harbor Drive
Orlando, FL   32887
                                800-531-5015
                               FAX 800-699-9459
                        http://www.steckvaughn.com
                        e-mail: info@steckvaughn.com
Steck-Vaughn Staff, Author
Tim McEwen, President/CEO
Jeff Johnson, Dir Marketing Communications
Chris Lehmann, Team Coordinator

Keep students engaged in building vocabulary through crossword puzzles and cloze passages, and by using words in context and making analogies. Lessons build around thematically organized literature and nonfiction selections provide meaningful context for essential vocabulary words.

836 Vocabulary Play by Play

LinguiSystems
3100 4th Avenue
East Moline, IL   61244
                                800-776-4332
                               FAX 309-755-2377
                               TDY:800-933-8331
                        http://www.linguisystems.com
                        e-mail: service@linguisystems.com
Caolyn LoGiudice, Mike LoGiudice, Author
Linda Bowers, Owner
Rosemary Huisingh, Owner

Students with language-learning disabilities need ten times more encounters with new vocabulary words than their nondisabled peers. Vocabulary Play by Play gives students the built-in encounters with vocabulary they need for school success. *$44.95*

Ages 9-15

837 Vowel Patterns

Sunburst Technology
400 Columbus Avenue
Valhalla, NY   10595   914-747-3310
                              800-321-7511
                             FAX 914-747-4109
                        http://www.sunburst.com
                        e-mail: service@sunburst.com

Some vowels are neither long nor short. In this investigation, students explore and learn to use abstract vowels.

838 Vowel Scramble

LinguiSystems
3100 4th Avenue
East Moline, IL   61244

800-776-4332
FAX 309-755-2377
TDY:800-933-8331
http://www.linguisystems.com
e-mail: service@linguisystems.com

Carolyn LoGiudice, Author
Linda Bowers, Owner
Rosemary Huisingh, Owner

Your student will love this fun new way to practice spelling and phonological awareness skills. Players earn points by using letter tiles to complete words on the game board. *$44.95*

Ages 7-12

839 Warmups and Workouts

The Speech Bin
1965 25th Avenue
Vero Beach, FL   32960

772-770-0007
FAX 772-770-0006
http://www.speechbin.com
e-mail: info@speechbin.com

Easy-to-follow step-by-step instructions demonstrate how to help children achieve reliable production of r sounds, practice them in words of increasing complexity, and improve their phonic skills simultaneously. Item number 1486. *$26.95*

840 Weekly Language Practice

Harcourt Achieve
6277 Sea Harbor Drive
Orlando, FL   32887

800-531-5015
FAX 800-699-9459
http://www.steckvaughn.com
e-mail: info@steckvaughn.com

Keely Hoffman, Ken Bowser, Author
Tim McEwen, President/CEO
Jeff Johnson, Dir Marketing Communications
Chris Lehmann, Team Coordinator

Each activity page features five activity strips, one for each day of the week, and is backed up by a convenient answer key for the teacher that includes explanations and extensions.

841 Winning in Speech

The Speech Bin
1965 25th Avenue
Vero Beach, FL   32960

772-770-0007
FAX 772-770-0006
http://www.speechbin.com
e-mail: info@speechbin.com

Michelle Waugh, Author
Jan J Binney, Editor-in-Chief

This delightful workbook gives your 7-14 year olds a wealth of information about stuttering and how to handle it. Winning in Speech shows them how they can modify their stuttering behaviors through everyday experiences. Item number 1594. *$22.95*

40 pages
ISBN 0-937857-29-7

842 Wizard of Rs

The Speech Bin
1965 25th Avenue
Vero Beach, FL   32960

772-770-0007
FAX 772-770-0006
http://www.speechbin.com
e-mail: info@speechbin.com

This wizard makes those troublesome r problems diappear like magic! It gives you a practical approach with a wide range of scripted activities and helpful criterion-referenced testing, oral-motor exercises, remedial techniques and review of musculature. Item number P756. *$22.00*

843 Workbook for Aphasia

The Speech Bin
1965 25th Avenue
Vero Beach, FL   32960

772-770-0007
FAX 772-770-0006
http://www.speechbin.com
e-mail: info@speechbin.com

This book gives you materials for adults who have recovered a significant degree of speaking, reading, writing, and comprehension skills. It includes 106 excercises divided into eight target areas. Item number W331. *$48.95*

844 Workbook for Language Skills

The Speech Bin
1965 25th Avenue
Vero Beach, FL   32960

772-770-0007
FAX 772-770-0006
http://www.speechbin.com
e-mail: info@speechbin.com

This workbook features 68 real-world exercises designed for use with mildly to severely cognitive and language-impaired individuals. The workbook is divided in seven target areas: Sentence Completion; General Knowledge; Word Recall; Figurative Language; Sentence Comprehension; Sentence Construction and Spelling. Item number W333. *$48.95*

845 Workbook for Verbal Expression

The Speech Bin
1965 25th Avenue
Vero Beach, FL   32960

772-770-0007
FAX 772-770-0006
http://www.speechbin.com
e-mail: info@speechbin.com

Is a book of 100s of excerises from simple naming, automatic speech sequences, and repetition exercises to complex tasks in sentence formulation and abstract verbal reasoning. Item number 1435. *$43.95*

846 Writing Trek Grades 4-6

Sunburst Technology
400 Columbus Avenue
Valhalla, NY   10595

914-747-3310
800-321-7511
FAX 914-747-4109
http://www.sunburst.com
e-mail: service@sunburst.com

Enhance your students' experience in your English language arts classroom with twelve authentic writing projects that build students' competence while encouraging creativity.

847 Writing Trek Grades 6-8

Sunburst Technology
400 Columbus Avenue
Valhalla, NY   10595   914-747-3310
                              800-321-7511
                              FAX 914-747-4109
                              http://www.sunburst.com
                              e-mail: service@sunburst.com

Twelve authentic language arts projects, activities, and assignments develop your students' writing confidence and ability.

848 Writing Trek Grades 8-10

Sunburst Technology
400 Columbus Avenue
Valhalla, NY   10595   914-747-3310
                              800-321-7511
                              FAX 914-747-4109
                              http://ww.sunburst.com
                              e-mail: service@sunburst.com

Help your students develop a concept of genre as they become familiar with the writing elements and characteristics of a variety of writing forms.

849 Your Child's Speech and Language

The Speech Bin
1965 25th Avenue
Vero Beach, FL   32960   772-770-0007
                              FAX 772-770-0006
                              http://www.speechbin.com
                              e-mail: info@speechbin.com

This delightfully illustrated 52- page book provides helpful information about speech and language development from infancy through five years. It shows how to determine if speech is developing normally and ways to stimulate its growth. It's ideal for parent training and baby showers too! Item number P652. *$17.00*

Life Skills

850 Ablenet

1081 10th Avenue SE
Minneapolis, MN   55414   612-379-0956
                              800-322-0956
                              FAX 612-379-9143
                              http://www.ablenetinc.com
                              e-mail: customerservice@ablenetinc.com
Cheryl Volkman, Chief Developmental Officer

Simple assistive technology for teaching children with disabilities including communication aids, switches, environmental control, literacy and teacher resources, kits and more.

851 Activities for the Elementary Classroom

Curriculum Associates
PO Box 2001
North Billerica, MA   01862
                              800-225-0248
                              FAX 800-366-1158
                              http://www.curriculumassociates.com
                              e-mail: ca@infocurriculumassociates.com
Ernest L Kern, Editor

Challenge your students to make a hole in a 3" x 5" index card large enough to poke their heads through. Or offer to pour them a glass of air. You'll have their attenion — the first step toward learning — when you use the high-interest, hands-on activities in these exciting teacher resource books.

852 Activities of Daily Living: A Manual of Group Activities and Written Exercises

Therapro
225 Arlington Street
Framingham, MA   01702   508-872-9494
                              800-257-5376
                              FAX 508-875-2062
                              http://www.theraproducts.com
                              e-mail: info@theraproducts.com
Karen McCarthy COTA/L, Author
Karen Conrad, President

Designed to provide group leaders easy access to structured plans for Activities of Daily Living (ADL) Groups. Organized into five modules: Personal Hygiene; Laundry Skills; Money Management; Leisure Skills and Nutrition. Each includes introduction, assessment guidelines, worksheets to copy, suggested board work, and wrap-up discussions. Appropriate for adult or adolescent programs, school systems and programs for the learning disabled. *$25.00*

136 pages

853 Aids and Appliances for Indepentent Living

Maxi
PO Box 3209
Farmingdale, NY   11735   631-752-0521
                              800-522-6294
                              FAX 631-752-0689
                              TDY:631-752-0738
                              http://www.maxiaids.com
Elliot Zaretsky, President

Thousands of products to make life easier. Eating, dressing, communications, bed, bath, kitchen, writing aids and more.

854 Artic-Action

The Speech Bin
1965 25th Avenue
Vero Beach, FL   32960   772-770-0007
                              FAX 772-770-0006
                              http://www.speechbin.com
                              e-mail: info@speechbin.com
Denise Grigas, Author
Jan J Binney, Editor-in-Chief

Take the doldrums out of speech drills with this terrific collection of ideas! Clever tasks facilitate learning through hands-on experiences and provide a rich language learning environment for K-5 children. Activities encourage cooperative learning, turn taking, conversational discourse and social interaction. Item number 1524. *$18.95*

144 pages
ISBN 0-937857-37-8

855 Barnaby's Burrow: An Auditory Processing Game

LinguiSystems
3100 4th Avenue
East Moline, IL   61244

800-776-4332
FAX 309-755-2375
TDY:800-933-8331
http://www.linguisystems.com
e-mail: service@linguisystems.com
Barb Truman, Author
Linda Bowers, Owner
Rosemary Huisingh, Owner

Your students will practice good auditory processing skills as they help Barnaby the rabbit get to his burrow. This delightful game gives you tons of auditory processing tasks at increasing levels of difficulty. 300 game cards provide you stimulus items for phonological awareness, following directions, absurdities, and identifying main ideas and details. *$44.95*

Ages 4-9

856 Boredom Rx

The Speech Bin
1965 25th Avenue
Vero Beach, FL   32960
772-770-0007
FAX 772-770-0006
http://www.speechbin.com
e-mail: info@speechbin.com
Kristel Aderholdt, Author
Jan J Binney, Editor-in-Chief

Fun-filled tasks help school-age kids improve their practical skills in listening, pragmatics, remembering, and following directions. Item number 1583. *$29.95*

857 Brainopoly: A Thinking Game

LinguiSystems
3100 4th Avenue
East Moline, IL   61244

800-776-4332
FAX 309-755-2377
TDY:800-933-8331
http://www.linguisystems.com
e-mail: service@linguisystems.com
LinguiSystems Staff, Author
Linda Bowers, Owner
Rosemary Huisingh, Owner

Target all the critical thinking, problem-solving, and decision-making skills your older students need to meet the demands of the classroom curriculum. Each game section has 50 questions divided into two levels of difficulty. That's 450 total questions! Students will practice using predicting, inferring, deduction skills, and more! *$44.95*

Ages 10-15

858 Categorically Speaking

The Speech Bin
1965 25th Avenue
Vero Beach, FL   32960
772-770-0007
FAX 772-770-0006
http://www.speechbin.com
e-mail: info@speechbin.com

This game for two to four players or two teams gives 6-10 year-olds experience in asking questions, evaluating information they receive, and using it to solve problems. To play, they must use specified question formats to get clues about pictures, recognize similarities and differences, identify salient features of objects, and encode and decode messages. Item number Q849. *$51.00*

859 Changes Around Us CD-ROM

Harcourt Achieve
6277 Sea Harbor Drive
Orlando, FL   32887

800-531-5015
FAX 800-699-9459
http://www.steckvaughn.com
e-mail: info@steckvaughn.com
Steck-Vaughn Staff, Author
Tim McEwen, President/CEO
Jeff Johnson, Dir Marketing Communications
Chris Lehmann, Team Coordinator

Nature is the natural choice for observing change. By observing and researching dramatic visual sequences such as the stages of development of a butterfly, children develop a broad understanding of the concept of change. As they search this multimedia database for images and information about plant and animal life cycles and seasonal change, students strengthen their abilities in research, analysis, problem-solving, critical thinking and communication.

860 Classroom Visual Activities

Therapro
225 Arlington Street
Framingham, MA   01702
508-872-9494
800-257-5376
FAX 508-875-2062
http://www.theraproducts.com
e-mail: info@theraproducts.com
Regina G Richards MA, Author
Karen Conrad, President

This work presents a wealth of activities for the development of visual skills in the areas of pursuit, scanning, aligning, and locating movements; eye hand coordination, and fixation activity. Each activity lists objectives and criteria for success and gives detailed instuctions. *$15.00*

80 pages

861 Cognitive Strategy Instruction for Middle & High Schools

Brookline Books
PO Box 97
Newton Upper Falls, MA   02464
800-666-2665
FAX 617-558-8011
http://www.brooklinebooks.com
e-mail: info@brooklinebooks.com
Eileen Wood, Vera Woloshyn, Teena Willoughby, Author

Presents cognitive strategies empirically validated for middle and high school students, with an emphasis for teachers on how to teach and support the strategies. *$26.95*

286 pages
ISBN 1-571290-07-9

862 Complete Guide to Running, Walking and Fitness for Kids

Therapro
225 Arlington Street
Framingham, MA   01702   508-872-9494
                               800-257-5376
                          FAX 508-875-2062
                  http://www.theraproducts.com
                  e-mail: info@theraproducts.com
Tim Erson MS PT, Author
Karen Conrad, President

This should be every child's first book of fitness. Many tips on how to get started, such as stretching, dressing wisely, where to run, racing, aerobics and more. Includes a logbook and journal for 1 year, with weekly goals, encouraging messages, training notes, and so on. *$18.95*

263 pages

863 Coping for Kids Who Stutter

The Speech Bin
1965 25th Avenue
Vero Beach, FL   32960   772-770-0007
                          FAX 772-770-0006
                    http://www.speechbin.com
                    e-mail: info@speechbin.com
Coping for Kids Who Stutter educates people of all ages about the confusing and frustrating communication disorder of stuttering. This matter-of-fact book presents a muiltitude of facts about stuttering and gives lots of good advice about what to do about it in a nonthreatening, convincing manner. Item number 1543. *$18.95*

864 Definition Play by Play

LinguiSystems
3100 4th Avenue
East Moline, IL   61244
                               800-776-4332
                          FAX 309-755-2377
                          TDY:800-933-8331
                    http://www.linguisystems.com
                  e-mail: service@linguisystems.com
Sharon Spencer, Author
Linda Bowers, Owner
Rosemary Huisingh, Owner

Teach your students to give accurate, cohesive definitions by identifying and organizing critical attributes of words. As players move along the board, they describe an object card by these attributes: function; what goes with it; size/shape; color; parts; what it's made of; and location. *$44.95*

Ages 8-14

865 Effective Listening

The Speech Bin
1965 25th Avenue
Vero Beach, FL   32960   772-770-0007
                          FAX 772-770-0006
                    http://www.speechbin.com
                    e-mail: info@speechbin.com

Effective Listening gives you creative lessons in a stimulating format that takes the drudgery out of listening drills. Its LISTEN techniques provide structured strategies to improve auditory processing skills. Item number 1355. *$ 25.95*

866 Fine Motor Activities Guide and Easel Activities Guide

Therapro
225 Arlington Street
Framingham, MA   01702   508-872-9494
                               800-257-5376
                          FAX 508-875-2062
                  http://www.theraproducts.com
                  e-mail: info@theraproducts.com
Jane Berry OTR/L, Author
Karen Conrad, President

These guides have always been included in the above kits and can now be purchased separately. Useful for activity plans or teacher-educator-parent consultations. Perfect hand-outs as part of your inservice packet (no need to write out ideas, photocopy materials, etc). Package of 10 booklets.

867 Fine Motor Fun

Therapro
225 Arlington Street
Framingham, MA   01702   508-872-9494
                               800-257-5376
                          FAX 508-875-2062
                  http://www.theraproducts.com
                  e-mail: info@theraproducts.com
Maryanne Bruni BS OT, Author
Karen Conrad, President

Fine motor skills are the hand skills that allow us to do things like hold a pencil, cut with scissors, eat with a fork, and use a computer. This practical guide shows parents and professionals how to help children with Down Syndrome from infancy to 12 years improve fine motor functioning. *$16.95*

191 pages   Ages Birth-12

868 Finger Frolics: Fingerplays

Therapro
225 Arlington Street
Framingham, MA   01702   508-872-9494
                               800-257-5376
                          FAX 508-875-2062
                  http://www.theraproducts.com
                  e-mail: info@theraproducts.com
Liz Cromwell, Dixie Hibner, Author
Karen Conrad, President

Invaluable for occupational therapists, speech/language pathologists and teachers. Over 350 light and humorous fingerplays help children with rhyming and performing actions which develop fine motor and language skills. *$10.95*

869 Follow Me!

LinguiSystems
3100 4th Avenue
East Moline, IL   61244

800-776-4332
FAX 309-755-2377
TDY:800-933-8331
http://www.linguisystems.com
e-mail: service@linguisystems.com

Grace W Frank, Author
Linda Bowers, Owner
Rosemary Huisingh, Owner

Lessons are organized by grade level so you can control the lesson complexity as your students listen and follow oral directions. Get 91 listen-and-do lessons, each with a reproducible student worksheet to teach concepts such as location, association, exclusion, sequencing, and more. *$34.95*

187 pages   Ages 5-9

870 Follow Me! 2

LinguiSystems
3100 4th Avenue
East Moline, IL   61244

800-776-4332
FAX 309-755-2377
TDY:800-933-8331
http://www.linguisystems.com
e-mail: service@linguisystems.com

Grace Frank, Author
Linda Bowers, Owner
Rosemary Huisingh, Owner

These activities are relevant to classroom listening demands. The directions relate specifically on an accompanying worksheet. It's a pick-up-and-use-now resource to teach the vocabulary of language arts, math, social studies and more. *$34.95*

201 pages   Ages 7-11

871 HELP Elementary

LinguiSystems
3100 4th Avenue
East Moline, IL   61244

800-776-4332
FAX 309-755-2377
TDY:800-933-8331
http://www.linguisystems.com
e-mail: service@linguisystems.com

Andrea Lazzari, Patricia Peters, Author
Linda Bowers, Owner
Rosemary Huisingh, Owner

The look and content of these activities appeal specifically to your elementary-aged students. The no-frills, ready-to-use approach fits your precious time. These worksheets are perfect for oral or written practice. Help students improve question comprehension, association, specific word-finding, grammar, and more. *$39.95*

207 pages   Ages 6-12

872 HELP for Memory

LinguiSystems
3100 4th Avenue
East Moline, IL   61244

800-776-4332
FAX 309-755-2377
TDY:800-933-8331
http://www.linguisystems.com
e-mail: service@linguisystems.com

Andrea Lazzari, Author
Linda Bowers, Owner
Rosemary Huisingh, Owner

Help clients and students acquire memory strategies they'll use in daily life. These exercises incorporate attention, discrimination, categorization, and association to cover the broad range of memory skills. These functional memory tasks are arranged in a hierarchy to build skill upon skill. Help clients organize and retrieve information through exercises for coding and grouping items for recall, applying memory techniques to daily life skills, and more. *$39.95*

178 pages   Ages 8-Adult

873 HELP for Middle School

LinguiSystems
3100 4th Avenue
East Moline, IL   61244

800-776-4332
FAX 309-755-2377
TDY:800-933-8331
http://www.linguisystems.com
e-mail: service@linguisystems.com

Andrea Lazzari, Author
Linda Bowers, Owner
Rosemary Huisingh, Owner

Get ready-to-use activities relevant to middle school students. Your students will tune in and make progress! Middle school clinicians are singing the praises of this great resource. You'll get IEP goals and great language activities for vocabulary, grammer, question comprehension, following directions, test taking, and expression. *$39.95*

183 pages   Ages 10-15

874 Hands-On Activities for Exceptional Students

Peytral Publications
PO Box 1162
Minnetonka, MN   55345

952-949-8707
877-739-8725
FAX 952-906-9777
http://www.peytral.com
e-mail: help@peytral.com

Beverly Thorne, Author
Peggy Hammeken, Owner/Publisher

This execptional new release is developed for educators of students who have cognitive delays who will eventually work in a sheltered employment environment. If you need new ideas at your fingertips, this practical book is for you. *$19.95*

112 pages   Special Ed
ISBN 1-890455-31-8

875   Health

Harcourt Achieve
6277 Sea Harbor Drive
Orlando, FL   32887

800-531-5015
FAX 800-699-9459
http://www.steckvaughn.com
e-mail: info@steckvaughn.com

Steck-Vaughn Staff, Author
Tim McEwen, President/CEO
Jeff Johnson, Dir Marketing Communications
Chris Lehmann, Team Coordinator

Lessons and projects focus on nutrition, outdoor safety, smart choices, and exercise. Designed to make children more health conscious. Activity formats include fill in the blank, word puzzles, multiple choice, crosswords, and more.

876   Hidden Senses: Your Balance Sense & Your Muscle Sense

Therapro
225 Arlington Street
Framingham, MA   01702

508-872-9494
800-257-5376
FAX 508-875-2062
http://www.theraproducts.com
e-mail: info@theraproducts.com

Jane Koomar PhD, Barbara Friedman MA, Author
Karen Conrad, President

These movement books are back in print! Help children discover the crucial, yet seldom mentioned body awareness senses that help them in movement, coordination, strength and perception. The authors, both practicing OTs, explain simply and clearly how the body senses work. Colorful and vibrant images bring the explanations to life.

877   It's All in Your Head: A Guide to Understanding Your Brain and Boosting Your Brain Power

Therapro
225 Arlington Street
Framingham, MA   01702

508-872-9494
800-257-5376
FAX 508-875-2062
http://www.theraproducts.com
e-mail: info@theraproducts.com

Susan L Barrett, Author
Karen Conrad, President

By popular demand from therapists, we are carrying this popular book for children. An owners manual on the brain, written especially for kids, this upbeat, engaging book is great for ages 9-14. *$9.95*

151 pages

878   Just for Me! Concepts

LinguiSystems
3100 4th Avenue
East Moline, IL   61244

800-776-4332
FAX 309-755-2377
TDY:800-933-8331
http://www.linguisystems.com
e-mail: service@linguisystems.com

Margaret Warner, Author
Linda Bowers, Owner
Rosemary Huisingh, Owner

These fun color, cut, fold and play pages will keep youngsters busy learning basic concepts. Teach basic concepts in four areas: spatial, attributes, quantity, and temporal. *$24.95*

150 pages   Ages 3-6

879   Key Concepts in Personal Development

Marsh Media
8025 Ward Parkway Plaza
Kansas City, MO   64114

816-523-1059
800-821-3303
FAX 866-333-7421
http://www.marshmedia.com
e-mail: info@marshmedia.com

Joan K Marsh, President

Our videos, books, and teaching guides bring character education to the classrom. These kits are invaluable aids in teaching everyday values like honesty, anger control, trustworthiness, perseverance, understanding and respect. They help you prepare youngsters to meet challenges and greet opportunities with skill and optimism.

880   LD Teacher's IEP Companion Software

LinguiSystems
3100 4th Avenue
East Moline, IL   61244

800-776-4332
FAX 309-755-2377
TDY:800-933-8331
http://www.linguisystems.com
e-mail: service@linguisystems.com

Molly Lyle, Author
Linda Bowers, Owner
Rosemary Huisingh, Owner

Create customized, professional reports with these terrific academic goals and objectives. You'll have individual objectives from nine skill areas at the click of your mouse! Save time with the software version of the best-selling book! For both PC and Macintosh. *$69.95*

Ages 5-18

881   Life Management Skills I

Therapro
225 Arlington Street
Framingham, MA   01702

508-872-9494
800-257-5376
FAX 508-875-2062
http://www.theraproducts.com
e-mail: info@theraproducts.com

Therapro Staff, Author
Karen Conrad, President

Topics include: assertion; discharge planning; emotion identification; exercise; goal setting; leisure; motivation; nutrition; problem solving; risk taking; self awareness; self esteem; sleep; stress management; support systems; time management; and values clarification. *$39.95*

882 **Life Management Skills II**

Therapro
225 Arlington Street
Framingham, MA   01702   508-872-9494
                                800-257-5376
                            FAX 508-875-2062
                    http://www.theraproducts.com
                    e-mail: info@theraproducts.com
Therapro Staff, Author
Karen Conrad, President

Topics include: activities of daily living; anger management; assertion; verbal and nonverbal communication; coping skills; grief/loss; humor; life balance; money management; parenting; reminiscence; safety issues; self esteem; image; steps to recovery; stress management; support systems and time management. *$41.95*

883 **Life Management Skills III**

Therapro
225 Arlington Street
Framingham, MA   01702   508-872-9494
                                800-257-5376
                            FAX 508-875-2062
                    http://www.theraproducts.com
                    e-mail: info@theraproducts.com
Therapro Staff, Author
Karen Conrad, President

Using the same format as books I and II, this new book has 50 handouts including 5 forms on both men's and women's issues. Includes 9 pages of generic forms that everyone can use. Topics include: aging; body image; communication; conflict resolution; coping skills; creative expression; healthy living; job readiness; nurturance; relapse prevention; relationships and many more. *$41.95*

884 **Life Management Skills IV**

Therapro
225 Arlington Street
Framingham, MA   01702   508-872-9494
                                800-257-5376
                            FAX 508-875-2062
                    http://www.theraproducts.com
                    e-mail: info@theraproducts.com
Therapro Staff, Author
Karen Conrad, President

Topics include: activities of daily living; combating stigma; communication; coping with serious mental illness; home management; humor; job readiness; journalizing; leisure; parenting; relationships; responsibility; self esteem; sexual health; social skills; stress mangagement; suicide isues and values. *$41.95*

885 **Life-Centered Career Education: Daily Living Skills**

Council for Exceptional Children
1110 N Glebe Road
Arlington, VA   22201   703-620-3660
                                888-232-7733
                            FAX 703-264-9494
                    http://www.cec.sped.org
                    e-mail: service@cec.sped.org
Donn Brolin, Author
Dr Drew Allbritten, Executive Director
Genee Norbert, LCCE Program Manager

LCCE teaches you to prepare students to function independently and productively as family members, citizens, and workers, and to enjoy fulfilling personal lives. LCCE is a motivating and effectiev classroom, home, and community-based curriculum.

886 **Listening for Basic Concepts All Year' Round**

LinguiSystems
3100 4th Avenue
East Moline, IL   61244
                                800-776-4332
                            FAX 309-755-2377
                            TDY:800-933-8331
                    http://www.linguisystems.com
                    e-mail: service@linguisystems.com
Brenda Brumbaugh, Nan Thompson-Trenta, Author
Linda Bowers, Owner
Rosemary Huisingh, Owner

Mastering concepts is guaranteed with this book because you teach them in fun, themed contexts. Teach 86 space, quanity, and attribute concepts. Concept tests give you built-in accountablility. *$39.95*

186 pages   Ages 5-8

887 **Living Skills**

The Speech Bin
1965 25th Avenue
Vero Beach, FL   32960   772-770-0007
                            FAX 772-770-0006
                    http://www.speechbin.com
                    e-mail: info@speechbin.com

Living Skills meets the challenges and special needs of children and adolescents with traumatic brain injury. A wealth of activities help restore cognitive, perceptual, and functional skills. Item number 1350. *$39.95*

888 **MORE: Integrating the Mouth with Sensory & Postural Functions**

Therapro
225 Arlington Street
Framingham, MA   01702   508-872-9494
                                800-257-5376
                            FAX 508-875-2062
                    http://www.theraproducts.com
                    e-mail: info@theraproducts.com
Particia Oetter OTR/L, Eileen Richter OTR, Author
Karen Conrad, President

MORE is an acronym for Motor components, Oral organization, Respiratory demands and Eye contact and control; elements of toys and items that can be used to facilitate integration of the mouth with sensory and postural development, as well as self-regulation and attention. A theoretical framework for the treatment of both sensorimotor and speech/language problems is presented, methods for evaluating therapeutic potential of motor toys, and activities designed to improve functions. *$46.00*

889   Memory Workbook

Therapro
225 Arlington Street
Framingham, MA   01702   508-872-9494
                                800-257-5376
                        FAX 508-875-2062
            http://www.theraproducts.com
            e-mail: info@theraproducts.com
Therapro Staff, Author
Karen Conrad, President

Recalling daily activities, seasons, months of the year, shapes, words and pictures. *$10.50*

890   One-Handed in a Two-Handed World

Therapro
225 Arlington Street
Framingham, MA   01702   508-872-9494
                                800-257-5376
                        FAX 508-875-2062
            http://www.theraproducts.com
            e-mail: info@theraproducts.com
Tommye K Mayer, Author
Karen Conrad, President

A personal guide to managing single handed. Written by a woman who has lived one-handed for many years, this book shares a methodology and mindset necessary for managing. It details a wide array of topics including personal care, daily chores, office work, traveling, sports, relationships and many more. A must for patients and therapists. *$19.95*

250 pages

891   Peabody Developmental Motor Scales-2

The Speech Bin
1965 25th Avenue
Vero Beach, FL   32960   772-770-0007
                                800-477-3324
                        FAX 888-329-2246
            http://www.speechbin.com
            e-mail: info@speechbin.com
Rhonda Folio, Rebecca Fewell, Author

PDMS-2 gives you in-depth standardized assessment of motor skills in children birth to six years. Subtests include: fine motor object manipulation; grasping; gross motor; locomotion; reflexes; visual-motor integration and stationary. Item number P624. *$413.00*

Ages Birth-6

892   People at Work

AGS Publishing
4201 Woodland Road
Circle Pines, MN   55014   651-287-7220
                                800-328-2560
                        FAX 800-471-8457
            http://www.agsnet.com
            e-mail: agsmail@agsnet.com
Karen Dahlen, Associate Director
Matt Keller, Marketing Manager

With an interest level of High School through Adult, ABE and ESL and a reading level of Grades 3-4, this program is a simple, thorough teaching plan for every day of the school year. The program's 180 sessions are divided into eighteen study units that each survey an entire occupational cluster of eight jobs while focusing on one or two writing skills. *$26.95*

893   Putting the Pieces Together: Volume 4

The Speech Bin
1965 25th Avenue
Vero Beach, FL   32960   772-770-0007
                        FAX 772-770-0006
            http://www.speechbin.com
            e-mail: info@speechbin.com

This helpful volume gives you enjoyable materials and effective strategies for conceptualization, problem-solving, inductive and deductive reasoning, organization, judgement sequencing, attention/concentration, visual field neglect, and cognitve system reintegration. Item number V360. *$47.95*

894   Reading and Writing Workbook

Therapro
225 Arlington Street
Framingham, MA   01702   508-872-9494
                                800-257-5376
                        FAX 508-875-2062
            http://www.theraproducts.com
            e-mail: info@theraproducts.com
Therapro Staff, Author
Karen Conrad, President

Writing checks and balancing a checkbook, copying words and sentences, and writing messages and notes. Helps with recognition and understanding of calendars, phone books and much more. *$10.50*

895   Real World Situations

Harcourt Achieve
6277 Sea Harbor Drive
Orlando, FL   32887
                                800-531-5015
                        FAX 800-699-9459
            http://www.steckvaughn.com
            e-mail: info@steckvaughn.com
Steck-Vaughn Staff, Author
Tim McEwen, President/CEO
Jeff Johnson, Dir Marketing Communications
Chris Lehmann, Team Coordinator

Practice the practical problem-solving skills students need every day.

896   Responding to Oral Directions

The Speech Bin
1965 25th Avenue
Vero Beach, FL   32960   772-770-0007
                        FAX 772-770-0006
            http://www.speechbin.com
            e-mail: info@speechbin.com

Help children of all ages who function at first through sixth-grade levels learn to identify unclear directions and ask for clarification. Nine units teach them how to handle: recognizing directions, carryover and generalization; unreasonable, distorted, vague, unfamiliar, lenngthy, unknown, and mixed directions. Item number 975. *$49.00*

897 SEALS II Self-Esteem and Life Skills II

Therapro
225 Arlington Street
Framingham, MA   01702   508-872-9494
                                800-257-5376
                            FAX 508-875-2062
                    http://www.theraproducts.com
                    e-mail: info@theraproducts.com
Therapro Staff, Author
Karen Conrad, President

Adapted from Life Management Skills III and IV, this book is for youth, ages 12-18 with age-appropriate language, graphics, and illustrations. Includes 80 activity-based handouts related to body image, communication, conflict resolution, coping skills, creative expression, humor, job readiness, leisure skills, nurturance and more. *$43.95*

898 Scissors, Glue, and Concepts, Too!

LinguiSystems
3100 4th Avenue
East Moline, IL   61244
                                800-776-4332
                            FAX 309-755-2377
                            TDY:800-933-8331
                    http://www.linguisystems.com
                    e-mail: service@linguisystems.com
Susan Boegler, Debbie Abruzzini, Author
Linda Bowers, Owner
Rosemary Huisingh, Owner

Your young students will learn to follow directions and understand basic concepts in context. Concepts for each activity are grouped as they naturally occur in our language. Teach over 50 concepts including right/left, above/below, empty/full, and more. *$39.95*

199 pages Ages 5-8

899 Sensory Motor Issues in Autism

The Speech Bin
1965 25th Avenue
Vero Beach, FL   32960   772-770-0007
                            FAX 772-770-0006
                    http://www.speechbin.com
                    e-mail: info@speechbin.com

This resource for professionals and parents explains sensory processing disorders and their relationship to autism. It shows how to improve a child's responses to sensation, teach motor skills using daily living activities, and provide an effective learning environment. Item number C971. *$20.95*

900 So What Can I Do?

Therapro
225 Arlington Street
Framingham, MA   01702   508-872-9494
                                800-257-5376
                            FAX 508-875-2062
                    http://www.theraproducts.com
                    e-mail: info@theraproducts.com
Gail Kushnir, Author
Karen Conrad, President

A book to help children develop their own solutions to everyday problems. Cartoon illustrations feature common situations for children to analyze. The adult asks the child, so what can you do? The child is then encouraged to think of creative solutions, developing their emotional intelligence and improving coping skills. 58 problems to solve. *$10.95*

901 Special Needs Program

Learning for Life
3330 S Lancaster Road
Dallas, TX   75216   214-371-0474
                            FAX 214-371-3933
Cecilia Castillo, Director

The special needs curriculum teaches students with disabilities the life skills they need to achieve self-sufficiency. The program focuses on and enhances coping skills.

902 Stepwise Cookbooks

Therapro
225 Arlington Street
Framingham, MA   01702   508-872-9494
                                800-257-5376
                            FAX 508-875-2062
                    http://www.theraproducts.com
                    e-mail: info@theraproducts.com
Beth Jackson OTR, Author
Karen Conrad, President

A chance for children and adults at all developmental levels to participate in fun-filled hands-on cooking activities while developing independence. These cookbooks were developed by an OT working with children and teenagers with cognitive and physical challenges. Only one direction is presented on a page to reduce confusion. Recipes are represented by large Boardmaker symbols from Mayer Johnson. Large, easy-to-read text with dividing lines for visual clarity.

903 Strategies for Problem-Solving

Harcourt Achieve
6277 Sea Harbor Drive
Orlando, FL   32887
                                800-531-5015
                            FAX 800-699-9459
                    http://www.steckvaughn.com
                    e-mail: info@steckvaughn.com
Yellin, Author
Tim McEwen, President/CEO
Jeff Johnson, Dir Marketing Communications
Chris Lehmann, Team Coordinator

Show students more than one way to approach a problem, and you hand them the key to effective problem solving. These reproducible activities build math reasoning and critical thinking skills, reinforce core concepts, and reduce math anxiety too. *$8.49*

904 **Survey of Teenage Readiness and Neurodevelopmental Status**

Educators Publishing Service
31 Smith Place
Cambridge, MA 02139
617-547-6706
800-225-5750
FAX 888-440-2665
http://www.epsbooks.com
e-mail: eps@epsbooks.com

Melvin D Levine MD FAAP, Author
Nick Gaehde, President

Developed by Dr. Mel Livine and Dr.Stephen Hooper, The Survey of Teenage Readiness and Neurodevelopmental Status capitalizes on adolescents' evolving metacognitive abilities by directly asking them for their perceptions of how they are functioning in school and how they process information across a variety of neurocognitive and psychosocial domains.

905 **Swallow Right**

The Speech Bin
1965 25th Avenue
Vero Beach, FL 32960
772-770-0007
FAX 772-770-0006
http://www.speechbin.com
e-mail: info@speechbin.com

This 12-session program evaluates and treats oral myofunctional disorders. 40 reproducible sequential exercises train individuals from five years to adult how to swallow correctly. Easy-to-use evaluation and tracking forms, checklist, and carryover strategies make this book a real time-saver! Item number Q858. *$44.00*

906 **TARGET**

The Speech Bin
1965 25th Avenue
Vero Beach, FL 32960
772-770-0007
FAX 772-770-0006
http://www.speechbin.com
e-mail: info@speechbin.com

TARGET is the kind of resource aphasia clinicians beg for — a practical resource that answers not only the what and how questions of treatment but also the why. It describes dozens of treatment methods and gives you practical exercises and activities to implement each technique. Item number 1434. *$49.95*

907 **TOPS Kit- Adolescent: Tasks of Problem Solving**

LinguiSystems
3100 4th Avenue
East Moline, IL 61244
800-776-4332
FAX 309-755-2377
TDY:800-933-8331
http://www.linguisystems.com
e-mail: service@linguisystems.com

Linda Bowers, Rosemary Huisingh, Mark Barrett, Author
Linda Bowers, Owner
Rosemary Huisingh, Owner

Teach your teens how to use their language skills to think, think, think. We combine literacy, thinking, writing, humor, and language arts practice to cover these thinking skills: using content to make references; analyzing information; taking another's point of view; and more. It's a literacy-based approach that gets dramatic results! *$59.95*

192 pages Ages 12-18

908 **TOPS Kit-Elementary: Tasks of Problem Solving**

LinguiSystems
3100 4th Avenue
East Moline, IL 61244
800-776-4332
FAX 800-577-4555
http://www.linguisystems.com
e-mail: service@linguisystems.com

Linda Bowers, Owner
Rosemary Huisingh, Owner

Reveal thinking and language skills your students didn't know they had with this remarkable kit. TOPS Kit-Elementary combines thinking and expressive language skills to develop better communications.

Ages 6-12

909 **Target Spelling**

Harcourt Achieve
6277 Sea Harbor Drive
Orlando, FL 32887
800-531-5015
FAX 800-699-9459
http://www.steckvaughn.com
e-mail: info@steckvaughn.com

Scarborough, Author
Tim McEwen, President/CEO
Jeff Johnson, Dir Marketing Communications
Chris Lehmann, Team Coordinator

You can differentiate instructions to address a variety of learning styles and profiles and meet the needs of special education students.

910 **Teaching Dressing Skills: Buttons, Bows and More**

Therapro
225 Arlington Street
Framingham, MA 01702
508-872-9494
800-257-5376
FAX 508-875-2062
http://www.theraproducts.com
e-mail: info@theraproducts.com

Marcy Coppelman Goldsmith OTR/L BCP, Author
Karen Conrad, President

Consists of 5 fold-out pamphlets for teaching children and adults of varying abilities the basic dressing skills: shoe tying, buttoning, zippering, dressing and undressing. Each task is broken down with every step clearly illustrated and specific verbal directions given to avoid confusion and to eliminate excess verbiage that can distract the learner. The author, an experienced OT, has included the needed prerequisites for each task, many great teaching tips and more. *$12.95*

5 Pamphlets

911 That's Life Picture Stories

AGS Publishing
4201 Woodland Road
Circle Pines, MN 55014   651-287-7223
                                   800-328-2560
                            FAX 800-471-8457
                         http://www.agsnet.com
                      e-mail: agsmail@agsnet.com
Tana Reiff, Vince Clews, Author
Karen Dahlen, Associate Director
Matt Keller, Marketing Manager

With an interest level of high school through adult, ABE and ESL and a reading level of Grades 3-4, these eight picture stories describe how four families face daily challenges and solve practical problems. Features comic-book-style art and speech balloons. Families represent varied ethnic backgrounds. DramaTape cassettes featuring professional actors, music and sound effects available. *$105.99*

912 That's Life! Social Language

LinguiSystems
3100 4th Avenue
East Moline, IL 61244
                                   800-776-4332
                            FAX 309-755-2377
                            TDY:800-933-8331
                     http://www.linguisystems.com
                   e-mail: service@linguisystems.com
Carolyn LoGiudice, Nancy McConnell, Author
Linda Bowers, Owner
Rosemary Huisingh, Owner

Teach your students to be effective and appropriate communicators in a wide variety of situations. Through direct instruction, role-playing activities, and discussion, your students will learn the how and why of social language interaction. *$37.95*

176 pages   Ages 12-18

913 That's Life: A Game of Life Skills

LinguiSystems
3100 4th Avenue
East Moline, IL 61244
                                   800-776-4332
                            FAX 309-755-2344
                            TDY:800-933-8331
                     http://www.linguisystems.com
                   e-mail: service@linguisystems.com
Patricia Smith, Author
Linda Bowers, Owner
Rosemary Huisingh, Owner

Help your older students refine their language skills to negotiate the real-world with this fun game. Get 100 thinking and language questions for each of these life areas: consumer affairs; government; health concerns; money matters; going places; and homemaking. *$44.95*

Ages 12-18

914 ThemeWeavers: Animals Activity Kit

Riverdeep
500 Redwood Boulevard
Novato, CA 94947   415-763-4700
                                   800-362-2890
                            FAX 415-763-4385
                         http://www.edmark.com
                      e-mail: info@riverdeep.net
Barry O'Callaghan, Chairman/CEO
Simon Calver, COO
John Rim, VP CFO

ThemeWeavers: Animals is the essential companion for theme-based teaching. Dozens of animal-themed, interactive activities immediately engage your students to practice fundamental skills in math, language arts, science, social studies and more. Easy-to-use tools allow you to modify these activities or create your own to meet specific classroom needs.

915 ThemeWeavers: Nature Activity Kit

Riverdeep
500 Redwood Boulevard
Novato, CA 94947   415-763-4700
                                   800-362-2890
                            FAX 415-763-4385
                         http://www.edmark.com
                      e-mail: info@riverdeep.net
Barry O'Callaghan, Chairman/CEO
Simon Calver, COO
John Rim, VP CFO

ThemeWeavers: Nature Activity Kit is an all-in-one solution for theme-based teaching. In just a few minutes, you can select from dozens of ready-to-use activities centering on the seasons and weather and be ready for the next day's lesson! Interactive and engaging activities cover multiple subject areas such as language arts, math, science, social studies and art.

916 Thinkin' Science ZAP

Riverdeep
500 Redmond Boulevard
Novato, CA 94947   415-763-4700
                                   800-362-2890
                            FAX 415-763-4385
                         http://www.edmark.com
                      e-mail: info@riverdeep.net
Barry O'Callaghan, Chairman/CEO
Simon Calver, COO
John Rim, CFO

It is a dark and stormy night as you step backstage to be guest director at the Wonder Dome, the world-famous auditorium of light, sound, and electricity. But great zotz! The Theater has been zapped by lightning, and the Laser Control System is on the fritz! Can you learn all about light, sound and electricity to rescue the show? *$69.95*

917 Time: Concepts & Problem-Solving

Harcourt Achieve
6277 Sea Harbor Drive
Orlando, FL 32887
                                   800-531-5015
                            FAX 800-699-9459
                      http://www.steckvaughn.com
                   e-mail: info@steckvaughn.com
Steck-Vaughn Staff, Author
Tim McEwen, President/CEO
Jeff Johnson, Dir Marketing Communications
Chris Lehmann, Team Coordinator

Develop concepts of telling time, identifying intervals, calculating elapsed time, and solving problems that deal with time changes, lapses, and changes over the AM/PM cusp.

918   Tips for Teaching Infants & Toddlers

The Speech Bin
1965 25th Avenue
Vero Beach, FL   32960   772-770-0007
                               FAX 772-770-0006
                          http://www.speechbin.com
                          e-mail: info@speechbin.com

This multisensory approach to Early Intervention is a whole year's worth of weekly thematic lessons which let children see, hear, feel, manipulate, smell, and taste. Item number 1235. *$45.95*

919   Travel the World with Timmy Deluxe

Riverdeep
500n Redmond Boulevard
Novato, CA   94947   415-763-4700
                                 800-362-2890
                               FAX 415-763-4385
                          http://www.edmark.com
                          e-mail: info@riverdeep.net
Barry O'Callaghan, Chairman/CEO
Simon Calver, COO
John Rim, CFO

France and Russia are the newest destinations for Edmark's favorite world traveler, Timmy! In this delightful and improved program, students will enjoy expanding their understanding of the world around them. With wonderful stories, songs, games, and printable crafts, early learners discover how their international neighbors live, dress, sing, eat and play.

920   Visual Perception and Attention Workbook

Therapro
225 Arlington Street
Framingham, MA   01702   508-872-9494
                                 800-257-5376
                               FAX 508-875-2062
                          http://www.theraproducts.com
                          e-mail: info@theraproducts.com
Therapro Staff, Author
Karen Conrad, President

Simple mazes, visual discrimination and visual form constancy task, telling time and much more! *$10.50*

921   Workbook for Cognitive Skills

The Speech Bin
1965 25th Avenue
Vero Beach, FL   32960   772-770-0007
                               FAX 772-770-0006
                          http://www.speechbin.com
                          e-mail: info@speechbin.com

This workbook of perceptual and problem-solving exercises provides challenging material that's easy to read. Designed for adults and adolescents who have cognitive disorders. Item number W336. *$48.95*

922   Workbook for Memory Skills

The Speech Bin
1965 25th Avenue
Vero Beach, FL   32960   772-770-0007
                               FAX 772-770-0006
                          http://www.speechbin.com
                          e-mail: info@speechbin.com

Helpful in treating individuals with deficits in attention and memory skills secondary to: traumatic brain injury; cognitive disorganization; early stage dementia; brain damage; learning disability; and progressive disease. Item number 1488. *$44.95*

923   Workbook for Reasoning Skills

The Speech Bin
1965 25th Avenue
Vero Beach, FL   32960   772-770-0007
                               FAX 772-770-0006
                          http://www.speechbin.com
                          e-mail: info@speechbin.com

This workbook is designed for adults and children who need practice in reasoning, thinking, and organizing. Includes 67 exercises created for individuals with closed head injuries and mild to moderate cognitive deficits. Item number W332. *$48.95*

924   Workbook for Word Retrieval

The Speech Bin
1965 25th Avenue
Vero Beach, FL   32960   772-770-0007
                               FAX 772-770-0006
                          http://www.speechbin.com
                          e-mail: info@speechbin.com
Beth M Kennedy, Author
Jan J Binney, Editor-in-Chief

Helpful materials treat individuals with deficits in attention and memory skills secondary to: Traumatic brain injury, Cognitive disorganization, Early stage dementia, Brain damage, Learning disability and Progressive disease. Item number 1523. *$42.95*

248 pages

925   Working With Words-Volume 3

The Speech Bin
1965 25th Avenue
Vero Beach, FL   32960   772-770-0007
                               FAX 772-770-0006
                          http://www.speechbin.com
                          e-mail: info@speechbin.com

Stimulate the reasoning skills of your brain-injured patients with this large print workbook of puzzles and word games. Activities include word builders, word hunters, word puzzlers, and word games challenging exercises for older children and adults. Item number V371. *$38.95*

926   Working for Myself

AGS Publishing
4201 Woodland Road
Circle Pines, MN   55014   651-287-7220
                                 800-328-2560
                               FAX 800-471-8457
                          http://www.agsnet.com
                          e-mail: agsmail@agsnet.com
Tana Reiff, Author
Karen Dahlen, Associate Director
Matt Keller, Marketing Manager

With an interest level of High School through Adult, ABE and ESL and a reading level of Grades 3-4, this series of ten easy-to-read books tells the stories of ordinary people who successfully build small businesses. Students will learn that energy, problem-solving skills and thorough preparation can make the difference between success and failure.

Math

927 Algebra Stars

Sunburst Technology
400 Columbus Avenue
Valhalla, NY   10595   914-747-3310
                          800-321-7511
                    FAX 914-747-4109
              http://www.sunburst.com
        e-mail: service@sunburst.com

Students build their understanding of algebra by constructing, categorizing, and solving equations and classifying polynomial expressions using algebra tiles.

928 American Guidance Service Learning Disabilities Resources

Instruction & Assessment AGS Special Needs Catolog
PO Box 716
Bryn Mawr, PA   19010   610-525-8336
                            800-869-8336
                      FAX 610-525-8337
              http://www.ldonline.org
Dr. Richard Cooper, Author

A collection of alternative techniques which Dr. Cooper has found useful in teaching arithmetic to individuals with learning problems. *$9.95*

929 Attack Math

Educators Publishing Service
31 Smith Plaza
Cambridge, MA   02139   617-547-6706
                            800-225-5750
                      FAX 888-440-2665
              http://www.epsbooks.com
        e-mail: eps@epsbooks.com
Carol Greenes, George Immerzeel, Linda Shulman, Author
Nick Gaehde, President

This series, for grades 1-6, teaches the four arithmetic operations: addition, subtraction, multiplication and division. Each operation is covered in three books, with book one teaching the basic facts and books two and three teaching multi-digit computation with whole numbers. A checkpoint and testpoint monitor progress at the middle and end of each book.

930 Awesome Animated Monster Maker Math

Sunburst Technology
400 Columbus Avenue
Valhalla, NY   10595   914-747-3310
                          800-321-7511
                    FAX 914-747-4109
              http://www.sunburst.com
        e-mail: service@sunburst.com

With an emphasis on building core math skills, this humorous program incorporates the monstrous and the ridiculous into a structured learning environment. Students choose from six skill levels tailored to the 3rd to 8th grade.

931 Awesome Animated Monster Maker Math & Monster Workshop

Sunburst Technology
400 Columbus Avenue
Valhalla, NY   10595   914-747-3310
                          800-321-7511
                    FAX 914-747-4109
              http://www.sunburst.com
        e-mail: service@sunburst.com

Students develop money and strategic thinking skills with this irresistable game that has them tinker about making monsters.

932 Awesome Animated Monster Maker Number Drop

Sunburst Technology
400 Columbus Avenue
Valhalla, NY   10595   914-747-3310
                          800-321-7511
                    FAX 914-747-4109
              http://www.sunburst.com
        e-mail: service@sunburst.com

Your students will think on their mathematical feet estimating and solving thousands of number problems in an arcade-style game designed to improve their performance in numeration, money, fractions, and decimals.

933 Basic Essentials of Mathematics

Harcourt Achieve
6277 Sea Harbor Drive
Orlando, FL   32887
                          800-531-5015
                    FAX 800-699-9459
              http://www.steckvaughn.com
        e-mail: info@steckvaughn.com
Shea, Author
Tim McEwen, President/CEO
Jeff Johnson, Dir Marketing Communications
Chris Lehmann, Team Coordinator

Ideal for basic math skill instruction, test practice, or any situation requiring a thorough, confidence-building review. It provides a complete lesson - instruction, examples, and computation exercises.

934 Basic Math for Job and Personal Use

AGS Publishing
4201 Woodland Road
Circle Pines, MN   55014   651-287-7220
                                 800-328-2560
                        FAX 800-471-8457
                        http://www.agsnet.com
                        e-mail: agsmail@agsnet.com
Merle Wood, Jeanette Powell, Author
Karen Dahlen, Associate Director
Matt Keller, Marketing Manager

With an interest level of high school through adult, and a reading level of Grade 3-4, this series has modules in addition, subtraction, multiplication and division.

935 Building Mathematical Thinking

Educators Publishing Service
31 Smith Place
Cambridge, MA   02139   617-547-6706
                               800-225-5750
                      FAX 888-440-2665
                      http://www.epsbooks.com
                      e-mail: eps@epsbooks.com
Marsha Stanton, Author

In this new math program, the units covered are presented as a series of Skinny Concepts that serve as manageable building blocks that eventually become entire topics. The Students Journal provides exercises for each Skinny Concept, encourages students to seek their own conclusions for problem solving, and provides space for the students ideas.

936 Building Perspective

Sunburst Technology
400 Columbus Avenue
Valhalla, NY   10595   914-747-3310
                             800-321-7511
                    FAX 914-747-4109
                    http://www.sunburst.com
                    e-mail: support@sunburst.com

Develop spatial perception and reasoning skills with this award-winning program that will sharpen your students' problem-solving abilities.

937 Building Perspective Deluxe

Sunburst Technology
400 Columbus Avenue
Valhalla, NY   10595   914-747-3310
                             800-321-7511
                    FAX 914-747-4109
                    http://www.sunburst.com
                    e-mail: support@sunburst.com

New visual thinking challenges await your students as they engage in three spacial reasoning activities that develop their 3D thinking, deductive reasoning and problem solving skills

938 Calculator Math for Job and Personal Use

4201 Woodland Road
Circle Pines, MN   55014   651-287-7220
                                 800-328-2560
                        FAX 800-471-8457
                        http://www.agsnet.com
                        e-mail: agsmail@agsnet.com

With an interest level of high school through adult, and a reading level of Grade 3-4, this series has modules in basic math with a calculator and fractions, decimals, and percentages using a calculator.

939 Combining Shapes

Sunburst Technology
400 Columbus Avenue
Valhalla, NY   10595   914-747-3310
                             800-321-7511
                    FAX 914-747-4109
                    http://www.sunburst.com
                    e-mail: support@sunburst.com

Students discover the properties of simple geometric figures through concrete experience combining shapes. Measurements, estimating and operation skills are part of this fun program.

940 Combining and Breaking Apart Numbers

Sunburst Technology
400 Columbus Avenue
Valhalla, NY   10595   914-747-3310
                             800-321-7511
                    FAX 914-747-4109
                    http://www.sunburst.com
                    e-mail: support@sunburst.com

Students develop their number sense as they engage in "real life" dilemmas, which demonstrates the basic concepts of operations.

941 Comparing with Ratios

Sunburst Technology
400 Columbus Avenue
Valhalla, NY   10595   914-747-3310
                             800-321-7511
                    FAX 914-747-4109
                    http://www.sunburst.com
                    e-mail: support@sunburst.com

Students learn that ratio is a way to compare amounts by using multiplication and division. Through five engaging activities, students recognize and describe ratios, develop proportional thinking skills, estimate ratios, determine equivalent ratios, and use ratios to analyze data.

942 Concert Tour Entrepreneur

Sunburst Technology
400 Columbus Avenue
Valhalla, NY 10595   914-747-3310
                                   800-321-7511
                                   FAX 914-747-4109
                                   http://www.sunburst.com
                                   e-mail: support@sunburst.com

Your students improve math, planning and problem solving skills as they manage a band in this music management business simulation.

943 Creating Patterns from Shapes

Sunburst Technology
400 Columbus Avenue
Valhalla, NY 10595   914-747-3310
                                   800-321-7511
                                   FAX 914-747-4109
                                   http://www.sunburst.com
                                   e-mail: support@sunburst.com

Students discover patterns by exploring the properties of radiating and tiling patterns through Native American basket weaving and Japanese fish print themes.

944 Data Explorer

Sunburst Technology
101 Castleton Street
Poleasantville, NY 10570   914-747-3310
                                   800-321-7511
                                   FAX 914-747-4109
                                   http://www.sunburst.com
                                   e-mail: support@nysunburst.com

This easy-to-use CD-ROM provides the flexibility needed for eleven different graph types including tools for long-term data analysis projects.

945 Decimals and Percentages for Job and Personal Use

AGS Publishing
4201 Woodland Road
Circle Pines, MN 55014   651-287-2560
                                   800-328-2560
                                   FAX 800-471-8457
                                   http://www.agsnet.com
                                   e-mail: agsmail@agsnet.com
Merle Wood, Jeanette Powell, Author
Karen Dahlen, Associate Director
Matt Keller, Marketing Manager

With an interest level of high school through adult, and a reading level of Grade 3-4, this series has modules in decimals, fractions and percentages.

946 Decimals: Concepts & Problem-Solving

Harcourt Achieve
6277 Sea Harbor Drive
Orlando, FL 32887
                                   800-531-5015
                                   FAX 800-699-9459
                                   http://www.steckvaughn.com
                                   e-mail: info@steckvaughn.com
Steck-Vaughn Staff, Author
Tim McEwen, President/CEO
Jeff Johnson, Dir Marketing Communications
Chris Lehmann, Team Coordinator

This easy to implement, flexible companion to the classroom mathematics curriculum emcompasses decimal concepts such as values and names, equivalent decimals, mixed decimals, patterns, comparing, ordering, estimating and more. *$ 8.49*

947 ESPA Math Practice Tests D

Harcourt Achieve
6277 Sea Harbor Drive
Orlando, FL 32887
                                   800-531-5015
                                   FAX 800-699-9459
                                   http://www.steckvaughn.com
                                   e-mail: info@steckvaughn.com
Steck-Vaughn Staff, Author
Tim McEwen, President/CEO
Jeff Johnson, Dir Marketing Communications
Chris Lehmann, Team Coordinator

If you are concerned about your students' performance on the math portion of the ESPA, these workbooks can give them the boost they need. Each follows the New Jersey State standards in mathematics, giving students additional practice with the same kinds of questions they will face on the test day. Workbooks include three practice tests, with 50 multiple choice and open-ended questions each.

948 ESPA Success in Mathematics

Harcourt Achieve
6277 Sea Harbor Drive
Orlando, FL 32887
                                   800-531-5015
                                   FAX 800-699-9459
                                   http://www.steckvaughn.com
                                   e-mail: info@steckvaughn.com
Steck-Vaughn Staff, Author
Tim McEwen, President/CEO
Jeff Johnson, Dir Marketing Communications
Chris Lehmann, Team Coordinator

Ensure a positive experience on the ESPA with the preparatory program that follows the New Jersey State standards in mathematics, including instruction and practice in all five content clusters. Modeled instruction provides strategies to help students get the right answer on both multiple choice and open-ended questions.

949 Elementary Math Bundle

Sunburst Technology
400 Columbus Avenue
Valhalla, NY 10595   914-747-3310
                                   800-321-7511
                                   FAX 914-747-4109
                                   http://www.sunburst.com
                                   e-mail: support@sunburst.com

Number sense and operations are the focus of the Elementary Math Bundle. Students engage in activities that reinforce basic addition and subtraction skills. This product comes with Splish Splash Math, Ten Tricky Tiles and Numbers Undercover.

950 Equation Tile Teaser

Sunburst Technology
400 Columbus Avenue
Valhalla, NY 10595
914-747-3310
800-321-7511
FAX 914-747-4109
http://www.sunburst.com
e-mail: support@sunburst.com

Students develop logic thinking and pre-algebra skills solving sets of numbers equations in three challenging problem-solving activities.

951 Equivalent Fractions

Sunburst Technology
400 Columbus Avenue
Valhalla, NY 10595
914-747-3310
800-321-7511
FAX 914-747-4109
http://www.sunburst.com
e-mail: support@sunburst.com

This exciting investigation develops students' conceptual understanding that every fraction can be named in many different but equivalent ways.

952 Estimation

Harcourt Achieve
6277 Sea Harbor Drive
Orlando, FL 32887
800-531-5015
FAX 800-699-9459
http://www.steckvaughn.com
e-mail: info@steckvaughn.com

Steck-Vaughn Staff, Author
Tim McEwen, President/CEO
Jeff Johnson, Dir Marketing Communications
Chris Lehmann, Team Coordiantor

Students learn to make sensible estimates, educated guesses, and logical choices, then use tools to check their estimates for accuracy. Practice includes estimation in measurement of length, weight, capacity, temperature, time and money.

953 Factory Deluxe

Sunburst Technology
400 Columbus Avenue
Valhalla, NY 10595
914-747-3310
800-321-7511
FAX 914-747-4109
http://www.sunburst.com
e-mail: support@sunburst.com

Five activities explore shapes, rotation, angles, geometric attributes, area formulas, and computation. Includes journal, record keeping, and on-screen help. This program helps sharpen geometry, visual thinking and problem solving skills.

954 Focus on Math

Harcourt Achieve
6277 Sea Harbor Drive
Orlando, FL 32887
800-531-5015
FAX 800-699-9459
http://www.steckvaughn.com
e-mail: info@steckvaughn.com

Steck-Vaugh Staff, Author
Tim McEwen, President/CEO
Jeff Johnson, Dir Marketing Communications
Chris Lehmann, Team Coordinator

Consists of four sections and in each you will learn more about addition and subtraction, multiplication and division, fractions, decimals, measurements, geometry and problem solving.

955 Follow Me! 2

LinguiSystems
3100 4th Avenue
East Moline, IL 61244
800-776-4332
FAX 309-755-2377
TDY:800-933-8331
http://www.linguisystems.com
e-mail: service@linguisystems.com

Grace Frank, Author
Linda Bowers, Owner
Rosemary Huisingh, Owner

These activities are relevant to classroom listening demands. The directions relate specifically on an accompanying worksheet. It's a pick-up-and-use-now resource to teach the vocabulary of language arts, math, social studies, and more. *$34.95*

201 pages   Ages 7-11

956 Fraction Attraction

Sunburst Technology
400 Columbus Avenue
Valhalla, NY 10595
914-747-3310
800-321-7511
FAX 914-747-4109
http://www.sunburst.com
e-mail: support@sunburst.com

Build the fraction skills of ordering, equivalence, relative sizes and multiple representations with four, multi-level, carnival style games.

957 Fraction Operations

Sunburst Technology
400 Columbus Avenue
Valhalla, NY 10595
914-747-3310
800-321-7511
FAX 914-747-4109
http://www.sunburst.com
e-mail: support@sunburst.com

Students build on their concepts of fraction meaning and equivalence as they learn how to perform operations with fractions.

958   Fractions: Concepts & Problem-Solving

Harcourt Achieve
6277 Sea Harbor Drive
Orlando, FL   32887

800-531-5015
FAX 800-699-9459
http://www.steckvaughn.com
e-mail: info@steckvaughn.com

Steck-Vaughn Staff, Author
Tim McEwen, President/CEO
Jeff Johnson, Dir Marketing Communications
Chris Lehmann, Team Coordinator

This companion to the classroom mathematics curriculum emcompasses many of the standards established at each grade level. Each activity page targets a specific skill to help bolster students who need additional work in a particular area of fractions.

959   Funny Monster for Tea

Sunburst Technology
400 Columbus Avenue
Valhalla, NY   10595

914-747-3310
800-321-7511
FAX 914-747-4109
http://www.sunburst.com
e-mail: support@sunburst.com

This interactive, read-along rhyme features six activities for young students to learn about time, practice spelling, investigate math and explore poetry, music and art.

960   GEPA Success in Language Arts Literacy and Mathematics

Harcourt Achieve
6277 Sea Harbor Drive
Orlando, FL   32887

800-531-5015
FAX 800-699-9459
http://www.steckvaughn.com
e-mail: info@steckvaughn.com

Steck-Vaughn Staff, Author
Tim McEwen, President/CEO
Jeff Johnson, Dir Marketing Communications
Chris Lehmann, Team Coordinator

Build skills as you improve scores on the GEPA. Better test scores don't always mean better skills. With these workbooks, you can ensure that your students are becoming more proficient users of language and math as well as more skilled test-takers. Your students will gain valuable practice answering the types of questions found on the GEPA, such as open-ended and enhanced multiple-choice items.

961   Geometry for Primary Grades

Harcourt Achieve
6277 Sea Harbor Drive
Orlando, FL   32887

800-531-5015
FAX 800-699-9459
http://www.steckvaughn.com
e-mail: info@steckvaughn.com

Steck-Vaughn Staff, Author
Tim McEwen, President/CEO
Jeff Johnson, Dir Marketing Communications
Chris Lehmann, Team Coordinator

Self-explanatory lessons ideal for independent work or as homework. Transitions from concrete to pictorial to abstract.

962   Get Up and Go!

Sunburst Technology
400 Columbus Avenue
Valhalla, NY   10595

914-747-3310
800-321-7511
FAX 914-747-4109
http://www.sunburst.com
e-mail: support@sunburst.com

Students interpret and construct timelines through three descriptive activities in the animated program. Students are introduced to timelines as they participate in an interactive story.

963   Grade Level Math

Harcourt Achieve
6277 Sea Harbor Drive
Orlando, FL   32887

800-531-5015
FAX 800-699-9459
http://www.steckvaughn.com
e-mail: info@steckvaughn.com

Steck-Vaughn Staff, Author
Tim McEwen, President/CEO
Jeff Johnson, Dir Marketing Communications
Chris Lehmann, Team Coordinator

Easy to understand practice exercises help students build conceptual knowledge and computation skills together. Each book addresses essential grade appropriate math areas.

964   Graphers

Sunburst Technology
400 Columbus Avenue
Valhalla, NY   10595

914-747-3310
800-321-7511
FAX 914-747-4109
http://www.sunburst.com
e-mail: support@sunburst.com

Students develop data analysis skills with this easy to use graphing tool. With over 30 pictorial data sets and 16 lessons, students learn to construct and interpret six different graph types.

965   Green Globs & Graphing Equations

Sunburst Technology
400 Columbus Avenue
Valhalla, NY   10595

914-747-3310
800-321-7511
FAX 914-747-4109
http://www.sunburst.com
e-mail: support@sunburst.com

As students explore parabolas, hyperbolas, and other graphs, they discover how altering an equation changes a graph's shape or position.

966 Grouping and Place Value

Sunburst Technology
400 Columbus Avenue
Valhalla, NY   10595   914-747-3310
                             800-321-7511
                          FAX 914-747-4109
                      http://www.sunburst.com
                    e-mail: support@sunburst.com

Students develop their understanding of our number system, learning to think about numbers in groups of ones, tens, and hundreds, and discovering the meaning of place value.

967 Hidden Treasures of Al-Jabr

Sunburst Technology
400 Columbus Avenue
Valhalla, NY   10595   914-747-3310
                             800-321-7511
                          FAX 914-747-4109
                      http://www.sunburst.com
                    e-mail: support@sunburst.com

Beginning algebra students undertake three challenges that develop skills in the areas of solving linear equations, substituting variables, grouping like variables, using systems of equations and translating algebra word problems into equations.

968 High School Math Bundle

Sunburst Technology
400 Columbus Avenue
Valhalla, NY   10595   914-747-3310
                             800-321-7511
                          FAX 914-747-4109
                      http://www.sunburst.com
                    e-mail: support@sunburst.com

Each program in this bundle focuses on a specific area to ensure that your students master the math skills they need. This bundle allows students to master basics of Algebra, explore equations and graphs, practice learning with algebra graphs, use trigonometric functions, apply math concepts to practical situations and improve problem solving and data analysis skills.

969 Higher Scores on Math Standardized Tests

Harcourt Achieve
6277 Sea Harbor Drive
Orlando, FL   32887

                             800-531-5015
                          FAX 800-699-9459
                     http://www.steckvaughn.com
                   e-mail: info@steckvaughn.com
Steck-Vaughn Staff, Author
Tim McEwen, President/CEO
Jeff Johnson, Dir Marketing Communications
Chris Lehmann, Team Coordinator

These grade level math test preparation series provide focused practice in areas where students have shown a weakness in previous standardized tests. Improves test scores by zeroing in on the skills requiring remediation.

970 Hot Dog Stand: The Works

Sunburst Technology
400 Columbus Avenue
Valhalla, NY   10595   914-747-3310
                             800-321-7511
                          FAX 914-747-4109
                      http://www.sunburst.com
                    e-mail: support@sunburst.com

Students practice math, problem-solving, and communication skills in a multimedia business simulation that challenges students with unexpected events.

971 How the West Was 1+3x4

Sunburst Technology
400 Columbus Avenue
Valhalla, NY   10595   914-747-3310
                             800-321-7511
                          FAX 914-747-4109
                      http://www.sunburst.com
                    e-mail: support@sunburst.com

Students use order of operations to construct equations and race along number line trails.

972 I Can See 1, 2, 3

Teddy Bear Press
3639 Midway Drive
San Diego, NV   92110   619-223-7311
                            FAX 619-255-2158
                    http://www.teddybearpress.net
                  e-mail: fparker@teddybearpress.net
Fran Parker, Author
Fran Parker, President

Introduces number concepts 1-10 using the pre-primer words found in the I Can Read series. *$20.00*

973 Ice Cream Truck

Sunburst Technology
400 Columbus Avenue
Valhalla, NY   10595   914-747-3310
                             800-321-7511
                          FAX 914-747-4109
                      http://www.sunburst.com
                    e-mail: support@sunburst.com

Elementary students learn important problem solving, strategic planning and math operation skills, as they become owners of a busy ice cream truck.

974 Intermediate Geometry

Harcourt Achieve
6277 Sea Harbor Drive
Orlando, FL   32887

                             800-531-5015
                          FAX 800-699-9459
                     http://www.steckvaughn.com
                   e-mail: info@steckvaughn.com
Steck-Vaughn Staff, Author
Tim McEwen, President/CEO
Jeff Johnson, Dir Marketing Communications
Chris Lehmann, Team Coordinator

Prepares intermediate and middle school students for a successful experience in high school geometry. Intermediate geometry provides a study of the concepts, computation, problem-solving, and enrichment of topics identified by NCTM standards. This three-book series links the informal explorations of geometry in primary grades to more formalized processes taught in high school.

975   Introduction to Patterns

Sunburst Technology
400 Columbus Avenue
Valhalla, NY   10595

914-747-3310
800-321-7511
FAX 914-747-4109
http://www.sunburst.com
e-mail: support@sunburst.com

Students discover patterns found in art and nature, exploring linear and geometric designs, predicting outcomes and creating patterns of their own.

976   It's Elementary!

Educators Publishing Service
31 Smith Place
Cambridge, MA   02139

617-547-6706
800-225-5750
FAX 888-440-2665
http://www.epsbooks.com
e-mail: eps@epsbooks.com

M J Owen, Author
Nick Gaehde, President

These new books helps make math word problems less intimidating for students in grades 2 through 5 by teaching them how to identify key words, draw pictures, and disregard unnecessary information. Captivating illustrations provide visual reinforcement of addition, subtraction, multiplication and division problems.

977   Maps & Navigation

Sunburst Technology
400 Columbus Avenue
Valhalla, NY   10595

914-747-3310
800-321-7511
FAX 914-747-4109
http://www.sunburst.com
e-mail: support@sunburst.com

This exciting nautical simulation provides students with opportunities use their math and science skills.

978   Mastering Math

Harcourt Achieve
6277 Sea Harbor Drive
Orlando, FL   32887

800-531-5015
FAX 800-699-9459
http://www.steckvaughn.com
e-mail: info@steckvaughn.com

Steck-Vaughn Staff, Author
Tim McEwen, President/CEO
Jeff Johnson, Dir Marketing Communications
Chris Lehmann, Team Coordinator

Now low level readers can succeed at math with this easy to read presentation. Makes basic math concepts accessible to all students.

979   Math Assessment System

Harcourt Achieve
6277 Sea Harbor Drive
Orlando, FL   32887

800-531-5015
FAX 800-699-9459
http://www.steckvaughn.com
e-mail: info@steckvaughn.com

Steck-Vaughn Staff, Author
Tim McEwen, President/CEO
Jeff Johnson, Dir Marketing Communications
Chris Lehmann, Team Coordinator

This easy-to-administer program generates individual scores, class scores, and an item analysis two times per year, providing a benchmark and two clear indicators of student progress.

980   Math Detectives

Harcourt Achieve
6277 Sea Harbor Drive
Orlando, FL   32887

800-531-5015
FAX 800-699-9459
http://www.steckvaughn.com
e-mail: info@steckvaughn.com

Steck-Vaughn Staff, Author
Tim McEwen, President/CEO
Jeff Johnson, Dir Marketing Communications
Chris Lehmann, Team Coordinator

Put student sleuths on the trail of mathematical problem solving and critical thinking with short mysteries even limited readers can manage. Use these motivating, grade-level mysteries as individual assignments, math center materials, group projects, or whole-class activities.

981   Math Enrichment

Harcourt Achieve
6277 Sea Harbor Drive
Orlando, FL   32887

800-531-5015
FAX 800-699-9459
http://www.steckvaughn.com
e-mail: info@steckvaughn.com

Steck-Vaughn Staff, Author
Tim McEwen, President/CEO
Jeff Johnson, Dir Marketing Communications
Chris Lehmann, Team Coordinator

Features alternate ways to help children become mathematical thinkers and master the basic rules and concepts. It has relevance to the reader, promoting and expanding critical thinking skills through puzzles, mazes, games, charts, tables, symbols and codes, and more.

982   Math Scramble

LinguiSystems
3100 4th Avenue
East Moline, IL   61244

800-776-4332
FAX 309-755-2377
TDY:800-933-8331
http://www.linguisystems.com
e-mail: service@linguisystems.com

Paul F Johnson, Author
Linda Bowers, Owner
Rosemary Huisingh, Owner

It's great for students with learning disabilities who need a different approach to learning and memorizing basic math facts. Students can play with your guidance or as independent practice. *$44.95*

Ages 5-12

983   Mathematics Skills Books

Harcourt Achieve
6277 Sea Harbor Drive
Orlando, FL   32887

800-531-5015
FAX 800-699-9459
http://www.steckvaughn.com
e-mail: info@steckvaughn.com

Steck-Vaughn Staff, Author
Tim McEwen, President/CEO
Jeff Johnson, Dir Marketing Communications
Chris Lehmann, Team Coordinator

Affordable, focused reviews of fundamental math principles. Six 48 page books. Complete series of focused books offers practice in all basic mathematics skill areas with a consistent approach.

984   Maximize Math Success for the Special Populations You Serve

Saxon Publishers
2600 John Saxon Boulevard
Norman, OK   73071

405-329-7071
800-284-7019
FAX 405-360-4205
http://www.saxonpublishers.com
e-mail: info@saxonpublishers.com

Gerard Smith, President/CEO

An adaptation that helps special populations with math where other teaching methods have failed.

985   Maya Math

Sunburst Technology
400 Columbus Avenue
Valhalla, NY   10595

914-747-3310
800-321-7511
FAX 914-747-4109
http://www.sunburst.com
e-mail: support@sunburst.com

Students discover the importance of place value and the number zero as they learn a different number and calendar system.

986   Measurement: Practical Applications

Harcourt Achieve
6277 Sea Harbor Drive
Orlando, FL   32887

800-531-5015
FAX 800-699-9459
http://www.steckvaughn.com
e-mail: info@steckvaughn.com

Steck-Vaughn Staff, Author
Tim McEwen, President/CEO
Jeff Johnson, Dir Marketing Communications
Chris Lehmann, Team Coordinator

Concentrated practice on the measurement skills we use on a daily basis. This practical presentation of both customary and metric units helps the student to understand the importance of measurement skills in everyday life. Hands on activities and real life situations create logical applications so measurements make sense.

987   Memory Fun!

Sunburst Technology
400 Columbus Avenue
Valhalla, NY   10595

914-747-3310
800-321-7511
FAX 914-747-4109
http://www.sunburst.com
e-mail: support@sunburst.com

Welcome to Tiny's attic where students build memory, matching, counting and money sense through a variety of fun matching activities.

988   Middle School Geometry: Basic Concepts

Harcourt Achieve
6277 Sea Harbor Drive
Orlando, FL   32887

800-531-5015
FAX 800-699-9459
http://www.steckvaughn.com
e-mail: info@steckvaughn.com

Steck-Vaughn Staff, Author
Tim McEwen, President/CEO
Jeff Johnson, Dir Marketing Communications
Chris Lehmann, Team Coordinator

Provides students with enough comprehensive, skill specific practice in the key areas of geometry to ensure mastery. Ideal for junior high or high school students in need of remediation.

989   Middle School Math

Harcourt Achieve
6277 Sea Harbor Drive
Orlando, FL   32887

800-531-5015
FAX 800-699-9459
http://www.steckvaughn.com
e-mail: info@steckvaughn.com

Steck-Vaughn Staff, Author
Tim McEwen, President/CEO
Jeff Johnson, Dir Marketing Communications
Chris Lehmann, Team Coordinator

This skill-specific series reinforces and enhances the middle school math curriculum. It provides teachers and parents with a tool to focus on the skills that students need to review and reinforce. The lessons provide step-by-step instructions, sample problems, and practices that enable students to work independently.

990 Middle School Math Bundle

Sunburst Technology
400 Columbus Avenue
Valhalla, NY   10595
914-747-3310
800-321-7511
FAX 914-747-4109
http://www.sunburst.com
e-mail: support@sunburst.com

This bundle helps improve student's logical thinking, number sense and operation skills. This product comes with Math Arena, Building Perspective Deluxe, Equation Tile Teasers and Easy Sheet.

991 MindTwister Math

Riverdeep
500 Redmond Boulevard
Novato, CA   94947
415-763-4700
800-362-2890
FAX 415-763-4385
http://www.edmark.com
e-mail: info@riverdeep.net
Barry O'Callaghan, Chairman/CEO
Simon Calver, COO
John Rim, CFO

MindTwister Math provides a challenging review of third grade math and problem-solving skills in a fast-paced, multi-player game show format. Thousands of action-packed challenges encourage students to practice essential math facts including addition, subtraction, mutiplication and division and develop more advanced mathematical problem-solving skills such as visualization, deduction, sequencing, estimating and pattern recognition.

992 Mirror Symmetry

Sunburst Technology
400 Columbus Avenue
Valhalla, NY   10595
914-747-3310
800-321-7511
FAX 914-747-4109
http://www.sunburst.com
e-mail: support@sunburst.com

Students advance their understanding of geometric properties and spatial relationships by exploring lines of symmetry within a single geometric shape.

993 Multiplication & Division

Harcourt Achieve
6277 Sea Harbor Drive
Orlando, FL   32887
800-531-5015
FAX 800-699-9459
http://www.steckvaughn.com
e-mail: info@steckvaughn.com
Steck-Vaughn Staff, Author
Tim McEwen, President/CEO
Jeff Johnson, Dir Marketing Communications
Chris Lehmann, Team Coordinator

Skill specific activities focus on the concepts and inverse relationships of multiplication and division. Explains in simplified terms how the process of multiplication undoes the process of division, and vice versa.

994 My Mathematical Life

Sunburst Technology
400 Columbus Avenue
Valhalla, NY   10595
914-747-3310
800-321-7511
FAX 914-747-4109
http://www.sunburst.com
e-mail: support@sunburst.com

Students discover the math involved in everyday living as they take a character from high school graduation to retirement, advising on important health, education, career, and financial decisions.

995 Number Meanings and Counting

Sunburst Technology
400 Columbus Avenue
Valhalla, NY   10595
914-747-3310
800-321-7511
FAX 914-747-4109
http://www.sunburst.com
e-mail: support@sunburst.com

Students develop their understanding of number meaning and uses with experiences practicing estimating, using number meanings, and making more-and-less comparisons.

996 Number Sense & Problem Solving CD-ROM

Sunburst Technology
400 Columbus Avenue
Valhalla, NY   10595
914-747-3310
800-321-7511
FAX 914-747-4109
http://www.sunburst.com
e-mail: support@sunburst.com

Build number and operation skills with these three programs: How the West Was One + Three x Four, Divide and Conquer and Puzzle Tanks.

997 Numbers Undercover

Sunburst Technology
400 Columbus Avenue
Valhalla, NY   10595
914-747-3310
800-321-7511
FAX 914-747-4109
http://www.sunburst.com
e-mail: support@sunburst.com

As children try to solve the case of missing numbers, they practice telling time, measuring and estimating, counting, and working with money.

998 Patterns Across the Curriculum

Harcourt Achieve
6277 Sea Harbor Drive
Orlando, FL 32887

800-531-5015
FAX 800-699-9459
http://www.steckvaughn.com
e-mail: info@steckvaughn.com

Steck-Vaughn Staff, Author
Tim McEwen, President/CEO
Jeff Johnson, Dir Marketing Communications
Chris Lehmann, Team Coordinator

Develop students awareness and understanding of patterns in the real world. Exercises allow students to identify, complete, extend, and create patterns. Developed across four curriculum areas: math, language, social studies, and science. Flexible organization allows teachers to utilize content specific activities in coordination with other classroom assignments, providing additional richness in learning.

999 Penny Pot

Sunburst Technology
400 Columbus Avenue
Valhalla, NY 10595

914-747-3310
800-321-7511
FAX 914-747-4109
http://www.sunburst.com
e-mail: support@sunburst.com

Students learn about money as they count combinations of coins in this engaging program.

1000 Problemas y mas

Harcourt Achieve
6277 Sea Harbor Drive
Orlando, FL 32887

800-531-5015
FAX 800-699-9459
http://www.steckvaughn.com
e-mail: info@steckvaughn.com

Tim McEwen, President/CEO
Jeff Johnson, Dir Marketing Communications
Chris Lehmann, Team Coordinator

This ESL math practice and strategy tool is in three levels the same as Problems Plus, but expressly for your Spanish fluent ESL learners.

1001 Problems Plus Levels B-H

Harcourt Achieve
6277 Sea Harbor Drive
Orlando, FL 32887

800-531-5015
FAX 800-699-9459
http://www.steckvaughn.com
e-mail: info@steckvaughn.com

Steck-Vaughn Staff, Author
Tim McEwen, President/CEO
Jeff Johnson, Dir Marketing Communications
Chris Lehmann, Team Coordinator

A one-of-a-kind guide to solving open-ended math problems. Doesn't just give answers to test questions. With its innovative problem-solving plan, this series teaches math thinking and problem attack strategies, plus offers practice in higher order thinking skills students need to solve open-ended math problems successfully.

1002 Puzzle Tanks

Sunburst Technology
400 Columbus Avenue
Valhalla, NY 10595

914-747-3310
800-321-7511
FAX 914-747-4109
http://www.sunburst.com
e-mail: support@sunburst.com

A problem-solving program that uses logic puzzles involving liquid measurements.

1003 Representing Fractions

Sunburst Technology
400 Columbus Avenue
Valhalla, NY 10595

914-747-3310
800-321-7511
FAX 914-747-4109
http://www.sunburst.com
e-mail: support@sunburst.com

In this investigation students work with one interpretation of a fraction and the relationship between parts and wholes by working with symbolic and visual representations.

1004 Sequencing Fun!

Sunburst Technology
400 Columbus Avenue
Valhalla, NY 10595

914-747-3310
800-321-7511
FAX 914-747-4109
http://www.sunburst.com
e-mail: support@sunburst.com

Text, pictures, animation, and video clips provide a fun-filled program that encourages critical thinking skills.

1005 Shape Up!

Sunburst Technology
400 Columbus Avenue
Valhalla, NY 10595

914-747-3310
800-321-7511
FAX 914-747-4109
http://www.sunburst.com
e-mail: support@sunburst.com

Students actively create and manipulate shapes to discover important ideas about mathematics in an electronic playground of two and three dimensional shapes.

1006   Shapes Within Shapes

Sunburst Technolgy
400 Columbus Avenue
Valhalla, NY   10595

914-747-3310
800-321-7511
FAX 914-747-4109
http://www.sunburst.com
e-mail: service@sunburst.com

Students identify shapes within shapes, then rearrange them to develop spatial sense and deepen their understanding of the properties of shapes.

1007   Soaring Scores AIMS Mathematics

Harcourt Achieve
6277 Sea Harbor Drive
Orlando, FL   32887

800-531-5015
FAX 800-699-9459
http://www.steckvaughn.com
e-mail: info@steckvaughn.com

Steck-Vaughn Staff, Author
Tim McEwen, President/CEO
Jeff Johnson, Dir Marketing Communications
Chris Lehmann, Team Coordinator

Emphasize problem-solving and conceptual understanding to succeed with Arizona mathematics standards such as number sense, data analysis and probability, patterns, algebra and functions, measurement and discrete mathematics, and mathematics structure.

1008   Soaring Scores in Math Assessment

Harcourt Achieve
6277 Sea Harbor Drive
Orlando, FL   32887

800-531-5015
FAX 800-699-9459
http://www.steckvaughn.com
e-mail: info@steckvaughn.com

Steck-Vaughn Staff, Author
Tim McEwen, President/CEO
Jeff Johnson, Dir Marketing Communications
Chris Lehmann, Team Coordinator

Students get 48 pages of modeled instruction and practice tests covering exactly the types of questions they'll face on assessments, which include open-ended, multiple choice, and free response problems with fill in grids. A review test helps assess, diagnose, and prescribe additional work quickly.

**1009   Soaring Scores on the CMT in Mathematics &
Soaring Scores on the CAPT in Mathematics**

Harcourt Archieve
6277 Sea Harbor Drive
Orlando, FL   32887

800-531-5015
FAX 800-699-9459
http://www.steckvaughn.com
e-mail: info@steckvaughn.com

Steck-Vaughn Staff, Author
Tim McEwen, President/CEO
Jeff Johnson, Dir Marketing Communications
Chris Lehmann, Team Coordinator

Build the skills, strategies, and confidence your students need to do their best on the mathematics portion of the CMT and CAPT with this focused test preparation program. The instructional portion offers hints and strategies for each type of question students will face. Content standards and strands accompany each modeled problem.

1010   Soaring Scores on the CSAP Mathematics Assessment

Harcourt Achieve
6277 Sea Harbor Drive
Orlando, FL   32887

800-531-5015
FAX 800-699-9459
http://www.steckvaughn.com
e-mail: info@steckvaughn.com

Steck-Vaughn Staff, Author
Tim McEwen, President/CEO
Jeff Johnson, Dir Marketing Communications
Chris Lehmann, Team Coordinator

Make the most of your CSAP test preparation. The best way to prepare your students for Colorado's unique achievement assessment is to use the program designed specifically for that purpose.

1011   Soaring Scores on the ISAT Mathematics

Harcourt Achieve
6277 Sea Harbor Drive
Orlando, FL   32887

800-531-5015
FAX 800-699-9459
http://www.steckvaughn.com
e-mail: info@steckvaughn.com

Steck-Vaughn Staff, Author
Tim McEwen, President/CEO
Jeff Johnson, Dir Marketing Communications
Chris Lehmann, Team Coordinator

Developed to ensure peak performance on Illinois new math assessment. This test preparation product offers grade specific materials and authentic practice designed to help students approach the ISAT in mathematics strategically and confidently.

1012   Soaring Scores on the MEAP Math Test

Harcourt Achieve
6277 Sea Harbor Drive
Orlando, FL   32887

800-531-5015
FAX 800-699-9459
http://www.steckvaughn.com
e-mail: info@steckvaughn.com

Steck-Vaughn Staff, Author
Tim McEwen, President/CEO
Jeff Johnson, Dir Marketing Communications
Chri Lehmann, Team Coordinator

Focus your MEAP math preparation where it will do the most good. This targeted test preparation program delivers the instruction, strategies, and practice your students need to be accomplished test takers.

Classroom Resources/Math

1013 Spatial Relationships

Sunburst Technology
400 Columbus Avenue
Valhalla, NY   10595   914-747-3310
                                    800-321-7511
                                FAX 914-747-4109
                          http://www.sunburst.com
                      e-mail: support@sunburst.com

Students explore location by identifying the positions
of objects and creating paths between places. Children
develop spatial abilities and language needed to communicate about our world.

1014 Spatial Sense CD-ROM

Sunburst Technology
400 Columbus Avenue
Valhalla, NY   10595   914-747-3310
                                    800-321-7511
                                FAX 914-747-4109
                          http://www.sunburst.com
                      e-mail: support@sunburst.com

Your students will strenghten their spatial perception,
spatial reasoning and problem-solving skills with
three great programs now on one CD-ROM.

1015 Splish Splash Math

Sunburst Technology
400 Columbus Avenue
Valhalla, NY   10595   914-747-3310
                                    800-321-7511
                                FAX 914-747-4109
                          http://www.sunburst.com
                      e-mail: support@sunburst.com

Students learn and practice basic operation skills as
they engage in this high interest program that keeps
them motivated. Great visual rewards and three levels
of difficulty keep students challanged.

1016 Statistics & Probability

Harcourt Achieve
6277 Sea Harbor Drive
Orlando, FL   32887
                                    800-531-5015
                                FAX 800-699-9459
                         http://www.steckvaughn.com
                      e-mail: info@steckvaughn.com
Steck-Vaughn Staff, Author
Tim McEwen, President/CEO
Jeff Johnson, Dir Marketing Communications
Chris Lehmann, Team Coordinator

A working knowledge of statistics and probability increases problem solving skills, and provides students
with the skills to be able to more effectively gather,
describe, organize, and interpret information in their
world.

1017 Strategic Math Series

Edge Enterprises
708 W 9th Street
Lawrence, KS   66044   785-749-1473
                                    877-767-1487
                                FAX 785-749-0207
                          e-mail: edge@midusa.net
Cecil D Mercer and Susan Peterson Miller, Author
Jacqueline Schafer, Managing Editor

The Strategic Math Series are a group of seven manuals designed for any aged student who needs to learn
basic math facts and operations. Each manual is built
upon the concrete-representational-abstract method
of instruction. Within this approach, understanding of
mathematics is developed through the use of concrete
objects, representational drawings and an
easy-to-learn strategy that turns all students into active problem-solvers. Available as a series or individually.

1018 Strategies for Problem-Solving

Harcourt Achieve
6277 Sea Harbor Drive
Orlando, FL   32887
                                    800-531-5015
                                FAX 800-699-9459
                         http://www.steckvaughn.com
                      e-mail: info@steckvaughn.com
Steck-Vaughn Staff, Author
Tim McEwen, President/CEO
Jeff Johnson, Dir Marketing Communications
Chris Lehmann, Team Coordinator

Show students more than one way to approach a problem, and you hand them the key to effective problem
solving. These reproducible activities build math reasoning and critical thinking skills, reinforce core concepts, and reduce math anxiety, too.

1019 Strategies for Success in Mathematics

Harcourt Archieve
6277 Sea Harbor Drive
Orlando, FL   32887
                                    800-531-5015
                                FAX 800-699-9459
                         http://www.steckvaughn.com
                      e-mail: info@steckvaughn.com
Steck-Vaughn Staff, Author
Tim McEwen, President/CEO
Jeff Johnson, Dir Marketing Communications
Chris Lehmann, Team Coordinator

Teach your students specific problem-solving skills
and test taking strategies for success with math and
math assessments. Practice thoroughly covers five
math clusters: numerical operations, patterns and
functions, algebraic concepts, measurement and geometry, and data analysis.

1020 Sunbuddy Math Playhouse

Sunburst Technology
400 Columbus Avenue
Valhalla, NY   10595   914-747-3310
                                   800-321-7511
                              FAX 914-747-4109
                         http://www.sunburst.com
                         e-mail: support@sunburst.com

An entertaining play, hidden math-related animations, and four multi-level interactive activities encourage children to explore math and reading.

1021 Take Off With...

Harcourt Achieve
6277 Sea Harbor Drive
Orlando, FL   32887
                                   800-531-5015
                              FAX 800-699-9459
                         http://www.steckvaughn.com
                         e-mail: info@steckvaughn.com
Steck-Vaughn Staff, Author
Tim McEwen, President/CEO
Jeff Johnson, Dir Marketing Communications
Chris Lehmann, Team Coordinator

Youngsters build number sense with concepts such as counting, sequencing and dividing, sorting, sets, and graphing, memory games, board games, and guessing games.

1022 Ten Tricky Tiles

Sunburst Technology
400 Columbus Avenue
Valhalla, NY   10595   914-747-3310
                                   800-321-7511
                              FAX 914-747-4109
                         http://www.sunburst.com
                         e-mail: support@sunburst.com

Students develop their arithmetic and logic skills with three levels of activities that involve solving sets of numbers sentences.

1023 Weekly Math Practice

Harcourt Achieve
6277 Sea Harbor Drive
Orlando, FL   32887
                                   800-531-5015
                              FAX 800-699-9459
                         http://www.steckvaughn.com
                         e-mail: info@steckvaughn.com
Steck-Vaughn Staff, Author
Tim McEwen, President/CEO
Jeff Johnson, Dir Marketing Communications
Chris Lehmann, Team Coordinator

Keep students sharp throughout the year with 36 weeks of brief, daily activities in math. Each activity page features five activity strips, one for each day of the week, and is backed up by a convenient answer key for the teacher that includes explanations and extensions.

1024 Zap! Around Town

Sunburst Technology
400 Columbus Avenue
Valhalla, NY   10595   914-747-3310
                                   800-321-7511
                              FAX 914-747-4109
                         http://www.sunburst.com
                         e-mail: support@sunburst.com

Students develop mapping and direction skills in this easy-to-use, animated program featuring Shelby, your friendly Sunbuddy guide.

Preschool

1025 2's Experience Fingerplays

Therapro
225 Arlington Street
Framingham, MA   01702   508-872-9494
                                   800-257-5376
                              FAX 508-875-2062
                         http://www.theraproducts.com
                         e-mail: info@theraproducts.com
Liz Wilmes, Dick Wilmes, Author
Karen Conrad, President

A wonderful collection of fingerplays, songs and rhymes for the very young child. Fingerplays are short, easy to learn, and full of simple movement. Chant or sing the fingerplays and then enjoy the accompanying games and activities. *$12.95*

159 pages

1026 28 Instant Song Games

Therapro
225 Arlington Street
Framingham, MA   01702   508-872-9494
                                   800-257-5376
                              FAX 508-875-2062
                         http://www.theraproducts.com
                         e-mail: info@theraproducts.com
MaBoAubLo, Barbara Sher, Author
Karen Conrad, President

Gets kids up and moving in no time! Includes numerous games of body awareness, movement play, self expression, imagination and language play. Booklet and 75 minute audio tape. *$21.00*

Audio Tape

1027 Artic Shuffle

LinguiSystems
3100 4th Avenue
East Moline, IL   61244
                                   800-776-4332
                              FAX 309-755-2377
                         TDY:800-933-8331
                         http://www.linguisystems.com
                         e-mail: service@linguisystems.com
Tobie Nan Kaufman, Author
Linda Bowers, Owner
Rosemary Huisingh, Owner

Why are these card decks best-sellers? Because they're real playing cards! Your students can play Go Fish, Crazy Eights, or Concentration while they practice their target sounds. Use them for vocabulary drills or naming practice. *$89.95*

Ages 5-Adult

1028 Curious George Preschool Learning Games

Sunburst Technology
400 Columbus Avenue
Valhalla, NY   10595   914-747-3310
                             800-321-7511
                        FAX 914-747-4109
                    http://www.sunburst.com
                    e-mail: support@sunburst.com

Join Curious George in Fun Town and play five arcade-style games that promote the visual and auditory discrimination skills all students need before they begin to read. Mac/Win CD-ROM

1029 Devereux Early Childhood Assessment (DECA)

Kaplan Early Learning Company
PO Box 609
Lewisville, NC   27023   336-766-7374
                             800-334-2014
                        FAX 800-452-7526
                    http://www.kaplanco.com
                    e-mail: info@kaplanco.com
Hal Kaplan, President/CEO

Strength-based standardized, norm-referenced behavior rating scale designed to promote resilience and measure protective factors in children ages 2-5. Through the program, early childhood professionals and families learn specific strategies to support young children's social and emotional development and to enhance the ovall quality of early childhood programs.

1030 Devereux Early Childhood Assessment: Clinical Version (DECA-C)

Kaplan Early Learning Company
PO Box 609
Lewisville, NC   27023   336-766-7374
                             800-334-2014
                        FAX 800-452-7526
                    http://www.kaplanco.com
                    e-mail: info@kaplanco.com
Paul LeBuffe, Author
Hal Kaplan, President/CEO
Paul A LeBuffe, Assistant Director
Pat Conte, Publishing Director

DECA-C is designed to support early intervention efforts to reduce or eliminate significant emotional and behavioral concerns in preschool children. This can be used for guide interventions, identify children needing special services, assess outcomes and help programs meet Head Start, IDEA, and similar requirements. Kit includes: 1 Manual, 30 Record Forms, and 1 Norms Reference Card. *$125.95*

1031 Early Movement Skills

Therapro
225 Arlington Street
Framingham, MA   01702   508-872-9494
                             800-257-5376
                        FAX 508-875-2062
                    http://www.theraproducts.com
                    e-mail: info@theraproducts.com
Naomi Benari, Author
Karen Conrad, President

Easy to follow, reproducible gross motor activities are graded from very simple (even for the passive child) to more demanding (folk dancing). Each of the 150 pages offers an activity with its objective, a clear instruction of the activity, rationale, and alternative movements and games. Many activities involve music and rythm. A great source for early intervention and early childhood programs. *$58.00*

1032 Early Screening Inventory: Revised

Harcourt
19500 Bulverde Road
San Antonio, TX   78259
                             800-872-1726
                        FAX 800-232-1223
                    http://www.harcourt
Gail Ribalta, VP Marketing

A developmental screening instrument for 3-to-6-year olds. Provides a norm-referenced overview of visual-motor/adaptive, language and cognition, and gross motor development. Meets IDEA and Head Start requirements for early identification and parental involvement. Test in English or Spanish in 15-20 minutes. Training video and materials available.

1033 Early Sensory Skills

Therapro
225 Arlington Street
Framingham, MA   01702   508-872-9494
                             800-257-5376
                        FAX 508-875-2062
                    http://www.theraproducts.com
                    e-mail: info@theraproducts.com
Jackie Cooke, Author
Karen Conrad, President

A wonderful book filled with practical and fun activities for stimulating vision, touch, taste and smell. Invaluable for anyone working with children 6 months to 5 years, this manual outlines basic principals followed by six sections containing activities, games and topics to excite the senses. Introductions are easy to follow, and materials for the sensory work are readily accessible in the everyday environment. *$52.50*

1034 Early Visual Skills

Therapro
225 Arlington Street
Framingham, MA   01702   508-872-9494
                             800-257-5376
                        FAX 508-875-2062
                    http://www.theraproducts.com
                    e-mail: info@theraproducts.com
Diana Williams, Author
Karen Conrad, President

A beautifully designed, easy to follow reproducible book for working with young children on visual perceptual skills. Most of the activities are nonverbal and can be used with children who have limited language. Each section has both easy and challenging activities for school and for parents working with children at home. Activities include sorting, color and shape matching, a looking walk, games to develop visual memory and concentration and many more. *$52.50*

208 pages

1035 Family Literacy Package

Harcourt Achieve
6277 Sea Harbor Drive
Orlando, FL   32887

800-531-5015
FAX 800-699-9459
http://www.steckvaughn.com
e-mail: info@steckvaughn.com

Steck-Vaughn Staff, Author
Tim McEwen, President/CEO
Jeff Johnson, Dir Marketing Communications
Chris Lehmann, Team Coordinator

Parent Package: includes materials that provide valuable academic and life coping resources for parents. Manual and companion video tapes prepare staff members for effective implementation. Child Package: includes materials that develop reading readiness and encourage positive parent-child interaction. Manual and companion video tapes prepare staff members to direct preschool learning and to facilitate supportive new relationships.

1036 Fluharty Preschool Speech & Language Screening Test-2

The Speech Bin
1965 25th Avenue
Vero Beach, FL   32960

772-770-0007
FAX 772-770-0006
http://www.speechbin.com
e-mail: info@speechbin.com

Carefully normed on 705 children, the Fluharty yields standard scores, percentiles, and age equivalents. The form features space for speech-language pathologist to note phonological processes, voice quality, and fluency; a Teacher Questionnaire is also provided. Item number P882 *$153.00*

1037 For Parents and Professionals: Preschool

LinguiSystems
3100 4th Avenue
East Moline, IL   61244

800-776-4332
FAX 309-755-2377
TDY:800-933-8331
http://www.linguisystems.com
e-mail: service@linguisystems.com

Marilyn A Ianni, Karin A Mullin, Author
Linda Bowers, Owner
Rosemary Huisingh, Owner

Get tips and activities to facilitate developing communication skills in young children. You'll target social development, fine and gross motor development, cognitive growth, and receptive and expressive language skills. Each activity gives you three levels of increasing complexity for children functioning at different developmental levels. *$37.95*

181 pages   Ages 2-5

1038 Funology Fables

The Speech Bin
1965 25th Avenue
Vero Beach, FL   32960

772-770-0007
FAX 772-770-0006
http://www.speechbin.com
e-mail: info@speechbin.com

Funology Fables targets specific phonemes and critical early concepts, such as matching, sequencing, opposites, comparisons, quantity, size, and space. Reproducible Talking Tales and activities include 32 six-part sequence stories. Item number 1484. *$45.00*

1039 Goal Oriented Gross & Fine Motor Lesson Plans for Early Childhood Classes

Therapro
225 Arlington Street
Framingham, MA   01702

508-872-9494
800-257-5376
FAX 508-875-2062
http://www.theraproducts.com
e-mail: info@theraproducts.com

Donna Weiss MA OTR, Author
Karen Conrad, President

Practical and convinient format covers 224 activities grouped into 12 monthly units, making it easy to incorporate gross and fine motor activities into a daily class schedule. Provides challenges for groups whose abilities span early childhood, from 2.5 to 5.5 years of age. *$32.00*

77 pages

1040 HELP for Preschoolers at Home

Therapro
225 Arlington Street
Framingham, MA   01702

508-872-9494
800-257-5376
FAX 508-875-2062
http://www.theraproducts.com
e-mail: info@theraproducts.com

Therapro Staff, Author
Karen Conrad, President

Three hundred pages of practical, home-based activities that can be easily administered by the parents or the child's home-care provider. Upon completion of their assessments, teachers and therapists provide parents with these handouts to help them work on skills at home in conjunction with the program. *$72.50*

Ages 3-6

1041 IEP Companion Software

LinguiSystems
3100 4th Avenue
East Moline, IL 61244

800-776-4332
FAX 309-755-2377
TDY:800-933-8331
http://www.linguisystems.com
e-mail: service@linguisystems.com

Carolyn Wilson, Janet Lanza, Jeannie Evans, Author
Linda Bowers, Owner
Rosemary Huisingh, Owner

Get IEP goals from the best-selling book with the click of your mouse. Writing complete reports is easy! You'll get to choose from hundreds of individual and classroom goals and objectives for all the important speech and language areas. Just click on the specific goals you want to create your individualized report. *$69.95*

Birth-Adult

1042 Just for Me! Grammar

LinguiSystems
3100 4th Avenue
East Moline, IL 61244

800-776-4332
FAX 309-755-2377
TDY:800-933-8331
http://www.linguisystems.com
e-mail: service@linguisystems.com

Margaret Warner, Author
Linda Bowers, Owner
Rosemary Huisingh, Owner

Teach oral grammar to your youngest students! Through a variety of engaging activities, your students will become familiar with basic parts of speech, correct word order, and simple grammar concepts. These activities provide a solid foundation for later formal grammar training in the classroom. *$24.95*

150 pages   Ages 3-6

1043 LAP-D Kindergarten Screen Kit

Kaplan Early Learning Company
PO Box 609
Lewisville, NC 27023

336-766-7374
800-334-2014
FAX 800-452-7526
http://www.kaplanco.com
e-mail: info@kaplanco.com

Hal Kaplan, President/CEO
Pat Conte, Publishing Director

Concise, standardized screening deice normed on 5 year old children. Tasks are in four domains: fine, motor, gross motor, cognititve, and language. The Kindergarten Kit includes the technical manual, examiners, manual, and materials to assist in determining pure outcomes. *$124.95*

1044 LILAC

Specch Bin
1965 25th Avenue
Vero Beach, FL 32960

570-770-0007
FAX 561-770-0006

LILAC uses direct and naturalistic teaching in a creative approach that links spoken language learning to reading and writing. Activities to develop semantic, syntactic, expressive, and receptive language skills are presented sequentially from three-to-five-year old developmental levels. *$21.95*

1045 Learning Accomplishment Profile Diagnostic Normed Screens for Age 3-5

Kaplan Early Learning Company
PO Box 609
Lewisville, NC 27023

336-766-7374
800-334-2014
FAX 800-452-7526
http://www.kaplanco.com
e-mail: info@kaplanco.com

Hal Kaplan, President/CEO
Pat Conte, Publishing Director

For 3-5 years. Create reliable developmental snapshots in fine motor, gross motor, cognitive, language, personal/social, and self-help skill domains. *$349.95*

1046 Learning Accomplishment Profile (LAP-R) KIT

Kaplan Early Learning Company
PO Box 609
Lewisville, NC 27023

336-766-7374
800-334-2014
FAX 800-452-7526
http://www.kaplanco.com
e-mail: info@kaplanco.com

Hal Kaplan, President/CEO
Pat Conte, Publishing Director

A criterion-referenced assessment instrument measuring development in six domains: gross motor, fine motor, cognitive, language, self-help and social/emotional. Kit includes all materials necessary for assessing 20 children. *$299.95*

1047 Learning Accomplishment Profile Diagnostic Normed Assessment (LAP-D)

Kaplan Early Learning Company
PO Box 609
Lewisville, NC 27023

336-766-7374
800-334-2014
FAX 800-452-7526
http://www.kaplanco.com
e-mail: info@kaplanco.com

Hal Kaplan, President/CEO
Pat Conte, Publishing Director

A comprehensive developemtal assessment tool for children between the ages of 30 and 72 months. LAP-D consists of a hierarchy of developmental skills arranged in four developmental domains: fine motor, gross motor, cognitive and language. *$624.95*

1048 Linamood Program (LIPS Clinical Version)-Phoneme Sequencing Program for Reading, Spelling,Speech

LinguiSystems
3100 4th Avenue
East Moline, IL   61244

800-776-4332
FAX 309-755-2377
TDY:800-933-8331
http://www.linguisystems.com
e-mail: service@linguisystems.com
Patricia Linamood, Phyllis Linamood, Author
Linda Bowers, Owner
Rosemary Huisingh, Owner

Help your students develop phoneme awareness for competence in reading, spelling, and speech. This multisensory program meets the needs of the many children and adults who don't develop phonemic awareness through traditional methods. *$247.00*

Birth-Adult

1049 Make Every Step Count: Birth to 1 Year

Therapro
225 Arlington Street
Framingham, MA   01702

508-872-9494
800-257-5376
FAX 508-875-2062
http://www.theraproducts.com
e-mail: info@theraproducts.com
Stephanie Parks MA, Author
Karen Conrad, President

A great book with many ideas for parents to use at home to foster child development. *$16.50*

94 pages

1050 Make It Today for Pre-K Play

Therapro
225 Arlington Street
Framingham, MA   01702

508-872-9494
800-257-5376
FAX 508-875-2062
http://www.theraproducts.com
e-mail: info@theraproducts.com
Joyce Hamman, Author
Karen Conrad, President

Many ideas for making and using toys for motor development. Includes a nice checklist for balance, directional terms, body awareness, and gross and fine motor skills. For each piece of equipment, specific directions are given on how to make it; teaching tips, many ideas for using in curriculum integration. *$7.95*

1051 Mouth Madness

The Speech Bin
1965 25th Avenue
Vero Beach, FL   32960

772-770-0007
FAX 772-770-0006
http://www.speechbin.com
e-mail: info@speechbin.com

This unique manual uses oral imitation, motor planning, and breath control activities to improve the articulation and feeding skills of preschool and primary children. Games, manipulative tasks, silly sentences, rhymes, and funny faces target higher organizational levels of motor planning. Item number C758. *$51.95*

1052 Partners for Learning (PFL)

Kaplan Early Learning Company
PO Box 609
Lewisville, NC   27023

336-766-7374
800-334-2014
FAX 800-452-7526
http://www.kaplanco.com
e-mail: info@kaplanco.com
Hal Kaplan, President/CEO
Pat Conte, Publishing Director

This resource uses cards, books, posters, and support materials to supply teaching ideas and to support child development. PARTNERS for Learning encourages cognitive, social, motor, and language development. The kit provides materials for curriculum planning and self-assessment. *$199.95*

1053 Preschool

Harcourt Achieve
6277 Sea Harbor Drive
Orlando, FL   32887

800-531-5015
FAX 800-699-9459
http://www.steckvaughn.com
e-mail: info@steckvaughn.com
Davis, Author
Tim McEwen, President/CEO
Jeff Johnson, Dir Marketing Communications
Chris Lehmann, Team Coordinator

This series provides age appropriate activities to foster childrens' desire to read and create a print rich classroom to enhance their emergent literacy. Multiple lesson plans save teachers time by providing suggested lessons that cover the purpose, materials, direct teaching, and application of new skills. This is a great resource for center ideas that provide opportunities for children to think creatively, explore new ideas, and use problem-solving skills.

1054 Preschool Motor Speech Evaluation & Intervention

The Speech Bin
1965 25th Avenue
Vero Beach, FL   32960

772-770-0007
FAX 772-770-0006
http://www.speechbin.com
e-mail: info@speechbin.com

This comprehensive criterion-based assessment tool differentiates motor-based speech disorders from those of phonology and determines if speech difficulties of children 18 months to six years old are characteristic of: oral nonverbal apraxia; dysarthria; developmental verbal dyspraxia; hypersensitivity; differences in tone and hyposensitivity. Item number J322. *$59.00*

1055 Promoting Communication in Infants & Children

The Speech Bin
1965 25th Avenue
Vero Beach, FL   32960   772-770-0007
                                      FAX 772-770-0006
                              http://www.speechbin.com
                              e-mail: info@speechbin.com

Promoting Communication in Infants and Young Children gives you down-to-earth information, activities, and step-by-step suggestions for stimulating children's speech and language skills. Topics are conveniently organized, concisely presented, and written in easy-to-understand language. Item number 1512. *$14.95*

1056 RULES

The Speech Bin
1965 25th Avenue
Vero Beach, FL   32960   772-770-0007
                                      FAX 772-770-0006
                              http://www.speechbin.com
                              e-mail: info@speechbin.com

Faced with young children whose speech is unintelligible? RULES is the perfect program for these preschool and elementary children. It remediates the processes: cluster reduction; final consonant deletion; stopping and prevocalic voicing. Item number 1557. *$43.95*

1057 Receptive One-Word Picture Vocabulary Test (ROWPVT-2000)

The Speech Bin
1965 25th Avenue
Vero Beach, FL   32960   772-770-0007
                                      FAX 772-770-0006
                              http://www.speechbin.com
                              e-mail: info@speechbin.com

This administered, untimed measure assesses the vocabulary comprehension of 0-2 through 11-18 years. New full-color test pictures are easy to recognize; many new test items have been added. It is ideal for children unable or reluctant to speak because only a gestural response is required. Item number A305. *$140.00*

1058 Right from the Start: Behavioral Intervention for Young Children with Autism: A Guide

Therapro
225 Arlington Street
Framingham, MA   01702   508-872-9494
                                      800-257-5376
                                      FAX 508-875-2062
                              http://www.theraproducts.com
                              e-mail: info@theraproducts.com
Mary Jane Weiss PhD, Sandra Harris PhD, Author
Karen Conrad, President

This informative and user-friendly guide helps parents and service providers explore programs that use early intensive behavioral intervention for young children with autism and related disorders. Within these programs, many children improve in intellectual, social and adaptive functioning, enabling them to move on to regular elementary and preschools. Benefits all children, but primarily useful for children age five and younger. *$14.95*

138 pages

1059 SPARC Artic Junior

LinguiSystems
3100 4th Avenue
East Moline, IL   61244
                                      800-776-4332
                                      FAX 309-755-2377
                                      TDY:800-933-8331
                              http://www.linguisystems.com
                              e-mail: service@linguisystems.com
Beverly Plass, Author
Linda Bowers, Owner
Rosemary Huisingh, Owner

Reach intelligibility goals faster with these take-home exercises. The practice words have been carefully selected to control the phonetic context. It's a programmed, research-based approach that will get results. Activities are divided by primary and secondary phonological processes. *$39.95*

211 pages   Ages 3-7

1060 Sensory Motor Activities for Early Development

Therapro
225 Arlington Street
Framingham, MA   01702   508-872-9494
                                      800-257-5376
                                      FAX 508-875-2062
                              http://www.theraproducts.com
                              e-mail: info@theraproducts.com
Chia Swee Hong, Helen Gabriel, Cathy St John, Author
Karen Conrad, President

A complete package of tried and tested gross and fine motor activities. Many activities to stimulate sensory and body awareness, encourage basic movement, promote hand skills, and enhance spatial/early perceptual skills. Master handouts throughout to give to parents for home practice activities for working in small groups. *$44.50*

1061 Silly Sentences

The Speech Bin
1965 25th Avenue
Vero Beach, FL   32960   772-770-0007
                                      FAX 772-770-0006
                              http://www.speechbin.com
                              e-mail: info@speechbin.com

Children love to have fun. Silly Sentences lets them have fun while they play these engaging card games to learn: subject verb agreement; speech sound articulation; S+ V+ O sentences; questioning and answering; humor and absurdities; and present progressive verbs. Item number P506. *$41.00*

1062 Sound Connections

The Speech Bin
1965 25th Avenue
Vero Beach, FL   32960   772-770-0007
                                      FAX 772-770-0006
                              http://www.speechbin.com
                              e-mail: info@speechbin.com

This program teaches the critical connections between the sounds kids hear and speaking, reading, and writing. Dozens of activities and worksheets, 19 phoneme-based stories, and 100s of pictures. Item number 1487. *$41.95*

1063 Source for Early Literacy Development

LinguiSystems
3100 4th Avenue
East Moline, IL 61244

800-776-4332
FAX 309-755-2377
TDY:800-933-8331
http://www.linguisystems.com
e-mail: service@linguisystems.com
Linda K Crowe, Sara S Reichmuth, Author
Linda Bowers, Owner
Rosemary Huisingh, Owner

This great resource gives you the latest information on children's emergent reading and writing from birth through age eight. You'll also get helpful strategies to facilitate literacy development for future academic success! *$41.95*

151 pages Birth-8

1064 Stuttering: Helping the Disfluent Preschool Child

The Speech Bin
1965 25th Avenue
Vero Beach, FL 32960

772-770-0007
FAX 772-770-0006
http://www.speechbin.com
e-mail: info@speechbin.com

Written in the warm encouraging style for which this author is known, Stuttering: Helping the Disfluent Preschool Child is the perfect tool for parents and teachers of young stuttering children. It uses a Speech Thermometer to show them ways to turn talking into an area of strength. Item number 1489. *$13.95*

1065 Take Home: Preschool Language Development

LinguiSystems
3100 4th Avenue
East Moline, IL 61244

800-776-4332
FAX 309-755-2377
TDY:800-933-8331
http://www.linguisystems.com
e-mail: service@linguisystems.com
Martha Drake, Author
Linda Bowers, Owner
Rosemary Huisingh, Owner

Home follow-up is essential for your little ones with speech and language delays. Get everything you need for a comprehensive take-home program with this time saver! Each take-home lesson is easy to follow. *$31.95*

191 pages Ages 1-5

1066 Test for Auditory Comprehension of Language: TACL-3

The Speech Bin
1965 25th Avenue
Vero Beach, FL 32960

772-770-0007
FAX 772-770-0006
http://www.speechbin.com
e-mail: info@speechbin.com

The newly revised TACL-3 evaluates the 0-3 to 9-11-year old's understanding of spoken language in three subtests: Vocabulary, Grammatical Morphemes and Elaborated Phrases and Sentences. Each test item is a word or sentence read aloud by the examiner; the child responds by pointing to one of three pictures. Item number P792. *$261.00*

1067 Tips for Teaching Infants & Toddlers

The Speech Bin
1965 25th Avenue
Vero Beach, FL 32960

772-770-0007
FAX 772-770-0006
http://www.speechbin.com
e-mail: info@speechbin.com

This multisensory approach to Early Intervention is a whole year's worth of weekly thematic lessons which let children see, hear, feel, manipulate, smell, and taste. Item number 1235. *$45.95*

1068 What Am I? Game

Harcourt Achieve
6277 Sea Harbor Drive
Orlando, FL 32887

800-531-5015
FAX 800-699-9459
http://www.steckvaughn.com
e-mail: info@steckvaughn.com
Steck-Vaughn Staff, Author
Tim McEwen, President/CEO
Jeff Johnson, Dir Marketing Communications
Chris Lehmann, Team Coordinator

Turn animal identity into a guessing game. Children guess the identities of amazing animals from a series of clues and up close views. A world map pinpoints each animal's habitat, and a quick quiz reinforces fun facts.

1069 When Pre-Schoolers are Not on Target: Guide for Parents & Early Childhood Educators

Learning Disabilities Association of America
LDA Literary Depository
Pittsburgh, PA 15234

412-341-1515
FAX 412-344-0224
http://www.ldanatl.org
e-mail: ldanatl@usaor.net

New booklet provides information on early identification of learning disabilities and appropriate intervention strategies to professionals who work with preschool children. Available in Spanish. Discounts for multiples. *$4.00*

1070 Your Child's Speech and Language

The Speech Bin
1965 25th Avenue
Vero Beach, FL 32960

772-770-0007
FAX 772-770-0006
http://www.speechbin.com
e-mail: info@speechbin.com

This delightfully illustrated 52-page book provides helpful information about speech and language development from infancy through five years. It shows how to determine if speech is developing normally and ways to stimulate its growth. It's ideal for parent training and baby showers too! Item number P652. *$17.00*

Reading

1071 100% Reading: 2-Book Intermediate Set

LinguiSystems
3100 4th Avenue
East Moline, IL   61244

800-776-4332
FAX 309-755-2377
TDY:800-933-8331
http://www.linguisystems.com
e-mail: service@linguisystems.com
LinguiSystems Staff, Author
Linda Bowers, Owner
Rosemary Huisingh, Owner

Our reading series uses a developmental approach based on the latest research in phonological awareness and early reading skills. Intermediate books are for ages 8-10. Great as a reading curriculum or to supplement your current reading program. *$69.90*

200 pages   Ages 8-10

1072 100% Reading: 3-Book Primary Set

LinguiSystems
3100 4th Avenue
East Moline, IL   61244

800-776-4332
FAX 309-755-2377
TDY:800-933-8331
http://www.linguisystems.com
e-mail: service@linguisystems.com
LinguiSystems Staff, Author
Linda Bowers, Owner
Rosemary Huisingh, Owner

Our reading series uses a developmental approach based on the latest research in phonological awareness and early reading skills. Primary books are for ages 5-7. Great as a reading curriculum or to supplement your current reading program. *$104.85*

200 pages   Ages 5-7

1073 100% Reading: Decoding and Word Recognition: 5-book set

LinguiSystems
3100 4th Avenue
East Moline, IL   61244

800-776-4332
FAX 309-755-2377
TDY:800-933-8331
http://www.linguisystems.com
e-mail: service@linguisystems.com
LinguiSystems Staff, Author
Linda Bowers, Owner
Rosemary Huisingh, Owner

Our reading series uses a developmental approach based on the latest research in phonological awareness and early reading skills. Primary books are for ages 5-7. Intermediate books are for ages 8-10. Great as a reading curriculum or to supplement your current reading program. *$174.75*

200 pages   Ages 5-10

1074 100% Reading: Intermediate Book 1

LinguiSystems
3100 4th Avenue
East Moline, IL   61244

800-776-4332
FAX 309-755-2377
TDY:800-933-8331
http://www.linguisystems.com
e-mail: service@linguisystems.com
LinguiSystems Staff, Author
Linda Bowers, Owner
Rosemary Huisingh, Owner

Our reading series uses a developmental approach based on the latest research in phonological awareness and early reading skills. Great as a reading curriculum or to supplement your current reading program. Intermediate Book 1 covers: schwa, vowel sounds, consonant sounds, hard and soft c and g sound, and silent letters. *$34.95*

211 pages   Ages 8-10

1075 100% Reading: Intermediate Book 2

LinguiSystems
3100 4th Avenue
East Moline, IL   61244

800-776-4332
FAX 309-755-2377
TDY:800-933-8331
http://www.linguisystems.com
e-mail: service@linguisystems.com
LinguiSystems Staff, Author
Linda Bowers, Owner
Rosemary Huisingh, Owner

Our reading series uses a developmental approach based on the latest research in phonological awareness and early reading skills. Great as a reading curriculum or to supplement your current reading program. Intermediate Book 2 covers: syllables, root words and affixes, plurals and possessive, contractions, homonyms, and word endings. *$34.95*

221 pages   Ages 8-10

1076 100% Reading: Primary Book 1

LinguiSystems
3100 4th Avenue
East Moline, IL   61244

800-776-4332
FAX 309-755-2377
TDY:800-933-8331
http://www.linguisystems.com
e-mail: service@linguisystems.com
LinguiSystems Staff, Author
Linda Bowers, Owner
Rosemary Huisingh, Owner

Our reading series uses a developmental approach based on the latest research in phonological awareness and early reading skills. Primary books are ages 5-7. Great as a reading curriculum or to supplement your current reading program. Primary Book 1 covers: sight words, short vowels, long vowels, and sorry vowels oo, ow, oi, aw, er. *$34.95*

194 pages   Ages 5-7

1077 100% Reading: Primary Book 2

LinguiSystems
3100 4th Avenue
East Moline, IL   61244

800-776-4332
FAX 309-755-2377
TDY:800-933-8331
http://www.linguisystems.com
e-mail: service@linguisystems.com

LinguiSystems Staff, Author
Linda Bowers, Owner
Rosemary Huisingh, Owner

Our reading series uses a developmental approach based on the latest research in phonological awareness and early reading skills. Primary books are ages 5-7. Great as a reading curriculum or to supplement your current reading program. Primary Book 2 covers: sight words, beginning consonants, and ending constants. *$34.95*

200 pages   Ages 5-7

1078 100% Reading: Primary Book 3

LinguiSystems
3100 4th Avenue
East Moline, IL   61244

800-776-4332
FAX 309-755-2377
TDY:800-933-8331
http://www.linguisystems.com
e-mail: service@linguisystems.com

LinguiSystems Staff, Author
Linda Bowers, Owner
Rosemary Huisingh, Owner

Our reading series uses a developmental approach based on the latest research in phonological awareness and early reading skills. Primary books are ages 5-7. Great as a reading curriculum or to supplement your current reading program. Primary Book 3 covers: intial blends, final blends, consonant digraphs, vowel digraphs, vowel dipthongs, sounds of y. *$34.95*

233 pages   Ages 5-7

1079 125 Ways to Be a Better Reader

LinguiSystems
3100 4th Avenue
East Moline, IL   61244

800-776-4332
FAX 309-755-2377
TDY:800-933-8331
http://www.linguisystems.com
e-mail: service@linguisystems.com

Elizabeth M Wadlington, Paula S Currie, Author
Linda Bowers, Owner
Rosemary Huisingh, Owner

Get 125 strategies to improve decoding and conprehension skills. You'll improve reading abilities and attitudes in seven major areas including: getting ready to read, decoding, comprehension, content area reading, reading for test, reading reference materials, and the reading-writing connection. *$35.95*

180 pages   Ages 10-16

1080 Ablenet

1081 10th Avenue SE
Minneapolis, MN   55414

612-379-0956
800-322-0956
FAX 612-379-9143
http://www.ablenetinc.com
e-mail: customerservice@ablenetinc.com

Cheryl Volkman, Chief Developmental Officer

Simple assistive technology for teaching children with disabilities including communication aids, switches, environmental control, mounting systems, literacy and teacher resources, kits and more.

1081 Animals of the Rain Forest: Steadwell

Harcourt Achieve
6277 Sea Harbor Drive
Orlando, FL   32887

800-531-5015
FAX 800-699-9459
http://www.steckvaughn.com
e-mail: info@steckvaughn.com

Steck-Vaughn Staff, Author
Tim McEwen, President/CEO
Jeff Johnson, Dir Marketing Communications
Chris Lehmann, Team Coordinator

When reading is a struggle, academic success is even harder to achieve. Now you can put social studies and science curriculum content within reach of every student with this series. Designed specifically for limited readers.

1082 Ants in His Pants: Absurdities and Realities of Special Education

Peytral Publications
PO Box 1162
Minnetonka, MN   55345

952-949-8707
877-739-8725
FAX 952-906-9777
http://www.peytral.com
e-mail: help@peytral.com

Michael F Giangreco, Author
Kevin Ruelle, Illustrator
Peggy Hammeken, Owner/Publisher

With wit, humor and profound one liners, Michael Giagreco will transform your thinking as you take a lighter look at the sometimes comical and occasionally harsh truths in the ever changing field of special education. *$19.95*

128 pages
ISBN 1-890455-42-3

1083 AppleSeeds

Cobblestone Publishing - Division of Cane Pub. Co.
30 Grove Street
Peterborough, NH   03458

603-924-7209
800-821-0115
FAX 603-924-7380
http://www.cobblestonepub.com
e-mail: custsvc@cobblestone.mv.com

John S Olbrych, Publisher
Susan Buckley, Editor
Lou Waryncia, Editorial Director

A delightful way to develop the love of nonfiction reading. Each full color issue comes jam-packed with fascinating articles, photographs, illustrations, time lines, maps, activities and contests. *$29.95*

36 pages   9 times a year

1084   Basic Level Workbook for Aphasia

The Speech Bin
1965 25th Avenue
Vero Beach, FL   32960
772-770-0007
FAX 772-770-0006
http://www.speechbin.com
e-mail: info@speechbin.com

If you work with adolescents and adults with mild to moderate language deficits or limited, impaired, or emerging reading skills, this workbook is what you've been waiting for! The mMaterial is relevant to their lives, interests, experiences, and vocabulary. Item number W324. *$48.95*

1085   Beyond the Code

Educators Publishing Service
31 Smith Place
Cambridge, MA   02139
617-547-6706
800-225-5750
FAX 888-440-2665
http://www.epsbooks.com
e-mail: eps@epsbooks.com

Nancy M Hall, Author
Nick Gaehde, President

Beyond the Code gives beginning readers experience reading original stories as well as thinking about what they have read. This companion series follows the same phonetic progression as the frist 4 books of the popular Explode the Code program.

1086   Book Reports Plus

Harcourt Achieve
6277 Sea Harbor Drive
Orlando, FL   32887
800-531-5015
FAX 800-699-9459
http://www.steckvaughn.com
e-mail: info@steckvaughn.com

Steck-Vaughn Staff, Author
Tim McEwen, President/CEO
Jeff Johnson, Dir Marketing Communications
Chris Lehmann, Team Coordinator

Readers of all levels and abilities will be able to participate in activities that allow them to respond to literature in nontraditional ways. Six units include written and oral reports, dramatizations, and other expressive media. Multiple graphic organizers reinforce the habits of planning and preparing for reading, writing, and presenting.

96 pages

1087   Bridges to Reading Comprehension

Harcourt Achieve
6277 Sea Harbor Drive
Orlando, FL   32887
800-531-5015
FAX 800-699-9459
http://www.steckvaughn.com
e-mail: info@steckvaughn.com

Steck-Vaughn Staff, Author
Tim McEwen, President/CEO
Jeff Johnson, Dir Marketing Communications
Chris Lehmann, Team Coordinator

Lets your readers build skills in the context of high quality fiction and nonfiction selections.

1088   Careers

Harcourt Achieve
6277 Sea Harbor Drive
Orlando, FL   32887
800-531-5015
FAX 800-699-9459
http://www.steckvaughn.com
e-mail: info@steckvaughn.com

Heyworth, Author
Tim McEwen, President/CEO
Jeff Johnson, Dir Marketing Communications
Chris Lehmann, Team Coordinator

Develop reading skills while expanding students frames of reference in employment. A highly accessible preview of vocational, technical, and professional career opportunities on both today's and tomorrow's job market. Eight thematic units per title present overviews of careers in health, science, community service, agriculture and forestry circuitry, communications, entertainment and the creative industries.

1089   Claims to Fame

Educators Publishing Service
31 Smith Place
Cambridge, MA   02139
617-547-6706
800-225-5750
FAX 888-440-2665
http://www.epsbooks.com
e-mail: eps@epsbooks.com

Carol Einstein, Author
Nick Gaehde, President

The three exercises after each reading are tailored to the content of each story. In Thinking About What You Have Read, students check and extend their understanding of the story. Working with Words asks students to think about and experiment with vaious word meanings.

1090   Clues to Meaning

Educators Publishing Service
31 Smith Place
Cambridge, MA   02139
617-547-6706
800-225-5750
FAX 888-440-2665
http://www.epsbooks.com
e-mail: eps@epsbooks.com

Ann L Staman, Author

A versatile series which teaches beginning readers to use the sounds of letters as one strategy among many in learning to read.

1091   Connect-A-Card

The Speech Bin
1965 25th Avenue
Vero Beach, FL   32960   772-770-0007
                                FAX 772-770-0006
                          http://www.speechbin.com
                          e-mail: info@speechbin.com

How to teach your 6-12 year olds how to build tons of sentences, each using two illustrated phrase cards plus a common conjunction. Word cards feature four coordinating and, but, or, yet and eleven subordinating after, although, because, before, if, since, so that, unless, until, when, while conjunctions; clear black and white picture cards foster creative sentence construction. Item number Q974. *$35.00*

1092   Cosmic Reading Journey

Sunburst Technology
400 Columbus Avenue
Valhalla, NY   10595   914-747-3310
                              800-321-7511
                         FAX 914-747-4109
                         http://www.sunburst.com
                         e-mail: support@sunburst.com

This reading comprehension program provides meaningful summary and writing activities for the 100 books that early readers and their teachers love most.

1093   Creepy Cave Initial Consonants

Sunburst Technology
400 Columbus Avenue
Valhalla, NY   10595   914-747-3310
                              800-321-7511
                         FAX 914-747-4109
                         http://www.sunburst.com
                         e-mail: support@sunburst.com

Help your students develop letter recognition and phonemic awareness skills matching words with the same initial consonant letter in a Creepy Cave.

**1094   Curious Creatures Program:
        Owls-Spiders-Wolves-Snakes-Bats**

Curriculum Associates
PO Box 2001
North Billerica, MA   01862
                              800-225-0248
                         FAX 800-366-1158
                    http://www.curriculumassociates.com/
                    e-mail: ca@infocurriculumassociates.com
Louis Jame Taris, James Robert Taris, Author

Users of this award-winning multimedia program say awesome! They learn little known facts about animals that make most of us cringe. Designed to encourage reluctant readers in grades 4 and above, the program is also appropriate for on-level students in grades 2-3. Students learn the language of life science as they strengthen their reading and comprehension skills.

1095   Decoding Games

LinguiSystems
3100 4th Avenue
East Moline, IL   61244
                              800-776-4332
                         FAX 309-755-2377
                         TDY:800-933-8331
                    http://www.linguisystems.com
                    e-mail: service@linguisystems.com
Tina Sanford, Author
Linda Bowers, Owner
Rosemary Huisingh, Owner

Get three fun games in one handy case. These colorful games target tricky decoding skills your students need for strong reading skills. *$39.95*

Ages 6-10

1096   Dyslexia Training Program

Educators Publishing Service
31 Smith Place
Cambridge, MA   02139   617-547-6706
                               800-225-5750
                          FAX 888-440-2665
                          http://www.epsbooks.com
                          e-mail: eps@epsbooks.com
Texas Scottish Rite Hospital For Children, Author

Introduces reading and writing skills to dyslexic children through a two-year, cumulative series of daily one-hour videotaped lessons and accompanying student's books and teacher's guides.

1097   Earobics Step 1 Home Version

The Speech Bin
1965 25th Avenue
Vero Beach, FL   32960   772-770-0007
                                FAX 772-770-0006
                          http://www.speechbin.com
                          e-mail: info@speechbin.com

Step 1 offers hundreds of levels of play, appealing graphics, and entertaining music to train the critical auditory skills young children need for success in learning. Item number C481. *$59.00*

1098   Earobics Step 1 Specialist/Clinician Version

The Speech Bin
1965 25th Avenue
Vero Beach, FL   32960   772-770-0007
                                FAX 772-770-0006
                          http://www.speechbin.com
                          e-mail: info@speechbin.com

Earobics is a dazzling software that teaches phonological awareness and auditory processing. It systematically — anf enjoyably — trains these critical skills for development ages four to seven years. Item number C482. *$299.00*

1099 Earobics for Adolescents & Adults Home Version

The Speech Bin
1965 25th Avenue
Vero Beach, FL   32960   772-770-0007
                               FAX 772-770-0006
                               http://www.speechbin.com
                               e-mail: info@speechbin.com

Two users may use the Home Version which offers hundreds of levels of play, age-appropriate graphics, and entertaining music. This level is also available in a professional version for specialists and clinicians. Item number C485. *$59.00*

1100 Earobics for Adolescents & Adults Specialist/Clinician Version

The Speech Bin
1965 25th Avenue
Vero Beach, FL   32960   772-770-0007
                               FAX 772-770-0006
                               http://www.speechbin.com
                               e-mail: info@speechbin.com

The Clinician/Specialist Version has twelve name slots per workstation and goal writing and charting capability to save professional time. This level is also available in a Home Version limited to two users. Both versions offer hundreds of levels of play, appealing graphics, and entertaining music. Item number C486. *$299.00*

1101 Emergent Reader

Sunburst Technology
400 Columbus Avenue
Valhalla, NY   10595   914-747-3310
                               800-321-7511
                               FAX 914-747-4109
                               http://www.sunburst.com
                               e-mail: support@sunburst.com

This story-reading program supports the efforts of beginning readers by developing their sight word vocabularies.

1102 Every Child a Reader

Sunburst Technology
400 Columbus Avenue
Valhalla, NY   10595   914-747-3310
                               800-321-7511
                               FAX 914-747-4109
                               http://www.sunburst.com
                               e-mail: support@sunburst.com

Traditional reading strategies in a rich literary context. Designed to promote independent reading and develop oral and written language expression.

1103 Explode the Code

Educators Publishing Service
31 Smith Place
Cambridge, MA   02139   617-547-6706
                               800-225-5750
                               FAX 888-440-2665
                               http://www.epsbooks.com
                               e-mail: eps@epsbooks.com
Nancy M Hall, Rena Price, Author
Nick Gaehde, President

Explode the Code provides a sequential, systematic approach to phonics in which students blend sounds to build vocabulary and read words, phrases, sentences, and stories.

1104 Expressway to Reading

Harcourt Achieve
6277 Sea Harbor Drive
Orlando, FL   32887
                               800-531-5015
                               FAX 800-699-9459
                               http://www.steckvaughn.com
                               e-mail: info@steckvaughn.com
Davis, Author
Tim McEwen, President/CEO
Jeff Johnson, Dir Marketing Communications
Chris Lehmann, Team Coordinator

Now parents can make everyday activities fun exercises in reading. These skill building and practice activities turn ordinary errands into opportunities for progress.

1105 Funology Fables

The Speech Bin
1965 25th Avenue
Vero Beach, FL   32960   772-770-0007
                               FAX 772-770-0006
                               http://www.speechbin.com
                               e-mail: info@speechbin.com

Funology Fables targets specific phonemes and critical early concepts, such as matching, sequencing, opposites, comparisons, quantity, size, and space. Reproducible Talking Tales and activities include 32 six-part sequence stories. Item number 1484. *$45.00*

1106 Great Series

Harcourt Achieve
6277 Sea Harbor Drive
Orlando, FL   32887
                               800-531-5015
                               FAX 800-699-9459
                               http://www.steckvaughn.com
                               e-mail: info@steckvaughn.com
Billings, Author
Tim McEwen, President/CEO
Jeff Johnson, Dir Marketing Communicatins
Chris Lehmann, Team Coordinator

Human drama makes beginning reading worth the effort. Eight exciting titles build confidence as they build skills. Short, easy-to-read selections enable limited readers to succeed with material that matters.

1107 Handprints

Educators Publishing Service
31 Smith Place
Cambridge, MA   02139   617-547-6706
                               800-225-5750
                               FAX 888-440-2665
                               http://www.epsbooks.com
                               e-mail: eps@epsbooks.com
Ann L Staman, Author
Nick Gaehde, President

Handprints is a set of 50 storybooks and 4 workbooks for beginning readers in kindergarten and first grade. The storybooks increase in difficulty very gradually and encourage the new readers to use meaning, language, and print cues as they read.

1108 High Interest Nonfiction

Harcourt Achieve
6277 Sea Harbor Drive
Orlando, FL 32887

800-531-5015
FAX 800-699-9459
http://www.steckvaughn.com
e-mail: info@steckvaughn.com
Steck-Vaughn Staff, Author
Tim McEwen, President/CEO
Jeff Johnson, Dir Marketing Communications
Chris Lehmann, Team Coordinator

Whether you want to promote the joy of reading or the thrill of reading riveting nonfiction, this series does the job. Amazing stories of adventure, mystery, escape, disaster, rescue, challenge, firsts, and heroes capture and hold student interest.

1109 High Interest Nonfiction for Primary Grades

Harcourt Achieve
6277 Sea Harbor Drive
Orlando, FL 32887

800-531-5015
FAX 800-699-9459
http://www.steckvaughn.com
e-mail: info@steckvaughn.com
Steck-Vaughn Staff, Author
Tim McEwen, President/CEO
Jeff Johnson, Dir Marketing Communications
Chris Lehmann, Team Coordinator

Introduce students to a new type of reading in which the reader gains information! As students read nonfiction, they continue to develop and build reading comprehension skills and reading strategies. Fun and exciting stories are organized into four units that support the curriculum, such as people, animals, Earth and space , and more.

1110 High Noon Books

Academic Therapy Publications
20 Commercial Boulevard
Novato, CA 94949

415-883-3314
800-422-7249
FAX 888-287-9975
http://www.academictherapy.com
e-mail: sales@academictherapy.com

Serving the field of learning disabilities for 35 years. High-interest books for reluctant readers, phonic remedial reading lessons, streamlined Shakespeare, etc.

1111 I Can Read

Teddy Bear Press
3639 Midway Drive
San Diego, CA 92110

619-223-7311
FAX 619-255-2158
http://www.teddybearpress.net
e-mail: fparker@teddybearpress.net
Fran Parker, Author
Fran Parker, President

A series of 7 reading books and 7 workbooks, a set of 52 flashcards and teacher manual which uses a sight word approach to teach beginning readers. These teacher created books and workbooks present an easy to use beginning reading program which provides repetition, visual motor, visual discrimination and word comprehension activities. It was created to teach young, learning disabled children and has been successfully employed to teach beginning readers of varying ages and abilities. *$80.00*

1112 I Can See the ABC's

Teddy Bear Press
3639 Midway Drive
San Diego, CA 92110

619-223-7311
FAX 619-255-2158
http://www.teddybearpress.net
e-mail: fparker@teddybearpress.net
Fran Parker, Author
Fran Parker, President

A big 11x17 which contains the pre-primer words found in the I Can Read program while introducing the alphabet. *$20.00*

1113 Inclusion: Strategies for Working with Young Children

Peytral Publications
PO Box 1162
Minnetonka, MN 55345

952-949-8707
877-739-8725
FAX 952-906-9777
http://www.peytral.com
e-mail: help@peytral.com
Lorraine O Moore PhD, Author
Peggy Hammeken, Owner/Publisher

This exceptional resource is a gold mine of developmentally based ideas to help children between the ages of 3-7 or older students who may be developmentally delayed. This is a very practical and easy-to-use publication which is appropriate for early childhood teachers, K-2 general and special education teachers. *$21.95*

185 pages Educators
ISBN 1-890455-33-4

1114 Island Reading Journey

Sunburst Technology
400 Columbus Avenue
Valhalla, NY 10595

914-747-3310
800-321-7511
FAX 914-747-4109
http://www.sunburst.com
e-mail: support@sunburst.com

Enhance your reading program with meaningful summary and extension activities for 100 intermediate level books. Students read for meaning while they engage in activities that test for comprehension, build writing skills with reader response and essay questions, develop usage skills with cloze activities and improve vocabulary/word attack skills.

Classroom Resources/Reading

1115 It's a...Safari: Software

The Speech Bin
1965 25th Avenue
Vero Beach, FL   32960   772-770-0007
                              FAX 772-770-0006
                         http://www.speechbin.com
                         e-mail: info@speechbin.com

It's a Safari improves these critical skills: auditory processing; reading; spelling and comprehension. This unique Locu Tour language software presents a total of 100 short stories which describe the animals and people of Africa. Item number L190. *$29.00*

1116 Just for Me! Phonological Awareness

LinguiSystems
3100 4th Avenue
East Moline, IL   61244
                              800-776-4332
                              FAX 309-755-2377
                              TDY:800-933-8331
                         http://www.linguisystems.com
                         e-mail: service@linguisystems.com
Margaret Warner, Author
Linda Bowers, Owner
Rosemary Huisingh, Owner

Youngsters will love this cut, color, and create approach to sound awareness. You'll love how they begin to learn strong reading and literacy skills. The hands-on activities help students learn rhyming, syllables, compound words, beginning and ending sounds, short and long vowels, and beginning blends. *$24.95*

154 pages   Ages 3-6

1117 Kids Media Magic 2.0

Sunburst Technology
400 Columbus Avenue
Valhalla, NY   10595   914-747-3310
                              800-321-7511
                              FAX 914-747-4109
                         http://www.sunburst.com
                         e-mail: service@sunburst.com

The first multimedia word processor designed for young children. Help your child become a fluent reader and writer. The Rebus Bar automatically scrolls over 45 vocabulary words as students type.

1118 LD Teacher's IEP Companion

LinguiSystems
3100 4th Avenue
East Moline, IL   61244
                              800-776-4332
                              FAX 309-755-2377
                              TDY:800-933-8331
                         http://www.linguisystems.com
                         e-mail: service@linguisystems.com
Molly Lyle, Author
Linda Bowers, Owner
Rosemary Huisingh, Owner

These IEP goals are organized developmentally by skill area with individual objectives and classroom activity suggestions. Goals and objectives cover these academic areas: math; reading; writing; literacy concepts; attention skills; study skills; classroom behavior; social interaction; and transition skills. *$39.95*

169 pages   Ages 5-18

1119 Learning 100 Computerized Reading Skills

Harcourt Achieve
6277 Sea Harbor Drive
Orlando, FL   32887
                              800-531-5015
                              FAX 800-699-9459
                         http://www.steckvaughn.com
                         e-mail: info@steckvaughn.com
Steck-Vaughn Staff, Author
Tim McEwen, President/CEO
Jeff Johnson, Dir Marketing Communications
Chris Lehmann, Team Coordinator

Now you can determine each individual's precise reading level and mastery of individual comprehension skills automatically with this extraordinary accurate, easy-to-use program. Computer-administered cloze and criterion referenced tests yield the results you need as well as personalized prescriptions.

1120 Learning 100 Computerized Reading Skills: Inventory

Harcourt Achieve
6277 Sea Harbor Drive
Orlando, FL   32887
                              800-531-5015
                              FAX 800-699-9459
                         http://www.steckvaughn.com
                         e-mail: info@steckvaughn.com
Steck-Vaughn Staff, Author
Tim McEwen, President/CEO
Jeff Johnson, Dir Marketing Communications
Chris Lehmann, Team Coordinator

Planning and placement without the guesswork. Now you can determine each individual's precise reading level and mastery of individual comprehension skills automatically with this extraordinary accurate, easy-to-use program.

1121 Learning 100 Go Books

Harcourt Achieve
6277 Sea Harbor Drive
Orlando, FL   32887
                              800-531-5015
                              FAX 800-699-9459
                         http://www.steckvaughn.com
                         e-mail: info@steckvaughn.com
Steck-Vaughn Staff, Author
Tim McEwen, President/CEO
Jeff Johnson, Dir Marketing Communications
Chris Lehmann, Team Coordinator

Go Books offer readers at all levels the opportunity to experience reading success with real-life content in an enjoyable environment. Softcover anthologies offer variety. Each book contains stories dealing with real-life situations in both fiction and nonfiction presentations.

1122 Learning 100 Language Clues Software

Harcourt Achieve
6277 Sea Harbor Drive
Orlando, FL 32887

800-531-5015
FAX 800-699-9459
http://www.steckvaughn.com
e-mail: info@steckvaughn.com

Steck-Vaughn Staff, Author
Tim McEwen, President/CEO
Jeff Johnson, Dir Marketing Communications
Chris Lehmann, Team Coordinator

When learners have control over their instruction, they are motivated to succeed. This program lets users customize instruction to their individual needs. They can control the speed of presentation, the number of times a word is used, and the length of time each word appears.

1123 Learning 100 System

Harcourt Achieve
6277 Sea Harbor Drive
Orlando, FL 32887

800-531-5015
FAX 800-699-9459
http://www.steckvaughn.com
e-mail: info@steckvaughn.com

Steck-Vaughn Staff, Author
Tim McEwen, President/CEO
Jeff Johnson, Dir Marketing Communications
Chris Lehmann, Team Coordinator

Deliver research-based reading strategies in the context of real-life stories. If your readers need extra motivation, this program is a must. Compelling, relevant stories coupled with audio instruction build vocabulary, comprehension, and confidence. Built on findings from 40 years of reading research, Learning 100 Reading Strategies is a proven performer for low-level readers.

1124 Learning 100 Write and Read

Harcourt Achieve
6277 Sea Harbor Drive
Orlando, FL 32887

800-531-5015
FAX 800-699-9459
http://www.steckvaughn.com
e-mail: info@steckvaughn.com

Steck-Vaughn Staff, Author
Tim McEwen, President/CEO
Jeff Johnson, Dir Marketing Communicatins
Chris Lehmann, Team Coordinator

Helps learners succeed with reading and writing opportunities they encounter every day. Learners improve grammar, mechanics, usage, style, and paragraphing skills through a proven program based on more than 40 years of research.

1125 Let's Go Read 1: An Island Adventure

Riverdeep
500 Redmond Boulevard
Novato, CA 94947

415-763-4700
800-362-2890
FAX 415-763-4385
http://www.edmark.com
e-mail: info@riverdeep.net

Barry O'Callaghan, Chairman/CEO
Simon Calver, COO
John Rim, CFO

Take off with Robby the Raccoon, Emily the Squirrel and the Reading Rover on an exciting adventure to an island inhabited by the alphabet. Motivated by the delight of mastering new challenges, your child will play through more than 35 fun activties that install and reinforce the essential skills for successful reading.

1126 Let's Go Read 2: An Ocean Adventure

Riverdeep
500 Redmond Boulevard
Novato, CA 94947

415-763-4700
800-362-2890
FAX 415-763-4385
http://www.edmark.com
e-mail: info@riverdeep.net

Barry O'Callaghan, Chairman/CEO
Simon Calver, COO
John Rim, CFO

Building upon your child's mastery of letters, Let's Go Read: 2 explores how letters combine to form words, and how words combine to express meaning. Dozens of captivating, skill-building activities teach your child the skills to sound out, recognize, build and comprehend hundreds of new words. It's an endlessly fun voyage toward reading fluency!

1127 Let's Read

Educators Publishing Service
31 Smith Place
Cambridge, MA 02139

617-547-6706
800-225-5750
FAX 888-440-2665
http://www.epsbooks.com
e-mail: eps@epsbooks.com

Leonard Bloomfield, Clarence and Robert
Barnhart, Author
Nick Gaehde, President

Using a linguistic approach to teaching reading skills, this series emphasizes relationship of spelling to sound, presenting the concepts together, and providing nine reading books and accompanying workbooks for practice. Provides classroom directions and suggestions for supplementary exercises.

1128 Lighthouse Low Vision Products

Lighthouse International
111 East 59th Street
New York, NY 10022

212-821-9740
800-829-0500
FAX 212-821-9707
http://www.lighthouse.org
e-mail: info@lighthouse.com

Wendy Maurice, Managing Director
Barbara Silverstone, President/CEO

Helping people who are blind or partially sighted to lead independent and productive lives.

1129 Linamood Program (LIPS Clinical Version):Phoneme Sequencing Program for Reading, Spelling,Speech

LinguiSystems
3100 4th Avenue
East Moline, IL 61244

800-776-4332
FAX 309-755-2377
TDY:800-933-8331
http://www.linguisystems.com
e-mail: service@linguisystems.com
Patricia Linamood, Phyllis Linamood, Author
Linda Bowers, Owner
Rosemary Huisingh, Owner

Help your students develop phoneme awareness for competence in reading, spelling, and speech. This multisensory program meets the needs of the many children and adults who don't develop phonemic awareness through traditional methods. *$247.00*

Birth-Adult

1130 Mastering Reading Series

AGS Publishing
4201 Woodland Road
Circle Pines, MN 55014

651-287-7220
800-328-2560
FAX 800-471-8457
http://www.agsnet.com
e-mail: agsmail@agsnet.com
Karen Dahlen, Associate Director
Matt Keller, Marketing Manager

With an interest level of High School through Adult, and a reading level of Grade 3-7, this series will help your students build reading and life skills while learning about specific occupations. Each series features four books of increasing complexity in reading level, allowing learners to work at their own pace to master essential reading skills. The five series titles are: Office Work; Health Care; Commercial Trucking; Food Service and Manufacturing.

1131 Megawords

Educators Publishing Service
31 Smith Place
Cambridge, MA 02139

617-547-6706
800-225-5750
FAX 888-440-2665
http://www.epsbooks.com
e-mail: eps@epsbooks.com
Kristin Johnson, Polly Baird, Author
Nick Gaehde, President

A series with a systematic, multisensory approach to learning the longer words encountered from fourth grade on. Students first work with syllables, then combine the syllables into words, use them in context, and work to increase their reading and spelling proficiency. Teacher's Guide and Answer Key available.

1132 Mike Mulligan & His Steam Shovel

Sunburst Technology
400 Columbus Avenue
Valhalla, NY 10595

914-747-3310
800-321-7511
FAX 914-747-4109
http://www.sunburst.com
e-mail: service@sunburst.com

This CD-ROM version of the Caldecott classic lets students experience interactive book reading and participate in four skills-based extension activities that promote memory, matching, sequencing, listening, pattern recognition and map reading skills.

1133 More Primary Phonics

Educators Publishing Service
31 Smith Place
Cambridge, MA 02139

617-547-6706
800-225-5750
FAX 888-440-2665
http://www.epsbooks.com
e-mail: eps@epsbooks.com
Barbara Makar, Author
Nick Gaehde, President

Reinforces and expands skills developed in Primary Phonics. Workbooks and storybooks contain the same phonetic elements, sight words and phonetic sequences as workbooks 1 and 2.

1134 Mythopoly

LinguiSystems
3100 4th Avenue
East Moline, IL 61244

800-776-4332
FAX 309-755-2377
TDY:800-933-8331
http://www.linguisystems.com
e-mail: service@linguisystems.com
Mike LoGiudice, Carolyn LoGiudice, Author
Linda Bowers, Owner
Rosemary Huisingh, Owner

Boost your student's reading and listening comprehension skills with this wonderful game. Engaging stories from classical mythology help students understand references to mythological concepts in literature and everyday life. The reading level of the 25 stories ranges from grades 3.5 to 5.2. *$44.95*

Ages 10-18

1135 New Way: Learning with Literature

Harcourt Achieve
6277 Sea Harbor Drive
Orlando, FL 32887

800-531-5015
FAX 800-699-9459
http://www.steckvaughn.com
e-mail: info@steckvaughn.com
Steck-Vaughn Staff, Author
Tim McEwen, President/CEO
Jeff Johnson, Dir Marketing Communications
Chris Lehmann, Team Coordinator

Do you need additional literature your primary readers can read independently? Steck-Vaughn offers a large collection of developmentally appropriate titles at attractive prices.

1136 Next Stop

Educators Publishing Service
31 Smith Place
Cambridge, MA 02139

617-547-6706
800-225-5750
FAX 888-440-2665
http://www.epsbooks.com
e-mail: eps@epsbooks.com

Tanya Auger, Author
Nick Gaehde, President

Increase reading and language skills while exploring different literacy genres. This series is intended for students who are ready to move beyond phonetically controlled readers to the nest stop-real chapter books that will help prepare them for the more challenging literature they will encounter in later grades.

1137 PATHS

The Speech Bin
1965 25th Avenue
Vero Beach, FL 32960

772-770-0007
FAX 772-770-0006
http://www.speechbin.com
e-mail: info@speechbin.com

PATHS gives you a step-by-step comprehensive program for students who have experienced difficulty in academic learning. It targets skills critical for academic achievements: phonological awareness; phonemic relationships; phonemic processing; and listening and memory. Item number 1491. *$21.95*

1138 Patterns of English Spelling

AVKO Dyslexia Research Foundation
3084 W Willard Road
Clio, MI 48420

810-686-9283
FAX 810-686-1101
http://www.avko.org
e-mail: avkoemail@aol.com

Don McCabe, Author
Don McCabe, Research Director

Use the index to locate the page upon which you can find all the words that share the same patterns. If you look up the word cat, you will find all the pages where all the at words are located. If you look up the word precious you will find all the words ending in cious. There are ten volumes which can be purchased all together or separately. *$119.95*

Whole set

1139 Phonemic Awareness: The Sounds of Reading

Peytral Publication
PO Box 1162
Minnetonka, MN 55345

952-949-8707
877-739-8725
FAX 952-906-9777
http://www.peytral.com
e-mail: help@peytral.com

Victoria Groves Scott, Author

In this dynamic new video, Dr. Scott demonstrates the principal components of phonemic awareness: identification; comparison; segmentation; blending and rhyming. This video will help you to better understand phonemic awareness training and will show you how to apply these components not only to the reading curriculum but to all subjects through the school day. Filmed in actual classroom settings. *$59.95*

25 minute video
ISBN 1-890455-29-6

1140 Phonological Awareness Kit

LinguiSystems
3100 4th Avenue
East Moline, IL 61244

800-776-4332
FAX 309-755-2377
TDY:800-933-8331
http://www.linguisystems.com
e-mail: service@linguisystems.com

Carolyn Robertson, Wanda Salter, Author
Linda Bowers, Owner
Rosemary Huisingh, Owner

Help your students learn to use phonological information to process oral and written language with this fantastic kit. Written by an SLP and special educator, this best-seller links sound awareness, oral language, and early reading and writing skills. The kit uses a multisensory approach to ensure success for all learning styles. *$69.95*

115 pages   Ages 5-8

1141 Poetry in Three Dimensions: Reading, Writing and Critical Thinking Skills through Poetry

Educators Publishing Service
31 Smith Place
Cambridge, MA 02139

617-547-6706
800-225-5750
FAX 888-440-2665
http://www.epsbooks.com
e-mail: eps@epsbooks.com

Carol Clark, Alison Draper, Author
Nick Gaehde, President

Help your students improve their reading comprehension and writing through the study of poetry in this collection of multicultural poems. With poems and questions on facing pages, students are encouraged to annotate the text of the poem and to go back to the text to respond to the questions.

1142 Polar Express

Sunburst Technology
400 Columbus Avenue
Valhalla, NY 10595

914-747-3310
800-321-7511
FAX 914-747-4109
http://www.sunburst.com
e-mail: service@sunburst.com

Share the magic and enchantment of the holiday season with this CD-ROM version of Chris Van Allsburg's Caldecott-winning picture book.

1143 Prehistoric Creaures Then & Now: Steadwell

Harcourt Achieve
6277 Sea Harbor Drive
Orlando, FL   32887

800-531-5015
FAX 800-699-9459
http://www.steckvaughn.com
e-mail: info@steckvaughn.com

Steck-Vaughn Staff, Author
Tim McEwen, President/CEO
Jeff Johnson, Dir Marketing Communications
Chris Lehmann, Team Coordinator

When reading is a struggle, academic success is even harder to achieve. Now you can put social studies and science curriculum content within reach of every students with Steadwell Books — the series designed specifically for limited readers. Attention-getting photos and informative illustrations, maps, and time lines communicate the social studies and science concepts found in the text.

1144 Primary Phonics

Educators Publishing Service
31 Smith Place
Cambridge, MA   02139

617-547-6706
800-225-5750
FAX 888-440-2665
http://www.epsbooks.com
e-mail: eps@epsbooks.com

Barbara Makar, Author
Nick Gaehde, President

This revised program of storybooks and coordinated workbooks teaches reading for grades K-2. There is a set of ten storybooks to go with each of the first five workbooks. A Primary Phonics Picture Dictionary contains 2,500 commonly used words, including most of the words in the series. This series' individualized nature permits students to progress at their own speed. Teacher's manual available.

1145 Racing Through Time on a Flying Machine

Harcourt Achieve
6277 Sea Harbor Drive
Orlando, FL   32887

800-531-5015
FAX 800-699-9459
http://www.steckvaughn.com
e-mail: info@steckvaughn.com

Elizabeth Werley-Prieto, Mike Lester, Author
Tim McEwen, President/CEO
Jeff Johnson, Dir Marketing Communications
Chris Lehmann, Team Coordinator

Traveling through time to visit Thomas Edison and Leonardo da Vinci inspires young Keene to become an inventor himself.

1146 Read On! Plus

Sunburst Technology
400 Columbus Avenue
Valhalla, NY   10595

914-747-3310
800-321-7511
FAX 914-747-4109
http://www.sunburst.com
e-mail: support@sunburst.com

Promote skills and strategies that improve reading comprehension, and build appreciation for literature and the written word.

1147 Read-A-Bit

LinguiSystems
3100 4th Avenue
East Moline, IL   61244

800-776-4332
FAX 309-755-2377
TDY:800-933-8331
http://www.linguisystems.com
e-mail: service@linguisystems.com

Dagmar Kafka, Author
Linda Bowers, Owner
Rosemary Huisingh, Owner

Get 15 games in one box! Six decks of cards with different levels of reading difficulty work with and without the colorful game board to give you plenty of flexibility. You'll work through a hierarchy of reading skills from primer to grade 3. Students practice consonants, vowels, controlled R sounds, sight words, and more. *$41.95*

Ages 5-9

1148 Reader's Quest I

Sunburst Technology
400 Columbus Avenue
Valhalla, NY   10595

914-747-3310
800-321-7511
FAX 914-747-4109
http://www.sunburst.com
e-mail: support@sunburst.com

These reading workshops provide students with direct reading instruction, interactive practice activities, and practical strategies to ensure reading success.

1149 Reader's Quest II

Sunburst Technology
400 Columbus Avenue
Valhalla, NY   10595

914-747-3310
800-321-7511
FAX 914-747-4109
http://www.sunburst.com
e-mail: support@sunburst.com

These reading workshops provide students with direct reading instruction, interactive practice activities, and practical strategies to ensure reading success.

1150   Reading Comprehension Bundle

Sunburst Technology
400 Columbus Avenue
Valhalla, NY   10595   914-747-3310
                             800-321-7511
                         FAX 914-747-4109
                    http://www.sunburst.com
                    e-mail: support@sunburst.com

This collection for the intermediate-level classroom develops the skills students need to read for meaning and understanding.

1151   Reading Comprehension Game Intermediate

LinguiSystems
3100 4th Avenue
East Moline, IL   61244
                            800-776-4332
                        FAX 309-755-2377
                        TDY:800-933-8331
                http://www.linguisystems.com
                e-mail: service@linguisystems.com
*Linda Bowers, Rosemary Huisingh, Carolyn
LoGiudice, Author
Linda Bowers, Owner
Rosemary Huisingh, Owner*

This game gives you fun, repetitive practice in three essential reading comprehension skills. The first is Reading for Details including cloze, referents, sequencing, describing, and more! The second is Reading for Understanding including main idea, paraphrasing, context clues, defining, and more. The thrid area is Going Beyond including making references, predicting, and making associations. *$44.95*

Ages 12-18

1152   Reading Comprehension Materials (Volume 5)

The Speech Bin
1965 25th Avenue
Vero Beach, FL   32960   772-770-0007
                         FAX 772-770-0006
                    http://www.speechbin.com
                    e-mail: info@speechbin.com

Three hundred and fifty-one pages of practical large-print materials give older children and adults practice thinking about words, following directions, and telling what/who stories, stories in part, short stories, and more. Stories are either high-interest factual stories or relate to everyday experiences. Tasks are versatile and a variety of difficulties for maximum use. Item number V372. *$49.95*

1153   Reading Comprehension Series

Harcourt Achieve
6277 Sea Harbor Drive
Orlando, FL   32887
                            800-531-5015
                        FAX 800-699-9459
                    http://www.steckvaughn.com
                    e-mail: info@steckvaughn.com
*Resnick, Author
Tim McEwen, President/CEO
Jeff Johnson, Dir Marketing Communications
Chris Lehmann, Team Coordinator*

Develop basic reading skills! Short stories sustain interest! Brief, captivating selections feature children and animals in contemporary situations. Exercises build comprehension skills! Exercises cover all aspects of reading comprehension, including main idea, sequencing, facts, and inferences.

1154   Reading Comprehension in Varied Subject Matter

Educators Publishing Service
31 Smith Plaza
Cambridge, MA   02139   617-547-6706
                             800-225-5750
                         FAX 888-440-2665
                    http://www.epsbooks.com
                    e-mail: eps@epsbooks.com
*Jane Ervin, Author
Nick Gaehde, President*

Ten workbooks that present a wide range of people and situations with new reading selections, new vocabulary, and a new writing exercise. Each book contains 31 selections in the subject areas of social studies, science, literature, mathematics, philosophy, logic, language, and the arts.

1155   Reading Pen

Wizcom Technologies
257 Great Road
Acton, MA   01720   978-635-5357
                             888-777-0552
                         FAX 978-929-9228
                    http://www.wizcomtech.com
                    e-mail: usasales@wizcomtech.com

Portable assitive reading device that reads words aloud and can be used anywhere. Scans a word from printed text, displays the word in large characters, reads the word aloud from built-in speaker or ear phones and defines the word with the press of a button. Displays syllables, keeps a history of scanned words, adjustable for left or right-handed use. Includes a tutorial video and audio cassette. Not recommended for persons with low vision or impaired fine motor control. *$279.00*

1156   Reading Power Modules Books

Harcourt Achieve
6277 Sea Harbor Drive
Orlando, FL   32887
                            800-531-5015
                        FAX 800-699-9459
                    http://www.steckvaughn.com
                    e-mail: info@steckvaughn.com
*Tim McEwen, President/CEO
Jeff Johnson, Dir Marketing Communications
Chris Lehmann, Team Coordinator*

Supplementary reading based on 4 decades of reading research. Companion books give students and teachers a choice of formats. High interest stories reinforce reading comprehension skills while building vocabulary, spelling skills, reading fluency, and speed.

1157 Reading Power Modules Software

Harcourt Achieve
6277 Sea Harbor Drive
Orlando, FL 32887

800-531-5015
FAX 800-699-9459
http://www.steckvaughn.com
e-mail: info@steckvaughn.com

Steck-Vaughn Staff, Author
Tim McEwen, President/CEO
Jeff Johnson, Dir Marketing Communications
Chris Lehmann, Team Coordinator

This program provides practice and reinforcement of reading comprehension skills while building spelling and reading skills and vocabulary. Exercises include requiring learners to type the new vocabulary word after it flashes on the screen, fill-in-the-blank exercises, timed reading exercises, comprehension checks, vocabulary review in multiple-choice format, and vocabulary games.

1158 Reading Readiness

Harcourt Achieve
6277 Sea Harbor Drive
Orlando, FL 32887

800-531-5015
FAX 800-699-9459
http://www.steckvaughn.com
e-mail: info@steckvaughn.com

Steck Vaughn Staff, Author
Tim McEwen, President/CEO
Jeff Johnson, Dir Marketing Communications
Chris Lehmann, Team Coordinator

Build a firm foundation for reading success with thematic workbooks that introduce readiness skills through literature. Fun-filled nursery rhymes, riddles, and tongue twisters focus on the key words and sound/letter patterns that precede decoding skills.

1159 Reading Skills Bundle

Sunburst Technology
400 Columbus Avenue
Valhalla, NY 10595

914-747-3310
800-321-7511
FAX 914-747-4109
http://www.sunburst.com
e-mail: support@sunburst.com

Teach beginning reading with teacher-developed programs that sequentially present phonics, phonemic awareness, word recognition, and reading comprehension concepts.

1160 Reading Who? Reading You!

Sunburst Technology
400 Columbus Avenue
Valhalla, NY 10595

914-747-3310
800-321-7511
FAX 914-747-4109
http://www.sunburst.com
e-mail: support@sunburst.com

Teach beginning reading skills effectively with phonics instruction built into engaging games and puzzles that have children asking for more.

1161 Reading and Writing Workbook

Therapro
225 Arlington Street
Framingham, MA 01702

508-872-9494
800-257-5376
FAX 508-875-2062
http://www.theraproducts.com
e-mail: info@theraproducts.com

Therapro Staff, Author
Karen Conrad, President

Writing checks and balancing a checkbook, copying words and sentences, and writing messages and notes. Helps with recognition and understanding of calendars, phone books and much more. *$10.50*

1162 Reading for Content

Educators Publishing Service
31 Smith Place
Cambridge, MA 02139

617-547-6706
800-225-5750
FAX 888-440-2665
http://www.epsbooks.com
e-mail: eps@epsbooks.com

Carol Einstein, Author
Nick Gaehde, President

Reading for Content is a series of 4 books designed to help students improve their reading comprehension skills. Each book contains 43 pasages followed by 4 questions. Two questions ask for a recall of main ideas, and two ask the student to draw conclusions from what they have just read.

1163 Reading for Job and Personal Use

AGS Publishing
4201 Woodland Road
Circle Pines, MN 55014

651-287-7220
800-328-2560
FAX 800-471-8457
http://www.agsnet.com
e-mail: agsmail@agsnet.com

Joyce Hing-McGowan, Author
Karen Dahlen, Associate Director
Matt Keller, Marketing Manager

The practical, real-life exercises in these texts teach students how to read and comprehend catalogs, training manuals, letters and memos, signs, reports, charts, and more. *$14.95*

1164 Ready to Read

Educators Publishing Service
31 Smith Place
Cambridge, MA 02139

617-547-6706
800-225-5750
FAX 888-440-2665
http://www.epsbooks.com
e-mail: eps@epsbooks.com

Phyllis Bertin, Eileen Perlman, Author
Nick Gaehde, President

Ready to Read contains activities for teaching sound/symbol association, blending, word recognition, reading, spelling and handwriting, including individual words, phrases, sentences, and connected text.

1165 Reasoning & Reading Series

Educators Publishing Service
31 Smith Place
Cambridge, MA   02139   617-547-6706
800-225-5750
FAX 888-440-2665
http://www.epsbooks.com
e-mail: eps@epsbooks.com
Joanne Carlisle, Author
Nick Gaehde, President

These workbooks develop basic language and thinking skills that build the foundation for reading comprehension. Exercises reinforce reading as a critical reasoning activity. Many exercises encourage students to come up with their own response in instances where there is no single correct answer. In other cases, exercises lend themselves to students working collaboratively to see how many different answers satisfy a question.

1166 Right into Reading: A Phonics-Based Reading and Comprehension Program

Educators Publishing Service
31 Smith Place
Cambridge, MA   02139   617-547-6706
800-225-5750
FAX 888-440-2665
http://www.epsbooks.com
e-mail: eps@epsbooks.com
Jane Ervin, Author
Nick Gaehde, President

Right into Reading introduces phonics skills in a carefully ordered sequence of bite-size lessons so that students can progress easily and successfully from one reading level to the next. The stories and selections are unusually diverse and interactive.

1167 Roots, Prefixes & Suffixes

Sunburst Technology
400 Columbus Avenue
Valhalla, NY   10595   914-747-3310
800-321-7511
FAX 914-747-4109
http://www.sunburst.com
e-mail: support@sunburst.com
Students learn to decode difficult and more complex words as they engage in six activities where they construct and dissect words with roots, prefixes and suffixes.

1168 See Me Add

Teddy Bear Press
3639 Midway Drive
San Diego, CA   92110   619-223-7311
FAX 619-255-2158
http://www.teddybearpress.net
e-mail: fparker@teddybearpress.net
Fran Parker, Author
Fran Parker, President

Introduces the concept of addition using simple story problems and the basic sight word vocabulary found in the I Can Read and Reading Is Fun programs. *$20.00*

1169 See Me Subtract

Teddy Bear Press
3639 Midway Drive
San Diego, CA   92110   619-223-7311
FAX 619-255-2158
http://www.teddybearpress.net
e-mail: fparker@teddybearpress.net
Fran Parker, Author
Fran Parker, President

Introduces the concept of subtraction using simple story problems. *$20.00*

1170 Short Classics

Harcourt Achieve
6277 Sea Harbor Drive
Orlando, FL   32887
800-531-5015
FAX 800-699-9459
http://www.steckvaughn.com
e-mail: info@steckvaughn.com
Steck-Vaughn Staff, Author
Tim McEwen, President/CEO
Jeff Johnson, Dir Marketing Communications
Chris Lehmann, Team Cooridnator

These shortened easy-to-read presentations use carefully controlled vocabulary while maintaining the style of the original authors. Your students can broaden their horizons and build self-esteem as they succeed with literary classics.

1171 Soaring Scores CTB: TerraNova Reading and Language Arts

Harcourt Achieve
6277 Sea Harbor Drive
Orlando, FL   32887
800-531-5015
FAX 800-699-9459
http://www.steckvaughn.com
e-mail: info@steckvaughn.com
Steck-Vaughn Staff, Author
Tim McEwen, President/CEO
Jeff Johnson, Dir Marketing Communciations
Chris Lehmann, Team Coordinator

Through a combination of targeted instructional practice and testing-taking tips, these workbooks help students build better skills and improve CTB-TerraNova tests scores. Initial lessons address reading comprehension and language arts. The authentic practice test mirrors the CTB's format and content.

1172 Soaring Scores on the ISAT Reading and Writing

Harcourt Achieve
6277 Sea Harbor Drive
Orlando, FL   32887

800-531-5015
FAX 800-699-9459
http://www.steckvaughn.com
e-mail: info@steckvaughn.com

Steck-Vaughn Staff, Author
Tim McEwen, President/CEO
Jeff Johnson, Dir Marketing Communications
Chris Lehmann, Team Cooridnator

Highly targeted instruction and practice tests help students approach the ISAT strategically and confidently. Writing prompts ask students to write a persuasive, expository, or narrative essay. Modeled questions practice both multiple-choice and open-ended queries.

1173 Sounds Abound Program

LinguiSystems
3100 4th Avenue
East Moline, IL   61244

800-776-4332
FAX 309-755-2377
TDY:800-933-8331
http://www.linguisystems.com
e-mail: service@linguisystems.com

Orna Lenchner PhD, Blanche Podhajski PhD, Author
Linda Bowers, Owner
Rosemary Huisingh, Owner

This program boosts emergent reading and beginning literacy through a hierarchy of skills. Activities target rhyming, syllables, sound recognition, sound production, sound blending, phoneme-grapheme correspondence, and more phonological skills. *$109.95*

112 pages   Ages 4-8

1174 Source for Aphasia Therapy

LinguiSystems
3100 4th Avenue
East Moline, IL   61244

800-776-4332
FAX 309-755-2377
TDY:800-933-8331
http://www.linguisystems.com
e-mail: service@linguisystems.com

Lisa A Arnold, Author
Linda Bowers, Owner
Rosemary Huisingh, Owner

Therapy exercises are organized into three groups: receptive language, reading comprehension, and expressive language. Each section is organized in a hierarchy to meet each client's individual needs. You'll cover imitating gestures, following commands, understanding symbols and signs, naming and describing objects, and much more! *$41.95*

183 pages   Adults

1175 Source for Dyslexia and Dysgraphia

LinguiSystems
3100 4th Avenue
East Moline, IL   61244

800-776-4332
FAX 309-755-2377
TDY:800-933-8331
http://www.linguisystems.com
e-mail: service@linguisystems.com

Regina G Richards, Author
Linda Bowers, Owner
Rosemary Huisingh, Owner

From diagnosis to developmental strategies to how-to techniques, this is the definitivie SOURCE on students who have difficulty with the reading and writing process. *$41.95*

308 pages   Ages 6-18

1176 Source for Early Literacy Development

LinguiSystems
3100 4th Avenue
East Moline, IL   61244

800-776-4332
FAX 309-755-2377
TDY:800-933-8331
http://www.linguisystems.com
e-mail: service@linguisystems.com

Linda K Crowe, Sara S Reichmuth, Author
Linda Bowers, Owner
Rosemary Huisingh, Owner

This great resource gives you the latest information on children's emergent reading and writing from birth through age eight. You'll also get helpful strategies to facilitate literacy development for future academic success! *$41.95*

151 pages   Birth-8

1177 Specialized Program Individualizing Reading Excellence (SPIRE)

Educators Publishing Service
31 Smith Place
Cambridge, MA   02139

800-225-5750
FAX 207-985-3878
http://www.espbooks.com
e-mail: spire@espbooks.com

Sheila Clark-Edmonds, President

SPIRE is a comprehensive multisensory reading and language arts program for students with learning differences.

1178 Starting Comprehension

Educators Publishing Service
31 Smith Place
Cambridge, MA   02139

617-547-6706
800-225-5750
FAX 888-440-2665
http://www.epsbooks.com
e-mail: eps@epsbooks.com

Ann L Staman, Author
Nick Gaehde, President

A reading series of 12 workbooks that develops essential comprehension skills at the earliest reading level. It is divided into two different strands, one for students who have a strong visual sense, the other for those who learn sounds easily. Vocabulary introduced within context of exercises, using most of the words in the books. Student relates the details of the passage to the main idea.

1179 Stories and More: Animal Friends

Riverdeep
500 Redmond Boulevard
Novato, CA   94947

415-763-4700
800-362-2890
FAX 415-763-4385
http://www.elmark.com
e-mail: info@riverdeep.net

Barry O'Callaghan, Chairman/CEO
Simon Calver, COO
John Rim, CFO

Stories and More: Animal Friends features three well-known stories — The Gunnywolf, The Trek, and Owl and the Moon — with engaging activities that strengthen students reading comprehension. A scaffolding of pre-reading, reading, and post-reading activities for each story helps kindergarten and 1st grade students practice prediction and sequencing skills; appreciate the importance of character and setting; and respond to literature through writing, drawing, and speaking. *$ 69.95*

1180 Stories and More: Time and Place

Riverdeep
500 Redwod Boulevard
Novato, CA   97947

415-763-4700
800-362-2890
FAX 415-763-4385
http://www.edmark.com
e-mail: info@riverdeep.net

Barry O'Callaghan, Chairman/CEO
Simon Calver, COO
John Rim, CFO

Stories and More: Time and Place combines three well-loved stories — The House on Maple Street, Roxaboxen, and Galimoto — with — engaging activities that strengthen students' reading comprehension. In these books, the setting plays a primary role. Second and third grade students learn the importance of time, culture, and place in our lives.

1181 Success Stories 1, 2

Educators Publishing Service
31 Smith Plaza
Cambridge, MA   02139

617-547-6706
800-225-5750
FAX 888-440-2665
http://www.epsbooks.com
e-mail: eps@epsbooks.com

Elizabeth H Butcher, Nancy A Simonetti, Author
Nick Gaehde, President

These workbooks contain high-interest phonetically structured stories. Each book contains 60 stories, each story focusing on an individual grapheme or syllable pattern.

1182 Take Me Home Pair-It Books

Harcourt Achieve
6277 Sea Harbor Drive
Orlando, FL   32887

800-531-5015
FAX 800-699-9459
http://www.steckvaughn.com
e-mail: info@steckvaughn.com

Park, Author
Tim McEwen, President/CEO
Jeff Johnson, Dir Marketing Communications
Chris Lehmann, Team Coordinator

Make reading time a family favorite. Our most popular Pair-It Book titles in convenient take-home packages make it easy to get parents involved in reinforcing reading.

1183 Taking Your Camera To...Steadwell

Harcourt Achieve
6277 Sea Harbor Drive
Orlando, FL   32887

800-531-5015
FAX 800-699-9459
http://www.steckvaughn.com
e-mail: info@steckvaughn.com

Park, Author
Tim McEwen, President/CEO
Jeff Johnson, Dir Marketing Communications
Chris Lehmann, Team Coordinator

Give limited readers unlimited access to major countries! Each title devotes a spread to the land, the people, major cities, lifestyles, places to visit, government and religion, earning a living, sports and school, food and holidays, quick facts, statistics and maps, and the future.

1184 That's LIFE! Reading Comprehension

LinguiSystems
3100 4th Avenue
East Moline, IL   61244

800-776-4332
FAX 309-755-2377
TDY:800-933-8331
http://www.linguisystems.com
e-mail: service@linguisystems.com

LinguiSystems Staff, Author
Linda Bowers, Owner
Rosemary Huisingh, Owner

Get two programs in one. Each high-interest reading passage is written at an upper and lower reading level to meet your students' needs. These lessons are great for individuals or classroom istruction. Each story is followed by thought-provoking comprehension questions, including multiple choice, fill-in-the-blank, true/false, and critical thinking questions. *$37.95*

191 pages   Ages 11-18

1185   Tic-Tac-Read and Match: Fun Phonics Games

LinguiSystems
3100 4th Avenue
East Moline, IL   61244

800-776-4332
FAX 309-755-2377
TDY:800-933-8331
http://www.linguisystems.com
e-mail: service@linguisystems.com

Carol A Vaccariello, Author
Linda Bowers, Owner
Rosemary Huisingh, Owner

Two-books set offers fun activities to reinforce reading. Use the whole page to play Read and Match. Use the nine shaded areas to play Tic-Tac-Read. Students move progressively through a hierarchy of phonics skills as they read the words aloud while playing. *$38.90*

160 pages   Ages 7-14

1186   Transition Stage 2-3

Harcourt Achieve
6277 Sea Harbor Drive
Orlando, FL   32887

800-531-5015
FAX 800-699-9459
http://www.steckvaughn.com
e-mail: info@steckvaughn.com

Steck-Vaughn Staff, Author
Tim McEwen, President/CEO
Jeff Johnson, Dir Marketing Communications
Chris Lehmann, Team Coordinator

A series of 20 books, each containing 16 pages, that provide readers with a gradual transition into early fluency. All stories are available on audio cassette, and four are available in big book format.

1187   Understanding Me

Churchill School
1035 Price School Lane
Saint Louis, MO   63124

314-997-4343
FAX 314-997-2760
http://churchillschool.org
e-mail: churchill@churchillschool.org

Sandra K Gilligan, Director
Jenny Hyde Carney, Outreach Coordinator

A student workbook of activities that have been developed to reinforce the language and vocabulary found in 'Keeping Ahead in School' by Dr. Melvin Levine. The workbook is comprised of blackline masters which can be reproduced. *$ 20.00*

1188   Vocabulary

Harcourt Achieve
6277 Sea Harbor Drive
Orlando, FL   32887

800-531-5015
FAX 800-699-9459
http://www.steckvaughn.com
e-mail: info@steckvaughn.com

Steck-Vaughn Staff, Author
Tim McEwen, President/CEO
Jeff Johnson, Dir Marketing Communications
Chris Lehmann, Team Coordinator

Improve reading comprehension where it matters most by introducing new words in the context of content area articles. Twenty-five highly visual lessons include a high-interest story with vocabulary words highlighted, a full-page graphic application activity, and reinforcement and extension activities presented as computer pull-down menus.

1189   Vowels: Short & Long

Sunburst Technology
400 Columbus Avenue
Valhalla, NY   10595

914-747-3310
800-321-7511
FAX 914-747-4109
http://www.sunburst.com
e-mail: support@sunburst.com

Introduce students to vowels and the role they play in the structure of words. By engaging in word building activities, students learn to identify short and long vowels and regular spelling patterns.

1190   Warmups and Workouts

The Speech Bin
1965 25th Avenue
Vero Beach, FL   32960

772-770-0007
FAX 772-770-0006
http://www.speechbin.com
e-mail: info@speechbin.com

Easy-to-follow step-by-step instructions demonstrate how to help children achieve reliable production of r sounds, practice them in words of increasing complexity, and improve their phonic skills simultaneously. Item number 1486. *$26.95*

1191   Wilson Language Training

Wilson Reading System
175 W Main Street
Millbury, MA   01527

508-865-5699
800-899-8454
FAX 508-865-9644
http://www.wilsonlanguage.com
e-mail: info@wilsonlanguage.com

Judith Nicholas, Administrator Training

Our mission is to instruct teachers, or other professionals in a related field, how to succeed with students who have not learned to read, write and spell despite great effort. Established in order to provide training in the Wilson Reading System, the Wilson staff provides Two-Day Overview Workshops as well as certified Level I and II training.

1192   Word Parts

Sunburst Technology
400 Columbus Avenue
Valhalla, NY   10595

914-747-3310
800-321-7511
FAX 914-747-4109
http://www.sunburst.com
e-mail: support@sunburst.com

Students build skills with compound and polysyllabic words by learning to chunk big words into manageable parts.

1193 Word Scramble 2

LinguiSystems
3100 4th Avenue
East Moline, IL 61244

800-776-4332
FAX 309-755-2377
TDY:800-933-8331
http://www.linguisystems.com
e-mail: service@linguisystems.com

Paul F Johnson, Author
Linda Bowers, Owner
Rosemary Huisingh, Owner

Customers loved the best-selling Word Scramble game and kept asking for more. Take your students to a new level of decoding practice with Word Scramble 2. This game is perfect for your students who've mastered CVC words and are ready for more challenging decoding practice. *$44.95*

Ages 7-14

1194 Wordly Wise 3000 ABC 1-9

Educators Publishing Service
31 Smith Place
Cambridge, MA 02139

617-547-6706
800-225-5750
FAX 888-440-2665
http://www.epsbooks.com
e-mail: eps@epsbooks.com

Kenneth Hodkinson, Sandra Adams, Author
Nick Gaehde, President

Three thousand new and carefully selected words taken from literature, textbooks and SAT-prep books, are the basis of this new series that teaches vocabulary through reading, writing, and a variety of exercises for grades 4-12.

1195 Wordly Wise ABC 1-9

Educators Publishing Service
31 Smith Place
Cambridge, MA 02139

617-547-6706
800-225-5750
FAX 888-440-2665
http://www.epsbooks.com
e-mail: eps@epsbooks.com

Kenneth Hodkinson, Author
Nick Gaehde, President

Vocabulary workbook series employs crossword puzzles, riddles, word games and a sense of humor to make the learning of new words an interesting experience.

1196 Workbook for Aphasia

The Speech Bin
1965 25th Avenue
Vero Beach, FL 32960

772-770-0007
FAX 772-770-0006
http://www.speechbin.com
e-mail: info@speechbin.com

This book gives you materials for adults who have recovered a significant degree of speaking, reading, writing, and comprehension skills. It includes 106 excercises divide into eight target areas. Item number W331. *$48.95*

Science

1197 Ablenet

1081 10th Avenue SE
Minneapolis, MN 55414

612-379-0956
800-322-0956
FAX 612-379-9143
http://www.ablenetinc.com
e-mail: customerservice@ablenetinc.com

Cheryl Volkman, Chief Developmental Officer

Simple assistive technology for teaching children with disabilities including communication aids, environmental control, mounting systems, literacy and teacher resources, kits and more.

1198 Animals and Their Homes CD-ROM

Harcourt Achieve
6277 Sea Harbor Drive
Orlando, FL 32887

800-531-5015
FAX 800-699-9459
http://www.steckvaughn.com
e-mail: info@steckvaughn.com

Steck-Vaughn Staff, Author
Tim McEwen, President/CEO
Jeff Johnson, Dir Marketing Communications
Chris Lehmann, Team Coordinator

This interactive simulation encourages students to explore animals habitats and environmental needs and create appropriate environments for a variety of animals. Students use the Animal Book to create a customized habitat display and write or record their own observations and ideas.

1199 Animals in Their World CD-ROM

Harcourt Achieve
6277 Sea Harbor Drive
Orlando, FL 32887

800-531-5015
FAX 800-699-9459
http://www.steckvaughn.com
e-mail: info@steckvaughn.com

Steck-Vaughn Staff, Author
Tim McEwen, President/CEO
Jeff Johnson, Dir Marketing Communications
Chris Lehmann, Team Coordinator

This multimedia database motivates children to explore, compare, and contrast habitats, behaviors, and physicl characteristics of 58 animals in nine categories, such as carnivore or herbivore, hatched or born, and with or without backbone.

**1200 Curious Creatures Program:
Owls-Spiders-Wolves-Snakes-Bats**

Curriculum Associates
PO Box 2001
North Billerica, MA 01862

800-225-0248
FAX 800-366-1158
http://www.curriculumassociates.com/
e-mail: ca@infocurriculumassociates.com

Louis James Taris, James Robert Taris, Author

Classroom Resources/Science

Users of this award-winning multimedia program say awesome! They learn little known facts about animals that make most of us cringe. Designed to encourage reluctant readers in grades 4 and above, the program is also appropriate for on-level students in grades 2-3. Students learn the language of life science as they strengthen their reading and comprehension skills.

1201 Deep in the Rain Forest

Harcourt Achieve
6277 Sea Harbor Drive
Orlando, FL   32887

800-531-5015
FAX 800-699-9459
http://www.steckvaughn.com
e-mail: info@steckvaughn.com

Pirotta, Author
Tim McEwen, President/CEO
Jeff Johnson, Dir Marketing Communications
Chris Lehmann, Team Coordinator

Now even young readers can investigate the wonder and importance of the rain forest. Hands-on activities, large photos, and meaningful tests in each of these titles relate rain forest facts to a child's world and introduce conservation and environmental protection issues.

1202 Dive to the Ocean Deep: Voyages of Exploration and Discovery

Harcourt Achieve
6277 Sea Harbor Drive
Orlando, FL   32819

800-531-5015
FAX 800-699-9459
http://www.steckvaughn.com
e-mail: info@steckvaughn.com

Steck-Vaughn Staff, Author
Tim McEwen, President/CEO
Jeff Johnson, Dir Marketing Communications
Chris Lehmann, Team Coordinator

These exciting titles draw readers in with true tales of discovery using a documentary approach. Renowned scientists show real world science at work in the depths of the ocean. *$27.11*

64 pages

1203 Harcourt Brace: The Science Book of....

Harcourt Achieve
6277 Sea Harbor Drive
Orlando, FL   32887

800-531-5015
FAX 800-699-9459
http://www.steckvaughn.com
e-mail: info@steckvaughn.com

Ardley, Author
Tim McEwen, President/CEO
Jeff Johnson, Dir Marketing Communications
Chris Lehmann, Team Coordinator

Encourage independent scientific inquiry. Set up a classroom library of 16 hardcover titles that offer dozens of exploration opportunities with basic science principles. Ordinary classroom or household materials are all you need. Full-color photos of preparations and experiments are ideal for independent work. Practical examples relate each experiment to real world.

1204 Learn About Life Science: Animals

Sunburst Technology
400 Columbus Avenue
Valhalla, NY   10595

914-747-3310
800-321-7511
FAX 914-747-4109
http://www.sunburst.com
e-mail: service@sunburst.com

Learn about animal classification, adaptation to climate, domestication and special relationships between humans and animals.

1205 Learn About Life Science: Plants

Sunburst Technology
400 Columbus Avenue
Valhalla, NY   10595

914-747-3310
800-321-7511
FAX 914-747-4109
http://www.sunburst.com
e-mail: service@sunburst.com

Students explore the world of plants. From small seeds to tall trees students learn what plants are and what they need to grow.

1206 Learn About Physical Science: Simple Machines

Sunburst Technology
400 Columbus Avenue
Valhalla, NY   10595

914-747-3310
800-321-7511
FAX 914-747-4109
http://www.sunburst.com
e-mail: service@sunburst.com

Students delve into the mechanical world learning about the ways simple machines make our work easier.

1207 Life Cycles

Harcourt Achieve
6277 Sea Harbor Drive
Orlando, FL   32887

800-531-5015
FAX 800-699-9459
http://www.steckvaughn.com
e-mail: info@steckvaughn.com

Hogan, Author
Tim McEwen, President/CEO
Jeff Johnson, Dir Marketing Communications
Chris Lehmann, Team Coordinator

Dramatic photos tell the story of animal growth and development. This softcover series enriches any classroom science curriculum. Animal development is a complex subject but this series makes it understandable for young readers with simple text and informative images that follow each animal from birth to maturity.

1208 Maps & Navigation

Sunburst Technology
400 Columbus Avenue
Valhalla, NY 10595   914-747-3310
     800-321-7511
     FAX 914-747-4109
     http://www.sunburst.com
     e-mail: support@sunburst.com

This exciting nautical simulation provides students with opportunities to use their math and science skills.

1209 Our Universe: Steadwell

Harcourt Achieve
6277 Sea Harbor Drive
Orlando, FL 32887
     800-531-5015
     FAX 800-699-9459
     http://www.steckvaughn.com
     e-mail: info@steckvaughn.com
Vogt, Author
Tim McEwen, President/CEO
Jeff Johnson, Dir Marketing Communications
Chris Lehmann, Team Coordinator

Unravel the mysteries of space! A complex universe becomes amazingly clear in these easy-to-read titles.

1210 Patterns Across the Curriculum

Harcourt Achieve
6277 Sea Harbor Drive
Orlando, FL 32887
     800-531-5015
     FAX 800-699-9459
     http://www.steckvaughn.com
     e-mail: info@steckvaughn.com
Steck-Vaughn Staff, Author
Tim McEwen, President/CEO
Jeff Johnson, Dir Marketing Communications
Chris Lehmann, Team Coordinator

Develop students awareness and understanding of patterns in the real world! Exercises allow students to identify, complete, extend, and create patterns. Developed across four curriculum areas: Math, Language, Social Studies, and Science. Flexible organization allows teachers to utilize content-specific activities in coordination with other classroom assignments, providing additional richness in learning.

1211 Prehistoric Creaures Then & Now: Steadwell

Harcourt Achieve
6277 Sea Harbor Drive
Orlando, FL 32887
     800-531-5015
     FAX 800-699-9459
     http://www.steckvaughn.com
     e-mail: info@steckvaughn.com
Steck-Vaughn Staff, Author
Tim McEwen, President/CEO
Jeff Johnson, Dir Marketing Communications
Chris Lehmann, Team Coordinator

Now limited readers can dig into the details of dinosaurs! Each information-packed title includes a special spread with a project, a profile of a dinosaur expert, or a description of a recent dinosaur discovery.

1212 Space Academy GX-1

Riverdeep
500 Redmond Boulevard
Novato, CA 94947   415-763-4700
     800-362-2890
     FAX 415-763-4385
     http://www.elmark.com
     e-mail: info@riverdeep.net
Barry O'Callaghan, Chairman/CEO
Simon Calver, COO
John Rim, CFO

Explore the solar system with Space Academy GX-1! Fully aligned with national science standards and state curricula, Space Academy GX-1, students investigate the astronomical basis for seasons, phases of the moon, gravity, orbits, and more. As students succeed, Grow Slides adjust to offer more advanced topics and problems.

1213 Steck-Vaughn Science Centers

Harcourt Achieve
6277 Sea Harbor Drive
Orlando, FL 32887
     800-531-5015
     FAX 800-699-9459
     http://www.harcourtachieve.com
     e-mail: info@harcourtachieve.com
Steck-Vaughn Staff, Author
Tim McEwen, President/CEO
Jeff Johnson, Dir Marketing Communications
Chris Lehmann, Team Coordinator

Organized by theme, these books will supplement the study of weather, prehistoric life, plants, animals of the ocean, animals of the rain forest, earth and space, and energy.

1214 Talking Walls

Riverdeep
500 Redmond Boulevard
Novato, CA 94947   415-763-4700
     800-362-2890
     FAX 415-763-4385
     http://www.elmark.com
     e-mail: info@riverdeep.net
Barry O'Callaghan, Chairman/CEO
Simon Calver, COO
John Rim, CFO

The Talking Walls Software Series is a wonderful springboard for a student's journey of exploration and discovery. This comprehensive collection of researched resources and materials enables students to focus on learning while conducting a guided search for information.

1215 Talking Walls: The Stories Continue

Riverdeep
500 Redmond Boulevard
Novato, CA 94947   415-763-4700
     800-362-2890
     FAX 415-763-4385
     http://www.elmark.com
     e-mail: info@riverdeep.net
Barry O'Callaghan, Chairman/CEO
Simon Calver, COO
John Rim, CFO

Using the Talking Walls Software Series, students discover the stories behind some of the world's most fascinating walls. The award-winning books, interactive software, carefully chosen Web sites, and suggested classroom activities build upon each other, providing a rich learning experience that includes text, video, and hands-on projects.

1216   ThemeWeavers: Nature Activity Kit

Riverdeep
500 Redmond Boulevard
Novato, CA   94947   415-763-4700
                               800-362-2890
                           FAX 415-763-4385
                        http://www.elmark.com
                     e-mail: info@riverdeep.net
Barry O'Callaghan, Chairman/CEO
Simon Calver, COO
John Rim, CFO

ThemeWeavers: Nature Activity Kit is an all-in-one solution for theme-based teaching. In just a few minutes, you can select from dozens of ready-to-use activities centering on the seasons and weather and be ready for the next day's lesson! Interactive and engaging activities cover multiple subject areas such as language arts, math, science, social studies and art.

1217   Thinkin' Science

Sunburst Technology
400 Columbus Avenue
Valhalla, NY   10595   914-747-3310
                               800-321-7511
                           FAX 914-747-4109
                        http://www.sunburst.com
                     e-mail: service@sunburst.com

Five environments introduce students to the scientific methods and concepts needed to understand basic earth, life and physical sciences. Students learn to think like scientists as they solve problems using hypothesis, experimentation, observation and deduction.

1218   Thinkin' Science ZAP!

Sunburst Technology
400 Columbus Avenue
Valhalla, NY   10595   914-747-3310
                               800-321-7511
                           FAX 914-747-4109
                        http://www.sunburst.com
                     e-mail: service@sunburst.com

Working with laser beams, electrical circuits, and "visible" sound waves, students practice valuable thinking skills, observation, prediction, dedutive reasoning, conceptual modeling, theory building and hypothesis testing while experimenting within scientifically accurate learning environment.

1219   True Tales

Harcourt Achieve
6277 Sea Harbor Drive
Orlando, FL   32887
                               800-531-5015
                           FAX 800-699-9459
                        http://www.steckvaughn.com
                     e-mail: info@steckvaughn.com
Billings, Author
Tim McEwen, President/CEO
Jeff Johnson, Dir Marketing Communications
Chris Lehmann, Team Coordinator

If you have been looking for reading comprehension materials for limited readers, your search is over. True Tales presents powerful real-lfe events with direct connections to geography and science at reading level 3. Gripping accounts of personal triumph and tragedy put geography and science in a very real context. Accompanying activities develop reading and language arts, science, and geography skills students need to boost test scores.

1220   Turnstone Explorer Kits

Harcourt Achieve
6277 Sea Harbor Drive
Orlando, FL   32887
                               800-531-5015
                           FAX 800-699-9459
                        http://www.steckvaughn.com
                     e-mail: info@steckvaughn.com
Steck-Vaughn Staff, Author
Tim McEwen, President/CEO
Jeff Johnson, Dir Marketing Communications
Chris Lehmann, Team Coordinator

Encourage inquiry with an insider's look at science exploration! Energize discovery-based learning through nonfiction literature, hands-on exploration, and challenging application projects. Put budding scientists in touch with real thing. Action-packed kits bring the experience of scientific exploration to life.

1221   Untamed World

Harcourt Achieve
6277 Sea Harbor Drive
Orlando, FL   32887
                               800-531-5015
                           FAX 800-699-9459
                        http://www.steckvaughn.com
                     e-mail: info@steckvaughn.com
Karen Dudley, Marie Levine, Patricia Schroeder,
Author
Tim McEwen, President/CEO
Jeff Johnson, Dir Marketing Communications
Chris Lehmann, Team Coordinator

A vivid view of wild animals through science and literature! Awe-inspiring creatures of the land and sea are as fascinating in fact as in folklore. These titles offer both views, combining a thorough nonfiction resource with riveting reading. Topics include life span, classification, the food chain, social organization, communication, and seasonal activities.

1222 Virtual Labs: Electricity

Riverdeep
500 Redmond Boulevard
Novato, CA   94947   415-763-4700
                                     800-362-2890
                              FAX 415-763-4385
                           http://www.elmark.com
                         e-mail: info@riverdeep.net
Barry O'Callaghan, Chairman/CEO
Simon Calver, COO
John Rim, CFO

Five environments introduce students to the scientific
methods and conepts needed to understand basic
Earth, life, and physical sciences. Students will learn
to think like scientists as they solve problems using
hypothesis, experimentation, observation, and deduction. *$69.95*

1223 Virtual Labs: Light

Riverdeep
500 Redmond Boulevard
Novato, CA   94947   415-763-4700
                                     800-362-2890
                              FAX 415-763-4385
                           http://www.elmark.com
                         e-mail: info@riverdeep.net
Barry O'Callaghan, Chairman/CEO
Simon Calver, COO
John Rim, CFO

Designed to integrate directly into the physcial science curricula, Virtual Labs: Light combines
easy-to-use experiments and highly accurate simulations with over 40 reproducible lab worksheets. Carefully sequenced levels of virtual experiments — basic,
extension, and challenge — provide a safe means for
students to perform hands-on activities with lasers
and an assortment of optical tools.

Social Skills

1224 2's Experience Fingerplays

Therapro
225 Arlington Street
Framingham, MA   01702   508-872-9494
                                     800-257-5376
                              FAX 508-875-2062
                         http://www.theraproducts.com
                       e-mail: info@theraproducts.com
Liz Wilmes, Dick Wilmes, Author
Karen Conrad, President

A wonderful collection of fingerplays, songs and
rhymes for the very young child. Fingerplays are
short, easy to learn, and full of simple movement.
Chant or sing the fingerplays and then enjoy the accompanying games and activities. *$12.95*

159 pages

1225 28 Instant Song Games

Therapro
225 Arlington Street
Framingham, MA   01702   508-872-9494
                                     800-257-5376
                              FAX 508-875-2062
                         http://www.theraproducts.com
                       e-mail: info@theraproducts.com
MaBoAubLo, Barbara Sher, Author
Karen Conrad, President

Gets kids up and moving in no time! Includes numerous games of body awareness, movement play, self
expression, imagination and language play. Booklet
and 75 minute audio tape. *$21.00*

Audio Tape

1226 Ablenet

1081 10th Avenue SE
Minneapolis, MN   55414   612-379-0956
                                     800-322-0956
                              FAX 612-379-9143
                          http://www.ablenetinc.com
                  e-mail: customerservice@ablenetinc.com
Cheryl Volkman, Chief Developmental Officer

Simple assistive technology for teaching children
with disabilities including communication aids,
switches, environmental control, mounting systems,
literacy and teacher resources, kits and more.

1227 Active Learning Series

Therapro
225 Arlington Street
Framingham, MA   01702   508-872-9494
                                     800-257-5376
                              FAX 508-875-2062
                         http://www.theraproducts.com
                       e-mail: info@theraproducts.com
Therapro Staff, Author
Karen Conrad, President

A favorite of parents and caregivers. Over 300 innovative and easy-to-do activities in each book. The activities are easy to read and can be done with one child in a
group. Helps caregivers to choose the right activities
for each child. Ideas on setting up environments, and
an easy system for writing plans, helps caregivers set
the stage for a good activity program. Each book contains a complete planning guide. Activities for listening, talking, physical development and more.

1228 Activities Unlimited

Therapro
225 Arlington Street
Framingham, MA   01702   508-872-9494
                                     800-257-5376
                              FAX 508-875-2062
                         http://www.theraproducts.com
                       e-mail: info@theraproducts.com
A Cleveland, B Caton, L Adler, Author
Karen Conrad, President

Helps young children develop fine and gross motor
skills, increase their language, become self-reliant
and play cooperatively. An innovative resource that
immediately attracts and engages children. Short of
time? Need a good idea? Count on Activites Unlimited. *$19.95*

1229 Activities for a Diverse Classroom: Connecting Students

PEAK Parent Center
611 N Weber
Colorado Springs, CO 80903   719-531-9400
                                    800-284-0251
                              FAX 719-531-9452
                              TDY:719-531-5403
                    http://www.peakparent.org
                    e-mail: info@peakparent.org
Leah Katz, Caren Sax, Douglas Fisher, Author

Offers elementary school teachers 18 fun and enriching do it tomorrow activities designed to build acceptance, belonging, and friendships among all students throughout the academic year. Each activity includes extension ideas for linking students' learning to the general education curriculum. *$10.00*

80 pages
ISBN 1-884720-20-X

1230 Activity Schedules for Children with Autism: Teaching Independent Behavior

Therapro
225 Arlington Street
Framingham, MA 01702   508-872-9494
                              800-257-5376
                        FAX 508-875-2062
                http://www.theraproducts.com
                e-mail: info@theraproducts.com
Lynn McClannahan PhD, Patricia Krantz PhD, Author
Karen Conrad, President

An activity schedule is a set of pictures or words that cue a child to follow a sequence of activities. When mastered, the children are more self-directed and purposeful at home, school and leisure activites. In this book, parents and professionals can find detailed instructions and examples, assess a child's readiness to use activity schedules, and understand graduated guidance and progress monitoring. Great for promoting independence in children with autism. *$14.95*

117 pages

1231 Alert Program With Songs for Self-Regulation

Therapro
225 Arlington Street
Framingham, MA 01702   508-872-9494
                              800-257-5376
                        FAX 508-875-2062
                http://www.theraproducts.com
                e-mail: info@theraproducts.com
Mary Sue Williams OTR, Sherry Shellenberger OTR, Author
Karen Conrad, President

This program compares the body to an engine, running either high, low, or just right. Side A is an overview, Side B has 15 songs for self-regulation. Extremely successful in helping kids recognize and change their own engine speeds.

Audio Tape

1232 An Introduction to How Does Your Engine Run?

Therapro
225 Arlington Street
Framingham, MA 01702   508-872-9494
                              800-257-5376
                        FAX 508-875-2062
                http://www.theraproducts.com
                e-mail: info@theraproducts.com
Mary Sue Williams OTR, Sherry Shellenberger OTR, Author
Karen Conrad, President

Introduces the entire Alert Program, which explains how we regulate our arousal states. Describes the use of sensorimotor strategies to manage levels of alertness. This program is fun for students and the adults working with them, and translates easily into real life. *$40.00*

1233 Andy and His Yellow Frisbee

Therapro
225 Arlington Street
Framingham, MA 01702   508-872-9494
                              800-257-5376
                        FAX 508-875-2062
                http://www.theraproducts.com
                e-mail: info@theraproducts.com
Mary Thompson, Author
Karen Conrad, President

A heartwarming story about Andy, a boy with autism. Like many children with autism, Andy has a fascination with objects in motion. His talent for spinning his Frisbee and a new classmate's curiosity set this story in motion. Rosie, the watchful and protective sister, supplies backround on Andy and autism, as well as a sibling's perspective. *$14.95*

19 pages

1234 Artic-Riddles

The Speech Bin
1965 25th Avenue
Vero Beach, FL 32960   772-770-0007
                            FAX 772-770-0006
                    http://www.speechbin.com
                    e-mail: info@speechbin.com

Tired of the same old games? Artic-Riddles is a collection of speech materials with a tantalizing new twist! Each deck of twenty cards has an eye-catching picture on the front and five riddle clues on the back. Games provide speech sound practice; at the same time, they develop and reinforce skills in listening, turn taking, recalling, reasoning, vocabulary, naming, inferring, answering questions, and drawing conclusions. Item number 1401. *$54.95*

1235 Autism & PDD: Primary Social Skills Lessons

LinguiSystems
3100 4th Avenue
East Moline, IL 61244
                                  800-776-4332
                            FAX 309-755-2377
                            TDY:800-933-8331
                    http://www.linguisystems.com
                    e-mail: service@linguisystems.com
Pam Britton Reese, Nena C Challenner, Author
Linda Bowers, Owner
Rosemary Huisingh, Owner

These structured lessons teach social skills through rebus stories. The pictures help students read the lesson with you. Here are just some of the social skill areas you'll address: using a quiet voice, self-care skills, school behavior, hurting self or others, table social skills, getting a check-up. *$109.75*

60 pages   Ages 3-8

1236   Autism & PPD: Adolescent Social Skills Lessons

LinguiSystems
3100 4th Avenue
East Moline, IL   61244

800-776-4332
FAX 309-755-2377
TDY:800-933-8331
http://www.linguisystems.com
e-mail: service@linguisystems.com
Pam Britton Reese, Nena C Challenner, Author
Linda Bowers, Owner
Rosemary Huisingh, Owner

These lessons target the social skills your students with autism need to succeed in school and in life. From school schedule changes to staying healthy to job skills, you'll cover all the important skills your students need. Each book includes instructional and behavioral lessons. *$109.75*

65 pages   Ages 12-18

1237   Autism & PPD: Adolescent Social Skills Lessons-Health & Hygiene

LinguiSystems
3100 4th Avenue
East Moline, IL   61244

800-776-4332
FAX 309-755-2377
TDY:800-933-8331
http://www.linguisystems.com
e-mail: service@linguisystems.com
Pam Britton Reese, Nena C Challenner, Author
Linda Bowers, Owner
Rosemary Huisingh, Owner

Use these rebus story lessons to teach your students important social skills related to health and hygiene. The instructional lessons teach what to say or do in social situations that are sometimes overwhelming to the student with autism and PPD. The behavioral lessons target specific social problems that need to be stopped. *$21.95*

63 pages   Ages 12-18

1238   Breakthroughs Manual: How to Reach Students with Autism

Therapro
225 Arlington Street
Framingham, MA   01702   508-872-9494
800-257-5376
FAX 508-875-2062
http://www.theraproducts.com
e-mail: info@theraproducts.com
Karen Sewell, Author
Karen Conrad, President

This manual features practical suggestions for everyday use with preschool through high school students. Covers communication, behavior, academics, self-help, life and social skills. Includes reproducible lesson plans and up to date listing of classroom materials and catalog supply companies. *$59.00*

243 pages

1239   Broccoli-Flavored Bubble Gum

Harcourt Achieve
6277 Sea Harbor Drive
Orlando, FL   32887

800-531-5015
FAX 800-699-9459
http://www.steckvaughn.com
e-mail: info@steckvaughn.com
Justin McGivern, Patrick Girouard, Author
Tim McEwen, President/CEO
Jeff Johnson, Dir Marketing Communications
Chris Lehmann, Team Coordinator

A young boy gains fame and fortune encouraging kids to eat their vegetables.

32 pages

1240   Busy Kids Movement

Therapro
225 Arlington Street
Framingham, MA   01702   508-872-9494
800-257-5376
FAX 508-875-2062
http://www.theraproducts.com
e-mail: info@theraproducts.com
Therapro Staff, Author
Karen Conrad, President

Full of ideas for developing youngsters' gross motor skills. Games, dramatics, action songs, music and rythm activities. *$9.95*

64 pages

1241   Calm Down and Play

Childswork
135 Dupont Street
Plainview, NY   11803

800-962-1141
FAX 800-262-1886
http://www.childswork.com
e-mail: www.guidancechannel.com

Filled with fun and effective activities to help children: calm down and control their impulses; focus, concentrate, and organize their thoughts; identify and verbalize feelings; channel and release excess energy appropriately; and build self-esteem and confidence. *$17.95*

Ages 5-12

1242   Case of the Crooked Candles

Harcort Achieve
6277 Sea Harbor Drive
Orlando, FL   32887

800-531-5015
FAX 800-699-9459
http://www.steckvaughn.com
e-mail: info@steckvaughn.com
Jonathan Conn, Author
Tim McEwen, President/CEO
Jeff Johnson, Dir Marketing Communications
Chris Lehmann, Team Coordinator

A pair of felonious fruit bats is no match for Detective Dog and his alert animal assistants.

32 pages

1243 Cooperative Thinking Strategies

Edge Enterprises
708 W 9th Street
Lawrence, KS   66044   785-749-1473
                                          FAX 785-749-0207
                                   e-mail: edge@midusa.net
D Sue Vernon, Donald Deshler, Jean Schumaker, Author
Jacqueline Schafer, Managing Editor

Cooperative Thinking Strategies are a group of strategies students can use to think, learn and work together productively. The strategies are designed to improve the students' ability to interact and work with others as they restructure and manipulate information in group tasks. Instruction in these strategies has been designed to be delivered in general education classes in which a diversity of students are enrolled, including students with disabilities. Available as a series or individually.

1244 Courageous Pacers Classroom Chart

Therapro
225 Arlington Street
Framingham, MA   01702   508-872-9494
                                             800-257-5376
                                      FAX 508-875-2062
                             http://www.theraproducts.com
                              e-mail: info@theraproducts.com
Therapro Staff, Author
Karen Conrad, President

Highly recommended to accompany the Courageous Pacers Program. Assists in keeping record of 12 students' progress in walking and lifting. A great visual tool to view progress.

1245 Courageous Pacers Program

Therapro
225 Arlington Street
Framingham, MA   01702   508-872-9494
                                             800-257-5376
                                      FAX 508-875-2062
                             http://www.theraproducts.com
                              e-mail: info@theraproducts.com
Tim Erson MS PT, Author
Karen Conrad, President

This fun and easy program was developed to help students become more active. Research shows that students who are more active, do better in school. The goal of the program is simple: get students to walk 100 miles and lift 10,000 pounds in a year.

92 pages

1246 Dance Land

Therapro
225 Arlington Street
Framingham, MA   01702   508-872-9494
                                             800-257-5376
                                      FAX 508-875-2062
                             http://www.theraproducts.com
                              e-mail: info@theraproducts.com
Fitz-Taylor, McDonald, Hicman, Lande, Wiz, Author
Karen Conrad, President

Safe fun for kids of all abilities. Engages listeners in rythmic expression, which is fundamental to physical, cognitive and emotional development. Dance activities designed by physical and occupational therapists. 33 page book included. Many sensory motor activites included. 50 minute audio tape. *$21.00*

Audio Tape

1247 Eden Family of Services

Eden Services
One Eden Way
Princeton, NJ   08540   609-987-0099
                                      FAX 609-987-0243
                              http://www.edenservices.org
                               e-mail: info@edenservices.org
David L Holmes EdD, Executive Director/President
Joani Truch, Administration/Communications

Provides year round educational services, early intervention, parent training, respite care, outreach services, community based residential services and employment opportunities for individuals with autism.

1248 Emotions Activity Manuals

Therapro
225 Arlington Street
Framingham, MA   01702   508-872-9494
                                             800-257-5376
                                      FAX 508-875-2062
                             http://www.theraproducts.com
                              e-mail: info@theraproducts.com
Therapro Staff, Author
Karen Conrad, President

Great new manuals to use with the EMOTIONS products (poster, cards and flashcards). 63 different tried and true activities from therapists, educators and counselors form the US and Canada. Simply produced, includes an EMOTIONS page.

1249 Expression Connection

The Speech Bin
1965 25th Avenue
Vero Beach, FL   32960   772-770-0007
                                      FAX 772-770-0006
                              http://www.speechbin.com
                               e-mail: info@speechbin.com

This criterion-referenced assessment protocol and structured instructional program moves elementary school children from simple narratives to complex stories and establishes the critical concepts that underline coherent oral expression. Item number 1586. *$43.95*

1250 Expressive Language Kit

LinguiSystems
3100 4th Avenue
East Moline, IL   61244

800-776-4332
FAX 309-755-2377
TDY:800-933-8331
http://www.linguisystems.com
e-mail: service@linguisystems.com

*Linda Bowers, Rosemary Huisingh, Carolyn
LoGiudice, Author
Linda Bowers, Owner
Rosemary Huisingh, Owner*

It's our biggest language therapy kit ever. The focus is on strengthening expressive language skills so your students will become effective communicators. A combination of colorful photographs, picture cards, and activity sheets work together to create an outstanding expressive language program. A comprehension therapy manual is included to help you direct this incredibly wide variety of language activities. *$149.95*

250 pages   Ages 5-11

1251 Face to Face: Resolving Conflict Without Giving in or Giving Up

National Association for Community Mediation
1527 New Hampshire Avenue, NW
Washington, DC   20036
202-667-9700
FAX 202-466-8629
http://www.nafcm.org\nafcm
e-mail: nafcm@nafcm.org

*Jan Bellard,Hilda Gutierrez Baldoquin,Andrew
Sachs, Author
Linda Baron, Executive Director
Joanne Galindo, Associate Director*

Modular curriculum for training program for AmeriCorps members. Addresses conflict at the personal level, interpersonal level, and group collaboration. Includes workbook. *$69.95*

266 pages

1252 Forms for Helping the ADHD Child

Childswork
135 Dupont Street
Plainview, NY   11803

800-962-1141
FAX 800-262-1886
http://www.childswork.com
e-mail: www.guidancechannel.com

Forms, charts, and checklists for treating children with Attention Deficit Hyperactivity Disorder cover a wide range of approaches. Includes effective aids in assessing, treating, and monitoring the progress of the ADHD child. *$ 31.95*

100 pages

1253 Friendzee: A Social Skills Game

LinguiSystems
3100 4th Avenue
East Moline, IL   61244

800-776-4332
FAX 309-755-2377
TDY:800-933-8331
http://www.linguisystems.com
e-mail: service@linguisystems.com

*Diane A Figula, Author
Linda Bowers, Owner
Rosemary Huisingh, Owner*

This game uses a communication-based approach to teaching social skills. Skills are taught through the themes of home, school, and community. Stimulus items teach these social skills: body language; tone of voice; polite forms; giving information; listening; asking questions; and problem solving. *$39.95*

Ages 7-11

1254 Funsical Fitness With Silly-cise CD: Motor Development Activities

Therapro
225 Arlington Street
Framingham, MA   01702
508-872-9494
800-257-5376
FAX 508-875-2062
http://www.theraproducts.com
e-mail: info@theraproducts.com

Karen Conrad, President

This unique blending of developmentally appropriate gross motor, sensory integration, and aerobic activities is guaranteed to build children's strength, balance endurance, coordination, and self confidence. Leads children through four 15-minute classes of Wacky Walking, Grinnastics, Brain Gym, Warm Ups, Adventurobics, and Chill Out activities. *$15.00*

Ages 3-9

1255 Games We Should Play in School

Therapro
225 Arlington Street
Framingham, MA   01702
508-872-9494
800-257-5376
FAX 508-875-2062
http://www.theraproducts.com
e-mail: info@theraproducts.com

*Frank Aycox, Author
Karen Conrad, President*

Includes over 75 interactive, fun, social games; describes how to effectively lead Social Play sessions in the classroom. Students become more cooperative, less antagonistic and more capable of increased attentiveness. Contains the secrets to enriching the entire school environment. *$16.50*

154 pages

1256   Goal Oriented Gross & Fine Motor Lesson Plans for Early Childhood Classes

Therapro
225 Arlington Street
Framingham, MA   01702   508-872-9494
                                800-257-5376
                           FAX 508-875-2062
                  http://www.theraproducts.com
                  e-mail: info@theraproducts.com
Donna Weiss MA OTR, Author
Karen Conrad, President

Practical and convinient format covers 224 activities grouped into 12 monthly units, making it easy to incorporate gross and fine motor activities into a daily class schedule. Provides challenges for groups whose abilities span early childhood, from 2.5 to 5.5 years of age. *$32.00*

77 pages

1257   Hidden Child: Linwood Method for Reaching the Autistic Child

Therapro
225 Arlington Street
Framingham, MA   01702   508-872-9494
                                800-257-5376
                           FAX 508-875-2062
                  http://www.theraproducts.com
                  e-mail: info@theraproducts.com
Jeanne Simmons, Sabine Oiski PhD, Author
Karen Conrad, President

This book provides an explanation of autism, then a step-by-step analysis of the Linwood method of establishing relationships, patterning good behavior, overcoming compulsions, developing skills, and fostering social and emotional development. This guidebook for teachers and therapists also has a message for parents.

1258   High Interest Sports

Harcourt Achieve
6277 Sea Harbor Drive
Orlando, FL   32887
                                800-531-5015
                           FAX 800-699-9459
                  http://www.steckvaughn.com
                  e-mail: info@steckvaughn.com
Fetty, Author
Tim McEwen, President/CEO
Jeff Johnson, Dir Marketing Communications
Chris Lehmann, Team Coordinator

Exercise is an important part of a healthy lifestyle. By providing a variety of activities, games, and sports, we give students as opportunity to choose the exercise that fits their personal needs. These books provide the basic framework of a variety of sports and schoolyard games, making it an excellent resource for the classroom teacher.

1259   Inclusive Early Childhood Classroom: Easy Ways to Adapt Learning Centers for All Children

Therapro
225 Arlington Street
Framingham, MA   01702   508-872-9494
                                800-257-5376
                           FAX 508-875-2062
                  http://www.theraproducts.com
                  e-mail: info@theraproducts.com
Patti Gould, Joyce Sullivan, Author
Karen Conrad, President

A great inclusion resource! This long awaited book by two experienced occupational therapists offers many concrete suggestions that are easy to implement. Gives teachers tools to make classrooms more effective environments for ALL students. *$24.95*

203 pages

1260   Jarvis Clutch: Social Spy

Educators Publishing Service
31 Smith Place
Cambridge, MA   02139   617-547-6706
                                800-225-5750
                           FAX 888-440-2665
                  http://www.epsbooks.com
                  e-mail: eps@epsbooks.com
Melvin D Levine MD FAAP, Author
Nick Gaehde, President

In Jarvis Clutch social spy, Dr. Mel Levine teams up with eight grader Jarvis Clutch for an insider's look at life on the middle school social scene. Jarvis's wry and insightful observations of student interactions at Eastern Middle School bring to light the myriad social challenges that adolescents face every day, including peer pressure, the need to seem cool, the perils of dating., Include the commentary in Jarivs' Spy Notes!

1261   Kids with Special Needs: Information & Activities to Promote Awareness & Understanding

Therapro
225 Arlington Street
Framingham, MA   01702   508-872-9494
                                800-257-5376
                           FAX 508-875-2062
                  http://www.theraproducts.com
                  e-mail: info@theraproducts.com
Dee Konczal, Veronica Getskow, Author
Karen Conrad, President

Children with disabilities have a need to be accepted and understood by other children. This book provides simulation activities to better understand what it's like to have a disability. Background information about communicative developmental, physical and learning disabilities is also offered. Includes a comprehensive resource list. *$16.95*

200 pages

1262 Learning in Motion

Therapro
225 Arlington Street
Framingham, MA   01702   508-872-9494
                                800-257-5376
                           FAX 508-875-2062
              http://www.theraproducts.com
              e-mail: info@theraproducts.com
Angermeir, Krzyzanowski, Keller-Moir, Author
Karen Conrad, President

Written by 3 OTs, this book is for the busy therapist or teacher of preschoolers to second graders. Provides group activities using gross, fine andsensory motor skills in theme based curricula. Every lesson plan contains goals, objectives, materials and adaptations to facilitate inclusion and multilevel instructions. Includes 130 lesson plans with corresponding parent letters that explain the lesson and provide home follow-up activities. *$50.00*

379 pages

1263 Look At It This Way

Therapro
225 Arlington Street
Framingham, MA   01702   508-872-9494
                                800-257-5376
                           FAX 508-875-2062
              http://www.theraproducts.com
              e-mail: info@theraproducts.com
Roma Lee, Author
Karen Conrad, President

Although the play and toy activities in this book are designed for children with visual impairment, they can be used with other children as well. Chapters include Learning to Look, Learning to Listen, Learning to Feel, and Using the Sense of Smell. *$32.00*

129 pages

1264 Maxwell's Manor: A Social Language Game

LinguiSystems
3100 4th Avenue
East Moline, IL   61244
                                800-776-4332
                           FAX 309-755-2377
                           TDY:800-933-8331
              http://www.linguisystems.com
              e-mail: service@linguisystems.com
Carolyn LoGiudice, Nancy McConnell, Author
Linda Bowers, Owner
Rosemary Huisingh, Owner

This fun game will teach your students the social skills they need to get along with others, be more accepted by their peers, and be successful in the classroom. Maxwell, the loveable dog, leads the way as your students practice positive social language skills. *$44.95*

Ages 4-9

1265 Moving Right Along

Therapro
225 Arlington Street
Framingham, MA   01702   508-872-9494
                                800-257-5376
                           FAX 508-875-2062
              http://www.theraproducts.com
              e-mail: info@theraproducts.com
Barbara Sher MA OTR, Author
Karen Conrad, President

A collection of 264 easy, spur of the moment, movement games for young children to increase coordination, balance, rythm and enhance their sense of mastery. Great resource for parents, teachers, PT's and OT's. *$14.50*

1266 Moving and Learning Across the Curriculum: 315 Games to Make Learning Fun

Therapro
225 Arlington Street
Framingham, MA   01702   508-872-9494
                                800-257-5376
                           FAX 508-875-2062
              http://www.theraproducts.com
              e-mail: info@theraproducts.com
Rae Pica, Author
Karen Conrad, President

Gives children the chance to be physically involved in the experience of learning concepts. A great way to include gross motor skills across 6 major content areas: art; language arts; mathematics; music; science and social studies. *$4.00*

1267 New Language of Toys: Teaching Communication Skills to Children with Special Needs

Therapro
225 Arlington Street
Framingham, MA   01702   508-872-9494
                                800-257-5376
                           FAX 508-875-2062
              http://www.theraproducts.com
              e-mail: info@theraproducts.com
Sue Schwarz PhD, Joan Heller Miller EdM, Author
Karen Conrad, President

Play time becomes a fun and educational experience with this revised hands-on approach for developing communication skills using everyday toys. Includes a fresh assortment of toys, books and new chapters on computer technology, language learning, videotapes and television. *$16.95*

289 pages   Ages Birth-6

1268 Patterns Across the Curriculum

Harcourt Achieve
6277 Sea Harbor Drive
Orlando, FL   32887
                                800-531-5015
                           FAX 800-699-9459
              http://www.steckvaughn.com
              e-mail: info@steckvaughn.com
Steck-Vaughn Staff, Author
Tim McEwen, President/CEO
Jeff Johnson, Dir Marketing Communications
Chris Lehmann, Team Coordinator

Develop students' awareness and understanding of patterns in the real world! Exercises allow students to identify, complete, extend, and create patterns. Developed across four curriculum areas: Math; Language; Social Studies; and Science. Flexible organization allows teachers to utilize content-specific activities in coordination with other classroom assignments, providing additional richness in learning.

1269 Peer Pals

AGS Publishing
4201 Woodland Road
Circle Pines, MN   55014   651-287-7220
                                      800-328-2560
                                 FAX 800-471-8457
                           http://www.agsnet.com
                         e-mail: agsmail@agsnet.com
Robert P Bowman, John N Chanaca, Author
Karen Dahlen, Associate Director
Matt Keller, Marketing Manager

A peer helping program designed to improve study skills, self-esteem, and decision making. The program uses a big sister/big brother approach, as grade 3-6 students are paired with grade K-2 students. *$33.99*

ISBN 0-886711-62-2

1270 Play Helps: Toys and Activities for Children with Special Needs

Therapro
225 Arlington Street
Framingham, MA   01702   508-872-9494
                                    800-257-5376
                               FAX 508-875-2062
                         http://www.theraproducts.com
                         e-mail: info@theraproducts.com
Roma Lear, Author
Karen Conrad, President

This unique book features many homemade ideas for all ages, including the very young child. All the toys can be adapted to meet individual needs. The text is divided into sections on each of the five senses: sight, hearing, touch, taste and smell. Anyone working with children will find this book indispensable. *$42.00*

200 pages   3rd Edition

1271 Reaching Out, Joining In: Teaching Social Skills to Young Children with Autism

Therapro
225 Arlington Street
Framingham, MA   01702   508-872-9494
                                    800-257-5376
                               FAX 508-875-2062
                         http://www.theraproducts.com
                         e-mail: info@theraproducts.com
Mary Jane Weiss PhD BCBA, Sandra Harris PhD, Author
Karen Conrad, President

Describes how to help young children diagnosed within the autism spectrum with one of their most challenging areas of development, social behavior. Focuses on four broad topics: play skills; the language of social skills; undestanding another person's perspective; and using these skills in an inclusive classroon. The authors present concrete strategies to teach basic play skills, how to play with others, to recognize social cues and engage in social conversation. Practical and accessible. *$16.95*

215 pages

1272 Right from the Start: Behavioral Intervention for Young Children with Autism: A Guide

Therapro
225 Arlington Street
Framingham, MA   01702   508-872-9494
                                    800-257-5376
                               FAX 508-875-2062
                         http://www.theraproducts.com
                         e-mail: info@theraproducts.com
Mary Jane Weiss PhD BCBA, Sandra Harris PhD, Author
Karen Conrad, President

This informative and user-friendly guide helps parents and service providers explore programs that use early intensive behavioral intervention for young children with autism and related disorders. Within these programs, many children improve in intellectual, social and adaptive functioning, enabling them to move on to regular elementary and preschools. Benefits all children, but primarily useful for children age five and younger. *$14.95*

138 pages

1273 Room 14

LinguiSystems
3100 4th Avenue
East Moline, IL   61244
                                      800-776-4332
                                 FAX 309-755-2377
                                  TDY:800-933-8331
                         http://www.linguisystems.com
                         e-mail: service@linguisystems.com
Carolyn Wilson, Author
Linda Bowers, Owner
Rosemary Huisingh, Owner

Build social skills by offering a variety of teaching approaches to meet the language and learning needs of your students. Through stories, comprehension activities, and organized lessons, students learn to: make and keep friends: fit in at school; handle feelings; and be responsible for their actions. *$59.95*

198 pages   Ages 6-10

1274 S'Cool Moves for Learning: A Program Designed to Enhance Learning Through Body-Mind

Therapro
225 Arlington Street
Framingham, MA   01702   508-872-9494
                                    800-257-5376
                               FAX 508-875-2062
                         http://www.theraproducts.com
                         e-mail: info@theraproducts.com
Debra Heiberger MA, Margot Heiniger-White MA, Author
Karen Conrad, President

The movement activities described in this book are organized in a way that is easy to integrate into the class routine throughout the day. The Minute Moves for the Classroom included in several chapters is a handy reference of movement activities which help make the transition from one activity to another fun and smooth. *$35.00*

1275   Self-Perception: Organizing Functional Information Workbook

Therapro
225 Arlington Street
Framingham, MA   01702   508-872-9494
                                        800-257-5376
                                   FAX 508-875-2062
                         http://www.theraproducts.com
                         e-mail: info@theraproducts.com
Therapro Staff, Author
Karen Conrad, President

Recognizing human and animal body parts, discriminating between right and left, and exploring attitudes, emotions, humor and personal problem-solving. *$10.50*

1276   Simple Steps: Developmental Activities for Infants, Toddlers & Two Year-Olds

Therapro
225 Arlington Street
Framingham, MA   01702   508-872-9494
                                        800-257-5376
                                   FAX 508-875-2062
                         http://www.theraproducts.com
                         e-mail: info@theraproducts.com
Karen Miller, Author
Karen Conrad, President

Three hundred activities linked to the latest research in brain development. Outlines a typical developmental sequence in 10 domains: social/emotional, fine motor; gross motor; language; cognition; sensory; nature; music and movement; creativity and dramatic play. Chapters on curriculum development and learning environment also included. *$24.95*

293 pages

1277   Solutions Kit for ADHD

Childswork
135 Dupont Street
Plainview, NY   11803
                                          800-962-1141
                                      FAX 800-262-1886
                             http://www.childswork.com
                          e-mail: www.guidancechannel.com

This comprehensive kit is packed with hands-on materials for a multi-modal approach to working with ADHD kids aged 5 through 12. *$105.00*

Ages 5-12

1278   Song Games for Sensory Integration

Therapro
225 Arlington Street
Framingham, MA   01702   508-872-9494
                                        800-257-5376
                                   FAX 508-875-2062
                         http://www.theraproducts.com
                         e-mail: info@theraproducts.com
Aubrey Carton, Lois Hickman, Author
Karen Conrad, President

For young children with sensory processing challenges, 15 play-along routines help remediate everything from bilateral skills to vestibular dysfunction. Narrative is helpful for parents. Includes a 51 page book filled with ideas for extending therapeutic value of these activites. 87 minute audio tape. *$21.00*

Audio Tape

1279   Source for Syndromes

LinguiSystems
3100 4th Avenue
East Moline, IL   61244
                                          800-776-4332
                                     FAX 309-755-2377
                                     TDY:800-933-8331
                           http://www.linguisystems.com
                          e-mail: service@linguisystems.com
Gail J Richard, Debra Reichert Hoge, Author
Linda Bowers, Owner
Rosemary Huisingh, Owner

Do you often wish someone would just tell you what to do with a specific youngster on your caseload? The Source for Syndromes can do just that. Learn about the speech-language characteristics for each sydrome with a focus on communication issues. This resource covers pertinent information for such sydromes such as Angelman, Asperger's, Autism, Rett's Tourette's, Williams, and more. *$41.95*

117 pages   Ages Birth-18

1280   Start to Finish: Developmentally Sequenced Fine Motor Activities for Preschool Children

Therapro
225 Arlington Street
Framingham, MA   01702   508-872-9494
                                        800-257-5376
                                   FAX 508-875-2062
                         http://www.theraproducts.com
                         e-mail: info@theraproducts.com
Nory Marsh, Author
Karen Conrad, President

Seventy stimulating activities target 4 areas of fine motor development normally acquired between 3 and 5: hand manipulation, pencil grasp, scissors skill and grasp, and visual motor skills. Each 30 minute activity has skills, projected goal, supplies needed, instructions and modifications provided and needs limited preparation time. *$57.50*

1281 Stop, Relax and Think

Childswork
135 Dupont Street
Plainview, NY   11803

800-962-1141
FAX 800-262-1886
http://www.childswork.com
e-mail: www.guidancechannel.com

In this board game, active impulsive children learn motor control, relaxation skills, how to express their feelings, and how to problem-solve. Can be used both as a diagnostic and a treatment tool, and behaviors learned in the game can be generalized into the home or classroom. *$52.00*

Ages 6-12

1282 Stop, Relax and Think Ball

Childswork
135 Dupont Street
Plainview, NY   11803

800-962-1141
FAX 800-262-1886
http://www.childswork.com
e-mail: www.guidancechannel.com

This ball teaches children to control their impulsivity by helping them understand and control their actions. *$22.00*

1283 Stop, Relax and Think Card Game

Childswork
135 Dupont Street
Plainview, NY   11803

800-962-1141
FAX 800-262-1886
http://www.childswork.com
e-mail: www.guidancechannel.com

Players are dealt Stop, Relax and Think cards and also Stressed Out, Confused, and Discouraged cards. As they acquire more cards, they must choose different self-control skills, and they learn the value of patience and cooperating with others to achieve a goal. *$21.95*

Ages 6-12

1284 Stop, Relax and Think Scriptbook

Childswork
135 Dupont Street
Plainview, NY   11803

800-962-1141
FAX 800-262-1886
http://www.childswork.com
e-mail: www.guidancechannel.com

In this uniquely designed book, children can practice what to say and how to act in eight different scenarios common to children with behavioral problems. The counselor and the child sit across from each other and read the scripts. *$24.95*

Ages 8-12

1285 Stop, Relax and Think Workbook

Childswork
135 Dupont Street
Plainview, NY   11803

800-962-1141
FAX 800-262-1886
http://www.childswork.com
e-mail: www.guidancechannel.com

This new workbook contains more than 60 paper and pencil activities that teach children such important skills as: thinking about consequences, staying focused and completing a task, engaging in quiet activities without disturbing others, and more. *$19.95*

Ages 6-12

1286 Successful Movement Challenges

Therapro
225 Arlington Street
Framingham, MA   01702

508-872-9494
800-257-5376
FAX 508-875-2062
http://www.theraproducts.com
e-mail: info@theraproducts.com

Jack Capon, Author
Karen Conrad, President

Extensive and exciting movement activities for children in preschool, elementary and special education. Includes movement exploration challenges using parachutes, balls, hoops, ropes, bean bags, rythm sticks, scarves and much more. This popular publication also includes body conditioning, mat activities and playground apparatus activities. Everyone enjoys the creative and carefully designed movement experiences. *$14.25*

127 pages

1287 Surface Counseling

Edge Enterprises
708 W 9th Street
Lawrence, KS   66044

785-749-1473
FAX 785-749-0207
e-mail: edge@midusa.net

Joe N Crank, Donald D Deshler, Jean B Schumaker, Author
Jacqueline Schafer, Managing Editor

Details a set of relationship-building skills necessary for establishing a trusting, cooperative relationship between adults and youths and a problem-solving strategy that youths can learn to use by themselves. Includes study guide questions, model dialogues and role-play activities. Useful for any adult who has daily contact with children and adolescents.

60 pages   Paperback

1288 Survival Guide for Kids with LD

Therapro
225 Arlington Street
Framingham, MA   01702

508-872-9494
800-257-5376
FAX 508-875-2062
http://www.theraproducts.com
e-mail: info@theraproducts.com

Gary Fisher PhD, Rhonda Cummings EdD, Author
Karen Conrad, President

Popular book that is highly reccommended. Contains vital information, practical advice, step-by-step strategies, and encouragement for children labeled Learning Disabled. *$9.95*

1289   Taking Part

AGS Publishing
4201 Woodland Road
Circle Pines, MN   55014   651-287-7220
                                  800-328-2560
                              FAX 800-471-8457
                          http://www.agsnet.com
                      e-mail: agsmail@agsnet.com
Gwendolyn Cartledge, James Kleefield, Author
Karen Dahlen, Associate Director
Matt Keller, Marketing Manager

A social skills program for students in preschool to grade 3 that teaches skills identified by research to be essential to social development: expressing oneself; playing with peers; responding to aggression; cooperating with peers; communicating nonverbally and making conversation. The program focuses on cooperative or group play skills and conflict resolution. Materials include a manual, puppets, stickers and posters. *$90.99*

ISBN 0-886714-21-4

1290   That's Life! Social Language

LinguiSystems
3100 4th Avenue
East Moline, IL   61244
                                  800-776-4332
                              FAX 309-755-2377
                             TDY:800-933-8331
                      http://www.linguisystems.com
                  e-mail: service@linguisystems.com
Linda Bowers, Owner
Rosemary Huisingh, Owner

Teach your students to be effective and appropriate communicators in a wide variety of situations. Through direct instruction, role-playing activities, and discussion, your students will learn the how and why of social language interaction.

Ages 12-18

1291   Tools for Students Video

Therapro
225 Arlington Street
Framingham, MA   01702   508-872-9494
                                  800-257-5376
                              FAX 508-875-2062
                       http://www.theraproducts.com
                    e-mail: info@theraproducts.com
Therapro Staff, Author
Karen Conrad, President

This 30 minute video is a fun and participatory how-to video which provides solutions to the problems indentified in the Tools for Teachers Video. It can be used by teachers in the classroom and by parents at home. There are 25 sensory tools for movement, proprioception, mouth and hand fidgets, calming and recess. Pencil-holding and hand games to develop hand manipulation skills are also demonstrated. *$25.95*

Video

1292   Tools for Teachers Video

Therapro
225 Arlington Street
Framingham, MA   01702   508-872-9494
                                  800-257-5376
                              FAX 508-875-2062
                       http://www.theraproducts.com
                    e-mail: info@theraproducts.com
Therapro Staff, Author
Karen Conrad, President

This video, designed by an OT to provide a logical approach to sensory integration and hand skill strategies for anyone to use, is ideal for in-services. Within 20 minutes, you'll learn how to help students calm down, focus, and increase their self-awareness. This is a great tool for teachers and therapists (shows how to inplement sensory diet into classroom), administrators and parents. *$25.95*

Video

1293   Understanding Argumentative Communication: How Many Ways Can You Ask for a Cookie?

Therapro
225 Arlington Street
Framingham, MA   01702   508-872-9494
                                  800-257-5376
                              FAX 508-875-2062
                       http://www.theraproducts.com
                    e-mail: info@theraproducts.com
Christine Derse MEd, Janice Lopes MSEd, Author
Karen Conrad, President

Ten uncomplicated lesson plans for classroom use. Teach a complete overview of all that Argumentative Communication encompasses or give students a brief awareness lesson about just one type of communication. Lessons can be used either consecutively or singly. Includes defining communication, gestures, sign language, object boards, picture boards, headsticks, eye pointing, scanning with picture boards, picture boards in sentence format and computers for argumentative communication. *$17.95*

142 pages

1294   Updown Chair

Rehab and Educational Aids for Living
187 N Main Street
Dolgeville, NY   13329
                                  800-696-7041
                              FAX 315-429-3071
                          http://www.realdesign.inc
                     e-mail: rdesign@twcny.rr.com
Kris Wohnsen, Co-Owner

The updown chair is designed for children from 43"-63" in height. It combines optimal positioning and sitting comfort with ease of adjustment. Changing the seat height can be done quickly and safely with our exclusive foot lever activation which uses a pneumatic cylinder assist. Children can be elevated to just the right position for floor or table top activities.

5-15 years

1295 What's Up? A That's LIFE! Game of Social Language

LinguiSystems
3100 4th Avenue
East Moline, IL   61244

800-776-4332
FAX 309-755-2377
TDY:800-933-8331
http://www.linguisystems.com
e-mail: service@linguisystems.com

Carolyn LoGiudice, Nancy McConnell, Author
Linda Bowers, Owner
Rosemary Huisingh, Owner

Here's a game with strategy, fast action, and competition. Your older students will love it! Teach appropriate social communication with this game. Peer evaluation is built-in so students can track progress. *$44.95*

Ages 12-16

1296 Who Cares?

Therapro
225 Arlington Street
Framingham, MA   01702

508-872-9494
800-257-5376
FAX 508-875-2062
http://www.theraproducts.com
e-mail: info@theraproducts.com

Therapro Staff, Author
Karen Conrad, President

This series of small handbooks for children teaches them about diversity. *$7.99*

32 pages   Hardcover

1297 Wikki Stix Hands On-Learning Activity Book

Therapro
225 Arlington Street
Framingham, MA   01702

508-872-9494
800-257-5376
FAX 508-875-2062
http://www.theraproducts.com
e-mail: info@theraproducts.com

Therapro Staff, Author
Karen Conrad, President

Loaded with great ideas for using Wikki Stix. For all ages and curriculums. *$3.50*

1298 Workbook for Verbal Expression

The Speech Bin
1965 25th Avenue
Vero Beach, FL   32960

772-770-0007
FAX 772-770-0006
http://www.speechbin.com
e-mail: info@speechbin.com

A book of 100s of excercises from simple naming, automatic speech sequences, and repetition exercises to complex tasks in sentence formulation and abstract verbal reasoning. Item number 1435. *$43.95*

Social Studies

1299 A Knock at the Door

Harcourt Achieve
6277 Sea Harbor Drive
Orlando, FL   32887

800-531-5015
FAX 800-699-9459
http://www.steckvaughn.com
e-mail: info@steckvaughn.com

Eric Sonderling, Wendy Wassink Ackison, Author
Tim McEwen, President/CEO
Jeff Johnson, Dir Marketing Communications
Chris Lehmann, Team Coordinator

The frightened stranger's identity remains a secret until the day a Nazi soldier knocks on the door.

1300 A World So Different

Harcourt Achieve
6277 Sea Harbor Drive
Orlando, FL   32887

800-531-5015
FAX 800-699-9459
http://www.steckvaughn.com
e-mail: info@steckvaughn.com

Steck-Vaughn Staff, Author
Tim McEwen, President/CEO
Jeff Johnson, Dir Marketing Communications
Chris Lehmann, Team Coordinator

As generations of family members recall how dramatically technology has changed everyday life, Sarah wonders what changes are in store for her generation.

1301 American Government Today: Steadwell

Harcourt Achieve
6277 Sea Harbor Drive
Orlando, FL   32887

800-531-5015
FAX 800-699-9459
http://www.steckvaughn.com
e-mail: info@steckvaughn.com

Sanders, Author
Tim McEwen, President/CEO
Jeff Johnson, Dir Marketing Communications
Chris Lehmann, Team Coordinator

Give limited readers unlimited access to social studies and citizenship topics! Whether applying for citizenship or studying for GED Test, learners need to know about our nation's capital and the democracy it hosts. In this series, even limited readers can get a clear picture of a complex system.

1302 Calliope

Cobblestone Publishing
30 Grove Street
Peterborough, NH   03458

603-924-7209
800-821-0115
FAX 603-924-7380
http://www.cobblestonepub.com
e-mail: custsvc@cobblestone.mv.com

Rosalie Baker, Editor
Malcom Jensen, Publisher
Charles Baker, Editor

Winner of the coveted 1998 Educational Press Association's Golden Lamp Award. Calliope brings to the classroom a fresh and exciting look at world history, one theme at a time. *$29.95*

52 pages 9 times anually

1303 Discoveries: Explore the Desert Ecosystem

Sunburst Technology
400 Columbus Avenue
Valhalla, NY 10595
914-747-3310
800-321-7511
FAX 914-747-4109
http://www.sunburst.com
e-mail: service@sunburst.com

This program invites students to explore the plants, animals, culture and georgraphy of the Sonoran Desert by day and by night.

1304 Discoveries: Explore the Everglades Ecosystem

Sunburst Technology
400 Columbus Avenue
Valhalla, NY 10595
914-747-3310
800-321-7511
FAX 914-747-4109
http://www.sunburst.com
e-mail: service@sunburst.com

This multi curricular research program takes students to the Everglades where they anchor their exploration photo realistic panaramas of the habitiat.

1305 Discoveries: Explore the Forest Ecosystem

Sunburst Technology
400 Columbus Avenue
Valhalla, NY 10595
914-747-3310
800-321-7511
FAX 914-747-4109
http://www.sunburst.com
e-mail: service@sunburst.com

This theme based CD-ROM enables students of all abilities to actively research a multitude of different forest ecosystems in the Appalachian National Park.

1306 Easybook Deluxe Writing Workshop: Colonial Times

Sunburst Technology
400 Columbus Avenue
Valhalla, NY 10595
914-747-3310
800-321-7511
FAX 914-747-4109
http://www.sunburst.com
e-mail: service@sunburst.com

Writing workshops combine theme-based activities with the award-winning EasyBook Deluxe.

1307 Easybook Deluxe Writing Workshop: Immigration

Sunburst Technology
400 Columbus Avenue
Valhalla, NY 10595
914-747-3310
800-321-7511
FAX 914-747-4109
http://www.sunburst.com
e-mail: support@sunburst.com

Writing workshops combine theme-based activities with the award-winning EasyBook Deluxe.

1308 Easybook Deluxe Writing Workshop: Rainforest & Astronomy

Sunburst Technology
400 Columbus Avenue
Valhalla, NY 10595
914-747-3310
800-321-7511
FAX 914-747-4109
http://www.sunburst.com
e-mail: support@sunburst.com

Writing workshops combine theme-based activities with the award-winning EasyBook Deluxe.

1309 Explorers & Exploration: Steadwell

Harcourt Achieve
6277 Sea Harbor Drive
Orlando, FL 32887
800-531-5015
FAX 800-699-9459
http://www.steckvaughn.com
e-mail: info@steckvaughn.com

Steck-Vaughn Staff, Author
Tim McEwen, President/CEO
Jeff Johnson, Dir Marketing Communications
Chris Lehmann, Team Coordinator

Long ago adventures are still a thrill in these vividly illustrated titles. Maps, diagrams, and contemporary prints lend an authenic air. A time line and list of events in the appropriate century put history in perspective.

1310 First Biographies

Harcourt Achieve
6277 Sea Harbor Drive
Orlando, FL 32887
800-531-5015
FAX 800-699-9459
http://www.steckvaughn.com
e-mail: info@steckvaughn.com

Steck-Vaughn Staff, Author
Tim McEwen, President/CEO
Jeff Johnson, Dir Marketing Communications
Chris Lehmann, Team Coordinator

True stories of true legends! Legendary figures triumph over tough challenges in these brief biographies. Beginning readers learn about favorite heroes and heroines in books they can read for themselves.

1311 Footsteps

Cobblestone Publishing
30 Grove Street
Peterborough, NH   03458   603-924-7209
                                 800-821-0115
                                 FAX 603-924-7380
         http://www.footstepsmagazine.com
         e-mail: custsvc@cobblestone.mv.com
John S Olbrych, Publisher
Charles F Baker III, Editor

Celebrate the heritage of African-Americans and explore their contributions to the development of our culture from the Colonial period through today. Interviews from descendents of figures from the past, maps, illustrations, and photographs complement the nonfiction articles. *$23.95*

52 pages   5 times a year

1312 Imagination Express Destination Time Trip USA

Sunburst Technology
400 Columbus Avenue
Valhalla, NY   10595   914-747-3310
                             800-321-7511
                             FAX 914-747-4109
         http://www.sunburst.com
         e-mail: service@sunburst.com

Student's travel through time to explore the history and development of a fictional New England town. An online scrapbook lets them learn about architecture, fashion, entertainment and events of the six major periods in U.S. history.

1313 Make-a-Map 3D

Sunburst Technology
400 Columbus Avenue
Valhalla, NY   10595   914-747-3310
                             800-321-7511
                             FAX 914-747-4109
         http://www.sunburst.com
         e-mail: support@sunburst.com

Students learn basic mapping, geography and navigation skills. Students design maps of their immediate surroundings by dragging and dropping roads and buildings and adding landmarks, land forms and traffic signs.

1314 Maps & Navigation

Sunburst Technology
400 Columbus Avenue
Valhalla, NY   10595   914-747-3310
                             800-321-7511
                             FAX 914-747-4109
         http://www.sunburst.com
         e-mail: support@sunburst.com

This exciting nautical simulation provides students with opportunities to use their math and science skills.

1315 Patterns Across the Curriculum

Harcourt Achieve
6277 Sea Harbor Drive
Orlando, FL   32887
                             800-531-5015
                             FAX 800-699-9459
         http://www.steckvaughn.com
         e-mail: info@steckvaughn.com
Steck-Vaughn Staff, Author
Tim McEwen, President/CEO
Jeff Johnson, Dir Marketing Communications
Chris Lehmann, Team Coordinator

Develop students' awareness and understanding of patterns in the real world. Exercises allow students to identify, complete, extend, and create patterns. Developed across math, language, social studies, and science. This flexible organization allows teachers to utilize content specific activities in coordination with other classroom assignments, providing additional richness in learning.

1316 Prehistoric Creaures Then & Now: Steadwell

Harcourt Achieve
6277 Sea Harbor Drive
Orlando, FL   32887
                             800-531-5015
                             FAX 800-699-9459
         http://www.steckvaughn.com
         e-mail: info@steckvaughn.com
Steck-Vaughn Staff, Author
Tim McEwen, President/CEO
Jeff Johnson, Dir Marketing Communications
Chris Lehmann, Team Coordinator

Now limited readers can dig into the details of dinosaurs! Each information-packed title includes a special spread with a project, a profile of a dinosaur expert, or a description of a recent dinosaur discovery.

1317 Story of the USA

Educators Publishing Service
31 Smith Place
Cambridge, MA   02139   617-547-6706
                               800-225-5750
                               FAX 888-440-2665
         http://www.epsbooks.com
         e-mail: eps@epsbooks.com
Franklin Escher Jr, Author
Nick Gaehde, President

A series of four workbooks for grades 4-8 which presents basic topics in American History: Book 1, Explorers and Settlers - Book 2, A Young Nation Solves Its Problems - Book 3, America Becomes A Giant - and Book 4, Modern America. A list of vocabulary words introduces each chapter and study questions test students' knowledge.

1318   Talking Walls Bundle

Sunburst Technology
400 Columbus Avenue
Valhalla, NY   10595   914-747-3310
                                         800-321-7511
                                  FAX 914-747-4109
                              http://www.sunburst.com
                        e-mail: service@sunburst.com

Broaden students' perspective of cultures around the world with this two program CD-ROM bundle. From the Great Wall of China to the Berlin Wall to the Vietnam Memorial, students explore 28 "walls" that represent examples of the greatest human achievements to the most intimate expressions of individuality.

1319   Test Practice Success: American History

Harcourt Achieve
6277 Sea Harbor Drive
Orlando, FL   32887
                                         800-531-5015
                                  FAX 800-699-9459
                           http://www.steckvaughn.com
                         e-mail: info@steckvaughn.com
Steck-Vaughn Staff, Author
Tim McEwen, President/CEO
Jeff Johnson, Dir Marketing Communications
Chris Lehmann, Team Coordinator

When you are trying to meet history standards, standardized test preparation is hard to schedule. Now you can do both at the same time. Steck-Vaughn/Berrent Test Practice Success: American History refreshes basic skills, familiarizes students with test formats and directions, and teaches test-taking strategies, while drawing on the material students are studying in class.

1320   True Tales

Harcourt Achieve
6277 Sea Harbor Drive
Orlando, FL   32877
                                         800-531-5015
                                  FAX 800-699-9459
                           http://www.steckvaughn.com
                         e-mail: info@steckvaughn.com
Billings, Author
Tim McEwen, President/CEO
Jeff Johnson, Dir Marketing Communications
Chris Lehmann, Team Coordinator

If you have been looking for reading comprehension materials for limiteed readers, your search is over. True Tales presents powerful real-lfe events with direct connections to geography and science at reading level 3. Gripping accounts of personal triumph and tragedy put geography and science in a very real context. Accompanying activities develop reading and language arts, science, and geography skills students need to boost test scores.

Study Skills

1321   125 Ways to Be a Better Student

LinguiSystems
3100 4th Avenue
East Moline, IL   61244
                                         800-776-4332
                                  FAX 309-755-2377
                                  TDY:800-933-8331
                          http://www.linguisystems.com
                       e-mail: service@linguisystems.com
Paula Currie, Mary deBrueys, Jill Exnicios, Author
Linda Bowers, Owner
Rosemary Huisingh, Owner

Eliminate poor study habits! Help your students develop positive attitudes toward school with these study strategies. Students will get organized and take responsibility for their classroom attitude with these terrific lessons. Lessons are complete with key vocabulary, informative handouts, and practice activities. *$35.95*

136 pages   Ages 10-18

1322   125 Ways to Be a Better Test-Taker

LinguiSystems
3100 4th Avenue
East Moline, IL   61244
                                         800-776-4332
                                  FAX 309-755-2377
                                  TDY:800-933-8331
                          http://www.linguisystems.com
                       e-mail: service@linguisystems.com
Andrea M Lazzari, Judy W Wood, Author
Linda Bowers, Owner
Rosemary Huisingh, Owner

Help your students with test-taking strategies they can use right away. Through activities and practice tests, students learn test-taking strategies including: looking for key words in true/false questions;, answering the multiple-choice questions you know first;, drawing lines through answers you've used in matching questions, re-reading passages for comprehension tasks;, and adding details to a main idea in an essay test. *$35.95*

150 pages   Ages 12-18

1323   Crash Course for Study Skills

LinguiSystems
3100 4th Avenue
East Moline, IL   61244
                                         800-776-4332
                                  FAX 309-755-2377
                                  TDY:800-933-8331
                          http://www.linguisystems.com
                       e-mail: service@linguisystems.com
Marty Soper, Author
Linda Bowers, Owner
Rosemary Huisingh, Owner

These helpful study strategies teach your students to take responsibility for their own learning. It's a practical, motivating approach that works! Students will learn to set goals, manage time, take notes, improve study habits, and understand their personal learning styles. *$35.95*

172 pages   Ages 12-18

1324 Experiences with Writing Styles

Harcourt Achieve
6277 Sea Harbor Drive
Orlando, FL 32887

800-531-5015
FAX 800-699-9459
http://www.steckvaughn.com
e-mail: info@steckvaughn.com

Steck-Vaughn Staff, Author
Tim McEwen, President/CEO
Jeff Johnson, Dir Marketing Communications
Chris Lehmann, Team Coordinator

Give your students experience applying the writing process in nine relevant situations, from personal narratives to persuasive paragraphs to research reports. Units provide a clear definition of each genre and plenty of practice with prewriting, writing, revising, proofreading, and publishing.

1325 INSPECT: A Strategy for Finding and Correcting Spelling Errors

Edge Enterprises
708 W 9th Street
Lawrence, KS 66044

785-749-1473
FAX 785-749-0207
e-mail: edge@midusa.net

David B McNaughton and Charles A Hughes, Author
Jacqueline Schafer, Managing Editor

A strategy for detecting and correcting spelling errors in work generated with a word processing-based spell-checker. Can also be adapted for use with hand-held spellcheckers. The manual comes with IBM and Macintosh computer disks containing practice passages appropriate for upper elementary-aged students, junior-high students and high-school students. The passages can be used with such word processing programs as MS Word, Claris Works and MS Works.

36 pages Paperback

1326 Keyboarding Skills

Educators Publishing Service
31 Smith Place
Cambridge, MA 02139

617-547-6706
800-225-5750
FAX 888-440-2665
http://www.epsbooks.com
e-mail: eps@epsbooks.com

Diana Hanbury King, Author
Nick Gaehde, President

This innovative touch typing method enables students of all ages to learn to type quickly and easily. After learning the alphabet, students can practice words, phrases, numbers, symbols and punctuation.

1327 LD Teacher's IEP Companion

LinguiSystems
3100 4th Avenue
East Moline, IL 61244

800-776-4332
FAX 309-755-2377
TDY:800-933-8331
http://www.linguisystems.com
e-mail: service@linguisystems.com

Molly Lyle, Author
Linda Bowers, Owner
Rosemary Huisingh, Owner

These IEP goals are organized developmentally by skill area with individual objectives and classroom activity suggestions. Goals and objectives cover these academic areas: math, reading, writing, literacy concepts, attention skills, study skills, classroom behavior, social interaction, and transition skills. *$39.95*

169 pages Ages 5-18

1328 Learning Strategies Curriculum

Edge Enterprises
708 W 9th Street
Lawrence, KS 66044

785-749-1473
FAX 785-749-0207
e-mail: edge@midusa.net

Jacqueline Schafer, Managing Editor

A learning strategy is an individual's approach to a learning task. It includes how a person thinks and acts when planning, executing and evaluating performance on the task and its outcomes. In short, learning strategy instruction focuses on how to learn and how to effectively use what has been learned. Manuals range from sentence writing to test taking. All require training. For information, contact the Kansas Center for Research on Learning, 3061 Dole Center, Lawrence 66045 (785-864-4780)

1329 Peer Pals

AGS Publishing
4201 Woodland Road
Circle Pines, MN 55014

651-287-7720
800-328-2560
FAX 800-471-8457
http://www.agsnet.com
e-mail: agsmail@agsnet.com

Robert P Bowman, John N Chanaca, Author
Karen Dahlen, Associate Director
Matt Keller, Marketing Manager

A peer helping program designed to improve study skills, self-esteem, and decision-making. The program uses a big sister/big brother approach, as grade 3-6 students are paired with grade K-2 students. *$33.99*

ISBN 0-886711-62-2

1330 SLANT: A Starter Strategy for Class Participation

Edge Enterprises
708 W 9th Street
Lawrence, KS 66044

785-749-1473
FAX 785-749-0207
e-mail: edge@midusa.net

Edwin S Ellis, Author
Jacqueline Schafer, Managing Editor

An easy-to-learn strategy that students of all ages can use to combine nonverbal, cognitive and verbal behaviors to increase their class participation. Specifically, students learn how to use appropriate posture, track the speaker, activate their thinking and contribute information. Once exposed to this strategy, students not only increase their amount of class participation, but understand how their use of positive participation behaviors can influence the reactions of others.

8 pages   Pamphlet

1331   School Power: Strategies for Succeeding in School

Therapro
225 Arlington Street
Framingham, MA   01702   508-872-9494
                                            800-257-5376
                              FAX 508-875-2062
            http://www.theraproducts.com
            e-mail: info@theraproducts.com
Jeanne Schumm PhD, Marguite Radencich PhD, Author
Karen Conrad, President

A great book for students, parents and teachers. Helps students get organized, take notes, study smarter, write better, handle homework and more. Includes 17 reproducible handout masters. *$16.95*

136 pages

1332   Study Skills and Learning Strategies for Transition

HEATH Resource Center
2121 K Street NW
Washington, DC   20036   202-973-0904
                                            800-544-3284
                              FAX 202-973-0908
            http://www.bobcat-ace.nche.edu
                e-mail: heath@ace.nche.edu
Dan Gardner, Information Specialist

The curriculum guide provides students with learning disabilities the skills and strategies they will need to increase their level of success within the high school curriculum. *$15.00*

1333   Super Study Wheel: Homework Helper

Therapro
225 Arlington Street
Framingham, MA   01702   508-872-9494
                                            800-257-5376
                              FAX 508-875-2062
            http://www.theraproducts.com
            e-mail: info@theraproducts.com
Therapro Staff, Author
Karen Conrad, President

The fun and simple way to find study tips. Developed by learning specialists and an occupational therapist, the Super Study Wheel is an idea-packed resource (with 101 tips) to improve study skills in 13 areas. As a visual, motor and kinesthetic tool, it is very helpful to students with unique learning styles. *$6.95*

Toys & Games, Catalogs

1334   Ablenet

1081 10th Avenue SE
Minneapolis, MN   55414   612-379-0956
                                            800-322-0956
                              FAX 612-379-9143
            http://www.ablenetinc.com
        e-mail: customerservice@ablenetinc.com
Cheryl Volkman, Chief Developmental Officer

Simple assistive technology for teaching children with disabilities including communication aids, switches, mounting systems, environmental control, literacy and teacher resources, kits and more.

1335   Childswork/Childsplay Catalog

Guidance Channel
135 Dupont Street
Plainview, NY   11803   516-349-5520
                                          800-962-1141
                            FAX 800-262-1886
            http://www.childswork.com
            e-mail: info@childswork.com
Ed Werz, President

The most complete source for toys, books and games to help children with their mental health needs, including hundreds of items that deal with ADD, behavior problems, learning disabilities, physical disabilities, sleep disorders, stress and more.

1336   Enabling Devices/Toys for Special Children

Enabling Devices
385 Warburton Avenue
Hastings On Hudson, NY   10706   914-478-0960
                                            800-832-8697
                              FAX 914-478-7030
            http://www.enablingdevices.com
            e-mail: info@enablingdevices.com
Steven E Kanor PhD, President/CEO
Karen O'Connor, VP Operations

A designer, manufacturer and distributor of unique and affordable assitive and adaptive technologies for the physically and mentally challenged, ED/TFSC's products are sought by parents, teachers, and professionals alike.

1337   Maxi Aids

42 Executive Blouevard
Farmingdale, NY   11735   631-752-0521
                                            800-522-6294
                              FAX 631-752-0689
                          TDY:516-752-0738
            http://www.maxiaids.com
            e-mail: sales@maxiaids.com
Aids and appliances for independent living with products designed especially for the visually impaired, blind, hard of hearing, deaf, deaf-blind, arthritic and the physically challenged. New educational games and toys section.

1338 PCI Educational Publishing

PO Box 34270
San Antonio, TX   78265

800-594-4263
FAX 210-377-1121
http://www.pcieducation.com
e-mail: info@pcieducation.com

Jeff McLane, President/CEO
Janie Haugen-McLane, Senior VP/Founder
Richard Resnik, VP Sales/Marketing

Offers 14 programs in a gameboard format to improve life and social skills including Cooking Class, Community Skills, Looking Good, Eating Skills, Workplace Skills, Behavior Skills, Time Skills, Money Skills, Safety Skills, Household Skills, Social Skills, Health Skills, Survival Skills and Recreation Skills. Also offers a Life Skills catalog with over 140 additional products.

1339 Therapro

225 Arlington Street
Framingham, MA   01702

508-872-9494
800-257-5376
FAX 508-875-2062
http://www.theraproducts.com
e-mail: info@theraproducts.com

Karen Conrad, President

Therapro offers for families and professionals a 100+ page catalog with the following: handwriting and fine motor products; perceptual, cognitive and language activities; publications and assessments.

116 pages

Toys & Games, Products

1340 Animal Match-Ups

Therapro
225 Arlington Street
Framingham, MA   01702

508-872-9494
800-257-5376
FAX 508-875-2062
http://www.theraproducts.com
e-mail: info@theraproducts.com

Therapro Staff, Author
Karen Conrad, President

A wonderful visual memory game designed to appeal to young children. Learn to recognize 28 animals by collecting matching pairs from remembered positions. Develops attention and memory. *$8.95*

Ages 3+

1341 Artic Shuffle

LinguiSystems
3100 4th Avenue
East Moline, IL   61244

800-776-4332
FAX 309-755-2377
TDY:800-933-8331
http://www.linguisystems.com
e-mail: service@linguisystems.com

Tobie Nan Kaufman, Author
Linda Bowers, Owner
Rosemary Huisingh, Owner

Why are these card decks best-sellers? Because they're real playing cards! Your students can play Go Fish, Crazy Eights, or Concentration while they practice their target sounds. Use them for vocabulary drills or naming practice. *$89.95*

Ages 5-Adult

1342 ArticBURST Articulation Practice for S, R, Ch, and Sh

LinguiSystems
3100 4th Avenue
East Moline, IL   61244

800-776-4332
FAX 309-755-2377
TDY:800-933-8331
http://www.linguisystems.com
e-mail: service@linguisystems.com

LinguiSystems Staff, Author
Linda Bowers, Owner
Rosemary Huisingh, Owner

Here's a fun quick-thinking game for your older students and clients who continue to need articulation therapy. You'll get a set of cards for each of the toughest sounds. Players have to think of a word with their target sound in these four areas: rhyming, compounds, antonyms, and synonyms. *$37.95*

Ages 10-Adult

1343 BUSY BOX Activity Centers

Enabling Devices
385 Warburton Avenue
Hastings On Hudson, NY   10706

914-478-0960
800-832-8697
FAX 914-478-7030
http://www.enablingdevices.com
e-mail: info@enablingdevices.com

Steven E Kanor PhD, President/CEO
Karen O'Connor, VP Operations

With their bright colors and exciting variety of textures and shapes that are designed to invite exploration that results in rewards including buzzers, music box melodies, radio, vibrations, puffs of air, flashing lights, and even a model that talks. Encourages hand-eye coordination, fine motor skills, gross arm movement. A full line of activity centers are available to meet the needs of the learning disabled, hearing impaired, visually impaired and multisensory impaired.

1344 Barnaby's Burrow: An Auditory Processing Game

LinguiSystems
3100 4th Avenue
East Moline, IL   61244

800-776-4332
FAX 309-755-2377
TDY:800-933-8331
http://www.linguisystems.com
e-mail: service@linguisystems.com

Barb Truman, Author
Linda Bowers, Owner
Rosemary Huisingh, Owner

Your students will practice good auditory processing skills as they help Barnaby the rabbit get to his burrow. This delightful game gives you tons of auditory processing tasks at increasing levels of difficulty. 300 game cards provide stimulus items for: phonological awareness; following directions; absurdities; and identifying main idea and details. *$44.95*

Ages 4-9

1345 Beads and Baubles

Therapro
225 Arlington Street
Framingham, MA 01702   508-872-9494
                                               800-257-5376
                                     FAX 508-875-2062
                        http://www.theraproducts.com
                        e-mail: info@theraproducts.com
Therapro Staff, Author
Karen Conrad, President

A basic stringing activity great for developing fine motor skills. Over 100 pieces in various shapes, colors, and sizes to string on a lace. Three laces included. *$7.50*

1346 Beads and Pattern Cards: Complete Set

Therapro
225 Arlington Street
Framingham, MA 01702   508-872-9494
                                               800-257-5376
                                     FAX 508-875-2062
                        http://www.theraproducts.com
                        e-mail: info@theraproducts.com
Therapro Staff, Author
Karen Conrad, President

Colorful wooden sphers, cubes, cylinders and laces provide pre-reading/early math practice and help develop shape/color sorting and recognition skills. *$26.50*

1347 Big-Little Pegboard Set

Therapro
225 Arlington Street
Framingham, MA 01702   508-872-9494
                                               800-257-5376
                                     FAX 508-875-2062
                        http://www.theraproducts.com
                        e-mail: info@theraproducts.com
Therapro Staff, Author
Karen Conrad, President

Kids love to play with this set of 25 safe, brightly colored hardwood pegs and a durable foam rubber board. *$16.99*

1348 Blend It! End It!

LinguiSystems
3100 4th Avenue
East Moline, IL 61244
                                           800-776-4332
                                FAX 309-755-2377
                                TDY:800-933-8331
                        http://www.linguisystems.com
                        e-mail: service@linguisystems.com
Heather Koepke, Author
Linda Bowers, Owner
Rosemary Huisingh, Owner

Get this fun, quick-thinking game to work on phonics and spelling skills. Players write as many words as they can that include a specific initial blend or word ending. You get 36 initial word blends including: bl-, cr-, spl-. sk-, th-, tw-. *$42.95*

Ages 7-14

1349 Brainopoly: A Thinking Game

LinguiSystems
3100 4th Avenue
East Moline, IL 61244
                                           800-776-4332
                                FAX 309-755-2377
                                TDY:800-933-8331
                        http://www.linguisystems.com
                        e-mail: service@linguisystems.com
LinguiSystems Staff, Author
Linda Bowers, Owner
Rosemary Huisingh, Owner

Target all the critical thinking, problem-solving, and decision-making skills your older students need to meet the demands of the classroom curriculum. Each game section has 50 questions divided into two levels of difficulty. That's 450 total questions! Students will practice using predicting, inferring, deduction skills, and more! *$44.95*

Ages 10-15

1350 Categorically Speaking

The Speech Bin
1965 25th Avenue
Vero Beach, FL 32960   772-770-0007
                                     FAX 772-770-0006
                        http://www.speechbin.com
                        e-mail: info@speechbin.com

This game for two to four players or two teams gives 6-10 years-olds experience in asking questions, evaluating information they receive, and using it to solve problems. To play, they must use specified question formats to get clues about pictures, recognize similarities and differences, identify salient features of objects, and encode and decode messages. Item number Q849. *$49.00*

1351 Children's Cabinet

1090 S Rock Boulevard
Reno, NV 89502   775-856-6200
                              FAX 775-856-6208
                     http://www.childrenscabinet.org
                     e-mail: mail@childrenscabinet.org
Mary Ann Brown, Executive Director

The Children's Cabinet is our community's stand to ensure every child and family has the services and resources to meet fundamental development, care, and learning needs.

1352 Clip Art Collections: The Environment & Space

Sunburst Technology
Elgin, IL 60123
                                           800-321-7511
                                FAX 888-800-3028
Mark Sotir, CEO
Morton Cohen, VP/CFO
Daniel Figurski, VP Sales

This thematic clip art collection is a perfect creativity tool for the classroom.

1353 Clip Art Collections: The US & The World

Sunburts Technology
101 Castleton Street
Pleasantville, NY   10570   914-747-3310
                                   FAX 914-747-4109

This thematic clip art collection is a perfect tool for the classroom.

1354 Colored Wooden Counting Cubes

Therapro
225 Arlington Street
Framingham, MA   01702   508-872-9494
                                800-257-5376
                         FAX 508-875-2062
              http://www.theraproducts.com
              e-mail: info@theraproducts.com
Therapro Staff, Author
Karen Conrad, President

100 cubes in 6 colors are perfect for counting, patterning, and building activities. Activity Guide included. *$19.95*

1355 Come Play with Me

Therapro
225 Arlington Street
Framingham, MA   01702   508-872-9494
                                800-257-5376
                         FAX 508-875-2062
              http://www.theraproducts.com
              e-mail: info@theraproducts.com
Therapro Staff, Author
Karen Conrad, President

This three-dimensional game is so much fun while working on language, matching and visual observation skills. Toys are everywhere! Balls in the livingroom, trains in the kitchen, bears in the bedroom. Look, I found the blocks! Can you be the first to collect all of the toys you need for your toybox? *$19.95*

Ages 3-6

1356 Communication Aids

Enabling Devices
385 Warburton Avenue
Hastings On Hudson, NY   10706   914-478-0960
                                 800-832-8697
                         FAX 914-478-7030
Steven E Kanor PhD, President/CEO
Karen O'Connor, VP Operations

Designed to encourage independence by allowing the user to speak your pre-recorded messages.

1357 Create-A-Story

The Speech Bin
1965 25th Avenue
Vero Beach, FL   32960   772-770-0007
                         FAX 772-770-0006
              http://www.speechbin.com
              e-mail: info@speechbin.com

Here's a powerful language learning game that simplifies the creative process of story-telling and writing for 5-99 years-olds. It fosters their imaginations, organizes their thoughts, and boosts their confidence as they build a narrative. The game can be played by 1-6 players as groups or individuals. Item number C151. *$44.95*

1358 Decoding Games

LinguiSystems
3100 4th Avenue
East Moline, IL   61244
                                800-776-4332
                         FAX 309-755-2377
                       TDY:800-933-8331
              http://www.linguisystems.com
              e-mail: service@linguisystems.com
Tina Sanford, Author
Linda Bowers, Owner
Rosemary Huisingh, Owner

Get three fun games in one handy case. These colorful games target tricky decoding skills your students need for strong reading skills. *$39.95*

Ages 6-10

1359 Definition Play by Play

LinguiSystems
3100 4th Avenue
East Moline, IL   61244
                                800-776-4332
                         FAX 309-755-2377
                       TDY:800-933-8331
              http://www.linguisystems.com
              e-mail: service@linguisystems.com
Sharon Spencer, Author
Linda Bowers, Owner
Rosemary Huisingh, Owner

Teach your students to give accurate, cohesive definitions by identifying and organizing critical attributes of words. As players move along the board, they describe an object card by these attributes: function; what goes with it; size/shape; color; parts; what it's made of; and location. *$44.95*

Ages 8-14

1360 Disc-O-Bocce

Therapro
225 Arlington Street
Framingham, MA   01702   508-872-9494
                                800-257-5376
                         FAX 508-875-2062
              http://www.theraproducts.com
              e-mail: info@theraproducts.com
Therapro Staff, Author
Karen Conrad, President

Requested by therapists working with adults, this item is also great for children. Hundreds of uses include tossing the discs onto the ground and stepping on them to follow their path, tossing and trying to hit the same color disc on the floor, or using the discs to toss in a game of tic-tac-toe on the floor. Includes 12 colorful bocce discs in a storage box with handle. *$17.95*

1361   Earobics Step 1 Home Version

The Speech Bin
1965 25th Avenue
Vero Beach, FL   32960   772-770-0007
                              FAX 772-770-0006
                         http://www.speechbin.com
                         e-mail: info@speechbin.com

Step 1 offers hundreds of levels of play, appealing graphics, and entertaining music to train the critical auditory skills young children need for success in learning. Item number C481. *$59.00*

1362   Earobics Step 2 Home Version

The Speech Bin
1965 25th Avenue
Vero Beach, FL   39260   772-770-0007
                              FAX 772-770-0006
                         http://www.speechbin.com
                         e-mail: info@speechbin.com

Step 2 teaches critical language comprehension skills and trains the critical auditory skills children need for success in learning. It offers hundreds of levels of play, appealing graphics, and entertaining music to train the critical auditory skills young children need for success in learning. Item number C483. *$59.00*

1363   Earobics Step 2 Specialist-Clinician Version

The Speech Bin
1965 25th Avenue
Vero Beach, FL   32960   772-770-0007
                              FAX 772-770-0006
                         http://www.speechbin.com
                         e-mail: info@speechbin.com

Earobics features: Tasks and Level Counter with real time display, adaptive training technology for individualized programs and reporting to track and evaluate each individual's progress. Step 2 teaches critical language comprehension skills and trains the critical auditory skills children need for success in learning. Item number C484. *$299.00*

1364   Eye-Hand Coordination Boosters

Therapro
225 Arlington Street
Framingham, MA   01702   508-872-9494
                              800-257-5376
                         FAX 508-875-2062
                         http://www.theraproducts.com
                         e-mail: info@theraproducts.com
Therapro Staff, Author
Karen Conrad, President

A book of 92 masters that can be used over and over again with work sheets that are appropriate for all ages. These are perceptual motor activities that involve copying and tracing in the areas of visual tracking, discrimination and spatial relationships. *$14.00*

92 pages

1365   Familiar Things

Therapro
225 Arlington Street
Framingham, MA   01702   508-872-9494
                              800-257-5376
                         FAX 508-875-2062
                         http://www.theraproducts.com
                         e-mail: info@theraproducts.com
Therapro Staff, Author
Karen Conrad, President

Identify and match shapes of common objects with these large square, rubber pieces. *$19.99*

1366   Fishing!

Therapro
225 Arlington Street
Framingham, MA   01702   508-872-9494
                              800-257-5376
                         FAX 508-875-2062
                         http://www.theraproducts.com
                         e-mail: info@theraproducts.com
Therapro Staff, Author
Karen Conrad, President

Encourages eye-hand coordination. Rubber hook safely catches velcro on chipboard fish. *$6.95*

1367   Flagship Carpets

1546 Progress Road
Ellijay, GA   30540   706-695-4055
                              800-848-4055
                         FAX 706-276-1980
                         http://www.flagshipcarpets.com
                         e-mail: info@flagshipcarpets.com
Vicki Winkler, Director Sales

Offers a variety of carpet games like hopscotch, the alphabet, geography maps, custom logo mats and more.

1368   Geoboard Colored Plastic

Therapro
225 Arlington Street
Framingham, MA   01702   508-872-9494
                              800-257-5376
                         FAX 508-875-2062
                         http://www.theraproducts.com
                         e-mail: info@theraproducts.com
Therapro Staff, Author
Karen Conrad, President

Teach eye/hand coordination skills while strengthening pincher grasp with rubber bands. *$3.25*

1369   Geometrical Design Coloring Book

Therapro
225 Arlington Street
Framingham, MA   01702   508-872-9494
                              800-257-5376
                         FAX 508-875-2062
                         http://www.theraproducts.com
                         e-mail: info@theraproducts.com
Spyros Horemis, Author
Karen Conrad, President

Color these 46 original designs of pure patterns and abstract shapes for a striking and beautiful result, regardless of skill level. Most designs are made of a combination of small and large areas. *$3.95*

48 pages

1370 Geosafari

Lakeshore Learning Materials
2695 E Dominguez Street
Carson, CA 90810   310-537-8600
    800-421-5354
    FAX 800-537-5403
Michael Kaplan, VP

A fast-paced electronic game teaching geography in an exciting new way. *$99.50*

Item #ED8700

1371 Get in Shape to Write

Therapro
225 Arlington Street
Framingham, MA 01702   508-872-9494
    800-257-5376
    FAX 508-875-2062
    http://www.theraproducts.com
    e-mail: info@theraproducts.com
Phillip Bongiorno MA OTR, Author
Karen Conrad, President

Practice the visula perceptual motor skills needed for writing with these colorful, fun, and engaging activities. The 23 reusuable activities will keep a student's interest while they learn to process auditory, visual, and motoor movement patterns. In addition, learn concepts of matching and sorting colors, shapes and familiar objects. *$12.95*

Ages 3+

1372 Gram's Cracker: A Grammar Game

LinguiSystems
3100 4th Avenue
East Moline, IL 61244
    800-776-4332
    FAX 309-755-2377
    TDY:800-933-8331
    http://www.linguisystems.com
    e-mail: service@linguisystems.com
Julie Cole, Author
Linda Bowers, Owner
Rosemary Huisingh, Owner

Gram the mouse is in the house! Students will love helping Gram get to his mouse hole as they practice these grammar skills: pronouns; plurals; possessives; past tense verbs; comparatives and superlatives; copulas; present progressives; has and have; and negatives. *$44.95*

Ages 4-9

1373 Grammar Scramble: A Grammar and Sentence-Building Game

LinguiSystems
3100 4th Avenue
East Moline, IL 61244
    800-776-4332
    FAX 309-755-2377
    TDY:800-933-8331
    http://www.linguisystems.com
    e-mail: service@linguisystems.com
Rick Bowers, Linda Bowers, Author
Linda Bowers, Owner
Rosemary Huisingh, Owner

Students will improve their grammar and thinking skills as they form intersecting sentences in crossword style. Students receive word tiles divide into these parts of speech: nouns; verbs; pronouns; adjectives; adverbs; articles; interrogatives; prepositions; and conjunctions. *$44.95*

Ages 8-Adult

1374 Gramopoly: A Parts of Speech Game

LinguiSystems
3100 4th Avenue
East Moline, IL 61244
    800-776-4332
    FAX 309-755-2377
    TDY:800-933-8331
    http://www.linguisystems.com
    e-mail: service@linguisystems.com
Raelene Hudson, Author
Linda Bowers, Owner
Rosemary Huisingh, Owner

This best-selling game turns on the grammar lights for your older students. Assign each player a sentence from three levels of difficulty. Players must purchase parts of speech to complete their sentence. *$44.95*

Ages 10-15

1375 Half and Half Design and Color Book

Therapro
225 Arlington Street
Framingham, MA 01702   508-872-9494
    800-257-5376
    FAX 508-875-2062
    http://www.theraproducts.com
    e-mail: info@theraproducts.com
Therapro Staff, Author
Karen Conrad, President

Geometric designs appropriate for all ages. The client draws over dotted lines to finish the other half of the printed design. *$15.00*

72 pages

1376 Hands, Feet and Arrows

Therapro
225 Arlington Street
Framingham, MA 01702   508-872-9494
    800-257-5376
    FAX 508-875-2062
    http://www.theraproducts.com
    e-mail: info@theraproducts.com
Therapro Staff, Author
Karen Conrad, President

This kit has many possibilities for working on gross motor, sensory integration and academic skills. Its variety and ability to easily change to new tasks challenges all levels of abilities. Includes: 12 round sturdy plastic pieces (3 red, 3 yellow, 3 blue and 3 green) and stickers to go on the plastic pieces (3 right & 3 left feet, 3 right & 3 left hands, and 3 arrows). Guaranteed to provide many hours of fun. *$52.95*

1377 Hooray I Can Read!

Therapro
225 Arlington Street
Framingham, MA   01702   508-872-9494
                               800-257-5376
                          FAX 508-875-2062
              http://www.theraproducts.com
               e-mail: info@theraproducts.com
Ravensburger, Author
Karen Conrad, President

Have fun learning letters, sounds and more with 200 age appropriate questions and answers. Turn the dial until a question appears in the window, choose an answer and flip up the question mark to check it. 1-2 Players. *$18.95*

Ages 6-8

1378 Huffy Woofers

Therapro
225 Arlington Street
Framingham, MA   01702   508-872-9494
                               800-257-5376
                          FAX 508-875-2062
              http://www.theraproducts.com
               e-mail: info@theraproducts.com
Therapro Staff, Author
Karen Conrad, President

Safe giant ring toss game. Great for either indoor or outdoor activity. Includes a foam base and 6 rings, 3 red and 3 blue. *$18.95*

1379 Idiom Game

LinguiSystems
3100 4th Avenue
East Moline, IL   61244
                               800-776-4332
                          FAX 309-755-2377
                        TDY:800-933-8331
              http://www.linguisystems.com
               e-mail: service@linguisystems.com
Dave Wisniewski, Author
Linda Bowers, Owner
Rosemary Huisingh, Owner

Idioms give our language richness but confuse our students! Give your students practice with 800 of the most commonly used idiomatic expressions in our language. Each card provides multiple-choice questions at a lower and upper level. *$44.95*

Ages 10-16

1380 Just for Me! Game

LinguiSystems
3100 4th Avenue
East Moline, IL   61244
                               800-776-4332
                          FAX 309-755-2377
                        TDY:800-933-8331
              http://www.linguisystems.com
               e-mail: service@linguisystems.com
Margaret Warner, Author
Linda Bowers, Owner
Rosemary Huisingh, Owner

Follow-up on the early language skills from all five Just for Me! books with this fun new game. It's a hands-on approach as youngsters mix up specially-designed puzzle pieces to make funny faces. Each piece gives you five questions. That's 360 questions in all! Each puzzle piece covers an early language skill and corresponds to one part of the face. *$37.95*

Ages 4-7

1381 LanguageBURST: A Language and Vocabulary Game

LinguiSystems
3100 4th Avenue
East Moline, IL   61244
                               800-776-4332
                          FAX 309-755-2377
                        TDY:800-933-8331
              http://www.linguisystems.com
               e-mail: service@linguisystems.com
Lauri Whiskeyman, Author
Linda Bowers, Owner
Rosemary Huisingh, Owner

Expand your students' language and vocabulary skills with this quick- thinking game. Many of the items are based on the curriculum for grades 3-8 so your therapy is classroom-relevent. Students think quickly as they practice skills in four key language areas: fill-in-the-blank; categories; comparing and contrasting; and attributes. *$37.95*

Ages 9-15

1382 Link N' Learn Activity Book

Therapro
225 Arlington Street
Framingham, MA   01702   508-872-9494
                               800-257-5376
                          FAX 508-875-2062
              http://www.theraproducts.com
               e-mail: info@theraproducts.com
Therapro Staff, Author
Karen Conrad, President

A nice accompaniment to the color rings. There are great cognitive activities included. *$8.95*

80 pages

1383   Link N' Learn Activity Cards

Therapro
225 Arlington Street
Framingham, MA   01702   508-872-9494
                                800-257-5376
                            FAX 508-875-2062
                    http://www.theraproducts.com
                    e-mail: info@theraproducts.com
Therapro Staff, Author
Karen Conrad, President

Learn patterning, sequencing and color discrimination and logic skills with this set of 20 cards that show life-sized links. An instructor's guide is included. *$6.95*

1384   Link N' Learn Color Rings

Therapro
225 Arlington Street
Framingham, MA   01702   508-872-9494
                                800-257-5376
                            FAX 508-875-2062
                    http://www.theraproducts.com
                    e-mail: info@theraproducts.com
Therapro Staff, Author
Karen Conrad, President

These easy to hook and separate colorful 1-1/2" plastic rings can be used in color sorting, counting, sequencing, and other perceptual/cognitive activities. *$6.95*

1385   Magicatch Set

Therapro
225 Arlington Street
Framingham, MA   01702   508-872-9494
                                800-257-5376
                            FAX 508-875-2062
                    http://www.theraproducts.com
                    e-mail: info@theraproducts.com
Therapro Staff, Author
Karen Conrad, President

This Velcro catch game offers a much higher degree of success and feeling of security than traditional ball tossing games. 7 1/2 inch neon catching paddles and 2 1/2 inch ball, in a mesh bag. No latex. *$7.50*

1386   Magnetic Fun

Therapro
225 Arlington Street
Framingham, MA   01702   508-872-9494
                                800-257-5376
                            FAX 508-875-2062
                    http://www.theraproducts.com
                    e-mail: info@theraproducts.com
Therapro Staff, Author
Karen Conrad, President

One swipe of the magic wand can pick up small objects without the need for a refined pincher grasp. *$13.95*

1387   Maxwell's Manor: A Social Language Game

LinguiSystems
3100 4th Avenue
East Moline, IL   61244
                                800-776-4332
                            FAX 309-755-2377
                            TDY:800-933-8331
                    http://www.linguisystems.com
                    e-mail: service@linguisystems.com
Carolyn LoGiudice, Nancy McConnell, Author
Linda Bowers, Owner
Rosemary Huisingh, Owner

This fun game will teach your students the social skills they need to get along with others, be more accepted by their peers, and be successful in the classroom. Maxwell, the loveable dog, leads the way as your students practice positive social language skills. *$44.95*

Ages 4-9

1388   Maze Book

Therapro
225 Arlington Street
Framingham, MA   01702   508-872-9494
                                800-257-5376
                            FAX 508-875-2062
                    http://www.theraproducts.com
                    e-mail: info@theraproducts.com
Therapro Staff, Author
Karen Conrad, President

Significantly more challenging than the ABC Mazes; rich in perceptual activities. *$10.00*

32 pages

1389   Myrtle's Beach: A Phonological Awareness and Articulation Game

LinguiSystems
3100 4th Avenue
East Moline, IL   61244
                                800-776-4332
                            FAX 309-755-2377
                            TDY:800-933-8331
                    http://www.linguisystems.com
                    e-mail: service@linguisystems.com
LinguiSystems Staff, Author
Linda Bowers, Owner
Rosemary Huisingh, Owner

Myrtle's Beach is a fun place to practice phonologial awareness, articulation, and language skills. The flexible format allows you to meet the varied needs of all the students in your speech and language groups. *$44.95*

Ages 4-9

1390   Opposites Game

Therapro
225 Arlington Street
Framingham, MA   01702   508-872-9494
                                800-257-5376
                            FAX 508-875-2062
                    http://www.theraproducts.com
                    e-mail: info@theraproducts.com
Therapro Staff, Author
Karen Conrad, President

Children can explore the concept of opposites by matching and then joining these tiles. Self correcting feature allows for both independent and supervised play. Helps build observation and recognition skills. *$8.50*

1391 PLAID

The Speech Bin
1965 25th Avenue
Vero Beach, FL   32960   772-770-0007
                             FAX 772-770-0006
                        http://www.speechbin.com
                      e-mail: info@speechbin.com

PLAID is a top-notch clinical tool that gives you practical practice materials featuring twenty different phonemes — just what you need for your apraxic and aphasic adults — all in one resource. Item number 1424. *$29.95*

1392 Parquetry Blocks & Pattern Cards

Therapro
225 Arlington Street
Framingham, MA   01702   508-872-9494
                                800-257-5376
                             FAX 508-875-2062
                        http://www.theraproducts.com
                      e-mail: info@theraproducts.com
Therapro Staff, Author
Karen Conrad, President

Encourages visual perceptual skills and challenges a person's sense of design and color with squares, triangles, and rhombuses in six colors.

1393 Patty's Cake: A Describing Game

LinguiSystems
3100 4th Avenue
East Moline, IL   61244
                                800-776-4332
                             FAX 309-755-2377
                             TDY:800-933-8331
                        http://www.linguisystems.com
                      e-mail: service@linguisystems.com
Julie Cole, Author
Linda Bowers, Owner
Rosemary Huisingh, Owner

Teach describing skills with Patty's Cake. Two levels of play in this fun game give you flexibility to meet individual students' learning needs. Players describe age-appropriate picture vocabulary cards by naming attributes such as category, function, shape, color, or location. Your students will improve their skills in: listening; memory; word retrieval; categorizing; naming attributes; formulating sentences; and giving descriptions. *$44.95*

Ages 4-9

1394 Peabody Articulation

The Speech Bin
1965 25th Avenue
Vero Beach, FL   32960   772-770-0007
                             FAX 772-770-0006
                        http://www.speechbin.com
                      e-mail: info@speechbin.com

You'll use these colorful stimulus cards in dozens of games and activities. Ten PAD decks — 480 cards — feature 18 frequently misarticulated consonants and blends. Each deck includes 40 picture cards, word list, two response cards, and five blank cards. Item number A180. *$140.99*

1395 Pegboard Set

Therapro
225 Arlington Street
Framingham, MA   01702   508-872-9494
                                800-257-5376
                             FAX 508-875-2062
                        http://www.theraproducts.com
                      e-mail: info@theraproducts.com
Therapro Staff, Author
Karen Conrad, President

Pegboard has 100 holes and measures 5-3/4 inch square. The pegs come in six bright colors. The 20 double-sided pattern cards or 40 different patterns present 5 levels of difficulty. *$14.99*

1396 Phonology: Software

The Speech Bin
1965 25th Avenue
Vero Beach, FL   32960   772-770-0007
                             FAX 772-770-0006
                        http://www.speechbin.com
                      e-mail: info@speechbin.com

This unique software gives you six entertaining games to treat children's phonological disorders. The program uses target patterns in a pattern cycling approach to phonological processes. Item number L183. *$99.00*

1397 Plastic Cones

Therapro
225 Arlington Street
Framingham, MA   01702   508-872-9494
                                800-257-5376
                             FAX 508-875-2062
                        http://www.theraproducts.com
                      e-mail: info@theraproducts.com
Therapro Staff, Author
Karen Conrad, President

The 12-inch versions of the construction project cones are bright orange and made of lightweigth vinyl. Hole in top. *$5.95*

1398 Plunk's Pond: A Riddles Game for Language

LinguiSystems
3100 4th Avenue
East Moline, IL 61244

800-776-4332
FAX 309-755-2377
TDY:800-933-8331
http://www.linguisystems.com
e-mail: service@linguisystems.com

LinguiSystems Staff, Author
Linda Bowers, Owner
Rosemary Huisingh, Owner

Encourage divergent thinking, sharpen listening skills, and improve vocabulary with this fun riddle game. With a picture on one side and three clues on the other, these cards are great for all kinds of therapy games. Target attributes such as function, color, category, and more! *$44.95*

Ages 4-9

1399 Primer Pak

Therapro
225 Arlington Street
Framingham, MA 01702

508-872-9494
800-257-5376
FAX 508-875-2062
http://www.theraproducts.com
e-mail: info@theraproducts.com

Therapro Staff, Author
Karen Conrad, President

A challenging sampler of manipulatives. Four Fit-A-Space disk puzzles with basic shapes, an 8x8 Alphabet Puzzle, three Lacing Shapes for primary lacing, and 24 Locktagons to form structures. *$14.99*

1400 Punctuation Play-by-Play

LinguiSystems
3100 4th Avenue
East Moline, IL 61244

800-776-4332
FAX 309-755-2377
TDY:800-933-8331
http://www.linguisystems.com
e-mail: service@linguisystems.com

Carolyn LoGiudice, Mike LoGiudice, Author
Linda Bowers, Owner
Rosemary Huisingh, Owner

Punctuation Play-by-Play engages students in a lively game as they practice essential punctuation skills including: capitalization; end marks; apostrophes; commas; quotation marks; colons; semicolons. Question cards are divided into two levels of difficulty. *$44.95*

Ages 10-18

1401 Read-A-Bit

LinguiSystems
3100 4th Avenue
East Moline, IL 61244

800-776-4332
FAX 309-755-2377
TDY:800-933-8331
http://www.linguisystems.com
e-mail: service@linguisystems.com

Dagmar Kafka, Author
Linda Bowers, Owner
Rosemary Huisingh, Owner

Get 15 games in one box! Six decks of cards with different levels of reading difficulty work with and without the colorful game board to give you plenty of flexibility. You'll work through a hierarchy of reading skills from primer to grade 3. Students practice consonants, vowels, controlled R sounds, sight words, and more. *$41.95*

Ages 5-9

1402 Reading Comprehension Game Intermediate

LinguiSystems
3100 4th Avenue
East Moline, IL 61244

800-776-4332
FAX 309-755-2377
TDY:800-933-8331
http://www.linguisystems.com
e-mail: service@linguisystems.com

Linda Bowers, Rosemary Huisingh, Carolyn LoGiudice, Author
Linda Bowers, Owner
Rosemary Huisingh, Owner

This game gives you fun, repetitive practice in three essential reading comprehension skills. The first is Reading for Details including cloze, referents, sequencing, describing, and more! The second is Reading for Understanding including main idea, paraphrasing, context clues, defining, and more. The third area is Going Beyond including making references, predicting, and making associations. *$44.95*

Ages 12-18

1403 Rhyming Sounds Game

Therapro
225 Arlington Street
Framingham, MA 01702

508-872-9494
800-257-5376
FAX 508-875-2062
http://www.theraproducts.com
e-mail: info@theraproducts.com

Therapro Staff, Author
Karen Conrad, President

Introduces 32 different rhyming sounds as players match the ending sound of the picture tile to the corresponding object on the category boards. Includes sorting/storage tray, 56 picture tiles, and 4 category cards with self-checking feature. No reading required. *$9.95*

1404 Rocky's Mountain: A Word-finding Game

LinguiSystems
3100 4th Avenue
East Moline, IL 61244

800-776-4332
FAX 309-755-2377
TDY:800-933-8331
http://www.linguisystems.com
e-mail: service@linguisystems.com

Gina Williamson, Susan Shields, Author
Linda Bowers, Owner
Rosemary Huisingh, Owner

Tackle stubborn word-finding problems with this fun game! Game cards are organized by four word-finding strategies so you can pick the strategy that best meets your students' needs. Teach these strategies for word-finding: visual imagery; word association; sound/letter cueing; and categories. *$44.95*

Ages 4-9

1405 SPARC for Grammar

LinguiSystems
3100 4th Avenue
East Moline, IL   61244

800-776-4332
FAX 309-755-2377
TDY:800-933-8331
http://www.linguisystems.com
e-mail: service@linguisystems.com
Susan Thomsen, Kathy Donnelly, Author
Linda Bowers, Owner
Rosemary Huisingh, Owner

Teach grammar in meaningful contexts! The lessons provide a wealth of opportunities for your students to hear, repeat, answer questions and tell stories using targeted language structures. *$39.95*

165 pages   Ages 4-10

1406 Self-Control Games & Workbook

Western Psychological Services
12031 Wilshire Boulevard
Los Angeles, CA   90025

310-478-2061
800-648-8857
FAX 310-478-7838
Berthold Berg, PhD, Author

This game is designed to teach self-control in academic and social situations. Addresses a total of 24 impulsive, inattentive and hyperactive behaviors. The companion workbook reinforces the use of positive self-statements, and problem-solving techniques, instead of expressing anger. *$62.50*

1407 Sequenced Inventory of Communication Development Revised(SICD)

The Speech Bin
1965 25th Avenue
Vero Beach, FL   32960

772-770-0007
800-477-3324
FAX 888-329-2246
http://www.speechbin.com
e-mail: info@speechbin.com
Dona Hedrick, Elizabeth Prather, Annette Tobin, Author

SICD uses appealing toys to assess communication skills of children at all levels of ability including those with impaired hearing or vision. SICD looks at child and environment, measuring receptive and expressive language. Item number W710. *$395.00*

1408 Shape and Color Sorter

Therapro
225 Arlington Street
Framingham, MA   01702

508-872-9494
800-257-5376
FAX 508-875-2062
http://www.theraproducts.com
e-mail: info@theraproducts.com
Therapro Staff, Author
Karen Conrad, President

This simple and safe task of perception includes 25 crepe foam rubber pieces to sort by shape or color. Comes in five bright colors, each color representing a shape. Shapes fit nicely onto five large pegs. *$14.99*

1409 Shapes

Therapro
225 Arlington Street
Framingham, MA   01702

508-872-9494
800-257-5376
FAX 508-875-2062
http://www.theraproducts.com
e-mail: info@theraproducts.com
Therapro Staff, Author
Karen Conrad, President

This 8 1/2 x 11 inch high quality coloring book will help children learn to recognize shapes while improving their fine motor and perceptual skills. *$1.50*

30 pages

1410 Silly Sentences

The Speech Bin
1965 25th Avenue
Vero Beach, FL   32960

772-770-0007
FAX 772-770-0006
http://www.speechbin.com
e-mail: info@speechbin.com

Children love to have fun. Silly Sentences lets them have fun while they play these engaging card games to learn: subject + verb agreement; speech sound articulation; S+ V+ O sentences; questioning and answering; humor and absurdities and present progressive verbs. Item number P506. *$41.00*

1411 Snail's Pace Race Game

Therapro
225 Arlington Street
Framingham, MA   01702

508-872-9494
800-257-5376
FAX 508-875-2062
http://www.theraproducts.com
e-mail: info@theraproducts.com
Therapro Staff, Author
Karen Conrad, President

This classic, easy color game is back and is fun for all to play. Roll the colored dice to see which wooden snail will move closer to the finish line. Promotes color recognition, understanding of taking turns, and sharing. *$19.95*

1412 Sounds Abound Game

LinguiSystems
3100 4th Avenue
East Moline, IL 61244

800-776-4332
FAX 309-755-2377
TDY:800-933-8331
http://www.linguisystems.com
e-mail: service@linguisystems.com
Orna Lenchner PhD, Blanche Podhajski PhD, Author
Linda Bowers, Owner
Rosemary Huisingh, Owner

Teach critical features about sounds in words for better language skills. Your students will love this fun game because it's easy to play. This game targets the sounds students use the most — f, s, p, t, and m. These essential sounds are critical for early literacy success. *$109.95*

112 pages   Ages 4-8

1413 Speech & Language & Voice & More...

The Speech Bin
1965 25th Avenue
Vero Beach, FL 32960

772-770-0007
FAX 772-770-0006
http://www.speechbin.com
e-mail: info@speechbin.com

Contains 88 practically perfect reproducible games and activities ideal for your K-5 clients. It gives you: manipulable activities to keep active leaners learning; tasks to match a multitude of interests and abilities and vocal hygiene worksheets targeted to reduce vocal abuse. Item number 1496. *$19.95*

1414 Speech Sports

The Speech Bin
1965 25th Avenue
Vero Beach, FL 32960

772-770-0007
FAX 772-770-0006
http://www.speechbin.com
e-mail: info@speechbin.com

Speech Sports makes every child in your caseload a shining sports star. Reproducible gamesboards and language activities feature 19 different sports from boating to skating, bowling to running, basketball to soccer. Item number 1590. *$24.95*

1415 Speech-Language Delights

The Speech Bin
1965 25th Avenue
Vero Beach, FL 32960

772-770-0007
FAX 772-770-0006
http://www.speechbin.com
e-mail: info@speechbin.com

Cook up lots of fun with Speech-Language Delights! Delectably delicious speech and language activities and games provide rich opportunities and hands-on activities with food-related themes to enrich K-8 kids. Item number 1541. *$ 29.95*

1416 Spider Ball

Therapro
225 Arlington Street
Framingham, MA 01702

508-872-9494
800-257-5376
FAX 508-875-2062
http://www.theraproducts.com
e-mail: info@theraproducts.com
Therapro Staff, Author
Karen Conrad, President

Easy to catch, won't roll away! This foam rubber ball has rubber legs that make it incredibly easy to catch. Invented by a PE teacher to help children improve their ball playing skills. The Spiderball's legs act as brakes bringing it to a stop when rolled and minimizing the time needed to chase a missed ball. 2 1/4 inch diameter. *$4.50*

1417 Squidgie Flying Disc

Therapro
225 Arlington Street
Framingham, MA 01702

508-872-9494
800-257-5376
FAX 508-875-2062
http://www.theraproducts.com
e-mail: info@theraproducts.com
Therapro Staff, Author
Karen Conrad, President

This is a great flexible flying disc that is amazingly easy to throw and travels over long distances. It is soft and easy to catch. It will even float in the pool! *$4.95*

1418 String-A-Long Lacing Activity

Therapro
225 Arlington Street
Framingham, MA 01702

508-872-9494
800-257-5376
FAX 508-875-2062
http://www.theraproducts.com
e-mail: info@theraproducts.com
Therapro Staff, Author
Karen Conrad, President

A lacing activity that develops hand eye coordination and concentration as children create 2 colorful bead buddies. Each buddy has 4 laces attached to its painted heal now build the body with 23 beads! *$18.00*

Ages 4+

1419 That's Life: A Game of Life Skills

LinguiSystems
3100 4th Avenue
East Moline, IL 61244

800-776-4332
FAX 309-755-2377
TDY:800-933-8331
http://www.linguisystems.com
e-mail: service@linguisystems.com
Patricia Smith, Author
Linda Bowers, Owner
Rosemary Huisingh, Owner

Help your older students refine their language skills to negotiate the real world with this fun game. Get 100 thinking and language questions for each of these life area: consumer affairs, government, health concerns, money matters, going places, and homemaking. *$44.95*

Ages 12-18

1420 Things in My House: Picture Matching Game

Therapro
225 Arlington Street
Framingham, MA   01702   508-872-9494
800-257-5376
FAX 508-875-2062
http://www.theraproducts.com
e-mail: info@theraproducts.com
Therapro Staff, Author
Karen Conrad, President

Strengthen visual discrimination, sorting, and organizing skills. Young children enjoy finding correct matches in this fun first game. The colorful graphics depicting familiar household objects and activities encourage verbalization and imaginative play. *$10.95*

1421 Tic-Tac-Artic and Match

LinguiSystems
3100 4th Avenue
East Moline, IL   61244
800-776-4332
FAX 309-755-2377
TDY:800-933-8331
http://www.linguisystems.com
e-mail: service@linguisystems.com
Carol A Vaccariello, Author
Linda Bowers, Owner
Rosemary Huisingh, Owner

Tic-Tac-Artic and Match gives you five games on every page and tons of practice per session. Each page has 16 pictures for one target phoneme. To play Tic-Tac-Artic, use the special game template to create four different tic-tac-toe style games. *$34.95*

Ages 4-12

1422 Toddler Tote

Therapro
225 Arlington Street
Framingham, MA   01702   508-872-9494
800-257-5376
FAX 508-875-2062
http://www.theraproducts.com
e-mail: info@theraproducts.com
Therapro Staff, Author
Karen Conrad, President

Offers one Junior Fit-A-Space panel that has large geometric shapes; 4 Shape Squares providing basic shapes in a more challenging size; 2 Peg Play Vehicles and Pegs introducing early peg board skills; 3 Familiar Things and 2 piece puzzles and a handy take-along bag. *$14.99*

1423 Tools of the Trade Game

Therapro
225 Arlington Street
Framingham, MA   01702   508-872-9494
800-257-5376
FAX 508-875-2062
http://www.theraproducts.com
e-mail: info@theraproducts.com
Therapro Staff, Author
Karen Conrad, President

Introduces 32 different occupations and the tools they use. Tool picture tiles are sorted into compartments which correspond to the category card, showing people dressed for their jobs. Includes sorting tray, 56 tool tiles and 4 category cards with self-checking feature. No reading required. *$9.95*

1424 Vowel Scramble

LinguiSystems
3100 4th Avenue
East Moline, IL   61244
800-776-4332
FAX 309-755-2377
TDY:800-933-8331
http://www.linguisystems.com
e-mail: service@linguisystems.com
Carolyn LoGiudice, Author
Linda Bowers, Owner
Rosemary Huisingh, Owner

Your student will love this fun new way to practice spelling and phonological awareness skills. Players earn points by using letter tiles to complete words on the game board. *$44.95*

Ages 7-12

1425 Whistle Set

Therapro
225 Arlington Street
Framingham, MA   01702   508-872-9494
800-257-5376
FAX 508-875-2062
http://www.theraproducts.com
e-mail: info@theraproducts.com
Therapro Staff, Author
Karen Conrad, President

The whistles in this collection are colorful and sturdy. Most feature moving parts as well as noise-makers to stimulate both ocular and oral motor skills. Includes nine whistles. Respiratory demand ranges from easy to difficult. *$17.50*

1426 Wikki Stix-Neon & Primary

Therapro
225 Arlington Street
Framingham, MA   01702   508-872-9494
800-257-5376
FAX 508-875-2062
http://www.theraproducts.com
e-mail: info@theraproducts.com
Therapro Staff, Author
Karen Conrad, President

Colorful, nontoxic waxed strings which are easily molded to create various forms, shapes and letters. Combine motor planning skill with fine motor skill by following simple shapes with Wikki Stix and then coloring in the shape. *$ 4.95*

Each

1427 Wonder Ball

Therapro
225 Arlington Street
Framingham, MA   01702   508-872-9494
                                800-257-5376
                         FAX 508-875-2062
                   http://www.theraproducts.com
                   e-mail: info@theraproducts.com
Therapro Staff, Author
Karen Conrad, President

This 3 inch ball made of many small suction cups feels good in the palm of the hand and, when thrown against a smooth surface, will firmly stick. Pulling it from the surface requires strength, resulting in proprioceptive stimulation. *$1.95*

1428 Wooden Pegboard

Therapro
225 Arlington Street
Framingham, MA   01702   508-872-9494
                                800-257-5376
                         FAX 508-875-2062
                   http://www.theraproducts.com
                   e-mail: info@theraproducts.com
Therapro Staff, Author
Karen Conrad, President

This 10 inch square, laquer-finished wooden board has 100 drilled holes. *$10.95*

1429 Wooden Pegs

Therapro
225 Arlington Street
Framingham, MA   01702   508-872-9494
                                800-257-5376
                         FAX 508-875-2062
                   http://www.theraproducts.com
                   e-mail: info@theraproducts.com
Therapro Staff, Author
Karen Conrad, President

Smooth 2 inch pegs in 6 colors for use in design and pattern making with the wooden pegboard above. Set of 100 pegs. *$4.95*

1430 WriteOPOLY

LinguiSystems
3100 4th Avenue
East Moline, IL   61244
                                800-776-4332
                         FAX 309-755-2377
                         TDY:800-933-8331
                   http://www.linguisystems.com
                   e-mail: service@linguisystems.com
Paul F Johnson, Author
Linda Bowers, Owner
Rosemary Huisingh, Owner

End writer's block for even your most reluctant writers with this fun game. Improve written language skills with WriteOPOLY. Students travel around a colorful game board buying properties and filling out Writing Plan sheets. *$44.95*

Ages 9-14

Writing

1431 100% Grammar

LinguiSystems
3100 4th Avenue
East Moline, IL   61244
                                800-776-4332
                         FAX 309-755-2377
                         TDY:800-933-8331
                   http://www.linguisystems.com
                   e-mail: service@linguisystems.com
Mike LoGiudice, Carolyn LoGiudice, Author
Linda Bowers, Owner
Rosemary Huisingh, Owner

Make the link between grammar and communication skills with this incredible resource. You'll get relevant, fun activities to develop clear, accurate, excellent communication skills. 100% Grammar thoroughly covers all the essential grammar areas including: nouns; pronouns; complements; verbals; clauses; and fine points. *$37.95*

174 pages   Ages 9-14

1432 100% Grammar LITE

LinguiSystems
3100 4th Avenue
East Moline, IL   61244
                                800-776-4332
                         FAX 309-755-2377
                         TDY:800-933-8331
                   http://www.linguisystems.com
                   e-mail: service@linguisystems.com
Mike LoGiudice, Carolyn LoGiudice, Author
Linda Bowers, Owner
Rosemary Huisingh, Owner

Teach one grammar concept at a time. Compared to 100% Grammar, this resource is lighter in the amount of content per page and contextual demands of the practice items. The fun art and light approach will appeal to your hardest-to-teach students. The book is divided into two sections covering parts of speech and sentence structures. *$37.95*

178 pages   Ages 4-19

1433 100% Punctuation

LinguiSystems
3100 4th Avenue
East Moline, IL   61244
                                800-776-4332
                         FAX 309-755-2377
                         TDY:800-933-8331
                   http://www.linguisystems.com
                   e-mail: service@linguisystems.com
Mike LoGiudice, Carolyn LoGiudice, Author
Linda Bowers, Owner
Rosemary Huisingh, Owner

Good written language requires the appropriate touches. On-target punctuation is essential for clear writing. This resource puts fun, zip, and humor into teaching this necessary skill. Each unit gives you a teacher guide, a skill overview, light-hearted activity sheets, and a handy quiz for accountability. *$37.95*

179 pages   Ages 9-14

1434   100% Punctuation LITE

LinguiSystems
3100 4th Avenue
East Moline, IL   61244

800-776-4332
FAX 309-755-2377
TDY:800-933-8331
http://www.linguisystems.com
e-mail: service@linguisystems.com
LinguiSystems Staff, Author
Linda Bowers, Owner
Rosemary Huisingh, Owner

Good punctuation is essential for clear written communication. This light approach makes it fun to teach and fun to learn. Get practice pages for: capitals; end marks; apostrophes; commas; quotation marks; letters; abbreviations; colons; and semicolons. *$37.95*

183 pages   Ages 9-14

1435   100% Spelling

LinguiSystems
3100 4th Avenue
East Moline, IL   61244

800-776-4332
FAX 309-755-2377
TDY:800-933-8331
http://www.linguisystems.com
e-mail: service@linguisystems.com
LinguiSystems Staff, Author
Linda Bowers, Owner
Rosemary Huisingh, Owner

Demystify spelling by helping students tackle one pattern at a time. Your students will discover and retain spelling rules by searching for spelling patterns. Each set of three lessons targets a specific spelling pattern. These activity sheets are great for independent work, group work, and take-home practice. *$37.95*

187 pages   Ages 8-14

1436   100% Story Writing

LinguiSystems
3100 4th Avenue
East Moline, IL   61244

800-776-4332
FAX 309-755-2377
TDY:800-933-8331
http://www.linguisystems.com
e-mail: service@linguisystems.com
Dave Wisniewski, Katarina Hempstead, Author
Kathleen Van Horn

Your students experience success with writing because you give them strategies to sequence, plan, and write a great story! You'll get 50 well-developed topics for your students to choose from. Work on organizing thoughts before writing, sequencing story events, writing paragraphs, and using storyboards to visualize a story. *$37.95*

149 pages   Ages 9-14

1437   100% Writing 4-book Set

LinguiSystems
3100 4th Avenue
East Moline, IL   61244

800-776-4332
FAX 309-755-2377
TDY:800-933-8331
http://www.linguisystems.com
e-mail: service@linguisystems.com
Dave Wisniewski, Author
Linda Bowers, Owner
Rosemary Huisingh, Owner

Awaken the slumbering interest in writing that your students unknowingly possess. This set of books shows students how to organize thoughts into cohesive, interesting writing. Even students who hate to write will produce solidly-crafted products. *$131.80*

150 pages   Ages 12-15

1438   100% Writing: Comparison and Contrast

LinguiSystems
3100 4th Avenue
East Moline, IL   61244

800-776-4332
FAX 309-755-2377
TDY:800-933-8331
http://www.linguisystems.com
e-mail: service@linguisystems.com
Dave Wisniewski, Author
Linda Bowers, Owner
Rosemary Huisingh, Owner

Help your students to learn to write comparison and contrast with this helpful resource. Chapters walk students through introductory, body, and concluding paragraphs. Along the way they'll practice helpful strategies of identifying workable comparisons and meaningful contrasts. *$37.95*

183 pages   Ages 12-15

1439   100% Writing: Exposition

LinguiSystems
3100 4th Avenue
East Moline, IL   61244

800-776-4332
FAX 309-755-2377
TDY:800-933-8331
http://www.linguisystems.com
e-mail: service@linguisystems.com
Dave Wisniewski, Author
Linda Bowers, Owner
Rosemary Huisingh, Owner

Get helpful handouts, instructions, and practice sheets to help students learn all about expository writing. Chapters cover introductory paragraph, building body paragraphs, concluding paragraph, using quotations in definition, and much more! *$37.95*

143 pages   Ages 12-15

1440 100% Writing: Narration

LinguiSystems
3100 4th Avenue
East Moline, IL   61244

800-776-4332
FAX 309-755-2377
TDY:800-933-8331
http://www.linguisystems.com
e-mail: service@linguisystems.com

Dave Wisniewski, Author
Linda Bowers, Owner
Rosemary Huisingh, Owner

Your students will learn all they need to know about narrative writing with this incredible resource. Chapters cover introducing narration, consistency of tense, use of dialogue sequencing an incident, using specific vocabulary, variety in sentence structure, character and setting development, and much more! *$37.95*

187 pages   Ages 12-15

1441 100% Writing: Persuasion

LinguiSystems
3100 4th Avenue
East Moline, IL   61244

800-776-4332
FAX 309-755-2377
TDY:800-933-8331
http://www.linguisystems.com
e-mail: service@linguisystems.com

Dave Wisniewski, Author
Linda Bowers, Owner
Rosemary Huisingh, Owner

Teach all the basics of writing persuasion. Students will learn how to write a simple five-paragraph persuasion, understand fact vs. opinion, circling in persuasion, appealing to logic and emotion, and much more. *$37.95*

143 pages   Ages 12-15

1442 125 Ways to Be a Better Writer

LinguiSystems
3100 4th Avenue
East Moline, IL   61244

800-776-4332
FAX 309-755-2377
TDY:800-933-8331
http://www.linguisystems.com
e-mail: service@linguisystems.com

Paul F Johnson, Author
Linda Bowers, Owner
Rosemary Huisingh, Owner

Your students will be eager to write in these fun, relevant contexts. Train functional, confident writers with 125 strategies for better writing skills. Easy-to-grasp strategies and practice pages help your students learn the writing process, express their thoughts clearly, write better sentences and paragraphs, and more. *$35.95*

166 pages   Ages 12-18

1443 125 Writing Projects

LinguiSystems
3100 4th Avenue
East Moline, IL   61244

800-776-4332
FAX 309-755-2377
TDY:800-933-8331
http://www.linguisystems.com
e-mail: service@linguisystems.com

Paul F Johnson, Author
Linda Bowers, Owner
Rosemary Huisingh, Owner

Help your students discover themselves as successful writers. This handy resource gives you activities arranged in a hierarchy to meet the needs of all the levels you teach. *$35.95*

171 pages   Ages 10-17

1444 Author's Toolkit

Sunburst Technology
400 Columbus Avenue
Valhalla, NY   10595

914-747-3310
800-321-7511
FAX 914-747-4109
http://www.sunburst.com
e-mail: support@sunburst.com

Students can use this comprehensive tool to organize ideas, make outlines, rough drafts, edit and print all their written work.

1445 Blend It! End It!

LinguiSystems
3100 4th Avenue
East Moline, IL   61244

800-776-4332
FAX 309-755-2377
TDY:800-933-8331
http://www.linguisystems.com
e-mail: service@linguisystems.com

Heather Koepke, Author
Linda Bowers, Owner
Rosemary Huisingh, Owner

Get this fun quick-thinking game to work on phonics and spelling skills. Players write as many words as they can including a specific initial blend or word ending. You get 36 initial word blends including: bl-, cr-, spl-. sk-, th-, tw-. *$42.95*

Ages 7-14

1446 Callirobics: Advanced Exercises

Therapro
225 Arlington Street
Framingham, MA   01702

508-872-9494
800-257-5376
FAX 508-875-2062
http://www.theraproducts.com
e-mail: info@theraproducts.com

Therapro Staff, Author
Karen Conrad, President

Allows those who have finished earlier Callirobics programs to continue improving their handwriting in a fun and creative way. Callirobics Advanced lets one create shapes to popular music from around the world. *$27.95*

Book and CD

1447 Callirobics: Exercises for Adults

Therapro
225 Arlington Street
Framingham, MA   01702   508-872-9494
                                800-257-5376
                         FAX 508-875-2062
             http://www.theraproducts.com
             e-mail: info@theraproducts.com
Therapro Staff, Author
Karen Conrad, President

Callirobics-for-Adults is a program designed to help adults regain handwriting skills to music. The music assists as an auditory cue in initiating writing movements, and will help develop a sense of rhythm in writing. The program consists of two sections: exercises of simple graphical shapes that help adults gain fluency in the writing movement, and exercises of various combinations of cursive letters. *$30.95*

1448 Callirobics: Handwriting Exercises to Music

Therapro
225 Arlington Street
Framingham, MA   01702   508-872-9494
                                800-257-5376
                         FAX 508-875-2062
             http://www.theraproducts.com
             e-mail: info@theraproducts.com
Therapro Staff, Author
Karen Conrad, President

Ten structured sessions, each with 2 exercises and 2 pieces of music. Includes stickers and a certificate book. *$27.95*

Book and CD

1449 Callirobics: Prewriting Skills with Music

Therapro
225 Arlington Street
Framingham, MA   01702   508-872-9494
                                800-257-5376
                         FAX 508-875-2062
             http://www.theraproducts.com
             e-mail: info@theraproducts.com
Therapro Staff, Author
Karen Conrad, President

These 11 handwriting exercises are a series of simple and enjoyable graphical patterns to be traced by the child while listening to popular melodies. *$27.95*

Book and CD

1450 Caps, Commas and Other Things

Academic Therapy Publications
20 Commercial Boulevard
Novato, CA   94949   415-883-3314
                                 800-422-7249
                          FAX 888-287-9975
             http://www.academictherapy.com
             e-mail: sales@academictherapy.com
Sheryl Pastorek, Author
Betty Lou Kratoville, Editor

A writing program for regular, remedial and EST students in grades 3 through 12 and adults in basic education classes remedial ESL. Six levels on capitalization and punctuation, four levels on written expression. Specific lesson plans with reproducible worksheets. *$20.00*

264 pages
ISBN 0-878793-25-9

1451 Create-A-Story

The Speech Bin
1965 25th Avenue
Vero Beach, FL   32960   772-770-0007
                          FAX 772-770-0006
             http://www.speechbin.com
             e-mail: info@speechbin.com

Here's a powerful language learning game that simplifies the creative process of storytelling and writing for 5-99 year olds. It fosters their imaginations, organizes their thoughts, and boosts their confidence as they build a narrative. The game can be played by 1-6 players as groups or individuals. Item number C151. *$44.95*

1452 D'Nealian Handwriting from A to Z

Therapro
225 Arlington Street
Framingham, MA   01702   508-872-9494
                                800-257-5376
                         FAX 508-875-2062
             http://www.theraproducts.com
             e-mail: info@theraproducts.com
Donald Thurber, Author
Karen Conrad, President

Up to date books for D'Nealian manuscript and cursive handwriting. In the manuscript children master each lowercase and uppercase letter in natural progressive stages first by tracing with their fingers, then by writing the letters, and finally by writing words that begin with the letter. *$9.95*

1453 Daily Starters: Quote of the Day

LinguiSystems
3100 4th Avenue
East Moline, IL   61244
                                 800-776-4332
                          FAX 309-755-2377
                         TDY:800-933-8331
             http://www.linguisystems.com
             e-mail: service@linguisystems.com
Dave Wisniewski, Author
Linda Bowers, Owner
Rosemary Huisingh, Owner

Get your students off to a focused start in therapy or in the classroom. These quick activities help older students integrate several language arts skills at once including writing, thinking, grammar, punctuation, vocabulary, and more. *$21.95*

142 pages   Ages 12-18

1454   Do-A-Dot Activity Books

Therapro
225 Arlington Street
Framingham, MA   01702   508-872-9494
                                 800-257-5376
                          FAX 508-875-2062
                http://www.theraproducts.com
                e-mail: info@theraproducts.com
Therapro Staff, Author
Karen Conrad, President

Do-A-Dot Activity Books are great for pre-writing skill books, printed on heavy paper stock, with each page perforated for easy removal. They promote eye-hand coordination and visual recognition. *$4.95*

1455   Draw-Write-Now, A Drawing and Handwriting Course for Kids

Therapro
225 Arlington Street
Framingham, MA   01702   508-872-9494
                                 800-257-5376
                          FAX 508-875-2062
                http://www.theraproducts.com
                e-mail: info@theraproducts.com
Therapro Staff, Author
Karen Conrad, President

A great way to incorporate visual motor skills and handwriting with curriculum studies. Based on a teacher's idea that handwriting utilizes many of the same skills as drawing, these books feature easy to follow drawing lessons that are broken down into a series of steps. Students can use the practice text provided to write about their drawings. The books cover a variety of themes and subjects. *$10.95*

1456   Dysgraphia: Why Johnny Can't Write: 3rd Edition

Therapro
225 Arlington Street
Framingham, MA   01702   508-872-9494
                                 800-257-5376
                          FAX 508-875-2062
                http://www.theraproducts.com
                e-mail: info@theraproducts.com
D Cavey, Author
Karen Conrad, President

Dysgraphia is a serious writing difficulty. This book provides guidelines for recognizing dysgraphic children and explains their special writing needs. Offers valuable tips, ideas and methods to promote success and self regard. *$15.95*

61 pages

1457   Easybook Deluxe

Sunburst Technology
400 Columbus Avenue
Valhalla, NY   10595   914-747-3310
                                 800-321-7511
                          FAX 914-747-4109
                   http://www.sunburst.com
                e-mail: service@sunburst.com

Designed to support the needs of a wide range of writers, this book publishing tool provides students with a creative environment to write, design and illustrate stories and reports, and to print their work in book formats.

1458   Easybook Deluxe Writing Workshop: Colonial Times

Sunburst Technology
400 Columbus Avenue
Valhalla, NY   10595   914-747-3310
                                 800-321-7511
                          FAX 914-747-4109
                   http://www.sunburst.com
                e-mail: service@sunburst.com

Writing workshops combine theme-based activities with the award-winning EasyBook Deluxe.

1459   Easybook Deluxe Writing Workshop: Immigration

Sunburst Technology
400 Columbus Avenue
Valhalla, NY   10595   914-747-3310
                                 800-321-7511
                          FAX 914-747-4109
                   http://www.sunburst.com
                e-mail: support@sunburst.com

Writing workshops combine theme-based activities with the award-winning EasyBook Deluxe.

1460   Easybook Deluxe Writing Workshop: Rainforest & Astronomy

Sunburst Technology
400 Columbus Avenue
Valhalla, NY   10595   914-747-3310
                                 800-321-7511
                          FAX 914-747-4109
                   http://www.sunburst.com
                e-mail: support@sunburst.com

Writing workshops combine theme-based activities with the award-winning EasyBook Deluxe.

1461   Easybook Deluxe Writing Workshop: Whales & Oceans

Sunburst Technology
400 Columbus Avenue
Valhalla, NY   10595   914-747-3310
                                 800-321-7511
                          FAX 914-747-4109
                   http://www.sunburst.com
                e-mail: support@sunburst.com

Writing workshops combine theme-based activities with the award-winning EasyBook Deluxe.

1462 Experiences with Writing Styles

Harcourt Achieve
6277 Sea Harbor Drive
Orlando, FL   32887

800-531-5015
FAX 800-699-9459
http://www.steckvaughn.com
e-mail: info@steckvaughn.com

Steck-Vaughn Staff, Author
Tim McEwen, President/CEO
Jeff Johnson, Dir Marketing Communications
Chris Lehmann, Team Coordinator

Give your students experience applying the writing process in nine relevant situations, from personal narratives to persuasive paragraphs to research reports. Units provide a clear definition of each genre and plenty of practice with prewriting, writing, revising, proofreading, and publishing.

1463 Fonts 4 Teachers

Therapro
225 Arlington Street
Framingham, MA   01702

508-872-9494
800-257-5376
FAX 508-875-2062
http://www.theraproducts.com
e-mail: info@theraproducts.com

Therapro Staff, Author
Karen Conrad, President

A software collection of 31 True Type fonts for teachers, parents and students. Fonts include Tracing, lined and unlined Traditional Manuscript and Cursive (similar to Zaner Blouser and D'Nealian), math, clip art, decorative, time, American Sign Language symbols and more. The included manual is very informative, with great examples of lesson plans and educational goals. *$39.95*

Windows/Mac

1464 From Scribbling to Writing

Therapro
225 Arlington Street
Framingham, MA   01702

508-872-9494
800-257-5376
FAX 508-875-2062
http://www.theraproducts.com
e-mail: info@theraproducts.com

Suzanne Naville, Pia Marbacher, Author
Karen Conrad, President

Ideas, exercises and practice pages for all children preparing to write. Contains line drawing exercises, forms to complete, and forms for encouraging good flow of movement during writing. *$29.95*

99 pages

1465 Fun with Handwriting

Therapro
225 Arlington Street
Framingham, MA   01702

508-872-9494
800-257-5376
FAX 508-875-2062
http://www.theraproducts.com
e-mail: info@theraproducts.com

Therapro Staff, Author
Karen Conrad, President

One hundred and one ways to improve handwriting. Includes key to writing legibly, chalkboard activities, evaluation tips, and real world handwriting projects. *$16.00*

160 pages   Spiral-bound

1466 Getting It Write

Therapro
225 Arlington Street
Framingham, MA   01702

508-872-9494
800-257-5376
FAX 508-875-2062
http://www.theraproducts.com
e-mail: info@theraproducts.com

LouAnne Audette OTR, Anne Karson OTR, Author
Karen Conrad, President

A 6-week course for individuals or groups of 4-10 children, 6-12 years. Weekly, 1/2 hour classes begin with a short orientation followed by 25 minutes of games and sensory motor activities, from prewriting to writing practice, from basic strokes to letter formation. Reproducible manuscript and cursive worksheets are included along with homework assignments. *$58.95*

215 pages

1467 Getting Ready to Write: Preschool-K

Therapro
225 Arlington Street
Framingham, MA   01702

508-872-9494
800-257-5376
FAX 508-875-2062
http://www.theraproducts.com
e-mail: info@theraproducts.com

Therapro Staff, Author
Karen Conrad, President

A wonderful little book for any handwriting program. Includes many basic skills needed for beginning writing such as matching like objects, finding differences, writing basic strokes, left to right sequence, etc. *$6.50*

97 pages

1468 Grammar Scramble: A Grammar and Sentence-Building Game

LinguiSystems
3100 4th Avenue
East Moline, IL   61244

800-776-4332
FAX 309-755-2377
TDY:800-933-8331
http://www.linguisystems.com
e-mail: service@linguisystems.com

Rick Bowers, Linda Bowers, Author
Linda Bowers, Owner
Rosemary Huisingh, Owner

Students will improve their grammar and thinking skills as they form intersecting sentences in crossword style. Students receive word tiles divided into these parts of speech: nouns; verbs; pronouns; adjectives; adverbs; articles; interrogatives; prepostions; and conjunctions. *$44.95*

Ages 8-Adult

1469 Grammar and Writing for Job and Personal Use

AGS Publishing
4201 Woodland Road
Circle Pines, MN 55014   651-287-7220
800-328-2560
FAX 800-471-8457
http://www.agsnet.com
e-mail: agsmail@agsnet.com

Joyce Hing-McGowan, Author
Karen Dahlen, Associate Director
Matt Keller, Marketing Manager

With an interest level of high school through adult, and a reading level of Grade 5-6, this series has modules in Improving Basic Grammar and Writing Skills and Writing for Employment. Self-paced texts are filled with exercises that teach students the basic rules of English grammar and how to apply them to actual writing situations.

1470 Gramopoly: A Parts of Speech Game

LinguiSystems
3100 4th Avenue
East Moline, IL 61244

800-776-4332
FAX 309-755-2377
TDY:800-933-8331
http://www.linguisystems.com
e-mail: service@linguisystems.com

Raelene Hudson, Author
Linda Bowers, Owner
Rosemary Huisingh, Owner

This best-selling game turns on the grammar lights for your older students. Assign each player a sentence from three levels of difficulty. Players must purchase parts of speech to complete their sentence. *$44.95*

Ages 10-15

1471 HELP for Grammar

LinguiSystems
3100 4th Avenue
East Moline, IL 61244

800-776-4332
FAX 309-755-2377
TDY:800-933-8331
http://www.linguisystems.com
e-mail: service@linguisystems.com

Andrea Larazzi, Author
Linda Bowers, Owner
Rosemary Huisingh, Owner

Get in-depth grammar practice arranged in developmental order so skill builds upon skill. Get grammar training and practice with oral and written language exercises including identifying and matching grammar types, categorizing grammar types, applying grammar skills in context, and more. *$39.95*

191 pages Ages 8-Adult

1472 Handwriting Readiness for Preschoolers

Therapro
225 Arlington Street
Framingham, MA 01702   508-872-9494
800-257-5376
FAX 508-875-2062
http://www.theraproducts.com
e-mail: info@theraproducts.com

Donald Thurber, Author
Karen Conrad, President

As teacher recites directions, children trace lower case manuscript letters with finger (Book 1) or crayon (Book 2), developing letter recognition skills and writing readiness. *$9.95*

32 pages

1473 Handwriting Without Tears

8801 MacArthur Boulevard
Cabin John, MD 20818   301-263-2700
888-983-8409
FAX 301-263-2707
http://www.hwtears.com
e-mail: Jan@hwtears.com

Jan Olsen, Occupational Therapist

An easy and fun method for children of all abilities to learn printing and cursive.

1474 Handwriting without Tears Workbooks

Therapro
225 Arlington Street
Framingham, MA 01702   508-872-9494
800-257-5376
FAX 508-875-2062
http://www.theraproducts.com
e-mail: info@theraproducts.com

Therapro Staff, Author
Karen Conrad, President

These workbooks are excellent for both classroom and individual instruction. Minimal preparation time is needed to use the clear and easy-to-follow lesson guides. *$5.95*

1475 Handwriting: Cursive ABC Book

Therapro
225 Arlington Street
Framingham, MA 01702   508-872-9494
800-257-5376
FAX 508-875-2062
http://www.theraproducts.com
e-mail: info@theraproducts.com

Therapro Staff, Author
Karen Conrad, President

The perfect at-home reinforcement with fully illustrated excerpts from children's literature, model letters, practice space and tear-out alphabet cards. *$9.95*

56 pages

1476 Handwriting: Manuscript ABC Book

Therapro
225 Arlington Street
Framingham, MA   01702   508-872-9494
                                      800-257-5376
                               FAX 508-875-2062
                           http://www.theraproducts.com
                           e-mail: info@theraproducts.com
Therapro Staff, Author
Karen Conrad, President

Illustrated rhymes, practice letters and words, coloring and tear out alphabet cards teach letter formation. *$9.95*

56 pages

1477 Home/School Activities Manuscript Practice

Therapro
225 Arlington Street
Framingham, MA   01702   508-872-9494
                                      800-257-5376
                               FAX 508-875-2062
                           http://www.theraproducts.com
                           e-mail: info@theraproducts.com
Therapro Staff, Author
Karen Conrad, President

Directions for forming lower and upper case letters, and numbers, with space for practice. Activities use letters in words and sentences. *$9.95*

64 pages

1478 Introduction to Journal Writing

Harcourt Achieve
6277 Sea Harbor Drive
Orlando, FL   32887
                                      800-531-5015
                               FAX 800-699-9459
                           http://www.steckvaughn.com
                           e-mail: info@steckvaughn.com
Steck-Vaughn Staff, Author
Tim McEwen, President/CEO
Jeff Johnson, Dir Marketing Communications
Chris Lehmann, Team Coordinator

The more students write as young children, the higher quality their writing will be, now and as they go on through life. Journal Writing is not about spelling and grammar. It's a highly personal outpouring of thoughts and experiences.

1479 Just for Kids: Grammar

LinguiSystems
3100 4th Avenue
East Moline, IL   61244
                                      800-776-4332
                               FAX 309-755-2377
                               TDY:800-933-8331
                           http://www.linguisystems.com
                           e-mail: service@linguisystems.com
Janet Lanza, Lynn Flahive, Author
Linda Bowers, Owner
Rosemary Huisingh, Owner

This kid-friendly approach to grammar teaches the parts of speech your students need to know. The practice centers around natural, meaningful activities. Each chapter includes: a pre-and post-test, picture cards, sequence story, rebus story, and family letter. *$39.95*

186 pages   Ages 4-9

1480 LD Teacher's IEP Companion

LinguiSystems
3100 4th Avenue
East Moline, IL   61244
                                      800-776-4332
                               FAX 309-755-2377
                               TDY:800-933-8331
                           http://www.linguisystems.com
                           e-mail: service@linguisystems.com
Molly Lyle, Author
Linda Bowers, Owner
Rosemary Huisingh, Owner

These IEP goals are organized developmentally by skill area with individual objectives and classroom activity suggestions. Goals and objectives cover these academic areas: math; reading; writing; literacy concepts; attention skills; study skills; classroom behavior; social interaction; and transition skills. *$39.95*

169 pages   Ages 5-18

1481 Learning 100 Writing Strategies

Harcourt Achieve
6277 Sea Harbor Drive
Orlando, FL   32887
                                      800-531-5015
                               FAX 800-699-9459
                           http://www.steckvaughn.com
                           e-mail: info@steckvaughn.com
Steck-Vaughn Staff, Author
Tim McEwen, President/CEO
Jeff Johnson, Dir Marketing Communications
Chris Lehmann, Team Coordinator

Use the writing process as a tool to build reading comprehension, writing proficiency, and learner confidence. Help learners make a successful connection between reading and writing. Writing Strategies gives learners thorough instruction in the writing process and challenges them to apply their new skills in an everyday writing task that provides ongoing success and encouragement.

1482 Learning Grammar Through Writing

Educators Publishing Service
31 Smith Place
Cambridge, MA   02139   617-547-6706
                                      800-225-5750
                               FAX 888-440-2665
                           http://www.epsbooks.com
                           e-mail: eps@epsbooks.com
Sandra M Bell, James I Wheeler, Author
Nick Gaehde, President

Learning Grammar through Writing contains grammar and composition rules explained and reference-numbered. Basic grammatical rules, common stylistic and grammatical writing errors, and commonly confused words and expressions are a few of the topics.

1483 Let's Write Right: Teacher's Edition

AVKO'S Dyslexia Research Foundation
3084 W Willard Road
Clio, MI   48420   810-686-9283
                                    FAX 810-686-1101
                                    http://www.avko.org
                            e-mail: avkoemail@aol.com
Don McCabe, Author
Don McCabe, Research Director

This is a teacher's lesson plan book which uses an approach designed specifically for dyslexics to teach reading and spelling skills through the side door of penmanship exercises with an empasis on legibility. Student books are handy but are not required. *$19.95*

1484 Let's-Do-It-Write: Writing Readiness Workbook

Therapro
225 Arlington Street
Framingham, MA   01702   508-872-9494
                                     800-257-5376
                                FAX 508-875-2062
                      http://www.theraproducts.com
                      e-mail: info@theraproducts.com
Gail Kushnir, Author
Karen Conrad, President

A great variety of prewriting activities and exercises focusing on development of eye-hand coordination and motor, sensory and cognitive skills. Also, helps improve sitting posture, cutting skills, pencil grasp, spatial orientation and problem-solving. Written by an occupational therapist who is a special educator. *$19.95*

112 pages

1485 Linamood Program (LIPS Clinical Version):Phoneme Sequencing Program for Reading, Spelling,Speech

LinguiSystems
3100 4th Avenue
East Moline, IL   61244
                                     800-776-4332
                                FAX 309-755-2377
                            TDY:800-933-8331
                      http://www.linguisystems.com
                   e-mail: service@linguisystems.com
Patricia Linamood, Phyllis Linamood, Author
Linda Bowers, Owner
Rosemary Huisingh, Owner

Help your students develop phoneme awareness for competence in reading, spelling, and speech. This multisensory program meets the needs of the many children and adults who don't develop phonemic awareness through traditional methods. *$247.00*

Birth-Adult

1486 MAXI

Aids and Appliances for Independant Living
PO Box 3209
Farmingdale, NY   11735   516-752-0521
                                     800-522-6294
                                FAX 516-752-0689
                            TDY:516-752-0738
                      http://www.maxiaids.com
Elliot Zaretsky, President

Thousands of products to make life easier. Eating, dressing, communications, bed, bath, kitchen, writing aids and more.

1487 Manual for Learning to Use Manuscript and Cursive Handwriting

Educators Publishing Service
31 Smith Place
Cambridge, MA   02139   617-547-6706
                                     800-225-5750
                                FAX 888-440-2665
                      http://www.epsbooks.com
                      e-mail: eps@epsbooks.com
Beth Slingerland, Author
Nick Gaehde, President

This multisensory handwriting program is divided into two parts, manuscript and cursive, which can be used either consecutively or independently.

1488 Media Weaver 3.5

Sunburst Technology
400 Columbus Avenue
Valhalla, NY   10595   914-747-3310
                                     800-321-7511
                                FAX 914-747-4109
                      http://www.sunburst.com
                      e-mail: support@sunburst.com

Publishing becomes a multimedia event with this dynamic word processor that contains hundreds of media elements and effective process writing resources.

1489 Middle School Writing: Expository Writing

Harcourt Achieve
6277 Sea Harbor Drive
Orlando, FL   32887
                                     800-531-5015
                                FAX 800-699-9459
                      http://www.steckvaughn.com
                      e-mail: info@steckvaughn.com
Steck-Vaughn Staff, Author
Tim McEwen, President/CEO
Jeff Johnson, Dir Marketing Communications
Chris Lehmann, Team Coordinator

An effective comprehensive review and reinforcement of the writing and research skills students will need. Effectively used in both school and home setting. Ideal for junior high or high school students in need of remediation.

1490 My Handwriting Word Book

Therapro
225 Arlington Street
Framingham, MA   01702   508-872-9494
                                     800-257-5376
                                FAX 508-875-2062
                      http://www.theraproducts.com
                      e-mail: info@theraproducts.com
Therapro Staff, Author
Karen Conrad, President

Children practice writing everyday words — two letter words, words for days, months, numbers, family names and more. *$9.95*

64 pages

1491 PAF Handwriting Programs for Print, Cursive (Right or Left-Handed)

Educators Publishing Service
31 Smith Place
Cambridge, MA   02139   617-547-6706
                                   800-225-5750
                              FAX 888-440-2665
                         http://www.epsbooks.com
                         e-mail: eps@epsbooks.com
Phyllis Bertin, Eileen Perlman, Author
Nick Gaehde, President

These workbooks can be used in conjunction with the PAF curriculum or independently as a classroom penmanship program. They were specifically designed to accommodate all students including those with fine-motor, visual-motor and graphomotor weaknesses. The workbooks contain both large models for introducing motor patterns and smaller models to facilitate the transition to primary and loose-leaf papers. A detailed instruction booklet accompanies each workbook.

1492 PATHS

The Speech Bin
1965 25th Avenue
Vero Beach, FL   32960   772-770-0007
                              FAX 772-770-0006
                        http://www.speechbin.com
                        e-mail: info@speechbin.com

PATHS gives you a step-by-step comprehensive program for students who have experienced difficulty in academic learning. It targets skills critical for academic achievements: phonological awareness, phonemic relationships, phonemic processing and listening and memory. Item number 1491. *$21.95*

1493 Phonological Awareness Kit

LinguiSystems
3100 4th Avenue
East Moline, IL   61244
                                   800-776-4332
                              FAX 309-755-2377
                              TDY:800-933-8331
                        http://www.linguisystems.com
                        e-mail: service@linguisystems.com
Carolyn Robertson, Wanda Salter, Author
Linda Bowers, Owner
Rosemary Huisingh, Owner

Help your students learn to use phonological information to process oral and written language with this fantastic kit. Written by an SLP and special educator, this best-seller links sound awareness, oral language, and early reading and writing skills. The kit uses a multisensory approach to ensure success for all learning styles. *$69.95*

115 pages   Ages 5-8

1494 Phonological Awareness Kit: Intermediate

LinguiSystems
3100 4th Avenue
East Moline, IL   61244
                                   800-776-4332
                              FAX 309-755-2377
                              TDY:800-933-8331
                        http://www.linguisystems.com
                        e-mail: service@linguisystems.com
Carolyn Robertson, Wanda Salter, Author
Linda Bowers, Owner
Rosemary Huisingh, Owner

Now there's hope for your older students who have struggled with reading through their early school years. Give them strategies to crack the reading code with this comprehensive program. Great for students with deficits in auditory processing, decoding, and written language. *$69.95*

116 pages   Ages 9-14

1495 Prewriting Curriculum Enrichment Series

Therapro
225 Arlington Street
Framingham, MA   01702   508-872-9494
                                    800-257-5376
                              FAX 508-875-2062
                        http://www.theraproducts.com
                        e-mail: info@theraproducts.com
Peggy Hundley Spitz OTR, Author
Karen Conrad, President

This series offers a wide variety of thematically related developmental activities: Trace & Draw; Crafts and Costumes; Cooking; Stories to Color & Read; and Games. Enough activities for several years. Many reproducable worksheets are included. Ideal for preschool programs. Helps all levels of development with hand skills, eye-hand coordination, perception and sensory motor awareness. *$22.50*

180 pages

1496 Punctuation Play-by-Play

LinguiSystems
3100 4th Avenue
East Moline, IL   61244
                                   800-776-4332
                              FAX 309-755-2377
                              TDY:800-933-8331
                        http://www.linguisystems.com
                        e-mail: service@linguisystems.com
Carolyn LoGiudice, Mike LoGiudice, Author
Linda Bowers, Owner
Rosemary Huisingh, Owner

Punctuation Play-by-Play engages students in a lively game as they practice essential punctuation skills including: capitalization; end marks; apostrophes; commas; quotation marks; colons; semicolons. Question cards are divides into two levels of difficulty. *$44.95*

Ages 10-18

1497 Punctuation, Capitalization, and Handwriting for Job and Personal Use

AGS Publishing
4201 Woodland Road
Circle Pines, MN 55014   651-287-7220
                                 800-328-2560
                            FAX 800-471-8457
                         http://www.agsnet.com
                      e-mail: agsmail@agsnet.com

Renae B Humberg, Author
Karen Dahlen, Associate Director
Matt Keller, Marketing Manager

With an interest level of high school through adult, and a reading level of Grade 5-6, this series has modules in Punctuation, Capitalization and Handwriting. *$299.00*

1498 Reading and Writing Workbook

Therapro
225 Arlington Street
Framingham, MA 01702   508-872-9494
                               800-257-5376
                          FAX 508-875-2062
                    http://www.theraproducts.com
                   e-mail: info@theraproducts.com

Therapro Staff, Author
Karen Conrad, President

Writing checks and balancing a checkbook, copying words and sentences, and writing messages and notes. Helps with recognition and understanding of calendars, phone books and much more. *$10.50*

1499 Report Writing

Harcourt Achieve
6277 Sea Harbor Drive
Orlando, FL 32887

                               800-531-5015
                          FAX 800-699-9459
                    http://www.steckvaughn.com
                  e-mail: info@steckvaughn.com

Steck-Vaughn Staff, Author
Tim McEwen, President/CEO
Jeff Johnson, Dir Marketing Communications
Chriss Lehmann, Team Coordinator

Here is the complete, step-by-step guide to learning the tools, skills, and time management techniques necessary for researching, organizing, outlining, and writing reports.

1500 SLP's IDEA Companion

LinguiSystems
3100 4th Avenue
East Moline, IL 61244

                               800-776-4332
                          FAX 309-755-2377
                          TDY:800-933-8331
                    http://www.linguisystems.com
                 e-mail: service@linguisystems.com

Shaila Lucas, Author
Linda Bowers, Owner
Rosemary Huisingh, Owner

Get goals and objectives that match the guidelines outlined in the individuals with Disabilities Education Act. You'll be able to link your therapy goals to the classroom curriculum, determine appropriate benchmarks for students, and determine levels of performance using the baseline measures provided in the book. *$39.95*

162 pages   Ages 5-18

1501 Soaring Scores on the ISAT Reading and Writing

Harcourt Achieve
6277 Sea Harbor Drive
Orlando, FL 32887

                               800-531-5015
                          FAX 800-699-9459
                    http://www.steckvaughn.com
                  e-mail: info@steckvaughn.com

Steck-Vaughn Staff, Author
Tim McEwen, President/CEO
Jeff Johnson, Dir Marketing Communications
Chris Lehmann, Team Coordinator

Highly targeted instruction and practice tests help students approach the ISAT strategically and confidently. Writing prompts ask students to write a persuasive, expository, or narrative essay. Modeled questions practice both multiple-choice and open-ended queries.

1502 Spelling Charts: Intermediate

LinguiSystems
3100 4th Avenue
East Moline, IL 61244

                               800-776-4332
                          FAX 800-577-4555
                    http://www.linguisystems.com
                 e-mail: service@linguisystems.com

Linda Bowers, Owner
Rosemary Huisingh, Owner

Good spelling doesn't stop in the primary grades. Help your older students understand word families with this great resource. It's a valuable tool for spelling, writing, and vocabulary skills. You get 45 full-color cards to use as charts, overheads, or take-home practice.

1503 Spelling Charts: Primary

LinguiSystems
3100 4th Avenue
East Moline, IL 61244

                               800-776-4332
                          FAX 800-577-4555
                    http://www.linguisystems.com
                 e-mail: service@linguisystems.com

Linda Bowers, Owner
Rosemary Huisingh, Owner

Tap into phonological awareness skills with these full-color charts. Use them as classroom charts, overheads, or take-home practice. They're great for large group, small group, or individual teaching. Each chart features words grouped by rhyming families or similar word endings.

1504 Spelling for Job and Personal Use

AGS Publishing
4201 Woodland Road
Circle Pines, MN   55014   651-287-7220
                                 800-328-2560
                            FAX 800-471-8457
                         http://www.agsnet.com
                      e-mail: agsmail@agsnet.com
Merle Wood, Author
Karen Dahlen, Associate Director
Matt Keller, Marketing Manager

With an interest level of high school through adult, and a reading level of Grade 5-6, this series has modules in Using the Dictionary, Guides to Spelling and Spelling the 100 Most Used Words.

1505 StartWrite

Therapro
225 Arlington Street
Framingham, MA   01702   508-872-9494
                                800-257-5376
                           FAX 508-875-2062
                      http://www.theraproducts.com
                   e-mail: info@theraproducts.com
Therapro Staff, Author
Karen Conrad, President

With this easy-to-use software package, you can make papers and handwriting worksheets to meet individual student's needs. Type letters, words, or numbers and they appear in a dot format on the triple line guide. Change letter size, add shading, turn on or off guide lines and arrow strokes and place provided clipart. Fonts include Manuscript and Cursive, Modern Manuscript and Cursive and Italic Manuscript and Cursive. Useful manual included. *$39.95*

Windows/Mac

1506 Strategies for Success in Writing

Harcourt Achieve
6277 Sea Harbor Drive
Orlando, FL   32887
                                800-531-5015
                           FAX 800-699-9459
                      http://www.steckvaughn.com
                   e-mail: info@steckvaughn.com
Steck-Vaughn Staff, Author
Tim McEwen, President/CEO
Jeff Johnson, Dir Marketing Communications
Chriss Lehmann, Team Coordinator

Help your students gain success and master all the steps in writing through essay-writing strategies and exercises in proofreading, editing, and revising written work. This program also helps students approach tests strategically.

1507 Sunbuddy Writer

Sunburst Technology
400 Columbus Avenue
Valhalla, NY   10595   914-747-3310
                                800-321-7511
                           FAX 914-747-4109
                       http://www.sunburst.com
                    e-mail: support@sunburst.com

An easy-to-use picture and word processor designed especially for young writers.

1508 TOPS Kit: Adolescent-Tasks of Problem Solving

LinguiSystems
3100 4th Avenue
East Moline, IL   61244
                                800-776-4332
                           FAX 309-755-2377
                           TDY:800-933-8331
                      http://www.linguisystems.com
                   e-mail: service@linguisystems.com
Linda Bowers, Rosemary Huisingh, Mark Barrett, Author
Linda Bowers, Owner
Rosemary Huisingh, Owner

Teach your teens how to use their language skills to think, think, think. We combine literacy, thinking, writing, humor, and language arts practice to cover these thinking skills: using content to make references; analyzing information; taking another's point of view; and more. It's a literacy- based approach that gets dramatic results! *$59.95*

192 pages   Ages 12-18

1509 The Getty-Dubay Italic Handwriting Series: The Natural Way to Write

Therapro
225 Arlington Street
Framingham, MA   01702   508-872-9494
                                800-257-5376
                           FAX 508-875-2062
                      http://www.theraproducts.com
                   e-mail: info@theraproducts.com
Barbara Getty, Inga Dubay, Author
Karen Conrad, President

This method produces fast and legible handwriting by consistently using an elliptical shape and letter slope (5 degrees) which conforms to natural hand movements and requires very few pencil lifts. A great handwriting program for all children and for adults. Also, use this method with student's handwriting problems. You will see an immediate difference. Has long term effects, when the practice stops, the good handwriting continues!

Video available

1510 Tool Chest: For Teachers, Parents and Students

Therapro
225 Arlington Street
Framingham, MA   01702   508-872-9494
                                800-257-5376
                           FAX 508-875-2062
                      http://www.theraproducts.com
                   e-mail: info@theraproducts.com
Henry OT Services, Author
Karen Conrad, President

Ideas for self-regulation and handwriting skills. 26+ activities, each on its own page, with rationale, supplies needed, instructions and related projects. Provides a fast way to prepare for OT activities. Supports the videotapes Tools for Teachers and Tools for Students. *$19.95*

1511   Type-It

Educators Publishing Service
31 Smith Place
Cambridge, MA   02139   617-547-6706
                              800-225-5750
                        FAX 888-440-2666
                    http://www.epsbooks.com
                    e-mail: eps@epsbooks.com

Joan Duffy, Author
Nick Gaehde, President

A linguistically oriented beginning 'touch-system' typing manual. A progress chart allows students to pace their progress in short, easily attainable units, often enabling them to proceed with little or no supervision.

1512   Vowel Scramble

LinguiSystems
3100 4th Avenue
East Moline, IL   61244
                              800-776-4332
                        FAX 309-755-2377
                        TDY:800-933-8331
                http://www.linguisystems.com
                e-mail: service@linguisystems.com

Carolyn LoGiudice, Author
Linda Bowers, Owner
Rosemary Huisingh, Owner

Your student will love this fun new way to practice spelling and phonological awareness skills. Players earn points by using letter tiles to complete words on the game board. *$44.95*

Ages 7-12

1513   Workbook for Aphasia

The Speech Bin
1965 25th Avenue
Vero Beach, FL   32960   772-770-0007
                        FAX 772-770-0006
                    http://www.speechbin.com
                    e-mail: info@speechbin.com

This book gives you materials for adults who have recovered a significant degree of speaking, reading, writing, and comprehension skills. It includes 106 exercises divided into eight target areas. Item number W331. *$48.95*

1514   Write On! Plus: Beginning Writing Skills

Sunburst Technology
400 Columbus Avenue
Valhalla, NY   10595   914-747-3310
                              800-321-7511
                        FAX 914-747-4109
                    http://www.sunburst.com
                    e-mail: support@sunburst.com

This classic process writing series teaches a wide range of core writing and literature skills through hundreds of motivating and challenging activities.

1515   Write On! Plus: Elementary Writing Skills

Sunburst Technology
400 Columbus Avenue
Valhalla, NY   10595   914-747-3310
                              800-321-7511
                        FAX 914-747-4109
                    http://www.sunburst.com
                    e-mail: support@sunburst.com

This classic process writing series teaches a wide range of core writing and literature skills through hundreds of motivating and challenging activities.

1516   Write On! Plus: Essential Writing

Sunburst Technology
400 Columbus Avenue
Valhalla, NY   10595   914-747-3310
                              800-321-7511
                        FAX 914-747-4109
                    http://www.sunburst.com
                    e-mail: support@sunburst.com

This classic process writing series teaches a wide range of core writing and literature skills through hundreds of motivating and challenging activities.

1517   Write On! Plus: Growing as a Writer

Sunburst Technology
400 Columbus Avenue
Valhalla, NY   10595   914-747-3310
                              800-321-7511
                        FAX 914-747-4109
                    http://www.sunburst.com
                    e-mail: support@sunburst.com

This classic process writing series teaches a wide range of core writing and literature skills through hundreds of motivating and challenging activities.

1518   Write On! Plus: High School Writing Skills

Sunburst Technology
400 Columbus Avenue
Valhalla, NY   10595   914-747-3310
                              800-321-7511
                        FAX 914-747-4109
                    http://www.sunburst.com
                    e-mail: support@sunburst.com

This classic process writing series teaches a wide range of core writing and literature skills through hundreds of motivating and challenging activities.

1519 Write On! Plus: Literature Studies

Sunburst Technology
400 Columbus Avenue
Valhalla, NY   10595   914-747-3310
                             800-321-7511
                          FAX 914-747-4109
                     http://www.sunburst.com
                  e-mail: support@sunburst.com

This classic process writing series teaches a wide range of core writing and literature skills through hundreds of motivating and challenging activities.

1520 Write On! Plus: Middle School Writing Skills

Sunburst Technology
400 Columbus Avenue
Valhalla, NY   10595   914-747-3310
                             800-321-7511
                          FAX 914-747-4109
                     http://www.sunburst.com
                  e-mail: support@sunburst.com

This classic process writing series teaches a wide range of core writing and literature skills through hundreds of motivating and challenging activities.

1521 Write On! Plus: Responding to Great Literature

Sunburst Technology
400 Columbus Avenue
Valhalla, NY   10595   914-747-3310
                             800-321-7511
                          FAX 914-747-4109
                     http://www.sunburst.com
                  e-mail: support@sunburst.com

This classic process writing series teaches a wide range of core writing and literature skills through hundreds of motivating and challenging activities.

1522 Write On! Plus: Spanish/ English Literacy Series

Sunburst Technology
400 Columbus Avenue
Valhalla, NY   10595   914-747-3310
                             800-321-7511
                          FAX 914-747-4109
                     http://www.sunburst.com
                  e-mail: support@sunburst.com

This classic process writing series teaches a wide range of core writing and literature skills through hundreds of motivating and challenging activities.

1523 Write On! Plus: Steps to Better Writing

Sunburst Technology
400 Columbus Avenue
Valhalla, NY   10595   914-747-3310
                             800-321-7511
                          FAX 914-747-4109
                     http://www.sunburst.com
                  e-mail: support@sunburst.com

This classic process writing series teaches a wide range of core writing and literature skills through hundreds of motivating and challenging activities.

1524 Write On! Plus: Writing with Picture Books

Sunburst Technology
400 Columbus Avenue
Valhalla, NY   10595   914-747-3310
                             800-321-7511
                          FAX 914-747-4109
                     http://www.sunburst.com
                  e-mail: support@sunburst.com

This classic process writing series teaches a wide range of core writing and literature skills through hundreds of motivating and challenging activities.

1525 Write from the Start

Therapro
225 Arlington Street
Framingham, MA   01702   508-872-9494
                                800-257-5376
                             FAX 508-875-2062
                     http://www.theraproducts.com
                  e-mail: info@theraproducts.com
Ion Teodorescu, Lois M Addy, Author
Karen Conrad, President

This program addresses the handwriting process in two ways. First, it assists in developing the intrinsic muscles of the hand to gain the control required to form letter shapes and to create appropriate spaces between words. Secondly, it helps to develop perceptual skills that are required to orient letters and organize the page. Each book has sections to be copied. Two books consisting of eye hand, spatial organization, graphic and perceptual challenges.

128 pages

1526 WriteOPOLY

LinguiSystems
3100 4th Avenue
East Moline, IL   61244
                                800-776-4332
                             FAX 309-755-2377
                             TDY:800-933-8331
                     http://www.linguisystems.com
                  e-mail: service@linguisystems.com
Paul F Johnson, Author
Linda Bowers, Owner
Rosemary Huisingh, Owner

End writer's block for even your most reluctant writers with this fun game. Improve written language skills with WriteOPOLY. Students travel around a colorful game board buying properties and filling out Writing Plan sheets. *$44.95*

Ages 9-14

1527 Writer's Resources Library 2.0

Sunburst Technology
400 Columbus Avenue
Valhalla, NY   10595   914-747-3310
                             800-321-7511
                          FAX 914-747-4109
                     http://www.sunburst.com
                  e-mail: service@sunburst.com

Students quickly access seven reference resources with this indispensable writing tool.

1528 Writestart

Therapro
225 Arlington Street
Framingham, MA   01702   508-872-9494
                                    800-257-5376
                             FAX 508-875-2062
                 http://www.theraproducts.com
                 e-mail: info@theraproducts.com
Therapro Staff, Author
Karen Conrad, President

A great prewriting kit with 30 beautifully illustrated 8x8 reusable cards. The activities progress from simple pre-writing activities such as mazes and tracking, up to formation of upper and lower case letters, all hosted by a green dinosaur. Includes a special pencil and triangular grip. *$16.95*

1529 Writing Trek Grades 4-6

Sunburst Technology
400 Columbus Avenue
Valhalla, NY   10595   914-747-3310
                                800-321-7511
                         FAX 914-747-4109
                 http://www.sunburst.com
                 e-mail: service@sunburst.com

Enhance your students' experience in your English language arts classroom with twelve authentic writing projects that build students' competence while encouraging creativity.

1530 Writing Trek Grades 6-8

Sunburst Technology
400 Columbus Avenue
Valhalla, NY   10595   914-747-3310
                                800-321-7511
                         FAX 914-747-4109
                 http://www.sunburst.com
                 e-mail: service@sunburst.com

Twelve authentic language arts projects, activities, and assignments develop your students' writing confidence and ability.

1531 Writing Trek Grades 8-10

Sunburst Technology
400 Columbus Avenue
Valhalla, NY   10595   914-747-3310
                                800-321-7511
                         FAX 914-747-4109
                 http://ww.sunburst.com
                 e-mail: service@sunburst.com

Help your students develop a concept of genre as they become familiar with the writing elements and characteristics of a variety of writing forms.

Learning Disabilities

1532 AHEAD Exposition

Association on Higher Education and Disability
PO Box 54066
Waltham, MA   02454   781-788-0003
                                   FAX 781-788-0033
                                   http://www.ahead.org
                                   e-mail: ahead@ahead.org
Stephan Smith, Executive Director
Tri Do, Member Services
Rhonda Rapp, Training Program

Gathering of disability service providers in higher education internationally. Features keynote speakers, workshops, exhibits and receptions.

   July

1533   Access Expo and Conference

Fairfield Factor
30 Main Street
Danbury, CT   06810   203-798-8850
                                   FAX 203-798-8779
                                   http://www.fairfieldfactor.com
                                   e-mail: mail@fairfieldfactor.com

Offers information on the latest technology, assistive devices and more for the disabled.

1534   Active Parenting Workshops

Active Parenting Publishers
1955 Vaughn Road NW
Kennesaw, GA   30144   770-429-0565
                                   800-825-0060
                                   FAX 770-429-0334
                                   http://www.activeparenting.com
                                   e-mail: cservice@activeparenting.com
Michael H Popkin PhD, President
Virginia Murray, Marketing

Conducts nationwide parenting workshops recognized by the National Board of Certified Counselors. Offers parenting education curriculum for parents of ADD/ADHD children.

1535   American Council on Rural Special Education Conference

Utah State University
2865 Old Main Hill
Logan, UT   84322   801-626-6268
                                   FAX 801-626-7427
                                   http://www.extension.usu.edu/acres
                                   e-mail: jmayhew@weber.edu
Dr. Jack Mayhew, Program Chair

Conference of special educators, teachers and professors working with exceptional needs students. Keynote speakers, silent auction.

   March

1536   American Counseling Association Convention

ACA Membership Division
5999 Stevenson Avenue
Alexandria, VA   22304   703-823-0252
                                   800-347-6647
                                   FAX 703-823-0252
                                   http://www.counseling.org
                                   e-mail: webmaster@counseling.org
Dr. Mark Pope, President
Debra Bass, Marketing
Robin Hayes, Convention/Meetings

Keynote speakers and workshops as well as exhibits are offered.

   April

1537   American Speech-Language-Hearing Association Annual Convention

10801 Rockville Pike
Rockville, MD   20852   301-897-5700
                                   800-638-8255
                                   FAX 301-571-0457
                                   http://www.asha.org
Eileen Pietrarton, Executive Director
Cheyrl Russel, Convention/Meetings

Topics addressed include hearing impairments, special education and speech communication. 10,000 attendees.

   November

1538   Annual Postsecondary Learning Disability Training Institute Workshop

University of Connecticut
362 Fairfield Road
Storrs, CT   06269   860-486-3321
                                   FAX 860-486-5799
                                   http://www.cped.uconn.edu
                                   e-mail: carrol.waite@uconn.edu
Stan Shaw, Institute Coordinator
Carrol Waite, Program Assistant

Focus of the Institute's workshop is to assist concerned professionals to meet the unique needs of college students with learning disabilities and other hidden disabilities.

   June

1539   Assessing Learning Problems Workshop

Learning Disabilities Resources
PO Box 716
Bryn Mawr, PA   19010   610-525-8336
                                   800-869-8336
                                   FAX 610-525-8337
                                   http://www.ldonline.org

This workshop includes behavioral manifestations of information processing problems and how to relate these to learning processes.

1540   Association Book Exhibit: Brain Research

8525A Cooper Road
Alexandria, VA   22309   703-619-5030
                                   FAX 703-619-5035
                                   http://www.bookexhibit.com
                                   e-mail: info@bookexhibit.com
Mark Trocchi, President

Attendence is 800-1,000. Every serious publisher of Neuroscience material represented.

1541 CACLD Spring & Fall Conferences

Connecticut Assoc. for Children & Adults with LD
25 Van Zant Street
East Norwalk, CT   06855   203-838-5010
                                 FAX 203-866-6108
                                 http://www.CACLD.org
                                 e-mail: cacld@juno.com
Marie Armstrong, Conference Coordinator
Beryl Kaufman, Executive Director

Offers speakers, workshops, presentations and more for professionals and parents dealing with learning disability and attention disorder in their daily life. Also offers a stand on college for students with LD and ADD, exhibitors and a giant bookstore.

1542 CEC Federation Conference: Arkansas

Council for Exceptional Children
105 N 6th Street
Heber Springs, AR   72543   501-362-2404
                                 FAX 501-329-7409
                                 e-mail: dido@ozarkisp.net
Annual conference held in November at Hot Springs Convention Centerin Hot Springs, AR.

1543 CEC Federation Conference: Kansas

Council for Exceptional Children
1011 Price Boulevard
Atchison, KS   66002   785-462-2940
                                 http://www.kscec.org
                                 e-mail: jstewart719@yahoo.com
Janette Stewart, President

Exhibits and workshop sessions for educators building a brighter tomorrow.

October

1544 CEC Federation Conference: Pennsylvania

Council of Exceptional Children
West Chester University
West Chester, PA   19383   610-436-1060
                                 FAX 610-436-3102
                                 http://www.pfcec.org
                                 e-mail: vmcginley@wcupa.edu
Dr. Vicki McGinley, Convention Chair

Annual conference for parents and educators involved with the Pennsylvania Council of Exceptional Children.

November

1545 CEC Federation Conference: Virginia

Council for Exceptional Children
1110 N Glede Road
Arlington, VA   22201   703-264-9454
                                 FAX 703-264-1637
                                 http://www.cec.sped.org
                                 e-mail: victore@cec.sped.org
Victor Erickson, Exhibits Manager

Find a wealth of information targeted just for educators. Choose from more than 600 workshops, lectures, demonstrations, mini workshops, panels and poster sessions.

April

1546 Center on Disabilities Conference

California State University
401 Golden Shore
Long Beach, CA   90802   562-951-4000
                                 FAX 562-951-4986
                                 http://www.csun.edu
                                 e-mail: ctrdis@csun.edu
Harry Murphy PhD, Registration

Focuses on issues pertaining to the disabled learner and gifted education. 2,000 attendees.

1547 Closing the Gap Conference

PO Box 68
Henderson, MN   56044   507-248-3294
                                 FAX 507-248-3810
                                 http://www.closingthegap.com
                                 e-mail: info@closingthegap.com
Jan Latzke, Registration

Annual international conference with over 100 exhibitors concerned with the use of computer technology in special education and rehabilitation.

October

1548 College Students with Learning Disabilities Workshop

Learning Disabilities Resources
PO Box 716
Bryn Mawr, PA   19010   610-525-8336
                                 800-869-8336
                                 FAX 610-525-8337
                                 http://www.ldonline.org

This workshop is designed to provide both information and motivation to both students and college personnel.

1549 Communication Aid Manufacturers Association (CAMA) Workshops

205 W Randolf Street
Evanston, IL   60204
                                 800-441-2262
                                 FAX 847-869-5689
                                 http://www.aacproducts.org
                                 e-mail: cama@northshore.net
James Neils, Association Administrator
Chris Murin, Workshop Coordinator

CAMA sponsors workshops throughout the US and Canada that demonstrates a variety of communication products from leading manufacturers. The Association strives to keep up with the latest in augmentative and alternative communication (ACC) technology, and promotes understanding of software and hardware, appropriate for clients with learning disabilities. Members teach functional use in a variety of speaking situations.

1550 ConnSENSE Conference

University of Connecticut
233 Glenbrook Road
Storrs, CT   06269   860-486-2020
                                  FAX 860-486-4412
                                   TDY:8604862077
                          http://www.csd.uconn.edu
                    e-mail: jennifer.lucia@uconn.edu
Donna Korbel, Director
Jennifer Lucia, Associate Director
Christine Morello, Associate Director

Annual conference on technology for people with special needs.

1551 Council for Exceptional Children: Teacher Education Division Conference

Peabody College/Vanderbilt University
2201 W End Avenue
Nashville, TN   37235   615-322-7311
                                  FAX 615-343-5555
Patricia Cegelka, Contact

Topics addressed include personnel, productivity and teacher education.

1552 Council for Learning Disabilities International Conference

Council for Learning Disabilities
PO Box 40303
Overland Park, KS   66204   571-258-1010
                                  FAX 571-258-1011
                       http://www.cldinternational.org
                          e-mail: info@mcs-amc.com
Andrea Falzarano, Executive Director

Focuses on all aspects pertaining to learning disabled individuals from a teaching and research perspective. Over 1000 attendees.

October

1553 Council of Administrators of Special Education Conference

Fort Valley State University
1005 State University Drive
Fort Valley, GA   31030   478-825-7667
                                       800-585-1753
                                  FAX 478-825-7811
                           http://www.casecec.org
                         e-mail: casecec@ad.com
Brenda Heiman, President
Luann Purcell, Executive Director

Our mission is to provide leadership and support to members by shaping policies and practices that impact the quality of education.

January

1554 Counseling Individuals with Learning Disabilities Workshop

Learning Disabilities Resources
PO Box 716
Bryn Mawr, PA   19010   610-525-8336
                                       800-869-8336
                                  FAX 610-525-8337
                           http://www.ldonline.org

In this workshop, Dr. Cooper discusses reasons why some individuals with learning disabilities often do respond well to traditional therapies.

1555 Creative Mind Workshop: Making Magic with Children and Art

P Buckley Moss Foundation for Children's Education
601 Shenandoah Village Drive
Waynesboro, VA   22980   540-932-1728
                                  FAX 540-941-8865
                        http://www.mossfoundation.org
                 e-mail: foundation@mossfoundation.org
Randy Myers, President

Instructional and collaborative strategies for including the visual and performing arts in the education of students with special needs.

1556 Eden Family of Services

Eden Services
One Eden Way
Princeton, NJ   08540   609-987-0099
                                  FAX 609-987-0243
                          http://www.edenservices.org
                        e-mail: info@edenservices.org
David L Holmes EdD, Executive Director/President
Anne Holmes, Director Outreach Support Svcs
Joani Truch, Administration/Communications

Provides year-round educational services, early intervention, parent training and workshops, respite care, outreach services, community based residential services and employment opportunities for individuals with autism.

1557 Educating Children: Summer Training Institute at Muskingum College

Ecsti Administrative Services
824 S Main Street
Ada, OH   45810   419-634-9232
                                  FAX 419-634-9232
                           http://www.muskingum.edu
                      e-mail: rschmitz@muskingum.edu
Rolf G Schmitz, Medical Doctor

For public or private school, child care center or family day care teachers, parents, administrators, Head Start, undergraduate/graduate students and other education-related professionals.

1558 Educational Computer Conference

Annual International Conference
19 Calvert Court
Piedmont, CA   94611   510-594-1249
                                       888-594-1249
                                  FAX 510-594-1838
                              http://www.trld.com
                      e-mail: registration@trld.com
Diane Frost, CEO

Focusing on actual classroom and administrative applications for technology, reading and learning difficulties. Hands on workshops are featured.

January

1559 Hearsay Workshops

1325 Ramblewood Trail
S Euclid, OH   44121   216-382-0383
                                  FAX 216-382-0385
                              http://hearsayinfo.com
                      e-mail: mlandis@hearsayinfo.com
Marilyn Landis, President

Hearsay offers a variety of training programs and workshops for those working with the hearing impaired population. Workshops and seminars are individualized to meet the special needs of each program. Follow up and online coaching available.

1560 Inclusion of Learning Disabled Students in Regular Classrooms Workshop

Learning Disabilities Resources
PO Box 716
Bryn Mawr, PA   19010   610-525-8336
                              800-869-8336
                    FAX 610-525-8337
                    http://www.ldonline.org

This workshop provides teachers with practical suggestions and techniques for including students with learning problems.

1561 Innovative Instructional Techniques Workshop

Learning Disabilities Resources
PO Box 716
Bryn Mawr, PA   19010   610-525-8336
                              800-869-8336
                    FAX 610-525-8337
                    http://www.ldonline.org

In this workshop, Dr. Cooper provides an overview of the various techniques he has developed for helping students with learning problems in reading, writing, spelling and math.

1562 Interest-Driven Learning Workshop

383 DeSoto Drive
New Smyna Beach, FL   32169   386-427-4473
                              800-245-5733
                    FAX 386-427-4473
                    http://www.drpeet.com
                    e-mail: drpeet@drpeet.com
Dr. Bill Peet, CEO

Provides affordable low and high-tech tools that will help people of all ages and abilities learn to read, write and communicate with support from assistive technology as needed.

1563 International Adolescent Conference: Programs for Adolescents

Behavioral Institute for Children and Adolescents
3585 Lexington Avenue N
Arden Hills, MN   55126   651-484-5510
                    FAX 651-483-3879
                    http://www.behavioralinstitute.org
Sheldon Braaten, Executive Director

Information on programs for the developmental needs of children and adolescents with behavioral disorders. Transdisciplinary knowledge and skill, training related, to serve children and youth who have emotional/behavioral disorders.

1564 International Dyslexia Association Conference: Maryland

8600 Lasalle Road, Chester Building
Baltimore, MD   21286   410-296-0232
                              800-ABC-D123
                    FAX 410-321-5069
                    http://www.interdys.org
                    e-mail: info@interdys.org
J Thomas Viall, Executive Director
Judith Dudek, Director Marketing
Cindy Ciresi, Director Conference

Each year IDA sponsors an international conference typically in early November. Sessions meet the needs and interests of a wide range of consumers.

1565 International Dyslexia Association Conference: Illinois

751 Roosevelt Road, Building 7
Glen Ellyn, IL   60137   630-469-6900
                    FAX 630-469-6810
Susan Hill, President

This conference will be held in November with approximately 500 attendees and 20 exhibitors.

1566 LDR Workshop: What Are Learning Disabilities, Problems and Differences?

Learning Disabilities Resources
PO Box 716
Bryn Mawr, PA   19010   610-525-8336
                              800-869-8336
                    FAX 610-525-8337
                    http://www.ldonline.org

In this workshop, Dr. Cooper draws on personal experiences with a learning disability and on his clinical work with thousands of individuals with a wide variety of learning problems to provide the participants with an understanding of the positive and negative aspects of being, living and learning differently.

1567 Landmark Outreach Program Workshops

Landmark School
429 Hale Street
Prides Crossing, MA   01965   978-236-3010
                    FAX 978-927-7268
                    http://www.landmarkschool.org
                    e-mail: outreach@landmarkschool.org
Dan Ahearn, Program Director
Trish Newhall, Associate Director

Provides consultation and training to public and private schools, professional organizations, parent groups, and businesses on topics related to individuals with learning disabilities. Services are individually designed to meet the client's specific needs and can range from a two-hour workshop to a year-long training project. Options include: consulting services; training workshops; summer training program; seminars; and parent workshops.

1568 Learning Disabilities Association Conference: International

4156 Library Road
Pittsburgh, PA   15234   412-341-1515
                    FAX 412-344-0224
                    http://www.ldanatl.org
                    e-mail: info@ldaamerica.org
Jane Browning, Executive Director
Andrea Turkheimer, Conference Coordinator

Topics addressed at the conference include advocacy, adult literacy and learning disabled education.

March

1569 Learning Disabilities Association of Texas Conference

1011 W 31st Street
Austin, TX   78705   512-458-8234
                            800-604-7500
                    FAX 512-458-3826
        http://www.ourworld.compuserve.com
                e-mail: ldatexas@cs.com
Ann Robinson, State Coordinator

Promotes the educational and general welfare of individuals with learning disabilities.

1570 Learning Disabilities and the World of Work Workshop

Learning Disabilities Resources
PO Box 716
Bryn Mawr, PA   19010   610-525-8336
                            800-869-8336
                    FAX 610-525-8337
            http://www.ldonline.org

This workshop is designed for employers, parents or professionals working with individuals with learning disabilities.

1571 Learning Problems and Adult Basic Education Workshop

Learning Disabilities Resources
Bryn Mawr, PA   19010   610-525-8336
                            800-869-8336
                    FAX 610-525-8337
            http://www.ldonline.org

This workshop for adult educators discusses the manifestations of learning problems in adults.

1572 Life After High School for the Student with LD/ADD Conference

Connecticut Assoc. for Children & Adults with LD
25 Van Zant Street
East Norwalk, CT   06855   203-838-5010
                        FAX 203-866-6108
            http://www.CACLD.org
        e-mail: cacld@optonline.net
Beryl Kaufman, Executive Director
Marie Armstrong, Conference Coordinator

Conference held every spring for parents, students and professionals. Features workshops, panels, exhibitors and a bookstore.

1573 Life Lines in the Classroom: LR Consulting & Workshops

925 S Mason Road
Katy, TX   77450   281-395-4978
                        FAX 281-392-8379
            http://www.lrconsulting.com
Marlene Johnson, Curriculum and Instruction
Mary Fitzgerald, Special Education

Offers a variety of staff development training options regarding inclusive and special educational issues.

1574 Lindamood-Bell Research & Training Conferences

Lindamood-Bell Learning Processes
416 Higuera Street
San Luis Obispo, CA   93401   805-541-3836
                                    800-233-1819
                            FAX 805-541-8756
                http://www.lblp.com
                e-mail: rbell@lblp.com
Rodney Bell, Training Coordinator

Offers workshops nationwide for educators using Lindamood-Bell teaching methods. Twenty or more workshops annually. Inservices also available.

1575 Melvin-Smith Learning Center Annual Conference

EDU-Theraputics
775 Kimball Avenue
Seaside, CA   93955   831-620-1908
                                800-505-3276
                        FAX 831-620-1907
        http://www.edu-theraputics.com
                e-mail: edu-t@erc1.com

National conference entitled Strategies for Success in Overcoming Learning Handicaps. Special Sessions: 1) Strategic Planning for Learning Centers; 2) Administration and Interpretation of Receptive Expressive Observation of Memory Skills. Workshops: 1) Reading for Nonreaders; 2) Setting Structure for Homework Success; 3) Developing Attention Focus Skills and many more. Call for conference program. Exhibitors welcome.

1576 National Center for Family Literacy Conference

325 W Main Street
Louisville, KY   40202   502-584-1133
                                877-famlit-1
                        FAX 502-584-0172
                http://www.famlit.org
                e-mail: ncfl@famlit.org
Sharon Darling, President

National Center for Family Literacy will be holding a conference with approximately 40-50 exhibitors and 2,000-2,400 attendees.

March

1577 National Head Start Association Academy Workshop

1651 Prince Street
Alexandria, VA   22314   703-739-0875
                        FAX 703-739-0878
                http://www.nhsa.org
            e-mail: rlewisriar@nhsa.org
Diane Whitehead, Program Development
Ruby Lewis-Riar, Conferences
Cheyrl Thompson, Conferences

Both Adminstrator and Mid-Manager credentials are offered in a six day, institute style setting, workshop. Family Services and Health credentials are offered through a self study format.

September

1578 National Head Start Association Parent Conference

1651 Prince Street
Alexandria, VA 22314 703-739-0875
FAX 703-739-0878
http://www.nhsa.org
e-mail: rlewisriar@nhsa.org
Diane Whitehead, Program Development
Ruby Lewis-Riar, Conferences
Cheyrl Thompson, Conferences

Newest information on enhancing parent involvement, child development, and sharpening parenting skills. More than 100 workshops.

1579 New England Joint Conference on Specific Learning Disabilities

58 Prince Street
Needham, MA 02492 781-455-9895
FAX 781-449-1332
http://addinfonetwork.org
e-mail: adin@gis.net
Linda Downer, Conference Coordinator

Dynamic, informative conference with the goal being to improve services for language/learning-disabled individuals by encouraging dialogue among the many disciplines, organizations and professions involved in the field of learning disabilities.

1580 North American Montessori Teachers' Association Conference

13693 Butternut Road
Buton, OH 44021 440-834-4011
FAX 440-834-4016
http://www.montessori-namta.org
e-mail: staff@montessori-namta.org
Cindy Eppich, Conference Coordinator

Montessori method of teaching is discussed as well as topics pertaining to all levels of special education. This and other conferences are held in different locations and months throughout the year. Please contact us for more information.

Quarterly

1581 Pacific Rim Conference on Disabilities

University of Hawaii Center on Disability Studies
1776 University Avenue
Honolulu, HI 96822 808-956-9810
FAX 808-956-7878
http://www.pacrim.hawaii.edu
e-mail: cds@pacrim.hawaii.edu
Martha Guinan, Organizer
Valerie Shearer, Organizer

Participants from the US and other Pacific Rim nations study such topics as lifelong inclusion in education and community, new technology, family support, employment and adult services.

March

1582 Pennsylvania Training and Technical Assistance Network Workshops

6340 Flank Drive
Harrisburg, PA 17112 717-541-4960
800-360-7282
FAX 717-541-4968
http://www.pattan.k12.pa.us
e-mail: fwarkomski@pattan k12pa.us
Fran Warkomski, Executive Director

Works collaboratively with intermediate units in the areas of professional development, technical assistance and information dissemination to support school districts throughout the Commonwealth. Training and resources are available regarding assistive technology services, short term loans, demonstrations, and production of large print and Braille for student use.

1583 Social Skills Workshop

Learning Disabilities Resources
PO Box 716
Bryn Mawr, PA 19010 610-525-8336
800-869-8336
FAX 610-525-8337
http://www.ldonline.org

This workshop is relevant for individuals with learning disabilities, parents or professionals.

1584 Son-Rise Program Start-Up Workshops

Autism Treatment Center of America
2080 S Undermountain Road
Sheffield, MA 01257 413-229-2100
800-714-2779
FAX 413-229-8931
http://www.son-rise.org
e-mail: information@son-rise.org
Sean Fitzgerald, Assistant Director

Since 1983, the Autism Treatment Center of America has provided innovative training programs for parents and professionals caring for children challenged by autism, autism spectrum disorders, pervasive developmental disorder (PDD) and other developmental difficulties. The Son-Rise Program teaches a specific yet comprehensive system of treatment and education designed to help families and caregivers enable their children to dramatically improve in all areas of learning.

1585 Symposium Series on Assistive Technology

Center on Disabilities/California State University
1811 Nordhoff Street
Northridge, CA 91330 818-677-2578
FAX 818-677-4929
http://www.csun.edu
e-mail: ctrdis@csun.edu
Joanne Moreno, Coordinator
Sonya Hernandez, Coordinator

Series of workshops that will address specific areas of assistive technology through in depth one and two day training workshops.

1586 TASH Annual Conference

29 W Susquehanna Avenue
Baltimore, MD   21204   410-828-8274
                              FAX 410-828-6706
                              http://www.tash.org
                              e-mail: knelson@tash.org
Nancy Weiss, Executive Director
Kelly Nelson, Conference Coordinator

Progressive international conference that focuses on strategies for achieving full inclusion for people with disabilities. This invigorating conference, which brings together the best hearts and minds in the disability movement, features over 450 breakout sessions, exhibits, roundtable discussions, poster sessions and much more.

December

1587 Teaching Math Workshop

Learning Disabilities Resources
PO Box 716
Bryn Mawr, PA   19010   610-525-8336
                              800-869-8336
                              FAX 610-525-8337
                              http://www.ldonline.org

A workshop for teachers on how to teach math to individuals with learning problems.

1588 Teaching Reading Workshop

Learning Disabilities Resources
PO Box 716
Bryn Mawr, PA   19010   610-525-8336
                              800-869-8336
                              FAX 610-525-8337
                              http://www.ldonline.org

This workshop explains how to teach individuals with reading problems, dyslexia, ADD, and specific learning disabilities.

1589 Teaching Spelling Workshop

Learning Disabilities Resources
PO Box 716
Bryn Mawr, PA   19010   610-525-8336
                              800-869-8336
                              FAX 610-525-8337
                              http://www.ldonline.org

Spelling is a problem which directly affects an individual's ability to write.

1590 Technology and Persons with Disabilities Conference

California State University, Northridge
18111 Nordhoff Street
Northridge, CA   91330   818-677-2578
                               FAX 818-677-4929
                               http://www.csun.edu/cod
                               e-mail: ctrdis@csun.edu
Joanne Moreno, Exhibits Coordinator
Sonya Hernandez, Speakers Coordinator

Comprehensive, international conference where technologies across all ages, disabilities, levels of education and training, employment and independent living are addressed.

March

1591 Tic Tac Toe: Math Training Workshop

Learning Disabilities Resources
PO Box 716
Bryn Mawr, PA   19010   610-525-8336
                              800-869-8336
                              FAX 610-525-8337
                              http://www.ldonline.org

This two hour workshop provides teachers with instruction in Tic Tac Toe Math and how to teach it.

1592 US International Council on Disabilities Conference

1630 Connecticut Avenue NW
Washington, DC   20009   202-429-2706
                               FAX 202-429-9574
                               http://www.usid.org
                               e-mail: usid.org@verizon.net
Ilene R Zeitzer, Interim Executive Director

Annual conference offers information for professionals in the areas of rehabilitation research, assistive technology and more.

September

1593 Wilson Language Training

Wilson Reading System
175 W Main Street
Millbury, MA   01527   508-865-5699
                             FAX 508-865-9644
                             http://www.wilsonlanguage.com
                             e-mail: info@wilsonlanguage.com
Judith Nicholas, Administrator Training

Our workshops instruct teachers, or other professionals in a related field, how to succeed with students who have not learned to read, write and spell despite great effort. Established in order to provide training in the Wilson Reading System, the Wilson staff provides Two-Day Overview Workshops as well as certified Level I and II training.

1594 Wilson Reading System

Wilson Language Training
175 W Main Street
Millbury, MA   01527   508-865-5699
                             800-899-8454
                             FAX 508-865-9644
                             http://www.wilsonlanguage.com
Judith Nicholas, Administrator Training
Duane Armstrong

Wilson Reading System workshops are research-based programs designed for individuals who have difficulty with written language in the areas of decoding and spelling. Wilson Language Training was established in order to provide training in the Wilson Reading System. The Wilson staff provides two-day Overview Workshops as well as certified Level I and Level II training. A noncertified Level I training is now offered on line.

**1595 Young Adult Institute Conference on
Developmental Disabilities**

460 W 34th Street
New York, NY   10001   212-273-6100
                              FAX 212-629-4113
                              http://www.yai.org
                              e-mail: ahorowitz@yai.org

Ben Nivin, Conference Director
Abbe Wittenberg, Conference Manager
Aimee Horowitz, Project Director

Annual conference of developmental disabilities.
In-depth sessions on the keys to success in developmental and learning disabilities.

   May

Assistive Devices

1596 ABLEDATA

8630 Fenton Street
Silver Spring, MD 20910　　301-608-8998
800-227-0216
FAX 301-608-8958
TDY:301-608-8912
http://www.abledata.com
e-mail: abledata@oremacro.com
Katherine Belknap, Project Director
Janice Benton, Information Services
David Johnson, Publications Director

Database contains descriptions of more than 30,000 commercially available, one-of-a-kind, and do-it-yourself products for rehabilitation and independent living. A wealth of information on assistive technology.

1597 ARTIC Technologies

1000 John R Road
Troy, MI 48083　　248-588-7370
FAX 248-588-1424
http://www.artictech.com
e-mail: info@artictech.com

Manufacturers of speed boards for the blind and visually impaired. Accessibility appliances for low vision and blindness.

1598 Ablenet

1081 10th Avenue SE
Minneapolis, MN 55414　　612-379-0956
800-322-0956
FAX 612-379-9143
http://www.ablenetinc.com
e-mail: customerservice@ablenetinc.com
Cheryl Volkman, Chief Developmental Officer

Simple assistive technology for teaching children with disabilities including communication aids, switches, environmental control, mounting systems, literacy and teacher resources, kits and more.

1599 Adaptive Device Locator System (ADLS)

Academic Software
3504 Tates Creek Road
Lexington, KY 40517　　859-552-1020
FAX 859-273-1943
http://www.acsw.com
e-mail: asistaff@acsw.com
Warren Lacefield, President
Penny D Ellis, COO

System describes thousands of devices, cross references over 600 vendors and illustrates devices graphically. The ADLS databases include a full spectrum of living aids, products ranging from specialized eating utensils to dressing aids, electronic switches, computer hardware and software, adapted physical education devices and much more. Now accessible on the internet through Adaptworld.com and Acsw.com *$195.00*

1600 Arcade Adventure

Dunamis
Lawrenceville, GA 30044　　770-279-1144
800-828-2443
FAX 770-279-0809
http://www.dunamisinc.com
e-mail: info@dunamisinc.com
Ben Satterfield, President
Matt Satterfield, College/LD Sales

Game-style program helps more advanced switch users build hand-eye coordination and problem solving skills. *$50.00*

1601 Braille' n Speak Classic

American Printing House for the Blind
1839 Frankfort Avenue
Louisville, KY 40206　　502-895-2405
800-223-1839
FAX 502-899-2274
http://www.aph.org
Fred Gissoni, Customer Support

This computerized, talking device has many features useful to student and adult braille users (word processors, print-to-braille translator, talking clocks/calculators and much more). *$929.95*

1602 CCT Telephone Interface

Consultants for Communication Technology
508 Bellevue Terrace
Pittsburgh, PA 15202　　412-761-6062
FAX 412-761-7336
http://www.concommtech.com
e-mail: kathy@concommtech.com
Kathleen Miller PhD, Speech Pathologist

Device allows output from your communication software to be transmitted directly through the telephone. Requires CCT software. *$300.00*

1603 Communication Aids: Manufacturers Association

205 W Randolph
Chicago, IL 60606
800-441-2262
FAX 312-229-5445
http://www.aacproducts.org
e-mail: cama@northshore.net
James Neils, President

A nonprofit organization of the world's leading manufacturers of augmentative and alternative communication software and hardware.

1604 Compu-Lenz

Florida New Concepts Marketing
PO Box 261
Port Richey, FL 34673　　727-842-3231
800-456-7097
FAX 727-842-3231
http://www.gulfside.com/compulenz
e-mail: compulnz@gte.net
Carol Lezark, Customer Service

A powerful lens which will more than double the size of computer screen characters without distortion or light refraction. *$204.95*

1605 Connect Outloud

Freedon Scientific
11800 31st Court N
St.Petersburg, FL   33716   727-803-8000
                                   800-444-4443
                              FAX 727-803-8001
            http://www.freedomscientific.com
            e-mail: info@freedomscientific.com
Lee Hamilton, CEO

Designed to allow beginners through experienced blind or low vision computer users to access the Internet through speech and Braille output. Based on our JAWS for Windows technology, and offers additional access to Windows XP. *$ 249.00*

1606 Consultants for Communication Technology

508 Bellevue Terrace
Pittsburgh, PA   15202   412-761-6062
                          FAX 412-761-7336
            http://www.concommtech.com
            e-mail: cct@concommtech.com
Kathleen Miller PhD, Speech Pathologist

Manufactures and distributes a line of augmentative communication products for persons with speech impairments. In addition we have software products for environmental control, word processing and phone management. All products can be used with only one muscle movement or from the full keyboard.

1607 Controlpad 24

Genovation
17741 Mitchell N
Irvine, CA   92614   949-833-3355
                           800-822-4333
                      FAX 949-833-0322
            http://www.genovation.com
            e-mail: sales@genovation.com
Edward Lopez, Project Manager
Chris Fructus, Director Marketing

Fully programmable 24 key pad. Its principal purpose is to provide single keystroke macros.

1608 Creature Games Series

Dunamis
3545 Cruse Road
Lawrenceville, GA   30044   770-279-1144
                                   800-828-2443
                              FAX 770-279-0809
            http://www.dunamisinc.com
            e-mail: info@dunamisinc.com
Ben Satterfield, President
Matt Satterfield, College/LD Sales

Everybody loves computer games, but these games are unique. They can be enjoyed by children with severe/profound disabilities, including those functioning as low as 4 months of age. *$80.00*

1609 Dunamis

3545 Cruse Road
Lawrenceville, GA   30044   770-279-1144
                                   800-828-2443
                              FAX 770-279-0809
            http://www.dunamisinc.com
            e-mail: info@dunamisinc.com
Ben Satterfield, President
Matt Satterfield, College/LD Sales

Since 1984 we have been committed to helping you find the technology you need to accomplish your goals and realize your dreams. We offer assistive technology that is the most appropriate available, at the highest quality and the most competitive price possible.

1610 DynaVoxDyna Vox Systems

2100 Wharton Street
Pittsburgh, PA   15203   412-381-4883
                                800-344-1778
                           FAX 412-381-5241
            http://www.dynavoxsys.com
            e-mail: sale@dynavoxsys.com
Joanne Kaufmann, Corporate Communications

Dynamic display, touch screen augmentative communication devices that allow the user to create messages by choosing preprogrammed items, or create novel messages. Each device comes with DynaSyms, a comprehensive, language-based system with more than 2600 symbols. Word and symbol prediction helps individuals construct long messages quickly by offering a continuous stream of logical words and/or symbols. A built-in environmental control unit (ECU) allows users to access TVs, VCRs, and computers. *$4500.00*

1611 EZ Keys/Key Wiz

Words+
1220 W Avenue J
Lancaster, CA   93534   661-723-6523
                               800-869-8521
                          FAX 661-723-2114
            http://www.world-plus.com
            e-mail: info@world-plus.com

Assistance program that provides keyboard control, dual word prediction, abbreviation-expansion and speech output while running standard software. *$695.00*

1612 Franklin Language Master

Freedon Scientific
11800 31st Court N
St. Petersburg, FL   33716   727-803-8000
                                    800-444-4443
                               FAX 727-803-8001
            http://www.freedomscientific.com
            e-mail: info@freedomscientific.com
Lee Hamilton, CEO

Versatile hand-held dictionary full speech controls to read screens or speak individual words at the speed you choose. At less than 6 inches square, this lightweight tool is designed for maximum efficiency. Large-type display, high contrast screen and black on white QWERTY keyboard. For blind users, orientation features include active screen announcing and raised dots on location keys. *$450.00*

1613 Genie Color TV

TeleSensory
520 Almanor Avenue
Sunnyvale, CA 94043   408-616-8700
800-227-8418
FAX 408-616-8753
http://www.telesensory.com
e-mail: info@telesensory.com
David Wrench, Marketing
Beth Thomlinson, Marketing

Brings clarity and comfort to reading and writing.
Since many people with low vision find that specific
color combinations enhance legibility, VersiColor offers 24 customized foreground and background color
combinations to choose from in addition to a full color
mode. Genie can also connect to a computer for use
with Telesensory's Vista screen magnification system. *$2995.00*

1614 Genovation

17741 Mitchell N
Irvine, CA 92614   949-833-3355
800-822-4333
FAX 949-822-4333
http://www.genovation.com
e-mail: sales@genovation.com
Edward Lopez, Project Manager
Chris Fructus, Director Marketing

Produces a wide variety of computer input devices for
data-entry, and custom applications. Produces the
Function Keypad 682 for people with limited dexter-
ity. It is programmable, allowing the user to store macros (selected patterns of key strokes) into memory,
and relegendable keys allow easy labeling of user-pro-
grammed functions. Additional options such as larger
keys (1x2), allow reconfiguration to meet the user's
needs. Call toll-free for pricing and availability.

1615 Home Row Indicators

Hooleon Corporation
417 Building A, S 6th Street
Cottonwood, AZ 86326   928-634-7515
800-937-1337
FAX 928-634-4620
http://www.hooleon.com
e-mail: sales@hooleon.com
Joan Crozier, President

Plastic adhesive labels with a raised bump in the center allowing the user to designate home row keys, or
any other key, for quick recognition.

1616 Hub

Alliance for Technology Access
1304 Southpoint Boulevard
Petaluma, CA 94954   707-778-3011
FAX 707-765-2080
TDY:707-778-3015
http://www.ataccess.org
e-mail: atainfo@ataccess.org
Mary Lester, Executive Director

Interactive information service provides quick and efficient access to information on assistive technology
tools and services to consumers, families and service
providers.

1617 IBM Independence Series

IBM
11400 Burnet Road
Austin, TX 78758   800-426-4832
FAX 512-838-9367
http://www.IBM.com/sns
Dennis T O'Brien, Product Manager

A group of products designed to help individuals with
disabilities to achieve greater personal and professional independence through the use of technology.
Products include Keyguard, AccessDOS, THINK-
able/2, Screen Reader/2, Screen Magnifier/2,
SpeechViewer II, THINKable/DOS and Screen
Reader/DOS.

1618 IntelliKeys

IntelliTools
1720 Corporate Circle
Petaluma, CA 94954   707-773-2000
800-899-6687
FAX 707-773-2001
http://www.intellitools.com
e-mail: info@intellitools.com
Beth Davis, Sales

Alternative, touch-sensitive keyboard. Plugs into any
MAC, APPLE, or IBM compatible computer, no interface needed. *$395.00*

1619 JAWS for Windows

Freedon Scientific
11800 31st Court N
St.Petersburg, FL 33716   727-803-8000
800-444-4443
FAX 727-803-8001
http://www.freedomscientific.com
e-mail: info@freedomscientific.com
Lee Hamilton, CEO

Works with your PC to provide access to today's software applications and the internet. With its internal
software speech synthesizer and the computer's
sound card, information from the screen is read aloud,
providing technology to access a wide variety of information, education and job related applications.

1620 Large Print Keyboard

Hooleon Corporation
417 Building 3565, S 6th Street
Cottonwood, AZ 86326   928-634-7515
800-937-1337
FAX 928-634-4620
http://www.hooleon.com
e-mail: sales@hooleon.com
Joan Crozier, President

Keyboard with 104 keys features large print on all the
keys.

1621 Large Print Lower Case Labels

Hooleon Corporation
417 Building A, S 6th Street
Cottonwood, AZ   86326   928-634-7515
                                          800-937-1337
                                      FAX 928-634-4620
                                  http://www.hooleon.com
                               e-mail: sales@hooleon.com
Joan Crozier, President

For children learning the keyboard.

1622 Lekotek of Georgia Shareware

Lekotek of Georgia
1955 Cliff Valley Way NE
Atlanta, GA   30329   404-633-3430
                                      FAX 404-633-1242
                                 http://www.lekotekga.org
                              e-mail: email@lekotekga.org
Helena Prokesh, Executive Director
Margaret Deavours, Tech Specialist

Software created by our staff using Intellipics,
Intellipics Studio or Hyperstudio. Players are included to run this shareware. Color overlays for
intellemusic are included. Input methods are mouse,
switch, touch window, head mouse and intellikeys if
applicable. Subjects are colors and emotions, early
childhood music in English and Spanish, shapes and
sounds, pictures and letters.

1623 Micro IntroVoice

Voice Connection
17971 Skypark Circle
Irvine, CA   92614   949-261-2366
                                      FAX 949-261-8563
                                  http://www.voicecnx.com
                                e-mail: voicecnx@aol.com
Shirley Dworak, VP Marketing

A complete voice input/output system which provides
voice recognition of 1,000 words with accuracy of 98
percent and unlimited text-to-speech and recorded
speech for voice prompting and varification. Micro
IntroVoice works with DOS and Windows applications for entering commands or data. *$1095.00*

1624 Open Book

Freedon Scientific
11800 31st Court N
St.Petersburg, FL   33716   727-803-8000
                                          800-444-4443
                                      FAX 727-803-8001
                           http://www.freedomscientific.com
                         e-mail: info@freedomscientific.com
Lee Hamilton, CEO

Allows you to convert printed documents or graphic
based text into an electronic text format using accurate optical character recognition and quality speech.
The many powerful low vision tools allow you to customize how the document appears on your screen,
while other features provide portability. *$995.00*

1625 OutSPOKEN

Alva Access Group
436 14th Street
Oakland, CA   94612   510-451-2582
                                          888-318-2582
                                      FAX 510-451-0878
                                   http://www.aagi.com
                                 e-mail: info@aagi.com
Gives blind and learning disabled persons access to
mainstream Macintosh software via speech output.
$395.00

1626 Personal Communicating Device

ABOVO
96 Rhinebeck Avenue
Springfield, MA   01129   413-594-5279
                                      FAX 413-594-5809

A portable, handheld electronic device designed for
single finger communication by people who wish to
communicate through typing.

1627 Phonic Ear Auditory Trainers

Phonic Ear
3880 Cypress Drive
Petaluma, CA   94954   707-769-1110
                                          800-227-0735
                                      FAX 707-769-9624
                                 http://www.phonicear.com
                          e-mail: marketing@phonicear.com
Paul Hickey, VP Sales
J Merline, Director Marketing
Cindy Pedersen, Customer Service Manager

A line of learning disabled communication equipment.

1628 QuicKeys

CE Software
PO Box 65580
West Des Moines, IA   50265   515-221-1801
                                      FAX 515-221-1806
                                   http://www.cesoft.com
                                 e-mail: sales@cesoft.com
John S Kirk, Controller

Assigns Macintosh functions to one keystroke.

1629 Reading Pen

Wizcom Technologies
257 Great Road
Acton, MA   01720   978-635-5357
                                          888-777-0552
                                      FAX 978-929-9228
                                http://www.wizcomtech.com
                              e-mail: sales@wizcomtech.com
Portable assistive reading device that reads words
aloud and can be used anywhere. Scans a word from
printed text, displays the word in large characters,
reads the word aloud from built-in speaker or ear
phones and defines the word with the press of a button.
Displays syllables, keeps a history of scanned words,
adjustable for left or right-handed use. Includes a tutorial video and audio cassette. Not recommended for
persons with low vision or impaired fine motor control.

1630 Scan It-Switch It

UCLA Intervention Program for Handicapped Children
1000 Veteran Avenue
Los Angeles, CA   90095   310-825-4821
                          FAX 310-206-7744
                          http://www.bol.ucla.edu
Sharon Cislo, Administrative Assistant

Helps teach horizontal and vertical scanning using a
single switch or TouchWindow. Instruction progresses through five levels of difficulty from captur-
ing a single object with a moving box to using
scanning to select matching items. *$45.00*

1631 Self-Adhesive Braille Keytop Labels

Hooleon Corporation
411 S 6th Street, Building B
Cottonwood, AZ   86326   520-634-7515
                          800-937-1337
                          FAX 520-634-4620
                          http://www.hooleon.com
                          e-mail: sales@hooleon.com
Joan Crozier, President

Transparent with raised braille allows both sighted
and nonsighted users to use same keyboard.

1632 Switch Accessible Trackball

Lekotek of Georgia
1955 Cliff Valley Way NE
Atlanta, GA   30329   404-633-3430
                          FAX 404-633-1242
                          http://www.lekotekga.org
                          e-mail: email@lekotekga.org
Helena Prokesh, Executive Director
Margaret Deavours, Tech Specialist

Universal to Mac or Windows, this device aids computer navigation where traditional devices are not
used. Trackball guards available. *$125.00*

1633 Switch It Software Bundle

Dunamis
3423 Fowler Boulevard
Lawrenceville, GA   30044   770-279-1144
                          800-828-2443
                          FAX 770-279-0809
                          http://www.dunamisinc.com
                          e-mail: info@dunamisinc.com
Ben Satterfield, President
Matt Satterfield, College/LD Sales

Collection of 4 software programs that follow a developmental learning sequence.

1634 Talking Typer

American Printing House for the Blind
1839 Frankfort Avenue
Louisville, KY   40206   502-895-2405
                          800-223-1839
                          FAX 502-899-2274
                          http://www.aph.org
Fred Gissoni, Customer Support

Designed to reinforce keyboarding skills for visually
impaired Apple VI users and their teachers.

1635 Talking Utilities for DOS 3.3

American Printing House for the Blind
1839 Frankfort Avenue
Louisville, KY   40206   502-895-2405
                          800-223-1839
                          FAX 502-899-2274
                          http://www.aph.org
Fred Gissoni, Customer Support

A talking version of System Master with features
added for speech synthesis users. *$15.00*

1636 Talking Utilities for ProDOS

American Printing House for the Blind
1839 Frankfort Avenue
Louisville, KY   40206   502-895-2405
                          800-223-1839
                          FAX 502-899-2274
                          http://www.aph.org
Fred Gissoni, Customer Support

A speech-accessible version of Apple's ProDOS
User's Disk. *$10.00*

1637 Text 2000

American Printing House for the Blind
1839 Frankfort Avenue
Louisville, KY   40206   502-895-2405
                          800-223-1839
                          FAX 502-899-2274
                          http://www.aph.org
Fred Gissoni, Customer Support

Allows students to read textbooks in a number of
ways, including synthetic speech, large type sized to
the screen and refreshable braille. *$112.00*

1638 Ufonic Voice System

Jostens Learning Systems
7878 N 16th Street
Phoenix, AZ   85020   602-678-7272
                          800-551-1121
                          FAX 602-230-7034

Consists of the interface card, amplifier/speaker with
dual headphones and volume control, and provides
human sounding speech in instructional software developed for this use. *$245.00*

1639 Unicorn Expanded Keyboard

IntelliTools
1720 Corporate Circle
Petaluma, CA   94954   707-773-2000
                          800-899-6687
                          FAX 707-773-2001
                          http://www.intellitools.com
                          e-mail: info@intellitools.com
Beth Davis, Sales

Alternative keyboard with large, user-defined keys,
requires interface. Smaller version is also available.
$315.00

1640 Unicorn Smart Keyboard

IntelliTools
55 Leveroni Court
Novato, CA   94949

800-899-6687
FAX 415-382-5950

Works with any standard keyboard and offers seven overlays and a cable for one type of computer.

1641 Universal Numeric Keypad

Genovation
17741 Mitchell N
Irvine, CA   92614

949-833-3355
800-822-4333
FAX 949-833-4333
http://www.genovation.com
e-mail: sales@genovation.com

Chris Fructus, Director Marketing
Edward Lopez, Product Manager

A 21 key numeric keypad that works with any laptop or portable computer.

1642 Up and Running

IntelliTools
1720 Corporate Circle
Petaluma, CA   94954

707-773-2000
800-899-6687
FAX 707-773-2001
http://www.intellitools.com

A custom overlay kit for the Unicorn Keyboard that provides instant access to a wide range of software including over 60 popular educational programs. *$69.95*

1643 VISTA

TeleSensory
520 Almanor Avenue
Sunnyvale, CA   94086

408-616-8700
800-227-8418
FAX 408-616-8720
http://www.telesensory.com
e-mail: info@telesensory.com

David Wrench, Marketing
Beth Thomlinson, Marketing

Image enlarging system that magnifies the print and graphics on the screen from three to 16 times. *$2495.00*

1644 Visagraph II Eye-Movement Recording System

Taylor Associated Communications
200 E 2nd Street
Huntington Station, NY   11746

631-549-3000
800-732-3587
FAX 631-549-3156
http://www.ta-comm.com
e-mail: info@ta-comm.com

Stanford Taylor, President

Measures reading performance efficiency, visual and functional proficiency, perceptual development, and information processing competence.

1645 VoiceNote

Pulse Date Human Ware
175 Mason Circle
Concord, CA   94520

925-680-7100
800-722-3393
FAX 925-681-4630
http://www.pulsedata.com
e-mail: usa@pulsedata.com

Speech synthesizer without a braille display. Most of the great features that are on BrailleNote are here, but on a smaller and lighter unit. Choose from either a braille key or a QWERTY input, depending on your preference.

1646 Window-Eyes

GW Micro
725 Airport N Office Park
Fort Wayne, IN   46825

260-489-3671
FAX 260-489-2608
http://www.gwmicro.com
e-mail: support@gwmicro.com

Dan Weirich, President

Screen reader that is adaptable to your specific needs and preferances. Works automatically so you can focus on your application program, not so much on operating the screen reader.

Books & Periodicals

1647 AppleWorks Education

AACE
PO Box 3728
Norfolk, VA   23514

757-623-7588
FAX 703-997-8760
http://www.aace.org
e-mail: info@aace.org

Gary Marks, Publisher

Covers educational uses of AppleWorks software. *$25.00*

1648 AppleWorks Manuals: Special Editions

American Printing House for the Blind
1839 Frankfort Avenue
Louisville, KY   40206

502-895-2405
800-223-1839
FAX 502-899-2274
http://www.aph.org

Fred Gissoni, Customer Support

Designed for visually impaired users. Includes AppleWorks tutorials on cassette and AppleWorks Reference Manual on computer diskette. *$23.90*

1649 Art Express and the Literacy Curriculum

Center for Best Practices in Early Childhood
Western Illnois University
Macomb, IL   61455

309-298-1634
FAX 309-298-2305
http://www.mprojects.wiu.edu
e-mail: PL-Hutinger@wiu.edu

Patricia Hutinger EdD, Director
Joyce Johanson, Coordinator

Make your classroom come alive with art, music, movement, and dramatic play. Innovative, yet practical guide for helping teachers implement a comprehensive expressive arts curriculum in their classrooms include tips for arranging the environment. *$20.00*

16-20 pages

1650 Bibliography of Journal Articles on Microcomputers & Special Education

Special Education Resource Center
25 Industrial Park Road
Middletown, CT 06457   860-632-1485
                              FAX 860-632-8870
Stephen Kramer, Compiler

This pamphlet offers information on a wide variety of professional journals in the fields of microcomputers and special education.

1651 Closing the Gap Newsletter

PO Box 68
Henderson, MN 56044   507-248-3294
                             FAX 507-248-3810
              http://www.closingthegap.com
              e-mail: info@closingthegap.com
Jan Latzke, Communications

Bimonthly newsletter on the use of computer technology in special education and rehabilitation. CTG also sponsors an annual international conference. *$34.00*

40 pages
ISSN 0886-1935

1652 Computer Access-Computer Learning

Special Needs Project
324 State Street
Santa Barbara, CA 93105   805-962-8087
                                 800-333-6867
                            FAX 805-962-5087
              http://www.specialneeds.com
              e-mail: books@specialneeds.com
Ginny LaVine, Author

A resource manual in adaptive technology. *$22.50*

226 pages

1653 Computers in Head Start Classrooms

Learning Disabilities Association of America
4156 Library Road
Pittsburgh, PA 15234   412-341-1515
                              FAX 412-344-0224
                    http://www.ldanatl.org
                    e-mail: ldanatl@usaor.net

$7.00

1654 MACcessories: Guide to Peripherals

Western Illinois University: Macomb Projects
27 Horrabin Hall
Macomb, IL 61455   309-298-1634
                          FAX 309-298-2305
                  http://www.mprojects.wiu.edu
                  e-mail: PL-Hutinger@wiu.edu
Patricia Hutinger EdD, Director
Joyce Johanson, Coordinator

Designed to help the Macintosh user understand peripheral devices. Includes descriptions of each device, advantages and disadvantages of each, procedures for installation, troubleshooting tips, suggested software and company resources. *$15.00*

41 pages

1655 Opening Windows: A Talking and Tactile Tutorial for Microsoft Windows

American Printing House for the Blind
1839 Frankfort Avenue
Louisville, KY 40206   502-895-2405
                              800-223-1839
                          FAX 502-895-1509
                          http://www.aph.org
Fred Gissoni, Customer Support

Includes raised line graphics, cassette and computer diskette designed to acquaint visually impaired computer users with Windows 3.1 operating environment. *$50.00*

1656 Switch to Turn Kids On

Western Illinois University: Macomb Projects
27 Horrabin Hall
Macomb, IL 61455   309-298-1634
                          FAX 309-298-2305
                  http://www.mprojects.wiu.edu
                  e-mail: PL-Hutinger@wiu.edu
Patricia Hutinger EdD, Director
Joyce Johanson, Coordinator

Guide to homemade switches gives information on conducting a switch workshop and constructing a battery interrupter as well as various kinds of switches (tread switches, ribbon switches, mercury switches, pillow switches). Contains illustrations and step-by-step instructions. *$12.00*

47 pages

Centers & Organizations

1657 Activating Children Through Technology (ACCT)

Western Illinois University: Macomb Projects
27 Horrabin Hall
Macomb, IL 61455   309-298-1634
                          FAX 309-298-2305
                  http://www.mprojects.wiu.edu
                  e-mail: PL-Hutinger@wiu.edu
Patricia Hutinger EdD, Director
Joyce Johanson, Coordinator

ACTT integrates assistive technology into early childhood services for children with disabilities from birth to 8 years old. It helps them gain control over their environment, develop autonomy, communicate, develop problem-solving skills and participate in an inclusive environment. ACTT provides training to families and educators and has written materials and software available. *$16.00*

1658 Adaptive Technology Laboratory

Southern Connecticut State University
501 Crescent Street
New Haven, CT 06515   203-392-6790
FAX 203-392-5796
http://www.southernct.edu
e-mail: webmaster@computerethics.org
Janice Hecht, Adaptive Technology Coordinator

Helps individuals with visual, orthopedic and learning disabilities to gain computer access through the use of the latest technology.

1659 Artificial Language Laboratory

Michigan State University
405 Computer Center
East Lansing, MI 48824   517-353-5399
FAX 517-353-4766
http://www.ms.uedu/~artlang/
e-mail: artlang@pilot.msu.edu
John B Eulenberg PhD, Director
Stephen Blosser, Rehab Engineer

Multidisciplinary teaching and research center involved in basic and applied research concerning the computer processing of formal linguistic structures.

1660 Assistive Technology Information Network

IA University Assistive Technology
University Hospital School
Iowa City, IA 52242   319-355-4463
800-331-3027
FAX 319-356-8284
http://www.uiowa.edu
e-mail: jane-gay@uiowa.edu
Jane Gray, Director
Mary Quigley, Director

Computer accesssed solutions for physically challenged students.

1661 Association for Educational Communications and Technology

1800 N Stonelake Drive
Bloomington, IN 47408   812335767580
FAX 812-335-7678
http://www.aect.org
e-mail: rxaver@aect.org
Dr. Phillip Harris, Executive Director
Richard Xaver, Electronic Services

Provides leadership in educational communications and technology by linking professionals holding a common interest in the use of educational technology and its application to the learning process.

1662 Birmingham Alliance for Technology Access Center

Birmingham Independent Living Center
206 13th Street S
Birmingham, AL 35233   205-251-2223
FAX 205-251-0605
e-mail: mikenorris@mindspring.net
Mike Norris, Director

Information dissemination, network, referral service, support services, and training. Disabilities served are cognitive, hearing, learning, physical, speech and vision.

1663 Bluegrass Technology Center

961 Beasley Street
Lexington, KY 40509   859-294-4343
800-209-7769
FAX 859-294-0704
TDY:800-209-7767
http://www.bluegrass-tech.org
e-mail: office@bluegrass-tech.org
Jean Isaacs, Director Technology
Debbie Sharon, Director Education
Penny Ellis, Assistive Technology Consultant

Provides support to all persons with disabilities in their efforts to access technology and to increase awareness and understanding of how that technology can enhance their abilities to participate more fully in their community, assisting individuals directly or indirectly by working with their caregivers, therapists, vocational counselors, case managers, educators, employers, and community members.

1664 CAST

40 Harvard Mills Square
Wakefield, MA 01880   781-245-2212
888-858-9994
FAX 781-245-5212
http://www.cast.org
e-mail: djordon@cast.org
Dr. David Rose, Co-Executive Director
David Gordon, Communications

Nonprofit organization whose mission is to expand educational opportunities for all children through innovative uses of computer technology. Provides direct services to individuals, offers consultation and training, conducts research and develops software and implementation models for education.

1665 CITE Technology Access Center

215 E New Hampshire Street
Orlando, FL 32804   407-898-2483
FAX 407-895-5255
http://www.centralfloridalighthouse.org
e-mail: jgideons@cite-fl.com
Lee Nasehi, Executive Director
Karen Morehouse, Children's Services

Community based technology resource center seeks to redefine human potential by making technology a regular part of the lives of people with disabilities. Dedicated to increasing the use of technology by children and adults with disabilities, their families, educators and employers. CITE exists to solve the problem of where people can find out about the power of technology and get the expertise and assistance they need to make computers work for them.

1666 CMECSU Technology Project for Learners with Low Incidence Disabilities

3335 W St. Germain Street
Saint Cloud, MN 56301   763-255-4913
Dixie Waller Anderson

A regional educational organization that works within a nine county region. Maintains a demonstration center with about 500 public domain software programs. Offers specialized equipment for loan to students.

1667   Carolina Computer Access Center

401 E 9th Street
Charlotte, NC   28202   704-342-3004
                                         FAX 704-342-1513
                                         http://ccac.ataccess.org
                                         e-mail: ccacnc@aol.com
Linda Schilling, Director

Demonstrations, assessments, workshops, and information on assistive technologies.

1668   Center for Accessible Technology

2547 8th Street
Berkeley, CA   94710   510-841-3224
                                         FAX 510-841-7956
                                         http://www.cforat.org
                                         e-mail: info@cforat.org
Dimitri Belser, Executive Director

Provides access to the tools of expression for people with disabilities. Offers information and traning on assistive computer technology and adapted art programs, allowing people with disabilities to participate fully in work, school, and community activities.

1669   Center for Enabling Technology

College of New Jersey
Forcina 102
Ewing, NJ   08628   609-771-3016
                                         FAX 609-637-5172
                                         http://www.tcnj.edu
                                         e-mail: educat@tcnj.edu
Terry O'Connor, Dean
Christine Schindler, Director

Ongoing projects that match assistive devices to the children who need them. Training and educational workshops.

1670   Comprehensive Services for the Disabled

Belmar Boulevard & Woodfield Avenue
Wall, NJ   07719   732-681-5632
                                         800-784-2919
                                         FAX 732-681-5632
Donald J DeSanto, Executive Director
Anthony J Aquilino, Director
Jennifer DeSanto, Administrative Assistant

Helps special students realize their potential and bring college admission a step closer. Program designed to meet the needs and maximize the unique talents of each individual. The staff consists of highly qualified teachers who see beyond labels and reach the person inside. By pacing scholastics to each student's ability, the college increases understanding and makes learning a positive experience. Instruction is tailored to each individual.

1671   Computer Access Center

6234 W 87th Street
Los Angeles, CA   90045   310-338-5977
                                         FAX 310-338-9318
                                         http://www.cac.org
                                         e-mail: cac@cac.org
Mary Ann Glicksman, Director

Computer resource center serving primarily as a place where people with all types of disabilities can preview equipment. Workshops, seminars, after school clubs for children and individual consultations are provided.

1672   Computer Accommodation Lab

Woodrow Wilson Rehab Center
Box 1500
Fishersville, VA   22939   540-332-7000
                                         800-345-9972
                                         FAX 540-332-7132
                                         http://www.wwrc.net
                                         e-mail: colemawl@wwrc.state.va.us
Twana Afton, Resource Specialist

Provides assessments for adolescents and adults in appropriate access to computers, including alternative input strategies, mouse applications, and software solutions.

1673   Computer Learning Foundation

47 Northgate Boulevard
Sacramento, CA   95834   916-595-4766
                                         FAX 916-565-0220
                                         http://www.computerlearning.org
                                         e-mail: clf@computerlearning.org
Sally Bowman Alden, Executive Director

An international nonprofit educational foundation, dedicated to improving the quality of education and preparation of youth for the workplace through the use of technology. To accomplish its mission, the foundation provides numerous projects and materials to help parents and educators use technology effectively with children.

1674   DIRECT LINK for the Disabled

PO Box 1036
Solvang, CA   93464   805-626-5285
                                         FAX 805-688-1603
                                         e-mail: Suharry@terminus.com
Linda Harry, Executive Director

Provides technical assistance for making job accommodations and worksite adaptations for individuals with disabilities. Maintains database providing information on financial assistance, attendant care services, adaptive equipment, transportation, job training, job placement services and vocational rehabilitation. 7,000 entries.

1675   Dialog Information Services

11000 Regency Parkway
Cary, NC   27511   919-462-8600
                                         800-334-2564
                                         FAX 919-468-9890
                                         http://www.dialog.com
                                         e-mail: customer@dialog.com
Roy Martin, President

Offers access to over 390 data bases containing information on various aspects of disabling conditions and services to disabled individuals.

1676   Disabled Children's Computer Group

2547 8th Street
Berkeley, CA   94710   510-841-3224
                                FAX 510-841-7956
                                http://www.cforat.org
                                e-mail: info@cforat.org
Lisa Lahl, Program Director
Dimitri Belser, Executive Director

Resource center for parents, professionals, developers and individuals with disabilities, filled with computers, software, adapted toys and adaptive technology.

1677   Eastern Tennessee Technology Access Center

4918 N Broadway
Knoxville, TN   37918   423-219-0130
                                http://www.korrnet.org/ettac
                                e-mail: etstactn@aol.com
Louis Symington, Director

Assistive technology resource and information center for individuals with disabilities, their families and professionals who work with them. Workshops, consultations, tutoring, information and product reviews available.

1678   Enabling Technologies of Kentuckiana

Louisville Free Public Library
301 York Street
Louisville, KY   40203   502-574-1637
                                800-890-1840
                                FAX 502-582-2448
        http://www.kde.state.ky.us/oct/customer/at/ente
                                e-mail: entech@iglou.com
Robin Stacy, Project Director

Strives to support all people with disabilities in their efforts to access technology and to increase awareness and understanding of how technology can enhance their abilities to participate more fully in the community.

1679   Exceptional Child Education Resource (ECER)

Council for Exceptional Children
1110 N Glebe Road
Arlington, VA   22201   703-620-3660
                                888-232-7733
                                FAX 703-264-9494
                                http://www.cec.sped.org/
Kathleen McClane, Associate Director
Janet Drill, Acquisitions Coordinator

This database contains citations and abstracts of print and nonprint materials dealing with exceptional children, those who have disabilities and those who are gifted. Resources in all areas of special education and related services (including services provided by audiologists, speech therapists, occupational therapists, physical therapists, and educational psychologists) are covered in ECER.

1680   High Tech Center for the Disabled of the California Community Colleges

Foothill-DeAnza Community College District
21050 McClellan Road
Cupertino, CA   95014   408-996-4636
                                800-411-8954
                                FAX 408-996-6042
                                http://www.htctu.fhda.edu
                                e-mail: cbrown@htctu.net
Carl Brown, Director

Provides training for faculty and staff of the California community colleges in access technologies.

1681   Learning Independence Through Computers

LINC
1001 Eastern Avenue
Baltimore, MD   21202   410-659-5462
                                FAX 410-659-5472
                                http://www.linc.org
                                e-mail: lincmd@aol.com
Mary Salkever, Executive Director
Susan Pompa, Director Program Management

Resource center that offers specially adapted computer technology to children and adults with a variety of disabilities. State-of-the-art systems allow consumers to achieve their potential for productivity and independence at home, school, work and in the community. Also offers a quarterly newsletter called Connections.

1682   National Technology Center

American Foundation for the Blind
11 Penn Plaza
New York, NY   10001   212-502-7600
                                800-232-5463
                                FAX 212-502-7777
                                http://www.afb.org
                                e-mail: afbinfo@afb.net
Carl R Augusto, President

Demonstrates and evaluates equipment and publishes evaluations in the Journal of Visual Impairment & Blindness.

1683   New Breakthroughs

89911 Greenwood Drive
Eugene, OR   97402   541-741-5070
                                FAX 541-896-0123
Carol Lee Berger, Contact

Facilitated communication and information in all areas of assistive, alternative communication. Technological education materials, workshops and training in new special education advancements are available.

1684   Northern Illinois Center for Adaptive Technology

3615 Louisiana Road
Rockford, IL   61108   815-229-2163
                                FAX 815-229-2135
                                http://www.nicat.ataccess.org
                                e-mail: davegrass@earthlink.net
Dave Grass, Director

Nonprofit computer and adaptive devices resource center operated by parents, consumers, volunteers and professionals dedicated to providing information, seminars and individual needs technology. It is the goal of the center to help people with disabilities reach their full potential by providing them with information on the latest technology and by matching adaptive devices to their disabilities allowing them to more effectively interface with their environment.

1685 Project TECH

Massachusetts Easter Seal Society
484 Main Street
Worcester, MA   01608   508-757-2756
                               800-922-8290
                          FAX 508-831-9768
     http://www.eastersealma.org/index/general
          e-mail: maryd@eastersealma.org
Kirk Joslin, President
Mary D'Antonio, Information Specialist

Assistive technology services, suited to an individual's needs. Transition from school to work, employment planning, occupational skills and more are coached here.

1686 RESNA Technical Assistance Project

Rehabilitation Engineering & Asst Technology: NA
1700 N Moore Street
Arlington, VA   22209   703-524-6686
                          FAX 703-524-6630
                          TDY:703-524-6639
                 http://www.resna.org
          e-mail: membership@resna.org
Larry Pencak, Executive Director
Shannon Marullo, Professional Services
Nell Bailey, Director Projects

Provides technical assistance to states in the development and implementation of consumer responsive statewide programs of technology-related assistance under the Technology Related Assistance for Individuals with Disabilities Act of 1988.

1687 Special Awareness Computer Center

Rehabilitation Center
2975 N Sycamore Drive
Simi Valley, CA   93065   805-582-1881
                          FAX 805-582-2855
               e-mail: saccca@aol.org
Suzanne Feit, Director

Nonprofit resource center helping people with disabilities to learn how technology can lead them to more independent lives. Offers workshops, training and community presentations.

1688 Special Education Preview Center

Ruth Eason School
648 Old Mill Road
Millersville, MD   21108   410-222-3815
                          FAX 410-222-3817

1689 Tech-Able

1114 Brett Drive SW
Conyers, GA   30094   770-922-6768
                        FAX 770-992-6769
                http://www.techable.org
            e-mail: techable@techable.org
Carolyn M McGonagill, Director
Pat Hanus, Assistant Director
Joe Tedesco, Assistive Tech. Practitioner

Assistive technology demonstration and information center. Provides demonstrations of computer hardware and software specially designed to assist people with disabilities. Serves a wide range of disabilities and virtually all age groups. Also custom fabrication of key guards and switches.

1690 Technology Access Center

2222 Metrocenter Boulevard
Nashville, TN   37228   615-248-6733
                               800-368-4651
                          FAX 615-259-2536
                          TDY:615-248-6733
                 http://www.tac.ataccess.org
          e-mail: techaccess@mindstate.com
Bob Kibler, Director
Lynn Magner, Service Coordinator

Serves the community as a resource center and carries out specific projects related to assistive technology.

1691 Technology Access Foundation

3803 S Edmunds Street
Seattle, WA   98112   206-725-9095
                        FAX 206-725-9097
                http://www.techaccess.org
            e-mail: taf@techaccess.org
Trish Millines-Dziko, Executive Director
Sherry Williams, Program Manager

Provides information, consultation and technical assistance on assistive technology for people with disabilities, including computer hardware and software technology, and adaptive and assistive equipment.

1692 Technology Assistance for Special Consumers

915 Monroe Street
Huntsville, AL   35804   256-532-5996
                          FAX 256-532-2355
                 http://www.tasc.ataccess.org
            e-mail: tasc@hiwaay.net
Lisa Snyder, Resource Center Specialist

Offers a computer resource center which has both computers and software for use at the center or for short-term.

1693 Technology Utilization Program

National Aeronautics and Space Administration
500 Independence Avenue SW
Washington, DC   20546   202-358-0000
                          FAX 202-358-4338

Adapts aerospace technology to the development of equipment for the disabled, sick and elderly persons.

1694 Technology for Language and Learning

PO Box 327
East Rockaway, NY 11518   516-625-4550
                          FAX 516-621-3321
Joan Tanenhaus, Executive Director

An organization dedicated to advancing the use of computers and technology for children and adults with special language and learning needs. Public domain computer software for special education.

1695 Tidewater Center for Technology Access

Special Education Annex
960 Windsor Oaks Boulevard
Virginia Beach, VA 23462   757-474-8650
                           FAX 757-474-8648

Offers resources and information, equipment loans, hands-on exploration of assistive technologies, equipment and software awareness, consultations and interagency collaborations.

1696 West Tennessee Special Technology AccessResource Center

60 Lynoak Cove
Jackson, TN 38305   731-668-3888
                     FAX 731-668-1666
             http://www.starcenter.tn.org
             e-mail: jduke@starcenter.tn.org
Judy Duke, Manager Information & Outreach

Technology center for people with disabilities. Some of the services are: music therapy, art therapy, augmentative communication evaluation and training, vocational evaluation, job placement, vision department, environmental controls.

Games

1697 A Day at Play

Don Johnston
26799 W Commerce Drive
Volo, IL 60073   847-740-0749
                  800-999-4660
             FAX 847-740-7326
             http://www.donjohnston.com
             e-mail: info@donjohnston.com
Christine Filler, Marketing/Channel Development

A Day at Play and Out and About, programs in the UKanDu Little Books Series, are early literacy programs that consist of several create-your-own four-page animated stories that help build language experience for early readers. Students fill in the blanks to complete a sentence on each page and then watch the page come alive with animation and sound. After completing the story, students can print it out to make a book which can be read over and over again.

1698 Academic Drill Builders: Wiz Works

SRA Order Services
220 E Danieldale Road
DeSoto, TX 75115
                     800-843-8855
             FAX 972-228-1982
Jerry Chaffin, Author

A program using an arcade game format for the creation, editing, pacing and monitoring of 36 drill and practice games. Grades K-8. *$49.00*

1699 Alpine Tram Ride

Merit Software
132 W 21 Street
New York, NY 10011   212-675-8567
                      800-753-6488
             FAX 212-675-8607
             http://www.meritsoftware.com
             e-mail: sales@meritsoftware.com

Teaches cognitive redevelopment skills. *$12.95*

1700 Blocks in Motion

Don Johnston
26799 W Commerce Drive
Volo, IL 60073   847-740-0749
                  800-999-4660
             FAX 847-740-7326
             http://www.donjohnston.com
             e-mail: info@donjohnston.com
Christine Filler, Marketing/Channel Development

An art and motion program that makes drawing, creating and animating fun and educational for all users. Based on the Piagetian theory for motor-sensory development, this program promotes the concept that the process is as educational and as much fun as the end result. Good fine motor skills are not required for students to be successful and practice critical thinking. *$99.00*

1701 CONCENTRATE! On Words and Concepts

Laureate Learning Systems
110 E Spring Street
Winooski, VT 05404   802-655-4755
                      800-562-6801
             FAX 802-655-4757
             http://www.laureatelearning.com
             e-mail: info@lauretelearning.com
Mary Sweig Wilson, President
Bernard Fox, VP

A series of educational games that reinforces the lessons of the Words and Concepts Series while developing short term memory skills. *$105.00*

1702 Camp Frog Hollow

Don Johnston
26799 W Commerce Drive
Volo, IL 60073   847-740-0749
                  800-999-4660
             FAX 847-740-7326
             http://www.donjohnston.com
             e-mail: info@donjohnston.com
Christine Filler, Marketing/Channel Development

Camp Frog Hollow chronicles the further adventures of K.C. and Clyde as they head off to summer camp. This entertaining approach to reading, literacy and learning can be beneficial for individual reading lessons or large group activities. The journaling feature provides students the opportunity to record their thoughts and feelings while the tracking feature provides a record of progress for the teacher/parent.

1703 Create with Garfield

SRA Order Services
220 E Danieldale Road
DeSoto, TX   75115

800-843-8855
FAX 972-228-1982

For students to create cartoons, posters and labels by choosing a variety of backgrounds, props and Garfield characters.

1704 Create with Garfield: Deluxe Edition

SRA Order Services
220 E Danieldale Road
DeSoto, TX   75115

800-843-8855
FAX 972-228-1982

Ahead Designes, Author

A program to be used by children to create and print cartoons, posters or labels featuring Garfield and his friends.

1705 Crystal Rain Forest

Terrapin Software
10 Holworthy Street
Cambridge, MA   02138

617-547-5646
800-972-8200
FAX 617-492-4610

This computer learning adventure for grades 3-8 is set in a tropical rain forest. As students explore the town and rain forest, they encounter a series of math challenges. In solving these challenges, they learn to use the Logo programming language. The built-in Crystal Logo language can be used separately after the adventure is over. Two levels of difficulty and an easy-user interface make this program suitable for a wide range of users (Available in Mac or IBM). *$ 59.95*

1706 Dino-Games

Academic Software
331 W 2nd Street
Lexington, KY   40507

859-552-1020
FAX 859-231-0725
http://www.acsw.com
e-mail: asistaff@acsw.com

Penny D Ellis, COO
Warren Lacefield, President

Single switch software programs designed for early switch practice. CD-ROM for Mac or PC. Visit web site for demonstrations. *$39.00*

1707 Dinosaur Days

Queue
338 Commerce Drive
Fairfield, CT   06432

203-335-0906
800-232-2224
FAX 203-336-2481

Students can create their own unique dinosaurs choosing from hundreds of prehistoric parts. *$49.95*

1708 Early Games for Young Children

Software to Go-Gallaudet University
PO Box 77800
Washington, DC   20013

202-651-5705
FAX 202-651-5109

Ken Kurlychek, Project Coordinator

1709 Eden Institute Curriculum Adaptive Physical Education

One Eden Way
Princeton, NJ   08540

609-987-0099
FAX 609-987-0243
http://www.edenservices.org
e-mail: info@edenservices.org

David L Holmes, Executive Director and President
Anne Holmes, Director Outreach Support Svcs

This volume contains teaching programs in the area of sensory integration and adaptive physical education for students with autism. *$50.00*

1710 Eency-Weency Spider Game

UCLA Intervention Program for Handicapped Children
1000 Veteran Avenue
Los Angeles, CA   90095

310-825-4821
FAX 310-206-7744
http://www.bol.ucla.edu

Sharon Cislo, Administrative Assistant

Board game with spiders moving up the drain spout to win. The scanner randomly selects the sun (move up one space) or rain (move down one space). Scan speed can be modified to allow children with various abilities to compete more equally. *$35.00*

1711 Every Day Is a Holiday: Summer/Fall

UCLA Intervention Program for Handicapped Children
1000 Veteran Avenue
Los Angeles, CA   90095

310-825-4821
FAX 310-206-7744
http://www.bol.ucla.edu

Sharon Cislo, Administrative Assistant

Explore the major holidays of the year. Summer/Fall includes July 4th, Birthday, Halloween and Thanksgiving. *$45.00*

1712 Every Day Is a Holiday: Winter/Spring

UCLA Intervention Program for Handicapped Children
1000 Veteran Avenue
Los Angeles, CA   90095

310-825-4821
FAX 310-206-7744
http://www.bol.ucla.edu

Sharon Cislo, Administrative Assistant

Explore the major holidays of the year. Winter/Spring includes Hanukkah, Christmas, Valentine's Day and Easter. *$45.00*

1713 Fast Food Game

UCLA Intervention Program for Handicapped Children
1000 Veteran Avenue
Los Angeles, CA   90095   310-825-4821
                                FAX 310-206-7744
                                http://www.bol.ucla.edu
Sharon Cislo, Administrative Assistant

Board game activity where players advance by selecting Fast Food items. The children press their switches
to spin a spinner which randomly points to a fast food
item or sick face. Press the switch to move to the next
square with the selected item on it. If you get a sick
face you lose your turn. *$35.00*

1714 Garfield Trivia Game

SRA Order Services
220 E Danieldale Road
DeSoto, TX   75115
                                800-843-8855
                                FAX 972-228-1982

Jerry Chaffin, Author

Designed for the student's creative side. Students can
apply their knowledge to 300 intriguing questions
about Garfield and his friends.

1715 Incredible Adventures of Quentin

Queue
338 Commerce Drive
Fairfield, CT   06432   203-335-0906
                               800-232-2224
                               FAX 203-336-2481

Students can interact with the story on a screen, with
wonderful visual and sound effects, animation and
music, for a multisensory learning experience.
$225.00

1716 KC & Clyde in Fly Ball

Don Johnston
26799 W Commerce Drive
Volo, IL   60073   847-740-0749
                               800-999-4660
                               FAX 847-740-7326
                               http://www.donjohnston.com
                               e-mail: info@donjohnston.com
Christine Filler, Marketing/Channel Development

In the UKanDu Series of interactive software which is
designed to promote learning, independence, and accommodate special needs. Word interaction and context are stressed as students progress through the story
and make decisions on how the storyline will advance.
Active interaction at the word level is encouraged by
UKanDu the wordbird, the tour guide to language in
this story. *$95.00*

1717 Listen with Your Ears

UCLA Intervention Program for Handicapped Children
1000 Veteran Avenue
Los Angeles, CA   90095   310-825-4821
                                ·FAX 310-206-7744
                                http://www.bol.ucla.org
Sharon Cislo, Administrative Assistant

Auditory discrimination game in which the user identifies an object or action by the sound it makes.
Twenty-four choices include: snoring, laughing, cat,
doorbell, fire truck, dog, cow, and many more. *$45.00*

1718 Logo Plus

Terrapin Software
10 Holworthy Street
Cambridge, MA   02138   617-547-5646
                               800-972-8200
                               FAX 617-492-4610
Andre Rossi, Marketing Director

An enhanced version of Logo, the classic learning language, will have kids exploring in minutes. Logo enables learners at all ability levels to discover the
rewards of logical thinking, creative problem-solving, and successful communication. Logo gives students a hands-on, enjoyable way to practice math and
programming, inspiring them to experiment and
learn. *$119.00*

1719 Logo Works: Lessons in Logo

Terrapin Software
10 Holworthy Street
Cambridge, MA   02138   617-547-5646
                               800-972-8200
                               FAX 617-492-4610
Andre Rossi, Marketing Director

Curriculum support materials designed to integrate
Logo into the classroom. Requires Logo software
from Terrapin for use. *$24.95*

1720 Maze-O

Software to Go by Gallaudet University
PO Box 77800
Washington, DC   20013   202-651-5705
                               FAX 202-651-5109
Ken Kurlychek, Project Coordinator

1721 Mind Over Matter

Learning Well
111 Kane Street
Baltimore, MD   21224   516-326-2101
                               800-645-6564
                               FAX 800-413-7442
Michael Heins, Author

A game program that challenges students to solve 185
visual word puzzles or create their own puzzles, using
symbols and graphics.

1722 Monkey Business

Merit Software
132 W 21st Street
New York, NY   10011   212-675-8567
                               800-753-6488
                               FAX 212-675-8607
                               http://www.meritsoftware.com
                               e-mail: sales@meritsoftware.com

Choose one of the three levels of difficulty and play
until a minimum score is reached. *$10.95*

1723 Monsters & Make-Believe

Queue
338 Commerce Drive
Fairfield, CT   06432   203-335-0906
                                         800-232-2224
                                   FAX 203-336-2481

Children of all ages will love making monsters from over 100 body parts. Use the text processor to write about characters and add speech bubbles and type to the dialogue. *$49.95*

1724 Monty Plays Scrabble

Software to Go-Gallaudet University
PO Box 77800
Washington, DC   20013   202-651-5705
                                   FAX 202-651-5109

Ken Kurlychek, Project Coordinator

1725 Multi-Scan

Academic Software
3504 Tates Creek Road
Lexington, KY   40517   859-552-1020
                                   FAX 859-273-1943
                                http://www.acsw.com
                           e-mail: asistaff@acsw.com

Warren Lacefield, President
Penny D Ellis, COO

Single switch activity center containing educational games such as numerical dot to dot, concentration, mazes, and matching, for PCs and Macintosh CD-ROM. Handbook for adaptive switches available. *$149.00*

1726 Note Speller

Electronic Courseware Systems
1713 S State Street
Champaign, IL   61820   217-359-7099
                                     800-832-4965
                                   FAX 217-359-6578
                                http://www.ecsmedia.com
                           e-mail: Sales@ecsmedia.com

Jodie Varner, Director Marketing/Sales

A drill-and-practice game designed to teach notes presented on the alto, treble, or bass staff. Note Speller has four levels of difficulty. This is one of eighty music education titles published by Electronic Courseware Systems *$39.95*

1727 On a Green Bus

Don Johnston
26799 W Commerce Drive
Volo, IL   60073   847-740-0749
                                     800-999-4660
                                   FAX 847-740-7326
                               http://www.donjohnston.com
                           e-mail: info@donjohnston.com

Christine Filler, Marketing/Channel Development

An early literacy program in the UKandDu Little Books Series consisting of several create-your-own four-page animated stories that help build language experience for early readers. Students fill in the blanks, completing sentences on each page. After completing the story, students can print it out to make a book which can be read over and over again.

1728 PC-Quizzer for Windows

Data Assist
659 Lakeview Plaza Boulevard
Columbus, OH   43085   614-888-8088
                                     800-326-8088
                                   FAX 614-888-8072

Brian Lockrey, President

A computer-based testing and training package designed for easy use while retaining many of the features found in expensive CBT packages. The product allows the user to easily create lessons and quizzes without having to learn a complex programming package. PC-Quizzer lessons are text files which contain questions, answers and commands. Offers various options to the student and the instructor.

1729 Path Tactics

Software to Go-Gallaudet University
PO Box 77800
Washington, DC   20013   202-651-5705
                                   FAX 202-651-5109

Ken Kurlychek, Project Coordinator

1730 Pitch Explorer

Electronic Courseware Systems
1210 Lancaster Drive
Champaign, IL   61821   217-359-7099
                                     800-832-4965
                                   FAX 217-359-6578
                                http://www.ecsmedia.com
                           e-mail: sales@ecsmedia.com

Jodie Varner, Director Education/Marketing

Enables a computer to detect pitches produced by voice or instruments. Comes with microphone and is geared towards elementary and junior high students. Available for Mac or IBM. *$295.00*

1731 Seek and Find

UCLA Intervention Program for Handicapped Children
1000 Veteran Avenue
Los Angeles, CA   90095   310-825-4821
                                   FAX 310-206-7744
                                http://www.bol.ucla.edu

Sharon Cislo, Administrative Assistant

Game promoting matching, figure/ground, and auditory discrimination utilizing four scenes: park; campground; city; play room. *$55.00*

1732 Ships Ahoy

Software to Go-Gallaudet University
PO Box 77800
Washington, DC   20013   202-651-5705
                                   FAX 202-651-5109

Ken Kurlychek, Project Coordinator

1733 Son of Seek and Find

UCLA Intervention Program for Handicapped Children
1000 Veteran Avenue
Los Angeles, CA   90095   310-825-4821
                              FAX 310-206-7744
                              http://www.bol.ucla.edu
Sharon Cislo, Administrative Assistant

Game promoting matching, figure/ground, and auditory discrimination utilizing three scenes: farm; classroom; house. *$55.00*

1734 Switch It-See It

UCLA Intervention Program for Handicapped Children
1000 Veteran Avenue
Los Angeles, CA   90095   310-825-4821
                              FAX 310-206-7744
                              http://www.bol.ucla.edu
Sharon Cislo, Administrative Assistant

Colorful animated graphics and sound effects encourage visual tracking from left to right, up and down, and on the diagonal. Graphics include: bear; fish; mouse; rocket; and others. *$35.00*

   Mac

1735 Teddy Barrels of Fun

SRA Order Services
220 E Danieldale Road
DeSoto, TX   75115
                              800-843-8855
                              FAX 972-228-1982
A graphic design program that includes over 200 pieces of art for creating pictures, posters and labels, and word processing capabilities to develop writing skills and creative thinking. *$42.00*

1736 Tennis Anyone?

Software to Go-Gallaudet University
PO Box 77800
Washington, DC   20013   202-651-5705
                              FAX 202-651-5109
Ken Kurlychek, Project Coordinator

1737 Tune It II: Music Pitch Matcher

Electronic Courseware Systems
1713 S State Street
Champaign, IL   61820   217-359-7099
                              800-832-4965
                              FAX 217-359-6578
                              http://www.ecsmedia.com
                              e-mail: sales@ecsmedia.com
Jodie Varner, Director Education/Marketing

A fun program designed to help students practice in matching pitches. Two pitches are played with the second one sounding out of tune with the first. The student adjusts the second pitch until it matches the first. Records are kept for students' scores. Tune It II is one of 80 programs in music education published by Electronic Courseware Systems.

1738 Worm Squirm

UCLA Intervention Program for Handicapped Children
1000 Veteran Avenue
Los Angeles, CA   90095   310-825-4821
                              FAX 310-206-7744
                              http://www.bol.ucla.edu
Sharon Cislo, Administrative Assistant

Maze game designed to teach directionality. A worm is directed through the maze by pushing the appropriate arrows on the overlay. *$35.00*

1739 Zoo Time

UCLA Intervention Program for Handicapped Children
1000 Veteran Avenue
Los Angeles, CA   90095   310-825-4821
                              FAX 310-206-7744
                              http://www.bol.ucla.edu
Sharon Cislo, Administrative Assistant

Five familiar zoo animals: kangaroo, elephant, monkey, giraffe and bird are depicted on an overlay. Level I, the child selects any animal. Level II, the child selects an animal by name. Level III, the child selects an animal by its actions. *$35.00*

Language Arts

1740 A to Zap!

Sunburst Technology
400 Columbus Avenue
Valhalla, NY   10595   914-747-3310
                              800-321-7511
                              FAX 914-747-4109
                              http://www.sunburst.com
                              e-mail: service@sunburst.com

When users select an A, little airplanes that fly madly about appear. Users select T and students have their own telephone to talk to any one of nine animated friends. This program for prereaders has an activity for every letter.

1741 Aesop in ASL: Four Fables Told in American Sign Language

Harris Communications
15155 Technology Drive
Eden Prairie, MN   55344   952-906-1180
                              800-825-6758
                              FAX 952-906-1099
                              TDY:952-906-1198
                              http://www.harriscomm.com
                              e-mail: mail@harriscomm.com
Texas School for the Deaf, Author

Colorful picture book of four popular fables with fun animation on CD-ROM. Has the option to have the story voiced, with computer highlighting words as they are spoken. *$79.95*

   CD-ROM

1742　Alphabet Circus

SRA Order Services
220 E Danieldale Road
DeSoto, TX　75115
　　　　　　　　　　　　　　800-843-8855
　　　　　　　　　　　　FAX 972-228-1982

Software to teach letter recognition. *$35.00*

1743　Alphabetizing

Aquarius Instructional
PO Box 128
Indian Rocks Beach, FL　34655　　727-595-7890
　　　　　　　　　　　　　　800-338-2644
　　　　　　　　　　　　FAX 727-595-2685

Teaches language arts skills to early childhood students. *$45.00*

1744　American Sign Language Dictionary on CD-ROM

Harris Communications
15155 Technology Drive
Eden Prairie, MN　55344　　　　952-906-1180
　　　　　　　　　　　　　　800-825-6758
　　　　　　　　　　　　FAX 952-906-1099
　　　　　　　　　　　　TDY:952-906-1180
　　　　　　　　　　　　http://www.harriscomm.com

Martin Sternberg, Author

Combines text, video, and animation to create a leading interactive reference tool that makes learning ASL easy and fun. Contains 2400 signs, searching capabilities in 5 languages, new learning games, and expanded sections in fingerspelling. *$79.95*

　　　　　448 pages　CD-ROM

1745　American Sign Language Dictionary: Software

The Speech Bin
1965 25th Avenue
Vero Beach, FL　32960　　　　772-770-0007
　　　　　　　　　　　　FAX 772-770-0006
　　　　　　　　　　　http://www.speechbin.com
　　　　　　　　　　　e-mail: info@speechbin.com

The CD includes captivating video clips that show 2,500+ words, phrases, and idioms in sign language. The videos may be played at normal speed, slow motion, and stop action. Animations explain origins of selected signs; drills and games are provided to reinforce learning. Item number M545 for Windows $24.95 Item number M540 for MAC. *$29.95*

1746　Auditory Skills

Psychological Software Services
6555 Carrollton Avenue
Indianapolis, IN　46220　　　　317-257-9672
　　　　　　　　　　　　FAX 317-257-9674

Four computer programs designed to aid in the remediation of auditory discrimination problems. *$50.00*

1747　Basic Language Units: Grammar

Continental Press
520 E Bainbridge Street
Elizabethtown, PA　17022
　　　　　　　　　　　　800-233-0759
　　　　　　　　　　　　FAX 888-834-1303
　　　　　　　　　http://www.continentalpress.com

Robyn Fitzpatrick

Sentence disks include sentence types, subjects and predicates and phrases and clauses (Apple).

1748　Basic Skills Products

EDCON Publishing Group
30 Montauk Boulevard
Oakdale, NY　11769　　　　631-567-7227
　　　　　　　　　　　　888-553-3266
　　　　　　　　　　　　FAX 631-567-8745
　　　　　　　　　http://www.edconpublishing.com
　　　　　　　　　e-mail: info@edconpublishing.com

Deals with basic math and language arts. Free catalog available.

1749　Blackout! A Capitalization Game

Software to Go-Gallaudet University
PO Box 77800
Washington, DC　20013　　　　202-651-5705
　　　　　　　　　　　　FAX 202-651-5109

Ken Kurlychek, Project Coordinator

1750　Boppie's Great Word Chase

SRA Order Services
220 E Danieldale Road
DeSoto, TX　75115
　　　　　　　　　　　　800-843-8855
　　　　　　　　　　　　FAX 972-228-1982

Stephen Schlapp, Author

A program that helps refine spelling and word recognition skills.

1751　Bubblegum Machine

Heartsoft
3101 N Hemlock Circle
Broken Arrow, OK　74012　　　918-251-1066
　　　　　　　　　　　　800-285-4018
　　　　　　　　　　　　FAX 800-285-4018
　　　　　　　　　　　http://www.heartsoft.com/
　　　　　　　　　　　e-mail: sales@heartsoft.com

A vocabulary enrichment program that challenges students to rhyme, build words out of provided vocabulary or a user-created one. *$39.95*

1752　Capitalization Plus

Software to Go-Gallaudet University
PO Box 77800
Washington, DC　20013　　　　202-651-5705
　　　　　　　　　　　　FAX 202-651-5109

Ken Kurlychek, Project Coordinator

1753 Circletime Tales Deluxe

Don Johnston
26799 W Commerce Drive
Volo, IL   60073   847-740-0749
                                          800-999-4660
                                   FAX 847-740-7326
                          http://www.donjohnston.com
                          e-mail: info@donjohnston.com
Christine Filler, Marketing/Channel Development

An interactive CD-ROM that introduces and reinforces pre-literacy concepts using nursery rhymes and songs familiar to many children. This English/Spanish program emphasizes listening to and learning basic concepts such as opposites, directionality, colors and counting.

1754 Cognitive Rehabilitation

Technology for Language and Learning
PO Box 327
East Rockaway, NY   11518   516-625-4550
                                   FAX 516-621-3321
A series of public domain programs that strengthen cognitive skills, memory, language and visual motor skills. *$20.00*

1755 Construct-A-Word I & II

SRA Order Services
220 E Danieldale Road
DeSoto, TX   75115
                                        800-843-8855
                                   FAX 972-228-1982
Students blend beginnings and endings to create words. *$99.00*

1756 Crypto Cube

Software to Go-Gallaudet University
PO Box 77800
Washington, DC   20013   202-651-5705
                                   FAX 202-651-5109
Ken Kurlychek, Project Coordinator

1757 Curious George Pre-K ABCs

Sunburst Technology
400 Columbus Avenue
Valhalla, NY   10595   914-747-3310
                                        800-321-7511
                                   FAX 914-747-4109
                          http://www.sunburst.com
                          e-mail: support@sunburst.com

Children go on a lively adventure with Curious George visiting six multi level activities that provide an animated introduction to letters and their sounds. Students discover letter names and shapes, initial letter sounds, letter pronunciations, the order of the alphabet and new vocabulary words during the fun exursions with Curious George. Mac/Win CD-ROM

1758 Double-Up

Research Design Associates
5 Main Street
Freeville, NY   13068   607-844-4601
                                   FAX 607-844-3310
Takes one or two sentences and puts words in alphabetical order. *$139.95*

1759 Dr. Peet's Talk Writer for Windows & Mac

Interest Driven Learning
383 DeSoto Drive
New Smryna Beach, FL   32169   386-427-4473
                                        800-245-5733
                                   FAX 386-426-0100
                          http://www.drpeet.com
                          e-mail: drpeet@drpeet.com
Dr. Bill Peet, CEO

For developmental ages 3-8. Price ranges from $39.95 to $59.95.

1760 Easy as ABC

Software to Go-Gallaudet University
PO Box 77800
Washington, DC   20013   202-651-5705
                                   FAX 202-651-5109
Ken Kurlychek, Project Coordinator

1761 Eden Institute Curriculum: Classroom

One Eden Way
Princeton, NJ   08540   609-987-0099
                                   FAX 609-987-0243
                          http://www.edenservices.org
                          e-mail: info@edenservices.org
David L Holmes, Executive Director/President
Anne Holmes, Director Outreach Support Svcs

This volume is geered toward students with autism who have mastered some basic academic skills and are able to learn in a small group setting. Teaching programs include academics, domestic and social skills. *$100.00*

1762 Elephant Ears: English with Speech

Ballard & Tighe
480 Atlas Street
Brea, CA   92821   714-990-4332
                                        800-321-4332
                                   FAX 714-255-9828
                          e-mail: info@ballard-tighe.com
Features instruction and assessment of prepositions in a 3-part diskette. *$49.00*

1763 Emerging Literacy

Technology for Language and Learning
PO Box 327
East Rockaway, NY   11518   516-625-4550
                                   FAX 516-621-3321
A five-volume set of stories. *$25.00*

1764 English 4-Pack

Dataflo Computer Services
531 US Route 4
Lebanon, NH 03766   603-448-2223

These programs provide various spelling problems through word scrambling, letter substitution and spelling bee simulation. *$39.95*

1765 English Info

Phillip Roy
13064 Indian Rocks Road
Largo, FL 33774   727-593-2700
                               800-255-9085
                           FAX 727-595-2685
Stephanie Dipple
Ruth Bragman

Offers informational disks on teaching nouns, pronouns, adjectives and more. *$350.00*

1766 Essential Learning Systems

Creative Education Institute
5000 Lakewood Drive
Waco, TX 76710   254-751-1188
                              800-234-7319
                          FAX 254-751-1199
                   http://www.cei-waco.com
                   e-mail: info@cei-waco.com
Jane Wilkinson, President
Marva Howlett, Marketing Director

Enables special education, learning disabled and dyslexic students to develop the skills they need to learn. Using computer exercises to appropriately stimulate the brain's language areas, the lagging learning skills can be developed and patterns of correct language taught.

1767 First Phonics

Sunburst Technology
400 Columbus Avenue
Valhalla, NY 10595   914-747-3310
                                  800-321-7511
                              FAX 914-747-4109
                       http://www.sunburst.com
                   e-mail: support@sunburst.com
Targets the phonics skills that all children need to develop, sounding out the first letter of a word. This program offers four different engaging activities that you can customize to match each child's specific need.

1768 Grammar Examiner

Software to Go-Gallaudet University
PO Box 77800
Washington, DC 20013   202-651-5705
                                FAX 202-651-5109
Ken Kurlychek, Project Coordinator

1769 Grammar Toy Shop

Software to Go-Gallaudet University
PO Box 77800
Washington, DC 20013   202-651-5705
                                FAX 202-651-5109
Ken Kurlychek, Project Coordinator

1770 Gremlin Hunt

Merit Software
132 W 21 Street
New York, NY 10011   212-675-8567
                                  800-753-6488
                              FAX 212-675-8607
                   http://www.meritsoftware.com
               e-mail: sales@meritsoftware.com
Gremlins test visual discrimination and memory skills at three levels. *$9.95*

1771 High Frequency Vocabulary

Technology for Language and Learning
PO Box 327
East Rockaway, NY 11518   516-625-4550
                                   FAX 516-621-3321
Each volume of the series has 10 stories that teach specific vocabulary. *$35.00*

1772 Hint and Hunt I & II

SRA Order Services
220 E Danieldale Road
DeSoto, TX 75115
                                   800-843-8855
                               FAX 972-228-1982
With these programs, students can actually see and hear how changing vowels can make a new word. *$99.00*

1773 Homonyms

Software to Go-Gallaudet University
PO Box 77800
Washington, DC 20013   202-651-5705
                                FAX 202-651-5109
Ken Kurlychek, Project Coordinator

1774 HyperStudio Stacks

Technology for Language and Learning
PO Box 327
East Rockaway, NY 11518   516-625-4550
                                   FAX 516-621-3321
Offers various volumes in language arts, social studies and reading. *$10.00*

1775 Hyperlingua

Research Design Associates
5 Main Street
Freeville, NY 13068   607-844-4601
                               FAX 607-844-3310
Allows teachers to create on-screen printing language drills. *$69.95*

1776 IDEA Cat I, II and III

Ballard & Tighe
480 Atlas Street
Brea, CA   92821   714-990-4332
                                             800-321-4332
                                    FAX 714-255-9828
                        e-mail: info@ballard-tighe.com

Computer-assisted teaching of English language lessons reinforces skills of Level I, II, and III of the IDEA Oral Program. *$142.00*

1777 Individualized Keyboarding: Improving Reading/Spelling Skills via Keyboard

AVKO Educational Research Foundation
3084 W Willard Road
Clio, MI   48420   810-686-9283
                                    FAX 810-686-1101
                   http://www.avko.org/indiv_key.htm
                        e-mail: avkoemail@aol.com

Don McCabe, Author
Don McCabe, Research Director

Students learn spelling patterns and acquire important word recognition skills as they slowly and methodically learn proper fingering and keystrokes on a typewriter or computer keyboard. *$12.95*

ISBN 1-564004-01-5

1778 Katie's Farm

Lawrence Productions
1800 S 35th Street
Galesburg, MI   49053   269-665-7075
                                             800-421-4157
                                    FAX 269-665-7060
                                    http://www.lpi.com
                                    e-mail: sales@lpi.com

Edwin Wright, President

Designed to encourage exploration and language development. *$29.95*

1779 Key Words

Humanities Software
PO Box 950
Hood River, OR   97031   541-386-6737
                                             800-245-6737
                                    FAX 541-386-1410

Karen Withrow, Marketing Assistant
Charlotte Arnold, Marketing Director

Learning to keyboard goes hand-in-hand with language play, learning word families, and phonics rules. Six original passages at each of sixteen levels provide reading pleasure and finger dances that pop. You'll tell your students to stop. Key Words is available in versions for all your needs — elementary, high school, emergent literacy and remedial education. One computer, lab pack and school community site and network license. *$49.00*

1780 Keys to Success: Computer Keyboard Skills for Blind Children

Life Science Associates
1 Fennimore Road
Bayport, NY   11705   631-472-2111
                                    FAX 631-472-8146
                        e-mail: lifesciassoc@pipeline.com

Joe Frank, Manager

A talking program that provides keyboard tutorial, keyboard practice, timed keyboard practice and a timed game for two players.

1781 Kid Pix

Broderbund Software
500 Redwood Boulevard
Novato, CA   94947   415-382-4400
                                    FAX 415-763-4828

Joseph Durett, President

A painting program that combines special effect art tools, sounds and magic screen transformations. *$59.95*

1782 Kids Media Magic 2.0

Sunburst Technology
400 Columbus Avenue
Valhalla, NY   10595   914-747-3310
                                             800-321-7511
                                    FAX 914-747-4109
                                    http://www.sunburst.com
                        e-mail: service@sunburst.com

The first multimedia word processor designed for young children. Help your child become a fluent reader and writer. The Rebus Bar automatically scrolls over 45 vocabulary words as students type.

1783 Language Carnival I

SRA Order Services
220 E Danieldale Road
DeSoto, TX   75115
                                             800-843-8855
                                    FAX 972-228-1982

David Ertmer, Author

A diskette of four games using humor to help students develop language and thinking skills.

1784 Language Carnival II

SRA Order Services
220 E Danieldale Road
DeSoto, TX   75115
                                             800-843-8855
                                    FAX 972-228-1982

David Ertmer, Author

A diskette of four games using humor to help students develop language and thinking skills.

1785 Language Master: MWD-640

Franklin Learning Resources
1 Franklin Plaza
Burlington, NJ   08016

800-525-9673
FAX 609-387-1787

A language master without speech defining over 83,000 words, spelling correction capability, pick/edit feature, vocabulary enrichment activities and advanced word list. *$79.95*

1786 Learn to Match

Technology for Language and Learning
PO Box 327
East Rockaway, NY   11518
516-625-4550
FAX 516-621-3321

Ten volume set of picture-matching disks. *$50.00*

1787 Letter Sounds

Sunburst Technology
400 Columbus Avenue
Valhalla, NY   10595
914-747-3310
800-321-7511
FAX 914-747-4109
http://www.sunburst.com
e-mail: service@sunburst.com

Students develop phonemic awareness skills as they make the connection between consonant letters and their sounds.

1788 Letters and First Words

C&C Software
5713 Kentford Circle
Wichita, KS   67220
316-683-6056
800-752-2086

Carol Clark, President

Helps children learn to identify letters and recognize their associated sounds. *$30.00*

1789 Level III - Phonics Based Reading: Grades 1, 2 & 3

Lexia Learning Systems
2 Lewis Street
Lincoln, MA   01773
781-259-8752
800-435-3942
FAX 781-259-1349

Five activity areas with 64 branching units and practice with 535 one-syllable words and 90 two-syllable words, sentences and stories. *$250.00*

1790 Look! Listen! & Learn Language!: Software

The Speech Bin
1965 25th Avenue
Vero Beach, FL   32960
772-770-0007
FAX 772-770-0006
http://www.speechbin.com
e-mail: info@speechbin.com

Interactive activities for children with autism, PDD, Down syndrome, language delay, or apraxia include: hello; Match Same to Same; Quack; Let's talk About It; visual scanning/attention and match ups! Item number L177. *$99.00*

1791 M-SS-NG L-NKS

Sunburst Technology
400 Columbus Avenue
Valhalla, NY   10595
914-747-3310
800-321-7511
FAX 914-747-4109
http://www.sunburst.com
e-mail: service@sunburst.com

This award-winning program is an engrossing language puzzle. A passage appears with letters or words missing. Students complete it based on their knowledge of word structure, spelling, grammar, meaning in context, and literary style.

1792 Make It Go

KidTECH
4181 Pinewood Lake Drive
Bakersfield, CA   93309
661-396-8676
FAX 661-396-8760

A collection of seven original cause and effect programs. *$20.00*

1793 Make-A-Flash

Teacher Support Software
3542 NW 97th Boulevard
Gainesville, FL   32606
352-332-6404
800-228-2871
FAX 352-332-6779
http://www.tssoftware.com
Ruth Smith, Educational Software Consultant

A flash card program displaying and printing large, easy-to-read letters or numbers. *$69.95*

1794 Mark Up

Research Design Associates
5 Main Street
Freeville, NY   13068
607-844-4601
FAX 607-844-3310

A sentence reconstruction program which presents learners with four options for the study of grammar. *$49.95*

1795 Max's Attic: Long & Short Vowels

Sunburst Technology
400 Columbus Avenue
Valhalla, NY   10595
914-747-3310
800-321-7511
FAX 914-747-4109
http://www.sunburst.com
e-mail: service@sunburst.com

Filled to the rafters with phonics fun, this animated program builds your students' vowel recognition skills.

1796 McGee

Lawrence Productions
1800 S 35th Street
Galesburg, MI   49053
269-665-7075
800-421-4157
FAX 269-665-7060
http://www.lpi.com
e-mail: sales@lpi.com

Edwin Wright, President

An independent exploration with no words. Available in IBM, Mac and IIGS formats. *$34.95*

1797 Memory I

Psychological Software Services
6555 Carrollton Avenue
Indianapolis, IN   46220   317-257-9672
                                 FAX 317-257-9674

Consists of four computer programs designed to provide verbal and nonverbal memory exercises. *$110.00*

1798 Memory II

Psychological Software Services
6555 Carrollton Avenue
Indianapolis, IN   46220   317-257-9672
                                 FAX 317-257-9674

These programs allow for work with encoding, categorizing and organizing skills. *$150.00*

1799 Microcomputer Language Assessment and Development System

Laureate Learning Systems
110 E Spring Street
Winooski, VT   05404   802-655-4755
                                 800-562-6801
                             FAX 802-655-4757

Mary Sweig Wilson, President
Bernard Fox, VP

A series of seven diskettes designed to teach over 45 fundamental syntactic rules. Students are presented two or three pictures, depending on the grammatical construction being trained with optional speech and/or text and asked to select the picture which represents the correct construction. *$775.00*

1800 Mike Mulligan & His Steam Shovel

Sunburst Technology
400 Columbus Avenue
Valhalla, NY   10595   914-747-3310
                                 800-321-7511
                             FAX 914-747-4109
                        http://www.sunburst.com
                        e-mail: service@sunburst.com

This CD-ROM version of the Caldecott classic lets students experience interactive book reading and participate in four skills-based extension activities that promote memory, matching, sequencing, listening, pattern recognition and map reading skills.

1801 Mosaix/VGA

Data Assist
659 Lakeview Plaza Boulevard
Columbus, OH   43085   614-888-8088
                                 800-326-8088
                             FAX 614-888-8072

Brian Lockrey, President
Teri Weaver, Marketing Manager

An electronic jigsaw puzzle program that uses digitized photographic images as its puzzles. *$59.00*

1802 My Action Book

KidTECH
4181 Pinewood Lake Drive
Bakersfield, CA   93309   661-396-8676
                             FAX 661-396-8760

Designed to teach familiar action vocabulary through live voice, song and animation. *$30.00*

1803 Old MacDonald II

UCLA Intervention Program for Handicapped Children
1000 Veteran Avenue
Los Angeles, CA   90095   310-825-4821
                             FAX 310-206-7744
                         http://www.bol.ucla.edu
Sharon Cislo, Administrative Assistant

An early preposition program involving in, on top, behind, in front of, next to and between depicted in a farm scene. *$35.00*

1804 Optimum Resource

18 Hunter Road
Hilton Head Island, SC   29926   843-689-8000
                                 888-784-2592
                             FAX 843-689-8008
                        http://www.stickybear.com
                        e-mail: stickyb@stickybear.com
Christopher J Gintz, COO
Robert Stangroom, Product Manager

An educational software publishing company for grades K-12. Our software titles are available in Consumer, School, Labpack or Site License versions. Please call for further details. Prices range from $59.95 for Consumer to $699.95 for Site Licenses.

1805 Padded Food

UCLA Intervention Program for Handicapped Children
1000 Veteran Avenue
Los Angeles, CA   90095   310-825-4821
                             FAX 310-206-7744
                         http://www.bol.ucla.edu
Sharon Cislo, Administrative Assistant

Program overlay depicts familiar foods and can be used as a matching or categorizing program. *$35.00*

   Mac

1806 Phonology: Software

The Speech Bin
1965 25th Avenue
Vero Beach, FL   32960   772-770-0007
                             FAX 772-770-0006
                        http://www.speechbin.com
                        e-mail: info@speechbin.com

This unique software gives you six entertaining games to treat children's phonological disorders. The program uses target patterns in a pattern cycling approach to phonological processess. Item number L183. *$99.00*

1807 Prefixes

American Printing House for the Blind
1839 Frankfort Avenue
Louisville, KY 40206   502-895-2405
     800-223-1839
     FAX 502-899-2274
     http://www.aph.org
Fred Gissoni, Customer Support

An interactive software program that teaches about five common prefixes — un, re, dis, pre, and in — for Apple II computers. *$34.95*

1808 Python Path Phonics Word Families

Sunburst Technology
400 Columbus Avenue
Valhalla, NY 10595   914-747-3310
     800-321-7511
     FAX 914-747-4109
     http://www.sunburst.com
     e-mail: service@sunburst.com

Your child improves their word-building skills by playing three fun strategy games that involve linking one-or two-letter consonant beginnings to basic word endings.

1809 Read, Write and Type Learning System

Talking Fingers
1 St. Vincents Street
San Rafael, CA 94903   415-472-3104
     800-674-9126
     FAX 415-472-7812
     http://www.readwritetype.com
     e-mail: info@talkingfingers.com

This 40-lesson adventure is a powerful tool for 6-8 year-olds just learning to read, for children of other cultures learning to read and write in English, and for students of any age who are struggling to become successful readers and writers.

1810 Reading Riddles with the Boars

Queue
338 Commerce Drive
Fairfield, CT 06432   203-335-0906
     800-232-2224
     FAX 203-336-2481

Children are naturally curious about pictures. This program uses pictures to teach over 1,000 vocabulary words. *$39.95*

1811 Reading Rodeo

Heartsoft
3101 N Hemlock Circle
Broken Arrow, OK 74012
     800-285-4018
     FAX 800-285-3475
     e-mail: sales@heartsoft.com

Utilizes over 100 artist drawn pictures to show students how to distinguish between words beginning with different initial consonant sounds. *$39.95*

1812 Rhubarb

Research Design Associates
5 Main Street
Freeville, NY 13068   607-844-4601
     FAX 607-844-3310

Allows teachers to quickly and easily enter reading passages tailored to needs of their classes. *$69.95*

1813 Same or Different

Merit Software
132 W 21 Street
New York, NY 10011   212-675-8567
     800-753-6488
     FAX 212-675-8607
     http://www.meritsoftware.com
     e-mail: sales@meritsoftware.com

Requires students to make important visual discriminations which involve shape, color and whole/part relationships. *$9.95*

1814 Sensible Speller: Talking APH Edition

American Printing House for the Blind
1839 Frankfort Avenue
Louisville, KY 40206   502-895-2405
     800-223-1839
     FAX 502-899-2274
     http://www.aph.org
Fred Gissoni, Customer Support

A speech output version of the spelling checker program from Sensible Software, for Apple IIs using the ProDOS Operating System. *$65.00*

1815 Sequencing Fun!

Sunburst Technology
400 Columbus Avenue
Valhalla, NY 10595   914-747-3310
     800-321-7511
     FAX 914-747-4109
     http://www.sunburst.com
     e-mail: service@sunburst

Text, pictures, animation and video clips provide a fun filled program that encourages critical thinking skills.

1816 Show Time

Software to Go - Gallaudet University
PO Box 77800
Washington, DC 20013   202-651-5705
     FAX 202-651-5109
Ken Kurlychek, Project Coordinator

1817 Sight Words

UCLA Intervention Program for Handicapped Children
1000 Veteran Avenue
Los Angeles, CA 90095   310-825-4821
     FAX 310-206-7744
     http://www.bol.ucla.edu
Sharon Cislo, Administrative Assistant

Early sight vocabulary program with six categories to choose from: school; outside; home; toys; food; clothing. Teacher options include: scan speed selection; switch or spacebar selection. *$35.00*

Mac

1818 Soft Tools

Psychological Software Services
6555 Carrollton Avenue
Indianapolis, IN   46220   317-257-9672
                                 FAX 317-257-9674

Menu-driven disk versions of the computer programs published in the Cognitive Rehabilitation Journal. *$50.00*

1819 Solving Word Problems

Phillip Roy
PO Box 130
Indian Rocks Beach, FL   33785   727-593-2700
                                     800-255-9085
                                 FAX 727-595-2685

Stephanie Dipple
Ruth Bragman

Offers 3 disks on how to solve word problems. *$115.00*

1820 Sound Match

Enable/Schneier Communication Unit
1603 Court Street
Syracuse, NY   13208   315-455-7591
                             FAX 315-455-1230

Presents a variety of sounds/noises requiring gross levels of auditory discrimination and matching. *$25.00*

1821 Speaking Speller

American Printing House for the Blind
1839 Frankfort Avenue
Louisville, KY   40206   502-895-2405
                                 800-223-1839
                             FAX 502-899-2274
                             http://www.aph.org

Fred Gissoni, Customer Support

A spelling program with speech output for students and teachers. For Apple II computers using either ProDOS or DOS 3.3. *$28.95*

1822 Spell a Word

RJ Cooper & Associates
27601 Forbes Road #39
Laguna Niguel, CA   92677
                                 800-752-6673
                             FAX 949-582-3169
                             http://www.rjcooper.com
                             e-mail: info@rjcooper.com

RJ Cooper, Owner/Developer

A large print, talking, spelling program. It uses an errorless learning method. It has both a drill and test mode, which a supervisor can set. Letters, words or phrases are entered by a supervisor and recorded by supervisor, peer, or sibling. Available for Apple II, Mac, Windows. *$99.00*

1823 Spell-a-Saurus

First Byte
19840 Pioneer Avenue
Torrance, CA   90503   310-793-0610
                                 800-523-2983
                             FAX 310-793-0611

Children enter their own spelling lists, and with limited test-to-speech, play four challenging games to reinforce learning. *$54.95*

1824 Spellagraph

Software to Go-Gallaudet University
PO Box 77800
Washington, DC   20013   202-651-5705
                             FAX 202-651-5109

Ken Kurlychek, Project Coordinator

1825 Spelling Ace

Franklin Learning Resources
1 Franklin Plaza
Burlington, NJ   08016
                                 800-525-9673
                             FAX 609-387-1787

The basic spelling corrector with 80,000 words. Sound-Alikes feature identifies commonly confused words. *$25.00*

1826 Spelling Mastery

SRA Order Services
220 E Danieldale Road
DeSoto, TX   75115
                                 800-843-8855
                             FAX 972-228-1982

Six animated games offer practice for spelling in grades 1 to 3. *$49.00*

1827 Stanley Sticker Stories

Edmark Corporation
PO Box 97021
Redmond, WA   98073   206-556-8400
                                 800-362-2890
                             FAX 260-556-8430

Kids love Mille, Bailey, Sammy and Trudy, the characters from Edmark's award-winning Early Learning Series. Now they can feature these and other Edmark characters in their very own animated storybooks building spelling and writing skills and expanding creativity along the way. The fun-filled program from the educational software experts at Edmark gives kids the power to build stories that come to life right on screen. *$59.95*

1828 Stickybear Software

Optimum Resource
18 Hunter Road
Hilton Head Island, SC   29926   843-689-8000
                                  888-784-2592
                             FAX 843-689-8008
                             http://www.stickybear.com
                             e-mail: stickyb@stickybear.com

Christopher J Gintz, COO
Robert Stangroom, Product Manager

An educational software publishing company for grades K-12. Our software titles are available in Consumer, School, Labpack or Site License versions. Please call for further details. Prices range from $59.95 for Consumer to $699.95 for Site Licenses.

1829 Sunken Treasure Adventure: Beginning Blends

Sunburst Technology
400 Columbus Avenue
Valhalla, NY 10595 914-747-3310
800-321-7511
FAX 914-747-4109
http://www.sunburst.com
e-mail: service@sunburst.com

Focus on beginning blends sounds and concepts with three high-spirited games that invite students to use two letter consonant blends as they build words.

1830 Syllasearch I, II, III, IV

SRA Order Services
220 E Danieldale Road
DeSoto, TX 75115
800-843-8855
FAX 972-228-1982

Students learn how to read multi-syllable words accurately and automatically with this new game that uses actual human speech for instruction and correction. *$99.00*

1831 Talking Nouns

Laureate Learning Systems
110 E Spring Street
Winooski, VT 05404 802-655-4755
800-562-6801
FAX 802-655-4757

Mary Sweig Wilson, President
Bernard Fox, VP

An interactive communication product that helps build expressive language and augmentative communication skills. *$130.00*

1832 Talking Nouns II

Laureate Learning Systems
110 E Spring Street
Winooski, VT 05404 802-655-4755
800-562-6801
FAX 802-655-4757

Mary Sweig Wilson, President
Bernard Fox, VP

Designed to build expressive language and augmentative communication skills. *$130.00*

1833 Talking Riddles

Cross Educational Software
Morada 504 E Kentucky Avenue
Ruston, LA 71270 318-255-8921
800-768-1969
FAX 800768-1969
e-mail: MarkCross@aol.com

Contains three programs in Hangman format. *$24.95*

1834 Talking Verbs

Laureate Learning Systems
110 E Spring Street
Winooski, VT 05404 802-655-4755
800-562-6801
FAX 802-655-4757

Mary Sweig Wilson, President
Bernard Fox, VP

Builds expressive language and augmentative communication skills. *$130.00*

1835 Twenty Categories

Laureate Learning Systems
110 E Spring Street
Winooski, VT 05404 802-655-4755
800-562-6801
FAX 802-655-4757
http://www.laureatelearning.com
Mary S Wilson, Author

Designed to use with children and adults, these two diskettes provide instruction in both abstracting the correct category for a noun and placing a noun in the appropriate category. *$100.00*

1836 Type to Learn 3

Sunburst Technology
400 Columbus Avenue
Valhalla, NY 10595 914-747-3310
800-321-7511
FAX 914-747-4109
http://www.sunburst.com
e-mail: service@sunburst

With the 25 lessons in this animated update of Type to Learn, students embark on time travel missions to learn keyboarding skills.

1837 Type to Learn Jr.

Sunburst Technology
400 Columbus Avenue
Valhalla, NY 10595 914-747-3310
800-321-7511
FAX 914-747-4109
http://www.sunburst.com
e-mail: service@sunburst

One of the first steps to literacy is learning how to use the keyboard. Age appropriate instruction and three practice activities help students use the computer with greater ease.

1838   Type to Learn Jr. New Keys for Kids

Sunburst Technology
400 Columbus Avenue
Valhalla, NY   10595   914-747-3310
                                        800-321-7511
                                    FAX 914-747-4109
                                    http://www.sunburst.com
                                    e-mail: service@sunburst

With new keys to learn, your early keyboarders focus on using the letter and number keys, the shift key, home row and are introduced to selected internet symbols.

1839   Vowel Patterns

Sunburst Technology
400 Columbus Avenue
Valhalla, NY   10595   914-747-3310
                                        800-321-7511
                                    FAX 914-747-4109
                                    http://www.sunburst.com
                                    e-mail: service@sunburst.com

Some vowels are neither long nor short. In this investigation, students explore and learn to use abstract vowels.

1840   Word Invasion: Academic Skill Builders in Language Arts

SRA Order Services
220 E Danieldale Road
DeSoto, TX   75115
                                        800-843-8855
                                    FAX 972-228-1982
Jerry Chaffin, Author

A program using an arcade game format to provide practice in identifying words representing six parts of speech: nouns; pronouns; verbs; adjectives; adverbs and prepositions. *$49.00*

1841   Word Master: Academic Skill Builders in Language Arts

SRA Order Services
220 E Danieldale Road
DeSoto, TX   75115
                                        800-843-8855
                                    FAX 972-228-1982
Jerry Chaffin, Author

A program using arcade game format to provide practice in identifying parts of antonyms, synonyms or homonyms at three difficulty levels. *$49.00*

1842   Word Wise I and II: Better Comprehension Through Vocabulary

SRA Order Services
220 E Danieldale Road
DeSoto, TX   75115
                                        800-843-8855
                                    FAX 972-228-1982
Isabel Beck, Author

A series of two software programs for developing and improving reading comprehension by building vocabulary knowledge.

Life Skills

1843   Big/Little I

UCLA Intervention Program for Handicapped Children
1000 Veteran Avenue
Los Angeles, CA   90095   310-825-4821
                                    FAX 310-206-7744
                                    http://www.bol.ucla.edu
Sharon Cislo, Administrative Assistant

Program for one to four players in which a little bear scans big and little objects commonly seen by young children. *$35.00*

   Mac

1844   Big/Little II

UCLA Intervention Program for Handicapped Children
1000 Veteran Avenue
Los Angeles, CA   90095   310-825-4821
                                    FAX 310-206-7744
                                    http://www.bol.ucla.edu
Sharon Cislo, Administrative Assistant

Children construct a big or little bear by choosing the appropriate size body parts and articles of clothing.

1845   Boars Tell Time

Queue
338 Commerce Drive
Fairfield, CT   06432   203-335-0906
                                        800-232-2224
                                    FAX 203-336-2481

The Boars help youngsters to learn both analog and digital time. *$39.95*

1846   Bozons' Quest

Laureate Learning Systems
110 E Spring Street
Winooski, VT   05404   802-655-4755
                                        800-562-6801
                                    FAX 802-655-4757
Mary Sweig Wilson, President
Bernard Fox, VP

A computer game designed to teach cognitive skills and strategies and left/right discrimination skills. *$32.50*

1847 Braille 'n Speak Scholar

American Printing House for the Blind
1839 Frankfort Avenue
Louisville, KY   40206   502-895-2405
                               800-223-1839
                               FAX 502-899-2274
                               http://www.aph.org
                               e-mail: info@aph.org
Roseann Broome, Marketing

This portable, computerized, talking device has many
features useful to student and adult braille users (word
processors, print-to-braille translator, talking
clocks/calculators and much more). *$929.95*

1848 Buddy's Body

UCLA Intervention Program for Handicapped Children
1000 Veteran Avenue
Los Angeles, CA   90095   310-825-4821
                                 FAX 310-206-7744
                                 http://www.bol.ucla.edu
Sharon Cislo, Administrative Assistant

Body parts program containing two levels with animation. Level I contains facial features. Level II contains
larger body parts. In each level, children are asked to
identify body parts by pressing the part on the overlay.
Each level has its own overlay. *$35.00*

1849 Calendar Fun with Lollipop Dragon

SVE & Churchill Media
677 N NW Highway
Chicago, IL   60631   773-775-9550
                             FAX 773-775-5091
                             http://www.SVEmedia.com
Young students learn the calendar basics. *$84.00*

1850 Coin Changer

Heartsoft
3101 N Hemlock Circle
Broken Arrow, OK   74012   918-251-1066
                                  800-285-4018
                                  FAX 800285-4018
                                  http://www.hearsoft.com
                                  e-mail: sales@hearsoft.com
Uses large coin graphics which help teach money
skills. *$39.95*

1851 Comparison Kitchen

SRA Order Services
220 E Danieldale Road
DeSoto, TX   75115
                             800-843-8855
                             FAX 972-228-1982
Strengthens students' visual perception of sizes and
amounts as well as their visual discrimination of objects by color, shape and size. *$35.00*

1852 Contemporary Living

Aquarius Instructional
PO Box 128
Indian Rocks Beach, FL   33785   727-595-7890
                                        800-338-2644
                                        FAX 727-595-2685
Through the use of high-interest, low-reading levels,
these programs promote self-concept. *$115.00*

1853 Critical Thinking for Contemporary Lifestyles

Phillip Roy
PO Box 130
Indian Rocks Beach, FL   33785   727-593-2700
                                        800-255-9085
                                        FAX 727-595-2685
Stephanie Dipple
Ruth Bragman

This program of 14 titles offers to help improve employment, independent living, and community life
skills. *$825.00*

1854 Eden Institute Curriculum: Volume I

Eden Services
One Logan Drive
Princeton, NJ   08540   609-987-0099
                               FAX 609-987-0243
                  http://www.members.aol.com/edensvcs
                               e-mail: info@edenservices.org
David L Holmes, Executive Director/President
Anne Holmes, Director Outreach Support Svcs

Learning readiness, preacademic, academic,
prevocational, self-care, domestic, social and play
skills programs for young students with autism.
$200.00

1855 Electric Crayon

Merit Software
132 W 21 Street
New York, NY   10011   212-675-8567
                              800-753-6488
                              FAX 212-675-8607
                  http://www.meritsoftware.com
                  e-mail: sales@meritsoftware.com

A tool to help preschool and primary aged children
learn about and enjoy the computer. *$14.95*

1856 Family Fun

UCLA Intervention Program for Handicapped Children
1000 Veteran Avenue
Los Angeles, CA   90095   310-825-4821
                                 FAX 310-206-7744
                                 http://www.bol.ucla.edu
Sharon Cislo, Administrative Assistant

Family members and household items (TV, table, tub,
crib, etc.) are represented graphically on an overlay.
The program can be utilized as a matching activity or
for representational play. *$35.00*

1857 Feelings

UCLA Intervention Program for Handicapped Children
1000 Veteran Avenue
Los Angeles, CA   90095   310-825-4821
                                 FAX 310-206-7744
                                 http://www.bol.ucla.edu
Sharon Cislo, Administrative Assistant

Five feelings: happy, sad, scared, love and tired, are
depicted on an overlay. Level I describes each emotion. Level II, the child associates an emotion with an
action. Level III, the child chooses a picture to describe his or her feelings. *$35.00*

1858 First Categories

Laureate Learning Systems
110 E Spring Street
Winooski, VT   05404   802-655-4755
                                         800-562-6801
                                    FAX 802-655-4757
Mary Sweig Wilson, President
Bernard Fox, VP

A program that trains categorization skills with a natural sounding voice and pictures of 60 nouns in six categories. *$100.00*

1859 First R

Milliken Publishing
11643 Lilburn Park Road
Saint Louis, MO   63146   314-991-4220
                                     800-325-4136
                                FAX 314-991-4807
                         http://www.millikenpub.com
                  e-mail: webmaster@millikenpub.com
A phonetically-based word recognition program with emphasis on comprehension. *$325.00*

1860 First Verbs

Laureate Learning Systems
110 E Spring Street
Winooski, VT   05404   802-655-4755
                                         800-562-6801
                                    FAX 802-655-4757
Mary Sweig Wilson, President
Bernard Fox, VP

A program that trains and tests 40 early developing verbs using animated pictures and a natural sounding female voice. *$225.00*

1861 First Words

Laureate Learning Systems
110 E Spring Street
Winooski, VT   05404   802-655-4755
                                         800-562-6801
                                    FAX 802-655-4757
Mary Sweig Wilson, President
Bernard Fox, VP

A talking program that trains and tests 50 early developing nouns presented within 10 categories. *$225.00*

1862 First Words II

Laureate Learning Systems
110 E Spring Street
Winooski, VT   05404   802-655-4755
                                         800-562-6801
                                    FAX 802-655-4757
Mary Sweig Wilson, President
Bernard Fox, VP

Continues the training of First Words with training and testing of an additional 50 early developing nouns presented within the same 10 categories as used in First Words. *$225.00*

1863 Fish Scales

SRA Order Services
220 E Danieldale Road
DeSoto, TX   75115
                                         800-843-8855
                                    FAX 972-228-1982
Graphics, animation and sound will capture players' attention as they learn how things are measured for height, length and distance. *$35.00*

1864 Following Directions: Left and Right

Laureate Learning Systems
110 E Spring Street
Winooski, VT   05404   802-655-4755
                                         800-562-6801
                                    FAX 802-655-4757
Mary Sweig Wilson, President
Bernard Fox, VP

Provides practice in following directions and exercises short-term memory while reinforcing left/right discrimination concepts. *$165.00*

1865 Following Directions: One and Two Level Commands

Laureate Learning Systems
110 E Spring Street
Winooski, VT   05404   802-655-4755
                                         800-562-6801
                                    FAX 802-655-4757
Eleanor Semel, Author

Designed for a broad range of students experiencing difficulty in processing, remembering and following oral commands, a program of exercises on short and long-term memory highlighting specific spatial, directional and ordinary vocabulary.

1866 Food Facts

American Printing House for the Blind
1839 Frankfort Avenue
Louisville, KY   40206   502-895-2405
                                         800-223-1839
                                    FAX 502-899-2274
                                     http://www.aph.org
Fred Gissoni, Customer Support

An interactive software program for Apple II computer that teaches about nutrition of common foods. *$39.70*

1867 Getting Clean with Herkimer I

UCLA Intervention Program for Handicapped Children
1000 Veteran Avenue
Los Angeles, CA   90095   310-825-4821
                                FAX 310-206-7744
                         http://www.bol.ucla.edu
Sharon Cislo, Administrative Assistant

Help Herkimer, the visitor from outer space, find the things he can use to get clean and look good in the bath, at the sink, or in the shower. Grooming items such as brush, comb, soap, towel, washcloth, toothbrush, tooth paste, sponge and bubble bath are illustrated. *$75.00*

1868 Getting Clean with Herkimer II

UCLA Intervention Program for Handicapped Children
1000 Veteran Avenue
Los Angeles, CA 90095 310-825-4821
FAX 310-206-7744
http://www.bol.ucla.edu
Sharon Cislo, Administrative Assistant

Find the things that Herkimer cannot use to get clean or look good. *$45.00*

1869 Getting Clean with Herkimer III

UCLA Intervention Program for Handicapped Children
1000 Veteran Avenue
Los Angeles, CA 90095 310-825-4821
FAX 310-206-7744
http://www.bol.ucla.edu
Sharon Cislo, Administrative Assistant

Emphasis is on grooming items, with cooking and health care items also shown. Teaches children to categorize objects according to their functions. *$45.00*

1870 Information Station

SVE & Churchill Media
677 N NW Highway
Chicago, IL 60631 773-775-9550
FAX 773-775-5091
http://www.SVEmedia.com
Students who boot up this software will find themselves floating miles above the earth orbiting the planet in an information station satellite. *$144.00*

1871 Job Readiness Software

Lawrence Productions
1800 S 35th Street
Galesburg, MI 49053 269-665-7075
800-421-4157
FAX 269-665-7060
e-mail: sales@lpi.com

Edwin Wright, President

Four programs: Job Attitudes: Assessment and Improvement; Filling Out Job Applications; Successful Job Interviewing; and Resumes Made Easy. *$99.00*

CD

1872 Knowledgeworks

Milliken Publishing
11643 Lilburn Park Road
Saint Louis, MO 63146 314-991-4220
800-325-4136
FAX 314-991-4807
http://www.millikenpub.com
e-mail: webmaster@millikenpub.com
Diane Love, Manager-Sales

Math and reading software for on track and remediation.

Price varies

1873 Let's Go Shopping I

UCLA Intervention Program for Handicapped Children
1000 Veteran Avenue
Los Angeles, CA 90095 310-825-4821
FAX 310-206-7744
http://www.bol.ucla.edu
Sharon Cislo, Administrative Assistant

Classification game in which children select the appropriate items that belong in the corresponding store (toy or grocery). *$35.00*

1874 Let's Go Shopping II: Clothes & Pets

UCLA Intervention Program for Handicapped Children
1000 Veteran Avenue
Los Angeles, CA 90095 310-825-4821
FAX 310-206-7744
http://www.bol.ucla.edu
Sharon Cislo, Administrative Assistant

Classification game in which children select the appropriate items that belong in the corresponding store (clothes or pet).

1875 Lion's Workshop

Merit Software
132 W 21 Street
New York, NY 10011 212-675-8567
800-753-6488
FAX 212-675-8607
http://www.meritsoftware.com
e-mail: sales@meritsoftware.com
Presents various objects with parts missing or with like objects to be matched. *$9.95*

1876 Marsh Media

Marshware
PO Box 8082
Shawnee Mission, KS 66208 816-523-1059
800-821-5309
FAX 816-333-7421
http://www.marshmedia.com
e-mail: order@marshmedia.com
Joan K Marsh, President

Marsh Media publishes closed captioned health and guidance videos for the classroom and school library. Catalog available.

1877 Math Spending and Saving

Media Materials
111 Kane Street
Baltimore, MD 21224 410-633-0730
FAX 410-633-2758

Paul Edwards, Author

Designed for secondary students and adults, this program focuses on personal financial management, comparison shopping and calculation of essential banking transactions.

1878 Money Skills

MarbleSoft
12301 Central Avenue NE
Blaine, MN 55434   763-755-1402
                                FAX 763-862-2920
                            http://www.marblesoft.com
                            e-mail: sales@marblesoft.com
Valerie Reit, Sales

Money Skills 2.0 includes five activities that teach counting money and making change: Coins and Bills; Counting Money; Making Change; how much change? and the Marblesoft Store. Teaches American, Canadian and European money using clear, realistic pictures of the money. Single and dual-switch scanning options on all difficulty levels. Runs on Macintosh and Windows computers. *$60.00*

1879 My House: Language Activities of Daily Living

Laureate Learning Systems
110 E Spring Street
Winooski, VT 05404   802-655-4755
                                FAX 802-655-4757

A language-simulation program designed for communicatively low-functioning clients. *$1200.00*

1880 NOMAD Talking Touch Pad

American Printing House for the Blind
1839 Frankfort Avenue
Louisville, KY 40206   502-895-2405
                                800-223-1839
                                FAX 502-899-2274
                            http://www.aph.org
Fred Gissoni, Customer Support

Connects to a computer to make tactile pictures talk. Uses include teaching about tactile graphics, training in orientation and mobility, and a talking directory for buildings and campuses. *$750.00*

1881 Occupations

UCLA Intervention Program for Handicapped Children
1000 Veteran Avenue
Los Angeles, CA 90095   310-825-4821
                                FAX 310-206-7744
                            http://www.bol.ucla.edu
Sharon Cislo, Administrative Assistant

Companion game to Community Vehicles. Game identifying 6 community helpers: Fireman, teacher, police officer, gas station attendant, dentist, and doctor. Level I, the child selects any community helper. Level II, the child chooses the community helper associated with the scene. *$36.00*

1882 Optimum Resource

18 Hunter Road
Hilton Head Island, SC 29926   843-689-8000
                                888-784-2592
                                FAX 843-689-8008
                            http://www.stickybear.com
                            e-mail: stickyb@stickybear.com
Christopher J Gintz, COO
Robert Stangroom, Product Manager

An educational software publishing company for grades K-12. Our software titles are available in Consumer, School, Labpack or Site License versions. Please call for further details. Prices range from $59.95 for Consumer to $699.95 for Site Licenses.

1883 PAVE: Perceptual Accuracy

Software to Go-Gallaudet University
PO Box 77800
Washington, DC 20013   202-651-5705
                                FAX 202-651-5109
Ken Kurlychek, Project Coordinator

1884 Padded Vehicles

UCLA Intervention Program for Handicapped Children
1000 Veteran Avenue
Los Angeles, CA 90095   310-825-4821
                                FAX 310-206-7744
                            http://www.bol.ucla.edu
Sharon Cislo, Administrative Assistant

Children Identify 10 Vehicles — airplane, helicopter, motorcycle, police car, truck, ambulance, garbage truck, school bus, fire engine and tractor, which are illustrated on the overlay. Level I, the child selects any vehicle, Level II, the child selects the vehicle by name. *$36.00*

1885 Paper Dolls I: Dress Me First

UCLA Intervention Program for Handicapped Children
1000 Veteran Avenue
Los Angeles, CA 90095   310-825-4821
                                FAX 310-206-7744
                            http://www.bol.ucla.edu
Sharon Cislo, Administrative Assistant

Five articles of clothing (shoes, socks, jacket, pants, and T-shirt for boy, overall and dress for girl) are depicted on an overlay to dress the paper doll. *$36.00*

1886 Paper Dolls II: Dress Me Too

UCLA Intervention Program for Handicapped Children
1000 Veteran Avenue
Los Angeles, CA 90095   310-825-4821
                                FAX 310-206-7744
                            http://www.bol.ucla.edu
Sharon Cislo, Administrative Assistant

Twelve articles of clothing are depicted on an overlay to dress the paper doll (boy or girl). Options include dressing for: school day; sunny day; rainy day; or silly day. *$36.00*

1887 Pic Talk

UCLA Intervention Program for Handicapped Children
1000 Veteran Avenue
Los Angeles, CA 90095   310-825-4821
                                FAX 310-206-7744
                            http://www.bol.ucla.edu
Sharon Cislo, Administrative Assistant

Developed as a pre-primer for an alternative communication device for nonreaders who are severely physically disabled. Program includes 6 categories— places, things, action, foods, and feelings — with 54 picture vocabulary. *$ 35.00*

1888 Pick a Meal

UCLA Intervention Program for Handicapped Children
1000 Veteran Avenue
Los Angeles, CA 90095   310-825-4821
                                FAX 310-206-7744
                                http://www.bol.ucla.edu
Sharon Cislo, Administrative Assistant

This game is designed to promote good nutrition for children and/or individuals who are low functioning. Level I teaches the 4 basic food groups. Level II helps the individual learn how to select balanced meals for each meal of the day. There is no printout data collection, but scan speed selection is available. *$35.00*

1889 Print Shop

Broderbund Software
500 Redwood Boulevard
Novato, CA 94948   415-382-4400
                            FAX 415-763-4828
David Valsam, Author
Jospeh Durett, President

A program allowing the user to automatically design and print greeting cards, letterhead stationery, banners, signs and other graphic designs on regular computer paper.

1890 Print Shop Companion

Broderbund Software
500 Redwood Boulevard
Novato, CA 94948   415-382-4400
                            FAX 415-763-4828
Roland Gustafsson, Author
Joseph Durett, President

A program designed to expand the capabilities of The Print Shop with 12 new printing fonts, 50 new borders, additional graphic design options, custom calendar production and more.

1891 Print Shop Graphics Library

Broderbund Software
500 Redwood Boulevard
Novato, CA 94948   415-382-4400
                            FAX 415-763-4828
David Balsam, Author
Joseph Durett, President

Designed to be used with The Print Shop, this program with 120 additional graphic designs focuses on holidays, zodiac signs, animals, sports, school children and creative patterns.

1892 Print Shop Graphics Library: Disk 2

Broderbund Software
500 Redwood Boulevard
Novato, CA 94948   415-382-4400
                            FAX 415-763-4828
David Balsam, Author
Joseph Durett, President

Designed to supplement The Print Shop, this diskette with 120 additional graphics and a graphic editor focuses on graphics used on the job, as hobbies, places, travel, health, animals, sports and music.

1893 Puzzle Works Readiness

Continental Press
520 E Bainbridge Street
Elizabethtown, PA 17022
                            800-233-0759
                            FAX 888-834-1303
This series of five disks uses colorful graphics and reward techniques that are especially suited to the interests and needs of special learners. *$25.95*

1894 Quiz Castle

Software to Go-Gallaudet University
PO Box 77800
Washington, DC 20013   202-651-5705
                                FAX 202-651-5109
Ken Kurlychek, Project Coordinator

1895 Remembering Numbers and Letters

Aquarius Instructional
PO Box 128
Indian Rocks Beach, FL 33785   727-595-7890
                                  800-338-2644
                                  FAX 727-595-2685
Students work at their own pace and select their own numbers and letters with which to work. *$29.95*

1896 Resumes Made Easy

Lawrence Productions
1800 S 35th Street
Galesburg, MI 49053   269-665-7075
                              800-421-4157
                              FAX 269-665-7060
                              http://www.lpi.com
                              e-mail: sales@lpi.com
George Spengler, Author
Edwin Wright, President

An interactive program covering what a resume is, how a resume is prepared and what is to be included in a resume. *$29.95*

1897 Seasons

UCLA Intervention Program for Handicapped Children
1000 Veteran Avenue
Los Angeles, CA 90095   310-825-4821
                                FAX 310-206-7744
                                http://www.bol.ucla.edu
Sharon Cislo, Administrative Assistant

Game is designed to help teach children and/or low functioning individuals to identify attributes of the four seasons. Students select a season from the menu, then objects from each season scan the bottom of the screen. The child selects items matching the season using the mouse, switch, space bar, or TouchWindows. When a season is completed, there is an option to type a brief statement about the scene. *$45.00*

1898 Secondary Print Pack

Failure Free
140 W Cabarrus Avenue
Concord, NC   28025

800-221-1274
FAX 314-569-2834
e-mail: ffsales@concord.nc.com

Thousands of independent activities teaching over 750 words. *$1929.00*

1899 Stickybear Software

Optimum Resource
18 Hunter Road
Hilton Head Island, SC   29926

843-689-8000
888-784-2592
FAX 843-689-8008
http://www.stickybear.com
e-mail: stickyb@stickybear.com
Christopher J Gintz, COO
Robert Stangroom, Product Manager

An educational software publishing company for grades K-12. Our software titles are available in Consumer, School, Labpack or Site License versions. Please call for further details. Prices range from $59.95 for Consumer to $699.95 for Site Licenses.

1900 Switch It-Change It

UCLA Intervention Program for Handicapped Children
1000 Veteran Avenue
Los Angeles, CA   90095

310-825-4821
FAX 310-206-7744
http://www.bol.ucla.edu
Sharon Cislo, Administrative Assistant

Switch-activated cause and effect program presents colorful, common objects. Designed to be paired with three-dimensional objects for matching, identification and selection. Geared toward the young and/or low functioning. *$35.00*

Mac

1901 Tea Party

UCLA Intervention Program for Handicapped Children
1000 Veteran Avenue
Los Angeles, CA   90095

310-825-4821
FAX 310-206-7744
http://www.bol.ucla.edu
Sharon Cislo, Administrative Assistant

Follow-up classification game to Let's Go Shopping. Children shop at four different stores to select items for a tea party. *$36.00*

1902 Teenage Switch Progressions

RJ Cooper & Associates
27601 Forbes Road #39
Laguna Nigel, CA   92677

800-752-6673
FAX 949-582-3169
http://www.rjcooper.com
e-mail: info@rjcooper.com
RJ Cooper, Owner/Developer

Five activities for teenage persons working on switch training, attention training, life skills simulation and following directions. *$75.00*

1903 TeleSensory

520 Almanor Avenue
Sunnyvale, CA   94043

408-616-8700
800-227-8418
FAX 408-616-8720
http://www.telesensory.com
e-mail: info@telesensory.com
David Wrench, Marketing
Beth Thomlinson, Marketing

Helps visually impaired people become more independent with the most comprehensive products available anywhere for reading, writing, taking notes and using computers.

1904 This Is the Way We Wash Our Face

UCLA Intervention Program for Handicapped Children
1000 Veteran Avenue
Los Angeles, CA   90095

310-825-4821
FAX 310-206-7744
http://www.bol.ucla.edu
Sharon Cislo, Administrative Assistant

Familiar Nursery song with singing and animation depicted in picture form on an overlay. Five verses are: washing your face; brushing your teeth; combing your hair; getting dressed; and eating. *$36.00*

1905 Tools for Life

Oakwood Solutions LLC/Conover Company
2926 Hidden Hollow Road
Oshkosh, WI   54904

920-231-4667
800-933-1933
FAX 920-231-4809
http://www.conovercompany.com
e-mail: conover@execpc.com
Terry Schonitz, President

Tools for life software assists in the transition from school to the community and workplace. Functional literary, functional life skills, functional social skills, functional work skills. *$2535.00*

Math

1906 2+2

RJ Cooper & Associates
27601 Forbes Road #39
Laguna Nigel, CA   92677

800-752-6673
FAX 949-582-3169
http://www.rjcooper.com
e-mail: info@rjcooper.com
RJ Cooper, Owner/Developer

This large print, talking, early academic program is for drilling math facts, including addition, subtraction, multiplication and division. It uses an errorless learning method. *$89.00*

1907 Access to Math

Don Johnston
26799 W Commerce Drive
Volo, IL   60073

847-740-0749
800-999-4660
FAX 847-740-7326
http://www.donjohnston.com
e-mail: info@donjohnston.com
Christine Filler, Marketing/Channel Development

The Macintosh talking math worksheet program that's two products in one. For teachers, it makes customized worksheets in a snap. For students who struggle, it provides individualized on-screen lessons.

1908 Algebra Stars

Sunburst Technology
400 Columbus Avenue
Valhalla, NY   10595

914-747-3310
800-321-7511
FAX 914-747-4109
http://www.sunburst.com
e-mail: service@sunburst.com

Students build their understanding of algebra by constructing, categorizing, and solving equations and classifying polynomial expressions using algebra tiles.

1909 Alien Addition: Academic Skill Builders in Math

SRA Order Services
220 E Danieldale Road
DeSoto, TX   75115

800-843-8855
FAX 972-228-1982
Jerry Chaffin, Author

A program using an arcade game format to provide practice in addition of numbers 0 through 9. *$49.00*

1910 Awesome Animated Monster Maker Math

Sunburst Technology
400 Columbus Avenue
Valhalla, NY   10595

914-747-3310
800-321-7511
FAX 914-747-4109
http://www.sunburst.com
e-mail: service@sunburst.com

With an emphasis on building core math skills, this humorous program incorporates the monstrous and the ridiculous into a structured learning environment. Students choose from six skill levels tailored to the 3rd to 8th grade.

1911 Awesome Animated Monster Maker Math & Monster Workshop

Sunburst Technology
400 Columbus Avenue
Valhalla, NY   10595

914-747-3310
800-321-7511
FAX 914-747-4109
http://www.sunburst.com
e-mail: service@sunburst.com

Students develop money and strategic thinking skills with this irresistable game that has them tinker about making monsters.

1912 Awesome Animated Monster Maker Number Drop

Sunburst Technology
400 Columbus Avenue
Valhalla, NY   10595

914-747-3310
800-321-7511
FAX 914-747-4109
http://www.sunburst.com
e-mail: service@sunburst.com

Your students will think on their mathematical feet estimating and solving thousands of number problems in an arcade-style game designed to improve their performance in numeration, money, fractions, and decimals.

1913 Basic Math Competency Skill Building

Educational Activities Software
PO Box 754
Baldwin, NY   11520

516-867-7878
800-645-2796
FAX 516-379-7429
Michael Conlon, Author
Alan Stern, Sales Director
Melissa Slevin, Assistant

An interactive, tutorial and practice program to teach competency with arithmetic operations, decimals, fractions, graphs, measurement and geometric concepts. *$369.00*

1914 Basic Skills Products

EDCON Publishing Group
30 Montauk Boulevard
Oakdale, NY   11769   631-567-7227
                                       888-553-3266
                                   FAX 631-567-8745
                http://www.edconpublishing.com
                e-mail: info@edconpublishing.com

Deals with basic math and language arts. Free catalog
available.

1915 Big: Calc

Don Johnston
26799 W Commerce Drive
Volo, IL   60073   847-740-0749
                                       800-999-4660
                                   FAX 847-740-7326
                http://www.donjohnston.com
                e-mail: info@donjohnston.com
Christine Filler, Marketing/Channel Development

A Macintosh calculator program for people with special needs but also beneficial for users who need the
auditory reinforcement of a talking calculator. Features include big numbers, high-quality speech and
versatile layouts. Encourages math motivation.

1916 Boars 1, 2, 3! Counting with the Boars

Queue
338 Commerce Drive
Fairfield, CT   06432   203-335-0906
                                       800-232-2224
                                   FAX 203-336-2481

The Boars teach young learners basic keyboard skills
while they identify numbers from 1-10 and count familiar objects in a variety of colorful scenes. *$39.95*

1917 Boars Store

Queue
338 Commerce Drive
Fairfield, CT   06432   203-335-0906
                                       800-232-2224
                                   FAX 203-336-2481

Shopping at the Boars Store offers students an exciting way to learn to count money and make change.
$39.95

1918 Building Perspective

Sunburst Technology
400 Columbus Avenue
Valhalla, NY   10595   914-747-3310
                                       800-321-7511
                                   FAX 914-747-4109
                http://www.sunburst.com
                e-mail: support@sunburst.com

Develop spatial perception and reasoning skills with
this award-winning program that will sharpen your
students' problem-solving abilities.

1919 Building Perspective Deluxe

Sunburst Technology
400 Columbus Avenue
Valhalla, NY   10595   914-747-3310
                                       800-321-7511
                                   FAX 914-747-4109
                http://www.sunburst.com
                e-mail: support@sunburst.com

New visual thinking challenges await your students as
they engage in three spacial reasoning activities that
develop their 3D thinking, deductive reasoning and
problem solving skills

1920 Combining Shapes

Sunburst Technology
400 Columbus Avenue
Valhalla, NY   10595   914-747-3310
                                       800-321-7511
                                   FAX 914-747-4109
                http://www.sunburst.com
                e-mail: support@sunburst.com

Students discover the properties of simple geometric
figures through concrete experience combining
shapes. Measurements, estimating and operation
skills are part of this fun program.

1921 Combining and Breaking Apart Numbers

Sunburst Technology
400 Columbus Avenue
Valhalla, NY   10595   914-747-3310
                                       800-321-7511
                                   FAX 914-747-4109
                http://www.sunburst.com
                e-mail: support@sunburst.com

Students explore part-whole relationships and develop number sense by combining and breaking apart
numbers in a variety of problem-solving situations.

1922 Comparing with Ratios

Sunburst Technology
400 Columbus Avenue
Valhalla, NY   10595   914-747-3310
                                       800-321-7511
                                   FAX 914-747-4109
                http://www.sunburst.com
                e-mail: support@sunburst.com

Students learn that ratio is a way to compare amounts
by using multiplication and division. Through five engaging activities, students recognize and describe ratios, develop proportional thinking skills, estimate
ratios, determine equivalent ratios, and use ratios to
analyze data.

1923 Conceptual Skills

Psychological Software Services
6555 Carrollton Avenue
Indianapolis, IN   46220   317-257-9672
                                   FAX 317-257-9674

Twelve programs designed to enhance skills involved
in relationships, comparisons and number concepts.
$50.00

1924 Concert Tour Entrepreneur

Sunburst Technology
400 Columbus Avenue
Valhalla, NY 10595   914-747-3310
                           800-321-7511
                           FAX 914-747-4109
                           http://www.sunburst.com
                           e-mail: support@sunburst.com

Your students improve math, planning and problem solving skills as they manage a band in this music management business simulation.

1925 Counters

Software to Go-Gallaudet University
PO Box 77800
Washington, DC 20013   202-651-5705
                           FAX 202-651-5109
Ken Kurlychek, Project Coordinator

1926 Counting Critters

Software to Go-Gallaudet University
PO Box 77800
Washington, DC 20013   202-651-5705
                           FAX 202-651-5109
Ken Kurlychek, Project Coordinator

1927 DLM Math Fluency Program: Addition Facts

SRA Order Services
220 E Danieldale Road
DeSoto, TX 75115
                           800-843-8855
                           FAX 972-228-1982
Ted Hasselbring, Author

A program using drill and practice, arcade games, student record keeping, worksheet production and testing to develop the ability to recall basic addition math facts. *$32.00*

1928 DLM Math Fluency Program: Division Facts

SRA Order Services
220 E Danieldale Road
DeSoto, TX 75115
                           800-843-8855
                           FAX 972-228-1982
Ted Hasselbring, Author

A series of 10-minute sessions in this diskette program easily retrieves answers to basic division facts up to 144 divided by 12.

1929 DLM Math Fluency Program: Multiplication Facts

SRA Order Services
220 E Danieldale Road
DeSoto, TX 75115
                           800-843-8855
                           FAX 972-228-1982
Ted Hasselbring, Author

A series of 10-minute sessions easily retrieves answers to basic multiplication facts up to 12x12. *$32.00*

1930 DLM Math Fluency Program: Subtraction Facts

SRA Order Services
220 E Danieldale Road
DeSoto, TX 75115
                           800-843-8855
                           FAX 972-228-1982
Ted Hasselbring, Author
Terry Avon, Head Supervisor

A series of sessions that easily retrieve answers to basic subtraction facts up to 24x12. *$32.00*

1931 Data Explorer

Sunburst Technology
101 Castleton Street
Poleasantville, NY 10570   914-747-3310
                           800-321-7511
                           FAX 914-747-4109
                           http://www.sunburst.com
                           e-mail: support@nysunburst.com

This easy-to-use CD-ROM provides the flexibility needed for eleven different graph types including tools for long-term data analysis projects.

1932 Dragon Mix: Academic Skill Builders in Math

SRA Order Services
220 E Danieldale Road
DeSoto, TX 75115
                           800-843-8855
                           FAX 214-228-1982
Jerry Chaffin, Author

A program providing practice in multiplication of numbers 0 through 9 and division of problems with answers 0 through 9. *$49.00*

1933 Eighth Through Tenth-Grade MathCompetencies

Phillip Roy
PO Box 130
Indian Rocks Beach, FL 33785   727-593-2700
                                800-255-9085
                                FAX 727-595-2685
Stephanie Dipple
Ruth Bragman

Offers 59 disks on reading numerals and comparing, solving word problems with fractions, word problems, measurement, averages, geometry, graphs and more. *$1775.00*

1934 Elementary Math Bundle

Sunburst Technology
400 Columbus Avenue
Valhalla, NY 10595   914-747-3310
800-321-7511
FAX 914-747-4109
http://www.sunburst.com
e-mail: support@sunburst.com

Number sense and operations are the focus of the Elementary Math Bundle. Students engage in activities that reinforce basic addition and subtraction skills. This product comes with Splish Splash Math, Ten Tricky Tiles and Numbers Undercover.

1935 Elements of Mathematics

Electronic Courseware Systems
1713 S State Street
Champaign, IL 61820   217-359-7099
800-832-4965
FAX 217-359-6578
http://www.ecsmedia.com
e-mail: sales@ecsmedia.com
Jodie Varner, Director Education/Marketing

This program includes two lessons and a test in the addition of simple and complex fractions. Test results are stored for both student and instructor accessibility. Includes such graphics as pie slices. Elements of Mathematics is one of several programs published by Electronic Courseware Systems.

1936 Equation Tile Teaser

Sunburst Technology
400 Columbus Avenue
Valhalla, NY 10595   914-747-3310
800-321-7511
FAX 914-747-4109
http://www.sunburst.com
e-mail: support@sunburst.com

Students develop logic thinking and pre-algebra skills solving sets of numbers equations in three challenging problem-solving activities.

1937 Equations

Software to Go-Gallaudet University
PO Box 77800
Washington, DC 20013   202-651-5705
FAX 202-651-5109
Ken Kurlychek, Project Coordinator

1938 Equivalent Fractions

Sunburst Technology
400 Columbus Avenue
Valhalla, NY 10595   914-747-3310
800-321-7511
FAX 914-747-4109
http://www.sunburst.com
e-mail: support@sunburst.com

This exciting investigation develops students' conceptual understanding that every fraction can be named in many different but equivalent ways.

1939 Excelling in Mathematics

Phillip Roy
PO Box 130
Indian Rocks Beach, FL 33785   727-593-2700
800-255-9085
FAX 727-595-2685

Stephanie Dipple
Ruth Bragman

A series of tutorial math programs designed to provide instruction for above average math students to prepare them for college math. *$795.00*

1940 Factory Deluxe

Sunburst Technology
400 Columbus Avenue
Valhalla, NY 10595   914-747-3310
800-321-7511
FAX 914-747-4109
http://www.sunburst.com
e-mail: support@sunburst.com

Five activities explore shapes, rotation, angles, geometric attributes, area formulas, and computation. Includes journal, record keeping, and on-screen help. This program helps sharpen geometry, visual thinking and problem solving skills.

1941 Fast-Track Fractions

SRA Order Services
220 E Danieldale Road
DeSoto, TX 75115   800-843-8855
FAX 214-228-1982

Students solve problems that compare, add, subtract, multiply and divide fractions. *$46.00*

1942 Fifth Through Seventh Grade Math Competencies

Aquarius Instructional
PO Box 128
Indian Rocks Beach, FL 33785   727-595-7890
800-338-2644
FAX 727-595-2685

Offers 32 disks on reading money values, ordering numbers, multiplying whole numbers, dividing whole numbers, adding and subtracting decimals and more. *$995.00*

1943 Fraction Attraction

Sunburst Technology
400 Columbus Avenue
Valhalla, NY 10595   914-747-3310
800-321-7511
FAX 914-747-4109
http://www.sunburst.com
e-mail: support@sunburst.com

Build the fraction skills of ordering, equivalence, relative sizes and multiple representations with four, multi-level, carnival style games.

1944 Fraction Fairy Tales with the Boars

Queue
338 Commerce Drive
Fairfield, CT   06432   203-335-0906
                              800-232-2224
                          FAX 203-336-2481

The Boars teach students about fractions in their favorite fairy tale surroundings. *$39.95*

1945 Fraction Fuel-Up

SRA Order Services
220 E Danieldale Road
DeSoto, TX   75115
                              800-843-8855
                          FAX 214-228-1982

Players practice reducing, renaming, finding equivalent fractions and adding/subtracting fractions. *$46.00*

1946 Fraction Operations

Sunburst Technology
400 Columbus Avenue
Valhalla, NY   10595   914-747-3310
                              800-321-7511
                          FAX 914-747-4109
                   http://www.sunburst.com
                e-mail: support@sunburst.com

Students build on their concepts of fraction meaning and equivalence as they learn how to perform operations with fractions.

1947 Get Up and Go!

Sunburst Technology
400 Columbus Avenue
Valhalla, NY   10595   914-747-3310
                              800-321-7511
                          FAX 914-747-4109
                   http://www.sunburst.com
                e-mail: support@sunburst.com

Students interpret and construct timelines through three descriptive activities in the animated program. Students are introduced to timelines as they participate in an interactive story.

1948 Handling Money

Aquarius Instructional
PO Box 128
Indian Rocks Beach, FL   33785   727-595-7890
                                   800-338-2644
                               FAX 727-595-2685

This program teaches students how to count money and make change in paper and coin. *$75.00*

1949 Hey, Taxi!

Queue
338 Commerce Drive
Fairfield, CT   06432   203-333-7268
                              800-232-2224
                          FAX 203-336-2481
                e-mail: jck@queueine.com

Children maneuver their cab through the city streets to pick up passengers that solve basic math facts problems to collect their fares. *$39.95*

1950 Learning About Numbers

C&C Software
5713 Kentford Circle
Wichita, KS   67220   316-683-6056
                             800-752-2086
Carol Clark, President

Three segments use computer graphics to provide students with an experience in working with numbers. *$25.00*

1951 Math Machine

Software to Go-Gallaudet University
PO Box 77800
Washington, DC   20013   202-651-5705
                          FAX 202-651-5109
Ken Kurlychek, Project Coordinator

1952 Math Masters: Addition and Subtraction

SRA Order Services
220 E Danieldale Road
DeSoto, TX   75115
                             800-843-8855
                         FAX 214-228-1982
Jerry Chaffin, Author

Designed to supplement math curriculum, this program covers addition and subtraction for all numbers from 0 through 25.

1953 Math Masters: Multiplication and Division

SRA Order Services
220 E Danieldale Road
DeSoto, TX   75115
                             800-843-8855
                         FAX 214-228-1982
Jerry Chaffin, Author

Designed to supplement math curriculum, this program covers multiplication and division for all numbers from 0 through 25.

1954 Math Shop

Software to Go-Gallaudet University
PO Box 77800
Washington, DC   20013   202-651-5705
                          FAX 202-651-5109
Ken Kurlychek, Project Coordinator

1955 Math Skill Games

Software to Go-Gallaudet University
PO Box 77800
Washington, DC   20013   202-651-5705
                          FAX 202-651-5109
Ken Kurlychek, Project Coordinator

1956 Math Spending and Saving

Media Materials
111 Kane Street
Baltimore, MD 21224   410-633-0730
                      FAX 410-633-2758

Paul Edwards, Author

Designed for secondary students and adults, this program focuses on personal financial management, comparison shopping and calculation of essential banking transactions.

1957 Math for All Ages: A Sequential MathProgram

Phillip Roy
PO Box 130
Indian Rocks Beach, FL 33785   727-593-2700
                      800-255-9085
                 FAX 727-595-2685

Stephanie Dipple
Ruth Bragman

Offers 16 disks on adding, subtracting, multiplication and division.

1958 Math for Everyday Living

Educational Activities
PO Box 392
Freeport, NY 11520   516-223-4666
                   800-645-3739
            FAX 516-379-7429
       e-mail: learn@edact.com

Ann Edson, Author
Alan Stern, VP
Rose Falco, Sales/Marketing

Designed for secondary students, a tutorial and practice program with simulated activities for applying math skills in making change, working with sales slips, unit pricing, computing gas mileage and sales tax. *$129.00*

1959 Mighty Math Astro Algebra

Edmark Corporation
PO Box 97021
Redmond, WA 98073   206-556-8400
                   800-362-2890
            FAX 206-556-8430

In Astro Algebra, you're the captain of the Algebra Centauri spaceship! Traveling through the galaxy, you meet fascinating alien species and use algebra to help them out of predicaments. Four expert crew members Skler, Max, Mialee and Tyric are standing by to help you understand, strategize, calculate and check your work. *$59.95*

1960 Mighty Math Calculating Crew

Edmark Corporation
PO Box 97021
Redmond, WA 98073   206-556-8400
                   800-362-2890
            FAX 206-556-8430

Calculating Crew teaches your 3rd, 4th, 5th, or 6th grader the concepts, facts and thinking skills necessary to build math confidence and develop a strong, lasting understanding of math! Wanda Wavelet, Captain Nick Knack and Dr. Gee guide your child through thousands of skill-building problems! *$59.95*

1961 Mighty Math Cosmic Geometry

Edmark Corporation
PO Box 97021
Redmond, WA 98073   206-556-8400
                   800-362-2890
            FAX 206-556-8430

Cosmic Gemetry teaches you the concepts and problem-solving skills you need to master geometry and build math confidence! Polyhedral characters such as Dodeca, Hexa and Lcosa are your guides on this fun-filled exploration of Planet Geometry. *$59.95*

1962 Mighty Math Countdown

Edmark Corporation
PO Box 97021
Redmond, WA 98073   206-556-8400
                   800-362-2890
            FAX 206-556-8430

Kids love to visit Carnival Countdown, where addition, subtraction, early multiplication, division and logic are always center ring! This breakthrough math progam offers your child three years of math learning and ensures math success by teaching kindergarten through 2nd grade math concepts and problem-solving. With Carnival Countdown, learning math is as much fun as a trip to the circus! *$59.95*

1963 Mighty Math Number Heroes

Edmark Corporation
PO Box 97021
Redmond, WA 98073   206-556-8400
                   800-362-2890
            FAX 206-556-8430

Number Heroes teaches kids the basics and problem-solving skills they need to succeed in math. With the help of Fraction Man, Star Brilliant and other math superheroes, kids understand dozens of math concepts and solve thousands of problems while learning multiplication and division, fractions, 2D geometry and probability. Help your children master 3rd through 6th-grade math with the Number Heroes! *$59.95*

1964 Mighty Math Zoo Zillions

Edmark Corporation
PO Box 97021
Redmond, WA 98073   206-556-8400
                   800-362-2890
            FAX 206-556-8430

Mighty Math Zoo Zillions teaches your kindergartener, 1st grader or 2nd grader the concepts, facts and thinking skills necessary to build math confidence and develop a strong, lasting understanding of math! Armadillo Annie, the Otter Twins and other animal friends guide your child on this exciting mathematical adventure! *$59.95*

1965 Millie's Math House

Edmark Corporation
PO Box 97021
Redmond, WA   98073   206-556-8400
                             800-362-2890
                        FAX 206-556-8430
Tina Martin, Education Marketing

Now featuring addition, subtraction and counting to 30, the award-winning Millie's Math House has been enhanced to offer even more learning! In seven activities, children explore numbers, shapes, sizes, patterns, addition and subtraction as they build mouse houses, create wacky bugs, count animated critters, make jellybean cookies and answer math challenges posed by Dorothy the Duck! *$59.95*

1966 Number Farm

Software to Go-Gallaudet University
PO Box 77800
Washington, DC   20013   202-651-5705
                           FAX 202-651-5109
Ken Kurlychek, Project Coordinator

1967 Number Please

Merit Software
132 W 21 Street
New York, NY   10011   212-675-8567
                              800-753-6488
                         FAX 212-675-8607
                http://www.meritsoftware.com
           e-mail: sales@meritsoftware.com
Students are challenged to remember combinations of 4, 7 and 10 digit numbers. *$9.95*

1968 Number Sense & Problem Solving CD-ROM

Sunburst Technology
400 Columbus Avenue
Valhalla, NY   10595   914-747-3310
                              800-321-7511
                         FAX 914-747-4109
                  http://www.sunburst.com
           e-mail: support@sunburst.com

Build number and operation skills with these three programs: How the West Was One + Three x Four, Divide and Conquer and Puzzle Tank.

1969 Number Stumper

Software to Go-Gallaudet University
PO Box 77800
Washington, DC   20013   202-651-5705
                           FAX 202-651-5109
Ken Kurlychek, Project Coordinator

1970 Optimum Resource

18 Hunter Road
Hilton Head Island, SC   29926   843-689-8000
                                    888-784-2592
                               FAX 843-689-8008
                      http://www.stickybear.com
              e-mail: stickyb@stickybear.com
Christopher J Gintz, COO
Robert Stangroom, Product Manager

An educational software publishing company for grades K-12. Our software titles are available in Consumer, School, Labpack or Site License versions. Please call for further details. Prices range from $59.95 for Consumer to $699.95 for Site Licenses.

1971 Race Car 'rithmetic

Software to Go-Gallaudet University
PO Box 77800
Washington, DC   20013   202-651-5705
                           FAX 202-651-5109
Ken Kurlychek, Project Coordinator

1972 Read and Solve Math Problems #1

Educational Activities
PO Box 392
Freeport, NY   11520   516-223-4666
                              800-645-3739
                         FAX 516-379-7429
                  e-mail: learn@edact.com
Ann Edson, Author
Alan Stern, VP
Rose Falco, Sales/Marketing

A tutorial and practice program for students which focuses on recognition of key words in solving arithmetic word problems, writing equations and solving word problems. *$109.00*

1973 Read and Solve Math Problems #2

Educational Activities
PO Box 392
Freeport, NY   11520   516-223-4666
                              800-645-3739
                         FAX 516-379-7429
                  e-mail: learn@edact.com
Ann Edson, Author
Alan Stern, VP
Rose Falco, Sales/Marketing

A tutorial and practice program for students which focuses on recognition of key words in solving two-step arithmetic problems, writing equations and solving two-step word problems. *$109.00*

1974 Read and Solve Math Problems #3 Fractions, Two-Step Problems

Educational Activities
PO Box 392
Freeport, NY   11520   516-223-4666
                                     800-645-3739
                                FAX 516-379-7429
                          e-mail: learn@edact.com

Ann Edson, Author
Alan Stern, VP
Rose Falco, Sales/Marketing

Designed for students, this tutorial and practice program provides initial instruction and experience in critical thinking and problem-solving using fractions and mixed numbers. *$109.00*

1975 Shape Up!

Sunburst Technology
400 Columbus Avenue
Valhalla, NY   10595   914-747-3310
                                     800-321-7511
                                FAX 914-747-4109
                          http://www.sunburst.com
                      e-mail: support@sunburst.com

Students actively create and manipulate shapes to discover important ideas about mathematics in an electronic playground of two and three dimensional shapes.

1976 Spatial Sense CD-ROM

Sunburst Technology
400 Columbus Avenue
Valhalla, NY   10595   914-747-3310
                                     800-321-7511
                                FAX 914-747-4109
                          http://www.sunburst.com
                      e-mail: support@sunburst.com

Your students will strenghten their spatial perception, spatial reasoning and problem-solving skills with three great programs now on one CD-ROM.

1977 Splish Splash Math

Sunburst Technology
400 Columbus Avenue
Valhalla, NY   10595   914-747-3310
                                     800-321-7511
                                FAX 914-747-4109
                          http://www.sunburst.com
                      e-mail: support@sunburst.com

Students learn and practice basic operation skills as they engage in this high interest program that keeps them motivated. Great visual rewards and three levels of difficulty keep students challanged.

1978 Third and Fourth Grade Math Competencies

Phillip Roy
PO Box 130
Indian Rocks Beach, FL   33785   727-593-2700
                                     800-255-9085
                                FAX 727-595-2685

Stephanie Dipple
Ruth Bragman

Offers various programs of 40 disks on geometry, money, measurement, adding whole numbers, subtracting whole numbers and more. *$1175.00*

1979 This Old Man

UCLA Intervention Program for Handicapped Children
1000 Veteran Avenue
Los Angeles, CA   90095   310-825-4821
                                FAX 310-206-7744
                          http://www.bol.ucla.edu
Sharon Cislo, Administrative Assistant

Uses the song This Old Man in singing and signing to teach numbers and counting 1-10. *$35.00*

1980 Zap! Around Town

Sunburst Technology
400 Columbus Avenue
Valhalla, NY   10595   914-747-3310
                                     800-321-7511
                                FAX 914-747-4109
                          http://www.sunburst.com
                      e-mail: support@sunburst.com

Students develop mapping and direction skills in this easy-to-use, animated program featuring Shelby, your friendly Sunbuddy guide.

Preschool

1981 Creature Series

Laureate Learning Systems
110 E Spring Street
Winooski, VT   05404   802-655-4755
                                     800-562-6801
                                FAX 802-655-4757

Mary Sweig Wilson, President
Bernard Fox, VP

Programs designed to improve visual and auditory attention and teach cause and effect, turn taking, and switch use. *$95.00*

1982 Curious George Visits the Library

Software to Go-Gallaudet University
PO Box 77800
Washington, DC   20013   202-651-5705
                                FAX 202-651-5109
Ken Kurlychek, Project Coordinator

1983   Dinosaur Game

UCLA Intervention Program for Handicapped Children
1000 Veteran Avenue
Los Angeles, CA   90095   310-825-4821
                                 FAX 310-206-7744
                                 http://www.bol.ucla.edu
Sharon Cislo, Administrative Assistant

Game board format where dinosaurs race each other
home. Children press their switches to spin a spinner
which randomly selects the color of the square.
Children then move their dinosaurs by pressing their
switches. Accommodates 1-4 players. *$35.00*

1984   Early Discoveries: Size and Logic

Software to Go-Gallaudet University
PO Box 77800
Washington, DC   20013   202-651-5705
                                 FAX 202-651-5109
Ken Kurlychek, Project Coordinator

1985   Early Emerging Rules Series

Laureate Learning Systems
110 E Spring Street
Winooski, VT   05404   802-655-4755
                                 800-562-6801
                                 FAX 802-655-4757
Mary Sweig Wilson, President
Bernard Fox, VP

Three programs that introduce early developing grammatical constructions and facilitate the transition
from single words to word combinations. *$175.00*

1986   Early Learning I

MarbleSoft
12301 Central Avenue NE
Blaine, MN   55434   763-755-1402
                                 FAX 763-862-2920
                                 http://www.marblesoft.com
                                 e-mail: sales@marblesoft.com
Valerie Reit, Sales

Early Learning 2.0 includes four activities that teach
prereading skills. Single and dual-switch scanning are
built in and special prompts allow blind students to
use all levels of difficulty. Includes Matching Colors,
Learning Shapes, Counting Numbers and Letter
Match. Runs on Macintosh and Windows computers.
$70.00

1987   Early Music Skills

Electronic Courseware Systems
1210 Lancaster Drive
Champaign, IL   61821   217-359-7099
                                 800-832-4965
                                 FAX 217-359-6578
                                 http://www.ecsmedica.com
                                 e-mail: sales@ecsmedia.com
Jodie Varner, Director Education/Marketing

Covers four basic music reading skills. *$39.95*

1988   Early and Advanced Switch Games

RJ Cooper & Associates
27601 Forbes Road #39
Laguna Nigel, CA   92677
                                 800-752-6673
                                 FAX 949-582-3169
                                 http://www.rjcooper.com
                                 e-mail: info@rjcooper.com
RJ Cooper, Owner/Developer

Thirteen single switch games that start at cause/effect,
work through timing and selection and graduate with
matching and manipulation tasks. *$75.00*

**1989   Edustar's Early Childhood Special Education
Programs**

Edustar America
6220 S Orange Blossom Trail
Orlando, FL   32809
                                 800-952-3041
                                 FAX 561-330-0849
David Zeldin, Marketing Manager
Stewart Holtz, Curriculum Director

Integrated software program that incorporates
manipulatives and special tables for learning early
childhood subjects. Features include an illuminated
six key keyboard. A special U-shaped touch table for
the physically challenged and changeable mats and
keys for different subject areas.

1990   Electric Coloring Book

Heartsoft
3101 N Hemlock Circle
Broken Arrow, OK   74012
                                 800-285-4018
                                 FAX 800-285-3475
                                 e-mail: sales@heartsoft.com
Teaches young students the alphabet, numbers and basic keyboarding skills by using a graphic coloring
concept. *$39.95*

1991   If You're Happy and You Know It

UCLA Intervention Program for Handicapped Children
1000 Veteran Avenue
Los Angeles, CA   90095   310-825-4821
                                 FAX 310-206-7744
                                 http://www.bol.ucla.edu
Sharon Cislo, Administrative Assistant

A nursery school song with five verses depicted in
picture form. *$35.00*

1992   Joystick Games

Technology for Language and Learning
PO Box 327
East Rockaway, NY   11518   516-625-4550
                                 FAX 516-621-3321

Five volumes of public domain joystick programs.
$28.50

1993 Kindercomp Gold

Software to Go-Gallaudet University
PO Box 77800
Washington, DC   20013   202-651-5705
                                      FAX 202-651-5109
Ken Kurlychek, Project Coordinator

1994 Old MacDonald's Farm

KidTECH
4181 Pinewood Lake Drive
Bakersfield, CA   93309   661-396-8676
                                 FAX 661-396-8760

Utilizes the all-time favorite children's song to teach
vocabulary and animal sounds to young children.
$30.00

1995 Old MacDonald's Farm I

UCLA Intervention Program for Handicapped Children
1000 Veteran Avenue
Los Angeles, CA   90095   310-825-4821
                                 FAX 310-206-7744
                                 http://www.bol.ucla.edu
Sharon Cislo, Administrative Assistant

Nursery School song depicting a farmer, his wife, and
6 farm animals — cow, sheep, rooster, pig, and duck
— displayed on as overlay. Level I, the child selects
any animal. Level II, the child selects an animal by
name. Level III, the child selects an animal by its
sound. *$35.00*

1996 Optimum Resource

18 Hunter Road
Hilton Head Island, SC   29926   843-689-8000
                                     888-784-2592
                                 FAX 843-689-8008
                                 http://www.stickybear.com
                                 e-mail: stickyb@stickybear.com
Christopher J Gintz, COO
Robert Stangroom, Product Manager

An educational software publishing company for
grades K-12. Our software titles are available in Consumer, School, Labpack or Site License versions.
Please call for further details. Prices range from
$59.95 for Consumer to $699.95 for Site Licenses.

1997 Padded Vehicles

UCLA Intervention Program for Handicapped Children
1000 Veteran Avenue
Los Angeles, CA   90095   310-825-4821
                                 FAX 310-206-7744
                                 http://www.bol.ucla.edu
Sharon Cislo, Administrative Assistant

Children identify 10 vehicles — airplane, helicopter,
motorcycle, police car, truck, ambulance, garbage
truck, school bus, fire engine, and tractor — which are
depicted on an overlay. Level I, the child selects any
vehicle. Level II, the child selects the vehicle by
name. *$35.00*

1998 Shape and Color Rodeo

SRA Order Services
220 E Danieldale Road
DeSoto, TX   75115
                                     800-843-8855
                                 FAX 214-228-1982

Children learn recognition and identification of common shapes and color discriminations. *$35.00*

1999 Silly Sandwich

UCLA Intervention Program for Handicapped Children
1000 Veteran Avenue
Los Angeles, CA   90095   310-825-4821
                                 FAX 310-206-7744
                                 http://www.bol.ucla.edu
Sharon Cislo, Administrative Assistant

Build a silly sandwich selecting from six to twelve different items depicted on a PowerPad overlay. *$35.00*

2000 Switch It - Change It

UCLA Intervention Program for Handicapped Children
1000 Veteran Avenue
Los Angeles, CA   90095   310-825-4821
                                 FAX 310-206-7744
                                 http://www.bol.ucla.edu
Sharon Cislo, Administrative Assistant

Cause and effect program presents color-animated
common objects. *$35.00*

Mac

2001 Trudy's Time and Place House

Edmark Corporation
PO Box 97021
Redmond, WA   98073   206-556-8400
                                     800-362-2890
                                 FAX 206-556-8430

In Trudy's Time and Place House, children enjoy exploring geography and time with Trudy's whimsical
friends! Ann and Dan, Joe Crow and Nellie the Elephant invite kids to: build time-telling skills; develop
mapping and direction skills; and travel the world
learning about continents, oceans and landmarks.
$59.95

2002 Wheels on the Bus I: Intellipics Activity

UCLA Intervention Program for Handicapped Children
1000 Veteran Avenue
Los Angeles, CA   90095   310-825-4821
                                     800-899-6687
                                 FAX 310-206-7744
                                 http://www.bol.ucla.edu
Sharon Cislo, Administrative Assistant

This native Macintosh activity requires Intellipics to
run. It includes 6 verses (Baby, Bus, Doors, Horn,
Kids, Mommy) with digitalized sound and color animations. It can be used with intellipics options such as
color and a number selection, and includes both free
choice and quiz options. *$25.00*

2003 Wheels on the Bus II

UCLA Intervention Program for Handicapped Children
1000 Veteran Avenue
Los Angeles, CA   90095   310-825-4821
                                FAX 310-206-7744
                          http://www.bol.ucla.edu
Sharon Cislo, Administrative Assistant

Popular nursery school song that is activated to sing 5 verses by pressing the corresponding picture on an overlay. Verses are driver, wheel, wiper, windows, daddy. *$36.00*

2004 Wheels on the Bus III

UCLA Intervention Program for Handicapped Children
1000 Veteran Avenue
Los Angeles, CA   90095   310-825-4821
                                FAX 310-206-7744
                          http://www.bol.ucla.edu
Sharon Cislo, Administrative Assistant

Popular nursery school song that is activated to sing 5 verses of the song by pressing the corresponding picture on an overlay. Verses are: People, money, brakes, seatbelt, wheelchair lift. *$36.00*

2005 Where is Puff?

UCLA Intervention Program for Handicapped Children
1000 Veteran Avenue
Los Angeles, CA   90095   310-825-4821
                                FAX 310-206-7744
                          http://www.bol.ucla.edu
Sharon Cislo, Administrative Assistant

Early preposition program that includes six prepositions illustrated by Puff the cat: in, on, next to, under, in front of, in back of. Features include: scan speed selection and data collection. *$35.00*

2006 Word Pieces

Software to Go-Gallaudet University
PO Box 77800
Washington, DC   20013   202-651-5705
                                FAX 202-651-5109
Ken Kurlychek, Project Coordinator

Problem Solving

2007 Captain's Log Cognitive Training System for Windows

BrainTrain
727 Twinridge Lane
Richmond, VA   23235   804-320-0105
                              800-822-0538
                        FAX 804-320-0242
                  http://www.braintrain.com
                  e-mail: info@braintrain.com
Ginger Sandford, VP Sales/Marketing

A comprehensive, multilevel computerized mental gym to help people with brain injuries, learning disabilities, developmental disabilities, ADD, ADHD and psychiatric disorders improve their cognitive skills. *$2695.00*

ISBN 3-490019-95-0

2008 Changes Around Us CD-ROM

Steck-Vaughn Company
PO Box 690789
Orlando, FL   32819
                                800-531-5015
                          FAX 800-699-9459
                  http://www.steck-vaughn.com
                  e-mail: info@steck-vaughn.com
Chris Lehman, Team Coordinator

Nature is the natural choice for observing change. By observing and researching dramatic visual sequences such as the stages of development of a butterfly, children develop a broad understanding of the concept of change. As they search this multimedia database for images and information about plant and animal life cycles and seasonal change, students strengthen their abilities in research, analysis, problem-solving, critical thinking and communication.

2009 Factory Deluxe

Sunburst Technology
400 Columbus Avenue
Valhalla, NY   10595   914-747-3310
                              800-321-7511
                        FAX 914-747-4109
                  http://www.sunburst.com
                  e-mail: support@sunburst.com

Five activities explore shapes, rotation, angles, geometric attributes, area formulas, and computation. Includes journal, record keeping, and on-screen help. This program helps sharpen geometry, visual thinking and problem solving skills.

2010 Freddy's Puzzling Adventures

SRA Order Services
220 E Danieldale Road
DeSoto, TX   75115
                                800-843-8855
                          FAX 214-228-1982

Helps students acquire problem solving and logical thinking skills with three activities. *$34.00*

2011 Guessing and Thinking

Software to Go-Gallaudet University
PO Box 77800
Washington, DC   20013   202-651-5705
                                FAX 202-651-5109
Ken Kurlychek, Project Coordinator

2012 High School Math Bundle

Sunburst Technology
400 Columbus Avenue
Valhalla, NY   10595
914-747-3310
800-321-7511
FAX 914-747-4109
http://www.sunburst.com
e-mail: support@sunburst.com

Each program in this bundle focuses on a specific area to ensure that your students master the math skills they need. This bundle allows students to master basics of Algebra, explore equations and graphs, practice learning with algebra graphs, use trigonometric functions, apply math concepts to practical situations and improve problem solving and data analysis skills.

2013 Ice Cream Truck

Sunburst Technology
400 Columbus Avenue
Valhalla, NY   10595
914-747-3310
800-321-7511
FAX 914-747-4109
http://www.sunburst.com
e-mail: support@sunburst.com

Elementary students learn important problem solving, strategic planning and math operation skills, as they become owners of a busy ice cream truck.

2014 Lesson Maker: Do-It-Yourself Computer Program

Harris Communications
15155 Technology Drive
Eden Prairie, MN   55344
952-906-1180
800-825-6758
FAX 952-906-1099
TDY:952-906-1198
http://www.harriscomm.com
e-mail: mail@harriscomm.com
Bill Williams, National Sales Manager

For teachers, parents and students who want to create their own computer lessons. Choose any topic from Vocabulary to Volcanoes. For each lesson enter eight of your own questions or prompts with eight answers or desired responses. Lesson Maker automatically inputs information into 4 separate fun games for each lesson: Spinmeister; Matching; Paired Squares; and Pop Quiz. Up to 15 individual lessons can be made for one Unit. *$24.95*

Diskettes

2015 Memory Match

Software to Go-Gallaudet University
PO Box 77800
Washington, DC   20013
202-651-5705
FAX 202-651-5109
Ken Kurlychek, Project Coordinator

2016 Memory: A First Step in Problem Solving

Software to Go-Gallaudet University
PO Box 77800
Washington, DC   20013
202-651-5705
FAX 202-651-5109
Ken Kurlychek, Project Coordinator

2017 Middle School Math Bundle

Sunburst Technology
400 Columbus Avenue
Valhalla, NY   10595
914-747-3310
800-321-7511
FAX 914-747-4109
http://www.sunburst.com
e-mail: support@sunburst.com

This bundle helps improve student's logical thinking, number sense and operation skills. This product comes with Math Arena, Building Perspective Deluxe, Equation Tile Teasers and Easy Sheet.

2018 Nordic Software

PO Box 83499
Lincoln, NE   68501
402-475-5300
800-306-6502
FAX 402-488-2914
http://www.nordicsoftware.com
Tammy Kear, Sales/Marketing

Develops and publishes entertaining, educational software. Children ages three and up can build math skills, expand their vocabulary and increase proficiency in spelling, among other subjects. *$59.95*

2019 Number Sense & Problem Solving CD-ROM

Sunburst Technology
400 Columbus Avenue
Valhalla, NY   10595
914-747-3310
800-321-7511
FAX 914-747-4109
http://www.sunburst.com
e-mail: support@sunburst.com

Build number and operation skills with these three programs: How the West Was One + Three x Four, Divide and Conquer and Puzzle Tank.

2020 Problem Solving

Psychological Software Services
6555 Carrollton Avenue
Indianapolis, IN   46220
317-257-9672
FAX 317-257-9674

Nine computer programs designed to challenge high functioning patients/students with tasks requiring logic. *$150.00*

2021 Puzzle Storybook

First Byte
19840 Pioneer Avenue
Torrance, CA   90503
310-793-0610
800-523-2983
FAX 310-793-0611
http://www.fbyte.com
e-mail: info@fbyte.com

Helps students build early problem solving skills. *$49.95*

2022 Scrambled Eggs

Merit Software
132 W 21 Street
New York, NY   10011   212-675-8567
                              800-753-6488
                         FAX 212-675-8607
              http://www.meritsoftware.com
              e-mail: sales@meritsoftware.com

Deductive logic and problem solving are the primary skills developed in the variation of the game MAS-TERMIND. *$9.95*

2023 Single Switch Games

MarbleSoft
12301 Central Avenue NE
Blaine, MN   55434   763-755-1402
                      FAX 763-862-2920
              http://www.marblesoft.com
              e-mail: sales@marblesoft.com

Valerie Reit, Sales

There's a lot of educational software for single switch users, but how about something that's just for fun? We've taken some games similar to the ones you enjoyed as a kid and made them work just right for single switch users. Includes Single Switch Maze, A Frog's Life, Switching Lanes, Switch Invaders, Slingshot Gallery and Scurry. Runs on Macintosh and Windows computers. *$30.00*

2024 Sliding Block

Merit Software
132 W 21 Street
New York, NY   10011   212-675-8567
                              800-753-6488
                         FAX 212-675-8607
              http://www.meritsoftware.com
              e-mail: sales@meritsoftware.com

Learners rearrange one of the four pictures which can be scrambled at five separate levels to test visual discrimination and problem solving skills. *$9.95*

2025 SoundSmart

BrainTrain
727 Twinridge Lane
Richmond, VA   23235   804-320-0105
                              800-822-0538
                         FAX 804-320-0242
              http://www.braintrain.com
              e-mail: info@braintrain.com

Ginger Sandford, VP Sales/Marketing

Auditory Attention Building software to help improve phonenic awareness, listening skills, working memory, mental processing speech and self-control. *$549.00*

2026 Strategy Challenges Collection: 1

Edmark Corporation
PO Box 97021
Redmond, WA   98073   206-556-8400
                              800-362-2890
                         FAX 206-556-8430

Play Mancala, Go-Muku and Nine Men's Morris- the three games in Strategy Challenges Collection 1 against Game Masters from around the world! Why? Because you'll learn important problem-solving and strategies thinking skills you can use throughout life in games, in school and in jobs. *$39.95*

2027 Strategy Challenges Collection: 2

Edmark Corporation
PO Box 97021
Redmond, WA   98073   206-556-8400
                              800-362-2890
                         FAX 206-556-8430

Strategy Challenges Collection: 2 — featuring Jungle Chess, Surakarta and Tablut — boosts your thinking power! How does it work? Six diverse Opponents challenge you to build a repertoire of powerful problem-solving strategies and skills. You'll also meet Strategy Coaches who offer offensive and defensive tips that can improve your game and be applied throughout life. *$39.95*

2028 Switch Arcade

UCLA Intervention Program for Handicapped Children
1000 Veteran Avenue
Los Angeles, CA   90095   310-825-4821
                           FAX 310-206-7744
                 http://www.bol.ucla.edu

Sharon Cislo, Administrative Assistant

Three switch games are presented: Tug of War; Racing; Fishing. The racing game allows children to choose from several racers including cars, wheelchairs, and animals using a single switch. The game is designed for two players using two switches to play competitive, cooperative games together. Can be used to promote social interaction and eye-hand coordination. *$45.00*

Mac

2029 Thinkin' Things: All Around Frippletown

Edmark Corporation
PO Box 97021
Redmond, WA   98073   206-556-8400
                              800-362-2890
                         FAX 206-556-8430

Welcome to FrippleTown, where dozens of fun-loving Fripples will tickle your funny bone and challenge your brain. Discover and use the best of your creative thinking skills! Think through problems and explore solutions to furnish the Fripples with artful flags, crazy cookies, door-to-door surprises and more. Every visit to FrippleTown is a chance to discover something new.

2030 Thinkin' Things: Collection 1

Edmark Corporation
PO Box 97021
Redmond, WA 98073   206-556-8400
    800-362-2890
    FAX 206-556-8430

Good thinkers learn quickly, adapt to change easily and accomplish remarkable things. That's why we created Thinkin' Things Collection 1, a powerful set of tools and toys to help children strengthen observation and memory, improve problem solving and encourage creativity. Thinkin' Things Collection 1 will help your child build a solid foundation for successful learning!

2031 Thinkin' Things: Collection 2

Edmark Corporation
PO Box 97021
Redmond, WA 98073   206-556-8400
    800-362-2890
    FAX 206-556-8430

In this rapidly changing world, kids with strong thinking skills will thrive and excel. That's why the educators at Edmark developed Thinkin' Things Collection 2, a powerful set of tools and toys that strengthen observation and analysis, develop spatial awareness, improve memory and foster creativity. With a strong grasp of these skills, your child is ready to succeed!

2032 Thinkin' Things: Collection 3

Edmark Corporation
PO Box 97021
Redmond, WA 98073   206-556-8400
    800-362-2890
    FAX 206-556-8430

Become a strong thinker with Thinkin' Things Collection 3 and build thinking skills you can use wherever you are in anything you do! Make trades with brokers from around the world, program a half-time show and solve the Case of the Empty Fripple House. You'll improve deductive and inductive reasoning, synthesis and analysis, while building problem-solving skills essential for success!

2033 Thinkin' Things: Galactic Brain Benders

Edmark Corporation
PO Box 97021
Redmond, WA 98073   206-556-8400
    800-362-2890
    FAX 206-556-8430

Your brain power is needed all across the galaxy! Develop logic, sequencing and decision-making skills as you organize Fripples in space, experiment with special effects tools and program a half-time show at the Intergalactic Rocket Bowl.

2034 Thinkin' Things: Sky Island Mysteries

Edmark Corporation
PO Box 97021
Redmond, WA 98073   206-556-8400
    800-362-2890
    FAX 206-556-8430

Inspector Cluestoe needs help cracking 14 zany mysteries to nab a slew of crafty culprits. Visit each island and put your best thinking skills to work to collect the clues! Prioritize tasks, apply your powers of observation and logic, and draw valid conclusions to solve the mysteries of the Sky Islands.

2035 Thinkin' Things: Toony the Loon's Lagoon

Edmark Corporation
PO Box 97021
Redmond, WA 98073   206-556-8400
    800-362-2890
    FAX 206-556-8430

Toony the Loon's Lagoon sparkles with dozens of fun loving characters and activities that help kids learn how to be better thinkers. Toony, Oranga and other jungle friends guide your child toward success in six unique locations — plus there's a fun, new online puzzle each week.

Professional Resources

2036 Accurate Assessments

1823 Harney Street
Omaha, NE 68102   402-341-8880
    800-324-7966
    FAX 402-341-8911
http://www.accurateassessments.com
e-mail: info@accurateassessments.com

Accurate Assessments offers a full range of superior innovative technological services and expertise to the behavioral health industry. Our premier product, AccuCare Behavioral Healthcare System, was developed by teams of experts in their respective fields, insuring our products are truly useful to clinicians and are easy to use. This innovative software program is a comprehensive and adaptable approach to the behavioral health practice environment.

2037 Analytic Learning Disability Assessment Computer Report

Southern Micro Systems
203 Woodley Avenue
Pratville, AL 36066   334-365-6560
    FAX 334-365-6464
http://www.smsi.net

This software provides an interpretation of the ALDA assessment results. The report describes to the professional the most efficient method for this child to learn the basic subjects of Reading, Spelling, Math and Handwriting. The report can be given to the professional or parent and may be used to design remedial approaches and improve academic functioning. *$195.00*

2038 Beyond Drill and Practice: Expanding the Computer Mainstream

Council for Exceptional Children
1110 N Glebe Road
Arlington, VA 22201   703-620-3660
    888-232-7733
    FAX 703-264-9494
http://www.cec.sped.org/

Provides informative guidelines and examples for teachers who want to expand the use of the computer as a learning tool. *$10.00*

120 pages

250

2039 CE Software

PO Box 65580
West Des Moines, IA   50265   515-221-1801
                                    FAX 515-221-1806
                                    http://www.cesoft.com
                                    e-mail: sales@cesoft.com
John S Kirk, Controller

International software developer. Many products for adaptive technology.

2040 CRISP

National Institute of Health
6701 Rockledge Drive
Bethesda, MD   20892   301-435-0650
                                    FAX 301-480-2845
                      http://www.commons.cit.nih.gov\crisp
                                    e-mail: commons@od.nih.gov
Dorrette Finch, Dir. Div. Research Documentation

A major scientific information system containing data on the research programs supported by the US Public Health Service.

2041 Claris Corporation

5201 Patrick Henry Drive
Santa Clara, CA   95054
                                     800-325-2747
                                    FAX 408-987-3932
Company that produces a variety of Macintosh Documentation.

2042 Classification Series

Aquarius Instructional
PO Box 128
Indian Rocks Beach, FL   33785   727-595-7890
                                     800-338-2644
                                    FAX 727-595-2685

Curriculum-based programs are learning units containing matching, sorting, form and object, and familiar settings. *$75.00*

2043 Compass Learning

9920 Pacific Heights Boulevard
San Diego, CA   92121   858-587-0087
                                     800-422-4339
                                    FAX 858-587-1629
                      http://www.compasslearning.com
Polly Irwin, Receptionist

Educational software for teachers of K-12.

2044 Conover Company

2926 Hidden Hollow Road
Oshkosh, WI   54904   920-231-4667
                                    FAX 920-231-4809
                      http://www.conovercompany.com
                      e-mail: conover@execpc.com

2045 DC Health and Company

125 Spring Street
Lexington, MA   02421   617-351-5000
                                    FAX 800-235-3565

Helping people with learning disabilities.

2046 Edmark Corporation

PO Box 97021
Redmond, WA   98073   425-556-8400
                                     800-362-2890
                                    FAX 425-556-8430
                                    http://www.edmark.com
                                    e-mail: edmarkteam@edmark.com
Ellie McCormack, Director of Public Relations

2047 Filling Out Job Applications

Lawrence Productions
1800 S 35th Street
Galesburg, MI   49053   269-665-7075
                                     800-421-4157
                                    FAX 269-665-7060
                                    http://www.lpi.com
                                    e-mail: sales@lpi.com
Holly Argue, Author
Edwin Wright, President

Designed for adolescents and adults in basic education classes providing one step analysis and completion of typical job applications. *$29.95*

2048 Higher Education with Adult Training for People with Handicaps

HEATH Resource Center
2121 K Street NW
Washington, DC   20036   202-973-0904
                                     800-544-3284
                                    FAX 202-973-0908
                      http://gopher://bobcat-ace.nche.edu
                                    e-mail: heath@ace.nche.edu
Dan Gardner, Information Specialist

$1.00

2049 IEP Companion Software

LinguiSystems
3100 4th Avenue
East Moline, IL   61244
                                     800-776-4332
                                    FAX 309-755-2377
                                    TDY:800-933-8331
                                    http://www.linguisystems.com
                                    e-mail: service@linguisystems.com
Carolyn Wilson, Janet Lanza, Jeannie Evans, Author
Linda Bowers, Owner
Rosemary Huisingh, Owner

Get IEP goals from the best-selling book with the click of your mouse. Writing complete reports is easy! You'll get to choose from hundreds of individual and classroom goals and objectives for all the important speech and language areas. Just click on the specific goals you want to create your individualized report. *$69.95*

Birth-Adult

2050 Interest Driven Learning

383 DeSoto Drive
New Smyna Beach, FL   32169   386-427-4473
                                 800-245-5733
                                 FAX 386-426-0100
                                 http://www.drpeet.com
                                 e-mail: drpeet@drpect.com

Dr. Bill Peet, CEO

Our mission is to provide affordable low and high-tech tools that will help people of all ages and abilities learn to read, write and communicate with support from assistive technology as needed.

2051 International Society for Technology in Education

University of Oregon
15th Avenue & Kincaid
Eugene, OR   97403   541-346-4705
                         FAX 541-346-0987
                         http://www.iste.org
                         e-mail: iste@iste.org

A nonprofit professional organization dedicated to promoting appropriate uses of information technology to support and improve learning, teaching, and administration in K-12 education and teacher education.

2052 Keyboard Assessment Program

Assistive Device Center, School of Engineering
600 J Street
Sacramento, CA   95819   916-278-6422
                            FAX 916-278-5949

Software program gathers and compiles data about track time, select time and multiple key selection. *$41.65*

2053 KidDesk

Edmark Corporation
PO Box 97021
Redmond, WA   98073   206-556-8400
                         800-362-2890
                         FAX 206-556-8430

A hard disk security program, KidDesk makes it easy for kids to launch their programs, but impossible for them to access adult programs. Includes interactive desktop accessories including desktop-to-desktop electronic mail, and voice mail. *$24.95*

2054 KidDesk: Family Edition

Edmark Corporation
PO Box 97021
Redmond, WA   98073   206-556-8400
                         800-362-2890
                         FAX 206-556-8430

Now kids can launch their programs, but can't access yours! With KidDesk Family Edition, you can give your children the keys to the computer without putting your programs and files at risk! The auto-start option provides constant hard drive security — any time your computer is turned on, KidDesk will appear. *$24.95*

2055 Kinderlogo

Terrapin Software
10 Holworthy Street
Cambridge, MA   02138   617-547-5646
                           800-972-8200
                           FAX 617-492-4610

Andre Rossi, Marketing Director

A Logo curriculum based on single keystroke commands that teaches prereaders to explore computer literacy and early learning. Developmentally designed so kids can progress at their own pace. Organized into five levels with activities (Available in Apple or Mac). *$49.95*

2056 LD Teacher's IEP Companion Software

LinguiSystems
3100 4th Avenue
East Moline, IL   61244
                         800-776-4332
                         FAX 309-755-2377
                         TDY:800-933-8331
                         http://www.linguisystems.com
                         e-mail: service@linguisystems.com

Molly Lyle, Author
Linda Bowers, Owner
Rosemary Huisingh, Owner

Create customized, professional reports with these terrific academic goals and objectives. You'll have individual objectives from nine skill areas at the click of your mouse! Save time with the software version of the best-selling book! For both PC and Macintosh. *$69.95*

Ages 5-18

2057 Laureate Learning Systems

110 E Spring Street
Winooski, VT   05404   802-655-4755
                          800-652-6801
                          FAX 802-655-4757

Provides resources for people with learning disabilities.

2058 Learning Company

6493 Kaiser Drive
Fremont, CA   94555   415-792-2101
                         800-852-2255
                         FAX 510-792-9628

2059 Microsoft Corporation

1 Microsoft Way
Redmond, WA   98052   425-882-8088
                         800-227-4679
                         FAX 425-936-7329
                         http://www.microsoft.com

Mission is to enable people and businesses throughout the world to realize their full potential.

2060 Print Module

Failure Free
140 Cabarrus Avenue W
Concord, NC   28025
                         800-221-1274
                         FAX 314-569-2834
                         e-mail: ffsales@concord.nc.com

Includes teacher's manual, instructional readers, flashcards, independent activities and illustrated independent reading booklets. *$499.00*

2061 PsycINFO Database

American Psychological Association
750 1st Street NE
Washington, DC 20002   202-336-5650
                                800-374-2722
                          FAX 202-336-5633
                          TDY:202-336-6123
                    http://www.apa.org/psycinfo
                    e-mail: psycinfo@apa.org

An online abstract database that provides access to citations to the international serial literature in psychology and related disciplines from 1887 to present. Available via PsycINFO Direct at www.psycinfo.com.

2062 Public Domain Software

Kentucky Special Ed TechTraining Center
229 Taylor Education Building
Lexington, KY 40506   859-257-4713
                          FAX 859-257-1325
                          TDY:859-257-4714
                    http://www.serc.gws.uky.edu

Entire collections of Macintosh, MS-DOS or Apple II software.

2063 Pugliese, Davey and Associates

Adaptive Technology Institutes
5 Bessom Street
Marblehead, MA 01945   781-639-1930
                          FAX 781-631-9928
                          TDY:781-224-2521

Offers computer lab courses for Apple IIGS and Macintosh LC.

2064 Scholastic

2931 E McCarty Street
Jefferson City, MO 65101   573-636-5271
                                800-541-5513
                          FAX 573-632-5271

2065 Sunburst Communications

101 Castleton Street
Pleasantville, NY 10570   914-747-3310
                                800-338-3457
                          FAX 914-747-4109
                    http://www.sunburst.com
                    e-mail: service@nysunburst.com

2066 Testmaster

Research Design Associates
5 Main Street
Freeville, NY 13068   607-844-4601
                          FAX 607-844-3310

A new concept in question and answer testing with an Exploratory Mode which allows students to explore a range of answers. *$199.95*

2067 The Speech Bin

1965 25th Avenue
Vero Beach, FL 32960
                                800-477-3324
                          FAX 888-329-2246
                    http://www.speechbin.com
                    e-mail: info@speechbin.com
Jan J Binney, President

The Speech Bin offers materials to help persons of all ages who have special needs. We specialize in products for children and adults who have communication disorders.

2068 WPS Automated IEP System

Western Psychological Services
12031 Wilshire Boulevard
Los Angeles, CA 90025   310-478-2061
                                800-648-8857
                          FAX 310-478-7838

This computer program substantially reduces the time educators spend on preparing Individualized Educational Plans (IEPs). The system allows the user to use any IEP format. Simply type the format into the computer, and the program will customize the system to your district's specifications. *$115.00*

Reading

2069 Adaptive Technology Tools

Freedom Scientific
11800 31st Court N
 St. Petersburg, FL 33716   727-803-8000
                                800-444-4443
                          FAX 727-803-8001
                    http://www.freedomscientific.com
Lee Hamilton, CEO

A wide variety of adaptive technology tools for the visually or reading impaired person.

2070 An Open Book

Arkenstone
1390 Borregas Avenue
Sunnyvale, CA 94089   408-752-2200
                                800-444-4443
                          FAX 408-745-6739
James R Fruchterman, President

The stand-alone reading machine, An Open Book, is an easy-to-use appliance for noncomputer users that comes equipped with a Hewlett Packard ScanJet IIP scanner, DECtalk PC speech synthesizer and a 17 key keypad. An Open Book uses Calera WordScan optical character recognition (OCR) to convert pages into text, then reads it aloud with a speech synthesizer.

2071 An Open Book Unbound

Arkenstone
1390 Borregas Avenue
Sunnyvale, CA 94089   408-752-2200
                                800-444-4443
                          FAX 408-745-6739
James R Fruchterman, President

PC-based OCR and reading software. Together with a scanner and a speech synthesizer, this software provides everything needed to make an IBM-compatible PC into a talking reading machine. The system includes automatic page orientation, automatic contrast control, decolumnization of multicolumn documents and recognition of a wide variety of type fonts and sizes. *$995.00*

2072 Bailey's Book House

Edmark Corporation
PO Box 97021
Redmond, WA 98073 206-556-8400
800-362-2890
FAX 206-556-8430
Tina Martin, Education Marketing

The award-winning Bailey's Book House now features 2 new activities! Bailey and his friends encourage young children to build important literacy skills while developing a love for reading. In seven activities, kids explore the sounds and meanings of letters, words, sentences, rhymes and stories. No reading skills are required: all directions and written words are spoken. *$59.95*

2073 Banner Books

Queue
338 Commerce Drive
Fairfield, CT 06432 203-335-0906
800-232-2224
FAX 203-336-2481
This is a format students and teachers will love. Students select a variety of backgrounds and watch as they move by on the screen. Students then add clip art and text to create their own Banner Book pages. Offers various programs. *$49.95*

2074 Basic Reading Skills

Phillip Roy
PO Box 130
Indian Rocks Beach, FL 33785 727-593-2700
800-255-9085
FAX 727-595-2685
Stephanie Dipple
Ruth Bragman

These programs are designed to encourage students to learn and use critical thinking skills. *$550.00*

21 disks

2075 Boars in Camelot

Queue
338 Commerce Drive
Fairfield, CT 06432 203-335-0906
800-232-2224
FAX 203-336-2481
Written in an upbeat and amusing style to capture students' interest as they interact with the story by answering questions about what they have read. *$45.00*

2076 Comprehension Connection

Milliken Publishing
11643 Lilburn Park Road
St. Louis, MO 63146 314-991-4220
FAX 314-991-4807

Comprehension Connection improves reading comprehension by stressing basic skills that combine the reading process with relevant activities and interesting, thought-provoking stories. This award-winning software package spans six reading levels that increase in difficulty. Passages range from 150-300 words. *$150.00*

2077 Cosmic Reading Journey

Sunburst Technology
400 Columbus Avenue
Valhalla, NY 10595 914-747-3310
800-321-7511
FAX 914-747-4109
http://www.sunburst.com
e-mail: support@sunburst.com

This reading comprehension program provides meaningful summary and writing activities for the 100 books that early readers and their teachers love most.

2078 Dinosaur Discovery Kit

First Byte
19840 Pioneer Avenue
Torrance, CA 90503 310-793-0610
800-523-2983
FAX 310-793-0611

Offers children help with reading and prereading skills. *$49.95*

2079 Don Johnston Reading

Don Johnston
26799 W Commerce Drive
Volo, IL 60073 847-740-0749
800-999-4660
FAX 847-740-7326
http://www.donjohnston.com
e-mail: info@donjohnston.com
Christine Filler, Marketing/Channel Development

Don Johnston Inc. is a provider of quality products and services that enable people with special needs to discover their potential and experience success. Products are developed for the areas of computer access and for those who struggle with reading and writing.

2080 Failure Free Reading

140 Cabarrus Avenue W
Concord, NC 28025
800-221-1274
FAX 314-569-2834
Bill Sedergren, VP
Bob Fowles, VP Sales

Curriculum areas covered: reading for those with learning disabilities and moderate mentally disabled/emotionally disabled.

2081 Judy Lynn Software

PO Box 373
East Brunswick, NJ   08816   732-390-8845
                                         FAX 732-390-8845
                                  http://www.judylynn.com
                            e-mail: webmaster@judylynn.com
Elliot Pludwinski, President
Myra Pludwinski, VP

Offers switch computer programs for windows. The
programs are geared towards children with a cognitive
age level from 9 months to 4 years. Programs use
bright colorful animation with captivating sounds to
maintain attention span. Programs are reasonably
priced from $20-$39. Recipient of a Parents' Choice
Honor.

2082 Kurzweil 3000

Kurzweil Educational Systems
14 Crosby Drive
Bedford, MA   01730   781-203-5000
                                  800-894-5374
                             FAX 781-276-0650
                         http://www.kurzweiledu.com
                           e-mail: info@kurzweiledu.cc
Christina B Newman, Marketing Communications
Manager

Kurzweil Educational's flagship product for struggling readers and writers. It is widely recognized as
the most comprehensive and integrated solution for
addressing language and literacy difficulties. The
software uses a multisensory approach — presenting
printed or electronic text on the computer screen with
added visual and audible accessibility. The product
incorporates a host of dynamic features including
powerful decoding, study skills tools and test taking
tools.

**2083 Level II: Strategies for Older Students/Reading
SOS**

Lexia Learning Systems
2 Lewis Street
Lincoln, MA   01773   781-259-8752
                                  800-435-3942
                             FAX 781-259-1349

Five units with 65 branching activities and practice
with 295 one-syllable words. *$250.00*

2084 Level III: Phonics Based Reading-Grades 1, 2 & 3

Lexia Learning Systems
2 Lewis Street
Lincoln, MA   01773   781-259-8752
                                  800-435-3942
                             FAX 781-259-1349

Five activity areas with 64 branching units and practice with 535 one-syllable words and 90 two-syllable
words. *$50.00*

**2085 Level IV: Reading Strategies for Older Students
Grades 4, 5 & 6**

Lexia Learning Systems
2 Leis Street
Lincoln, MA   01773   781-259-8752
                                  800-435-3942
                             FAX 781-259-1349

Four units with 60 branching activities focusing on
two-syllable words with six syllable types, hard and
soft c and g, construction of three-syllable words,
reading comprehension with word attack strategies.
$250.00

**2086 Lexia Early Reading: Lexia Phonics Based
Reading, Reading Stategies for Older Students**

Lexia Learning Systems
PO Box 466
Lincoln, MA   01773   781-259-8752
                                  800-435-3942
                             FAX 781-259-1349
                        http://www.lexialearning.com
                         e-mail: info@lexialearning.com

Lexia's skill development assessment software helps
children and adults with learning disabilities master
their core reading skills. Based on the
Orton-Gillingham method, Lexia Early reading, Phonics Based Reading and S.O.S. (Strategies for Older
Students) apply phonics principles to help students
learn essential sound-symbol correspondence and decoding skills.

2087 Math and Reading Bonus Pack

Compu-Teach
PMB 137, 16541 Redmond Way
Redmond, WA   98052   425-885-0517
                                  800-448-3224
                             FAX 425-883-9169
                         http://www.compu-teach.com
                          e-mail: info@compu-teach.com
David Urban, President

Higher resolution graphics, digitized voice, MIDI
music, animation and sound effects make this program one of America's favorites. Children have never
had so much fun learning the basics of reading, language and math! Includes letter recognition, counting, adding and sentence structure. This wonderful
series will provide an exciting learning experience for
any child between the ages of 2 and 7. The bonus pack
contains six separate learning activities which have
won many software awards. *$59.95*

Ages 4-7

2088 Mike Mulligan & His Steam Shovel

Sunburst Technology
400 Columbus Avenue
Valhalla, NY   10595   914-747-3310
                                    800-321-7511
                                    FAX 914-747-4109
                                    http://www.sunburst.com
                                    e-mail: service@sunburst.com

This CD-ROM version of the Caldecott classic lets students experience interactive book reading and participate in four skills-based extension activities that promote memory, matching, sequencing, listening, pattern recognition and map reading skills.

2089 Optimum Resource

18 Hunter Road
Hilton Head Island, SC   29926   843-689-8000
                                   888-784-2592
                                   FAX 843-689-8008
                                   http://www.stickybear.com
                                   e-mail: stickyb@stickybear.com
Christopher J Gintz, COO
Robert Stangroom, Product Manager

An educational software publishing company for grades K-12. Our software titles are available in Consumer, School, Labpack or Site License versions. Please call for further details. Prices range from $59.95 for Consumer to $699.95 for Site Licenses.

2090 Polar Express

Sunburst Technology
400 Columbus Avenue
Valhalla, NY   10595   914-747-3310
                                   800-321-7511
                                   FAX 914-747-4109
                                   http://www.sunburst.com
                                   e-mail: service@sunburst.com

Share the magic and enchantment of the holiday season with this CD-ROM version of Chris Van Allsburg's Caldecott-winning picture book.

2091 Prolexia

4726 13th Avenue NW
Rochester, MN   55901
                                   888-776-5394
                                   FAX 507-252-0131
                                   http://www.prolexia.com
                                   e-mail: info@prolexia.com

Reading education softeare simulating actual Orton-Gillingham one-on-one tutoring.

2092 Read On! Plus

Sunburst Technology
400 Columbus Avenue
Valhalla, NY   10595   914-747-3310
                                   800-321-7511
                                   FAX 914-747-4109
                                   http://www.sunburst.com
                                   e-mail: support@sunburst.com

Promote skills and strategies that improve reading comprehension, and build appreciation for literature and the written word.

2093 Read, Write and Type Learning System

Talking Fingers
1 St. Vincents Street
San Rafael, CA   94903   415-472-3104
                                   800-674-9126
                                   FAX 415-472-7812
                                   http://www.readwritetype.com
                                   e-mail: info@talkingfingers.com

A 40-level software adventure providing highly motivating instruction and practice in phonics, reading, writing, spelling and typing. This multisensory program includes 9 levels of assessment and reports. Classroom packs available.

2094 Reading Power Modules Books

Steck-Vaughn Company
PO Box 690789
Orlando, FL   32819
                                   800-531-5015
                                   FAX 512-343-6854
                                   http://www.steck-vaughn.com
                                   e-mail: info@steck-vaughn.com

Supplementary reading based on 4 decades of reading research. Companion books give students and teachers a choice of formats. High interest stories reinforce reading comprehension skills while building vocabulary, spelling skills, reading fluency, and speed.

2095 Reading Realities Elementary Series

Teacher Support Software
3542 NW 97th Boulevard
Gainesville, FL   32606   352-332-6404
                                   800-228-2871
                                   FAX 352-332-6779
                                   http://www.tssoftware.com
Ruth Smith, Educational Software Consultant

Students will read about topics that focus on issues they face in their everyday lives. Over 1000 students contributed stories that make up the program. Students will benefit from prereading, reading and follow-up activities in a directed reading-thinking format. The manager tracks reading ability and class and student progress. Vocabulary support and speech make this a nonthreatening atmosphere for sharing and learning.

2096 Reading Skills Bundle

Sunburst Technology
400 Columbus Avenue
Valhalla, NY   10595   914-747-3310
                                   800-321-7511
                                   FAX 914-747-4109
                                   http://www.sunburst.com
                                   e-mail: support@sunburst.com

Teach beginning reading with teacher-developed programs that sequentially present phonics, phonemic awareness, word recognition, and reading comprehension concepts.

2097 Reading Who? Reading You!

Sunburst Technology
400 Columbus Avenue
Valhalla, NY   10595   914-747-3310
                                   800-321-7511
                              FAX 914-747-4109
                         http://www.sunburst.com
                         e-mail: support@sunburst.com

Teach beginning reading skills effectively with phonics instruction built into engaging games and puzzles that have children asking for more.

2098 Roots, Prefixes & Suffixes

Sunburst Technology
400 Columbus Avenue
Valhalla, NY   10595   914-747-3310
                                   800-321-7511
                              FAX 914-747-4109
                         http://www.sunburst.com
                         e-mail: support@sunburst.com

Students learn to decode difficult and more complex words as they engage in six activities where they construct and dissect words with roots, prefixes and suffixes.

2099 Sentence Master: Level 1, 2, 3, 4

Laureate Learning Systems
110 E Spring Street
Winooski, VT   05404   802-655-4755
                                   800-562-6801
                              FAX 802-655-4757
Mary Sweig Wilson, President
Bernard Fox, VP

A revolutionary way to teach beginning reading. Avoiding the confusing rules of phonics and the complexity of whole language, The Sentence Master focuses on the most frequently-used words of our language; i.e. the, is, but, and, etc., by truly teaching these little words, The Sentence Master gives students control over the majority of text they will ever encounter. *$475.00*

2100 Simon Sounds It Out

Don Johnston
26799 W Commerce Dive
Volo, IL   60073   847-740-0749
                                   800-999-4660
                              FAX 847-740-7326
                         http://www.donjohnston.com
                         e-mail: info@donjohnston.com
Christine Filler, Marketing/Channel Development

Struggling students who can recite the alphabet and recognize letters on a page may still have trouble making connections between letters and sounds. This creates a barrier to recognizing and learning words which prevents your students from reading and writing successfully. Simon Sounds It Out provides the vital practice and repetition they need to overcome the letter-to-sound barrier. *$59.00*

2101 Stickybear Software

Optimum Resource
18 Hunter Road
Hilton Head Island, SC   29926   843-689-8000
                                   888-784-2592
                              FAX 843-689-8008
                         http://www.stickybear.com
                         e-mail: stickyb@stickybear.com
Christopher J Gintz, COO
Robert Stangroom, Product Manager

An educational software publishing company for grades K-12. Our software titles are available in Consumer, School, Labpack or Site License versions. Please call for further details. Prices range from $59.95 for Consumer to $699.95 for Site Licenses.

2102 Time for Teachers Online

Stern Center for Language and Learning
135 Allen Brook Lane
Williston, VT   05495   802-878-2332
                                   800-544-4863
                              FAX 802-878-0230
                         http://www.sterncenter.org
                         e-mail: learning@sterncenter.org
Jakie Earle Cruickshanks

A 45 hour course completed entirely on the internet, designed to help teachers implement research-based best practices in reading instruction. *$525.00*

Science

2103 Changes Around Us CD-ROM

Steck-Vaughn Company
PO Box 690789
Orlando, FL   32819
                                   800-531-5015
                              FAX 800-699-9459
                         http://www.steck-vaughn.com
                         e-mail: info@steck-vaughn.com
Chris Lehman, Team Coordinator

Nature is the natural choice for observing change. By observing and researching dramatic visual sequences such as the stages of development of a butterfly, children develop a broad understanding of the concept of change. As they search this multimedia database for images and information about plant and animal life cycles and seasonal change, students strengthen their abilities in research, analysis, problem-solving, critical thinking and communication.

2104 Exploring Heat

TERC
2067 Massachusetts Avenue
Cambridge, MA   02140   617-547-0430
                              FAX 617-349-3535
                         http://www.terc.edu
                         e-mail: communications@terc.edu

A combination of lessons, software, temperature probes and activity sheets, specifically designed for the learning disabled child. *$160.00*

2105 Field Trip Into the Sea

Sunburst Technology
400 Columbus Avenue
Valhalla, NY   10595

914-747-3310
800-321-7511
FAX 914-747-4109
http://www.sunburst.com
e-mail: service@sunburst

Visit a kelp forest and the rocky shore with this information packed guide that lets your students learn about the plants, animals and habitats of coastal environments.

2106 Field Trip to the Rain Forest

Sunburst Technology
400 Columbus Avenue
Valhalla, NY   10595

914-747-3310
800-321-7511
FAX 914-747-4109
http://www.sunburst.com
e-mail: service@sunburst

Visit a Central American rainforest to learn more about its plants and animals with this dynamic research program that includes a useful information management tool.

2107 Learn About Life Science: Animals

Sunburst Technology
400 Columbus Avenue
Valhalla, NY   10595

914-747-3310
800-321-7511
FAX 914-747-4109
http://www.sunburst.com
e-mail: service@sunburst.com

Learn about animal classification, adaptation to climate, domestication and special relationships between humans and animals.

2108 Learn About Life Science: Plants

Sunburst Technology
400 Columbus Avenue
Valhalla, NY   10595

914-747-3310
800-321-7511
FAX 914-747-4109
http://www.sunburst.com
e-mail: service@sunburst.com

Students explore the world of plants. From small seeds to tall trees students learn what plants are and what they need to grow.

2109 Milliken Science Series: Circulation and Digestion

Milliken Publishing
11643 Liburn Park Raod
Saint Louis, MO   63132

314-991-4220
FAX 314-991-4807

Delores Boufard, Author

A program designed to introduce students to two subsystems of the human body. Provides practice using the correct terms for the various organs that make up each system, illustrating how the parts of each subsystem work together, and ensuring that students can explain the functions of the subsystems and their parts.

2110 NOMAD Graphics Packages

American Printing House for the Blind
1839 Frankfort Avenue
Louisville, KY   40206

502-895-2405
800-223-1839
FAX 502-899-2274
http://www.aph.org

Fred Gissoni, Customer Support

Offers a variety of ready-made graphics as well as pre-programmed computer files, for use with NOMAD Talking Touch Pad. Topics include geography, orientation and mobility, and Star Trek.

2111 Sammy's Science House

Edmark Corporation
PO Box 97021
Redmond, WA   98073

206-556-8400
800-691-2986
FAX 206-556-8430

Tina Martin, Education Marketing

Developed by early learning experts, the award-winning Sammy's Science House builds important early science skills, encourages wonder and joy as children discover the world of science around them. Five engaging activities help children practice sorting, sequencing, observing, predicting and constructing. They'll learn about plants, animals, minerals, fun seasons and weather, too! *$59.95*

2112 Talking Walls

Riverdeep
500 Redmond Boulevard
Novato, CA   94947

415-763-4700
800-362-2890
FAX 415-763-4385
http://www/elmark.com
e-mail: info@riverdeep.net

Barry O'Callaghan, Chairman/CEO
Simon Calver, COO
John Rim, CFO

The Talking Walls Software Series is a wonderful springboard for a student's journey of exploration and discovery. This comprehensive collection of researched resources and materials enables students to focus on learning while conducting a guided search for information.

2113 Talking Walls: The Stories Continue

Riverdeep
500 Redmond Boulevard
Novato, CA   94947

415-763-4700
800-362-2890
FAX 415-763-4385
http://www.elmark.com
e-mail: info@riverdeep.net

Barry O'Callaghan, Chairman/CEO
Simon Calver, COO
John Rim, CFO

Using the Talking Walls Software Series, students discover the stories behind some of the world's most fascinating walls. The award-winning books, interactive software, carefully chosen Web sites, and suggested classroom activities build upon each other, providing a rich learning experience that includes text, video, and hands-on projects.

Social Studies

2114   Discoveries: Explore the Desert Ecosystem

Sunburst Technology
400 Columbus Avenue
Valhalla, NY   10595   914-747-3310
                                    800-321-7511
                              FAX 914-747-4109
                        http://www.sunburst.com
                        e-mail: service@sunburst.com

This program invites students to explore the plants, animals, culture and georgraphy of the Sonoran Desert by day and by night.

2115   Discoveries: Explore the Everglades Ecosystem

Sunburst Technology
400 Columbus Avenue
Valhalla, NY   10595   914-747-3310
                                    800-321-7511
                              FAX 914-747-4109
                        http://www.sunburst.com
                        e-mail: service@sunburst.com

This multi curricular research program takes students to the Everglades where they anchor their exploration photo realistic panaramas of the habitiat.

2116   Discoveries: Explore the Forest Ecosystem

Sunburst Technology
400 Columbus Avenue
Valhalla, NY   10595   914-747-3310
                                    800-321-7511
                              FAX 914-747-4109
                        http://www.sunburst.com
                        e-mail: service@sunburst.com

This theme based CD-ROM enables students of all abilities to actively research a multitude of different forest ecosystems in the Appalachian National Park.

2117   Imagination Express: Castle

Edmark Corporation
PO Box 97021
Redmond, WA   98073   206-556-8400
                                    800-691-2986
                              FAX 206-556-8430

Kids enter a medieval kingdom where knights, jesters, wild boars and falconers become actors in their own interactive stories. As kids cast characters, develop plots, narrate and write and record dialogue, they become enthusiastic writers, editors, producers and publishers! *$59.95*

2118   Imagination Express: Neighborhood

Edmark Corporation
PO Box 97021
Redmond, WA   98073   206-556-8400
                                    800-691-2986
                              FAX 206-556-8430

In Destination: Neighborhood, familiar settings and characters encourage kids to write about actual or imagined adventures. Kids enjoy developing creativity, writing and communication skills as they explore the neighborhood and all the people who live there. As kids select scenes, choose and animate stickers, write, narrate, add music and record dialogue, their stories, journals, letters and poems come alive! *$59.95*

2119   Imagination Express: Ocean

Edmark Corporation
PO Box 97021
Redmond, WA   98073   206-556-8400
                                    800-691-2986
                              FAX 206-556-8430

The fascinating shores and depths of Destination: Ocean inspire kids to create interactive stories and movies. Using exciting new technology, kids make stickers move across each scene: sharks swim through the sea kelp while dolphins leap above waves! With Destination: Ocean, your child's writing and creativity will soar! *$59.95*

2120   Imagination Express: Pyramids

Edmark Corporation
PO Box 97021
Redmond, WA   98073   206-556-8400
                                    800-691-2986
                              FAX 206-556-8430

Kids can create interactive electronic books and movies featuring pharaohs, mummies and life on the Nile. Builds writing, creativity and communication skills as they learn about and explore this captivating destination. Kids select scenes, choose and animate characters, plan plots, write stories, narrate pages and add music, dialogue and sound effects to make their own adventures. *$59.95*

2121   Imagination Express: Rain Forest

Edmark Corporation
PO Box 97021
Redmond, WA   98073   206-556-8400
                                    800-691-2986
                              FAX 206-556-8430

Rain Forest invites kids to step into a Panamanian rain forest, where they craft exciting, interactive adventures filled with exotic plants, insects, waterfalls and Kuna Indians. Kids build essential communication skills as they select scenes and characters, plan plots, write, narrate, animate and record dialogue to create remarkable adventures! *$59.95*

2122 Imagination Express: Time Trip USA

Edmark Corporation
PO Box 97021
Redmond, WA 98073   206-556-8400
     800-691-2986
     FAX 206-556-8430

Children will love traveling through time to create interactive electronic books and movies set in a fictional New England town. As students select scenes, cast charcters, develop plots, narrate, write and record dialogue, they'll bring the town's history to life through their own exciting adventures. *$59.95*

2123 NOMAD Graphics Packages

American Printing House for the Blind
1839 Frankfort Avenue
Louisville, KY 40206   502-895-2405
     800-223-1839
     FAX 502-899-2274
     http://www.aph.org
Fred Gissoni, Customer Support

Offers a variety of ready-made graphics as well as preprogrammed computer files, for use with NOMAD Talking Touch Pad. Topics include geography, orientation and mobility, and Star Trek.

Speech

2124 Eden Institute Curriculum: Speech and Language, Volume IV

One Eden Way
Princeton, NJ 08540   609-987-0099
     FAX 609-987-0243
     http://www.edenservices.org
     e-mail: info@edenservices.org
David L Holmes, Executive Director/President
Anne Holmes, Director Outreach Support Svcs

Peceptive, expressive and pragmatic language skills programs for students with autism. *$170.00*

2125 Spectral Speech Analysis: Software

The Speech Bin
1965 25th Avenue
Vero Beach, FL 32960   772-770-0007
     FAX 772-770-0006
     http://www.speechbin.com
     e-mail: info@speechbin.com

This exciting new software uses visual feedback as an effective speech treatment tool. Speech-language pathologists can record speech and corresponding visual displays for clients who then try to match either auditory or visual targets. These built-in visual patterns can be displayed as either sophisticated spectrograms or real-time waveforms. Item number P227. *$159.95*

Word Processors

2126 Braille' n Speak Classic

American Printing House for the Blind
1839 Frankfort Avenue
Louisville, KY 40206   502-895-2405
     800-223-1839
     FAX 502-899-2274
     http://www.aph.org
Fred Gissoni, Customer Support

This computerized, talking device has many features useful to student and adult braille users (word processors, print-to-braille translators, talking clocks/calculators and much more). *$929.95*

2127 Kids Media Magic 2.0

Sunburst Technology
400 Columbus Avenue
Valhalla, NY 10595   914-747-3310
     800-321-7511
     FAX 914-747-4109
     http://www.sunburst.com
     e-mail: service@sunburst.com

The first multimedia word processor designed for young children. Help your child become a fluent reader and writer. The Rebus Bar automatically scrolls over 45 vocabulary words as students type.

2128 Media Weaver 3.5

Sunburst Technology
400 Columbus Avenue
Valhalla, NY 10595   914-747-3310
     800-321-7511
     FAX 914-747-4109
     http://www.sunburst.com
     e-mail: support@sunburst.com

Publishing becomes a multimedia event with this dynamic word processor that contains hundreds of media elements and effective process writing resources.

2129 Sunbuddy Writer

Sunburst Technology
400 Columbus Avenue
Valhalla, NY 10595   914-747-3310
     800-321-7511
     FAX 914-747-4109
     http://www.sunburst.com
     e-mail: support@sunburst.com

An easy-to-use picture and word processor designed especially for young writers.

2130 Write: Outloud

Don Johnston
26799 W Commerce Drive
Volo, IL 60073   847-740-0749
     800-999-4660
     FAX 847-740-7326
     http://www.donjohnston.com
     e-mail: info@donjohnston.com
Christine Filler, Marketing/Channel Development

A flexible and user-friendly talking word processor that offers multisensory learning and positive reinforcement for writers of all ages and ability levels. Powerful features include a talking spell checker, on-screen speech and file management and color capabilities that allow for customization to meet individual needs or preferences. Requires Macintosh computer. Voted Best Special Needs Product by the Software Publishers Association. *$99.00*

Writing

2131 Abbreviation/Expansion

Zygo Industries
PO Box 1008
Portland, OR   97207   503-297-1724
                                        800-234-6006
                                        FAX 503-684-6011

Allows the individual to define and store word/phrase abbreviations to achieve efficiency and accelerated entry rate of text. *$95.00*

2132 Author's Toolkit

Sunburst Technology
400 Columbus Avenue
Valhalla, NY   10595   914-747-3310
                                        800-321-7511
                                        FAX 914-747-4109
                                        http://www.sunburst.com
                                        e-mail: support@sunburst.com

Students can use this comprehensive tool to organize ideas, make outlines, rough drafts, edit and print all their written work.

2133 Dr. Peet's Picture Writer

Dr. Peet's Software
4241 Aldrich Avenue
Minneapolis, MN   55409   612-827-8060
                                        800-354-2950
                                        FAX 386-426-0100
                                        http://www.drpeet.com
                                        e-mail: wpeet@drpeet.com

A talking picture-writer. It guides novice writers, regardless of age, motivation or ability, in creating simple talking picture sentences about things that are interesting and important to them. *$500.00*

2134 Easybook Deluxe

Sunburst Technology
400 Columbus Avenue
Valhalla, NY   10595   914-747-3310
                                        800-321-7511
                                        FAX 914-747-4109
                                        http://www.sunburst.com
                                        e-mail: service@sunburst.com

Designed to support the needs of a wide range of writers, this book publishing tool provides students with a creative environment to write, design and illustrate stories and reports, and to print their work in book formats.

2135 Fonts 4 Teachers

Therapro
225 Arlington Street
Framingham, MA   01702   508-872-9494
                                        800-257-5376
                                        FAX 508-875-2062
                                        http://www.theraproducts.com
                                        e-mail: info@theraproducts.com
Karen Conrad, President

A software collection of 31 True Type fonts for teachers, parents and students. Fonts include Tracing, lined and unlined Traditional Manuscript and Cursive (similar to Zaner Blouser and D'Nealian), math, clip art, decorative, time, American Sign Language symbols and more. The included manual is very informative, with great examples of lesson plans and educational goals. *$39.95*

Windows/Mac

2136 Great Beginnings

Teacher Support Software
3542 NW 97th Boulevard
Gainesville, FL   32606   352-332-6404
                                        800-228-2871
                                        FAX 352-332-6779
                                        http://www.tssoftware.com
                                        e-mail: tssoftware.com
Ruth Smith, Educational Software Consultant

From a broad selection of topics and descriptive words, students may create their own stories and illustrate them with colorful graphics. *$69.95*

2137 Language Experience Recorder

Teacher Support Software
3542 NW 97th Boulevard
Gainesville, FL   32606   352-332-6404
                                        800-228-2871
                                        FAX 352-332-6779
                                        http://www.tssoftware.com
                                        e-mail: tssoftware.com
Ruth Smith, Educational Software Consultant

This program provides students with the opportunity to read, write and hear their own experience stories. Analyzes student writing. Cumulative word list, word and sentence counts and readability estimate. *$99.95*

2138 Once Upon a Time Volume I: Passport to Discovery

Compu-Teach
PMB 137, 16541 Redmond Way
Redmond, WA   98052   425-885-0517
                                        800-448-3224
                                        FAX 425-883-9169
                                        http://www.compu-teach.com
                                        e-mail: info@compu-teach.com
David Urban, President

Features familiar objects associated with three unique themes. These graphic images offer limitless possibilities for new stories and illustrations. As children author books from one to hundreds of pages, they can either display them on screen or print them out. Themes: Farm Life; Down Main Street; and On Safari. *$59.95*

Ages 4-12

2139 Once Upon a Time Volume II: Worlds of Enchantment

Compu-Teach
PMB 137, 16541 Redmond Way
Redmond, WA   98052
425-885-0517
800-448-3224
FAX 425-883-9169
http://www.compu-teach.com
e-mail: info@compu-teach.com
David Urban, President

Makes writing, reading and vocabulary skills easy to learn. While building their illustrations, children experiment with perspective and other spatial relationships. This volume features familiar objects associated with three unique themes: Underwater; Dinosaur Age; and Forest Friends. *$59.95*

Ages 4-12

2140 Once Upon a Time Volume III: Journey Through Time

Compu-Teach
PMB 137, 16541 Redmond Way
Redmond, WA   98052
425-885-0517
800-448-3224
FAX 425-883-9169
http://www.compu-teach.com
e-mail: info@compu-teach.com
David Urban, President

Makes writing, reading and vocabulary skills easy to learn. With imagination as a youngster's only guide, the important concepts of story creation and illustration are naturally discovered. Themes: Medieval Times, Wild West and Outer Space. *$59.95*

Ages 4-12

2141 Once Upon a Time Volume IV: Exploring Nature

Compu-Teach
PMB 137, 16541 Redmond Way
Redmond, WA   98052
425-885-0517
800-448-3224
FAX 425-883-9169
http://www.compu-teach.com
e-mail: info@compu-teach.com
David Urban, President

The latest in award-winning creative writing series. Kids just hear, click and draw as the state of the art graphics and digitized voice make writing, reading and vocabulary skills easy to learn. Themes: Rain Forest; African Grasslands; Ocean; Desert; and Forest. *$59.95*

2142 Raised Dot Computing Mega Dots

Duxbury Systems
270 Littleton Road
Westford, MA   01886
978-692-3000
800-347-9594
FAX 978-692-7912
http://www.duxsys.com
e-mail: joe@duxsys.com

MegaDots is a mature DOS braille translator with powerful features for the volume transcriber and producer. Its straightforward, style based system and automated features let you create great braille with only a few keystrokes, yet it is sophisticated enough to please the fussiest braille producers. You can control each step MegaDots follows to format, translate and produce braille documents. *$540.00*

2143 Read, Write and Type Learning System

Talking Fingers, California Neuropsych Services
1st St. Vincents Street
San Rafael, CA   94903
415-472-3104
800-674-9126
FAX 415-472-7812
http://www.readwritetype.com
e-mail: info@talkingfingers.com

A 40-level software adventure providing highly motivating instruction and practice in phonics, reading, writing, spelling and typing. This multisensory program includes 9 levels of assessment and reports. Classroom packs available.

2144 StartWrite

Therapro
225 Arlington Street
Framingham, MA   01702
508-872-9494
800-257-5376
FAX 508-875-2062
http://www.theraproducts.com
e-mail: info@theraproducts.com
Therapro Staff, Author
Karen Conrad, President

With this easy-to-use software package, you can make papers and handwriting worksheets to meet individual student's needs. Type letters, words, or numbers and they appear in a dot format on the triple line guide. Change letter size, add shading, turn on or off guide lines and arrow strokes and place provided clipart. Fonts include Manuscript and Cursive, Modern Manuscript and Cursive and Italic Manuscript and Cursive. Useful manual included. *$39.95*

Windows/Mac

2145 Wish Writer

Consultants for Communication Technology
508 Bellevue Terrace
Pittsburgh, PA   15202
412-761-6062
FAX 412-761-7336
e-mail: 70272.1034@compuserve.com
Kathleen H Miller PhD, Partner/Speech Pathologist
Jaime Olivia, Partner

Wish Writer is a word processing program designed to be used by keyboard or single switch users. Word Prediction feature produces documents with fewer keystrokes. When used with the K, S, or multivoice synthesizers, text typed into the PC can be spoken or printed. *$300.00*

2146 Write

Computers to Help People
825 E Johnson Street
Madison, WI   53703   608-257-5917
                                     FAX 608-257-3480
John J Boyer, Executive Director/Founder
Dee Dee Collette, Administrative Director

Enter up to 20 words/sentences which are displayed in large letters word-by-word for the pupil. We specialize in Verbal Math, Large Print, and Braille Translations of Math and Science textbooks. *$50.00*

2147 Writing Trek Grades 4-6

Sunburst Technology
400 Columbus Avenue
Valhalla, NY   10595   914-747-3310
                                     800-321-7511
                                     FAX 914-747-4109
                                     http://www.sunburst.com
                                     e-mail: service@sunburst.com

Enhance your students' experience in your English language arts classroom with twelve authentic writing projects that build students' competence while encouraging creativity.

2148 Writing Trek Grades 6-8

Sunburst Technology
400 Columbus Avenue
Valhalla, NY   10595   914-747-3310
                                     800-321-7511
                                     FAX 914-747-4109
                                     http://www.sunburst.com
                                     e-mail: service@sunburst.com

Twelve authentic language arts projects, activities, and assignments develop your students' writing confidence and ability.

2149 Writing Trek Grades 8-10

Sunburst Technology
400 Columbus Avenue
Valhalla, NY   10595   914-747-3310
                                     800-321-7511
                                     FAX 914-747-4109
                                     http://ww.sunburst.com
                                     e-mail: service@sunburst.com

Help your students develop a concept of genre as they become familiar with the writing elements and characteristics of a variety of writing forms.

General

2150 American Institute for Foreign Study

River Plaza
Stamford, CT 06902   203-399-5000
FAX 203-399-5590
http://www.aifs.com
e-mail: info@aifs.com
William Gertz, Executive Vice President

Provides summer travel programs overseas and in the US ranging from one week to a full academic year.

2151 American Universities International Program

Colorado University
307 S College Avenue
Fort Collins, CO 80523   970-495-0869
888-692-2847
FAX 970-484-6997
http://www.auip.com
e-mail: info@auip.com

One hundred colleges and universities throughout the USA and Canada that participate in exchange programs.

2152 American-Scandinavian Foundation

58 Park Avenue
New York, NY 10016   212-879-9779
FAX 212-686-2115
http://www.amscan.org
e-mail: info@amscan.org
Jean Prahl, Director Training

Offers young US citizens the opportunity to live in Scandinavia and train in their professional field.

2153 Association for International Practical Training

10400 Little Patuxent Parkway
Columbia, MD 21044   410-997-2200
FAX 410-992-3924
http://www.aipt.org
e-mail: aipt@aipt.org
Dr. Jackson Janes, Executive Director
Dr. Cathleen Fisher, Associate Director
Lynn Van Norstrand, Financial Officer

Be a leader in international human resource development by conducting high-quality international experiential training exchanges that enhance the ability of individual participants, employers, and host organizations to meet the opportunities and challenges of the global economy.

2154 Earthstewards Network

PO Box 10697
Bainbridge Island, WA 98110   206-842-7986
800-561-2909
FAX 206-842-8918
http://www.earthstewards.org
e-mail: outreach@earthstewards.org
Beverly Duperly Boos, Vice President
Chuck Meadows, Treasurer

Hundreds of active, caring people in the US, Canada and other countries. Puts North American teenagers working alongside Northern Irish teenagers and more.

2155 Educational Foundation for Foreign Study

1 Education Street
Cambridge, MA 02141
800-447-4273
FAX 617-619-1401
http://www.effoundation.org
Asa Fanelli, President

Offers an opportunity to study and live for a year in a foreign country for students between the ages of 15 and 18.

2156 Higher Education Consortium for Urban Affairs

2233 University Avenue W
Saint Paul, MN 55114   651-646-8831
800-554-1089
FAX 651-659-9421
http://www.hecua.org
e-mail: info@hecua.org
Michael Eaton, Director of Enrollment Services
Judy Sharken Simon, Assistant to Director
Phil Hatlie, Director of Operations

Consortium of 15 Midwest colleges and universities offering undergraduate, academic programs, both international and domestic that incorporate field study and internships in the examination of urban and global issues.

2157 International Summerstays

620 SW 5th Avenue
Portland, OR 97204   503-274-1776
800-274-6007
FAX 503-274-9004
http://www.summerstays.org
e-mail: info2summerstays.org
Melinda Samis, Director
Patty Hayashi, Assistant Director

Offers summer homestays in a different country for teenagers from Oregon only to Spain, Germany and France.

2158 Lisle Fellowship

900 County Road
Leander, TX 78641   512-259-7621
800-477-1538
FAX 512-259-0392
http://www.lisleinternational.org
e-mail: lisle@utnet.utoledo.edu
Mark Kinney, Executive Director

Educational organization which works toward world peace and a better quality of human life through increased understanding between persons of similar and different cultures.

2159 National Society for Experiential Education

515 King Street
Alexandria, VA 22314   703-706-9552
FAX 703-684-6048
http://www.nsee.org
e-mail: info@nsee.org
Dr. Linda Goff, Director
Albert Cabral, Vice President
Carole Rogin, Executive Director

National nonprofit membership organization which supports the use of learning through experience for intellectual development, civic and social responsibility, career exploration and ethical development. Fosters the effective use of experience as an integral part of education.

2160 No Barriers to Study

Lock Haven University
401 N Fairview Street
Lock Haven, PA 17745   570-893-2157
800-223-8978
FAX 570-893-2659
Russell C Jameson Jr, Resident Hall Director
Dr. Roger B Johnson, Dean

A regional consortium committed to facilitating study abroad for college students with disabilities.

2161 People to People International

501 E Armour Boulevard
Kansas City, MO 64109   816-531-4701
FAX 816-561-7502
http://www.ptpi.org
e-mail: ptpi@ptpi.org
Mary Eisenhower, President
Marc L Bright, Executive Vice President
Rosanne Rosen, Senior Vice President Operations

Nonpolitical, nonprofit organization working outside the government to advance the cause of international understanding through international contact.

2162 United States Information Agency

301 4th Street SW
Washington, DC 20547   202-619-4355
FAX 202-619-6988
http://www.usia.gov
Frances Sullinger, Acting Director

Programs are designed to increase mutual understanding between the people of the US and the people of other countries.

2163 World Experience

2440 S Hacienda Boulevard
Hacienda Heights, CA 91745   626-336-3638
800-633-6653
FAX 626-333-4914
http://www.worldexperience.org
e-mail: weworld@weworld.com

Nonprofit organization which sponsors, develops and carries out international student exchange programs for study and service abroad.

2164 Youth for Understanding USA

6400 Goldsboro Road
Bethesda, MD 20817   240-235-2100
866-493-8872
FAX 240-235-2104
http://www.YouthForUnderstanding.org
e-mail: admissions@yfu.org
Mike Finnell, President

Nonprofit international exchange program, prepares young people for their responsibilities and opportunities in todays changing, interdependent world through homestay exchange programs. Offers year, semester, and summer study abroad and scholarship opportunities in 34 countries worldwide.

Federal

2165 Administration on Children, Youth and Families: US Department of Education

330 C Street SW
Washington, DC 20447 202-205-8347
FAX 202-205-9721
http://www.acf.hhs.gov
Frank Fuentes, Deputy Commissioner

Programs under the Administration include the Children's Bureau, Head Start, Child Care Bureau, and The Family and Youth Services Bureau.

2166 Civil Rights Division: US Department of Justice

Coordination and Review Section
950 Pennsylvania Avenue NW
Washington, DC 20530 202-307-2222
FAX 202-307-0595
TDY:800-514-0383
R Alexander Costa, Assistant Attorney General

Coordinates the reinforcement of Section 504 which prohibits discrimination on the basis of disability in all federally conducted programs and activities, and in the programs and activities that receive federal financial assistance.

2167 Clearinghouse on Adult Education and Literacy

US Department of Education
400 Maryland Avenue SW
Washington, DC 20202 202-401-2000
800-872-5327
FAX 202-401-0689
http://www.ed.gov

The Clearinghouse was established in 1981 to link the adult education community with existing resources in adult education, provide information which deals with state administered adult education programs funded under the Adult Education and Family Literacy Act, and provide resources that support adult education activities.

2168 Developmental Disability Services: US Department of Health & Human Services

200 Independence Avenue SW
Washington, DC 20201 202-619-0257
877-696-6775
FAX 202-690-7203
http://www.hhs.gov
Scott Whittaker, Chief of Staff
Andrew Knapp, Deputy Chief of Staff

Councils in each state provide training and technical assistance to local and state agencies, employers and the public, improving services to people with developmental disabilities.

2169 Employment Standards Administration: US Department of Labor

Frances Perkins Building
Washington, DC 20210 202-693-5000
866-487-2365
FAX 202-693-0218
http://www.dol.gov
Elaine L Chao, Secretary of Labor
Steven J Law, Deputy Secretary

Develops policy and implements legislation for all workers in the nation.

2170 Employment and Training Administration: US Department of Labor

Frances Perkins Building
200 Constitution Avenue NW
Washington, DC 20210 202-693-2700
877-872-5627
FAX 202-693-2725
http://www.doleta.gov
Grace Kilbane, Administrator

Through more than 1,700 state and local offices nationwide, provides employment services to job seekers, including employability assessments, job counseling, occupational training referral, job placement, and trained specialists to work with the specific needs of job-seekers with disabilities.

2171 Equal Employment Opportunity Commission

1801 L Street NW
Washington, DC 20507 202-663-4900
800-669-4000
FAX 202-663-4639

Cari M Dominguez, Chair
Naomi C Earp, Vice Chair
Paul Steven Miller, Commissioner

Enforces Section 501 which prohibits discrimination on the basis of disability in Federal employment, and requires that all Federal agencies establish and implement affirmative action programs for hiring, placing and advancing individuals with disabilities. Also oversees Federal sector equal employment opportunity complaint processing system.

2172 National Institute of Child Health and Human Development

1 Center Drive
Bethesda, MD 20892 301-496-4000
800-370-2943
FAX 301-496-7101
http://www.nih.gov/nichd
e-mail: nihinfo@gov
Elias A Zerhouni MD, Director

Its mission is science in pursuit of fundamental knowledge about the nature and behavior of living systems and the application of that knowledge to extend healthy life and reduce the burdens of illness and disability.

2173 National Institute of Mental Health

6001 Executive Boulevard
Bethesda, MD   20892   301-443-4513
                                        866-615-6464
                              FAX 301-443-5158
                      http://www.nimh.nih.gov
                      e-mail: nimhinfo@nih.gov
Thomas R Insel MD, Director
Richard K Nakamura PhD, Deputy Director
William T Fitzsimmons, Executive Officer

Mission is to diminish the burden of mental illness
through research. This public health mandate demands that we harness powerful scientific tools to
achieve better understanding, treatment and eventually prevention of mental illness.

2174 National Institute on Disability and Rehabilitation Research

US Department of Education
400 Maryland Avenue
Washington, DC   20202   202-205-5465
                              FAX 202-205-9252
                      http://www.ed.gov/offices
Rod Paige, US Secretary Education
Anne Radice, Chief of Staff
Philip Link, Executive Secertariat Director

Offers information about special education programs,
vocational rehabilitation programs and information
about national and international research regarding
disabilities and rehabilitation.

2175 National Library Services for the Blind and Physically Handicapped

Library of Congress
1291 Taylor Street NW
Washington, DC   20011   202-707-5100
                                     800-424-8567
                              FAX 202-707-0712
                              TDY:202-707-0744
                      http://www.nls@loc.gov
                      e-mail: nls@loc.gov
Frank Kurt Cylke, Director
Marvine R Wanamaker, Assistant Director

Administers a free program that loans recorded and
braille books and magazines, music scores in braille
and large print, and specially designed playback
equipment to residents of the United States who are
unable to read or use standard print materials because
of visual or physical impairment.

2176 National Technical Information Service

US Department of Commerce
5285 Port Royal Road
Springfield, VA   22161   703-605-6000
                                     800-553-6867
                              FAX 703-605-6900
                              TDY:703-487-4639
                      http://www.ntis.gov
                      e-mail: info@ntis.fedworld.gov
Ron Lawson, Director

Our mission supports the nation's economic growth
by providing access to information that stimulates innovation and discovery.

2177 National Technical Information Service: US Department of Commerce

5285 Port Royal Road
Springfield, VA   22161   703-487-4650
                              FAX 703-321-8547
                      http://www.ntis.gov

Maintains a worldwide database for research, development and engineering reports on a range of topics,
including architectural barrier removal, employing
individuals with disabilities, alternative testing formats, job accommodations, school-to-work transition
for students with disabilities, rehabilitation engineering, disability law and transportation.

2178 Office of Civil Rights: US Department of Health and Human Services

US Department of Health & Human Services
200 Independence Avenue SW
Washington, DC   20201   202-619-0403
                                     800-368-1019
                              FAX 202-619-3437
                              TDY:800-537-7697
Richard Campanelli, Director

Responsible for investigating discrimination on the
basis of race, color, national origin and religion in
programs receiving financial assistance from the US
Department of Health and Human Services.

2179 Office of Civil Rights: US Department of Education

330 C Street SW
Washington, DC   20202   202-205-5413
                                     800-421-3481
                              FAX 202-205-9862
                              TDY:877-521-2172
                      http://www.ed.gov
                      e-mail: ocr@ed.gov
Rod Paige, US Secretary of Education

Our mission is to ensure access to education and to
promote educational excellence throughout the nation
through vigorous enforecement of civil rights.

2180 Office of Disability Employment Policy

US Department of Labor
200 Constitution Avenue NW
Washington, DC   20210   202-693-7880
                                     866-487-2365
                              FAX 202-693-7888
                      http://www.dol.gov/odep
                      e-mail: infoodep@dol.gov
Elaine L Chao, Secretary of Labor
Steven J Law, Deputy Secretary
Ruth D Knouse, Executive Secretariat Director

Provides national leadership to increase employment
opportunities for adults and youth with disabilities,
while striving to eliminate barriers to employment.

2181 Office of Federal Contract Compliance Programs: US Department of Labor

Frances Perkins Building
Washington, DC   20210   202-693-0101
                                     866-487-2365
                              FAX 202-693-1304
                      http://www.dol.gov/esa/ofccp
William E Doyle Jr, Deputy Assistant Secretary
Shawn Hooper, Chief of Staff

Administers a variety of federal labor laws including those that guarantee worker's rights to safe and healthful working conditions; a minimum hourly wage and overtime pay; freedom from employment discrimination; unemployment insurance; and other income support.

2182   Office of Personnel Management

Office of Human Resources & EEO
1900 E Street NW
Washington, DC   20415   202-606-1800
                                FAX 202-606-1732
Kay Coles James, Director
Ruth E McGinn, Special Assistant to Director
Dan G Blair, Deputy Director

The central personnel agency of the federal government. Provides information on the selective placement program for persons with disabilities.

2183   Office of Program Operations: US Department of Education

400 Maryland Avenue SW
Washington, DC   20202
                                800-872-5327
                                FAX 202-401-0689
                                http://www.ed.gov
                                e-mail: customerservice@inet.ed.gov

Programs in each state provide information and assistance to individuals seeking or receiving services under the Rehabilitation Act of 1973.

2184   Rehabilitation Services Administration State Vocational Program

US Department of Education
400 Maryland Avenue SW
Washington, DC   20202
                                800-872-5327
                                FAX 202-401-0689

State and local vocational rehabilitation agencies provide comprehensive services of rehabilitation, training and job-related assistance to people with disabilities and assist employers in recruiting, training, placing, accommodating and meeting other employment-related needs of people with disabilities.

2185   Social Security Administration

Office of Public Inquiries
Windsor Park Building
Baltimore, MD   21235
                                800-772-1213
                                FAX 202-395-7298
                                http://www.ffagov
Jo Anne B Barnhart, Commissioner

Provides financial assistance to those with disabilities who meet eligibility requirements.

2186   US Bureau of the Census

4700 Silver Hill Road
Washington, DC   20233   301-457-4090
                                FAX 301-457-2778
                                http://www.census.gov
                                e-mail: pio@census.gov
Charles L Kincannon, Director
Betty Ann Saucier, Executive Assistant
Herman Habermann, Deputy Director, COO

The principal statistical agency of the federal government. It publishes data on persons with disabilities, as well as other demographic data derived from censuses and surveys.

Alabama

2187   Alabama Department of Industrial Relations

649 Monroe Street
Montgomery, AL   36130   334-242-8003
                                FAX 334-242-8843
                                http://www.dir.state.al.us
                                e-mail: webmaster@dir.state.al.us

2188   Alabama Disabilities Advocacy Program

University of Alabama
Tuscaloosa, AL   35487   205-348-4928
                                800-826-1675
                                FAX 205-348-3909
                                TDY:205-348-9484
                                http://www.adap.net
                                e-mail: adap@law.ua.edu
Reuben W Cook, Director

2189   Council for Developmental Disabilities

100 N Union Street
Montgomery, AL   36130   334-242-3973
                                800-232-2158
                                FAX 334-242-0797
                                e-mail: addpc@mh.state.al.us
Sheryl R Matney, Executive Director

The council provides systems change, capacity building and advocacy efforts throughout the state for people with the most significant disabilities.

2190   Employment Service Division: Alabama

Department of Industrial Relations
649 Monroe Street
Montgomery, AL   36131   334-242-8003
                                FAX 334-242-8012
                                e-mail: shorton@dir.state.al.us

Alaska

2191   Alaska Department of Labor: Employment Security Division

Department of Labor
PO Box 25509
Juneau, AK   99802   907-465-2712
                                FAX 907-465-2101

2192 Assistive Technology: Metro Region

Anchorage Metro Branch Office
1251 Muldoon Road
Anchorage, AK 99504   907-269-3550
     800-478-3387
     FAX 907-269-3630
     e-mail: mshiffer@educ.state.ak.us
Shari Lee, Vocational Rehab Manager

Information and referral to Alaska residents with disabilities about adaptive aids and equipment that will better their lives.

2193 Center for Community

700 Katlian Street
Sitka, AK 99835   907-747-6960
     800-478-6962
     FAX 907-747-4868
Margaret Andrews, Director Services

Center for Community is a multiservice agency that provides early intervention, respite, futures planning, functional skills training, and vocational assistance for people with disabilities.

2194 Correctional Education Division: Alaska

Department of Corrections/Division of Institutions
4500 Diplomacy Drive
Anchorage, AK 99508   907-269-7416
     FAX 907-269-7420
     http://www.correct.state.ak.us/
     e-mail: webmaster@correct.state.ak.us
Rose Munago, Criminal Justice Planner

2195 Disability Law Center of Alaska

3330 Arctic Boulevard
Anchorage, AK 99503   907-565-1002
     800-478-1234
     FAX 907-565-1000
     http://www.dlcak.org
     e-mail: akpa@dlcak.org
David C Fleurant, Executive Director

2196 Fair Employment Practice Agency

Alaska State Commission for Human Rights
800 A Street
Anchorage, AK 99501   907-274-4692
     800-478-4692
     FAX 907-278-8588
     TDY:907-276-3177

2197 State Department of Adult Education

Department of Education
801 W 10th Street
Juneau, AK 99801   907-465-2800
     FAX 907-465-4156
     http://www.eed.state.ak.us/
     e-mail: mpartlow@aduc.state.ak.us
Marsha Partlow, State Supervisor

2198 State Department of Education

801 W 10th Street
Juneau, AK 99801   907-465-2900
     FAX 907-465-3452
     http://www/educ.state.ak.us/
Vince Barry, Director, EPS

2199 State GED Administration: GED Testing Program

Alaska Department of Education
801 W 10th Street
Juneau, AK 99801   907-465-8707
     FAX 907-465-3240
Constance Munro, Administrator

2200 State of Alaska Community & Regional Affairs Department: Administrative Services

150 3rd Street
Juneau, AK 99801   907-465-4708
     FAX 907-465-3519

Arizona

2201 Adult & Family Literacy Education

Arizona Department of Education
1535 W Jefferson Street
Phoenix, AZ 85007   602-258-2410
     FAX 602-258-4986
     http://www.literacynet.org
     e-mail: kliersc@ade.az.gov
Karen Liersch, State Director

2202 Arizona Center for Law in the Public Interest

18 E Ochoa
Tucson, AZ 85701   520-529-1798
     FAX 520-529-2927
     http://www.NAU.edu\~ihd/acdl.html
     e-mail: info@aclpi.org
Leslie Cohen, Executive Director

2203 Arizona Department of Economic Security

Rehabilitation Services Administration
1789 W Jefferson Street 930-A
Phoenix, AZ 85007   602-542-3794
     800-563-1221
     FAX 602-542-3778
     http://www.de.state.az.us

2204 Arizona Department of Education

1535 W Jefferson Street
Phoenix, AZ   85007   602-542-5460
                             800-352-8400
                         FAX 602-542-5440
                    http://www.ade.state.az.us
                    e-mail: ADE@ade.az.gov
Dr. Kathryn Lund, Special Education Director

2205 Arizona Governor's Committee on Employment of the Handicapped

5040 E Shea Boulevard
Scottsdale, AZ   85254   480-609-3888
                            FAX 480-556-9927
                        http://www.alsaz.org
                        e-mail: daniel@alsaz.org

2206 Correctional Education

Arizona Department of Corrections
1601 W Jefferson Street
Phoenix, AZ   85007   602-542-5810
                         FAX 602-364-0259
                  e-mail: bkilian@adc.state.az.us
Barbara Kilian MA NCC, Special Education Coordinator

2207 Fair Employment Practice Agency

Office of the Arizona Attorney General
1275 W Washington Street
Phoenix, AZ   85007   602-542-5263
                             877-491-5742
                         FAX 602-542-8885
                         TDY:602-542-5002
            http://www.attorney_general.state.az.us

2208 GED Testing Services

Arizona Department of Education
3rd Street Virginia
Phoenix, AZ   85007   602-258-2410
                         FAX 602-258-2410
              http://www.ade.state.az.us/adult-ed/

2209 Governor's Council on Developmental Disabilities

1717 W Jefferson Street
Phoenix, AZ   85007   602-542-4049
                             800-889-5893
                         FAX 602-542-5320
                         TDY:602-542-8920
Dr. Michael Ward, Executive Director

2210 Protection & Advocacy Agency

Arizona Center for Law in the Public Interest
100 N Stone Avenue
Tucson, AZ   85701   520-327-9547
                            800-922-1447
                        FAX 520-884-0992
                http://www.nau.edu/~ihd/acdl
                e-mail: center@acdl.com
Leslie Cohen, Executive Director

Arkansas

2211 Arkansas Department of Education

1401 W Capitol
Little Rock, AR   72201   501-682-2379
                             FAX 501-682-5159
                    http://www.arkedu.state.ar.us
                 e-mail: Mtolson@arkedu.k12.ar.us
Marcia Harding, Associate Director

2212 Arkansas Department of Human Services: Division of Rehabilitation Services

PO Box 1437
Little Rock, AR   72203   501-682-8707
                             FAX 501-682-8679
                    http://www.state.ar.us/dhs

2213 Arkansas Department of Special Education

54 Capitol Mall
Little Rock, AR   72201   501-371-2161
                             FAX 501-682-5159
                 e-mail: dsydoriak@arkedu.k12.ar.us
Dr. Diane Sydoriak, Associate Director

2214 Arkansas Department of Workforce Education

3 Capitol Mall
Little Rock, AR   72201   501-682-1970
                             FAX 501-682-1509
                    http://www.work-ed.state.ar.us
                 e-mail: steve.franks@mial.state.ar.us
Garland Hankins, Deputy Director

2215 Arkansas Employment Security Department

1 Pershing Circle
North Little Rock, AR   72114   501-682-3105
                                   FAX 501-682-3748
                                   TDY:501-296-1669
                         http://www.state.ar.us/esd
                 e-mail: ed.rolle.aesd@mial.state.ar.us
Albessie Thompson, Equal Opportunity Manager

2216 Arkansas Governor's Developmental Disabilities Council

5800 W 10th Street
Little Rock, AR   72204   501-661-2589
                                 FAX 501-661-2399
                                 TDY:501-661-2736
Wilma Stewart, Director

2217 Assistive Technology Project

Increasing Capabilities Access Network
2201 Brookwood Drive
Little Rock, AR   72202   501-666-8868
                                 800-828-2799
                                 FAX 501-666-5319
                  e-mail: sgaskin@compuserve.com
Sue Gaskin, Project Director

A consumer responsive statewide program promoting assistive technology devices and sources for persons of all ages with disabilities.

2218 Client Assistance Program (CAP): Arkansas Division of Persons with Disabilities

Disability Rights Center
1100 N University Avenue
Little Rock, AR   72207   501-296-1775
                                 800-482-1174
                                 FAX 501-296-1779
                 http://www.arkdisabilityrights.org
             e-mail: panda@arkdisabilityrights.org
Eddie Miller, CAP Director

The Client Assistance Program is mandated by the Federal Rehabilitation Act. It provides free services to consumers and applicants for projects, programs, and facilities funded under the Rehabilitation Act. CAP analyzes issues a consumer/applicant may have and provides advocacy services regarding Rehabilitation Act funded services.

2219 Department of Correction School District

8000 Correction Circle
Pine Bluff, AR   71603   870-267-6725
                                 FAX 870-267-6731
                  e-mail: allenc@adcsd.k12.ar.us
Charles F Allen PhD, Supervisor of Education Services

2220 Increasing Capabilities Access Network

ACES Project
2201 Brookwood Drive
Little Rock, AR   72202   501-603-0781
                                 FAX 501-603-0798
                                 TDY:501-666-8868
                  e-mail: jswilson@ars.state.ar.us
Sue Gaskin, Project Director

2221 Office of the Governor

State Capitol
Little Rock, AR   72201   501-682-3642
                                 FAX 501-682-1382
Julie Rhodes

2222 Protection & Advocacy Agency

Advocacy Services
1100 N University Avenue
Little Rock, AR   72207   501-296-1775
                                 800-482-1174
                                 FAX 501-296-1779
                    http://www.advocacyservices.org
             e-mail: panda@arkdisabilityrights.org
Nan Ellen East, Executive Director

2223 State GED Administration

Department of Workforce Education
3 Capitol Mall
Little Rock, AR   72201   501-682-1980
                                 FAX 501-682-1982
          http://www.work-ed.state.ar.us/ged/index.html
           e-mail: janice.hanlon@mail.state.ar.us
Janice Hanlon, GED Test Administrator

California

2224 California Department of Fair Employment and Housing

2014 T Street
Sacramento, CA   95814   916-227-0551
                                 FAX 916-227-2859
                                 http://www.dfeh.ca.gov

2225 California Department of Rehabilitation

PO Box 944222
Sacramento, CA   94244   916-263-7365
                                 FAX 916-263-7474
                                 TDY:916-263-7477
                                 http://www.rehab.cahwnet.gov

The mission of the Department of Rehabilitation is to assist Californians with disabilities in obtaining and retaining employment and maximizing their ability to live independently in their communities.

2226 California Department of Special Education

721 Capitol Mall
Sacramento, CA   95814   916-323-4768
                                 FAX 916-327-3516

2227 California Employment Development Department

800 Capitol Mall
Sacramento, CA   95814   916-654-8210
                                FAX 916-657-5294

Robert L Garcia

2228 California State Board of Education

1430 N Street
Sacramento, CA   95814   916-319-0827
                                FAX 916-319-0175
                        http://www.cde.ca.gov/board
Reed Hastings, President

2229 California State Council on Developmental Disabilities

2000 O Street
Sacramento, CA   95814   916-322-8481
                                FAX 916-443-4957
                                TDY:916-324-8420
                        http://www.scdd.ca.gov
                        e-mail: scdd@dss.ca.gov
Judy McDonald, Executive Director

2230 Career Assessment and Placement Center Whittier Union High School District

9401 S Painter Avenue
Whittier, CA   90602   562-698-8121
                                FAX 562-693-5354
Daniel Hubert

Provides job placement programs, remunerative work services and work adjustment training programs.

2231 Clearinghouse for Specialized Media

California Department of Education
560 J Street
Sacramento, CA   95814   916-445-5103
                                FAX 916-323-9732
                        http://www.cde.ca.gov
                        e-mail: rbrawley@cde.ca.gov
Rod Brawley, Specialist Educator Consultant

Supports access to general education curriculum by students with disabilities. This unit of the state special schools and services division produces accessible versions of textbooks, workbooks, and literature books adopted for all public schools by the State Board of Education.

2232 Education & Inmate Programs Unit

1515 S Street
Sacramento, CA   94283   916-445-8035
                                800-952-5544
                                FAX 916-324-1416
Gary L Sutherland

2233 Employment Development Department: Employment Services Woodland

California Health and Human Services Agency
825 E Street
Woodland, CA   95776   530-661-2600
                                FAX 530-668-3152
                                http://www.edd.ca.gov
Bill Burke, Contact

2234 Employment Development Department: Employment Services W Sacramento

California Health and Human Services Agency
500-A W Jefferson Boulevard
W Sacramento, CA   95605   916-375-6288
                                FAX 916-375-6310
                                http://www.edd.ca.gov
Bill Burke, Contact

2235 Pacific Disability and Business Technical Assistance Center

555 12th Street
Oakland, CA   94607   510-848-2980
                                800-949-4232
                                FAX 510-848-1981
                                TDY:510-848-1840
                        http://www.pacdbtac.org
                        e-mail: info@pdbtac.com
Erica Jones, Program Director

One of 10 federally funded regional resource centers of the Americans with Disabilities Act. We provide information, problem solving assistance and referrals for implementing the ADA.

2236 Region IX: Office of Federal Contract Compliance

US Department of Labor
200 Constitution Avenue NW
Washington, DC   20210   888-376-3227
                                866-487-2365
                                FAX 202-693-1304
                        http://www.dol.gov/esa/ofccp
Charles E James, President

These regional offices of agencies enforce laws prohibiting employment discrimination on the basis of disability.

2237 Region IX: US Department of Education-Office of Civil Rights

US Department of Education
50 UN Plaza
San Francisco, CA   94012   415-556-4120
                                FAX 415-437-7540
                                http://www.ed.gov
                        e-mail: loni_hancock@ed.gov
Emory Lee, Acting Director

The Office of Federal Contract Compliance Programs is part of the US Department of Labor's Employment Standards Administration. It has a national network of six regional offices, each with district and area offices in major metropolitan centers.

2238 Region IX: US Department of Health and Human Services-Office of Civil Rights

US Department of Health & Human Services
50 UN Plaza
San Francisco, CA 94102   415-437-8310
                                 FAX 415-437-8329

These regional offices of agencies enforce laws prohibiting employment discrimination on the basis of disability.

2239 Sacramento County Office of Education

9738 Lincoln Village Drive
Sacramento, CA 95827   916-228-2500
                              FAX 916-228-2403
Carole Talan, Executive Director

Colorado

2240 Client Assistance Program (CAP): California Division of Persons with Disabilities

PO Box 944222
Sacramento, CA 94244   916-263-7367
                              800-952-5544
                        FAX 916-263-7464
http://www.dor.ca.gov/public/contacts
           e-mail: capinfo@dor.ca.gov
Sheila Conlon Mentkowski, Director

The CAP is mandated by the Federal Rehabilitation Act. CAP provides free services to consumers and applicants for projects, programs, and facilities funded under the Rehabilitation Act. CAP services involve the analysis of issues a consumer/applicant may have and provision of advocacy services regarding Rehabilitation Act funded services.

2241 Colorado Assistive Technology Project

1245 E Colfax
Denver, CO 80218   303-315-1280
                          FAX 303-837-1208
                   http://www.uchsc.edu/atp
Cathy Bodine, Director

Designed to support capacity building and advocacy activities, and to assist states in maintaining permanent, comprehensive statewide programs of technology related assistance for all people with disabilities living in Colorado.

2242 Colorado Civil Rights Division

1560 Broadway
Denver, CO 80202   303-894-2997
                          FAX 303-894-7830

2243 Colorado Department of Labor and Employment

1515 Arapahoe
Denver, CO 80202   303-318-8886
                          FAX 303-318-8870
                   http://www.state.co.us

2244 Colorado Developmental Disabilities

3824 W Princeton Circle
Denver, CO 80236   303-866-7450
                      FAX 303-866-7470
                      TDY:303-866-7471
                e-mail: cddpc@aol.com
Donald St. Louis, Executive Director

2245 Correctional Education Division: Colorado

Colorado Department of Corrections
2862 S Circle Drive
Colorado Springs, CO 80906   719-540-4862
                                FAX 719-226-4565
         http://www.doc.state.co.us/programs.htm
                e-mail: pio@doc.state.co.us
Eric Brookens, Director Academic Education

2246 Increasing Capabilities Access Network (ICAN)

2201 Brookwood Drive
Little Rock, AR 72202   501-683-3014
                               800-828-2799
                          FAX 501-666-5319
                          TDY:501-666-8868
              http://www.arkansas-ICAN.org
          e-mail: sogaskin@ars.state.ar.us
Sue Gaskin, Project Director

ICAN is a federally funded program of the Arkansas Rehabilitation Service, designed to make technology information available and accessible for all who need it. The program provides information on new and existing technology free to any person regardless of age or disability.

2247 Region VIII: US Department of Education

Office of Civil Rights
1244 Spear Boulevard
Denver, CO 80204   303-844-3544
                          FAX 303-844-2524

These regional offices of agencies enforce laws prohibiting employment discrimination on the basis of disability.

2248 Region VIII: US Department of Health andHuman Services

Office of Civil Rights
1961 Stout Street
Denver, CO 80294   303-844-5101
                          FAX 303-844-6665

These regional offices of agencies enforce laws prohibiting employment discrimination on the basis of disability.

2249 Region VIII: US Department of Labor-Office of Federal Contract Compliance

US Department of Labor
1809 California
Denver, CO 80202   303-844-1600
                          FAX 303-844-1616

These regional offices of agencies enforce laws prohibiting employment discrimination on the basis of disability.

2250 State Department of Education

201 E Colfax Avenue
Denver, CO 80203   303-866-6609
FAX 303-830-0793
e-mail: howerter_c@cde.state.co.us
Diane Bates, Contact

Connecticut

2251 Assistive Technology Project

Connecticut State Department of Social Services
25 Sigourney Street, 11th Floor
Hartford, CT 06106   806-424-5008
800-537-2549
FAX 860-424-4850
TDY:860-424-4839
http://www.techact.uconn.edu/
e-mail: cttap@aol.com
John M Ficarro, Project Director

2252 Bureau of Special Education & Pupil Services

Department of Education
25 Industrial Park Road
Middletown, CT 06457   860-807-2025
FAX 860-807-2047
http://www.stat.ct.us/sde/
e-mail: george.dowaliby@po.state.ct.us

Offers information on educational programs and services. The Complaint Resolution Process Office answers and processes parent complaints regarding procedural violations by local educational agencies and facilities. The Due Process Office is responsible for the management of special education and due process proceedings which are available to parents and school districts.

2253 CHILD FIND of Connecticut

25 Industrial Park Road
Middletown, CT 06457
800-632-1455
FAX 860-632-8870
http://www.serc.rh.edu

A service under the direction of The Connecticut State Department of Education and operated by the Special Education Resource Center. The primary goal is the identification, diagnosis and programming of all unserved disabled children.

2254 Connecticut Bureau of Rehabilitation Services

State of Connecticut
25 Sigourney Street
Hartford, CT 06105   860-424-4844
800-537-2549
FAX 860-424-4850
TDY:860-424-4839
http://www.dss.state.ct.us/
e-mail: evelynknight@po.state.ct.us

Offers vocational rehabilitation and independent living services to individuals who are physically or mentally disabled.

2255 Connecticut Department of Social Services

25 Sigourney Street
Hartford, CT 06106   860-424-5881
800-842-1508
FAX 860-424-4952
http://www.dss.state.ct.us/contact.htm
e-mail: mary.plaskonka@po.state.ct
Joyce A Thomas, Commissioner

2256 Connecticut Office of Protection & Advocacecy for Handicapped & DD Persons

Office of Protection & Advocacy
60 W Street
Hartford, CT 06120   860-297-4300
800-842-7303
FAX 860-566-8714
TDY:860-566-2102
http://www.state.ct.us/opapd
e-mail: james.mcgaughey@po.state.ct.us
Jim McGaughey, Executive Director

Supports families and individuals who are affected by developmental disabilities.

2257 Connecticut State Department of Education

Bureau of Adult and Education Training
165 Capital Avenue
Hartford, CT 06145   860-713-6740
FAX 860-713-7018
http://www.state.ct.us/sde/
e-mail: frances.rabimowitz@po.state.ct.us
Roberta Pawloski, Bureau Chief

2258 Correctional Education Division

Unified School District #1
24 Wolcott Hill Road
Wethersfield, CT 06109   860-692-7536
FAX 860-692-7538
http://www.state.ct.us/doc/
Angela Jalbert, Contact

2259 Protection & Advocacy Agency

Office of P&A for Persons with Disabilities
60B Weston Street
Hartford, CT 06120   860-297-4300
800-842-7303
FAX 860-566-8714
TDY:860-566-2102
http://www.state.ct.us/opapd
e-mail: linda.Mizzi@state.ct.us
Eliot Dober, Executive Director

The mission of the Office of Protection and Advocacy is to advance the cause of equal rights for persons with disabilities and their families.

2260 State GED Administration

Bureau of Adult Education and Training
25 Industrial Park Road
Middletown, CT   06457   860-807-2110
                              FAX 860-807-2112
        e-mail: roberta.pawloski@po.state.ct.us
Carl Paternostro

2261 State of Connecticut Board of Education & Services for the Blind

184 Windsor Avenue
Windsor, CT   06095   860-602-4000
                            800-842-4510
                        FAX 860-602-4020
            http://www.besb.state.ct.us/
Donna Balaski, Executive Director

Provides educational, vocational and communications services to legally blind persons of all ages. Services are free to registered clients

2262 State of Connecticut: Board of Education for the Visually Impaired

184 Windsor Avenue
Windsor, CT   06095   860-602-4000
                            800-842-4510
                        FAX 860-602-4020
                        TDY:860-602-4002
        http://www.besb.state.ct.us/addresses.htm
                e-mail: besb@po.state.ct.us
George Precourt, Executive Director

Delaware

2263 Client Assistance Program (CAP): Maryland Division of Persons with Disabilities

254 E Camden Wyoming Avenue
Camden, DE   19934   302-698-9336
                            800-640-9336
                        FAX 302-698-9338
        http://www.protectionandadvocacy.com
                e-mail: info@magpage.com
Melissa Shahun, Director

Provides free services to consumers and applicants for projects, programs and facilities funded under the Rehabilitation Act.

2264 Correctional Education Division

Department of Corrections
245 McKee Road
Dover, DE   19904   302-739-5601
                        FAX 302-739-7215
        http://www.state.de.us/correct/ddoc/default.htm
                e-mail: jryan@state.de.us
Dr. Bruce Hobler, Contact

2265 Delaware Assistive Technology Initiative

University of DE/duPont Hospital for Children
1600 Rockland Road
Wilmington, DE   19899   302-651-6790
                                800-870-DATI
                            FAX 302-651-6793
                            TDY:302-651-6794
                http://www.asel.udel.edu/dati
                    e-mail: dati@asel.udel.edu
Beth Mineo Mollica PhD, Project Director
Sonja L Simowitz, Project Coordinator

Focuses on improving public awareness, public access to information, funding for assistive technology devices and services, training and technical assistance, and coordination of statewide activities. The project has established Assistive Technology Resource Centers in each of Delaware's three counties. These barrier-free centers are open to the public and house assistive technology devices and materials that are available for demonstration and short-term loan.

2266 Delaware Department of Labor

4425 N Market Street
Wilmington, DE   19802   302-761-8000
                            FAX 302-761-6621

2267 Protection & Advocacy Agency

Community Legal Aid/Disabilities Law Program
100 W 10th Street
Wilmington, DE   19801   302-575-0690
                                800-292-7980
                            FAX 302-575-0840
                        http://www.declasi.org

2268 State Department of Adult & Community Education

Department of Public Instruction
PO Box 1402
Dover, DE   19903   302-739-3743
                        FAX 302-739-1318
            e-mail: ftracymumf@state.de.us
Fran Tracy Mumford, Director Adult Education

2269 State GED Administration

Department of Public Instruction
PO Box 1402
Dover, DE   19903   302-739-3743
                        FAX 302-739-1318
            e-mail: ftracymumf@state.de.us
Fran Tracy Mumford, Director Adult Education

District of Columbia

2270 Client Assistance Program (CAP): District of Columbia

University Legal Services
2001 Street NE
Washington, DC   20002   202-547-0198
                                      FAX x02-547-2083
                          http://www.dcpanda.org
                          e-mail: info@napas.org
Jane Brown, Executive Director
Kelly Bagby, Legal Director
Joseph Cooney, Information Ext 116

Provides free services to consumers and applicants for projects, programs and facilities funded under the Rehabilitation Act.

2271 District of Columbia Department of Employment Services

77 P Street NE
Washington, DC   20002   202-671-1633
                                      FAX 202-673-3795

2272 District of Columbia Fair Employment Practice Agencies

DC Office of Human Rights
1889 F Street NW
Washington, DC   20006   202-458-6002
                                      FAX 202-458-3992

2273 District of Columbia Office of Human Rights

441 4th Street NW
Washington, DC   20001   202-727-3900
                                      FAX 202-727-9589
                                      e-mail: ohr@dc.gov

The DC Office of Human Rights is an agency of the District of Columbia government that seeks to eradicate discrimination, increase equal opportunity, and protect human rights in the city.

2274 State Department of Adult Education

University of The District of Columbia
4200 Connecticut Avenue NW
Washington, DC   20008   202-274-7181
                                      FAX 202-274-7188
                          e-mail: kbrisbane213@hotmail.com
Dr. Sandra Lee Anderson, Director

2275 State GED Administration

DC Public Schools Vocational & Adult Education
1709 3rd Street NE
Washington, DC   20002   202-576-6308
                                      FAX 202-576-7899
Dr. Cynthia Bell, Director
Clive Smith, GED Chief Examiner

Helps individuals over the age of 16 prepare for and take the General Equivalency Diploma. Classes offered in local schools all over the area.

Florida

2276 Client Assistance Program (CAP): Florida Division of Persons with Disabilities

2671 Executive Center Circle W
Tallahassee, FL   32301   904-488-9071
                                           800-342-0823
                                      FAX 850-488-8640
                          http://www.advocacycenter.org
Elizabeth Holifield, Board President

Provides free services to consumers and applicants for projects, programs and facilities funded under the rehabilitation act.

2277 Florida Department of Labor and Employment Security

2571 Executive Center
Tallahassee, FL   32399   850-921-1459
                                      FAX 850-921-1459

2278 Florida Fair Employment Practice Agency

Florida Commission on Human Relations
2009 Apalachee Parkway
Tallahassee, FL   32301   850-488-7082
                                      FAX 850-488-5291
                          http://www.fchr.state.fl.us
                          e-mail: fchrinfo@dmsstate.fl.us
Derick Daniel, Executive Director

2279 Florida GED Administration: Bureau of Adult & Community Education

Department of Education
325 W Gaines Street, FED Building
Tallahassee, FL   32399   850-487-7033
                                      FAX 850-487-0419
                          e-mail: bob.wofford@fldoe.org
Bob Wofford, Sr Education Program Director

2280 Florida State Department of Adult Education: Division of Applied Technology & Adult Education

325 W Gaines Street
Tallahassee, FL   32399   850-487-7033
                                      FAX 850-487-3601
Bob Wofford, Sr Education Program Director

Research in the societal and economic contributions of Adult and Community education; development and validation of vocational educator competencies; design model of competency-based vocational teacher training curriculum, etc.

2281 State Department of Education

Division of Applied Tech & Adult Education
325 W Gaines Street
Tallahassee, FL   32399   850-922-9750
                                      FAX 850-413-0026
                          e-mail: millerc@mail.doe.state.fl.us
Carl Miller, Contact

2282 State GED Administration

Bureau of Adult & Community Education
325 W Gaines Street, Room 1244
Tallahassee, FL   32399   904-487-4929

Georgia

2283 Assistive Technology

Tools for Life/Division of Rehabilitation Services
2 Peachtreet Street 35-415
Atlanta, GA   30303   404-657-0698
                                800-497-8665
                           FAX 404-657-3086
                           TDY:404-657-3085
Christopher Lee, Contact

**2284 Client Assistance Program (CAP): Georgia
Division of Persons with Disabilities**

123 N McDonough Street
Decatur, GA   30030   404-373-2040
                                800-822-9727
                           FAX 404-373-4110
              http://www.theombudsman.com/CAP
      e-mail: GaCAPDirector@dueOmbudsman.com
Charles Martin, Director
Anil Lewis, Counselor

Provides free services to consumers and applicants for
projects, programs and facilities funded under the Rehabilitation Act.

**2285 Georgia Department of Technical & Adult
Education**

1800 Century Place
Atlanta, GA   30345   404-679-1600
                           FAX 404-679-1710
                     http://www.dtae.org
              e-mail: mdelaney@dtae.org
Tony Bruehl, Director

The Georgia Department of Technical and Adult Education oversees the state's system of technical colleges, the adult literacy program, and a host of
economic and workforce development programs

2286 Governor's Council on Developmental Disabilities

2 Peachtree Street NW
Atlanta, GA   30303   404-657-2126
                                888-275-4633
                           FAX 404-657-2132
                           TDY:404-657-2133
                     http://www.godd.org
              e-mail: tharris@dhr.state.ga.us
Eric E Jacobson, Executive Director
Marcey Dolgoff, Progam Director
Tonya L Harris, Executive Assistant

Council collaborates with consumers, their families,
advocacy organizations, and policymakers to promote
public policies that enhance the quality of life for people with developmental disabilities and their families
through advocacy and education, funding and project
implementation, research and policy analysis.

2287 Protection & Advocacy Center

Georgia Advocacy Office
100 Cresent Centre Parkway
Atlanta, GA   30084   404-885-1234
                                800-537-2329
                           FAX 770-414-2948

Joyce Ringer, Director

2288 Region IV: Office of Civil Rights

US Department of Health & Human Services
101 Marietta Tower
Atlanta, GA   30323   404-562-7886
                           FAX 404-331-1807

These regional offices of agencies enforce laws prohibiting employment discrimination on the basis of
disability.

2289 State Department of Education

Department of Technical and Adult Education
2051 Twin Towers E
Atlanta, GA   30334   404-657-7410
                                800-331-3627
                           FAX 404-657-6978
                     http://www.doe.k12.ga.us
              e-mail: stateboard@doe.k12.ga.us
Dr. Jean DeVard-Kemp, Assistant Commissioner

2290 State GED Administration

1800 Century Place NE
Atlanta, GA   30345   404-679-1621
                           FAX 404-679-4911
                     e-mail: klee@dtae.org
Robert Wofford, GED Administrator

Hawaii

2291 Correctional Education

Department of Public Safety
919 Ala Moana Boulevard
Honolulu, HI   96814   808-587-1279
                           FAX 808-587-1280
                     e-mail: coredhi@pixi.net
Maureen L Tito, Program Manager

2292 Protection & Advocacy Agency

1580 Makaloa Street
Honolulu, HI   96814   808-949-2922
                                 800-882-1057
                           FAX 808-949-2928
              http://www.dss.org/nta/states.HI.htm
Gary Smith, Director

2293 State Council on Developmental Disabilities
919 Ala Moana Boulevard
Honolulu, HI 96814   808-586-8100
                                    FAX 808-586-7543
                                e-mail: hiddc@pixi.com
Waynette KY Cabral, Administrator

2294 State Department of Education
Department of Adult Education
PO Box 2360
Honolulu, HI 96813   808-586-3230
                                    FAX 808-586-3234
                                http://www.doe.k12.hi.us/
Arthur Kaneshiro, Director

2295 State GED Administration
Building C-203
Honolulu, HI 96816   808-733-9124
Art Kaneshiro, Director

Idaho

2296 Adult Education Office: Idaho Department of Education
PO Box 83720
Boise, ID 83720   208-332-6931
                                    FAX 208-334-4664
                            e-mail: stspence@sde.state.id.us
Shirley Spencer, Director Adult Education

2297 Division of Vocational Rehabilitation
State of Idaho
650 W State
Boise, ID 83720   208-334-3390
                                    FAX 208-334-5305
                    http://www2.state.id.us/idvr/idvrhome.htm
                        e-mail: scook@idvr.state.id.us
Michael Graham, Administrator
Sue Payne, Chief Field Services
Sue Cook, Assistant Chief Field Services

Helping individuals become more independent at home, in the community and at work. Direct services to people with disabilities, including learning disabilities. Services may include evaluation and diagnosis, counseling, guidance and referral services. Transportation to vocational training and assistive devices are available.

2298 Idaho Center on Developmental Disabilities
ID Assistive Technology Project
129 W 3rd Street
Moscow, ID 83843   208-885-3559
                                         800-432-8324
                                    FAX 208-885-3628
                            http://www.educ.uidaho.edu/idatech
                                e-mail: rseiler@uidaho.edu
Ron Seiler, Director
Yvonne Write
Sue

Assistive Technology Project at the University of Idaho, established 1994, offers alternatie financing (loan) programs for the purchase of assistive technology for the benefit of persons with disabilities in the state. The loan programs offer individuals with disabilities and their families low interest rates on loans for assistive technology and the option of securing a loan guarantee or a principle buy-down arrangement.

2299 Idaho Fair Employment Practice Agency
Idaho Human Rights Commission
1109 Main Street
Boise, ID 83720   208-334-2873
                                    FAX 208-334-2873
                                http://www.state.id.us/ihrc

2300 Idaho Human Rights Commission
1109 Main Street, 4th Floor
Boise, ID 83720   208-334-2873
                                    FAX 208-334-2664
                                http://www.state.id.us/ihrc

2301 Protection & Advocacy Agency
4477 Emerald Street
Boise, ID 83706   208-336-5353
                                         800-632-5125
                                    FAX 208-336-5396
                                TDY:208-336-5353
                        e-mail: coadinc@mcleodusa.net
James R Baugh, Executive Director

Gives assistance to incapacitated people to protect, promote and advance their legal rights.

2302 State Department of Education: Special Education
650 W State Street
Boise, ID 83720   208-332-6917
                                    FAX 208-334-4664
Jerry L Evans, Superintendent

2303 State GED Administration
PO Box 83720
Boise, ID 83720   208-332-6931
                                    FAX 208-334-4664
                            http://www.sde.stateaid.us/Dept/
                        e-mail: etspence@sde.state.id.us
Dr. Shirley T Spencer, Director

Illinois

2304 Assistive Technology

1 W Old State Capitol Plaza
Springfield, IL   62701   217-522-7985
                                 800-852-5110
                            FAX 217-522-8067
                            http://www.iltech.org
Wilhelmina Gunther, Director

2305 Board of Education of Chicago

1819 W Pershing Road
Chicago, IL   60609   773-553-1000
                            FAX 773-553-1501
                            http://www.cps.k12.il.us/
Offers instruction and information services, curriculum information and government relations advocacy.

2306 Client Assistance Program (CAP): Illinois Division of Persons with Disabilities

100 N 1st Street
Springfield, IL   62702   217-782-5374
                            FAX 217-524-1790
                    http://www.dhs.state.IL.us/ors/CAP
                    e-mail: cmeadows@dhs.state.il.us
Cathy Meadows, Director

Provides free services to consumers and applicants for projects, programs and facilities funded under the Rehabilitation Act.

2307 Correctional Education

Illinois Department of Corrections
1301 Concordia Court
Springfield, IL   62794   217-522-2666
                                 800-546-0844
                            FAX 217-557-7902
                    http://www.idoc.state.il.us/
                    e-mail: webmaster@idoc.state.il.us
John R Castro, Director

2308 Great Lakes Disability and Business Technical Assistance Center

1640 W Roosevelt Road
Chicago, IL   60608   312-413-1407
                                 800-949-4232
                            FAX 312-413-1856
                            TDY:800-949-4232
                    http://www.uic.edu/orgs/ada-greatlakes
                    e-mail: gldbtac@uic.edu
Robin A Jones, Project Director
Peter Berg, Technical Assistance

Provides information, training and technical assistance to employers, people with disabilities and other entities with responsibilities under the ADA. These centers act as a one-stop central source of information, direct technical assistance, training and referral on ADA issues concerning employment, public accommodations, public services and communications.

2309 Illinois Affiliation of Private Schools for Exceptional Children

Lawrence Hall Youth Services
4833 N Francisco Avenue
Chicago, IL   60625   773-769-3500
                            FAX 773-769-0106
                    http://www.lawrencehall.org
Sharri Demitrowicz, Director Education

2310 Illinois Council on Developmental Disabilities

830 S Spring Street
Springfield, IL   62704   217-782-9696
                            FAX 217-524-5339
                    http://www.state.il.us
Sheila T Romano EdD, Director

2311 Illinois Department of Commerce and Community Affairs

JTPA Programs Division
620 E Adams Street
Springfield, IL   62701   217-782-7500
                                 800-785-6055
                            FAX 800-785-6055
              http://www.spinotew.commerce.state.il.us

2312 Illinois Department of Employment Security

401 S State Street
Chicago, IL   60605   312-793-5700

2313 Illinois Department of Human Rights

James R Thompson Center
Chicago, IL   60601   312-814-6200
                            FAX 312-814-6251
                    http://www.state.il.us/dhr
                    e-mail: David_Espionza@cms.state.il.us

2314 Illinois Department of Rehabilitation Services

1200-1 W Jackson
McComb, IL   61455   309-833-4573
                            FAX 309-833-5953
              http://www.state.il.us/agency/dhs/rsnp.html
                    e-mail: ors@dhs.state.il.us
Audrey L McCrimon, Contact Person

2315 Illinois Fair Employment Practice Agency

James R Thompson Center
Chicago, IL   60601   312-814-6245
                            TDY:312-263-1579
                    http://www.state.il.us/dhr
                    e-mail: David_Espionza@cms.state.il.us

2316 Illinois Office of Rehabilitation Services

Illinois Department of Human Services
100 S Grand Avenue E
Springfield, IL   62762   217-557-1601
                    e-mail: ors@dhs.state.il.us
Teyonda Wertz, Chief of Staff
Dylan Livingearth, Manager of Information Services

DHS' Office of Rehabilitation Services is the state's lead agency serving individuals with disabilities.

2317 Illinois State Board of Education: Division of Certificate Renewal

E 315 100 N 1st Street
Springfield, IL   62777   217-557-8393
                        FAX 217-557-8392
                    http://www.isbe.state.il.us/

2318 Region V: Civil Rights Office

US Department of Health & Human Services
233 N Michidan Avenue
Chicago, IL   60601   312-886-2359
                        FAX 312-866-1807
                        http://www.hhs.gov

These regional offices of agencies enforce laws prohibiting employment discrimination on the basis of disability.

2319 Region V: US Department of Labor-Office of Federal Contract Compliance

US Department of Labor
230 S Dearborn Street
Chicago, IL   60604   312-353-8927
                        FAX 312-353-1509

These regional offices of agencies enforce laws prohibiting employment discrimination on the basis of disability.

2320 Region V: US Small Business Administration

500 W Madison Street
Chicago, IL   60606   312-353-6070
                        FAX 312-353-3426

These regional offices of agencies enforce laws prohibiting employment discrimination on the basis of disability.

2321 State Department of Adult Education

State Board of Education
100 N 1st Street
Springfield, IL   62777   217-782-3370
                        FAX 217-782-9224
        http://www.isbe.net/partnerships/def.cult.htm
                    e-mail: jll.lit@isbe.net
Daniel J Miller, Administrator

Indiana

2322 Assistive Technology

2346 Lynhurst Drive
Indianapolis, IN   46241   317-486-8808
                            800-528-8246
                        FAX 317-486-8809
                    http://www.attaininc.org
                    e-mail: attain@attaininc.org
Gary R Hand, Executive Director

Assistive technology. To insure that all people with disabilities in Indiana have access to assistive technology.

2323 Corrections Agency: Indiana Department of Correction

302 W Washington Street
Indianapolis, IN   46204   317-232-5715
                        FAX 317-232-6798
Carolyn Hagersty-Heier, Department Correction

The mission of the Department of Correction is to protect the public by incarcerating offenders and complying with established means for preparing them for reentry into the community.

2324 Indiana ATTAIN Project

Indiana Family and Social Services Administration
PO Box 7083
Indianapolis, IN   46207   317-233-3394
        http://www.state.in.us/gpcpd/html/publications

2325 Indiana Employment Services and Job Training Program Liaison

10 N Senate Avenue
Indianapolis, IN   46204   317-232-6702
                        FAX 317-233-1670
                        TDY:317-232-7560

2326 Protection & Advocacy Agency

Indiana Advocacy Services
4701 N Keystone Avenue
Indianapolis, IN   46205   317-722-5555
                            800-622-4845
                        FAX 317-722-5564
                    e-mail: info@ipas.state.in.us
Tom Gallagher, Director

2327 State Department of Education

State House
Indianapolis, IN   46204   317-232-0808
                        FAX 317-233-6326
                    http://www.ideanet.doe.state.in.us/
                    e-mail: webmaster@doe.state.in.us
Suellen K Reed, Superintendent

2328 State GED Administration

State House
Indianapolis, IN   46204   317-232-0522
                                    FAX 317-233-0859
                              e-mail: pmhill@doe.state.in.us

Iowa

**2329 Client Assistance Program (CAP): Iowa Division
of Persons with Disabilities**

321 E 12th Street
Des Moines, IA   50319   515-242-6172
                                    888-219-0471
                                  FAX 515-242-6119
                    http://www.state.ia.us/government
                  e-mail: harlietta.helland@dhr.state.ia.us
Harlietta Helland, Director
Jill Fulitano-Avery, Administrator

Designed to help people who are seeking or receiving
rehabilitation services from an agency funded under
the Rehabilitation Act. Provides information on all
available services under the Act to any individual with
disabilities in Iowa. This includes the Department for
the Blind, the Division of Vocational Rehabilitation
Services and seven centers for independent living.

2330 Governor's Council on DevelopmentalDisabilities

617 E 2nd Street
Des Moines, IA   50309   515-281-9082
                                    800-452-1936
                                  FAX 515-281-9087
                    http://www.state.ia.us/ddcouncil/
                      e-mail: akillin@dhs.state.ia.us
Becky Harker, Director

The council identifies, develops and promotes public
policy and support through capacity building, advocacy, and systems-changing activities. The purpose is
to ensure that people with developmental disabilities
and their families are included in planning, decision
making, and development of policy related to services
and supports that affect their quality of life and full
participation in communities of their choice.

2331 Iowa Employment Service

1000 E Grand Avenue
Des Moines, IA   50319   515-281-9619
                                  FAX 515-281-9650
                    http://www.state.ic.us/jobs/
                e-mail: IWD.customerservice@iwd.state.ic.us

2332 Iowa Welfare Programs

Iowa Department of Human Services
Hoover State Building
Des Moines, IA   50319   515-281-5452
                                  FAX 515-281-4597
                    http://www.state.ia.us/government/dhs/

To provide assistance to families in need in the Des
Moines area.

2333 Iowa Workforce Investment Act

Department of Economic Development
200 E Grand Avenue
Des Moines, IA   50309   515-242-4700
                                  FAX 515-242-4809
                      http://www.state.ia.us/ided
                  e-mail: iowasmart@ided.state.ia.us
Mike Blouin, Director

Job placement and training services. Especially for
those workers who have been laid off, or have other
barriers to steady employment.

2334 Learning Disabilities Association of Iowa

321 E 6th Street
Des Moines, IA   50329   515-280-8558
                                    888-690-5324
                      http://www.lda-ia.org

Vicki Goshon, President
Connie Sullivan, Secretary

The Learning Disabilities Association of Iowa advances the education and general welfare of children
and youth of normal, near-normal, and potentially
normal intelligence who have learning disabilities.

2335 Protection & Advocacy Agency

3015 Merle Hay Road
Des Moines, IA   50310   515-278-2502
                                    800-779-2502
                                  FAX 515-281-6544
                                  TDY:515-278-0571
                              e-mail: info@ipna.org
Mervin L Roth, Director

2336 State Department of Adult Education

Grimes State Office Building
Des Moines, IA   50319   515-281-3636
                                  FAX 515-281-6544
                    http://www.state.ia.us/educate
                  e-mail: john.hartwig@ed.state.ia.us
Miriam Temple, Director

2337 State Department of Education

Grimms State Office Building
Des Moines, IA   50319   515-281-5294
                                  FAX 515-242-5988
                    http://www.state.ia.us/educate/
                  e-mail: webmaster@ed.state.ia.us
Al Ramirez, Director

Kansas

2338 Client Assistance Program (CAP):Kansas Division of Persons with Disabilities

2914 SW Plass Court
Topeka, KS   66611   785-266-8193
                            800-432-2326

Mary Reyer, Director

Provides free services to consumers and applicants for projects, programs and facilities funded under the rehabilitation act.

2339 Community College: Kansas State Department of Education

120 SE 10th Avenue
Topeka, KS   66612   785-296-4936
                       FAX 785-296-7933
               http://www.ksbe.state.ks.us
               e-mail: pplamann@ksde.org
David Moore PhD, Consultant

2340 Kansas Adult Education Association

Barton County Community College
245 NE 30th Road
Great Bend, KS   67530   620-792-2701
                            800-748-7594
               http://www.barton.cc.ks.us
Angie Reid, Public Relations
Vikki Jo Stewart

The Kansas Adult Education Association has been the professional association for adult educators at community colleges, school districts, and non-profit organizations.

2341 Kansas Advocacy Protective Services

3745 SW Wanamaker Road
Topeka, KS   66610   785-273-9661
                            877-776-1541
                       FAX 785-273-9414
James L Germer, Executive Director
Michelle Rola, Director Operations
Tim Voth, Outreach Coordinator

KAPS is the protection and advocacy system in Kansas. It provides legal, administrative and other advocacy services for Kansans with disabilities.

2342 Kansas Department of Human Resources

401 SW Topeka Boulevard
Topeka, KS   66603   785-296-5025
                       FAX 785-291-3425
               http://www.hr.state.ks.us
               e-mail: uitax@hr.state.ks.us

2343 Kansas Department of Social and Rehabilitation Services

915 SW Harrison
Topeka, KS   66612   785-296-3959
                       FAX 785-296-2173
               http://www.srskansas.org

2344 Kansas Human Rights Commission

South Landon State Office Building
900 SW Jackson Street
Topeka, KS   66612   785-296-3206
                       FAX 785-296-0983
               http://www.ink.org/public/khrc/
               e-mail: khrc@ink.org

2345 Kansas Welfare Programs: Kansas Social and Rehabilitative Services

915 SLD Harrison
Topeka, KS   66612   785-296-3713
                       FAX 785-296-6960
               http://www.srskansas.org
Trudy Racine, Chief of Staff
Margaret Zillinger, Community Support Director

To protect children and promote adult self-sufficiency.

2346 Office of Disability Services

Witchita State University
1845 Fairmont
Wichita, KS   67260   316-978-3309
                       FAX 316-978-3114
                       TDY:316-978-3309
               http://www.twsu.edu/~disserv
Grady L Landrum, Director

Serving students with learning disabilities, including ADD, ADHD, and dyslexia.

2347 State Department of Adult Education

Kansas Board of Regents
1000 SW Jackson Street
Topeka, KS   66612   785-296-7159
                       FAX 785-296-0983
               http://www.ksbe.state.ks.us/welcome.html
Janet Stotts, Director

2348 State GED Administration: Kansas State Department of Education

120 E 10th Street
Topeka, KS   66612   785-296-7159
                       FAX 785-296-0983
Janet Stotts, GED Administrator

Promotes adult education.

2349 Western Kansas Community Service Consortiuum

348 NE SR
Pratt, KS   67124   620-672-6251
               http://www.wkcsc.org
               e-mail: dedram@genmail.pcc.cc.ks.us
Dedra Manes, Executive Director

Mission is to provide cooperative community services to Western Kansas. Total service area includes 73 counties and nearly 3/4 of the state's geographic area.

Kentucky

2350 Assistive Technology Office

8412 Westport Road
Louisville, KY 40242
502-327-0022
800-327-5287
FAX 502-327-9974
http://www.katsnet.org
e-mail: katsnet@iglou.com
Chase Forrester, Director

2351 Assistive Technology Service Network

427 Versailles Road
Frankfort, KY 40601
502-573-4665
800-327-5287
FAX 502-573-4665
Chase Forrester, Director

A statewide network of organizations and individuals connecting to enhance and incorporate assistive technology (AT) into service which improves the quality and productivity of life. Through advocacy activities and systems-changing efforts, the mission of the consumer driven, collaborative KATS Network is to make available assistive technology information and services.

2352 Client Assistance Program (CAP): Kentucky Division of Persons with Disabilities

209 Saint Clair Street
Frankfort, KY 40601
502-564-8035
800-633-6283
FAX 502-564-2951
http://www.kycwd.org
e-mail: vickil.staggs@mail.state.ky.gov
Gerry Gordon-Brown, Director
Vicki Staggs, Administrative Specialist III

Provides advocacy for persons with disabilities who are clients or applicants of the Department of Vocational Rehabilitation or the Department for the Blind and are having problems receiving services.

2353 Correctional Education

Department of Corrections
PO Box 2400
Frankfort, KY 40242
502-564-4726
FAX 502-564-5037
http://www.cor.state.ky.us/
Wendell McCourt, Education Program Manager

2354 Kentucky Bureau of Education

500 Mero Street
Frankfort, KY 40601
502-564-4770
800-533-5372
FAX 502-564-5680
http://www.desde.sky.org

2355 Learning Disabilities Association of Kentucky

2210 Goldsmith Lane
Louisville, KY 40218
502-473-1256
877-587-1256
FAX 502-473-4695
http://www.ldaofky.org
e-mail: LDAofky@aol.com
Catherine Senn, Director

2356 Protection & Advocacy Agency

Department for Public Advocacy
100 Fair Oaks Lane
Frankfort, KY 40601
502-564-5967
800-372-2988
FAX 502-564-0848
TDY:502-372-2988
http://www.kypa.sky1.net
Maureen Fizgerald, Director

2357 State Department of Adult Education

Department for Adult Education & Literacy
500 Mero Street
Frankfort, KY 40601
502-564-5114
800-928-7323
FAX 502-564-5436
http://adulted.state.ky.us/
e-mail: reecied.stagnolia@mail.state.ky.us
Sandy Degado, Contact
Harlan Stubbs, Director

2358 State Department of Education

500 Mero Street
Frankfort, KY 40601
502-564-4770
800-533-5372
FAX 502-564-5680
e-mail: sdelgado@mail.state.ky.us
Thomas C Boysen, Commissioner

Promotes quality education.

Louisiana

2359 Client Assistance Program (CAP): Shreveport Division of Persons with Disabilities

Advocacy Center
2620 Centenary Boulevard
Shreveport, LA 71104
318-227-6186
800-960-7703
FAX 318-227-1841
TDY:318-227-6186
http://www.advocacycenter@advocacyla.org
e-mail: dmirvis@advocacyla.org
Diane Mirvis, Director

Advocacy services for applicants and clients of Louisiana Rehabilitation Services (LRS) and American Indian Rehabilitation Services (AIRS). No fee.

2360 Client Assistance Program (CAP): Louisiana HDQS Division of Persons with Disabilities

Advocacy Center
225 Baronne Street
New Orleans, LA 70112   504-522-2337
                              800-960-7705
http://www.advocacycenter@advocacyla.org
e-mail: info@advocacyla.org
Lois Simpson, Director

Advocacy services to applicants and clients of Louisiana Rehabilitation Services (LRS) and American Indian Rehabilitation Services (AIRS). No fee. Committed to the belief in the dignity of every life and the freedom of everyone to experience the highest degree of self-determination. Exists to protect and advocate for human and legal rights of the elderly and disabled. Umbrella organization for Advocacy Centers in Baton Rouge, Lafayette, Shreveport, Monroe, Pineville, Jackson, and Mandeville.

2361 Correctional Education

Louisiana Department of Education
PO Box 94064
Baton Rouge, LA 70804   225-342-3530
                          FAX 225-342-0193
http://www.doe.state.la.us
Cosby Joiner, Director

Promotes quality correctional education.

2362 Louisiana Assistive Technology Access Network

3042 Old Forge Drive
Baton Rouge, LA 70808   225-952-9500
                              800-270-6185
                          FAX 225-925-9560
http://www.latan.org
Julie M Nesbit, Executive Director

2363 State Department of Adult Education

Department of Education
PO Box 94064
Baton Rouge, LA 70804   225-342-3336
                          FAX 225-219-4439
http://www.doe.state.la.us
e-mail: wmeaux@mail.doe.state.la.us
W Wayne Meaux, Contact

2364 State GED Administration

Louisiana Department of Education
PO Box 94604
Baton Rouge, LA 70804   225-342-3510
                          FAX 225-342-0193
Glen Gosett, Director

Promotes quality education.

Maine

2365 Adult Education Team

Maine Department of Education
23 State House Station
Augusta, ME 04333   207-624-6730
                       FAX 207-624-6731
e-mail: andy.mcmahan@state.me.us
Andrew McMahan, Contact

2366 Consulting Advocacy Research Evaluation Services (CARES) and Client Assistance Program (CAP)

47 Water Street
Hallowell, ME 04347   207-622-7055
                              800-773-7055
                          FAX 207-621-1869
http://www.caresinc.org
e-mail: capsite@aol.com
Steve Beam, Director

Consulting, advocacy research and evaluation services.

2367 Developmental Disabilities Council

139 State House Station
Augusta, ME 04333   207-287-4213
                              800-244-3999
                          FAX 207-287-8001
                          TDY:800-244-3999
http://www.state.me.us/dmhmrsas/ddcouncil
e-mail: tania.boterf@state.me.us
Tania Boterf, Program Planner

2368 Maine Department of Labor: Bureau of Rehabilitation Services

Department of Human Services
2 Anthony Avenue
Augusta, ME 04333   207-624-5950
                          FAX 207-624-5980
http://www.state.me.us/dhs
e-mail: webmaster_dhs@state.me.us

2369 Maine Department of Labor: Employment Services

Bureau of Employment Security
20 Union Street
Augusta, ME 04330   207-287-2271
                          FAX 207-287-2947

2370 Maine Human Rights Commission

51 State House Station
Augusta, ME 04333   207-624-6050
                          FAX 207-624-6063
                          TDY:207-624-6064
                          http://www.state.me.us
                          e-mail: cheryl.foote@state.me.us

The Commission investigates charges of unlawful discrimination in employment, housing, public accommodation, credit extension and education.

2371 Protection & Advocacy Agency

Disability Rights Center
24 Stone Street
Augusta, ME 04338   207-626-2774
                          800-452-1948
                          FAX 207-621-1419
                          e-mail: advocate@drcme.org
Kim Moody, Executive Director

Maryland

2372 Client Assistance Program (CAP): Maryland Division of Persons with Disabilities

Division of Rehabilitation Services
2301 Argonne Drive
Baltimore, MD 21218   410-554-9361
                            800-638-6243
                            FAX 410-554-9362
                            http://www.dors.state.md.us
                            e-mail: cap@dors.state.md.us
Beth Lash, Director
Robert A Burns, Assistant Superintendent Rehab

Provides free services for consumers and applicants of projects, programs and facilities funded under the Rehabilitation Act.

2373 Correctional Education

State Department of Education
200 W Baltimore Street
Baltimore, MD 21201   410-767-0100
                            FAX 410-333-6033
                            http://www.msde.state.md.us/
John Linton, Director

2374 Maryland Developmental Disabilities Council

300 W Lexington Street
Baltimore, MD 21201   410-333-3688
                            800-305-6441
                            FAX 410-333-3686
                            http://www.md-council.org
                            e-mail: info@md-council.org
Brian Cox, Executive Director

2375 Maryland Technology Assistance Program

2301 Argonne Drive
Baltimore, MD 21218   410-554-9230
                            800-832-4827
                            FAX 410-554-9237
                            http://www.mdtap.com
                            e-mail: mdtap@mdtap.org
Jessica Vollmer, Office Manager

Offers information and referrals, reduced rate loan program for assistive technology, five regional display centers, presentations and training on request.

2376 State Department of Education

200 W Baltimore Street
Baltimore, MD 21201   410-767-0100
                            FAX 410-333-6033
Charles Talbert, Director

The mission of MSDE is to provide leadership, support, and accountabilty for effective systems of public education, library services, and rehabilitation services.

Massachusetts

2377 Assistive Technology Partnership Center

MATP Center
1295 Boylston Street
Boston, MA 02215   617-355-7820
                          800-848-8867
                          FAX 617-355-6345
Pat Hill, I&R Specialist
Judy Brewer, Project Director

Provides information and referral on assistive technology products and services for all Massachusetts residents.

2378 Autism Support Center: Northshore Arc

6 Southside Road
Danvers, MA 01923   978-777-9135
                          800-7-autism
                          FAX 978-762-3980
                          http://www2.primushost.com
                          e-mail: asc@nsarc.org   glcastorf@nsarc.org
Gail M Kastorf, Director

Supports parents/professionals who need information and support about autism, PDD and Asperger's disorder. Directed by a Parent Advisory Policy Committee of parents of children with autism/PDD. Funded through Mass Department of Mental Retardation, we empower families by providing current, accurate and unbiased information about service referrals, resources, research trends and educational opportunities. We promote networking, increase community awareness and advocate for service and opportunity.

2379 Client Assistance Program (CAP): Massachusetts Division of Persons with Disabilities

1 Ashburton Place
Boston, MA   02108   617-727-7440
                                      800-322-2020
                                 FAX 617-727-0965
http://www.state.ma.us/mod/ClientAssistance
e-mail: barbara.lybarger@mod.state.ma.us
Barbara Lybarger, Esq., Director

If you have a disability and want to work but have trouble getting vocational rehabilitation services, or want a lifestyle which is more self-reliant but are having trouble getting independent living services, contact CAP. All dealings with us are confidential. CAP is independent of the vocational rehab and independent living agencies, run by Massachusetts Office of Disability, an indepedent state agency. MOD is responsible for promoting the rights of people with disability in Massachusetts.

2380 Department of Corrections

Inmate Training & Education
50 Maple Street
Milford, MA   01757   508-422-3314
                                 FAX 508-422-3383
http://www.state.maus/doc/default.htm
e-mail: docinfo@doe.state.maus
Carolyn J Vicari, Director

Protects the public by operating a safe corrections system.

2381 Massachusetts Assistive Technology Partnership (MATP)

MATP Children's Hospital
1295 Boylston Street
Boston, MA   02215   617-355-7820
                                 http://www.matp.org
e-mail: mjackowitz@matp.org
Judy Brewer, Project Director
Michael Jackowitz, Coordinator of Public Awareness
Howard Shane, PhD, Principal Investigator

Funded under Tech Act/NIDRR to increase access to assistive technology for all ages and disabilities. Affiliated with Communication Enhancement Center, Dept of Otolaryngology, Children's Hospital. Conducts statewide project activities such as needs assessment, awareness, information referral, technical training/assistance and advocacy. Two peer programs are based at Stavros Center, Springfield (W Mass) and Cape Organization for Rights of the Disabled, Hyannis (E Mass).

2382 Massachusetts Commission Against Discrimination

1 Ashburton Place
Boston, MA   02108   617-994-6000
                                 FAX 617-994-6024
http://www.state.maus/mcad/
Works for fair employment within Massachusetts.

2383 Massachusetts GED Administration: Massachusetts Department of Education

350 Main Street
Malden, MA   02148   781-338-6604
http://www.doe.mass.edu
e-mail: rderfler@doe.mass.edu
Ruth Derfler, Director

Thirty-three test centers operate state-wide to serve the needs of the adult population in need of a high school credential.

2384 Massachusetts Rehabilitation Commission

27-43 Wormwood Street
Boston, MA   02210   617-204-3600
                                      800-245-6543
                                 FAX 617-727-1354
http://www.state.maus/mrc.htm

2385 Office of Federal Contract Compliance: Boston District Office

US Department of Labor
JFK Federal Building
Boston, MA   02203   617-624-6780
                                 FAX 617-624-6702
                                 TDY:617-565-9869
http://www.dol.gov/dol/esa
Reba Beatty, Assistant District Director

Enforces laws prohibiting employment discrimination on the basis of disability.

2386 Protection & Advocacy Agency

Disability Law Center
11 Beacon Street
Boston, MA   02108   617-723-8455
                                      800-872-9992
                                 FAX 617-723-9125
                                 TDY:617-227-9464
http://www.dlc-ma.org
e-mail: mail@dlc-ma.org

2387 Region I: Office for Civil Rights

US Department Health & Human Services
JF Kennedy Federal Building
Boston, MA   02203   617-565-1340
                                 FAX 617-439-4482
These regional offices of agencies enforce laws prohibiting employment discrimination on the basis of disability.

2388 Region I: US Small Business Administration

Massachusetts District Office
10 Causeway Street
Boston, MA   02222   617-565-5590
                                 FAX 617-565-5598
http://www.sBA.gov
These regional offices of agencies enforce laws prohibiting employment discrimination on the basis of disability.

2389 State Department of Adult Education
Adult and Community Learning Services
350 Main Street
Malden, MA 02148 781-388-3300
FAX 781-388-3394
http://www.doe.mass.edu
e-mail: rbickerton@doe.mass.edu
Bob Dickerton, Director

Michigan

2390 Assistive Technology
Michigan Jobs Commission
119 Pere Maegutte Drive
Lansing, MI 48917 517-485-4477
FAX 517-485-4488
http://www.publicpolicy.com/nyc.html
e-mail: ppa@publicpolicy.com
Mary Barnes, Director

2391 Client Assistance Program (CAP): Michigan Department of Persons with Disabilities
409 Legacy Parkway
Lansing, MI 48911 517-373-8193
800-292-0827
FAX 517-373-0565
http://www.mpas.org
Elmer Cerano, Executive Director

Provides information and advocacy, without charge, to people with disabilities who are receiving, or want to receive, services under the Rehabilitation Act. CAP is operated by Michigan Protection and Advocacy Services, which receives money from the Michigan Department of Career Development to provide these services.

2392 Correctional Education: Department of Corrections
BCF Treatment & Education
PO Box 30003
Lansing, MI 48909 517-373-3605
FAX 517-335-0045
http://www.state.mi.us/mdoc
e-mail: spencede@state.mi.us
Diane Spence, Director

2393 Michigan Assistive Technology: Michigan Rehabilitation Services
Michigan Jobs Commission
119 Pere Marquette Drive
Lansing, MI 48912 517-485-4477
FAX 517-485-4488
http://www.publicpolicy.com
e-mail: ppa@publicpolicy.com
Jeffrey D Padden, President
Nancy C Hewat, Executive Director

2394 Michigan Developmental Disabilities Council
Lewis Cass Building, 320 Walnut St
Lansing, MI 48913 517-334-6123
FAX 517-334-7353
TDY:517-334-7354
http://www.mdch.state.mi.us/mddc
e-mail: collinsve@state.mi.us
Vendella Collins, Executive Director
Bud Kraft, Advocacy Director
Terry Hunt, Community Services Consultant

An advocacy organization that engages in advocacy, capacity building and systemic change activities that promote self-determination, independence, productivity, integration and inclusion in all facets of community life for people with developmental disabilities.

2395 Michigan Employment Security Commission
7310 Woodward Avenue
Detroit, MI 48202 313-876-5000
FAX 313-876-5304

Brings people and jobs together.

2396 Michigan Protection and Advocacy Service
4095 Legacy Parkway
Lansing, MI 48911 517-487-1755
800-288-5923
FAX 517-487-0827
http://www.mpas.org
e-mail: tmassea@mpas.org
Elmer Cerano, Executive Director

Advocates for people with disabilities and gives information and advice about their rights as a person with disabilities.

2397 State Department of Adult Education
Department of Education
608 W Allegan Street
Lansing, MI 48909 517-241-0162
FAX 517-335-0592
http://www.moe.state.mi.us
e-mail: equity@ed.mde.state.mi.us
James Folkening, Interim Director

Promotes quality adult education.

2398 State GED Administration
201 N Washington Square, 3rd Floor
Lansing, MI 48909 517-373-1692
FAX 517-335-3461
http://www.michigan.gov/mdcd
e-mail: williamsb4@michigan.gov
Ben Williams, GED State Administrator
Amy Heckman, Department Technician

Promotes adult education.

Minnesota

2399 Assistive Technology

Minnesota STAR Program
50 Sherburne Avenue
Saint Paul, MN 55155 651-296-2771
800-657-3863
FAX 651-282-6671
http://www.admin.state.mn.us
e-mail: star.program@state.mn.us
Mary Brogdon, Executive Director

Promotes independent living through technology.

2400 Minnesota Department of Children, Families & Learning

1500 Highway 36 W
Roseville, MN 55113 651-582-8200
FAX 651-582-8202
http://www.educ.state.mn.us/
Works to help communities to improve the well-being of children through programs that focus on education.

2401 Minnesota Department of Human Rights

Army Corps of Engineers
190 E 5th Street
St. Paul, MN 55101 651-296-5663
800-657-3704
FAX 651-296-9064
http://www.humanrights.state.mn.us
e-mail: webmaster@therightsplace.net

2402 Minnesota Governor's Council on Developmental Disabilities

370 Centennial Office Building
Saint Paul, MN 55155 651-296-9964
877-348-0505
FAX 651-297-7200
TDY:612-296-9962
http://www.partnersinpolicymaking.com
e-mail: admin.dd@state.mn.us
Colleen Wieck PhD, Executive Director

To teach best practices in disability, and to teach the competencies of influencing and communication.

2403 Minnesota Life Work Center

1000 La Salle Avenue
Minneapolis, MN 55403 651-962-4763
http://www.stthomas.edu
e-mail: lifework@stthomas.edu
Brian Dusbiber, Director
Mary Kay Kernan, Career Counselor

Supporting the educational goals, personal growth and career management needs of graduate students, education students, and alumni, through professional services and comprehensive resources.

2404 Protection & Advocacy Agency

Minnesota Disability Law Center
430 1st Avenue N
Minneapolis, MN 55401 612-332-1441
800-292-4150
FAX 612-334-5755
TDY:612-332-4668
http://www.mnlegalservices.org/mdlc
e-mail: lcohen@midmnlegal.org
Pamela Huopes, Legal Director
Lisa Cohen, Administrator

2405 State Department of Adult Education

Department of Children, Families & Learning
1500 Highway 36 W
Roseville, MN 55113 651-582-8200
FAX 651-582-8727
http://www.edu.state.mn.us
e-mail: barry.shaffer@state.mn.us
Barry Shaffer, Director Adult Education

Mississippi

2406 Client Assistance Program (CAP): Mississippi Division of Persons with Disabilities

Easter Seals Society
3226 N State Street
Jackson, MS 39216 601-982-7051
888-982-7051
FAX 601-982-1951
http://members.aol.com/msess1/cap.htm
Presley Posey, Director

Provides free services to consumers and applicants of projects, programs and facilities funded under the rehabilitation act.

2407 Correctional Education

PO Box A
Parchman, MS 38738 662-745-6611
FAX 601-745-3101
http://www.mdoc.state.ms.us
Buddy Conger, Director

2408 Mississippi Employment Security Commission

PO Box 1699
Jackson, MS 39215 601-961-7425
FAX 601-961-7448
http://www.mesc.state.ms.us/
e-mail: lmi-info@mesc.state.ms.us
Brings people and jobs together.

2409 Mississippi Project START

Division of Rehabilitation Services
PO Box 1698
Jackson, MS 39215 601-987-4872
800-852-8238
FAX 601-364-2349
Stephen Power, Director

The purpose of Project START is to expand the availability of assistive technology through a comprehensive, consumer-responsive, statewide program of technology-related services. The activities include providing technical assistance, conducting systems analysis, information and referral service, conducting training seminars, performing needs assessment and maintaining an equipment loan program.

2410 State Department of Adult Education

State Board for Community & Jr Colleges
359 NW Street
Jackson, MS 39205 601-359-3498
FAX 601-359-2198
e-mail: dbowman@mdek12.state.ms.us
Eloise Richardson, Director Literacy

Promotes adult education.

2411 State Department of Education

359 NW Street
Jackson, MS 39205 601-359-3498
FAX 601-359-2198
e-mail: dbowman@mdek12.state.ms.us
Promotes quality education.

Missouri

2412 Assistive Technology

4731 S Cochnise
Independence, MO 64055 816-373-5193
800-647-8557
FAX 816-373-9314
http://www.dolir.state.mo.us/matp/
e-mail: matpmo@swbell.net
Diane Golden, Director

2413 Assistive Technology Project

University of Missouri-Kansas City
5100 Rockhill Road
Kansas City, MO 64110 816-235-2660
FAX 517-373-8439
http://www.umka.edu
Promotes independent living through technology.

2414 Correctional Education

Department of Corrections
PO Box 236
Jefferson City, MO 65102 573-751-2389
FAX 573-526-3009
http://www.corrections.state.mo.us/divis
Dr. John J Bell, Director

2415 Equal Employment Opportunity Commission

1222 Spruce Street
St. Louis, MO 63103 314-539-5100
FAX 314-539-7895

These regional offices of agencies enforce laws prohibiting employment discrimination on the basis of disability.

2416 Great Plains Disability and Business Technical Assistance Center (DBTAC)

100 Corparte Lake Drive
Columbia, MO 65203 573-882-3600
800-949-4232
FAX 573-884-4925
http://www.adaproject.org
e-mail: ada@missouri.edu
Jim Dejong, Executive Director

Mission is to provide accurate, up-to-date technical information and links to resources regarding the Americans with Disabilities Act. The ADA Project has provided technical assistance since 1991 as one of ten regional Disability and Technical Assistance Centers (DBTAC) established by the National Institute for Disability and Rehabilitation Research (NIDDR)

2417 Learning Disabilities Association of Missouri

PO Box 3303
Springfield, MO 65808 417-864-5110
FAX 417-864-7290
http://www.ldamo.org
e-mail: ldamo@cland.net
Eleanor Scherff, Director

2418 Missouri Commission on Human Rights

906 Olive Street
St. Louis, MO 63101 314-444-7590
FAX 314-340-7238
http://www.dohir.state.mo.us/hr

2419 Missouri Protection & Advocacy Services

925 S Country Club Drive
Jefferson City, MO 65109 573-893-3333
800-392-8667
FAX 573-893-4231
http://www.moadvocacy.org
e-mail: mopasjc@earthlink.com
Shawn de Loyola, Executive Director

Protects the rights of individuals with disabilities by providing advocacy and legal services. With branch offices in St. Louis 800-233-3958; Kansas City 800-233-3959; Cape Girardeau 800-356-3163; De Soto 877-321-4419; and Springfield 888-632-9551.

2420 Protection & Advocacy Agency

925 S Country Club Drive
Jefferson City, MO 65109 573-893-3333
800-392-8667
FAX 573-893-4231
Shawn Deloyola, Director

Protects the rights of individuals with disabilities by providing advocacy and legal services.

2421 Region VII: US Department of Health and Human Services

Office of Civil Rights
601 E 12th Street
Kansas City, MO   64106   816-426-7278
                                 800-368-1019
                          FAX 816-426-3686
                          TDY:816-426-7065
                http://www.hhs.gov/region7

The office for Civil Rights investigates complaints of discrimination against hospitals, nursing homes, social service agencies, mental health facilities, and other federally funded providers of health and social services. The office enforces Title II of the Americans with Disabilities Act with respect to all state and local government entities providing health and social services. This includes public medical and other health training schools and state-provided child care.

Montana

2422 Assistive Technology Project

Rural Institute on Disabilities
52 Corbin Hall
Missoula, MT   59812   406-243-5467
                       FAX 406-243-4730

William Lamb

This statewide program at the University of Montana promotes assistive devices and services for persons of all ages with disabilities.

2423 Correctional Education

Department of Corrections & Human Services
1539 11th Avenue
Helena, MT   19620   406-444-3930
                     FAX 406-444-4920
        http://www.cor.state.mt.us/css/default.csp
Jack Powers, Director

2424 Developmental Disabilities Planning and Advisory Council

111 N Last Chance Gulch, Unit 1C
Helena, MT   59624   406-444-1334
                            800-337-9942
                     FAX 406-444-5999
        e-mail: dswingley@state.mt.us
Deborah Swingley, Executive Director

2425 MonTECH

634 Eddy Avenue
Missoula, MT   59812   406-243-5676
                              800-732-0323
                       FAX 406-243-4730
        http://www.ruralinstitute.umt.edu
        e-mail: montech@selway.umt.edu

2426 Montana Department of Labor & Industry

PO Box 1728
Helena, MT   59624   406-444-3555
                            800-922-2873
                     FAX 406-444-1394

Promotes well being of Montana's workers, employees and citizens.

2427 Montana Office of Public Instruction

PO Box 202501
Helena, MT   59620   406-444-3680
                            888-231-9393
                     FAX 406-444-3924
      http://www.asd.com/asd/edconn/tfrdoe.htm

Supports schools so that students acheive high standards.

2428 Office of Adult Basic and Literacy Education

Montana Office of Public Instruciton
PO Box 202501
Helena, MT   59620   406-444-4443
                     FAX 406-444-1373
            http://www.metnet.state.mt.us
Becky Bird, Director

Nebraska

2429 Answers4Families: Center on Children, Families, Law

121 S 13th Street
Lincoln, NE   68588
                http://www.answers4families.org/nrrs
                e-mail: chayek@answers4families.org
Connie K Hayek, Director
Sharon Bloechle, Omaha Parent Coordinator

A project of the Center on Children, Families and Law at University of Nebraska. Mission is to provide info, opportunities, education and support to Nebraskans through Internet resources. The Center serves individuals with special needs and mental health disorders, foster families, caregivers, assisted living, and school nurses.

2430 Assistive Technology Project

Department of Education
5143 S 48th Street
Lincoln, NE   68516   402-471-0734
                             888-806-6287
                      FAX 402-471-6052
      http://www.nde.state.ne.us/ATP/TECHome.html
          e-mail: mschultz@atp.state.ne.us

Government Agencies/Nevada

2431 Client Assistance Program (CAP): Nebraska Division of Persons with Disabilities

Nebraska Department of Education
301 Centennial Mall S
Lincoln, NE 68509   402-471-3656
     800-742-7594
     FAX 402-471-0117
http://www.nde.state.ne.us
e-mail: victoria@cap.state.ne.us

The Client Assistance Program helps individuals who have concerns or difficulties when applying for or receiving rehabilitation services funded under the Rehabilitation Act.

2432 Nebraska Department of Labor

550 S 16th Street
Lincoln, NE 68508   402-471-2600
     FAX 402-471-9867
http://www.dol.state.ne.us/
e-mail: lme_ne@dol.state.ne.us

2433 Nebraska Equal Opportunity Commission

1313 Farnam on the Mall
Omaha, NE 68102   402-595-2028
     FAX 402-595-1205
e-mail: mclancy@ops.org

2434 State Department of Education

301 Centennial Mall S
Lincoln, NE 68509   402-471-2295
     FAX 402-471-0117
http://www.nde.state.ne.us

Mission to lead and support the preparation of all Nebraskans for learning, earning, and living.

2435 State GED Administration

Department of Eduction: Adult & Community
301 Centennial Mall S
Lincoln, NE 68509   402-471-4807
     FAX 402-471-0117

Vicki Bauer, Director

Promotes adult education.

2436 Vocational Rehabilitation Services for Central/East Nebraska

3335 W Capital Avenue
Grand Island, NE 68803   308-385-6200
     FAX 402-471-0788
http://www.nchtm.okstate.edu
e-mail: Idaafneb@yahoo.com

Helps individuals with disabilites to secure employment through career planning, education and training, and restorative services as necessarsy to help secure employment. Other county offices are: Columbus 402-562-8065; North Platte 308-535-8100; Central East 308-385-6200; Omaha 402-595-2100; Kearney 308-865-5343; Scottsbluff 308-632-1321; Lincoln 402-471-2331; South Sioux City 402-494-2265; Norfolk 402-370-3200.

Nevada

2437 Assistive Technology

Office of Community Based Services
711 S Stewart Street
Carson City, NV 89701   775-687-4452
     FAX 775-687-3292
     TDY:701-687-3388
e-mail: kvogel@gov.mail.state.nv.us
Donny Loux, Chief
Ken Vogel, Director
George Brown, Chairperson

Promotes independent living through technology.

2438 Client Assistance Program (CAP): Nevada Division of Persons with Disability

2450 Wrondel Way
Reno, NV 89502   702-486-6888
     800-633-9879
http://www.detr.state.nv.us/rehab/reh_cap
e-mail: detrcap@nvdtr.orgte.nv.us

Provides free services to consumers and applicants of projects, programs and facilities funded under the rehabilitation act.

2439 Correctional Education

State Department of Prisons
PO Box 607
Carson City, NV 89702   775-887-8588
     FAX 775-887-3420
http://www.prisons.state.nu.us/
e-mail: ndopinfo@goumail.state.nu.us
George Weeks, Director

To continue and expand an educational training program which contains literacy, ESL, numeracy, community outreach, and vocational training that will provide long-term benefits to both inmates and the Nevada community in general.

2440 Nevada Bureau of Disability Adjudication

1050 E Williams Street
Carson City, NV 89701   775-687-4430
http://www.detr.state.nv.us/rehab

Evaluates applications from individuals with permanent disabilities to determine if they are eligible for federal Supplemental Security Income or Social Security Disability Insurance (SSDI).

2441 Nevada Employment Security Department

500 E 3rd Street
Carson City, NV 89713   775-684-3909
     FAX 775-684-3910
http://www.detr.state.nv.us/es/es_index.htm
e-mail: bakeresd@govmail.state.nv.us

2442 Nevada Employment Services: Department of Employment, Training and Rehabilitation

Employment Security Division
500 E 3rd Street
Carson City, NV 89713   775-687-4635
     FAX 775-684-8681

291

2443 Nevada Equal Rights Commission: Fair Employment Practice Agency

Tropicana Avenue
Las Vegas, NV 89119   702-486-7161
                                   FAX 702-486-7054
                                   TDY:702-486-7164
                        http://www.detr.state.nu.us/nerc/
                        e-mail: detrnerc@goumail.state.nu.us

To foster the rights of all persons to seek, obtain and maintain employment, and to access services in places of public accommodation without discrimination, distinction, exclusion or restriction because of race, religion, creed, color, age, sex, disability, national origin or ancestry.

2444 Nevada Governor's Council on Developmental Disabilities

711 S Stewart Street
Carson City, NV 89701   775-687-4452
                                   FAX 775-687-3292
                                   TDY:702-687-3388
                        e-mail: kvogel@govmail.state.nv.us
George Brown, Chairperson
Ken Vogel, Director

2445 Nevada Governor's Council on Rehabilitation & Employment of People with Disabilities

1325 Corporate Boulevard
Reno, NV 89502   775-688-1111
                        e-mail: mailto:kfbarth@nvdetr.org
Donna Sanders, Executive Director

To help insure vocational rehabilitation programs are consumer oriented, driven and result in employment outcomes for Nevadans with disabilities. Funding for innovation and expansions grants

2446 Protection & Advocacy Agency

State Disability and Law Center
6039 Eldora Avenue
Las Vegas, NV 89146   702-257-8150
                                        888-349-3843
                                   FAX 702-257-8170
                                http://www.ndalc.org
                        e-mail: ndalc@earthlink.net
Jack Mayes, Executive Director

Nevada's protection and advocacy system for individuals with disabilities.

2447 State Department of Adult Education

Nevada Department of Education
700 E 5th Street
Carson City, NV 89701   775-687-9200
                                   FAX 775-687-9101
                        e-mail: mkmoen@nsn.142.nu.us/
David Sheffield, President

2448 State Department of Education

700 E 5th Street
Carson City, NV 89701   775-687-9200
                                   FAX 775-687-9101
                        http://www.nde.state.nu.us/

New Hampshire

2449 Client Assistance Program: Governor's Commission on Disability

57 Regional Drive
Concord, NH 03301   603-271-2773
                                        800-852-3405
                                   FAX 603-271-2837
William G McGonagle, Education Director

Provides information about vocational rehabilitation services.

2450 Granite State Independent Living Foundation

21 Chennell Drive
Concord, NH
                                http://www.gsil.org
Clyde Terry, Executive Director

A private, non-profit organization committed to equality of opportunity for all people with disabilities. GSIL is a statewide information, advocacy, and direct-services organization run by and for people with disabilities.

2451 Institute on Disability

New Hampshire Technology Partnership Project
Morrill Hall
Durham, NH 03820   603-862-0561
                                   FAX 603-862-0034
                http://www.NHassistivetechnology.org
                        e-mail: Twillkomm@NHATT.MV.com
Marion Pawlek, Project Coordinator

2452 New Hampshire Commission for Human Rights

2 Chenell Drive
Concord, NH 03301   603-271-2767
                                   FAX 603-271-6339
                        e-mail: humanrights@nhsa.state.nh.us
Raymond S Perry Jr, Executive Director

Investigates complaints of discrimination in employment, housing and public accommodations based on a person's, race, color, religion, national origin, sex, age, marital status, disability or sexual orientation.

2453 New Hampshire Developmental Disabilities Council

267 Forest Street
Concord, NH 03301   603-271-3236
                        800-852-3345
                        FAX 603-271-1156
                        TDY:800-735-2964
                        http://www.nhddc.com
                        e-mail: nhddcncl@aol.com
Alan Robichaud, Executive Director

2454 New Hampshire Employment Security

32 S Main Street
Concord, NH 03301   603-224-3311
                        800-852-3400
                        FAX 603-228-4145
                        TDY:800-735-2964
                        http://www.nhes.state.nh.us
Sandy Smith Dupree, Public Information Officer

Refers individuals with disabilities to organizations and agencies that assist people with disabilities without charge.

2455 New Hampshire Governor's Commission on Disability

57 Regional Drive
Concord, NH 03301   603-271-2773
                        800-852-3405
                        FAX 603-271-2837
                        http://www.state.nh.us/disability
                        e-mail: cnadeau@gov.state.nh.us
Carole A Nadeau, Executive Director
Maureen Stimpson, Project Specialist

The goal is to remove the barriers, architectural or attitudinal, which bar persons with disabilities from participating in the mainstream of society. Formulates an integrated, comprehensive statewide plan to address the needs of individuals with disabilities. Responds to requests wtih answers to service providers, legislators, state and local officials and the many laws and regulations that affect disability issues. Weekly newpaper column, Beyond the Barriers, and newsletter, The Blue Sheet.

2456 Parent Information Center: New Hampshire Coalition for Citizens With Disabilities

PO Box 2405
Concord, NH 03302   603-224-7005
                        800-947-7005
                        FAX 603-224-4365
                        http://www.parentinformationcenter.org
Heather Thallheimer, Executive Director

Works with families through parent training sessions, educational consultations about special ed needs and workshops, provides information, support, and an educational surrogate-parent training and mediation. Governed by a Board comprised of families with members with disability. Established Advisory Council to adsive the staff of community needs. Additional offices in Gorham, 800-286-3006, Mollie White; Manchester, 603-624-8082, Lynn Bolser; Nashua, 603-598-8012; Rochester, 603-330-0896.

2457 Protection & Advocacy Agency

PO Box 3660
Concord, NH 03302   603-228-0432
                        800-834-1721
                        FAX 603-225-2077
Donna Woodfin, Executive Director

2458 ServiceLink

555 Auburn Street
Manchester, NH 03103   603-644-2240
                        866-634-9412
                        FAX 603-625-1148
                        http://www.state.nh.us/servicelink
Grace Ryan

Provides community information and assistance to adults with disabilities in accessing services for caregiver support, financial and legal concerns, home care services, housing information, prescription drug options, recreational and social events, volunteer opportunities, wellness education. Offices in Laconia, Chocorua, Keene, Berlin, Littleton, Manchester, Lebanon, Nashua, Concord, Portsmouth, Rochester, Claremont and more satellites in each county, all reached through the toll-free number.

2459 State Department of Education: Division of Vocational Rehabilitation and State GED Administration

101 Pleasant Street
Concord, NH 03301   603-271-3759
                        FAX 603-271-1953
                        TDY:603-271-6698
                        http://www.ed.state.nh.us
                        e-mail: pleatuer@ed.state.nh.us
Paul K Leather, Administrator

Provides assistance to eligible persons with disabilities in the State of New Hampshire to gain and retain employment outcomes through the provision of direct vocational rehabilitation services, as funded under the Rehabilitation Act Amendments of 1992.

2460 The Institute on Disability at theUniversity of New Hampshire

105 Pleasant Street
Concord, NH 03301   603-271-8349
                        FAX 603-271-5265
                        http://www.iod.unh.edu
Jan Nisbet, Director
Mary Schuh, Associate Director

Establishsed to provide a coherent university-based focus for the improvement of knowledge, policy and practice related to persons with disabilities. Our mission is to promote their full inclusion into their communities through areas of Early Childhood, High School/Post Secondary, Adult Community Living, Technology, Public Policy, Leadership Training/Professional Development and publications. Workshops/seminars contact The Concord Center, Unit 14, 10 Ferry Street, Concord NY 03301, 800-238-2048

New Jersey

2461 Assistive Technology

State Technology Assisted Resource Program
210 S Broad Street
Trenton, NJ 08608   609-292-9742
    800-382-7765
    FAX 609-777-0187

2462 New Jersey Department of Education: Special Education

Office of Special Education Programs
100 Riverview Plaza
Trenton, NJ 08625   609-292-0147
    800-322-8174
    FAX 609-984-8422
    http://www.state.nj.us
Barbara Gantwerk, Director

The office is resonsible for administering all federal funds received for educating people with disabilities ages 3 through 21. Also monitors the delivery of special education programs operated under state authority, provides mediation services to parents and school districts, processes hearings and conducts complaint investigations. Also funds four learning resource centers (LRCs) that provide information, circulate materials, offer technical assistance/consultation and production services.

2463 New Jersey Department of Law and Public Safety

New Jersey Division on Civil Rights
31 Clinton Street
Newark, NJ 07102   973-648-2700
    FAX 973-648-4405

The Division on Civil Rights enforces the New Jersey Law Against Discrimination which prohibits discrimination in employment, housing and public accommodations because of race, creed, color, national origin, ancestry, sex, affectional and sexual orientation, marital status, nationality or handicap.

2464 Protection & Advocacy Agency

NJ Protection & Advocacy
210 S Broad Street
Trenton, NJ 08608   609-292-9742
    800-922-7233
    FAX 609-777-0187
    TDY:800-852-7899
Rick Considine, Director Outreach/Communication

NJP&A is a private nonprofit consumer driven organization established to advocate for and protect the civil, human and leagal rights of citizens of New Jersey with disabilities.

2465 State Department of Adult Education

Department of Education
100 Riverview Plaza
Trenton, NJ 08625   609-633-9627
    FAX 609-633-9825
    http://www.state.nj.us/education
Arlene Roth, Director Adult Education

2466 State GED Administration: Office of Specialized Populations

New Jersey Department of Education
100 River View Plaza
Trenton, NJ 08625   609-633-9627
    FAX 609-633-9825
Arlene Roth, Director

New Mexico

2467 Client Assistance Program (CAP): New Mexico Protection and Advocacy System

1720 Louisiana Boulevard NE
Albuquerque, NM 87110   505-256-3100
    800-432-4682
    http://www.nmpanda.org/selfadv/cap/capman
James Jackson, Executive Director

Helps persons with disabilities who have concerns about agencies in New Mexico that provide rehabilitation or independent living services. The kind of help may be information or advocacy. For questions about Division of Vocational Rehabilitation, Commission for the Blind, Independent Living Centers and Preojects With Industsry CAP can help.

2468 New Jersey Programs for Children with Disabilities: Ages 3 - 5

Office of Special Education Programs
135 E Street
Trenton, NJ 08625   609-292-2912
    FAX 609-292-7276

Programs for young children with learning disabilities.

2469 New Jersey Programs for Infants and Toddlers with Disabilities: Early Intervention System

Division of Family Health Services
PO Box 364
Trenton, NJ 08625   609-777-7734
    FAX 609-292-0296
    http://www.state.nj.us/health/fhs/eiphome.htm
Terry Harrison, Coordinator

Implements a statewide system of service for infants and toddlers, birth to age three, with developmental delays or disabilities. Maintains Services-Case Management in each county as entry into the system. Here a service coordinator talks with the family about their concerns and offers referral information if needed. If developmental evaluation is indicated, the coordinator will facilitate a multidisciplinary evaluation and assessment with no cost to the parents.

2470 New Mexico Department of Labor: Employment Services and Job Training Programs

PO Box 1928
Albuquerque, NM 87103   505-841-8409
                                    FAX 505-841-8491
        http://www3.state.nm.us/dol/dol_esd.html

Currently composed of two bureaus and under the supervision of a Division Director responsible for the design, administration, management and implementation of the Workforce Investment Act in New Mexico and any successor legislation. Within this capacity, the Division serves on behalf of the Governor with respect to statewide oversight and compliance, and as the principle support staff to the State Workforce Development Board.

2471 New Mexico Developmental Disabilities Plan

435 Saint Michaels Drive
Santa Fe, NM 87505   505-827-7590
                                 FAX 505-827-7589

Patrick Putnam, Director

2472 New Mexico Human Rights Commission Education Bureau

1596 Pacheo Street
Santa Fe, NM 87505   505-827-6838
                                 FAX 505-827-6878
        http://www.user.gov/crd/cds_all.htm

2473 New Mexico Technology-Related Assistance Program

Department of Education
300 Don Gaspar Avenue
Santa Fe, NM 87503   505-954-8521
                                 FAX 505-827-5066
        e-mail: mlandazuri@ade.state.nm.us
Andrew Winnegar, Project Director

2474 Northeast Disability & Business Technical Assistance Center (NeDBTAC)

354 S Broad Street
Trenton, NJ 08608

                                 800-949-4232
                                 FAX 609-392-3505
                                 TDY:609-392-7044
        http://www.disabilityact.com
Huntly Forester, Project Director

Offers training and information on the Americans with Disabilities Act (ADA). The Center is a technical assistance program which provides important information and training to all businesses, employers, government agencies and persons with disabilities, plus tax incentive information. Free quarterly newsletter: EVERYBODY'S BUSINESS.

2475 Protection & Advocacy System

1720 Louisiana Boulevard
Albuquerque, NM 87110   505-256-3100
                                 800-432-4682
                                 FAX 505-256-3184
        http://www.nmprotection-advocacy.com
        e-mail: nmpacurtiss@hotmail.com
James Jackson, Executive Director

2476 State Department of Adult Education

Department of Education
300 Don Gaspar Avenue
Santa Fe, NM 87501   505-827-6672
                                 FAX 505-623-8220
        http://www.sde.state.nm.us
Patricia M Chavez, Contact

2477 State Department of Education

300 Don Gaspar Avenue
Santa Fe, NM 87503   505-827-6788
                                 FAX 505-827-6696
        e-mail: mlandazuri@sde.state.nm.us
Patricia M Chavez

2478 State GED Administration

Assessment & Evaluation
300 Don Gaspar Avenue
Santa Fe, NM 87503   505-827-6788
                                 FAX 505-827-6696
        e-mail: mlandazuri@sde.state.nm.us
Dr. Carroll Hall, Director

New York

2479 Client Assistance Program

CAP Director, NY Commission on Quality of Care
99 Washington Avenue
Albany, NY 12210   518-473-7378
                                 FAX 800-624-4143

Provides free services to consumers and applicants for projects, programs and facilities funded under the rehabilitation act.

2480 Department of Correctional Services

1220 Washington Avenue
Albany, NY 12226   518-457-8126
                                 FAX 518-457-7252
        http://www.docs.state.ny.us/
George Newman

2481 New York Department of Human Rights

1 Fordham Plaza
Bronx, NY   10458   718-741-8400
                                          FAX 718-935-2531
                                          http://www.nysdhr.com

2482 New York Department of Labor: Employment Services & Job Training

State Office Building Campus
Albany, NY   12240   518-457-6369
                                          FAX 518-485-1773
              http://www.labor.state.ny.us/html/dolemp.htm
                      e-mail: nysdol@labor.state.ny.us

2483 New York Office of Advocates: TRAID Project

1 Empire State Plaza
Albany, NY   12223   518-474-2825
                                          800-522-4369
                                       FAX 518-473-6005
                 http://www.advoc4disabled.state.ny.us
        e-mail: oapwdinfo@advoc4disabled.state.ny.us
Lisarah Rosano-Kackowski, Project Manager

A statewide systems advocacy program promoting assistive technology devices and services to persons of all ages with all disabilities.

2484 New York State Developmental Disabilities Council

155 Washington Avenue
Albany, NY   12210   518-486-7505
                                          800-395-3372
                                       FAX 518-402-3505
                                       TDY:800-395-3372
                      e-mail: grants@ddpc.stste.ny.us
Sheila M Carey, Executive Director

2485 New York State Office of Vocational & Educational Services for Individuals with Disabilities

301 Manchester Road
Poughkeepsie, NY   12603   845-452-5325
                                       FAX 845-452-5336
                                       TDY:845-452-5336
Bruce Solomkin, District Office Manager

The Office of Vocational and Educational Services for Individuals with Disabilities (VESID), helps people with disabilities find and maintain employment. Services include job placement, training at colleges, tuition assistance based on economic need, home and vehicle modifications, vocational guidance and counseling.

2486 Office of Advocacy for Persons with Disabilities

One Empire State Plaza
Albany, NY   12223   518-474-2825
                                       FAX 518-473-6005
                                       TDY:518-473-4231
Deborah V Buck, Project Manager

2487 Office of Curriculum & Instructional Support

State Department of Adult Education
Washington Avenue
Albany, NY   12234   518-474-8892
                                       FAX 518-474-0319
              http://www.emsc.nysed.gov/workforce
                      e-mail: jstevens@mail.nysed.gov
Jean C Stevens, Assistant Commisioner

Works with those seeking General Educational Development diplomas and technical training.

2488 Programs for Children with Disabilities: Ages 3 - 5

State Education Department
1 Commerce Plaza
Albany, NY   12234   518-473-6108
                                       FAX 518-473-4057

2489 Programs for Children with Special Health Care Needs

Bureau of Child & Adolescent Health
Corning Tower Building
Albany, NY   12237   518-486-4966
                                       FAX 518-474-5445

2490 Programs for Infants and Toddlers with Disabilities

Early Intervention Program
Bureau of Child & Adolescent Health
Albany, NY   12237   518-473-7016
                                       FAX 518-473-8673

2491 Protection & Advocacy Agency

NY Commission on Quality of Care
99 Washington Avenue
Albany, NY   12210   518-473-7378
                                       FAX 800-624-4143

2492 Region II: US Department of Health and Human Services

Office of Civil Rights
26 Federal Plaza
New York, NY   10278   212-264-3313
                                       FAX 212-264-3039

These regional offices of agencies enforce laws prohibiting employment discrimination on the basis of disability.

2493 State Developmental Disabilities Planning Council

NYS DD Planning Council
Tower Building
Albany, NY   12237   518-474-2084
                                       FAX 518-473-8673

2494 State GED Administration

State Education Department
PO Box 7348
Albany, NY   12224   518-474-3852
                                       FAX 518-474-3041
              http://www.emsc.nysed.gov/workforce/ged
                      e-mail: ged@mail.nysed.gov
Patricia Mooney, GED Administrator

Instruction and testing for those over the age of 16 to earn the General Educational Development diploma.

2495 Vocational & Educational Services for Individuals with Disabilities

New York State Education Department
One Commerce Plaza
Albany, NY 12234   518-474-7566
800-222-5627
FAX 518-473-9466
http://www.vesid.nysed.gov
e-mail: nlauria@mail.nysed.gov
Richard P Mills, Commissioner
Nancy Lauria, Director

Promotes educational equality and excellence for students with disabilities while ensuring that they receive the rights and protection to which they are entitiled. Assures appropriate continuity between the child and adult services systems, and provides the highest quality vocational rehabilitation and independent living services to all eligible people.

North Carolina

2496 Assistive Technology Program

Department of Human Resources
1110 Navaho Drive
Raleigh, NC 27609   919-850-2787
FAX 919-850-2792
TDY:919-850-2787
http://www.ncatp.org
Yeu-Li Yeung, Consumer Resource Specialist

Provides free, statewide assistive technology services such as demonstration, loan, training, funding, resources, awareness and outreach presentations to persons of all ages and abilities.

2497 Client Assistance Program (CAP): North Carolina Division of Persons with Disabilities

2801 Mail Service Center
Raleigh, NC 27699   919-855-3600
800-215-2772
FAX 919-715-2456
e-mail: kathy.brack@ncmail.net
Kathy Brack, Director

The Client Assistance Program helps people understand and use rehabilitation services.

2498 North Carolina Council on Developmental Disabilities

1001 Navaho Drive
Raleigh, NC 27609   919-850-2833
800-357-6916
FAX 919-850-2895
TDY:800-357-6916
http://www.nc-ddc.org
e-mail: hriddle@ddc.dhr.state.nc.us
William B Morris III, Council Chair
Holly Riddle JD MEd, Executive Director

2499 North Carolina Division of Employment and Training

313 Chapanoke Road
Raleigh, NC 27604   919-661-6010
800-562-6333
FAX 919-662-4770
http://www.ncdet.com
Alan Alexander, Director

2500 North Carolina Division of Vocational Rehabilitation

Department of Human Resources
2801 Mail Service Center
Raleigh, NC 27699   919-855-3500
FAX 919-733-7968
http://www.dvr.dhhs.state.nc.us
e-mail: gmccoy@dhr.state.nc.us
Carmen Hooker-Odom, Secretary Health/Human Services
George McCoy, Director

Vocational rehabilitation counselors work with business and community agencies to help them prepare their worksites to accommodate employees who have physical or mental disabilities. The division also provides services that encourage and reinforce independent living for the disabled.

2501 North Carolina Employment Security Commission

PO Box 27625
Raleigh, NC 27605   919-733-7522
FAX 919-733-0773

2502 North Carolina Office of Administrative Hearings: Civil Rights Division

PO Box 27447
Raleigh, NC 27611   919-733-0431
FAX 919-733-4866

2503 Office of the Governor

116 W Jones Street
Raleigh, NC 27603   919-733-7061
FAX 919-733-0640
Jane S Patterson, Senior Advisor for Policy

2504 State Department of Adult Education

North Carolina Community College System
Caswell Building
Raleigh, NC 27603   919-733-7051
FAX 919-733-0680
e-mail: randyw@ncccs.cc.nc.us
Dr. Randy Whitfield, Associate VP

North Dakota

2505 Client Assistance Program (CAP): Nebraska Division of Persons with Disabilities

600 S 2nd Street
Bismarck, ND   58504
701-328-8947
800-207-6122
FAX 701-328-8968
http://www.state.nd.us/cap/
e-mail: cap@state.nd.us

Dennis Lyon, Director

Provides free services to consumers and applicants for projects, programs and facilities funded under the rehabilitation act.

2506 North Dakota Department of Human Services

Vocational Rehabilitation
600 S 2nd Street
Bismarck, ND   58504
701-328-8950
800-755-2745
FAX 701-328-8969
http://www.dnotes.state.nd.us/dhs/dhsweb.nsf
e-mail: soperc@state.nd.us

2507 North Dakota Department of Labor: Fair Employment Practice Agency

600 E Boulevard Avenue
Bismarck, ND   58505
701-328-2660
800-582-8032
FAX 701-328-2031
http://www.state.nd.us/labor/
e-mail: labor@state.nd.us

Provides information and enforces laws related to labor standards and discrimination in employment, housing, public services, public accommodations and lending. The department also issues sub minimum wage certificates, verifies independent contractor status and licenses employment agencies.

2508 North Dakota State Council on Developmental Disabilities

ND Department of Human Services
600 E Boulevard Avenue
Bismarck, ND   58505
701-328-8953
FAX 701-328-8969
e-mail: sowalt@state.nd.us

Tom Wallner, Executive Director

2509 State GED Administration

Division of Adult Education
600 E Boulevard Avenue
Bismarck, ND   58505
701-328-2393
FAX 701-328-4770
http://www.dpi.state.nd.us
e-mail: dmassey@sendit.nodak.edu

David Massey, Director Adult Education

Ohio

2510 Assistive Technology

JL Camera Center
2050 Kenny Road
Columbus, OH   43212
614-292-3158
800-784-3425
FAX 614-292-5866
http://www.atohio.org
e-mail: huntt.1@osu.edu

Douglas Hunt, Director

2511 Client Assistance Program (CAP): Ohio Division

Gov Office of Advocacy for People w/Disabilities
Long Street
Columbus, OH   43266
614-466-7264
800-228-5405
FAX 614-644-1888
http://www.stc.te.oh.us

Arthur Schlesinger, Contact

Provides free services to consumers and applicants for projects, programs and facilities funded under the Rehabilitation Act.

2512 Correctional Education

Department of Rehabilitation & Correction
1050 Freeway Drive N
Columbus, OH   43228
614-752-1162
FAX 614-752-1086
http://www.drc.state.oh.us
e-mail: publicinfo@odrc.state.oh.us

Dr. Jerry McGlone, Director

2513 Ohio Adult Basic and Literacy Education

Ohio Department of Education
Mail Stop 406
Columbus, OH   43215
614-466-5015
FAX 614-752-1640
http://www.ode.state.oh.us/ctae/able
e-mail: jim.bowling@ode.state.oh.us

Jim Bowling, State Director

2514 Ohio Bureau of Employment Services and Job Training Program Liaison

145 S Front Street
Columbus, OH   43216
614-466-2100
FAX 614-466-5025

2515 Ohio Civil Rights Commission

1111 E Broad Street
Columbus, OH   43205
614-466-5928
FAX 614-466-6250
http://www.state.oh.us/crc/
e-mail: harringtonc@ocrc.state.oh.us

Beleta Ebron, Regional Director

2516 Ohio Developmental Disabilities Council

8 E Long Street
Columbus, OH 43215 614-466-5205
800-766-7426
FAX 614-466-0298
TDY:614-644-5530
http://www.ohio.gov/ddc
Kay Treanor, Children's Issues Committee

A federal program under the DD Act which strives to develop innovative programs and services to support individuals with disabilities, and to make them more a part of their own communities.

2517 Ohio Governor's Office of Advocacy for People With Disabilities

8 E Long Street
Columbus, OH 43266 614-466-9956
FAX 614-644-1888
Vicky Jenkins, Director

Helps children and adults with disabilities.

2518 Protection & Advocacy Agency

Ohio Legal Rights Service
8 E Long Street
Columbus, OH 43215 614-466-7264
800-282-9181
FAX 614-644-1888
http://www.state.oh.us/drs
e-mail: hn7149@handsnet.org
Advocacy services.

2519 State Department of Education

65 S Front Street
Columbus, OH 43215 614-466-0224
877-644-6338
FAX 614-728-2338
http://www.ode.state.oh.us
e-mail: jeanne.Lance@ode.state.oh.us
Frank New, Director

2520 State GED Administration

State Department of Education
65 S Front Street
Columbus, OH 43215 614-466-0224
FAX 614-728-2338
David Fischer, GED Administrator

Oklahoma

2521 Assistive Technology

OK ABLE Tech/OSU-Wellness Center
1514 W Hall Of Fame
Stillwater, OK 74078 405-744-9864
800-257-1705
FAX 405-744-2487
TDY:888-885-5588
http://www.okabletech.okstate.edu
e-mail: mljwell@okstate.edu
Linda Jaco, Program Manager

2522 Client Assistance Program (CAP): Oklahoma Division

Office of Handicapped Concerns
2712 Villa Promenade, Shepard Mall
Oklahoma City, OK 73107 405-521-3756
800-522-8224
FAX 405-522-6695
TDY:405-522-6706
http://www.state.ok.us/~ohc/cap.html
e-mail: CAP@ohc.state.ok.us
Steven Stokes, Director

The purpose of this program is to advise and inform clients and client applicants of all services and benefits available to them through programs authorized under the Rehabilitation Act of 1973. Assist and advocates for clients and client applicants in their relationships with projects, programs, and community rehabilitation programs providing services under the Act.

2523 Correctional Education

Department of Corrections
PO Box 11400
Oklahoma City, OK 73136 405-425-2500
FAX 405-425-2578
http://www.doc.state.ok.us
James L Saffle, Director

2524 Oklahoma Disability Law Center

Oklahoma City Office
2915 Classen Boulevard
Oklahoma City, OK 73106 405-525-7755
800-880-7755
FAX 405-525-7759
http://www.oklahomadisabilitylaw.org
e-mail: kbower1@flash.net
Kayla A Bower JD, Director

Protection and advocacy system for people with disabilities.

2525 Protection & Advocacy Agency

Disability Law Center
2915 Classen Boulevard
Oklahoma City, OK 73106 405-525-7755
800-880-7755
FAX 405-525-7759
Kayla Bower, Executive Director

2526 Secretary of Education

2500 N Lincoln Boulevard
Oklahoma City, OK   73105   405-521-3311
                                   FAX 405-521-2971
        http://www.ron_west@mail.sde.state.ok.us
Tim Tall, Director

2527 State Department of Adult Education

Department of Education
2500 N Lincoln Boulevard
Oklahoma City, OK   73105   405-521-4873
                                   800-405-0355
                                   FAX 405-522-3503
              http://www.sde.state.ok.us
        e-mail: linda_young@mail.sde.state.ok.us
Linda Young, Director

2528 State GED Administration

State Department of Education
2500 N Lincoln Boulevard
Oklahoma City, OK   73105   405-521-4873
                                   FAX 405-522-3503

Linda Young, Director

Oregon

**2529 Department of Community Colleges and
Workforce Development**

255 Capitol Street NE
Salem, OR   97310   503-378-8666
                                   FAX 503-378-8444
            http://www.literacynet.org/oregon/
     e-mail: Sharlene.walker@odccwd.state.or.us
*Sharlene Walker, Human Resource Partnerships
Team*

2530 Oregon Advocacy Center

620 SW 5th Avenue
Portland, OR   97204   503-243-2081
                                   800-452-1694
                                   FAX 503-243-1738
              http://www.oradvocacy.org
Robert Joondeph, Director

**2531 Oregon Bureau of Labor and Industry: Fair
Employment Practice Agency**

800 NE Oregon Street
Portland, OR   97232   503-731-4200
                                   FAX 503-731-4208
              http://www.boli.state.or.us

2532 Oregon Council on Developmental Disabilities

540 24th Place NE
Salem, OR   97301   503-945-9941
                                   800-292-4154
                                   FAX 503-945-9947
              http://www.oddc.org
              e-mail: oddc@aol.com
Janna Starr, Executive Director

**2533 Oregon Department of Education:
School-to-Work**

255 Capitol Street NW
Salem, OR   97310   503-378-3584
                                   FAX 503-373-7968
              http://www.ode.state.or.us
        e-mail: ode.frontdesk@ode.state.or.us
Robert Larson, Policy & Research Director
Patrick Burk, Education Policy Deputy

School-to-Work is a federally funded initiative that
provides funding for state and local implementation
of the Oregon Educational Act for the 21st Century.

**2534 Oregon Department of Human Resource Adult &
Family Services Division**

500 Summer Street NE
Salem, OR   97310   503-945-5733
                                   FAX 503-378-2897
              http://www.dhs.state.or.us
              e-mail: dhr.info@state.or.us
Ramona Foley, Assistant Director
Mickey Serice, Deputy

This group combines programs from the former Adult
& Family Services Division and the State Office for
Services to Children and Families.

2535 Oregon Employment Department

875 Union Street NE
Salem, OR   97311   503-947-1394
                                   800-237-3710
                                   FAX 503-947-1668
              http://www.emp.state.or.us
Deborah Lincoln, Director
Greg Hickman, Deputy Director
Odie Vogel, Assistant to Director

Supports economic stability for Oregonians and communities during times of unemployment through the
payment of unemployment benefits. Serves businesses by recruiting and referring the best qualified
applicants to jobs, and provides resources to diverse
job seekers in support of their employment needs.

2536 State Department of Adult Education

Department of Community Colleges
255 Capitol Street NE
Salem, OR   97310   503-378-8648
                                   FAX 503-378-8434
              http://www.odccwd.state.or.us
        e-mail: sharlene.walker@state.or.us
Sharlene Walker, Contact

2537   Technology Access for Life Needs Project

Access Technologies
3070 Lancaster Drive NE
Salem, OR   97305   503-361-1201
                                     FAX 503-370-4530
                                     http://www.taln.org
Laurie Brooks, Executive Director

A statewide program promoting services and assistive
devices for people with disabilities.

2538   Vocational Rehabilitation Division

Department of Human Services
500 Summer Street NE
Salem, OR   97301   503-945-5944
                                     877-277-0513
                                     FAX 503-378-2897
          http://www.dhs.state.or.us/vr/index.html
                          e-mail: info.vr@state.or.us
Jean Thorne, Director Human Services
Stephanie Parrish-Taylor, Program Director

Uses state and federal funds to assist Oregonians who
have disabilities to achieve and maintain employment
and independence.

Pennsylvania

**2539   Client Assistance Program (CAP): Pennsylvania
Division**

1617 JFK Boulevard
Philadelphia, PA   19103   215-557-7112
                                     888-745-2357
                                     FAX 215-557-7602
                                     TDY:215-577-7112
                  http://www.equalemployment.org
                  e-mail: info@equalemployment.org
Steve Pennington, Director

CAP is an advocacy program for people with disabilities administered by the Center for Disability Law and
Policy. CAP helps people who are seeking services
from the Office of Vocational Rehabilitation, Blindness and Visual Services, Centers for Independent
Living and other programs funded under federal law.
CAP services are provided at no charge.

2540   Correctional Education

Bureau of Correction Education
75 Utleg Drive
Camp Hill, PA   17011   717-731-7823
                                     FAX 717-731-7830
                  e-mail: bmaden@cor.state.pa.us
William Mader, Director

2541   Developmental Disabilities Council

Commonwealth Avenue
Harrisburg, PA   17120   717-787-6057
                                     FAX 717-772-0738
                                     http://www.paddc.org
                                     e-mail: info@paddc.org
Graham Mulholland, Executive Director

**2542   Pennsylvania Human Rights Commission and
Fair Employment Practice**

101 S 2nd Street
Harrisburg, PA   17101   717-787-4410
                                     FAX 717-787-0420
                                     TDY:717-783-9308
Homer C Floyd, Executive Director

The PHRC enforces the State's antidiscrimination
laws in employment, housing, public accommodations and education. It receives, investigates, re-
solves and litigates formal complaints filed by
aggrieved persons in three regional offices: Pittsburgh, Harrisburg and Philadelphia.

2543   Pennsylvania Initiative on Assistive Technology

1301 Cecil Moore Avenue
Philadelphia, PA   19122   215-204-1356
                                     FAX 215-204-6336
                                     TDY:215-204-1356
          http://www.temple.edu/ins_disabilities
          e-mail: dianeb@astro.ocis.temple.edu
Amy Goldman, Director

Mission to increase access to assistive technology for
all Pennsylvanians with disabilities.

2544   Pennsylvania's Initiative on Assistive Technology

Institute on Disabilities at Temple University
423 Ritter Annex
Philadelphia, PA   19122   800-204-7428
                                     800-750-7428
                                     FAX 215-204-9371
          http://www.disabilities.temple/edu/piat
          e-mail: piat@temple.edu
Carol Kann, Information Coordinator

2545   Protection & Advocacy Agency

1414 N Cameron Street
Harrisburg, PA   17101   717-236-8110
                                     800-692-7443
                                     FAX 717-236-0192
                                     http://www.ppainc.org
Kevin Casey, Executive Director

Provides information and referral to persons with disabilities and mental health issues.

**2546   Region III: US Department of Health and Human
Services, Civil Rights Office**

US Department of Health & Human Services
3535 Market Street
Philadelphia, PA   19104   215-596-5831
                                     FAX 215-796-5195

These regional offices of agencies enforce laws prohibiting employment discrimination on the basis of
disability.

2547   State Department of Adult Education

333 Market Street
Harrisburg, PA   17101   570-722-3737
                                     FAX 717-783-0583
          http://www.pde.psu.edu/able/index.html
          e-mail: ckeenan@state.pa.us
Cheryl Keenan, Director

2548 State Department of Education

333 Market Street
Harrisburg, PA   17101   717-787-5820
                         FAX 717-787-7222
                  http://www.pde.state.edu
                  e-mail: pde@psupen.psu.edu
Donald M Carroll, Secretary

2549 State GED Administration

Pennsylvania Department of Education
333 Market Street
Harrisburg, PA   17101   717-787-5820
                         FAX 717-787-7222
                  http://www.pde.state.pa
                  e-mail: pde@psupen.psu.edu
Lawrence B Goodwin, Director

Rhode Island

2550 Correctional Education

Rhode Island Department of Corrections
PO Box 8312
Cranston, RI   02920   401-462-1000
                         FAX 401-464-2509
Timothy Murphy, Administrator Education Services

2551 Protection & Advocacy Agency

Rhode Island Disability Law Center
349 Eddy Street
Providence, RI   02903   401-831-3150
                         FAX 401-274-5568
Raymond L Bandusky, Executive Director

2552 Rhode Island Commission for Human Rights

10 Abbott Park Place
Providence, RI   02903   401-277-2661
                         FAX 401-222-2616

**2553 Rhode Island Department of Elementary and
Secondary Education**

Rhode Island Department of Education
400 W Westminister Street
Providence, RI   02903   401-222-4600
                         FAX 401-222-6030
                  e-mail: ccast@ride.ri.net

**2554 Rhode Island Department of Employment
Services & Job Training**

101 Friendship Street
Providence, RI   02903   401-277-3732
                         FAX 401-277-1473
                  http://www.dlt.state.ri.us

2555 Rhode Island Developmental Disabilities Council

Rhode Island Department of Education
400 Bald Hill Road
Warwick, RI   02886   401-737-1238
                         FAX 401-737-3395
                  e-mail: riddc@riddc.org
Marie V Citrone, Executive Director
Mary E Okero, Associate Director
Sylvia Klien, Secretary

2556 State Department of Adult Education

400 W Westminster Street
Providence, RI   02903   401-222-4600
                         FAX 701-222-6030
Robert Mason, Adult Education Specialist

South Carolina

2557 Assistive Technology Program

South Carolina Developmental Disabilities Council
1205 Pendleton Street
Columbia, SC   29201   803-734-0465
                         FAX 803-734-0241
                  http://www.scddc.state.sc.us
Charles Lang, Director

A statewide project established to provide an opportunity for individuals with disabilities to lead the fullest, most productive lives possible.

2558 Protection & Advocacy Agency

3710 Landmark Drive
Columbia, SC   29204   803-782-0639
                              800-922-5225
                         FAX 803-790-1946
                  e-mail: scpa@sc-online.net
Gloria M Prevost, Executive Director

2559 South Carolina Department of Corrections

4444 Broad River Road
Columbia, SC   29221   803-896-8555
                         FAX 803-896-1220
                  http://www.state.sc.us
                  e-mail: corrections.info@doc.state.sc.us

2560 **South Carolina Developmental Disabilities Council**

1205 Pendleton Street
Columbia, SC   29201   803-734-0465
                              FAX 803-734-0241
Charles B Lang, Executive Director

2561 **South Carolina Employment Services and Job Training Services**

PO Box 995
Columbia, SC   29202   803-737-2617
                              FAX 803-737-2642
                  e-mail: mmungo@sces.org

2562 **South Carolina Governor's Committee on Employment of the Handicapped**

1410 Boston Avenue
West Columbia, SC   29171   803-822-5324
                                   FAX 803-822-5386

2563 **South Carolina Human Affairs Commission**

2611 Forest Drive
Columbia, SC   29204   803-737-7800
                              800-521-0725
                        FAX 803-253-4191
                     http://www.state.sc.us
        e-mail: information@schac.state.sc.us
Dr. Willis Ham, Contact

2564 **State Department of Adult Education**

1429 Senate Street
Columbia, SC   29201   803-734-8071
                              FAX 803-734-2780
             http://www.sde.state.sc.us/sde
            e-mail: cldaniel@sde.state.sc.us
Ramona Williams Carr, Interim Director

2565 **State GED Administration**

Department of Education
1429 Senate Street
Columbia, SC   29201   803-734-0322
                              FAX 803-734-6142
David Stout, GED Administrator

South Dakota

2566 **Client Assistance Program (CAP): South Dakota Division**

South Dakota Advocacy Services
221 S Central Avenue
Pierre, SD   57501   605-224-8294
                            800-658-4782
                      FAX 605-224-5125
                http://www.sdadvocacy.com
           e-mail: sdas@sdadvocacy.com
Brady L Kerkman, Director

Provides free services to consumers and applicants for projects, programs and facilities funded under the rehabilitation act.

2567 **Department of Correction: Education Coordinator**

Solem Public Safety Center
3200 E Highway 34
Pierre, SD   57501   605-773-3478
                            FAX 605-773-3194
                      http://www.state.sd.us/
          e-mail: DOCInternetinfo@state.sd.us

2568 **South Dakota Council on DevelopmentalDisabilities**

Department of Human Services
Hillsview Plaza, E Highway 34
Pierre, SD   57501   605-773-6339
                            FAX 605-773-5483
                      TDY:605-773-5990
            http://www.state.sd.us/dhs/ddc
       e-mail: info@DCC.dhs.state.sd.us
Arlene Poncelet, Executive Director

Established by the Developmental Disabilities Assistance Act, the council is made up of 21 members appointed by the Governor. The council works toward independence, productivity, integration and inclusion of individuals with developmental disabilities and their families.

2569 **South Dakota Department of Labor: Employment Services & Job Training**

700 Governors Drive
Pierre, SD   57501   605-773-5071
                            FAX 605-773-4211
             http://www.state.sd.us/dol/dol.htm
            e-mail: miker@dol.pr.state.sd.us
Michael Ryan, Administrator

Job training programs provide an important framework for developing public-private sector partnerships. We help prepare South Dakotans of all ages for entry or re-entry into the labor force.

2570 **South Dakota Division of Human Rights**

118 W Capitol Avenue
Pierre, SD   57501   605-773-4493
                            FAX 605-773-6893
                http://www.state.sd.us/dor/hr/
          e-mail: marianne.gabriel@state.sd.us

2571 South Dakota Division of Special Education

Department of Education
700 Governors Drive
Pierre, SD   57501   605-773-3678
                                        FAX 605-773-3782
http://www.state.sd.us/deca/special/special.htm
e-mail: michelle.powers@state.sd.us
Deborah Barnett, Director

The Office of Special Education advocates for the
availability of the full range of personnel, programming, and placement options, including early intervention and transition services, required to assure that
all individuals with disabilities are able to achieve
maximum independence upon exiting from school.

2572 State GED Administration

Department of Labor
700 Governors Drive
Pierre, SD   57501   605-773-5821
                                        FAX 605-773-6184
e-mail: roxie.thielen@state.sd.us
Marcia Hess, Adult Education/Literacy

2573 Youth Dakota Advocacy Services

221 S Central
Pierre, SD   57501   605-224-8294
                                               800-658-4782
                                        FAX 605-224-5125
e-mail: sdas@iw.net
Robert Kean, Executive Director
Nancy Schade, Director

Tennessee

2574 Council on Developmental Disabilities

425 5th Avenue N
Nashville, TN   37243   615-532-6615
                                        FAX 615-532-6964
                                        TDY:615-741-4562
e-mail: wwillis@mail.state.tn.us
Wanda Willis, Executive Director

**2575 Department of Human Services: Division of
Rehabilitation Services**

400 Deaderick Street
Nashville, TN   37248   615-313-4714
                                        FAX 615-741-4165
http://www.state.tn.us/humanserv/
e-mail: carlbrown@mail.state.tn.usa
Carl Brown, Assistant Commissioner

Agency takes an active leadership role in removing
the barriers to employment due to disabilities.

2576 State Department of Education

710 James Robertson Parkway
Nashville, TN   37243   615-741-2731
                                        FAX 615-532-4791
http://www.state.tn.us/education
e-mail: phobbins@mail.state.tn.us
Phil White, Contact

2577 State GED Administration

State Department of Education
Andrew Johnson Tower
Nashville, TN   37210   615-741-2731
                                        FAX 615-532-4791
Phil White, GED Administrator

2578 Tennessee Division of Rehabilitation Services

Tennessee Department of Human Services
400 Deaderick Street
Nashville, TN   37248   615-313-4918
                                        FAX 615-741-6508
http://www.state.tn.us/humanserv/
e-mail: Human-Services.Webmaster@state.tn.us
Gina Lodge, Commissioner Human Services
Philip Wagster, Director Vocational Rehab

Federal and state funded services to help individuals
with disabilities enter or return to employment.

2579 Tennessee Technology Access Project

400 Deadrick Street
Nashville, TN   37243   615-532-3122
                                               800-732-5059
                                        FAX 615-532-4685
http://www.state.tn.us
e-mail: ttap@mail.state.tn.us
Rob Roberts, Project Director

Texas

2580 Advocacy

7800 Shoal Creek Boulevard
Austin, TX   78757   512-454-4816
                                               800-252-9108
                                        FAX 512-323-0902
e-mail: hn2414@handsnet.org
Mary Faithfull, Interm Executive Director
Karenh Stanfill, CAP Coordinator

2581 LAUNCH

Department of Special Education
Commerce, TX   75428   903-886-5594
                                        FAX 903-886-5510

An organization that provides resources for learning
disabled individuals, coordinates efforts of other local, state and national LD organizations.

2582 Learning Disabilities Association

1011 W 31st Street
Austin, TX   78705   512-458-8234
800-604-7500
FAX 512-458-3826
http://www.ourworld.compuserve.com
e-mail: ldatexas@cs.com
Ann Robinson

Provides information, support and referrals.

2583 Southwest Texas Disability & Business Technical Assistance Center: Region VI

2323 S Shepherd Drive
Houston, TX   77019   713-520-0232
800-949-4232
FAX 713-520-5785
http://www.bcm.tmc.edu/ilru/dbtac/index.html

Southwest DBTA is the resource for trainings, technical assistance and materials on the ADA in Federal Region VI. Authorized to provide training information, materials and technical assistance to individuals and entities that are protected or have obligations under the Americans with Disabilities Act. Project staff with expertise in all areas of the ADA are available.

2584 State GED Administration

Texas Education Agency
1701 Congress Avenue
Austin, TX   78701   512-463-9292
FAX 512-305-9493
http://www.tea.state.tx.us
e-mail: proussos@mail.tea.state.tx.us
Dr. Walter Tillman, Education Services

2585 Texas Commission on Human Rights

6330 Highway 290 E
Austin, TX   78711   512-437-3450
888-452-4778
FAX 512-437-3478
e-mail: tchr.net@mail.carpnet.stste.tx.us

2586 Texas Department of Commerce: Work Force Development Division

PO Box 12728
Austin, TX   78711   512-320-9439
FAX 512-320-0433

2587 Texas Department of Criminal Justice

Windham School District
PO Box 99
Huntsville, TX   77342   936-295-6371
http://www.tdcj.state.tx.us/
e-mail: webmaster@tdcj.state.tx.us

2588 Texas Education Agency

1701 Congress Avenue
Austin, TX   78701   512-463-9734
FAX 512-463-9838
http://www.tea.state.tx.us
e-mail: proussos@mail.tea.state.tx.us
Pavlos Roussos, Program Director

2589 Texas Employment Services and Job Training Program Liaison

15th & Congress Avenue
Austin, TX   78778   512-463-2652

2590 Texas Planning Council for Developmental Disabilities

4900 N Lamar Boulevard
Austin, TX   78751   512-424-4080
FAX 512-424-4097
TDY:512-424-4099
http://www.txddc.state.tx.us/menus/fset_cecl-1.
Roger A Webb, Executive Director

The mission of the Texas Council for Developmental Disabilities is to create change so that all people are fully included in their communities and exercise control over their own lives.

2591 Texas Rehabilitation Commission: Vocational Rehabilitation

4900 N Lamar Boulevard
Austin, TX   78751   512-483-4240
800-628-5115
FAX 512-483-4245
http://www.rehab.state.tx.us

2592 University of Texas at Austin

Sanchez Building
Austin, TX   78713   512-471-4161
FAX 512-471-2471
http://www.edb.utexas.edu/coe/depts
e-mail: heike@mail.utexas.edu
Penny Seay

Utah

2593 Assistive Technology Center

1595 W 500 S
Salt Lake City, UT   84106   801-887-9500
FAX 801-485-8675
Craig Boogaard, Director

The fundamental goal is to improve the lives of children and adults with disabilities by introducing them and their families to the many ways in which microcomputer technology can enhance their jobs, careers and education.

2594 Assistive Technology Program
6588 Old Main Hill
Logan, UT 84322 435-797-3824
FAX 435-797-2355
http://www.uatpat.org/
e-mail: jmholt2@home.com

A program that helps ensure people with disabilities will be secure.

2595 Center for Persons with Disabilities
Utah State University
Logan, UT 84322 435-797-3681
866-284-2821
FAX 435-797-3944
http://www.cpd.usu.edu/
e-mail: sharon@cpd2.usu.edu
Marvin Fifield, Director

A University Center for excellence in developmental disabilities education, research and services. The Center for Persons with Disabilities provides interdisciplinary training, research, exemplary services, and technical assistance to agencies related to people with disabilities.

2596 Disability Law Center
455 E 400 S
Salt Lake City, UT 84111 801-363-1347
800-662-9080
FAX 801-363-1437
http://www.disabilitylawcenter.org
e-mail: info@disabilitylawcenter.org
Fraser Nelson, Legal Director

Nonprofit organization designated by the governor to protect the rights of people with disabilities in Utah.

2597 State GED Administration
1236 S State Street
Salt Lake City, UT 84101 801-578-8356
FAX 801-578-8198
Dr. Brent Gubler, State GED Administrator

Promotes adult education.

2598 State Office of Education
250 E 500 S
Salt Lake City, UT 84111 801-538-7894
FAX 801-538-7882
http://www.usoe.k12.ut.us
e-mail: sgrant@usoe.k12.ut.us
Sandra Grant, Specialist
Dave Steele, State Director

2599 Utah Governor's Council for People with Disabilities
555 E 300 S
Salt Lake City, UT 84102 801-553-4128
FAX 801-533-5305
TDY:801-533-4128
http://www.gcpd.state.ut.us/images/default.htm
e-mail: cchamble@email.state.ut.us
Catherine E Chambless, Executive Director

The mission of the Utah Governor's Council for People with Disabilities is to create an environment in which people with disabilities direct their own lives and participate in the community. The council achieves this through: facilitating interagency and citizen planning, identifying policy, promoting partnerships and more.

2600 Utah Labor Commission: Utah Anti-discrimination and Labor Division
PO Box 146630
Salt Lake City, UT 84111 801-530-6801
800-222-1238
FAX 435-830-7609
http://www.labor.state.ut.us/utah
Joseph Gallegos Jr, Program Director

State agency responsible for enforcing laws which prohibit employment discrimination. The agency is also charged with enforcing laws which prohibit housing discrimination. Additionally, the agency is responsible for enforcing state laws which require the payment of wages, govern the employment of youth and establish Utah's minimum wage law.

2601 Utah Work Force
140 E Broadway
Salt Lake City, UT 84111 801-526-9675
FAX 801-526-9211

Vermont

2602 Assistive Technology Project
Agency of Human Services
103 S Main Street
Waterbury, VT 05671 802-241-2620
800-639-1522
FAX 802-241-2174
e-mail: tomf@dad.state.vt.us
Lynne Cleveland, Project Director

Provides a revolving loan fund for assistive technology, a used equipment recycling project, as well as training and technical assistance in computer and augmentative communications access.

2603 Learning Disabilities Association of Vermont
PO Box 1041
Manchester Center, VT 05255 802-362-3127
FAX 802-362-3128
Christina Thurston, President

A nonprofit organization whose members are individuals with learning disabilities, their families, and the professionals who work with them.

2604 Protection & Advocacy Agency
141 Main Street
Montpelier, VT 05602 802-229-1355
800-834-7890
FAX 802-229-1359
http://www.vtpa.org
e-mail: info@vtpa.org

Mission is to defend and advance the rights of people who have been labeled mentally ill.

2605 REACH-UP Program: Department of Social Welfare

State Office Building Division
103 S Main Street
Waterbury, VT   05671   802-241-2800
                                             FAX 802-241-2830
Karen Ryder

2606 State Department of Education

120 State Street
Montpelier, VT   05602   802-828-3134
                                             FAX 802-828-3146
          e-mail: srobinson@doe.state.vt.us
Sandra Robinson, Director

Promotes quality education.

2607 State GED Administration

Department of Education,Career & Lifelong Learning
120 State Street
Montpelier, VT   05602   802-828-3134
                                             FAX 802-828-3146
          e-mail: srobinson@doe.state.vt.us
Kay Charron, Contact

Promotes adult education.

2608 Vermont Agency of Human Services

Vocational Rehabilitation Division
103 S Main Street
Waterbury, VT   05671   802-241-2189
                                   http://www.ahs.state.ut.us

2609 Vermont Assistive Technology Project: Department of Aging and Disabilities

Agency of Human Services
103 S Main Street, Weeks Building
Waterbury, VT   05671   802-241-2620
                                             800-750-6355
                                             FAX 802-241-2174
          e-mail: jtucker@dad.state.vt.us
Julie L Tucker, Project Director
Gail Koehler, Information/Training
Betsy Ross, Administrative Assistant

2610 Vermont Department of Employment & Training

5 Green Mountain Drive
Montpelier, VT   05601   802-828-4000
                                             FAX 802-828-4022
                                 http://www.det.state.vt.us
          e-mail: mcalcagni@det.state.vt.us
Mike Calcagni, Director Jobs/Training
Mike Griffin, Labor Market Information

Represents Vermont's efforts to provide services, information and support both to individuals to obtain and keep good jobs, and to employers to recruit and maintain a productive workforce.

2611 Vermont Department of Welfare

103 S Main Street
Waterbury, VT   05671   802-241-2834
                                             FAX 802-241-2830
Steve Gold, Director

2612 Vermont Developmental Disabilities Council

103 S Main Street
Waterbury, VT   05671   802-241-2612
                                             888-317-2006
                                        FAX 802-241-2989
          e-mail: vtddc@wpgate1.ahs.state.vt.us
Thomas A Pumbar, Executive Director

2613 Vermont Disability Law Project

Protection and Advocacy Agency
PO Box 1367
Burlington, VT   05402   802-863-2881
                                             FAX 802-863-7152
Judith Dickson, Project Director

Works in partnership with persons with disabilities to protect, advocate for, and advance their human, legal, and service rights.

2614 Vermont Governor's Office

109 State Street
Montpelier, VT   05609   802-828-3333
                                             FAX 802-828-3339
                                 http://www.state.vt.us/stw/
          e-mail: jbagalio@state.vt.us
Jim Douglas, Governor

2615 Vermont Legal Aid Client Assistance Program and Disability Law Project

PO Box 1367
Burlington, VT   05402   802-863-2881
                                             800-747-5022
                                        FAX 802-863-7152
Laura Philipps, Co-Director
Judy Dickson, Co-Director

Program assists people with disabilities seeking information on vocational rehabilitation and independent living services from state agencies. Offers advisement of employment rights and services available under the ADA.

2616 Vermont REACH-UP Program

Department of Social Welfare
103 S Main Street
Waterbury, VT   05671   802-241-2800
                                             FAX 802-241-2830
Karen Ryder

2617 Vermont Special Education

120 State Street
Montpelier, VT   05602   802-828-3130
                                             FAX 802-828-3140
Theodore Riggen, Executive Director

Promotes the quality of special education.

Virginia

2618 Adult and Employment Training: Virginia Department of Education
PO Box 2120
Richmond, VA 23218   804-225-2075
FAX 804-225-3352
e-mail: imclendo@pen.k12.va.us
Employment training for individuals in Virginia.

2619 Assistive Technology System
Department of Rehabilitative Services
8004 Franklin Farms Drive
Richmond, VA 23288   804-662-9998
FAX 804-622-9478
http://www.uats.org

Helps people with disabilities know that they will be secure.

2620 Correctional Education
101 N 14th Street
Richmond, VA 23219   804-225-3310
FAX 804-225-3255
http://www.dce.state.va.us/
e-mail: webmaster@dce.state.va.us

2621 District of Columbia Department of Corrections
1923 N Vermont Street
Arlington, VA 22207   703-643-1357
John Thomas, Deputy Director for Programs

Protects the public by operating a safe, secure, humane and efficient corrections system.

2622 State Department of Education
PO Box 2120
Richmond, VA 23218   804-225-2075
FAX 804-225-3352
http://www.pen.k12.va.us
Lennox McLedon, Associate Director Adult Ed

Promotes quality education.

2623 State GED Administration
Department of Education: Office of Adult Education
PO Box 2120
Richmond, VA 23218   804-225-2075
FAX 804-225-3352
Dr. Patricia Ta'ani, Specialist

Promotes quality education for adults.

2624 Virginia Board for People with Disabilities
202 N 9th Street
Richmond, VA 23219   804-786-0016
FAX 804-786-1118
TDY:800-846-4464

Brian S Parsons, Director

Washington

2625 Client Assistance Program (CAP): Washington Division
PO Box 22510
Seattle, WA 98122   206-721-5999
800-544-2121
FAX 206-721-4537
e-mail: capseattle@adccomsys.net
Jerry Johnsen, Director

Provides information and advocacy for persons seeking services from the Department of Services for the Blind and the Division of Vocational Rehabilitation. Approximately 25 percent of cases involve assistive technology issues.

2626 Correctional Education
Department of Corrections
PO Box 41100
Olympia, WA 98504   360-753-2500
FAX 360-586-3676
http://www.wa.gov/doc/
e-mail: jimstewart@doc1.wa.gov
Jean M Stewart, Director

Protects the public by operating a safe corrections system.

2627 Developmental Disabilities Council
PO Box 48314
Olympia, WA 98504   360-586-3560
FAX 360-586-2424
TDY:800-634-4473
http://www.wa.gov/ddc
e-mail: cathyt@cted.wa.gov
Edward M Holen, Executive Director

2628 Employment & Training
614 Division Street
Port Orchard, WA 98366   360-337-4873
FAX 360-337-7187
e-mail: bpotter@co.kitsap.wa.us

2629 Region X: US Department of Education Office for Civil Rights
US Department of Education
915 2nd Avenue
Seattle, WA 98174   206-220-7800
FAX 206-220-7806

These regional offices of agencies enforce laws prohibiting employment discrimination on the basis of disability.

2630 Region X: US Department of Health and Human Services, Office of Civil Rights
US Department of Health & Human Services
2201 6th Avenue
Seattle, WA 98121   206-553-7483
FAX 206-553-6612

These regional offices of agencies enforce laws prohibiting employment discrimination on the basis of disability.

2631 Region X: US Department of Labor Office of Federal Contract Compliance

US Department of Labor
1111 3rd Avenue
Seattle, WA 98101   206-553-4543
                           FAX 206-553-0098

These regional offices of agencies enforce laws prohibiting employment discrimination on the basis of disability.

2632 State Department of Adult Education

PO Box 47206
Olympia, WA 98504   360-725-6025
                           FAX 360-586-2357
            e-mail: imendozac@sbeta.ctc.edu
Israel Mendoza, Director

Promotes the quality of adult education.

2633 State GED Administration

State Board for Community & Technical Colleges
PO Box 47206
Olympia, WA 98504   360-725-6025
                           FAX 360-586-2357
Janet Anderson

Promotes adult education.

2634 Washington Employment Services & Job Training Programs

605 Wood Drive SE
Lacey, WA 98503   360-438-3168
                         FAX 360-438-3208

Employment services and training programs provided to those working in Washington state.

2635 Washington Human Rights Commission

711 S Capitol Way
Olympia, WA 98504   425-753-6770
                           800-233-3247
                        FAX 360-586-2282
                  http://www.wc.gov/hrc

2636 Washington Protection and Advocacy System

180 W Dayton
Edmonds, WA 98020   425-776-1199
                           800-562-2702
                        FAX 425-776-0601
               http://www.wpas-rights.org
             e-mail: wpas@wpas-rights.org
Mark Stroh, Director

Focuses on individuals with disabilities and mental illness. Services include information and referral, legal assistance, training and systemic advocacy. Investigates abuse and neglect at residential and treatment facilities.

West Virginia

2637 Assistive Technology

955 Hartman Run Road
Morgantown, WV 26505   304-293-4692
                              800-841-8436
                           FAX 304-293-7294
               http://www.uacdd.wuu.edu/wuats
                  e-mail: jstweart@wuu.edu
Jack Stewart, Director

2638 Client Assistance Program (CAP): West Virginia Division

West Virginia Advocates
1207 Quarrier Street, Litton Bldg
Charleston, WV 25311   304-346-0867
                           FAX 304-346-0867
                  http://www.wvadvocates.org
Susan Edwards, Director

The Client Assistance Program (CAP), mandated in 1984 to provide advocacy to individuals seeking services from the State Division of Rehabilitation Services, Centers for Independent Living, supports employment programs and sheltered workshops under the federal Rehabilitation Act.

2639 Correctional Education

State Department of Education
1900 Kanawha Boulevard E
Charleston, WV 25305   304-558-8833
                           FAX 304-558-5042
Frank D Andrews, Director

2640 State Department of Adult Education

Department of Education
1900 Kanawha Boulevard E
Charleston, WV 25305   304-558-6318
                 e-mail: kpolis@access.k12.wv.us
Kathy Polis, Director

2641 State Department of Education

1900 Washington Street E
Charleston, WV 25305   304-558-2584
                           FAX 304-558-0304
                  http://www.wvde.state.wv.us
William Capehart, Director

Promotes quality education.

2642 State GED Administration

1900 Kanawha Boulevard E
Charleston, WV 25305   304-558-6315
                           FAX 304-558-4874
              e-mail: pabston@access.k12.wv.us
Debra Kimbler, GED Administrator

Our organization's goal is to provide reasonable accommodations to qualifying GED candidates.

2643 West Virginia Human Rights Commission
1321 Plaza E
Charleston, WV 25301   304-348-2616
                             888-676-5546
                        FAX 304-558-0085
http://www.sate.wu.us/wuhrc/default.htm
e-mail: wvhrc@wvhrc.state.wv.us

Wisconsin

2644 Assistive Technology Project
State Grants Program
1 W Wilson Street, Room 450R
Madison, WI 53707   608-266-1794
                        FAX 608-267-3203
                        TDY:608-267-9880
                    http://www.wistech.org
e-mail: abbeysu@dhfs.state.wi.us
Susan Abbey, Manager

A statewide program promoting assistive technology and services for people with disabilities.

2645 Correctional Education
Department of Corrections
149 E Wilson Street
Madison, WI 53707   608-266-2473
                        FAX 608-267-5069
                    http://www.wi.doc.com
e-mail: joh.brueggemann@doc.state.wi.us
Tracy K Bredeson, Director

2646 Protection & Advocacy Agency
Coalition for Advocacy
16 N Carroll Street
Madison, WI 53703   608-267-0214
                             800-928-8778
                        FAX 608-267-0368
e-mail: lynnb@wca.org
Lynn Breedlove, Director

2647 State Capitol
Room 115 East
Madison, WI 53702   608-266-7493
                        FAX 608-267-8983
William Coslt, Policy Advisor

2648 State Department of Education
310 Price Place
Madison, WI 53707   608-266-1770
                        FAX 608-266-1285
                    http://www.dpi.state.wi.us
e-mail: webadmin@dpi.state.wi.us
Edward Chin, Director

Promotes quality education.

2649 State GED Administration
Deptartment of Public Instruction
310 Price Place
Madison, WI 53707   608-266-1770
                        FAX 608-266-1285
Kathleen Cole, Contact

Promotes quality adult education.

2650 Wisconsin Council on Developmental Disabilities
600 Williamson Street
Madison, WI 53707   608-266-7826
                        FAX 608-267-3906
                        TDY:608-266-6660
                    http://www.wcdd.org
e-mail: hfswiswcdd@dhfs.state.wi.us
Jennifer Ondrejka, Executive Director

A statewide advocacy organization working on system change for people with developmental disabilities.

2651 Wisconsin Department of Workforce Development
PO Box 7946
Madison, WI 53707   608-267-4400
                        FAX 608-266-1784
Janet Pugh, Librarian

Provides information on equal rights, employment and training programs, labor, market statistics, unemployment compensation and workers' compensation.

2652 Wisconsin Equal Rights Division
PO Box 53708
Madison, WI 537-2   608-267-9678
                        FAX 307-334-2254
http://www.state.wy.us/~corr/corrections

2653 Wisconsin Governor's Commission for People with Disabilities
PO Box 7850
Madison, WI 53707   608-267-4896
                             800-362-1290
                        FAX 608-264-9832
Paul Yochum, Director

Wyoming

2654 Adult Basic Education
Wyoming Community College Commission
2020 Carey Avenue
Cheyenne, WY 82002   307-777-3545
                        FAX 307-777-6567
http://www.commission.wcc.edu@wccc.ABE/
e-mail: kmilmont@commission.wcc.edu
Karen Ross Milmont, Director

**2655   Client Assistance Program (CAP): Wyoming
Division**

320 W 25th Street
Cheyenne, WY   82001   307-638-7668
                                        FAX 307-638-0815
                                e-mail: wypanda@vcn.com
Kriss Smith, Director

Provides free services to consumers and applicants for
projects, programs and facilities funded under the rehabilitation act.

**2656   Correctional Education: Wyoming Women's
Center**

1000 W Griffith
Lusk, WY   82225   307-334-3693
                                        FAX 307-334-2254
                              e-mail: cthaye@state.wy.us
Virginia Pullen, Educational Director

The Wyoming Women's Center is a full service, secure correctional facility for female offenders and the
sole adult female facility in the State of Wyoming. In
October 2000, WWC opened a self-contained 16 bed
intensive addiction treatment unit, a is highly structured long term 7-9 month program based upon the
therapeutic community treatment model. It is tailored
to provide gender specific services and is funded with
a combination of state and federal resources.

2657   Protection & Advocacy Agency

320 W 25th Street
Cheyenne, WY   82001   307-632-3496
                                           800-624-7648
                                        FAX 307-638-0815
                        http://www.ucn.com/~wypan.da
                                e-mail: wypanda@ucn.com
Jeanne A Thobro, Director

2658   State Department of Education

2300 Capitol Avenue
Cheyenne, WY   82002   307-777-7675
                                        FAX 307-777-6234
                    http://www.k12.wy.us/wdehome.html
                          e-mail: jcatch@www.k12.wy.us
Lynn Simons, Superintendent

2659   State GED Administration

State Department of Education
Hathaway Building
Cheyenne, WY   82002   307-777-7675
                                        FAX 307-777-6234
                             e-mail: jcatch@state.wy.us
Karen Ross Milmont, Director

Promotes quality adult education.

**2660   Wyoming Department of Employment Services
and Job Training Programs**

Herschler Building
Cheyenne, WY   82002   307-777-7672
                                           888-996-9226
                                        FAX 307-777-5805
                             http://www.wydoe.state.wy.us

Employment training for persons working in Wyoming.

National Programs

2661 Academic Institute

13400 NE 20th
Bellevue, WA 98005

888-385-2977
FAX 928-244-1315

Sherrill O'Saughnessy

Advising families and teens who have special needs.

2662 American Association for Adult and Continuing Education

4380 Forbes Boulevard
Lanham, MD 20706

301-918-1913
FAX 301-918-1846
http://www.aaace.org
e-mail: aaace10@aol.com

Stephen J Steurer PhD, Managing Director
Cle Anderson, Executive Administrator

Mission is to provide leadership for the field of adult and continuing education: by expanding opportunities for adult growth and development; unifying adult educators; fostering the development and dissemination of theory, research, information and best practices; promoting identity and standards for the profession; and advocating relevant public policy and social change initiatives.

2663 American Literacy Council

148 W 117th Street
New York, NY 10026

800-781-9985
http://www.americanliteracy.com
e-mail: fyi@americanliteracy.com

Dr Edward Lias, President

Provides resources and assistance to persons and organizations who are involved in the literacy crisis in America. The organization provides software and publications that seek to promote solutions to the problem of illiteracy in English speaking countries. One primary product of the Council is Sound-Write (TM), a Windows-based writing program with instant audiovisual feedback and a 25,000 word vocabulary.

2664 Association of Educational Therapists

1804 W Burbank Boulevard
Burbank, CA 91506

818-843-1181
800-286-4267
FAX 818-843-7423
http://aetcaetonline.org
e-mail: aetla@aol.com

A national professional organization dedicated to establishing ethical professional standards, defining the roles and responsibilities of the educational therapist, providing opportunities for professional growth, and to studying techniques and technologies, philosophies and research related to the practice of educational therapy.

2665 Association on Higher Education and Disability

100 Morrissey Boulevard
Waltham, MA 02454

781-788-0003
FAX 781-788-0033
http://www.AHEAD.org
e-mail: AHEAD@ahead.org

Stephan Smith, Executive Director

An international, muiticultural organization of professionals committed to full participation in higher education for persons with disabilities. The Association is a vital resource, promoting excellence through education, communication and training.

2666 Career College Association (CCA)

10 G Street NE
Washington, DC 20002

202-336-6700
FAX 202-336-6828
http://www.career.org
e-mail: cca@career.org

Nick Glakas, President

Represents more than 1,000 private for profit post secondary schools, institutes, colleges and universities.

2667 Center for the Improvement of Early Reading Achievement CIERA

University of Michigan School of Education
Rm 1600 SEB
Ann Arbor, MI 48109

734-647-6940
FAX 734-615-4858
http://www.ciera.org
e-mail: ciera@umich.edu

Karen Wixson, Director
Joanne Carlisle, Co Director

CIERA is a national center for research on early reading, representing a consortium of educators from five universities.

2668 Council for Educational Diagnostic Services

Council for Exceptional Children
1110 N Glebe Road
Arlington, VA 22201

703-620-3660
800-224-6830
FAX 703-264-9494
http://www.cec.sped.org
e-mail: cathym@cec.sped.org

The mission of the Council for Educational Diagnostic Services is: to promote the most appropriate education of children and youth through appraisal, diagnosis, educational intervention, implementation, and continuous evaluation of a prescribed educational program.

2669 Distance Education and Training Council (DETC)

1601 18th Street NW
Washington, DC 20009

202-234-5100
FAX 202-332-1386
http://www.detc.org
e-mail: detc@detc.org

Michael P Lambert, Executive Director

Nonprofit educational association located in Washington, DC. DETC serves as a clearinghouse of information about the distance study/correspondence field and sponsors a nationally recognized accrediting agency called the Accrediting Commission of the Distance Education and Training Council.

2670 Division for Children's Communication Development

Council for Exceptional Children
1110 N Glebe Road
Arlington, VA 22201　　　　　703-620-3660
　　　　　　　　　　　　　　　800-224-6830
　　　　　　　　　　　　FAX 703-264-9494
　　　　　　　　　http://www.cec.sped.org
　　　　　　　e-mail: service@cec.sped.org

Dedicated to improving the education of children with communication delays and disorders and hearing loss. Members include professionals serving individuals with hearing, speech and language disorders in the areas of receptive and expressive, verbal and nonverbal spoken, written and sign communication. Members receive a quarterly journal and newsletter three times a year.

2671 Division for Culturally and Linguistically Diverse Learners

Council for Exceptional Children
1110 N Glebe Road
Arlington, VA 22201　　　　　703-620-3660
　　　　　　　　　　　　　　　888-232-7733
　　　　　　　　　　　　FAX 703-620-2521
　　　　　　　　　http://www.cec.sped.org
Nancy D Safer, Executive Director
Bruce A Ramirez, Deputy Executive Director
Gwendolyn Webb-Johnson, Division President

Dedicated to advancing and improving educational opportunities for culturally and linguistically diverse learners with disabilites and/or who are gifted, their families and the professionals who serve them.

2672 Division for Research

Council for Exceptional Children
1110 N Glebe Road
Arlington, VA 22201　　　　　703-620-3660
　　　　　　　　　　　　　　　888-232-7733
　　　　　　　　　　　　FAX 703-264-9494
　　　　　　　　　http://www.cec.sped.org
　　　　　　　e-mail: cathym@cec.sped.org

Devoted to the advancement of research related to the education of individuals with disabilities and/or who are gifted. Members include university, public and private school teachers, researchers, administrators, psychologists, speech/language clinicians, parents of children with special learning needs and other related professionals and service personnel. Members receive quarterly journal and newsletter three times a year.

2673 Educational Advisory Group

2222 E Lake Avenue E
Seattle, WA 98102　　　　　　206-323-1838
　　　　　　　　　　　　FAX 206-267-1325
　　　　　　　　　http://www.eduadvisory.com
Yvonne Jones, Associate
Paul Auchterlonie, Associate

Specializes in matching children with the learning environments that are best for them and works with families to help them identify concerns and establish priorities about their child's education.

2674 HEATH Resource Center: The George Washington University

2121 K Street NW
Washington, DC 20037　　　　202-973-0904
　　　　　　　　　　　　　　　800-544-3284
　　　　　　　　　　　　FAX 202-973-0908
　　　　　　　　　http://www.heath.gwu.edu
　　　　　　　e-mail: askheath@heath.gwu.edu
Dr. Pamela Ekpone, Director

Support from the US Department of Education enables the center to serve as an information exchange about educational services, policies, procedures, adaptations, and opportunities at American campuses, vocational-technical schools, and other postsecondary training entities.

2675 Institute for Educational Leadership

1001 Connecticut Avenue NW
Washington, DC 20036　　　　202-822-8405
　　　　　　　　　　　　FAX 202-872-4050
　　　　　　　　　　http://www.iel.org
　　　　　　　　　e-mail: iel@iel.org
Elizabeth L Hale, President
Louise A Clarke, Chief Administrator
Bert Berkley, Chairman of the Board

Mission is to improve education and the lives of children and their families through positive and visionary change. Everyday, we face that challenge by bringing together diverse constituencies and empowering leaders with knowledge and applicable ideas.

2676 Institute for the Study of Adult Literacy

Pennsylvania State Univ. College of Education
102 Rackley Building
University Park, PA 16802　　　814-863-3777
　　　　　　　　　　　　FAX 814-863-6108
　　　　　　　　　　http://www.ed.psu.edu
　　　　　　　　　e-mail: bdo1@psu.edu
Dr Eunice Askov, Co-Director

The Institute for the Study of Adult Literacy's goals include development and dissemination of sound conceptual and research base in the field of adult literacy; improvement of practice in the field of adult literacy; and leadership and coordination of a comprehensive approach to the delivery of adult literacy.

2677 International Dyslexia Association: National Headquarters

8600 Lasalle Road, Chester Building
Baltimore, MD 21286　　　　410-296-0232
　　　　　　　　　　　　　　　800-223-3123
　　　　　　　　　　　　FAX 410-321-5069
　　　　　　　　　http://www.interdys.org
　　　　　　　e-mail: MBIDA4@hotmail.com
Cathy Rosemond, President

Nonprofit, scientific and educational organization dedicated to the study and treatment of dyslexia. Focus is educating parents, teachers and professionals in the field of dyslexia in effective teaching methodologies. Programs and services include: information and referral; public awareness; medical and educational research; governmental affairs; conferences and publications.

2678 International Reading Association

800 Barksdale Road
Newark, DE 19714   302-731-1600
                                800-628-8508
                        FAX 302-731-1057
                    http://www.reading.org
                e-mail: pubinfo@reading.org
Alan E Farstrup, Executive Director

A professional association with more than 80,000
members in nearly 100 countries dedicated to promoting higher achievement levels in literacy, reading and
communications worldwide.

2679 Learning Resource Network

1130 Hostetler
Manhattan, KS 66502   785-539-5376
                                800-678-5376
                        FAX 785-539-7766
                    http://www.lern.org
                e-mail: rebel@lern.org
William Draves, Director

This network for educators provides resources to adult
education and adult basic education service providers.

2680 Literacy Volunteers of America

1320 Jamesville Avenue
Syracuse, NY 13203   315-422-9121
                                800-448-8878
                        FAX 315-472-8878
                http://www.proliteracy.com
                e-mail: info@proliteracy.org
Robert Wedgeworth, President

Literacy Volunteers of America is a fully integrated
national network of local, state, and regional literacy
providers that give adults and their families the opportunity to acquire skills to be effective in their roles as
members of their families, communities, and
workplaces.

**2681 National Adult Education Professional
Development Consortium**

444 N Capitol Street NW
Washington, DC 20001   202-624-5250
                        FAX 202-624-1497
                    http://www.naepdc.org
                e-mail: dc1@naepdc.org
Patricia Bennett MD, Chairman
Dr Lennox McLendon, Executive Director

The Consortium, incorporated in 1990 by state adult
education directors, provides professional development, policy analysis, and dissemination of information important to state staff in adult education.

**2682 National Adult Literacy & Learning Disabilities
Center (NALLD)**

Academy for Educational Development
1825 Connecticut Avenue NW
Washington, DC 20009   202-884-8178
                                800-953-2553
                        FAX 202-884-8400
                    http://www.aed.org
                e-mail: admindc@aed.org
Denise Glyn Borders, Senior VP/Director
Edward W Russell, Chairman

The center is a national resource for information on
learning disabilities in adults and on the relationship
between learning disabilities and low-level literacy
skills.

**2683 National Association for Adults with Special
Learning Needs**

PO Box 716
Bryn Mawr, PA 19010   610-525-8336
                                800-869-8336
                        FAX 610-446-6129
                    http://www.ldonline.org
            e-mail: 75250.1273@compuserv.com

A nonprofit organization designed to organize, establish, and promote an effective national and international coalition of professionals, advocates, and
consumers of lifelong learning for the purpose of educating adults with special learning needs.

**2684 National Association of Private Special Education
Centers**

1522 K Street NW
Washington, DC 20005   202-408-3338
                        FAX 202-408-3340
                    http://www.napsec.com
                e-mail: napsec@aol.com
Sherry L Kolbe, Executive Director/CEO
Alison Figi, Communications Coordinator
Dr. Mike Rice, President

A nonprofit association whose mission is to ensure access for individuals to private special education as a
vital component of the continuum of appropriate
placement and services in American education. The
association consists solely of private special education schools that serve both privately and publicly
placed children with disabilities.

**2685 National Center for ESL Literacy Education
(NCLE)**

4646 40th Street NW
Washington, DC 20016   202-362-0700
                        FAX 202-363-7204
                    http://www.cal.org
                e-mail: ncle@cal.org
Joy Kreeft Peyton, Director
Miriam Burt, Associate Director

A national organization focusing on literacy education for adults and out of school youth learning English as a second language. NCLE publishes many
documents on its web site.

2686 National Center for Family Literacy

325 W Main Street
Louisville, KY 40202   502-584-1133
                        FAX 502-584-0172
                    http://www.famlit.org
                e-mail: ncfl@famlit.org
Sharon Darling, President

Provides leadership for family literacy development
nationwide; promotes policies at the national and
state level to support family literacy; designs, develops and demostrates new family literacy practices that
addresses the need of families in a changing social,
economic and political landscape; delivers high quality, dynamic, research-based training, staff development and technical assistance; conducts research to
expand the knowledge base of family literacy.

2687 National Center for Learning Disabilities (NCLD)

381 Park Avenue S
New York, NY 10016   212-545-7510
888-575-7373
FAX 212-545-9665
http://www.ld.org
e-mail: help@ncld.org
John G Gantz Jr, Chairman of the Board/President
James H Wendorf, Executive Director

Increases opportunities for all individuals with learning disabilities to achive their potential. NCLD accomplishes its mission by increasing public awareness and understanding of learning disabilities, conducting educational programs and services that promote research-based knowledge, and providing national leadership in shaping public policy. Provides solutions that help people with LD participate fully in society.

2688 National Center for the Study of Adult Learning & Literacy

Harvard Graduate School of Education
Nichols House
Cambridge, MA 02138   617-495-4843
FAX 617-495-4811
http://www.gse.harvard.edu
e-mail: ncsall@gse.harvard.edu
John P Comings, Director

The National Center for the Study of Adult Learning & Literacy both informs and learns from practice. Its rigorous, high quality research increases knowledge and gives those teaching, managing, and setting policy in adult literacy education a sound basis for making decisions.

2689 National Center on Adult Literacy (NCAL)

University of Pennsylvania
3910 Chestnut Street
Philadelphia, PA 19104   215-898-2100
FAX 215-898-9804
http://www.literserve.literacy.upenn.edu
e-mail: editor@literacy.upenn.edu
Dr. Daniel A Wagner, Director

NCAL's mission incorporates three primary goals: to improve understanding of youth and adult learning; to foster innovation and increase effectiveness in youth and adult basic education and literacy work; and to expand access to information and build capacity for literacy and basic skills service.

2690 National Education Association (NEA)

1201 16th Street NW
Washington, DC 20036   202-833-4000
FAX 202-822-7974
http://www.nea.org
Rug Weaver, President

NEA is a volunteer-based organization supported by a network of staff at the local, state and national level. At the local level, NEA affiliates are active in a wide variety of activities, everything from conducting professional workshops on discipline and other issues that affect faculty and school support staff to bargaining contracts for school district employees. At the state level, NEA affiliate activities are equally wide-ranging.

2691 National Institute for Literacy (NIFL)

1775 I Street NW
Washington, DC 20006   202-233-2025
FAX 202-233-2050
http://www.nifl.gov
e-mail: sbaxter@nifl.gov
June Crawford, Program Director

NIFL's mission is to ensure that the highest quality of literacy services is available to adults. By fostering communication, collaboration, and innovation, NIFL works to build and strengthen a comprehensive, unified system for literacy in the US. NIFL maintains a database of over 7,000 literacy programs across the country and operates a hotline seven days a week.

2692 National Lekotek Center

3204 W Armitage Avenue
Chicago, IL 60647   773-276-5164
800-366-7529
FAX 773-276-8644
http://www.lekotek.org
e-mail: lekotek@lekotek.org
Helen Hilken McCarthy, Executive Director

The mission of the National Lekotek Center is driven by the philosophy that children learn best when play is a family-centered activity that includes all children, regardless of their abilities or disabilities, in family and community activities. We offer play-centered services to children with disabilities and supportive services to their families. We also offer computer play, parent support and national resources for families and professionals.

2693 New England ADA & Accessible IT Center

Adaptive Environments
374 Congress Street
Boston, MA 02210   617-695-1225
800-949-4232
FAX 617-482-8099
TDY:617-695-1225
http://www.adaptiveenvironments.org
e-mail: info@adaptiveenvironments.org
Valerie Fletcher, Executive Director
Andy Washburn, Information Specialist

Adaptive Environments promotes design that works for everyone across the spectrum of ability and age and enhances human experience.

2694 Office of Special Education Programs

US Department of Education
330 C Street SW
Washington, DC 20202   202-205-5507
http://www.ed.gov/offices/osers/osep/index.html

Administers programs and projects relating to the free appropriate public education of all children and young adults with disabilities, from birth through age 21; provides information and publications about disabilities and special education.

2695 Reach for Learning

1221 Marin Avenue
Albany, CA 94706   510-524-6455
FAX 510-524-5154
Corinne Gustafson, Director

Educational center providing diagnosis, instruction, consultation for children, youth, adults with learning disabilities or under achievement.

2696 Thinking and Learning Connection

239 Whitclem Court
Palo Alto, CA 94306 650-493-3497
FAX 650-494-3499
Lynne D Stietzel, Co-Director
Eric R Stietzel, Co-Director

A group of independent associates committed to teaching students to learn new paths of knowledge and understanding. Our primary focus is working with dyslexic and dyscalculia. Individualized educational programs utilize extensive multisensory approaches to teach reading, spelling, handwriting, composition, comprehension, and mathematics. The students are actively involved in learning processes that integrate visual, auditory, and tactile techniques.

Publications

2697 ALL Points Bulletin: Department of Education

Division of Adult Education and Literacy
600 Independence Avenue SW
Washington, DC 20202 202-205-9720
FAX 202-205-8973

The quarterly newsletter of the division of adult education and literacy. Issues focus on selected areas of interest in the field of adult education, current research, new publications, and upcoming events. Special sections concentrate on ESL and workplace literacy issues.

2698 Adult Basic Education: An Interdisciplinary Journal for Adult Literacy Educators

Commission on Adult Basic Education (COABE)
Piedmont College
Demorest, GA 30535 706-778-3000
FAX 706-776-0133
e-mail: melichar@piedmnt.edu
Ken Melichar, Editor

Adult Basic Education: An Interdisciplinary Journal for Adult Literacy Educators is a double blind, peer review, scholarly journal with a practical intent devoted to improving the efforts of adult educators working with low literally disadvantaged, and educationally oppressed people. *$25.00*

3x/year

Alabama

2699 Alabama Adult Literacy Resource Center

PO Box 30201
Montgomery, AL 36130 334-242-8182
FAX 334-242-2236
http://www.slincs.coe.utk.edu/alabama
e-mail: macaluso@sdenet.alsde.edu
Joe Macaluso, Contact

The Alabama Adult Literacy Resource Center serves as a clearinghouse for literacy information linking local providers with literacy clearinghouses.

2700 Alabama Commission on Higher Education

100 N Union Street
Montgomery, AL 36130 334-242-1998
FAX 334-242-0268
http://www.ache.state.al.us
e-mail: tvick@ache.state.al.us
Dr. Michael Malone, Executive Director
Tim Vick, Associate Executive Director

The Commission on Higher Education has the statutory responsibility for the overall statewide planning and coordination of higher education in Alabama, the administration of various student aid programs and the performance of designated regulatory functions.

Alaska

2701 Alaska Literacy Program

Nine Star Enterprises
125 West 5th Avenue
Fairbanks, AK 907-279-7827
800-478-7587
FAX 907-279-3299
http://www.ninestar.com
e-mail: amyy@ninestar.com
Amy Young, Contact
Arva Carlson, Literacy Contact

Evaluates student needs and addresses those needs through specialized lesson plans, private tutoring and personal attention.

2702 Arkansas Adult Basic Education

SERRC
210 Ferry Way
Juneau, AK 99801 907-586-5718
FAX 907-586-5971
e-mail: carins@serrc.org
Carin Smolin, Contact

The mission of the Adult Basic Education program is to provide instruction in the basic skills of reading, writing, and mathematics to adult learners in order to prepare them for transitioning into the labor market or higher academic or vocational training.

2703 Literacy Council of Alaska

823 3rd Avenue
Fairbanks, AK 99701 907-456-6212
FAX 907-456-4302
http://www.literacycouncilofalaska.org
e-mail: lca@literacycouncilofalaska.org
Teriscoukya Smith, Contact
Mike Donaldson, Contact

The Literacy Council of Alaska is a private, nonprofit educational agency. Our mission is to promote literacy for people of all ages in Fairbanks and the interior.

Arizona

2704 Adult Education Division of the Arizona Department of Education

1535 W Jefferson Street
Phoenix, AZ   85007   602-542-3813
                                                       800-352-4558
                                                 FAX 602-542-5440
                             http://www.ade.az.gov/adult-ed/
                             e-mail: ade@mail1.ade.state.az.us
Karen Liersch, State Director Adult Education

To ensure that learners 16 years of age and older have access to quality educational opportunities that will support them in their employment, job training, assist them in acquiring the knowledge and skills necessary for effective participation in society.

2705 Literacy Volunteers of America: MaricopaCounty

1500 E Thomas Road
   85007   602-274-3430
                                                 FAX 602-542-5440
                        http://www.literacyvolunteers-maricopa.org
                                        e-mail: lvmc@lvmc.net
Lynn Reed, Executive Director

To ensure that learners 16 years of age and older have access to quality educational opportunities that will support them in their employment, job training, assist them in acquiring the knowledge and skills necessary for effective participation in society.

2706 Literacy Volunteers of America: Santa CruzCounty

21 E Court Street
Nogales, AR   85621   520-287-0111
                                                 FAX 520-287-0704
                             e-mail: lruiz@co.santa-cruz.az.us
Lizzette Ruiz, Director
Ross Levine, Project Coordinator

Literacy Volunteers of America is a national organization with over 1000 chapters teaching adult literacy throughout the United States. The Santa Cruz County Chapter is run out of the Nogales-Santa Cruz County Public Library, and relies on the work of local volunteer tutors and Americorps volunteers.

Arkansas

2707 Arkansas Adult Learning Resource Center

3905 Cooperative Way
Little Rock, AR   72209   501-907-2490
                                                 FAX 501-907-2492
                                      http://www.aalrc.org
                                      e-mail: info@aalrc.org
Marsha Taylor, Director
Klaus Neu, Media Coordinator

The Arkansas Adult Learning Resource Center was established in 1990 to provide a source for identification, evaluation, and dissemination of materials and information to adult education/literacy programs within the state.

2708 Arkansas Literacy Council: Laubach Literacy Action

4942 W Markham
Little Rock, AR   72205   501-663-4321
                                                       800-264-7323
                                                 FAX 501-663-3041
                             http://www.arkansasliteracy.org
                             e-mail: alcouncil@aol.com
Theresa Long, Executive Director

Arkansas Literacy Council is a statewide 501 (c) (3) nonprofit agency on focusing strengthening learning efforts across Arkansas.

2709 Literacy League of Craighead County

301 South Main
Jonesboro, AR   71401   870-910-6511
                                                 FAX 870-910-0552
                             e-mail: llcc@newsources.net
Thomas Templeton, Contact

Offering information and resources on literacy throughout the area.

California

2710 Butte County Library Adult Reading Program

1820 Mitchell Avenue
Oroville, CA   95966   530-538-7642
                             http://www.buttecounty.net/bclibrary
                             e-mail: lib@buttecounty.net
Nancy Brower, Library Director

Tutoring at no charge in reading, writing and math. Participants will learn the basics and more with one-on-one tutoring. A volunteer tutor will meet with participants at any branch library in Butte County.

2711 California Association of Special Education & Services

CASES Executive Office
1722 J Street
Sacramento, CA   95814   916-447-7061
                                                 FAX 916-447-1320
                                      http://www.capses.com
                                      e-mail: info@capses.com
Barbara Browning, Executive Director

The purposes are to serve as a liaison between the public and private sectors and to lend support for a continuum of programs and objectives which improve the delivery of services provided to the exceptional individual.

2712 California Department of Education

Office of the Secretary for Education
1121 L Street
Sacramento, CA   95814   916-323-0611
                                                 FAX 916-323-3753
                                      http://www.ose.ca.gov
Richard Riordan, Education Secretary

The Office of the Secretary for Education is responsible for advising and making policy recommendations to the Governor on education issues.

2713 California Literacy

133 N Altadena Drive
Pasadena, CA 91107   626-395-9989
                                       800-894-7323
                                   FAX 626-395-9987
                              http://www.caliteracy.org
                              e-mail: office@caliteracy.org
Lisa Bennett-Garrison, Executive Director
Archana Carey, Operations Director

California Literacy was founded in 1956 and is the nation's oldest and largest statewide adult volunteer literacy organization. Its purpose is to establish literacy programs and to support them through tutor training, consulting, and ongoing education.

2714 Lake County Literacy Coalition

Lake County Library
1425 N High Street
Lakeport, CA 95422   707-263-7633
                              http://www.co.lake.ca.us
                              e-mail: dianaf@co.lake.ca.us
Mary Amendola, Contact

We provide free, basic literacy instruction to adult learners through confidential one-on-one study sessions that are geared to what the student wants to learn.

2715 Literacy Program: County of Los AngelesPublic Library

7400 East Imperial Highway
Downey, CA 90241   562-940-8511
                              http://www.colapublib.org
                              e-mail: hilda@colapl.org
Margaret Donnellan, Librarian
Barbara Hirsch, Contact

The Literacy Centers of the County of Los Angeles Public Library offer a variety of literacy services for adults and families at no charge. Literacy services include one-to-one basic literacy tutoring, English as a Second Language group instruction, Family Literacy and self-help instruction on audio cassettes, videocassettes and computer-based training. The literacy program is an affiliate of Literacy Volunteers of America, Inc.

2716 Literacy Volunteers of America: ImperialValley

2695 S 4th Street
El Centro, CA 92243   760-352-8541
                              e-mail: lva@icoet.org
Norma Gomez, Contact

Literacy Volunteers of America is affiliated with ProLiteracy of America and provides the opportunity to acquire skills to be effective in their roles as members of their families, communities and workplaces.

2717 Literacy Volunteers of America: WillitsPublic Library

390 E Commercial Street
Willits, CA 95490   707-459-5098
                              http://www.mendolibrary.org/willits
                              e-mail: lvawillits@pacific.net
Donna Kerr, Branch Librarian
Pamela Shilling, Contact

The Literacy program offers one-on-one reading, writing and tutoring for adults in the area.

2718 Marin Literacy Program

San Rafael Public Library
1100 E Street
San Rafael, CA 94901   415-485-3318
                                   FAX 415-485-3112
                              http://www.marinliteracy.org
                              e-mail: marinliteracy@marinliteracy.org
Barbara Barwood, Contact

The Marin Literacy Program offers reading, writing and English conversation through professionally trained volunteers to Marin County adults who skills are too low to be helped by other services in the county.

2719 Merced Adult School

50 E 20th Street
Merced, CA 95344   209-385-6524
                                   FAX 209-385-6430
                              e-mail: croberds@muhsd.k12.ca.us
Carole Roberds, Contact
Kimberly Cohen, Contact

To empower and educate our adult students to discover their own unique, productive place in our dynamic world and encourage them to be lifelong learners.

2720 Metropolitan Adult Education Program

760 Hillsdale Avenue
San Jose, CA 95136   404-723-6464
                                   FAX 404-723-6449
                              http://www.metroed.net
                              e-mail: jmondo@metroed.net
Joyce Mondo, Public Information Officer
Nancy Arnold, Principal

MetroED is the largest career-oriented educational organization in Santa Clara County. We provide vocational and adult education programs for the high school students and adults in their geographic areas.

2721 Mid City Adult Learning Center

Belmont Community Adult School
1510 Cambria Street
Los Angeles, CA 90017   213-483-8689
                                   FAX 213-413-1356
                              e-mail: midcity@otan.dni.us
Judy Griffin, Regional Center Manager

Provides adult education on ESL, basic reading, language and literacy programs.

2722 Newport Beach Public Library LiteracyServices

1000 Avocado Avenue
Newport Beach, CA 92660   949-717-3874
                              http://www.citynewportbeachlibrary.org
                              e-mail: literacy@city.newport-beach.ca.us
Diane Moseley, Program Coordinator
Sheila Tierney, Program Assistant

The mission of the Literacy Services Program is to help English-speaking adults improve their reading and writing skills.

2723 Pomona Public Library Literacy Services

625 S Garey Avenue
Pomona, CA   91766   909-620-2035
                                       FAX 909-620-3713
                   http://www.youseemore.com/pomona
                   e-mail: library@ci.pomona.ca.us
Muriel Spill, Contact

The Pomona Literacy Service provides free adult literacy services to the City of Pomona. Volunteers provide tutorial programs to adults (16 years and older) who do not have basic literacy skills or whose literacy skills are so limited that they are not able to function independently in daily life or acquire employment or higher education.

2724 Recording for the Blind & Dyslexic: Los Angeles

5022 Hollywood Boulevard
Los Angeles, CA   90027   323-664-5525
                                       800-499-5525
                                       FAX 323-664-1881
                         http://www.rfbdla.org
                         e-mail: los_angeles@rfbdla.org
Carol Smith, Executive Director
Stacey Eubank, Outreach Director

A national, nonprofit organization providing recorded textbooks, library services and other educational materials to students who cannot read standard print because of a visual, physical or learning disability. $50.00 registration fee and a $25.00 annual renewal fee. No fee for students whose schools are members.

2725 Recording for the Blind & Dyslexic: Northern California Unit

488 W Charleston Road
Palo Alto, CA   94306   650-493-3717
                                       800-221-4792
                                       FAX 650-493-5513
                         http://www.rfbd.org
John Stevenson, Executive Director
Valley Brown, Outreach Director

A national network of thirty three studios with headquarters in Princeton, NJ. The sole purpose is to provide educational materials in recorded and computerized formats at every academic level. The materials are for all people unable to read standard print because of a visual, perceptual (dyslexia), or other physical disability.

2726 Recording for the Blind & Dyslexic: Santa Barbara Chapter

3970 La Colina Road
Santa Barbara, CA   93110   805-687-6393
                                       FAX 805-682-8197
                         http://www.rfbd.org
                         e-mail: jkarpenko@rfbd.org
Julie Karpenko, Interim Executive Director

The Santa Barbara Unit was founded in 1976. Over 300 volunteers produce textbooks on tape for students at local schools and around the country.

2727 Recording for the Blind and Dyslexic: Inland Empire-Orange County Unit

1844 W 11th Street
Upland, CA   91786   909-949-4316
                                       FAX 909-981-8457
                         http://www.rfbd.org
                         e-mail: mdavis@rfbd.org
Maureen Ahearn, Production Director
Mike Davis, Executive Director
Maggie Tupman, Educational Outreach Director

Volunteers record texts on audio cassettes and computer disks for the visually, physically and perceptually disabled.

2728 Regional Resource Center for San Diego: Imperial Counties

6401 Linda Vista Road
San Diego, CA   92111   858-292-3754
                                       FAX 858-268-9726
                    e-mail: linda.carlton@suhsd.k12.ca.us
Linda Carlton, Manager

The center assists regional adult education and literacy providers as they work to provide high quality and effective services to adult learners.

2729 Sacramento Public Library Literacy Service

828 I Street
Sacramento, CA   95814   916-264-2891
                                       800-561-4636
                                       FAX 916-264-2755
                    http://www.saclibrary.org/literacy
                    e-mail: contact@saclibrary.org
Jackie Miller, Literacy Coordinator
Judith Alvi, Literacy Service Representative
Anne Marie Gold, Library Director

The Literacy Service is committed to helping adults attain the skills they need to achieve their goals and develop their knowledge and potential. Free one-on-one tutoring is provided to English speaking adults who want to improve their basic reading and writing skills.

2730 Sweetwater State Literacy Regional Resource Center

Adult Resource Center
458 Moss Street
Chula Vista, CA   91911   619-691-5624
                                       FAX 619-425-8728
                    http://www.literacynet.org/slrc/sweetwater
                    e-mail: hurley@otan.dni.us
Alice Hurley, Regional Manager

The Sweetwater State Literacy Resource Center is located at the Adult and Continuing Education Division of the Sweetwater Union High School District. The Division is the fourth largest adult education program in the State of California, serving over 32,000 adult learners yearly.

2731 Vision Literacy of California

40 N Milpitas Boulevard
Milpitas, CA   95035   408-262-1349
                                       FAX 408-262-5806
                         http://www.visionliteracy.org
                         e-mail: info@visionliteracy.org
Pat Lawson-North, Literacy Contact

Vision Literacy is dedicated to enriching the community in which we live by helping adults improve their literacy skills.

Colorado

2732 Colorado Adult Education and Family Literacy

Colorado Department of Education
201 East Colfax Avenue
Denver, CO 80203   303-866-6884
                          FAX 303-830-0793
                          http://www.cde.state.co.us
                          e-mail: smith p@cde.state.co.us
Pamela Smith, State Director
Debra Fawcett, Contact

To assist adults to become literate in English and obtain the knowledge and skills necessary for employment and self-sufficiency.

2733 Learning Disabilities Association of Colorado

4596 E Iliff Avenue
Denver, CO 80222   303-894-0992
                          FAX 303-830-1645
                          http://www.ldanatl.org
                          e-mail: info@ldacolorado.com
Tim Carroll, Public Relations

A non-profit volunteer organization dedicated to advocacy and education of learning disabled children and adults.

2734 Literacy Coalition of Jefferson County

10125 West 6th Avenue
Lakewood, CO 80215   303-271-6387
                          FAX 303-854-4001
                          http://www.literacyjeffco.org
                          e-mail: marcie.hanson@judicial.state.co.us
Marcie Hanson, Contact

The purpose of the organization is to promote and foster increased literacy in Jefferson County, Colorado.

2735 Literacy Volunteers of America: Colorado Literacy Outreach

413 9th Avenue
Glenwood Springs, CO 81601   970-945-5282
                          FAX 970-945-7723
                          http://www.literacyvolunteers.org/who/states
                          e-mail: mfred@coloradomtn.edu
Martha Fredendall, Contact

Literacy Volunteers of America is a fully integrated national network of local, state and regional literacy providers that give adults and their families the opportunity to acquire skills to be effective in their roles as members of their families, communities, and workplaces.

Connecticut

2736 Connecticut Institute for Cultural Literacy and Wellness

60 Connolly Parkway, Building 12
Hamden, CT 06514   203-281-1347
                          FAX 203-281-1386
Fredrick Chappelle, Executive Director

Offers adult education and literacy programs, as well as other programs that touch on other aspects of a well-rounded education.

2737 Connecticut Literacy Resource Center

CREC/ATDW
111 Charter Oak Avenue
Hartford, CT 06106   860-247-2732
                          FAX 860-246-3304
                          http://www.crec.org/lc/index.shtml
                          e-mail: atyskiewicz@crec.org
Bruce Douglas, Executive Director

The Literacy Center offers services that foster literacy development from early childhood to adult. Technical assistance and training are available in the following areas: School Readiness; k-12; and Family Literacy.

2738 LEARN: Connecticut Reading Association

44 Hatchetts Hill Road
Old Lyme, CT 06371   860-434-4800
                          FAX 860-434-4837
                          http://www.learn.k12.ct.us
                          e-mail: director@learn.k12.ct.us
Dr. Virginia Seccombe, Executive Director

LEARN initiates, supports and provides a wide range of programs and services that enhance the quality and expand the opportunities for learning in the educational community.

2739 Literacy Volunteers of Greater Hartford

30 Arbor Street
Hartford, CT 06106   860-233-3853
                          http://www.lvgh.org
                          e-mail: susan.roman@lvgh.org
Susan Roman, Executive Director
George Demetrion, Outreach Manager

Literacy Volunteers of Greater Hartford has trained volunteers to provide free English literacy instruction to Hartford area adults.

Delaware

2740 Delaware Department of Education: AdultCommunity Education

John G Townsend Building
401 Federal Street
Dover, DE 19903   302-739-3743
                          FAX 302-739-1318
                          http://www.doe.state.de.us
                          e-mail: ftracy-mumf@doe.k12.de.us
Valerie A Woodruff, Education Secretary
Dr. Fran Tracy-Mumford, State Director

Provides students with opportunities to develop skills needed to qualify for further education, job training, and better employment.

2741 Literacy Volunteers of America: Wilmington Library

10th and Market Street
Wilmington, DE 19899
http://www.wilmlib.org
e-mail: litvolunteers@aol.com
Carmen A Knox, Contact

An organization of volunteers that provide a variety of services locally to enable people to achieve personal goals through literacy programs.

2742 State of Delaware Adult and CommunityEducation Network

PO Box 639
Dover, DE 19903
302-739-5556
FAX 302-739-5565
http://www.acenetwork.org
e-mail: acedir@yahoo.com
Paul Hughey, Statewide Coordinator

The ACE Network is a service agency that supports adult education and literacy providers through training and resource development.

District of Columbia

2743 District of Columbia Department of Education: Vocational & Adult Education

400 Maryland Avenue SW
Washington, DC 20202
202-205-5451
800-872-5327
FAX 202-205-8748
http://www.ed.gov/offices/OVAE
e-mail: ovae@ed.gov

To help all people achieve the knowledge and skills to be lifelong learners, to be successful in their chosen careers, and to be effective citizens.

2744 District of Columbia Literacy Resource Center

Martin Luther King Memorial Library
901 G Street NW
Washington, DC 20001
202-727-3157
FAX 202-727-1129
e-mail: marcia_harrington@csgi.com
Marcia Harrington, ABE Specialist

As part of the State Library, the State Resource Center provides electronic and print resources.

2745 District of Columbia Public Schools

825 N Capitol Street NE
Washington, DC 20202
202-442-4800
FAX 202-442-5517
http://www.k12.dc.us
e-mail: callcenter@k12.dc.us
Dr. Elfreda Massie, Superintendent

The public school system is committed to constant improvements in the achievement of all students today in preparation for their world tomorrow.

2746 Literacy Volunteers of the NationalCapital Area

PO Box 73275
Washington, DC 20056
202-387-1772
http://www.lvanca.org
e-mail: dlewis@lvanca.org
Donna Lewis, Contact

Literacy Volunteers of the National Capital Area is an affiliate of ProLiteracy Network and provides free tutoring to illiterate adults in the Washington, D.C./National Capital Area.

Florida

2747 Florida Coalition

Florida Literacy Coalition
934 N Magnolia Avenue
Orlando, FL 32803
407-246-7110
800-237-5113
FAX 407-246-7104
http://www.floridaliteracy.org
e-mail: info@floridaliteracy.org
Greg Smith, Executive Director

A nonprofit organization funded through private and corporate donations, state of Florida grants, and a diverse membership.

2748 Florida GED Administration: Bureau of Adult & Community Education

Department of Education
325 W Gaines Street, FED Building
Tallahassee, FL 32399
850-487-7033
FAX 850-487-0419
e-mail: bob.wofford@fldoe.org
Bob Wofford, Sr Education Program Director

2749 Florida Laubach Literacy Action

52 E Main Street
Apopka, FL 32703
407-889-0100
FAX 407-889-5576
Teresa McElwee, President

Laubach Literacy is a nonprofit educational corporation dedicated to helping adults of all ages improve their lives and their communities by learning reading, writing, math and problem solving skills.

2750 Florida Literacy Coalition

934 N Magnolia Avenue
Orlando, FL 32803
407-246-7110
800-237-5113
FAX 407-246-7104
http://www.floridaliteracy.org
e-mail: info@floridaliteracy.org
Kelley Weppner, Education & Training Coordinator

A nonprofit organization funded through private and corporate donations, state of Florida grants, and a diverse membership.

2751   Florida Literacy Resource Center

Adult & Community Educators of Florida
912 S Martin Luther King Jr
Tallahassee, FL   32301   850-922-5343
                              FAX 850-922-5352
                        http://www.ace-leon.org
                    e-mail: ace@aceofflorida.org
Veronica Sehrt, Project Manager

As part of the State Library, the State Resource Center
provides electronic and print resources.

**2752   Florida Protection & Advocacy Agency for
Persons with Disabilities**

2671 Executive Center Circle W
Tallahassee, FL   32301   850-488-9071
                                 800-342-0823
                              FAX 850-488-8640
Marcia Beach, Executive Director

Offers help for people with disabilities.

**2753   Florida State Department of Adult Education:
Division of Applied Technology & Adult
Education**

325 W Gaines Street
Tallahassee, FL   32399   850-487-7033
                              FAX 850-487-3601
Bob Wofford, Sr Education Program Director

Research in the societal and economic contributions
of Adult and Community education; development and
validation of vocational educator competencies; design model of competency-based vocational teacher
training curriculum, etc.

**2754   Florida Vocational Rehabilitation Agency:
Division of Vocational Rehabilitation**

2002 Old Street Augustine Road
Tallahassee, FL   32399   850-488-6210
                              FAX 850-921-7217
                         http://www.fndfl.org
Loretta Costin, Director

A statewide employment resource for businesses and
people with disabilities that enables individuals with
disabilities to obtain and keep employment.

2755   Florida Workforce Investment Act

Department of Labor & Employment Security
1320 Executive Center Drive
Tallahassee, FL   32399   904-488-7228
                              FAX 850-413-7587
Kathleen L McLeskey, Acting Director

Provides job-training services for economically disadvantaged adults and youth, dislocated workers and
others who face significant employment barriers.

2756   Learning Disabilities Association of Florida

331 E Henry Street
Punta Gorda, FL   33950   941-637-8957
                              FAX 941-637-0617
                         http://www.lda-fl.org
                    e-mail: ldaf00@sunline.net
Cheryl Kron, Executive Secretary

The Learning Disabilities Association of Florida is a
nonprofit volunteer organization of parents, professionals and LD adults.

Georgia

2757   Gainesville/Hall County Alliance for Literacy

PO Box 58
Gainesville, GA   30503   770-531-4337
                              FAX 770-531-6406
                     http://www.northeastga.com
Marci Hipp, Director

A nonprofit agency designed to SUPPORT the literacy providers of Hall County. The Alliance for Literacy promotes education for adults, ages 16 and older.

2758   Georgia Department of Education

Department of Technical & Adult Education
1800 Century Place
Atlanta, GA   30345   404-679-1600
Ken Breeden, Commissioner

To oversee the state's system of technical colleges,
the adult literacy program, and a host of economic
workforce development programs.

**2759   Georgia Department of Technical & Adult
Education**

Office of Adult Literacy
1800 Century Place
Atlanta, GA   30345   404-679-1600
                          FAX 404-679-1710
                       http://www.dtae.org
                   e-mail: mdelaney@dtae.org
Tony Bruehl, Director

The Georgia Department of Technical and Adult Education oversees the state's system of technical colleges, the adult literacy program, and a host of
economic and workforce development programs

**2760   Georgia Literacy Resource Center: Office of
Adult Literacy**

1800 Century Place NE
Atlanta, GA   30345   404-679-1600
                          FAX 404-679-1630
                       http://www.dtae.org
                   e-mail: mdelaney@dtae.org
Tony Bruehl, Director

The mission of the adult literacy programs is to enable
every adult learner in Georgia to acquire the necessary
basic skills in reading, writing, computation, speaking, and listening to compete successfully in today's
workplace, strengthen family foundations, and exercise full citizenship.

2761   Literacy Volunteers of America: Forsyth County

PO Box 1097
Cumming, GA   30028   770-887-0074
                   e-mail: focoliteracy@juno.com
Eddith DeVeau, Executive Director

Dedicated to teaching adults to read in the Forsyth
County region.

2762 Literacy Volunteers of America: Metropolitan Atlanta

246 Sycamore Street
Decatur, GA   30030   404-377-7323
                                FAX 404-377-8662
                             http://www.lvama.org
                  e-mail: lva_ma@mindspring.com
Katie Wilson, Executive Director

An organization dedicated to teaching adults to read in the Atlanta area.

2763 Literacy Volunteers of America: Tift County

211 Chestnut Avenue
Tifton, GA   31794   229-382-0505
                                FAX 229-387-0442
                  e-mail: tiftlva@surfsouth.com
Mary Laster, Contact

2764 Literacy Volunteers of America: Troup County

PO Box 1087
La Grange, GA   30241   706-883-7837
                                FAX 706-882-5114
                   e-mail: lvatc@mindspring.com
Charlotte Anderson, Executive Director

The Literacy Volunteers of America is a fully integrated national network of local, state and regional literacy providers that give adults and their families the opportunity to acquire skills to be effective in their roles as members of their families, communities and workplace.

2765 Nancy Hart Literacy Council of Georgia

150 Benson Street, Suite 2
Hartwell, GA   30643   706-376-5534
                                FAX 706-856-2655
Emily S Gunnells

To organize volunteers for the purpose of improving literacy.

2766 Toccoa/Stephens County Literacy Council

PO Box 63
Toccoa, GA   30577   706-282-5171
                                FAX 706-282-7633
                  e-mail: mwalters3@yahoo.com
Maggie Walters, Tutor Coordinator

Hawaii

2767 Hawaii Laubach Literacy Action

Hawaii Literacy
200 N Vineyard Boulevard
Honolulu, HI   96817   808-537-6706
                                FAX 808-528-1690
                   http://www.literacynet.org/hilit
                       e-mail: hiliteracy@aol.com
Millie A Gorecki, Executive Director

Laubach Literacy Action is a nonprofit educational corporation dedicated to helping adult of all ages improve their lives and their communities by learning reading, writing, math and problem-solving skills.

2768 Hawaii Literacy Resource Center

Office of State Libraries
3225 Salt Lake Boulevard
Honolulu, HI   96818   808-831-6878
                                FAX 808-831-6882
                http://www.literacynet.org/hawaii/home
                  e-mail: susann@lib.state.hi.us
Sue Berg, State Literacy Director

As part of the state library, the state resource center provides electronic and print resources.

Idaho

2769 Idaho Adult Education Office

Idaho Department of Education
650 W State Street
Boise, ID   83720   208-332-6800
                                FAX 208-334-4664
                             http://www.sde.state.id.us
                  e-mail: Shoehler@sde.state.id.us
Sue Oehler, Office Specialist

2770 Idaho Coalition for Adult Literacy

325 W State Street
Boise, ID   83702   208-334-2150
                                00-458-3271
                                FAX 208-334-4016
                                http://www.lili.org
Peggy McClendon, Literacy Coodinator

An nonprofit organization which raise public awareness about the importance of a literate society.

2771 Idaho Council: International Reading Assocation

3401 S Indiana
Caldwell, ID   83602   208-455-3304
                                FAX 208-455-3256
                             http://www.sde.state.id.us
                  e-mail: mhealy@sde131.k12.id.us
Margo Healy

The International Reading Association is a professional membership organization dedicated to promoting high levels of literacy for all by improving the quality of reading instruction, disseminating research and information about reading, and encouraging the lifetime reading habit.

2772 Idaho Department of Corrections

1299 N Orchard Street
Boise, ID   83706   208-658-2000
                             http://www.corr.state.id.us
                  e-mail: inquiry@corr.state.id.us
Doug R Gray, Education Bureau Chief

The Education Bureau of the Idaho Department of Correction operates prison education programs in seven facilities across the state.

2773 Idaho State Library

325 W State Street
Boise, ID   83702   208-334-2150
                                       800-458-3271
                                    FAX 208-334-4016
                                    http://www.lili.org
                              e-mail: lili@isL.state.id.us
Stephanie Bailey-White, Public Information Officer
Charles Bolles, State Librarian

Offers a history of pioneering new frontiers in library
services.

2774 Idaho Workforce Investment Act

Idaho Department of Labor
317 Main Street
Boise, ID   83735   208-332-3570
                                    FAX 208-334-6300
                                http://www.jobservice.us
                         e-mail: cbrush@labor.state.id.us
Cheryl Brush, Chief

Provides vocational training services for economically disadvantaged adults and youth, dislocated
workers and others who face significant employment
barriers.

**2775 Temporary Assistance for Needy Families: Idaho
Department of Health and Welfare**

450 W State Street
Boise, ID   83720   208-334-0606
                                    FAX 208-334-6581
                                 http://www.2.state.id.us
                           e-mail: BCEH@idhw.state.id.us
Penny Robbe, Cheif TAFI

Provides assistance and work opportunities to needy
families by granting states the federal funds and wide
flexibility to develop and implement their own welfare programs.

Illinois

2776 Illinois Laubach Literacy Action

6910 N Rockvale Drive
Peoria, IL   61614   309-691-0292
                                    FAX 309-691-6118
                       e-mail: ralphkroehler@prodigy.net
Marge Krohler, President

Laubach Literacy is a nonprofit, educational corporation dedicated to helping adults of all ages improve
their lives and their communities by learning reading,
writing, math and problem-solving skills.

2777 Illinois Library Association

33 W Grand Avenue
Chicago, IL   60610   312-644-1896
                                    FAX 312-644-1899
                                    e-mail: ila@ila.org

Bob Doyle, Contact

The Illinois Library Association is the voice for Illinois Libraries and the millions who depend on them. It
provides leadership for the development, promotion,
and improvement of library services in Illinois and for
the library community.

2778 Illinois Literacy Resource Center

IL Network of Literacy/Adult Education Resources
431 S 4th Street
Springfield, IL   62701   217-785-6921
                                       800-665-5576
                                    FAX 217-785-6927
                                    TDY:800-526-0844
Judith Rake, Literacy Program Director

As part of the State Library, the State Resource Center
provides electronic and print resources.

2779 Illinois Literacy Resource Development Center

209 W Clark Street
Champaign, IL   61820   217-355-6068
                                    FAX 217-355-6347
                                    http://www.ilrdc.org
                               e-mail: tbudz@ilrdc.org
Suzanne Knell, Executive Director
Janet Scogins, Associate Director

The Illinois Literacy Resource Development Center is
dedicated to improving literacy policy and practice at
the local, state, and national levels. It is a nonprofit organization supporting literacy and adult education efforts throughout Illinois and the nation. One key to its
success has been its ability to build partnerships
among the organizations, individuals and agencies
working in the literacy arena from the local to the national level.

2780 Illinois Office of Rehabilitation Services

Illinois Department of Human Services
100 S Grand Avenue E
Springfield, IL   62762   217-557-1601
                               e-mail: ors@dhs.state.il.us
Teyonda Wertz, Chief of Staff
*Dylan Livingearth, Manager of Information Ser-
vices*

DHS' Office of Rehabilitation Services is the state's
lead agency serving individuals with disabilities.

**2781 Illinois Protection & Advocacy Agency:Equip for
Equality**

11 E Adams Street
Chicago, IL   60603   312-341-0022
                                       800-537-2632
                                    FAX 312-341-0295
                                    TDY:312-341-0022
                           http://www.equipforequality.org
                             e-mail: hn6177@handsnet.org
Peter Grosz, Relations Manager

Equip for Equality is a not-for-profit Federally-funded organization that advocates for disability rights in the state of Illinois.

2782 Literacy Chicago

70 E Lake Street
Chicago, IL   60601   312-870-1100
                                  FAX 312-870-4488
                    http://www.literacychicago.org
                    e-mail: info@literacychicago.org

Literacy Chicago is dedicated to improving the literacy skills of Chicago-area adults and families.

2783 Literacy Volunteers of America: Illinois

30 E Adams Street
Chicago, IL   60603   312-857-1582
                                  FAX 312-857-1586
              http://www.literacyvolunteersillinois.org
                              e-mail: LVAILL@aol.com
Dorothy Miaso, Executive Director

Literacy Volunteers of Illinois is a statewide organization committed to developing and supporting volunteer literacy programs that help families, adults and out-of-school teens increase their literacy skills.

Indiana

2784 Indiana Literacy & Technical Education Resource Center

Indiana State Library
140 N Senate Avenue
Indianapolis, IN   46204   317-232-3727
                                       800-233-4572
                                  FAX 317-232-3728
                       http://www.ciesck.in.us
                  e-mail: ilterc@statelib.lib.in.us

Provides literacy, technical, and career education resources to meet basic adult educational needs. Adult education materials include GED, learning disabilities and ESL resources. A thirty day loan period is provided to literacy, business and industry, goverment, schools and other adult education programs as well as to individual Indiana residents.

2785 Indiana Literacy Foundation

1920 W Morrison
Indianapolis, IN   46221   317-639-6106
                                  FAX 317-639-2782
                    http://www.indianaliteracy.org
                 e-mail: psiemant@indianaliteracy.org

Indiana Literacy Foundation is a non-profit organization dedicated to strengthening basic skills among children and adults working with and through volunteer literacy programs across Indiana.

2786 Indiana Workforce Literacy

10 N Senate Avenue
Indianapolis, IN   46204   317-232-4785
                                  FAX 317-232-1815
                 http://www.in.gov/dwd/information
                  e-mail: tmartin@dwd.state.in.us

The Office of Workforce Literacy is dedicated to strengthening the skills of Indiana's workforce and to increasing the competitive edge of Indiana employers. Workforce Literacy grants provide on-site, customized, specific job related training. Employers and workers alike report that knowledge, skills, work attitudes, and productivity improves as a result of job-specific training.

2787 Indy Reads: Indianapolis/Marion County Public Library

PO Box 211
Indianapolis, IN   46206   317-269-1700
                                  FAX 317-269-5220
                        http://www.imcpl.org
                  e-mail: lgabrielson@imcpl.org
Linda Gabrielson, Manager

Indy Reads, a nationally recognized not-for-profit affiliate of the Indianapolis-Marion County Public Library, exists to improve the reading and writing skills of adults in Marion County who read at or below the sixth grade level.

2788 Literacy Volunteers of America: Cass County

847 S Cicott Street
Logansport, IN   46947   219-722-6809
                                  FAX 219-722-6810
Jane Miller, Contact

Literacy Volunteers of America is a fully integrated national network of local, state and regional literacy providers that gives adults and their families the opportunity to acquire skills to be effective in their roles as members of their families, communities, and workplaces.

2789 Literacy Volunteers of America: White County

1001 S Main
Monticello, IN   47960   574-583-0789
                                  FAX 219-943-3533
Judy Hickman, Contact

A not-for-profit organization which provides a variety of free services to help people achieve personal goals through literacy.

2790 Morrisson/Reeves Library Literacy Resource Center

80 N 6th Street
Richmond, IN   47374   765-966-8291
                                  FAX 765-962-1318
                        http://www.mrl.lib.org
                  e-mail: library@mrlinfo.org

The Literacy Resource Center provides free training for volunteers to tutor adults in Wayne County who want to learn to read, write and do basic math.

2791 Steuben County Literacy Coalition

Community Center
317 S Wayne
Angola, IN   46703   260-665-1414
                                  FAX 260-665-1414
              http://www.steubencountyliteracycoalition.org
                          e-mail: sclc@locl.net
Rebecca Fifer, President
Kathleen Armstrong, Director

The Steuben County Literacy Coalition helps adults and families develop their potential through improved literacy, education, and training.

2792 Three Rivers Literacy Alliance
709 Clay Street
Fort Wayne, IN   46802   260-426-7323
                                  FAX 260-424-0371
                                  http://www.tria.org
                                  e-mail: trlafw@yahoo.com
Kathleen Benson-Chaney, Literacy Coordinator

Three Rivers Literacy Alliance addresses literacy issues with the adult population of Fort Wayne and the surrounding community.

Iowa

2793 Iowa Bureau of Community Colleges
Department of Education
Grimes State Office Building
Des Moines, IA   50319   515-281-3125
                                  FAX 515-281-6544
            http://www.state.ia.us/educate/commcoll.html
                   e-mail: sally.schroeder@ed.state.ia.us
Sally Schroeder, Contact

2794 Iowa Department of Education: Iowa Literacy Council Programs
Grimes State Office Building
Des Moines, IA   50319   515-281-5294
                                  FAX 515-242-5988
            http://www.state.ia.us/educate/commcoll
                   e-mail: sally.schroeder@ed.state.ia.us
Sally Schroeder, Contact
Ted Stilwater, Director, Family Literacy

Helps adults and families develop their potential through improved literacy, education, and training.

2795 Iowa JOBS Program: Division of Economic Assistance
Department of Human Services
Hoover State Building
Des Moines, IA   50319   515-281-8629
                                  FAX 515-281-7791
Doug Howard, Administrator

2796 Iowa Literacy Resource Center
Iowa Literacy Resource Center
415 Commercial Street
Waterloo, IA   50701   319-233-1200
                                       800-772-2023
                                  FAX 319-233-1964
                                  http://www.readiowa.org
                                  e-mail: riesberg@neilsa.org
Eunice Riesberg, Director
Denise Luppen, Administrative Assistant

The Center provides a link to resource materials in Iowa and at a regional and national level for adult literacy practitioners and students.

2797 Iowa Vocational Rehabilitation Agency
Department of Education
Grimes State Office Building
Des Moines, IA   50319   515-281-5294
                                  FAX 515-281-4703
            http://www.state.ia.us/educate/directory.html
Steve Wooderson, Administrator

2798 Iowa Workforce Investment Act
Department of Economic Development
200 E Grand Avenue
Des Moines, IA   50309   515-242-4700
                                  FAX 515-242-4809
                                  http://www.state.ia.us/ided
                                  e-mail: iowasmart@ided.state.ia.us
Mike Blouin, Director

Job placement and training services. Especially for those workers who have been laid off, or have other barriers to steady employment.

2799 Learning Disabilities Association of Iowa
321 E 6th Street
Des Moines, IA   50329   515-280-8558
                                       888-690-5324
                                  http://www.lda-ia.org
Vicki Goshon, President
Connie Sullivan, Secretary

The Learning Disabilities Association of Iowa advances the education and general welfare of children and youth of normal, near-normal, and potentially normal intelligence who have learning disabilities.

2800 Library Literacy Programs: State Library of Iowa
1112 E Grand Avenue
Des Moines, IA   50319   515-281-4105
                                  FAX 515-281-6171
                                  http://www.silo.lib.ia.us
Helen Dagley, Information Services

Kansas

2801 Client Assistance Program (CAP):Kansas Division of Persons with Disabilities
2914 SW Plass Court
Topeka, KS   66611   785-266-8193
                                       800-432-2326
Mary Reyer, Director

Provides free services to consumers and applicants for projects, programs and facilities funded under the rehabilitation act.

2802 Kansas Adult Education Association
Barton County Community College
245 NE 30th Road
Great Bend, KS   67530   620-792-2701
                                       800-748-7594
                                  http://www.barton.cc.ks.us
Angie Reid, Public Relations
Vikki Jo Stewart

The Kansas Adult Education Association has been the professional association for adult educators at community colleges, school districts, and non-profit organizations.

2803 Kansas Correctional Education

900 SW Jackson
Topeka, KS 66612　　　　785-296-3317
　　　　　　　　　　　　888-317-8204
http://www.docnet.dc.state.ks.us
Roger L Haden, Secretary of Programs & Staff

The provision of correctional education programming to inmates.

2804 Kansas Department of Corrections

900 SW Jackson
Topeka, KS 66612　　　　785-296-3317
　　　　　　　　　　　　888-317-8204
　　　　　　　　FAX 785-296-3317
http://www.dc.state.ks.us
Correctional education programming to inmates.

2805 Kansas Human Resource Investment Council

Kansas Department of Human Resources
401 SW Topeka Boulevard
Topeka, KS 66603　　　　785-296-3974
　　　　　　　　FAX 785-296-8177
http://www.hr.state.ks.us
e-mail: sandra.brown@hr.state.ks.us
Deann Tiede, State Council Coordinator
Sandra Brown, On-Site Coordinator

Cultivates a job ready workforce and a workplace environment to fuel economic growth for Kansas.

2806 Kansas Laubach Literacy Action

PO Box 1071
Arkansas City, KS 67005　　620-442-1107

A non-profit educational corporation dedicated to helping adults of all ages improve their lives and their communities by learning reading, writing, math and problem-solving skills.

2807 Kansas Library Literacy Programs: Kansas State Library

200 Arco Place, Suite 309
Independence, KS 67301　　620-331-8218
　　　　　　　　FAX 620-331-9087
e-mail: vikkijo@kslib.info
Vikki Jo Stewart, Management Coordinator

The goal of the Kansas Library Literacy Program is to provide Kansans with current volunteer management information to assist in their effort to use volunteers to meet a mission, e.g., libraries, literacy programs, etc. and to provide Kansans with current literacy information to assist in their effort to help adults and youth to read better, e.g., community-based literacy programs, traditional adult education, etc.

2808 Kansas Literacy Resource Center

Kansas Board of Regents/Literacy Resource Center
1000 SW Jackson Street
Topeka, KS 66612　　　　785-296-0175
　　　　　　　　FAX 785-296-0983
http://www.literacy.kent.edu
e-mail: dglass@ksbor.org
Dianne S Glass, State Director Adult Education
Diane K Whitley, Associate Director

The Kansas Literacy Resource Center enhances systems, both private and public, that provide basic skills education across Kansas.

2809 Kansas Literacy Volunteers of America

Kansas State Library
State Capital Building
Topeka, KS 66612　　　　785-296-3296
　　　　　　　　　　　　800-432-3919
　　　　　　　　FAX 785-296-6650
http://www.skyways.org
e-mail: KSST15LB@INK.ORG
Vikki Stewart, Literacy Program Director

To give adults and their families the opportunity to acquire skills to be effective in their roles as members of their families, communities and workplaces.

2810 Kansas State Department of Adult Education

120 E 10th Street
Topeka, KS 66612　　　　785-296-3201
　　　　　　　　FAX 785-296-7933

To assist adults to become literate and obtain the knowledge and skills necessary for employment and self-sufficiency.

2811 Kansas State Literacy Resource Center: Kansas State Department of Education

120 SE 10th
Topeka, KS 66612　　　　913-296-7159
　　　　　　　　FAX 913-296-7933
Janet Stotts, Co-Director
Dianne Glass, Co-Director

The State Literacy Resource Center can assist adult education practitioners across the nation in locating and accessing the most current materials in their issue area.

2812 Kansas Vocational Rehabilitation Agency

300 SW Oakley, Biddle Building
Topeka, KS 66606　　　　785-296-3911
　　　　　　　　FAX 785-368-6688
Joyce A Cussimanio, Commissioner

To assist people with disabilities achieve suitable employment and independence.

2813 Western Kansas Community Service Consortiuum

348 NE SR
Pratt, KS 67124　　　　620-672-6251
http://www.wkcsc.org
e-mail: dedram@genmail.pcc.cc.ks.us
Dedra Manes, Executive Director

Mission is to provide cooperative community services to Western Kansas. Total service area includes 73 counties and nearly 3/4 of the state's geographic area.

Kentucky

2814 Kentucky Laubach Literacy Action

Department for Adult Education & Literacy
Capital Plaza Tower, 3rd Floor
Frankfort, KY   40601   502-564-5114
FAX 502-564-5436
http://www.win.net
e-mail: dvislisel@mail.state.ky.us
Dave Vislisel, Director

Dedicated to helping adults of all ages improve their lives and their communities by learning reading, writing, match and problem-solving skills.

2815 Kentucky Literacy Resource Center

Center for Adult Education & Literacy
1049 US 127 S
Frankfort, KY   40601   502-564-4062
FAX 502-564-6407
http://www.win.net
e-mail: scallaway@mail.state.ky.us
Sare Callaway, Contact

As part of the State Library, the State Resource Center provides electronic and print resources.

2816 Kentucky Literacy Volunteers of America

Capital Plaza Tower, 3rd Floor
Frankfort, KY   40601   502-564-5114
FAX 502-564-5436
e-mail: dvislsel@mail.state.ky.us
Dave Vislisel, Director

Promotes literacy for people of all ages.

Louisiana

2817 Literacy Volunteers of America: Centenary College Program

2911 Centenary Boulevard
Shreveport, LA   71134   318-869-2411
FAX 318-869-2474
e-mail: lvacent@softdisk.com
Sue Lee, Contact

2818 Louisiana Literacy Resource Center: Adult Education and Training

PO Box 94064
Baton Rouge, LA   70802   504-342-9442
877-453-2721
FAX 504-219-4439
http://www.leeric.lsu.edu
e-mail: pdwall@aol.com
Pamela Wall, Director

To provide professional development and technical assistance for literacy and adult education/programs throughout the state.

2819 Louisiana State Literacy Resource Center: State Department of Education

Office of School & Community Support
626 N 4th Street
Baton Rouge, LA   70804   225-342-3340
877-453-2721
FAX 225-219-4439
http://www.louisianaschools.net
e-mail: mbryant@la.gov

The Center provides a link to resource materials in Louisiana and at a regional and national level for adult literacy, practitioners and students.

Maine

2820 Center for Adult Learning and Literacy: University of Maine

5749 Merrill Hall
Orono, ME   04469   207-581-2498
FAX 207-581-1517
http://www.umaine.edu
e-mail: evelyn.beaulieu@umit.maine.edu
Evelyn Beaulieu, Director
Carol Wynne, Project Coordinator

The Center for Adult Learning and Literacy offers quality, research-based professional development and resources, based on funded initiatives to improve the quality of services within the Maine Adult Education System.

2821 Maine Bureau of Applied Technical Adult Learning: Adult Career and Technical Education

23 State House Station
Augusta, ME   04333   207-624-6730
FAX 207-624-6731
http://www.maine.gov/education
e-mail: yvonne.davis@maine.gov
Yvonne Davis, Coordinator

2822 Maine Literacy Resource Center

University of Maine
5749 Merrill Hall
Orono, ME   04469   207-581-2498
http://www.umaine.edu
e-mail: evelyn.beaulieu@umit.maine.edu
Evelyn Beaulieu, Director

As part of the State Library, the State Resource Center provides electronic and print resources.

2823 Maine Literacy Volunteers of America

142 High Street, #529
Portland, ME   04101   207-780-1352
http://www.lvaportland.org
e-mail: lvportland@gwi.net
Suzanne Hunt, Director

A non-profit organization that provides free tutoring to adults who cannot read and to adults whose native language is not English.

Maryland

2824 Howard University School of Continuing Education

1100 Wayne Avenue
Silver Spring, MD   20910   301-585-2295
                                          FAX 301-585-8911
                    http://www.con-ed.howard.edu
                    e-mail: paberry@howard.edu
Peggy A Berry, Director

Howard University Continuing Education was established in April 1986 to meet the education and training needs of professionals, administrators, entrepreneurs, technical personnel, paraprofessionals and other adults on an individual or group basis.

2825 Maryland Literacy Coalition

Howard County Library
10375 Little Patuxent Parkway
Columbia, MD   21044   410-313-7900
                                          FAX 410-313-7811
Janet Carsetti, President

2826 Maryland Literacy Resource Center

UMBC, Department of Education
1000 Hilltop Circle
Baltimore, MD   21250   410-455-1000
                                          800-358-3010
                                          FAX 410-455-1139
                    http://www.umbc.edu
                    e-mail: help@umbc.edu
Katherine Ira, Director

As part of the State Library, the State Resource Center provides resources and information for adult literacy providers and students in Maryland.

Massachusetts

2827 Adult Center at PAL: Curry College

1071 Blue Hill Avenue
Milton, MA   02186   617-333-0500
                                          FAX 617-333-2114
                    http://www.curry.edu/pal
                    e-mail: pal@curry.edu
Jane Utley Adelizzi PhD, Contact

The Adult Center at PAL (Program for Advancement of Learning) is the first program to offer academic and socio-emotional services to adults with LD/ADHD/Dyslexia in a college setting in the New England area. The ACD offers one-to-one academic tutorials; small support groups that meet weekly; and Saturday Seminars that explore issues that impact the lives of adults with LD/ADHD.

2828 Eastern Massachusetts Literacy Council

400 High Street
Medford, MA   02155   781-395-2374
                                          FAX 781-395-3281
                    http://www.emlc.org
                    e-mail: volunteer@emlc.org

The Eastern Massachusetts Literacy Council is a private non-profit affiliate of ProLiteracy Worldwide, the largest nonprofit volunteer adult literacy organization in the world. The EMLC trains volunteers to assist adults who are learning English as another language and adults who wish to strengthen their basic reading skills.

2829 JOBS Program: Massachusetts Employment Services Program

Dept of Transitional Assistance/Office of Health
600 Washington Street
Boston, MA   02111   617-348-8400
                                          FAX 617-348-8575
                    http://www.state.ma.us/dta/index.htm

The Employment Services Program is a joint federal and state funded program whose primary goal is to provide a way to self-sufficiency for TAFDC families ESP is an employment-oriented program that is based on a work-first approach.

2830 Literacy Volunteers of Massachusetts

15 Court Square
Boston, MA   02108   617-367-8894
                    http://www.volunteerssolutions.org
                    e-mail: volunteers@uwmb.org
Amy Todeschini, Coordinator

The Literacy Volunteers of Massachusetts helps adults learn to read and write or speak English by matching them with trained volunteer tutors.

2831 Massachusetts Correctional Education: Inmate Training & Education

Department of Correction
2 Clark Street
Norfolk, MA   02056   617-727-9170
                                          FAX 617-727-7262
                    http://www.state.ma.us
Carolyn J Vicari, Director

To establish departmental policy regarding inmates' involvement in academic and vocational training programs.

2832 Massachusetts Family Literacy Consortium

Massachusetts Department of Education
350 Main Street
Malden, MA   02148   781-338-3300
                                          FAX 781-338-3394
                    http://www.doe.mass.edu
                    e-mail: MFLC@doe.mass.edu
Kathy Rodriguez, MFLC Coordinator
Arlene Dale, State Coordinator

The Massachusetts Family Literacy Consortium is a statewide initiative with the mission of forging effective partnerships among state agencies, community organizations, and other interested parties to expand and strengthen family literacy and support.

2833 Massachusetts GED Administration: Massachusetts Department of Education

350 Main Street
Malden, MA 02148   781-338-6604
http://www.doe.mass.edu
e-mail: rderfler@doe.mass.edu
Ruth Derfler, Director

Thirty-three test centers operate state-wide to serve the needs of the adult population in need of a high school credential.

2834 Massachusetts Job Training Partnership Act: Department of Employment & Training

CF Hurley Building, 3rd Floor
Boston, MA 02114   617-626-6600
Nils L Nordberg, Commissioner

Supplies information on the local labor market and assists companies in locating employees.

Michigan

2835 Genesee County Literacy Coalition

Zimmerman Center
2421 Corunna Road
Flint, MI 48503   810-760-5182
FAX 810-760-1215
http://www.flint.lib.mi.us

The Genesee County Literacy Coalition is a non-profit organization dedicated to promoting literacy in Genesee County.

2836 Literacy Volunteers of America: Lansing Area Literacy Coalition

1028 E Saginaw
Lansing, MI 48906   517-485-4949
FAX 517-485-1924
http://www.thereadingpeople.org
e-mail: mail@thereadingpeople.org
Lois Bader, Executive Director
Di Clark, Assistant Director

The Capital Area Literacy Coalition helps children and adults learn to read, write and speak English with an ultimate goal of helping individuals achieve self-sufficiency.

2837 Literacy Volunteers of America: Sanilac Council

Grace Temple
46 N Jackson Street
Sandusky, MI 48471   810-648-2200

Helps children and adults learn to read, write and speak English with self sufficiency as the ultimate goal.

2838 Michigan Adult Learning & Technology Center

Central Michigan University
219 Ronan Hall
Mount Pleasant, MI 48859   989-774-3337
FAX 989-714-7713
http://www.malt.cmich.edu
e-mail: malt@cmich.edu
Michael Kent, Special Projects Coordinator

A professional development center that extends support services and resources to adult education providers, volunteers, and students. These efforts include: disseminating research information; conducting and sponsoring training for tutors and educators; coordinating conferences; aiding in the utilization of technology in professional development and the classroom; providing grants or sponsoring research projects related to the field of education.

2839 Michigan Assistive Technology: Michigan Rehabilitation Services

Michigan Jobs Commission
119 Pere Marquette Drive
Lansing, MI 48912   517-485-4477
FAX 517-485-4488
http://www.publicpolicy.com
e-mail: ppa@publicpolicy.com
Jeffrey D Padden, President
Nancy C Hewat, Executive Director

2840 Michigan Laubach Literacy Action

2157 University Park Drive
Okemos, MI 48864   517-349-7511
FAX 517-349-6667
http://www.michiganliteracy.org
e-mail: mli@voyager.net
Levona Whitakersident, Contact

Dedicated to advancing basic literacy skills throughout Michigan and beyond.

2841 Michigan Libraries and Adult Literacy

717 W Allegan Street
Lansing, MI 48909   517-373-1297
FAX 517-373-5853
e-mail: swatkins@libraryofmichigan.org
Christine McGinley, Contact

2842 Michigan State Department of Adult Education: Office of Extended Learning Services

Department of Education
608 W Allegan
Lansing, MI 48933   517-241-3946
FAX 517-335-0592
http://www.michigan.gov
e-mail: kingsley@state.mi.us
Maria Kingsley, Educational Consultant

2843 Michigan Workforce Investment Act

Michigan Jobs Commission
119 Pere Marquette Drive
Lansing, MI 48912   517-485-4477
FAX 517-485-4488
http://www.publicpolicy.com
e-mail: ppa@publicpolicy.com
Jeffrey D Padden, President
Nancy C Hewat, Executive Officer

Minnesota

2844 Minnesota Department of Adult Education: Adult Basic Education

Department of Children, Families & Learning
986 Capitol Square Building
Saint Paul, MN 55101   651-596-5616
                              FAX 651-634-5154
Brian Kanes, Coordinator

2845 Minnesota Department of Employment and Economic Development

Minnesota Workforce Center
390 N Robert Street
St. Paul, MN 55101   612-296-6061
                               800-657-3858
                          FAX 651-296-0994
                    http://www.mnwfc.org
e-mail: mdes.customerservice@state.mn.us
Bonnie Elsey, Director

The Department of Employment and Economic Development is Minnesota's principal economic development agency, with programs promoting business expansion and retention, workforce development, international trade, community development and tourism.

2846 Minnesota GED Administration

997 Capitol Square Building
St. Paul, MN 55101   612-296-2704
                          FAX 612-668-3805
Patrick Rupp, GED Director

State of Minnesota General Educational Development.

2847 Minnesota LDA Learning Disabilities Center

4301 Highway 7
Minneapolis, MN 55416   952-922-8374
                               866-891-0601
                          FAX 952-922-8102
                http://www.ldaminnesota.org
Kitty Christiansen, Executive Director
Victoria Weinberg, Program Director

The LDA Learning Center maximizes the potential of children, youth and adults with learning disabilities or related learning difficulties so that they and their families lead more productive and fulfilled lives.

2848 Minnesota LINCS: Literacy Council

756 Transfer Road
St. Paul, MN 55114   651-645-2277
                               800-225-7323
                          FAX 651-645-2272
                    http://www.themic.org
Cathy Grady, Program Director
Eric Nesheim, Executive Director

Makes information available to literacy and other educators throughout Minnesota. The system is a result of cooperation between numerous agencies and organizations in Minnesota that realize the benefit of using the internet to provide information to the public. The system allows literacy and other educators to locate information at one central site or follow links to connect to wherever the information resides.

2849 Minnesota Life Work Center

1000 La Salle Avenue
Minneapolis, MN 55403   651-962-4763
                    http://www.stthomas.edu
              e-mail: lifework@stthomas.edu
Brian Dusbiber, Director
Mary Kay Kernan, Career Counselor

Supporting the educational goals, personal growth and career management needs of graduate students, education students, and alumni, through professional services and comprehensive resources.

2850 Minnesota Literacy Training Network

University of St. Thomas
1000 La Salle
Minneapolis, MN 55403   651-962-4000
                               800-328-6819
                    http://www.stthomas.edu
Deborah Simmons, Director

Literacy Training Network offers noncredit learning opportunities for adult basic education and literacy training staff in Minnesota.

2851 Minnesota Vocational Rehabilitation Agency: Rehabilitation Services Branch

Department of Economic Security
390 N Robert Street
Saint Paul, MN 55101   651-296-5616
                               800-328-9095
                          FAX 651-297-5159
          http://www.mnworkforcecenter.org
          e-mail: Howard.Glad@state.mn.us
Howard Glad, Contact

Provides basic vocational rehabilitation services to consumers including vocational counseling, planning, guidance and placement, as well as certain special services based on individual circumstances.

Mississippi

2852 Mississippi Literacy Resource Center

Governor's Office of Literacy
3825 Ridgewood Road
Jackson, MS 39211   601-982-6519
                          FAX 601-982-6449
               http://www.ihl.state.ms.us
          e-mail: judy@gol.state.ms.us
Judy Williams, Director

A central clearinghouse of information for literacy groups in Mississippi.

Missouri

2853 Literacy Investment for Tomorrow: Missouri

500 NW Plaza
Saint Ann, MO   63074   314-291-4443
                                     800-729-4443
                               FAX 314-291-7385
                    http://www.literacy.kent.edu
                        e-mail: lift@icon-stl.net
Sarah Beaman-Jones, Literacy Program Developer
Tim O'Dea, Executive Director

LIFT develops and promotes resources to increase literacy skills of Missourians so all individuals can reach their personal and economic potential.

2854 Literacy Kansas City

205 W 65th Street
Kansas City, MO   64113   816-333-9332
                               FAX 816-444-6628
                        http://www.literacykc.org
                        e-mail: info@literacykc.org
Janis Doty, Program Director
Marge Gasnick, Program Director

Literacy Kansas City is a 501 (c) (3) not-for-profit organization that helps adults from greater metropolitan Kansas City improve their basic literacy skills.

Montana

2855 Literacy Volunteers of America: Montana

304 N Main Street
Butte, MT   59701   406-723-7905
                                     888-606-7905
                               FAX 406-723-6196
                      e-mail: lvabulit@in-tch.com
Paula Anerson, Contact

We provide adults and their families the opportunity to acquire skills to be effective in their roles as members of their families, communitites, and workplaces.

2856 Montana Literacy Resource Center

Montana State Library
1515 E 6th Avenue
Helena, MT   59620   406-444-3004
                               FAX 406-444-5612
                        http://www.msl.state.mt.us
                        e-mail: kstrege@state.mt.us
Karen Strege, State Librarian
Kris Schmitz, Central Services Manager

A state-wide literacy support network.

Nebraska

2857 Answers4Families: Center on Children, Families, Law

121 S 13th Street
Lincoln, NE   68588
                    http://www.answers4families.org/nrrs
                    e-mail: chayek@answers4families.org
Connie K Hayek, Director
Sharon Bloechle, Omaha Parent Coordinator

A project of the Center on Children, Families and Law at University of Nebraska. Mission is to provide info, opportunities, education and support to Nebraskans through Internet resources. The Center serves individuals with special needs and mental health disorders, foster families, caregivers, assisted living, and school nurses.

2858 Client Assistance Program (CAP): Nebraska Division of Persons with Disabilities

Nebraska Department of Education
301 Centennial Mall S
Lincoln, NE   68509   402-471-3656
                                     800-742-7594
                               FAX 402-471-0117
                        http://www.nde.state.ne.us
                    e-mail: victoria@cap.state.ne.us

The Client Assistance Program helps individuals who have concerns or difficulties when applying for or receiving rehabilitation services funded under the Rehabilitation Act.

2859 State Literacy Resource Center for Nebraska: Institute for the Study of Adult Literacy

Department of Vocational and Adult Education
University of Nebraska-Lincoln
Lincoln, NE   68588   402-472-5924
                               FAX 402-472-5907
                    http://www.literacy.kent.edu
                        e-mail: bsparks1@unl.edu
Barbara Sparks PhD, Director
Qian Geng, Coordinator

As the State Literacy Resource Center for Nebraska, NISAL provides a central point of contact for researchers, decision makers and literacy providers in Nebraska and serves as a vital link between providers and user groups, community based organizations, state agencies and business and industry. The institute enhances existing practice by promoting and providing information and resources to enhance and encourage best practices.

Nevada

2860 Nevada Department of Adult Education

Nevada Department of Education
700 E 5th Street
Carson City, NV   89701   775-687-9200
                               FAX 775-687-9101
                        http://www.nde.state.nv.us
Mary K Moen, Adult Education Director

Provides adult basic education and literacy services in order to assist adults to become literate and obtain the knowledge and skills necessary for employment and self-sufficiency.

2861   Nevada Economic Opportunity Board: Community Action Partnership

PO Box 270880
Las Vegas, NV   89127   702-647-1510
                               FAX 702-647-6639
                               http://www.eobcc.org
Marcia Walker, Executive Director

Located in one of the fastest growing and most diverse communities in the United States, the Economic Opportunity Board of Clark County is a highly innovative Community Action Agency. Our mission is to eliminate poverty by providing programs, resources, services, and advocacy for self-sufficiency and economic empowerment.

2862   Nevada Literacy Coalition: State Literacy Resource Center

Nevada State Library and Archives
100 N Stewart Street
Carson City, NV   89710   775-684-3340
                                800-445-9673
                          FAX 775-684-3311
                http://www.dmia.clan.lib.nv.us
                e-mail: nslref@clan.lib.nv.us
Susan Graf, Literacy Coordinator

The Nevada State Literacy Resource Center has books, newsletters and a wide variety of multi-media resources such as videos, audiotapes and games for literacy instruction and programs for literacy students, trainers and tutors.

2863   Northern Nevada Literacy Council

680 Greenbrae Drive
Sparks, NV   89431   775-356-1007
                          FAX 775-356-1009
                          http://www.nnlc.org
                e-mail: director@nnlc.org
Vicki Newell, Executive Director

Provides a framework that assists Nevada's communities in addressing their literacy needs at the local level.

New Hampshire

2864   New Hampshire Literacy Volunteers of America

Manchester City Library
405 Pine Street
Manchester, NH   03104   603-624-6550
                          FAX 603-624-6559
                http://www.manchesternh.gov
Elizabeth Sabol, Program Director
Gwen Brown, Assistant Director

This program is the only nationally accredited adult literacy program in New Hampshire. Provides free confidential one-to-one tutoring for adults who want to learn to write and read for lifelong learning.

2865   New Hampshire Second Start Adult Education

17 Knight Street
Concord, NH   03301   603-228-1341
                          FAX 603-228-3852
                http://www.second-start.org
                e-mail: ABE@second-start.org

Provides basic reading, writing and math skills for people who want to achieve educational goals, participate in the life of the community, gain independence and become lifelong learners.

New Jersey

2866   New Jersey Literacy Volunteers of America: Peoplecare Center

120 Finderne Avenue
Bridgewater, NJ   08807   908-203-4582
                                800-848-0048
                          FAX 908-203-4585
                e-mail: lvanj@aol.com
Doryce Wheeler, Center

Literacy Volunteers of America-New Jersey (LVA-NJ) is a nonprofit, education organization providing training, technical assistance, communications, and program support to adult literacy organizations in New Jersey. It directs most of its services to its affiliated community based organizations located in twenty counties of the state.

New Mexico

2867   Deming Literacy Program

2301 S Tin Street
Deming, NM   88030   505-546-7571
                          FAX 505-546-1356
                e-mail: dlp@zianet.com
Marisol Perez, Contact

The Literacy Home Mentoring and After School Project will encourage parents to read to their children at home, as well as provide mentors to help children with their reading skills after school.

2868   Literacy Center of Albuquerque

PO Box 30393
Albuquerque, NM   87190   505-266-7202
                          FAX 505-884-3129
                          http://www.lcbq.org
                e-mail: info@lcbq.org
Kathleen Salas, Program Coordinator

The Literacy Center of Albuquerque is a non-profit organization of students, tutors and supporters working together to enhance the lives of people with English as a Second Language and addresses literacy needs by providing programs through volunteers and community resources.

2869 Literacy Volunteers of America: Cibola County
PO Box 306
Grants, NM   87020   505-285-5995
                                    FAX 505-285-5995
                              http://www.7cities.net
                        e-mail: lvagrants@7cities.net
Charlotte Otts, Executive Director

Offers basic reading and ESL tutoring at no charge to
adults in Cibola County.

**2870 Literacy Volunteers of America: Dona Ana
County**
Dona Ana Branch Community College
3400 S Espina Street
Las Cruces, NM   88003   505-527-7640
                                      800-903-7540
                                    FAX 505-527-7515
                         http://www.dabcc-www.nmsu.edu
Harry H Pearson, Coordinator

The Literacy Volunteers of America is designed to
help people who cannot read or write the English language. This program gives adults a new opportunity to
learn reading through the sixth-grade level.

**2871 Literacy Volunteers of America: Las Vegas, San
Miguel**
PO Box 516
Las Vegas, NM   88701   505-454-8043
                              http://www.nmhu.edu
Ann Costello, Director

Las Vegas/San Miquel Literacy Volunteers are a part
of the national non-profit organization Literacy Volunteers of America, which is dedicated to promoting
literacy throughout the country.

2872 Literacy Volunteers of America: Otero County
New Mexico State University at Alamogordo
2400 N Scenic Drive
Alamogordo, NM   88310   505-439-3600
                                    FAX 505-439-3643
                           http://www.alamo.nmsu.edu
                      e-mail: reynolds@nmsua.nmsu.edu
Anita C Raynor, Contact

Can provide volunteer tutors to work one-on-one with
adult non-readers and non-English speaking adults.
All these services are provided free of charge to
adults.

2873 Literacy Volunteers of America: Read West
PO Box 44058
Rio Rancho, NM   87174   505-892-1131
                                    FAX 505-892-1131
                              http://www.uwcnm.org
                        e-mail: readwest@hubwest.com
Susan Markin-Ryerson, Executive Director

Programs that assist adults in reading development.
English as a second language program offered. Family
literacy workshops for parents.

2874 Literacy Volunteers of America: Santa Fe
6401 Richards Avenue
Santa Fe, NM   87505   505-428-1353
                                    FAX 505-428-1237
                              http://www.lvsf.net
                        e-mail: pete681@msn.com
Letty Naranjo, Manager
Catherine Johnson, Program Coordinator

Literacy Volunteers of Santa Fe was established to
provide free tutoring services for adults in the Santa
Fe area seeking to improve their reading skills or learn
English as a second language.

2875 Literacy Volunteers of America: Socorro County
PO Box 1431
Socorro, NM   87801   505-835-4659
                                    FAX 505-835-1182
Margaret Aquilar-Rhodes, Contact

Promotes literacy for people of Socorro County.

2876 New Mexico Coalition for Literacy
PO Box 6085
Sante Fe, NM   87502   505-982-3997
                                      800-233-7587
                                    FAX 505-982-4095
                              http://www.nmcl.org
                        e-mail: info@nmcl.org
David Godsted, Executive Director
Rena Paradis, Training Coordinator

The Coalition encourages and supports community-based literacy programs and is the New Mexico
affiliate and coordinator for the national program of
ProLiteracy America.

2877 Valencia County Literacy Council
Belen Public Library
333 Becker Avenue
Belen, NM   87002   595-864-3511
                                    FAX 505-864-7798
                           http://www.youseemore.com
                        e-mail: joglesby@unm.edu
Jill Oglesby, Executive Director

Promotes and supports literacy in the area.

New York

**2878 Literacy Volunteers of America: Middletown,
New York**
25 Orchard Street
Middletown, NY   10940   845-341-5460
                                    FAX 845-343-7191
                        http://www.literacymiddletown.org
                     e-mail: baclvamdtn@frontiernet.net
Barbara A Clifford, Executive Director
Rowena M Reich, Program Coordinator

An organization of volunteers which provides a variety of services to enable people to achieve personal goals through literacy. We believe that the ability to read is critical to personal freedom and maintenance of a democratic society. These beliefs have led us to make the following commitments: the personal growth of our students; the effective use of our volunteers; the improvement of society and strengthening and improving our organization.

2879 New York Laubach Literacy International

ProLiteracy Worldwide
1320 Jamesville Avenue
Syracuse, NY   13210   315-422-9121
                                            888-528-2224
                                       FAX 315-422-6369
                                http://www.proliteracy.org
Robert Wedgeworth, President

The Syracuse chapters of the world's two largest adult volunteer literacy organization merged and Laubach Literacy International and Literacy Volunteers of America became ProLiteracy Worldwide. This organization sponsors educational programs and services for adults and their families. These programs assist participants to acquire the literacy practices and skills needed to function more effectively in their daily lives and participate in their societies.

2880 New York Literacy Assistance Center

32 Broadway
New York, NY   10004   212-803-3300
                                       FAX 212-785-3685
                                   http://www.lacnyc.org
Winston Lawrence, Coordinator of Adult Literacy
Ira Yankwitt, Director of Adult Literacy

Founded in 1983, a not-for-profit organization that provides essential referral, training information and technical assistance services to hundreds of adult and youth literacy programs in New York. Our mission is to support and promote the expansion of quality literacy services in New York.

2881 New York Literacy Partners

30 E 33rd Street
New York, NY   10016   212-725-9200
                                       FAX 212-725-9744
                              http://www.literarypartners.org
Susan A McLean, Executive Director
Doris P Meister, Executive VP

Literacy Partners, is a not-for-profit organization, providing free community-based adult and family literacy programs to ensure that all adults have the access to quality education needed to fully realize their potential as individuals, parents, and citizens.

2882 New York Literacy Resource Center

State University of New York
135 Western Avenue
Albany, NY   12222   518-442-5372
                                            800-331-0931
                                       FAX 518-442-5021
                                   http://www.albany.edu
Maritza Ramirez-Vallinas, Director

State Literacy Resource Center is a statewide literacy information network throughout the state.

2883 New York Literacy Volunteers of America

Literacy Volunteers of New York State
777 Maryvale Drive
Buffalo, NY   14225   716-631-5282
                                       FAX 716-631-0657
                                  http://www.lvanys.org
                             e-mail: buffalo@lvanys.org
Janice Cuddahee, Associate Executive Director
Rosalinde Mecca, Program Director

Literacy Volunteers of America in New York State is a nonprofit educational organization that provides training and technical assistance to 48 local, community-based literacy programs in New York. In addition, LVA-NYS offers consultation services and support to literacy organizations nationally.

2884 Resources for Children with Special Needs

116 E 16th Street
New York, NY   10003   212-677-4650
                                       FAX 212-254-4070
                             http://www.resourcesnyc.org
                           e-mail: info@resourcesnyc.org
Karen Thoreson Schlesinger, Executive Director
Helene F Crane, Associate Director

An independent, nonprofit organization that provides information and referral, case management and support, individual and systemic advocacy, parent and professional training and library services to New York City parents and caregivers of children with disabilities and special needs and to professionals who work with them. Our publications include: Camps 2003; After School and more; The Comprehensive Directory; and Schools for Children with Autism Spectrum Disorders.

North Carolina

2885 Blue Ridge Literacy Council

PO Box 1728
Hendersonville, NC   28793   828-696-3811
                                       FAX 828-696-3887
                                http://www.litcouncil.org
                             e-mail: info@litcouncil.org

The Blue Ridge Literacy Council provides Henderson County adult students the English communication and literacy skills they need to reach their full potential as individuals, parents, workers and citizens.

2886 Buncombe County Literacy Council

86 Victoria Road
Asheville, NC   28801   828-254-3442
                                        FAX 828-254-1742
                                http://www.main.nc.us
                     e-mail: literacy@main.buncombe.nc.us

Promotes increased adult literacy in Buncombe County through effective use of trained tutors; to provide support services for tutors and learners; and to collaborate with individuals, groups, or other community organizations desiring to foster increased adult literacy.

2887 Durham County Literacy Council

1410 W Chapel Hill Street
Durham, NC   27701   919-489-8383
                                  800-562-2139
                              FAX 919-489-1456
                          http://www.duhamlit.org
                         e-mail: durhamlit@aol.com
Lucy E Haagen, Executive Director

The Durham County Literacy Council provides training in adult basic education (including reading, writing and mathematics), English for Speakers of Other Languages, GED examination preparation, Family Literacy, workplace literacy, and technology.

2888 Gastonia Literacy Council

116 S Marietta
Gastonia, NC   28052   704-868-4815
                              FAX 704-867-7796
                      http://www.clt.quik.com/literacy
                        e-mail: literacy@quik.com
Kaye Gribble, Executive Director

The Gaston Literacy Council is dedicated to improving literacy throughout the Gastonia area.

2889 Literacy Volunteers of America: Pitt County

504-A Dexter Street
Greenville, NC   27834   252-353-6578
                              FAX 252-353-6868
                     e-mail: lva-pc@greenvillenc.com
Laura Smith, Executive Director

The mission of LVA-PC is to teach adults to read or improve their reading, writing or English speaking skills through free, confidential, and small group instruction by trained volunteers.

2890 North Carolina Literacy Resource Center

North Carolina Community College
200 W Jones Street
Raleigh, NC   27699   919-807-7144
                              FAX 919-807-7164
                         http://www.ncccs.cc.nc.us
                     e-mail: ALLENB@ncccs.cc.nc.us
Bob Allen, Coordinator

North Carolina Community College Literacy Resource Center collects and disseminates information about literacy resources and organizations.

2891 Reading Connections of North Carolina

122 N Elm Street
Greensboro, NC   27401   336-230-2223
                              FAX 336-230-2203
                      http://www.Readingconnections.org
                    e-mail: info@readingconnections.org
Phyllis Ledbetter, Executive Director
Wanda Parker, Program Coordinator

The mission of Reading Connections is to help adults live more independently by providing free and confidential basic literacy services, to increase community awareness of adult literacy needs and to serve as a resource for the provision of basic literacy services.

North Carolina

2892 North Dakota Adult Education and Literacy Resource Center

1609 4th Avenue NW
Minot, ND   58703   701-857-4467
                              FAX 701-857-4489
                     http://www.dpi.state.nd.us/adulted/
Deb Sisco, Coordinator

The purpose of the North Dakota Adult Education Resource Center is to provide training for adult education staff and volunteer personnel engaged in programs designed to carry out the purposes of the National Literacy Act.

2893 North Dakota Department of Career and Technical Education

600 E Boulevard Avenue
Bismarck, ND   58505   701-328-3180
                              FAX 701-328-1255
                           http://www.state.nd.us
                      e-mail: mwilson@state.nd.us
Mark Wilson, Assistant State Director

The mission of the Board for Vocational and Technical Education is to work with others to provide all North Dakota citizens with the technical skills, knowledge, and attitudes necessary for successful performance in a globally competitive workplace.

2894 North Dakota Department of Corrections

3100 Railroad Avenue
Bismarck, ND   58501   701-328-6390
                              FAX 701-328-6651
                           http://www.state.nd.us
                       e-mail: elittle@state.nd.us
Elaine Little, Director

Mission is to protect the public while providing a safe and humane environment for both adults and juveniles placed in the department's care and custody.

2895 North Dakota Department of Human Services: Welfare & Public Assistance

State Capitol
600 E Boulevard Avenue
Bismarck, ND   58505   701-328-2310
                                  800-472-2622
                              FAX 701-328-2359
                       e-mail: dhseo@state.nd.us
Carol K Olson, Executive Director
Yvonne Smith, Deputy Director
Tove Mandigo, Administrative Assistant

To provide services and support for poor, disabled, ill, elderly or juvenile clients in North Dakota.

2896 North Dakota Department of Public Instruction

Division of Adult Education and Literacy
600 E Boulevard Avenue
Bismarck, ND   58505   701-328-2393
                              FAX 701-328-4770
                      http://www.dpi.state.nd.us/adulted
                  e-mail: dmassey@mail.dpi.state.nd.us
David Massey, Assistant State Superintendent
Jolli Marcellais, Administrative Assistant

This unit provides funding and technical assistance to local programs and monitors progress of each funded project. This unit is also responsible for the administration of the GED Testing Program.

2897   North Dakota Reading Association

2420 2nd Avenue SW
Minot, ND 58701
701-857-4642
FAX 701-857-8761
http://www.ndreading.utma.com
e-mail: Paula.Rogers@sendit.nodak.edu
Pam Rettig, President
Paula Rogers, VP

North Dakota Reading Association's mission is to provide a variety of professional development opportunities.

2898   North Dakota Workforce Development Council

North Dakota Department of Commerce
1600 E Century Avenue, Suite 2
Bismarck, ND 58502
701-328-5300
FAX 701-328-5320
http://www.growingnd.com/services/workforce
e-mail: jhirsch@state.nd.us
James Hirsch, Director

The role of the North Dakota Workforce Development Council is to advise the Governor and the Public concerning the nature and extent of workforce development in the context of North Dakota's economic development needs, and how to meet these needs effectively while maximizing the efficient use of available resources and avoiding unnecessary duplication of effort.

2899   Project Advancing Literacy in North Carolina

2110 Library Circle
Grand Forks, ND 58201
701-772-6344
FAX 701-772-1379
http://www.grandforksgov.com/readpal
e-mail: info@grandforksgov.com
Diane Bell, President
Dennis Page, Treasurer

Project Advancing Literacy (PAL) is a basic literacy support program among adults in the Greater Grand Forks area. PAL provides one-to-one tutoring support to those who have identified a need to increase basic literacy.

Ohio

2900   Literacy Council of Medina County

Project Learn
222 S Broadway
Medina, OH 44256
330-723-1314
FAX 330-764-9305
http://www.projectlearnmedina.org
e-mail: dmorawski@zoominternet.net
Diane Morawski

Our program helps individuals 14 and older improve basic reading, writing, spelling and comprehensive skills necessary to meet the challenges they encounter in the workplace and other aspects of their daily lives. It provides the only one-on-one tutoring available free of charge to anyone interested in improving basic skills.

2901   Literacy Volunteers of America: Washington County

701 Wayne Street
Marietta, OH 45750
740-374-6548
FAX 740-376-2457
e-mail: ma_mkern@seovec.ohio.gov
Rene Rudd

Literacy Volunteers of America - Ohio provides training and technical assistance to literacy programs in Ohio. We offer consultation services and support to literacy organizations nationally.

2902   Ohio Literacy Network

1500 W Lane Avenue
Columbus, OH 43221
614-486-7757
800-228-7323
FAX 614-486-1527
http://www.literacy.kent.edu
e-mail: KSOLN@cs.com
Karen Scheid, Executive Director

The Ohio Literacy Network is an association of organizations and individuals dedicated to helping adults achieve effectively in today's society, and to promote public awareness of adult literacy issues and needs.

2903   Ohio Literacy Resource Center

Kent State University
Research 1-1100 Summit Street
Kent, OH 44242
330-672-2007
800-765-2897
FAX 330-672-4841
http://www.literacy.kent.edu/oasis/
e-mail: olrc@literacy.kent.edu
Jean Stephens, Director

Mission is to stimulate joint planning and coordination of literacy services at the local, regional and state levels and to enhance the capacity of state and local organizations and services delivery systems.

2904   Project LEARN of Summit County

1040 E Tallmadge Avenue
Akron, OH 44310
330-434-9461
FAX 330-643-9195
http://www.projectlearnsummit.org
e-mail: info@projectlearnsummit.org
Rick McIntosh, Executive Director
Darla Earnest, Literacy Instructor
Doris Zene, Program Assistant

Project LEARN is a nonprofit, community-based organization providing Summit County's nonreading adult population with free, confidential, small group classes and tutoring.

Oklahoma

2905 Creek County Literacy Program

Sapulpa Public Library
27 W Dewey Avenue
Sapulpa, OK   74066   918-224-9647
                              FAX 918-224-3546
                    http://www.cityofsapulpa.net
                    e-mail: spl@oklahoma.net
Barbara Belk, Executive Director

Free one-on-one tutoring services for those residents
of Creek County who wish to improve reading skills.

**2906 Literacy Volunteers of America: Tulsa City
County Library**

400 Civic Center
Tulsa, OK   74103   918-596-7977
                              FAX 918-596-7907
            http://www.tulsalibrary.org/central
                    e-mail: jgreb@tccl.lib.ok.us

We offer one-on-one tutoring to adults and young
adults who wish to improve their reading and writing
skills.

2907 Northwest Oklahoma Literacy Council

1500 Main Street
Woodward, OK   73801   580-254-8582
                              FAX 580-254-8546
            e-mail: nwoklitcouncil@woodward.lib.ok.us
Cindy Colclasure, Coordinator
Patty McGuire, Contact

Mission is to break the intergenerational cycle of illiteracy by broadening the learner and service base to include family members. Services include literacy and
parenting instruction, as a compliment to ESL, adult
basic education, and learning disabilities programs.

2908 Oklahoma Literacy Resource Center

Oklahoma Department of Libraries
200 NE 18th Street
Oklahoma City, OK   73105   405-522-3205
                              FAX 405-525-7804
            http://www.odl.state.ok.us/literacy/
                    e-mail: lgelders@oltn.state.ok.us
Leslie Gelders, Literacy Coordinator
Rebecca Barker, Literacy & ESL Consultant
Colleen Woolery, Family Literacy Coordinator

Dedicated to supporting Oklahoma's library and community based literacy programs and their volunteer tutors. The office has been serving the literacy
community in Oklahoma since 1983, first as the ODL
Literacy Office, and now as the Oklahoma Literacy
Resource Office.

Oregon

2909 Oregon Department of Corrections

2575 Center Street NE
Salem, OR   97301   503-945-9090
                              FAX 503-945-1173
                    http://www.doc.state.or.us
                    e-mail: DOCinfo@doc.state.or.us
Max Williams, Director
Mitch Morrow, Deputy Director

The Oregon Department of Corrections is responsible
for the management and administration of all adult
correctional institutions and other functions related to
state programs for adult corrections.

**2910 Oregon Department of Education:
School-to-Work**

255 Capitol Street NW
Salem, OR   97310   503-378-3584
                              FAX 503-373-7968
                    http://www.ode.state.or.us
                    e-mail: ode.frontdesk@ode.state.or.us
Robert Larson, Policy & Research Director
Patrick Burk, Education Policy Deputy

School-to-Work is a federally funded initiative that
provides funding for state and local implementation
of the Oregon Educational Act for the 21st Century.

**2911 Oregon Department of Human Resource Adult &
Family Services Division**

500 Summer Street NE
Salem, OR   97310   503-945-5733
                              FAX 503-378-2897
                    http://www.dhs.state.or.us
                    e-mail: dhr.info@state.or.us
Ramona Foley, Assistant Director
Mickey Serice, Deputy

This group combines programs from the former Adult
& Family Services Division and the State Office for
Services to Children and Families.

2912 Oregon Employment Department

875 Union Street NE
Salem, OR   97311   503-947-1394
                              800-237-3710
                              FAX 503-947-1668
                    http://www.emp.state.or.us
Deborah Lincoln, Director
Greg Hickman, Deputy Director
Odie Vogel, Assistant to Director

Supports economic stability for Oregonians and communities during times of unemployment through the
payment of unemployment benefits. Serves businesses by recruiting and referring the best qualified
applicants to jobs, and provides resources to diverse
job seekers in support of their employment needs.

**2913 Oregon GED Administrator: Office of
Community College Services**

255 Capitol Street NE
Salem, OR   97310   503-378-8648
                              FAX 503-378-3365
            e-mail: Sharlene.WALKER@state.or.us
Sharlene Walker, GED Administrator

2914   Oregon Literacy

1001 SW 5th Avenue
Portland, OR   97204   503-244-3898
                                    800-322-8715
                               FAX 503-244-9147
                     http://www.oregonliteracy.org
                     e-mail: info@oregonliteracy.org
Meg Young, Executive Director
Elizabeth Raymond, Tutor Helpline Coordinator

Mission is to increase the capacity and effectiveness
of literacy services through partnerships with community-based programs across the state.

2915   Oregon Office of Education and Workforce Policy

State Capitol Building
Salem, OR   97301   503-378-4582
                               FAX 503-378-4863
                    http://www.arcweb.sos.state.or.us
                     e-mail: annette.talbott@state.or.us
Annette Talbott, Workforce Policy Coordinator
Danny Santos, Education Policy Coordinator

The Governor's Office of Education and Workforce
Policy was established to assist the Governor in examining education and workforce efforts with a view to
supporting and strengthening what is working well.
The goal is to have Oregonians prepared to meet the
education and workforce needs of Oregon businesses
rather than having to recruit from outside the state to
fill quality jobs.

2916   Oregon State Library

250 Winter Street NE
Salem, OR   97310   503-378-4243
                               FAX 503-588-7119
                         http://www.osl.state.or.us
                     e-mail: leann.bromeland@state.or.us
LeAnn Bromeland, Volunteer Coordinator
Denise Davis, Program Manager
Jim Scheppke, State Librarian

Mission is to provide quality information services to
Oregon state government, to provide reading materials to blind and print-disabled Oregonians, and to provide leadership, grants, and other assistance to
improve local library service for all Oregonians.

2917   Oregon State Literacy Resource Center

Department of Community Colleges & Workforce
255 Capitol Street NE
Salem, OR   97310   503-378-8648
                               FAX 503-378-8434
                      http://www.odccwd.state.or.us
                     e-mail: ric.latour@state.or.us
Richard LaTour, Coordinator
Sharlene Walker, Unit Leader

To contribute leadership and resources to increase the
skills, knowledge and career opportunities of Oregonians.

2918   Project Literacy Douglas County

1034 SE Oak Avenue
Roseburg, OR   97470   541-957-9072
                               FAX 541-957-9072
                     e-mail: PLUR@rosenet.net
Patricia Yeager

2919   Salem Literacy Council

189 Liberty Street NE
Salem, OR   97301   503-588-0307
                               FAX 503-588-0307
                  http://www.angelfire.com/or/salemliteracy/

Pennsylvania

2920   Delaware County Literacy Council

2217 Providence Avenue
Chester, PA   19013   610-876-4811
                               FAX 610-876-5414
Patricia R Gaul, Executive Director

The Delaware County Literacy Council is a private,
nonprofit, educational agency that provides
one-on-one, free literacy instruction to non- and
low-reading adults through a county-wide network of
trained volunteer tutors. It is unique among the limited options available to adult residents of Delaware
County who require help with their basic reading and
writing skills in that it remains the only organization
whose sole mission is adult literacy.

2921   Learning Disabilities Association: Pennsylvania

Toomey Building
Uwchland, PA   19480   610-458-8193
                               FAX 412-344-0224
                         http://www.ldanatl.org
Anna Mary McHugh, President

LDAP is a nonprofit organization whose purpose is to
advance the education and general well-being of persons with normal, potentially normal or above normal
intelligence who have learning disabilities.

2922   Literacy Council of Lancaster/Lebanon

38 W King Street
Lancaster, PA   17603   717-295-5523
                               FAX 717-295-5342
                     e-mail: mary@adultlit.org
Mary Hohensee, Contact

Mission is to promote literacy for adults and children.

2923   Pennsylvania Adult Literacy

110 E Bald Eagle Street
Lock Haven, PA   17745   570-893-4038
                               FAX 570-748-1598
                     e-mail: vedmonst@lhup.edu
Ginney Seay, Facilitator

2924   Pennsylvania Literacy Resource Center

ADVANCE Clearinghouse & Resource Center
333 Market Street
Harrisburg, PA   17101   717-783-9192
                                    800-992-2283
                               FAX 717-783-5420
                     http://www.cas.psu.edu/docs
Evelyn Werner, Director

As part of the State Library, the State Resource Center
provides electronic and print resources.

2925 Project Literacy US (PLUS) in Pennsylvania

4802 5th Avenue
Pittsburgh, PA   15213   412-622-1492
                                      FAX 412-622-1492
         http://www.dyslexia-add.org/plus.htm
Margot Woodwell, Project Director
Herb Stein, Assistant Director

PLUS promotes adult literacy. A joint project of the Public Broadcasting Service and the American Broadcasting Corporation, PLUS uses media to increase awareness of literacy issues and to recruit individuals into literacy training programs.

2926 York County Literacy Council

800 E King Street
York, PA   17403   717-845-8719
                                 FAX 717-843-4082
                           e-mail: yclcpa@aol.com
Gail L Dennis, Contact

Rhode Island

2927 Family Independence Program of Rhode Island

Department of Human Services
600 New London Avenue
Cranston, RI   02920   401-462-1300
                                 FAX 401-462-6504
Donald M Carlson

2928 Learning Disabilities Association: Rhode Island

PO Box 6685
Providence, RI   02940   401-232-3822
Norma Veresko, President

2929 Literacy Volunteers of America: Rhode Island

260 W Exchange Street
Providence, RI   02903   401-861-0815
                                 FAX 401-861-0863
              http://www.literacyvolunteers.org
                        e-mail: lvaricindy@aol.com
Cindy Mlyniec, Executive Director

The mission of LVA-RI is to advance adult literacy in Rhode Island by: providing training and support services to local LVA-RI affiliates, volunteer tutors and adult literacy services; providing the state with information about adult literacy and with appropriate referral services; collaborating with other organizations to promote adult literacy in Rhode Island.

2930 Literary Resources Rhode Island

Brown University
PO Box 1974
Providence, RI   02912   401-863-2839
                                 FAX 401-863-3094
                        http://www.brown.edu
              e-mail: janet_isserlis@brown .edu
Howard L Dooley Jr, Director

Literacy Resources Rhode Island was established in 1997. Its goals include: expand existing professional capacity within the state's adult education community; increase educator and learner capacity to use and interact with online technology; and assist in improving delivery of services to adult learners, thereby strengthening adult education provision across the state.

2931 Rhode Island Department of Employment and Training

101 Friendship Street
Providence, RI   02914   401-277-4922
                                 FAX 401-861-8030

2932 Rhode Island Department of Human Services

600 New London Avenue
Cranston, RI   02920   401-464-3071
                                 FAX 405-462-6353
                        http://www.dhs.state.ri.us
              e-mail: rcarroll@ors.state.ri.us
Raymond A Carroll, Acting Administrator

2933 Rhode Island Department of State Library Services

1 Capitol Hill
Providence, RI   02903   401-222-1220
                                 FAX 401-222-2083
John O'Brien, Executive Director

2934 Rhode Island Human Resource Investment Council

1511 Pontiac Avenue
Cranston, RI   02920   401-462-8860
                                 FAX 401-462-8865
              e-mail: larnodd@dlt.state.ri.us
Dr. Lee Arnold, Director

2935 Rhode Island READS: Public Education Fund

15 Westminster Street
Providence, RI   02903   401-454-1054
                                 FAX 401-454-1059
                 http://www.ri.net/PEF/RIREADS/
              e-mail: info@rhodeislandreads.org
JoAnn Johnson, Director

2936 Rhode Island Vocational and Rehabilitation Agency

Rhode Island Department of Human Services
40 Fountain Street
Providence, RI   02903   401-421-7005
                                 FAX 401-222-3574
                              TDY:401-421-7016
                        http://www.ors.state.ri.us
              e-mail: rcarroll@ors.state.ri.us
Raymond A Carroll, Administrator

Assists people with disabilities to become employed and to live independently in the community. In order to achieve this goal, we work in partnership with the State Rehabilitation Council, our customers, staff and community.

2937 Rhode Island Workforce Literacy Collaborative

260 W Exchange Street
Providence, RI   02903   401-861-0815
FAX 401-861-0863
http://www.riwlc.org/
e-mail: LVARIYVETT@aol.com

Mission is to create a framework for an ongoing, comprehensive, seamless system for delivering adult workforce literacy services in Rhode Island.

South Carolina

2938 Greenwood Literacy Council

PO Drawer 1467
Greenwood, SC   29648   864-223-1303
FAX 864-223-0475
e-mail: sowens@greenwood.net
Sandra Owens

Provides ongoing, comprehensive adult literacy programs in Greenwood, for illiterate adults and their families.

2939 Literacy Volunteers of the Lowcountry

9 Town Center Court
Hilton Head, SC   29928   843-686-6655
FAX 843-686-6949
e-mail: lvlhhi@hargray.com
Rebecca Morris, Contact

2940 Resource Center for Literacy Technology & Parenting

South Carolina Department of Education
1429 Senate Street
Columbia, SC   29201   803-734-8500
FAX 803-734-8624
Diana Deadrick, Contact

Combines literacy programs with parenting instruction.

2941 South Carolina Adult Literacy Educators

PO Box 185
Blackville, SC   29817   803-284-4424
FAX 803-284-1444
Vickie Zissette, President

2942 South Carolina Department of Education

1429 Senate Street
Columbia, SC   29201   803-734-8815
FAX 803-734-3389
http://www.sclrc.org/page1.htm

2943 South Carolina Literacy Resource Center

1722 Main Street
Columbia, SC   29201   803-929-2563
FAX 803-929-2571
http://www.sclrc.org
e-mail: info@sclrc.org

The mission of the South Carolina Resource Center is to provide leadership in literacy to South Carolina's adults and their families, in conjunction with state and local public and private nonprofit efforts. The Center serves as a site for training for adult literacy providers, as a reciprocal link with the National Institute for Literacy for the purpose of sharing information to service providers, and as a clearinghouse for state-of-the-art literacy materials and technology.

2944 Spartanburg Aware

PO Box 308
Spartanburg, SC   29304   864-476-5928
FAX 864-596-3518
e-mail: spartanburgaware@mindspring.com
Therese Brewton

Provides literacy programs for adults whose goal it is to acquire the basic skills necessary to continue their education and function in society.

South Dakota

2945 South Dakota GED: Literacy Department of Education & Cultural Affairs

700 Governors Drive
Pierre, SD   57501   605-773-5017
FAX 605-773-6184
http://www.state.sd.us./dol/abe/index.html
e-mail: miken@dol.pr.state.sd.us
Marcia Hess, State Administrator

Adult Education & Literacy instruction is designed to teach persons 16 years of age or older to read and write English and to substantially raise their educational level. The purpose of the program is to expand the educational opportunities for adults and to establish programs that will enable all adults to acquire basic skills necessary to function in society and allow them to continue their education to at least the level of completion of secondary school.

2946 South Dakota Literacy Council

PO Box 219
Pierre, SD   57501   605-224-1595
FAX 605-224-1595
Bonnie London

2947 South Dakota Literacy Resouce Center

800 Governors Drive
Pierre, SD   57501   605-773-3131
800-423-6665
FAX 605-773-6969
http://www.state.sd.us/deca/literacy/
e-mail: dan.boyd@state.sd.us
Dan Boyd, Coordinator

The mission of the SD Literary Resource Center is to establish a state wide on-line computer catalog of all existing literacy materials within South Dakota and a South Dakota Literacy Resource Center home page with links to other literacy sites within South Dakota, regionally and nationally.

Tennessee

2948   Center for Literary Studies Tennessee

University of Tennessee: Knoxville
600 Henley Street
Knoxville, TN   37996   865-974-4109
                              FAX 865-974-3857
                    http://www.cls.coc.utk.edu
                    e-mail: mziegler@utk.edu
Mary Ziegler, Director

The Center for Literacy Studies strengthens adult literacy education in order to equip adults with the knowledge and skills they need to be lifelong learners and effective members of their families, communities and workplaces. The Center links theory and practice through research, professional development, partnerships, and building and sharing the knowledge of the field.

2949   Claiborne County Adult Reading Experience

Claiborne County Schools
PO Box 800
Tazewell, TN   37879   423-626-2273
                              FAX 423-626-5945
Sherri Claiborne, President

2950   Department of Human Services: Division of Rehabilitation Services

400 Deaderick Street
Nashville, TN   37248   615-313-4714
                              FAX 615-741-4165
              http://www.state.tn.us/humanserv/
              e-mail: carlbrown@mail.state.tn.usa
Carl Brown, Assistant Commissioner

Agency takes an active leadership role in removing the barriers to employment due to disabilities.

2951   Nashville READ

1701 W End Avenue
Nashville, TN   37203   615-255-4982
                              FAX 615-255-4783
              e-mail: literacy@nashvilleread.org
Carol Thigpin, Contact

2952   Protection and Advocacy Agency: Tennessee

PO Box 121257
Nashville, TN   37212   615-298-1080
                              800-342-1660
                              FAX 615-298-2046
Shirley Shea, Executive Director

2953   Tennessee Department of Education

710 James Robertson Parkway
Nashville, TN   37243   615-741-2731
                              800-531-1515
                              FAX 615-532-4899
                    http://www.state.tn.us
              e-mail: education.comments@state.tn.us
Phil White, Director

Mission is to take Tennessee to the top in education. Guides administration of the state's K-12 public schools.

2954   Tennessee Department of Labor & Workforce Development: Office of Adult Education

500 James Robertson Parkway
Nashville, TN   37243   615-741-7054
                              FAX 615-532-4899
Phil White, Director

2955   Tennessee Literacy Coalition

Cohn Adult Learning Center
Nashville, TN   37209   615-298-4738
                              800-323-6986
                              FAX 615-298-8444
                    http://www.tnliteracy.org
              e-mail: mnugent@tnliteracy.org

2956   Tennessee School-to-Work Office

710 James Robertson Parkway
Nashville, TN   37243   615-532-4725
                              FAX 615-532-8226
                    http://www.state.tn.us
              e-mail: awilks@mail.state.tn.us
Alberta Wilks, Consultant

2957   Tennessee State Library and Archives

403 7th Avenue N
Nashville, TN   37243   615-741-3158
                              FAX 615-741-6471
Nancy Weatherman, Special Projects Coordinator

Texas

2958   Adult Literacy Council of the Tom Green County

3111 SW Boulevard
San Angelo, TX   76904   915-947-1536
                              FAX 915-947-1875
                    e-mail: adlitl@gte.net
Mary Ann Cochran, Contact

Promote adult literacy.

2959   Commerce Library Literacy Program

PO Box 308
Commerce, TX   75429   903-886-5279
Pricilla Donovan

2960   Greater Orange Area Literacy Services
PO Box 221
Orange, TX   77631   409-886-4311
                           FAX 409-886-0149
                           e-mail: goals@pnx.com

Joyce Corrati

2961   Irving Public Library Literacy Program
440 S Nursery
Irving, TX   75060   972-721-3722
                           FAX 972-721-3724
Gwen Bates, Contact

Promotes literacy among people of all ages.

2962   Literacy Austin
2002 A Manor Road
Austin, TX   78722   512-478-7323
                           FAX 512-479-7323
                           e-mail: literacy@io.com

Mandy Shooter, Contact

2963   Literacy Center of Marshall: Harrison County
700 W Houston Street
Marshall, TX   75670   903-935-0962
Joyce Hammers

2964   Literacy Council of Bowie and Miller Counties
600 Walnut Street
Texarkana, TX   75505   903-838-8521
                           FAX 870-774-2078
                           e-mail: RMagee@cableone.net

Robbye Magee, Contact

2965   Literacy Volunteers of America: Bastrop
1201 Church Street
Bastrop, TX   78602   512-321-6686
                           e-mail: suemunster@aol.com
Sue Steinbring

Provides literacy training and pre-GED for students, English as a Second Language, tutoring and tutor training.

2966   Literacy Volunteers of America: Bay City
1921 5th Street
Bay City, TX   77414   979-244-9544
                           FAX 979-244-9566
                           e-mail: lvabc@wcnet.net
Linda Brown, Contact

Promotes literacy for people of all ages.

2967   Literacy Volunteers of America: Beaumont Public Library
PO Box 3827
Beaumont, TX   77704   409-835-7324
                           FAX 409-838-6734
                           e-mail: bbeard@bpls.lib.tx.us
Barbara Bear, Contact

2968   Literacy Volunteers of America: Brazos Valley
801 E 29th Street
Bryan, TX   77805   979-779-3743
                           FAX 979-823-2071
                           e-mail: lva@bvcog.org
Bobbee Pennington, Contact

Provides tutors for 18+ adults in reading, writing, math, and computer literacy. Lessons are one on one, free of charge.

2969   Literacy Volunteers of America: Calhoun County
1104 Broadway
Port Lavaca, TX   77979   361-552-6364
                           FAX 361-552-6364
Donna Boyd, Contact

Promotes literacy for people of all ages.

2970   Literacy Volunteers of America: Cleburne
212 E Chambers
Cleburne, TX   76031   817-641-3187
                           FAX 817-556-3444
                           e-mail: dlajean@juno.com
Alita Rice, Contact

Promotes literacy for people of all ages.

2971   Literacy Volunteers of America: Houston
Heights Learning Center
1111 Lawrence
Houston, TX   77008   972-721-3722
                           FAX 972-721-3724
Sabrina Haselhorst, Contact

Promotes literacy for people of all ages.

2972   Literacy Volunteers of America: Laredo
W End Washington Street
Laredo, TX   78042   956-724-5207
                           FAX 956-725-4253
                           e-mail: lvlaredo@grandecom.net
Lourdes Castaneda, Contact

Promotes literacy for people of all ages.

2973   Literacy Volunteers of America: Montgomery County
709 W Montgomery
Willis, TX   77378   936-890-0635
                           888-878-9400
                           FAX 936-494-0635
Twillia Liles

As part of the national literacy organization, combats illiteracy in Montgomery County through volunteer tutoring.

2974   Literacy Volunteers of America: Port Arthur Literacy Support
4615 9th Avenue
Port Arthur, TX   77642   409-982-7257
Deborah Campbell

2975 Literacy Volunteers of America: READ of Brazoria County

210 Commerce Street
Clute, TX   77553   979-233-6155
                                    FAX 979-297-2195
Beulah Taylor

2976 Literacy Volunteers of America: Wimberley Area

PO Box 135
Wimberley, TX   78676   512-847-8953
                   e-mail: johngray@wimberley-tx.com
Jack Anderson, President
Linda Mueller, Accreditation Manager
Annette Harrington, Treasurer

Nonprofit, volunteer organization which exists to improve the reading, writing, speaking, cultural and life skills of adults reading at or below the sixth grade level and/or those for whom English is not their native language. Provides GED instruction. All services are free.

2977 Texas Center for Adult Literacy & Learning

Texas A&M University
College Station, TX   77843
                                    800-441-7323
                                    FAX 979-845-0952
                   http://www.cdlr.tamu.edu/tcall
Victoria Hoffman, Director

2978 Texas Families and Literacy

719 Hill Country Drive
Kerrville, TX   78028   830-896-8787
                                    FAX 830-896-3639
                   e-mail: famlit@maverickbbs.com
Jimmy Sparks

2979 Victoria Adult Literacy

802 E Crestwood Drive
Victoria, TX   77901   361-573-7323
                                    FAX 361-582-4348
                   e-mail: valctx@yahoo.com
Donna Bentley, Contact

2980 Weslaco Public Library

525 S Kansas Avenue
Weslaco, TX   78596   956-968-4533
                                    FAX 956-969-4069
                   e-mail: volcntr@ccwf.cc.utexas.edu
Virginia Allain, Director

Utah

2981 Literacy Volunteers of America: Wasatch Front

175 N 600 W
Salt Lake City, UT   84116   801-328-5608
                                    FAX 801-328-5637
                   http://www.LVA2000.org
                   e-mail: erikaj29@yahoo.com
Erika Johnson

2982 Utah Literacy Action Center

1234 S Main Street
Salt Lake City, UT   84101   801-521-9050
                                    FAX 801-578-8577
Eileen Smart, Director

2983 Utah Literacy Resource Center

State Office of Education
250 E 500 S
Salt Lake City, UT   84111   801-538-7824
                                    800-451-9500
                                    FAX 801-538-7882
        http://www.usoe.k12.ut.us/adulted/home.htm
                   e-mail: dsteele@usoe.k12.ut.us
David Steele, Coordinator
Sandra Grant, Specialist
Shauna South, Specialist

As part of the State Library, the State Resource Center provides electronic and print resources.

Vermont

2984 ABE Career and Lifelong Learning: Vermont Department of Education

120 State Street
Montpelier, VT   05602   802-828-3134
                                    FAX 802-828-3146
                   e-mail: srobinson@doe.state.vt.us
Sandra Robinson, Director

Promotes quality education.

2985 Learning Disabilities Association of Vermont

PO Box 1041
Manchester Center, VT   05255   802-362-3127
                                    FAX 802-362-3128
Christina Thurston, President

A nonprofit organization whose members are individuals with learning disabilities, their families, and the professionals who work with them.

2986 Vermont Assistive Technology Project: Department of Aging and Disabilities

Agency of Human Services
103 S Main Street, Weeks Building
Waterbury, VT   05671   802-241-2620
                                    800-750-6355
                                    FAX 802-241-2174
                   e-mail: jtucker@dad.state.vt.us
Julie L Tucker, Project Director
Gail Koehler, Information/Training
Betsy Ross, Administrative Assistant

2987 Vermont Department of Corrections

103 S Main Street
Waterbury, VT   05671   802-241-2276
                                    FAX 802-241-2565
Robert Lucenti, Superintendant Education Svcs

2988   Vermont Department of Welfare

103 S Main Street
Waterbury, VT   05671   802-241-2834
                              FAX 802-241-2830

Steve Gold, Director

2989   Vermont Human Resources Investment Council

5 Green Mountain Drive
Montpelier, VT   05601   802-828-4156
                              FAX 802-828-4022
                              e-mail: aevans@pop.det.state.vt.us

2990   Vermont Literacy Resource Center: Department of Education

120 State Street
Montpelier, VT   05602   802-828-5148
                              FAX 802-828-0573
                              http://www.state.vt.us/educ/vlrc/
                              e-mail: wross@doe.state.vt.us

Wendy Ross, Director Literacy Board

The Vermont Literacy Resource Center links Vermont to national, regional, and state literacy organizations, provides staff development and serves as a clearinghouse for the literacy community. The Vermont Literacy Resource Center is located at the Vermont Department of Education.

2991   Vermont REACH-UP Program

Department of Social Welfare
103 S Main Street
Waterbury, VT   05671   802-241-2800
                              FAX 802-241-2830

Karen Ryder

2992   Vermont Workforce Reinvestment Act

Vermont Department of Employment & Training
5 Green Mountain Drive
Montpelier, VT   05601   802-828-4000
                              FAX 802-828-4181
                              http://www.det.state.vt.us
                              e-mail: mcalcagni@det.state.vt.us

Anne V Ginevan, Commissioner
Mike Calcagni, Jobs/Training

Vocational training and job listings for displaced workers or others with difficulty finding regular employment.

2993   VocRehab Vermont

Agency of Human Services
103 S Main Street
Waterbury, VT   05671   802-241-2186
                              866-879-6757
                              FAX 802-241-3359
                              http://www.vocrehabvermont.org
                              e-mail: janetr@dad.state.vt.us

Diana Dalmasse, Director

Works in close partnership with the Vermont Association of Business and Industry Rehabilitation to assist Vermonters with disabilities and maintain meaningful employment in their communities.

Virginia

2994   Charlotte County Literacy Program

395 Thomas Jefferson Highway
Charlotte Court House, VA   23923   434-542-5782
                              e-mail: charcolit@hovac.com

Mary A Jones

Offers basic and family literacy programs, ESL and computer, parenting and work skills.

2995   DCE-LVA Virginia Institutions

101 N 14th Street
Richmond, VA   23219   804-692-0282
                              FAX 804-786-0559
                              e-mail: sjoyner@saturn.vcu.edu

2996   Highlands Educational Literacy Program

334 Rose Street
Abingdon, VA   24212   540-676-4355
                              FAX 540-676-0677
                              e-mail: garretsj@jaxs.net

Sallie Garrett, Executive Director

2997   Literacy Volunteers of America: Campbell County Public Library

684 Village Highway
Lynchburg, VA   24588   434-332-9561
                              FAX 434-332-9697
                              e-mail: rgjo@aol.com

Becky Olsen, Program Manager
Carolyn Cothron, Program Coordinator

Provides tutoring for basic literacy and English as a second language.

2998   Literacy Volunteers of America: Charlottsville/Albemarle

PO Box 1156
Charlottesville, VA   22902   434-977-3838
                              FAX 434-979-7846
                              http://www.avenue.org/lva
                              e-mail: lva@avenue.org

Anne Jellen, Administrative Director
Mary Mullen, Program Director

Promotes literacy for people of all ages.

2999   Literacy Volunteers of America: Fishersville

26 John Lewis Road
Fishersville, VA   22939   540-949-6134
                              FAX 540-245-5115
                              e-mail: lvaaa.cfw.com

Candida Clark

Provides free and confidential one-to-one tutoring in basic reading and ESL to persons not in the school system.

3000   Literacy Volunteers of America: Gloucester

PO Box 981
Gloucester, VA   23061   804-693-1306
                              e-mail: jmes223@aol.com

Shelby W Friend

3001 Literacy Volunteers of America: Louisa County

2128 S Lakeshore Drive
Louisa, VA 23093   540-967-1051
                    FAX 540-967-1051
Terry McElhone

3002 Literacy Volunteers of America: Nelson County

195 Callohill Drive
Lovingston, VA 22949   434-263-8228
                    FAX 434-263-4378
               e-mail: grahame@cville.net
Art Grahame

3003 Literacy Volunteers of America: New River Valley

195 W Main Street
Christiansburg, VA 24073   540-382-7262
                    FAX 540-382-7262
               e-mail: lvanrv@aol.com
E Randall Wertz, Executive Director

The empowerment of every adult in the New River Valley through the provision of opportunities to achieve independence through literacy.

3004 Literacy Volunteers of America: Northern Neck Chapter

2172 Northumberland Highway
Lottsburg, VA 22511   804-580-3152
                    FAX 804-580-3152
Tonya Creasy

3005 Literacy Volunteers of America: Prince William

4326 Dale Boulevard
Woodbridge, VA 22193   703-670-5702
                    FAX 703-583-0703
               http://www.pwcweb.com/lva
               e-mail: lvapw@aol.com
Janet Sorlin-Davis

Promotes literacy for people of all ages.

3006 Literacy Volunteers of America: Shenandoah County

PO Box 303
Woodstock, VA 22664   540-459-2446
Terry Chambers

3007 One-on-One Literacy Program: Wythe and Grayson Counties

PO Box 905
Independence, VA 24348   276-655-9931
                    FAX 276-773-0028
               e-mail: joanbolduc@ls.net
Joan Bolduc, Director

3008 Skyline Literacy Coalition

290 Mill Street
Dayton, VA 22821   540-879-2833
                    FAX 540-879-2033
               http://www.home.rica.net/slc
               e-mail: skylitjay@aol.com
Jay Morgan Bungard

3009 Virginia Adult Education Centers for Professional Development

Adult Education and Literacy Resource Center
1015 W Main Street
Richmond, VA 23284   804-828-6521
                    800-237-0178
               FAX 804-828-7539
               http://www.vcv.edu/aelweb/
               e-mail: vdesk@vcu.edu
Evelyn Nunes, Director

We provide adult education and literacy resources, information, and professional development in Virginia.

3010 Virginia Council of Administrators of Special Education

1110 N Glebe Road
Arlington, VA 22201   703-620-3660
                    800-224-6830
               FAX 703-264-9494
               http://www.cec.sped.org
               e-mail: feedback@vcase.org

The Virginia Council of Administrators of Special Education is organized to promote professional leadership, provide opportunity for the study of problems common to its members, and to communicate through discussions and publications information that will develop improved services for children with disabilities.

3011 Virginia Literacy Coalition

11503 Allecingie Parkway
Richmond, VA 23235   804-225-8777
                    FAX 804-225-1859
Jean Proffitt, Organizational Liaison

Washington

3012 Division of Vocational Rehabilitation

Po Box 45340
Olympia, WA 98504   360-438-8045
                    FAX 360-407-3915
               e-mail: ruddyl@dshs.wa.gov

3013 Literacy Council of Kitsap

612 5th Street
Bremerton, WA 98337   360-373-1539
                    FAX 360-373-6859
               e-mail: literacy@krl.org
Helen Robinson, Executive Director

3014 Mason County Literacy Council

207 N 9th Street
Shelton, WA 98584   360-426-9733
                    FAX 360-427-8610
               e-mail: lbusacca@shelton.wednet.edu
Lynn E Busacca, Contact

3015 Northwest Regional Literacy Resource Center

2120 S Jackson Street
Seattle, WA 98144   360-586-3527
                       FAX 360-586-3529
                       http://www.literacynet.org
                       e-mail: nwrlrc@literacynet.org
Donna Miller-Parker, Director
Nick d'Alonzo, Instuctional Coordinator

Provides resources and technical support to adult basic skills instructors in Alaska, Idaho, Oregon, Montana, Washington and Wyoming.

3016 People's Learning Center of Seattle

PO Box 28084
Seattle, WA 98198   206-325-8308
Georgia Rogers

3017 South King County Multi-Service Center

1200 S 336th Street
Federal Way, WA 98003   253-836-6810
                       FAX 253-874-7831
Stephanie Boschee, Contact

3018 St. James ESL Program

St. James Cathedral
804 9th Avenue
Seattle, WA 98104   206-382-4511
                       FAX 206-622-5303
          e-mail: ckoehler@stjamescatherdral.org
Christopher Koehler, Contact

Helps promote literacy among the community.

3019 Washington Department of Corrections

PO Box 41100
Olympia, WA 98504   360-753-2500
                       FAX 360-586-3676

3020 Washington Employment & Training

614 Division Street
Port Orchard, WA 98366   360-337-4873
                       FAX 360-337-7187
          e-mail: bpotter@co.kitsap.wa.us

3021 Washington Laubach Literacy Action

Washington Literacy
220 Nickerson Street
Seattle, WA 98109   206-461-3623
                       800-323-2556
                       FAX 206-284-7895
                       http://www.waliteracy.org
                       e-mail: WALT@aol.com
Brenda Gray, Executive Director

3022 Work First Division: Washington Department of Social and Health Services

PO Box 45480
Olympia, WA 98504   360-413-3371

West Virginia

3023 Division of Technical & Adult Education Services: West Virginia

State Department of Education
1900 Kanawha Boulevard E, Bldg 6
Charleston, WV 25305   304-558-6318
                       FAX 304-558-3946
                       http://wvabe.state.k12.wv.us
                       e-mail: lbmiller@access.k12.wv.us
Promotes the quality of adult education.

3024 Laubach Literacy Action: West Virginia

3942 39th Street E
Nitro, WV 25143   304-755-1476
                       800-642-2670
                       FAX 304-766-7915

David Coccari

3025 West Virginia Adult Education Network

RESA III/Nitro-Putnam
3942 39th Street E
Nitro, WV 25143   304-766-7655
                       800-642-2670
                       FAX 304-766-2824
                       http://www.nuemedia.net
                       e-mail: cshank@access.k12.wv.us
Charles Nichols, Executive Director
Linda Andersen, Administrative Assistant

Offers services for literacy and adult basic education including literacy hotline, networks newsletter, resources for English as a second language, beginning literacy, learning disabilities and other special learning needs.

3026 West Virginia Department of Education

1900 Kanawha Boulevard E, Bldg 6
Charleston, WV 26501   304-558-6317
                       800-642-2670
                       FAX 304-558-3946
                       http://www.wvabe.state.k12.wv.us/
Preston Browning, Assistant Director

3027 West Virginia Literacy Volunteers of America

501 22nd Street
Dunbar, WV 25064   304-766-7851
                       800-642-2670
                       FAX 304-766-7915
David Greenstreet, Director

Wisconsin

3028 Laubach Literacy Action: Wisconsin

Literacy Plus-Grant County
PO Box 447
Lancaster, WI 53813   608-723-2136
                       FAX 608-723-4834
Arlene D Siss, Director

Includes Grant County.

3029 Literacy Volunteers of America: Eau Claire

221 W Madison Street
Eau Claire, WI   54703   715-834-0222
                                      FAX 715-834-2546
                                      e-mail: info@lvacv.org
Carol Gabler, Contact

Promotes literacy for people of all ages.

3030 Literacy Volunteers of America: Marquette County

PO Box 671
Montello, WI   53949   608-297-8900
                                      FAX 608-297-2673
                                      e-mail: vjhawk@maqs.net
Vicki Huffman, Executive Director

Promotes literacy for people of all ages.

3031 Literacy Volunteers of America: Trempealeau County

36084 Walnut Street
Independance, WI   54747   715-985-3392
                                      FAX 715-985-2580
                                      e-mail: braggerc@hotmail.com
Promotes literacy for people of all ages.

3032 Literacy Volunteers of America: Wisconsin

3099 W Washington Avenue
Madison, WI   53707   608-267-9660
                                      FAX 608-266-5069
                                      e-mail: peggy.meyers@doc.state.wi.us
Peggy Meyers, Contact

Promotes literacy for people of all ages.

3033 Price County Area Literacy Council

211 N Lake Avenue
Phillips, WI   54555   715-339-3939
                                      FAX 715-339-3909
                                      e-mail: rgstueber@yahoo.com
Ruth Stueber

3034 Western Wisconsin Literacy Services

W7077 US Highway 12
Black River Falls, WI   54615   715-284-3361
                                      FAX 715-284-9681
                                      e-mail: jacksonlva@hotmail.com
Judith Bronson, Contact

3035 Wisconsin Literacy Resource Center

Board of Vocational, Technical & Adult Education
310 Price Place
Madison, WI   53705   608-266-3497
                                      FAX 608-266-1690
                                      http://www.board.tec.wi.us
                                      e-mail: mvellej@boardtec.wi.us
Mark Johnson, Director

As part of the state library, the State Resource Center provides electronic and print resources.

3036 Wisconsin Literacy Services

518 Hill Street
Green Lake, WI   54941   920-294-0144
                                      FAX 920-294-6055
                                      e-mail: glclc@hotmail.com
Rena Beyer, Contact

Wyoming

3037 Literacy Volunteers of Casper

125 College Drive
Casper, WY   82601   307-268-2453
                                      FAX 307-268-3021
                                      e-mail: lmixer@caspercollege.edu
Lisa Mixer

3038 Literacy Volunteers of Douglas

203 N 6th Street
Douglas, WY   82633   307-358-5622
                                      FAX 307-358-5629
                                      e-mail: slunsford@wewc.cc.wy.us
Shannon Lunsford, Director

Promotes adult literacy among the people in the community.

3039 Literacy Volunteers of Powell North College

231 W 6th Street
Powell, WY   82435   307-754-6280
                                      FAX 307-754-6700
                                      e-mail: bushnelr@nwc.cc.wy.us
Rom Bushnell, Director

Promotes literacy for people of all ages.

3040 Literacy Volunteers of Rock Springs

PO Box 428
Rock Springs, WY   82902   307-382-1829
                                      FAX 307-382-1823
http://www.wwcc.cc.wy.us/college/alc/index.html
                                      e-mail: jbentley@wwcc.cc.wy.us
Jami Bentley

3041 Literacy Volunteers of Sheridan/Northern Wyoming

102 S Connor Street
Sheridan, WY   82801   307-673-2813
                                      FAX 307-672-6157
                                      e-mail: wa@fiberpipe.net
Jolene Olson, Contact

Promotes literacy for people of all ages.

3042 Wyoming Literacy Resource Center

Division of Lifelong Learning & Instruction
College of Education, Room 46
Laramie, WY   82071   307-766-3970
                                      FAX 307-766-6668
                                      e-mail: dstithem@uwyo.edu
Diana Stithem, Director

As part of the state library, the State Resource Center provides electronic and print resources.

Adults

3043 A Miracle to Believe In

Option Indigo Press
2080 S Undermountain Road
Sheffield, MA   01257
413-229-8727
800-562-7171
FAX 413-229-8727
http://www.optionindio.com
e-mail: indigo@bcn.net
Barry Neil Kaufman, Author

A group of people from all walks of life come together and are transformed as they reach out, under the direction of Kaufman, to help a little boy the medical world had given up as hopeless. This heartwarming journey of loving a child back to life will not only inspire, but presents a compelling new way to deal with life's traumas and difficulties. *$7.99*

ISBN 0-449201-08-2

3044 Closer Look: Perspectives & Reflections on College Students with LD

Curry College Bookstore
1071 Blue Hill Avenue
Milton, MA   02186
617-333-2322
FAX 617-333-2018
e-mail: dgoss@curry.edu
Jane Adelizzi, Diane Goss, Author
Diane Goss, Editor
Jane Adelizzi, Editor

This book is a collection of personal accounts by teachers and learners. It's a sensitive portrayal of the real world of teaching and learning, particularly as it impacts on those with learning differences. Topics include connections between theory and practice, emotions and learning disabilities, classroom trauma, learning disabilities and social deficits, metacognitive development, ESL and learning disabilities, models for inclusion and practical strategies. *$24.95*

240 pages
ISBN 0-964975-20-3

3045 Dyslexia in Adults: Taking Charge of Your Life

Taylor Publishing
1550 W Mockingbird Lane
Dallas, TX   75235
214-637-2800
800-677-2800
FAX 214-819-8580
http://images.amazon.com
Kathleen Nosek, Author

Adult dyslexics are experts at hiding reading, writing, and spelling difficulties long after high school. Dyslexia in Adults is a perfect guidebook for adult dyslexias to use in coping with day-to-day problems that are complicated by their learning disability. *$12.95*

192 pages   Paperback
ISBN 0-878339-48-5

3046 Faking It: A Look into the Mind of a Creative Learner

Heinemann/Boynton Cook Publishers
361 Hanover Street
Portsmouth, NH   03801
800-541-2086
FAX 800-354-2004
http://www.heinemann.com
e-mail: custserv@heinemann.com
Christopher Lee, Author
Rosemary Jackson, Author

Engage in professional dialog with Heinemann's celebrated authors and colleagues!

181 pages   paperback
ISBN 0-867092-96-3

3047 How to Get Services by Being Assertive

Family Resource Center on Disabilities
20 E Jackson Boulevard
Chicago, IL   60604
312-939-3513
800-952-4199
FAX 312-939-7297
http://www.ameritech.net/users/frcdptiil
e-mail: FRCDPTIIL@ameritech.net
Charlotte DesJardins, Executive Director

A 100 page manual that demonstrates positive assertiveness techniques. Price includes postage & handling. *$12.00*

3048 Language in Motion: Exploring the Nature of Sign

Harris Communications
15155 Technology Drive
Eden Prairie, MN   55344
952-906-1180
800-825-6758
FAX 952-906-1099
TDY:952-906-1198
http://www.harriscomm.com
e-mail: mail@harriscomm.com
David A Stewart, Author
Jerome D Schein, Author
Bill Williams, National Sales Manager

Explore the nature of American Sign Language and its relationship to other sign languages and sign systems used around the world. An enlightening book about deaf people and their culture and a useful guide to interacting and communicating with deaf and hard-of-hearing people. *$24.95*

221 pages   Hardcover

3049 Out of Darkness

Connecticut Assoc. for Children and Adults with LD
25 Van Zant Street
East Norwalk, CT   06855
203-838-5010
FAX 203-866-6108
http://www.CACLD.org

Article by an adult who discovers at age 30 that he has ADD. *$1.00*

4 pages

3050 Painting the Joy of the Soul

Learning Disabilities Association of America
4156 Library Road
Pittsburgh, PA 15234   412-341-1515
FAX 412-344-0224
http://www.ldanatl.org
e-mail: ldanatl@usaor.net

The first comprehensively researched and written book on the art and life of America's beloved artist, P. Buckley Moss, whose passion for painting is equal only to her passion for people, especially those with learning disabilities. Inspirational book about a woman who succeeded not in spite of her disability, but because of it. Contains 168 full color pages, over 100 art images. *$50.00*

168 pages $5.00 postage

3051 Son-Rise: The Miracle Continues

Option Indigo Press
2080 S Undermountain Road
Sheffield, MA 01257   413-229-8727
800-562-7171
FAX 413-229-8727
http://www.optionindio.com
e-mail: indigo@bcn.net

This book documents Raun Kaufman's astonishing development from a lifeless, autistic, retarded child into a highly verbal, lovable youngster with no traces of his former condition. It includes details of Raun's extraordinary progress from the age of four into young adulthood. It also shares moving accounts of five families that successfully used the Son-Rise Program to reach their own special children. An awe-inspiring reminder that love moves mountains. *$14.95*

ISBN 0-915811-61-8

3052 Succeeding with LD

Free Spirit Publishing
217 5th Avenue N
Minneapolis, MN 55401   612-338-2068
800-735-7323
FAX 612-337-5050
http://www.freespirit.com
e-mail: help4kids@freespirit.com
Jill Lauren, MA, Author
Betsy Gabler, Sales Manager

Twenty talented adults and children with LD share their stories, struggles, achievements, and tips for success. *$14.95*

160 pages Illustrated
ISBN 1-575420-12-0

3053 You Don't Outgrow It: Living with Learning Disabilities

Academic Therapy Publications
20 Commercial Boulevard
Novato, CA 94949   415-883-3314
800-422-7249
FAX 415-883-3720
http://www.atpub.com
Marnell L. Hayes, Author

Offers information to help the learning disabled adult. Uses strengths creatively to work around learning disabilities to reach a goal, get and hold a job, etc. Comprehensive glossary, related readings and recommended resources. *$6.00*

ISBN 0-878799-67-2

Children

3054 123 Sign with Me

Harris Communications
15155 Technology Drive
Eden Prairie, MN 55344   952-906-1180
800-825-6758
FAX 952-906-1099
TDY:952-906-1198
http://www.harriscomm.com
e-mail: mail@harriscomm.com
Bill Williams, National Sales Manager

The Sign with Me number book is a book for all children. It is designed to teach basic counting skills, the numerals 1-10, and their manual counterparts in sign language. The book offers a unique opportunity to introduce sign language to young children through the natural process of reading. *$12.00*

24 pages Paperback
ISBN 0-939849-01-1

3055 ABC Sign with Me

Harris Communications
15155 Technology Drive
Eden Prairie, MN 55344   952-906-1180
800-825-6758
FAX 952-906-1099
TDY:952-906-1198
http://www.harriscomm.com
e-mail: mail@harriscomm.com
Bill Williams, National Sales Manager

The Sign with Me alphabet book is a book for all children. It is designed to teach the 26 letters of the alphabet and the corresponding manual alphabet in sign language. The book provides early exposure to letter recognition plus a unique opportunity to introduce sign language to young children. *$12.00*

32 pages Paperback
ISBN 0-939849-00-3

3056 Adam Zigzag

Bantam Doubleday Dell
1540 Broadway
New York, NY 10036   212-782-9000
800-323-9872
FAX 212-302-7985
Barbara Barrie, Author

Dyslexia affects Adam's self-esteem and the lives of his family.

ISBN 0-385311-72-9

3057 An Alphabet of Animal Signs

Harris Communications
15155 Technology Drive
Eden Prairie, MN   55344   952-906-1180
                                  800-825-6758
                            FAX 952-906-1099
                            TDY:952-906-1198
                     http://www.harriscomm.com
                     e-mail: mail@harriscomm.com
S Harold Collins, Author
Bill Williams, National Sales Manager

A fun sign language starter book that presents an animal sign for each letter of the alphabet. *$5.95*

13 pages   Paperback

3058 Basic Vocabulary: American Sign Language for Parents and Children

Harris Communications
15155 Technology Drive
Eden Prairie, MN   55344   952-906-1180
                                  800-825-6758
                            FAX 952-906-1099
                            TDY:952-906-1198
                     http://www.harriscomm.com
                     e-mail: mail@harriscomm.com
Terrence J O'Rourke, Author
Bill Williams, National Sales Manager

A child's first dictionary of signs. Arranged alphabetically, this book incorporates developmental lists helpful to both deaf and hearing children with over 1,000 clear illustrations. *$8.95*

228 pages   Paperback
ISBN 0-932666-00-0

3059 Beginning Signing Primer

Harris Communications
15155 Technology Drive
Eden Prairie, MN   55344   952-906-1180
                                  800-825-6758
                            FAX 952-906-1099
                            TDY:952-906-1198
                     http://www.harriscomm.com
                     e-mail: mail@harriscomm.com
Bill Williams, National Sales Manager

A set of 100 cards designed especially for beginning signers. The cards present seven topics with words and signs. The topics: Color; Creatures; Family; Months; Days; Time and Weather. *$5.95*

3060 Best Way Out

Harcourt Brace Jovanovich
6277 Sea Harbor Drive
Orlando, FL   32887   407-345-2000
                       FAX 407-352-1318
                http://www.harcourtcollege.com
Karyn Follis Cheatham, Author
John D Benson, VP

A fictional story of thirteen-year-old Haywood Romby who faces the same real life academic and social problems faced daily by teenagers with learning disabilities.

168 pages

3061 Christmas Bear

Teddy Bear Press
3639 Midway Drive
San Diego, CA   92110   619-223-7311
                         FAX 619-255-2158
                http://www.teddybearpress.net
            e-mail: fparker@teddybearpress.net
Fran Parker, President

An 11x17 big book with color illustrations and a large print format uses the same simple sentence structure fount in I Can Read and Reading Is Fun programs. This story adds seasonal words to the developing sight vocabulary found in our reading programs. *$25.95*

12 pages
ISBN 1-928876-11-0

3062 Don't Give Up Kid

Verbal Images Press
19 Fox Hill Drive
Fairport, NY   14450   585-377-3807
                              800-888-4741
                        FAX 716-377-5401
Jeanne Gehret, MA, Author
Victoria Harmison, Marketing Director

A picture book for children with dyslexia and other learning differences gives a clear understanding of their difficulties and the necessary courage to live with them. Young Alex finds in his hero, Thomas Edison, the strength to keep trying and to experiment with different ways to learn. Recommended by LDA and CHADD. *$9.95*

40 pages   Paperback
ISBN 1-884281-10-9

3063 Fundamentals of Autism

Slosson Educational Publications
538 Buffalo Road
East Aurora, NY   14052   888-756-7766
                                 800-828-4800
                           FAX 800-655-3840
                      http://www.slosson.com
                  e-mail: slosson@slosson.com
Georgina Moynihan, TTFM

A handbook for those who work with children diagnosed as autistic.

3064 Funny Bunny and Sunny Bunny

Teddy Bear Press
3639 Midway Drive
San Diego, CA   92110   619-223-7311
                         FAX 619-255-2158
                http://www.teddybearpress.net
            e-mail: fparker@teddybearpress.net
Fran Parker, President

An 11x17 big book with color illustrations and a large print format uses the same simple sentence structure fount in I Can Read and Reading Is Fun programs. This story adds seasonal words to the developing sight vocabulary found in our reading programs. *$25.95*

17 pages
ISBN 1-928876-14-5

3065 Halloween Bear

Teddy Bear Press
3639 Midway Drive
San Diego, CA   92110   619-223-7311
                              FAX 619-255-2158
                         http://www.teddybearpress.net
                      e-mail: fparker@teddybearpress.net
Fran Parker, President

An 11x17 big book with color illustrations and a large print format uses the same simple sentence structure fount in I Can Read and Reading Is Fun programs. This story adds seasonal words to the developing sight vocabulary found in our reading programs. *$25.95*

> *13 pages*
> *ISBN 1-928876-15-3*

3066 Handmade Alphabet

Harris Communications
15155 Technology Drive
Eden Prairie, MN   55344   952-906-1180
                                  800-825-6758
                              FAX 952-906-1099
                              TDY:952-906-1198
                         http://www.harriscomm.com
                         e-mail: mail@harriscomm.com
Laura Rankin, Author
Bill Williams, National Sales Manager

An alphabet book which celebrates the beauty of the manual alphabet. Each illustration consists of the manual representation of the letter linked with an item beginning with that letter. *$16.99*

> *32 pages   Hardcover*
> *ISBN 0-803709-74-9*

3067 I Can Read Charts

Teddy Bear Press
3639 Midway Drive
San Diego, CA   92110   619-223-7311
                              FAX 619-255-2158
                         http://www.teddybearpress.net
                      e-mail: fparker@teddybearpress.net
Fran Parker, President

Designed to accompany the I Can Read program is an 11x17 big book containing 54 charts which can be used to assist in introducing new words to students. These charts also provide review for previously taught words with either individual student or a small group. *$54.95*

> *54 pages*

3068 Josh: A Boy with Dyslexia

Waterfront Books
85 Crescent Road
Burlington, VT   05401   802-658-7477
                                800-639-6063
                              FAX 802-860-1368
                         http://www.waterfrontbooks.com
                      e-mail: helpkids@waterfrontbooks.com
Caroline Janover, Author
Sherrill N Musty, Owner/Publisher

This is an adventure story for kids with a section in the back of facts about learning disabilities and a list of resources for parents and teachers. *$11.95*

> *100 pages   Hardcover*
> *ISBN 0-914525-18-2*

3069 Jumpin' Johnny Get Back to Work: A Child's Guide to ADHD/Hyperactivity

Connecticut Association Children & Adults with LD
25 Van Zant Street
East Norwalk, CT   06855   203-838-5010
                              FAX 203-866-6108
                         http://www.CACLD.org
                         e-mail: cacld@juno.com
Michael Gordon PhD, Author
Marie Armstrong, Information Specialist

Written primarily for elementary age youngsters with ADHD, this book helps them to understand their disability. Also valuable as an educational tool for parents, siblings, friends and classmates. The author's text reflects his sensitivity toward children with ADHD. *$12.50*

> *$2.50 shipping*

3070 Leo the Late Bloomer

Connecticut Assoc. for Children and Adults with LD
25 Van Zant Street
East Norwalk, CT   06855   203-838-5010
                              FAX 203-866-6108
                         http://www.CACLD.org
                         e-mail: cacld@juno.com
Robert Kraus, Author
Marie Armstrong, Information Specialist

A wonderful book for the young child who is having problems learning. Children follow along with Leo as he finally blooms. *$6.50*

> *$2.50 shipping*

3071 Mandy

Harris Communications
15155 Technology Drive
Eden Prairie, MN   55344   952-906-1180
                                  800-825-6758
                              FAX 952-906-1099
                              TDY:952-906-1198
                         http://www.harriscomm.com
                         e-mail: mail@harriscomm.com
Barbar D Booth, Author
Jim La Marche, Illustrator
Bill Williams, National Sales Manager

This book is presented in a lively, picture-book format and will give readers an understanding of the joys of sound and what it would be like not to be able to hear. Mandy, a young deaf girl, shares her perception of the world and her wonder of what sound actually is. Mandy is a fluent speechreader but also uses sign language occasionally in the text. *$5.35*

> *32 pages   Hardcover*

3072 My Brother Matthew

Woodbine House
6510 Bells Mill Road
Bethesda, MD   20817

301-897-3570
800-843-7323
FAX 301-897-5838
http://www.woodbinehouse.com
e-mail: info@woodbinehouse.com

Mary Thompson, Author
Mary Thompson, Illustrator

Narrated by a young boy who describes the ups and downs of day-to-day life as he and his family adjust to his new brother, Matthew, who is born with a disability. *$14.95*

28 pages   Hardcover
ISBN 0-933149-47-6

3073 My First Book of Sign

Harris Communications
15155 Technology Drive
Eden Prairie, MN   55344

952-906-1180
800-825-6758
FAX 952-906-1099
TDY:952-906-1198
http://www.harriscomm.com
e-mail: mail@harriscomm.com

Pamela J Baker, Author
Patricia Bellan Gillen, Illustrator

This book is an excellent source to teach children and even adults sign language. The illustrations are accurate in their representation of sign. It is colorful and visually attractive which makes it easy to read. The black and white manual alphabet, the fingerspelling, and aspects of sign provide exellent directions and pointers to signing correctly. The sign descriptions are a great supplement to the illustrations. *$11.96*

76 pages   Hardcover

3074 My Signing Book of Numbers

Harris Communications
15155 Technology Drive
Eden Prairie, MN   55344

952-906-1180
800-825-6758
FAX 952-906-1099
TDY:952-906-1198
http://www.harriscomm.com
e-mail: mail@harriscomm.com

Patricia Bellan Gillen, Author
Bill Williams, National Sales Manager

Learn signs for numbers 0 through 20, and 30 through 100 by tens. *$14.95*

56 pages   Hardcover

3075 Rosey: The Imperfect Angel

Special Needs Project
324 State Street
Santa Barbara, CA   93105

805-962-8087
800-333-6867
FAX 805-962-5087
e-mail: books@specialneeds.com

Sandra Lee Peckinpah, Author
Trisha Moore, Illustrator

Rosie, an angel with a cleft palate, works hard in her heavenly garden after the Boss Angel declares her disfigured mouth as lovely as a rose petal. Her reward is to be born on earth, as a baby with a cleft. *$15.95*

3076 Scare Bear

Teddy Bear Press
3639 Midway Drive
San Diego, CA   92110

619-223-7311
FAX 619-255-2158
http://www.teddybearpress.net
e-mail: fparker@teddybearpress.net

Fran Parker, President

An 11x17 big book with color illustrations and a large print format uses the same simple sentence structure fount in I Can Read and Reading Is Fun programs. This story adds seasonal words to the developing sight vocabulary found in our reading programs. *$25.95*

13 pages
ISBN 1-928876-16-1

3077 Signing is Fun: A Child's Introduction to the Basics of Sign Language

Harris Communications
15155 Technology Drive
Eden Prairie, MN   55344

952-906-1180
800-825-6758
FAX 952-906-1099
TDY:952-906-1198
http://www.harriscomm.com

Mickey Flodin, Author

The author of Signing for Kids offers children their first glimpse at a whole new world. Starting with the alphabet and working up to everyday phrases, this volume uses clear instructions on how to begin using American Sign Language and features an informative introduction to signing and its importance. One hundred and fifty illustrations. *$9.00*

95 pages   Paperback

3078 Sixth Grade Can Really Kill You

Penquin Putnam Publishing Group
375 Hudson Street
New York, NY   10014

212-366-2000
800-788-6262
FAX 212-366-2666

Barthe DeClements, Author

Helen's learning difficulties cause her to act up and are threatening to keep her from passing sixth grade. *$4.60*

Paperback
ISBN 0-670806-56-0

3079 Snowbear

Teddy Bear Press
3639 Midway Drive
San Diego, CA   92110

619-223-7311
FAX 619-255-2158
http://www.teddybearpress.net
e-mail: fparker@teddybearpress.net

Fran Parker, President

An 11x17 big book with color illustrations and a large print format uses the same simple sentence structure fount in I Can Read and Reading Is Fun programs. This story adds seasonal words to the developing sight vocabulary found in our reading programs. *$25.95*

13 pages
ISBN 1-928876-12-9

3080 Someone Special, Just Like You

Special Needs Project
324 State Street
Santa Barbara, CA   93105   805-962-8087
                                   800-333-6867
                              FAX 805-962-5087
          e-mail: books@specialneeds.com
Tricia Brown, Author
Fran Ortiz, Photographer

A handsome photo-essay including a range of youngsters with disabilities at four preschools in the San Francisco Bay area. *$6.25*

19 pages

3081 Unicorns Are Real!

Learning Disabilities Association of America
4156 Library Road
Pittsburgh, PA   15234   412-341-1515
                              FAX 412-344-0224
                         http://www.ldanatl.org
                    e-mail: ldanatl@usaor.net

This mega best-seller provides 65 practical, easy-to-follow-lessons to develop the much ignored right brain tendencies of children. These simple yet dramatically effective ideas and activities have helped thousands with learning difficulties. Includes an easy-to-administer screening checklist to determine hemisphere dominance, engaging instructional activities that draw on the intuitive, nonverbal abilities of the right brain, a list of skills associated with each brain hemisphere and more. *$14.95*

3082 Valentine Bear

Teddy Bear Press
3639 Midway Drive
San Diego, CA   92110   619-223-7311
                              FAX 619-255-2158
                      http://www.teddybearpress.net
                e-mail: fparker@teddybearpress.net
Fran Parker, President

An 11x17 big book with color illustrations and a large print format uses the same simple sentence structure fount in I Can Read and Reading Is Fun programs. This story adds seasonal words to the developing sight vocabulary found in our reading programs. *$25.95*

13 pages
ISBN 1-928876-13-7

3083 Zipper, the Kid with ADHD

Woodbine House
6510 Bells Mill Road
Bethesda, MD   20817   301-897-3570
                                  800-843-7323
                              FAX 301-897-5838
                  http://www.woodbinehouse.com
              e-mail: info@Woodbinehouse.com
Caroline Janover, Author
Rick Powell, Illustrator

Readers will enjoy this middle-grade novel's amusing but realistic portrayal of the effect of attention deficit hyperactivity disorder on a young person's life. Zipper, the Kid with ADHD will encourage other kids to find ways to manage their behavior, and give their friends a look at what it's like to have this disorder. *$11.95*

108 pages   Paperback
ISBN 0-933149-95-6

Law

3084 ADA Quiz Book: 3rd Edition

Rocky Mountain Dis. & Bus. Technical Assistance
3630 Sinton Road
Colorado Springs, CO   80907   719-444-0268
                                  800-949-4232
                              FAX 719-444-0269
                   http://www.adainformation.org
               e-mail: regionviii@mtc-inc.com
Jana Copeland, Editor

A collection of puzzles, quizzes, questions and case studies on the Americans with Disabilities Act of 1990 and accessible information technology. Features sections on ADA basics, employment, state and local governments, public accommodations, architectural accessibility, disability etiquette, effective communication, and electronic and information technology. *$9.95*

81 pages   4.00 shipping

3085 Americans with Disabilities Act Management Training Program

RPM Press
PO Box 31483
Tucson, AZ   85751   520-886-1990
                                  888-810-1990
                              FAX 520-886-1990
                       http://www.rpmpress.com/
Jan Stonebraker, Operations Manager

Provides authoritative information on the Americans with Disabilities Act and compliance requirements for employers, schools and other entities which provide employment, education or related opportunities to persons with disabilities. *$142.95*

3086 Approaching Equality: Education of the Deaf

T-J Publishers
817 Silver Spring Avenue
Silver Spring, MD   20910   301-585-4440
                                   800-999-1168
                                   FAX 301-585-5930
                                   TDY:301-585-4440
                                   e-mail: tjpubinc@aol.com

Frank Bowe, Author
Angela K Thames, President
Jerald A Murphy, VP

Public education laws guarantee special education for all deaf and learning disabled children, but many find the special education system confusing, or are unsure of their rights under current laws. For anyone with interest in education, advocacy and the disabled community, this book reviews dramatic developments in education of special children, youth and adults. *$12.95*

112 pages
ISBN 0-932666-39-6

3087 Attention Deficit Disorder and the Law

JKL Communications
PO Box 40157
Washington, DC   20016   202-223-5097
                                FAX 202-223-5096
                                http://www.lathamlaw.org
                                e-mail: plath3@his.com

$29.00

3088 Discipline

Special Education Resource Center
25 Industrial Park Road
Middletown, CT   06457   860-632-1485
                                FAX 860-632-8870

JJ Jennings
CL Weatherly

A general analysis of the problems encountered in the discipline of students with disabilities. Discussion of the legal principles of discipline that have evolved pursuant to Public Law 94-142.

3089 Dispute Resolution Journal

American Arbitration Association
335 Madison Avenue
New York, NY   10017   212-716-3972
                              FAX 212-716-5906
                              e-mail: OConnorR@adr.org
Ted Pons, Director of Publications

Provides information on mediation, arbitration and other dispute resolution alternatives. *$100.00*

100 pages

3090 Documentation and the Law

JKL Communications
PO Box 40157
Washington, DC   20016   202-223-5097
                                FAX 202-223-5096
                                http://www.lathamlaw.org
                                e-mail: plath3@his.com

$29.00

3091 Education of the Handicapped: Laws

William Hein & Company
1285 Main Street
Buffalo, NY   14209   716-882-2600
                             800-828-7871
                             FAX 716-883-8100
                             http://www.wshein.com/
Bernard D Reams Jr, Author

Focuses on elementary and secondary Education Act of 1965 and its amendment, Education For All Handicapped Children Act of 1975 and its amendments and acts providing services for the disabled.

3092 Ethical and Legal Issues in School Counseling

American School Counselor Association
801 N Fairfax Street
Alexandria, VA   22314   703-683-2722
                                800-306-4722
                                FAX 703-683-1619
                                http://www.schoolcounselor.org
                                e-mail: asca@schoolcounselor.org
Stephanie Will, Office Manager

Perhaps the increase in litigation involving educators and mental health practitioners is a factor. Certainly the laws are changing or at least are being interpreted differently, requiring counselors to stay up-to-date. The process of decision-making and some of the more complex issues in ethical and legal areas are summarized in this digest. *$40.50*

ISBN 1-556200-55-2

3093 Individuals with Disabilities: Implementing the Newest Laws

Corwin Press
2455 Teller Road
Thousand Oaks, CA   91320   805-499-9734
                                   800-818-7243
                                   FAX 805-499-5323
                                   http://www.corwinpress.com
                                   e-mail: order@corwinpress.com
Patricia F First & Joan L Curcio, Author
Kimberly Gonzales, Marketing Director
Robb Clouse, Senior Acquisitions Editor

Aimed at school administrators, this highly readable book covers the three major pieces of legislation: Americans with Disabilities Act of 1990; Individuals with Disabilities Education Act; and the Rehabilitation Act of 1973. Suitable for lay public use, anyone needing an overview of the laws affecting education and disabilities. *$12.95*

64 pages
ISBN 0-803960-55-7

3094 Learning Disabilities and the Law

JKL Communications
PO Box 40157
Washington, DC   20016   202-223-5097
                                FAX 202-223-5096
                                http://www.lathamlaw.org
                                e-mail: plath3@his.com

$29.00

3095 Least Restrictive Environment

Special Education Resource Center
25 Industrial Park Road
Middletown, CT 06457   860-632-1485
                             FAX 860-632-8870

JJ Jennings
CL Weatherly

A general discussion and analysis of the mandate to educate students with disabilities to the maximum extent appropriate with nondisabled students.

3096 Legal Notes for Education

Oakstone Legal and Business Publishing
6801 Cahaba Valley Road
Burmingham, AL 35242   205-991-5188
                              800-365-4900
                         FAX 205-995-1926
              e-mail: info@andrewspub.com
Nancy McMeekin, CEO

Summaries of court decisions dealing with education law. *$122.00*

3097 Legal Rights of Persons with Disabilities: An Analysis of Federal Law

LRP Publications
747 Dresher Road
Horsham, PA 19044   215-784-0941
                           800-341-7874
                      FAX 215-784-9639
                      TDY:215-658-0938
                      http://www.lrp.com
                 e-mail: custserv@lrp.com
Bonnie P Tucker & Bruce A Goldstein, Author
Honora McDowell, Product Group Manager

This book will provide professionals working with the disabled a comprehensive analysis of the rights accorded individuals with disabilities under federal law. *$185.00*

> 2226 pages   +$7.50
> ISBN 0-934753-46-6

3098 New Directions

Association of State Mental Health Program Direct.
66 Canal Center Plaza
Alexandria, VA 22314   703-739-9333
                         FAX 703-548-9517
                      http://www.nasddds.org

A newsletter offering information on laws, amendments, and legislation affecting the disabled. *$55.00*

3099 New IDEA Amendments: Assistive Technology Devices and Services

Special Education Resource Center
25 Industrial Park Road
Middletown, CT 06457   860-632-1485
                         FAX 860-623-8870

JJ Jennings
CL Weatherly

A discussion of new mandates created by the 1990 Amendments to Public Law 94-142. An overview of the requirement for the provision of assistive technology devices and services as well as a discussion on the transition services that are to be provided to disabled adolescents.

3100 Numbers That Add Up to Educational Rights for Children with Disabilities

Children's Defense Fund
25 E Street NW
Washington, DC 20001   202-628-8787
                         FAX 202-662-3510
              http://www.childrensdefense.org
Information on the laws 94-142 and 504.

3101 Opening Doors: Connecting Students to Curriculum, Classmate, and Learning

PEAK Parent Center
611 N Weber
Colorado Springs, CO 80903   719-531-9400
                                    800-284-0251
                               FAX 719-531-9452
                               TDY:719-531-5403
                       http://www.peakparent.org
                   e-mail: info@peakparent.org
Barbara Buswell, Editor
Beth Schaffner, Editor
Alison Seyler, Editor

Written for educators and parents about including all students in general education classes and activities. Chapter topics, coauthored by leading education experts, include instructional strategies, curriculum modifications, behavior, standards, literacy, and providing supports. *$13.00*

> ISBN 0-884720-12-9

3102 Parent's Guide to the Social Security Administration

Eden Services
One Eden Way
Princeton, NJ 08540   609-987-0099
                         FAX 609-987-0243
              http://www.members.aol.com/edensvcs
                   e-mail: info@edenservices.org
David L Holmes EdD, Executive Director/President
Anne Holmes, Director Outreach Support Svcs

A parents' guide to the Social Security Administration and Social Security Work Incentive Programs. *$16.00*

3103 Procedural Due Process

Special Education Resource Center
25 Industrial Park Road
Middletown, CT 06457   860-632-1485
                         FAX 860-632-8870

JJ Jennings
CL Weatherly

Analyzes the importance of the procedural safeguards afforded to parents and their children with disabilities by the Public Law 94-142. Safeguards are discussed and possible legal implications are addressed.

3104 Public Law 94-142: An Overview

Special Education Resource Center
25 Industrial Park Road
Middletown, CT   06457   860-632-1485
                                    FAX 860-632-8870
JJ Jennings
CL Weatherly

An overview of the general provisions of the Individuals with Disabilities Education Act, commonly referred to as Public Law 94-142. Designed to provide the less-experienced viewer with a fundamental understanding of the Public Law and its significance.

3105 Purposeful Integration: Inherently Equal

Federation for Children with Special Needs
1135 Tremont Street
Boston, MA   02120   617-236-7210
                                   800-331-0688
                              FAX 617-572-2094
                              TDY:617-236-7210
                              http://www.fcsn.org
                           e-mail: fcsninfo@fcsn.org
Richard J Robison, Executive Director

This publication covers integration, mainstreaming, and least restrictive environments. *$8.00*

55 pages

3106 Section 504 of the Rehabilitation Act

Special Education Resource Center
25 Industrial Park Road
Middletown, CT   06457   860-632-1485
                                    FAX 860-632-8870
JJ Jennings
CL Weatherly

A general overview of the legal implications of the Rehabilitation Act and its implementing regulations, a law that is often forgotten in the process of appropriately educating children with disabilities.

3107 Section 504: Help for the Learning Disabled College Student

Connecticut Assoc. for Children and Adults with LD
25 Van Zant Street
East Norwalk, CT   06855   203-838-5010
                                    FAX 203-866-6108
                              http://www.CACLD.org
                           e-mail: cacld@juno.com
Joan Sedita, Author
Marie Armstrong, Information Specialist

Provides a review of Section 504 of the Vocational Rehabilitation Act as it relates specifically to the learning disabled. *$3.25*

$2.50 shipping

3108 So You're Going to a Hearing: Preparing for Public Law 94-142

Learning Disabilities Association of America
4156 Library Road
Pittsburgh, PA   15234   412-341-1515
                                    FAX 412-344-0224
                              http://www.ldanatl.org
                           e-mail: ldanatl@usaor.net

A public informational source offering legal advice to children and youth with learning disabilities. *$5.50*

3109 Special Education Law Update

Data Research
4635 Nicols Road
Eagan, MN   55122   651-452-8267
                                  800-365-4900
                             FAX 651-452-8694
                       http://www.dataresearchinc.com
Bruce Montgomery

Monthly newsletter service. Cases, legislation, administrative regulations and law review articles dealing with special education law. Annual index and binder included. *$159.00*

3110 Special Education in Juvenile Corrections

Council for Exceptional Children
1110 N Glebe Road
Arlington, VA   22201   703-620-3660
                                  888-232-7733
                             FAX 703-264-9494
                       http://www.cec.sped.org/
Peter E Leone, Author
Robert B Rutherford Jr, Author

This topic is of increasing concern. This book describes the demographics of incarcerated youth and suggests some promising practices that are being used. *$8.90*

26 pages
ISBN 0-865862-03-6

3111 Special Law for Special People

Smith, Howard & Ajax
3333 Peachtree Road NE
Atlanta, GA   30326
                                    FAX 404-239-1930
Julie J Jennings, Contact
Charles L Weatherly, Contact

A ten-tape video series that is designed to assist in educating regular education personnel as to the legal requirements of IDEA and Section 504.

3112 Statutes, Regulations and Case LawProtecting Disabled Individuals

Data Research
4635 Nicols Road
Eagan, MN   55122   651-452-8267
                                  800-365-4900
                             FAX 651-452-8694
                       http://www.dataresearchinc.com
Bruce Montgomery

Annum book presenting annotated statutes and regulations relevant to disability law issues. *$125.00*

3113 Stories Behind Special Education Case Law

Special Needs Project
324 State Street
Santa Barbara, CA 93105 805-962-8087
800-333-6867
FAX 805-962-5087
e-mail: books@specialneeds.com
Ree Martin, Author

The personal stories behind ten leading court cases that shaped the basic principles of special education law. *$12.95*

150 pages

3114 Students with Disabilities and SpecialEducation

Data Research
4635 Nicols Road
Eagan, MN 55122 651-452-8267
800-365-4900
FAX 651-452-8694
http://www.dataresearchinc.com

Annual book presenting case summaries, citations, statutes and regulations relevant to special education. *$139.00*

500+ pages
ISBN 0-939675-44-7

3115 Technology, Curriculum, and ProfessionalDevelopment

Corwin Press
2455 Teller Road
Thousand Oaks, CA 91320 805-499-9734
800-818-7243
FAX 805-499-5323
http://www.corwinpress.com
e-mail: order@corwinpress.com
John Woodward, Larry Cuban, Author
Kimberly Gonzales, Marketing Director
Robb Clouse, Senior Acquisitions Editor

Adapting schools to meet the needs of students with disabilities. The history of special education technologies, the requirements of IDEA'97, and the successes and obstacles for special education technology implementation. *$34.95*

264 pages
ISBN 0-761977-43-0

3116 Testing Students with Disabilities

Corwin Press
2455 Teller Road
Thousand Oaks, CA 91320 805-499-9734
800-818-7243
FAX 805-499-5323
http://www.corwinpress.com
e-mail: order@corwinpress.com
Martha Thurloiw, Judy Elliott, James Ysseldyke, Author
Kimberly Gonzales, Marketing Director
Robb Clouse, Senior Acquisitions Editor

Practical strategies for complying with district and state requirements. Helps translate the issues surrounding state and district testing of students with disabilities, including IDEA, into what educators need to know and do. *$ 34.95*

296 pages
ISBN 0-803965-52-4

3117 US Department of Justice: DisabilitiesRights Section

PO Box 66738
Washington, DC 20035
800-514-0301
FAX 202-307-1198
http://www.usd.j.gov/crt/ada/adahoml.htm

Information concerning the rights people with learning disabilities have under the Americans with Disabilities Act.

Parents & Professionals

3118 125 Brain Games for Babies

Therapro
225 Arlington Street
Framingham, MA 01702 508-872-9494
800-257-5376
FAX 508-875-2062
http://www.theraproducts.com
e-mail: info@theraproducts.com
Jackie Silberg, Author

Packed with everyday opportunities to enhance brain development of children from birth to 12 months. Each game includes notes on recent brain research in practical terms.

3119 A Miracle to Believe In

Option Indigo Press
2080 S Undermountain Road
Sheffield, MA 01257 413-229-8727
800-562-7171
FAX 413-229-8727
http://www.optionindio.com
e-mail: indigo@bcn.net
Barry Neil Kaufman, Author

A group of people from all walks of life come together and are transformed as they reach out, under the direction of Kaufman, to help a little boy the medical world had given up as hopeless. This heartwarming journey of loving a child back to life will not only inspire, but presents a compelling new way to deal with life's traumas and difficulties. *$7.99*

ISBN 0-449201-08-2

3120 A Practical Parent's Handbook on TeachingChildren with Learning Disabilities

Charles C Thomas Publisher
2600 S 1st Street
Springfield, IL 62704 217-789-8980
800-258-8980
FAX 217-789-9130
http://www.ccthomas.com
Shelby Holley, Author

Gives enough information for an adult with no previous teaching experience to design and implement an effective remedial program. Books sent on approval. $68.95

308 pages   Paper $43.95
ISBN 0-398059-03-9

3121   ADHD in Adolescents: Diagnosis andTreatment

Guilford Publications
72 Spring Street
New York, NY   10012   212-431-9800
                              800-365-7006
                         FAX 212-966-6708
                      http://www.guilford.com
                      e-mail: info@guilford.com
Arthur L Robin, Author

Here Dr. Robin teaches us not only about the facts of the disorder, but also about its nature and the proper means of clinically evaluating it. Includes numerous reproducible forms for clinicians and clients, among them rating scales and detailed checklists for psychological testing, interviewing, treatment planning, and school and family interventions. $46.95

461 pages   Hardcover
ISBN 1-572303-91-3

3122   About Dyslexia: Unraveling the Myth

Connecticut Assoc. for Children and Adults with LD
25 Van Zant Street
East Norwalk, CT   06855   203-838-5010
                            FAX 203-866-6108
                         http://www.CACLD.org
Priscilla Vail, Author

This book focuses on the communication patterns of strength and weaknesses in dyslexic people from early childhood through adulthood. $7.95

49 pages
ISBN 0-935493-34-4

3123   Absudities of Special Education: The Best of Ants....Flying and Logs

Peytral Publicatons
PO Box 1162
Minnetonka, MN   55345   952-949-8707
                               877-739-8725
                          FAX 952-906-9777
                        http://www.peytral.com
                        e-mail: help@peytral.com
Michael F Giangreco, Author

Now available in this full color edition. Create beautiful transperances or use in PowerPoint presentations for staff development. Also a great gift for parents of educators. $39.95

114 pages
ISBN 1-890455-40-7

3124   Access Aware: Extending Your Reach to People with Disabilities

Alliance for Technology Access
1304 Southpoint Boulevard
Petaluma, CA   94954   707-778-3011
                         FAX 707-765-2080
                      http://www.ataccess.org
                      e-mail: atainfo@ataccess.org
Mary Lester, Executive Director

This easy-to-use manual is designed to help any organization become more accessible for people with disabilities. $45.00

219 pages
ISBN 0-897933-00-1

3125   Activity Schedules for Children with Autism: A Guide for Parents and Professionals

Woodbine House
6510 Bells Mill Road
Bethesda, MD   20817   301-897-3570
                              800-843-7323
                         FAX 301-897-5838
                      http://www.woodbinehouse.com
                      e-mail: info@woodbinehouse.com
Lynn E McClannahan PhD, Author
Patricia J Krantz PhD, Author

Detailed instructions and examples help parents prepare their child's first activity schedule, then progress to more varied and sophisticated schedules. The goal of this system is for children with autism to make effective use of unstructured time, handle changes in routine, and help them choose among an established set of home, school, and leisure activities independently. $14.95

117 pages   Paperback
ISBN 0-933149-93-X

3126   Alternate Assessments for Students with Disabilities

Corwin Press
2455 Teller Road
Thousand Oaks, CA   91320   805-499-9734
                                   800-818-7243
                              FAX 805-499-5323
                         http://www.corwinpress.com
                         e-mail: order@corwinpress.com
Sandra J Thompson, Rachel F Quenemoen, Author
Kimberly Gonzales, Marketing Director
Robb Clouse, Senior Acquisitions Editor

Distinguished group of experts in a landmark book, co-published with the Council for Exceptional Children show you how to shift to high expectations for all learners, improve schooling for all. $29.95

168 pages
ISBN 0-761977-74-0

3127 American Sign Language Concise Dictionary

Harris Communications
15155 Technology Drive
Eden Prairie, MN 55344   952-906-1180
                                800-825-6758
                                FAX 952-906-1099
                                TDY:952-906-1198
                                http://www.harriscomm.com
Martin Sternberg, Author

A portable version containing 2,000 of the most commonly used words and phrases in ASL. Illustrated with easy-to-follow hand, arm and facial movements. *$11.95*

737 pages   Paperback

3128 American Sign Language Dictionary: A Comprehensive Abridgement

Harris Communications
15155 Technology Drive
Eden Prairie, MN 55344   952-906-1180
                                800-825-6758
                                FAX 952-906-1099
                                TDY:952-906-1198
                                http://www.harriscomm.com
Martin Sternberg, Author

An abridged version of American Sign Language. A comprehensive dictionary with 4,400 illustrated signs. It has 500 new signs and 1,500 new illustrations. Third edition. *$24.00*

772 pages   Paperback

3129 American Sign Language: A Comprehensive Dictionary

Harris Communications
15155 Technology Drive
Eden Prairie, MN 55344   952-906-1180
                                800-825-6758
                                FAX 952-906-1099
                                TDY:952-906-1198
                                http://www.harriscomm.com
Martin Sternberg, Author

Contains over 5,000 entries and cross-references, an extensive bibliography and seven foreign language indexes. Contains clear illustrations and easily understood directions for forming and using each sign. *$75.00*

1132 pages

3130 Another Door to Learning

Crossroad Publishing
481 8th Avenue
New York, NY 10001   212-868-1801
                            FAX 212-868-2171
        e-mail: sales@crossroadpublishing.com
Judy Schwartz, Author
John Jones, Executive Manager

Stories of eleven atypical learners who got the help they needed to make a lasting difference in their lives.

ISBN 0-824513-85-1

3131 Answers to Distraction

Pantheon Books
201 E 50th Street
New York, NY 10022   212-751-2600
                            800-638-6460
                            FAX 212-572-8700
Edward M Hallowell, Author
John Ratey, Author

Responses to common questions the authors' audiences have asked, organized by topic.

ISBN 0-679439-73-0

3132 Ants in His Pants: Absurdities and Realities of Special Education

Peytral Publication
PO Box 1162
Minnetonka, MN 55345   952-949-8707
                              877-739-8725
                              FAX 612-906-9777
                              http://www.peytral.com
                              e-mail: help@peytral.com
Michael F Giangreco, Author

With wit, humor, and profound one liners, this book will transform your thinking as you take a lighter look at the often comical and occasionally harsh truth in the field of special education. This carefully crafted collection of 101 cartoons can be made into transparencies for staff development and training. *$19.95*

128 pages
ISBN 1-890455-42-3

3133 Assessment & Instruction of Culturally & Linguistically Diverse Students

Books on Special Children
PO Box 305
Congers, NY 10920   845-638-1236
                           FAX 845-638-0847
                           http://www.boscbooks.com/
                           e-mail: irene@boscbooks.com
Sam Goldstein, PhD, Author

Appropriate assessments and educational models and practices are discussed. Also, educational environment and how to help problems, understanding diversity and disability, legal aspects. *$49.00*

254 pages   hardcover
ISBN 0-205156-29-0

3134 Attention-Deficit Hyperactivity Disorder

Slosson Educational Publications
538 Buffalo Road
East Aurora, NY 14052   716-652-0930
                               800-828-4800
                               FAX 800-655-3840
                               http://www.slosson.com
                               e-mail: slosson@slosson.com
Sue Larson, Author

The book addresses issues of theory and practice quickly, with compassion and practicality and, most importantly, is very effective. Well-grounded answers and suggestions which would facilitate behavior, learning, social-emotional functioning, and other factors in preschool and adolescence are discussed.

3135 Attention-Deficit Hyperactivity Disorder: A Handbook for Diagnosis and Treatment, 2nd Edition

Guilford Publications
72 Spring Street
New York, NY   10012   212-431-9800
                              800-365-7006
                         FAX 212-966-6708
                      http://www.guilford.com
                      e-mail: info@guilford.com
Russell A Barkley, Author

Incorporates the latest findings on the nature, diagnosis, assessment, and treatment of ADHD. Clinicians, researchers, and students will find practical and richly referenced information on nearly every aspect of the disorder. *$ 55.00*

628 pages

3136 Autism and the Family: Problems, Prospects and Coping with the Disorder

Charles C Thomas Publisher
2600 S 1st Street
Springfield, IL   62704   217-789-8980
                                 800-258-8980
                            FAX 217-789-9130
David E Gray, Author

Explores aspects of the family's experience of autism, offering a sociological account of what it is like to be parents of an autistic child. *$45.95*

210 pages   Cloth
ISBN 0-398068-42-9

3137 Backyards & Butterflies: Ways to Include Children with Disabilities

Brookline Books
PO Box 1047
Cambridge, MA   02238   617-868-0360
                               800-666-2665
                          FAX 617-868-1772

72 pages

3138 Behavior Management Applications for Teachers and Parents

Prentice Hall Publishing Company
One Lake Street
Upper Saddle River, NJ   07458
                               800-382-3419
                          FAX 201-236-7141
                       http://www.prenhall.com
Thomas J Zirpoli, Author

A clear, extensive presentation of the technical basis and appropriate implementation strategies for managing behavior in classrooms, day care centers, even at home.

ISBN 0-135205-37-9

3139 Behavior Technology Guide Book

One Eden Way
Princeton, NJ   08540   609-987-0099
                          FAX 609-987-0243
                      http://www.edenservices.org
                      e-mail: info@edenservices.org
David L Holmes, Executive Director/President
Anne Holmes, Director Outreach Support Svcs

Techniques for increasing and decreasing behavior using the principles of applied behavior analysis and related teaching strategies — discrete trial, shaping, task analysis and chaining. *$50.00*

3140 Beyond the Rainbow

Learning Disabilities Association of America
4156 Library Road
Pittsburgh, PA   15234   412-341-1515
                           FAX 412-344-0224
                       http://www.ldanatl.org
                       e-mail: ldanatl@usaor.net
Patricia Dodds, Author

A guide for parents with children with dyslexia and other disabilities. *$16.00*

3141 Bridges to Reading

Parents & Educators Resource Center
PO Box 389
Brisbane, CA   94005   650-655-2410
                              800-471-9545
                         FAX 650-655-2411
Helps parents identify, understand, and address reading problems. Includes eight booklets, national resources, and information on tutoring and Attention Deficit/Hyperactivity Disorder. *$20.00*

3142 Building Healthy Minds

Perseus Publishing
5500 Central Avenue
Boulder, CO   80301
                               800-386-5656
                          FAX 800-822-4090
Stanley Greenspan, MD, Author

Explains what sorts of games, conversations and other interactions foster cognitive, emotional and moral development. *$17.00*

398 pages   Paperback
ISBN 0-738203-56-4

3143 Building a Child's Self-Image: A Guide for Parents

Learning Disabilities Association of America
4156 Library Road
Pittsburgh, PA   15234   412-341-1515
                           FAX 412-344-0224
                       http://www.ldanatl.org
                       e-mail: ldanatl@usaor.net

$9.25

3144 Care of the Neurologically Handicapped Child

Special Needs Project
324 State Street
Santa Barbara, CA   93105   805-962-8087
                                   800-333-6867
                              FAX 805-962-5087
               e-mail: books@specialneeds.com
Arthur Prensky, Author

This book describes normal and abnormal development, what to expect from the various specialists parents may consult, and seven of the most common neurological disorders. *$32.95*

331 pages

3145 Caring for Your Baby and Young Child: Birth to Age 5

Bantam
400 Hahn Road
Westminster, MD   21157
                                   800-726-0600
                              FAX 800-659-2436
Sponsored by the American Academy of Pediatrics, Author

Reliable information on child rearing, with particular emphasis on health issues. *$32.95*

736 pages   Hardcover
ISBN 0-553110-45-4

3146 Children with Autism

Special Needs Project
324 State Street
Santa Barbara, CA   93105   805-962-8087
                                   800-333-6867
                              FAX 805-962-5087
               e-mail: books@specialneeds.com
Michael Powers, Author

Recommended as the first book that parents should read, this book provides a complete introduction to autism, while easing a family's fears and concerns as they adjust and cope with their child's disorder. *$14.95*

368 pages

3147 Children with Cerebral Palsy: A Parent's Guide

Therapro
225 Arlington Street
Framingham, MA   01702   508-872-9494
                                   800-257-5376
                              FAX 508-875-2062
               http://www.theraproducts.com
               e-mail: info@theraproducts.com
Elaine Geralis, Editor

This book explains what cerebral palsy is, and discusses its diagnosis and treatment. It also offers information and advice concerning daily care, early intervention, therapy, educational options and family life.

3148 Children with Special Needs: A Resource Guide for Parents, Educators, Social Workers...

Charles C Thomas Publisher
2600 S 1st Street
Springfield, IL   62704   217-789-8980
                                   800-258-8980
                              FAX 217-789-9130
Karen L Lungu, Author

Writing from her own experience as the parent of a special needs child and with the background of both a therapist and educator, the author presents a most readable text discussing developmental disabilities, emotional and intellectual challenges, neurological disabilities, communication and learning disorders, attention deficit disorders and more. *$49.95*

234 pages   Cloth
ISBN 0-398069-33-6

3149 Children with Tourette Syndrome

Woodbine House
6510 Bells Mill Road
Bethesda, MD   20817   301-897-3570
                                   800-843-7323
                              FAX 301-897-5838
               http://www.woodbinehouse.com
               e-mail: info@Woodbinehouse.com
Tracy Haerle, Editor

A guide for parents of children and teenagers with Tourette syndrome. Covers medical, educational, legal, family life, daily care, and emotional issues, as well as explanations of related conditions. *$14.95*

352 pages   Paperback
ISBN 0-933149-39-5

3150 Classroom Success for the LD and ADHD Child

Therapro
225 Arlington Street
Framingham, MA   01702   508-872-9494
                                   800-257-5376
                              FAX 508-875-2062
               http://www.theraproducts.com
               e-mail: info@theraproducts.com
Suzanne H Stevens, Author

Helpful book for parents and therapists who work with children with learning disabilities. It addresses specific issues such as organization, homework and concentration. Stevens offers practical suggestions on adjusting teaching techniques, adapting texts, adjusting classroom management procedures and testing and grading fairly.

Revised

3151 Common Ground: Whole Language & Phonics Working Together

Modern Learning Press
PO Box 167
Rosemont, NJ   08556   609-397-2214
                                   800-627-5867
                              FAX 609-397-3467
Priscilla L Vail, Author

Media: Books/Parents & Professionals

Offers guidelines for reading instruction in the primary grades that combines whole language with multisensory phonics instruction. *$9.95*

ISBN 0-935493-27-1

3152 Common Sense About Dyslexia

Special Needs Project
324 State Street
Santa Barbara, CA   93105   805-962-8087
                                          800-333-6867
                                     FAX 805-962-5087
                    e-mail: books@specialneeds.com
Ann Marshall Huston, Author

Offers important, need-to-know information about dyslexia. *$16.95*

300 pages

3153 Communication Skills in Children with Down Syndrome

Woodbine House
6510 Bells Mill Road
Bethesda, MD   20817   301-897-3570
                                    800-843-7323
                               FAX 301-897-5838
                    http://www.woodbinehouse.com
                    e-mail: info@Woodbinehouse.com
Libby Kumin, PhD, CCC-SLP, Author

Accessible information, advice and practical home activities for children and adolescents with Down syndrome. *$14.95*

256 pages   Paperback
ISBN 0-933149-53-0

3154 Complete IEP Guide: How to Advocate for Your Special Ed Child

NOLO
950 Parker Street
Berkeley, CA   94710   510-549-1976
                                    800-955-4775
                               FAX 510-548-5902
                          http://www.nolo.com
Attorney Lawrence M Siegel, Author
Maira Dizgalvis, Trade Customer Service Manager
Susan McConnell, Director Sales
Natasha Kaluza, Sales Assistant

This book has all the plain-English suggestions, strategies, resources and forms to develop an effective IEP. *$17.47*

300 pages   paperback
ISBN 0-873376-07-2

3155 Complete Learning Disabilities Resource Library

Slosson Educational Publications
538 Buffalo Road
East Aurora, NY   14052   888-756-7766
                                       800-828-4800
                                  FAX 800-655-3840
                          http://www.sloss.com
                    e-mail: slosson@slosson.com
Joan M Harwell, Author

These volumes provide easy-to-use tips, techniques, and activities to help students with learning disabilities at all grade levels. *$29.95*

3156 Computer & Web Resources for People with Disabilities: A Guide to...

Alliance for Technology Access
1304 Southpoint Boulevard
Petaluma, CA   94954   707-778-3011
                               FAX 707-765-2080
                          http://www.ataccess.org
                    e-mail: atainfo@ataccess.org
Mary Lester, President

This highly acclaimed book includes detailed descriptions of software, hardware and communication aids, plus a gold mine of published and online resources. *$20.75*

364 pages

3157 Conducting Individualized Education Program Meetings that Withstand Due Process

Charles C Thomas Publisher
2600 S 1st Street
Springfield, IL   62704   217-789-8980
                                       800-258-8980
                                  FAX 217-789-9130
                          http://www.ccthomas.com
                    e-mail: books@ccthomas.com
James N Hollis, Author

Written to help parents, school administrators, teachers and assessment professionals meet basic requirements of conducting an IEP team meeting in a way that produces defensible IEP decisions in a litigious environment. *$41.95*

180 pages   Cloth

3158 Contemporary Intellectual Assessment: Theories, Tests and Issues

Guilford Publications
72 Spring Street
New York, NY   10012   212-431-9800
                                    800-365-7006
                               FAX 212-966-6708
                          http://www.guilford.com
                    e-mail: info@guilford.com
Dawn P Flanagan, Editor
Judy L Genshaft, Editor
Patti L Harrison, Editor

This unique volume provides a comprehensive conceptual and practical overview of the current state of the art of intellectual assessment. The book covers major theories of intelligence, methods of assessing human cognitive abilities, and issues related to the validity of current intelligence test batteries. *$60.00*

597 pages

3159 Controversial Issues Confronting Special Education

Books on Special Children
PO Box 305
Congers, NY   10920   845-638-1236
                              FAX 845-638-0847
                         http://www.boscbooks.com/
                    e-mail: irene@boscbooks.com
William Stainback, Author

The book has divergent perspectives from many contributors on twelve important controversial issues. Inclusive education, talented and gifted, classification and labeling, assessments, classroom management, research, adult services and more. *$59.00*

314 pages softcover
ISBN 0-205182-66-6

3160 Deciding What to Teach and How to Teach It Connecting Students through Curriculum and Instruction

PEAK Parent Center
611 N Weber
Colorado Springs, CO   80903   719-531-9400
800-284-0251
FAX 719-531-9452
TDY:719-531-5403
http://www.peakparent.org
e-mail: info@peakparent.org
E Castagnera, D Fisher, K Rodifer, C Sax, Author

Provides exciting and practical resource tips to ensure that all students participate and learn successfully in secondary general education classrooms. Lead the reader through a step-by-step process for starting with general curriculum, making accommodations and modifications, and providing appropriate supports. Planning grids and concrete strategies make this an essential tool for both secondary educators and families. *$13.00*

3161 Defiant Children

Guilford Publications
72 Spring Street
New York, NY   10012   212-431-9800
800-365-7006
FAX 212-966-6708
http://www.guilford.com
e-mail: info@guilford.com
Russell A Barkley, Author
Christine M Benton, Author

This book is written expressly for parents who are struggling with an unyielding or combative child, helping them understand what causes defiance, when it becomes a problem, and how it can be resolved. Its clear eight-step program stresses consistency and co-operation, promoting changes through a system of praise, rewards, and mild punishment. Filled with helpful sidebars, charts, and checklists. *$35.00*

255 pages Hardcover
ISBN 1-572301-23-6

3162 Developing Fine and Gross Motor Skills

Therapro
225 Arlington Street
Framingham, MA   01702   508-872-9494
800-257-5376
FAX 508-875-2062
http://www.theraproducts.com
e-mail: info@theraproducts.com
Donna Staisiunas Hurley, Author

This new home exercise program has dozens of beautifully illustrated, reproducible handouts for the parent, therapists, health care and child care workers. Each interval of 3 to 6 months in the child's development is divided into a fine motor and a gross motor section. Each section has several exercise sheets that guide parents in ways to develop specific motor skills that typically occur at that age level. Also includes practical information on how to guide parents when doing the exercises.

Ages Birth-3

3163 Diamonds in the Rough

Slosson Educational Publications
538 Buffalo Road
East Aurora, NY   14052   716-652-0930
888-756-7766
FAX 800-655-3840
http://www.slosson.com
e-mail: slosson@slosson.com
Peggy Strass Dias, Author
Steven W Slosson, President
John Slosson, VP

An invaluable multidisciplinary reference guide to learning disabilities. It is an indispensable resource for educators, health specialists, parents and librarians. The author has printed a clear picture of the archetypical learner with a step-by-step view of the learning disabled child. *$53.00*

3164 Dictionary of Special Education & Rehabilitation: 4th Editon

Books on Special Children
PO Box 305
Congers, NY   10920   845-638-1236
FAX 845-638-0847
http://www.boscbooks.com/
e-mail: irene@boscbooks.com
ML Anderegg, Author

A reference of definitions of terminology and jargon in special education and rehabilitation fields. Latest language in the field clearly defined. For those new or inexperienced in special ed and rehabilitation. Includes abbreviations, acronyms, legal terms lists of associations and national centers, periodicals, journals and sources of legal assistance. *$32.95*

210 pages softcover
ISBN 0-891082-43-3

3165 Directive Group Play Therapy: 2nd Edtion

Books on Special Children
PO Box 305
Congers, NY   10920   845-638-1236
FAX 845-638-0847
http://www.boscbooks.com/
e-mail: irene@boscbooks.com
N Leben, Author

Morning Glory Treatment Center for Children is a licensed therapeutic foster group home of about 10 children of ages 5-17. These games are played as part of therapy milieu. Each game contains objectives, supplies used. *$28.00*

96 pages spiralbound

3166   Directory for Exceptional Children: 14th Edition

Porter Sargent Publishers
11 Beacon Street
Boston, MA   02108   617-523-1670
                                        800-342-7470
                                    FAX 617-523-1021
                        http://www.portersargent.com
                        e-mail: info@portersargent.com
Dan McKeever, Senior Editor
John Yonce, General Manager
Leslie Weston, Production Editor

A comprehensive survey of 3000 schools, facilities
and organizations across the USA, serving children
and young adults with developmental, emotional,
physical and medical disabilities. An invaluable aid to
parents and professionals. *$75.00*

> *1056 pages   trienniel*
> *ISBN 0-875581-41-2*

3167   Dr. Larry Silver's Advice to Parents on AD-HD

Learning Disabilities Association of America
4156 Library Road
Pittsburgh, PA   15234   412-341-1515
                                    FAX 412-344-0224
                              http://www.ldanatl.org
                              e-mail: ldanatl@usaor.net
Dr. Larry B Silver, Author

Offers information on parenting children with Attention Deficit and Hyperactivity Disorders. *$19.95*

**3168   Early Childhood Special Education: Birth to
Three**

Connecticut Assoc. for Children and Adults with LD
25 Van Zant Street
East Norwalk, CT   06855   203-838-5010
                                    FAX 203-866-6108
                              http://www.CACLD.org
J Jordan, Author

Resources on early childhood education.

3169   Educating Deaf Children Bilingually

Harris Communications
15155 Technology Drive
Eden Prairie, MN   55344   952-906-1180
                                         800-825-9187
                                    FAX 952-906-1099
                                    TDY:952-906-1198
                              http://www.harriscomm.com
                              e-mail: mail@harriscomm.com
Bill Williams, National Sales Manager

Perspectives and practices in educating deaf children
with the goal of grade-level achievement in fluency in
the languages of the deaf community, general society
and of the home are discussed in this book. *$19.95*

> *262 pages*

**3170   Educating Students Who Have Visual
Impairments with Other Disabilities**

Brookes Publishing Company
PO Box 10624
Baltimore, MD   21285   410-337-9580
                                         800-638-3775
                                    FAX 410-337-8539
                              http://www.info@pbrookes.com
                              e-mail: sales@pbrookes.com
Sharon Z Sacks PhD, Editor
Rosanne K Silberman EdD, Editor

This text provides techniques for facilitating functional learning in students with a wide range of visual
impairments and multiple disabilities. *$49.95*

> *528 pages   Paperback*
> *ISBN 1-557662-80-0*

**3171   Effective Instructions for Students withLearning
Difficulties**

Books on Special Children
PO Box 305
Congers, NY   10920   845-638-1236
                                    FAX 845-638-0847
                              http://www.boscbooks.com/
                              e-mail: irene@boscbooks.com
PT Cegelka, Author

The book is designed to help teach students and prevent academic failure. Overview of effective education: identify; measure; then manage behavior.
Classroom structure to meet individual needs and
teach reading, spelling written language skills, math.
How to plan transition to adulthood. Each chapter has
objectives outline and summary charts and forms.
$68.00

> *469 pages   softcover*
> *ISBN 0-205162-68-1*

3172   Effective Teaching Methods for Autistic Children

Charles C Thomas Publisher
2600 S 1st Street
Springfield, IL   62704   217-789-8980
                                         800-258-8980
                                    FAX 217-789-9130
                              e-mail: books@ccthomas.com
Rosalind C Oppenheim, Author

> *124 pages   Hardcover $30.95*
> *ISBN 0-398028-58-3*

3173   Emergence-Labeled Autistic

Therapro
225 Arlington Street
Framingham, MA   01702   508-872-9494
                                         800-257-5376
                                    FAX 508-875-2062
                              http://www.theraproducts.com
                              e-mail: info@theraproducts.com
*Temple Grandin, PhD as told by Margaret
Scariano, Author*

In this autobiography, Temple tells the story of her emergence from her fear-gripped, autistic childhood to becoming a successful professional. This astonishing, true story will give new insight into autism and show it from the 'inside'.

180 pages

3174   Emergence: Labeled Autistic

Academic Therapy Publications
20 Commercial Boulevard
Novato, CA   94949   415-883-3314
                                      800-422-7249
                                 FAX 415-883-3720
              http://www.academictherapy.com
              e-mail: sales@academictherapy.com
Temple Grandin and Margaret M. Scariano, Author
Anna Arena, President

A recovered autistic individual shares her history, and includes her own suggestions for parents and professionals. Technical Appendix, which overviews recent treatment methods and more. *$13.00*

184 pages
ISBN 0-878795-24-3

3175   Endangered Minds: Why Our Children Don't Think

Learning Disabilities Association of America
4156 Library Road
Pittsburgh, PA   15234   412-341-1515
                                 FAX 412-344-0224
                    http://www.ldanatl.org
                    e-mail: ldanatl@usaor.net

J Healy, Author

$13.00

3176   Essential ASL: The Fun, Fast, and Simple Way to Learn American Sign Language

Harris Communications
15155 Technology Drive
Eden Prairie, MN   55344   952-906-1180
                                      800-825-6758
                                 FAX 952-906-1099
                               TDY:952-906-1198
Martin LA Sternberg, EdD, Author

This pocket version contains more than 700 frequently used signs with 2,000 easy-to-follow illustrations. Also, 50 common phrases. *$7.95*

322 pages   Paperback

3177   Evaluation of the Association for Children with Learning Disabilities

National Center for State Courts
300 Newport Avenue
Williamsburg, VA   23185   757-253-2000
                                 FAX 757-220-0449
                    http://www.ncsonline.org
                    e-mail: webmaster@ncsc.dni.us

Final report on children with learning disabilities training institute. *$6.96*

3178   Family Communication

Harris Communications
15155 Technology Drive
Eden Prairie, MN   55344   952-906-1180
                                      800-825-6758
                                 FAX 952-906-1099
                               TDY:952-906-1198
                    http://www.harriscomm.com

A broad range of topics that affect communication in the home and classroom, including support for families, and ways parents and school can work together toward language literacy development. *$10.95*

62 pages

3179   Family Guide to Assistive Technology

Federation for Children with Special Needs
1135 Tremont Street
Boston, MA   02120   617-236 7210
                                      800-331-0688
                                 FAX 617-572-2094
                       http://www.fcsn.org
                       e-mail: fcsninfo@fcsn.org
Richard J Robison, Executive Director

This guide is intended to help parents learn more about assistive technology and how it can help their children. Includes tips for getting started, ideas about how and where to look for funding and contact information for software and equipment. *$10.00*

143 pages

3180   Family Place in Cyberspace

Alliance for Technology Access
1304 Southpoint Boulevard
Petaluma, CA   94954   707-778-3011
                                 FAX 707-765-2080
                       http://www.ataccess.org
                       e-mail: atainfo@ataccess.org
Mary Lester, Executive Director

Includes We Can Play, a variety of suggestions and ideas for making play activities accessible to all. Available in English and Spanish. Access in Transition. Information and resources for students with disabilities who are facing the transition from public school to the next stage in life. Includes links and resources. Assistive Technology in K-12 Schools gives a range of information about integrating assistive technology into schools.

3181   Fine Motor Skills in Children with Downs Syndrome: A Guide for Parents and Professionals

Therapro
225 Arlington Street
Framingham, MA   01702   508-872-9494
                                      800-257-5376
                                 FAX 508-875-2062
                    http://www.theraproducts.com
                    e-mail: info@theraproducts.com
Maryanne Bruni B.Sc., OT(C), Author

Fine motor skills are the hand skills that allow us to do the things like hold a pencil, cut with scissors, eat with a fork, and use a computer. This practical guide shows parents and professionals how to help children with Downs syndrome from infancy to 12 years improve fine motor functioning. Includes many age appropriate activities for home or school, with step by step instructions and photos. Invaluable for families and professionals.

3182 Fine Motor Skills in the Classroom: Screening & Remediation Strategies

Therapro
225 Arlington Street
Framingham, MA 01702   508-872-9494
                                 800-257-5376
                            FAX 508-875-2062
                    http://www.theraproducts.com
                    e-mail: info@theraproducts.com
Jayne Berry, OTR/L, Author

The Give Yourself a Hand program, revised. Developed as a tool to facilitate consultation in the classroom. The manual consists of training modules, a screening to administer to an entire class, report formats for teachers and parents, and classroom and home remediation activities. The program is designed to include everyone involved in the education process and to make them aware of the opportunites offered by occupational therapy in the classroom.

96 pages

3183 Flying By the Seat of Your Pants: More Absurdities and Realities of Special Education

Peytral Publication
PO Box 1162
Minnetonka, MN 55345   952-949-8707
                                 877-739-8725
                            FAX 952-906-9777
                       http://www.peytral.com
                       e-mail: help@peytral.com
Michael F Giangreco, Author

In the sequel to Ants in His Pants, Giangreco continues to stimulate the reader to think differently about some of our current educational practices and raise questions about specific issues surrounding special education. Whether an educator, parent or advocate for persons with disabilities, you will smile, laugh aloud and ponder the hidden truths playfully captured in these carefully crafted cartoons. Transparencies may be created directly from the book. *$19.95*

126 pages
ISBN 1-890455-41-5

3184 For Parents and Professionals: Down Syndrome

LinguiSystems
3100 4th Avenue
East Moline, IL 61244
                                 800-776-4332
                            FAX 800-577-4555
                  http://www.linguisystems.com
                 e-mail: service@linguisystems.com
Linda Bowers, Owner
Rosemary Huisingh, Owner

This comprehensive resource gives you valuable information, helpful tips, and great activities to share with parents, teachers, and other caregivers. Packed with examples and activities, chapters cover: getting to know the child with Down syndrome; applying teaching and learning strategies, oral-motor and feeding skills, impact on overall communication skills, getting through the school years and more.

3185 Gross Motor Skills Children with Down Syndrome: A Guide For Parents and Professionals

Therapro
225 Arlington Street
Framingham, MA 01702   508-872-9494
                                 800-257-5376
                            FAX 508-875-2062
                    http://www.theraproducts.com
                    e-mail: info@theraproducts.com
Patricia C Winders, PT, Author

Children with Down syndrome master basic gross motor skills, everything from rolling over to running, just as their peers do, but may need additional help. This guide describes and illustrates more than 100 easy to follow activities for parents and professionals to practice with infants and children from birth to age six. Checklists and statistics allow readers to track, plan and maximize a child's progress.

3186 Guide for Parents on Hyperactivity in Children

Learning Disabilities Association of America
4156 Library Road
Pittsburgh, PA 15234   412-341-1515
                            FAX 412-344-0224
                       http://www.ldanatl.org
                    e-mail: ldanatl@usaor.net
Klaus K Minde, Author

Describes difficulties faced by a child with ADHD. Elaborates on types of management and ends with a section called 'A Day With a Hyperactive Child: Possible Problems'. *$2.00*

23 pages

3187 Guidelines and Recommended Practices for Individualized Family Service Plan

Association for the Care of Children's Health
7910 Woodmont Avenue
Bethesda, MD 20814
                            FAX 301-986-4553
B Johnson, Author

Presents a growing consensus about best practices for comprehensive family-centered early intervention services as required by Part H of the Individuals with Disabilities Education Act. *$15.00*

208 pages

3188 Handbook for Implementing Workshops for Siblings of Special Needs Children

Special Needs Project
324 State Street
Santa Barbara, CA 93105   805-964-8087
                                 800-333-6867
                            FAX 805-962-5087
                    e-mail: books@specialneeds.com
Donald Meyer, Author

Based on three years of professional experience working with siblings ages 8 through 13 and their parents, this handbook provides guidelines and technologies for those who wish to start and conduct workshops for siblings. *$40.00*

65 pages

3189 Handling the Young Child with Cerebral Palsy at Home

Therapro
225 Arlington Street
Framingham, MA   01702   508-872-9494
                                 800-257-5376
                          FAX 508-875-2062
                  http://www.theraproducts.com
                  e-mail: info@theraproducts.com
Nancie R Finnie, Author

This guide for parents remains a classic book on handling their cerebral palsied child during all activities of daily living. It has been said that its message is so important that it should be read by all those caring for such children including doctors, therapists, teachers and nurses. Many simple line drawings illustrate handling problems and solutions.

3rd Edition

3190 Help Build a Brighter Future: Children at Risk for LD in Child Care Centers

Learning Disabilities Association of America
4156 Library Road
Pittsburgh, PA   15234   412-341-1515
                          FAX 412-344-0224
                  http://www.ldanatl.org
                  e-mail: ldanatl@usaor.net

Offers information for parents and professionals caring for the learning disabled child. *$3.00*

3191 Help Me to Help My Child

Little Brown & Company
3 Center Plaza
Boston, MA   02108   617-227-0730
                          FAX 617-263-2871
Jill Bloom, Author

Contains nontechnical information on testing, advocacy, legal issues, instructional practices, and social-emotional development, as well as a resource list and bibliography.

ISBN 0-316099-82-1

3192 Help for the Hyperactive Child: A Good Sense Guide for Parents

Learning Disabilities Association of America
4156 Library Road
Pittsburgh, PA   15234   412-341-1515
                          FAX 412-344-0224
                  http://www.ldanatl.org
                  e-mail: ldanatl@usaor.net

A practical guide; offering parents of ADHD children alternatives to Ritalin. *$16.95*

3193 Help for the Learning Disabled Child

Slosson Educational Publications
538 Buffalo Road
East Aurora, NY   14052   888-756-7766
                                    800-828-4800
                          FAX 800-655-3840
                  http://www.slosson.com
                  e-mail: slosson@slosson.com
Lou Stewart, Author
Steven W Slosson, President
John Slosson, VP

An easy-to-read text describes observable behaviors, offers remediation techniques, materials, and specific test to assist in further diagnosis. *$38.00*

3194 Helping Young Writers Master the Craft

Brookline Books
PO Box 1047
Cambridge, MA   02238   617-868-0360
                                    800-666-2665
                          FAX 617-868-1772
                  e-mail: brooklinebks@delphi.com
K Harris, Author
S Graham, Author

Strategy instruction and self-regulation in the writing process.

3195 Helping Your Child Achieve in School

Academic Therapy Publications
20 Commercial Boulevard
Novato, CA   94949   415-883-3314
                                    800-422-7249
                          FAX 415-883-3720
                  http://www.apub.com
Betty Lou Kratoville, Editor

A wealth of simple and enjoyable at-home educational activities. Special emphasis is given to developing reading skills in primary-aged children and to building comprehension skills of middle-grade children. *$12.50*

264 pages
ISBN 0-878794-65-4

3196 Helping Your Child with Attention-Deficit Hyperactivity Disorder

Learning Disabilities Association of America
4156 Library Road
Pittsburgh, PA   15234   412-341-1515
                          FAX 412-344-0224
                  http://www.ldanatl.org
                  e-mail: ldanatl@usaor.net
M Fowler, Author

$12.95

3197 Helping Your Hyperactive Child

Connecticut Assoc. for Children and Adults with LD
25 Van Zant Street
East Norwalk, CT   06855   203-838-5010
                          FAX 203-866-6018
                  http://www.CACLD.org
John Taylor, Author

A large, comprehensive book for parents, covering everything from techniques pertaining to sibling rivalry to coping with marital stresses. Contains thorough discussions of various treatments: nutritional, medical and educational. Also is an excellent source of advice and information for parents of kids with ADHD. *$2195.00*

483 pages

3198 Hidden Child: Linwood Method for Reaching the Autistic Child

Therapro
225 Arlington Street
Framingham, MA   01702   508-872-9494
                                 800-257-5376
                             FAX 508-875-2062
                  http://www.theraproducts.com
                  e-mail: info@theraproducts.com
Jeanne Simmons and Sabine Oiski, PhD, Author

This book provides an explanation of autism, then a step-by-step analysis of the Linwood method of establishing relationships, patterning good behavior, overcoming compulsions, developing skills, and fostering social and emotional development. This guidebook for teachers and therapists also has a message for parents.

3199 Higher Education Services for Students with LD or ADD a Legal Guide

JKL Communications
PO Box 40157
Washington, DC   20016   202-223-5097
                             FAX 202-223-5096
                  http://www.lathamlaw.org
                  e-mail: plath3@his.com

$29.00

3200 How the Special Needs Brain Learns

Corwin Press
2455 Teller Road
Thousand Oaks, CA   91320   805-499-9734
                                 800-818-7243
                             FAX 805-499-5323
                  http://www.corwinpress.com
                  e-mail: order@corwinpress.com
David A Sousa, Author
Kimberly Gonzales, Marketing Director
Robb Clouse, Senior Acquisitions Editor

Research on the brain function of students with various learning challenges. Practical classroom activities and strategies, such as how to build self-esteem, how to work in groups, and strategies for engagement and retention. Focuses on the most commmon challenges to learning for many students. *$34.95*

248 pages
ISBN 0-761978-51-8

3201 How to Get Services by Being Assertive

Family Resource Center on Disabilities
20 E Jackson Boulevard
Chicago, IL   60604   312-939-3513
                             800-952-4199
                         FAX 312-939-7297
                         TDY:312-939-3519
Family Resource Center on Disabilities, Author

A manual that demonstrates positive assertiveness techniques for staffing, IEP meetings, due process hearings and other special education meetings. *$10.00*

100 pages

3202 How to Organize Your Child and Save Your Sanity

Learning Disabilities Association of America
4156 Library Road
Pittsburgh, PA   15234   412-341-1515
                             FAX 412-344-0224
                  http://www.ldanatl.org
                  e-mail: ldanatl@usaor.net
Brown/Connelly, Author

$3.00

3203 How to Organize an Effective Parent-Advocacy Group and Move Bureaucracies

Family Resource Center on Disabilities
20 E Jackson Boulevard
Chicago, IL   60604   312-939-3513
                             800-952-4199
                         FAX 312-939-7297
                         TDY:312-939-3519
Charlotte Desjardins, Author

A 100-page handbook that gives step-by-step directions for organizing parent support groups from scratch. *$10.00*

100 pages

3204 How to Own and Operate an Attention Deficit Disorder

Learning Disabilities Association of America
4156 Library Road
Pittsburgh, PA   15234   412-341-1515
                             FAX 412-344-0224
                  http://www.ldanatl.org
                  e-mail: ldanatl@usaor.net

Clear, informative and sensitive introduction to ADHD. Packed with practical things to do at home and school, the author offers her insight as a professional and mother of a son with ADHD. *$8.95*

43 pages

3205 Hyperactive Children Grown Up

Guilford Publications
72 Spring Street
New York, NY   10012   212-431-9800
                             800-365-7006
                         FAX 212-966-6708
                  http://www.guilford.com
                  e-mail: info@guilford.com
Gabrielle Weiss, Author
Lily Trokenberg Hechtman, Author

Long considered a standard in the field, this book explores what happens to hyperactive children when they grow into adulthood. Updated and expanded, this second edition describes new developments in ADHD, current psychological treatments of ADHD, contemporary perspectives on the use of medications, and assessment, diagnosis and treatment of ADHD adults. *$26.00*

473 pages   Paperback
ISBN 0-898625-96-3

3206   Hyperactivity, Attention Deficits, and School Failure: Better Ways

Learning Disabilities Association of America
4156 Library Road
Pittsburgh, PA   15234   412-341-1515
FAX 412-344-0224
http://www.ldanatl.org
e-mail: ldanatl@usaor.net

WG Crook, Author

$6.00

3207   If it is to Be, It is Up to Me to Do it!

AVKO Educational Research Foundation
3084 W Willard Road
Clio, MI   48420   810-686-9283
FAX 810-686-1101
http://www.avko.org/upto.htm
e-mail: DonMcCabe@aol.com

Don McCabe, Author
Don McCabe, Research Director

This is a tutors' book that can be used by anyone who can read this paragraph. It also contains the student's response pages. It is especially good to use to help an older child or adult. It uses the same basic format as Sequential Spelling I except it has the sentences to be read along with the word to be spelled. The students get to correct their own mistakes immediately. This way they quickly learn that mistakes are opportunities to learn. *$19.95*

96 pages
ISBN 1-564007-42-1

3208   In Their Own Way: Discovering and Encouraging Your Child's Learning

Special Needs Project
324 State Street
Santa Barbara, CA   93101   805-962-8087
800-333-6867
FAX 805-962-5087
e-mail: books@specialneeds.com
Dr. Thomas Armstrong, Author

An unconventional teacher has written a very popular book for a wide audience. It's customary to be categorical about youngsters who learn conventionally/are normal/are OK — and those who don't/who need special ed/are learning disabled. *$8.37*

224 pages   Paperback

3209   In Time and with Love

Special Needs Project
324 State Street
Santa Barbara, CA   93105   805-962-8087
800-333-6867
FAX 805-962-5087
e-mail: books@specialnedds.com

Play and parenting techniques for children with disabilities. *$12.95*

19 pages

3210   In the Mind's Eye

Prometheus Books
59 John Glenn Drive
Amherst, NY   14228   716-691-0133
800-421-0351
FAX 716-691-0137
http://www.prometheusbooks.com
e-mail: mrogers@prometheusmail.com
TR West, Author
Marcia Rogers, Sales Manager

Visual thinkers, gifted people with learning difficulties, computer images, and the ironies of creativity. Be concerned with results, not uniformity of learning style. *$28.00*

397 pages
ISBN 1-573921-55-6

3211   Inclusion: 450 Strategies for Success

Peytral Publication
PO Box 1162
Minnetonka, MN   55345   952-949-8707
877-739-8725
FAX 952-906-9777
http://www.peytral.com
e-mail: help@peytral.com
Peggy A Hammeken, Author

This perennial best seller is written for general and special educators in inclusive education settings. Topics include step-by-step guidelines to help develop and improve the inclusive setting, hundreds of practical teacher tested ideas, adaptations, and modifications covering both curriculum and instruction. Many reproducibles. General and special educators, ESL, Chapter one. *$23.95*

190 pages
ISBN 1-890455-25-3

3212   Inclusion: A Practical Guide for Parents

Peytral Publication
PO Box 1162
Minnetonka, MN   55345   952-949-8707
877-739-8725
FAX 952-906-9777
http://www.peytral.com
e-mail: help@peytral.com
Lorraine O Moore, Author

This comprehensive resource answers parent questions related to inclusive education and provides the tools to promote and enhance their child's learning. This publication includes practical strategies, exercises, questionnaires and do-it-yourself graphs to assist parents with their child's learning. Beneficial for parents, psychologists, social workers, and educators. *$19.95*

192 pages
ISBN 0-964427-13-3

3213 Inclusion: An Essential Guide for the Paraprofessional

Peytral Publication
PO Box 1162
Minnetonka, MN   55345   952-949-8707
                                877-739-8725
                         FAX 952-906-9777
                         http://www.peytral.com
                         e-mail: help@peytral.com
Peggy A Hammeken, Author

This practical, simple, and easy-to-use resource provides ready-to-use information, ideas and strategies which can be put into practice immediately. Topics include special education background information, the paraprofessional's role, ideas to help with scheduling, communications, substitute lesson plans and monitoring of students. Hundreds of ideas and strategies for specific subject areas will help the paraprofessional in the classroom. Excellent training tool. *$21.95*

142 pages
ISBN 0-964427-16-8

3214 Inclusion: Strategies for Working with Young Children

Peytral Publication
PO Box 1162
Minnetonka, MN   55345   952-949-8707
                                877-739-8725
                         FAX 952-906-9777
                         http://www.peytral.com
                         e-mail: help@peytral.com
Lorraine O Moore, Author

Developed for early childhood through grade two educators and parents, this comprehensive developmentally focused publication focuses on the whole child. Hundreds of developmentally-based strategies help young children learn about feelings, empathy, resolving conflicts, communication, large/small motor development, prereading, writing and math strategies are included, plus much more. Excellent training tool. *$21.95*

185 pages
ISBN 0-964427-13-3

3215 Individual Education Plan: Involved Effective Parents

PEAK Parent Center
611 N Weber
Colorado Springs, CO   80903   719-531-9400
                                  800-284-0251
                           FAX 719-531-9452
                           TDY:719-531-5403
                           http://www.peakparent.org
                           e-mail: info@peakparent.org
Alison B Seyler, Barbara E Buswell, Author

An essential tool for both families and educators as they develop and implement Individual Education plans. Explains what occurs before, during, and after the development of an IEP, and provides a continuity process for transferring information from year to year. Includes innovative forms for parents and educators. Complements the IEP video. *$10.00*

3216 Innovations in Family Support for People with Learning Disabilities

Brookes Publishing Company
PO Box 10624
Baltimore, MD   21285   410-337-9580
                               800-638-3775
                         FAX 410-337-8539
                         http://www.pbrookes.com
                         e-mail: custerv@pbrookes.com
Barbara Coyne Cutler, EdD, Author

272 pages   Paperback $22.00
ISBN 1-870335-15-5

3217 Interventions for ADHD: Treatment in Developmental Context

Guilford Publications
72 Spring Street
New York, NY   10012   212-431-9800
                              800-365-7006
                        FAX 212-966-6708
                        http://www.guilford.com
                        e-mail: info@guilford.com
Phyllis Anne Teeter, Author

This book takes a lifespan perspective on ADHD, dispelling the notion that it is only a disorder of childhood and enabling clinicians to develop effective and appropriate interventions for preschoolers, school-age children, adolescents, and adults. The author reviews empirically-and clinically-based treatment interventions including psychopharmacology, behavior management, parent/teacher training, and self-management techniques. *$40.00*

378 pages   Hardcover
ISBN 1-572303-84-0

3218 Invisible Disability: Understanding Learning Disabilities in the Context of Health & Edu.

Learning Disabilities Association of America
4156 Library Road
Pittsburgh, PA   15234   412-341-1515
                          FAX 412-344-0224
                          http://www.ldanatl.org
                          e-mail: ldanatl@usaor.net
Pasquale Accardo, Author

$9.00
ISBN 0-937846-39-2

3219 It's Your Turn Now

Harris Communications
15155 Technology Drive
Eden Prairie, MN   55344   952-906-1180
                                            800-825-6758
                                            FAX 952-906-1099
                                            TDY:952-906-1198
                                            http://www.harriscomm.com
                                            e-mail: mail@harriscomm.com
Cindy Bailes, Author
Susan Searls, Author
Jean Slobodzian, Author
Jana Staton, Author

Using dialogue journals with deaf students help the students learn to enjoy communicating ideas, information, and feelings through reading and writing. The book reviews teacher's questions and answers, frustrations and successes. *$14.95*

130 pages

3220 Key Concepts in Personal Development

Marsh Media
8082 Ward Parkway Plaza
Kansas City, MO   64114   816-523-1059
                                            800-821-3303
                                            FAX 866-333-7421
                                            http://www.marshmedia.com
                                            e-mail: info@marshmedia.com
Joan Marsh, President
Liz Sweeney, Editorial Assistant

Our videos, books, and teaching guides bring character education to the classrom. These kits are invaluable aids in teaching everyday values like honesty, anger control, trustworthiness, perseverance, understanding and respect. They help you prepare youngsters to meet challenges and greet opportunities with skill and optimism.

3221 Ladders to Literacy: A Kindergarten Activity Book

Brookes Publishing Company
PO Box 10624
Baltimore, MD   21285   410-337-9580
                                            800-638-3775
                                            FAX 410-337-8539
                                            http://www.info@pbrookes.com
                                            e-mail: sales@pbrookes.com
Rollanda E O'Connor, PhD, et. al., Author

The kindergarten activities are designed for higher developmental levels, focusing on preacademic skills, early literacy development, and early reading development. Goals and scaffolding are more intense as children learn to recognize letters, match sounds with letters, and develop phonological awareness and the alphabetic principle. *$32.16*

272 pages   Spiral bound
ISBN 1-557663-18-1

3222 Ladders to Literacy: A Preschool Activity Book

Brookes Publishing Company
PO Box 10624
Baltimore, MD   21285   410-337-9580
                                            800-638-3775
                                            FAX 410-337-8539
                                            http://www.info@pbrookes.com
                                            e-mail: sales@pbrookes.com
Angela Notari-Syverson, PhD, et. al., Author

The preschool activity book targets basic preliteracy skills such as orienting children toward printed materials and teaching letter sounds. It also provides professionals (and parents) with developmentally appropriate and ecologically valid assessment procedures — informal observation guidelines, structured performance samples, and a checklist — for measuring children's learning. *$34.96*

352 pages   Spiral bound
ISBN 1-557663-17-3

3223 Landmark Study Skills Guide

Landmark School
429 Hale Street
Prides Crossing, MA   01965   978-236-3216
                                            FAX 978-927-7268
                                            http://www.landmarkschool.org
                                            e-mail: outreach@landmarkschool.org
Joan Sedita, Author
Dan Ahearn, Program Director
Trish Newhall, Associate Director
Kathryn Frye, Administrative Assistant

Provides practical teaching strategies for teachers and parents working with students who are unable to organize themselves, take adequate notes, use their textbooks efficiently or study on a regular basis. Includes chapters on organizing, main ideas, note-taking, summarizing, textbook skills, test preparation, and report-writing skills. Sample assignments and How To lists for students to follow are included throughout. *$30.00*

125 pages
ISBN 0-962411-90-6

3224 Language-Related Learning Disabilities

Brookes Publishing Company
PO Box 10624
Baltimore, MD   21285   410-337-9580
                                            800-638-3775
                                            FAX 410-337-8539
                                            http://www.pbrookes.com
                                            e-mail: custerv@pbrookes.com
Adele Gerber, MA, Author

384 pages   Paperback $47.00
ISBN 1-557660-53-0

3225 Learning Difficulties and Emotional Problems

Temeron Books
Bellingham, WA   98227
                                            FAX 360-738-4016
                                            http://www.temerondetselig.com
                                            e-mail: temeron@telusplanet.net
Roy Brown and Maurice Chazan , Editors, Author

International authorities shed light on recent research. *$18.95*

> *239 pages Paperback*
> *ISBN 0-920490-89-1*

3226 Learning Disabilities & ADHD: A Family Guide to Living and Learning Together

John Wiley & Sons
10475 Crosspoint Road
Indianapolis, IN   46256
201-748-6000
FAX 800-597-3299
http://www.wiley.com
Betty B Osman, Author

> *228 pages paperback $14.95*
> *ISBN 0-471155-10-1*

3227 Learning Disabilities A to Z

Simon and Schuster
PO Box 11071
Des Moines, IA   50336
515-284-6751
800-223-2348
FAX 515-284-2607
http://www.simonandschuster.com
Smith, Corinne and Lisa Strick, Author

Brings the best of recent research and educational experience to parents, teachers and caregivers who are responsible for children with information processing problems. Corinne Smith and Lisa Strick provide a comprehensive guide to the causes, indentification and treatment of learning disabilities. You will learn how these subtle neurological disorders can have a major impact on a child's development, both in and out of school. *$25.00*

> *416 pages*
> *ISBN 0-684827-38-7*

3228 Learning Disabilities: Lifelong Issues

Brookes Publishing Company
PO Box 10624
Baltimore, MD   21285
410-337-9580
800-638-3775
FAX 410-337-8539
http://www.info@pbrookes.com
e-mail: sales@pbrookes.com
Shirley C Cramer, Editor
William Ellis, Editor

Based on the diverse, representative viewpoints of educators, practitioners, policy makers, and adults with learning disabilities, this volume sets forth an agenda for improving the educational and ultimately, social and economic, futures of people with learning disabilities. *$36.00*

> *352 pages Paperback*
> *ISBN 1-557662-40-1*

3229 Learning Disabilities: Literacy, and Adult Education

Brookes Publishing Company
PO Box 10624
Baltimore, MD   21285
410-337-9580
800-638-3775
FAX 410-337-8539
http://www.info@pbrookes.com
e-mail: sales@pbrookes.com
Susan A Vogel PhD, Editor
Stephen Reder PhD, Editor

This book focuses on adults with severe learning disabilities and the educators who work with them. *$49.95*

> *400 pages Paperback*
> *ISBN 1-557663-47-5*

3230 Learning Disabilities: Theories, Diagnosis and Teaching Strategies

Houghton-Mifflin
222 Berkeley Street
Boston, MA   02116
617-351-5468
FAX 617-351-1119
http://www.houghtonmifflinbooks.com
J Lerner, Author

Theories on learning disabilities.

> *ISBN 0-395796-85-7*

3231 Learning Journey

Temeron Books
Bellingham, WA   98227
FAX 360-738-4016
http://www.temerondetselig.com
e-mail: temeron@telusplanet.net
Malcom Jeffreys and Robert Gall, Author

Enhancing lifelong learning and self-determination for people with special needs, this book presents a detailed view of emerging trends and models of service that promise a better future in terms of self-determination for the developmentally disabled. *$18.95*

> *204 pages Paperback*
> *ISBN 1-550591-22-3*

3232 Let's Learn About Deafness

Harris Communications
15155 Technology Drive
Eden Prairie, MN   55344
952-906-1180
800-825-6758
FAX 952-906-1099
TDY:952-906-1198
http://www.harriscomm.com
Rachel Stone, Author

Hands-on activities, games, bulletin board displays, surveys, quizzes, craft projects, and skits used to help teachers and their students become more aware of deafness and its implications are included in this book. *$16.95*

> *82 pages*

3233 Life Beyond the Classroom: Transition Strategies for Young People with Disabilities

Books on Special Children
PO Box 305
Congers, NY 10920
845-638-1236
FAX 845-638-0847
http://www.boscbooks.com/
e-mail: irene@boscbooks.com
P Wehman, Author

Community living, leisure activities, personal relationships as well as employment. Planning with community, individualized, state and local governments, curriculum for transition, job development and placement, independent living plans for people with mild MR, severe disabilities, LD, physical and health impairments, and traumatic brain injury. *$59.95*

533 pages   softcover
ISBN 1-557662-48-7

3234 Living with a Learning Disability

Southern Illinois University Press
PO Box 3697
Carbondale, IL   62902
618-453-2281
800-346-2680
FAX 800-346-2681
http://www.siu.edu/nsiupress
e-mail: townsend@siu.edu
Barbara Cordoni, Author
Larry Townsend, Director Sales/Marketing

This book presents the kinds of adaptations needed for educating, communicating with, and parenting the child, the adolescent, and the young adult with learning disabilities. Deals with such issues as relationships, the legal process, implications for the professional, juvenile delinquency, and the future.

17.5 pages
ISBN 0-809316-68-4

3235 Making Sense of Sensory Integration

Therapro
225 Arlington Street
Framingham, MA   01702
508-872-9494
800-257-5376
FAX 508-875-2062
http://www.theraproducts.com
e-mail: info@theraproducts.com
Koomar, Szklut, Cermak and Silver, Author

A discussion for parents and caregivers about sensory integration (SI), how it affects children throughout their lives, how diagnosis is made, appropriate treatment, recognizing red flags, and how SI difficulties affect child and family in their everyday lives. Informative 33 page book included. 75 minute audio tape.

Audio Tape

3236 McGraw Hill Companies

2 Penn Plaza
New York, NY   10003
212-904-5448
FAX 212-904-5974
http://www.mcgraw-hill.com
e-mail: elizabeth_schacht@mcgraw-hill.com
Corrective reading program, helps students master the essential decoding and comprehension skills.

3237 Me! A Curriculum for Teaching Self-Esteem Through an Interest Center

Connecticut Assoc. for Children and Adults with LD
25 Van Zant Street
East Norwalk, CT   06855
203-838-5010
FAX 203-866-6108
http://www.CACLD.org
e-mail: cacld@juno.com
Jo Ellen Hartline, Author
Marie Armstrong, Information Specialist

A curriculum for the professional. *$18.50*

$2.50 shipping

3238 Meeting the Needs of Students of ALL Abilities

Corwin Press
2455 Teller Road
Thousand Oaks, CA   91320
805-499-9734
800-818-7243
FAX 805-499-5323
http://www.corwinpress.com
e-mail: order@corwinpress.com
Collleen Capper, Elise Frattura, Maureen Keyes, Author
Kimberly Gonzales, Marketing Director
Robb Clouse, Senior Acquisitions Editor

Step-by-step handbook offers practical strategies for administrators, teachers, policymakers and parents who want to shift from costly special learning programs for a few students, to excellent educational services for all students and teachers, and adapting curriculum and instruction. *$32.95*

224 pages
ISBN 0-761975-01-2

3239 Misunderstood Child

Connecticut Assoc. for Children and Adults with LD
25 Van Zant Street
East Norwalk, CT   06855
203-838-5010
FAX 203-866-6108
http://www.CACLD.org
LB Silver, Author

A guide for parents of learning disabled children. *$8.95*

3240 Moving Violations, A Memoir: War Zones, Wheelchairs, and Declarations of Independence

Books on Special Children
PO Box 305
Congers, NY   10920
845-638-1236
FAX 845-638-0847
http://www.boscbooks.com/
e-mail: irene@boscbooks.com
J Hockenberry, Author

He is a newspaper man, out to get his story, wherever. What sets him apart is his inability to move his legs. He does what he must in a wheelchair. This is his remarkable story, told with humor and without self-pity. *$26.95*

371 pages   hardcover
ISBN 0-786860-78-2

3241 Negotiating the Special Education Maze 3rd Edition

Woodbine House
6510 Bells Mill Road
Bethesda, MD   20817   301-897-3570
                           800-843-7323
                       FAX 301-897-5838
              http://www.woodbinehouse.com
              e-mail: info@woodbinehouse.com

Winifred Anderson, Author
Stephen Chitwood, Author
Deidre Hayden, Author

Now in its third edition, Negotiating the Special Education Maze isone of the best tools available to parents and teachers for developing an effective special education program for their child or student. Every step is explained, from eligibility and evaluation to the Individualized Education Program and beyond. *$16.95*

264 pages   Paperback 7x10
ISBN 0-933149-72-7

3242 New Language of Toys

Woodbine House
6510 Bells Mill Road
Bethesda, MD   20817   301-897-3570
                           800-843-7323
                       FAX 301-897-5838
              http://www.woodbinehouse.com
              e-mail: info@woodbinehouse.com

Sue Schwartz PhD, Author
Joan E Heller Miller EdM, Author

This revised and updated edition presents a fun, hands-on approach to developing communication skills in children with disabilities using everyday toys. There's a fresh assortment of toys and books, as well as newe chapters on computer technology and language learning, videotapes and television. *$16.95*

289 pages   Paperback 7x10
ISBN 0-933149-73-5

3243 No One to Play with: The Social Side of Learning Disabilities

Connecticut Assoc. for Children and Adults with LD
25 Van Zant Street
East Norwalk, CT   06855   203-838-5010
                            FAX 203-866-6108
                   http://www.CACLD.org
                   e-mail: cacld@juno.com

Betty Osman, Author
Marie Armstrong, Information Specialist

Your child suffers from a learning disability and you have read reams on how to improve on her academic skills and now want to address his or her social needs. *$13.00*

$2.50 shipping

3244 Nobody's Perfect: Living and Growing with Children who Have Special Needs

Books on Special Children
PO Box 305
Congers, NY   10920   845-638-1236
                       FAX 845-638-0847
              http://www.boscbooks.com/
              e-mail: irene@boscbooks.com

NB Miller, Author

Study of four families with children who have special needs. How they all adapted in surviving, how they care for the child, family, parents and siblings. How families react and relate. What it is like in community and extended family? Basic issues dicussed: self-esteem, separating parent from the adult with special needs and other issues. *$24.00*

307 pages   softcover
ISBN 1-557661-43-X

3245 Optimizing Special Education: How Parents Can Make a Difference

Insight Books
233 Spring Street
New York, NY   10013   212-620-8000
                           800-221-9369
                       FAX 212-807-1047
                http://www.plenum.com
                e-mail: info@plenum.com

N Wilson, Author

The author shows families how to use education laws to increase services or change services to suit a child's needs. Book contains personal anecdotes and balanced viewpoint of parent and professional relationships. *$26.50*

300 pages
ISBN 0-306443-23-6

3246 Out of the Mouths of Babes: Discovering the Developmental Significance of the Mouth

Therapro
225 Arlington Street
Framingham, MA   01702   508-872-9494
                             800-257-5376
                         FAX 508-875-2062
               http://www.theraproducts.com
               e-mail: info@theraproducts.com

Frick, Frick, Oetter and Richter, Author

Help children who have difficulty with focusing, staying alert, or being calm with these simple techniqes and activities. Learn how behavior is affected by suck/swallow/breathe (SSB) synchrony with suggestions for correcting specific problems. This informal writing style and many illustrations make it a great resource for parents, teachers and therapists.

3247 Parent Manual

Federation for Children with Special Needs
1135 Tremont Street
Boston, MA   02120   617-236-7210
                         800-331-0688
                     FAX 617-572-2094
                     TDY:617-236-7210
                http://www.fcsn.org
                e-mail: fcsninfo@fcsn.org

Richard J Robison, Executive Director

Outlines parents' and children's rights in special education as guaranteed by Chapter 766, the Massachusetts special education law, and the Individuals with Disabilities Education Act (IDEA), the federal special education law *$ 25.00*

75 pages

3248 Parenting Children with Special Needs

AGC/United Learning
1560 Sherman Avenue
Evanston, IL 60201

800-328-6700
FAX 847-328-6706
http://www.agcunitedlearning.com
e-mail: info@agcunited.com

Bill Wagonseller, Author
Jim McColl, VP Sales

This program deals exclusively with the subject of parenting children with mental or physical disabilities. Particular emphasis is placed on children from infancy through early childhood. The content includes important topics such as: Birth and diagnosis of a child with disabilities Impact on the family system Psychological stages that most parents of children with disabilities will experience Importance of early intervention programs. *$95.00*

3249 Parenting to Make a Difference: Your One to Four Year-Old

Therapro
225 Arlington Street
Framingham, MA 01702

508-872-9494
800-257-5376
FAX 508-875-2062
http://www.theraproducts.com
e-mail: info@theraproducts.com

Brenda Hussey-Gardner, MA, MPH, Author

Covers twelve key topics to help parents foster the developmental growth of their young children.

3250 Physical Side of Learning

Therapro
225 Arlington Street
Framingham, MA 01702

508-872-9494
800-257-5376
FAX 508-875-2062
http://www.theraproducts.com
e-mail: info@theraproducts.com

Leela C Zion, Author

Assist preschool, elementary and special children with academic subjects by utilizing simple physical activities that are fun, easy to understand, and perform, all of which are clearly illustrated in this book. Explains the connection between movement/perception and learning, with special attention to promoting body awareness, directionality, balance, body concept, self-esteem and body mastery in general. Help prepare children for success in school through physical activities.

3251 Play Therapy

Books on Special Children
PO Box 305
Congers, NY 10920

845-638-1236
FAX 845-638-0847
http://www.boscbooks.com/
e-mail: irene@boscbooks.com

KJ O'Connor, Author

Leading authorities present various theoretical models of play therapy treatment and application. Case studies on how various treatments are applied. *$44.95*

416 pages hardcover
ISBN 0-471106-38-0

3252 Positive Self-Talk for Children

Books on Special Children
PO Box 305
Congers, NY 10920

845-638-1236
FAX 845-638-0847
http://www.boscbooks.com/
e-mail: irene@boscbooks.com

D Bloch, Author

This book teaches positive talk and ideas to achieve positive self-esteem. Use this as a refererence in specific situations: ie: fears on 1st day of school, doctor's visit. Covers cases, includes specific dialogue. *$12.95*

331 pages softcover
ISBN 0-553351-98-2

3253 Practical Parent's Handbook on Teaching Children with Learning Disabilities

Charles C Thomas Publisher
2600 S 1st Street
Springfield, IL 62704

217-789-8980
800-258-8980
FAX 217-789-9130
http://www.ccthomas.com
e-mail: books@ccthomas.com

Shelby Holley, Author

Helps children who learn differently and who have been failing or underachieving in school by enabling adults with no previous teaching experience to design and implement an effective remedial program. Helps parents make realistic changes in the physical and emotional environment at home and at school, gives simple objective tests that show what a child knows and what he needs to learn and shows how to use the test findings. *$65.95*

308 pages Cloth
ISBN 0-398059-03-9

3254 Raising Your Child to be Gifted

Brookline Books
PO Box 1047
Cambridge, MA 02238

617-868-0360
800-666-2665
FAX 617-868-1772

Dr. James R Campbell, Author

Moving beyond the usual genetic eplanations for giftedness, Dr. James Campbell presents powerful evidence that it is parental involvement- very specific methods of working with and nurturing a child which increases the child's chances of being gifted. *$19.95*

275 pages
ISBN 1-571290-00-1

3255 Reading Writing & Rage: The Terrible Price Paid By Victims of School Failure

RWR Press
16800 Adlon Road
Encino, CA   91436   818-784-6561
                                              FAX 818-906-2158
                              e-mail: dotrwr@earthlink.net
Dorothy Ungerleider, Author

Offers the story of seeking help through the words and perceptions of one learning disabled teen, his parents, teachers and professionals. It reveals an often over-looked source of potential violence: pent-up rage from feeling powerless and misunderstood, school failure and ineffective interventions. *$19.95*

> *219 pages   2nd Ed. 1996*
> *ISBN 0-965025-20-9*

3256 Right from the Start: Behavioral Intervention for Young Children with Autism: A Guide

Therapro
225 Arlington Street
Framingham, MA   01702   508-872-9494
                                              800-257-5376
                                         FAX 508-875-2062
                          http://www.theraproducts.com
                          e-mail: info@theraproducts.com
Mary Jane Weiss, PhD,BCBA & Sandra Harris, PhD, Author

This informative and user-friendly guide helps parents and service providers explore programs that use early intensive behavioral intervention for young children with autism and related disorders. Within these programs, many children improve in intellectual, social and adaptive functioning, enabling them to move on to regular elementary and preschools. Benefits all children, but primarily useful for children age five and younger.

> *215 pages*

3257 SMARTS: A Study Skills Resource Guide

Connecticut Assoc. for Children and Adults with LD
25 Van Zant Street
East Norwalk, CT   06855   203-838-5010
                                         FAX 203-866-6108
                              http://www.CACLD.org
                              e-mail: cacld@juno.com
Susan Custer, Author
Marie Armstrong, Information Specialist

A comprehensive teachers handbook of activities to help students develop study skills. *$20.50*

> *$2.50 shipping*

3258 School-Based Home Developmental PE Program

Therapro
225 Arlington Street
Framingham, MA   01702   508-872-9494
                                              800-257-5376
                                         FAX 508-875-2062
                          http://www.theraproducts.com
                          e-mail: info@theraproducts.com
Barbara Wood, Author

A wire bound flip book. Comprehensive developmental physical education program indentifies and improves motor ability right down to the specific sensory and perceptual motor areas for children. Has what you need: assessment; parent involvement; understandable directions; examples; and sample letters to parents. Includes fun sheets that parents/professionals can use with children. Activities are for vestibular integration, body awareness, eye-hand coordination, and fine motor manipulation.

3259 Seeing Clearly

Therapro
225 Arlington Street
Framingham, MA   01702   508-872-9494
                                              800-257-5376
                                         FAX 508-875-2062
                          http://www.theraproducts.com
                          e-mail: info@theraproducts.com
Lois Hickman, MS, OTR FAOTA & Rebecca Hutchins, OD, Author

This booklet is chock-full of great information regarding vision andvisual perceptual problems and activities designed to improve visual skills of both adults and children. Begins with an overview of the development of vision with a checklist of warning signs of vision problems. 25 eye game activities are divided into those for Eye Movements, Suspended Ball, Chalkboard and Visualization (e.g. Pictures in your Mind, Spelling Comprehension, etc.)

3260 Sensory Defensiveness in Children Aged 2 to 12: An Intervention Guide for Parents/Caretakers

Therapro
225 Arlington Street
Framingham, MA   01702   508-872-9494
                                              800-257-5376
                                         FAX 508-875-2062
                          http://www.theraproducts.com
                          e-mail: info@theraproducts.com
Patricia Wilbarger and Julia Wilbarger, Author

This booklet defines and describes the symptoms and behaviors related to sensory defensiveness, treatment approaches and the rationale behind treatment strategies. Recommended for everyone administering the Wilbarger Protocol Pressure Program.

3261 Sensory Integration and the Child

Therapro
225 Arlington Street
Framingham, MA   01702   508-872-9494
                                              800-257-5376
                                         FAX 508-875-2062
                          http://www.theraproducts.com
                          e-mail: info@theraproducts.com
A Jean Ayres, PhD, Author

Designed to educate parents, students, and beginning therapists in sensory integration treatment.

3262 Sensory Integration: Theory and Practice

Therapro
225 Arlington Street
Framingham, MA   01702   508-872-9494
                                800-257-5376
                         FAX 508-875-2062
                    http://www.theraproducts.com
                    e-mail: info@theraproducts.com
Fisher, Murray, and Bundy, Author

This is the very latest in sensory integration theory and practice. The entire volume achieves an admirable balance between theory and practice, covering sensory integration theory, various kinds of sensory integrative dysfunction and comprehensive discussions of assessment, direct treatment, consultation and continuing research issues.

3263 Siblings of Children with Autism: A Guide for Families

Therapro
225 Arlington Street
Framingham, MA   01702   508-872-9494
                                800-257-5376
                         FAX 508-875-2062
                    http://www.theraproducts.com
                    e-mail: info@theraproducts.com
Sandra Harris, PhD, Author

An invaluable guide to understanding sibling relationships, how they are affected by autism, and what families can do to support their other children while coping with the intensive needs of the child with autism.

3264 Simple Steps: Developmental Activities for Infants, Toddlers & Two Year Olds

Therapro
225 Arlington Street
Framingham, MA   01702   508-872-9494
                                800-257-5376
                         FAX 508-875-2062
                    http://www.theraproducts.com
                    e-mail: info@theraproducts.com
Karen Miller, Author

300 activites linked to the latest research in brain development. Outlines a typical developmental sequence in 10 domains: social/emotional, fine motor, gross motor, language, cognition, sensory, nature, music & movement, creativity and dramatic play. Chapters on curriculum development and learning environment also included.

3265 Social Perception of People with Disabilities in History

Learning Disabilities Association of America
4156 Library Road
Pittsburgh, PA   15234   412-341-1515
                         FAX 412-344-0224
                    http://www.ldanatl.org
                    e-mail: ldanatl@usaor.net
Herbert C Covey, Author

Shows how historical factors shape some of our current perceptions about disability. Of interest to special educators, historians, students of the humanities and social scientists. *$62.95*

324 pages   Cloth
ISBN 0-398068-37-2

3266 Son Rise: The Miracle Continues

Option Indigo Press
2080 S Undermountain Road
Sheffield, MA   01257   413-229-8727
                               800-562-7171
                         FAX 413-229-8727
                    http://www.optionindio.com
                    e-mail: indigo@bcn.net
Barry Neil Kaufman, Author

This book documents Raun Kaufman's astonishing develpment from a lifeless, autistic, retarded child into a highly verbal, lovable youngster with no traces of his former condition. It details Raun's extraordinary progress from the age of four into young adulthood. It also shares moving accounts of five families that successfully used the Son-Rise Program to reach their own special children. An awe-inspiring reminder that love moves mountains. A must for any parent, professional or teacher. *$14.95*

ISBN 0-915811-61-8

3267 Source for Dysarthria

LinguiSystems
3100 4th Avenue
East Moline, IL   61244
                               800-776-4332
                         FAX 800-577-4555
                    http://www.linguisystems.com
                    e-mail: service@linguisystems.com
Linda Bowers, Owner
Rosemary Huisingh, Owner

You'll reach for this book as a therapy tool again and again. This outstanding manual gives you information on types of dysarthria, evaluation and treatment planning options, axamples of documentation, and much more.

Adults

3268 Special-Needs Reading List

Woodbine House
6510 Bells Mill Road
Bethesda, MD   20817   301-897-3570
                               800-843-7323
                         FAX 301-897-5838
                    http://www.woodbinehouse.com
                    e-mail: info@woodbinehouse.com
Wilma Sweeney, Author

In one easy-to-use volume, The Special-Needs reading List reviews and recommends the best books, journals, newsletters, organizations, and other information sources on children with disabilities. *$18.95*

300 pages   Paperback
ISBN 0-933149-74-3

3269 Study Skills: A Landmark School Student Guide

Landmark School
429 Hale Street
Prides Crossing, MA   01965   978-236-3216
                                     FAX 978-927-7268
                    http://www.landmarkschool.org
                    e-mail: outreach@landmarkschool.org
Diane Vener, Author
Dan Ahearn, Program Director
Trish Newhall, Associate Director
Kathryn Frye, Administrative Assistant

Designed to help all students learn to comprehend and organize the information they must learn in school, Study Skills: A Landmark School Student Guide offers instruction in how to apply specific comprehension and study skills including multiple exercises to practice each skill. Intended for reading levels of middle school and beyond. *$30.00*

187 pages
ISBN 0-962411-97-3

3270 Stuttering and Your Child: Questions and Answers

Stuttering Foundation of America
3100 Walnut Grove Road
Memphis, TN   38111   901-452-7343
                                 800-992-9392
                            FAX 901-452-3931
                    http://www.stutterSFA.org
                    e-mail: stutterSFA@vantek.net
June Fraser, Director
Anne Edwards, Office Coordinator

Provides help, information, and resources to those who stutter,   their families, schools day care centers, and all others who need help for a   stuttering problem. *$1.00*

3271 Substance Use Among Children and Adolescents

Books on Special Children
PO Box 305
Congers, NY   10920   845-638-1236
                            FAX 845-638-0847
                    http://www.boscbooks.com/
                    e-mail: irene@boscbooks.com
AM Pagliaro, Author

Exposure and use among infants, children and adolescents. Impact on mental and physical health. Ingestion of substances during pregnancy and effects on fetus and neonate. Drug abuse effects on learning, memory.. Preventing and treating children and adolescents. *$59.95*

405 pages   hardcover
ISBN 0-471580-42-2

3272 Supporting Children with Communication Difficulties In Inclusive Settings

Books on Special Children
PO Box 305
Congers, NY   10920   845-638-1236
                            FAX 845-638-0847
                    http://www.boscbooks.com/
                    e-mail: irene@boscbooks.com
L McCormick, Author

A collaboration of professionals and parents can achieve language communication competence in classroom and other settings. Essential background material, assessment and intervention and needs of special populations are discussed. Contains sectional headings and marginal comments, chapter summary. *$55.95*

530 pages   softcover
ISBN 0-023792-72-8

3273 Surface Counseling

Edge Enterprises
PO Box 1304
Lawrence, KS   66044   785-749-1473
                            FAX 785-749-0207
                    e-mail: edge@midusa.net
Joe N Crank, Donald D Deshler, Jean B Schumaker, Author
Jacqueline Schafer, Managing Editor

Details a set of relationship-building skills necessary for establishing a trusting, cooperative relationship between adults and youths and a problem-solving strategy that youths can learn to use by themselves. Includes study guide questions, model dialogues and role-play activities. Useful for any adult who has daily contact with children and adolescents. *$8.00*

60 pages   Paperback

3274 Survival Guide for Kids with LD

Therapro
225 Arlington Street
Framingham, MA   01702   508-872-9494
                                 800-257-5376
                            FAX 508-875-2062
                    http://www.theraproducts.com
                    e-mail: info@theraproducts.com
Gary Fisher, PhD & Rhonda Cummings, EdD, Author

Popular book that is highly reccommended. Contains vital information, practical advice, step-by-step strategies, and encouragement for children labeled Learning Disabled.

3275 Tactics for Improving Parenting Skills (TIPS)

Sopris West
4093 Specialty Place
Longmont, CO   80504
                                 800-547-6747
                            FAX 303-776-5934
Bob Algozzine, Author
Jim Ysseldyke, Author

Perhaps best described as a compilation of one-page parenting brochures, this helpful resource represents volumes of ideas and suggestions on topics of concern in today's families.

202 pages
ISBN 1-570350-35-3

3276 Tales from the Workplace ADD & LD

JKL Communications
PO Box 40157
Washington, DC   20016   202-223-5097
                    FAX 202-223-5096
                  http://www.lathamlaw.org
                  e-mail: plath3@his.com

$15.00

3277 Teach Me Language

Slosson Educational Publications
538 Buffalo Road
East Aurora, NY   14052   888-756-7766
                          800-828-4800
                    FAX 800-655-3840
                  http://www.sloss.com
                  e-mail: slosson@slosson.com
Joan M Harwell, Author

Teach Me Language is designed for teachers, therapists, and parents, and includes a step-by-step how to manual with 400 pages of instructions, explanations, examples, and games and cards to attack language weaknesses common to children with pervasive developmental disorders. *$29.95*

3278 Teaching Developmentally Disabled Children

Slosson Educational Publications
538 Buffalo Road
East Aurora, NY   14052   716-652-0930
                          800-828-4800
                    FAX 800-655-3840
                  http://www.slosson.com
                  e-mail: slosson@slosson.com
O Ivar Lovaas, Author

This instructional program for teachers, nurses, and parents is clear and concisely shows how to help children who are developmentally disabled function more normally at home, in school, and in the community. *$34.00*

250 pages

3279 Teaching Old Logs New Tricks: Absurdities and Realities of Education

Peytral Publications
PO Box 1162
Minnetonka, MN   55345   952-949-8707
                          877-739-8725
                    FAX 952-906-9777
                  http://www.peytral.com
                  e-mail: help@peytral.com
Michael F Giangreco, Author
Kevin Ruelle, Illustrator
Peggy Hammeken, Owner/Publisher

If you enjoyed Ants in His Pants and Flying by the Seat of your Pants - you'll love this book. This publication contains 100+ carefully crafted cartoons which may be reproduced as transparencies for staff development and training. This book is the third book in a series of three. *$19.95*

112 pages Educators
ISBN 1-890455-43-1

3280 Teaching Reading to Children with Down Syndrome

Woodbine House
6510 Bells Mill Road
Bethesda, MD   20817   301-897-3570
                          800-843-7323
                    FAX 301-897-5838
                  http://www.woodbinehouse.com
                  e-mail: info@woodbinehouse.com
Patricia Logan Oelwein, Author

Teach your child with Down syndrome to read using the author's nationally recognized, proven method. From introducing the alphabet to writing and spelling, the lessons are easy to follow. The many pictures and flash cards included appeal to visual learners and are easy to photocopy! *$16.95*

392 pages Paperback
ISBN 0-933149-55-7

3281 Teaching Students with Mild Disabilities

Books on Special Children
PO Box 305
Congers, NY   10920   845-638-1236
                    FAX 845-638-0847
                  http://www.boscbooks.com/
                  e-mail: irene@boscbooks.com
William N Bender, Author

Specific strategies for effective instruction in special ed. Basis for effective instruction, specialized instructional areas, strategies for curriculum content areas, information on indirect instructional responsibilities. Chapters have objectives, key words, chapter headings, interest boxes, tables, photos, sample questionaires. *$66.00*

388 pages softcover
ISBN 0-138927-20-0

3282 Teaching of Reading: A Continuum from Kindergarten through College

AVKO Educational Research Foundation
3084 W Willard Road
Clio, MI   48420   810-686-9283
                    FAX 810-686-1101
                  http://www.avko.org/teaching_of_reading.htm
                  e-mail: avkoemail@aol.com
Don McCabe, Author
Don McCabe, Research Director

This book covers concepts, techniques, and practical diagnostic tests not normally taught in regular college courses on reading. It is designed to be used by teachers, parents, tutors, and college reading instructors willing to try new approaches to old problems. *$49.95*

364 pages
ISBN 1-564006-50-6

3283 Teaching the Dyslexic Child

Slosson Educational Publications
538 Buffalo Road
East Aurora, NY   14052   716-652-0930
                          800-828-4800
                    FAX 800-655-3840
                  http://www.slosson.com
                  e-mail: slosson@slosson.com
Anita N Griffiths, Author

Teaching the Dyslexic Child talks about the frustrations that the dyslexic youngsters and their parents encounter in the day to day collisions with life's demand. *$12.00*

128 pages

3284 The Out of Sync Child: Recognizing and Coping with Sensory Integration Dysfunction

Therapro
225 Arlington Street
Framingham, MA   01702   508-872-9494
                                800-257-5376
                          FAX 508-875-2062
                     http://www.theraproducts.com
                     e-mail: info@theraproducts.com
Carol Stock Kranowitz, MA, Author

Finally, a parent-friendly book about sensory integration (SI) clearly written to explain SI dysfunction from the perspective of a teacher who has worked extensively with an OT. Part I deals with recognizing SI dysfunction. Part II addresses coping with SI dysfunction.

3285 Understanding Learning Disabilities: A Parent Guide and Workbook, Third Edition

York Press
PO Box 504
Timonium, MD   21094   410-560-1557
                              800-962-2763
                        FAX 410-560-6758
                   http://www.yorkpress.com
                     e-mail: york@abs.net
Mary Louise Trusdell & Inge Horowitz, Author
Elinor Hartwig, President

An invaluable resource for parents who are new to the field of learning disabilities. Easy to read and overflowing with helpful information and advice. *$25.00*

380 pages
ISBN 0-912752-67-X

3286 Understanding and Teaching Children with Autism

Books on Special Children
PO Box 305
Congers, NY   10920   845-638-1236
                        FAX 845-638-0847
                   http://www.boscbooks.com/
                   e-mail: irene@boscbooks.com
R Jordan, Author

The triad of impairment: social, language and communication and thought behavior aspects of development discussed. Difficulties in interacting, transfer of learning and bizarre behaviors are syndome. Many LD are associated with autism. *$57.00*

175 pages   hardcover
ISBN 0-471958-88-3

3287 Unlocking the Mysteries of Sensory Dysfunction

Therapro
225 Arlington Street
Framingham, MA   01702   508-872-9494
                                800-257-5376
                          FAX 508-875-2062
                     http://www.theraproducts.com
                     e-mail: info@theraproducts.com
Elizabeth Anderson & Pauline Emmons, Author

A must-read for therapists, parents and educators. Written by parents, this book is informative and insightful regarding children with sensory integration problems. The autors offer practical suggestions dealing with the often complex realities of living with a child who has sensory issues. A good explanation of sensory integration therapy and advice about how to access it.

3288 What to Expect: The Toddler Years

Workman Publishing
708 Broadway
New York, NY   10003
                                800-722-7202
                          FAX 800-521-1832
                     http://www.workman.com
Arlene Eisenberg, et al., Author
Jerry Mandel, Special Markets Director

They guided you through pregnancy, they guided you through baby's first year, and now they'll guide you through the toddler years. In a direct continuation of What to Expect When You're Expecting and What to Expect the Frist Year, American's bestselling pregnancy and childcare authors turn their uniquely comprehensive, lively, and reassuring coverage to years two and three. *$15.95*

928 pages   Paperback

3289 When Your Child Has LD

Free Spirit Publishing
217 5th Avenue N
Minneapolis, MN   55401   612-338-2068
                                 800-735-7323
                           FAX 612-337-5050
                     http://www.freespirit.com
                   e-mail: help4kids@freespirit.com
Rhoda Cummings and Gary Fisher, Author
Betsy Gabler, Sales Manager

Clear, reassuring advice and essential information for parents of children ages five and up who have a learning difference. *$12.95*

160 pages
ISBN 0-915793-87-3

Young Adults

3290 Assertive Option: Your Rights and Responsibilities

Research Press
PO Box 9177
Champaign, IL   61826

217-352-3273
800-519-2707
FAX 217-352-1221
http://www.researchpress.com
e-mail: rp@researchpress.com

Dr. Patricia Jakubowski, Dr. Arthur J Lange, Author
Ann Wendell, President

A self instructional assertiveness book, with many exercises and self tests. *$24.95*

348 pages
ISBN 0-878221-92-1

3291 Education of Students with Disabilities: Where Do We Stand?

National Council on Disability
1331 F Street NW
Washington, DC   20591

202-272-2004
FAX 202-272-2022
http://www.ncd.gov
e-mail: mquigley@ncd.ogv

3292 Keeping Ahead in School: A Students Book About Learning Disabilities & Learning Disorders

Educators Publishing Service
31 Smith Place
Cambridge, MA   02138

617-547-6706
800-225-5750
FAX 617-547-0412
http://www.epsbooks.com
e-mail: eps@epsbooks.com

Mel Levine, Author

Written for students 9 to 15 years of age with learning disorders. This book helps students gain important insights into their problems by combining realism with justifiable optimism. *$24.75*

ISBN 0-838820-09-7

3293 Modern Consumer Education: You and the Law

Educational Design
345 Hudson Street
New York, NY   10014

800-221-9372
FAX 866-805-5723
http://www.triumphlearning.com

Buz Traugot, Sales Representative

An instructional program to teach independent living, with emphasis on legal resources and survival skills. *$59.00*

3294 Phonemic Awareness: Lessons, Activities & Games

Peytral Publicatons
PO Box 1162
Minnetonka, MN   55345

952-949-8707
877-739-8725
FAX 952-906-9777
http://www.peytral.com
e-mail: help@peytral.com

Victoria Groves Scott, Author

Help struggling readers with Phonemic Awareness training. This all inclusive book iuncludes 48 scripted lessons. May be used as a prerequisite to reading or for stuggling students. Includes 49 reproductible masters. May be used with individual students or with groups. *$27.95*

176 pages

3295 Reading Is Fun

Teddy Bear Press
3639 Midway Drive
San Diego, CA   92110

619-223-7311
FAX 619-255-2158
http://www.teddybearpress.net
e-mail: fparker@teddybearpress.net

Fran Parker, President

Introduces 55 primer level words in six reading books and accompanting activity sheets. This easy to use reading program provides repition, visual motor, visual discrimination and word comprehension excersies. The manual and placement test. *$85.00*

ISBN 1-928876-01-3

3296 School Survival Guide for Kids with Learning Disabilities

Free Spirit Publishing
217 5th Avenue N
Minneapolis, MN   55401

612-338-2068
800-735-7323
FAX 612-337-5050
http://www.freespirit.com
e-mail: help4kids@freespirit.com

Rhoda Cummings & Gary Fisher, Author
Betsy Gabler, Sales Manager

Strategies and tips for building confidence in reading, writing, spelling, and math, managing time, coping with testing, gtting help, and more. *$12.95*

176 pages
ISBN 0-915793-32-6

3297 Succeeding in the Workplace

JKL Communications
PO Box 40157
Washington, DC   20016

202-223-5097
FAX 202-223-5096
http://www.lathamlaw.org
e-mail: plath3@his.com

$29.00

3298 Survival Guide for Teenagers with LD

Free Spirit Publishing
217 5th Avenue N
Minneapolis, MN   55401   612-338-2068
                                  800-735-7323
                             FAX 612-337-5050
                    http://www.freespirit.com
              e-mail: help4kids@freespirit.com
Rhoda Cummings and Gary Fisher, Author
Betsy Gabler, Sales Manager

A step-by-step handbook to help teens with LD succeed at school and prepare for life as adults. Also available in audio cassette format. *$12.95*

200 pages
ISBN 0-915793-51-2

3299 Winning at Math: Your Guide to Learning Mathematics Through Successful Study Skills

Academic Success Press
6023 26th Street
West Bradenton, FL   34207   941-359-2819
                                  800-444-2524
                             FAX 941-753-2882
                http://www.academicsuccess.com
          e-mail: academ@academicsuccess.com
P Nolting, Author
P Nolting, President

A guide that helps people with learning disabilities learn math easier.

3300 Winning the Study Game

Peytral Publicatons
PO Box 1162
Minnetonka, MN   55345   952-949-8707
                                  877-739-8725
                             FAX 952-906-9777
                       http://www.peytral.com
Lawrence J Greene, Author

A comprehensive study skills program for students with learning differences in grades 6-11. The student book has 16 units which will help students learn to study better, take notes, advance their thinking skills while stregthening their reading and writing. The student version is available in a reproducible or consumable format. Teachers guide sold separately. *$34.95*

2500 pages
ISBN 1-890455-48-2

3301 You Don't Have to be Dyslexic

Melvin-Smith Learning Center
7230 S Land Park Drive
Sacramento, CA   95831   916-392-6415
                                  800-50L-EARN
                             FAX 916-392-6453
Joan M Smith, Author

Dr. Smith has designed this user-friendly book to: Demystify the area of learning that is emotionally charged for many people, Provide teaching methods for teachers, professionals and parents. Depict actual case studies, describing various dyslexic learning styles. And use real-life cases which show excellent examples of how to remediate learning issues. *$19.95*

205 pages

General

3302 A Student's Guide to Jobs
NICHCY
PO Box 1492
Washington, DC   20013   202-884-8200
                                800-695-0285
                            FAX 202-884-8441
                            http://www.nichcy.org
                            e-mail: nichcy@ace.org
Susan Ripley, Information Specialist

Young people with mental retardation speak freely about their job-related experiences. *$2.00*

8 pages

3303 A Student's Guide to the IEP
NICHCY
PO Box 1492
Washington, DC   20013   202-884-8200
                                800-695-0285
                            FAX 202-884-8441
                            http://www.nichcy.org
                            e-mail: nichcy@ace.org
Susan Ripley, Information Specialist

A guide for students that features other students discussing their experiences as active members on their IEP team. *$2.00*

12 pages

3304 Accessing Parent Groups
NICHCY
PO Box 1492
Washington, DC   20013   202-884-8200
                                800-695-0285
                            FAX 202-884-8441
                            http://www.nichcy.org
                            e-mail: nichcy@ace.org
Susan Ripley, Information Specialist

Helps parents locate support groups where they can share information, give and receive emotional support, and address common concerns. *$2.00*

12 pages

3305 Accessing Programs for Infants, Toddlers and Preschoolers
NICHCY
PO Box 1492
Washington, DC   20013   202-884-8200
                                800-695-0285
                            FAX 202-884-8441
                            http://www.nichcy.org
                            e-mail: nichcy@ace.org
Susan Ripley, Information Specialist

This guide helps locate intervention services for infants and toddlers with disabilities. Also answers questions about educational programs for preschoolers. *$2.00*

20 pages

3306 Advocacy Services for Families of Children in Special Education
Arizona Department of Education
1535 W Jefferson Street
Phoenix, AZ   85007   602-542-4361
                                800-352-4558
                            FAX 602-542-5440
                            http://www.ade.state.az.us
                            e-mail: ADE@ade.az.gov

Information provided to families that have children in special education.

3307 Assessing Children for the Presence of a Disability
NICHCY
PO Box 1492
Washington, DC   20013   202-884-8200
                                800-695-0285
                            FAX 202-884-8441
                            http://www.nichcy.org
                            e-mail: nichcy@ace.org
Susan Ripley, Information Specialist

Describes the criteria and process preformed by school systems to determine if a child has a learning disabilty. *$4.00*

28 pages

3308 Assessing the ERIC Resource Collection
NICHCY
PO Box 1492
Washington, DC   20013   202-884-8200
                                800-695-0285
                            FAX 202-884-8441
                            http://www.nichcy.org
                            e-mail: nichcy@ace.org
Susan Ripley, Information Specialist

A nationwide network that gives access to education literature, this document explains how to search and retrieve documents from ERIC. Also explains how to find information about children with disabilites. *$2.00*

8 pages

3309 Can What a Child Eats Make Him Dull, Stupid or Hyperactive?
Learning Disabilities Association of America
4156 Library Road
Pittsburgh, PA   15234   412-341-1515
                            FAX 412-344-0224
                            http://www.ldanatl.org
                            e-mail: ldanatl@usaor.net

$2.00

3310 Children with Learning and Behavioral Disorders
Learning Disabilities Association of America
4156 Library Road
Pittsburgh, PA   15234   412-341-1515
                            FAX 412-344-0224
                            http://www.ldanatl.org
                            e-mail: ldanatl@usaor.net

$.50

3311 Complete Set of State Resource Sheets
NICHCY
PO Box 1492
Washington, DC 20013   202-884-8200
                              800-695-0285
                         FAX 202-884-8441
                      http://www.nichcy.org
                      e-mail: nichcy@ace.org
Susan Ripley, Information Specialist

Provides a sheet for every state and territory in the
United States. *$10.00*

200 pages

3312 Directory of Organizations
NICHCY
PO Box 1492
Washington, DC 20013   202-884-8200
                              800-695-0285
                         FAX 202-884-8441
                      http://www.nichcy.org
                      e-mail: nichcy@ace.org
Susan Ripley, Information Specialist

Lists many organizations and services *$4.00*

28 pages

3313 Ethical and Legal Issues in School Counseling
American School Counselor Association
801 N Fairfax Street
Alexandria, VA 22314   703-683-2722
                              800-306-4722
                         FAX 703-683-1619
                   http://www.schoolcounselor.org
                   e-mail: asca@schoolcounselor.org
Stephanie Will, Office Manager

Contains answers to many of the most controversial
and challenging questions school counselors face every day. *$40.50*

ISBN 1-556200-55-2

3314 Fact Sheet: Attention Deficit Hyperactivity Disorder
Learning Disabilities Association of America
4156 Library Road
Pittsburgh, PA 15234   412-341-1515
                         FAX 412-344-0224
                      http://www.ldanatl.org
                      e-mail: ldanatl@usaor.net
A pamphlet offering factual information on ADHD.

3315 Fundamentals of Autism
Slosson Educational Publications
538 Buffalo Road
East Aurora, NY 14052   716-652-0930
                              800-828-4800
                         FAX 800-655-3840
                      http://www.slosson.com
                      e-mail: slosson@slosson.com
Sue Larson, Author
Steven W Slosson, President
John Slosson, VP

Provides a quick, user friendly effective and accurate
approach to help in identifying and developing educationally related program objectives for children diagnosed as Autistic. These materials have been designed
to be easily and functionally used by teachers, therapists, special education/learning disability resource
specialists, psychologists, and others who work with
children diagnosed with similar disabilites.

3316 General Information about Autism
NICHCY
PO Box 1492
Washington, DC 20013   202-884-8200
                              800-695-0285
                         FAX 202-884-8441
                      http://www.nichcy.org
                      e-mail: nichcy@ace.org
Susan Ripley, Executive Director

Offers information about autism.

3317 General Information about Disabilities
NICHCY
PO Box 1492
Washington, DC 20013   202-884-8200
                              800-695-0285
                         FAX 202-884-8841
                      http://www.nichcy.org
                      e-mail: nichcy@ace.org
Susan Ripley, Information Specialist

A fact sheet offering information on the Education of
the Handicapped Act.

2 pages

3318 General Information about Speech and Language Disorders
NICHCY
PO Box 1492
Washington, DC 20013   202-884-8200
                              800-695-0285
                         FAX 202-884-8841
                      http://www.nichcy.org
                      e-mail: nichcy@ace.org
Susan Ripley, Information Specialist

Offers characteristics, educational implications and
associations in the area of speech and language disorders.

3319 IDEA Amendments
NICHCY
PO Box 1492
Washington, DC 20013   202-884-8200
                              800-695-0285
                         FAX 202-884-8441
                      http://www.nichcy.org
                      e-mail: nichcy@ace.org
Susan Ripley, Information Specialist

Examines the important changes that have occured in
the Individuals Education Act, amended in June of
1997. *$4.00*

40 pages

3320 If Your Child Stutters: A Guide for Parents

Stuttering Foundation of America
3100 Walnut Grove Road
Memphis, TN   38111   901-452-0995
                             800-992-9392
                         FAX 901-452-3931
                     http://www.stuttersfa.org
                     e-mail: stutter@vantek.net
Anne Edwards, Coordinator

A guide that enables parents to provide appropriate
help to children who stutter. *$1.00*

3321 Individualized Education Programs

NICHCY
PO Box 1492
Washington, DC   20013   202-884-8200
                              800-695-0285
                          FAX 202-884-8441
                      http://www.nichcy.org
                      e-mail: nichcy@ace.org
Susan Ripley, Information Specialist

Provides guidance regarding the legal requirement for
beginning a student's IEP. *$2.00*

32 pages

**3322 Interventions for Students with Learning
Disabilities**

NICHCY
PO Box 1492
Washington, DC   20013   202-884-8200
                              800-695-0285
                          FAX 202-884-8441
                      http://www.nichcy.org
                      e-mail: nichcy@ace.org
Susan Ripley, Information Specialist

A document that examines 2 different interventions
for students who have learning disabilities; the first
deals with strategies and the second with phonological
awareness. *$4.00*

16 pages

3323 National Resources

NICHCY
PO Box 1492
Washington, DC   20013   202-884-8200
                              800-695-0285
                          FAX 202-884-8441
                      http://www.nichcy.org
                      e-mail: nichcy@ace.org
Susan Ripley, Information Specialist

Lists different organizations that provide information
about different disabilities.

6 pages

3324 National Toll-free Numbers

NICHCY
PO Box 1492
Washington, DC   20013   202-884-8200
                              800-695-0285
                          FAX 202-884-8441
                      http://www.nichcy.org
                      e-mail: nichcy@ace.org
Susan Ripley, Information Specialist

Gives the names of organizations with toll-free numbers who specialize in different disabilities.

6 pages

**3325 Parenting a Child with Special Needs: A Guide to
Reading and Resources**

NICHCY
PO Box 1492
Washington, DC   20013   202-884-8200
                              800-695-0285
                          FAX 202-884-8441
                      http://www.nichcy.org
                      e-mail: nichcy@ace.org
Susan Ripley, Information Specialist

Provides information to families whose child has been
diagnosed with a disability. Also gives insight on how
disabilities can in turn affect the family. *$4.00*

24 pages

3326 Parents Guide

NICHCY
PO Box 1492
Washington, DC   20013   202-884-8200
                              800-695-0285
                          FAX 202-884-8841
                      http://www.nichcy.org
                      e-mail: nichcy@ace.org
Lisa Kupper, Editor
Susan Ripley, Information Specialist

Talks directly to parents about specific disability issues.

3327 Planning a Move: Mapping Your Strategy

NICHCY
PO Box 1492
Washington, DC   20013   202-884-8200
                              800-695-0285
                          FAX 202-884-8441
                      http://www.nichcy.org
                      e-mail: nichcy@ace.org
Susan Ripley, Information Specialist

This guide helps to make moving to a new place easier
for parents and their children by listing available services in the new area and compiling educational and
medical records. *$2.00*

12 pages

3328 Planning for Inclusion: News Digest

NICHCY
PO Box 1492
Washington, DC   20013   202-884-8200
                              800-695-0285
                          FAX 202-884-8441
                      http://www.nichcy.org
                      e-mail: nichcy@ace.org
Susan Ripley, Information Specialist

Provides a general guide to raising children with
learning disabilities in an educational setting. *$4.00*

32 pages

3329 Problem Sensitivity: A Qualitative Difference in the Learning Disabled

National Clearinghouse of Rehabilitation Materials
5202 N Richmond Hill Road
Stillwater, OK   74078   405-624-7650
                                          800-223-5219
                                      FAX 405-624-0695
                          http://www.nchrtm.okstate.edu

Presenting information that can be used in modifying the cognitive structure at the Problem Sensitivity level, this paper looks at the learning disabled adult from the viewpoint of cognitive psychology. Behavior is considered significantly deviant when a person's approach to a task is at a qualitatively different level than expected at the person's age.

21 pages

3330 Promising Practices and Future Directions for Special Education

NICHCY
PO Box 1492
Washington, DC   20013   202-884-8200
                                          800-695-0285
                                      FAX 202-884-8441
                              http://www.nichcy.org
                          e-mail: nichcy@ace.org
Susan Ripley, Information Specialist

Examines different research regarding the educational methods for children with learning disabilities. *$4.00*

24 pages

3331 Public Agencies Fact Sheet

NICHCY
PO Box 1492
Washington, DC   20013   202-884-8200
                                          800-695-0285
                                      FAX 202-884-8841
                              http://www.nichcy.org
                          e-mail: nichcy@ace.org
Susan Ripley, Information Specialist

General information on public agencies that serve the disabled individual.

2 pages

3332 Questions Often Asked about Special Education Services

NICHCY
PO Box 1492
Washington, DC   20013   202-884-8200
                                          800-695-0285
                                      FAX 202-884-8841
                              http://www.nichcy.org
                          e-mail: nichcy@ace.org
Susan Ripley, Informaton Specialist

Offers information regarding special education.

3333 Questions Often Asked by Parents About Special Education Services

NICHCY
PO Box 1492
Washington, DC   20013   202-884-8200
                                          800-695-0285
                                      FAX 202-884-8441
                              http://www.nichcy.org
                          e-mail: nichcy@ace.org
Susan Ripley, Information Specialist

A publication to help parents learn about the Individuals with Disabilities Education Act. Also discusses how student access special education and other related services.

12 pages

3334 Questions and Answers About the IDEA News Digest

NICHCY
PO Box 1492
Washington, DC   20013   202-884-8200
                                      FAX 202-884-8441
                              http://www.nichcy.org
                          e-mail: nichcy@ace.org
Susan Ripley, Information Specialist

Covers the more commonly asked questions from families and professionals about the IDEA. *$4.00*

28 pages

3335 Related Services for School-Aged Children with Disabilities

NICHCY
PO Box 1492
Washington, DC   20013   202-884-8200
                                          800-695-0285
                                      FAX 202-884-8441
                              http://www.nichcy.org
                          e-mail: nichcy@ace.org
Susan Ripley, Information Specialist

Examines the different services offered to children with disabilities such as speech-language pathology, transportation, occupational and physical therapy and special health services. *$4.00*

24 pages

3336 Resources for Adults with Disabilities

NICHCY
PO Box 1492
Washington, DC   20013   202-884-8200
                                          800-695-0285
                                      FAX 202-884-8441
                              http://www.nichcy.org
                          e-mail: nichcy@ace.org
Susan Ripley, Information Specialist

Helps adults with disabilities find organizations that will help them find employment, education, recreation and independent living. *$2.00*

16 pages

3337 Serving on Boards and Committees
NICHCY
PO Box 1492
Washington, DC   20013   202-884-8200
                               800-695-0285
                               FAX 202-884-8441
                               http://www.nichcy.org
                               e-mail: nichcy@ace.org
Susan Ripley, Information Specialist

Part of the Parent's Guide series, this publication examines the different boards and committees on which parents of children with disabilities often serve. Also suggests ways to go about becoming involved with such organizations. *$2.00*

   8 pages

3338 Special Education and Related Services: Communicating Through Letterwriting
NICHCY
PO Box 1492
Washington, DC   20013   202-884-8200
                               800-695-0285
                               FAX 202-884-8441
                               http://www.nichcy.org
                               e-mail: nichcy@ace.org
Susan Ripley, Information Specialist

Identifies the rights of parents and their children with disabilities and explains when and how to notify the school in writing about such conditions. *$2.00*

   20 pages

3339 State Capitals
PO Box 7376
Alexandria, VA   22307   703-768-2545
                               800-876-2545
                               FAX 703-768-9690
                    http://www.statecapitals.com
              e-mail: newsletters@statecapitals.com
Briefing on important selected state activities.

3340 State Resource Sheet
NICHCY
PO Box 1492
Washington, DC   20013   202-884-8200
                               800-695-0285
                               FAX 202-884-8441
                               http://www.nichcy.org
                               e-mail: nichcy@ace.org
Susan Ripley, Information Specialist

List numbers of different organizations that deal with disabilities by state.

3341 The Education of Children and Youth with Special Needs: What do the Laws Say?
NICHCY
PO Box 1492
Washington, DC   20013   202-884-8200
                               800-695-0285
                               FAX 202-884-8441
                               http://www.nichcy.org
                               e-mail: nichcy@ace.org
Susan Ripley, Information Specialist

Provides an overview of 3 laws that aid disabled children; 1. Section 504 of the Rehabilitation Act of 1973, 2. the Individuals with Disabilities Education Act, and 3. the Carl P. Perkins Vocational Educational Act. *$4.00*

   16 pages

3342 Underachieving Gifted
Council for Exceptional Children
1110 N Glebe Road
Arlington, VA   22201   703-620-3660
                               888-232-7733
                               FAX 703-264-9494
                               http://www.cec.sped.org/
Gerard Hurley, Contact

A collection of annotated references from the ERIC and Exceptional Child Evaluation Resources (171 abstracts). Note: Abstracts only. Not the complete research. *$1.00*

3343 What Every Parent Should Know about Learning Disabilities
Connecticut Assoc. for Children and Adults with LD
25 Van Zant Street
East Norwalk, CT   06855   203-838-5010
                               FAX 203-866-6108
                               http://www.CACLD.org
CL Bete, Author

What to do with a child with a learning disability.

3344 When Pre-schoolers are Not on Target: Guide for Parents & Early Childhood Educators
Learning Disabilities Association of America
LDA Literary Depository
Pittsburgh, PA   15234   412-341-1515
                               FAX 412-344-0224
                               http://www.ldanatl.org
                               e-mail: ldanatl@usaor.net

New booklet provides information on early identification of learning disabilities and appropriate intervention strategies to professionals who work with preschool children. Available in Spanish. Discounts for multiples. *$4.00*

3345 Who's Teaching Our Children with Disabilities?
NICHCY
PO Box 1492
Washington, DC   20013   202-884-8200
                               800-695-0285
                               FAX 202-884-8441
                               http://www.nichcy.org
                               e-mail: nichcy@ace.org
Susan Ripley, Information Specialist

Takes a detailed look at the people who are teaching children with disabilities. *$4.00*

   24 pages

3346 Your Child's Evaluation
NICHCY
PO Box 1492
Washington, DC 20013   202-884-8200
                               800-695-0285
                          FAX 202-884-8441
                          http://www.nichcy.org
                          e-mail: nichcy@ace.org
Susan Ripley, Information Specialist

This document describes the steps that the school system will use to determine if you child has a learning disability. *$2.00*

   4 pages

Adults

3347 Community Education Journal

National Community Education Association
3929 Old Lee Highway
Fairfax, VA 22030   703-359-8973
    FAX 703-359-0972
    e-mail: ncea@ids2.idsonline.com

A quarterly publication for people with disabilities.
$25.00

Quarterly

3348 Correctional Education Quarterly News: US Department of Education

Office of Correctional Education
400 Maryland Avenue SW
Washington, DC 20202   202-205-5621
    FAX 202-401-2615
    e-mail: oce@inet.ed.gov

Provides information about correctional education and the activities of the Office of Correctional Education in the US Department of Education. Free.

3349 International Dyslexia Association: Illinois Branch Newsletter

751 Roosevelt Road
Glen Ellyn, IL 60137   630-469-6900
    FAX 630-469-6810
    http://www.interdys.org
    e-mail: ilbranch_ida@ameritech.net
Donna Rafanello, Executive Director
Gail Oliphant, Office Manager

3350 International Dyslexia Association: Louisiana Branch Newsletter

2125 Coliseum Street
New Orleans, LA 70130   504-876-0034
    FAX 504-595-8848
Marqua Brunette, President

3351 Moving Forward

1186 East Avenue
Napa, CA 94559   510-337-2460
    FAX 510-934-9022
    http://www.iser.com/movingforward-CA.html
    e-mail: aia1@aol.com
Paul Aziz, Publisher/Editor
Agena Aziz, Publisher/Business Manager

A national newspaper for persons with disabilities offering convention information, book reviews, assistive technology, law and legislation information and more. *$11.50*

3352 NAASLN Newsletter

Nat'l Assn. af Adults with Special Learning Needs
PO Box 716
Bryn Mawr, PA 19010   610-525-8336
    http://www.ldonline.org

Newsletter focusing on issues related to teaching adults with special learning needs.

3353 NICHCY News Digest

NICHCY
PO Box 1492
Washington, DC 20013   202-884-8200
    800-695-0285
    FAX 202-884-8841
    http://www.nichcy.org
    e-mail: nichcy@ace.org
Lisa Kupper, Editor

Addresses a single disability issue in depth.

3354 Rural Education Forum

161 College Court Building
Manhattan, KS 66506   785-532-5560
    FAX 785-532-5637
    e-mail: wberryd@dce.ksu.edu

Provides information about rural education programs resources, research and events.

3355 Work America

National Alliance of Business (NAB)
1201 New York Avenue NW
Washington, DC 20005
    800-787-2848
    FAX 202-289-1303
    http://www.nab.com
    e-mail: info@nab.com

A monthly newsletter focused on model programs and information about employment and training.

Monthly

Children

3356 Calliope

Cobblestone Publishing Company
30 Grove Street
Peterborough, NH 03458   603-924-7209
    800-821-0115
    FAX 603-924-7380
    http://www.cobblestonepub.com
    e-mail: custsvc@cobblestone.mv.com
Rosalie Baker, Editor
Malcom Jensen, Publisher
Charles Baker, Editor

Winner of the coveted 1998 Educational Press Association's Golden Lamp Award. Calliope brings to the classroom a fresh and exciting look at world history, one theme at a time. *$29.95*

52 pages 9 times anually
ISSN 1050-7086

3357 KIND News

NAHEE
PO Box 362
East Haddam, CT   06423   860-434-8666
                                       FAX 860-434-9579
                                       http://www.nahee.org
                                       e-mail: nahee@nahee.org
Lesia Winiarskyj, Director Publications
Cathy Vincenti, Managing Editor
Jessica Vanase, Associate Editor

Four-page color newspaper with games, puzzles and entertaining, informative articles designed to install kindness to people, animals, and the enviroment and to make reading fun. *$30.00*

> *4 pages   9x school year*
> *ISSN 1050-9542*

3358 KIND News Jr: Kids in Nature's Defense

Kind News
PO Box 362
East Haddam, CT   06423   860-434-8666
                                       FAX 860-434-6282
                                       http://www.kindnews.org
                                       e-mail: nahee@nahee.org
Lesia Winiarsky, Director Publications
Cathy Vincenti, Managing Editor
Jessica Yanase, Associate Editor

Short, easy-to-read items on the environment and animal world with puzzles, contests and cartoons. Many illustrations, pictures.

3359 KIND News Primary: Kids in Nature's Defense

Kind News
PO Box 362
East Haddam, CT   06423   860-434-8666
                                       FAX 860-434-6282
                                       http://www.kindnews.org
                                       e-mail: nahee@nahee.org
Lesia Winiarsky, Director Publications
Cathy Vincenti, Managing Editor
Jessica Yanase, Associate Editor

Short, easy-to-read items on the environment and animal world with puzzles, pictures to color and cartoons. Many illustrations, pictures.

3360 KIND News Sr: Kids in Nature's Defense

NAHEE
PO Box 362
East Haddam, CT   06423   860-434-8666
                                       FAX 860-434-6282
                                       http://www.kindnews.org
                                       e-mail: nahee@nahee.org
Lesia Winiarsky, Director Publications
Cathy Vincenti, Managing Editor
Jessica Yanase, Associate Editor

Publication put out by the National Association for Humane and Environmental Education, KIND News Sr. is intended for children between grades 5 through 6. The magazine covers different pet issues such as how to care for,feed and play with pets.

3361 Koala Club News

San Diego Zoo Membership Department
PO Box 120551
San Diego, CA   92112   619-231-1515
                                       FAX 619-231-0249
                                       http://www.sandiegozoo.org
Georgeanne Irvine, Editor

A magazine about animals going to kids who are members of the Zoological Society of San Diego Koala Club. *$9.00*

3362 Let's Find Out

Scholastic
555 Broadway
New York, NY   10012
Jean Marzollo, Editor

Get your PreK and K classes off to a great start with Free-trail copies of Let's Find Out, and bring all this to your teaching program: monthly seasonal themes in 32 colorful weekly issues, activity pages to develop early reading and math skills. *$4.25*

3363 National Association for Humane and Environmental Education

PO Box 362
East Haddam, CT   06423   860-434-8666
                                       FAX 860-434-6282
                                       http://www.nahee.org
                                       e-mail: nahee@nahee.org
Lesia Winiarsky, Director Publications
Cathy Vincenti, Managing Editor
Jesica Yanase, Associate Editor

3364 Ranger Rick

National Wildlife Foundation/Membership Services
11100 Wild Life Center Drive
Reston, VA   20190
                                       800-822-9919
                                       FAX 703-438-6039
                                       http://www.nuf.org
Gerry Bishop, Editor

A magazine for children ages 6-12 that is dedicated to helping students gain a greater understanding and appreciation of nature. *$15.00*

3365 Sibling Forum

Family Resource Associates
35 Haddon Avenue
Shrewsbury, NJ   07702   732-747-5310
                                       FAX 732-747-1896
Susan Levine, Editor

Newsletter for siblings aged 10 through teens with brothers or sisters with disabilities. Includes library information, special definitions and feedback from readers. Each issue also has a Focusing on Feelings discussion. A useful tool for siblings, parents, educators, and special workers. *$12.00*

> *12 pages   4 Times/Sibling*

3366 Stone Soup: The Magazine by Young Writers and Artists

PO Box 83
Santa Cruz, CA   95063   831-426-5557
                                     800-447-4569
                                 FAX 831-426-1161
                          http://www.stonesoup.com
                       e-mail: editor@stonesoup.com
Gerry Mandel, Editor

A literary magazine publishing fiction, poetry, book reviews and art by children through age 13. *$32.00*

6x/year

Parents & Professionals

3367 ALL Points Bulletin: Department of Education

Division of Adult Education and Literacy
600 Independence Avenue SW
Washington, DC   20202
                                 FAX 202-205-8973

The quarterly newsletter of the division of adult education and literacy. Issues focus on selected areas of interest in the field of adult education, current research, new publications, and upcoming events. Special sections concentrate on ESL and workplace literacy issues.

3368 Adult Basic Education: An Interdisciplinary Journal for Adult Literacy Educators

Commission on Adult Basic Education (COABE)
Piedmont College
Demorest, GA   30535   706-778-3000
                                 FAX 706-778-2811
                  http://www.206.75.28/journal/abe.html
                    e-mail: kmelichar@piedmnt.edu
Ken Melichar, Editor

Adult Basic Education: An Interdisciplinary Journal for Adult Literacy Educators is a double-blind, peer review, scholarly journal with a practical intent devoted to improving the efforts of adult educators working with low-literally disadvantaged, and educationally oppressed people. *$25.00*

3x/year

3369 Association of Higher Education Facilities Officers Newsletter

1643 Prince Street
Alexandria, VA   22314   703-684-1446
                                 FAX 703-549-2772
                            http://www.appa.org

A newsletter whose purpose is to promote excellence in the administration, care, operation, planning, and development of higher education facilities.

3370 Children and Families

National Head Start Association
1651 Prince Street
Alexandria, VA   22314   703-739-0875
                                 FAX 703-739-0878

The magazine of the National Head Start Association.

3371 Connections: A Journal of Adult Literacy

Adult Literacy Resource Institute
989 Commonwealth Avenue
Boston, MA   02215   617-782-8956
                                 FAX 617-782-9011
                              http://www.alri.org

Connections is primarily intended to provide an opportunity for adult educators in the Boston area to communicate with colleagues.

3372 Council for Exceptional Children

1110 N Glebe Road
Arlington, VA   22201   703-620-3660
                                     888-232-7733
                                 FAX 703-264-9494
                         http://www.cec.sped.org
                   e-mail: cathym@cec.sped.org
Gerald Reynaud, President
Dave Edyburn, Editor
Nancy Safer, Executive Director

3373 Education Funding News

Education Funding Research Council
1725 K Street NW
Washington, DC   20006   202-872-4000
                                     800-876-0226
                                 FAX 800-926-2012
                  http://www.grantsandfunding.com
Emily Lechy, Editor

Provides the latest details on funding opportunities in education. *$298.00*

50 pages

3374 Exceptional Children

Council for Exceptional Children
1110 N Glebe Road
Arlington, VA   22201   703-620-3660
                                     888-232-7733
                                 FAX 703-264-9494
                         http://www.cec.sped.org

Peer review journal publishing original research on the education and development of toddlers, infants, children and youth with exceptionality and articles on professional issues of concern to special educators. Published quarterly.

3375 Federation for Children with Special Needs Newsletter

1135 Tremont Street
Boston, MA   02120   617-236-7210
                                 FAX 617-572-2094
                              http://www.fcsn.org
                      e-mail: fcsninfo@fcsn.org
Richard Robison, Executive Director

The mission of the Federation is to provide information, support, and assistance to parents of children with disabilities, their professional partners, and their communities. Major services are information and referrals and parent and professional training.

3376   International Dyslexia Association Quarterly Newsletter: Perspectives

IDA
8600 Lasalle Road
Baltimore, MD   21286   410-296-0232
                                          800-ABC-D123
                                         FAX 410-321-5069
                                    http://www.interdys.org
                                    e-mail: info@interdys.org
J Thomas Viall, Executive Director

Nonprofit, scientific and educational organization dedicated to the study and treatment of dyslexia. Focus is educating parents, teachers and professionals in the field of dyslexia in effective teaching methodologies. Programs and services include: information and referral; public awareness; medical and educational research; governmental affairs; conferences and publications.

50-56 pages   Free to Members

3377   International Dyslexia Association: Illinois Branch Newsletter

751 Roosevelt Road
Glen Ellyn, IL   60137   630-469-6900
                                         FAX 630-469-6810
                                    http://www.interdys.org
                              e-mail: ilbranch_ida@ameritech.net
Donna Rafanello, Executive Director
Gail Oliphant, Office Manager

3378   International Dyslexia Association: Louisiana Branch Newsletter

2125 Coliseum Street
New Orleans, LA   70130   504-876-0034
                                          FAX 504-595-8848
Marqua Brunette, President

3379   International Dyslexia Association: Philadelphia Branch Newsletter

PO Box 251
Bryn Mawr, PA   19010   610-527-1548
                                          FAX 610-527-5011
Jann Stuart Glider, President

An international 501(c)(3) nonprofit, scientific and educational organization dedicated to the study and treatment of dyslexia. All branches hold at least one public meeting, workshop or conference per year.

3380   International Reading Association Newspaper: Reading Today

PO Box 8139
Newark, DE   19714   302-731-1600
                                          FAX 302-731-1057
                                    http://www.reading.org
                                 e-mail: jbutler@reading.org
Janet Butler, Public Information Associate

The International Reading Association is a professional membership organization dedicated to promoting high levels of literacy for all by improving the quality of reading instruction, disseminating research and information about reading, and encouraging the lifetime reading habit. Our members include classroom teachers, reading specialistsss, consultants, administrators, supervisors, university faculty, researchers, psychologists, librarians, media specialists, and parents.

3381   Journal of Physical Education, Recreation and Dance

1900 Association Drive
Reston, VA   20191   703-476-3475
                                          FAX 703-476-9537
                                    http://www.aahpend.org

80 pages $9.00

3382   LDA Alabama Newsletter

Learning Disabilities Association Alabama
PO Box 11588
Montgomery, AL   36111   334-277-9151
                                          FAX 334-284-9357
                                    http://www.ldaal.org
                              e-mail: alabama@ldaal.org
Debbie Gibson, President

Educational, support, and advocacy group for individuals with learning disabilities and ADD.

3383   LDA Georgia Newsletter

Learning Disabilities Association Georgia
PO Box 1337
Roswell, GA   30077   678-461-4471
                                          FAX 678-461-4472
              http://www.accessatlanta.com/community/groups/
                                    e-mail: ldaga@aol.com
Vicki Hansberger, Executive Director

Information and helpful articles on learning disabilities. Mailed free four times a year to members. Members also receive National Association newsletter four times a year *$40.00*

3384   LDA Illinois Newsletter

Learning Disabilities Association Illinois
10101 S Roberts Road
Palos Hills, IL   60465   708-430-7532
                                          FAX 708-430-7592
                                http://www.idanatl.org/illinois
Sharon Schussler, Administrative Assistant

A non profit organization dedicated to the advancement of the education and general welfare of children and youth of normal or potentially normal intelligence who have perceptual, conceptual, coordinative or related learning disabilities.

3385 Learning Disabilities Association of Texas Newsletter

1011 W 31st Street
Austin, TX   78705   512-458-8234
                                      800-604-7500
                                  FAX 512-458-3826
http://www.ourworld.compuserve.com/homepages/
                                              LD
              e-mail: LDAT@compuserve.com
Ann Robinson, State Coordinator

Provides information, referral for services and support to those with learning disabilities.

3386 Link Newsletter

Parent Information Center of Delaware
700 Barksdale Road
Newark, DE   19711   302-366-0152
                                      888-547-4412
                                  FAX 302-366-0276
                                  TDY:State Relay
              e-mail: picofdel@picofdel.org
Marie-Anne Aghazadian, Director

20 pages   quarterly $12.00

3387 Literacy News

National Institute for Literacy
1775 I Street NW
Washington, DC   20006   202-233-2025
                                  FAX 202-233-2050
                  http://www.novel.nifl.gov

Provides current information on what the Institute is doing and its progress.

3388 Louisiana State Planning Council on Developmental Disabilities Newsletter

PO Box 3455
Baton Rouge, LA   70821   225-342-6804
                                      800-922-DIAL
                                  FAX 225-342-1970
Clarice Eichelberge, Executive Director
Shelia Bridgewater, DIAL Coordinator

To improve circumstances, programs, and systems for people with developmental disabilities.

3389 OSERS Magazine

Office of Special Education & Rehabilitative Svcs.
303 C Street SW
Washington, DC   20202   202-727-6436
                                      800-433-3243
                      http://www.ed.gov

Provides information, research and resources in the area of special learning needs.

Quarterly

3390 Resources in Education

US Government Printing Office
710 N Capitol Street NW
Washington, DC   20401   202-512-0132
                                  FAX 202-512-1355
                  http://www.access.gpo.gov
              e-mail: www.admine@gpo.gov

A monthly publication announcing education related documents.

3391 TASKS's Newsletter

100 W Cerritos Avenue
Anaheim, CA   92805   714-533-8275
                                  FAX 714-533-2533
              e-mail: taskca@yahoo.com
Marta Anchondo, Executive Director
Brenda Smith, Deputy Director

TASK's mission is to enable children with disabilities to reach their maximum potential by providing them, their families and the professionals whoserve them, with training, support information resources and referrals. and by providing community awarness programs.

28 pages   TASK members

3392 TESOL Journal

Teachers of English to Speakers of Other Languages
706 S Washington Street
Alexandria, VA   22314   703-836-0774
                                  FAX 703-836-7864
                  http://www.tesol.org
              e-mail: TJ@tesol.org

TESOL Journal articles focus on teaching and classroom research for classroom practitioners. The journal includes articles about adult education and literacy in every volume year. Subscriptions available to members only.

3393 TESOL Newsletter

Teachers of English to Speakers of Other Languages
700 S Washington Street
Alexandria, VA   22314   703-836-0774
                                  FAX 703-836-7864
              e-mail: info@tesol.org

TESOL produces the Adult Education Interest Section Newsletter and the Refugee Concerns Interest Section Newsletter. They provide news, ideas, and activities for ESL instructors. Subscriptions are available to members only.

3394 TESOL Quarterly

Teachers of English to Speakers of Other Languages
700 S Washington Street
Alexandria, VA   22314   703-836-0774
                                  FAX 703-836-7864
                  http://www.tesol.edu
              e-mail: info@tesol.org

TESOL Quarterly is a referred interdisciplinary journal teachers of English to speakers of other languages. Subscriptions available to members.

Young Adults

3395   Get Ready to Read!
National Center for Learning Disabilities
381 Park Avenue S
New York, NY   10016   212-545-7510
                                        888-575-7373
                               FAX 212-545-9665
                                    http://www.ld.org
                               e-mail: help@ncld.org
Amber Eden, Assistant Director Online Comm.
Hal Stucker, Managing Editor

Quarterly

3396   LD Advocate
National Center for Learning Disabilities
381 Park Avenue S
New York, NY   10016   212-545-7510
                                        888-575-7373
                               FAX 212-545-9665
                                    http://www.ld.org
                               e-mail: help@ncld.org
Amber Eden, Assistant Director Online Comm.
Hal Stucker, Managing Editor

Monthly

3397   LD News
National Center for Learning Disabilities
381 Park Avenue S
New York, NY   10016   212-545-7510
                                        888-575-7373
                               FAX 212-545-9665
                                    http://www.ld.org
                               e-mail: help@ncld.org
Amber Eden, Assistant Director Online Comm.
Hal Stucker, Managing Editor

Monthly

3398   Literary Cavalcade
Scholastic
555 Broadway
New York, NY   10012

Every issue makes literature come alive with captivating reading students will love, and skill-building activities that meet your teaching needs. *$8.95*

48 pages

3399   National Geographic World
1145 17th Street NW
Washington, DC   20036   202-857-7000
                                        800-647-5463
                               FAX 202-429-5712

Susan M Tejada, Editor

Features factual stories on outdoor adventures, natural history, sports, science and history. Special features include posters, games, crafts and mazes. *$17.95*

32 pages

3400   Our World
National Center for Learning Disabilities
381 Park Avenue S
New York, NY   10016   212-545-7510
                                        888-575-7373
                               FAX 212-545-9665
                                    http://www.ld.org
                               e-mail: help@ncld.org
Amber Eden, Assistant Director Online Comm.
Hal Stucker, Managing Editor

Quarterly

3401   Scholastic Action
Scholastic
555 Broadway
New York, NY   10012
Patrick Daley, Editor

Motivate your grades 7-12 below-level readers to read and improve their language arts skills with FREE-trial copies of Scholastic Action. *$7.95*

32 pages

3402   Sibling Forum
Family Resource Associates
35 Haddon Avenue
Shrewsbury, NJ   07702   732-747-5310
                               FAX 732-747-1896

Susan Levine, Editor

Newsletter for siblings aged 10 through teens with brothers or sisters with disabilities. Includes library information, special definitions and feedback from readers. Each issue also has a Focusing on Feelings discussion. A useful tool for siblings, parents, educators, and special workers. *$12.00*

12 pages   4 Times/Sibling

General

3403 Academic Communication Associates

Educational Book Division
4149 Avenida de la Plata
Oceanside, CA 92052   760-758-9593
888-758-9558
FAX 760-758-1604
http://www.acadcom.com
e-mail: acom@acadcom.com
Dr. Larry Mattes, Founder/President

Publishes hundreds of speech and language products, educational books and assessment materials for children and adults with speech, language, and hearing disorders, learning disabilities, developmental disabilities, and special learning needs. Products include books, software programs, learning games, augmentative communication materials, bilingual/multicultural materials, and special education resources.

Catalog

3404 Academic Success Press

6023 26th Street W
PO Box 132
Bradenton, FL 34207
888-822-6657
http://www.academicsuccess.com
Paul D Nolting PhD, Author

Publishes books and materials in the interest of making the classroom learning experience less difficult, while improving student learning, to transform the classroom into a more successful environment where educators and students can use inventive learning techniques based on sound academic research.

3405 Academic Therapy Publications

20 Commercial Boulevard
Novato, CA 94949   415-883-3314
800-422-7249
FAX 888-287-9975
http://www.academictherapy.com
e-mail: sales@academictherapy.com
John Arena, Founder

Publishes supplementary education materials for people with reading, learning and communication disabilities; features professional texts and reference books, curriculum materials, teacher/parent resources, and visual/perceptual training aids.

3406 Active Parenting Publishers

1955 Vaughn Road NW
Kennesaw, GA 30144   770-429-0565
800-825-0060
FAX 770-429-0334
http://www.activeparenting.com
e-mail: cservice@activeparenting.com
Michael H Popkin PhD, Founder/President
Harry Popkin, Secretary to the President

Publishes materials that teach parenting skills. Offers video-based training and program packages that include videos, guidebooks, CD-ROMs and additional items.

3407 Alexander Graham Bell Association for the Deaf and Hard of Hearing

3417 Volta Place NW
Washington, DC 20007   202-337-5220
FAX 202-337-8270
http://www.agbell.org
e-mail: publications@agbell.org
K Todd Houston PhD, Executive Director/CEO
Kathleen Daniel Sussman, President
Rachel Reed, Director Publication Projects

Publishes and distributes books, brochures, instructional materials, videos, CDs and audiocassettes relating to hearing loss.

Magazine

3408 American Guidance Service

4201 Woodland Road
Circle Pines, MN 55014   651-287-7220
800-328-2560
FAX 800-471-8457
http://www.agsnet.com
e-mail: agsmail@agsnet.com

Produces assessments, textbooks, and instructional materials for people with a wide range of needs; publishes individually administered tests to measure cognitive ability, achievement, behavior, speech and language skills, and personal and social adjustment.

3409 American Printing House for the Blind

1839 Frankfort Avenue
Louisville, KY 40206   502-895-2405
800-233-1839
FAX 502-899-2274
http://www.aph.org
e-mail: info@aph.org
Tuck Tinsley III, President
Fred Gissoni, Customer Support
Tony Grantz, Business Development Manager

Promotes independence of blind and visually impaired persons by providing specialized materials, products, and services needed for education and life.

3410 American Psychological Association

750 1st Street NE
Washington, DC 20002   202-336-5650
800-374-2722
FAX 202-336-5633
http://www.apa.org/psycinfo
e-mail: psycinfo@apa.org

Publishes periodicals, including PsycSCAN, a quarterly print abstract that provides citations to the journal literature on Learning Disorders and Mental Retardation, including theories, research, assessment, treatment, rehabilitation, and educational issues. Also publishes Psychological Abstracts, a monthly print reference tool containing summaries of journal articles, book chapters and books in the field of psychology and related disciplines.

3411 Associated Services for the Blind

919 Walnut Street
Philadelphia, PA 19107 215-627-0600
FAX 215-922-0692
http://www.asb.org
e-mail: asbinfo@asb.org
Dolores Ferrara-Godzieba, Director
Patricia C Johnson, CEO

Promotes self-esteem, independence and self-determination in blind and visually impaired people, providing educational materials, training and resources.

3412 BOSC Books on Special Children

BOSC Publishing
PO Box 3378
Amherst, MA 01004 413-256-8164
FAX 413-256-8896
http://www.boscbooks.com
e-mail: contact@boscbooks.com
Irene Slovak, Founder/Owner
Marcia Young, President

Offers books that cover all kinds of disabilities to librarians, other professionals and parents; publishes the BOSC Directory of programs, clinics, and centers for disabled individuals.

3413 Bethany House Publishers

11400 Hampshire Avenue S
Minneapolis, MN 55438 616-676-9185
800-877-2665
FAX 616-676-9576
http://www.bethanyhouse.com
e-mail: orders@bakerbooks.com
Teresa Fogarty, General Publicist

Publishes books in large-print format for the learning disabled.

3414 Blackwell Publishing

350 Main Street
Malden, MA 02148 781-388-8200
FAX 781-388-8210
http://www.blackwellpublishing.com
e-mail: dpeters@bos.blackwellpublishing.com
Rene Olivieri, Chief Executive
Dawn Peters, Media Contact

Publishes books and journals for the higher education, research and professional markets, including several journals on topics relating to learning disabilities.

3415 Brookes Publishing

PO Box 10624
Baltimore, MD 21285 410-337-9580
800-638-3775
FAX 410-337-8539
http://www.brookespublishing.com
e-mail: custserv@brookespublishing.com
Paul H Brookes, President
Melissa A Behm, VP

Publishes books, texts, curricula, videos, tools and a newsletter based on research in disabilities, education and child development, including learning disabilities, ADHD, communication and language, reading and literacy, and special education.

Catalog

3416 Brookline Books/Lumen Editions

PO Box 97
Newton Upper Falls, MA 02464 800-666-2665
FAX 617-558-8011
http://www.brooklinebooks.com
e-mail: milt@brooklinebooks.com

Publishes books on education, learning and topics relating to disabilities.

3417 Charles C Thomas Publisher

2600 S 1st Street
Springfield, IL 62704 217-789-8980
800-258-8980
FAX 217-789-9130
http://www.ccthomas.com
e-mail: books@ccthomas.com

Publishes books on education and special education for the blind and visually impaired, the gifted and talented, the developmentally disabled, and people with learning disabilities.

3418 City Creek Press

1422 W Lake Street #202
Minneapolis, MN 55408 612-823-2500
800-585-6059
FAX 612-823-5380
http://www.citycreek.com
Judy Liautaud, Owner

Publishes books and products offering a literature-based method of learning, such as books, clue cards, posters, magnetic math story boards, workbooks and audio tapes; the program is multisensory, interactive, and appeals to the visual, auditory and tactile learning styles.

3419 Connecticut Association for Children and Adults with Learning Disabilities

25 Van Zant Street
East Norwalk, CT 06855 203-838-5010
FAX 203-866-6108
http://www.cacld.org
e-mail: cacld@optonline.net

Offers over 300 books and titles to ensure access to the resources needed to help children and adults with learning disabilities and attention disorders achieve their full potential.

3428 Guilford Publications

72 Spring Street
New York, NY 10012   212-431-9800
800-365-7006
FAX 212-966-6708
http://www.guilford.com
e-mail: info@guilford.com
Seymour Weingarten, Editor-in-Chief
Chris Jennison, Senior Editor, Education
Robert Matloff, President

Publishes books for education on the subjects of literacy, general education, school psychology and special education. Also offers books, videos, audio cassettes and software, as well as journals, newsletters, and AD/HD resources.

3429 Harcourt Achieve

PO Box 690789
Orlando, FL 32819
800-531-5015
FAX 800-699-9459
http://www.harcourtachieve.com
Tim McEwen, President/CEO
Jeff Johnson, Director Marketing/Communication

Produces learning solutions and materials to help young and adult learners, based on a development philosophy that assesses learner's skills, matches them to appropriate content, and accelerates the ability of learners to meet and exceed expectations.

Catalog

3430 Hazelden Publishing and Educational Services

15251 Pleasant Valley Road
Center City, MN 55012
800-328-9000
FAX 651-213-4577
http://www.hazelden.org
e-mail: customersupport@hazelden.org
Nick Motu, VP/Publisher
Christine Anderson, Media Specialist

Publishes real-world resources that are accessible for all experience levels and learning styles, including audio and video formats, manuals for educators, workbooks for students, and a catalog of products.

Catalog

3431 Heinemann-Boynton/Cook

361 Hanover Street
Portsmouth, NH 03801   603-431-7894
800-225-5800
FAX 603-431-2214
http://www.boyntoncook.com
e-mail: custserv@heinemann.com
George Goldberg, VP Human Resources

Publishes professional resources and provides educational services for teachers, and offers nearly 100 titles related to learning disabilities.

3432 High Noon Books

20 Commercial Boulevard
Novato, CA 94949
800-422-7249
FAX 888-287-9975
http://www.academictherapy.com
e-mail: sales@academictherapy.com

Features over 35 sets of high-interest, low-level books written on a first through fourth grade reading level, for people with reading difficulties, ages nine and up.

3433 Holt, Rinehart and Winston

Language Arts Catalog
6277 Sea Harbor Drive
Orlando, FL 32887
800-225-5425
FAX 800-269-5232
http://www.hrw.com
e-mail: holtinfo@hrw.com

Publishes secondary educational material including curriculum-based textbooks, CD-ROMs, videodiscs, and other support and reference materials.

3434 JKL Communications

2700 Virginia Avenue NW #707
Washington, DC 20037   202-333-1713
FAX 202-333-1735
http://www.lathamlaw.org
e-mail: plath@lathamlaw.org
Peter S Latham JD, Director
Patricia Horan Latham JD, Director

Publishes books and videos on learning disabilities and ADD with a focus on legal issues in school, higher education and employment.

3435 Jewish Braille Institute of America

110 E 30th Street
New York, NY 10016   212-889-2525
800-433-1531
FAX 212-689-3692
http://www.jewishbraille.org
e-mail: eisler@jbilibrary.org
Dr. Ellen Isler, Executive VP
Israel Taub, Associate Director
Sandra Radinsky, Director of Development

Publishes magazines, a newsletter, and special resources available to the reading disabled who are themselves print-handicapped in varying degrees. Seeks the integration of Jews who are blind, visually impaired and reading disabled into the Jewish community and society.

Newsletter

3436 Learning Disabilities Association of America

4156 Library Road
Pittsburgh, PA 15234   412-341-1515
FAX 412-344-0224
http://www.ldanatl.org
e-mail: info@ldaamerica.org
Marianne Toombs, President
Suzanne Fornaro, First VP
Connie Parr, Second VP

Maintains a large inventory of publications, videos and other materials related to learning disabilities, and publishes two periodicals available by subscription as well as various books, booklets, brochures, papers and pamphlets on topics related to learning disabilities.

3437 Learning Disabilities Resources

6 E Eagle Road
Havertown, PA   19083   610-446-6126
                              800-869-8336
                         FAX 610-446-6129
           http://www.learningdifferences.com
           e-mail: rcooper-ldr@comcast.net
Dr. Richard Cooper, Author
Dr. Richard Cooper, Executive Director

Offers a variety of resources to help teach the learning disabled, including alternative ways to teach math, language, spelling, vocabulary, and also how to organize and study. Available in books, videos, and audio tapes.

Catalog

3438 Library Reproduction Service

LRS
14214 S Figueroa Street
Los Angeles, CA   90061   310-354-2610
                              800-255-5002
                         FAX 310-354-2601
              http://www.lrs-largeprint.com
                  e-mail: lrsprint@aol.com
Joan Hudson-Miller, President

Offers large print reproductions to special needs students in first grade through post-secondary, as well as adult basic and continuing education programs; also produces an extensive collection of large print classics for all ages as well as children's literature.

Catalog

3439 LinguiSystems

3100 Fourth Avenue
East Moline, IL   61244   309-755-2300
                               800-776-4332
                          FAX 800-577-4555
                          TDY:800-933-8331
                http://www.linguisystems.com
            e-mail: service@linguisystems.com
Linda Bowers, Co-Owner
Rosemary Huisingh, Co-Owner

Publishes a newsletter and speech-language materials for learning disabilities, ADD/ADHD, auditory processing and listening, language skills, fluency and voice, reading and comprehension, social skills and pragmatics, vocabulary and concepts, writing, spelling, punctuation and other specialized subjects.

Catalog

3440 Love Publishing Company

9101 E Kenyon Avenue
Denver, CO   80237   303-221-7333
                          FAX 303-221-7444
                http://www.lovepublishing.com
              e-mail: lpc@lovepublishing.com

Publishes titles for use in special education, counseling, social work, and individuals with learning differences.

Catalog

3441 Magination Press

750 First Street NE
Washington, DC   20002
                               800-374-2721
                          FAX 202-336-5502
              http://www.maginationpress.com
                e-mail: magination@apa.org

Publishes special books for children's special concerns, including starting school, learning disabilities, and other topics in psychology, development and mental health.

Catalog

3442 Marsh Media

8025 Ward Parkway Plaza
Kansas City, MO   64114
                               800-821-3303
                          FAX 866-333-7421
                 http://www.marshmedia.com
                e-mail: info@marshmedia.com

Offers educational videos, storybooks and language-intensive teaching guides with a focus on key character-building concepts, health and guidance.

3443 Mindworks Press

4019 Westerly Place
Newport Beach, CA   92660   949-266-3730
                          FAX 949-266-3770
               http://www.mindworkspress.com
            e-mail: mindworkspress@aol.com
Dr. Daniel Amen, Author

Features books, audio, video, and CD-ROMs addressing a range of disorders, including anxiety, depression, obsessive-compulsiveness and ADD.

Catalog

3444 Modern Learning Press

PO Box 9067
Cambridge, MA   02139
                               800-627-5867
                          FAX 888-558-7350
                   http://www.modlearn.com
                 e-mail: mlp@epsbooks.com

Publishes materials to help students, teachers and parents with literacy, school readiness and other important aspects of education and childhood.

3445 Music Section: National Library Service for the Blind and Physically Handicapped

Library of Congress
1291 Taylor Street NW
Washington, DC   20542   202-707-5100
                                800-424-8567
                            FAX 202-707-0712
                            TDY:202-707-0744
                      http://www.loc.gov/nls/music
                          e-mail: nlsm@loc.gov
John Hanson, Department Head

Offers a special music collection consisting of more than 30,000 braille and large print music scores, texts, and instructional recordings about music and musicians on cassette and audio disc.

3446 National Association for Visually Handicapped

22 W 21st Street
New York, NY   10010   212-889-3141
                          FAX 212-727-2931
                        http://www.navh.org
                       e-mail: staff@navh.org
Lorraine H Marchi, Founder/CEO

Publishes information about sight and sight problems for adults and children. Offers a product line of low-vision aids, a collection of articles about eye conditions, causes and treatment modalities, and a newsletter issued four times a year with information to assist people in dealing with low vision.

Newsletter

3447 National Bible Association

1865 Broadway
New York, NY   10023   212-408-1390
                          FAX 212-408-1448
                     http://www.nationalbible.org
                   e-mail: nba@nationalbible.org
Thomas May, President
Tamara Collins, VP Reading Program

Publishes Read it! A Journal for Bible Readers, which is issued three times a year. Also offers many versions of the Bible, including large-print editions and the easy-to-read Contemporary English Version.

3448 Northwest Media

326 W 12th Avenue
Eugene, OR   97401   541-343-6636
                            800-777-6636
                        FAX 541-343-0177
                   http://www.sociallearning.com
                  e-mail: nwm@northwestmedia.com
Lee White, President

Publishes material with a focus on independent living and foster care products.

3449 Oxton House Publishers

PO Box 209
Farmington, ME   04938   800-539-7323
                            FAX 207-779-0623
                        http://www.oxtonhouse.com
                     e-mail: oxtonhse@mainewest.com

Provides books and educational materials specializing in materials for teaching reading and mathematics and for dealing with learning disabilities.

3450 Performance Resource Press

1270 Rankin
Troy, MI   48083   800-453-7733
                      FAX 800-499-5718
                  http://www.prponline.net
              e-mail: customerservice@prponline.net

Publishes over 600 products, including catalogs, journals, digests, newsletters, books, videos, posters and pamplets with a focus on behavioral health.

Catalogs

3451 Peytral Publications

PO Box 1162
Minnetonka, MN   55345   952-949-8707
                                877-739-8725
                            FAX 952-906-9777
                        http://www.peytral.com
                       e-mail: help@peytral.com

Publishes and distributes special education materials which promote success for all learners.

3452 Phillip Roy

The Roy Building
Largo, FL   33774   727-593-2700
                            800-255-9085
                        FAX 727-595-2685
                    http://www.philliproy.com
                   e-mail: info@philliproy.com
Ruth Bragman PhD, President

Publishes educational materials written for students of any age with different learning abilities. Offers an alternative approach to traditional education. Free catalog upon request.

Catalog

3453 Reader's Digest Partners for Sight Foundation

Reader's Digest Road
Pleasantville, NY   10570   800-877-5293
                            http://www.rd.com
                    e-mail: partnersforsight@rd.com
Susan Olivo, VP/General Manager
Dianna Kelly-Naghizadeh, Program Manager

Offers large type editions of select books and large print editions of Readers Digest Magazines, as well as a foundation newsletter, Sightlines, which is published in large format with large type.

Newsletter

3454 Riggs Institute

4185 SW 102nd Avenue
Beaverton, OR   97005   503-646-9459
                              800-200-4840
                         FAX 503-644-5191
                    http://www.riggsinst.org
                 e-mail: riggs@riggsinst.org
Myrna McCulloch, Founder/Director/Author

Publishes materials to help remedial students using
the Orton method, a multisensory approach to learning. Offers a catalog of products, including teacher's
editions, phonogram cards, audio CDs for students,
student materials and classroom materials.

Catalog

3455 Scholastic

557 Broadway
New York, NY   10012   212-343-6100
                              800-246-2986
                    http://www.scholastic.com
Richard Robinson, Chairman/President/CEO
Barbara A Marcus, VP/President Children's Books
Richard M Spaulding, Executive VP Marketing

Produces educational materials to assist and inspire
students of all ages, including a range of special education books, software, and other products.

3456 Schwab Learning

1650 S Amphlett Boulevard
San Mateo, CA   94402   650-655-2410
                               800-230-0988
                          FAX 650-655-2411
                 http://www.schwablearning.org
              e-mail: media@schwablearning.org

Provides information, guidance, support and materials that address the emotional, social, practical and academic needs and concerns of children with learning
difficulties, and their parents.

3457 Slosson Educational Publications

538 Buffalo Road
East Aurora, NY   14052   716-652-0930
                                 888-756-7766
                            FAX 800-655-3840
                      http://www.slosson.com
                  e-mail: slosson@slosson.com

Publishes and distributes educational materials in the
areas of intelligence, aptitude, developmental disabilities, school screening and achievement, speech-language and assessment therapy, emotional/behavior,
and special needs. Offers a product line of testing and
assessment materials, books, games, videos, cassettes
and computer software intended for use by professionals, psychologists, teachers, counselors, students and
parents.

Catalog

3458 Teddy Bear Press

3639 Midway Drive
San Diego, CA   92110   619-223-7311
                          FAX 619-255-2158
                 http://www.teddybearpress.net
             e-mail: fparker@teddybearpress.net
Fran Parker, Author

Publishes books and reading materials designed with
the beginning reader in mind, written and illustrated
by a special education teacher specializing in elementary education, learning disabilities, and education
for the emotionally and mentally challenged.

3459 Therapro

225 Arlington Street
Framingham, MA   01702   508-872-9494
                                800-257-5376
                           FAX 508-875-2062
                  http://www.theraproducts.com
                e-mail: info@theraproducts.com
Karen Conrad ScD OTR/L, Co-Founder
Paul Weihrauch PhD, Co-Founder

Offers specialty products and publications for all ages
in the field of occupational therapy, including
assistive technology, evaluations, handwriting programs, sensory-motor awareness and alerting products, oral motor products, early learning products, and
perception, cognition and language resources.

Catalog

3460 Thomas Nelson Publishers

PO Box 141000
Nashville, TN   37214   615-889-9000
                               800-889-9000
                          FAX 615-391-5225
                 http://www.thomasnelson.com
             e-mail: publicity@thomasnelson.com
Sam Moore, Chairman/CEO/President/Director
Michael S Hyatt, Executive VP/Group Publisher
Phil Stoner, Executive VP/Group Publisher

Publishes books and other resources for the learning
disabled.

3461 Thomas T Beeler, Publisher

PO Box 310
Rollinsford, NH   03869   603-794-0392
                                 800-818-7574
                            FAX 888-222-3396
                     http://www.beelerpub.com
                e-mail: tombeeler@beelerpub.com
Thomas T Beeler, Publisher
David W O'Connor, President
Traci Watson, Editor

Publishes and distributes hardcover, large print editions of popular titles for all ages, printed in 16-point
type on acid-free paper and bound in sturdy, li-
brary-grade sewn binding with full color covers. Also
offers audiobooks.

3462 Thorndike Press

295 Kennedy Memorial Drive
Waterville, ME   04901
                               800-223-1244
                          FAX 800-558-4676
              http://www.galegroup.com/thorndike
Debbie Ludden, Director Marketing
Jill Leckta, General Manager/Publisher

Publishes and distributes over 900 new large-print
editions per year, with an emphasis on bestsellers and
genre fiction, as well as nonfiction titles.

3463 Transaction Publishers

Rutgers University
35 Berrue Circle
Piscataway, NJ   08854   732-445-2280
                                          888-999-6778
                                   FAX 732-445-3138
                   http://www.transactionpub.com
                   e-mail: trans@transactionpub.com
Irving Louis Horowitz, Chairman
Mary E Curtis, President
Scott B Bramson, President Express Book Division

Publishes over 70 books in large print, including new
large print titles, as well as selections from the best of
the company's backlist, with many classic titles from
well-known American authors. The large print format
makes selection easy for visually impaired readers.

3464 Ulverscroft Large Print Books

PO Box 1230
West Seneca, NY   14224   716-674-4270
                                          800-955-9659
                                   FAX 716-674-4195
                       http://www.ulverscroft.com
                   e-mail: enquiries@ulverscroft.co.uk
Jan McGowan, Director

Publishes large print books and audio products for
people hard of seeing.

3465 Wadsworth Publishing Company

10 Davis Drive
Belmont, CA   94002   650-595-2350
                                          800-354-9706
                                   FAX 650-637-7544
                       http://www.wadworth.com
       e-mail: dory.schaeffer@thomsonlearning.com
Dan Alpert, Acquisitions Editor
Dory Schaeffer, Marketing Manager

Publishes books on a wide range of topics in special
education, including behavior modification, language
disorders and development, and learning disabilities.

3466 Waterfront Books

85 Crescent Road
Burlington, VT   05401
                                          800-639-6063
                   http://www.waterfrontbooks.com
                   e-mail: helpkids@waterfrontbooks.com
Sherrill N Musty, President

Publishes and distributes informative books and materials serving professionals and parents who are concerned with children at home, at school and in the
workplace. Topics include overcoming barriers to
learning, family support and parenting, personal
safety, learning differences and special needs.

Catalog

3467 Woodbine House

6510 Bells Mill Road
Bethesda, MD   20817   301-897-3570
                                          800-843-7323
                                   FAX 301-897-5838
                   http://www.woodbinehouse.com
                   e-mail: info@woodbinehouse.com
Irv Shapell, Publisher

Specializes in books about children with special
needs; publishes sixty-five titles within the Special
Needs Collection, covering AD/HD, learning disabilities, special education, communication skills, and
other disabilities, for use by parents, children, therapists, health care providers and teachers.

3468 Xavier Society for the Blind

154 E 23rd Street
New York, NY   10010   212-473-7800
Gina Ballero, Secretary to Director

Provides resources for the visually impaired, including large-print, braille, and audio products.

3469 York Press

PO Box 504
Timonium, MD   21094
                                          800-962-2763
                                   FAX 410-560-6758
                       http://www.yorkpress.com
                       e-mail: info@yorkpress.com

Publishes books about language development and disabilities, especially dyslexia, and about hearing impairment.

Classroom Resources

3470 ADD From A to Z

Connecticut Assoc. for Children and Adults with LD
25 Van Zant Street
East Norwalk, CT   06855   203-838-5010
                                  FAX 203-866-6108
                                  http://www.CACLD.org
                                  e-mail: cacld@juno.com
Edward Hallowell MD, Presenter

Dr. Hallowell, child and adult psychiatrist on the faculty of the Harvard Medical School, is widely regarded as a leading authority on the subject of Attention Deficit Disorder. This video version of one of his classic lectures provides a comprehensive overview of this complicated and often misunderstood subject. Topics include symptoms to look for, how to tell if it is not ADD, twenty steps to diagnosis, methods of treatment (medical and nonmedical) and the Ritalin controversy. *$34.95*

$5.00 shipping

3471 ASCD Cooperative Learning Series

Assoc. for Supervision/Curriculum Development
1250 N Beauregard Street
Alexandria, VA   22311   703-578-9600
                                800-933-ASCD
                                FAX 703-575-5400
                                http://www.ascd.org
RE Slavin, Author

A facilitator's manual, book and five videotapes focusing on: providing a fundamental knowledge of cooperative learning and the benefits derived from its use, providing a basic understanding of how to plan and teach cooperative lessons and providing resources.

3472 Arts Express

KET, The Kentucky Network Enterprise Division
600 Cooper Drive
Lexington, KY   40502   859-258-7000
                               800-354-9067
                               FAX 859-258-7396

A delightful way to introduce elementary students to the visual arts, music and dance. Twenty 15 minute video programs available individually or on five videotapes of four programs each. *$320.00*

price/set

3473 Becoming a Proficient Cuer

Harris Communications
15155 Technology Drive
Eden Prairie, MN   55344   952-906-1180
                                  800-825-6758
                                  FAX 952-906-1099
                                  TDY:952-906-1198
                                  http://www.harriscomm.com
Melanie Metzger
Earl Fleetwood

Video lessons are combined with workbook drills to describe and teach Cued Speech, and prevent and eliminate errors. Designed for hearing people at all levels of Cued Speech proficiency. *$49.95*

19 pages   108-min. Video

3474 Collaboration in the Schools: The Problem-Solving Process

Pro-Ed
8700 Shoal Creek Boulevard
Austin, TX   78757   512-451-3246
                            800-897-3202
                            FAX 512-451-8542
                            http://www.proedinc.com
L Idol, Author

An inservice/preservice video that demonstrates the stages of the consultative/collaborative process, as well as many of the various communicative/interactive skills and collaborative problem solving skills. *$106.00*

3475 College Transition

Central Piedmont Community College
PO Box 35009
Charlotte, NC   28235   704-330-2722
                               FAX 704-330-6136
                               http://www.cpcc.cc.nc.us

A video developed for facilitators to show to audiences of high school students, college transfer students and college freshman.

3476 Cooperative Discipline: Classroom Management Promoting Self-Esteem

AGS
4201 Woodland Road
Circle Pines, MN   55014   763-786-4343
                                  800-328-2560
                                  FAX 763-786-9077
                                  http://www.agsnet.com
                                  e-mail: agsmail@agsnet.com
L Albert, Author

A leader's guide, teacher's guide, set of 23 blackline masters, 2 scripts and 2 videotapes comprise this comprehensive discipline training program that helps teachers achieve control and order in their classroom. *$495.00*

3477 Designing Clinical Strategies for Language Impaired Children

Purdue University Continuing Education
1586 Stewart Center
West Lafayette, IN   47907   765-494-7231
                                    800-359-2968
                                    FAX 765-494-0567
Jeanette S Leonard MS, Author
Laurence B Leonard, Author

Discusses the application of single subject designs involving therapy with language-impaired children in day-to-day clinical practices; values of the designs for monitoring a child's progress and for assessing clinical effectiveness. *$81.00*

3478 Educational Evaluation

Stern Center for Language and Learning
135 Allen Brook Lane
Williston, VT   05495   802-878-2332
                              800-544-4863
                         FAX 802-878-0230
               http://www.sterncenter.org
               e-mail: learning@sterncenter.org
Andrea Brown

The evaluation is an assessment of intelligence, academic achievement, language, and emotional and behavioral issues related to learning and includes pre- and post- evaluation conferences with parents and/ or students as well as an extensive written report detailing results and recommendations.

3479 Fundamentals of Reading Success

Educators Publishing Service
31 Smith Place
Cambridge, MA   02138   617-547-6706
                              800-225-5750
                         FAX 617-547-0412
               http://www.epsbooks.com
               e-mail: eps@epsbooks.com
Arlene W Sonday, Author

This Orton-Gillingham-based video series teaches a phonic or code-emphasis approach to reading, spelling, and handwriting, and provides the foundation for a multisensory phonics curriculum. May be used by teachers and tutors. *$ 480.00*

ISBN 0-838872-52-2

3480 Individual Instruction

Stern Center for Language and Learning
135 Allen Brook Lane
Williston, VT   05495   802-878-2332
                              800-544-4863
                         FAX 802-878-0230
               http://www.sterncenter.org
               e-mail: learning@sterncenter.org
Stefanie Mitchell

Individualized instruction to help students develop literacy skills and achieve academic success, building on learning strengths and compensating for areas of difficulty.

3481 Instructional Strategies for Learning Disabled Community College Students

Graduate School and University Center
365 5th Avenue
New York, NY   10036   212-817-7000
                         FAX 212-817-1503
               http://www.gc.cuny.edu

For working with a cross-section of types of individuals with learning problems. *$47.50*

3482 Key Concepts in Personal Development

Marsh Media
8082 Ward Parkway Plaza
Kansas City, MO   64114   816-523-1059
                                800-821-3303
                           FAX 866-333-7421
                 http://www.marshmedia.com
                 e-mail: info@marshmedia.com
Joan Marsh, President
Liz Sweeney, Editorial Assistant

Our videos, books, and teaching guides bring character education to the classrom. These kits are invaluable aids in teaching everyday values like honesty, anger control, trustworthiness, perseverance, understanding and respect. They help you prepare youngsters to meet challenges and greet opportunities with skill and optimism.

3483 New Room Arrangement as a Teaching Strategy

Teaching Strategies
PO Box 42243
Washington, DC   20015   202-362-7543
                                800-637-3652
                           FAX 202-364-7273
              http://www.TeachingStrategies.com
              e-mail: info@TeachingStrategies.com
Diane Trister Dodge

A manual and video present the impact of the early childhood classroom environment on how children learn, how they relate to others and how teachers teach. *$35.00*

3484 Now You're Talking: Extend Conversation

Educational Productions
9000 SW Gemini Drive
Beaverton, OR   97008   503-644-7000
                              800-950-4949
                         FAX 503-350-7000
               http://www.edpro.com
               e-mail: custserv@edpro.com
C Sharp, Author
Molly Krumm, Marketing Directror

Video. Teachers in a language-based preschool and speech-language pathologists model effective techniques that focus and extend conversations of young children. *$295.00*

3485 Phonemic Awareness: Lessons, Activities and Games

Peytral Publication
PO Box 1162
Minnetonka, MN   55345   952-949-8707
                                877-739-8725
                           FAX 612-906-9777
                 http://www.peytral.com
                 e-mail: help@peytral.com
Victoria Groves Scott, Author

Exceptional field tested guide to help educators who want to reach phonemic awareness as a prerequisite to reading, and/or to supplement the current curriculum. Special educators and speech clinicians will find this practical guide especially helpful as research indicates that deficits in phonemic awareness is often a major contributor to reading disabilities. This book contains fifty-eight scripted lessons, forty-nine reproducible blackline master and progress charts. Video also available *$27.95*

176 pages
ISBN 1-890455-28-8

3486 Planning Individualized Education Programs for Language-Impaired Children

Purdue University Continuing Education
1586 Stewart Center
West Lafayette, IN   47907   765-494-7231
                                    800-359-2968
                               FAX 765-494-0567
Nickola Wolf Nelson, PhD, Author

Stresses the need to select different kinds of intervention strategies and content for different types of language disorders.   Includes general consideration regarding the identification, writing and implementing of goals and short-term objectives. *$81.00*

3487 Professional Development

Stern Center for Language and Learning
135 Allen Brook Lane
Williston, VT   05495   802-878-2332
                               800-544-4863
                          FAX 802-878-0230
                     http://www.sterncenter.org
                 e-mail: learning@sterncenter.org
Jackie Earle Cruickshanks

Staff development programs for preschool through grade 12 designed in response to requests from teachers and administrators for cutting-edge information about different kinds of learners and the teaching strategies most successful for them.

3488 Restructuring America's Schools

Association for Supervision/Curriculum Development
1703 N Beaurguard Street
Alexandria, VA   22314   703-578-9600
                           FAX 703-549-3891
                          http://www.ascd.org
M D'Arcangelo, Author

A leader's guide and videotape designed for administrators, teachers, parents, school board members, and community leaders.

3489 Science Showtime! Videos

Steck-Vaughn Company
PO Box 690789
Orlando, FL   32819
                               800-531-5015
                          FAX 512-343-6854
                    http://www.steck-vaughn.com
                    e-mail: info@steck-vaughn.com

Interactive videos that bring science concepts to life. Programs of 6 to 12 minutes include Wonder Stops for classroom discussion. Additional Interactive Video Segments with activity sheets challenge listening, observing, and problem-solving skills.

3490 Skillstreaming Video: How to Teach Students Prosocial Skills

Research Press
PO Box 9177
Champaign, IL   61826   217-352-3273
                               800-519-2707
                          FAX 217-352-1221
                     http://www.researchpress.com
                     e-mail: rp@researchpress.com
Dr. AP Goldstein And Dr. Ellen McGinness, Author
Ann Wendell, President

A video and two books providing an overview of a training procedure for teaching elementary and secondary level students the skills they need for coping with typical social and interpersonal problems. *$365.00*

3491 Spelling Workbook Video

Learning Disabilities Resources
PO Box 716
Bryn Mawr, PA   19010   610-525-8336
                               800-869-8336
                          FAX 610-525-8337
                        http://www.ldonline.org

An instructional video which works through the spelling workbooks for teachers and students. *$16.00*

3492 Strategic Planning and Leadership

Assoc. for Supervision/Curriculum Development
1703 N Beauregard Street
Alexandria, VA   22311   703-578-9600
                                800-933-2723
                           FAX 703-575-5400
                          http://www.ascd.org

Designed to explain and illustrate effective approaches to dealing with change through strategic planning.

3493 Strategies Intervention Program

Special Education Resource Center
25 Industrial Park Road
Middletown, CT   06457   860-632-1485
                           FAX 860-632-8870
A Marks, Author

A video illustrating through an interview with five eighth grade students, the effectiveness of a program designed to develop specific learning strategies for adolescents with learning disabilities.

3494 Teaching Adults with Learning Disabilities

Stern Center for Language and Learning
135 Allen Brook Lane
Williston, VT   05495   802-878-2332
                               800-544-4863
                          FAX 802-878-0230
                     http://www.sterncenter.org
                 e-mail: bpodhajski@sterncenter.org
Blanche Podhajski PhD, President/Editor

A videotape training program and companion guide designed to help adult literacy teachers identify and instruct adults with learning disabilities. The focus of this five hour video series is on teaching basic reading and spelling skills. *$199.95*

3495 Teaching Math

Learning Disabilities Resources
PO Box 716
Bryn Mawr, PA   19010   610-525-8336
                                      800-869-8336
                               FAX 610-525-8337
                               http://www.ldonline.org

A video for educational professionals teaching math
to disabled children. *$12.00*

3496 Teaching People with Developmental Disabilities

Research Press
PO Box 9177
Champaign, IL   61826   217-352-3273
                                  800-519-2707
                           FAX 217-352-1221
                           http://www.researchpress.com
                           e-mail: rp@researchpress.com
Ann Wendell, President

A set of four videotapes and accompanying participant workbooks designed to help teachers, staff, volunteers, or family members master task analysis,
prompting, reinforcement and error correction.
$595.00

**3497 Teaching Strategies Library: Research Based
Strategies for Teachers**

Assoc. for Supervision/Curriculum Development
1250 Pitt Street
Alexandria, VA   22314   703-549-9110
                           FAX 703-549-3891
                           http://www.ascd.org
HF Silver, Author

A trainer's manual and five videotapes designed for
inservice education of teachers K-12 focusing on four
different types of learning expected of students: mastery, understanding, synthesis and involvement.

**3498 Teaching Students Through Their Individual
Learning Styles**

St. John's University, Learning Styles Network
8000 Utopia Parkway
Jamaica, NY   11439   718-990-6161
                           FAX 718-990-1882
                           http://www.learningstyles.net
R Dunn, Author

A set of six videotapes introducing the Dunn and Dunn
learning styles model. Explains the environmental,
emotional, sociological, physical and psychological
elements of style.

3499 Technology in the Classroom Kit

American Speech-Language-Hearing Association
10801 Rockville Pike
Bethesda, MD   20814   301-897-5700
                                   888-498-6699
                           FAX 301-571-0457
                           http://www.asha.org
Laurie Ward, Marketing Coordinator

This kit includes a collection of four written modules
and a videotape designed to help families and professionals implement assistive technology in the education programs of young children. Each module
provides a brief background in assistive technology
and covers specific topics in great detail. The technology is geared for children. *$104.00*

3500 Telling Tales

KET, The Kentucky Network Enterprise Division
600 Cooper Drive
Lexington, KY   40502   859-258-7000
                                   800-354-9067
                           FAX 859-258-7396

Resource for teachers, librarians and drama departments at all levels of instruction. Telling Tales can be
used to encourage creativity and self expression and
help students understand their cultural and language
arts skills, and develop openess to diverse cultures,
build self confidence and leadership skills, improve
communication and language arts skills and develop
oral history projects. *$30.00*

3501 Word Feathers

KET, The Kentucky Network Enterprise Division
600 Cooper Drive
Lexington, KY   40502   859-258-7000
                                   800-354-9067
                           FAX 859-258-7396

An activity-oriented language arts video series.

Parents & Professionals

**3502 3 R'S for Special Education: Rights, Resources,
Results**

Brookes Publishing Company
PO Box 10624
Baltimore, MD   21285   410-337-9580
                                   800-638-3775
                           FAX 410-337-8539
                           http://www.pbrookes.com
                           e-mail: sales@pbrookes.com
Grace Hanlon, Trevor

This video helps parents navigate the steps of the special education system and work towards securing the
best education and services for their children. *$49.95*

Video

3503 A Mind of Your Own

Fanlight Productions
4196 Washington Street
Boston, MA   02131   617-469-4999
                                   800-937-4113
                           FAX 617-469-3379
                           http://www.fanlight.com
                           e-mail: fanlight@fanlight.com
Sandy St. Louis, Contact

New video on learning disabilities from the National Film Board of Canada, follows four learning disabled students through their struggles academically and socially as well as their successes in learning to cope with their disabilities and develop their own unique talents. Amtec Award of Merit. 37 minutes. *$199.00*

Rental $60/day
ISSN DD29-0

3504 ABC's of ADD

JKL Communications
PO Box 40157
Washington, DC   20016   202-223-5097
                              FAX 202-223-5096
                      http://www.lathamlaw.org
                      e-mail: plath3@his.com

$29.00

3505 ABC's of Learning Disabilities

American Federation of Teachers
555 New Jersey Avenue NW
Washington, DC   20001   202-393-5674
                              FAX 202-879-4597
                              http://www.aft.org
                          e-mail: online@aft.org

This film illustrates the case histories of four learning disabled students with various learning disabilities.

3506 ADHD

Brookes Publishing Company
PO Box 10624
Baltimore, MD   21285   410-337-9580
                              800-638-3775
                          FAX 410-337-8539
                    http://www.pbrookes.com
                e-mail: custerv@pbrookes.com
Sandra Rief, Presenter

This video shows methods for helping students who have ADHD increase attention to tasks, improve listening skills, become better organized, and boost work production. *$99.00*

Video
ISBN 1-557661-15-4

3507 ADHD in Adults

Guilford Publications
72 Spring Street
New York, NY   10012   212-431-9800
                              800-365-7006
                          FAX 212-966-6708
                      http://www.guilford.com
                  e-mail: info@guilford.com
Russell A Barkley, Author

This program integrates information on ADHD with the actual experiences of four adults who suffer from the disorder. Representing a range of professions, from a lawyer to a mother working at home, each candidly discusses the impact of ADHD on his or her daily life. These interviews are augmented by comments from family members and other clinicians who treat adults with ADHD. *$95.00*

36-min VHS

3508 ADHD in the Classroom: Strategies for Teachers

Guilford Publications
72 Spring Street
New York, NY   10012   212-431-9800
                              800-365-7006
                          FAX 212-966-6708
                      http://www.guilford.com
                  e-mail: info@guilford.com
Russell A Barkley, Author

Viewers see the problems teachers encounter with children who suffer with ADHD, as well as instructive demonstrations of effective behavior management techniques including color charts and signs, point system, token economy, and turtle-control technique. Also includes a Leader's Guide and a 42-page Manual. *$95.00*

36-min. VHS

3509 ADHD: What Can We Do?

Guilford Publications
72 Spring Street
New York, NY   10012   212-431-9800
                              800-365-7006
                          FAX 212-966-6708
                      http://www.guilford.com
                  e-mail: info@guilford.com
Russell A Barkley, PhD, Author

A video program that introduces teachers and parents to a variety of the most effective techniques for managing ADHD in the classroom, at home, and on family outings. Includes Leader's Guide and 30-page Manual. *$95.00*

ISBN 0-898629-72-1

3510 ADHD: What Do We Know?

Guilford Publications
72 Spring Street
New York, NY   10012   212-431-9800
                              800-365-7006
                          FAX 212-966-6708
                      http://www.guilford.com
                  e-mail: info@guilford.com
RA Barkley, Author

An introduction for teachers and special education practitioners, school psychologists and parents of ADHD children. Topics outlined in this video include the causes and prevalence of ADHD, ways children with ADHD behave, other conditions that may accompany ADHD and long-term prospects for children with ADHD. *$95.00*

Video

3511 Adults with Learning Problems

Learning Disabilities Resources
PO Box 716
Bryn Mawr, PA   19010   610-525-8336
                              800-869-8336
                          FAX 610-525-8337
                      http://www.ldonline.org

Educational materials for adults with a learning disability.

3512 American Sign Language Phrase Book Videotape Series

Harris Communications
15155 Technology Drive
Eden Prairie, MN 55344　　952-906-1180
800-825-6758
FAX 952-906-1099
TDY:952-906-1198
http://www.harriscomm.com

Includes book and three videotapes, each 60 minutes long. In Volume 1 you will find everyday expressions, signing and deafness, getting acquainted, health and water; in Volume 2 you will find family, school, food and drink, clothing, sports and recreation; and in Volume 3 you will find travel, animal, colors, civics, religion, numbers, time, dates and money. *$134.95*

3513 Andreas: Outcomes of Inclusion

Center on Disability and Community Inclusion
499C Waterman Building
Burlington, VT 05401　　802-656-4031
FAX 802-656-1357
http://www.uvm.edu/zvapvt/timfox
e-mail: syuan@zoo.uvm.edu

Video portrays the academic, occupational, and social inclusion of a high school student with severe disabilities. Includes commentary of parents, administrators, teachers, support personnel, classmates.

3514 Anger Within Programs 1-4: Walking Through the Storm Life Space Crisis Intervention

NAK Production Associates
4304 E West Highway
Bethesda, MD 20814　　301-654-4777
FAX 301-654-7772
e-mail: NAK@makprod.com

NA Klotz, Author
Norman Klutz, Producer

Videos focusing on parental and professional perspectives, understanding of children's feelings, treatment models and techniques and skills for working with students with emotional problems.

3515 Around the Clock: Parenting the Delayed ADHD Child

Guilford Publications
72 Spring Street
New York, NY 10012　　212-431-9800
800-365-7006
FAX 212-966-6708
http://www.guilford.com
e-mail: info@guilford.com

Joan F Goodman
Susan Hoban

This videotape provides both professionals and parents a helpful look at how the difficulties facing parents of ADHD children can be handled. *$150.00*

45-min. VHS

3516 Art of Communication

United Learning
1560 Sherman Avenue
Evanston, IL 60201　　847-647-0600
800-424-0362
FAX 847-647-0918
http://www.unitedlearning.com
e-mail: info@unitedlearning.com

B Wagonseller, Author
Ronald Reed, VP Marketing

Designed for parents and professionals, this video focuses on: effective parent-child communication; non-verbal communication in children; effective listening; effects of negative and critical messages; and deterrents limiting child/parent communication. *$99.00*

3517 Attention Deficit Disorder

Pro-Ed
8700 Shoal Creek Boulevard
Austin, TX 78757　　512-451-3246
800-897-3202
FAX 512-451-8542
http://www.proedinc.com

DR Jordan, Author

A video and book providing helpful suggestions for both home and classroom management of students with attention deficit disorder. *$19.00*

3518 Augmentative Communication Without Limitations

Prentke Romich Company
1022 Heyl Road
Wooster, OH 44691　　330-262-1984
800-262-1984
FAX 330-263-4829
http://www.prentrom.com

Looks at the issues one must consider in the selection process. These include hardware, software, service and support.

3519 Avenues to Compliance

New England ADA Technical Assistance Center
374 Congress Street
Boston, MA 02210　　617-695-1225
800-949-4232
FAX 617-482-8099
http://www.adaptenu.org/neada/defaultasp

This training video provides information on the requirements of a Title II entity to provide program access (as required by the Americans with Disabilities Act).

3520 Behind the Glass Door: Hannah's Story

Fanlight Productions
4196 Washington Street
Boston, MA 02131　　617-469-4999
800-937-4113
FAX 617-469-3379
http://www.fanlight.com
e-mail: fanlight@fanlight.com

Karen Pascal, Producer
Sandy St. Louis, Contact

New video, produced in association with Vision TV, follows the Shepard family through five years of struggle, hardship and bittersweet success in raising their child, Hannah, who was diagnosed with autism. Offers insight into the stress families and educators face as they tackle this mysterious disorder. Offers hope and inspiration to parents. Recipient of Silver Screen Award; US International Film and Video Festival. *$245.00*

> *Rental $50/day*
> *ISBN 1-572952-92-1*

3521   Beyond the ADD Myth

Brookes Publishing Company
PO Box 10624
Baltimore, MD   21285   410-337-9580
800-638-3775
FAX 410-337-8539
http://www.pbrookes.com
e-mail: custerv@pbrookes.com
Dr. Thomas Armstrong, Author

This video builds on the theory that many of the behaviors associated with attention deficit disorder are not solely due to neurological dysfunction but actually result from a wide range of social, psychological, and educational causes. *$22.00*

> *Video*
> *ISBN 1-557661-15-4*

3522   Characteristics of the Learning Disabled Adult

Special Education Nazareth
4245 E Avenue
Rochester, NY   14618   716-389-2860
800-462-3944
FAX 585-389-2826

An awareness interactive video recognizing characteristics and instructional needs of learning disabled adults.

3523   Child Management

AGC/United Learning
1560 Sherman Avenue
Evanston, IL   60201
800-328-6700
FAX 847-328-6706
http://www.agcunitedlearning.com
e-mail: info@agcunited.com
B Wagonseller, Author
Ronald Reed, VP Marketing

For teachers, paraprofessionals, administrators, and special educators who deal with disruptive, inattentive, and hyperactive preschool and elementary age children. It gives teachers proven and practical strategies on how to manage these children, and importance of developing a network approach. *$99.00*

3524   Child Who Appears Aloof: Module 5

Educational Productions
9000 SW Gemini Drive
Beaverton, OR   97008   503-644-7000
800-950-4949
FAX 503-350-7000
http://www.edpro.com
e-mail: custserv@edpro.com
Molly Krumm, Marketing Directror

A 30 minute video and 60 page facilitation packet focusing on children who pull back, who avoid social contact. Teaches strategies to understand and support these children. Part of the Hand-in-Hand Series. *$295.00*

3525   Child Who Appears Anxious: Module 4

Educational Productions
9000 SW Gemini Drive
Beaverton, OR   97008   503-644-7000
800-950-4949
FAX 503-350-7000
http://www.edpro.com
e-mail: custserv@edpro.com
Molly Krumm, Marketing Directror

A 35 minute video and 60 page training facilitation packet examining the issues of anxious children and how a supporting adult can help bring them into play. Part of the Hand-in-Hand Series. *$295.00*

3526   Child Who Dabbles: Module 3

Educational Productions
9000 SW Gemini Drive
Beaverton, OR   97008   503-644-7000
800-950-4949
FAX 503-350-7000
http://www.edpro.com
e-mail: custserv@edpro.com
Molly Krumm, Marketing Directror

A 30-minute video and 60-page training facilitation guide that compares dabbling to quality, invested play and offers various strategies for adultsto help children build play skills. Part of Hand-in-Hand Series. *$295.00*

3527   Child Who Wanders: Module 2

Educational Productions
9000 SW Gemini Drive
Beaverton, OR   97008   503-644-7000
800-950-4949
FAX 503-350-7000
http://www.edpro.com
e-mail: custserv@edpro.com
Molly Krumm, Marketing Directror

A 30-minute video and 67-page training facilitation packet showing how to identify children who cannot engage in play so wander about the room. Shows creative interventions to help teach new skills. Part of Hand-in-Hand Series.

3528 Child Who is Ignored: Module 6

Educational Productions
9000 SW Gemini Drive
Beaverton, OR   97008   503-644-7000
                             800-950-4949
                         FAX 503-350-7000
                         http://www.edpro.vom
Molly Krumm, Marketing Directror

A 30 minute video and 60 page facilitation guide illustrating the children who are ignored by others and offering several interventions for them to learn social skills. Part of the Hand-in-Hand Series. *$295.00*

3529 Child Who is Rejected: Module 7

Educational Productions
9000 SW Gemini Drive
Beaverton, OR   97008   503-644-7000
                             800-950-4949
                         FAX 503-350-7000
                         http://www.edpro.com
                         e-mail: custserv@edpro.com
Molly Krumm, Marketing Directror

A 35-minute video and 60-page facilitation packet with strategies to help children whose behavior and/or appearance causes them to be rejected by other children. Part of Hand-in-Hand Series.

3530 Concentration Video

Learning Disabilities Resources
PO Box 716
Bryn Mawr, PA   19010   610-525-8336
                             800-869-8336
                         FAX 610-525-8337
                         http://www.ldonline.org

A 53 minute instructional video provides an optimistic perspective about attention problems ADD. Dr. Cooper discusses different types of attention problems causes and solutions. The second part of the video contains concentration exercises to help children and adults with attention problems. *$19.95*

Video

3531 Degrees of Success: Conversations with College Students with LD

New York University
240 Green Street
New York, NY   10012   212-998-4980
                         FAX 212-995-4114
                         http://www.nyu.edu/osl/csd

A new video which features college students with learning disabilities speaking in their own words about: making the decision to attend college, developing effective learning strategies, coping with frustrations and utilizing college support services. Includes resource packet with suggested discussion questions and list of other resources. *$49.95*

3532 Early Childhood STEP: Systematic Training for Effective Parenting

AGS
4201 Woodland Road
Circle Pines, MN   55014   763-786-4343
                             800-328-2560
                         FAX 763-786-9077
                         http://www.agsnet.com
                         e-mail: agsmail@agsnet.com

Parenting young children can be ususally rewarding, occasionally difficult, and always a challenge. The updated Early Childhood STEP can help parents meet the challenge. It adapts and expands the proven principles and techniques of STEP while vividly illustrating how they can be applied to babies, toddlers, and preschoolers. *$229.95*

3533 Enhancing the Communicative Abilities of Disabled Infants and Toddlers

Purdue University Continuing Education
1586 Stewart Center
West Lafayette, IN   47907   765-494-7231
                             800-359-2968
                         FAX 765-494-0567
M Jeanne Wilcox, PhD, Author

Communication is a key need of most infants and toddlers with disabilities. This video provides: a brief overview of specific communication difficulties encountered by young children, an overview of approaches to intervention, and strategies for using children's interactive partners to enhance and facilitate communication skills. *$64.00*

3534 FAT City

Connecticut Assoc. for Children and Adults with LD
25 Van Zant Street
East Norwalk, CT   06855   203-838-5010
                         FAX 203-866-6108
                         http://www.CACLD.org
                         e-mail: cacld@juno.com
Marie Armstrong, Information Specialist

Nationally acclaimed video designed to sensitize adults to the frustration, anxiety and tension that the learning disabled child experiences daily. Add $5.00 for shipping and handling. *$49.95*

3535 Getting Started with Facilitated Communication

Syracuse University, Institute on Communication
370 Huntington Hall
Syracuse, NY   13244   315-443-9657
                         FAX 315-443-2274
                         http://www.soeweb.syr.edu/thefair
                         e-mail: fcstaff@sued.syr.edu
D Biklen, Author

Describes in detail how to help individuals with autism and/or severe communication difficulties to get started with facilitated communication.

3536 Going to School with Facilitated Communication

Syracuse University, School of Education
805 S Krouse
Syracuse, NY   13244   315-443-2693
                         FAX 315-443-2562
D Biklen, Author

A video in which students with autism and/or severe disabilities illustrate the use of facilitated communication focusing on basic principles fostering facilitated communication.

3537 Help! This Kid's Driving Me Crazy!

Pro-Ed
8700 Shoal Creek Boulevard
Austin, TX 78757   512-451-3246
                                    800-897-3202
                                    FAX 512-451-8542
                                    http://www.proedinc.com
L Adkins, Author

Designed for parents and professionals working with children up to five years old, this videotape and booklet offers information about the nature, special needs, and typical behavioral characteristics for young children with attention deficit disorder. *$5.00*

3538 Helping Adults Learn: Learning Disabilities

Audio/Visual Services, PENN State University
1127 Fox Hill Road
University Park, PA 16803
                                    800-826-0132
                                    FAX 814-863-3102
Thomas McKenna, Coordinator Media

Intended for people who deal with adult learners. Focuses on the special needs of adults with learning disabilities. A printed guide accompanies this video package. *$28.00*

140 pages

3539 How Difficult Can This Be?

Connecticut Assoc. for Children and Adults with LD
18 Marshall Street
Norwalk, CT 06854   203-838-5010
                                    http://www.CACLD.org
Rick Lavoie, Author

This video for parents and professionals illustrates the frustration, anxiety and tension that learning disabled children face via simulations that recreate their experience firsthand. Video also comes with manual. *$49.95*

70 min. Video

3540 I Want My Little Boy Back

Autism Treatment Center of America
2080 S Undermountain Road
Sheffield, MA 01257   413-229-2100
                                    800-714-2779
                                    FAX 413-229-8931
                                    http://www.son-rise.org
                                    e-mail: information@son-rise.org
Lauren Astor, Public Relations Manager

This BBC documentary follows an English family with a child with autism before, during, and after their time at the Son-Rise Program. It uniquely captures the heart of the Son-Rise Program and is extremely useful in understanding its techniques. *$20.00*

3541 I'm Not Autistic on the Typewriter

Syracuse Univ./Facilitated Communication Institute
370 Huntington Hall
Syracuse, NY 13244   315-443-9657
                                    FAX 315-443-2274
                        http://www.soeweb.syr.edu/thefci/
                                    e-mail: fcstaff@sued.syr.edu
Douglas Biklen, Director/Professor

A video introducing facilitated communication, a method by which persons with autism express themselves. Focuses on the following elements: physical support; progression from initial training to practice, and finally to fluency; maintenance of focus on task; emotional support; and fading physical support. *$25.00*

3542 I'm Not Stupid

Learning Disabilities Association of America
4156 Library Road
Pittsburgh, PA 15234   412-341-1515
                                    FAX 412-344-0224
                                    http://www.ldanatl.org
                                    e-mail: ldanatl@usaor.net

This video depicts the constant battle of the learning disabled child in school. *$22.00*

3543 IEP: A Tool for Realizing Possibilities (Video)

PEAK Parent Center
611 N Weber
Colorado Springs, CO 80903   719-531-9400
                                    800-284-0251
                                    FAX 719-531-9452
                                    TDY:719-531-5403
                                    http://www.peakparent.org
                                    e-mail: info@peakparent.org
PEAK/Partnership with San Diego State University, Author

Highlights the importance and use of the IEP as the basic tool in designing and delivering supports and services for students with disabilities. Shows students successfully included in general education classrooms. Useful for building confidence in family members about their vital role in the IEP process. Available in English and Spanish. 20 minutes. *$15.00*

3544 Identifying Learning Problems

Learning Disabilities Resources
PO Box 716
Bryn Mawr, PA 19010   610-525-8336
                                    800-869-8336
                                    FAX 610-525-8337
                                    http://www.ldonline.org

Materials on how to identify a learning problem.

3545 Inclusion Series

Comforty Mediaconcepts
2145 Pioneer Road
Evanston, IL   60201   847-475-0791
                                    FAX 847-475-0793
                          e-mail: comforty@comforty.com

A series of video programs on inclusive education and
community life. Titles include: Choices, providing instruction for all audiences to the inclusion process; Inclusion: Issues for Educators, focusing on particular
teachers and administrators in Illinois schools; Families, Friends, Futures, emphasizing the need for early
inclusion; and Together We're Better, providing an
overview of this comprehensive program. Videos
available separately or as a set.

3546 Language Therapy

Purdue University Continuing Education
1586 Stewart Center
West Lafayette, IN   47907   765-494-7231
                                      800-359-2968
                                 FAX 765-494-0567
Laura L Lee, MA, Author

Discusses the clinical description of the typical preschool child manifesting a language disorder and observations that should be made by the clinician.
$64.00

3547 Language and the Retarded Child

Purdue University Continuing Education
1586 Stewart Center
West Lafayette, IN   47907   765-494-7231
                                      800-359-2968
                                 FAX 765-494-0567
Herold S Lillywhite, PhD, Author

Describes the speech and language functions of the
mentally retarded child; demonstrates problems in
hearing, speech, language, cognition, and general motor development. *$64.00*

3548 Latest Technology for Young Children

Western Illinois University: Macomb Projects
27 Horrabin Hall
Macomb, IL   61455   309-298-1634
                                 FAX 309-298-2305
                        http://www.mprojects.wiu.edu
                     e-mail: PL-Hutinger@wiu.edu
Patricia Hutinger EdD, Director
Joyce Johanson, Coordinator

This 25 minute videotape focuses on the Macintosh
LC and adaptations for young children and includes a
discussion of the features and advantages of the
Macintosh LC, software demonstrations, footage of
child applications, and ideas for off-computer activities. Videotape and written materials available.
$40.00

16-20 pages

3549 Learn to Read

KET, The Kentucky Network Enterprise Division
600 Cooper Drive
Lexington, KY   40502   859-258-7000
                                      800-354-9067
                                 FAX 859-258-7396

Offers 30 half-hour programs tailored for the adult
student.

**3550 Learning Disabilities and Discipline: Rick
Lavoie's Guide to Improving Children's Behavior**

Connecticut Assoc. for Children and Adults with LD
25 Van Zant Street
East Norwalk, CT   06855   203-838-5010
                                 FAX 203-866-6108
                             http://www.CACLD.org
                             e-mail: cacld@juno.com
Rick Lavoie, Presenter

In this video, Richard Lavoie, a nationally known expert on learning disabilities, offers practical advice on
dealing with behavioral problems quickly and effectively. Shows how preventive discipline can antici-
pate many problems before they start. Explains how
teachers and parents can create stable, predictable environments in which children with learning disabilities can flourish. 62 minutes. *$49.95*

$5.00 shipping

3551 Learning Disabilities and Self-Esteem

Connecticut Assoc. for Children and Adults with LD
25 Van Zant Street
East Norwalk, CT   06855   203-838-5010
                                 FAX 203-866-6108
                             http://www.CACLD.org
                             e-mail: cacld@juno.com

The 60 minute Teacher video contains program material for building self-esteem in the classroom. The 60
minute Parent video contains program material for
building self-esteem in the home. A 16 page Program
Guide accompanies each video. Dr. Robert Brooks, a
clinical psychologist, renowned speaker and nationally known expert on learning disabilities, is on the
faculty at Harvard Medical School and is the author of
The Self-Esteem Teacher. *$49.95*

$5.00 shipping

**3552 Learning Disabilities and Social Skills: Last One
Picked..First One Picked On**

Connecticut Assoc. for Children and Adults with LD
25 Van Zant Street
East Norwalk, CT   06855   203-838-5010
                                 FAX 203-866-6108
                             http://www.CACLD.org
                             e-mail: cacld@juno.com

Nationally recognized expert on learning disabilities,
Richard Lavoie, gives examples on how to help LD
children succeed in everyday social situations. Lavoie
helps students dissect their social errors to learn correct behavior. Mistakes are seen as opportunities for
learning. Available in parent (62 min.) or teacher (68
min.) version. *$49.95*

$5.00 shipping

3553 Learning Problems in Language

Learning Disabilities Resources
PO Box 716
Bryn Mawr, PA   19010   610-525-8336
                                 800-869-8336
                            FAX 610-525-8337
                       http://www.ldonline.org

Identifying learning problems in speech.

3554 Letting Go: Views on Integration

Iowa University Affiliated Programs
University Hospital School
Iowa City, IA   52242   319-353-6390
                            FAX 319-356-8284

A video designed for parents and professionals involved in special education, illustrating the fears that parents of special needs children have of letting go, of allowing their children to experience life.

3555 Lily Videos : A Longitudinel View of Lily with Down Syndrome

Davidson Films
668 Marsh Street
Son Lois Obispo, CA   93401   805-594-0422
                                 888-437-4200
                            FAX 805-594-0532
                    http://www.davidsonfilms.com
                    e-mail: dfi@davidsonfilms.com
Elaine Taunt, Manager

1. Lily: A Story About a Girl Like Me 2. Lily: A Sequal 3. Lily: At Thirty.

3556 Lost Dreams & Growth: Parents' Concerns

Resource Networks
Evanston, IL   60204   847-864-4522
K Moses, Author

A video designed for professionals and parents of children with developmental disabilities.

3557 Motivation to Learn: How Parents and Teachers Can Help

Assoc. for Supervision/Curriculum Development
1703 N Beauregard Street
Alexandria, VA   22311   703-578-9600
                                 800-933-2723
                            FAX 703-575-5400
                        http://www.ascd.org

Two videos intended for all those concerned about how educators and families can develop student motivation to learn, solve motivational problems, and effectively participate in parent-teacher conferences.

3558 Normal Growth and Development: Performance Prediction

Love Publishing Company
PO Box 22353
Denver, CO   80222   303-221-7333
                            FAX 303-221-7444
                    http://www.lovepublishing.com
               e-mail: lovepublishing@compuserve.com
Dan Love, Director

Teaches the age at which skills are normally achieved by children ages 0 to 48 months. *$140.00*

Video

3559 Oh Say What They See: Language Stimulation

Educational Productions
9000 SW Gemini Drive
Beaverton, OR   97008   503-644-7000
                                 800-950-4949
                            FAX 503-350-7000
                       http://www.edpro.com
                    e-mail: custserv@edpro.com
Molly Krumm, Marketing Directror

A complete video training program illustrating indirect language stimulation techniques to teachers, parents, students, child care staff, and other adult caregivers working with children.

3560 Parent Teacher Meeting

Learning Disabilities Resources
PO Box 716
Bryn Mawr, PA   19010   610-525-8336
                                 800-869-8336
                            FAX 610-525-8337
                       http://www.ldonline.org

Discusses learning differences and instructional techniques. *$12.00*

3561 Phonemic Awareness: The Sounds of Reading

Peytral Publicatons
PO Box 1162
Minnetonka, MN   55345   952-949-8707
                                 877-739-8725
                            FAX 952-906-9777
                       http://www.peytral.com
                    e-mail: help@peytral.com
Victoria Groves Scott, Author

This staff development video may be used with paraprofessionals and teachers to learn the techniques of teaching pnomemic awareness. *$59.95*

Video
ISBN 1-890455-29-6

3562 Regular Lives

WETA-TV, Department of Educational Activities
2775 S Quincy Street
Arlington, VA   22206   703-998-2600
                            FAX 703-998-3401
                       http://www.weta.com
                    e-mail: info@weta.com
DP Biklen, Author

Designed to show the successful integration of handicapped students in school, work and community settings. Demonstrates that sharing the ordinary routines of learning and living is essential for people with disabilities.

3563 **STEP/Teen: Systematic Training for Effective Parenting of Teens**

AGS
4201 Woodland Road
Circle Pines, MN   55014   763-786-4343
                                  800-328-2560
                                  FAX 763-786-9077
                                  http://www.agsnet.com
                                  e-mail: agsmail@agsnet.com

D Dinkmeyer, Author

A parent training program designed to help parents of teenagers in the following areas: understanding misbehavior; improving communication and family relationships; understanding and expressing emotions and feelings and discipline. *$229.50*

3564 **Sign Songs: Fun Songs to Sign and Sing**

Harris Communications
15155 Technology Drive
Eden Prairie, MN   55344   952-906-1180
                                  800-825-6758
                                  FAX 952-906-1099
                                  TDY:952-906-1198

Features performers John Kinstler, formerly with the National Theater of the Deaf, signing along to the lyrics of eleven kids' songs written and performed by Ken Lonnquist. Includes Public Performance rights and 10 lyric sheets for schools and public libraries. No captions. *$49.95*

29-min. video

3565 **Someday's Child: Special Needs Families**

Educational Productions
9000 SW Gemini Drive
Beaverton, OR   97008   503-644-7000
                                  800-950-4949
                                  FAX 503-350-7000

LL Pletcher, Author
Molly Krumm, Marketing Directror

A complete training video for parents and professionals working with young children with special needs: the personal accounts of three families with young children of their adjustment to and advocacy for their children. *$250.00*

3566 **Strengths and Weaknesses: College Students with Learning Disabilities**

Altschul Group
2832 S Wentworth Avenue
Chicago, IL   60616   312-326-6700
                                  FAX 312-326-6793

Four students share their feelings and four professionals explore possible adjustment and compensation relative to learning disabilities.

3567 **Study Skills: How to Manage Your Time**

Guidance Associates
100 S Bedford Road
Mount Kisco, NY   10549   914-666-4100
                                  800-431-1242
                                  FAX 914-666-5319
                                  http://www.guidanceassociates.com
                                  e-mail: info@guidanceassociates.com

Describes how to create a personal schedule that will help users get more accomplished each day and waste less time. *$61.00*

Video

3568 **Teach an Adult to Read**

KET, The Kentucky Network Enterprise Division
600 Cooper Drive
Lexington, KY   40502   859-258-7000
                                  800-354-9067
                                  FAX 859-258-7396

A video series for reading tutors and tutor trainers that will help your program solve problems and give insight on how to teach an adult to read.

3569 **Time Together: Adults Supporting Play**

Educational Productions
9000 SW Gemini Drive
Beaverton, OR   97008   503-644-7000
                                  800-950-4949
                                  FAX 503-350-7000
                                  http://www.edpro.com
                                  e-mail: custserv@edpro.com

Molly Krumm, Marketing Directror

A complete video training program for beginning childhood teachers,aides and parents illustrating when to join a child's play, how to enhance and extend the play, and when to step back.

3570 **Tomorrow's Children**

Vallejo City Unified School District
211 Valle Vista Avenue
Vallejo, CA   94590   707-556-8950
                                  FAX 707-556-8820
                                  http://www.uallejo.k12.ca.us

E Brower, Author

Addresses the needs for early intervention and comprehensive services for high risk and handicapped infants and preschool children.

3571 **Treatment of Children's Grammatical Impairments in Naturalistic Context**

Purdue University Continuing Education
1586 Stewart Center
West Lafayette, IN   47907   765-494-7231
                                  800-359-2968
                                  FAX 765-494-0567

Marc E Fey, PhD, Author

The basic assumption is challenged that language intervention which takes place in naturalistic settings will be more effective than intervention that occurs in settings that are more heavily constrained by a clinician or other intervention agent. The concept of naturalness will be described as a continuum that is influenced by a number of factors that can be manipulated by clinicians. Several effective intervention approaches that reflect different levels of naturalness are presented. *$64.00*

3572 Tutor Training Session

Learning Disabilities Resources
PO Box 716
Bryn Mawr, PA   19010   610-525-8336
                                800-869-8336
                           FAX 610-525-8337
                           http://www.ldonline.org

Educational meterials on how to tutor someone with a learning disability.

3573 Understanding Attention Deficit Disorder

Connecticut Assoc. for Children and Adults with LD
25 Van Zant Street
East Norwalk, CT   06855   203-838-5010
                             FAX 203-866-6108
                             http://www.CACLD.org
                             e-mail: cacld@juno.com

Simon Epstein MD

A video in an interview format for parents and professionals providing the history, symptoms, methods of diagnosis and three approaches used to ease the effects of attention deficit disorder. A comprehensive general introduction to ADHD. 45 minutes. *$20.00*

Video

3574 What About Me? Siblings Without Disabilities

Educational Productions
9000 SW Gemini Drive
Beaverton, OR   97008   503-644-7000
                                800-950-4949
                           FAX 503-350-7000
                           http://www.edpro.com
                           e-mail: custserv@edpro.com

S Butrille, Author
Molly Krumm, Marketing Directror

Designed for siblings, parents, professionals, community members and students about pre-teens and two teenagers who share their perspectives, theirworries, concerns and histories about living with a sibling with a disability. *$ 250.00*

3575 What Every Parent Should Know About ADD

AGC/United Learning
1560 Sherman Avenue
Evanston, IL   60201   800-328-6700
                         FAX 847-328-6706
                    http://www.agcunitedlearning.com
                         e-mail: info@agcunited.com

Bill Wagonseller, Author
Jim McColl, VP Sales

Part 1: Identification and Diagnosis, clearly defines what Attention Deficit Disorder is and is not, giving parents a virtual behavioral road map to determine if their children exhibit any one of the leading symptoms of these conditions. Part 2: Causes and Strategies, explains the possible causes of ADD, and includes a step-by-step approach on what to do if parents suspect their children have the disorder. *$99.00*

2/30 min Videos

3576 What Every Teacher Should Know About ADD

United Learning
6633 W Howard Street
Niles, IL   60714   847-647-0600
                            800-424-0362
                       FAX 847-647-0918
                       http://www.unitedlearning.com
                       e-mail: bistern@interaccess.com

Ronald Reed, VP Marketing

This program is a must for teachers, para-professionals, administrators, and special educators. It is written for and about educators who deal with disruptive, inattentive, and hyperactive pre-school and elementary age children. It gives teachers proven and practical strategies on how to manage these children, and the importance of developing a teamwork approach.

30-min. video

3577 When a Child Doesn't Play: Module 1

Educational Productions
9000 SW Gemini Drive
Beaverton, OR   97008   503-644-7000
                                800-950-4949
                           FAX 503-350-7000
                           http://www.edpro.com
                           e-mail: custserv@edpro.com

Molly Krumm, Marketing Directror

A 30 minute video with 100 pages of facilitation materials presentsdramatic footage of children with play problems and how they miss critical opportunities to learn. Illustrates supportive strategies for adults. Foundation program for Hand-in-Hand Series. *$350.00*

Vocational

3578 College: A Viable Option

HEATH Resource Center
2121 K Street NW
Washington, DC   20036   202-973-0904
                                 800-544-3284
                            FAX 202-973-0908
                    http://gopher://bobcat-ace.nche.edu
                         e-mail: heath@ace.nche.edu

Dan Gardner, Information Specialist

A video discussing what a learning disability is, learning strategies and compensatory techniques. *$23.00*

3579 Different Way of Learning

Brookes Publishing Company
PO Box 10624
Baltimore, MD   21285   410-337-9580
                                 800-638-3775
                          FAX 410-337-8539
                    http://www.pbrookes.com
                 e-mail: custerv@pbrookes.com

This video prepares students with learning disabilities for the transition from school to the workplace. *$49.00*

Video
ISBN 1-557663-49-1

3580 Direct Link, May I Help You?

Direct Link for the Disabled
PO Box 1036
Solvang, CA   93464   805-688-1603
                         FAX 805-686-5285

Introduces Direct Link and demonstrates practical ideas to include those with disabilities in the work force. *$25.00*

3581 Employment Initiatives Model: Job Coach Training Manual and Tape

Young Adult Institute
460 W 34th Street
New York, NY   10001   212-273-6100
                         FAX 212-629-4113
                      http://www.yai.org
                  e-mail: ahorowitz@yai.org
Stephen E Freeman, Assoc. Executive Director
Thomas A Dern, Assoc. Executive Director
Aimee Horowitz, Project Specialist

Video and manual providing an overview and orientation for staff members involved in transition services to ensure that they are well-grounded inthe concepts, responsibilities, and activities that are required to provide quality supported employment services.

3582 First Jobs: Entering the Job World

Educational Design
345 Hudson Street
New York, NY   10014
                               800-221-9372
                         FAX 212-675-8922

Career/vocational education with emphasis on job search skills, job interviews and survival skills. *$139.00*

3583 How Not to Contact Employers

Nat'l Clearinghouse of Rehab. Training Materials
Oklahoma State University
Stillwater, OK   405-624-7650
                               800-223-5219
                         FAX 405-624-0695
                 http://www.nchrtm.okstate.edu/
                      e-mail: index_3.html

A single vignette of what not to do when visiting perspective employers to secure positions for clients. *$10.00*

3584 Job Coaching Video Training Series

RPM Press
PO Box 31483
Tucson, AZ   85751   520-886-1990
                               888-810-1990
                         FAX 520-886-1990
Jan Stonebraker, Operations Manager

Multi-media professional training program designed for training educators, counselors, vocational rehabilitation personnel, employment specialists and paraprofessional staff in job coaching methods such as speed training, time sampling, fading, behavior observation and other methods. *$225.00*

3585 Job Interview Reality Seminar

Texas Commission for the Blind
4800 N Lamar Street
Austin, TX   78710   512-377-0500
                         FAX 512-459-2682
                    http://www.tcb.state.tx.us
                 e-mail: patw@tcb.state.tx.us

These tapes include job interview and feedback to the interviewee about his/her performance. *$20.00*

3586 KET Basic Skills Series

KET, The Kentucky Network Enterprise Division
600 Cooper Drive
Lexington, KY   40502   859-258-7000
                                800-354-9067
                          FAX 859-258-7396

Offers an independent learning system for workers who need retraining or help with basic skills.

3587 KET Foundation Series

KET, The Kentucky Network Enterprise Division
600 Cooper Drive
Lexington, KY   40502   859-258-7000
                                800-354-9067
                          FAX 859-258-7396

A highly effective basic skills series that is tailor-made for the needs of proprietary and vocational schools.

3588 KET/GED Series

KET, The Kentucky Network Enterprise Division
600 Cooper Drive
Lexington, KY   40502   859-258-7000
                                800-354-9067
                          FAX 859-258-7396

This nationally acclaimed instructional series helps adults prepare for the GED test.

3589 KET/GED Series Transitional Spanish Edition

KET, The Kentucky Network Enterprise Division
600 Cooper Drive
Lexington, KY   40502   859-258-7000
                                800-354-9067
                          FAX 859-258-7396

This award-winning series offers ESL students effective preparation for the GED test.

3590 **Life After High School for Students with Moderate and Severe Disabilities**

Beech Center on Families and Disability
3111 Haworth Hall
Lawrence, MA   66045   785-864-7600
                                        FAX 785-864-7605

A set of three videotapes and a participant handbook document, and a teleconference in which family members, people with disabilities, teachers, rehabilitation specialists, program administrators and policy makers focus on improving the quality of services in high school and supported employment programs.

3591 **On Our Own Transition Series**

Young Adult Institute
460 W 34th Street
New York, NY   10001   212-273-6100
                                        FAX 212-629-4113
                                        http://www.yai.org
                                        e-mail: ahorowitz@yai.org
Stephen E Freemen, Assoc. Executive Director
Thomas A Dern, Assoc. Executive Director
Aimee Horowitz, Project Specialist

Designed for parents and professionals, this series of 15 videotapes examines innovative transitional approaches that help create marketable skills, instill self-esteem and facilitate successful transition for individuals with developmental disabilities.

3592 **Social Skills on the Job: A Transition to the Workplace for Special Needs**

AGS
4201 Woodland Road
Circle Pines, MN   55014   763-786-4343
                                        800-328-2560
                                        FAX 763-786-9077
                                        http://www.agsnet.com
                                        e-mail: agsmail@agsnet.com

Presents 28 simulations to help students learn and practice 14 basic social skills that will allow them to compete successfully with their peers in the job market. *$299.95*

3593 **Succeeding in the Workplace**

JKL Communications
PO Box 40157
Washington, DC   20016   202-223-5097
                                        FAX 202-223-5096
                                        http://www.lathamlaw.org
                                        e-mail: plath3@his.com

   $49.00

3594 **Tools for Transition: Preparing Students with Learning Disabilities**

AGS
4201 Woodland Road
Circle Pines, MN   55014   763-786-4343
                                        800-328-2560
                                        FAX 763-786-9077
                                        http://www.agsnet.com
                                        e-mail: agsmail@agsnet.com
EP Aune, Author

Designed for learning disabled high school juniors and seniors, this program will prepare them for postsecondary education by focusing on: learningstyles, study skills, learning accommodations, self advocacy, career exploration, interpersonal relationships and choosing and applying to postsecondary schools. *$124.95*

General

3595 **National Technical Information Service: US Department of Commerce**

5285 Port Royal Road
Springfield, VA 22161   703-487-4650
                          FAX 703-321-8547
                          http://www.ntis.gov

Maintains a worldwide database for research, development and engineering reports on a range of topics, including architectural barrier removal, employing individuals with disabilities, alternative testing formats, job accommodations, school-to-work transition for students with disabilities, rehabilitation engineering, disability law and transportation.

3596 **PsycINFO Database**

American Psychological Association
750 1st Street NE
Washington, DC 20002   202-336-5650
                          800-374-2722
                     FAX 202-336-5633
                     TDY:202-336-6123
                http://www.apa.org/psycinfo
                e-mail: psycinfo@apa.org

An online abstract database that provides access to citations to the international serial literature in psychology and related disciplines from 1887 to present. Available via PsycINFO Direct at www.psycinfo.com.

3597 **Special Needs Project**

                http://www.specialneeds.com
A place to get books about disabilities.

3598 **www.abcparenting.com**

Information and resources related to learning disabilities.

3599 **www.adhdnews.com/sped.htm**

Guidance in writing IEPs, TIEPs for special education services.

3600 **www.ajb.dni.us**
America's Job Bank

Useful both for job seekers and employers; offers job announcements, talent banks and information about getting a job.

3601 **www.ala.org/roads**
Roads to Learning

Run by the American Library Association, this site works to raise public awareness about learning disabilities.

3602 **www.allaboutvision.com**
All About Vision

Vision information and resources, including articles on learning disabilities.

3603 **www.ataccess.org**
Alliance for Technology Access

                http://www.ataccess.org
                e-mail: atainfo@ataccess.org

Not sure where to begin your search for assistive technology information and tools? A wealth of information can be found here. ATA is a national network of assistive technology center, vendors, community based organizations, and individuals committed to increasing the use of technology by people with disabilities and junctioned invitations.

3604 **www.autismtreatment.com**
Autism Treatment Center of America

Since 1983, the Autism Treatment Center of America, has provided innovative training programs for parents and professionals caring for children challenged by Autism, Autism Spectrum Disorders, Pervasive Developmental Disorders (PDD) and other developmental difficulties. The Son-Rise Program teaches a specific yet comprehensive system of treatment and education designed to help families and caregivers enable their children to dramatically improve in all areas of learning.

3605 **www.babycenter.com**

Includes an easy-to-follow milestone chart, advice on when to call the doctor, chat rooms and an immunization scheduler.

3606 **www.career.com**
Career Connections

Posts a job announcement and an online application form, and hosts cyber job fairs.

3607 **www.childdevelopmentinfo.com**
Child Development Institute

Provides online information on child development, psychology, parenting, learning, health and safety as well as childhood disorders such as attention deficit disorder, dyslexia and autism. Provides comprehensive resources and practical suggestions for parents.

3608 **www.childparenting.about.com**

Information, research and resources for the learning disabled.

3609 www.disabilityinfo.gov
Disability Direct

Provides one-stop online access to resources, services, and information available throughout the federal government to Americans with disabilities, their families, employers and service providers; also promotes awareness of disability issues to the general public.

3610 www.disabilityresources.org

Information about learning disabilities and related subjects.

3611 www.discoveryhealth.com

Information on conditions that impact learning.

3612 www.dmoz.org
DMOZ Open Directory Project

Information on special education and learning disabilities.

3613 www.doleta.gov/programs/adtrain.asp
O'Net: Department of Labor's Occ. Information

Useful for job seekers, employers and teachers; has career information and links to government resources.

3614 www.drkoop.com
Former Surgeon-General Dr. C Everett Koop

Information on health and conditions that affect learning.

3615 www.dyslexia.com
Davis Dyslexia Association

Links to internet resources for learning. Includes dyslexia, Autism and Asperger's Syndrome, ADD/ADHD and other learning disabilities.

3616 www.familyvillage.wisc.edu
University of Wisconsin-Madison

A global community that integrates information, resources and communication opportunities on the Internet for all those involved with cognitive and other disabilities.

3617 www.funbrain.com
Quiz Lab

Internet education site for teachers and kids. Access thousands of assessment quizzes online. Assign paperless quizzes that are graded automatically by email. Teaching tools are free and easy to use.

3618 www.geocities.com

A site that informs and educates about common misconceptions associated with learning disabilities.

3619 www.healthanswers.com

Health information, including learning disabilities, etc.

3620 www.healthatoz.com
Medical Network

Health information, including ADD, ADHD, etc.

3621 www.healthcentral.com

Information and products for a healthier life. Includes conditions that impact learning.

3622 www.healthymind.com

Information on ADD and learning disabilities.

3623 www.hood.edu/seri/serihome.htm
Special Education Resources on the Internet

Contains links to information about definitions, legal issues, and teaching and learning related to learning disabilities.

3624 www.iamyourchild.org

From Rob Reiner's I Am Your Child Foundation, featuring information on child development.

3625 www.icpac.indiana.edu/infoseries/is-50.htm
Finding Your Career: Holland Interest Inventory

Includes information on self-assessing one's skills and matching them to careers.

3626 www.intelihealth.com

Includes information on learning disabilities.

3627 www.irsc.org
Internet Research for Special Children

Attention deficit and hyperactivity disorder help website, created so information, support and ADD coaching are available without having to pour over all 531,136 links that come up on a net search.

3628 www.jobhunt.org/slocareers/resources.html

Online Career Resources

Contains assessment tools, tutorials, labor market information, etc.

3629 www.kidsdirect.net/pd

Information on education and learning disabilities.

3630 www.ld-add.com

Attention Deficit Disorder (ADD or ADHD)

Do you think that you or your child has ADHD with or without learning disabilities? If the answer is yes, this webpage is for you.

3631 www.ldonline.org

The Learning Project at WETA

Learning disabilities information and resources.

3632 www.ldpride.net

LD Pride Online

Inspired by Deaf Pride, a site developed as an interactive community resource for youth and adults with learning disabilities and ADD.

3633 www.ldresources.com

Resources for people with learning disabilities.

3634 www.ldteens.org

Study Skills Web Site

Run by the New York State Chapter of the International Dyslexia Association; a site for students, created by students; provides helpful tips and links.

3635 www.marriottfoundation.org

Marriott Foundation

Provides information on job opportunities for teenagers and young adults with disabilities.

3636 www.my.webmd.com

Web MD Health

Medical website with information which includes learning disabilities, ADD/ADHD, etc.

3637 www.ocde.K12.ca.us/PAL/index2.html

Peer Assistance Leadership (PAL)

A California-based outreach program for elementary, intermediate and high school students.

3638 www.oneaddplace.com

One A D D Place

A virtual neighborhood of information and resources relating to ADD, ADHD and learning disorders.

3639 www.optimums.com

JR Mills, MS, MEd

Information on learning disabilities.

3640 www.pacer.org

Does My Child Have An Emotional Disorder

Our mission is to expand opportunities and enhance the quality of life of children and young adults with disabilities and their families, based on the concept of parents helping parents.

3641 www.parentpals.com

Ameri-Corp Speech and Hearing

Offers parents and professionals special education support, teaching ideas and tips, special education continuing education, disability-specific information and more.

3642 www.parentsplace.com

Shares the adventure of parenting through articles, newsletters, questions and answers and polls.

3643 www.peer.ca/peer.html

Peer Resources Network

A Canadian organization that offers training, educational resources, and consultation to those interested in peer helping and education. Their resources section has information on books, articles and videos.

3644 www.petersons.com

Peterson's Education and Career Center

Contains postings for full-and part-time jobs as well as summer job opportunities.

3645 www.schwablearnig.org

A parent's guide to helping kids with learning differences.

3646 **www.son-rise.org**
Autism Treatment Center of America

Since 1983, the Autism Treatment Center of America, has provided innovative training programs for parents and professionals caring for children challenged by Autism, Autism Spectrum Disorders, Pervasive Developmental Disorders (PDD) and other developmental difficulties. The Son-Rise Program teaches a specific yet comprehensive system of treatment and education designed to help families and caregivers enable their children to dramatically improve in all areas of learning.

3647 **www.specialchild.com**
Resource Foundation for Children with Challenges

Variety of information for parents of children with disabilities, including actual stories, family and legal issues, diagnosis search, etc.

3648 **www.therapistfinder.net**

Locate psychologists, psychiatrists, social workers, family counselors, and more specializing in disorders.

3649 **www.wrightlaw.com**
Wrightslaw

Provides information about advocacy.

3650 **www4.gvsu.edu**
Grand Valley State University

Information and resources for the learning disabled.

Counseling & Psychology

3651 American Psychologist

American Psychological Association
750 1st Street NE
Washington, DC   20002   202-336-5500
                                800-374-2721
                          FAX 202-336-5502
                          http://www.apa.org
                          e-mail: apeditor@apa.org
Raymond Fowler, Editor

Contains articles of broad interest to all psychologists that cut across all domains of the field of psychology. The articles are theoretical in nature.

3652 Association of Educational Therapists

1804 W Burbank Boulevard
Burbank, CA   91506   818-788-3850
                             800-286-4267
                       FAX 818-843-7423
                       http://www.aetonline.org
                       e-mail: aetla@aol.com
Janine Newell

Contains articles on such topics as clinical practice, current theory, research, reviews of testing methods and assessments of materials. A legislative summary is included. *$25.00*

3653 Case Manager

Mosby
10801 Executive Center Drive
Little Rock, AR   72211   501-223-0183
                                 800-325-4177
                           FAX 501-223-0519
                           http://www.mosby.com/casemgr
                           e-mail: nathania.sawyer@mosby.com
Nathania Sawyer, Associate Publisher
Catherine M Mullahy, Editor

Targeted to medical case managers and other related professionals who create and manage patient care in hospital, home, long-term care, rehabilitation, mental health, and managed care settings. Articles, columns, and departments provide the latest information in the field though coverage of the profession's hottest topics, including outcomes management, guidelines and standards of practice, reimbursement, trends in managed care, and ethical/ legal issues. *$45.00*

Bi-Monthly
ISSN 1061-9259

3654 Center Focus

Nat'l Center for Research in Vocational Education
2150 Shattuck Avenue
Berkeley, CA   94704   510-642-4004
                             800-762-4093
                       FAX 510-642-2124

Each issue provides a brief but thorough distillation of research, development, evaluation and practice knowledge about a specific topic.

Quarterly

3655 Journal of Social and Clinical Psychology

72 Spring Street
New York, NY   10012   800-365-7006
                        FAX 212-966-6708
Jody Falco, Managing Editor

Examines and reports the burgeoning areas of theory, research and practice. This journal was created to foster interdisciplinary communication and scholarship among practitioners of social and clinical psychology. It concentrates on presenting solid clinical and experimental reports on a wide range of topics crucial to the practice and study of mental health. *$37.50*

ISSN 0736-7236

3656 Learning Disabilities: Research and Practice

Lawrence Erlbaum Associates
10 Industrial Avenue
Mahwah, NJ   07430   800-926-6579
                       FAX 201-236-0072
Margo A Mastropieri, Co-Editor
Thomas E Scruggs, Co-Editor

Because learning disabilities is a multidisciplinary field of study, this important journal publishes articles addressing the nature and characteristics of learning disabled students, promising research, program development, assessment practices, and teaching methodologies from different disciplines. In so doing, LDRP provides information of great value to professionals involved in a variety of different disciplines including school psychology, counseling, reading and medicine. *$45.00*

ISSN 0938-8982

3657 School Psychology Quarterly: Official Journal of Div. 16 of the American Psychological Assoc

Guilford Publications
72 Spring Street
New York, NY   10012   212-431-9800
                              800-365-7006
                        FAX 212-966-6708
                        http://www.guilford.com
                        e-mail: info@guilford.com

This journal advances the latest research, theory, and practice and features a new book review section. Strengthening the relationship between school psychology and broad-based psychological science. *$35.00*

4 issues/year
ISSN 1045-3830

General

3658 ASCD Update

Assoc. for Supervision/Curriculum Development
1703 N Beauregard Street
Alexandria, VA 22311   703-578-9600
                              800-933-2723
                          FAX 703-575-5400
                          http://www.ascd.org
Ronald Brandt, Executive Editor
Marge Scherer, Managing Editor

News on contemporary education issues and information on ASCD programs.

**3659 Adult Basic Education: An Interdisciplinary
Journal for Adult Literacy Educators**

Commission on Adult Basic Education (COABE)
Piedmont College
Demorest, GA 30535   706-778-3000
                          FAX 706-776-0133
                  e-mail: melichar@piedmnt.edu
Ken Melichar, Editor

Adult Basic Education: An Interdisciplinary Journal for Adult Literacy Educators is a double blind, peer review, scholarly journal with a practical intent devoted to improving the efforts of adult educators working with low literally disadvantaged, and educationally oppressed people. *$25.00*

3x/year

3660 American Journal of Occupational Therapy

American Occupational Therapy Association
4720 Montgomery Lane
Bethesda, MD 20824   301-652-2682
                              800-377-8555
                          FAX 301-652-7711
                          http://www.aota.org
                  e-mail: ajotsis@aota.org
Liz Holcomb, Managing Editor

An official publication of the American Occupational Therapy Association, inc. This peer reviewed journal focuses on research, practice, and health care issues in the field of occupational therapy. *$50.00*

3661 American School Board Journal

National School Boards Association
1680 Duke Street
Alexandria, VA 22314   703-838-6739
                          FAX 703-549-6719
                          http://www.asbj.com
                  e-mail: editor@asbj.com
Sally Zakariya, Editor

American School Board Journal chronicles change, interprets issues, and offers readers — some 40,000 school board members and school administrators — practical advice on a broad range of topics pertinent to school go9vernance and management, policy making, student achievement, and the art of school leadership. In addition, regular departments cover education news, school law, research, and new books. *$54.00*

Monthly

3662 Annals of Otology, Rhinology and Laryngology

Annals Publishing Company
4507 Laclede Avenue
Saint Louis, MO 63108   314-367-4987
                          FAX 314-367-4988
                          http://www.annals.com
                  e-mail: manager@annals.com

Offers original manuscripts of clinical and research importance in otolaryngology - head and neck surgery, audiology, speech pathology, head and neck oncology and surgery, and related specialties. All papers are peer-reviewed *$ 179.00*

112 pages   Monthly

3663 Autism Research Review International

Autism Research Institute
4182 Adams Avenue
San Diego, CA 92116   619-281-7165
                          FAX 619-563-6840
              http://www.autismresearchinstitute.com
Mallie Odle, Directors Assistant
Bernard Rimland, Director

A quarterly newsletter that reviews current research pertaining to autism. *$16.00*

3664 CABE Journal

Connecticut Association of Boards of Education
81 Wolcott Hill Road
Wethersfield, CT 06109   860-571-7446
                              800-317-0033
                          FAX 860-571-7452
                          http://www.cabe.org
                  e-mail: admin@cabe.org
Bonnie Carney, Sr. Staff Associate
Robert Rader, Executive Director

Published for school board members and deals with a wide range of issues such as: legal, teaching and learning, finances and resources, at-risk youth and more.

3665 CASE Newsletter

Council of Administrators of Special Education
615 7th Street SW
Rochester, MN 55902   507-285-8738
Virginia Dixon, Editor

Information to CASE members on issues pertinent to education of youth with special needs. *$48.00*

8 pages

3666 CEC Today

Council for Exceptional Children
1110 N Glebe Road
Arlington, VA 22201   703-620-3660
                              888-232-7733
                          FAX 703-264-9494
                          http://www.cec.sped.org
                  e-mail: lyndav@cec.sped.org
Lynda Voyles, Editor

Newsletter of the Council for Exceptional Children. Available to members of the council.

10x per year

3667 Chalk Talk

Fresno Teachers Association
5334 N Fresno Street
Fresno, CA   93710   559-224-8430
                            FAX 559-224-1571
                            http://www.fresno.com/fta/
Pat Imperatrice, Editor

Improvement in public education and the condition of
the working environment of public school teachers.
$2.00

6 pages

3668 Child Assessment News

Guilford Publications
72 Spring Street
New York, NY   10012   212-431-9800
                              800-365-7006
                              FAX 212-966-6708
                              http://www.guilford.com
                              e-mail: info@guilford.com

Offers the easiest and most effective way possible for
busy professionals to learn about: the hottest news in
child assessment, brand new test materials, groundbreaking research developments, helpful clinical
techniques, expertopinions of well-known and respected researchers and clinicians, important legislation, and software updates. *$75.00*

Bimonthly
ISSN 1055-0518

3669 Classroom Computer Learning

Peter Li
330 Progress Road
Dayton, OH   45439   937-847-5900
                            FAX 937-847-5910
An educational magazine geared toward teachers.

3670 Comparative Education Review

University Center for International Education
1712 Neil Avenue, Oxley Hall
Columbus, OH   43210   614-292-9660
                              FAX 614-292-4273
Dr. Erwin Epstein, Editor

A scholarly journal that examines the application of
social science theories and methods to international
issues of education.

3671 Connections

National Center for Youth with Disabilities
420 Delaware Street
Minneapolis, MN   55440   612-626-2825
                                 800-333-6293
                                 FAX 612-626-2134
Elizabeth Latts MSW, Information Specialist

Newsletter that addresses key issues of youth with disabilities, current research, new programs, and training
materials.

3672 Creative Classroom Magazine

170 5th Avenue
New York, NY   10010   212-243-5750
                              FAX 212-242-5628
                              http://www.creativeclassroom.org
                              e-mail: ccmag@inch.com
Meg Bozzone, Editor
Robin Bromley, Associate Editor

Classroom ideas, lesson suggestions, materials listings, advice and articles on teaching students current
events such as environmental issues. Covers all subjects and includes a calendar of special events and
suggestions for projects.

Bimonthly

3673 Diagnostique

Council for Exceptional Children
1110 N Glebe Road
Arlington, VA   22201   703-620-3660
                               888-232-7733
                               FAX 703-264-9494
                               http://www.cec.sped.org/
Gerard Hurley, Contact

Offers information on preparation for postsecondary
success. *$28.00*

3674 Disability Compliance for Higher Education

LRP Publications
PO Box 24668
West Palm Beach, FL   33416   561-622-6520
                                     800-341-7874
                                     FAX 561-622-0757
                                     http://www.lfp.com
                                     e-mail: custerve@lrp.com
Ed Fllo, Author
Anna McMahon, Product Group Manager

This monthly newsletter combines analysis of disability law eith detaiols on innovative accommodations
for students and staff. *$190.00*

16 pages   Monthly

**3675 Division for Children with Communication
Disorders Newsletter**

Council for Exceptional Children
1110 N Glebe Road
Arlington, VA   22201   703-620-3660
                               888-232-7733
                               FAX 703-264-9494
                               http://www.cec.sped.org/
Penny Griffith, Editor

Information concerning the education and welfare of
children and youth with communication disorders; reports on division committee activities, highlights current research and programs.

12 pages

3676 Education Digest

College of Education
University of Illinois
Urbana, IL   61801   217-333-0260
                            FAX 217-244-7732
                            http://www.ed.uiuc.edu

3677 Education Technology News

Business Publishers
8737 Colesville Road
Silver Spring, MD   20910   301-587-6300
                                           800-274-0122
                                    FAX 301-585-9075
Howard Fields, Editor
Connie Arnold, Marketing Manager

Full coverage of innovations in technology that can be implemented in the classroom, including those which enhance learning for children with disabilities. Focus is on computer use in the classroom, and related subjects such as teacher training, new software, research findings, grants and other funding issues. *$267.00*

3678 Education Week

4301 Connecticut Avenue NW
Washington, DC   20008   202-364-4114
                                 FAX 202-464-1039
                                 http://www.edweek.org

Offers articles of interest to educators, teachers, professionals and special educators on the latest developments, laws, issues and more in the various fields of education. *$69.94*

3679 Educational Leadership

Assoc. for Supervision/Curriculum Development
1703 N Beauregard Street
Alexandria, VA   22311   703-578-9600
                                        800-933-2723
                                 FAX 703-575-5400
                                 http://www.ascd.org

3680 Educational Researcher

American Educational Research Association
1230 17th Street NW
Washington, DC   20036   202-223-9485
                                 FAX 202-775-1824
                                 http://www.aera.net

3681 Educational Staffing Program

International Schools Services
15 Roszel Road
Princeton, NJ   08543   609-452-0990
                                 FAX 609-452-2690
                                 http://www.iss.adu
                                 e-mail: edustaffing@iss.edu

Opportunities for K-12 teachers and administrators exist in private American and international schools around the world. International Schools Services has placed over 15,000 K-12 educators in overseas schools since 1955. Interviews are conducted at one of our US-based international Recruitment Centers (IRCs). *$5.00*

3682 Educational Technology

Educational Technology Publications
700 E Palisade Avenue
Englewood Cliffs, NJ   07632   201-871-4007
                                               800-952-BOOK
                                        FAX 201-871-4009
                                 http://www.bookstoread.com/ctp
                                 e-mail: edtecpubls@aol.com
L Lipsitz, Editor

Leading magazine covering the field of educational technology, including devices for people with learning disabilities. 6x annually. *$119.00*

64 pages

3683 Employment in the Mainstream

Mainstream
3 Bethesda Metro Center
Bethesda, MD   20814   301-654-2400
                                        800-424-8089
                                 FAX 301-654-2403
                                 e-mail: info@mainstream.com
Fritz Rumpel, Editor

A magazine offering information on employment issues of interest to rehabilitation professionals and employers. *$25.00*

3684 Faculty Inservice Education Kit

Association on Higher Education and Disability
PO Box 21192
Columbus, OH   43221   614-488-4972
                                 FAX 614-488-1174
                                 http://www.ahead.org
                                 e-mail: ahead@postbox.acs.ohio-state.edu

Lists all the handouts and documentation necessary to conduct inservice training for the postsecondary community regarding the inclusion of students with disabilities in campus life. *$45.95*

3685 GED Items

GED Testing Services
1 Dupont Circle NW
Washington, DC   20036   202-939-9490
                                 FAX 202-775-8578
               http://www.acenet.edu/programs/calec/ged/home
                                 e-mail: ged@ace.nche.edu
Lisa Richards Hone, Special Projects Manager
Fred Edwards, Director Partner Outreach

A newsletter for GED examiners and teachers as well as other adult education professionals. It provides information about GED policies and best practices.

5x/year

3686 Gander Publishing

412 Higuera Street
San Luis Obispo, CA   93401   805-541-3836
                                               800-233-1819
                                        FAX 805-782-0488
                                 http://www.ganderpub.com
                                 e-mail: wcook@ganderpub.com
Wendy Cook, Marketing Manager

Books, kits, videos and CD-ROMs used to train educators and parents in specific programs for helping people with learning disabilities.

3687 Gifted Child Today

Prufrock Press
PO Box 8813
Waco, TX   76714   254-756-3337
                                 800-998-2208
                                 FAX 254-756-3339

Joel M McIntosh, Publisher
Stephanie Stout, Editor

Provides teachers accurate, current information about the education of gifted and talented children. *$29.95*

3688 InfoTech Newsletter

InfoTech
University of Iowa
Iowa City, IA 52242

800-331-3027

A free publication covering topics relating to assistive technology, including announcements from Iowa's IPAT Program and from Minnesota's S.T.A.R. Program as well as Used Equipment Referral Service listing.

3689 Information from HEATH

HEATH Resource Center
2121 K Street NW
Washington, DC 20036

202-973-0904
800-544-3284
FAX 202-973-0908
http://gopher://bobcat-ace.nche.edu
e-mail: heath@ace.nche.edu
Dan Gardner, Information Specialist

A newsletter offering information on postsecondary education for individuals with disabilities. *$1.00*

3690 Journal of Learning Disabilities

Pro-Ed
8700 Shoal Creek Boulevard
Austin, TX 78757

512-451-3246
800-897-3202
FAX 512-451-8542
http://www.proedinc.com
Judith K Voress PhD, Periodicals Director

Bimonthly, international publication containing articles on practice research, and theory related to learning disabilities.

64 pages Bimonthly

3691 Journal of Postsecondary Education and Disability

Association on Higher Education and Disability
PO Box 21192
Columbus, OH 43221

614-488-4972
FAX 614-488-1174
http://www.ahead.org
e-mail: ahead@postbox.acs.ohio-state.edu

Provides in-depth examination of research, issues, policies and programs in postsecondary education.

3692 Journal of Rehabilitation

National Rehabilitation Association
633 S Washington Street
Alexandria, VA 22314

703-836-0850
888-258-4295
FAX 703-836-0848
http://www.nationalrehab.org
e-mail: info@nationalrehab.org
Michelle A Vaughan, Executive Director
Paul Alston, Editor
Carol Hamilla, Managing Editor

The Journal of Rehabilitation publishes articles by leaders in the fields of rehabilitation. The articles are written for rehabilitation professionals and students studying in the fields of rehabilitation *$18.00*

ISSN 0022-4154

3693 Journal of School Health

American School Health Association
7263 State Route 43
Kent, OH 44240

330-678-1601
FAX 330-678-4526
http://www.ashaweb.org
e-mail: asha@ashaweb.org

3694 Journal of Secondary Gifted Education

Prufrock Press
PO Box 8813
Waco, TX 76714

254-756-3337
800-998-2208
FAX 254-756-3339
Joel M McIntosh, Publisher
Tracy Cross, Editor

Publishes research and critical theory related to the education of adolescent gifted and talented students. *$35.00*

3695 Journal of Special Education Technology

Peabody College, Box 328
Vanderbilt University
Nashville, TN 37203

615-322-7311
FAX 615-322-8236
Herbert Rieth, Editor
Paulette Jackson, Administrative Assistant

Quarterly $40.00

3696 KDDWB Variety Family Center

University of Minnesota
200 Oak Street SE
Minneapolis, MN 55455

612-626-3087
800-276-8642
FAX 612-624-0997
http://www.allaboutkids.umn.edu
e-mail: lib-web@tc.umn.edu
Elizabeth Latts MSW, Resource Coordinator

A University Community partnership that provides family-centered services that promote physical, emotional, psychological and social health and well-being for children and youth at risk, including children and youth with disabilities.

3697 LDA Alabama Newsletter

Learning Disabilities Association of Alabama
PO Box 11588
Montgomery, AL 36111

334-279-9324
FAX 334-284-9357
Debbie Gibson, President

Educational support and advocacy for those with learning disabilities and Attention Deficit Disorder.

3698 LDA Rhode Island Newsletter

Learning Disabilities Association of Rhode Island
PO Box 8128
Cranston, RI   02920   401-946-6968
                                      FAX 401-946-6968
                                      TDY:401-946-6968
        http://www.worldville.com/lifestyles/ldari
                        e-mail: lindixx@email.com
Linda DiCecco, President

A nonprofit, volunteer organization whose members give their time and support to children with learning disabilities as well as share information with other parents, professionals and individuals with learning disabilities.

3699 Learning Disabilities Newsletter

Learning Disabilities Resources
PO Box 716
Bryn Mawr, PA   19010   610-525-8336
                                         800-869-8336
                                     FAX 610-525-8336
                        http://www.ldonline.org

Offers information on difficulties associated with learning disabilities. *$10.00*

3700 Learning Disabilities Quarterly

Council for Learning Disabilities
PO Box 40303
Overland Park, KS   66204   913-492-8755
                                     FAX 913-492-2546
                        http://www1.winthrop.ecu/cld

Offers information to professionals on working with learning disabled individuals.

3701 Learning Disabilities Research & Practice

Council for Exceptional Children
1110 N Glebe Road
Arlington, VA   22201   703-620-3660
                                         888-232-7733
                                     FAX 703-264-9494
                        http://www.cec.sped.org/
Gerard Hurley, Contact

Scholarly journal providing current research in the field of learning disabilities of importance to teachers, educators and researchers.

3702 Learning Disabilities: A Multidisciplinary Journal

Learning Disabilities Association of America
4156 Library Road
Pittsburgh, PA   15234   412-341-1515
                                      FAX 412-344-0224
                        http://www.ldanatl.org
                        e-mail: ldanatl@usaor.net
Janet Lerner PhD, Editor-in-Chief

A vehicle for disseminating the most current thinking on learning disabilities and to provide information on research, practice, theory, issues and trends regarding learning disabilities. *$25.00*

              Biannual

3703 Learning and Individual Differences

National Association of School Psychologists
4340 E West Highway
Bethesda, MD   20814   301-657-0270
                                     FAX 301-608-2514

A multidisciplinary journal in education.

3704 Mainstream

Johnson Press
2973 Beech Street
San Diego, CA   92102   619-234-3138
                                     FAX 619-234-3155

3705 Media & Methods Magazine

1429 Walnut Street
Philadelphia, PA   19102   215-563-6005
                                         800-555-5657
                                     FAX 215-563-6005
                http://www.media-methods.com
Michele Sokoloff, Publisher

The education source magazine that features how to use instructional technologies with all learning abilities. Practical and hands on teaching ideas and expectional resources.

3706 Mental Health Report

Business Publishers
8737 Colesville Road
Silver Spring, MD   20910   301-587-6300
                                         800-274-6737
                                     FAX 301-585-9075

Covers issues of interest to mental health program administrators including treatment of children with mental disorders and other special populations, tracks federal agency regulation and funding for programs nationwide, as well as court cases and state/federal law. *$325.00*

3707 NICHCY Briefing Paper

NICHCY
PO Box 1492
Washington, DC   20013   202-884-8200
                                         800-695-0285
                                     FAX 202-884-8841
                        http://www.nichcy.org
                        e-mail: nichcy@ace.org
Susan Ripley, Information Specialist

A newsletter offering information, guides, books and reference sources for the learning disabled.

3708 National Organization on Disability

910 16th Street NW
Washington, DC   20006   202-293-5960
                                         800-248-2253
                                     FAX 202-293-7999
                                     TDY:202-293-5968
Alan Reich, President

A newsletter offering information and articles on the organization.

3709 OT Practice

American Occupational Therapy Association
PO Box 31220
Bethesda, MD   20824   301-652-2682
                             800-SAY-AOTA
                             FAX 301-652-7711
Laura Collins, Editor

The clinical and professional magazine of AOTA. It provides professional information and news on all aspects of practice and encourages a dialogue among our members on professional concerns and views.

64 pages

3710 Occupational Outlook Quarterly

US Department of Labor
200 Constitution Avenue
Washington, DC   20212   202-693-6000
                               FAX 202-693-6140
                               http://www.dol.gov

Information on new educational and training opportunities, emerging jobs, prospects for change in the work world and the latest research findings.

3711 Rehabilitation Grants and Contracts Monitor

RPM Press
PO Box 31483
Tucson, AZ   85751   520-886-1990
                           888-810-1990
                           FAX 520-886-1990
Jan Stonebraker, Operations Manager

Newsletter providing a listing of grants and contracts available in the areas of special education, education, voc-ed special needs, vocational rehabilitation, mental health, job training, housing, transportation and a variety of other human service fields. *$97.00*

3712 Report on Disability Programs

Business Publishers
8737 Colesville Road
Silver Spring, MD   20910   301-587-6300
                                  800-274-6737
                                  FAX 301-585-9075

Public policy issues that affect people with disabilities, plus court cases, funding opportunities and national news. Focus is on laws including American with Disabilities Act, Rehabilitation Act, Fair Housing Amendments, Affirmative Action, Individuals with Disabilities Education Act, and other legislation. Also tracks education, housing, job training, rehabilitation, Social Security and SSI, Medicare, Medicaid, and more. Tracks court cases and news from 50 states as well as federal news. *$286.00*

3713 Report on Education of the Disadvantaged

Business Publishers
951 Pershing Drive
Silver Spring, MD   20910   301-587-6300
                                  FAX 301-585-9075
Clair Hill, Marketing Manager

Covers federal aid to education programs affecting the disadvantaged, including children with special education needs. Covers funding programs, court cases and national/local news. *$273.00*

8 pages

3714 Self-Advocacy Resources for Persons with Learning Disabilities

Learning Disabilities Association of America
4156 Library Road
Pittsburgh, PA   15234   412-341-1515
                               FAX 412-344-0224
                               http://www.ldanatl.org
                               e-mail: ldanatl@usaor.net

A newsletter offering information on resources and programs for the learning disabled. *$1.50*

3715 Teacher Magazine

6935 Arlington Road
Bethesda, MD   20814   301-280-3100
                             FAX 301-280-3200
                             http://www.edweek.org
Virginia Edwards, President

Offers articles and information on the latest programs, software, books, classroom materials and more for the teaching professional. *$17.94*

3716 Teaching Exceptional Children

Council for Exceptional Children
1110 N Glebe Road
Arlington, VA   22201   703-620-3660
                              888-232-7733
                              FAX 703-264-9494
                              http://www.cec.sped.org/

Published specifically for teachers and administrators of children with disabilities and children who are gifted. Features practical articles that present methods and materials for classroom use as well as current issues in special education teaching and learning. Also provides the latest data on technology, assistive technology, procedures and techniques with applications to students with exceptionalities.

6x per year

3717 Texas Key

Learning Disabilities Association of Texas
1011 W 31st Street
Austin, TX   78705   512-458-8234
                           800-604-7500
                           FAX 512-458-3826
http://www.ourworld.compuserve.com/homepages/
                                              LD
          e-mail: LDAT@compuserve.com
Ann Robinson, Editor

Quarterly newsletter providing information of intrest to parents and professionals in the field of learning.

16-24 pages

Language Arts

3718 ASHA Leader

American Speech-Language-Hearing Association
10801 Rockville Pike
Bethesda, MD   20814   301-897-5700
                             888-498-6699
                             FAX 301-897-7358
                             http://www.Asha.org
Laurie Ward, Marketing Coordinator

Pertains to the professional and administrative activities in the fields of speech-language pathology, audiology and the American Speech-Language-Hearing Association.

24X/year

3719 American Journal of Speech-Language Pathology: Clinical Practice

American Speech-Language-Hearing Association
10801 Rockville Pike
Bethesda, MD 20814   301-897-5700
888-498-6699
FAX 301-897-7358
http://www.asha.org
Laurie Ward, Marketing Coordinator

Addresses all aspects of clinical practice in speech-language pathology. 3x annually.

3720 Communication Outlook

Michigan University/Artificial Language Laboratory
405 Computer Center
East Lansing, MI 48824   517-353-0870
FAX 517-353-4766
John B Eulenberg, Director
Julie E Warren, Circulation/Advertising

An international quarterly magazine which covers technological developments for persons who experience communication handicaps due to neurological, sensory or neuromuscular conditions. Communication Outlook provides clear and concise information about this emerging technology. Communication Outlook explains where and how communication aids are developed and where they may be purchased. Readers also learn how augmentative and alternative communication is expanding internationally.

32 pages

3721 Journal of Speech, Language, and Hearing Research

American Speech-Language-Hearing Association
10801 Rockville Pike
Bethesda, MD 20814   301-897-5700
888-498-6699
FAX 301-897-7358
http://www.asha.org
Laurie Ward, Marketing Coordinator

An archival research publication that includes papers pertaining to the processes and disorders of hearing, language, speech and to the diagnosis and treatment of these disorders.

3722 Kaleidoscope, Exploring the Experience of Disability Through Literature and Fine Arts

701 S Main Street
Akron, OH 44311   330-762-9755
FAX 330-762-0912
TDY:330-379-3349
http://www.udsakron.org
e-mail: mshiplett@udsakron.org
Gail Willmott, Senior Editor, Author
Phyllis Boerner, Publication Director
Darshan Perusek PhD, Editor-in-Chief
Gail Willmott, Sr Editor

Creatively focuses on the experience of disability through diverse forms of literature and the fine arts. An award-winning magazine unique to the field of disability studies, it is open to writers with or without disabilities. KALEIDOSCOPE strives to express how disability does or does not affect society and individuals feelings and reactions to disability. Its portrayals of disability reflect a conscious effort to challenge and overcome stereotypical and patronizing attitudes. *$6.00*

64 pages $10.00/year

3723 Language Arts

National Council of Teachers of English
1111 W Kenyon Road
Urbana, IL 61801   217-328-3870
800-369-6283
FAX 217-328-9645

3724 National Council of Teachers of English

1111 W Kenyon Road
Urbana, IL 61801   217-328-3870
800-369-6283
FAX 217-278-3761
http://www.ncte.org
e-mail: lbianchini@ncte.org
Lori Bianchini, Communications Specialist

With 75,000 individual and institutional members worldwide, NCTE is dedicated to improving the teaching and learning of English and the language arts at all levels of education. Members include elementary, middle, and high school teachers, supervisors of English programs, college and university faculty, teacher educators, local and state agency English specialists, and professionals in related fields.

College Guides

3725 Assisting College Students with Learning Disabilities: A Tutor's Manual

Association on Higher Education and Disability
PO Box 21192
Columbus, OH   43221   614-488-4972
FAX 614-488-1174
http://www.ahead.org
e-mail: ahead@postbox.acs.ohio-state.edu

This manual is designed for use by service providers and tutors working with students with learning disabilities. *$26.00*

3726 Bridges to Career Success: A Model for Training Career Counselors

National Clearinghouse of Rehabilitation Materials
5202 N Richmond Hill Road
Stillwater, OK   74078   405-624-7650
800-223-5219
FAX 405-624-0695
TDY:405-624-7650
http://www.nchrtm.okstate.edu
Jamie Satcher, Author

This training package consists of materials for a one-day training program including an agenda outline, instructions and resource materials. Content encompasses services typically offered by college and university programs andresources to aid in career planning and placement. *$6.40*

54 pages

3727 College Relations Recruitment Survey

College Placement Council
62 Highland Avenue
Bethlehem, PA   18017   610-868-1421
800-544-5272
FAX 610-868-0208

Gives hard data on practitioners, budgets, the college relations and recruitment function, entry-level hiring, on-campus recruitment, new hires and much much more. *$46.95*

100+ pages

3728 Guide for Delivering Faculty Inservice on the LD College Student

HEATH Resource Center
2121 K Street NW
Washington, DC   20036   202-973-0904
800-544-3284
FAX 202-973-0908
http://gopher://bobcat-ace.nche.edu
e-mail: heath@ace.nche.edu
Dan Gardner, Information Specialist

The guide focuses on providing faculty inservice and training on how to work with students with learning disabilities. *$15.00*

3729 Guide to Community Colleges Serving Students with Learning Disabilities

National Clearinghouse of Rehabilitation Materials
5202 N Richmond Hill Road
Stillwater, OK   74078   405-624-7650
800-223-5219
FAX 405-624-0695
TDY:405-624-3156
http://www.nchrtm.okstate.edu
e-mail: brookdj@okway.okstate.edu
Sonja Burnhan And Jamie Satcher, Author

The guide lists two-year community colleges in Mississippi, Alabama, Georgia, Tennessee, and Florida and describes services and accommodations provided for students with learning disabilities. *$2.80*

18 pages   Item # 353.020

3730 Learning Disabilities Program at Family Service

166 4th Street E
Saint Paul, MN   55101   651-222-0311
FAX 651-222-8920
TDY:651-222-0175
http://www.familyinc.org
e-mail: familyservice@familyinc.org
Kristen Brown, LDP Educator

The Learning Disabilities Program is committed to ensuring that people with challenges to learning are valued, contributing members of their community. This program assists individuals by providing individual consultation, educational presentations, information and referrals.

3731 Postsecondary Learning Disabilities Primer

Carolina University
McKee Building
Cullowhee, NC   38723   828-227-7127
FAX 828-227-7078

A collection of service options and handouts for students/service providers. *$20.50*

3732 Project TAPE: Technical Assistance for Postsecondary Education

Northern Illinois University
DeKalb, IL   60115   815-753-0659
FAX 815-753-0355
Ernest Rose

Includes intervention strategies for persons with learning disabilities attending two-year community colleges.

3733 Service Operations Manual

HEATH Resource Center
2121 K Street NW
Washington, DC   20036   202-973-0904
800-544-3284
FAX 202-973-0908
http://gopher://bobcat-ace.nche.edu
e-mail: heath@ace.nche.edu
Dan Gardner, Information Specialist

This manual describes the system for delivering services to students with learning disabilities at community colleges. *$15.00*

3734 Study of Job Clubs for Two-Year College Students with Learning Disabilities

HEATH Resource Center
2121 K Street NW
Washington, DC 20036   202-973-0904
                               800-544-3284
                            FAX 202-973-0908
            http://gopher://bobcat-ace.nche.edu
                    e-mail: heath@ace.nche.edu
Dan Gardner, Information Specialist

This report describes the results of a study of how job clubs help two-year college students with learning disabilities improve their job-seeking skills. *$15.00*

Counseling & Psychology

3735 A Decision Making Model for Occupational Therapy in the Public Schools

Therapro
225 Arlington Street
Framingham, MA 01702   508-872-9494
                               800-257-5376
                            FAX 508-875-2062
               http://www.theraproducts.com
              e-mail: info@theraproducts.com
Wendy Drobnyk,MS,OTR/L & Sara Sicilliano,MS, OTR/L, Author

Designed to guide the often complex decision making process of initiating, continuing, and discontinuing occupational therapy in the public school. The first publication of its kind to describe entrance and exit criteria for students referred for occupational therapy services.

3736 Accommodations in Higher Education under the Americans with Disabilities Act (ADA)

Guilford Publications
72 Spring Street
New York, NY 10012   212-431-9800
                               800-365-7006
                            FAX 212-966-6708
                   http://www.guilford.com
                  e-mail: info@guilford.com
Michael Gordon, Editor
Shelby Keiser, Editor

Essential reading for any clinician evaluating students who are requesting educational accommodations under the ADA. It provides detailed information concerning how to conduct appropriate evaluations of mental disabilities, particularly attention-deficit/hyperactivity disorder and learning disabilities. Outlines a series of fundamental principles and actual clinical/administrative procedures, providing helpful diagnostic roadmaps, sample evaluations, and resource listings. *$35.00*

236 pages

3737 Affect and Creativity

Lawrence Erlbaum Associates
365 Broadway
Hillsdale, NJ 07642   201-666-4110
                               800-926-6579
                            FAX 201-666-2394
Sandra Walker Russ, Author

This volume offers information on the role of affect and play in the creative process. Designed as a required or supplemental text in graduate level courses in creativity, children's play, child development, affective/cognitive development and psychodynamic theory. *$36.00*

160 pages
ISBN 0-805809-86-4

3738 Behavior Analysis in Education

Brooks/Cole Publishing Company
511 Forest Lodge Road
Pacific Grove, CA 93950   831-373-0728
                            FAX 831-375-6414
Gardner, et. al., Author
Carolyn Crockett, Marketing Manager
Barbara Smallwood, Marketing Assistant

Summarizes the major issues, trends, and findings found in behavior analysis in education literature. The contributors are leaders in the behavior analytic field, and their chapter-length treatment of topics, such as the Future of Behavior Analysis in Education, Early Childhood Interventions, and Promoting Applied Behavior Analysis, provides a volume that allows the professor to cover a range of topics which emphasize measurably superior instruction.

512 pages
ISBN 0-534222-60-9

3739 Behavior Management System

Connecticut Assoc. for Children and Adults with LD
25 Van Zant Street
East Norwalk, CT 06855   203-838-5010
                            FAX 203-866-6108
                     http://www.CACLD.org
Ethyl Papa, Author

Offers information on behavior management for learning disabled students. *$5.95*

3740 Behavioral Technology Guidebook

Eden Services
One Eden Way
Princeton, NJ 08540   609-987-0099
                            FAX 609-987-0243
                 http://www.edenservices.org
                e-mail: info@edenservices.org
David L Holmes EdD, Executive Director/President
Anne Holmes, Director Outreach Support Svcs

Practical guide for behavior modification techniques. *$50.00*

3741 Best Practice Occupational Therapy: Community Service with Children and Families

Therapro
225 Arlington Street
Framingham, MA 01702   508-872-9494
                               800-257-5376
                            FAX 508-875-2062
               http://www.theraproducts.com
              e-mail: info@theraproducts.com
Winnie Dunn, PhD, OTR, FAOTA, Author

An invaluable resource for sudents and practitioners interested in working with children and families in early intervention programs and public schools. Includes screening, pre-assessment, the referral process, best practice assessments, designing best paractice services and examples of IEPs and IFSPs. Many of the forms (screenings, checklists for teachers, referral forms assessment planning guide, etc.) are reproducible. The case studies give good examples of reports.

3742 Cognitive-Behavioral Therapy for Impulsive Children: 2nd Edition

Guilford Publications
72 Spring Street
New York, NY   10012   212-431-9800
                              800-365-7006
                         FAX 212-966-6708
                      http://www.guilford.com
                      e-mail: info@guilford.com

Philip C Kendall, Author
Lauren Braswell, Author

The first edition of this book has been used successfully by thousands of clinicians to help children reduce impulsivity and improve their self-control. Building on the procedures reviewers call powerful tools and of great value to professionals who work with children. This second edition includes treatments, assessment issues and procedures and information on working with parents, teachers and groups of children. *$30.00*

239 pages

3743 Collaborative Problem Solving

Edge Enterprises
PO Box 1304
Lawrence, KS   66044   785-749-1473
                         FAX 785-749-0207
                      e-mail: edge@midusa.net
Knackendoffel, Robinson, Deshler and Schumaker, Author
Jacqueline Schafer, Managing Editor

Outlines the communication skills necessary for establishing a cooperative relationship between two parties and then shows how to incorporate these skills within a problem-solving process that can be used to structure meetings between professionals and parents or students. This is especially useful for professionals who are consulting with teachers about problems they are having in their classrooms. *$10.00*

74 pages   Paperback

3744 Curriculum Based Activities in Occupational Therapy: An Inclusion Resource

Therapro
225 Arlington Street
Framingham, MA   01702   508-872-9494
                                800-257-5376
                           FAX 508-875-2062
                    http://www.theraproducts.com
                    e-mail: info@theraproducts.com

This book is a comprehensive guide to classroom based occupational therapy. The authors have compiled over 162 classroom activities developed to provide a strong linkage between educational and therapeutic goals. Each structured activity is categorized into standard curriculum subsections (reading, math, written language, etc.). Designed for a 3rd and 4th grade classroom, it can be modified for use in lower grades.

3745 Disabled and Their Parents: A Counseling Challenge

Slack Incorporated
6900 Grove Road
Thorofare, NJ   08086   856-848-1000
                          FAX 856-853-5991
                     http://www.slackinc.com
Leo Buscaglia, Author

Offers information on inclusion and counseling services for the learning disabled student. *$8.95*

3746 Effective School Consultation: An Interactive Approach

Brooks/Cole Publishing Company
511 Forest Lodge Road
Pacific Grove, CA   93950   831-373-0728
                              FAX 831-375-6414
Sugai/Tindal, Author
Carolyn Crockett, Marketing Manager
Barbara Smallwood, Marketing Assistant

This book provides special educators with strategies they can use to solve academic and social behavior problems in consultation with parents and professionals in planning, implementing and evaluating programs for students with learning and/or behavior difficulties. The authors' approach, prescriptive case consultation, emphasizes modifying teacher behavior and classroom environments using social learning principles to assist consultees.

446 pages
ISBN 0-534193-02-1

3747 Emotional Disorders & Learning Disabilities in the Classroom

Corwin Press
2455 Teller Road
Thousand Oaks, CA   91320   805-499-9734
                                   800-818-7243
                              FAX 805-499-5323
                       http://www.corwinpress.com
                       e-mail: order@corwinpress.com
Jean Cheng Gorman, Author
Kimberly Gonzales, Marketing Director
Robb Clouse, Senior Acquisitions Editor

This unique book focuses on the interaction between learning disabilities and emotional disorders, fostering an understanding of how learning problems affect emotional well-being and vice-versa. This resource and practical classroom guide for all elementary school teachers includes an overview of common learning disabilities and emotional problems and a classroom-tested, research-based list of classroom interactions and interventions. *$27.95*

60 pages
ISBN 0-761976-20-5

3748 Emotionally Abused & Neglected Child

Books on Special Children
PO Box 305
Congers, NY   10920   845-638-1236
                                     FAX 845-638-0847
                            http://www.boscbooks.com/
                            e-mail: irene@boscbooks.com
D Iwaniec, Author

Describes emotional abuse and neglect and how it affects child's growth, development and well-being. Diagnosis, assessment and issues that should be addressed. *$31.95*

206 pages   softcover
ISBN 0-471955-79-5

3749 Ethical Principles of Psychologists and Code of Conduct

American Psychological Association
750 1st Street NE
Washington, DC   20002   202-336-5650
                                      800-374-2722
                                 FAX 202-336-5633

General ethical principles of psychologists and enforceable ethical standards.

3750 General Guidelines for Providers of Psychological Services

American Psychological Association
750 1st Street NE
Washington, DC   20002   202-336-5650
                                      800-374-2722
                                 FAX 202-336-5633

Offers information for the professional in the area of psychology.

3751 HELP...at Home

Therapro
225 Arlington Street
Framingham, MA   01702   508-872-9494
                                      800-257-5376
                                 FAX 508-875-2062
                          http://www.theraproducts.com
                          e-mail: info@theraproducts.com
Stephanie Parks, MA, Author

Practical and convenient format covers the 650 assesment skills from the Hawaii Early Learning Profile, with each page formatted as a separate, reproducible activity sheet. Therapist annotates, copies and hands out directly to parents to facilitate their involvement.

3752 Handbook of Psychological and Educational Assessment of Children

Guilford Publications
72 Spring Street
New York, NY   10012   212-431-9800
                                      800-365-7006
                                 FAX 212-966-6708
                            http://www.guilford.com
                            e-mail: info@guilford.com
Cecil R Reynolds, Editor
Randy W Kamphaus, Editor

Provides practitioners, researchers, professors, and students with an invaluable resource, this unique volume covers assessment of intelligence, learning styles, learning strategies, academic skills, and special populations, and discusses special topics in mental testing. Chapter contributions are by eminent psychologists and educators in the field of assessment with special expertise in research or practice in their topic areas. *$79.95*

814 pages

3753 Helping Students Become Strategic Learners

Brookline Books
PO Box 1047
Cambridge, MA   02238   617-868-0360
                                      800-666-2665
                                 FAX 617-868-1772
Karen Scheid, Author

The author demonstrates how teachers can implement cognitive theories of instruction in the classroom. *$26.95*

3754 Helping Students Grow

American College Testing Program
PO Box 168
Iowa City, IA   52243   319-337-1000
                                 FAX 319-339-3021
                            http://www.act.org
James Humphrey, Author

Designed to assist counselors in using the wealth of information generated by the ACT assessment.

3755 Overcoming Dyslexia in Children, Adolescents and Adults

Connecticut Assoc. for Children and Adults with LD
25 Van Zant Street
East Norwalk, CT   06855   203-838-5010
                                 FAX 203-866-6108
                            http://www.CACLD.org
Dale Jordan, Author

This book describes some forms of dyslexia in detail and then relates those problems to the social, emotional and personal development of dyslexic individuals. *$30.25*

3756 Pathways to Change: Brief Therapy Solutions with Difficult Adolescents

Guilford Publications
72 Spring Street
New York, NY   10012   212-431-9800
                              800-365-7006
                        FAX 212-966-6708
                     http://www.guilford.com
                     e-mail: info@guilford.com
Matthew D. Selekman, Author

Encouraging therapeutic improvisation and incorporating the use of humor, Selekman demonstrates how the clinician can capitalize on the strengths and resources of family members, peers, and other involved mental health professionhals to resolve the client's presenting problems rapidly. *$29.00*

186 pages
ISBN 0-898620-15-5

3757 Practitioner's Guide to Dynamic Assessment

Guilford Publications
72 Spring Street
New York, NY   10012   212-431-9800
                              800-365-7006
                        FAX 212-966-6708
                     http://www.guilford.com
                     e-mail: info@guilford.com
Carol S. Lidz, Author

An excellent text aimed at general practitioners offering information on assessment and intervention techniques. *$20.95*

210 pages   Paperback

3758 Prescriptions for Children with Learning and Adjustment Problems: A Consultant's Desk Reference

Charles C Thomas Publisher
2600 S 1st Street
Springfield, IL   62704   217-789-8980
                                 800-258-8980
                           FAX 217-789-9130
                        http://www.ccthomas.com
                        e-mail: books@ccthomas.com
Ralph F Blanco, David F Bogacki, Author

Third edition. Books sent on approval. Shipping charges: $5.50 US/6.50 Canada. Prices subject to change without notice.

264 pages   Cloth

3759 Problems in Written Expression: Assessment and Remediation

Guilford Publications
72 Spring Street
New York, NY   10012   212-431-9800
                              800-365-7006
                        FAX 212-966-6708
                     http://www.guilford.com
                     e-mail: info@guilford.com
Sharon Bradley-Johnson, Author
Jusi Lucas Lesiak, Author

A great resource for speech-language pathologists, counselors, resource specialists and other special educators. *$20.95*

178 pages   Paperback

3760 Reading and Learning Disability: A Neuropsychological Approach to Evaluation & Instruction

Charles C Thomas Publisher
2600 S 1st Street
Springfield, IL   62704   217-789-8980
                                 800-258-8980
                           FAX 217-789-9130
                        http://www.ccthomas.com
                        e-mail: books@ccthomas.com
Estelle L Fryburg, Author

This text utilizes the current knowledge of neuropsychology (brain-behavior relationships) and the concepts of cognitive psychology to provide an understanding of reading and learning disability which has a practical application to education. The primary goal of the book is to provide teachers, psychologists, physicians, concerned professionals, and parents with an interdisciplinary view of learning and schooling. *$79.95*

398 pages   Cloth
ISBN 0-398067-44-9

3761 Reflections Through the Looking Glass

Association on Higher Education and Disability
PO Box 21192
Columbus, OH   43221   614-488-4972
                        FAX 614-488-1174
                     http://www.ahead.org
           e-mail: ahead@postbox.acs.ohio-state.edu
A must for new professionals offering a philosophical review of the nature of the field written in first person by charter member and former Association President Richard Harris of Ball State University. *$5.50*

3762 Revels in Madness: Insanity in Medicine and Literature

University of Michigan Press
839 Greene Street
Ann Arbor, MI   48104   734-763-0163
                        FAX 734-763-0456
                  http://www.press.umich.edu
                  e-mail: pgarner@umich.edu
Allen Thiher, Author
Mary Erwin, Assistant Director

Revels in Madness offers a history of western culture's shifting understanding of insanity as evidenced in its literature and as influenced by medical knowledge. *$57.50*

368 pages   cloth
ISBN 0-472110-35-7

3763 Self-Advocacy Handbook for High School Students

Utah Department of Special Education
250 E 500 S
Salt Lake City, UT   84112   801-538-7711
                              FAX 801-538-7991
                     http://www.usoe.k12.ut.us/sans/
                     e-mail: mtaylor@usoe.k12.ut.us
Ann Jepsen, Author

This manual teaches the students to advocate for themselves.

3764 Self-Advocacy for Junior High School Students

Utah Department of Special Education
250 E 500 S
Salt Lake City, UT   84112   801-538-7711
                                    FAX 801-538-7991
                        http://www.usoe.k12.ut.us/sans/
                        e-mail: mtaylor@usoe.k12.ut.us

A program designed to increase students' verbal expressive skills in discussing learning disabilities, ADD and related characteristics.

**3765 Self-Injurious Behavior: A Somatosensory
Treatment Approach**

Therapro
225 Arlington Street
Framingham, MA   01702   508-872-9494
                                800-257-5376
                        FAX 508-875-2062
                        http://www.theraproducts.com
                        e-mail: info@theraproducts.com
Haru Hirama, EdD, OTR/L, Author

Practical account of treatment. Stimulation is given to counteract the somatosensory deprivation experienced by the self-injurious individual. Includes reviews/illustrations of the treatment.

**3766 Teaching Students with Learning and Behavior
Problems**

Pro-Ed
8700 Shoal Creek Boulevard
Austin, TX   78757   512-451-3246
                            800-897-3202
                        FAX 512-451-8542
                        http://www.proedinc.com
Donald Hammill, Author

This popular, classic text provides teachers with a comprehensive overview of the best practices in assessing and instructing students with mild-to-moderate learning and behavior problems. *$44.00*

520 pages
ISBN 0-890796-10-6

3767 Treating Troubled Children and Their Families

Books on Special Children
PO Box 305
Congers, NY   10920   845-638-1236
                             FAX 845-638-0847
                        http://www.boscbooks.com/
                        e-mail: irene@boscbooks.com
EF Wachtel, Author

In treating a child, learn about him or her as an individual, interview parents and family in separate units. Give caretaker various insights on treating this troubled child. Book has specific questions to ask, ways to interpret attitudes, explanations. Systemic and behavioral intervention formulated to specific needs of the child. *$38.00*

303 pages   hardcover
ISBN 0-898620-07-4

General

3768 A History of Disability

University of Michigan Press
839 Greene Street
Ann Arbor, MI   48104   734-763-0163
                               FAX 734-763-0456
                        http://www.press.umich.edu
                        e-mail: pgarner@umich.edu
Henri-Jacques Stiker, Author
Mary Erwin, Assistant Director

Published in 1997 in France as Corps Infirms et Societes and available now in excellent English translation, the book traces the history of Western cultural responses to disability, from ancient times to the present. *$52.50*

264 pages   cloth
ISBN 0-472110-63-2

**3769 A Human Development View of Learning
Disabilities: From Theory to Practice**

Charles C Thomas Publisher
2600 S 1st Street
Springfield, IL   62704   217-789-8980
                                 800-258-8980
                            FAX 217-789-9130
                        http://www.ccthomas.com
                        e-mail: books@ccthomas.com
Corrine E Kass and Cleborne D Maddux, Author

Presents a strategy for designing day-to-day individualized lessons for learning disabled students from kindergarten through adulthood. Books sent on approval. Shipping charges: $5.50 US/&6.50 Canada. Prices subject to change without notice. *$50.95*

222 pages   Cloth
ISBN 0-398058-86-5

**3770 A Manual of Sequential Art Activities for
Classified Children and Adolescents**

Charles C Thomas Publisher
2600 S 1st Street
Springfield, IL   62704   217-789-8980
                                 800-258-8980
                            FAX 217-789-9130
Rocco AL Fugaro, Author

246 pages   Spiral (paper) $41.95
ISBN 0-398050-85-6

**3771 A Practical Approach to RSP: A Handbook for
the Resource Specialist Program**

Charles C Thomas Publisher
2600 S 1st Street
Springfield, IL   62704   217-789-8980
                                 800-258-8980
                            FAX 217-789-9130
                        http://www.ccthomas.com
                        e-mail: books@ccthomas.com
Leslie A Williams and Lucile S Arntzen, Author

Valuable to resource specialists in training and in service, administrators and related professionals. Books sent on approval. *$33.95*

120 pages   Cloth
ISBN 0-398059-08-X

3772   Academic Skills Problems Workbook

Guilford Publications
72 Spring Street
New York, NY   10012   212-431-9800
                                        800-365-7006
                                   FAX 212-966-6708
                                http://www.guilford.com
                                e-mail: info@guilford.com
Edward S Shapiro, PhD, Author

This workbook is filled with reproducible forms, and features step-by-step instructions and practice exercises for school professionals that will facilitate observation, assessment, and intervention. *$19.95*

135 pages

3773   Academic Skills Problems: Direct Assessment and Intervention, 2nd Edition

Guilford Publications
72 Spring Street
New York, NY   10012   212-431-9800
                                        800-365-7006
                                   FAX 212-966-6708
                                http://www.guilford.com
                                e-mail: info@guilford.com
Edward S Shapiro, PhD, Author

This book shows how to use direct methods for establishing clear links to intervention strategies and determining the success of remedial efforts.   Contains reproducible forms and charts. *$32.00*

315 pages

3774   Academic and Developmental Learning Disabilities

Love Publishing Company
PO Box 22353
Denver, CO   80222   970-221-7333
                                   FAX 970-221-7444
                       e-mail: lovepublishing@compuserve.com
Samuel Kirk, Author

This text is intended to serve as a basis for classifying children and to help teachers diagnose and remediate children who have major disabilities in the learning process. *$39.95*

337 pages

3775   Accessing the General Curriculum Including Students with Disabilities in Standards-Based Reform

Corwin Press
2455 Teller Road
Thousand Oaks, CA   91320   805-499-9734
                                        800-818-7243
                                   FAX 805-499-5323
                               http://www.corwinpress.com
                               e-mail: order@corwinpress.com
Victor Noiet, Margaret J McLaughlin, Author
Kimberly Gonzales, Marketing Director
Robb Clouse, Senior Acquisitions Editor

Practical information and insight make it easier to design instruction that enables all students to access and make progress in inclusive K-12 environments. It also helps teachers, administrators, and curriculum development specialists design measures that can be used to assess the progress of special needs students, as well as develop effective collaborative relationships between general and special education instructors. *$29.95*

152 pages
ISBN 0-761976-70-1

3776   Adapted Physical Education for Students

Exceptional Parent Press
2600 S 1st Street
Springfield, IL   62704   217-789-8980
                                        800-258-8980
                                   FAX 217-789-9130
Kimberly Davis, Author

Focuses on the physical education needs and curriculum for autistic children. *$34.95*

142 pages

3777   An Introduction to Learning Disabilities

Scott Foresman Addison Wesley
1900 E Lake Avenue
Glenview, IL   60025   847-729-3000
                                   FAX 847-729-8910
                                   http://www.sf.aw.com
Howard Adelman, Author

This text is designed to introduce learning disabilities in a way that clarifies both instructional options and large educational issues.

354 pages

3778   An Introduction to the Nature and Needs of Students with Mild Disabilities

Charles C Thomas Publisher
2600 S 1st Street
Springfield, IL   62704   217-789-8980
                                        800-258-8980
                                   FAX 217-789-9130
                                http://www.ccthomas.com
                                e-mail: books@ccthomas.com
Carroll J Jones, Author

Mild mental retardation, behavior disorders, and learning disabilities are covered in this text. Designed as an introductory text for an undergraduate degree program in special education. Also included is information on the historical background of services in Europe, early-to-current services in the United States, landmark legislation, litigation relevant to each categorical area, with definitions and classification systems. *$50.95*

300 pages   Cloth
ISBN 0-398067-11-2

3779 Annals of Dyslexia

International Dyslexia Association
8600 LaSalle Road, Chester Building
Baltimore, MD 21286   410-296-0232
800-ABC-D123
FAX 410-321-5069
TDY:410-296-0232
http://www.interdys.org

The Society's scholarly journal contains updates on current research and selected proceedings from talks given at each ODS international conference. Issues of Annals are available from 1982 through the present year.

3780 Art as a Language for the Learning Disabled Child

Learning Disabilities Association of America
4156 Library Road
Pittsburgh, PA 15234   412-341-1515
FAX 412-344-0224
http://www.ldanatl.org
e-mail: ldanatl@usaor.net

A guide promoting art therapy in the classroom for the learning disabled student. $1.00

3781 Art for All the Children: Approaches to Art Therapy for Children with Disabilities

Charles C Thomas Publisher
2600 S 1st Street
Springfield, IL 62704   217-789-8980
800-258-8980
FAX 217-789-9130
http://www.ccthomas.com
e-mail: books@ccthomas.com
Frances E Anderson, Author

Tis edition is for art therapists in training and for in-service professionals in art therapy, art education and special education who have children with disabilities as a part of their case/class load. A major goal of this edition is to show the many ways that art can be adapted so that all children may have a meaningful encounter with art. The book will prepare the reader to understand children, their art, their disabilities and how to adapt art to meet their needs. $ 69.95

398 pages Cloth
ISBN 0-398057-97-4

3782 Art-Centered Education & Therapy for Children with Disabilities

Charles C Thomas Publisher
2600 S 1st Street
Springfield, IL 62704   217-789-8980
800-258-8980
FAX 217-789-9130
http://www.ccthomas.com
e-mail: books@ccthomas.com
Frances E Anderson, Author

To help both the regular education, and art and special education teachers, pre- and in-service, better understand the issues and realities of providing education and remediation to children with disabilities. Offers the concept that we must live, learn and develop through art - that art belongs at the core of the public school curriculum. $49.95

284 pages Cloth
ISBN 0-398058-96-2

3783 Assessment: The Special Educator's Role

Brooks/Cole Publishing Company
511 Forest Lodge Road
Pacific Grove, CA 93950   831-373-0728
FAX 831-375-6414
Cheri Hoy & Noel Gregg, Author
Carolyn Crockett, Marketing Manager
Barbara Smallwood, Marketing Assistant

Hoy and Gregg, two well-known professionals in the field, highlight the process of assessment of mild to moderate disabilities for a wide age range (preschool to adult). Aimed at those with no classroom experience in assessment, this book focuses on the integration of dynamic, curriculum-based, and non-referenced data for diagnostic decisions and program planning.

580 pages
ISBN 0-534211-32-1

3784 Attentional Deficit Disorder in Children and Adolescents

Charles C Thomas Publisher
2600 S 1st Street
Springfield, IL 62704   217-789-8980
800-258-8980
FAX 217-789-9130
http://www.ccthomas.com
e-mail: books@ccthomas.com
Jack L Fadely, Author
Virginia N Hosler, Author

This book presents an analysis of case studies of children and adolescents with attentional deficits and hyperactivity. The focus is to demonstrate CAUSAL factors in this disorder and to suggest treatment strategies both in psychological and medical practice. $56.95

292 pages Cloth
ISBN 0-398057-92-3

3785 Atypical Cognitive Deficits

Lawrence Erlbaum Associates
365 Broadway
Hillsdale, NJ 07642   201-666-4110
800-926-6579
FAX 201-666-2394
Sarah H Broman, Author
Jordan Grafman, Author

This volume is based on a conference held to examine what was known about cognitive behaviors and brain structure and function in three syndromes. $29.95

352 pages
ISBN 0-805811-80-0

3786 Auditory Processes

Academic Therapy Publications
20 Commercial Boulevard
Novato, CA 94949   415-883-3314
800-422-7249
FAX 415-883-3720
http://www.atpub.com
Pamela Gillel, Author
Betty Lou Kratoville, Editor

Explains how teachers, educational consultants and parents can identify auditory processing problems, understand their impact and implement appropriate instructional strategies to enhance learning. *$15.00*

120 pages
ISBN 0-878790-94-2

3787 Auditory Processes: Revised Edition

Therapro
225 Arlington Street
Framingham, MA   01702   508-872-9494
                                800-257-5376
                          FAX 508-875-2062
            http://www.theraproducts.com
            e-mail: info@theraproducts.com
Pamela Gillet, PhD, Author

This author clearly describes the sequence of auditory skill development as well as the symptomatic behavior of youngsters with auditory processing problems. Offers hundreds of tests and remedial exercises in areas such as auditory discrimination, auditory memory, auditiory perception deficit.

3788 Auditory Training

Harris Communications
15155 Technology Drive
Eden Prairie, MN   55344   952-906-1180
                                  800-825-6758
                            FAX 952-906-1099
                            TDY:952-906-1198
                http://www.harriscmm.com
Norman P Erber, Author

Written for parents, educators, and rehabilitative audiologists, who are concerned with auditory development of hearing impaired children. Auditory instruction strategies encourage children to learn to hear through whatever type of amplification device they are using. Covers research and developments in auditory training, speech perception, speech production, screening, training and practical suggestions. *$23.95*

197 pages   Paperback

3789 BOSC Directory: Facilities for People with Learning Disabilities

PO Box 305
Congers, NY   10920   845-638-1236
                        FAX 845-638-0847
            http://www.boscbooks.com
            e-mail: irene@boscbooks.com
Irene Slovak, Owner
Dr. Julius Kleiner, Marketing Director

Facilities that work with people with special needs; day and residential schools, independent living programs, centers and clinics, colleges and vocational training programs, agencies, and special consumer products. Specific and cumulative indexes with table of disabilities treated by the facility. *$70.00*

300+ pages
ISBN 0-961386-07-0

3790 Bilingualism and Learning Disabilities

Learning Disabilities Association of America
4156 Library Road
Pittsburgh, PA   15234   412-341-1515
                          FAX 412-344-0224
                http://www.ldanatl.org
                e-mail: ldanatl@usaor.net

A comprehensive guide on bilingualism in the classroom and on the job for learning disabled adults. *$21.95*

3791 Body and Physical Difference: Discourses of Disability

University of Michigan Press
839 Greene Street
Ann Arbor, MI   48104   734-763-0163
                          FAX 734-763-0456
                http://www.press.umich.edu
                e-mail: pgarner@umich.edu
David T Mitchell, Author
Mary Erwin, Assistant Director

For years the subject of human disability has engaged those in the biological, social and cognitive sciences, while at the same time, it has been curiously neglected within the humanitites. The Body and Physical Difference seeks to introduce the field of disability studies into the humanities by exploring the fantasies and fictons that have crystallized around conceptions of physical and cognitive difference. *$52.50*

320 pages   cloth
ISBN 0-472096-59-1

3792 Bridging the Family-Professional Gap: Facilitating Interdisciplinary Services

Charles C Thomas Publisher
2600 S 1st Street
Springfield, IL   62704   217-789-8980
                                800-258-8980
                          FAX 217-789-9130
                http://www.ccthomas.com
                e-mail: books@ccthomas.com
Billy Ogletree, Martin Fischer, Jane Schulz, Author

Facilitates family preparedness for interdisciplinary team functioning and promotes interdisciplinary professionals' awareness of family members' concerns and priorities. *$49.95*

300 pages   Cloth
ISBN 0-398069-88-3

3793 Brief Intervention for School Problems: Collaborating for Practical Solutions

Guilford Publications
72 Spring Street
New York, NY   10012   212-431-9800
                              800-365-7006
                        FAX 212-966-6708
                http://www.guilford.com
                e-mail: info@guilford.com
John J Murphy, Author
Barry L Duncan, Author

This book focuses on what works and spells out a compelling rationale and practical blueprint for time-efficient, collaborative problem solving in the schools. Extensive case examples and sample dialogues guide school practitioners and trainees through the interview and intervention process and tables and figures help illustrate the approach. *$26.95*

175 pages

3794   Case Studies of Exceptional Students: Handicapped and Gifted

Charles C Thomas Publisher
2600 S 1st Street
Springfield, IL   62704   217-789-8980
                                 800-258-8980
                             FAX 217-789-9130
Carroll J. Jones, Author

Clear, concise, educationally relevant case studies. *$56.95*

272 pages   Cloth
ISBN 0-398058-56-3

3795   Center Work

Center for Research in Vocational Education
2150 Shattuck Avenue
Berkeley, CA   94704
                                 800-762-4093

Profiles the center's current work and contains articles about policy issues, computer resources, NCRVE publications, and ERIC/ACVE digests.

Quarterly-Free

3796   Children, Problems and Guidelines, Special Ed

Slosson Educational Publications
538 Buffalo Road
East Aurora, NY   14052   888-756-7766
                                 800-828-4800
                             FAX 800-655-3840
                        http://www.slosson.com
                       e-mail: slosson@slosson.com
LaDeane Casey, Author
Steven W Slosson, President

A professional and responsible resource book which addresses many of the most common problems involving children and their homes or schools. *$45.00*

99 pages   Ages 6-16

3797   Classroom Management for Elementary Teachers: 4th Editon

Books on Special Children
PO Box 305
Congers, NY   10920   845-638-1236
                             FAX 845-638-0847
                        http://www.boscbooks.com/
                       e-mail: irene@boscbooks.com
ET Emmer, Author

Good classroom management just doesn't happen, it takes good planning and effective teachers organizing classroom rules and procedures, planning and conducting instructions. Appropriate student behavior, managing problem behavior and special groups are discussed. *$34.95*

228 pages   softcover
ISBN 0-205264-27-1

3798   Classroom Management for Secondary Teachers: 4th Editon

Books on Special Children
PO Box 305
Congers, NY   10920   845-638-1236
                             FAX 845-638-0847
                        http://www.boscbooks.com/
                       e-mail: irene@boscbooks.com
ET Emmer, Author

Good classroom management just doesn't happen, it takes good planning and effective teachers organizing classroom rules and procedures, planning and conducting instructions. Appropriate student behavior, managing problem behavior and special groups are discussed. *$34.95*

216 pages   softcover
ISBN 0-205264-28-X

3799   Classroom Notetaker: How to Organize a Program Serving Students with Hearing Impairments

Harris Communications
15155 Technology Drive
Eden Prairie, MN   55344   952-906-1180
                                 800-825-6758
                             FAX 952-906-1099
                             TDY:952-906-1198
                        http://www.harriscomm.com
Jimmie Joan Wilson, Author

Promotes classroom note taking and gives specifics on establishing a note taking program. Topics include proving the need for a note taking program, recruiting and training note takers, and the principles of note taking. *$25.95*

127 pages   Paperback

3800   Cognitive Approach to Learning Disabilities

Pro-Ed
8700 Shoal Creek Boulevard
Austin, TX   78757   512-451-3246
                                 800-897-3202
                             FAX 512-451-8542
                        http://www.proedinc.com
D Kim Reid, Author

This book is the first to bridge the gap between cognitive psychology and information processing theory in understanding learning disabilities. *$44.00*

686 pages
ISBN 0-890796-85-8

3801 Cognitive Retraining Using Microcomputers

Lawrence Erlbaum Associates
365 Broadway
Hillsdale, NJ   07642   201-666-4110
                                       800-926-6579
                                 FAX 201-666-2394
Veronica Bradley, Author
John L Welch, Author

This text reviews representative examples from the literature relating to the training of cognitive systems with the emphasis on studies describing the use of computerized methods. *$69.95*

> *304 pages*
> *ISBN 0-863772-02-1*

3802 Cognitive Strategy Instruction That Really Improves Children's Performance

Brookline Books
PO Box 1047
Cambridge, MA   02238   617-868-0360
                                       800-666-2665
                                 FAX 617-868-1772

A concise and focused work that summarily presents the few procedures for teaching strategies that aid academic subject matter learning that are empirically validated and fit well with the elementary school curriculum. *$27.95*

3803 Collaborative Practices for Educators Strategies for Effective Communication

Peytral Publication
PO Box 1162
Minnetonka, MN   55345   952-949-8707
                                       877-739-8725
                                 FAX 612-906-9777
                                 http://www.peytral.com
                                 e-mail: help@peytral.com
Patty Lee, EdD, Author

With inclusive education, general and special educators are expected to collaborate in ways never anticipated in the educational system. With more than sixty strategies and 180 practice activities from which to chose, you and your colleagues will be able to focus on specific areas or several areas simultaneously. Includes tip cards for effective communication. *$19.95*

> *85 pages*
> *ISBN 0-964427-13-3*

3804 Competencies for Teachers of Students with Learning Disabilities

Council for Exceptional Children
1110 N Glebe Road
Arlington, VA   22201   703-620-3660
                                       888-232-7733
                                 FAX 703-264-9494
                                 http://www.cec.sped.org/
Amme Graves, Author
Mary F Landers, Author
Jean Lockerson, Author

Lists 209 specific professional competencies needed by teachers of students with learning disabilities and provides a conceptual framework for the ten areas in which the competencies are organized. *$5.00*

> *25 pages*

3805 Complete Learning Disabilities Handbook

Learning Disabilities Association of America
4156 Library Road
Pittsburgh, PA   15234   412-341-1515
                                 FAX 412-344-0224
                                 http://www.ldanatl.org
                                 e-mail: ldanatl@usaor.net
JM Hartwell, Author

Offers complete coverage of persons with learning disabilities. *$29.95*

3806 Comprehensive Assessment in Special Education: Approaches, Procedures and Concerns

Charles C Thomas Publisher
2600 S 1st Street
Springfield, IL   62704   217-789-8980
                                       800-258-8980
                                 FAX 217-789-9130
                                 http://www.ccthomas.com
                                 e-mail: books@ccthomas.com
Rotatori, Fox, Sexton and Miller, Author

Books sent on approval. Shipping charges: $5.50, $6.50 Canada. Prices subject to change without notice. *$104.95*

> *578 pages*
> *ISBN 0-398056-45-5*

3807 Cooperative Learning and Strategies for Inclusion

Brookes Publishing Company
PO Box 10624
Baltimore, MD   21285   410-337-9580
                                       800-638-3775
                                 FAX 410-337-8539
                                 http://www.brookspublishing.com
                                 e-mail: custserv@brookespublishing.com
JoAnne W Putnam, PhD, Author

This book supplies educators, classroom support personnel, and administrators with numerous tools for creating positive, inclusive classroom environments for students from preschool through high school. *$37.00*

> *288 pages   Paperback*
> *ISBN 1-557663-46-7*

3808 Creating Positive Classroom Environments

Brooks/Cole Publishing Company
511 Forest Lodge Road
Pacific Grove, CA   93950   831-373-0728
                                 FAX 831-375-6414
Epanchin/Stoddard/Townsend, Author
Carolyn Crockett, Marketing Manager
Barbara Smallwood, Marketing Assistant

This book offers an approach to classroom management that encourages situation-specific decision-making. Presenting research-based information on how to establish an effective behavior management system in both regular and special education settings, this book centers on ways to help students manage their own behavior rather than on ways their behavior can be managed by others. Interventions focus on creating success.

> *448 pages*
> *ISBN 0-534222-54-4*

3809 Creative Curriculum for Early Childhood

Teaching Strategies
PO Box 42243
Washington, DC   20015   202-362-7543
                              800-637-3652
                           FAX 202-364-7273
              http://www.teachingstrategies.com
              e-mail: info@teachingstrategies.com
DT Dodge And LJ Collier, Author

Focuses on the developmentally appropriate program in early childhood education. Illustrates how preschool and kindergarten teachers set the stage for learning, and how children and teachers interact and learn in various interest areas. *$39.95*

390 pages
ISBN 1-879537-06-0

3810 Curriculum Development for Students with Mild Disabilities

Charles C Thomas Publisher
2600 S 1st Street
Springfield, IL   62704   217-789-8980
                              800-258-8980
                           FAX 217-789-9130
Carroll J Jones, Author

Many teachers of students with mild disabilities experience difficulty writing IEPs because they lack a foundation in the regular education curriculum of academic skills and sequences associated with each grade level. *$34.95*

258 pages   Spiral (paper)
ISBN 0-398070-18-0

3811 Curriculum Models and Strategies for Educating Individuals with Disabilities

Charles C Thomas Publisher
2600 S 1st Street
Springfield, IL   62704   217-789-8980
                              800-258-8980
                           FAX 217-789-9130
George Taylor, Author

Curriculum skills units developed as a guide to assist educators instructing disabled individuals in the areas of communication, math and science, socially effective and psychomotor skills, as well as morals and character. Also helpful to those working in community agencies with disabled individuals. *$48.95*

260 pages   Cloth
ISBN 0-398069-75-1

3812 Curriculum-Based Assessment: A Primer

Charles C Thomas Publisher
2600 S 1st Street
Springfield, IL   62704   217-789-8980
                              800-258-8980
                           FAX 217-789-9130
              http://www.ccthomas.com
              e-mail: books@ccthomas.com
Charles H Hargis, Author

The use of curriculum-based assessment (CBA) to ensure learning disabled and low achieving students adequate educational opportunity is the focus of this book. CBA requires an intimate relationship between teaching and testing. The author presents examples and methods of implementation through reading and arithmetic activities and discusses at length the issues involved in test validity and grading. *$33.95*

190 pages   Paperback
ISBN 0-398059-42-X

3813 Curriculum-Based Assessment: The Easy Way

Charles C Thomas Publisher
2600 S 1st Street
Springfield, IL   62704   217-789-8980
                              800-258-8980
                           FAX 217-789-9130
Carroll J Jones, Author

Practical and specific methods for developing and using CBA's in an educational setting. *$27.95*

176 pages   Spiral (paper)

3814 Curriculum-Based Evaluation: Teaching and Decision Making

Brooks/Cole Publishing Company
511 Forest Lodge Road
Pacific Grove, CA   93950   831-373-0728
                             FAX 831-375-6414
Howell/Fox/Morehead, Author
Carolyn Crockett, Marketing Manager
Barbara Smallwood, Marketing Assistant

Focusing on effective instruction, instructional decision making, and the various evaluation models useful in curriculum-based assessment, this book examines teacher-made tests and curriculum as they relate to a child's success or failure. Using a step-by-step approach, the authors show teachers how to use the curriculum to meet the child's needs, how to assess in an ongoing way, and how to recognize when instructional change is warranted.

526 pages
ISBN 0-534164-28-5

3815 Deal Me In: The Use of Playing Cards in Learning and Teaching

CT Association for Children and Adults with LD
25 Van Zant Street
East Norwalk, CT   06855   203-838-5010
                             FAX 203-866-6108
                           http://www.CACLD.org
                           e-mail: cacld@juno.com
M Golick, Author
Marie Armstrong, Information Specialist

A book of how to play cards with your learning disabled child. *$10.95*

$2.50 shipping

3816 Defects: Engendering the Modern Body

University of Michigan Press
839 Greene Street
Ann Arbor, MI   48104   734-763-0163
                                     FAX 734-763-0456
                                http://www.press.umich.edu
                                e-mail: pgarner@umich.edu
Helen Deutsch, Author
Mary Erwin, Assistant Director

Defects brings together essays on the emergence of
the concept of monstrosity in the eighteenth century
and the ways it paralleled the emergence of notions of
sexual difference. *$57.50*

   344 pages   cloth
   ISBN 0-472096-98-2

3817 Developmental Variation and Learning Disorders

Educators Publishing Service
31 Smith Place
Cambridge, MA   02138   617-547-6706
                                         800-225-5750
                                     FAX 617-547-0412
                                http://www.epsbooks.com
                                e-mail: eps@epsbooks.com
Dr. Melvin Levine, Author

Unique in its approach to learning disorders, this Second Edition combines what is known about normal
child development during the school years with insights into the nature of variation and dysfunction.
$69.00

   ISBN 0-838819-92-3

**3818 Dictionary of Special Education and
Rehabilitation**

Love Publishing Company
PO Box 22353
Denver, CO   80222   970-221-7333
                                     FAX 970-221-7444
                          e-mail: lovepublishing@compuserve.com
Glenn A Vergason, Author

A valuable basic resource in the field. It incorporates
hundreds of additions and changes. *$32.00*

3819 Directory for Exceptional Children

Porter Sargent Publishers
11 Beacon Street
Boston, MA   02108   617-523-1670
                                         800-342-7870
                                     FAX 617-523-1021
                                http://www.portersargent.com
                                e-mail: info@portersargent.com
Daniel McKeever, Sr Editor
John Yonce, General Manager
Leslie Weston, Production Editor

A comprehensive survey of 3000 schools, facilities,
and organizations across the USA. Serving children
and yound adults with developmental, physical, medical, and emotional disabilities. Aide to parents, consultants, educators, and other professionals. *$64.00*

   1312 pages
   ISBN 0-875581-31-5

**3820 Disability Awareness in the Classroom: A
Resource Tool for Teachers and Students**

Charles C Thomas Publisher
2600 S 1st Street
Springfield, IL   62704   217-789-8980
                                         800-258-8980
                                     FAX 217-789-9130
Lorie and Isabelle St. Onge Levison, Author

Dispels misconceptions that contribute to stereotyp-
ing. Provides training for general education teachers
and students preparing for inclusion or wanting to enhance their inclusion experiences. *$38.95*

   230 pages   Spiral (paper)
   ISBN 0-398069-53-0

**3821 Early Adolescence Perspectives on Research,
Policy and Intervention**

Lawrence Erlbaum Associates
365 Broadway
Hillsdale, NJ   07642   201-666-4110
                                         800-926-6579
                                     FAX 201-666-2394
Richard M Lerner, Author

This forthcoming volume brings together a diverse
group of scholars to write integratively about cutting-edge research issues pertinent to the study of
early adolescence. *$99.95*

   528 pages
   ISBN 0-805811-64-8

**3822 Eden Institute Curriculum: Adaptive Physical
Education, Volume V**

Eden Services
One Eden Way
Princeton, NJ   08540   609-987-0099
                                     FAX 609-987-0243
                                http://www.edenservices.org
                                e-mail: info@edenservices.org
David L Holmes EdD, Executive Director/President
Anne Holmes, Director Outreach Support Svcs

Teaching programs in the areas of sensory integration
and adaptive physical education for students with autism. *$50.00*

**3823 Eden Institute Curriculum: Classroom
Orienation, Volume II**

Eden Services
One Eden Way
Princeton, NJ   08540   609-987-0099
                                     FAX 609-987-0243
                                http://www.edenservices.org
                                e-mail: info@edenservices.org
David L Holmes EdD, Executive Director/President
Anne Holmes, Director Outreach Support Svcs

Academic and social skills programs for students with
autism. *$100.00*

3824 Eden Institute Curriculum: Core

Eden Services
One eden Way
Princeton, NJ 08540   609-987-0099
                             FAX 609-987-0243
                    http://www.edenservices.org
                    e-mail: info@edenservices.org
David L Holmes EdD, Executive Director/President
Anne Holmes, Director Outreach Support Svcs

Teaching programs for students with autism. *$200.00*

3825 Eden Institute Curriculum: Speech and Language, Volume IV

Eden Services
One Eden Way
Princeton, NJ 08540   609-987-0099
                             FAX 609-987-0243
                    http://www.edenservices.org
                    e-mail: info@edenservices.org
David L Holmes EdD, Executive Director/President
Anne Holmes, Director Outreach Support Svcs

Speech and language development programs for students with autism. *$170.00*

3826 Educating All Students Together

Corwin Press
2455 Teller Road
Thousand Oaks, CA 91320   805-499-9734
                               800-818-7243
                          FAX 805-499-5323
                    http://www.corwinpress.com
                    e-mail: order@corwinpress.com
Leonard C Burrello, Carl Lashley, Edith Beatty, Author
Kimberly Gonzales, Marketing Director
Robb Clouse, Senior Acquisitions Editor

A plan for unifying the separate and parallel systems of special and general education. Key concepts include: schools embracing special services personnel; the role of the community; program evaluation and incentives; brain and holographic design; collaboration between school administrators and teachers; and adapting curriculum; and instruction. *$32.95*

264 pages
ISBN 0-761976-98-1

3827 Educating Children with Multiple Disabilities, A Transdisciplinary Approach

Books on Special Children
PO Box 305
Congers, NY 10920   845-638-1236
                          FAX 845-638-0847
                    http://www.boscbooks.com/
                    e-mail: irene@boscbooks.com
FP Orelove, Author

Contributors discuss inclusive education for severely disabled students. Examines teamwork, needs of special students, designs curriculum needs, and special strategies for intervention. Discusses sensory disabilities, including new technology, and the need for working with family. *$42.00*

494 pages   softcover
ISBN 1-557662-46-0

3828 Educational Care

Educators Publishing Service
31 Smith Place
Cambridge, MA 02138   617-547-6706
                               800-225-5750
                          FAX 617-547-0412
                    http://www.epsbooks.com
                    e-mail: eps@epsbooks.com

Written for both parents and teachers, this is based on the view that education should be a system of care that looks after the specific needs of individual students. Using case studies, it identifies and illustrates twenty-six common behaviors or phenomena that often inhibit or interfere with school performance. These are arranged according to six different themes and include behaviors related to poorly regulated attention, reduced remembering. *$28.00*

340 pages
ISBN 0-838814-87-7

3829 Educator's Guide to Students with Epilepsy

Charles C Thomas Publisher
2600 S 1st Street
Springfield, IL 62704   217-789-8980
                               800-258-8980
                          FAX 217-789-9130
                    http://www.ccthomas.com
                    e-mail: books@ccthomas.com
Robert J Michael, Author

The purposes of the book are to: present relevant knowledge about epilepsy for the educator; create an awareness of and sensitivity to students with epilepsy; focus on the role of education with students with epilepsy; present the major educational issues associated with epilepsy; define the educator's responsibility to students with epilepsy; and present useful resources. *$44.95*

174 pages   Cloth
ISBN 0-398065-37-3

3830 Ending Discrimination in Special Education

Charles C Thomas Publisher
2600 S 1st Street
Springfield, IL 62704   217-789-8980
                               800-258-8980
                          FAX 217-789-9130
                    http://www.ccthomas.com
                    e-mail: books@ccthomas.com
Herbert Grossman, Author

For special educators, school administrators, pychologists and regular education teachers who need to acquire the competencies necessary to succeed with all disabled, gifted and talented students who will be included in their classrooms. Books sent on approval. Shipping charges: $5.50 US/&6.50 Canada. Prices subject to change without notice. *$18.95*

104 pages   Paper

3831 Enhancing Self-Concepts & Achievement of Mildly Handicapped Students

Charles C Thomas Publisher
2600 S 1st Street
Springfield, IL 62704

217-789-8980
800-258-8980
FAX 217-789-9130
http://www.ccthomas.com
e-mail: books@ccthomas.com

Carroll J Jones, Author

The self-concept theory is reviewed and examined from a chronological and developmental perspective, relating the impact of self concept on academic functioning. Includes approaches and techniques a teacher might choose, including interventions which are metacognitive, behavioral, social, or academic in nature. A valuable review of current best practices for understanding and intervening on behalf of mildly handicapped learners with emotionally fragile self-concepts. *$ 39.95*

294 pages Cloth
ISBN 0-398057-60-5

3832 Exceptional Child: An Introduction to Special Education

University of Sydney/School Educational Psychology
2011 New S Wales
Australia, NY

Susan Ruth Butler, PhD, Author

This comprehensive text, the first in Australia, covers all major special education topics. It features special contributions from professionals working with special disabilities. It has been edited to achieve a balance of substantive text (with medical and educational implications for each special need) as well as practical illustrative components and first-hand commentary from professionals and organizations in the field. *$36.95*

800 pages
ISBN 0-729503-72-0

3833 Exceptional Individuals: An Introduction

Brooks/Cole Publishing Company
511 Forest Lodge Road
Pacific Grove, CA 93950

831-373-0728
FAX 831-375-6414

Gearhart/Mullen/Gearhart, Author
Carolyn Crockett, Marketing Manager
Barbara Smallwood, Marketing Assistant

This book provides a direct, compassionate, and positive introduction to the characteristics and needs of exceptional individuals with disabilities and those who are gifted and talented. It looks at the role technology plays in meeting the needs of exceptional students, as well as the importance of early intervention, the impact of cultural and linguistic background and the role of the family as key factors in educational and social development.

548 pages

3834 Exceptional Teacher's Handbook: First Year Special Education Teacher's Guide for Success

Corwin Press
2455 Teller Road
Thousand Oaks, CA 91320

805-499-9734
800-818-7243
FAX 805-499-5323
http://www.corwinpress.com
e-mail: order@corwinpress.com

Carla F Shelton, Alice B Pollingue, Author
Kimberly Gonzales, Marketing Director
Robb Clouse, Senior Acquisitions Editor

This guide provides teachers with easily referenced tools for any situation and skill level, including skill development categories and icons showing which abilities are needed for each activity. An essential resource for both new and veteran teachers of students with special needs. *$32.95*

208 pages
ISBN 0-761977-40-6

3835 Exceptionality

Lawrence Erlbaum Associates
365 Broadway
Hillsdale, NJ 07642

201-666-4110
800-926-6579
FAX 201-666-2394

Edward J Sabornie, Author
Susan S Osborne, Co-Editor

Dedicated to the publication of original research and research reviews pertaining to individuals of all ages and disabilities as well as those who are gifted and talented. *$40.00*

ISSN 0936-2835

3836 Faculty Guidebook: Working with Students with Learning Disabilities

HEATH Resource Center
2121 K Street NW
Washington, DC 20036

202-973-0904
800-544-3284
FAX 202-973-0908
http://gopher://bobcat-ace.nche.edu
e-mail: heath@ace.nche.edu

Dan Gardner, Information Specialist

A compilation of articles written by various faculty members of New River Community College. Among others, topics addressed include suggestions for teaching general academic subjects, options for instruction in the social sciences, strategies and suggestions for math and data processing teachers and electrical/electronic technologies. *$7.50*

3837 Focus on Exceptional Children

Love Publishing Company
PO Box 22353
Denver, CO 80222

970-221-7333
FAX 970-221-7444
e-mail: lovepublishing@compuserve.com

Journal containing research and theory-based articles on special education topics, with an emphasis on application and intervention of interest to teachers, professors and administrators. *$30.00*

3838 Frames of Reference for the Assessment of Learning Disabilities

Brookes Publishing Company
PO Box 10624
Baltimore, MD   21285   410-337-9580
                                800-638-3775
                          FAX 410-337-8539
                    http://www.pbrookes.com
          e-mail: custserv@brookespublishing.com
G Reid Lyon PhD, Editor

This valuable reference offers an in-depth look at the fundamental concerns facing those who work with children with learning disabilities — assessment and identification.

672 pages   Hardcover
ISBN 1-557661-38-3

3839 General Educators Guide to Special Education

Peytral Publications
PO Box 1162
Minnetonka, MN   55345   952-949-8707
                                877-739-8725
                          FAX 952-906-9777
                      http://www.peytral.com
                    e-mail: help@peytral.com
Jody L Maanun, Author
Peggy Hammeken, Owner/Publisher

This valuable new resource is essential for educators who teach students with special needs or may refer students for special education placement. This new release is appropriate for educators at all levels. Very useful and practical. *$23.95*

192 pages   Educators
ISBN 1-890455-32-6

3840 HELP Activity Guide

Therapro
225 Arlington Street
Framingham, MA   01702   508-872-9494
                                800-257-5376
                          FAX 508-875-2062
                  http://www.theraproducts.com
              e-mail: info@theraproducts.com
Setan Furuns, PhD, Author

Takes you easily beyond assesment to offer the important next step, thousands of practical, task-analyzed curriculum activities and intervention strategies indexed by the 650 HELP skills. With up to ten activities and strategies per skill, this valuable resource includes definitions for each skill, illustrations, cross-references to skills in other developmental areas and a glossary. *$28.00*

190 pages

3841 HELP for Preschoolers Assessment and Curriculum Guide

Therapro
225 Arlington Street
Framingham, MA   01702   508-872-9494
                                800-257-5376
                          FAX 508-875-2062
                  http://www.theraproducts.com
              e-mail: info@theraproducts.com

Assessment procedure and instructional activities in one easy to use reference. Offers 6 sections of key information for each of the 622 skills: Definition, Materials, Assesment Procedures, Adaptions, Instructional Materials, and Instructional Activities.

3842 Handbook for Volunteer Tutors

HEATH Resource Center
1 Dupont Circle NW
Washington, DC   20036   202-939-9320
                                800-544-3284
                          FAX 202-833-4760
          http://gopher://bobcat-ace.nche.edu
                e-mail: askheath@heath.gwu.edu
Dan Gardner, Information Specialist

Filled with tips for both students and tutors, as well as materials to increase awareness and understanding of learning disabilities. *$25.00*

3843 Handwriting: Not Just in the Hands

Therapro
225 Arlington Street
Framingham, MA   01702   508-872-9494
                                800-257-5376
                          FAX 508-875-2062
                  http://www.theraproducts.com
              e-mail: info@theraproducts.com
Eileen Vreeland MS OTR/L, Author
Karen Conrad, President

Save time and provide professional services with this comprehensive resource and presentation manual! Reviews current literature and research providing an excellent knowledge base. Covers pre-writing skills, handwriting skills, handwriting instruction, ergonomics and informal assessment in the classroom, remedial and compensatory exercises. Compatible with any handwriting program, it includes reproducible handouts, ready-to-make overheads, group activities and more. *$ 80.00*

3 ring binder

3844 Helping Learning Disabled Gifted Children Learn Through Compensatory Active Play

Charles C Thomas Publisher
2600 S 1st Street
Springfield, IL   62704   217-789-8980
                                800-258-8980
                          FAX 217-789-9130
                    http://www.ccthomas.com
                e-mail: books@ccthomas.com
James H Humphrey, Author

About three percent of the school population is gifted and 5-8 percent suffer from learning disabilities. These children experience a great deal more trauma than the normal child. This text will help educators deal with learning disabilities more effectively. *$36.95*

164 pages   Cloth
ISBN 0-398056-95-1

3845   Helping Students Succeed in the Regular Classroom

Jossey-Bass
989 Market Street
San Francisco, CA   94104   415-433-1740
                                   FAX 415-433-0499
                                   http://www.josseybass.com
Joseph Zins, Author

The first book in a series from Jossey-Bass on psychoeducational interventions. Shows how to develop programs to help the learning disabled students integrate within the regular classroom situation and avoid costly and often ineffective special education classes. *$26.95*

3846   Hidden Youth: Dropouts from Special Education

Council for Exceptional Children
1110 N Glebe Road
Arlington, VA   22201   703-620-3660
                               888-232-7733
                               FAX 703-264-9494
                               http://www.cec.sped.org/
Donald L MacMillan, Author

Examines the characteristics of students and schools that place students at risk for early school leaving. Discusses the accounting procedures used by different agencies for estimating graduation and dropout rates and cautions educators about using these rates as indicators of educational quality. *$8.90*

37 pages
ISBN 0-865862-11-7

3847   How Difficult Can This Be?

CT Association for Children and Adults with LD
25 Van Zant Street
East Norwalk, CT   06855   203-838-5010
                                  FAX 203-866-6108
                                  http://www.CACLD.org
                                  e-mail: cacld@juno.com
Rick Lavoie, Presenter

FAT City Workshop video and discussion guide. Looks at the world through the eyes of a learning disabled child. Features a unique workshop attended by educators, psychologists, social workers, parents, siblings and a student with LD. They participate in a series of classroom activities which cause Frustration, Anxiety, and Tension-emotions all too familiar to the student with a learning disability. A discussion of topics ranging from school/home communication to social skills follows. *$49.95*

$5.00 shipping

3848   How Does Your Engine Run? A Leaders Guide to the Alert Program for Self Regulation

Therapro
225 Arlington Street
Framingham, MA   01702   508-872-9494
                                800-257-5376
                                FAX 508-875-2062
                                http://www.theraproducts.com
                                e-mail: info@theraproducts.com
Mary Sue Williams,OTR & Sherry Schellenberge,OTR, Author

Introduces the entire Alert Program. Explains how we regulate our arousal states and describes the use of sensorimotor strategies to manage levels of alertness. This program is fun for students and the adults working with them, and translates easily into real life.

3849   How Significant is Significant? A Personal Glimpse of Life with LD

Association on Higher Education and Disability
PO Box 21192
Columbus, OH   43221   614-488-4972
                              FAX 614-488-1174
                              http://www.ahead.org
                              e-mail: ahead@postbox.acs.ohio-state.edu
Carolee Reiling, Author

Provides a perspective not usually found in learning disability research material. *$3.50*

3850   How to Write an IEP

Academic Therapy Publications
20 Commercial Boulevard
Novato, CA   94949   415-883-3314
                            800-422-7249
                            FAX 415-883-3720
                            http://www.atpub.com
                            e-mail: atpub@aol.com
John Arena, Author

What goes into an Individual Education Plan for a special education student? This book gives detailed information.

ISBN 0-878790-72-1

3851   Human Development View of Learning Disabilities: From Theory to Practice

Charles C Thomas Publisher
2600 S 1st Street
Springfield, IL   62704   217-789-8980
                                 800-258-8980
                                 FAX 217-789-9130
                                 http://www.ccthomas.com
                                 e-mail: books@ccthomas.com
Corrine E Kass, Author
Cleborne D Maddux, Author

The ultimate purpose of this book is to present a strategy for designing day-to-day, individualized lessons for learning disabled students from kindergarten through adulthood. The book will have great appeal to teachers, clinicians, researchers, and graduate students who are interested in considering the field from a particular point of view for a holistic approach to the task of identifying and educating persons with learning disabilities. *$50.95*

222 pages   Cloth
ISBN 0-398058-86-5

3852   I'm Somebody Too Teachers' Manual

Verbal Images Press
19 Fox Hill Drive
Fairport, NY   14450   716-377-3807
                                       800-888-4741
                                   FAX 716-377-5401
Sarah Holmes, MA, Author

Designed for grades four and up, this guide provides everything you need to incorporate 'I'm Somebody Too' into the classroom. Includes chapter-by-chapter reading strategies, short answer questions, essay suggestions, and writing activities. *$10.95*

50 pages   Looseleaf
ISBN 1-884281-13-3

3853   IDEA: Resources from Sopris West

Sopris West
4093 Specialty Place
Longmont, CO   80504   303-651-2829
                             FAX 303-776-5934
                     http://www.sopriswest.com
IEP connections, IEP Tracker, Better IEP's, Self Directed IEP's

3854   Implementing Cognitive Strategy Instruction Across the School

Brookline Books
PO Box 1047
Cambridge, MA   02238   617-868-0360
                                  800-666-2665
                              FAX 617-868-1772
Irene Gaskins, Author

Describes a classroom based program planned and executed by teachers to focus and guide students with serious reading problems to be goal oriented, planful, strategic and self-assessing. *$24.95*

3855   Improving Test Performance of Students with Disabilities in the Classroom

Corwin Press
2455 Teller Road
Thousand Oaks, CA   91320   805-499-9734
                                  800-818-7243
                              FAX 805-499-5323
                     http://www.corwinpress.com
                  e-mail: order@corwinpress.com
Judy L Elliott, Martha L Thurlow, Author
Kimberly Gonzales, Marketing Director
Robb Clouse, Senior Acquisitions Editor

Elliott and Thurlow, long-time colleagues at the National Center on Educational Outcomes build on their highly respected work in accountability and assessment of students with disabilities to focus now on improving test performance — with an emphasis throughout on practical application. Common learning disabilities and emotional problems and a classroom-tested, research-based list of classroom interventions. *$39.95*

360 pages
ISBN 0-761975-59-4

3856   Including Students with Severe and Multiple Disabilities in Typical Classrooms

Brookes Publishing Company
PO Box 10624
Baltimore, MD   21285   410-337-9580
                                  800-638-3775
                              FAX 410-337-8539
                     http://www.pbrookes.com
                  e-mail: custerv@pbrookes.com
Mary A Favey, PhD, Author

This straightforward and jargon-free resource gives instructors the guidance needed to educate learners who have one or more sensory impairments in addition to cognitive and physical disabilities. *$32.95*

224 pages   Paperback
ISBN 1-557662-39-8

3857   Inclusion: 450 Strategies for Success

Peytral Publications
PO Box 1162
Minnetonka, MN   55345   952-949-8707
                                  877-739-8725
                              FAX 952-906-9777
                       http://www.peytral.com
                  e-mail: help@peytral.com
Peggy A Hammeken, Author
Peggy Hammeken, Owner/Publisher

Commences with step-by-step guidelines to help develop, expand and improve the existing inclusive education setting. Hundreds of practical teacher tested ideas and accommodations are conveniently listed by topic and numbered for quick, easy reference. *$23.95*

192 pages   Educators
ISBN 1-890455-25-3

3858   Inclusion: An Annotated Bibliography

National Clearinghouse of Rehabilitation Materials
5202 N Richmond Hill Road
Stillwater, OK   74078   405-624-7650
                                  800-223-5219
                              FAX 405-624-0695
                              TDY:405-624-3156
                     http://www.nchrtm.okstate.edu
                  e-mail: brookdj@okstate.edu
Caroline Moore, Susanne Carter, Author

This annotated bibliography is an initial compilation of recently published literature about what the special education community calls inclusion rather than mainstreaming. *$57.30*

563 pages   Item # 262.007A

3859 Inclusion: An Essential Guide for the Paraprofessional

Peytral Publications
PO Box 1162
Minnetonka, MN   55345
952-949-8707
877-739-8725
FAX 952-906-9777
http://www.peytral.com
e-mail: help@peytral.com

Peggy A Hammeken, Author
Peggy Hammeken, Owner/Publisher

This best-selling publication is developed specifically for paraprofessionals and classroom assistants. The book commences with a simplified introduction to inclusive education, handicapping conditions, due process, communication, collaboration, confidentiality and types of adaptations. Used by many schools and universities as a training tool for staff development. *$23.95*

205 pages   Assistants
ISBN 1-890455-34-2

3860 Inclusive Elementary Schools: Recipes for Success

PEAK Parent Center
611 N Weber
Colorado Springs, CO   80903
719-531-9400
800-284-0251
FAX 719-531-9452
TDY:719-531-5403
http://www.peakparent.org
e-mail: info@peakparent.org
Douglas Fisher, Nancy Frey, Caren Sax, Author

State-of-the-art step process to determine what and how to teach elementary students with disabilities in inclusive classrooms. This breakthrough publication highlights strategies for accommodating and modifying assignments and activities by using core curriculum. *$13.00*

3861 Individualizing Instruction for the Educationally Handicapped: Teaching Strategies

Charles C Thomas Publisher
2600 S 1st Street
Springfield, IL   62704
217-789-8980
800-258-8980
FAX 217-789-9130
http://www.ccthomas.com
e-mail: books@ccthomas.com

Jack Campbell, Author

Covers children that qualify for special education as well as those that are just on the cusp and do not. The author advocates that by clinically analyzing the child's learning ecology and modifying the instructional plan based on student performance, the teacher is able to design instruction appropriate for the unique needs of each child.

186 pages   Cloth
ISBN 0-398069-01-8

3862 Instructional Methods for Students

Allyn & Bacon
160 Gould Street
Needham Heights, MA   02494
781-455-1250
800-852-8024
FAX 781-455-1220

Patrick Joseph Schloss, Author

Instructional methods for students with learning and behavior problems.

3863 Intervention in School and Clinic

Pro-Ed
8700 Shoal Creek Boulevard
Austin, TX   78757
512-451-3246
800-897-3202
FAX 512-451-8542
http://www.proedinc.com

Features articles and instructional ideas to help teachers and therapists work with students with learning and behavior problems. *$20.00*

3864 KDES Health Curriculum Guide

Harris Communications
15155 Technology Drive
Eden Prairie, MN   55344
952-906-1180
800-825-6758
FAX 952-906-1099
TDY:952-906-1198
http://www.harriscomm.com
e-mail: mail@harriscomm.com

Sara Gillespie, Author
Doris Schwarz, Author
Bill Williams, National Sales Manager

Provides students with the information they need to make wise choices for healthy living. Divided into age-appropriate sections, there are four main areas covered: Health and Fitness, Safety and First Aid, Drugs, and Family Life.

125 pages

3865 Kids Who Hate School: A Survival Handbook on Learning Disabilities

Fawcett Book Group
201 E 50th Street
New York, NY   10022
212-751-2600
FAX 212-572-8700

Lawrence Greene, Author

Case studies, anecdotal material and educational data are used to tell parents of children with learning disabilities how to recognize the symptoms of a learning problem and what steps to take to see that their children receive the remediation needed. *$12.00*

255 pages

3866 LD Teacher's IDEA Companion (2BK Set)

LinguiSystems
3100 4th Avenue
East Moline, IL   61244
800-776-4332
FAX 800-577-4555
http://www.linguisystems.com
e-mail: service@linguisystems.com

Linda Bowers, Owner
Rosemary Huisingh, Owner

Help your special education students succeed in the regular classroom! Each book gives you page after page of goals and strategies to comply with current IDEA regulations. You'll get content standards, goals, benchmarks, and instructional modifications for several academic areas. You'll also get information on life skills and transition beyond high school.

Ages 5-18

3867 LD Teacher's IEP Companion

LinguiSystems
3100 4th Avenue
East Moline, IL   61244

800-776-4332
FAX 309-755-2377
TDY:800-933-8331
http://www.linguisystems.com
e-mail: service@linguisystems.com

Molly Lyle, Author
Linda Bowers, Owner
Rosemary Huisingh, Owner

These IEP goals are organized developmentally by skill area with individual objectives and classroom activity suggestions. Goals and objectives cover these academic areas: math; reading; writing; literacy concepts; attention skills; study skills; classroom behavior; social interaction; and transition skills. *$39.95*

169 pages   Ages 5-18

3868 Learning Disabilities Materials Guide: Secondary Level

Learning Disabilities Association of America
4156 Library Road
Pittsburgh, PA   15234

412-341-1515
FAX 412-344-0224
http://www.ldanatl.org
e-mail: ldanatl@usaor.net

$3.00

3869 Learning Disabilities in High School

Learning Disabilities Association of America
4156 Library Road
Pittsburgh, PA   15234

412-341-1515
FAX 412-344-0224
http://www.ldanatl.org
e-mail: ldanatl@usaor.net

$3.00

3870 Learning Disabilities: Information and Resources

Landmark Foundation
PO Box 227
Prides Crossing, MA   01965

978-236-3216
FAX 978-927-7268
http://www.landmarkschool.org
e-mail: outreach@landmarkschool.com

Joan Steinberg, Editor

A compilation of 28 of the best articles available on learning disabilities and a collection of resources for parents and educators, including an annotated bibliography, sources for video and audio material, government resources, and parent/professional organizations. *$25.00*

150 pages
ISBN 0-962411-94-9

3871 Learning Disabilities: The Interaction of Learner, Task and Setting

Learning Disabilities Association of America
4156 Library Road
Pittsburgh, PA   15234

412-341-1515
FAX 412-344-0224
http://www.ldanatl.org
e-mail: ldanatl@usaor.net

CR Smith, Author

$62.00

3872 Learning Disabilities: Theoretical and Research Issues

Lawrence Erlbaum Associates
365 Broadway
Hillsdale, NJ   07642

201-666-4110
800-926-6579
FAX 201-666-2394

H Lee Swanson, Author
Barbara Keogh, Author

This volume has been developed as a direct result of a conference sponsored by the International Academy for Research in Learning Disabilities, held at the University of California at Los Angeles. The test provides a review and critique achievement, and subtyping as they relate to learning disabilities. *$79.95*

384 pages
ISBN 0-805803-92-0

3873 Learning Disability: Social Class and the Construction of Inequality in American Education

Bergin & Gravey Greenwood
88 Post Road W
Westport, CT   06881

203-226-3571
800-225-5800
FAX 203-222-1502
http://www.greenwood.com
e-mail: dgoss@curry.edu

Diane Goss, Author

In straightforward, empathic tones, authors sensitively offer support to parents of children with LD/ADD. *$22.50*

248 pages
ISBN 0-964975-20-3

3874 Learning Problems & Learning Disabilities: Moving Forward

Brooks/Cole Publishing Company
511 Forest Lodge Road
Pacific Grove, CA   93950

831-373-0728
FAX 831-375-6414

Adelman/Taylor, Author
Carolyn Crockett, Marketing Manager
Barbara Smallwood, Marketing Assistant

Current trends and new ideas for improving practice and research are covered in this exploration of learning problems and learning disabilities. This book's broad scope and futuristic outlook emphasizes current and evolving assessment and intervention approaches, discussing motivational as well as developmental differences, deficiencies, and dysfunctions. In addition to key references, twenty specialized readings stimulate thought of critical issues and re-emphasize the need to move forward.

480 pages
ISBN 0-534187-56-0

3875 Mainstreaming Exceptional Students: A Guide for Classroom Teachers

Allyn & Bacon
160 Gould Street
Needham Heights, MA   02494   781-455-1250
                                     800-852-8024
                              FAX 781-455-1220
Schultz & Carpenter, Author

Provides a clear overview of mainstreaming and public law.

3876 Making School Inclusion Work

Brookline Books
PO Box 1047
Cambridge, MA   02238   617-868-0360
                               800-666-2665
                          FAX 617-868-1772

The authors explain true inclusion at the preschool/elementary level. *$24.95*

264 pages

3877 Meeting the Needs of Special Students: Legal, Ethical, and Practical Ramifications

Corwin Press
2455 Teller Road
Thousand Oaks, CA   91320   805-499-9734
                                   800-818-7243
                              FAX 805-499-5323
                    http://www.corwinpress.com
                    e-mail: order@corwinpress.com
Lawrence J Johnson & Anne M Bauer, Author
Kimberly Gonzales, Marketing Director
Robb Clouse, Senior Acquisitions Editor

The author gives administrators the information they need about the rights of students, federal guidelines and case law and precedents. *$17.00*

96 pages
ISBN 0-803960-21-2

3878 Mentoring Students at Risk: An Underutilized Alternative Education Strategy...

Charles C Thomas Publisher
2600 S 1st Street
Springfield, IL   62704   217-789-8980
                                 800-258-8980
                            FAX 217-789-9130
                    http://www.ccthomas.com
                    e-mail: books@ccthomas.com
Gary Reglin, Author

For K-12 teachers. Books sent on approval. Shipping charges: $5.50 US, $6.50 Canada. Prices subject to change without notice. *$17.95*

110 pages   Paper

3879 Myofascial Release and Its Application to Neuro-Developmental Treatment

Therapro
225 Arlington Street
Framingham, MA   01702   508-872-9494
                                800-257-5376
                           FAX 508-875-2062
                    http://www.theraproducts.com
                    e-mail: info@theraproducts.com
Regi Boehme, OTR, Author

This fully illustrated resource provides the therapist with techniques to approach myofascial restrictions which are secondary to tonal dysfunction in children and adults with neurological deficits. The Neuro-Developmental Treatment approach is included in the illustrated treatment rationale.

3880 Narrative Prosthesis: Disability and the Dependencies of Discourse

University of Michigan Press
839 Greene Street
Ann Arbor, MI   48104   734-763-0163
                          FAX 734-763-0456
                    http://www.press.umich.edu
                    e-mail: pgarner@umich.edu
David T Mitchell, Author
Mary Erwin, Assistant Director

This book develops a narrative theory of the pervasive use of disability as a device of characterization in literature and film. It argues that, while other marginalized identities have suffered cultural exclusion due to dearth of images reflecting their experience, the marginality of disabled people has occurred in the midst of the perpetual circulation of images of disability in print and visual media. *$49.50*

264 pages   cloth
ISBN 0-472097-48-2

3881 Otitis Media: Coping with the Effects in the Classroom

Harris Communications
15155 Technology Drive
Eden Prairie, MN   55344   952-906-1180
                                  800-825-6758
                             FAX 952-906-1099
                             TDY:952-906-1198
                    http://www.harriscomm.com
Dorinne S Davis, MA, CCC-A, Author

Designed to alert teachers and specialists to the potential for communication difficulties associated with children who are prone to recurrent middle ear infections. Ideas are provided to be used to assist children toward appropriate language skill development. *$28.95*

137 pages   Paperback

3882 Points of Contact: Disability, Art, and Culture

University of Michigan Press
839 Greene Street
Ann Arbor, MI 48104   734-763-0163
                             FAX 734-763-0456
                             http://www.press.umich.edu
                             e-mail: pgarner@umich.edu
Susan Crutchfield and Marcy Epstein, Author
Mary Erwin, Assistant Director

This book brings together contributions by leading writers, artists, scholars, and critics to provide a remarkably broad and consistently engaging look at the intersection of disability and the arts. *$47.50*

36 pages   cloth
ISBN 0-472097-11-3

3883 Prescriptions for Children with Learning and Adjustment Problems: A Consultant's Desk Reference

Charles C Thomas Publisher
2600 S 1st Street
Springfield, IL 62704   217-789-8980
                               800-258-8980
                         FAX 217-789-9130
                         http://www.ccthomas.com
                         e-mail: books@ccthomas.com
Ralph F Blanco, David F Bogacki, Author

Third edition. Books sent on approval. Shipping charges: $5.50 US, $6.50 Canada. Prices subject to change without notice. *$37.95*

264 pages   Cloth

3884 Preventing Academic Failure

Educators Publishing Service
31 Smith Place
Cambridge, MA 02138
                             800-225-5750
                         FAX 617-547-0412
Phyllis Bertin, Eileen Perlman, Author

This multisensory curriculum meets the needs of children with learning disabilities in regular classrooms by providing a four-year sequence of written language skills (reading, writing and spelling). PAF has a handwriting and numerical program. *$42.00*

ISBN 0-838852-71-8

3885 Project Success: Meeting the Diverse Needs of Learning Disabled Adults

Richland College of the Dallas Community College
12800 Abrams Road
Dallas, TX 75243   972-238-6106
                         FAX 972-238-3799
                         http://www.rlc.dcocd.edu

3886 Project Upgrade: Working with Adults Who Have Learning Disabilities

Manhattan Adult Learning and Resource Center
2031 Casement Road
Manhattan, KS 66502   785-589-2820

3887 Promoting Postsecondary Education for Students with Learning Disabilities

Pro-Ed
8700 Shoal Creek Boulevard
Austin, TX 78757   512-451-3246
                           800-897-3202
                     FAX 800-397-7633
                     http://www.proedinc.com
Loring C Brinckerhoff, Author
Stan F Shaw, Author
Joan McGuire, Author

This handbook is made up of comprehensive and practical chapters designed for the service provider. Contains an extensive reference section as well as 18 useful appendices. *$45.00*

440 pages
ISBN 0-890795-89-4

3888 Reach Them All: Adapting Curriculum & Instruction with Technology in Inclusive Classrooms

Indiana Institute on Disability and Community
2853 E 10th Street
Bloomington, IN 47408   812-855-6508
                           FAX 812-855-9630
                           TDY:812-855-9396

Manual designed as a resource tool to help teachers use technology appropriately to meet individual student learning needs. Contents include technology information and tips, learning styles and adaptations, a 12-step process for making adaptations, 10 types of adaptations, strategies for technology use with simple adaptations and reproducible lesson and recording forms. *$12.00*

3889 Rehabilitation of Clients with Specific Learning Disabilities

National Clearinghouse of Rehabilitation Materials
5202 N Richmond Hill Road
Stillwater, OK 74078   405-624-7650
                               800-223-5219
                         FAX 405-624-0695
                         TDY:405-624-3156
                    http://www.nchrtm.okstate.edu
                    e-mail: brookdj@okstate.edu
A Kansas RRTC, Author

Functional definitions on SLD that made adults eligible for vocational rehabilitation services are given. Three types of populations are examined and the implications for vocational rehabilitation are considered. Administrative issues are addressed to encourage rehabilitation professionals to think ahead and to develop policies for SLD. *$11.00*

100 pages   Item # 353.019

3890 Resourcing: Handbook for Special Education Resource Teachers

Council for Exceptional Children
1110 N Glebe Road
Arlington, VA 22201   703-620-3660
                              888-232-7733
                         FAX 703-264-9494
                         http://www.cec.sped.org/
Mary Yeomans Jackson, Author

Everything you need to know about how to be a resource for other teachers and support personnel who work with special education students. This book will teach how to be a resource to yourself, how to be a resource to others and how to access resources: people; telephone; parents; instructional materials; and national resources. *$11.40*

64 pages
ISBN 0-865862-19-2

3891 School Age Children with Special Needs

Special Needs Project
324 State Street
Santa Barbara, CA 93105 805-962-8087
800-333-6867
FAX 805-962-5087
e-mail: books@specialneeds.com
Dale Borman Fink, Author

The most comprehensive survey to date of child care practice for school aged children with a wide range of disabilities. *$12.95*

148 pages

3892 School-Home Notes: Promoting Children's Classroom Success

Guilford Publications
72 Spring Street
New York, NY 10012 212-431-9800
800-365-7006
FAX 212-966-6708
http://www.guilford.com
e-mail: info@guilford.com
Mary Lou Kelley, Author

A comprehensive guide to establish and maintain a regular school-home contact. *$20.95*

198 pages Paperback

3893 Scissors, Glue, and Concepts, Too!

LinguiSystems
3100 4th Avenue
East Moline, IL 61244
800-776-4332
FAX 800-577-4555
http://www.linguisystems.com
e-mail: service@linguisystems.com
Linda Bowers, Owner
Rosemary Huisingh, Owner

Your young students will learn to follow directions and understand basic concepts in context. Concepts for each activity are grouped as they naturally occur in our language. Teach over 50 concepts including right/left, above/below, empty/full, and more.

Ages 5-8

3894 Segregated and Second-Rate: Special Education in New York

Advocates for Children of New York
151 W 30th Street
New York, NY 10001 212-947-3089
FAX 212-947-9790
http://www.advocatesforchildren.org
e-mail: info@advocatesforchildren.org
Diane MTK Autin Esq., Author

Highlights the fact that New York rates last among all states in inclusive education. *$15.00*

3895 Self-Advocacy Strategy for Education and Transition Planning

Edge Enterprises
PO Box 1304
Lawrence, KS 66044 785-749-1473
FAX 785-749-0207
e-mail: edge@midusa.net
A Van Reusen, C Bos, J Schumaker, D Deshler, Author
Jacqueline Schafer, Managing Editor

This research-based instructor's manual features step-by-step instructions on how to teach students to advocate for themselves within the context of meetings with adults. Covered are the instruction of basic social skills, creating a personal inventory of strengths and weaknesses, creating a list of goals and using a strategy to communicate at the meeting. Individual Education Planning Conferences, Transition Planning conferences as well as other types of meetings are covered. *$15.00*

204 pages Paperback

3896 Sensory Integration: Theory and Practice

Therapro
225 Arlington Street
Framingham, MA 01702 508-872-9494
800-257-5376
FAX 508-875-2062
http://www.theraproducts.com
e-mail: info@theraproducts.com
Anne Fisher, Ann Bundy, Elizabeth Murray, Author
Karen Conrad, President

The very latest in sensory integration theory and practice. *$45.00*

418 pages

3897 Social and Emotional Development of Exceptional Students

Charles C Thomas Publisher
2600 S 1st Street
Springfield, IL 62704 217-789-8980
800-258-8980
FAX 217-789-9130
http://www.ccthomas.com
e-mail: books@ccthomas.com
Carroll J Jones, Author

Provides teachers with understandable information regarding the social and emotional development of exceptional students. *$41.95*

218 pages Cloth
ISBN 0-398057-81-8

3898 Source for Down Syndrome

LinguiSystems
3100 4th Avenue
East Moline, IL 61244
800-776-4332
FAX 800-577-4555
http://www.linguisystems.com
e-mail: service@linguisystems.com
Linda Bowers, Owner
Rosemary Huisingh, Owner

Get in-depth information on working with students with Down sydrome. Packed with helpful tips and therapy techniques, chapters cover characteristics of Down syndrome, feeding and oral motor skills, language development and intervention, augmentative communication, motor and sensorimotor skills, and much more.

3899 Source for Learning Disabilities

LinguiSystems
3100 4th Avenue
East Moline, IL   61244

800-776-4332
FAX 800-577-4555
http://www.linguisystems.com
e-mail: service@linguisystems.com
Linda Bowers, Owner
Rosemary Huisingh, Owner

This is the definitive source for information on learning disabilities. Get new information about federal mandates, teaming, transitioning, and involving parents. You'll also have a thorough discussion of the social and emotional aspects of LD and a glossary of terms.

3900 Source for Nonverbal Learning Disorders

LinguiSystems
3100 4th Avenue
East Moline, IL   61244

800-776-4332
FAX 800-577-4555
TDY:800-933-8331
http://www.linguisystems.com
e-mail: service@linguisystems.com
Sue Thompson, Author
Linda Bowers, Owner
Rosemary Huisingh, Owner

Not sure if you have a student with nonverbal learning disorder? See if this description sounds familiar: ignores nonverbal cues such as facial expressions; is clumsy for no apparent reason; makes inappropriate social remarks; and has difficulty with visual-spatial-organizational tasks. This resource provides you with useful checklists, anecdotes, and methods for dealing with this little understood disorder through the lifespan. *$41.95*

Birth-Adult

3901 Source for Treatment Methodologies in Autism

LinguiSystems
3100 4th Avenue
East Moline, IL   61244

800-776-4332
FAX 800-577-4555
http://www.linguisystems.com
e-mail: service@linguisystems.com
Linda Bowers, Owner
Rosemary Huisingh, Owner

Get basic, factual information on the leading treatment methodologies for autism in one handy resource. You'll get clear, helpful information to share with parents and other professionals faced with treatment decisions.

Ages Birth-18

3902 Special Education Technology: Classroom Applications

Brooks/Cole Publishing Company
511 Forest Lodge Road
Pacific Grove, CA   93950
831-373-0728
FAX 831-375-6414
Carolyn Crockett, Marketing Manager
Barbara Smallwood, Marketing Assistant

This exciting text helps pre- and in-service teachers understand how they can use technology to benefit individuals with disabilities in the classroom. Addressing the needs of a variety of populations, Lewis focuses on methods for adapting computers, as well as technologies such as environmental control devices; augmentative communication devices, mobility devices, systems that translate print for the blind and assistive listening devices.

552 pages
ISBN 0-534202-86-1

3903 Special Educators Guide to Regular Education

CT Association for Children and Adults with LD
25 Van Zant Street
East Norwalk, CT   06855
203-838-5010
FAX 203-866-6108
http://www.CACLD.org
L Lieberman, Author

Offers information on special education for learning disabled students. *$10.50*

3904 Strategy Assessment and Instruction for Students with Learning Disabilities

Pro-Ed
8700 Shoal Creek Boulevard
Austin, TX   78757
512-451-3246
800-897-3202
FAX 512-451-8542
http://www.proedinc.com
Lynn Meltzer, Author

The unifying theme of this volume is the view that strategic learning is a critical component of academic success and that inefficient strategy use characterizes many learning disabled students and prevents them from functioning at the level of their potential. *$41.00*

424 pages
ISBN 0-890795-40-1

3905 Subtypes of Learning Disabilities

Lawrence Erlbaum Associates
365 Broadway
Hillsdale, NJ   07642
201-666-4110
800-926-6579
FAX 201-666-2394
Lynne V Feagans, Author
Elizabeth Short, Author
Lynn Meltzer, Author

Although experts agree that various types of learning disabilities do exist, few attempts have been made to classify learning disabled children into subtypes. The editors of this collection feel that the lack of subcategorization has frustrated previous research efforts to obtain a generalizable body of knowledge in the field. *$59.95*

288 pages
ISBN 0-805806-02-4

3906 Survival Guide with Kids with LD

Free Spirit Publishing
217 5th Avenue N
Minneapolis, MN   55401   612-338-2068
                                 FAX 612-337-5050
                          http://www.freespirit.com
                       e-mail: help4kids@freespirit.com
Gary Fisher & Rhoda Cummings, Author

Vital information, practical advice, step-by-step strategies, and encouragement for children labeled learning disabled. *$9.95*

   104 pages
   ISBN 0-915793-18-0

3907 Take Part Art

CT Association for Children and Adults with LD
25 Van Zant Street
East Norwalk, CT   06855   203-838-5010
                                  FAX 203-866-6108
                             http://www.CACLD.org
                           e-mail: cacld@juno.com
Bob Gregson, Author
Marie Armstrong, Information Specialist

Offers information on art therapies and their inclusion
in learning disabled environments. *$19.50*

   $2.50 shipping

3908 Teachers Ask About Sensory Integration

Therapro
225 Arlington Street
Framingham, MA   01702   508-872-9494
                                800-257-5376
                                FAX 508-875-2062
                         http://www.theraproducts.com
                       e-mail: info@theraproducts.com
Carol Kranowitz, Stacey Szkult And David Silver,
Author

A narration and discussion for teachers and school
professionals about how to teach children with sensory integration problems. 60 page book included,
filled with checklists, idea sheets, sensory profiles
and resorces. 86 minute audio tape.

   Audio Tape

3909 Teaching Kids with LD in the Regular Classroom

Free Spirit Publishing
217 5th Avenue N
Minneapolis, MN   55401   612-338-2068
                                 800-735-7323
                                 FAX 612-337-5050
                          http://www.freespirit.com
                       e-mail: help4kids@freespirit.com
Susan Winebrenner, Author
Betsy Gabler, Sales Manager

Proven, classroom-tested, curriculum specific ways
to help teachers help special ed, slow and remedial students in their mixed ability classroom. *$27.95*

   248 pages
   ISBN 1-575420-04-X

3910 Teaching Learners with Mild Disabilities

Brooks/Cole Publishing Company
511 Forest Lodge Road
Pacific Grove, CA   93950   831-373-0728
                                   FAX 831-375-6414
Meese/Overton/Whitfield, Author
Meese Overton-Whitfield, Authors
Carolyn Crockett, Marketing Manager
Barbara Smallwood, Marketing Assistant

This very applied text introduces preservice teachers
to best practices for teaching learners with mild disabilities. The authors illustrate interactions among
regular teachers, special education teachers and students with mild disabilities through the use of eight
hypothetical case studies of students and teachers.

   496 pages
   ISBN 0-534211-01-0

3911 Teaching Students Ways to Remember

Brookline Books
PO Box 1047
Cambridge, MA   02238   617-868-0360
                               800-666-2665
                               FAX 617-868-1772
Dr. Margo Mastropieri, Author
Thomas Scruggs, Author

This book was written in response to the enormous interest in mnemonic instruction by teachers and administrators, telling them how it can be used with their
students. *$21.95*

3912 Teaching Visually Impaired Children

Charles C Thomas Publisher
2600 S 1st Street
Springfield, IL   62704   217-789-8980
                                 800-258-8980
                                 FAX 217-789-9130
                          http://www.ccthomas.com
                       e-mail: books@ccthomas.com
Virginia E. Bishop, Author

This book provides a comprehensive resource for the
classroom teacher who is working with a visually impaired child for the first time, as well as a systematic
overview of education for the specialist in visual disabilities. It approaches instructional challenges with
clear explanations and practical suggestions, and it
addresses common concerns of teachers in a reassuring and positive manner. The book is organized into
three sections: Vision, Learning, and Testing & Transitions. *$51.95*

   274 pages   Cloth
   ISBN 0-398065-95-0

**3913 Teaching the Learning Disabled Adolescent:
Strategies and Methods**

Learning Disabilities Association of America
4156 Library Road
Pittsburgh, PA   15234   412-341-1515
                                FAX 412-344-0224
                         http://www.ldanatl.org
                       e-mail: ldanatl@usaor.net
This book gives expert strategies and methods for
teaching learning disabled adolescents. *$58.00*

3914 Technology in the Classroom: Communication Module

American Speech-Language-Hearing Association
10801 Rockville Pike
Bethesda, MD   20814   301-897-5700
                              888-498-6699
                         FAX 301-897-7358
                      http://www.Asha.org
Laurie Ward, Marketing Coordinator

Provides a brief background of assistive technology and a detailed discussion on augmentative communication. Contains technology and strategies aimed at giving children who have disabilities, another way to communicate when speaking is difficult or impossible. *$40.00*

3915 Technology in the Classroom: Education Module

American Speech-Language-Hearing Association
10801 Rockville Pike
Bethesda, MD   20814   301-897-5700
                              888-498-6699
                         FAX 301-897-7358
                      http://www.Asha.org
Laurie Ward, Marketing Coordinator

Offers in-depth discussion as to how assistive technology can be used in educational settings. The technology is geared for children who have severe disabilities and provides a discussion of how to assess a child's needs for assistive technology in order to perform both pre-academic and academic tasks. *$40.00*

3916 Technology in the Classroom: Positioning, Access and Mobility Module

American Speech-Language-Hearing Association
10801 Rockville Pike
Bethesda, MD   20814   301-897-5700
                              888-498-6699
                         FAX 301-897-7358
                      http://www.asha.org
Laurie Ward, Marketing Coordinator

This manual emphasizes the importance of proper positioning that comfortably enables a child to perform activities of everyday life, and the technology which is available to help children move about when they are physically unable to do so. *$35.00*

3917 Test Accommodations for Students with Disabilities

Charles C Thomas Publisher
2600 S 1st Street
Springfield, IL   62704   217-789-8980
                                 800-258-8980
                            FAX 217-789-9130
                     http://www.ccthomas.com
                 e-mail: books@ccthomas.com
Edward Burns, Author

The purpose here is to consider legal questions, theoretical issues, and practical methods for meeting the assessment needs of students with disabilities. The ultimate goal of this book is to consider a variety of concerns and to provide several ideas for conceptualizing and implementing valid test accommodations. *$66.95*

340 pages   Cloth
ISBN 0-398068-44-5

3918 The Relationship of Learning Problems and Classroom Performance to Sensory Integration

Therapro
225 Arlington Street
Framingham, MA   01702   508-872-9494
                                800-257-5376
                           FAX 508-875-2062
                http://www.theraproducts.com
                e-mail: info@theraproducts.com
Norma Quirk, MS, OTR and Marie DiMatties, MS, OTR, Author

This is an invaluable resource written for therapists and teachers to explain how sensory integration deficits impact classroom performance.

3919 To Be Gifted and Learning Disabled: From Definitions to Practical Intervention Strategies

Creative Learning Press
PO Box 320
Mansfield Center, CT   06250   860-429-8118
                                      888-518-8004
                                 FAX 860-429-7783
              http://www.creativelearningpress.com
                             e-mail: clp@neca.com
Susan M Baum, Steven V Owen, John Dixon, Author
Kristina Morgan, Executive Director

The gifted and learning disabled child exhibits remarkable talents in some areas and disabling weakness in others. Covers everything a classroom or enrichment teacher must know in order to address the needs of gifted learning disabled youngsters, including identification, learning styles, and more. *$16.95*

149 pages
ISBN 0-936386-59-2

3920 To Teach a Dyslexic

AVKO Educational Research Foundation
3084 W Willard Road
Clio, MI   48420   810-686-9283
                     FAX 810-686-1101
           http://www.avko.org/upto.htm
           e-mail: avkoemail@aol.com
Don McCabe, Author
Don McCabe, Research Director

Just as it takes a thief to catch a thief, this is an autobiography of a dyslexic who discovered how to teach dyslexics. Common sense, logical approach, valuable to all who teach in our nation's classrooms. *$14.95*

ISBN 1-564000-04-4

3921 Tools for Transition

AGS
4201 Woodland Road
Circle Pines, MN   55014

763-786-4343
800-328-2560
FAX 763-786-9077
http://www.agsnet.com
e-mail: agsmail@agsnet.com

The materials in this kit offer a curriculum that is not always included in learning disabled programs. Comes with a teacher's manual, complete with instructions for each unit and a Student Workbook filled with skill-building activities. The accompanying video presents a variety of sciences to demonstrate plus an interview with college students who have learning disabilities.

3922 Understanding & Management of Health Problems in Schools

Temeron Books
Bellingham, WA   98227

FAX 360-738-4016
http://www.temerondetselig.com
e-mail: temeron@telusplanet.net

H Moghadam, Author

A guide for teachers of students with problems which are an obstacle to learning, this book offers information and suggestions teachers can use to help students learn. *$13.95*

152 pages   Paperback
ISBN 1-550591-21-5

3923 Understanding and Managing Vision Deficits

Therapro
225 Arlington Street
Framingham, MA   01702

508-872-9494
800-257-5376
FAX 508-875-2062
http://www.theraproducts.com
e-mail: info@theraproducts.com

Mitchell Scheiman, OD, Author

This book is a unique and comprehensive collaboration from OT's and optometrists developed to increase the understanding of vision. Learn to screen for common visual deficits and effectively manage patients with vision disorders. Provides recommendations for direct intervention techniques for a variety of vision problems and supportive and compensatory stratagies for visual field deficits and visual neglect.

3924 Vision and Learning Disabilities

Learning Disabilities Association of America
4156 Library Road
Pittsburgh, PA   15234

412-341-1515
FAX 412-344-0224
http://www.ldanatl.org
e-mail: ldanatl@usaor.net

$1.25

3925 Working Memory and Severe Learning Difficulties

Lawrence Erlbaum Associates
365 Broadway
Hillsdale, NJ   07642

201-666-4110
800-926-6579
FAX 201-666-2394

Charles Hulme, Author
Susie Mackenzie, Author

This monograph considers the development of working memory skills in children with severe learning difficulties. These children have marked difficulties with a wide range of cognitive tasks. The studies reported show that they also experience profound difficulties on verbal working memory tasks. *$29.95*

160 pages
ISBN 0-863770-75-4

3926 Working with Visually Impaired Young Students: A Curriculum Guide for 3 to 5 Year-Olds

Charles C Thomas Publisher
2600 S 1st Street
Springfield, IL   62704

217-789-8980
800-258-8980
FAX 217-789-9130
http://www.ccthomas.com
e-mail: books@ccthomas.com

Ellen Trief, Author

The purpose of this guide is to offer a curriculum model to preschool programs that provides services to visually impaired 3 to 5 year olds with emphasis on the need for psychological evaluations to establish the preschooler's cognitive and intellectual level of functioning, basic pre-braille concepts, orientation and mobility, activities that help facilitate speech and language learning, art therapy methods, and the application of music therapy to improve motor, language, and social skills.

218 pages   Paperback
ISBN 0-398068-75-5

Language Arts

3927 Clinical Interview: A Guide for Speech-Language Pathologists/Audiologists

American Speech-Language-Hearing Association
10801 Rockville Pike
Bethesda, MD   20814

301-897-5700
888-498-6699
FAX 301-897-7358
http://www.Asha.org

Laurie Ward, Marketing Coordinator

Integrates the components of the clinical interview within the context of the speech-language pathology and audiology helping process. *$9.00*

3928 **Closer Look: The English Program at the Model Secondary School for the Deaf**

Harris Communications
15155 Technology Drive
Eden Prairie, MN   55344   952-906-1180
                                 800-825-6758
                          FAX 952-906-1099
                          TDY:952-906-1198
                   http://www.harriscomm.com
                   e-mail: mail@harriscomm.com
MSSD English Teachers, Author

Features research-supported principles for incorporating the whole language philosophy into classroom routines, highlighting student-centered activities. Strategies are outlined for determining student levels based largely on the degree of teacher guidance needed. Reading and writing objectives are provided for grades 8-12. *$9.95*

67 pages

3929 **Communication Skills for Visually Impaired Learners**

Charles C Thomas Publisher
2600 S 1st Street
Springfield, IL   62704   217-789-8980
                                 800-258-8980
                          FAX 217-789-9130
                   http://www.ccthomas.com
                   e-mail: books@ccthomas.com
Randall Harley, Mila B. Truan & LaRhea D. San-ford, Author

Designed to provide a better understanding of teaching reading, writing, and listening skills to students with visual impairments. Intended for use by teachers who have a basic knowledge of the communication skills needed to teach students with normal vision and who have proficiencies in reading and writing the braille code, using large print, optical aids, and current technology such as microcomputers, access equipment, and closed caption TV. *$69.95*

322 pages   Cloth
ISBN 0-398066-92-2

3930 **First Start in Sign Language**

Harris Communications
15155 Technology Drive
Eden Prairie, MN   55344   952-906-1180
                                 800-825-6758
                          FAX 952-906-1099
                          TDY:952-906-1198
                   http://www.harriscomm.com
                   e-mail: mail@harriscomm.com
Amy J Strommer, Author

Fun pictures, stories, and activities are included in this book. Students first learn to sign words for people, animals, objects and actions. Then they learn to produce simple ententes and to sign stories. Reproducible activity pages included. *$32.00*

190 pages   Paperback

3931 **From Talking to Writing: Strategies for Scaffolding Expository Expression**

Landmark School
429 Hale Street
Prides Crossing, MA   01965   978-236-3216
                              FAX 978-927-7268
                   http://www.landmarkschool.org
                   e-mail: outreach@landmarkschool.org
Terrill Jennings and Charles Haynes, Author
Dan Ahearn, Program Director
Trish Newhall, Associate Director
Kathryn Frye, Administrative Assistant

Designed for teachers who work with students who have difficulty with writing and/or expressive language skills, this book provides practical strategies for teaching expository expression at the word, sentence, paragraph, and short essay levels. *$40.00*

191 pages
ISBN 0-962411-98-1

3932 **Helping Young Writers Master the Craft**

Brookline Books
PO Box 1047
Cambridge, MA   02238   617-868-0360
                               800-666-2665
                        FAX 617-868-1772
Karen R Harris, Author

This text for teachers will help the beginning writer, the unmotivated student and the learning disabled student to learn writing. *$24.95*

3933 **Landmark Method for Teaching Writing**

Landmark School
429 Hale Street
Prides Crossing, MA   01965   978-236-3216
                              FAX 978-927-7268
                   http://www.landmarkschool.org
                   e-mail: outreach@landmarkschool.org
Jean Gudaitis Tarricone, Author
Dan Ahearn, Program Director
Trish Newhall, Associate Director
Kathryn Frye, Administrative Assistant

This book provides practical strategies for teaching writing in the classroom. It emphasizes the integration of language and critical thinking skills within a five-step writing process. Paragraph framing, graphic organizing, multiparagraph writing, sample templates, and exercises that teachers can use in their classrooms are included. *$30.00*

92 pages
ISBN 0-962411-93-0

3934 **Language Learning Everywhere We Go**

Harris Communications
15155 Technology Drive
Eden Prairie, MN   55344   952-906-1180
                                 800-825-6758
                          FAX 952-906-1099
                          TDY:952-906-1198
                   http://www.harriscomm.com
Cecilia Casas, Author
Patricia Portillo, Author

Students learn the vocabulary associated with each situation that they encounter on their travels with Bernardo Bear. Questions and vocabulary lists are included in English and Spanish for each picture. The 103 situational pictures may all be reproduced. *$34.00*

209 pages   Paperback

3935   Multisensory Teaching Approach

Educators Publishing Service
31 Smith Place
Cambridge, MA   02138   617-547-6706
                                              800-225-5750
                                     FAX 617-547-0412
                          http://www.epsbooks.com
                          e-mail: eps@epsbooks.com
Margaret Taylor Smith, Author

MTA is a comprehensive, multisensory program in reading, spelling, cursive handwriting, and alphabet and dictionary skills for both regular and remedial instruction. Ungraded, MTA is based on the Orton-Gillingham techniques and Alphabetic Phonics.

3936   Problems in Written Expression: Assessment and Remediation

Guilford Publications
72 Spring Street
New York, NY   10012   212-431-9800
                                              800-365-7006
                                     FAX 212-966-6708
                          http://www.guilford.com
                          e-mail: info@guilford.com
Sharon Bradley-Johnson, Author
Jusi Lucas Lesiak, Author

A great resource for speech-language pathologists, counselors, resource specialists and other special educators. *$20.95*

178 pages   Paperback

3937   Report Writing in the Field of Communication Disorders

American Speech-Language-Hearing Association
10801 Rockville Pike
Bethesda, MD   20814   301-897-5700
                                              888-498-6699
                                     FAX 301-897-7358
                          http://www.Asha.org
Laurie Ward, Marketing Coordinator

Stresses the summarization and interpretation of vital information and highlights matters of ethics, privacy and more. *$7.00*

3938   Signs of the Times

Harris Communications
15155 Technology Drive
Eden Prairie, MN   55344   952-906-1180
                                                   800-825-6758
                                          FAX 952-906-1099
                                          TDY:952-906-1198
                          http://www.harriscomm.com

Contains 1,185 signs in 41 lessons. Each lesson contains clearly illustrated vocabulary, English glosses and synonyms, sample sentences to define vocabulary context, and sentences for practice. *$24.95*

433 pages   Paperback

3939   Slingerland-Multisensory Approach to Language Arts for Specific Language Disability Children

Educators Publishing Service
31 Smith Place
Cambridge, MA   02138   617-547-6706
                                              800-225-5750
                                     FAX 617-547-0412
                          http://www.epsbooks.com
                          e-mail: eps@epsbooks.com
Beth H Slingerland, Author

This adaptation of the Orton-Gillingham approach for classroom teachers provides a phonetically structured introduction to reading, writing and spelling. Books 1 and 2 are for first and second grade, Book 3 for primary classrooms and older students. Numerous supplementary materials are available.

3940   Source for Processing Disorders

LinguiSystems
3100 4th Avenue
East Moline, IL   61244
                                              800-776-4332
                                     FAX 800-577-4555
                          http://www.linguisystems.com
                          e-mail: service@linguisystems.com
Linda Bowers, Owner
Rosemary Huisingh, Owner

This great resource helps you differentiate between language processing disorders and auditory processing disorders. Chapters cover: the neurology of processing and learning; the central auditory processing model; the language processing model; and a lot more!

Ages 5-Adult

3941   Source for Syndromes

LinguiSystems
3100 4th Avenue
East Moline, IL   61244
                                              800-776-4332
                                     FAX 309-755-2377
                                     TDY:800-933-8331
                          http://www.linguisystems.com
                          e-mail: service@linguisystems.com
Gail J Richard, Debra Reichert Hoge, Author
Linda Bowers, Owner
Rosemary Huisingh, Owner

Do you often wish someone would just tell you what to do with a specific youngster on your caseload? The Source for Syndromes can do just that. Learn about the speech-language characteristics for each sydrome with a focus on communication issues. This resource covers pertinent information for such sydromes such as Angelman, Asperger's, Autism, Rett's, Tourette's, Williams, and more. *$41.95*

117 pages   Ages Birth-18

3942   Teaching Language-Deficient Children: Theory and Application of the Association Method

Educators Publishing Service
31 Smith Place
Cambridge, MA   02138   617-547-6706
                                 800-225-5750
                          FAX 617-547-0412
                    http://www.epsbooks.com
                  e-mail: eps@epsbooks.com
N Etoile duBard and Maureen K Martin, Author

This revised and expanded edition of Teaching Aphasics and Other Language Deficient Children offers information on its theory, implementation of the method and sample curriculum. *$42.00*

360 pages
ISBN 0-838823-40-8

3943   Thematic Instruction: Teacher's Primer for Developing Speaking & Writing Skill

Landmark Foundation
PO Box 227
Prides Crossing, MA   01965   978-236-3216
                          FAX 978-927-7268
                    http://www.landmarkschool.org
                  e-mail: outreach@landmarkschool.org
Terrill M Jennings, Author
Charles W Haynes, Author
Joan Sedita, Outreach Program

This book introduces teachers to a theme-centered approach to expressive language skills instruction. It is designed for classroom teachers who are teaching speaking and writing skills. It combines a structured, skills-based approach with thematic orientation. *$20.00*

3944   Visualizing and Verbalizing for Language Comprehension/Thinking

Academy of Reading
416 Higuera Street
San Luis Obispo, CA   93401   805-541-3836
                                 800-233-1819
                          FAX 805-541-8756
Nanci Bell, Author

This book identifies the important sensory connection that imagery provides and teaches specific techniques. Specific steps and sample dialog are presented. Summary pages after each step make it easy to implement the program in the classroom.

284 pages
ISBN 0-945856-01-6

Math

3945   Landmark Method for Teaching Arithmetic

Landmark School
429 Hale Street
Prides Crossing, MA   01965   978-236-3216
                          FAX 978-927-7268
                    http://www.landmarkschool.org
                  e-mail: outreach@landmarkschool.org
Christopher Woodin, Author
Dan Ahearn, Program Director
Trish Newhall, Associate Director
Kathryn Frye, Administrative Assistant

This book is written for teachers who work with students having difficulty learning math. It includes practical strategies for teaching multiplication, division, word problems, and math facts. It also introduces the reader to two learning tools developed at Landmark — Woodin Ladders and Woodmark Icons. Sample templates and exercises that teachers can copy and use in their classrooms are included. *$30.00*

145 pages
ISBN 0-962411-92-2

3946   Math and the Learning Disabled Student: A Practical Guide for Accommodations

Academic Success Press
6023 26th Strete
West Bradenton, FL   34206   941-359-2819
                                 800-444-2524
                          FAX 800-777-2525
P Nolting, Author

More and more learning disabled students are experiencing difficulty passing mathematics. The book is especially written for counselors and mathematics instructors of learning disabled students, and provides information on accommodations for students with different types of learning disabilities.

91 pages
ISBN 0-940287-23-4

3947   Moving Toward the Standards: A National Action Plan for Math Education Reform for the Deaf

Harris Communications
15155 Technology Drive
Eden Prairie, MN   55344   952-906-1180
                                 800-825-6758
                          FAX 952-906-1099
                          TDY:952-906-1198
                    http://www.harriscomm.com

Offers help for teachers working with students who are deaf and hard of hearing by presenting the most current, practical approaches to math instruction.

750 pages

3948   Teaching Mathematics to Students with Learning Disabilities

Pro-Ed
8700 Shoal Creek Boulevard
Austin, TX   78757   512-451-3246
                                 800-897-3202
                          FAX 512-451-8542
                    http://www.proedinc.com
Nancy Bley, Author

Offers information on problem-solving, estimation and the use of computers in teaching mathematics to the child with learning disabilities. *$38.00*

486 pages
ISBN 0-890796-03-3

Preschool

3949   Access for All: Integrating Deaf, Hard of Hearing, and Hearing Preschoolers

Harris Communications
15155 Technology Drive
Eden Prairie, MN   55344   952-906-1180
                                  800-825-6758
                              FAX 952-906-1099
                              TDY:952-906-1198
                          http://www.harriscomm.com

Gail Solit, Author
Angela Bednarczyk, Author
Maral Taylor, Author

Covers basic information needed to establish a successful preschool program for deaf and hearing children; interagency cooperation, staff training, and parental involvement. *$29.95*

169 pages   Video-90 min.

3950   Administrator's Policy Handbook for Preschool Mainstreaming

Brookline Books
PO Box 1047
Cambridge, MA   02238   617-868-0360
                               800-666-2665
                           FAX 617-868-1772

Barbara J Smith, Author

Prepared specifically for the public school administrator who is developing the policies and procedures to place young children with disabilities in mainstreamed settings. *$39.95*

3951   Early Intervention in Natural Environments

Brooks/Cole Publishing Company
511 Forest Lodge Road
Pacific Grove, CA   93950   831-373-0728
                               FAX 831-375-6414

Noonan and McCormick, Author
Carolyn Crockett, Marketing Manager
Barbara Smallwood, Marketing Assistant

Organized by topical area, this text offers the skills to adapt assessment and intervention methods to the needs of the child as well as the wishes of the parent. While emphasizing child independence, support, empowerment, and family enablement, the authors explore issues such as early intervention methods, procedures for infants, toddlers, preschoolers and their families, and the role of play as learning opportunities.

412 pages
ISBN 0-534144-42-0

3952   KDES Preschool Curriculum Guide

Harris Communications
15155 Technology Drive
Eden Prairie, MN   55344   952-906-1180
                                  800-825-6758
                              FAX 952-906-1099
                              TDY:952-906-1198
                          http://www.harriscomm.com

A complete, four-year program developed for preschool children who are deaf or hard of hearing. The guide offers a comprehensive scope and sequence of objectives, resource units and evaluation tools: a sample instructional unit; a bibliography; and a record-keeping system for student progress. Also contains general information for teachers and administrators, including how to modify the program for children with special needs.

327 pages

3953   When Slow Is Fast Enough: Educating the Delayed Preschool Child

Guilford Publications
72 Spring Street
New York, NY   10012   212-431-9800
                              800-365-7006
                          FAX 212-966-6708
                      http://www.guilford.com
                      e-mail: info@guilford.com

Joan F Goodman, Author
Robert Coles, Foreword

Bold and controversial book critiques early intervention programs that attempt to accelerate development in delayed young children. Goodman suggests that in pressuring these children to perform more, and sooner, we are undermining their capacity for independent development and depriving them of the freedom we insist upon for the nondelayed. *$18.95*

306 pages   Paperback

Reading

3954   Dyslogic Syndrome

Learning Disabilities Association of America
4156 Library Road
Pittsburgh, PA   15234   412-341-1515
                            FAX 412-344-0224
                        http://www.ldanatl.org
                        e-mail: ldanatl@usaor.net

$2.00

3955   Gillingham Manual

Educators Publishing Service
31 Smith Place
Cambridge, MA   02138   617-547-6706
                               800-225-5750
                           FAX 617-547-0412
                        http://www.epsbooks.com
                        e-mail: eps@epsbooks.com

Anna Gillingham Bessie W Stillman, Author

This classic in the field of specific language disability has now been completely revised and updated. The manual covers reading, spelling, writing and dictionary technique. It may be used with individuals or small groups. *$60.00*

352 pages
ISBN 0-838802-00-1

3956 Phonic Remedial Reading Lessons

Academic Therapy Publications
20 Commercial Boulevard
Novato, CA   94949   415-883-3314
                                       800-422-7249
                                   FAX 415-883-3720
Betty Lou Kratoville, Editor

A step-by-step program for teaching reading to children who failed to learn by conventional methods. Consistent sound-symbol relationships are presented and reinforced using a grapho-vocal method. *$15.00*

144 pages
ISBN 0-878795-08-1

3957 Phonology and Reading Disability

University of Michigan Press
839 Greene Street
Ann Arbor, MI   48104   734-764-4392
                                   FAX 800-876-1922
                          http://www.press.umich.edu
                  e-mail: umpress_orders@umich.edu
Donald Shankweiler, Author
Mary Erwin, Assistant Director

Argues the association of words with the sounds they represent is crucial to the learning process. *$47.50*

ISBN 1-472101-33-1

3958 Preventing Reading Difficulties in Young Children

National Academies Press
500 Fifth NW
Washington, DC   20055
                                       800-624-6242
                                   http://www.nap.edu
National Research Council, Author
Barbara Klein-Pope, Executive Director

Examines factors that put children at risk of poor reading. Explores in detail how literacy can be fostered from birth through kindergarten and the primary grades including evaluation of philosophies, systems and materials commonly used to teach reading.

3959 Readability Revisited: The New Dale-Chall Readability Formula

Brookline Books
PO Box 1047
Cambridge, MA   02238   617-868-0360
                                       800-666-2665
                                   FAX 617-868-1772
Information is given on reading difficulties in children with learning disabilities and how to overcome them.

168 pages
ISBN 1-571290-08-7

3960 Reading Brain: The Biological Basis of Dyslexia

Learning Disabilities Association of America
4156 Library Road
Pittsburgh, PA   15234   412-341-1515
                                   FAX 412-344-0224
                               http://www.ldanatl.org
                         e-mail: ldanatl@usaor.net

$35.00

3961 Reading Disabilities in College and High School

Learning Disabilities Association of America
4156 Library Road
Pittsburgh, PA   15234   412-341-1515
                                   FAX 412-344-0224
                               http://www.ldanatl.org
                         e-mail: ldanatl@usaor.net
Aaron and Baker, Author

Offers a comprehensive guide to information on reading disabled students in the college and high school arenas. *$23.00*

3962 Reading Problems: Consultation and Remediation

Guilford Publications
72 Spring Street
New York, NY   10012   212-431-9800
                                       800-365-7006
                                   FAX 212-966-6708
                               http://www.guilford.com
                         e-mail: info@guilford.com
PG Aaron, Author
R Malatesha Joshi, Author

Offers information to educators on consultation and remediation programs. *$30.00*

285 pages

3963 Reading Programs that Work: A Review of Programs From Pre-K to 4th Grade

Milken Family Foundation
1250 Fourth Street
Santa Monica, CA   90401   310-570-4800
                                   FAX 310-570-4801
                                   http://www.mff.org
Dr. John Schacter, Author

This 72 page publication tackles two questions, why are some students failing to learn to read and what reading programs are proven to be effective? Included in this reading report are analyses of 35 different reading programs and their impact on student achievement.

3964 Reading and Learning Disabilities: A Resource Guide

NICHCY
PO Box 1492
Washington, DC   20013   202-884-8200
                                       800-695-0285
                                   FAX 202-884-8841
                               http://www.nichcy.org
                         e-mail: nichcy@ace.org
Susan Ripley, Information Specialist

12 pages

3965 Reading and Learning Disability: A Neuropsychological Approach to Evaluation & Instruction

Charles C Thomas Publisher
2600 S 1st Street
Springfield, IL 62704   217-789-8980
                            800-258-8980
                        FAX 217-789-9130
                    http://www.ccthomas.com
                    e-mail: books@ccthomas.com
Estelle L Fryburg, Author

This text utilizes the current knowledge of neuropsychology (brain-behavior relationships) and the concepts of cognitive psychology to provide an understanding of reading and learning disability which has a practical application to education. The primary goal of the book is to provide teachers, psychologists, physicians, concerned professionals, and parents with an interdisciplinary view of learning and schooling. *$79.95*

398 pages   Cloth
ISBN 0-398067-44-9

3966 Reading-Writing-Rage: The Terrible Price Paid by Victims of School Failure

BL Winch/Jalmar Press
45 Hitching Post Drive
Rolling Hills Estates, CA 90274   310-547-1240
                                800-662-9662
                            FAX 310-547-1241
DF Ungerleider, Author

3967 Reading/Learning Disability: An Ecological Approach

Learning Disabilities Association of America
4156 Library Road
Pittsburgh, PA 15234   412-341-1515
                        FAX 412-344-0224
                    http://www.ldanatl.org
                    e-mail: ldanatl@usaor.net
Bartoli & Botel, Author

$9.00

3968 Starting Out Right: A Guide to Promoting Children's Reading Success

National Academies Press
500 Fifth NW
Washington, DC 20055
                            800-624-6242
                        http://www.nap.edu
National Research Council, Author
Barbara Klein-Pope, Executive Director

Discusses how best to help children succeed in reading. The book identifies the important questions and explores the authoritative answers on the topic of how children can grow into readers. A resource for any adult who wants to lay down a solid language and literacy foundation for every child.

3969 Teaching Reading to Disabled and Handicapped Learners

Charles C Thomas Publisher
2600 S 1st Street
Springfield, IL 62704   217-789-8980
                            800-258-8980
                        FAX 217-789-9130
                    http://www.ccthomas.com
                    e-mail: books@ccthomas.com
Harold D Love and Freddie W Litton, Author

Guides prospective and present special education teachers in assisting and teaching handicapped learners to read. Integrates traditional methods with newer perspectives. Books sent on approval. Shipping charges: $5.50 US, $6.50 Canada. Prices subject to change without notice. *$54.95*

260 pages   Cloth
ISBN 0-398059-09-8

3970 Teaching the Dyslexic Child

Academic Therapy Publications
20 Commercial Boulevard
Novato, CA 94949   415-883-3314
                        800-422-7249
                    FAX 415-883-3720
                    http://www.atpub.com
Anita Griffiths, Author
Betty Lou Kratoville, Editor

Dyslexia can be crushing to a child's self-image. The author shows teachers and parents how to focus on the child's ability and become a partner inlearning to help restore a positive self-image. *$13.00*

128 pages
ISBN 0-878792-05-8

3971 Textbooks and the Students Who Can't Read Them

Brookline Books
PO Box 1047
Cambridge, MA 02238   617-868-0360
                            800-666-2665
                        FAX 617-868-1772
Jean Ciborowski, Author

Based on a careful analysis of 10 textbook programs, 5 science and 5 social studies, the author concisely and sensibly indicates the procedure that facilitates teacher's use of regular grade level textbooks with low-reading students. *$21.95*

3972 Visual Processes in Reading and Reading Disabilities

Lawrence Erlbaum Associates
365 Broadway
Hillsdale, NJ 07642   201-666-4110
                        800-926-6579
                    FAX 201-666-2394
Dale M Willows, Author
Richard Kruk, Author
Evely Corcos, Author

The purpose of this book is to bring together a broad range of evidence that concerns the role of visual information in reading and reading disabilities. Because reading processes are of central interest to cognitive scientists, neuropsychologists, psycholinguists, clinicians, and educators, this book should draw a very broad readership. *$89.95*

504 pages
ISBN 0-805809-00-7

3973 Why Wait for a Criterion of Failure?

Educators Publishing Service
31 Smith Place
Cambridge, MA   02138   617-547-6706
                                800-225-5750
                           FAX 617-547-0412
                    http://www.epsbooks.com
                    e-mail: eps@epsbooks.com

B Slingerland, Author

A monograph concerning the teaching of reading to learning disabled students using the multi-sensory approach, which is the crux of the Orton-Gillingham approach. This book describes structured lessons, with sample word lists, and reading lessons. *$6.00*

48 pages
ISBN 0-838802-43-5

Social Skills

3974 ADHD in the Schools: Assessment andIntervention Strategies

Guilford Publications
72 Spring Street
New York, NY   10012   212-431-9800
                                800-365-7006
                           FAX 212-966-6708
                     http://www.guilford.com
                     e-mail: info@guilford.com

George J DuPaul, Author
Gary Stoner, Author

For psychologists, educators, and others who are involved in the treatment of children with ADD. Addresses such problems as academic under achievement, noncompliance with classroom rules, and problematic peer relationships. Tells school professionals how to identify and assess students who might have ADHD and how to develop and implement classroom-based programs. *$30.00*

269 pages

3975 Behavior Change in the Classroom: Self-Management Interventions

Guilford Publications
72 Spring Street
New York, NY   10012   212-431-9800
                                800-365-7006
                           FAX 212-966-6708
                     http://www.guilford.com
                     e-mail: info@guilford.com

Edward S Shapiro, Author
Christine L Cole, Author

This book presents practical approaches for designing and implementing self-management interventions in school settings. An excellent resource for school-based practitioners who wish to address the needs of all school-age children and adolescents. *$26.95*

204 pages

3976 Group Activities to Include Students with Special Needs

Corwin Press
2455 Teller Road
Thousand Oaks, CA   91320   805-499-9734
                                   800-818-7243
                              FAX 805-499-5323
                       http://www.corwinpress.com
                       e-mail: order@corwinpress.com

Julia Wilkins, Author
Kimberly Gonzales, Marketing Director
Robb Clouse, Senior Acquisitions Editor

This guide provides teachers with easily referenced tools for any situation and skill level, including skill development categories and icons showing which abilities are needed for each activity. An essential resource for both new and veteran teachers of students with special needs. *$34.95*

240 pages
ISBN 0-761977-26-0

3977 Joy of Listening

Harris Communications
15155 Technology Drive
Eden Prairie, MN   55344   952-906-1180
                                   800-825-6758
                              FAX 952-906-1099
                              TDY:952-906-1198
                       http://www.harriscomm.com

Janice Baliker Light, Author

Includes lessons that improve listening skills, auditory discrimination, attention span, and memory in hearing-impaired children and adults. Also recommended for learning-disabled children with auditory weaknesses. Many of the sections may be used for teaching lipreading skills. *$12.95*

148 pages   Paperback

3978 Key Concepts in Personal Development

Marsh Media
8082 Ward Parkway Plaza
Kansas City, MO   64114   816-523-1059
                                   800-821-3303
                              FAX 866-333-7421
                       http://www.marshmedia.com
                       e-mail: info@marshmedia.com

Joan Marsh, President
Liz Sweeney, Editorial Assistant

Our videos, books, and teaching guides bring character education to the classroom. These kits are invaluable aids in teaching everyday values like honesty, anger control, trustworthiness, perseverance, understanding and respect. They help you prepare youngsters to meet challenges and greet opportunities with skill and optimism.

3979 Progress Program

Edge Enterprises
PO Box 1304
Lawrence, KS   66044   785-749-1473
                             FAX 785-749-0207
                    e-mail: edge@midusa.net
*Jean Schumaker, Melbourne Hovell, James
Sherman, Author*
Jacqueline Schafer, Managing Editor

Describes how teachers, administrators and parents
can work together to use a Daily Report Card Program
to control disruptive student behavior and improve the
academic and social performance of students who are
at-risk for failure. This program is carefully sequenced to move from extrinsic control to student (intrinsic) control of behavior. *$10.00*

   96 pages   Paperback

3980 Social Perception and Learning Disabilities

Learning Disabilities Association of America
4156 Library Road
Pittsburgh, PA   15234   412-341-1515
                               FAX 412-344-0224
                       http://www.ldanatl.org
                  e-mail: ldanatl@usaor.net

   $6.00

**3981 Teaching Social Skills to Hearing Impaired
Students**

Harris Communications
15155 Technology Drive
Eden Prairie, MN   55344   952-906-1180
                                  800-825-6758
                          FAX 952-906-1099
                          TDY:952-906-1198
                  http://www.harriscomm.com
Patrick J Schloss PhD, Author
Maureen A Smith MA, Author

Provides teachers and parents with a comprehensive,
hands-on program to develop important social skills
in hearing-impaired children and young adults.
$24.95

   203 pages   Paperback

3982 Training for Independent Living Curriculum

RPM Press
PO Box 31483
Tucson, AZ   85751   520-886-1990
                            888-810-1990
                     FAX 520-886-1990
Jan Stonebraker, Operations Manager

Provides educators and rehabilitation personnel with
a 400 page curriculum designed to help teach developmentally disabled and other severely challenged persons essential independent living skills including
personal and social adjustment, money management,
meal preparation, money handling, personal safety,
grooming and more. *$79.95*

Publications

3983 Above and Beyond
AASCU
1 Dupont Circle NW
Washington, DC   20036   202-293-7070
                               FAX 202-833-4760
Jade Ann Gingerich, Author
Dan Gardner, Information Specialist

Describes college services for students with learning disabilities. *$8.00*

32 pages

3984 Assisting College Students with Learning Disabilities: A Tutor's Manual
Association on Higher Education and Disability
PO Box 21192
Columbus, OH   43221   614-488-4972
                              FAX 614-488-1174
                              http://www.ahead.org
                              e-mail: ahead@postbox.acs.ohio-state.edu

This resource manual is for service providers who want to take concrete action toward integrating women with disabilities into the mainstream of college life. *$9.95*

3985 Campus Opportunities for Students with Learning Differences
Octameron Associates
PO Box 2748
Alexandria, VA   22301   703-836-5480
                                FAX 703-836-5650
                                http://www.octameron.com
J Katz, Public Relations Director

A book about going to college for young adults with various types of learning disabilities. Details questions to ask in selecting a college. CAMPUS OPPORTUNITIES teaches how to be a self-advocate. *$7.00*

48 pages   Biannual
ISBN 1-575090-52-X

3986 Chronicle Financial Aid Guide
Chronicle Guidance Publications
66 Aurora Street
Moravia, NY   13118   315-497-0330
                             800-622-7284
                             FAX 315-497-3359
                             http://www.chronicleguidance.com
                             e-mail: janet@chronicleguidance.com
Janet Seemann, Managing Editor

Offers information on more than 1,950 financial aid programs, offering over 400,000 awards from current, verified sources. *$24.98*

424 pages   Annual
ISBN 1-556312-91-1

3987 College Placement Council Directory
College Placement Council
62 Highland Avenue
Bethlehem, PA   18017   215-868-1421
                               800-544-5272

Offers the who's who in the college placement/recruitment field. *$47.95*

3988 Colleges/Universities that Accept Students with Learning Disabilities
Learning Disabilities Association of America
4156 Library Road
Pittsburgh, PA   15234   412-341-1515
                                FAX 412-344-0224
                                http://www.ldanatl.org
                                e-mail: ldanatl@usaor.net

List of colleges by state. *$4.00*

3989 Directory of Catholic Special Education Programs and Facilities
National Catholic Education Association
1077 30th Street NW
Washington, DC   20007   202-337-6232
                                FAX 202-333-6706
                                http://www.ncea.org
                                e-mail: nceadmin@ncea.org
NCEA Publications Sales

A valuable resource for anyone seeking appropriate placements in Catholic settings. *$8.00*

100 pages
ISBN 1-558330-11-9

3990 Directory of Educational Facilities for Learning Disabled Students
Learning Disabilities Association of America
4156 Library Road
Pittsburgh, PA   15234   412-341-1515
                                FAX 412-344-0224
                                http://www.ldanatl.org
                                e-mail: ldanatl@usaor.net

A large directory offering information on educational facilities nationwide accepting and schooling learning disabled students. *$4.00*

3991 Dispelling the Myths: College Students and Learning Disabilities
381 Park Avenue S
New York, NY   10016   212-545-7510
                              888-575-7373
                              FAX 212-545-9665
                              http://www.ncld.org

A monograph for students and educators that explains what learning disabilities are and what faculty members can do to help students with learning disabilities achieve success in college.

3992 Four-Year College Databook

Chronicle Guidance Publications
PO Box 1190
Moravia, NY   13118   315-497-0330
                                       800-622-7284
                          FAX 315-497-3359
                  http://www.ChronicleGuidance.com
        e-mail: customerservice@ChronicleGuidance.com
Stephen D Thompson, Managing Editor
Nancy Carmody, Marketing

Chronicle Four-Year College Databook contains two
sections: The Four-Year College Majors section lists
2,160 institutions offering 790 four-year graduate and
professional majors. *$24.99*

> *487 pages   Annual*
> *ISBN 1-556312-92-X*

3993 From Access to Equity

Association on Higher Education and Disability
PO Box 21192
Columbus, OH   43221   614-488-4972
                          FAX 614-488-1174
                  http://www.ahead.org
        e-mail: ahead@postbox.acs.ohio-state.edu

This resource manual is for service providers who
want to take concrete action toward integrating
women with disabilities into the mainstream of college life. *$9.95*

3994 Getting LD Students Ready for College

HEATH Resource Center
2121 K Street NW
Washington, DC   20036   202-973-0904
                                       800-544-3284
                          FAX 202-973-0908
Carol Sullivan, Counselor

List offering parents, counselors, teachers and learning disabled students a reminder of helpful skills and
necessary steps to take as a high school student with a
learning disability moves toward college.

3995 Guide to Colleges for Learning Disabled Students

Academic Success Press
6023 26th Strete
West Bradenton, FL   34206   941-359-2819
                                       800-444-2524
                          FAX 800-777-2525
Mary Ann Liscio, Editor

**3996 Guide to Community Colleges Serving Students
with Learning Disabilities**

Project We Can, Mississippi State University
Department of Counselor Education
University, MS   38677   662-325-2640
                          FAX 662-325-8664
Sonja Burnham, Author

A list by state of two-year community colleges in Mississippi, Alabama, Georgia, Tennessee and Florida,
describing services and accommodations provided for
students with learning disabilities. *$1.50*

3997 HEATH Resource Directory

National Clearinghouse on Postsecondary Education
1 Dupont Circle NW
Washington, DC   20036   202-939-9300
                          FAX 202-833-4760
Dan Gardner, Information Specialist

Annotated listings of over 150 national organizations
which can provide additional information about
postsecondary education and individuals with disabilities. *$1.00*

> *30 pages*

3998 Higher Education Information Center

Boston Public Library
700 Boylston Street
Boston, MA   02116   617-536-0200
                                       800-442-1171
                          FAX 617-266-4673
                  http://www.bpl.org
                  e-mail: hr@bpl.org

Offers information on colleges and universities, voca-
tional/technical schools, financial aid and careers,
counseling on school selection and paying for educational costs.

**3999 How the Student with Hearing Loss Can Succeed
in College**

Harris Communications
15155 Technology Drive
Eden Prairie, MN   55344   952-906-1180
                                       800-825-6758
                          FAX 952-906-1099
                          TDY:952-906-1198
                  http://www.harriscomm.com
Carol Flexer PhD, Editor
Denise Wray PhD, Editor
Ron Leavitt MS, Editor

A handbook for students families and professionals.
Includes information on academic, financial, technological, and support services. *$28.95*

> *278 pages   Paperback*

4000 How to Succeed in College with Dyslexia

Learning Disabilities Association of America
4156 Library Road
Pittsburgh, PA   15234   412-341-1515
                          FAX 412-344-0224
                  http://www.ldanatl.org
                  e-mail: ldanatl@usaor.net
J Woods, Author

Offers information on college education for children
with dyslexia. *$19.95*

**4001 How to Succeed in College: A Handbook for
Students with Learning Disabilities**

National Center on Employment and Disability
201 IU Willets Road
Albertson, NY   11507   516-747-5400
                          FAX 516-747-5378

These two volumes demonstrate the advantages of cooperation between vocational rehabilitation and education. *$15.00*

4002 ISS Directory of International Schools

International Schools Services
15 Roszel Road
Princeton, NJ 08540   609-452-0990
                             FAX 609-452-2690
                             http://www.iss.edu
                             e-mail: directory@iss.edu

Comprehensive guide to over 550 American and international schools worldwide. *$45.95*

550 pages   Plus S&H
ISBN 0-913663-17-5

4003 K&W Guide to Colleges for the Learning Disabled

HarperCollins Publishers
10 E 53rd Street
New York, NY 10022   212-207-7000
                            800-331-3761
                            FAX 212-207-7145

Marybeth Kravets, Author
Imy Wax, Author

Offers information on support services for learning disabled college students. Includes learning disability services available, programs offered, college graduation requirements, admissions policies, costs, housing, tutorial help, learning resource centers and athletics.

4004 Learning to Care

ACTION
1100 Vermont Avenue NW
Washington, DC 20525   202-606-5135
                             800-424-8867
                             FAX 202-606-5135

A national directory of student community service programs.

4005 National Association of Private Schools for Exceptional Children

NAPSEC
1522 K Street NW
Washington, DC 20005   202-408-3338
                             FAX 202-408-3340

Sherry Kolbe, Executive Director

A membership directory listing NAPSEC'S members. Information given includes: disabilities served, program descriptions, school profiles, admissions procedures and funding approval. *$32.00*

300 pages

4006 National Directory of Colleges and Programs for Young People with Learning Disabilities

Partners in Publishing
PO Box 50347
Tulsa, OK 74150   918-835-8258
                        FAX 918-835-8258
                        e-mail: PLMFieldin@aol.com
PM Fielding, Editor

Gathered through questionnaires, this directory offers school name of four- and two-year colleges and post high school training programs, their size, type, address, telephone, contact person and what programs are offered for the learning disabled student. *$32.95*

4007 National Directory of Four Year Colleges, Two Year Colleges & High School Training Programs

Partners in Publishing
3332 E 4th Street
Tulsa, OK 74112   918-835-8258
                        FAX 918-835-8258
                        e-mail: PLMFieldin@aol.com
PM Fielding, Editor

Lists training programs at colleges and training centers for young people with learning disabilities.

4008 Peterson's Colleges with Programs for Students with Learning Disabilities or ADD

Peterson's
2000 Lenox Drive
Lawrenceville, NJ 08648   609-896-1800
                                800-338-3282
                                FAX 609-896-1811
                                http://www.petersons.com
                                e-mail: custsvce@petersons.com
Charles T Mangrum II, Author
Stephen S Strichart, Author

Directs special-needs students to educational programs and services at 1,000 two-and four-year colleges and universities in the US and Canada. *$29.95*

672 pages   Sixth Edition
ISBN 0-768904-55-2

4009 Questions to Aid in Selecting an Appropriate College Program for LD

CT Association for Children and Adults with LD
25 Van Zant Street
East Norwalk, CT 06855   203-838-5010
                               FAX 203-866-6108
                               http://www.CACLD.org
                               e-mail: cacld@juno.com
Marie Armstrong, Information Specialist

A collection of five one page information sheets, each from a different source. *$2.00*

$1.00 shipping

4010 Schoolsearch Guide to Colleges with Programs & Services for Students with LD

Schoolsearch Press
127 Marsh Street
Belmont, MA 02478   617-489-5785
                          FAX 617-489-5641
                          http://schoolsearch.com
                          e-mail: mlipkin@schoolsearch.com
Midge Lipkin, President

Lists more than 770 colleges and universities that offer programs and services to high school graduates with learning disabilities. *$39.95*

1660 pages   3rd Edition
ISBN 0-962032-67-0

4011 Shopper's Guide to Colleges Serving the Learning Disabled College Student

Learning Disabilities Association of America
4156 Library Road
Pittsburgh, PA 15234　　　　412-341-1515
　　　　　　　　　　　FAX 412-344-0224
　　　　　　　　　　　http://www.ldanatl.org
　　　　　　　　　　　e-mail: ldanatl@usaor.net
Fred Barbaro, Author

$3.00

4012 Two-Year College Databook

Chronicle Guidance Publications
66 Aurora Street
Moravia, NY 13118　　　　315-497-0330
　　　　　　　　　　　800-899-0454
　　　　　　　　　　　FAX 315-497-3359
　　　　http://www.chronicleguidance.com
　　　e-mail: customerservice@chronicleguidance.com
Stephen Thompson, Managing Editor

Comprehensive package offers students and counselors up-to-date information for selection colleges. The Chronical Two-Year Databook contains information on college majors, and on 2,432 institutions offering 760 occupational-career, associate, and transfer programs. *$24.97*

385 pages Annual
ISBN 1-556312-93-8

4013 Vocational School Manual

Chronicle Guidance Publications
66 Aurora Street
Moravia, NY 13118　　　　315-497-0330
　　　　　　　　　　　800-899-0454
　　　　　　　　　　　FAX 315-497-3359
　　　　http://www.chronicleguidance.com
　　　e-mail: customerservice@chronicleguidance.com
Stephen Thompson, Managing Editor

Offers information on occupational education programs currently available in the United States, Guam, and Puerto Rico. Programs consist of study or training leading to definite occupations. Prepares people for employment in recognized occupations, helps people make educated occupational choices, and upgrade and update their occupational skills. Includes data on vocational schools offering postsecondary occupational education. Accrediting associations are listed with contact information. *$24.96*

260 pages Annual
ISBN 1-556312-90-8

4014 World of Options: A Guide to International Education

Mobility International USA
PO Box 10767
Eugene, OR 97440　　　　541-343-1284
　　　　　　　　　　　FAX 541-343-6812
　　　　　　　　　　　http://www.miusa.org
　　　　　　　　　　　e-mail: info@miusa.org
Christa Bucks, Editor

Offers information on a wide variety of opportunities available to disabled participants including travel and international programs, and personal experience stories from people with disabilities who have had successful international experiences. *$35.00*

600 pages

Alabama

4015 Alabama Aviation and Technical College

Wallace Community College
PO Box 1209
Ozark, AL 36361　　　　334-774-5113
　　　　　　　　　　　800-624-3468
　　　　　　　　　　　FAX 334-774-6399
　　　　　　　　　　　http://www.wallace.edu
Carol Parker, Student Support

A public two-year college with 15 special education students out of a total of 600. Certified by the Federal Aviation Administration, and offers the only comprehensive aviation maintenance training program in the state of Alabama, with instruction in airframe, powerplant and avionics.

4016 Alabama Southern Community College

PO Box 2000
Monroeville, AL 36461　　　　334-575-3156
　　　　　　　　　　　FAX 334-575-5356
　　　　　　　　　　　http://www.asoc.edu
Theada Samuel

A public two-year college with 21 special education students out of a total of 1,127.

4017 Auburn University

Program for Students with Disabilities
1244 Haley Center
Auburn, AL 36849　　　　334-844-2096
　　　　　　　　　　　FAX 334-844-2099
　　　　　　　　　　　http://ww.auburn.edu
Four year college offering services to students with learning disabilities.

4018 Auburn University at Montgomery

Center for Special Services
Library Tower, 7th Floor
Montgomery, AL 36124　　　　334-244-3468
　　　　　　　　　　　FAX 334-244-3907
　　　　　　　　　　　TDY:3342443754
　　　　　　　　　　　http://www.aum.edu
　　　　e-mail: tmassey@mickey.aum.edu
Holly Brown, Acting Director
Tamara Massey-Garret, Student Services Coordinator

Offers a variety of services to students with disabilities including equipment, extended testing time, interpreting services, counseling services, and special accommodations.

4019 Birmingham-Southern College

900 Arkadelphia Road
Birmingham, AL   35254   205-226-4672
                               800-523-5793
                               FAX 205-226-4627
                               http://www.bsc.edu
Judith H Cox, Director Academic Advising
Sara Hoover, Director Personal Counseling

Offers a variety of services to students with disabilities including notetakers, extended testing time, counseling services, and special accommodations.

4020 Bishop State Community College

414 Stanton Street
Mobile, AL   36603   334-473-8692
                               FAX 334-473-7115
                               http://www.bscc.cc.al.us
                               e-mail: info@bscc.cc.al.us
Carrie Moore, Counselor

A public two-year college with 2 special education students out of a total of 2144.

4021 Chattahoochee Valley State Community College

2602 College Drive
Pheonix City, AL   36867   334-291-4900
                               FAX 334-291-4944
                               http://www.cvcc.cc.al.us
Jacquie Thacker, ADA Coordinator

Offers a variety of services to students with disabilities including note takers, extended testing time, counseling services and special accommodations.

4022 Douglas MacArthur State Technical College

1708 N Main Street
Opp, AL   36467   334-493-3573
                               FAX 334-493-7003
                               http://www.mstc.cc.al.us
L Wayne Bennett, Interim President
Peggy Linton, Interim Dean Instruction

A public two-year college with 102 special education students out of a total of 630. Provides postsecondary occupational education on a nondiscriminatory basis for individuals who desire to prepare for entry level employment, advancement, or retraining in a career field.

4023 George County Wallace State Community College

300 E Goodwin Parkway
Selma, AL   36702   334-876-9227
                               FAX 334-876-9250
                               http://www.wccs.cc.al.us
Effell Williams, Special Services

Offers a variety of services to students with disabilities including note takers, extended testing time, counseling services and special accommodations.

4024 Horizons School

2111 University Boulevard
Birmingham, AL   35233   205-322-6606
                               800-822-6242
                               FAX 205-322-6605
                               http://www.horizonsschool.org
                               e-mail: mcelheny@horizonsschool.org
Dr. Jade Carter, Director
Marie McElheny, Assistant Director

Serves students age 19-26 with specific learning disabilities and other mild learning problems. Gives students the opportunity to establish friendships, prepares students for successful transition to the community and offers courses in career, life and social skills.

4025 Jacksonville State University

700 Pelham Road N
Jacksonville, AL   36265   256-782-5400
                               FAX 256-782-5121
                               http://www.jsu.edu
                               e-mail: lbedford@jsucc.jsu.edu
Daniel Miller, Director

Offers a variety of services to students with disabilities including notetakers, extended testing time, counseling services, and special accommodations.

4026 James H Faulkner State Community College

1900 US Highway 31 S
Bay Minette, AL   36507   251-580-2100
                               800-231-3752
                               FAX 251-580-2226
                               http://www.faulknerstate.edu
Dr. Brenda Kennedy, Dean Student Development

A public two-year community college with approximately 125 students with disabilities out of a total student population of 4,350. Committed to the professional and cultural growth of each student without regard to race, color, qualified disability, gender, religion, creed, national origin, or age. Attempts to provide an educational environment that promotes development and learning through a wide variety of educational programs, adequate and comfortable facilities, and flexible scheduling.

4027 John M Patterson State Technical College

3920 Troy Highway
Montgomery, AL   36116   334-288-1080
                               FAX 334-284-9357
                               http://www.jptech.cc.al.us/
Jerry Joyce, Coordinator

A public two-year college with 101 special education students out of a total of 800.

4028 Marion Military Institute

1101 Washington Street
Marion, AL   36756   334-683-2306
                               800-664-1842
                               FAX 334-683-2383
                               http://www.mairon-institue.org
Col. James P Carruthers, Admissions Director

An independent two-year college with an academic advantage program for students with learning difficulties and for a limited number with diagnosed learning disabilities.

4029 Northeast Alabama Community College

138 Alabama Highway 35 E
Rainsville, AL   35986   256-638-4418
                                  FAX 256-228-6861
                          http://www.nacc.cc.al.us
Elaine Hayden, Assistant Dean Iinstruction

A public two-year college with support services for students with special needs that is consistant with the mission of the Alambama College System: to provide accessible quality educational opportunities, promote economic growth, and enhance the quality of life for people in Alabama.

4030 Troy State University Dothan

PO Box 8368
Dothan, AL   36304   334-983-6556
                                 FAX 334-983-6322
                             http://www.tsud.edu
                       e-mail: kseagle@tsud.edu
Keith Seagle, Director Counseling Services

Offers a variety of services to students with disabilities including notetakers, extended testing time, counseling services, and special accommodations.

4031 University of Alabama

PO Box 870132
Tuscaloosa, AL   35487   205-348-5666
                                 FAX 205-348-9046
                               http://www.ua.edu
Dr. Jim Saski, Manager LD/ADHD
Karen Clayton, Manager Physical Disabilities

A public four-year college with approximately 650 students identified with disabilities out of a total of 19,200.

4032 University of Alabama: Huntsville

301 Sparkman Drive
Huntsville, AL   35899   256-824-6070
                                 FAX 256-824-6073
                              http://www.uah.edu
                     e-mail: admitme@email.uah.edu
Delois H Smith, Director

Offers a variety of services and accommodations to assist students with disabilities in eliminating barriers they encounter in pursuing higher education.

4033 University of Montevallo

Station 6030
Montevallo, AL   35115   205-665-6000
                                 FAX 205-665-6042
                         http://www.montevallo.edu
Elaine Elledge, Special Services

Offers a variety of services to students with disabilities including notetakers, extended testing time, counseling services, and special accommodations.

4034 University of North Alabama

Box 5008
Florence, AL   35630   256-765-4248
                                 FAX 256-765-4904
                               http://www.una.edu
                    e-mail: jadams@unanov.una.edu
Jennifer Adams, Associate Director

Developmental services of UNA provides accommodation and supportive services to assist students with disabilities throughout their college expirence.

4035 University of South Alabama

182 Adminstration Building
Mobile, AL   36688   251-460-6211
                                 FAX 251-460-7827
                           http://www.usouthal.edu
                   e-mail: admiss@jaguar1.usouthal.edu
Keith Ayers, Director

Offers a variety of services to students with disabilities including note takers, extended testing time, counseling services, and special accommodations.

Alaska

4036 Alaska Pacific University

Disabled Student Services
4101 University Drive
Anchorage, AK   99508   907-564-8345
                                 FAX 907-564-8806
                         http://www.alaskapacific.edu
                   e-mail: tamera@alaskapacific.edu
Tamera Randolph, Coordinator Disability Support

Four-year college offering special services to students that are learning disabled.

4037 Juneau Campus: University of Alaska Southeast

11120 Glacier Highway
Juneau, AK   99801   907-465-6462
                                 877-465-4827
                                 FAX 907-465-6365
                           http://www.jun.alaska.edu
                   e-mail: uas.info@uas.alaska.edu
Roya Anseri, Learning Center

Offers a variety of services to students with disabilities including notetakers, extended testing time, counseling services, and special accommodations.

4038 Ketchikan Campus: University of Alaska Southeast

2600 7th Avenue
Ketchikan, AK   99901   907-225-6177
                                 FAX 907-225-3624
                          http://www.ketch.alaska.edu
                      e-mail: info@uas.alaska.edu
L Lee Naugen, Assistant Professor

Offers a variety of services to students with disabilities including note takers, extended testing time, counseling services and special accommodations.

4039 University of Alaska Anchorage: Disability Support Services

3211 Providence Drive
Anchorage, AK 99508   907-786-1480
                        FAX 907-786-4888
                        http://www.uaa.alaska.edu
                        e-mail: ayenrol@alaska.edu
Lyn Stoller, Director

Provides equal opportunites for students who experience disabilities.

4040 University of Alaska: Fairbanks

PO Box 757480
Fairbanks, AK 99775   907-474-7500
                        FAX 907-474-5379
                        http://www.uaf.edu
                        e-mail: fyapply@uaf.edu
Cindy Slats, Administrative Assistant

A public four-year college. Services provided to students with learning disabilities include: assistance determining accommodations, advocacy, testing accommodations, books on tape, peer support groups and individual counseling.

Arizona

4041 Arizona State University

Box 870112
Tempe, AZ 85287   480-965-7788
                        FAX 480-965-3610
                        http://www.asu.edu
                        e-mail: upgradingones@asu.edu
Tedde Scharf, Director

Four-year college that offers support to students with learning disabilities.

4042 Eastern Arizona College

3714 W Church Street
Thatcher, AZ 85552   520-428-8259
                        FAX 520-428-8462
                        http://www.eac.oc.az.us
Beverly Teague, Student Services

Offers a variety of services to students with disabilities including note takers, extended testing time, counseling services and special accommodations.

4043 Glendale Community College

6000 W Olive Avenue
Glendale, AZ 85302   603-845-3089
                        FAX 623-845-3329
                        http://www.gc.maricopa.edu
Mark Ferris, Coordinator Disability Service
Nancy Oreshack, LD Specialist

A public two-year college with 212 special education students out of a total of 15,200.

4044 Grand Canyon University

3300 W Camelback Road
Phoenix, AZ 85061   602-589-2855
                        FAX 602-589-2580
                        http://www.grand-canyon.edu
                        e-mail: admiss@grand-canyon.edu
Dr. Jane Castillo, Instructor Education

Offers a variety of services to students with disabilities including note takers, extended testing time, counseling services, and special accommodations.

4045 Mesa Community College

1833 W Southern Avenue
Mesa, AZ 85202   480-461-7870
                        FAX 480-461-7139
                        http://www.mc.maricopa.edu
Judith Taussig, Special Services

Offers a variety of services to students with disabilities including note takers, extended testing time, counseling services and special accommodations.

4046 Northern Arizona University

PO Box 4084
Flagstaff, AZ 86011   520-523-5511
                        FAX 520-523-6023
                        http://www.nau.edu
                e-mail: undergraduate.admissions@nau.edu
Marsha Fields, Director

A public four-year college.

4047 Phoenix College

1202 W Thomas Road
Phoenix, AZ 85013   602-285-7476
                        FAX 602-285-7700
                        TDY:602-285-7477
                        http://www.pc.maricopa.edu
Mitra Mehraban, Special Services

A public two-year college with 23 special education students out of a total of 14,327.

4048 Pima Community College

2202 W Anklam Road
Tucson, AZ 85709   520-206-6688
                        FAX 520-206-6071
Eric Morrison, Facility Advisor

A public two-year college offering special education classes for students with disabilities.

4049 Scottsdale Community College

9000 E Chaparral Road
Scottsdale, AZ 85256   480-423-6517
                        FAX 480-423-6200
Dee Duggan, Disability Resources/Service

Student Services office works closely with learning disabled students to provide the best accommodations possible.

4050 South Mountain Community College

7050 S 24th Street
Phoenix, AZ 85040   602-243-8119
                            FAX 602-243-8118
          http://www.smc.maricopa.edu
Henrietta Harris, Special Services

Offers a variety of services to students with disabilities including note takers, extended testing time, counseling services and special accommodations.

4051 Spring Ridge Academy

13690 S Burton Road
Spring Valley, AZ 86333   928-632-4602
                                  FAX 928-632-7661
          e-mail: sraemail@northlink.com
Jan Moss, Executive Director

4052 University of Advancing Computer Technology

2625 W Baseline Road
Tempe, AZ 85283   602-383-8228
                          800-658-5744
                       FAX 602-383-8222
          http://www.uact.edu
          e-mail: admissions@uat.edu
Daniel P Edwards, National Admissions

The University of Advancing Computer Technology has a program for you. Areas of study include digital animation production, game design, digital video production, interactive media, web design, graphic design, application development, computer programming, database programming, Internet development and administration, network engineering, game programming, network security, web site production, technology management, e-commerce marketing or internet database management.

4053 University of Arizona

PO Box 210040
Tucson, AZ 85721   520-621-3237
                           FAX 520-621-9799
          http://www.arizona.edu
          e-mail: appinfo@arizona.edu
Dr. Sue Kroeger, Director

The Strategic Alternative Learning Techniques (SALT) Center values the achievement of individuals with learning disabilities and provides an array of services to maximize student success.

4054 Yavapai College

Student Support Services
1100 E Sheldon Street
Prescott, AZ 86301   928-776-2117
                             FAX 928-776-2030
          http://www.yavapai.cc.az.us
Patricia Quinn-Kane, Learning Specialist

A public two-year college that offers a variety of services for students with disabilities.

Arkansas

4055 Arkansas Baptist College

1600 Bishop Street
Little Rock, AR 72202   501-374-7856
                                FAX 501-375-9257
          http://www.anicbapcol.edu
          e-mail: ahightower@swbell.net
Dr. Nile Smith, Director

An independent four-year college with 44 special education students out of a total of 418.

4056 Arkansas State University

Disability Services
2105 E Aggie Road
Jonesboro, AR 72467   870-972-3964
                              FAX 870-910-8048
                              TDY:870-972-3965
          http://www.astate.edu
          e-mail: phestand@chickasaw.astate.edu
Philip Hestand, Learning Disabilitty Specialist

Arranges for academic adjustments and auxiliary aids to be provided to qualified students and coordinates workplace accommodations. Will provide auxiliary aids, without cost, to those students with verified disabilities who require such services.

4057 Arkansas Tech University

1605 Coliseum Drive
Russellville, AR 72801   479-968-0389
                                 FAX 479-968-0208
          http://www.atu.edu
Janet Jones, Disabilities Coordinator

Provides equal opportunities for higher education to academically qualified individuals who are disabled. Students are integrated as completely as possible into the university community.

4058 Garland County Community College

101 College Drive
Hot Springs, AR 71913   501-760-4222
                                888-671-1229
                             FAX 501-760-4100
          http://www.gccc.cc.ar.us
Annette Smelser-Turk

Offers a variety of services to students with disabilities including note takers, extended testing time, counseling services and special accommodations.

4059 Harding University

900 E Center
Searcy, AR 72149   501-279-4028
                           800-477-4407
                        FAX 501-279-4217
          http://www.harding.edu
          e-mail: admission@harding.edu
Linda R Thompson, Dir. Student Support Services
Teresa McLead, Disabilities Specialist

Strives to deliver a program of services that will result in increasing the college retention and graduation rates of these students.

4060 Jones Learning Center

University of the Ozarks
415 N College Avenue
Clarksville, AR   72830

479-979-1403
800-264-8636
FAX 479-979-1429
http://www.ozarks.edu
e-mail: jlc@ozarks.edu

Julia Frost, Director
Debby Mooney, Assistant Director Center

An academic support unit that offers enhanced services to college students with diagnosed learning disabililtes or attention deficit disorder. Services are individualized and focus on the development of strategies and skills to build upon strengths and circumvent deficits. The ratio of professional full time staff to students is 1:4.

4061 Mississippi County Community College

PO Box 1109
Blytheville, AR   72316

870-762-1020
FAX 870-763-1654
http://www.mccc.cc.ar.us

Myles Jeffers, Special Services

Offers a variety of services to students with disabilities including note takers, extended testing time, counseling services and special accommodations.

4062 Philander Smith College

812 W 13th Street
Little Rock, AR   72202

501-370-5221
FAX 501-370-5225
http://www.philander.edu
e-mail: administrator@philander.edu

Dr. Dorothy Arnett, Director

Offers a variety of services to students with disabilities including notetakers, extended testing time, counseling services, and special accommodations.

4063 Sheldon Jackson College

801 Lincoln Street
Sitka, AK   99835

800-478-4556
FAX 907-747-6366
http://www.sj-alaska.edu
e-mail: yukonjohn@sj-alaska.edu

Alice Smith, Director

Seeks to help students find their forte, best learning modes, and best modes of expression; and seeks to help students prepare to find the greatest possible joy in vocation and service to others.

4064 Southern Arkansas University

PO Box 9371
Magnolia, AR   71753

870-235-4040
FAX 870-235-4931
http://www.saumag.edu
e-mail: pwwoods@saumag.edu

Paula Washington-Woods, Disability Support Services

Offers a variety of services to students with disabilities including notetakers, extended testing time, counseling services, and special accommodations.

4065 University of Arkansas

200 Silas Hunt Hall
Fayetteville, AR   72701

479-575-5346
800-377-8632
FAX 479-575-7515
http://www.uark.edu
e-mail: uafadmis@comp.uark.edu

Dawn Medley, Director Admissions

Offers a variety of services to students with disabilities including note takers, extended testing time, counseling services, and special accommodations.

4066 University of the Ozarks

415 College Avenue
Clarksville, AR   72830

501-979-1227
FAX 501-979-1355
http://www.ozarks.edu
e-mail: jdecker@ozarks.edu

Julia Frost, Director

A four-year college that provides a learning center for students with learning disabilities.

California

4067 Academy of Art College

Academy Resource Center
180 New Montgomery
San Francisco, CA   94015

415-263-8895
http://www.academyart.edu
e-mail: nhaughnes@academyart.edu

Natasha Haugnes, Academy Resource Director

4068 Allan Hancock College

800 S College Drive
Santa Maria, CA   93454

805-922-6966
FAX 805-922-3556

Mark Malangko, LAP Director

Students with mobility, visual, hearing and speech impairments, learning disabilities, acquired brain injury, developmental disabilities, psychological and other disabilities are eligible to receive special services which enable them to fully participate in the community college experience at Allan Hancock College.

4069 Antelope Valley College

3041 W Avenue K
Lancaster, CA   93536

661-722-6300
FAX 661-722-6361
http://www.avc.edu
e-mail: info@avc.edu

David Greenleaf, Learning Disability Specialist

A public two-year college with 228 learning disabled students out of a total of 11,105.

4070 Aria School

1601 Lane Street
San Francisco, CA   94124

415-330-3105
FAX 415-468-3273

Lorraine Petro, Contact

A two-year college that offers services and programs to disabled students.

4071   Bakersfield College

1801 Panorama Drive
Bakersfield, CA   93305   661-395-4011
                                 FAX 661-395-4500
                                 http://www.bc.cc.ca.us

Tim Bohan, Director

A public two-year college with 207 special education students out of a total of 12,312.

4072   Barstow Community College

Disabled Student Programs & Services
2700 Barstow Road
Barstow, CA   92311   619-252-2411
                                 FAX 619-252-1875
                                 http://www.barstow.cc.ca.us
                                 e-mail: dsps@barstow.cc.ca.us
Gene Pfeifer, Counselor
Gordon L Smith, LD Specialist

Educational support program for disabled students including special classes and support services for all disabled students.

4073   Bethany College

Special Advising
800 Bethany Drive
Scott Valley, CA   95066   408-438-3800
                                 800-843-9410
                                 FAX 408-438-4517
                                 http://www.bethany.edu
Kathy Tagg, Director
Barbara Van Beveren, Special Advising Counselor

An independent four-year college with support services for special education students.

4074   Biola University

13800 Biola Avenue
La Mirada, CA   90639   562-903-6000
                                 FAX 562-903-4709
                                 http://www.biola.edu
                                 e-mail: tom-engle@peter.biola.edu
Tim Engle, Coordinator

Christian liberal arts university responsible for all programs related to students with disabilities.

4075   Butte College

3536 Butte Campus Drive
Oroville, CA   95965   530-895-2511
                                 FAX 530-895-2345
                                 http://www.cin.butte.cc.ca.us
Richard Dunn, LD Specialist

A public two-year college with 223 special education students out of a total of 12,848.

4076   Cabrillo College

3500 Soquel Drive
Aptos, CA   95003   831-479-6390
                                 FAX 831-479-6393
                                 http://www.cabrillo.cc.ca.us
                                 e-mail: frlynch@cabrillo.cc.ca.us
Frank Lynch, Director

4077   California Lutheran University

60 W Olsen Road
Thousand Oaks, CA   91360   805-493-3260
                                 FAX 805-493-3114
                                 http://www.clunet.edu
                                 e-mail: cluadm@clunet.edu
Gerald Swanson

Offers a variety of services to students with disabilities including notetakers, extended testing time, counseling services, and special accommodations.

4078   California Polytechnic State University: San Luis Obispo

Disability Resource Center
1 Grand Avenue
San Luis Obispo, CA   93407   805-756-1111
                                 FAX 805-756-5400
                                 TDY:805-756-1395
                                 http://www.calpoly.edu
                                 e-mail: admissions@calpoly.edu
William Bailey, Director

Comprehensive program of academic advisement, disability management, and support services, including peer mentors; currently providing services to more than 350 students with learning disabilities, 700 students with various disabilities total.

4079   California State Polytechnic University: Pomona

3801 W Temple Avenue
Pomona, CA   91768   909-468-5020
                                 FAX 909-869-4529
                                 http://www.csupomona.edu
                                 e-mail: cppadmit@csupomona.edu
Fred Henderson, Director

Offers a variety of services to students with disabilities including notetakers, extended testing time, counseling services, and special accommodations.

4080   California State University: Bakersfield

Services for Students with Disabilities
9001 Stockdale Highway
Bakersfield, CA   93311   661-664-3360
                                 FAX 661-664-2171
                                 http://www.csubak.edu
                                 e-mail: jclausen@csub.edu
Janice Clausen, Director

Four year college which provides services to the learning disabled.

4081   California State University: Chico

400 W 1st Street
Chico, CA   95929   530-898-4428
                                 FAX 530-898-6456
Billie Jackson, Director

To facilitate accommodation requests and provide the support services necessary to ensure equal access to university programs for students with disabilities.

4082 California State University: Dominguez Hills

1000 E Victoria Street
Carson, CA   90747   310-243-3660
                                      FAX 310-516-4247
                                      http://www.csudh.edu
                                      e-mail: pwells@csudh.edu
Patricia Ann Wells, Director

The purpose of the Disabled Student Services (DSS) program is to make all of the University's educational, cultural social and physical facilities available to students with disabilities. The program serves as a centralized source of information for students with disabilities and those who work with them. By providing support services, DSS assists students with disabilities in the enhancement of their academic, career and personal development.

4083 California State University: Fresno

Services for Students with Disabilities
5200 N Barton
Fresno, CA   93740   559-278-6511
                                      FAX 559-278-4214
                                      http://ww.csufresno.edu
                                      e-mail: pat_blore@csufresno.edu
Four year college that provides students with services for the learning disabled.

4084 California State University: Fullerton

Disabled Student Services
University Hall 101
Fullerton, CA   92834   714-278-3117
                                      FAX 714-278-2408
                                      TDY:714-278-2786
                                      http://www.fullerton.edu
Doug Liverpool, Counselor
Debra Fletcher, Learning Disabilities Specialist

A public four-year college with 500 special education students out of a total of 29,000. The Office of Disabled Student Services aims to increase access and retention for students with permanent and temporary disabilities by ensuring equitable treatment in all aspects of campus life. Provides co-curricular and academically related services which empower students with disabilities to achieve academic and personal self-determination.

4085 California State University: Hayward

Student with Disability Resource Center
25800 Carlos Bee Boulevard
Hayward, CA   94542   520-885-3868
                                      FAX 510-885-7400
                                      http://www.csuhayward.edu
                                      e-mail: rwong@csuhayward.edu
Russell Wong, Learning Resources Counselor

4086 California State University: Long Beach

Stephen Benson Program
1250 Bellflower Boulevard
Long Beach, CA   90840   562-985-4430
                                      FAX 562-985-7183
                                      http://www.csulb.edu
                                      e-mail: bcarey@csulb.edu
Brian Carey MFT, Learning Disability Specialist

Four-year college offers a program for the learning disabled.

4087 California State University: Northridge

PO Box 1286
Northridge, CA   91328   818-677-3773
                                      FAX 818-677-4665
                                      http://www.csun.edu
                                      e-mail: lorraine.newlon@csun.edu
Lee Axelrod, Learning Disability Director

To assist students with learning disabilities in reaching their full potential, the program offers a comprehensive and well-coordinated system of educational support services that allow students to be judged on the basis of their ability rather than disability.

4088 California State University: Sacramento

Services to Students with Disabilities
6000 J Street
Sacramento, CA   95819   916-278-6955
                                      FAX 916-248-7825
                                      http://www.csus.edu
                                      e-mail: cronink@csus.edu
Kathleen A Cronin-Brown, Learning Disabilities Specialist

Offers a variety of services to students with disabilities including notetakers, extended testing time, counseling services, and special accommodations.

4089 California State University: San Bernardino

5500 University Parkway
San Bernardino, CA   92407   909-880-5000
                                      FAX 909-880-5200
                                      http://www.csusb.edu
                                      e-mail: cppadmit@csupomona.edu
Nicholas Erickson, Director

Dedicated to assuring each student an opportunity to experience equity in education .

4090 California State University: San Marcos

Disabled Student Services
San Marcos, CA   92096   760-750-4905
                                      FAX 760-750-3445
                                      http://www2.csusm.edu
                                      e-mail: kkornher@csusm.edu
Dr. Kara Kornher, Psychologist

Four year college that offers its learning disabled student support and services.

4091 California State University: Stanislaus

801 W Monte Vista Avenue
Turlock, CA   95382   209-667-3159
                                      FAX 209-667-3585
                                      http://www.csstan.edu
                                      e-mail: areith@stan.csustan.edu
Dr Anne Reith, Specialist

A public four-year college with 31 special education students out of a total of 4,293.

4092 Canada College

4200 Farm Hill Boulevard
Redwood City, CA   94061   650-306-3100
                                 FAX 650-306-3457
                    http://www.canadacollege.net
                    e-mail: hetrick@smccd.net
Jane Hetrick, DSPS Program Coordinator

Three unique programs that serve eligible students
with disabilities: the Physically Challenged Program,
the Learning Achievement Program and the Adaptive
P.E. Program.

4093 Cerritos College

11110 Alondra Boulevard
Norwalk, CA   90650   562-860-2451
                                 FAX 562-467-5071
                     http://www.cerritos.edu
Al Spetrino, Program Head

A public two-year college with 63 special education
students out of a total of 20,679.

4094 Chaffey Community College District

Disabled Students Programs and Services
5885 Haven Avenue
Rancho Cucamonga, CA   91737   909-941-2379
                                FAX 909-466-2834
                     http://www.chaffey.cc.ca.us
Sharlene Smith, Director

Chaffey College's Disabled Student Programs and
Services (DSP&S) offer instruction and support services to students with developmental, learning, physical, psychological disabilities or aquired brain injury.
Students can recieve a variety of services such as: test
facilitation, note taking, tutoring, adaptive physical
education, pre-vocational training, career preparation, and job placement.

4095 Chapman University

One University Drive
Orange, CA   92666   714-997-6828
                                 FAX 714-532-6079
                     http://www.chapman.edu

Anthony Garcia

Offers a variety of services to students with disabilities including note takers, extended testing time,
counseling services and special accommodations.

4096 College of Alameda

555 Atlantic Avenue
Alameda, CA   94501   510-522-7221
                                 FAX 510-769-6019
          http://www.peralta.cc.ca.us/coa/coa.htm
Pat Smith, LD Specialist

Accommodations, assessment and special classes are
provided for learning disabled students enrolled at
College Alameda, a 2 year college located by San
Francisco Bay.

4097 College of Marin

Disabled Students Program
Kentfield, CA   94904   415-485-9406
                                 FAX 415-457-4791
                     http://www.marin.cc.ca.us
                     e-mail: rfb@marin.cc.ca.us
Marie McCarthy, Coordinator

Offers a variety of services to students with disabilities including note takers, extended testing time,
counseling services, and special accommodations.
Also offers diagnostic testing and remedial classes for
learning disabled students.

4098 College of San Mateo

1700 W Hillsdale Boulevard
San Mateo, CA   94402   650-574-6433
                                 FAX 650-358-6806
                     http://www.smcccd.cc.ca.us
Marie Paparelli, LD Specialist

Primary objective of the Disabled Students Pro-
gram-Learning Disabilities Center is to assist the student in achieving academic, vocational, personal and
social success. This is best accomplished by integration into the mainstream of college classes and services. The learning disabilities program provides
support services in the following areas: assessment
and evaluation, specialized tutoring, test accommodations, computer access and more.

4099 College of the Canyons

27801 N Dickason Drive
Valencia, CA   91355   661-294-1188
                                 FAX 661-294-3828
                     http://www.coc.cc.ca.us
Dr. Nina Nashur, Coordinator

A public two-year college with 45 special education
students out of a total of 6,255.

4100 College of the Desert

43500 Monterey Avenue
Palm Desert, CA   92260   760-773-2596
                                 FAX 760-776-0128
                     http://www.desert.cc.ca.us/
Dr. Frank Siehien, LD Specialist

Offers a variety of services to students with disabilities including note takers, extended testing time,
counseling services and special accommodations.

4101 College of the Redwoods: Learning Skills Center

7351 Tompkins Hill Road
Eureka, CA   95501   707-476-4280
                                 800-641-0400
                                 FAX 707-476-4418
                                 TDY:707-476-4284
                     http://www.redwoods.cc.ca.us
Trish Blair, LD Specialist

Mission is to assist individual students in the development of a realistic self-concept, assist in the development of educational interests and employment goals,
provide the advice, counseling, and equipment necessary to facilitate success, starting with specialized assistance in the registration process.

4102 College of the Sequoias

Disabiity Resource Center
915 S Mooney Boulevard
Visalia, CA 93277   559-730-3805
                                           FAX 559-730-3803
Don Mast, Dean

A public two-year college with approximately 600
special education students out of a total of 10,300.

4103 College of the Siskiyous

800 College Avenue
Weed, CA 96094   530-938-4461
                                           FAX 530-938-5367
                                    http://www.siskiyous.edu
                                   e-mail: ar@siskiyous.edu
Karen Zeigler, Director

Dedicated to meeting the needs of students with disabilities.

4104 Columbia College

11600 Columbia College Drive
Sonora, CA 95370   209-533-5133
                                           FAX 209-588-5104
                          http://www.columbia.yosemite.cc.ca.us.
Suzanne Patterson, LD Specialist

Offers a variety of services to students with disabilities including note takers, extended testing time,
counseling services and special accommodations.

4105 Contra Costa College

2600 Mission Bell Drive
San Pablo, CA 94806   510-235-7800
                                           FAX 510-236-6768
                            http://www.contracosta.cc.ca.us/
Peggy Fleming, Learning Specialist

Offers a variety of services to students with disabilities including notetakers, extended testing time, counseling services, and special accommodations.

4106 Cosumnes River College

1410 Ethan Allan Way
Sacramento, CA 95823   916-563-3241
                                           FAX 916-563-3264
                             http://www.crc.bsrios.cc.ca.us
                             e-mail: rebrac@losrois.org
Paris Greenlee, Director

A public two-year college with 150 learning disabled
students out of a total of 10,000.

4107 Crafton Hills College

11711 Sand Canyon Road
Yucaipa, CA 92399   909-389-3209
                                           FAX 909-794-7881
                                    http://www.elac.cc.ca.us
Kristen Colvey, LD Specialist

A public two-year college with 52 special education
students out of a total of 5,732.

4108 Cuesta College

Disabled Student Programs & Services
PO Box 8106
San Luis Obispo, CA 93403   805-546-3148
                                           FAX 805-546-3930
                                    http://www.cuesta.cc.ca.us
                            e-mail: llong@bass.cuesta.cc.ca.us
Dr. Lynn Frady, Director

A public, two-year community college, offering instruction and services to students with learning disabilities since 1973. A comprehensive set of services
and special classes are available. Contact the program
for further information.

4109 De Anza College: Special Education Division

21250 Stevens Creek Boulevard
Cupertino, CA 95014   650-723-1066
                                           FAX 650-725-5301
                                    http://www.deanza.fhda.edu
Suzanne Caillat, Office Manager
Pauline Waathiq, Director

A public two-year college with 300 special education
students out of a total of 20,000.

4110 Diablo Valley College

321 Golf Club Road
Plesant Hill, CA 94523   925-685-1230
                                           FAX 925-687-1829
                                         http://www.dvc.edu
Terry Armstrong, Manager

Disabled Student Program & Services (DSPS) is a
program that is designed to ensure that students with
disabilities have equal access to all of the educational
offerings at Diablo Valley College. We facilitate
equal opportunity through the provision of appropriate support services, curriculum, instruction and
adaptive technology.

4111 East Los Angeles College

1301 Avenida Cesar Chavez
Monterey Park, CA 91754   323-265-8758
                                           FAX 323-265-8759
                                    http://www.elac.cc.ca.us
Marilyn Hutchens, Contact

A public two-year college with 44 special education
students out of a total of 14587. There is a an additional fee for the special education program in addition to the regular tuition.

4112 Educational Psychology Clinic

California State University, Long Beach
1250 N Bellflower Boulevard
Long Beach, CA 90840   562-985-4111
                                           FAX 562-985-5804
                            e-mail: magaddin@csulb.edu
Tami Shirron, Graduate Assistant
Dr. Michael Bernard, Clinic Director

A primary training site for the school psychology,
counseling, and special education programs while
providing comprehensive educational and psychological services to school age children and their families
at a moderate cost. Services at the clinic are provided
by graduate students under supervision by faculty in
the college of education.

4113 El Camino Community College

16007 Crenshaw Boulevard
Torrance, CA 90506   310-532-3670
FAX 310-660-3818
http://www.elcamino.edu
Dave Snowden, Admissions/Records

Offers a variety of services to students with disabilities including note takers, extended testing time, counseling services, and special accommodations.

4114 Evergreen Valley College

3095 Yerba Buena Road
San Jose, CA 95135   408-274-7900
FAX 408-223-9351
http://www.euc.edu
Bonnie Clark, LD Specialist

A public two-year college with 82 learning disabled students out of a total of 9,000.

4115 Excelsior Academy

7202 Princess View Drive
San Diego, CA 92120   619-583-6762
FAX 619-583-6764
http://www.excelsioracademy.com
e-mail: nanmag@earthlink.net

4116 Feather River College

570 Golden Eagle Avenue
Quincy, CA 95971   530-283-0202
FAX 530-283-3757
http://www.frcc.cc.ca.us
Maureen McPhee, Contact

Offers a variety of services to students with disabilities including note takers, extended testing time, counseling services and special accommodations.

4117 Foothill College

12345 El Monte Road
Los Altos Hills, CA 94022   650-949-7017
FAX 650-9171064
http://www.foothill.fhda.edu
e-mail: dobbinsmargo@fhda.edu
Margo Dobbins, Coordinator DSP

Offers a variety of services to students with disabilities including note takers, extended testing time, counseling services and special accommodations.

4118 Fresno City College

1101 E University Avenue
Fresno, CA 93741   559-442-8207
FAX 559-265-5784
http://www.fcc.cc.ca.us
e-mail: pio571@sccd.com
Jeanette Imperatrice, LD Specialist

A public two-year college with 259 special education students out of a total of 17,949.

4119 Fullerton College

Learning Resource Services
321 E Chapman Avenue
Fullerton, CA 92832   714-992-7270
FAX 714-447-4097
http://www.fullcoll.edu
Thomas Cantrell, Contact

A public two-year college with 281 special education students out of a total of 20,731.

4120 Gavilan College

5055 Santa Teresa Boulevard
Gilroy, CA 95020   408-848-4755
FAX 408-846-4944
http://www.gavilan..cc.ca.us
Dr. Carol Cooper, Coordinator

Offers a variety of services to students with disabilities including note takers, extended testing time, counseling services and special accommodations.

4121 Hartnell College

Learning Disability Services
156 Homestead Avenue
Salinas, CA 93901   831-755-6721
http://www.hartnell.cc.ca.us
Deborah Shulman, Enabler

A public two-year college with 72 special education students out of a total of 7,593.

4122 Humboldt State University

Disability Resource Center
Arcata, CA 95521   707-826-4678
FAX 707-826-5397
TDY:707-826-5392
http://www.sdrc.humboldt.edu
e-mail: rdm7001@humbolde.edu
Ralph McFarland, Director

A public four-year university which provides necessary services and assistance to students with disabilities, through their Disabled Students Services Program. Services are intended to offset the intrusiveness of the disability on a student's academic experience.

4123 Imperial Valley College

PO Box 158
Imperial, CA 92251   760-352-8320
FAX 760-355-2663
http://www.imperial.cc.ca.us
Norma Nava-Pinuleas, Instructional Specialist

A public two-year college with 44 special education students out of a total of 5,230.

4124 Institute for the Redesign of Learning

The Almansor Center
1137 Huntington Drive
South Pasadena, CA 91030   323-341-5580
FAX 323-257-0284
http://www.redesignlearning.org
Nancy Lavelle, Contact

A full day school serving 100 boys and girls, at-risk infants and children. Vocational Program serves adults and includes Supported Employment Services and an Independent Living Program.

4125 Irvine Valley College

5500 Irvine Center Drive
Irvine, CA   92618   949-451-5100
                                    FAX 949-451-5386
                              http://www.ivc.cc.ca.us
Julie Willard, LD Specialist

The goal is to effectivly provide assistance to all students with disabilities to achieve academic success while at Irvine Valley. The primary function is to accommodate a student's disability, whether it is a physical, communication, learning or psychological disability.

4126 Laney College

900 Fallon Street
Oakland, CA   94607   510-464-3162
                                    FAX 510-986-6906
                          http://www.laney.parita.cc.ca.us
Sondra Neiman, LD Specialist

A public two-year college with 58 special education students out of a total of 11,808.

4127 Long Beach City College Pacific Coast Campus

4351 Faculty Avenue
Long Beach, CA   90806   562-938-5020
                                    FAX 562-938-5030
                          http://www.dsps.lbcc.cc.ca.us
                            e-mail: dhansch@lbcc.ca.us
Mark Matsui, Disibility Student Service
Marvin Mastros, LD Specialist

Disabled Student Services (DSPS) is a program within Student Services at LBCC. DSPS provides many support services that enable students with disability related limitations to participate in the college's programs and activities. DSPS offers a wide range of services that compensate for a students limitations, like note taking assistance, interpretive services, alternative media, etc.

4128 Los Angeles City College

Learning Disabilities Program
855 N Vermont Avenue
Los Angeles, CA   90029   323-953-4208
                                    FAX 323-953-4526
                              http://www.lacc.cc.ca.us
Susan Matranga, LD Specialist

A public two-year college with 175 students with learning disabilities; total student body is 16,000. The Learning Disabilities Program provides assessment for eligibility in the program, support services, accommodations, and special classes in study skills and problem solving.

4129 Los Angeles Mission College: Disabled Student Programs and Services

13356 Eldridge Avenue
Sylmar, CA   91342   818-364-7732
                                    FAX 818-364-7755
                                     TDY:818-364-7861
                      http://www.lamission.cc.ca.us/front/dsps#
Dr. Rick Scuderi, Director

A support system that enables students to fully participate in the college's regular programs and activities. We provide a variety of services from academic and vocational support to assistance with finacial aid. All services are individulalized according to specific needs. They do not replace regular programs, but rather, accommodate students special requirements.

4130 Los Angeles Pierce College

6201 Winnetka Avenue
Woodland Hills, CA   91371   818-889-3055
                                    FAX 818-706-1350
                             http://www.peircecollege.com
David Phoenix, Contact

A public two-year college with 257 special education students out of a total of 19,207.

4131 Los Angeles Valley College

Disabled Student Programs & Services
5800 Fulton Avenue
Van Nuys, CA   91401   818-947-2600
                                    FAX 818-947-2680
                              http://www.lavc.cc.ca.us
Kathleen Sullivan, Coordinator

Provides specialized support services to students with disabilities which are in addition to the regular services provided to all students. Special accommodations and services are determined by the nature and extent of the disability related educational limitations of the student and are provided based upon the recommendation of DSPS.

4132 Los Medanos College

2700 E Leland Road
Pittsburg, CA   94565   925-439-2181
                                    FAX 925-427-1599
                              http://www.losmedanos.net
Dorrie Fisher, Contact

A public two-year college with 177 special education students out of a total of 7,784.

4133 Loyola Marymount University

7900 Loyola Boulevard
Los Angeles, CA   90045   310-338-2750
                                    FAX 310-338-2797
                                    http://www.lmu.edu
                         e-mail: admissns@lmumail.lmu.edu
Patricia Robbins, Director

Provides specialized assistance and resources that enable students with physical, perceptual, emotional and learning disabilities to achieve maximum independence while they pursue their educational goals.

4134 Master's College

21726 Placerita Canyon Road
Santa Clarita, CA 91321   661-362-5554
                                 FAX 661-362-5555
                                 http://www.master.edu
Donna Hall, Contact

An independent two-year college with 5 special education students out of a total of 850. There is an additional fee for the special education program in addition to the regular tuition.

4135 Mendocino College

PO Box 3000
Ukiah, CA 95482   707-468-3151
                             FAX 707-468-3120
                             http://www.mendocino.cc.ca.us
Kathleen Daigle, Specialist

A two-year public college that offers programs for the disabled.

4136 Menlo College

Academic Success Program
1000 El Camino Real
Atherton, CA 94027   650-688-3854
                             FAX 650-462-1932
                             http://www.menlo.edu
                             e-mail: admissions@menlo.edu
Mark Hager, Director

Four year college that offers a program for learning disabled students.

4137 Merced College

3600 M Street
Merced, CA 95348   209-384-6155
                             FAX 209-384-6103
                             http://www.merced.cc.ca.us

Students with physical, communicative, learning, and or psychological disabilities are encouraged to contact the Disabled Student Services Office. Students with verified disabilities are provided with services to meet their particular needs. These include, but are not limited to, counseling, instructional aids, interpeters for the deaf, registration assistance, computer access through the High Tech Center, learning strategies instruction, and test proctoring.

4138 Merritt College

Disabled Student Programs & Services
12500 Campus Drive
Oakland, CA 94619   510-531-4911
                            FAX 510-434-3870
                            http://www.merritt.edu
Mary McGrath, LD Specialist

A public two-year college with 78 special education students out of a total of 6,688.

4139 Mills College

5000 MacArthur Boulevard
Oakland, CA 94613   510-430-2264
                            FAX 510-430-3235
                            http://www.mills.edu
                            e-mail: ruthm@mills.edu
Ruth Masayko, Director

Services provided to disabled students.

4140 Miracosta College

1 Barnard Drive
Oceanside, CA 92056   760-757-2121
                             888-201-8480
                             FAX 760-967-6420
                             TDY:760-439-1060
                             http://www.miracosta.cc.ca.us
Nancy Schafer, LD Specialist

A community college which provides in-class academic accommodations to students with verified disabilities.

4141 Modesto Junior College

435 College Avenue
Modesto, CA 95350   209-575-6225
                             FAX 209-575-6852
                             TDY:209-575-6863
Derek Waring, Dean Special Services

The primary purposes of the Disability Services Center at Modesto Junior College are to provide students with disabilities access to post-secondary education and educational development opportunities, through supportive service and or instruction, depending on individual needs; and to improve campus and community understanding of the needs of students who have disabilities.

4142 Monterey Peninsula College

980 Fremont Street
Monterey, CA 93940   831-645-1357
                             FAX 831-645-1390
                             http://www.mpc.edu
Bill Jones, LD Coordinator

A public two-year college with 202 special education students out of a total of 8,502.

4143 Moorpark College

7075 Campus Road
Moorpark, CA 93021   805-378-1434
                             FAX 805-378-1563
                             http://www.moorpark.cc.ca.us
Joanna Dillon, Contact

A public two-year college with 154 special education students out of a total of 12,414.

4144 Mt. San Antonio Community College

Disabled Student Programs & Services
1100 N Grand Avenue
Walnut, CA 91789   909-594-5611
                             FAX 909-468-3943
                             http://dsps.mtsac.edu
                             e-mail: ghanson@mtsac.edu
Grace T Hanson, Director
James Andrews, Counselor LD Specialist
Clifford Stewart, LD Specialist

A public two-year college with 1,300 students with disabilities who receive special services. Total population of students is approximately 40,000.

4145 Mt. San Jacinto College

1499 N State Street
San Jacinto, CA   92583   909-487-6752
                                  FAX 909-487-1452
                                  http://www.msjc.cc.ca.us
Milly Douthit, LD Specialist

A public two-year college with 98 special education
students out of a total of 9,000 students.

4146 Napa Valley College

2277 Napa Valley Highway
Napa, CA   94558   707-253-3117
                                  800-826-1077
                                  FAX 707-253-3116
                                  http://www.nuc.cc.ca.us
Dr. Gwynne Katz, LD Specialist

Offers a variety of services to students with disabilities including note takers, extended testing time,
counseling services and special accommodations.

4147 Ohlone College

43600 Mission Boulevard
Fremont, CA   94539   510-659-7362
                                  FAX 510-6057
                http://www.ohlone.cc.ca.us/org/dsps
Fred Hilke, Special Services

The Ohlone College Disabled Student Services Program is designed to open doors to educational and occupational opportunities for students with physical or
medical disabilities. Our primary purpose is to provide an opportuninty for all individuals to gain
maximun benefit from their educational experience.
Ohlone College encourages students with physical or
medical disabilities to participate within the limits of
their disabilities in the same activies and courses as
other students.

4148 Orange Coast College

2701 Fairview Road
Costa Mesa, CA   92626   714-432-5047
                                  FAX 714-432-5609
                                  http://www.occ.cccd.edu
                                  e-mail: mcucurny@cccd.edu
Dr. Ken Ortiz, Associate Dean

A public two-year college with 350 special education
students out of a total of 27,960. There is a an additional fee for the special education program in addition to the regular tuition.

4149 Oxnard College

4000 S Rose Avenue
Oxnard, CA   93033   805-986-5800
                                  FAX 805-986-5806
                                  e-mail: ocinfo@vcccd.net
Carole Frick, LD Specialist
Ellen Young, Coordinator

Offers a complete repertoire of support services for
students with disabilities, including linkage with the
local department of rehabilitation. Special instruction
and high tech center available.

4150 Pacific Union College

One Angwin Avenue
Angwin, CA   94508   707-965-7364
                                  FAX 707-965-6797
                                  http://www.puc.edu
                                  e-mail: njacobo@puc.edu
Nancy Jacobo, Director Enrollment Services

Services provided to students with learning disabilities.

4151 Palomar College

1140 W Mission Road
San Marcos, CA   92069   760-744-1150
                                  FAX 760-591-9108
                                  http://www.palomar.edu
Ronald Haines, Disabled Student Programs

A public two-year college with 993 special education
students out of a total of 23,909.

4152 Pasadena City College

1570 E Colorado Boulevard
Pasadena, CA   91106   626-585-7127
                                  FAX 626-585-7566
                                  TDY:626-585-7052
                                  http://www.paccd.cc.ca.us
                                  e-mail: elweller@paccd.cc.ca.us
Dr. Emy Lu Weller, Teacher Specialist/Professor

A public two-year college with over 500 students with
learning disabilities of over 24,000 credit students.

4153 Pepperdine University

24255 Paific Coast Highway
Malibu, CA   90263   310-456-4269
                                  FAX 310-456-4827

4154 Porterville College

100 E College Avenue
Porterville, CA   93257   559-791-2200
                                  FAX 559-784-4779
                                  http://www.pc.cc.ca.us
                                  e-mail: dallen@pc.cc.ca.us
Diane Allen, LD Specialist

A public two-year college with 90 learning disabled
students. Services include assessment, special counseling, liaison with campus and community,
notetakers, readers, registration assistance, test taking assistance, transcription and tutoring.

4155 Rancho Santiago College

901 Esanta Ana Boulevard
Santa Ana, CA   92706   714-564-5250
                                  FAX 714-564-5479
                                  http://www.rsccd.org
Mary Kobane, LD Specialist

A public two-year college with 319 special education
students out of a total of 26,393.

4156 Rancho Santiago Community College
150 W 17th Street
Santa Ana, CA   92706   714-564-6000
                               FAX 714-564-5479
                               http://www.rsccd.org
Ann Vescial, Coordinator

The mission of Rancho Santiago Community College District is to respond to the educational needs of an everchanging community and to provide programs and services that reflect academic excellence. The district's two colleges promote open access and celebrate the diversity of both its students and staff, as well as the community.

4157 Raskob Learning Institute and Day School
3520 Mountain Boulevard
Oakland, CA   94619   510-436-1275
                             FAX 510-436-1106
                 e-mail: raskobinstitute@hnc.edu
Dr. Gary Yee, Executive Director
Rachel Hallanger, Head Teacher

A nonprofit, nondenominational service for children and adults with learning problems in the areas of reading, spelling, writing, language and mathematics. Diagnostic evaluation, remedial instruction, full-time comprehensive educational program. On the campus of Holy Names College in the Oakland Hills.

9-14 years old

4158 Reedley College
995 N Reed Avenue
Reedley, CA   93654   559-638-3641
                             FAX 559-638-5040
                http://www.reedleycollege.com
       e-mail: janice.emerzian@reedleycollege.edu
Dr. Janice Emerzian, District Director

Offer various services including: academic advising; adapted computer equipment; adapted physical education; books-on-tape and other educational aids; cooperative accommodations with instructors; educational limitations and accommodation notices to instructors; interpreters; learning disability assessment; liaison and referral to on-campus and off-campus resources; mobility assistance; notetakers; personal counseling and typing services.

4159 Roosevelt Center at Cypress College
9200 Valley View Street
Cypress, CA   90630   714-484-7104
                             FAX 714-826-4042
                             TDY:714-761-0961
Cindy Owens, LD Specialist

The Roosevelt Center provides testing to determine eligibility for LD services. For those students with verified learning disabilities, services including tutoring, test accommodations, and adapted software.

4160 Saint Mary's College of California
1928 Saint Mary's Road
Morago, CA   94575   925-631-4358
                            FAX 925-631-4835
                http://www.stmarys-ca.edu
           e-mail: jparfitt@stmarys-ca.edu
Jeannie Chavez-Parfitt, Director

Four year college that provides support and services to its disabled students.

4161 San Diego City College
1313 12th Avenue
San Diego, CA   92101   619-388-3400
                               FAX 619-388-3501
               http://www.city.sdccd.cc.ca.us
Ken Mayer, Counselor

Offers a variety of services to students with disabilities including note takers, extended testing time, counseling services, and special accommodations.

4162 San Diego Miramar College
Disabled Students Programs & Services
10440 Black Mountain Road
San Diego, CA   92126   858-536-7212
                               FAX 858-536-4302
                               TDY:858-536-4301
               http://www.intergate.miramar
               e-mail: kdoorly@sdccd.com
Kathleen Doorly, Program Coordinator
Sandra Smith, DSPS Counselor/LD Specialist
Kandice Walker, DSPS Counselor

A public two-year college with 500 learning disabled students. These students receive services and accommodations appropriate for their success in college. Individual counseling, class advising and LD assessments are also available. Special classes are offered to support college courses.

4163 San Diego State University
Learning Disability Services
San Diego, CA   92182   619-594-7800
                               FAX 619-594-4802
                               http://www.sdsu.edu
               e-mail: admissions@sdsu.edu
Margo Behr, Director
Sandra Cook, Admissions Director

A public four-year college with 520 disabled students out of a total of 25,658.

4164 San Francisco State University
Disability Resource Center
1600 Holloway Avenue
San Francisco, CA   94132   415-338-6356
                                   FAX 415-338-1041
                   http://www.sfsu.edu
                   e-mail: defreese@sfsu.edu
Deidre Defreese, Director

A public four-year college with 400 special education students out of a total of 21,044.

4165 San Jose City College

2100 Moorpark Avenue
San Jose, CA 95128   408-298-2181
                                       FAX 408-338-0412
                                       http://www.sjcc.edu
Martha Glazer, LD Specialist

Offers a variety of services to students with disabilities including note takers, extended testing time, counseling services and special accommodations.

4166 San Jose State University

Disability Resource Center
1 Washington Square
San Jose, CA 95192   408-924-6000
                                       FAX 408-924-5999
                                       http://www.sjsu.edu
                                       e-mail: marty@drc.sjsu.edu
Martin Schulter, Director
John Bradbury, Admissions Director

A four-year public university with 600 out of 20,679 receiving disability services.

4167 Santa Ana College

17th At Bristol
Santa Ana, CA 92706   714-564-6971
                                       FAX 714-836-6696
                                       http://www.sacollege.org
Cheryl Dunn-Hoanzl

Offers a variety of services to students with disabilities including note takers, extended testing time, counseling services and special accommodations.

4168 Santa Barbara City College

721 Cliff Drive
Santa Barbara, CA 93109   805-965-0581
                                       FAX 805-884-4966
                                       TDY:805-962-4084
                                       http://www.sbcc.net
                                       e-mail: dspshelp@sbcc.edu
Mary Lawson, LD Specialist
Gerry Lewin, LD Specialist

Offers complete repertoire of support services for students with disabilities, including linkage with local department of rehabilitation. Special instruction available. High tech center.

4169 Santa Clara University

Disability Resources
500 El Camino Real
Santa Clara, CA 95053   408-554-4111
                                       FAX 408-554-2709
                                       http://www.scu.edu
                                       e-mail: eravenscroft@scu.edu
Ann Ravenscroft, Coordinator
Sandra Hayes, Admissions Director

Designated by the University to ensure access for all students with disabilities to all academic programs and University resources. Types of disabilities include medical, physical, psychological, attention deficit and learning disabilities. Reasonable accommodations are provided to minimize the effects of a student's disability and to maximize the potential for success.

4170 Santa Monica College

1900 Pico Boulevard
Santa Monica, CA 90405   310-434-4000
                                       FAX 310-434-3694
                                       http://www.smc.edu
George Marcopulos, Learning Specialist

A public two-year college with 300 students with learning disabilities out of a total of 26,361.

4171 Santa Rosa Junior College

Disability Resource Department
1501 Mendocino Avenue
Santa Rosa, CA 95401   707-527-4278
                                       800-564-7752
                                       FAX 707-527-4798
                                       http://www.santarosa.edu
                                       e-mail: kvigeland@santarosa.edu
Kari Vigeland, Director
Ricardo Navarrette, Admissions Director

A public two-year college with 300 special education students out of a total of 28,223.

4172 Shasta College

11555 Old Oregon Trail
Redding, CA 96003   530-225-4912
                                       FAX 530-225-4952
                                       http://www.shasta.cc.ca.us
                                       e-mail: info@shastacollege.edu
Parker Pollock, Handicapped Director

A public two-year college with 104 special education students out of a total of 12,822.

4173 Sierra College

Learning Opportunities Center
5000 Rocklin Road
Rocklin, CA 95677   916-781-0599
                                       FAX 916-789-2967
                                       http://www.sierra.cc.ca.us
                                       e-mail: jhirschinger@scmail.sierra.cc.ca.us
Jim Hirschinger, Director
Mandy Davis, Admissions Director

A public two-year college with 400 special education students out of a total of 17,000.

4174 Skyline College

Developmental Skills Program
3300 College Drive
San Bruno, CA 94066   650-738-4193
                                       FAX 650-738-4299
                                       http://www.skylinecollege.net
Linda Van Sciver, Coordinator

A public two-year college with 103 special education students out of a total of 9,023.

4175 Solano Community College

4000 Suisun Valley Road
Suisun City, CA 94585   707-864-7136
                                       FAX 707-864-0361
                                       http://www.solano.cc.ca.us
Ron Nelson, Contact

The LD Center offers eligibility assessment (students with average to above average intelligence with severe processing deficit(s) and severe aptitude-achievement discrepancies), and instruction in strategies and interventions to help the student become more successful in regular college classes. Academic and personal counseling from Disabled Student Programs Counselors are available. Support services such as notetaking, extended test time and other modifications are available.

4176 Sonoma State University

Disabled Student Services
1801 E Cotati Avenue
Rohnert Park, CA   94928   707-664-2677
                                 FAX 707-664-2505
                                 TDY:707-664-2958
                                 http://www.sonoma.edu
                                 e-mail: bill.clopton@sonoma.edu
Linda Lipps, Director
Katharyn Crabbe, Admissions Director

A public four-year college with 230 disabled students out of a total of 6,211.

4177 Southwestern College

Diagnostic Learning Center
900 Otay Lakes Road
Chula Vista, CA   91910   619-482-6327
                                 FAX 619-482-6435
                                 http://www.swc.cc.ca.us
Diane Branman, Contact

A public two-year college with 99 special education students out of a total of 17,083.

4178 Spraings Academy

89 Moraga Way
Orinda, CA   94563   925-253-1906
                                 FAX 925-253-1907
Violet Spraings PhD, Director
Diane Emberlin, Assistant Director

This independent, nonprofit, co-educational day school serves students with learning disabilities and/or those needing a small, structured setting, individualization, and a low teacher/student ratio. Founded in 1967, it can help a few students find boarding situations so out of state and out of country students can attend the program.

4179 Springall Academy

6550 Soledad Mountain Road
La Jolla, CA   92037   858-459-9047
                                 FAX 858-459-4660
                                 http://www.springall.org
Dr. Arlene Baker, Executive Director

Offers a variety of services to students with disabilities including note takers, extended testing time, counseling services, and special accommodations. The academy is a nonprofit school for learning and behaviorally challenged students.

4180 Stanbridge Academy

515 E Poplar Avenue
San Mateo, CA   94401   650-375-5860
                                 FAX 650-375-5861
                                 http://www.stanbridgeacademy.org
                                 e-mail: info@stanbridgeacademy.org
Sanford Shapiro, Executive Director

4181 Stanford University

123 Meyer Library
Stanford, CA   94305   650-723-2273
                                 FAX 650-725-7411
                                 http://www.stanford.edu
Molly Sandperl, Special Services

An independent four-year college with 102 special education students out of a total of 6,527.

4182 Sterne School

2690 Jackson Street
San Francisco, CA   94115   415-922-6081
                                 FAX 415-922-1598
                                 http://www.sterneschool.org/
                                 e-mail: office@sterneschool.org

A private school serving students in 6-12 grade who have specific learning disabilities. Established in 1976.

4183 Taft College

29 Emmons Park Drive
Taft, CA   93268   661-763-7700
                                 FAX 661-763-7705
                                 http://www.taft.cc.ca.us/
Jeff Ross, Disabled Services

A public two-year college with 56 special education students out of a total of 952.

4184 UCLA Office for Students with Disabilities

405 Hilgard Avenue
Los Angeles, CA   90095   310-825-4321
                                 FAX 310-825-9656
                                 TDY:310-825-2833
                                 http://www.ucla.edu
                                 e-mail: jmorris@saonet.ucla.edu
Julie Morris, LD Program Coordinator

Offers a variety of services to students with disabilities including notetakers, accommodated testing, counseling services, assistive technology, support groups, advocacy to faculty, strategies, workshops and counseling.

4185 USC University Affiliated Program: Childrens Hospital at Los Angeles

University of Southern California
Mailstop #53
Los Angeles, CA   90054   213-740-2311
                                 FAX 323-663-6707
                                 http://www.usc.edu
Robert Jacobs, Director

The primary mission of the USC UAP is the continued improvement of the health and welfare of children and families who are affected by disabling conditions, chronic illness, or other special health care needs.

4186 United States International University

10455 Pomerado Road
San Diego, CA   92131   858-635-4598
                              FAX 858-635-4690
                              http://www.usiu.edu
Lorna Reese, Assistant Dean

Four year college offering services to disabled students.

4187 University Affiliated Mental Retardation Program

University of California at Los Angeles
760 Westwood Plaza
Los Angeles, CA   90095   310-825-8902
                                FAX 310-206-4446
James T McCracken, Director

4188 University of California-Davis: Student Disability Resource Center

One Shields Avenue
Davis, CA   95616   530-752-1011
                          FAX 530-752-0161
                          http://www.sdc.ucdavis.edu
Christine O'Dell, LD Specialist

Committed to ensuring equal educational opportunities for students with disabilities. Promotes independence and integrated participation in campus life for students with disabilities.

4189 University of California: Berkeley

Disabled Student's Program
110 Sproul Hall
Berkeley, CA   94720   510-642-0518
                             FAX 510-642-7333
                             http://www.berkeley.edu
                             e-mail: edrogers@uclink4.berkeley.edu
Ed Rogers, Director

A four-year public university.

4190 University of California: Irvine

Office for Disability Services
105 Administration Building
Irvine, CA   92697   949-824-7494
                           FAX 949-824-3083
                           TDY:949-824-6272
                           http://www.disability.uci.edu
                           e-mail: ods@uci.edu
Dr. Ron Blosser, Special Services

Our mission is to provide effective and reasonable academic accommodations and related disability services to UCI students, Extension and Summer Session students, and other program participants. Consults with and educates faculty about reasonable academic accommodations. Strives to improve access to UCI programs, activities, and facilities for students with disabilities. Advises and educates academic and administrative departments about access issues to programs or facilities.

4191 University of California: Irvine Campus

105 Administration Building
Irvine, CA   92717   949-824-3480
                           FAX 949-824-8566
                           http://www.uci.edu
Dr. Ron Blosser, Director

Offers a variety of services to students with disabilities including note takers, extended testing time, counseling services and special accommodations.

4192 University of California: Los Angeles

Office for Students with Disabilities
405 Hilgard Avenue
Los Angeles, CA   90095   310-825-1501
                                FAX 310-825-9656
                                http://www.ucla.edu
                                e-mail: kmolini@saonet.ucla.edu
Kathy Molini, Director
Joanne Woosley, Admissions Director

Served by a TWP learning disabilities specialist, UCLA offers a full range of accommodations and services. Services are individually designed, and include disability- related counseling, special test arrangements, notetaker services, readers, priority enrollment, adaptive technology, and individual small group and individual content area tutoring. An active support group and peer-mentor program provides opportunities for students to discuss mutual concerns and enhance learning strategies.

4193 University of California: Riverside

Disabled Student Services
900 University Avenue
Riverside, CA   92521   909-787-5330
                              FAX 909-787-4529
                              http://www.usr.edu
Marcia Theise Schiffer, Director DSS

A public four-year college with 25 learning disabled students out of a total of 8,000.

4194 University of California: San Diego

Office for Students with Disabilities
9500 Gilman Drive
La Jolla, CA   92093   858-534-4382
                             FAX 858-534-4650
                             http://www.ucsd.edu
                             e-mail: rgimblett@ucsd.edu
Roberta J Gimblett, Director
Mae Brown, Admissions Director
Naomi Levoy, Outreach Assistant

A public four-year college with 150 students receiving disability services out of 15,840.

4195 University of California: San Francisco

Office of Student Relations
500 Paranassus Avenue
San Francisco, CA   94143   415-476-4318
                                  FAX 415-476-7295
                                  TDY:415-476-4318
Eric Koenig, Director
Barbara Smith, Assistant Analyst
Candy Clemens, Adminstrative Assistant

The Office of Student Relations is responsible for coordinating Services for Students with Disabilities at UCSF.

4196 University of California: Santa Barbara

Disabled Student Program
1210 Cheadle Hall
Santa Barbara, CA   93106   805-893-2182
                                 FAX 805-893-7127
                                 TDY:805-893-2668
                                 http://www.ucsb.edu
                                 e-mail: batty-c@sa.ucsb.edu
Diane Glenn, Director

Works to increase the retention and graduation rates of students with disabilities and to foster student independence.

4197 University of California: Santa Cruz

140 Hahn
Santa Cruz, CA   95064   831-459-2743
                                 FAX 831-459-5077
                                 http://www.ucsc.edu
Sharyn Martin, Special Services

A public four-year college with 87 special education students out of a total of 9,162.

4198 University of Redlands

Academic Support Services/Disabled Student Service
1200 E Colton Avenue
Redlands, CA   92373   909-335-4079
                                 FAX 909-335-5297
                                 http://www.redlands.edu
                                 e-mail: judy.bowman@redlands.edu
Judy Bowman, Academic Support/Disabled Svcs.
Paul Driscoll, Admissions Director

Offers a variety of services to students with disabilities including notetakers, extended testing time, counseling services, and special accommodations.

4199 University of San Diego

9500 Gilman Drive
La Jolla, CA   92093   858-534-5149
                                 FAX 858-822-5407
                                 http://www.ucsd.edu
Dr. Tyler Gabriel, Academic Counseling

An independent four-year college with 35 special education students out of a total of 3,904.

4200 University of San Francisco

Learning Disability Services
2130 Fulton Street
San Francisco, CA   94117   415-422-6876
                                 FAX 415-422-5906
                                 http://www.usfca.edu
                                 e-mail: ongt@usfca.edu
Tom Merrell, Director

A four-year private college with 190 students recieving LD/ADHD services.

4201 University of Southern California

Disability Services and Programs
3601 Trousdale Parkway
Los Angeles, CA   90089   213-740-0776
                                 FAX 213-740-8216
                                 TDY:213-740-6948
                                 http://www.usc.edu
                                 e-mail: jeddy@usc.edu
Janet E Eddy PhD, LD Consultant
Laurel Tews, Admissions Director

An independent four-year university with 350 LD students out of a total of 15,705. The support structure for students with documented learning disabilities at USC is one that is totally individualized. Offers support at the student's request for such things as extended time for exams, proofreading papers and reports, and advocacy with faculty. There is no special admission process.

4202 University of the Pacific

Office of Special Services for Students with Dis.
3601 Pacific Avenue
Stockton, CA   95211   209-946-3221
                                 FAX 209-946-2278
                                 http://www.pacific.edu/education/ssd
                                 e-mail: hhouck@uop.edu
Lisa Cooper, Coordinator

Offers a variety of services to qualified students with disabilities on a case-by-case basis such as test proctoring services, note-taking assistance, priority registration or referrals to other campus services such as counseling and tuturial support.

4203 Vanguard University of Southern California

55 Fair Drive
Costa Mesa, CA   92626   714-556-3610
                                 FAX 714-966-5471
                                 http://www.vanguard.edu
                                 e-mail: jmireles@vanguard.edu
Jessica Mireles, Director

Four year college offers support for its disabled students.

4204 Ventura College

4667 Telegraph Road
Ventura, CA   93003   805-654-6400
                                 FAX 805-654-6466
                                 http://www.ventura.cc.ca.us
Dr. Jeff Barsch, LD Director

A public two-year college with 424 special education students out of a total of 12,153.

4205 Victor Valley College

18422 Bear Valley Road
Victorville, CA   92392   619-245-4271
                                 FAX 760-245-9744
                                 http://www.vvcconline.com
Susan Tillman, LD Specialist

Offers a variety of services to students with disabilities including note takers, extended testing time, counseling services and special accommodations.

4206 West Hills College

300 W Cherry Lane
Coalinga, CA 93210
559-935-0801
FAX 559-935-5655
http://www.westhills.cc.ca.us
Tom Winters, Contact

A public two-year college with 63 special education students out of a total of 3,530.

4207 West Los Angeles College

4800 Freshman Drive
Culver City, CA 90230
310-287-4200
FAX 310-287-4317
http://www.wlac.cc.ca.us
e-mail: regalaba@lacitycollege.edu
Frances Israel, Learning Specialist

A public two-year college with 104 special education students out of a total of 8,952.

4208 West Valley College

14000 Fruitvale Avenue
Saratoga, CA 95070
408-741-2564
FAX 408-867-5033
http://www.westvalley.edu/wcc/
Susan Bunch, LD Specialist

A public two-year college with 209 special education students out of a total of 1,429.

4209 Westmark School

5461 Louise Avenue
Encino, CA 91316
818-986-5045
FAX 818-986-2605
http://www.westmarkschool.org

4210 Whittier College

Learning Support Services
13406 Philadelphia Street
Whittier, CA 90608
562-907-4233
FAX 562-907-4980
http://www.whittier.edu
e-mail: tthomsen@whittier.edu
Jamie Shepard MA, Director

A four-year private college with 30 students recieving disability services out of 1,297.

Colorado

4211 Aims Community College

5401 W 20th Street
Greeley, CO 80632
970-330-8008
800-301-5388
FAX 970-339-6682
http://www.aims.edu
Donna Wright, LD Center

Offers a variety of services to students with disabilities including note takers, extended testing time, counseling services, and special accommodations.

4212 Arapahoe Community College

5900 S Santa Fe Drive
Littleton, CO 80120
303-797-0100
FAX 303-797-0127
http://www.arcpahoe.edu
Dr. Alex Labak, Contact

Offers a variety of services to students with disabilities including note takers, extended testing time, counseling services, and special accommodations.

4213 Colorado Christian University

Academic Support
160 S Garrison Street
Lakewood, CO 80226
303-963-3266
FAX 303-274-7560
http://www.ccu.edu
e-mail: jlambert@ccu.edu
Joanne Lambert, Assistance Coordinator

Four-year college that offers support to learning disabled students.

4214 Colorado Mountain College

Central Admissions Office
3000 County Road
Glenwood Springs, CO 81602
970-947-8253
800-621-8559
FAX 970-928-9668

The Disability Service Program at Colorado Mountain College is designed to assist students with disabilities to be successful in their programs. The program design offers students enhancement of basic skills, completion in a chosen area of study and removal of barriers in the classroom while preserving the integrity of the course objectives.

4215 Colorado Northwestern Community College

500 Kennedy Drive
Rangely, CO 81648
970-675-2261
800-562-1105
FAX 970-675-3330
http://www.cncc.cc.co.us
Mark Mascarenas, LD Director

A public two-year college with 11 special education students out of a total of 502.

4216 Colorado State University

Resources for Disabled Students
100 General Services
Fort Collins, CO 80523
970-491-6385
FAX 970-491-3457
TDY:970-491-6385
http://www.colostate.edu
e-mail: kivy@lamar.edu
Pat Hartman, Staff Assistant
Rosemary Creston, Director

The mission of Resources for Disabled Students (RDS) is to assist Colorado State University in ensuring that qualified students with disabilities are afforded and given access to the same, or equal, educational opportunities available to other university students.

4217 Community College of Aurora
16000 E Centre Tech Parkway
Aurora, CO 80011   303-360-4700
                          FAX 303-631-7432
                http://www.cca.cccoes.edu
Theresa Campbell, Contact

Offers a variety of services to students with disabilities including note takers, extended testing time, counseling services, and special accommodations.

4218 Community College of Denver
Special Learning Support Programs
PO Box 173363
Denver, CO 80217   303-556-2600
                          FAX 303-556-4563
Dr. Gary Macdonald, Coordinator

A public two-year college with 100 special education students out of a total of 6,000. There is an additional fee for the special education program in addition to the regular tuition.

4219 Denver Academy
1101 S Race Street
Denver, CO 80210   303-777-5870
                          FAX 303-777-5893
                http://www.denveracadamy.org
Lori Richardson

Denver Acadmy was founded in 1972 and is internationally recognized for the quality of its program. Our mission is to be a center of excellence for the education of students with learning differences in order to help them fully develop their intellectual, social, physical and moral potential thereby providing them with the necessary skill to be successful in life.

4220 Disability Services
University of Colorado at Colorado Springs
Main Hall 105
Colorado Springs, CO 80933   719-262-3354
                          FAX 719-262-3354
                http://www.uccs.edu/dss
                e-mail: disbserv@uccs.edu
Kaye Simonton MA, Coordinator Disability

Provides services and accommodations to students with disabilities, works closely with faculty and staff in an advisory capacity, assists in the development of reasonable accommodations for students and provides equal access for otherwise qualified individuals with disabilities.

4221 Fort Lewis College
1000 Rim Drive
Durango, CO 81301   970-247-7263
                          FAX 970-247-2703
                http://www.fortlewis.edu
                e-mail: admission@fortlewis.edu
Tim Slane, Disabled Student Director

Coordinates services at Fort Lewis for those students with disabilities, acts as liaison between students and faculty programs. Advises and directs those students to the appropriate services and academic advisors.

4222 Front Range Community College Progressive Learning
3645 W 112th Avenue
Westminster, CO 80031   303-460-1032
                          FAX 303-469-7143
                http://www.frcc.cc.co.us
Karol Janice Bennett, Education Assistant
Karen Hossack, Faculty

A public two-year college with a unique remedial program for all adults with learning disabilities. Enrollment is not necessary to attend Progressive Learning Program.

4223 John F Kennedy Child Development Center
University of Colorado Health Sciences Center
4200 E 9th Avenue
Denver, CO 80262   303-861-6410
                          FAX 303-764-8086
Cordelia Robinson, Director

4224 Lamar Community College
2401 S Main Street
Lamar, CO 81052   719-336-2248
                          800-968-6920
                          FAX 719-336-2448
                http://www.Icc.cccoes.edu
                e-mail: gary.hammar@lcc.ccoes.edu
Cynthia Baer, Director

Offers a variety of services to students with disabilities including notetakers, extended testing time, counseling services, and special accommodations.

4225 Morgan Community College
300 Main Street
Fort Morgan, CO 80701   970-867-3351
                          800-622-0216
                          FAX 970-867-3352
                http://www.mcc.cccoes.edu
Maxine Weimer, Developmental Education

A public two-year college with 11 special education students out of a total of 887.

4226 Northeastern Junior College
100 College Drive
Sterling, CO 80751   970-522-6600
                          800-626-4637
                          FAX 970-522-4945
                http://www.nejc.cc.co.us
Nancy Mann, Special Services

A public two-year college with 36 special education students out of a total of 2,042.

4227 Pikes Peak Community College
5675 S Academy Boulevard
Colorado Springs, CO 80906   719-540-7128
                          800-456-6847
                          FAX 719-540-7254
                http://www.ppcc.cocoes.edu
William Flynn, Coordinator

A public two-year college with 108 special education students out of a total of 6,517.

4228 Pueblo Community College

900 W Orman Avenue
Pueblo, CO 81004   719-549-3228
                    FAX 719-544-1179
                    http://www.pcc.cocoes.edu
Bob Van Alstyne, Contact

Offers a variety of services to students with disabilities including note takers, extended testing time, counseling services, and special accommodations.

4229 Red Rocks Community College

13300 W 6th Avenue
Lakewood, CO 80228   303-988-6160
                      FAX 303-914-6666
                      http://www.rrccc.cocoes.edu
Theona Hammond-Harns, Special Services

A public two-year college with 33 special education students out of a total of 6,300.

4230 Regis University

Disability Services
3333 Regis Boulevard
Denver, CO 80221   303-458-4941
                    FAX 303-964-3647
                    http://www.regis.edu
                    e-mail: koyler@regis.edu
KoKo Oyler, Director

A four-year private university with 110 students recieving disability services out of 1,022.

4231 Trinidad State Junior College

136 Main Street
Trinidad, CO 81082   719-846-5644
                      FAX 719-846-4550
                      http://www.tsjc.cccoes.edu/
John Giron, Special Services

Offers a variety of services to students with disabilities including note takers, extended testing time, counseling services, and special accommodations.

4232 University of Colorado at Boulder Disability Services

Academic Access and Resource Program (AAR)
107 UCB
Boulder, CO 80309   303-492-8671
                     FAX 303-492-5601
                     http://www.colorado.edu/disabilityservices
                     e-mail: dsinfo@colorado.edu
Jayne MacArthur, Coordinator AAR Program
Cindy Donahue, Director
Barbara Schneider, Admissions Director

Provides a variety of services to individuals with nonvisible disabilities, including individualized strategy sessions with a disability specialist, an assistive technology lab, a writing lab and a career program for students with disabilities. Disability specialists also assist with obtaining reasonable accommodations if documentation meets disability services requirements and supports the need for them.

4233 University of Colorado: Colorado Springs

Disability Services
PO Box 7150
Colorado Springs, CO 80933   719-262-3065
                              FAX 719-262-3354
                              http://www.uccs.edu
                              e-mail: ksimonto@mail.uccs.edu
Kaye Simonton, Director
Randy Kouba, Admissions Director

A four-year public university with 200 students receiving disability services out of 5,054.

4234 University of Denver

Learning Effectiveness Program
2199 S University Boulevard
Denver, CO 80208   303-871-2372
                    FAX 303-871-3938
                    http://www.du.edu
                    e-mail: tmay@du.edu
Ted F May, Director
John Dolan, Admissions Director

A fee for service program offering comprehensive, individualized services to University of Denver Students with learning disabilities and or ADHD. The LEP is part of a larger organization called University Disability Services.

4235 University of Northern Colorado

Disability Access Center
UNC Admissions Office
Greeley, CO 80639   970-351-2289
                     FAX 970-351-4166
                     http://www.unco.edu
                     e-mail: nlkauff@unco.edu
Nancy Kauffman, Director
Gary Gulickson, Admissions Director

Offers a variety of services to students with disabilities including notetakers, extended testing time, counseling services, and special accommodations.

4236 University of Southern Colorado

2200 Bonforte Boulevard
Pueblo, CO 81001   719-549-2581
                    877-872-9653
                    FAX 719-549-2195
                    http://www.uscolo.edu
                    e-mail: chambersp@uscolo.edu
Pam Chambers, Director
Pam Anastioussa, Admissions Director

Support services for special needs students are provided on an individual basis. The student must provide documentation of disability with a formal request for specific support services needed.

4237 Western State College of Colorado

600 N Adams Street
Gunnison, CO 81230   203-773-8539
                      800-876-5309
                      FAX 203-773-3117
                      http://www.western.edu
Jill Martinez, Advisor

A public four-year college with 59 special education students out of a total of 2,450.

Connecticut

4238 Albertus Magnus College

Director of the Academic Development Center
700 Prospect Street
New Haven, CT   06511   203-773-8590
                              FAX 203-773-3119
                              http://www.alberus.edu

Antonia Lewandowski

Offers a variety of services to students with disabilities including note takers, extended testing time, counseling services, and special accommodations.

4239 Asnuntuck Community Technical College

170 Elm Street
Enfield, CT   06082   860-253-3000
                              FAX 860-253-3063
                              http://www.acc.commnet.edu
Hassan Babatunji, Coordinator

The Academic Skills Center is offered to students with learning disabilities.

4240 Ben Bronz Academy

139 N Main Street
West Hartford, CT   06107   860-236-5807
                              FAX 860-233-9945
                              http://www.tli.com
                              e-mail: bba@tli.com

Aileen Stan-Spence, Director

Ben Bronz Acadamy is a day school for bright disabled students. Guides 60 students through an intensive school day that includes writing, mathematics, literature, science and social studies. Oral language is developed and stressed in all classes.

4241 Briarwood College

2279 Mount Vernon Road
Southington, CT   06489   860-628-4751
                              800-952-2444
                              FAX 860-628-6444
                              http://www.briarwood.edu
Cynthia Clarky, Disabilities Coordinator

Briarwood College is accredited by the New England Association of Schools and Colleges and the Connecticut State Board for Higher Education.   Indiviual progams are also accredited by organizations within their specific professions.

4242 Capitol Community-Tech College

401 Flatbush Avenue
Hartford, CT   06105   860-987-4891
                              FAX 860-987-4806

Virginia Foley-Psillas

Offers a variety of services to students with disabilities including note takers, extended testing time, counseling services, and special accommodations.

4243 Central Connecticut State University

1615 Stanley Street
New Britain, CT   06050   860-832-2278
                              FAX 860-832-2522
                              http://www.ccsu.edu

George Tenney, Director
Natalie Stimpson-Byers, Assistant Dean

Offers services and supports that promote educational equity for students with disabilities. Assistance includes arranging accommodations and auxillary aids that are necessary for students with disabilities to pursue their academic careers.

4244 Connecticut College

Office of Disability Services
270 Mohegan Avenue
New London, CT   06320   860-439-5428
                              FAX 860-439-5430
                              http://www.conncoll.edu
                              e-mail: slduq@conncoll.edu
Susan L Duques PhD, Director
Lee Coffin, Admissions Director

Offers a variety of services to students with disabilities including notetakers, extended testing time, counseling services, and special accommodations.

4245 Eastern Connecticut State University

Support Services Center
Willimantic, CT   06226   860-465-5573
                              FAX 860-465-0136
                              TDY:860-465-5799
                              http://www.ecsu.ctstateu.edu
                              e-mail: starrp@easternct.edu
Pamela Starr, Coordinator/Counselor

Academic support services are designed to provide equal access to the educational program. Each service must be approved by the OAS Coordinator and can be accessed by completing the appropriate service request form.

4246 Fairfield University

Office of Student Support Services
1073 N Benson Road
Fairfield, CT   06824   203-254-4000
                              FAX 203-254-4000
                              http://www.fairfield.edu
David Ryan-Soderlund, Assistant Director
Aloysius Kelley, President

Provides students with disabilities an equal opportunity to access the benefits, rights and privileges of Fairfield University's services, programs and activities in an accessible setting.

4247 Gateway Community-Tech College

60 Sargent Drive
New Haven, CT   06510   203-789-7071
                              FAX 203-777-8637
                              http://www.gwcc.commnet.edu
Shelley Heins RN, ADA Coordinator

Offers a variety of services to students with disabilities including extended testing time, counseling services, and special accommodations.

4248 Hartford College for Women

1265 Asylum Avenue
Hartford, CT   06105   860-236-1215
                                     FAX 860-768-5622
                   http://www.uhaweb.hartford.edu
                   e-mail: hcwinfo@mail.hartford.edu
Louise Loomis

Offers a variety of services to students with disabilities including note takers, extended testing time,
counseling services, and special accommodations.

4249 Housatonic Community Technical College

900 Lafayette Boulevard
Bridgeport, CT   06604   203-332-5000
                                     FAX 203-332-5123
                   http://www.hctc.commnet.edu
Peter G Anderheggen, Director

The Federally-funded Special Services Program
works to help students do well at Housatonic, stay in
college, and graduate. Students are eligible for the
Special Services Program based on criteria which include placement test scores, income levels, physical
handicap, limited English ability, or first generation
college student (neither parent has a bachelor's degree).

4250 Main Office: Technology and Media

University of Connecticut
Box U-64
Storrs, CT   06269   860-486-2530
                                     FAX 860-486-0210
                   http://www.ucimt.uconn.edu/
Richard Gorham, Director

Membership organization specializing in the education of people with special needs through technology
and media.

4251 Manchester Community Technical College

Great Path
Manchester, CT   06040   860-647-6000
                                     FAX 860-647-6238
                   http://www.mctc.commnet.edu
Dr. Mary White-Edger, LD Director

A public two-year college with 60 special education
students out of a total of 6,134.

4252 Mitchell College

Learning Resource Center
437 Pequot Avenue
New London, CT   06320   860-701-5141
                                     800-443-2811
                                     FAX 860-701-5099
Patricia A Pezzullo PhD, Director LRC

An independent two-year or four-year college with
275 special education students out of a total of 621.
There is a an additional fee for the special education
program in addition to the regular tuition.

4253 Naugatuck Community College

750 Chase Parkway
Waterbury, CT   06708   203-575-8040
                                     FAX 203-575-8001
                   http://www.nvcc.commnet.edu
Louise Meyers, Coordinator LD Program
Laurie Novi, Coordinator LD Services

Committed to providing equal educational opportunity and full participation for qualified students with
disabilities in accordance with the Americans with
Disabilities Act of 1990 (ADA). This includes equality of access, accommodations, auxilary aids and services determined to be appropriate to address those
functional limitations of the disability that adversely
affects educational opportunity.

4254 Northwestern Connecticut Community College

Park Place E
Winsted, CT   06098   860-738-6307
                                     FAX 860-379-4465
                                     TDY:860-738-6307
                   http://www.nwctc.commnet.edu
                   e-mail: rdennelien@nwcc.commnet.edu
Roseann Dennerlein, Counselor

Offers a variety of services to students with disabilities including notetakers, extended testing time, counseling services, and special accommodations.

4255 Norwalk Community-Technical College

188 Richards Avenue
Norwalk, CT   06854   203-857-7000
                                     FAX 203-857-3339
                   http://www.nctc.commnet.edu
Lori Orvetti, Developmental Studies Counselor

NCC is accessible to students with disabilites. Students who require accommodations are advised to notify the coodinator at least 6 weeks in advance.

4256 Paier College of Art

20 Gorham Avenue
Hamden, CT   06514   203-287-3031
                                     FAX 203-287-3021
                   http://www.paierart.com
Ronald Nonken, Dean

Offers a variety of services to students with disabilities including notetakers, extended testing time, counseling services, and special accommodations.

4257 Quinebaug Valley Community Technical College

742 Upper Maple Street
Danielson, CT   06239   203-774-1133
                                     FAX 203-774-6737
                   http://www.guctc.commnet.edu
Gary Hottinger, Director LD Center
Pam Abel, Learning Specialist

The Learning Assistance Center provides academic
support for students with disabilities. Such support
may include untimed tests, readers, proctors,
note-takers, tape recorders and so on. There is a Peer
Advocate for Students with Disabilities to assist disabled students; there is also a Learning Specialist
available ten hours a week to counsel and tutor disabled students.

4258 Quinnipiac University

275 Mount Carmel Avenue
Hamden, CT   06518   203-582-8200
                           800-462-1944
                        FAX 203-582-8970
e-mail: John.Jarvis@Quinnipiac.edu
John Jarvis, Coordinator Learning Services

Provides reasonable accommodations to those students who have self-disclosed and provided documentation of a disability.

4259 Sacred Heart University

5151 Park Avenue
Fairfield, CT   06432   203-365-4730
                            FAX 203-396-8049
http://www.sacredheart.edu
e-mail: angottaj@sacredheart.edu
Jill E Angotta, Director

Four year college that provides services to the learning disabled.

4260 Southern Connecticut State University

Disability Resource Office
501 Crescent Street
New Haven, CT   06515   203-392-6828
                               888-500-7278
                            FAX 203-392-6829
http://www.southernct.edu
e-mail: TuckerSl@southernct.edu
Suzanne Tucker, Director
Sharon Brennan, Admissions Director

Provides students, faculty and staff with assistance and information on issues of access and full participation for persons with disabilities. The major responsibility of the Disability Resource Office is to provide services and supports that promote educational equality for students with documented disabilities.

4261 St. Joseph College

1678 Asylum Avenue
West Hartford, CT   06117   860-232-4571
                                FAX 860-233-5695
http://www.sjc.edu

Judy Arzt, Director

Offers a variety of services to students with disabilities including notetakers, extended testing time, counseling services, and special accommodations.

4262 Thames Valley Campus of Three Rivers Community College

574 New London Turnpike
Norwich, CT   06360   860-885-2612
                             800-886-4960
                          FAX 860-886-6670
Dr. Linda Jacobsen, Counselor
Chris Scarborough, Learning Specialist

Offers associate degrees in computers, and engineering technologies (architectural, civil, electrical, general, manufacturing, mechanical and nuclear, business, general studies, liberal arts and sciences, nursing and others) and one-year certificates in architectural and CADD drafting and data processing.

4263 Trinity College

300 Summit Street
Hartford, CT   06106   860-297-2000
                           FAX 860-297-2287
http://www.trincoll.edu
Mary Thomas, Dean Student

Offers a variety of services to students with disabilities including notetakers, extended testing time, counseling services, and special accommodations.

4264 Tunxis Community College

271 Scott Swamp Road
Farmington, CT   06032   860-677-7701
                             FAX 860-676-8906
http://www.tunxis.commnet.edu
Dr. David Smith, LD Director

Offers a variety of services to students with disabilities including note takers, extended testing time, counseling services, and special accommodations.

4265 University of Bridgeport

Office of Special Services
60 Lafayette Street
Bridgeport, CT   06604   203-576-4454
                                800-392-3582
                             FAX 203-576-4941
http://www.bridgeport.edu
Barbara Maryak, Dean of Admissions

Committted to the development of all students. An advocate and liaison for the students with disabilities, as defined by the American with Disabilities Act. The goal is to provide supportive services for those students with special needs in order to promote sensitivity and equality for the entire University of Bridgeport community.

4266 University of Connecticut

University Program for College Students with LD
3621 Fairfield Road
Storrs, CT   06269   860-486-2020
                         FAX 860-486-1476
http://www.uconn.edu
e-mail: j.madaus@uconn.edu
Joseph W Madaus PhD, Director

Committed to assuring equal educational opportunity for students with learning disabilities who have the potential for success in a highly competitive university setting. Since 1984, a comprehensive program has been available to assist qualified students with learning disabilities to become independent and successful learners within the regular University curriculum.

4267 University of Hartford

Learning Plus
200 Bloomfield Avenue
W Hartford, CT   06117   860-768-4312
                                800-947-4303
                             FAX 860-768-4183
http://www.hartford.edu
e-mail: LDsupport@hartford.edu
Lynne Goldman, Director
Rosemarie Coleman

An academic support service available to any University of Hartford student who has submitted appropriate documentation showing evidence of a specific learning disability and/or attention disability.

4268 University of New Haven

300 Boston Post Road
W Haven, CT   06516   203-932-7331
                             800-324-5864
                        FAX 203-932-6082
                        TDY:203-932-7409
                      http://www.newhaven.edu
                   e-mail: lcokeke@newhaven.edu
Linda Cupney-Okeke, Director Disabilty Services
Jane C Sangeloty, Admissions Director

Persons who have special needs requiring accommodation should notify the Office for Students with Disabilities. The office handles all referrals regarding any student with a disability. The director provides guidance, assistance and information for students with disabilities and oversees the University's compliance with the Americans with Disabilities Act and the HEW Rehabilitation Act of 1973.

4269 VISTA Vocational & Life Skills Center

1356 Old Clinton Road
Westbrook, CT   06498   860-399-8080
                          FAX 860-399-3103
                   http://www.vistavocational.org
                e-mail: hbosch@vistavocational.org
Helen K Bosch, Executive Director

Building self-esteem and confidence in the lives of adults with disabilities through work, independence and friendship. Offers a post-secondary program for young adults with learning disabilities providing individualized training and support in career development, independent living skills, social skills development and community involvement.

4270 Wesleyan University

237 High Street
Middletown, CT   06459   860-685-2000
                           FAX 860-685-2201
                       http://www.wesleyan.edu
                  e-mail: vrutherford@wesleyan.edu
Vancenia Rutherford, Associate Dean
Richard Culliton, Associate Dean

Wesleyan University is committed to supporting all students in their academic and co-curricular endeavors. Although Wesleyan does not offer special academic programs for individuals with disabilities, the University does provide services and reasonable accommodations to all students who need and have a legal entitlement to such accommodations.

4271 Western Connecticut State University

Students with Disabilities Services
181 White Street
Danbury, CT   06810   203-837-8210
                             877-837-WCSU
                        FAX 203-837-8338
                        http://www.wcsu.edu
                   e-mail: admissions@wcsu.edu
James Roach, President

Offers a variety of services to students with disabilities including notetakers, extended testing time, counseling services, and special accommodations.

4272 Yale University

PO Box 208305
New Haven, CT   06520   203-432-2324
                           FAX 203-432-7884
                           TDY:203-432-8250
                           http://www.yale.edu
Judy York, LD Director

Offers a variety of services to students with disabilities including notetakers, extended testing time, counseling services, and special accommodations.

Delaware

4273 Atlantic Coast Special Educational Services

49 W Avenue
Ocean View, DE   19970   302-537-7263
                            877-785-7774
                   http://www.atlanticcoast.org
                   e-mail: lelling111@aol.com
Lloyd Elling, President/Owner

Full year, summer and respite care. Ages 18 and older.

4274 Delaware Technical and Community College: Terry Campus

100 Campus Drive
Dover, DE   19904   302-857-1000
                       FAX 302-857-1296
                http://www.terry.dtcc.edu/terry
Dr. Orlando George Jr, President

Offers a variety of services to students with disabilities including advocacy, readers, note takers, extended testing time, counseling services, and special accommodations.

4275 University Affiliated Program for Families & Individuals with Developmental Disabilities

University of Delaware
101 Alison Hall
Newark, DE   19716   302-831-6974
                        FAX 302-831-4690
                     e-mail: dkoch@udel.edu
Deborah Koch, Manager

Supports families and individuals who are affected by developmental disabilities.

4276 University of Delaware

Academic Services Center
5 W Main Street
Newark, DE   19716   302-831-1639
                        FAX 302-831-4128
                   http://www.udel.edu/ASC
                   e-mail: lysbet@udel.edu
Lysbet Murray, Associate Director

Provides accommodations for eligible students with disabilities or ADHD.

District of Columbia

4277 American University: Academic Support Center

Learning Services Program
4400 Massachusetts Avenue NW
Washington, DC 20016   202-885-3360
                               FAX 202-885-1042
                          http://www.american.edu
                     e-mail: hstein@american.edu
Melissa Scarfone, Learning Services Program Coord.
Kathy Schwartz, Director Academic Support Center

Focuses on assisting students with their transition from high school to college during their freshman year. It is a small, mainstream program offering weekly individual meetings with the coordinator of the Learning Services Program throughout the student's first year.

4278 Catholic University of America

Distict Support Services
620 Michigan Avenue NE
Washington, DC 20064   202-319-5211
                               FAX 202-319-5126
                     http://disabilityservices.cua.edu
                          e-mail: mcclellan@cua.edu
Bonnie McClellan, Director Disability Support
Christine Mica, Director Undergraduate Admiss.

Four-year college that has support services for students with learning disabilities.

4279 George Washington University

Disability Support Services
800 21st Street NW
Washington, DC 20052   202-944-8250
                               FAX 202-994-7610
                          http://www.gwu.edu
                     e-mail: cwillis@gwu.edu
Christy Willis, Director
Kathryn Napper, Admissions Director

An independent four-year college with 260 students with disabilities out of a total of 8,837.

4280 Georgetown University

Disability Support Services/Learning Services
37th & P Streets, NW
Washington, DC 20057   202-687-6985
                               FAX 202-687-6158
                          http://www.georgetown.edu
                     e-mail: gwr@georgetown.edu
Marcia Fulk, Director
Dean Charles Deacon, Admissions Director

A four-year private university with a total enrollment of 6,418.

4281 Howard University

2400 6th Street NW
Washington, DC 20059   802-806-6100
                               FAX 202-806-5934
                          http://www.howard.edu
Vincent Johns, Dean Special Services

Howard University is committed to compliance with the Americans with Disabilities Act, including providing special services to its disabled students such that they are able to achieve their academic goals. The Office of the Dean for Special Student Services (ODSSS) has been delegated the responsibility of providing reasonable accommodations for students with disabilities.

4282 Trinity College

125 Michigan Avenue
Washington, DC 20017   202-884-9647
                               FAX 202-884-9229
                          http://www.trinitydc.edu
                     e-mail: harrisk@trinitydc.edu
Kimberly Harris, Director

Four year college that provides services to students with a learning disability.

4283 University of the District of Columbia

4200 Connecticut Avenue NW
Washington, DC 20008   202-274-5336
                               FAX 202-274-6334
                          http://www.udc.edu
Dr. Madhuck Ohal, Senior Director

Offers a variety of services to students with disabilities including note takers, extended testing time, counseling services, and special accommodations.

Florida

4284 Barry University

Center for Advanced Learning
11300 NE 2nd Avenue
Miami Shores, FL 33161   305-899-3461
                               FAX 305-899-3778
                          http://www.barry.edu
                     e-mail: vcastro@mail.barry.edu
Vivian Castro, CAL Program Director

A comprehensive support program for students with learning disabilities and attention deficit disorders.

4285 Beacon College

105 E Main Street
Leesburg, FL 34748   352-787-7660
                               FAX 352-787-0721
                          http://www.beaconcollege.edu
                     e-mail: admissions@beaconcollege.edu
Betsy Stout Morrill, Admissions Director
Stephanie Knight, Admissions Counselor

Offering BA and AA degree programs exclusively for students with learning disabilities.

4286 Brevard Community College

1519 Clearlake Road
Cocoa, FL 32922   407-632-1111
                               FAX 321-634-3779
                          http://www.brevard.cc.fl.us
Brenda Fettrow, Director

A public two-year college with 602 students with disabilities out of a total of 15,033.

4287   Broward Community College

225 E Las Olas Boulevard
Fort Lauderdale, FL   33314   954-761-7465
                                     FAX 954-761-7309
                    http://www.broward.cc.fl.us/

Offers a variety of services to students with disabilities including note takers, extended testing time, counseling services, and special accommodations.

4288   Central Florida Community College

3001 SW College Road
Ocala, FL   34478   352-237-2111
                                     FAX 352-237-0510
                    http://www.cfcc.cc.fl.us
Charles Vassance, President

A public two-year college with 19 special education students out of a total of 5,616.

4289   Chipola College

3094 Indian Circle
Marianna, FL   32446   850-526-2761
                                     FAX 850-718-2240
                    http://www.chipola.edu
Gayle Duncan, Disabled Student Counselor

A public two-year college.

4290   DePaul School for Dyslexia

701 Orange Avenue
Clearwater, FL   34616   727-443-2711
                                     FAX 727-443-2604
                    http://www.webcoast.com/depaul/

4291   Disabled Student Services

Miami Dade Community College
11011 SW 104th Street
Miami, FL   33176   305-237-2767
                                     FAX 305-237-0880
          http://www.mdcc.edu/kendall/disabled/index.htm
Dianne Rossman, Coordinator

A public two-year college with 307 special education students out of a total of 30,013.

4292   Eckerd College

4200 54th Avenue S
Saint Petersburg, FL   33711   727-864-8331
                                     FAX 727-866-2304
                    http://www.eckerd.edu

Patricia Bowman

Offers a variety of services to students with disabilities including notetakers, extended testing time, counseling services, and special accommodations.

4293   Edison Community College

College Parkway SW
Fort Myers, FL   33906   941-489-9274
                                     800-749-2322
                                     FAX 941-489-9418
                    http://www.edison.edu
                    e-mail: inquiry@edison.edu
Andrea Anderson, Contact

Offers a variety of services to students with disabilities including note takers, extended testing time, counseling services, and special accommodations.

4294   Embry-Riddle Aeronautical University

600 S Clyde Morris Boulevard
Daytona Beach, FL   32114   386-226-6000
                                     FAX 386-226-6158
                    http://www.embryriddle.edu
Jim Hampton, Director

An independent four-year college with 19 special education students out of a total of 4,643.

4295   Florida Agricultural & Mechanical University

Learning Development & Evaluation Center
Foote-Hilyer Administration Center
Tallahassee, FL   32307   904-599-3180
                                     FAX 904-651-2513
                    http://www.famu.edu
                    e-mail: n.saabirjohnson@famu.edu
Sharon M Wooten, Director
Barbara Cox, Admissions Director

A four-year public school with 275 students receiving disability services out of 10,691.

4296   Florida Atlantic University

Office for Students with Disabilities
777 Glades Road
Boca Raton, FL   33431   561-297-3880
                                     FAX 561-297-2184
                    http://www.fau.edu
                    e-mail: nrokoi@fau.edu
Nicole Robes MEd, Director
Albert Colom, Admissions Director

Offers a variety of services to students with disabilities including notetakers, extended testing time, counseling services, and special accommodations.

4297   Florida Community College at Jacksonville

501 W State Street
Jacksonville, FL   32202   904-766-6769
                                     FAX 904-646-2204
                    http://www.fccj.org
Lucretia Childers, Disabled Student

A public two-year college with 80 special education students out of a total of 19,878.

4298   Florida Gulf Coast University

Office of Multi Access Services
10501 FGCU Boulevard
Fory Meyers, FL   33965   239-590-7956
                                     FAX 239-590-7975
                    http://www.fgcu.edu
                    e-mail: cwhiting@fgcu.edu
Cori Whiting, Coordinator

Four year college that offers students services for the disabled.

4299 Florida International University

Office of Disability Services
University Park GC 190
Miami, FL   33199   305-348-3532
                                   FAX 305-348-3850
                                   http://www.fiu.edu
                            e-mail: manheim@fiu.edu
Peter Manheimer, Director
Kathy Trionfo, Associate Director
Diane Russell, Assistant Director

A public four-year university with a north campus office, serving more than 30,000 students. Students with disabilities seeking assistance number about 500. Tuition is $63.73 per credit for undergraduate and $138.08 for graduate students.

4300 Florida State University

Student Disability Resource Center
2249 University Center
Tallahassee, FL   32306   850-644-9566
                                   FAX 850-644-7164
                                   http://www.fsu.edu
                               e-mail: sdrc@fsu.edu
Lauren Kennedy, Director
John Burnhill, Admissions Director

A public four-year college with 500 students with learning disabilities out of a total of 27,014.

4301 Gulf Coast Community College

5230 W Highway 98
Panama City, FL   32401   850-679-1551
                                   FAX 850-679-1556
                                http://www.gc.cc.fl.us
Linda Van Dalen, Coorindator

A public two-year college with 65 special education students out of a total of 7,374.

4302 Hillsborough Community College

10414 E Columbus Drive
Tampa, FL   33567   813-253-7914
                                   FAX 813-253-7910
                                   http://www.hccfl.edu
                          e-mail: dgiarrusso@hccfl.edu
Denise Giarrusso, Coordinator

A two-year college that provides services to the learning disabled.

4303 Indian River Community College

3209 Virginia Avenue
Fort Pierce, FL   34981   561-462-4328
                                 http://www.ircc.ccfl.edu
Rhoda Brant, Counselor

Two-year community college providing services for learning disabled students (i.e., unlimited tests, notetakers, etc.).

4304 Jacksonville University

2800 University Boulevard N
Jacksonville, FL   32211   904-256-7000
                                   FAX 904-256-7012
                                   http://www.ju.edu

John Grundig, Director

Offers a variety of services to students with disabilities including note takers, extended testing time, counseling services, and special accommodations.

4305 Johnson & Wales University: Florida

Student Success
1701 NE 127th Street
N Miami, FL   33181   305-892-7568
                                     800-232-2433
                                   FAX 305-892-7568
                                   http://www.jwu.edu

Martha Sacks, Director

4306 Lake City Community College

Route 19
Lake City, FL   32025   386-752-1822
                                   FAX 386-754-4594
                             http://www.lakecity.cc.fl.us
                    e-mail: mitchelln@mail.lakecity.cc.fl.us
Natasha R Mitchell, Coordinator

A public two-year college with 31 special education students out of a total of 2,553.

4307 Learning Development and Evaluation Center

Florida A&M University
677 Ardelia Court
Tallahassee, FL   32307   850-599-3180
                                   FAX 850-561-2513
                                   http://www.famu.edu
Dr. Sharon Wooten, Director
Donna Shell, Associate Director

Assists the students by providing a variety of supportive services for example counseling, academic advisement, learning strategies.

4308 Lynn University

Advancement Program
3601 N Military Trail
Boca Raton, FL   33431   561-237-7239
                                     800-888-5966
                                   FAX 561-237-7094
                                   http://www.lynn.edu
                            e-mail: melglines@lynn.edu
Gary Martin LMCH, Director
Allen Mullen, Admissions Director

Independent four-year college with 268 special education students out of a total of 1,633 full time undergraduates. There is an additional special education fee.

4309 Office of Disabled Students at Manatee Community College

5840 26th Street W
Bradenton, FL   34206   941-752-5000
                                   FAX 941-727-6380
                                   http://www.mcc.cc.fl.us
Paul Nolting, Adult Services

Provides reasonable accommodations to ensure the inclusive and total access of disabled students to credit courses at the college while, at the same time, maintaining the integrity and quality of the college's academic programs. Offers a variety of services to students with disabilities including note takers, extended testing time, counseling services and special accommodations.

4310   Okaloosa-Walton College

100 College Boulevard
Niceville, FL   32578   850-729-6079
                                          FAX 850-729-5323
                                          http://www.owcc.edu
                                          e-mail: swensonj@owcc.net
Jody Swenson, Coordinator Services

Offers a variety of services to students with disabilities including note takers, extended testing time, counseling services, and special accommodations.

4311   PACE-Brantley Hall School

3221 Sand Lake Road
Longwood, FL   32779   407-869-8882
                                          FAX 407-869-8717
                           http://www.pacebrantleyhall.org/

4312   Pensacola Junior College

1000 College Boulevard
Pensacola, FL   32504   850-484-1637
                                          FAX 850-484-2049
                                          TDY:850-484-2093
                                          http://www.pjc.cc.fl.us
                                          e-mail: jnickles@pjc.edu
Dr. James Nickles, Director
Linda Sheppard, Coordinator
Becky Adkins, Sign Language Interpretor
Provide services accommodations to students with disabilities enrolled in community college programs.

4313   Polk Community College

999 Avenue H NE
Winter Haven, FL   33881   863-297-1041
                                          FAX 863-297-1034
                                          http://www.polk.cc.fl.us/
James Dowdy, Special Services

Offers a variety of services to students with disabilities including note takers, extended testing time, counseling services, and special accommodations.

4314   Saint Leo University

PO Box 6665
Saint Leo, FL   33574   352-588-8464
                                          FAX 352-588-8605
                                          http://www.saintleo.edu
                                          e-mail: karen.hahn@saintleo.edu
Karen A Hahn, Director

Four year college that offers services to the disabled.

4315   Santa Fe Community College: Florida

3000 NW 83rd Street
Gainesville, FL   32606   352-295-4400
                                          FAX 352-395-4100
                                          http://www.sfcc.edu
                                          e-mail: drc@sfcc.edu
Larry Kiser, Disability Resource Counselor
Claudia Munnis, Disability Resource Counselor
Michael Hutley, Disability Resource Counselor

Located on the first floor of the Student Services Building in S-112. If you have a disability that impacts your academic success, please visit us.

4316   Seminole Community College

100 Weldon Boulevard
Sanford, FL   32773   407-328-4722
                                          FAX 407-328-2139
                                          http://www.seminole.cc.fl.us
                                          e-mail: admissions@scc-fl.edu
Dorothy Paishon, Coordinator

Disability Support Services can be reached at 407-328-2109. We provide learning aids, course substitutions, instructor notification and support, referral to area agencies and college services, interpreters, notetakers, talking texts and tutors. We also have workshops on identifying and creating positive learning environments for disabled students.

4317   Southeastern College of the Assemblies of God

1000 Longfellow Boulevard
Lakeland, FL   33801   863-667-5064
                                          FAX 863-667-5200
                                          http://www.secollege.edu
Ken Fanueff, Director

Offers a variety of services to students with disabilities including note takers, extended testing time, counseling services, and special accommodations.

4318   St. Johns River Community College

5001 Saint Johns Avenue
Palatka, FL   32177   386-312-4200
                                          FAX 386-312-4283
                                          http://www.sjrcc.cc.us
Annette Jones, Special Services

Students with disabilities are welcome at SJRCC, and are encouraged to contact the Counseling Center on their campus where special assistance is available with orientation, registration, academic planning, special supplies, and equipment. In addition, specialized services are available to students whose disability prevents them from participating fully in classroom activities.

4319   St. Petersburg Junior College

PO Box 13489
Saint Petersburg, FL   33733   727-341-3721
                                          http://www.spjc.edu
                                          e-mail: duncand@spcollege.edu
Dr. Susan Blanchard, Learning Specialist

A public two-year college with 890 special education students out of a total of 20,000+.

4320 Tallahassee Community College
444 Appleyard Drive
Tallahassee, FL 32304   850-201-6200
http://www.tallahassee.cc.fl.us/
Mark Linehan, Counselor
Margaret Handee, Educational Specialist

A public two-year college with 584 special education students out of a total of 10,400.

4321 Tampa Bay Academy
12012 Boyette Road
Riverview, FL 33569   813-677-6700
800-678-3838
FAX 813-671-3145
http://www.tampabay-acadamy.com
e-mail: james.merritt@tampa.yfcs.com
Andrea Smith, Contact

Offers a variety of services to students with disabilities including note takers, extended testing time, counseling services, and special accommodations.

4322 University of Florida
Office for Students with Disabilities
201 Criser Hall
Gainsville, FL 32611   352-392-1261
FAX 352-392-5566
http://www.ufl.edu
e-mail: osfield@ufl.edu
John Denny, Director
William Kolb, Admissions Director

A four-year public university with 100 students receiving disability services out of 32,680.

4323 University of Miami
PO Box 248106
Coral Gables, FL 33124   305-284-2374
FAX 305-284-1999
http://www.miami.edu
Judith Antinarella, Director

Offers a variety of services to students with disabilities including note takers, extended testing time, counseling services, and special accommodations.

4324 University of North Florida
4567 Saint Johns Bluff Road S
Jacksonville, FL 32216   904-620-2624
FAX 904-620-2414
http://www.unf.edu
Gary Albritton, Special Services

Offers a variety of services to students with disabilities including notetakers, extended testing time, counseling services, and special accommodations.

4325 University of Tampa
401 W Kennedy Boulevard
Tampa, FL 33606   813-253-3333
FAX 813-258-7208
http://www.ut.edu
e-mail: disability.services@ut.edu
Cheri Kittrell, Assistant Director Academic Cntr

A private, comprehensive university with an international reputation for excellence.

4326 University of West Florida
11000 University Parkway
Pensacola, FL 32514   850-474-2387
FAX 850-857-6188
http://www.uwf.edu
e-mail: bfitzpat@uwf.edu
Barbara Fitzpatrick, Assistant Director

A public four-year college with 8 special education students out of a total of 6793.

4327 Valencia Community College
PO Box 3028
Orlando, FL 32825   407-299-5000
FAX 407-293-8839
http://www.ualencia.cc.fl.us
Walter Johnson, Counselor
Peg Edmonds, Counselor

A public two-year college with 1,200 students with disabilities out of a total of 25,000.

4328 Webber College
PO Box 96
Babson Park, FL 33827   863-638-1431
800-741-1844
FAX 863-638-1591
http://www.webber.edu
Dr. Deborah Milliken, Director Admissions

An independent four-year college with 39 special education students out of a total of 354.

4329 Woodland Hall Academy-Dyslexia Research Institute
5746 Centerville Road
Tallahassee, FL 32309   850-893-2216
FAX 850-893-2440
http://www.dyslexia-add.org
e-mail: dri@talstar.com
Robyn Rennick, Program Coordinator

Participates in field research and offers testing materials for dyslexia, ADD, SLD children and adults.

6-20 years old

Georgia

4330 Albany State University
504 College Drive
Albany, GA 31705   229-430-4600
FAX 229-430-3936
http://www.asurams.edu
Portia Shields, President

Four-year college offering services and support to students with learning disabilities.

4331 Andrew College

413 College Street
Cuthbert, GA   39840   912-732-5908
                              FAX 912-732-5969
              http://www.andrewcollege.edu
              e-mail: focus@andrewcollege.edu
Sherri Taylor, Director

The FOCUS program offers an intensive level of academic support designed for and limited to documented learning disabilities or attention deficit disorder. While FOCUS supplements and complements the tutorial and advising to all students, the program also provides an additional level of professional assistance and mentoring. Those accepted into FOCUS are charged regular tuition andd fees, plus a FOCUS laboratory fee.

4332 Atlanta Speech School

Wardlaw School for Children with LD
3160 Northside Parkway NW
Atlanta, GA   30327   404-233-5332
                            FAX 404-266-2175
          http://www.atlantaspeechschool.org
          e-mail: jblalock@atlantaspeechschool.org
Jane Blalock, Director Professional Service
Sandra Mims, Coordinator Lower School
Maureen Demku, Coordinator, Upper School

Wardlaw School is for children with mild to moderate language and learning disabilities.

4333 Berry College

PO Box 490159
Rome, GA   30149   706-236-2215
                          FAX 706-236-2248
              http://www.berry.edu
Dr. Marshall Jenkins, Director

Offers a variety of services to students with disabilities including notetakers, extended testing time, counseling services, and special accommodations.

4334 Brandon Hall School

1701 Brandon Hall Drive
Atlanta, GA   30350   770-394-8177
                            FAX 770-804-8821
              http://www.brandonhall.org
              e-mail: pstockhammer@brandonhall.org
Paul R Stockhammer, President
Steve Boyce, Admissions Director

College preparatory, co-ed day and boys' boarding school for students in grades 4-12. Designed for academic underachievers and students with minor learning disabilities, attention deficit disorders and dyslexia. Enrollment 150 students; faculty 40, with 100% college acceptances. Interscholastic sports and numerous co-curriculum activities and summer programs.

4335 Brenau University

Learning Center
1 Centennial Circle
Gainesville, GA   30501   770-534-6134
                                800-252-5119
                            FAX 770-534-6221
              http://www.brenau.edu
              e-mail: vyamilkoski@lib.brenau.edu
Vincent Yamilkoski EdD, Learning Center Director
Christina Chocran, Women's College Admissions

Program for students with a diagnosed learning disability and who have average to above average intellectual potential. This program is designed to provide support services for learning disabled students as they attend regular college courses. Offers a more structured learning environment, as well as the freedom associated with college living.

4336 Brewton-Parker College

PO Box 2124
Mount Vernon, GA   30445   912-583-3222
                                 800-342-1087
                             FAX 912-583-4498
              http://www.bpc.edu
              e-mail: pweaver@bpc.edu
Pat Weaver, Director Counseling Service

An independent four-year college with 15 special education students out of a total of 1,942.

4337 Clayton College & State University

Disability Services
5900 N Lee Street
Morrow, GA   30260   770-961-3500
                           FAX 770-961-3752
              http://www.clayton.edu
Dr. Thomas Harden, President

Four-year college that offers programs for learning disabled students.

4338 Columbus State University

4225 University Avenue
Columbus, GA   31907   706-568-2330
                             FAX 706-569-3096
              http://www.colstate.edu
              e-mail: willliams_aracelis@colstate.edu
Aracelis Williams, Conatct

Offers a variety of services to students with disabilities including note takers, extended testing time, counseling services, and special accommodations.

4339 DeVry Institute of Technology

250 N Arcadia Avenue
Decatur, GA   30030   404-292-2645
                            FAX 404-292-7011
              http://www.atl.devry.edu
Andrea Rutherford, Academic Support

Offers a variety of services to students with disabilities including notetakers, extended testing time, counseling services, and special accommodations.

4340 East Georgia College

131 College Circle
Swainsboro, GA   30401   912-237-1011
                                 FAX 912-237-5161
                        http://www.ega.peachnet.edu
                     e-mail: rlosser@ega.peachnet.edu
Bennie Brinson, Student Services

Offers a variety of services to students with disabilities including note takers, extended testing time, counseling services, and special accommodations.

4341 Emory University

Office of Disability Services
Boisfeuillet Jones Center
Atlanta, GA   30322   404-727-6016
                                 FAX 404-727-1126
                          http://www.emory.edu
                        e-mail: gmccord@emory.edu
Gloria Weaver McCord, Director
Jane Jordon, Admissions Director

An independent four-year college with 150 special education students out of a total of 6,316.

4342 Fort Valley State University

Counseling & Career Development Center
PO Box 4091
Fort Valley, GA   31030   912-825-6202
                                 FAX 912-825-6471
                          http://www.fvsu.edu
                     e-mail: asmissap@mail.fvsu.edu
Dr. Myldred Hill, Director

Four-year college that provides counseling for learning disabled students.

4343 Gables Academy

811 Gordon Street
Stone Mountain, GA   30083   770-465-7500
                                 FAX 770-465-7700
                       http://www.gablesacademy.com
                     e-mail: info@gablesacademy.com
Jeff Sorgent, Register
Carol Clark, Administractive Assistant

Offers a variety of services to students with disabilities including notetakers, extended testing time, counseling services, and special accommodations.

4344 Georgia Affiliated Program for Persons with Developmental Disabilities

University of Georgia
Dawson Hall
Athens, GA   30602   706-542-3457
                                 FAX 706-542-4815
Zolinda Stoneman, Director

For students with developmental disabilities.

4345 Georgia College

231 W Hancock Street
Milledgeville, GA   31061   911-445-4577
                                 800-342-0471
                                 FAX 912-445-6582
                          http://www.gcsu.edu
                     e-mail: dcsmith@mail.gcsu.edu
Dr. Craig Smith, Chair

Offers a variety of services to students with disabilities including note takers, extended testing time, counseling services, and special accommodations.

4346 Georgia Institute of Technology

225 N Avenue
Atlanta, GA   30332   404-894-2564
                                 FAX 404-894-2564
                          http://www.gatech.edu
RoseMary Watkins, Contact

A public four-year college with 6 special education students out of a total of 9,587.

4347 Georgia Southern University

Student Disability Resource Center
PO Box 8037
Statesboro, GA   30460   912-871-1566
                                 FAX 912-871-1419
                          http://www.gasou.edu
                 e-mail: cwatkins@gsix2.cc.gasou.edu
Wayne Akins, Director
Teresa Thompsen, Admissions Director

Offers a variety of services to students with disabilities including note takers, extended testing time, counseling services, and special accommodations.

4348 Georgia State University

Disability Services
33 Gilmer Street, Unit 3
Atlanta, GA   30303   404-463-9044
                                 FAX 404-463-9049
                        http://www.gsu.edu/disability
                     e-mail: disleb@langate.gsu.edu
Louise Bedrossian, Cognitive Disability Specialist

An accessible campus with 149 students with disabilities. Support services include a staff of professionals and student aides who provide tutors, mobility assistance, test proctoring, extended time for exams, interpreters, transcribing, readers, reading machines, taped textbooks and class materials. Technology includes computers with voice output and zoom text, print magnification systems, Arkenstone and Kurzweil Readers, assistive listening devices, and specialized software programs.

4349 Life University

1269 Barclay Circle
Marietta, GA   30075   770-426-2725
                                 FAX 770-426-2728
                          http://www.life.edu
                        e-mail: adrake@life.edu
Dr. Ann Drake, Director

Four-year college offers academic support to students with disabilities.

4350 Macon State College
100 College Station Drive
Macon, GA   31206   912-471-2714
                          FAX 912-471-5730
                   http://www.mc.peachnet.edu
                   e-mail: sloyd@mail.maconstate.edu

Four-year college that provides services to those students who are disabled.

4351 Mercer University: Atlanta
Teaching Learning Center
Atlanta, GA   30341   478-301-2863
                          FAX 478-301-5329
Dorothy Roberts, Director

Offers a variety of services to students with disabilities including note takers, extended testing time, counseling services, and special accommodations.

4352 Mill Springs Academy
13660 New Providence Road
Alpharetta, GA   30004   770-360-1336
                          FAX 770-360-1341
                   http://www.millsprings.org/
Robert W Moore, Headmaster

4353 North Georgia College & State University
221 Barnes Hall
Dahlonega, GA   30597   706-867-2782
                          FAX 706-864-1404
                   http://www.ngcsu.edu
Rodney Pennamon, Coordinator

Four-year college that provides resources and programs for learning disabled students.

4354 Piedmont College
PO Box 10
Demorest, GA   30535   404-776-0103
                          FAX 706-776-6635
                   http://www.piedmont.edu
Nancy Adams, Special Services

Offers a variety of services to students with disabilities including notetakers, extended testing time, counseling services, and special accommodations.

4355 Reinhardt College
Academic Support Office
7300 Reinhardt College Circle
Waleska, GA   30183   770-720-5567
                          FAX 770-720-5602
                   http://www.reinhardt.edu
                   e-mail: srr@reinhardt.edu
Sylvia Robertson, Director Academic Support Office

An independent four-year college with 80 learning disabled students out of a total of 1,190 being served in academic support. There is an additional fee for the tutorial program in addition to the regular tuition.

4356 Savannah State University
Comprehensive Counseling Center
PO Box 20376
Savannah, GA   31404   912-356-2202
                          FAX 912-356-2464
                   http://www.savstate.edu
                   e-mail: akoredea@savstate.edu
Orlando Spencer, Coordinator

Four-year college has a comprehensive counseling center for students that are learning disabled.

4357 Shorter College
315 Shorter Avenue SW
Rome, GA   30165   706-291-2121
                          800-868-6980
                          FAX 706-236-1515
                   http://www.shorter.edu
Dr. Ed Schroeder, President

Offers a variety of services to students with disabilities including note takers, extended testing time, counseling services, and special accommodations.

4358 South Georgia College
100 W College Park Drive
Douglas, GA   31533   912-389-4220
                          800-342-6364
                          FAX 912-389-4392
                   http://www.sgc.peachnet.edu
Tommaline Key, Special Services

The Office of Disability Services, a division of Academic Affairs, is committed to providing an equal educational opportunity for all qualified students with disabilities. The Office of Disability Services is responsible for initiating and coordinating services for students with disabilities at South Georgia College.

4359 Southern College of Technology
1100 S Marietta Parkway
Marietta, GA   30060   404-528-7354
                          FAX 404-528-7409
Dr. Patricia Soper, Special Services

Offers a variety of services to students with disabilities including note takers, extended testing time, counseling services, and special accommodations.

4360 Southern Polytechnic State University
1100 S Marietta Parkway
Marietta, GA   30060   770-528-7226
                          FAX 770-528-6855
                   http://www.spsu.edu
                   e-mail: tcordle@spsu.edu
Terri Cordle, Counselor

Four-year college that offers counseling services to learning disabled students.

4361 State University of West Georgia
1237 Park Hall
Carrollton, GA   30118   770-836-6428
                          FAX 770-838-2562
                   http://www.westga.edu
                   e-mail: speacock@westga.edu
Shannon Peacock, Coordinator

Four-year college that provides services to disabled students.

4362 Toccoa Falls College
PO Box 777
Toccoa Falls, GA 30598 706-886-6831
FAX 706-886-6412
http://www.toccoafalls.edu
e-mail: wgardner@tfc.edu
Maily L Heu, Director

Four-year college that provides services to the learning disabled.

4363 University of Georgia
Learning Disabilities Center
331 Milledge Hall
Athens, GA 30602 706-542-7034
FAX 706-583-0001
http://www.uga.edu
Noel Gregg, Director
Elaine Manglitz, Service Head
Nancy McBuss, Admissions Director

A public four-year university with 276 students with learning disabilities out of a total of 24,213. There is no fee for the comprehensive service program. To be eligible for services, students must submit recent documentation which meets evaluation standards.

4364 Valdosta State University
1500 N Patterson Street
Valdosta, GA 31698 912-245-2498
800-872-2586
FAX 912-245-3788
http://www.valdosta.edu
e-mail: kgadden@valdosta.edu
Kimberly Gadden, Special Services Coordinator

A public four-year university with 90 learning disabled students out of a total of 9,000.

4365 West Georgia College
137 Mandeville Hall
Carrollton, GA 30118 770-845-4323
FAX 706-845-4339
http://www.westga.tec.ga.us
Dr. Ann Phillips, Special Services

A public four-year college with 34 special education students out of a total of 5,528.

Hawaii

4366 Brigham Young University: Hawaii
55-220 Kulanui Street
Laie, HI 96762 808-293-3211
FAX 808-293-3741
http://www.byuh.edu
Eric Scumway, President

Offers a variety of services to students with disabilities including note takers, extended testing time, counseling services, and special accommodations.

4367 Center on Disability Studies, University Affiliated Program: University of Hawaii
University of Hawaii at Manoa
1776 University Avenue
Honolulu, HI 96822 808-956-3162
FAX 808-956-5713
http://www.cds.hawaii.edu
e-mail: juana@hawaii.edu
Robert A Stodden, Director/Professor

Dedicated to supporting the quality of life, inclusion, and empowerment of all persons with disabilities and their families through partnerships in training, service, evaluation, research, dissemination, and technical assistance. Nurtures, sustains, and expands promising practices for people with disabilities.

4368 University of Hawaii: Honolulu Community College
874 Dillingham Boulevard
Honolulu, HI 96817 808-845-9282
FAX 808-847-9836
http://www.honolulu.hawaii.edu
e-mail: acess@hcc.hawaii.edu
Lorri Taniguchi, Disability Services Provider
Sheryl Legaspi, Disability Services Provider

Academic support provided for students with documented disabilities. Intake interview required to determine appropriate accommodations which may include taped books, testing accommodations, note takers, etc. Early notification requested.

4369 University of Hawaii: Kapiolani Community College
4303 Diamond Head Road
Honolulu, HI 96816 808-734-9111
FAX 808-734-9447
http://www.kcc.hawaii.edu
Mary Joan Haverly, Special Services

A public two-year college with 28 special education students out of a total of 6,529.

4370 University of Hawaii: Kauai Community College
3060 Eiwa Street
Lihue, HI 96766 808-274-3471
FAX 808-274-3474
http://www.kauaicc.hawaii.edu
Frances Dinnan, Special Services

Offers a variety of services to students with disabilities including note takers, extended testing time, counseling services, and special accommodations.

4371 University of Hawaii: Leeward Community College
Program for Adult Achievement
96-045 Ala Ike Street
Pearl City, HI 96782 808-455-0421
FAX 808-455-0471
http://www.lcc.hawaii.edu
e-mail: ewins@hawaii.edu
C Lynne Douglas

A public two-year college with 153 special education students out of a total of 6,345.

Idaho

4372 Boise State University

1910 University Drive
Boise, ID   83725   208-426-1156
                          FAX 208-426-3765
                          http://www.boisestate.edu
Charles Ruch, President

A public four-year college with 31 special education
students out of a total of 12,812.

4373 College of Southern Idaho

315 Falls Avenue
Twin Falls, ID   83303   208-733-9554
                            800-680-0274
                          FAX 208-736-3015
                          http://www.csi.cc.id.us/
Jim Palmer

Offers a variety of services to students with disabilities including note takers, extended testing time,
counseling services, and special accommodations.

4374 Idaho State University

ADA Disabilities Resource Center
Campus Box 8121
Pocatello, ID   83201   208-236-3599
                          FAX 208-236-4617
                          http://www.isu.edu
                          e-mail: lawsjona@isu.edu
Robert A Campbell, Director

Four-year college that provides information and resources to students with a learning disability.

4375 North Idaho College

1000 W Garden Avenue
Coeur d'Alene, ID   83814   208-769-7794
                          FAX 208-769-3300
                          http://www.nic.edu
Kristine Wold, Special Services

Offers a variety of services to students with disabilities including note takers, extended testing time,
counseling services, and special accommodations.

4376 University of Idaho

Student Disability Services
UI Admissions Office
Moscow, ID   83844   208-895-6746
                            888-884-3246
                          FAX 208-895-9404
                          http://www.uidaho.edu
                          e-mail: sds@widaho.edu
Diane Milhullin, Student Disability Services
Dan Davenport, Admissions Director

Provides disability support services for students with
temporary or permanent disabilities, in accordance
with the Americans with Disabilities Act, and the Rehabilitation Act. The Campus Guide for People with
Disabilities describes some of these services. About
100 people are served annually.

4377 University of Idaho: Idaho Center on Development

College of Education
129 W 3rd Street
Moscow, ID   83843   208-885-3559
                          FAX 208-885-3628
Lee Parks PhD, Director

Positive behavioral supports.

Illinois

4378 Acacia Academy

6425 Willow Springs Road
La Grange Highlands, IL   60525   708-579-9040
                                FAX 708-579-5872
                          e-mail: kfouks@acaciaacademy.com
Kathryn Fouks, Principal
Eileen Petzold, Dean

A school for grades K-12 for children with learning
disabilities. NCA accredited and approved for out of
district students in special education in the state of Illinois.

4379 Aurora University

347 S Gladstone Avenue
Aurora, IL   60506   630-892-6431
                            800-742-5281
                          FAX 630-844-5463
                          http://www.aurora.edu
                          e-mail: inquiry@aurora.edu
Eric Schwaerze, Co-Director Learning Center
Patsy Mahoney, Director Learning Center

An independent four-year college with an enrollment
near 2,000 students. The University Learning Center
provides accommodations, tutoring and support for
all students with physical or learning disabilities.

4380 Barat College of DePaul University

Learning Opportunities Program
700 E Westleigh Road
Lake Forest, IL   60045   847-234-3000
                          FAX 847-574-6000
                          http://www.barat.edu
                          e-mail: dwitikka@barat.edu
Debbie Sheade, Director

A four-year college with small classes and personalized education. There is a separate fee for the special
education program in addition to the regular tuition.
There is also a separate admissions procedure.

4381 Blackburn College

700 College Avenue
Carlinville, IL   62626   217-854-3231
                          FAX 217-854-3713
                          http://www.blackburn.edu
Patricia Kowal, Director

Offers a variety of services to students with disabilities including notetakers, extended testing time, counseling services, and special accommodations.

4382 Brehm Preparatory School

1245 E Grand Avenue
Carbondale, IL 62901 618-457-0371
FAX 618-529-1248
http://www.brehm.org
e-mail: everhart@bayou.com
Richard Collins PhD, Executive Director
Donna Collins, Director Admissions

A coeducational boarding school for students with learning differences. Services are provided for students in grades 6-12. A post-secondary program, OPTIONS, is also available.

4383 Center for Academic Development: National College of Education

2840 Sheridan Road
Evanston, IL 60201 312-475-1100
Annol Kim, Assistant Professor
Evanston Cad, Coordinator

Peer tutoring available- hours per week per course for documented Learning disability students who were regularly admitted and meet college entrance criteria.

4384 Chicago State University

Office of Student Development, Adm. 303
95th Street at King Drive
Chicago, IL 60628 773-995-2000
FAX 773-995-2563
http://www.csu.edu
Dr. Sandra Westbrooks, Assistant Provost
Bridget L Mason, Research Assistant

The Office of Student Development maintains a Student Support Services Program for the disabled students on the campus. Seeks to meet the needs and concerns of the disabled. Services, sources and suggestions are welcomed.

4385 College of DuPage

425 Fawell Boulevardt
Glen Ellyn, IL 60136 630-942-4259
FAX 630-858-5409
http://www.cod.edu
Mary Van DeWarker

Offers a variety of services to students with disabilities including note takers, extended testing time, counseling services, and special accommodations.

4386 College of Health & Human Development: Department of Disability & Human Development

University of Illinois at Chicago
1640 W Roosevelt Road
Chicago, IL 60608 312-413-1647
FAX 312-413-2918
http://www.uic.edu/depts/idhd
e-mail: DHD@uic.edu
David Braddock PhD, Professor

Dedicated to the scholarly, interdisciplinary study of disability and related aspects of human development. It critically examines current and prospective disability policies, conceptual models, and intervention strategies in terms of their historical development and their present merits.

4387 Columbia College Chicago

Student Support Services
600 S Michigan Avenue
Chicago, IL 60605 312-344-8132
FAX 312-344-8005
http://www.colum.edu
e-mail: mmalone@popmail.colum.edu
Marc K Malone, Director

Four-year college that offers support and services to special needs students.

4388 Danville Area Community College

2000 E Main Street
Danville, IL 61832 217-443-8747
FAX 217-431-0751
TDY:217-443-8853
http://www.dacc.ccil.us
e-mail: pmcconn@dacc.cc.il.us
Penny J McConnell, Assessment Center Coordinator

The college offers the associate's degree in 59 occupational programs and 36 transfer prgrams. DACC also offers 10 baccalaureate degree programs through cooperative agreements with Eastern Illinois University, Southern Illinois University, University at Carbondale, and Franklin University in Columbus, Ohio. Six of these four-year degree programs are offered online. Accommodations for students with disabilities.

4389 Eastern Illinois University

Office of Disability Services
600 Lincoln Avenue
Charleston, IL 61920 217-581-6583
FAX 217-581-7208
http://www.eiu.edu
e-mail: cfmpj@eiu.edu
Kathy Waggoner, Director
Dale Wolf, Admissions Director

A public four-year university with 90 students receiving disability services out of 9,346.

4390 Elgin Community College

1700 Spartan Drive
Elgin, IL 60123 847-697-1000
888-545-7222
FAX 847-669-9105
http://www.elgin.cc.il.us/
Annabelle Rhoades, Director LD

Offers a variety of services to students with disabilities including note takers, extended testing time, counseling services, and special accommodations.

4391 Governors State University

University Park, IL 60466 773-534-5000
http://www.govst.edu
e-mail: gsunow@govst.edu
Pamela Bax, Outreach Counselor

Provides assistance to GSU students with disabilities. Assistance includes coordination of untimed tests, notetakers, test readers, computerized testing and other assistance that will allow students equal access to the learning environment.

4392 Highland Community College
2998 W Pearl City Road
Freeport, IL 61032   815-599-3403
                              FAX 815-235-6130
Sue Wilson, Director

A public two-year college with 23 special education
students out of a total of 3,262.

4393 Illinois Central College
115 SW Adams Street
Peoria, IL 61635   309-999-4582
                            FAX 309-999-4549
                            http://www.icc.il.us
Denise Cioni, Special Needs Coordinator

A public two-year college with approximately 100
students with learning disabilities and/or attention
deficit disorder. Students may borrow tape recorders,
use note takers, access books on tape, request test accommodations and utilize tutorial labs and/or individual tutoring.

**4394 Illinois Eastern Community College/Lincoln Trail
College**
11220 State Highway I
Robinson, IL 62454   618-544-8657
                              FAX 618-544-7423
                              http://www.iecc.cc.il.us/iecc
                              e-mail: ltcadmissions@iecc.cc.il.us
Searoba Mascher, Learning Skills

A public two-year college with 4 special education
students out of a total of 1,040.

**4395 Illinois Eastern Community College/Olney Central
College**
305 NW Street
Olney, IL 62450   618-395-4351
                            FAX 618-392-5212
                            http://www.iecc.cc.il.us
                            e-mail: occadmissions.iecc.cc.il.us
Teresa Tagler, Learning Skills

Offers a variety of services to students with disabilities including note takers, extended testing time,
counseling services, and special accommodations.

**4396 Illinois Eastern Community
College/Wabash Valley College**
2200 College Drive
Mount Carmel, IL 62863   618-262-8641
                                  FAX 618-262-8962
                                  http://www.iecc.cc.il.us
                                  e-mail: wwvcadmissions@iecc.cc.il.us
Marj Doty, Learning Skills

Offers a variety of services to students with disabilities including note takers, extended testing time,
counseling services, and special accommodations.

**4397 Illinois Eastern Community Colleges/Frontier
Community College**
2 Frontier Drive
Fairfield, IL 62837   618-842-3711
                               FAX 618-842-4425
                               http://www.iecc.cc.il.us
                               e-mail: fccadmissions@iecc.cc.il.us
Beverly Fisher, Contact

Offers a variety of services to students with disabilities including note takers, extended testing time,
counseling services, and special accommodations.

4398 Illinois State University
Disability Concerns
350 Fell Hall
Normal, IL 61790   309-438-5853
                            FAX 309-438-7713
                            TDY:309-438-8620
                            http://www.ilstu.edu
                            e-mail: ableisu@ilstu.edu
Ann M Caldwell, Director
Steven Adams, Admissions Director

A public four-year university with 130 students with
learning disabilities and/or attention deficit (hyperactivity) disorder. Students may be eligible for services
such as notetakers, testing accommodations, books on
tape and e-text.

4399 John A Logan College
700 Logan College Road
Carterville, IL 62918   618-985-3741
                                 800-851-4720
                                 FAX 618-985-2867
                                 http://www.jal.cc.il.us
                                 e-mail: logan@jal.cc.il.us
Dr. Dollean York, Director

A public two-year college with 47 special education
students out of a total of 4,642.

4400 Joliet Junior College
1215 Houbolt Road
Joliet, IL 60431   815-729-9020
                            FAX 815-744-5507
                            http://www.jjc.cc.il.us
Mary Schafer, Special Needs Coordinator

Student Accommodations and Resources (StAR) is
the academic support department which provides support services to students with disabilities and students
enrolled in career and technical majors.

4401 Kaskaskia College
27210 College Road
Centralia, IL 62801   618-545-3011
                               800-642-0859
                               FAX 618-532-5313
                               http://www.kc.cc.il.us
Lisa Oelze, SNAP Coordinator

Offers a variety of services to students with disabilities including note takers, extended testing time,
counseling services, and special accommodations.

4402 Kendall College
2408 Orrington Avenue
Evanston, IL   60201   847-866-1300
                             FAX 847-866-1320
                             http://www.kendal.edu
Peter Pauletti, Admissions

An independent four-year college with 50 special education students out of a total of 400.

4403 Kishwaukee College
21193 Malta Road
Malta, IL   60150   815-825-2086
                             FAX 815-825-2072
                             http://www.kish.cc.il.us
Frances Loubere, Coordinator

Community college services for students with special needs. Students will be counseled and appropriate accommodations made on an individual basis.

4404 Knox College
2 ES Street
Galesburg, IL   61401   309-341-7397
                             FAX 309-341-7718
                             http://www.knox.edu
Karyn Halloran, Director

Offers a variety of services to students with disabilities including note takers, extended testing time, counseling services, and special accommodations.

4405 Lake Land College
5001 Lakeland Boulevard
Mattoon, IL   61938   217-234-5232
                             FAX 217-234-5390
                             TDY:217-234-5371
                             http://www.lakeland.cc.il.us
                             e-mail: dbeno@lakeland.cc.il.us
Donna Beno, Perkins/Title III Coordinator
Emily Hartke, Counselor

A public two-year college with 180 students with disabilities out of a total enrollment of approximately 5,000.

4406 Lewis and Clark Community College
5800 Godfrey Road
Godfrey, IL   62035   618-466-3411
                             FAX 618-466-1294
                             http://www.lc.cc.il.us
Patricia Dunn-Horn, Coordinator

Offers a variety of services to students with disabilities including note takers, extended testing time, counseling services, and special accommodations.

4407 Lincoln College
Supportive Educational Services
300 Keokuk
Lincoln, IL   62656
                             800-569-0556
                             FAX 207-732-7715
                             http://www.lincolncollege.com
                             e-mail: rumler@lincolncollege.com
Rod Rumler, Director

A private two-year college with 180 special education students out of a total of 725.

4408 Lincoln Land Community College
5250 Shepherd Road
Springfield, IL   62794   217-786-2267
                             800-727-4161
                             FAX 217-786-2866
                             TDY:217-786-2798
                             http://www.llcc.cc.il.us/
Linda Chriswell, Special Needs

A public two-year college with 75 special education students out of a total of 7,880.

4409 McHenry County College
8900 US Highway 14
Crystal Lake, IL   60012   815-455-3700
                             FAX 815-455-0718
                             http://www.mchenry.cc.il.us
Ed Eisner

Offers a variety of services to students with disabilities including note takers, extended testing time, counseling services, and special accommodations.

4410 Millikin University
1184 W Main Street
Decatur, IL   62522   217-424-3511
                             FAX 217-362-6497
                             http://www.millikin.edu
                             e-mail: webmaster@mail.millikin.edu
Elizabeth M Abrahamson, Director

Four-year college that provides programs for the learning disabled.

4411 Moraine Valley Community College
88th Avenue
Palos Hills, IL   60465   708-974-5469
                             FAX 708-974-0078
                             TDY:708-974-9556
                             http://www.moraine.cc.il.us
                             e-mail: moraine@moraine.valley.edu
Laura Vonborstel, Director

A public two-year college with 128 special education students out of a total of 13,958.

4412 Morton College
3801 S Central Avenue
Cicero, IL   60804   708-656-8000
                             FAX 708-656-3924
                             TDY:708-656-0389
                             http://www.morton.cc.il.us
George Russo, Special Populations Coordinator
Patti Demopoulos, Learning Assistant Specialist

A public two-year community college with 75 special education students out of a total of 5,044. Support services and accommodations are provided for students with disabilities. Tutoring is also available.

Schools & Colleges/Illinois

4413 National-Louis University

Center for Academic Devlopment
2840 Sheridan Road
Evanston, IL   60201   847-465-5829
                             FAX 847-465-5610
                             http://www.nl.edu
                   e-mail: aneukranz-butler@nl.edu
Andreen Neukranz-Butler, Diversity Director
Pat Patillo, Admissions Director

An independent four-year university with 10 special education students out of a total of 3,539. Two hours of tutoring per course per week available for documented LD Students.

4414 North Central College

30 N Brainard Street
Naperville, IL   60540   630-637-5100
                              FAX 630-637-5521
                              http://www.noctrl.edu
Mary Jean Lynch, Associate Dean

Offers a variety of services to students with disabilities including note takers, extended testing time, counseling services, and special accommodations.

4415 Northeastern Illinois University

5500 NS Louis Avenue
Chicago, IL   60625   773-583-4050
                            FAX 773-794-6243
                            http://www.neiu.edu
                  e-mail: v-amey-flippin@neiu.edu
Victoria Amey-Flippin, Special Services

A public four-year college with 38 special education students out of a total of 7,715.

4416 Northern Illinois University

Center for Access Ability Resources
Williston Hall 101, NIU
DeKalb, IL   60115   815-753-9734
                            FAX 815-753-9599
                            http://www.reg.niu.edu
                  e-mail: admissions-info@niu.edu
Nancy Kasinski, Director
Robert Burk, Admissions Director

A public four-year university with 150 students receiving disability services out of 16,893.

4417 Northwestern University

Services for Students with Disabilities
1801 Hinman Avenue
Evanston, IL   60204   847-467-5530
                            FAX 847-467-5531
                            http://www.northwestern.edu
                  e-mail: ckthom@northwestern.edu
Dannee Polomsky, Co-Director
Philip Romal, Co-Director
Carol Lunkenheimer, Admissions Director

Offers a variety of services to students with disabilities including notetakers, extended testing time, counseling services and special accommodations.

4418 Northwestern University Communicative Disorders

2299 N Campus Drive
Evanston, IL   60208   847-491-2416
                            FAX 847-467-2776
                            http://www.northwestern.edu
                  e-mail: ckthom@casbah.acns.nwu.edu
Mulhern Director

Offers speech/language and voice services, learning disabilities center and a hearing service.

4419 Oakton Community College

1600 E Golf Road
Des Plaines, IL   60016   847-635-1700
                             FAX 847-635-1764
                             http://www.oakton.edu
                   e-mail: tbers@oakton.edu

Students at Oakton Community College have the right to: Equal opportunity to participate; work and learn; reasonable accommodations; appropriate confidentiality; information about available services and accommodations; information about decisions made by the college regarding appropriate accommodations; accessible campus facilities and advocacy within the college community.

4420 Parkland College

2400 W Bradley Avenue
Champaign, IL   61821   217-351-2200
                            800-346-8089
                            FAX 217-351-2581
                            http://www.parkland.cc.il.us
Evelyn Brown, LD Specialist
Norm Lambert, Counselor

Services for students with disability is a part of the counseling department. These services are coordinated by a full-time counselor. Under the umbrella of these services is a targeted program (Learning Resource Services) for students with learning disabilities (LD) administered by an LD Specialist with type 10 LD certification. Provides accommodations for students with learning disabilities including extended test time, one-on-one tutoring, tape recorders, note takers and individual sessions.

4421 Productive Learning Strategies Program

DePaul University
2320 N Kenmore Avenue
Chicago, IL   60614   773-325-4239
                            FAX 773-325-4673
                  http://www.condor.depaul.edu/~plus
                  e-mail: smiras@depaul.edu
Stamatios Miras, Director

PLuS is a comprehensive program designed to assist students with specific learning disabilities and/or attention deficit disorders in experiencing academic success at DePaul University. Please visit PLuS' website for a description of services and application forms.

4422 Quincy University

1800 College Avenue
Quincy, IL 62301 217-228-5210
800-688-4295
FAX 217-228-5479
http://www.quincy.com
e-mail: admissions@quincy.edu
Kevin Brown, Admissions Director
Linda Godley, Dean Academic/Support Service

Offers a variety of services to students with disabilities including notetakers, extended testing time, counseling services, and special accommodations.

4423 Richland Community College

One College Park
Decatur, IL 62521 217-875-7200
FAX 217-875-6965
http://www.richland.cc.il.us
Mary Atkins, Coordinator
Margaret Shingleton, Secretary/DAS

Richland Community College is committed to providing accommodations to students with disabilities. Each individual has a basic right to an education in accordance with his/her aspirations, talents, and skills. Support services ensure students with disabilities an equal opportunity to participate fully in the total college experience.

4424 Robert Morris College

401 S State Street
Chicago, IL 60605 312-935-6892
FAX 312-935-6861
http://www.rmcil.edu
e-mail: bmylott@smtp.rmcil.edu
Brittany Mylott, Director

Four-year college offering programs to students who are disabled.

4425 Rockford College

5050 E State Street
Rockford, IL 61108 815-226-4000
800-892-2984
FAX 815-226-4119
http://www.rockford.edu
Jeanne Grey, Director

The L.R.C. is a nonprofit, educational resource center offering diagnostic testing, remedial tutoring in reading, writing, and mathematics, and enrichment workshops to enhance the learning experience.

4426 Roosevelt University

Learning and Support Services Program
430 S Michigan Avenue
Chicago, IL 60605 312-341-3810
FAX 312-341-3735
http://www.roosevelt.edu
e-mail: dessimm@admvsbk.roosevelt.edu
Nancy Litke, Director

The Disabled Student Services office serves all students with special needs. The use of services is voluntary and confidential. This office is a resource for students and faculty. The goal of this office is to ensure educational opportunity for all students with special needs by providing access to full participation in all aspects of campus life and increase awareness of disability issues on campus.

4427 Rosary College

7900 W Division Street
River Forest, IL 60305 708-366-2490
FAX 708-366-5360
Dr. Molly Burke, Special Services

Offers a variety of services to students with disabilities including note takers, extended testing time, counseling services, and special accommodations.

4428 Saint Xavier University

3700 W 103rd Street
Chicago, IL 60655 773-298-3540
FAX 773-779-3066
Mary K Sansore, LD Director

Offers a variety of services to students with disabilities including notetakers, extended testing time, counseling services, and special accommodations.

4429 School of the Art Institute of Chicago

37 S Wabash Avenue
Chicago, IL 60603 312-899-5100
800-232-7242
FAX 312-263-0141
http://www.artic.edu/said/life/sdd.html
e-mail: swhitlow@artic.edu
Susan Whitlow, Coordinator of Services

The Office of Services for Students with Disabilities attempts to ensure that students with disabilities have equal access to all programs and activities offered at the School of the Art Institute of Chicago. This can be accomplished by setting up needed accommodations and working to eliminate both attudinal and architectural barriers that exist at the school.

4430 Services for Students with Learning Disabilities at the University of Illinois at Urbana

1207 S Oak Street
Champaign, IL 61820 217-333-8705
FAX 217-333-0248
TDY:217-333-4603
http://www.rehab.uiuc.edu
e-mail: kwold2@uiuc.edu
Karen Wold, Learning Disabilities Specialist

Available accommodations may include, but are not restricted to: notetakers; alternate ways of completing exams and assignments; text conversion to an accessible format; access to assistive computer technologies; and consultation regarding learning strategies and disability management skills.

4431 Shawnee College
8364 College Road
Ullin, IL   62992   618-634-3300
                                       800-481-2242
                                   FAX 618-634-3300
                          http://www.shawnee.cc.il.us
Don Slayter, Special Services

Offers a variety of services to students with disabilities including notetakers, extended testing time, counseling services, and special accommodations.

4432 Shimer College
PO Box 500
Waukegan, IL   60079   847-623-8400
                                       800-215-7173
                                   FAX 847-249-8798
                              http://www.shimer.edu
                          e-mail: asolid@shimer.edu
Alan Solid, Director Admissions

A private four-year college with 3 special education students out of 100.

4433 Southeastern Illinois College
3575 College Road
Harrisburg, IL   62946   618-252-5400
                                       866-338-2742
                                   FAX 618-252-3062
                                 http://www.sic.edu
                      e-mail: lraymer@sic.cc.il.us
Dr. Mary Jo Oldham, President

A public two-year college with more than 50 special education and other special needs students out of a total of over 4,000.

4434 Southern Illinois University: Carbondale
Clinical Center Achieve Program
Carbondale, IL   62901   618-453-2369
                                   FAX 618-453-3711
                        http://www.siu.edu/~achieve
                             e-mail: admrec@siu.edu
Sally DeDecker MS, Director
Walker Allen, Admissions Director

The Achieve Program is a comprehensive academic support service for students with LD and/or ADHD. Students must apply to both Achieve and the University.

4435 Southern Illinois University: Edwardsville
Disability Support Services
PO Box 1047
Edwardsville, IL   62026   618-650-3782
                                   FAX 618-650-5691
                                http://www.siue.edu
                          e-mail: jfloydh@siue.edu
Jane Floyd-Hendey, Director
Boyd Bradshaw, Admissions Director

A public four-year college with 50 special education students out of a total of 9,576.

4436 Spoon River College
23235 N Co 22
Canton, IL   61520   309-647-4645
                                       800-334-7337
                                   FAX 309-649-6393
                             http://www.src.cc.il.us
                          e-mail: info@src.cc.il.us
Bradley Clark, SNAP/CAED

A public two-year college with 61 special education students out of a total of 2,312.

4437 Springfield College in Illinois
1500 N 5th Street
Springfield, IL   62702   217-525-1420
                                   FAX 217-789-1698
                                 http://www.sci.edu
Dr. Karen Hunter Anderson, Contact

Offers a variety of services to students with disabilities including note takers, extended testing time, counseling services, and special accommodations.

4438 University of Illinois at Springfield
1 University Plaza
Springfield, IL   62703   217-206-6600
                                       888-977-4847
                                   FAX 217-206-6511
                                 http://www.uis.edu
Chris Miller, Dean Students

A public four-year college with 26 special education students out of a total of 2,644.

4439 Waubonsee Community College
Route 47 Waubonsee Drive
Sugar Grove, IL   60554   630-466-7900
                                   FAX 630-466-4649
                               TDY:630-466-4649
                          http://www.waubonsee.edu
                      e-mail: ihansen@waubonsee.edu
Iris Hansen, Manager ACSD

A public two-year college with 400 special education students out of a total 10,000.

4440 Western Illinois University
Disability Support Services
1 University Circle
Macomb, IL   61455   309-298-2512
                                   FAX 309-298-2361
                                 http://www.wiu.edu
                  e-mail: joan_grren@ccmail.wiu.edu
Joan Green, Director
Karen Helmers, Admissions Director

A public four-year college with 135 special education students out of a total of 10,652.

4441 William Rainey Harper College
1200 W Algonquin Road
Palatine, IL   60067   847-925-6266
                                   FAX 847-925-6036
                             http://www.harper.cc.il.us
                      e-mail: pherrera@harper.cc.il.us
Pascuala Herrera, LD Specialist
Tom L Thompson, Director

A public two-year college with 550 students with disabilities out of a total of 24,00. Offer a special instructional program for students with LD or ADD for an additional fee. Offers a TRIO/SSS project for degree-seeking students (150 involved annually).

Indiana

4442 Ancilla College

9601 S Union Road
Donaldson, IN 46513
219-936-8898
FAX 219-935-1773
http://www.ancilla.edu

Kathryn Bigley, Director

An independent two-year college with three special education students out of a total of 667.

4443 Anderson University

Disabled Student Services
1100 E 5th Street
Anderson, IN 46012
765-641-4226
FAX 765-641-3851
http://www.anderson.edu
e-mail: rsvogel@anderson.edu
Rinda Vogelgesang, Director
Jim King, Admissions Director

An independent four-year college with 78 special education students out of a total of 1,977.

4444 Ball State University

Handicapped Services
Muncie, IN 47306
765-285-5293
800-482-4278
FAX 765-285-2606
http://www.bsu.edu

Richard Harris, Contact

Offers a variety of services to students with disabilities including note takers, extended testing time, counseling services, and special accommodations.

4445 Bethel College: Indiana

1001 W McKinley Avenue
Mishawaka, IN 46545
219-259-8511
FAX 219-257-3499
http://www.bethel-in.edu

Offers a variety of services to students with disabilities including note takers, extended testing time, counseling services, and special accommodations.

4446 Butler University

4600 Sunset Avenue
Indianapolis, IN 46208
317-283-9255
800-368-6852
FAX 317-940-9930
http://www.butler.edu
e-mail: info@butler.edu

Rick Tirman

Offers a variety of services to students with disabilities including notetakers, extended testing time, counseling services, and special accommodations.

4447 Earlham College

National Road W
Richmond, IN 47374
765-983-1200
800-327-5426
FAX 765-983-1497
http://www.earlham.edu

Kathy Bryne, Contact

Offers a variety of services to students with disabilities including note takers, extended testing time, counseling services, and special accommodations.

4448 Franklin College of Indiana

501 E Monroe Street
Franklin, IN 46131
317-738-8000
800-522-0232
FAX 317-738-8234
http://www.franklincoll.edu
e-mail: webmaster@franklincoll.edu
Dana Giles, Assistant Director

An independent four-year college with six special education students out of a total of 914.

4449 Goshen College

1700 S Main Street
Goshen, IN 46526
574-535-7535
800-348-7422
FAX 574-535-7660
http://www.goshen.edu

Marty Hooley, Director

An independent four-year college with 23 special education students out of a total of 1,042.

4450 Holy Cross College

PO Box 308
Notre Dame, IN 46556
219-239-8383
FAX 219-233-7427
http://www.hcc-nd.edu
e-mail: uduke@hcc-nd.edu

A two-year colege that provides programs for learning disabled students.

4451 Indiana Institute of Technology

Student Support Services
1600 E Washington Boulevard
Fort Wayne, IN 46803
260-422-5561
800-937-2448
FAX 260-422-1518
http://www.indtech.edu
e-mail: scudder@indtech.edu
Mary Scudder, Director Student Services

A program of academic support services, including appropriate tutoring, peer mentoring and academic assistance, which is provided to students meeting specific federal eligibility guidelines.

4452 Indiana Institute on Disability and Community at Indiana University

2853 E Tenth Street
Bloomington, IN   47408   812-855-6508
                                 FAX 812-855-9630
                          http://www.iidc.indiana.edu
                          e-mail: iidc@indiana.edu
David M Mank PhD, Director
Joel F Fosha, Coordinator Office Marketing

The Indiana Institute on Disability and Community (IIDC) at Indiana University, Bloomington is committed to providing Hoosiers with disability-related information and services that touch the entire life span, from birth through older adulthood. Through its collaborative efforts with institutions of higher education, state and local government agencies, community service providers, persons with disabilities and their families, and advocacy organizations.

4453 Indiana State University

210 N 7th Street
Terre Haute, IN   47809   812-237-4000
                                 FAX 812-237-7948
                          http://www.web.indstate.edu
Rita Worrell, Coordinator

Offers a variety of services to students with disabilities including note takers, extended testing time, counseling services, and special accommodations.

4454 Indiana University East

2325 Chester Boulevard
Richmond, IN   47374   765-973-8200
                                 800-959-3278
                                 FAX 765-973-8388
                          http://www.iue.indiana.edu
Sabrina Pennington, Student Support

A public four-year college with 21 special education students out of a total of 2,249.

4455 Indiana University Northwest

3400 Broadway
Gary, IN   46408   219-980-6500
                                 888-YOUR-IUN
                          http://www.iun.edu
Ronald Thornton, Student Coordinator

A public four-year college with 34 special education students out of a total of 5,000.

4456 Indiana University Southeast

4201 Grant Line Road
New Albany, IN   47150   812-941-2579
                                 FAX 812-941-2589
                          http://www.ius.edu
                          e-mail: jojames@ius.edu
Jodi James, Coordinator

Offers a variety of services to students with disabilities including note takers, extended testing time, counseling services, and special accommodations.

4457 Indiana University: Bloomington

Disabled Student Services
300 N Jordon Avenue
Bloomington, IN   47405   812-855-7578
                                 FAX 812-855-7650
                          http://www.indiana.edu
                          e-mail: dsscoord@indiana.edu
Martha P Jacques, Director
Mary Ellen Anderson, Admissions Director

A public four-year college with 225 special education students out of a total of 29,383.

4458 Indiana University: Kokomo

2300 S Washington Street
Kokomo, IN   46902   765-455-2000
                          http://www.iuk.edu
Gerry Stroman, Director

A combination of attitudes assistance, accommodations, classroom arrangements and technological aids that make it possible for learning disabled and physically disabled students to succeed in a degree program for which they are qualified.

4459 Indiana University: Purdue

425 University Boulevard
Indianapolis, IN   46202   317-274-4591
                                 FAX 317-274-4493
                          http://www.iupui.edu
Pamela King, Director

A public four-year college with 154 special education students out of a total of 21,165.

4460 Indiana Vocational Technical: Southeast Campus

Ivy Tech Drive
Madison, IN   47250   812-265-2580
                  http://www.tpub.com/college.indiana
Jane Vire, Support Services

Offers a variety of services to students with disabilities including notetakers, extended testing time, counseling services, and special accommodations.

4461 Indiana Wesleyan University

Student Support Services
1401 S Washington Street
Marion, IN   46953   765-677-2257
                                 FAX 765-677-2140
                          http://www.indwes.edu
                          e-mail: jharrell@indwas.edu
Jerry Harrell, Director
Gaytha Holloway, Admissions Director

Offers a variety of services to students with disabilities including notetakers, extended testing time, counseling services and special accommodations.

4462 Ivy Tech State College Southwest

3501 N 1st Avenue
Evansville, IN   47710   812-429-1386
                                 FAX 812-429-1483
                                 TDY:812-429-9803
                  http://www.faculty.ivytech.edu/~pehlen/
                          e-mail: pehlen@ivytech.edu
Peg Ehlen, Disability Services Coordinator

Provides reasonable and effective accommodations to qualified students with learning disabilities.

4463 Ivy Tech State College: Northcentral
220 Dean Johnson Boulevard
South Bend, IN   46601   574-289-7001
                            FAX 574-236-7178
                    http://www.ivytech.edu
              e-mail: amatthew@ivy.tec.in.us
Amy Matthews, Coordinator Disabilities Service
Gail S Craker, Support Services Coordinator

Accommodations based on individual needs.

4464 Manchester College
Services for Students with Disabilities
9601 S Union Road
Donaldson, IN   46513   219-982-5076
                            FAX 219-982-5043
                    http://www.manchester.edu
              e-mail: dshowe@manchester.edu
Denise LS Howe, Director
JoLane Rohr, Admissions Director

An independent four-year college with 50 special education students out of a total of 1,091.

4465 Purdue University
Schleman Hall
West Lafayette, IN   47907   765-494-4600
                            FAX 765-494-0307
                    http://www.purdue.edu
Sarah Templin, Special Services

A public four-year college with 232 special education students out of a total of 29,673.

4466 Riley Child Development Center
Indiana University School of Medicine
702 Barnhill Drive
Indianapolis, IN   46202   317-274-8167
                            FAX 317-274-9760
                    http://www.child-dev.com
John Rau, Director

The Child Development Center provides interdisciplinary assessment for academics, communication, motor, behavior, medical concerns, for children and their families.

4467 Rose-Hulman Institute of Technology
5500 Wabash Avenue
Terre Haute, IN   47803   812-877-1511
                            FAX 812-877-8175
                    http://www.rose-hulman.edu
Susan Smith, Director

Offers a variety of services to students with disabilities including note takers, extended testing time, counseling services, and special accommodations.

4468 Saint Joseph's College
Highway 231
Rensselaer, IN   47978   219-866-6000
                                800-447-8781
                            FAX 219-866-6355
                    http://www.saintjoe.edu
David Weed, Director

Offers a variety of services to students with disabilities including note takers, extended testing time, counseling services, and special accommodations.

4469 Saint Mary-of-the-Woods College
3301 Saint Mary-of-the-Woods
St. Mary-of-the-Woods, IN   47876   812-535-5151
                            FAX 812-535-4900
                    http://www.smwc.edu
              e-mail: smwc@smwc.edu
Kate Satchwill, VP

Offers a variety of services to students with disabilities including note takers, extended testing time, counseling services, and special accommodations.

4470 Southcentral Indiana Vocational Technical College
8204 Highway 311
Sellersburg, IN   47172   812-246-3301
                            FAX 765-973-8383
Jack Womack, Contact

Offers a variety of services to students with disabilities including note takers, extended testing time, counseling services, and special accommodations.

4471 Taylor University
236 W Reade Avenue
Upland, IN   46989   765-998-5523
                            FAX 765-998-5569
                    http://www.tayloru.edu
              e-mail: edwelch@tayloru.edu
Dr. R Edwin Welch, Coordinator

Four-year college that provides academic support to students with disabilities.

4472 University of Evansville
1800 Lincoln Avenue
Evansville, IN   47722   812-479-2500
                                800-423-8633
                            FAX 812-475-6429
                    http://www.evansville.edu
Dr. Nealon Gaskey, Contact

An independent four-year college with 60 special education students out of a total of 2,500.

4473 University of Indianapolis
Baccalaureate for University of Indianapolis
1400 E Hanna Avenue
Indianapolis, IN   46227   317-788-3536
                                800-232-8634
                            FAX 317-788-3300
                    http://www.uindy.edu
              e-mail: dspinney@uindy.edu
Deborah L Spinney, Director BUILD Program
Deb Kelly, Tutorial Coordinator
Ron Wilks, Admissions Director

A private four-year university with a comprehensive program for students with learning disabilities. The BUILD Program offers a variety of services including private tutoring, specialized college courses, course substitutions, testing accommodations and assistive technology. There is a fee for this specialized program in addition to the university tuition.

4474 University of Notre Dame

Office for Students with Disabilities
220 Main Building
Notre Dame, IN   46556   219-631-7141
                              FAX 219-631-7939
                              http://www.nd.edu
                e-mail: margaret.spitzer@uncu.edu
Scott Howland, Director
Dan Saracino, Admissions Director

An independent four-year college with 20 special education students out of a total of 8,038.

4475 University of Saint Francis

Student Learning Center
2701 Spring Street
Fort Wayne, IN   46808   219-434-7677
                              FAX 219-434-3183
                              http://www.sfc.edu
                         e-mail: mkruyer@sf.edu
Michelle Kruyer, Director
John Arruza, Director

Through the Student Learning Center, University of Saint Francis offers a support program providing comprehensive services for student with diagnosed disabilities in the university setting. Students who present appropriate documentation and qualify for support services will receive modifications and accommodations to facilitate academic success. These services are provided at no cost to the student.

4476 University of Southern Indiana

Counseling Center
8600 University Boulevard
Evansville, IN   47712   812-464-1867
                              FAX 812-464-1960
                              http://www.usi.edu
                         e-mail: lmsmith@usi.edu
Leslie Smith, Assistant Director Counseling
James Browning, Director Counseling
Eric Otto, Admissions Director

Offers a variety of services to students with disabilities including notetaker supplies, tutor referral, extended testing time, counseling services, advocacy, sign language services and special accommodations.

4477 Vincennes University

Students Transition into Education Program
1002 N 1st Street
Vincennes, IN   47591   812-888-4485
                              800-742-9198
                              FAX 812-888-5707
                              http://www.vinu.edu
                  e-mail: jkavanaugh@vinu.edu
Jane Kavanaugh, Education Director
Susan Laue, Associate Professor
Ann Skuce, Admissions Director

A public two-year college with 200 learning disabled students in the STEP Program. Total student enrollment is 6,000. There is a fee for the special education program.

Iowa

4478 Central College: Student Support Services

812 University Avenue
Pella, IA   50219   641-628-9000
                              FAX 641-628-7647
                              http://www.central.edu
                       e-mail: krosen@central.edu
Nancy Kroese, Director

Four-year college that provides student support for those with learning disabilities.

4479 Clinton Community College

1000 Lincoln Boulevard
Clinton, IA   52732   563-244-7183
                              800-637-0559
                              FAX 563-244-7005
                              http://www.eiccd.cc.ia.us
                        e-mail: bkunau@eicc.edu
Marilyn Lyons, Contact

Offers a variety of services to students with disabilities including note takers, extended testing time, counseling services, and special accommodations.

4480 Coe College

1220 1st Avenue NE
Cedar Rapids, IA   52402   319-399-8547
                              FAX 319-399-8503
                              http://www.coe.edu
                        e-mail: lkabela@coe.edu
Lois Kabela-Coates, Director

Services include: tutors, note takers, test proctoring for untimed and oral tests, assistance with accessing textbooks on tape, study skills and time management assistance, reading and writing assistance, personal and academic counseling, and assistance with course and instructor selection.

4481 Cornell College

600 1st Street W
Mount Vernon, IA   52314   319-895-4000
                              FAX 319-896-5188
                              http://www.cornell-iowa.edu
                e-mail: admissions@cornell-iowa.edu
An independent four-year college with 11 special education students out of a total of 1,114.

4482 DesMoines Area Community College

2006 S Ankeny Boulevard
Ankeny, IA   50021   515-964-6250
                              800-362-2127
                              FAX 515-964-7022
                              TDY:964-38101515
                              http://www.dmacc.cc.ia.us
                e-mail: webmaster@dmacc.cc.ia.us
DMACC is committed to providing an accessible environment that supports students with disabilities in reaching their full potential. Support services are available for students with disabilities to ensure equal access to educational opportunities.

4483   Dordt College

Academic Skills Center
498 4th Avenue NE
Sioux Center, IA   51250   712-722-6490
                                 FAX 712-722-4498
                                 http://www.dordt.edu
                        e-mail: admissions@dordt.edu
Lavonne Boer, Coordinator

Four-year college that offers academic services to students.

4484   Drake University

Student Disability Services
2507 University
Des Moines, IA   50311   515-271-3100
                                 800-443-7259
                                 FAX 515-271-3016
                                 TDY:515-271-2825
                                 http://www.drake.edu
                  e-mail: christal.stanley@drake.edu
Chrystal Stanley, Director
Thomas Willoughby, Admissions Director

Offers a variety of services to students with disabilities including formal academic accommodations and support services.

4485   Ellsworth Community College

1100 College Avenue
Iowa Falls, IA   50126   515-648-3128
                                 800-322-9235
                                 FAX 515-648-3128
                        http://www.iavalley.cc.ia.us
                    e-mail: lmulford@iavalley.cc.ia.us
Lori Mulford, Coordinator

Offers a variety of services to students with disabilities including note takers, extended testing time, counseling services and special accommodations.

4486   Graceland College

1 University Place
Lamoni, IA   50140   641-784-5000
                                 FAX 641-784-5698
                        http://www2.graceland.edu
JR Smith, Director

An independent four-year college with 27 special education students out of a total of 968. There is an additional fee for the special education program in addition to the regular tuition.

4487   Grand View College

1200 Grandview Avenue
Des Moines, IA   50316   515-263-2871
                                 FAX 515-263-2840
                                 http://www.gvc.edu
                        e-mail: cwassenaar@gve.edu
Carolyn Wassenaar, Director
Debbie Borger, Admissions Director

An independent four-year college with 15 special education students out of a total of 1,419.

4488   Grinnell College

Academic Advising Office
PO Box 805
Grinnell, IA   50112   641-269-3702
                                 FAX 641-269-3710
                                 http://www.grinnell.edu
                        e-mail: sternjm@grinnell.edu
Joyce M Stern, Associate Dean
Jim Sumner, Admissions Director

An independent four-year college which currently provides academic accommodations to students with learning disabilities and 15 students with ADHD out of a total of 1,344.

4489   Hawkeye Community College

1501 E Orange Road
Waterloo, IA   50704   319-296-2320
                                 FAX 319-296-4018
Kathy Linda, Developmental Studies Department
Ruben Carrion, Student Development Director

Offers a variety of services to students with disabilities including notetakers, extended testing time, tutoring, counseling services, and special accommodations.

4490   Indian Hills Community College

Success Center
525 Grandview Avenue
Ottumwa, IA   52501   641-683-5155
                                 800-726-2585
                                 FAX 641-683-5184
                                 http://www.ihec.cc.ia.us
                        e-mail: mstewart@ihcc.cc.ia.us
Judy Brickey, Coordinator
Mary Stewart, Special Needs Director
Sally Harris, Admissions Director

A public two-year college with 400 special education students out of a total of 3,166. There is a fee for the special education program in addition to the regular tuition.

4491   Iowa Central Community College

330 Avenue M
Fort Dodge, IA   50501   515-576-7201
                                 800-362-2793
                                 FAX 515-576-7206
        http://www.iccc.cc.ia.us/icc/home/default.htm
                  e-mail: lundeen@triton.iccc.cc.ia.us
Shelly Lundeen

A public two-year college with approximately 50 special needs students out of a total of 3,003.

4492   Iowa Lakes Community College: Emmetsburg Campus

3200 College Drive
Emmetsburg, IA   50536   712-852-3554
                                 800-242-5108
                                 FAX 712-852-2152
                                 http://www.ilcc.cc.ia.us/
Ann Petersen, Special Needs
Elizabeth Ankeny, SAVE Coordinator

Offers a variety of services to students with disabilities including notetakers, extended testing time, counseling services, and special accommodations, including secondary programs at post-secondary institutions.

4493 Iowa Lakes Community College: Success Centers

300 S 18th Street
Estherville, IA 51334   712-362-2604
                                800-521-5054
                           FAX 712-362-3969
                           http://www.iowalakes.edu
                           e-mail: info@iowalakes.edu
Colleen Peltz, Professor Developmental Educ.
Lynn Dodge, Assistant Professor Dev. Educ.
Linda Helmers, Counselor

Offers a variety of services to students with disabilities including note takers, extended testing time, counseling services, and special accommodations.

4494 Iowa State University

Disability Resources
100 Alumni Hall
Ames, IA 50011   515-294-0644
                         FAX 515-294-5670
                         http://www.iastate.edu
                         e-mail: online@iastate.edu
Gwen Woodward, Director
Marc Harding, Admissions Director

A public four-year university that has 80 students receiving disability services out of 21,503.

4495 Iowa Wesleyan College

601 N Main Street
Mount Pleasant, IA 52641   319-385-8021
                         FAX 319-385-6384
Linda Widmer, Director

An independent four-year college with four special education students out of a total of 1,000.

4496 Iowa Western Community College: Council Bluffs Campus

2700 College Road
Council Bluffs, IA 51502   712-325-3390
                              800-432-5852
                         FAX 712-388-0123
                         http://www.iwcc.cc.ia.us
                         e-mail: cholst@iwcc.cc.ia.us
Chris Holst, Coordinator

IWCC is committed to making individuals with disabilities full participants in its programs, services and activities. It is the policy of IWCC that no otherwise qualified individual with a disability shall be denied access to or participation in any program, service or activity offered by the college.

4497 Loras College

Learning Disabilities Program
1450 Alta Vista
Dubuque, IA 52004   319-588-7134
                         FAX 319-557-4080
                         http://www.loras.edu
                         e-mail: dgibson@loras.edu
Dianne Gibson, Director
Tim Hauber, Admissions Director

Private Catholic four-year college with 40 learning disabled students out of a total of 1,626. The Learning Disabilities Program charges a fee for the Enhanced program. Mandated services are free.

4498 Luther College

700 College Drive
Decorah, IA 52101   319-387-1270
                              800-458-8437
                         FAX 319-387-2519
                         http://www.luther.edu
                         e-mail: equalaccess@luther.edu
G Raymundo Rosales, Director
Janice Halsne, Services Director

In keeping with the mission of Luther College, the Student Academic Support Center (SASC) exists to support all students as they pursue a liberal arts education, and specifically to be an advocate for students with disabilities. SASC processes all student requests for accommodations to provide each student with a suitable learning environment. The accommodations provided are not remedial in nature, nor do they change or reduce the academic standard.

4499 Marshalltown Community College

3702 S Center Street
Marshalltown, IA 50158   515-752-7106
                         FAX 515-752-8149
Regina West, Coordinator

A two-year community college that offers programs for its learning disabled students.

4500 Morningside College

Achievement Center
Sioux City, IA 51106   712-274-5104
                              800-831-0806
                         FAX 712-274-5101
                         e-mail: rohlena@morningside.edu
Robbie Rohlena, Director
Karmen Jucht, LD Specialist

A comprehensive learning disabilities program which offers academic advisement accommodations, subject area tutoring, and supportive services.

4501 Mount Mercy College

1330 Elmhurst Drive NE
Cedar Rapids, IA 52402   319-363-8213
                         FAX 319-363-6341
                         http://www.mt mercy.edu
                         e-mail: nbrauhn@mmc.mtmercy.edu
Mary Jean Stanton, Director

Four-year college offering support and services to learning disabled students.

4502 Mount Saint Clare College

400 N Bluff Boulevard
Clinton, IA 52732   319-242-4023
                              800-242-4153
                         FAX 319-242-2003
                         http://www.clare.edu
Diane Cornilsen, Director

Offers a variety of services to students with disabilities including notetakers, extended testing time, counseling services, and special accommodations.

4503 **Muscatine Community College**

152 Colorado Street
Muscatine, IA 52761   563-288-6166
800-351-4669
FAX 563-288-6104
http://www.eiccd.cc.ia.us
e-mail: smewwiam@eicc.edu
Kathryn Trosen, Retention Specialist

A public two-year college with 29 special education students out of a total of 1,192.

4504 **North Iowa Area Community College**

500 College Drive
Mason City, IA 50401   614-422-4106
888-466-4222
FAX 614-422-4150
e-mail: ewerster@niaccicc.ia.us
Terri Benner Ewers, Director of Counseling

Offers a variety of services to students with disabilities including notetakers, extended testing time, counseling services, and special accommodations.

4505 **Northwestern College**

101 7th Street SW
Orange City, IA 51041   707-737-7307
FAX 707-737-7290
http://www.nwciowa.edu
Marcia Olson, Special Services

Offers a variety of services to students with disabilities including note takers, extended testing time, counseling services, and special accommodations.

4506 **Saint Ambrose College**

Services for Students with Disabilities
518 W Locus Street
Davenport, IA 52803   319-333-6161
FAX 319-333-6243
http://www.sau.edu
e-mail: aaqustin@saunix.sau.edu
Ann Austin, LD Specialist
Meg Flagherty, Admissions Director

An independent four-year college with 63 special education students out of a total of 2,022.

4507 **Scott Community College**

500 Belmont Road
Bettendorf, IA 52722   563-441-4000
FAX 563-441-4066
http://www.eiccd.cc.ia.us
Jerri Crabtree, Director

A public two-year college with 59 special education students out of a total of 3,611.

4508 **Southeastern Community College: North Campus**

1015 S Gear Avenue
West Burlington, IA 52655   319-752-2731
http://www.secc.cc.ia.us/
Dana Niggemeyer, Admissions Coordinator
Stacy White, Admissions Coordinator

Offers special services and student services to the learning disabled.

4509 **Southwestern Community College**

1501 Townline Road
Creston, IA 50801   641-782-7081
FAX 641-782-1334
http://www.swcc.cc.ia.us
Gary O'Daniels, Special Services

Offers a variety of services to students with disabilities including note takers, extended testing time, counseling services, and special accommodations.

4510 **University of Iowa**

Student Disability Services
107 Calvin Hall
Iowa City, IA 52242   319-335-1462
FAX 319-335-3973
http://www.uiowa.edu
e-mail: mary-richard@uiowa.edu
Mary Richard, Disability Services Coordinator
Michael Barron, Admissions Director

A public four-year college with 301 learning disabled students out of a total of 19,284.

4511 **University of Northern Iowa**

Disability Services
1222 W 27th Street
Cedar Falls, IA 50614   319-273-2676
FAX 319-273-6884
http://www.uni.edu
e-mail: jane.slykhuis@uni.edu
Jane Slykhuis, Coordinator
David Towle PhD, Director
Clark Elmer, Admissions Director

Four-year college that provides services to students with a learning disability.

4512 **Waldorf College**

Learning Disabilities Program
106 S 6th Street
Forest City, IA 50436   641-584-8207
800-292-1903
FAX 641-584-8194
http://www.waldorf.edu
e-mail: hillb@waldorf.edu
Rebecca Hill, Director
Steve Lovick, Admissions Director

An independent two-year college with 20 learning disabled students out of a total of 599. There is an additional fee for the learning disabled program in addition to the regular tuition.

4513 **Wartburg College**

222 9th Street NW
Waverly, IA 50677   319-352-8260
800-772-2085
FAX 319-352-8579
http://www.wartburg.edu
Debbie Heida, VP

An independent four-year college with 11 special education students out of a total of 1,454.

Kansas

4514 Allen County Community College

1801 N Cottonwood Street
Iola, KS   66749   316-365-5116
                                    FAX 316-365-3284
Rochelle Smith, Contact

Offers a variety of services to students with disabilities including note takers, extended testing time, counseling services, and special accommodations.

4515 Baker University

Learning Resource Center
8th & Grove
Baldwin City, KS   66006   785-894-8352
                                    FAX 785-594-8367
                                    http://www.bakeru.edu
                    e-mail: marian@harvey.bakeru.edu
Kathy Marian, Director
Paige Illum, Admissions Director

A private four-year college with a total of 923 students.

4516 Barton County Community College

245 NE 30th Road
Great Bend, KS   67530   316-792-2701
                                    FAX 316-792-3238
                        http://www.barton.cc.ks.us
                    e-mail: elliotts@barton.cc.ksus
Jackie Elliott, Director Student Support

A public two-year college with 12 special education students out of a total of 4,462.

4517 Bethel College

300 E 27th Street
North Newton, KS   67117   316-283-2500
                                    800-522-1887
                                    FAX 316-284-5286
                        http://www.bethelks.edu
Sandee Zerger

Offers a variety of services to students with disabilities including notetakers, extended testing time, counseling services, and special accommodations.

4518 Butler County Community College

College Drive
El Dorado, KS   16003   724-287-8711
                                    800-826-2829
                                    FAX 724-287-4961
Lora Rozeboom, Special Needs

A public two-year college with 93 special education students out of a total of 5,601.

4519 Center for Research on Learning

University of Kansas
1122 W Campus Road
Lawrence, KS   66045   785-864-4780
                                    FAX 785-864-5728
                                    http://www.ku-crl.org
                                    e-mail: cre@ku.edu
Don Deshler, Director

All of the research undertaken at the center adheres to a single mission that has been crafted to respond to these educational challenges: an information explosion in all content areas; a limited amount of instructional time; and increased expectations for student achievement.

4520 Colby Community College

1255 S Range Avenue
Colby, KS   67701   785-462-3984
                                    FAX 785-462-4600
                                    http://www.colby.cc.ks.us
Joyce Washburn, Academic Services

Offers a variety of services to students with disabilities including note takers, extended testing time, counseling services, and special accommodations.

4521 Cowley County Community College

125 S 2nd Street
Arkansas City, KS   67005   316-442-0430
                                    800-593-2222
                                    FAX 316-441-5350
                        http://www.cowleycollege.com
                    e-mail: watson@cowleycollege.com
Bruce D Watson, ADA Coordinator

Offers a variety of services to students with disabilities including notetakers, extended testing time, counseling services, and special accommodations.

4522 Donnelly College

608 N 18th Street
Kansas City, KS   66102   913-621-8764
                                    FAX 913-621-0354
                    e-mail: stephens@donnelly.cc.ks.us
Lee Stephenson, Director Student Services

An independent two-year college with 10 special education students out of a total of 381.

4523 Emporia State University

1200 Commercial Street
Emporia, KS   66801   620-341-5374
                                    FAX 620-341-5918
                                    http://www.emporia.edu
Dr. Keith Frank, Coordinator

Offers a variety of services to students with disabilities including note takers, extended testing time, counseling services, and special accommodations.

4524 Fort Scott Community College

2108 S Horton
Fort Scott, KS   66701   316-223-2700
                                    FAX 316-223-6530
            http://www.ftscott.cc.ks.us/fscchome.html
                    e-mail: beckyw@ftscott.cc.ks.us
Becky Weddle, Director CE/ETC/Mill

A public two-year college with 34 special education students out of a total of 1,928.

4525 Hutchinson Community College

1300 N Plum Street
Hutchinson, KS   67501   316-665-3500
                                      800-289-3501
                                      FAX 316-665-3310
                                      http://www.hutchcc.edu
                                      e-mail: info@hutchcc.edu

Mary Coplen, Director

Offers a variety of services to students with disabilities including notetakers, extended testing time, counseling services, and special accommodations.

4526 Kansas Community College: Kansas City

7250 State Avenue
Kansas City, KS   66112   913-334-1100
                                      FAX 913-596-9606
                                      http://www.kckcc.cc.ks.us
Valarie Webb, Disability Resource Center

A public two-year college with an enrollment of approximately 6,000 students. Thirty-five LD students request services each semester. Developmental courses and accommodations are offered for students with learning disabilities.

4527 Kansas State University

Disability Support Services
Holton Hall
Manhattan, KS   66506   785-532-6441
                                      FAX 785-532-6457
                                      http://www.ksu.edu
                                      e-mail: dss@ksu.edu

Gretchen Holden, Director
Andrea Blair, LD Specialist
Larry Moeder, Admissions Director

Dedicated to providing equal opportunity and access for every student. The staff provides a broad range of supportive services in an effort to ensure that the individual needs of each student are met. In addition, the staff functions as an advocate for students with disabilities on the K-State campus.

4528 Kansas University Center for Developmental Disabilities (KUCDD)

1000 Sunnyside Avenue
Lawrence, KS   66045   785-864-4950
                                      FAX 785-864-5323
                                      http://www.lsi.ku.edu
                                      e-mail: schroeder@ku.edu

Stephen R Schrander, Director

KUCDD develops alternatives to institutional care for persons with developmental disabilities. Helps families of persons with disabilities define their needs and find resources and plan and evaluate services on a cost-performance basis. Also provides in-service trainig to service providers.

4529 Labette Community College

200 S 14th Street
Parsons, KS   67357   620-421-6700
                                      FAX 620-421-0921
                                      http://www.labette.cc.ks.us

Viv Metcalf, Director

A public two-year college with 80 special education students out of a total of 2,598.

4530 Neosho County Community College

800 W 14th Street
Chanute, KS   66720   620-431-2820
                                      FAX 620-235-4030
                                      http://www.neosho.cc.ks.us
John Messenger, Instructor

Offers a variety of services to students with disabilities including note takers, extended testing time, counseling services, and special accommodations.

4531 Newman University

3100 McCormick Street
Wichita, KS   67213   316-942-4291
                                      FAX 316-942-4483
                                      http://www.newmanu.edu
                                      e-mail: niedensr@newmanu.edu
Rosemary Niedens, Dean of Students
Julie Wright Connolly, ADA Coordinator

Offers a variety of services to students with disabilities including notetakers, extended testing time, counseling services, and special accommodations.

4532 North Central Kansas Technical College

2205 Wheatland Drive
Hays, KS   67601   785-623-6155
                                      800-343-1195
                                      FAX 785-623-6152

4533 Ottawa University

1001 S Cedar Street
Ottawa, KS   66067   785-242-5200
                                      800-755-5200
                                      FAX 785-242-1008
                                      http://www.ottawa.edu
Karen Ohnesorge-Fick, Academic Achievement

An independent four-year college with 11 special education students out of a total of 546.

4534 Pittsburg State University

Learning Center
1701 S Broadway Street
Pittsburg, KS   66762   316-235-4966
                                      800-854-7488
                                      FAX 316-235-4520
                                      http://www.pittstate.edu
                                      e-mail: nhenry@pittstate.edu
Nick A Henry, Special Services
Ange Peterson, Admissions Director

A public four-year college with 74 special education students out of a total of 5,222.

4535 Saint Mary College

4100 S 4th Street
Leavenworth, KS   66048   913-682-5151
                                      FAX 913-758-6140
                                      http://www.smcks.edu
                                      e-mail: admiss@hub.smcks.edu
Dr. Carol Hinds, Academic Dean

Offers a variety of services to students with disabilities including note takers, extended testing time, counseling services, and special accommodations.

4536 Seward County Community College
1801 N Kansas Avenue
Liberal, KS 67905   316-624-1951
                                   800-373-9951
                             FAX 316-629-2715
                      http://www.scc.cc.ks.us/
Larry Philbeck, Academic Achievement

A public two-year college with 13 special education students out of a total of 1,522.

4537 Tabor College
400 S Jefferson
Hillsboro, KS 67063   620-947-3121
                                   800TABOR-99
                             FAX 620-947-2607
                        http://www.tabor.edu
Judy Heibert, Contact

Offers a variety of services to students with disabilities including note takers, extended testing time, counseling services, and special accommodations.

4538 University Affiliated Program
Kansas University
2601 Gabriel Avenue
Parsons, KS 67357   620-421-6550
                             FAX 620-421-1702
                      e-mail: dmoody@ku.edu
David Lindeman, Director

Mission is optimize the quality of life and extend the concept of independence, productivity, integration and inclusion of individuals with disabilities in all aspects of life. This can be accomplished by providing new options, meaningful choices, independence, self-reliance, dignity of risk, and the means to achieve enhanced personal productivity.

4539 University of Kansas
1502 Iowa Street
Lawrence, KS 66045   785-864-2620
                             FAX 785-864-4050
                        http://www.ku.edu
                      e-mail: lzimmer@ukans.edu
Lorna Zimmer, Director

Accommodates students with a learning disability by understanding the students ability.

4540 Washburn University of Topeka
University of Topeka
1700 SW College Avenue
Topeka, KS 66621   785-231-1010
                             FAX 785-234-3813
                        http://www.washburn.edu
Greg Moore, Contact

Offers a variety of services to students with disabilities including note takers, extended testing time, counseling services, and special accommodations.

4541 Wichita State University
1845 Fairmount Street
Wichita, KS 67260   316-978-3085
                                   800-362-2594
                             FAX 316-978-3016
                        http://www.wichita.edu
Grady Landrum, Special Services

A public four-year college with 11 special education students out of a total of 13,103.

Kentucky

4542 Bellarmine College
Disability Services
2001 Newburg Road
Louisville, KY 40205   502-452-8153
                             FAX 502-452-8050
                        http://www.bellarmine.edu
                      e-mail: rgarveynix@bellarmine.edu
Four-year college that provides services for the disabled.

4543 Berea College
CPO 2190 College Station
Berea, KY 40404   859-985-3000
                             FAX 859-985-3917
                        http://www.berea.edu
                      e-mail: webresponse@berea.edu
John Cook

Offers a variety of services to students with disabilities including note takers, extended testing time, counseling services, and special accommodations.

4544 Brescia University
717 Frederica Street
Owensboro, KY 42301   270-686-4259
                                   877-273-7242
                             FAX 270-686-4266
                        http://www.bresciu.edu
Mary Austin, Director Admissions

Provides the following for students with learning disabilities: developmental courses (English, mathematics and study skills); individual tutoring for all areas; and academic and career counseling.

4545 Clear Creek Baptist Bible College
300 Clear Creek Road
Pineville, KY 40977   606-337-3196
                             FAX 606-337-2372
                        http://www.ccbbc.edu
                      e-mail: ccbbc@ccbbc.edu
Georgia Mink

An independent four-year college with 11 special education students out of a total of 141.

4546 Eastern Kentucky University
Coates Box 2A
Richmond, KY   40475   859-622-1500
                              FAX 859-622-6395
                              http://www.eku.edu
                              e-mail: disbellu@acs.eku.edu
Teresa Belluscio, Director

Mission of project SUCCESS is to respond effectively and efficiently to the individual's educational needs.

4547 Jefferson Technical College
727 W Chestnut Street
Louisville, KY   40203   502-213-4100
                              FAX 502-213-4700
Carl Barnett, Director

Offers a variety of services to students with disabilities including note takers, extended testing time, counseling services, and special accommodations.

4548 Kentucky State University
103 Jackson Hall
Frankfort, KY   40601   502-597-6000
                              FAX 502-597-6407
                              http://www.kysu.edu
                              e-mail: bmorelock@gwmail.kysu.edu
Patricia Jones, Contact

Offers a variety of services to students with disabilities including note takers, extended testing time, counseling services, and special accommodations.

4549 Lexington Community College
103 Oswald Building
Lexington, KY   40506   859-257-4872
                              866-774-4872
                              FAX 859-323-7136
                              TDY:849-257-6068
                              http://www.uky.edu
                              e-mail: lccinfo@lsv.uky.edu
Veronica Miller, Director
Regina Johnson, SS Associate

Comprehensive community college on campus of University of Kentucky.

4550 Lindsey Wilson College
210 Lindsey Wilson Street
Columbia, KY   42728   270-384-8080
                              800-264-0138
                              FAX 270-384-8050
                              http://www.lindsey.edu
David Ludden, Learning Disabilities Coord.
Lilian Roland, Learning Disabilities Coord.

Offers a variety of services to students with disabilities including notetakers, extended testing time, counseling services, and special accommodations.

4551 Madisonville Community College: Universityof Kentucky
2000 College Drive
Madisonville, KY   42431   270-821-2250
                              FAX 270-825-8552
                              http://www.madcc.kctcs.net
                              e-mail: aimee.bullock@kctcs.edu
Nancy Douglas, Instructor

Offers a variety of services to students with disabilities including note takers, extended testing time, counseling services, and special accommodations.

4552 Murray State University
Lowry Center
Murray, KY   42071   270-762-2018
                              FAX 270-762-4339
                              http://www.murraystate.edu
                              e-mail: donna.harris@murraystate.edu
Cindy Clemson, Coordinator

Services and programs provided to the learning disabled.

4553 Northern Kentucky University
Nunn Drive
Highland Heights, KY   41099 606-572-5220
                              800-637-9948
                              FAX 606-572-5162
                              http://www.nku.edu
                              e-mail: admitnku@nku.edu
A Dale Adams, Special Services

Offers a variety of services to students with disabilities including note takers, extended testing time, counseling services, and special accommodations.

4554 Pikeville College
147 Sycamore Street
Pikeville, KY   41501   606-432-5250
                              FAX 606-218-5269
                              http://www.pc.edu
                              e-mail: webmaster@pc.edu
William Little

Offers a variety of services to students with disabilities including notetakers, extended testing time, counseling services, and special accommodations.

4555 Thomas More College
333 Thomas More Parkway
Crestview Hills, KY   41017   606-344-3521
                              FAX 606-344-3342
                              http://www.thomasmore.edu
                              e-mail: barb.davis@thomasmore.edu
Dr. Dale Meyers, Dean of Academic Affairs
Barbara Davis, Director Student Services

An independent four-year college with 50 special education students out of a total of 1,272.

4556 University of Kentucky: Interdisciplinary Human Development Institute

University of Kentucky
126 Mineral Industries Building
Lexington, KY   40506   859-257-1714
                               FAX 859-323-1901
                          http://www.ihdi.uky.edu
                       e-mail: mafar101@uky.edu
Melton C Martinson, Director

Mission is to promote independence, productivity, and integration of all people through numerous research, training and outreach activities.

4557 University of Louisville

Robbins Hall
Louisville, KY   40292   502-852-6938
                                FAX 502-852-0924
                           http://www.louisville.edu
Cathy Patus, Resource Center

A public four-year college with 60 learning disabled students out of a total of 22,000.

4558 Western Kentucky University

1 Big Red Way
Bowling Green, KY   42101   270-745-5121
                                   FAX 270-745-3199
                              http://www.wku.edu
                        e-mail: huda.melky@wku.edu
Huda Melky, Director

The goal of the program is to foster the participation of persons with disabilities.

Louisiana

4559 Human Development Center

Louisiana State University
1100 Florida Avenue
New Orleans, LA   70119   504-942-8202
                                 FAX 504-942-8305
                                 TDY:5049425900
                          http://www.hdc@lsuhsc.edu
Robert E Crow, Director

4560 Learning Disabilities Association of Louisiana

Northwestern State University
Teacher Education Center
Natchitoches, LA   71497   318-357-5154
                                  FAX 318-357-3275
                          e-mail: duchardt@nsula.edu
Dr. Barbara Duchardt, Associate Professor

4561 Louisiana College

Program to Assist Student Success
1140 College Drive
Pineville, LA   71360   318-487-7629
                          http://www.lacollege.edu
                       e-mail: pass@lacollege.edu
Betty P Matthews, Director

This highly individualized, limited enrollment program provides support services and personal attention to students who may need special academic guidance, tutoring, and classroom assistance.

4562 Louisiana State University Agricultural and Mechanical College

Johnston Hall
Baton Rouge, LA   70803   225-388-3202
                                 FAX 225-388-5982
                            http://www.lsu.edu
Tina Schultz

A public four-year college with 88 special education students out of a total of 21,245.

4563 Louisiana State University: Alexandria

8100 Highway 71 S
Alexandria, LA   71302   318-473-6545
                                888-473-6417
                                FAX 318-473-6580
                           http://www.lsua.edu
Dr. Dee Slavant, Director Student Services

Offers a variety of services to students with disabilities including extended testing time, counseling services, and special accommodations.

4564 Louisiana State University: Eunice

2048 Johnson Highway
Eunice, LA   70535   337-457-7311
                            888-367-5783
                            FAX 337-550-1445
                       http://www.lsue.edu
Dr. Marvette Thomas, Director TRIO

A public two-year college with 31 special education students out of a total of 2,595.

4565 Loyola University New Orleans

6363 St. Charles Avenue
New Orleans, LA   70118   504-865-2990
                                 FAX 504-865-3543
                            http://www.loyno.edu
                        e-mail: ssmith@loyno.edu
Sarah Mead Smith, Director

Four year college that provides services to disabled students.

4566 McNeese State University

4100 Ryan Street
Lake Charles, LA   70609   318-475-5820
                                  800-622-3352
                                  FAX 318-475-5924
                             http://www.mcneese.edu
Sena Theall, Director Special Project
Denise Leiato, Coordinator

Provides academic advising, arrangements for individual accommodations for disabilities, tutoring and computers and word processing equipment. All services are available to the students at no charge.

Maine

4567 Nicholls State University

PO Box 2050
Thibodaux, LA 70310 985-448-4214
FAX 985-448-4423
http://www.nich.edu
e-mail: nicholls@nich-nsunet.nich.edu
Carol Ronka, Director

Students with dyslexia are offered individual tutoring assistance and communicators.

4568 Southeastern Louisiana University

SLU 752
Hammond, LA 70402 504-549-2077
FAX 504-549-3640
http://www.selu.edu
e-mail: mhall@selu.edu
Dr. Michelle Hall, Interim Director

Four-year college that offers programs for students whom are disabled.

4569 Tulane University

6823 St. Charles Avenue
New Orleans, LA 70118 504-865-5113
FAX 504-862-8148
http://www.tulane.edu
e-mail: pr@tulane.edu
Kelley Hunter, Coordinator

Four-year college that provides services to those students who are learning disabled.

4570 University of Louisiana at Lafayette: Services of Students with Disabilities

PO Drawer 41650
Lafayette, LA 70504 337-482-5252
FAX 337-482-0195

The Mission of Services for Students with Disabilities is to provide extensive post secondary services for emotionally, physically and learning impaired students. Our goals are to facilitate the transition from high school to college, to assist students developing the necessary skills to succeed in college; and to provide counseling, including career counseling, and to assist in successful transition from college to employment.

4571 University of New Orleans

260 University Center
New Orleans, LA 70148 504-208-7284
FAX 504-280-3975
http://www.uno.edu
Amy A King, Coordinator

A public four-year college with 45 special education students out of a total of 12,441.

4572 ALLTech

University of Southern Maine
301 C Baily Hall
Gorham, ME 04038 207-780-5016
800-800-5016
FAX 207-780-5224
TDY:207-780-5016
http://www.alltech-tsi.org
e-mail: info@alltech-tsi.org
Deb Dimmick, Director

4573 Bates College

102 Lane Hall
Lewiston, ME 04240 207-786-6219
FAX 207-786-6219
http://www.bates.edu
e-mail: cba@branham@bates.edu
Celeste Branham, Dean

An independent four-year college with 17 special education students out of a total of 1,501.

4574 Bowdoin College

5000 College Station
Brunswick, ME 04011 207-725-3958
FAX 207-725-3764
http://www.bowdoin.edu
e-mail: help3030@bowdoin.edu
Mary McCann, Contact

Offers a variety of services to students with disabilities including note takers, extended testing time, counseling services, and special accommodations.

4575 Center for Community Inclusion (CCI): Maine's University Center for Excellence

University of Maine
5717 Corbett Hall
Orono, ME 04469 207-581-1084
800-203-6957
FAX 207-581-1231
http://www.ume.maine.edu/cci
e-mail: ccimail@umit.maine.edu
Lucille A Zeph, Director

CCI has four core functions: interdisciplinary education; community services, outreach education and technical assistance; research and evaluation; and dissemination.

4576 Eastern Maine Vocational-Technical Institute

354 Hogan Road
Bangor, ME 04401 207-941-4600
800-286-9357
FAX 207-941-4608
http://www.emtc.org
e-mail: admissions@emtc.org
Phillip Pratt

Offers a variety of services to students with disabilities including notetakers, extended testing time, counseling services, and special accommodations.

4577 Kennebec Valley Technical College

92 Western Avenue
Fairfield, ME 04937   207-453-5000
http://www.kvtc.net
e-mail: jhood@kvtc.net
Pat Ross, Students Services

A public two-year college with 13 special education students out of a total of 1,086.

4578 Mid-State College

88 E Hardscrabble Road
Auburn, ME 04210   207-783-1478
FAX 207-783-1477
http://www.midstatecollege.com
e-mail: info@midstatecollege.com
Richard Gross, Special Services

Offers a variety of services to students with disabilities including notetakers, extended testing time, counseling services, and special accommodations.

4579 Northern Maine Technical College

33 Edgemont Drive
Presque Isle, ME 04769   207-768-2787
800-535-NMTC
FAX 207-768-2831
http://www.nmtc.net
Iris Brewer, Special Services

A public two-year college with 33 special education students out of a total of 817.

4580 Southern Maine Technical College

2 Fort Road
South Portland, ME 04106   207-767-9536
FAX 207-767-9522
http://www.smtc.net
Mark Krogman, Disability Services Provider

Southern Maine Technical College is committed to helping qualified students with disabilities achieve their educational goals. Upon request and verification of the disability, SMTC will provide service coordination and reasonable accommodations to remediate the competitive disadvantage that a disability can create in the educational setting.

4581 Unity College

Unity, ME 04988   207-948-3131
FAX 207-948-6277
http://www.unity.edu
James Horan, Special Services

Offers a variety of services to students with disabilities including notetakers, extended testing time, counseling services, and special accommodations.

4582 University of Maine

Disability Support Services
Onward Building
Orono, ME 04469   207-581-2319
FAX 207-581-2969
http://www.umaine.edu
e-mail: ann.smith@umit.maine.edu
Ann Smith, Coordinator of Disability Svcs.
Sara Henry, Disability Counselor

The primary goal of the University of Maine Disability Support Services is to create educational access for students with disabilities at UMaine by providing a point of coordination, information and education for those students and the campus community.

4583 University of Maine: Fort Kent

Academic and Counseling Services
23 University Drive
Fort Kent, ME 04743   207-834-7500
888-879-8635
FAX 207-834-7503
TDY:207-834-7466
http://www.umfk.maine.edu
George Diaz, Director of Counseling Svcs.
Garland Caron, Counselor

Students with a documented disability, who need academic accommodations, are encouraged to meet with an Academic and Counseling Services representative to develop a plan for their accommodations.

4584 University of Maine: Machias

9 O'Brien Avenue
Machias, ME 04654   207-255-1228
FAX 207-255-4864
http://www.umm.maine.edu
e-mail: admissions@acd.umm.maine.edu
Jean Schild, Cordinator

Prepared to assist students with disabilities with reasonable accommodations to qualified individuals with disabilities upon request.

4585 University of New England: University Campus

Disability Services
11 Hills Beach Road
Biddeford, ME 04005   207-283-0171
800-477-4863
FAX 207-294-5931
http://www.une.edu
e-mail: schurch@une.edu
Susan Church, Coordinator
Diane Laverriere, Test Proctor

The Office for Students with Disabilities exists to ensure that the University fulfills the part of its mission that seeks to promote respect for individual differences and to ensure that no person who meets the academic and technical standards requisite for admisssion to, and continued enrollment at, the University is denied benefits or subjected to discrimination at UNE solely by reason of his or her disability.

4586 University of New England: Westbrook College Campus

716 Stevens Avenue
Portland, ME 04103   207-797-7261
FAX 207-282-6379
e-mail: Cehringhaus@mailbox.une.edu
Dr. Carolyn Ehringhaus, Director

Offers academic accommodations, as mandated under federal and state law, through the Office for Students with Disabilities (free of charge). General academic support services, such as tutoring and study strategies instruction, are available through the Learning Assistance Center. (Note: The Individual Learning Program is offered only on the Biddeford Campus).

4587 **University of Southern Maine: Office of Academic Support for Students with Disabilities**

96 Falmouth Street, Room 242
Portland, ME   04104   207-780-4706
                                        800-800-4USM
                                   FAX 207-780-4403
                          http://www.usm.maine.edu
Joyce Branaman, Coordinator

OASSD affirms the commitment of the University of Southern Maine to provide equal access to higher education for qualified students with disabilities. All services are provided with a philosophical framework that stresses student independence and self-reliance.

Maryland

4588 **Baltimore City Community College**

2901 Liberty Heights Avenue
Baltimore, MD   21215   410-462-8000
                              FAX 410-462-7677
                   http://www.bccc.state.md.us
A Qismat Gorham, Coordinator

Offers a variety of services to students with disabilities including notetakers, extended testing time, counseling services, and special accommodations.

4589 **Charles County Community College**

PO Box 910
La Plata, MD   20646   301-934-7765
                              FAX 301-934-7838
                     http://www.csm.cc.md.us/
               e-mail: bonnien@charles.cc.md.us
M Penelope Appel, Contact

A public two-year college with 600+ students with disabilities out of a total of 6,055.

4590 **Chelsea School**

711 Pershing Drive
Silver Spring, MD   20910   301-585-1430
                              FAX 301-585-5865
                  http://www.chelseaschool.edu
          e-mail: tocannor@chelseaschool.edu
Dr. Linda A Handy, Academic Head of School
Timothy Hall, Contact

Chelsea is a co-educational, residential or day school for bright, dyslexic students in grade K-12.

4591 **Chesapeake College**

Routes 50 and 213
Wye Mills, MD   21679   410-822-5400
                              FAX 410-827-9466
                              TDY:410-827-9164
                   http://www.chesapeake.edu
Becky Rader

Offers a variety of services to students with disabilities including notetakers, extended testing time, counseling services, and special accommodations.

4592 **College of Notre Dame of Maryland**

Disability Services
4701 N Charles Street
Baltimore, MD   21210   410-532-5379
                              FAX 410-532-5622
                          http://www.ndm.edu
                   e-mail: jsandmeyer@ndm.edu
Theresa Cannone, Marketing Manager

Disability Services attends to students' physical, emotional, and learning disabilities by ensuring that students with disabilities are afforded the accommodations that they need to help them succeed at the College of Notre Dame.

4593 **Columbia Union College**

7600 Flower Avenue
Takoma Park, MD   20912   301-891-4080
                              FAX 301-270-1618
                          http://www.cue.edu
Betty Howard, Assistant Dean

Offers a variety of services to students with disabilities including note takers, extended testing time, counseling services, and special accommodations.

4594 **Community College of Baltimore County**

800 S Rolling Road
Catonsville, MD   21228   410-455-4382
                              FAX 410-455-4504
          http://www.ccbc.cc.md.us/campuses/cat/htm
Mark Lieberman, Counselor
Jill Hodge, Counselor

Offers a variety of services to students with disabilities including notetakers, extended testing time, counseling services, and special accommodations.

4595 **Frostburg State University**

101 Braddock Road
Frostburg, MD   21532   301-687-4201
                              FAX 301-687-4597
                      http://www.frostburg.edu
Beth Hoffman, Coordinator

A public four-year college with 153 special education students out of a total of 4,472.

4596 **Hagerstown Junior College**

11404 Robinwood Drive
Hagerstown, MD   21742   301-790-2800
                              FAX 301-777-7504
Lynn Schlossberg, Coordinator

A public two-year college with 22 special education students out of a total of 3,364.

4597 **Harford Community College**

401 Thomas Run Road
Bel Air, MD   21015   410-836-4402
                              FAX 410-836-4200
                              TDY:410-836-4199
                   http://www.harford.cc.md.ud
               e-mail: pburton@harford.cc.md.us
Leigh Marshall, Special Services Coordinator

An open enrollment two-year college, with reasonable accommodations provided for students with documented disabilities through disability support services. Students may also receive academic advising, personal and career counseling, and study skills instruction.

4598   Hood College

Disabilities Services Office
401 Rosemont Avenue
Frederick, MD   21701   301-696-3421
                                    FAX 301-696-3952
                                    http://www.hood.edu
                    e-mail: webmaster@hood.edu
Lynn Schlossberg, Coordinator

Four-year college that provides services to disabled students.

4599   Howard Community College

10901 Little Patuxent Parkway
Columbia, MD   21044   410-772-4822
                                    FAX 410-772-4276
                                    http://www.howardcc.edu
                    e-mail: jmarks@howardcc.edu
Janice Marks, Director

A public two-year college with 225 students with disabilities using services out of a total of 5,500.

4600   Ivymount School

11614 Seven Locks Road
Rockville, MD   20854   301-469-0223
                                    FAX 301-469-0778
                    e-mail: lpender@ivymount.org
Janet Wintrol, Director
Stephanie deSibour, Assistant Director

Independent day-school serving students, 3-21, with disabilities including developmental delays, communication deficits, learning disabilities, and autism.

4601   James E Duckworth School

11201 Evans Trail
Beltsville, MD   20705   301-572-0620
                                    FAX 301-572-0628
            http://www.pgcps.pg.k12.md.us/~duckw/
                    e-mail: jedworth@pgcps.org
Lydia L Flynn, Principal

4602   Johns Hopkins University

3400 N Charles Hall
Baltimore, MD   21218   410-516-8000
                                    FAX 410-614-7251
Martha Rosemann, Associate Dean

Once a student with disabilities has been admitted to The Johns Hopkins School of Public Health it is important that he/she submits disability documentation to the school's disability services coordinator. This applies to both new students as well as current/continuing students who are requesting accommodation for the first time.

4603   Prince George's Community College

301 Largo Road
Largo, MD   20772   301-366-6000
                                FAX 301-322-0119
                                TDY:301-322-0122
                    http://www.pgweb.pg.cc.md.us
            e-mail: enrollmetnservices@pg.cc.md.us
Carrier Johnson, Special Services

Offers a variety of services to students with disabilities including note takers, extended testing time, counseling services, and special accommodations.

4604   Summit School

664 E Central Avenue
Edgewater, MD   21037   410-798-0005
                                    FAX 410-798-0008
                    http://www.thesummitschool.org
Dr. Jane R Snider, Founding Director

A school for children with language-based reading difficulties, particularly in the area of decoding, with average to above average cognitive ability, who are ultimately planning to attend a college-prep high school with limited support.

4605   Towson State University

8000 York Road
Towson, MD   21252   410-830-2638
                                  FAX 410-830-4247
                        http://www.towson.edu
                    e-mail: ruhland@towson.edu
Ronni Uhland, Director

A public four-year college with 134 special education students out of a total of 13,761.

4606   Towson University

8000 York Road
Towson, MD   21252   410-830-2638
                                  FAX 410-830-4247
                        http://www.towson.edu
                    e-mail: ruhland@towson.edu
Ronnie Uhland, Learning Disabilities Specialist

A four-year college that provides services to the learning disabled.

4607   University of Maryland: Baltimore County

1000 Hilltop Circle
Baltimore, MD   21250   410-455-2459
                                    FAX 410-455-1028
                        http://www.umbc.edu
                    e-mail: chill@umbc.edu
Lettie Bratcher, Office Manager
Cynthia M Hill, Director

The Office of Student Support Services provides services that are designed to improve the educational and personal development of disabled and returning students.

4608 University of Maryland: College Park

2111 Shoemaker Building
College Park, MD 20742   301-405-9969
FAX 301-314-9206
http://www.maryland.edu
e-mail: mh185@umail.umd.edu
Dr. William Scales, Director Disability Support
Peggy Hayestrip, LD Coordinator

The mission of the Disability Support Service is to ensure individuals with disabilities equal access to the University of Maryland College Park programs.

4609 University of Maryland: Eastern Shore

Blackbone Road
Princess Anne, MD 21853   410-651-6456
FAX 410-651-6322
http://www.umes.edu
Dr. Diann Showell, Director

Offers a variety of services to students with disabilities including note takers, extended testing time, counseling services, and special accommodations.

4610 Valley Academy

301 W Chesapeake Avenue
Towson, MD 21212   410-828-0620
FAX 410-828-0438
http://www.valleyacademy.org/
e-mail: UtzP@ValleyAcademy.org

4611 West Nottingham Academy

1079 Firetower Road
Colora, MD 21917   410-658-5556
800-962-1744
FAX 410-658-6790
http://www.wna.org
e-mail: admission@wna.org
Heidi KL Sprinkle, Director, Admissions
Tom Sorci, Director, Learning Center
Dr. John Watson, Headmaster

A college preparatory school dedicated to the intellectual, spiritual and social growth of each student. The academy equips students to become successful in all aspects of life through individual attention within a diverse community and a safe and caring environment.

4612 Western Maryland College: Academic Skills Center

2 College Hill
Westminster, MD 21157   410-857-2504
800-638-5005
FAX 410-857-2729
http://www.wmdc.edu
e-mail: dmarjaru@wmdc.edu
Denise Marjarum, Academic Skills Center
Susan Dorsey, Co-Director

The Academic Skills Center (ASC) provides reasonable accommodations and a range of services to meet the academic needs of students with learning disabilities or some type of documented learning problem.

4613 Wor-Wic Community College

32000 Campus Drive
Salisbury, MD 21801   410-334-2800
FAX 410-334-2952
http://www.worwic.cc.md.us
Suzanne Alexander, Counseling Director

A comprehensive two-year institution located on Maryland's eastern shore. The faculty and staff are dedicated to serving the unique needs of each student with a learning disability.

Massachusetts

4614 American International College: Supportive Learning Services Program

1000 State Street
Springfield, MA 01109   413-737-7000
800-242-3142
http://www.aic.edu
e-mail: inquiry@www.aic.edu
Mary Saltus

An independent four-year college with 95 special education students out of a total of 1,433. There is an additional fee for the special education program in addition to the regular tuition.

4615 Amherst College

PO Box 2206
Amherst, MA 01004   413-542-2529
FAX 413-542-2223
http://www.amherst.edu
e-mail: info@amherst.edu
Frances Tuleja, Director

Offers a variety of services to students with disabilities including note takers, extended testing time, counseling services, and special accommodations.

4616 Anna Maria College

50 Sunset Lane
Paxton, MA 01612   508-849-3300
800-344-4586
FAX 508-849-3319
http://www.annamaria.edu
Olivia Tarleton, Director

An independent four-year college with 12 special education students out of a total of 691.

4617 Atlantic Union College

Center for Academic Success
PO Box 1000
S Lancaster, MA 01561   978-368-2416
FAX 978-368-2015
http://www.atlanticuc.edu
e-mail: info@atlanticuc.edu
Elizabeth Anderson, Center Academic Success Director

4618   Babson College

Disability Services
Babson Park, MA   02457   781-239-4075
                                FAX 781-239-5567
                                http://www.babson.edu
Erin Evans, Coordinator/Disability Services

An independent four-year business-based college with 110 undergraduate and graduate students with disabilities. Accommodations are individualized for students presenting documentation and may include notetaking assistance, extended time, separate location for testing, books-on-tape and other special accommodations. Adaptive equipment, academic advising, counseling services and teaching of organizational and time management skills, study skills and test taking strategies are offered.

4619   Bentley College

175 Forest Street
Waltham, MA   02452   781-891-2000
                            FAX 781-891-2473
                            http://www.bentley.edu
                            e-mail: jgorgone@bentley.edu
Dr. Brenda Hawks, Contact

An independent four-year college with 13 special education students out of a total of 5181.

4620   Berkshire Center

18 Park Street
Lee, MA   01238   413-243-2576
                        FAX 413-243-3351
                        http://www.berkshirecenter.org
                        e-mail: gshaw@berkshirecenter.org
Dr. Mike McManmon, Executive Director
Grey Shaw, Admissions Director

A post secondary college business school or vocational program for young adults 18-27 with learning disabilities. A co-ed population from four countries and all regions of the United States. Students have individual academic tutorials, and courses in money management and vocational counseling. Students live in apartments and learn life skills.

4621   Boston College

140 Commonwealth Avenue
Chestnut Hill, MA   02467   617-552-8000
                                  FAX 617-552-2097
                                  http://www.bc.edu
Dr. Kathleen Duggan, Contact

An independent four-year college with 195 special education students out of a total of 14,230. There is an additional fee for the special education program in addition to the regular tuition.

4622   Boston University

Office of Disability Services
Martin Luther King Jr Center
Boston, MA   02215   617-353-3658
                           FAX 617-353-9646
                           http://www.bu.edu
                           e-mail: lwolf@bu.edu
Lorraine E Wolf, Clinical Director

Provides basic support services such as test taking accommodations, note taking assistance, etc. Provides comprehensive services that include learning strategies instruction for an additional fee. LDSS offers a six-week summer program, The Summer Transition Program, for high school graduates.

4623   Brandeis University

415 S Street
Waltham, MA   02454   781-736-4464
                            FAX 781-736-4466
                            http://www.brandeis.edu
                            e-mail: ddgratto@brandeis.edu
Laura Lyndon, Assist Dean/Student Disability

An independent four-year college with 67 special education students out of a total of 2,901. Brandeis is committed to providing reasonable accommodation/s to individuals with appropriately documented physical, learning and psychological disabilities.

4624   Bridgewater State College

Bridgewater, MA   02325   508-531-1276
                                FAX 508-531-6107
                                http://www.bridgew.edu
Martha D Jones, Dean Studies
Pamela Spillane, Learning Disabilities Specialist

Offers a variety of programs and services to students with disabilities including pre-college workshop, notetakers, extended testing time, counseling services, adaptive computing, peer tutors, supplemental instruction and special accommodations.

4625   Bristol Community College

777 Elsbree Street
Fall River, MA   02720   508-678-2811
                               FAX 508-730-3297
                               http://www.bristol.mass.edu
Susan Boissonneault

Located in Southeastern New England, serves the residents of Bristol County and Rhode Island, in offering Associate of Art Degrees and Associate of Science Degrees in career and transfer programs, as well as certificates in other programs. Offers the QUEST Project which is an academic support program for learning disabled students as they begin their college education. Builds academic skills and confidence in the student's ability to do college work. Advises students on career choices.

4626   Cape Cod Community College

2240 Lyanough Road
West Barnstable, MA   02668   503-362-2131
                                    877-846-3672
                                    FAX 508-362-3988
                                    http://www.capecod.mass.edu
                                    e-mail: info@capecod.mass.edu
Dr. Richard Sommers, LD Specialist

A public two-year college with 165 special education students out of a total of 2,141. A full range of accommodations are available to students with disabilities.

4627 Clark University

950 Main Street
Worcester, MA   01610   508-793-7431
                              800-GO-CLARK
                              FAX 508-793-8821
                              http://www.clarku.edu
                              e-mail: admissions@clarku.edu
Sharon De Klerk, Director Special Services

An independent four-year college with 84 special education students out of a total of 2151.

4628 Dean College

99 Main Street
Franklin, MA   02038   508-541-1764
                              FAX 508-541-1918
                              http://www.dean.edu
Paul Hastings, Director

Committed to maintaining a caring and nurturing environment for its students.

4629 Dearborn Academy

34 Winter Street
Arlington, MA   02174   781-641-5992
                               FAX 781-641-5997
                               http://www.spedschools.com

4630 Eagle Hill School

242 Old Petersham Road
Hardwick, MA   01037   413-477-6000
                              FAX 413-477-6837
                              http://www.eaglehillschool.com
                              e-mail: admission@eaglehillschool.com
George Thomson, Contact

Since 1967 has offered premier services to the special needs community. This co-educational, college preparatory, boarding program is designed to meet academic and social needs of students diagnosed with learning disabilities (LD) and Attention Deficit Disorder (ADD). Offers a success-oriented atmosphere, and a consistently structured and socially supportive environment. The program is ungraded and serves students ages 11-19.

4631 Eastern Nazarene College

23 E Elm Avenue
Quincy, MA   02170   617-745-3000
                            FAX 617-984-4901
                            http://www.enc.edu
Joyce Klittich, Director Academic Services

Offers a variety of services to students with disabilities including note takers, extended testing time, counseling services, and special accommodations.

4632 Endicott College

376 Hale Street
Beverly, MA   01915   978-927-0585
                             800-325-1114
                             FAX 978-232-2600
                             http://www.endicott.edu
Jane Lang, Student Support

An independent two-year college with 48 special education students out of a total of 793.

4633 Essex Agricultural and Technical Institute

562 Maple Street
Hawthorne, MA   01937   978-774-0050
                               FAX 978-774-6530
                               http://www.agtech.org
                               e-mail: rraucci@agtech.org
Craig Gray, Coordinator

A public two-year college with 74 special education students out of a total of 533.

4634 Fitchburg State College

Disability Services
160 Pearl Street
Fitchburg, MA   01420   978-665-4020
                               FAX 978-665-3021
                               http://www.fsc.edu
                               e-mail: jperkins@fsc.edu
Joni Perkins, Secretary

4635 Framingham State College

100 State Street
Framingham, MA   01701   508-620-1220
                                508-626-4598
                                http://www.framingham.edu

Offers a variety of services to students with disabilities including note takers, extended testing time, counseling services, and special accommodations.

4636 Hampshire College

Learning Disabilites Support Services
893 W Street
Amherst, MA   01002   413-559-5458
                             FAX 413-559-5695
                             http://www.hampshire.edu
Kayyl Lynch, Associate Dean

Four year college that offers students with learning disabilities services and support.

4637 Harvard University

677 Huntington Avenue
Boston, MA   02115   617-432-1032
                            FAX 617-432-2009
                            http://www.harvard.edu
Marie Trottier, Disability Coordinator

An independent four-year college with 45 special education students out of a total of 6,621. Disabled students are encouraged to take advantage of opportunities available to help them achieve their educational goals.

4638 Institute for Community Inclusion (ICI)

UMass Boston
100 Morrissey Boulevard
Boston, MA   02115   617-287-4300
                            FAX 617-287-4352
                            http://www.communityinclusion.org
                            e-mail: ici@umb.edu
William Kiernan, Director

ICI promotes the inclusion of people with disabilities in their communities through training, consultation, clinical and employment services and research.

4639 Landmark School Elementary and Middle School Program

429 Hale Street
Prides Crossing, MA   01965   978-236-3000
                                    FAX 978-927-7268
                    http://www.landmarkschool.org
                    e-mail: jtruslow@landmarkschool.org
Carolyn J Orsini, Director Admission

For students entering grades 2-8, of average to above average intelligence, who have a history of healthy emotional development, and who've been diagnosed with a specific language-based learning disability. Ten month programs include 1:1 daily tutorials.

4640 Landmark School High School Program

429 Hale Street
Prides Crossing, MA   01965   978-236-3000
                                    FAX 978-927-7268
                    http://www.landmarkschool.org
                    e-mail: jtruslow@landmarkschool.org
Carolyn J Orsini, Director Admission

For students entering grades 9-12, of average to above average intelligence, who have a history of healthy emotional development, and who've been diagnosed with a specific language-based learning disability. Ten month programs include 1:1 daily tutorials.

4641 Landmark School Preparatory Program

429 Hale Street
Prides Crossing, MA   01965   978-236-3000
                                    FAX 978-927-7268
                    http://www.landmarkschool.org
                    e-mail: jtruslow@landmarkschool.org
Carolyn J Orsini, Director Admission

Offers a secondary school level curriculum emphasizing organizational and study skills development in a traditional classroom setting, and is designed for college bound boys and girls who have progressed to within one year of expected grade level performance.

4642 Linden Hill School

154 S Mountain Road
Northfield, MA   01360   413-498-2906
                                     888-254-6336
                                FAX 413-498-2908
                    http://www.lindenhs.org
                    e-mail: mhollard@lindenhs.org
Michael P Hollard, Headmaster/Executive Director

An ungraded boarding school for boys between the ages of 9-15 with dyslexia or specific learning/language differences. Linden Hill also offers a formal freshman year program. The school's primary objective is to provide a comprehensive language training program in reading, spelling, and writing. The language program provides an alternative to the traditional approach by using the sight-recognition (whole word) method of learning.

4643 Massachusetts Bay Community College

50 Oakland Street
Wellesley, MA   02481   781-239-3000
                                FAX 781-239-1047
                    http://www.mbcc.mass.edu
Joseph O'Niel, LD Specialist

A public two-year college with 44 special education students out of a total of 4,684.

4644 Massachusetts College of Liberal Arts

375 Church Street
North Adams, MA   01247   413-662-5308
                                FAX 413-662-5319
Claire Smith, Coordinator Academic Support

Academic support services for students with disabilities.

4645 Massasoit Community College

1 Massasoit Boulevard
Brockton, MA   02302   508-588-9100
                                     800-CAREERS
                                FAX 508-427-1250
                                TDY:508-427-1240
                    http://www.massasoit.mass.edu
Peter Johnston, Director

A public two-year college with 164 special education students out of a total of 6,423.

4646 Middlesex Community College

591 Springs Road
Bedford, MA   01730   732-906-2546
                                     800-818-3434
                                FAX 732-906-2506
A public two-year college with 298 special education students out of a total of 4,028.

4647 Mount Ida College

777 Dedham Street
Newton Center, MA   02459   617-928-4535
                                FAX 617-928-4760
                    http://www.mountida.edu
Maya Evans, Associate Director

Designed and developed to provide additional support for students with learning disabilities. Services include individual tutoring by professional learning specialists, reduced course load, credit study skills course, specialized accommodations and community functions.

4648 Mount Wachusett Community College

444 Green Street
Gardner, MA   01440   978-630-9166
                                FAX 978-630-9559
Francine Meigs, Special Services

A public two-year college with 177 special education students out of a total of 2,202.

4649 Newbury College

129 Fisher Avenue
Brookline, MA   02445   617-730-7072
                              FAX 617-232-5139
                    http://www.newbury.edu/
                    e-mail: brookline@newbury.edu
Sara d'Anjou, Academic Services

An independent four-year college with 35 self identified special education students out of a total of 800.

4650 North Shore Community College

One Ferncroft Road
Danvers, MA   01923   978-762-4000
                              FAX 978-762-4038
Helen Halloran, Special Services

A public two-year college with 280 special education
students out of a total of 3,301.

4651 Northeastern University

Disability Resource Center
360 Huntington Avenue
Boston, MA   02115   617-373-2675
                              FAX 617-373-7800
                    http://www.neu.edu
                    e-mail: drcinfo@neu.edu
G Ruth Kukiela Bork, Dean/Director

Offers a variety of services to students with disabilities including note takers, extended testing time,
counseling services, and special accommodations.

4652 Pine Manor College

400 Heath Street
Chestnut Hill, MA   02467   617-731-7000
                              800-762-1357
                              FAX 617-731-7199
                    http://www.pmc.edu
                    e-mail: admision@pmc.edu
Sandra Robins, Dean of Admissions
Mary Walsh, Center Director

For students with learning disabilities, Pine Manor
College offers the Learning Resource Center. The
LRC supports and challenges students to realize their
maximum academic potential in the way that best suits
their individual learning styles.

4653 Program for Advancement of Learning

Curry College
1071 Blue Hill Avenue
Milton, MA   02186   617-333-2250
                              800-669-0686
                              FAX 617-333-2018
                    http://www.curry.edu
                    e-mail: spratt@curry.edu
Lisa Ijiri, Director
Susan Pratt, PAL Coordinator
Joan Manchester, Program Administrator

PAL is a program within Curry College, a co-educational, four-year liberal arts institution serving 2,000
students and located in the Boston suburb of Milton,
Massachusetts. For over 25 years, PAL has both
shaped and been shaped by Curry's distinctive philosophy of education. Serves college age students with
specific learning disabilities.

4654 Regis College: Massachusetts

235 Wellesley Street
Weston, MA   02493   781-768-7000
                              800-456-1820
                              FAX 781-768-8339
                    http://www.regiscollege.edu
S Marilyn MacGregor

Offers a variety of services to students with disabilities including notetakers, extended testing time, counseling services, and special accommodations.

4655 Riverview School

551 Route 6A
East Sandwich, MA   02537   508-888-0489
                              FAX 508-888-1315
                    e-mail: admissions@riverviewschool.org
Jeanne M Pachero, Director Admissions/Placement
Maureen B Brenner, Head School

An independent, residential school of international
reputation and service enrolling 183 male and female
students in its secondary and post-secondary programs. Students share a common history of lifelong
difficulty with academic achievement and the development of friendships. On measures of intellectual
ability, most students score within the 70-100 range
and have a primary diagnosis of learning disability
and/or complex language or learning disorder.

4656 Salem State College

325 Lafayeete Street
Salem, MA   01970   978-542-6217
                              FAX 978-542-6753
                    http://www.salem.mass.edu
                    e-mail: admissions@salemstate.edu
Eileen Berger, Director

Four year college offering a learning disabilities program for students.

4657 Simmons College

300 Fenway
Boston, MA   02115   617-521-2000
                              FAX 617-521-3190
Carolyn Holland, Special Services

An independent four-year college with 44 special education students out of a total of 1,399.

4658 Smith College

College Hall 7
Northampton, MA   01063   413-584-2700
                              FAX 413-585-4498
                    http://www.smith.edu
                    e-mail: admission@smith.edu
Laura Rausher, Director Disability Services

An independent four-year college with 42 special education students out of a total of 2,613.

4659 Springfield College

263 Alden Street
Springfield, MA 01109   413-748-3768
FAX 413-748-3937
http://www.spfldcol.edu
e-mail: ddickens@spfldcol.edu
Deb Dickins, Director

Four-year college that offers student support to students with learning disabilities.

4660 Springfield Technical Community College

One Armory Square
Springfield, MA 01105   413-781-7822
FAX 413-733-8403
Deena Shriver, Special Services

Offers a variety of services to students with disabilities including note takers, extended testing time, counseling services, and special accommodations.

4661 Stonehill College

320 Washington Street
Easton, MA 02357   508-565-1000
FAX 508-565-1500
TDY:508-565-1425
http://www.stonehill.edu
e-mail: academicservices@stonehill.edu
Richard Grant, Assistant Dean Academic Services
David Almeida PhD, Learning Disabilities Specialist

A small liberal arts-based college of 2000 students set in a quiet suburb of Boston sponsored by the Holy Cross Fathers. This Catholic college offers programs in the liberal arts, business, and the sciences and is committed to providing reasonable accommodations to students with disabilities.

4662 Suffolk University

41 Temple Street
Boston, MA 02114   617-573-8239
FAX 617-742-2582
TDY:617-557-4875
http://www.suffolk.edu
e-mail: jatkinso@admin.suffolk.edu
Nancy C Stoll, Dean Students

Offers a variety of services to students with disabilities including note takers, extended testing time, counseling services, special accommodations, assistive technology, and tutorial assistance.

4663 Threshold Program

Lesley University
29 Everett Street
Cambridge, MA 02138   617-349-8181
800-999-1959
FAX 617-349-8189
http://www.lesley.edu
e-mail: jwilbur@lesley.edu
James Wilbur, Director Admissions

The Threshold Program is a comprehensive, nondegree campus-based program at Lesley University for highly motivated young adults with diverse learning disabilities and other special needs.

4664 Tufts University

419 Boston Avenue
Medford, MA 02155   617-627-2000
FAX 617-627-4691
http://www.tufts.edu
e-mail: studentservices@ase.tufts.edu
Nadia Medina, Director ARC
Sandra Baer, Coordinator

Offers a variety of services to students with disabilities including note takers, extended testing time, counseling services, and special accommodations.

4665 University of Massachusetts: Amherst

Disabilities Services
231 Whitmore Administration Bldg
Amherst, MA 01003   413-545-0892
FAX 413-577-0691
http://www.umass.edu
e-mail: zygmont@acad.umass.edu
Madeline Peters, Director

A public four-year college with 192 special education students out of a total of 17,207.

4666 University of Massachusetts: Boston

Ross Center
Boston, MA 02125   617-287-7430
FAX 617-287-7436
http://www.umb.edu
e-mail: rosscenter.umb.edu
Sheila Petruccelli, Director

A public four-year college with 151 special education students out of a total of 8,598. Committed to the goal of providing equal access to its education programs, so that its students may achieve their academic potential.

4667 University of Massachusetts: Lowell

Office of Disability Services
McGauvran 363
Lowell, MA 01854   978-934-4338
FAX 508-934-3011
Noel Cartwright PhD, Director Disabilities
Chandrika Sharma EdD, Assistant Director
Kerry Donohoe, Disabilities Coordinator

Office of Disability Services has responsibility for assuring reasonable accommodations, program access and support to qualified physically and learning disabled students and students with psychiatric disabilities.

4668 Wellesley College

106 Central Street
Wellesley, MA 02481   781-283-1000
FAX 781-283-3644

An independent four-year college with 41 special education students out of a total of 2,325.

4669 Wheaton College

Norton, MA 02766   508-285-8215
FAX 508-285-8276
e-mail: mibledsor@wheatonma.edu
Martha Bredsu, Assistant Dean College Skills

An independent four-year college with 200 students with learning disabilities out of a total of 1450.

Michigan

4670 Adrian College
Academic Services Program
110 S Madison Street
Adrian, MI 49221
517-265-5161
FAX 517-264-3181
http://www.adrian.edu
e-mail: ctapp@adrian.edu
Carol Tapp, Learning Specialist

A private, co-educational liberal arts and sciences undergraduate college. The college strives to enroll a student body that reflects the wealth and diversity of our society and is committed to providing appropriate services to all students. There are 35 academic majors and 9 preprofessional programs.

4671 Alma College
614 W Superior Street
Alma, MI 48801
989-463-7111
FAX 989-463-7353
http://www.alma.edu
e-mail: perkins@alma.edu
Mindy Sargent, Interim Director

An independent four-year college with 5 special education students out of a total of 1,222.

4672 Andrews University
Old US 31
Berrien Springs, MI 49104
616-471-7771
FAX 616-471-9751
http://www.andrews.edu
Marion Swanpoel, Director

Offers a variety of services to students with disabilities including notetakers, extended testing time, counseling services, and special accommodations.

4673 Aquinas College
1607 Robinson Road SE
Grand Rapids, MI 49506
616-459-8281
FAX 616-732-4431
http://www.aquinas.edu
e-mail: admissions@aquinas.edu
Jane McCloskey, Director

An independent four-year college with 32 special education students out of a total of 2,141.

4674 Augmentative Communication Technology
Central Michigan University
441 Moore Hall
Mount Pleasant, MI 48859
989-774-4000
FAX 989-774-1727
Dr. Anne Ratcliffe, Director

Maintains a clinic for assessment and consultation for individuals needing special communication technology and/or augmentative communication strategies. Provides personnel preparation and in-servicing for professionals in practice.

4675 Bay De Noc Community College
2001 N Lincoln Road
Escanaba, MI 49829
906-786-5802
800-221-2001
FAX 906-789-6912
http://www.baydenoc.com
e-mail: paavilam@baydenoc.cc.mi.us
Marlene Paavilainen, Special Populations Director

A community college with 30 learning disabled students out of 2,500.

4676 Calvin College
Services to Students with Disabilities
3201 Burton Street SE
Grand Rapids, MI 49546
616-957-6077
FAX 616-957-8551
http://www.calvin.edu
e-mail: admission@calvin.edu
Margaret Vriend, Coordinator

4677 Central Michigan University
120 Park Library
Mount Pleasant, MI 48859
989-774-3018
FAX 989-774-1326
http://www.cmich.edu/student-disability
e-mail: sds@cmich.edu
Carol Wojcik, Director Student Services

Public four-year university offering students a choice of 24 degrees. Academic accommodations are available for students with documented learning disabilities.

4678 Charles Stewart Mott Community College
1401 E Court Street
Flint, MI 48503
810-762-0241
FAX 810-762-0159
http://www.mcc.edu
Delores Williams, Contact

Offers a variety of services to students with disabilities including note takers, extended testing time, counseling services, and special accommodations.

4679 College of Art and Design: Center for Creative Studies
15 E Kirby Street
Detroit, MI 48202
313-874-1955
FAX 313-872-8377
Rochana Koach

Offers a variety of services to students with disabilities including notetakers, extended testing time, counseling services, and special accommodations.

4680 Delta College
University Center, MI 48710
989-686-9000
FAX 989-686-8736
http://www.delta.edu
David Murley, Special Needs

Offers a variety of services to students with disabilities including note takers, extended testing time, counseling services, and special accommodations.

4681   Detroit College of Business

3488 N Jennings Road
Flint, MI   48504   810-789-2200
                                 FAX 810-789-2266
                                 http://www.dcb.edu
Fran Jarvis, Director

Offers a variety of services to students with disabilities including notetakers, extended testing time, counseling services, and special accommodations.

4682   Detroit College of Business: Warren Campus

27500 Dequindre Road
Warren, MI   48092   810-558-8700
                                 FAX 810-558-7868
                                 http://www.dcb.edu
Mary Cross, Associate Dean

Offers a variety of services to students with disabilities including note takers, extended testing time, counseling services, and special accommodations.

4683   Developmental Disabilities Institute: Wayne State University

4809 Woodward Avenue
Detroit, MI   48201   313-577-2654
                                 FAX 313-577-3770
                           http://www.wayne.edu.DDI
                        e-mail: B_Le_Roy@wayne.edu
Barbara LeRoy, Director

Contributes to the development of inclusive communities and quality of life for people with disabilities and their families through a culturally sensitive statewide program of interdisciplinary education, community support and services, research and dissemination of information.

4684   Eastern Michigan University

Access Services Office
203 King Hall
Ypsilanti, MI   48197   734-487-2470
                                 FAX 734-487-5784
                                 http://www.emich.edu
                    e-mail: vet_teehan@online.emich.edu
Robert E Teehan, Associate

Four year college that offers students with learning disabilities support and services.

4685   Eton Academy

1755 Melton Road
Birmingham, MI   48009   248-642-1150
                                 FAX 248-642-3670
                           http://www.etonacademy.org
                    e-mail: webmaster@etonacademy.org
Pete Pullen, Head Master
Sharon Morey, Admissions Director

A special purpose school dedicated to educating 1st through 12th grade students of average and above average academic potential who are experiencing specific learning disabilities.

4686   Ferris State University

420 Oak Street
Big Rapids, MI   49307   231-591-3772
                                 FAX 231-591-3686
                                 http://www.ferris.edu
                        e-mail: eunicemerwin@ferris.edu
Eunice Merwin, Director

Committed to a policy of equal opportunity for qualified students. Mission is to serve and advocate students with disabilities.

4687   Finlandia University

Program for Students with Learning Disabilities
601 Quincy Street
Hancock, MI   49930   906-487-7258
                                 FAX 906-487-7567
                                 http://www.suomi.edu
Carol Bates, Associate Professor/Director

4688   Glen Oaks Community College

62249 Shimmel Road
Centreville, MI   49032   616-467-9945
                                     888-994-7818
                                 FAX 616-467-9068
                    e-mail: daustin@glenoaks.cc.mi.us
Donna Austin, Special Populations Counselor

A public two-year college with 50 special education students out of a total of 1,416.

4689   Henry Ford Community College

5101 Evergreen Road
Dearborn, MI   48128   313-845-9600
                                     800-585-4322
                                 FAX 313-845-9700
                           http://www.henryford.cc.mi.us
Theodore Hunt Jr, Program Manager

A public two-year college with 36 special education students out of a total of 15,514.

4690   Hope College

35 E 12th Street
Holland, MI   49422   616-395-7860
                                 FAX 616-395-7118
                                 http://www.hope.edu

Jacqueline Heisler, Director

An independent four-year liberal arts college recognized for its strong academics (it is a Phi Beta Kappa School), excellent facilities and supportive Christian dimension. Students with learning disabilities are admitted according to regular admission criteria. Admitted students must then determine whether Hope's support services are adequate for their needs.

4691   Jackson Community College

2111 Emmons Road
Jackson, MI   49201   517-787-0800
                                 FAX 517-796-8632
                        e-mail: webmaster@jackson.cc.mi.us
Chris Kane, Chair

Offers a variety of services to students with disabilities including notetakers, extended testing time, counseling services, and special accommodations.

4692 Kalamazoo College

1200 Academy Street
Kalamazoo, MI 49006   616-337-7000
                                        FAX 616-337-7305
                                        http://www.kzoo.edu
                                        e-mail: cdombrow@kzoo.edu
Dr. Marilyn LaPlante, Dean Students

A selective, independent and undergraduate liberal arts college. The unique curricular plan weaves career development internships, study abroad programs and senior independent research projects with traditional liberal arts on campus programs.

4693 Kellogg Community College

450 N Avenue
Battle Creek, MI 49017   616-965-3931
                        e-mail: webmaster@kellogg.cc.mi.us
Janice McNearney, Support Services

Offers a variety of services to students with disabilities including notetakers, extended testing time, counseling services, and special accommodations.

4694 Kendall College of Art and Design

17 Fountain Street NW
Grand Rapids, MI 49503   616-451-2787
                                        FAX 616-451-9867
                                        http://www.kcad.edu
                                        e-mail: finaid@kcad.edu
Kathy Jordan, Counselor

An independent four-year college with 11 special education students out of a total of 657.

4695 Lake Michigan College

2755 E Napier Avenue
Benton Harbor, MI 49022   269-927-8100
                                        FAX 269-927-6847
                                http://www.raptor.lmc.cc.mi.us
Jean Christensen, Special Populations

A two-year community college offering students vocational/technical programs in business, health science, technology and the first two years of college credit toward transfer in a baccalaureate program. Tutors, readers, note takers and other support services are available to eligible disabled students.

4696 Lansing Community College

PO Box 40010
Lansing, MI 48901   517-483-1207
                                        FAX 517-483-1170
                                        http://www.lcc.edu
Kim Cory, LD Specialist

Offers a variety of services to students with disabilities including tutoring, extended testing time, counseling services, special services such as priority registration and classroom accommodations.

4697 Madonna University

36600 Schoolcraft
Livonia, MI 48150   734-432-5639
                                        FAX 734-432-5393
                                        http://www.munet.edu
                                        e-mail: sherron@madonna.edu

Four-year college that offers services to disabled students.

4698 Michigan State University

105b W Fee Hall
East Lansing, MI 48824   517-353-6654
                                        FAX 517-355-6473
                                        http://www.msu.edu
Dr. Elaine Cherney, Contact

Offers a variety of services to students with disabilities including note takers, extended testing time, counseling services, and special accommodations.

4699 Michigan Technological University

1400 Townsend Drive
Houghton, MI 49931   906-487-2212
                                        FAX 906-487-3060
                                        http://www.mtu.edu
                                        e-mail: gbmelton@mtu.edu
Gloria B Melton, Associate Dean

A public undergraduate and graduate university with programs in engineering, sciences, business, technology, forestry, social sciences, and humanities. In 2000/01, there were requests for services from 50 individuals with physical or learning disabilities. Services include extended testing time, books on tape, and counseling. Total student enrollment 6,336.

4700 Mid-Michigan Community College

1375 S Clare Avenue
Harrison, MI 48625   989-386-6622
                                        FAX 989-386-2411
                                        http://www.midmich.cc.mi.us
                                        e-mail: mmiller@midmich.edu
Susan Cobb, Counselor Special Populations

Tutoring, note taking, readers, writers, interpreters, text-on-tape, counseling, advising and career exploration available. Support services funded under the Carl D Perkins Vocational and Applied Technology Education Act for eligible students enrolled in vocational technical programs. Services for all other programs provided through college resources. Writing center and math lab available to students. Liaison with community services.

4701 Monroe County Community College

1555 S Rainesville Road
Monroe, MI 48161   734-242-7300
                                        FAX 734-242-9711
                        e-mail: swetzel@mail.monroe.cc.mi.us
Kim Hripko-Jacob, Special Services

Offers a variety of services to students with disabilities including notetakers, extended testing time, counseling services, and special accommodations.

4702 Montcalm Community College

2800 College Drive
Sidney, MI 48885   517-328-2111
                                   FAX 517-328-2950
                                   http://www.montcalm.cc
Charlotte Fokens, Special Needs

Offers a variety of services to students with disabilities including note takers, extended testing time, counseling services, and special accommodations.

4703 Northern Michigan University

1104 Bottum University Center
Marquette, MI 49855   906-227-1737
                                   FAX 906-227-1714
                                   http://www.nmu.edu
Lynn Walden, Coordinator

Disability services provides assistance for students who are qualified under the Americans with Disabilities Act to receive accommodations.

4704 Northwestern Michigan College

Instructional Support Center
1701 E Front Street
Traverse City, MI 49686   616-922-1000
                                   FAX 616-922-1073
                                   http://www.nmc.edu
Denny Everett, Instructional Center

Offers a wide range of services for students that have disabilities and need accommodations in order to achieve their academic goals.

4705 Northwood University

4000 Whitting Drive
Midland, MI 48640   517-837-4465
                                   FAX 517-837-4111
                                   http://www.northwood.edu
Michael Sullivan, Counselor

Four-year college that offers services to disabled students.

4706 Oakland Community College: Orchard Ridge Campus

27055 Orchard Lake Road
Farmington Hills, MI 48334   248-471-7643
                                   FAX 248-471-7767
                                   http://www.occ.cc.mi.us
Dr. Lawrence Gage, Learning Program
Dr. David Doidge, Academic Dean

Offers comprehensive services to students with learning disabilities including note takers, extended testing time, counseling services, special accommodations and advocacy support.

4707 Oakland University

157 N Foundation Hall
Rochester, MI 48309   248-370-2100
                                   FAX 248-370-2286
                                   TDY:248-370-3268
                                   http://www.oakland.edu

Offers a variety of services to students with disabilities including notetakers, extended testing time, priority registration, assistance with sign language interpreter services, assistive technology, and assistance with general needs and concerns.

4708 Office of Services for Students with Disabilities

University of Michigan
G-219 Angell Hall
Ann Arbor, MI 48109   734-763-3000
                                   FAX 734-936-3947
                                   TDY:734-763-3000
                          http://www.umich.edu/~sswd/ssd
Sam Grodin, Director
Stuart Segal, Coordinator LD Services
Joan E Smith, Coordinator Deaf Services

Offers selected student services, free of charge, which are not provided by other University offices or outside organizations. Assists students in negotiating disability-related barriers to the pursuit of their education. Strives to improve access to University programs, activities and facilities for students with disabilities. Promotes increased awareness of disability issues on campus.

4709 Saginaw Valley State University

7400 Bay Road
University Center, MI 48710   517-790-4168
                                   FAX 989-964-7838

4710 St. Clair County Community College

PO Box 5015
Port Huron, MI 48061   810-989-5555
                                   FAX 810-984-4730
                                   http://www.sc4.cc
Nancy Pecorilli, Counselor
Gerri Barber, Learning Center Coordinator

The learning center's supportive services are provided free of charge. These services include counseling, outreach and referrals, handicapped services, tutoring and study skills assistance, share information and financial aid assistance.

4711 University of Michigan: Dearborn

4901 Evergreen Road
Dearborn, MI 48128   313-593-5430
                                   FAX 313-593-3263
                                   http://www.umd.michigan.edu
                                   e-mail: dennisu@umd.umich.edu
Dr. Mary Ann Zawada, Counseling Director
Dennis Underwood, Coordinator

A public four-year college with 300 special education students out of a total of 8,000.

4712 University of Michigan: Flint
264 University Center
Flint, MI 48502
810-762-3456
FAX 810-762-3498
TDY:810-766-6727
http://www.flint.umich.edu
e-mail: tnhines@umich.edu
Trudie N Hines, Accessibility Coordinator

Provides support services and auxiliary aids for students with a variety of disabilities.

4713 Washtenaw Community College
4800 W Huron River Drive
Ann Arbor, MI 48106
824-973-3483
FAX 834-973-3711
Dr. Francie Helm Moorman, Special Services

A public two-year college with 78 special education students out of a total of 10,765.

4714 Western Michigan University
W Michigan Avenue
Kalamazoo, MI 49008
269-387-4440
FAX 269-387-4550
Kate Wesler, LD Director

A public four-year college with 79 special education students out of a total of 20,951.

Minnesota

4715 Alexandria Technical College
1601 Jefferson Street
Alexandria, MN 56308
320-762-0221
888-234-1222
FAX 320-762-4634
http://www.atc.tec.mn.us
Renee Larson, Support Services

Offers a variety of services to students with disabilities including note takers, extended testing time, counseling services, and special accommodations.

4716 Anoka-Ramsey Community College
11200 Mississippi Boulevard NW
Coon Rapids, MN 55433
763-427-2600
FAX 763-422-3341
http://www.an.cc.mn.us
Linda Tse, Director Disabilities

A public two-year college with 55 special education students out of a total of 6,900.

4717 Augsburg College
Center for Learning and Adaptive Student Services
2211 Riverside Avenue
Minneapolis, MN 55454
612-330-1648
FAX 612-330-1137
TDY:612-330-1749
http://www.augsburg.edu
e-mail: doljanac@augsburg.edu
Robert F Doljanac, Director
Karina Jones, Disability Specialist
Anne Lynd, Disability Specialist

The Center for Learning and Adaptive Student Services coordinates academics accommodations and services for students with learning, attentional and psychiatric disabilities.

4718 Bemidji State University
12 Sanford Hall
Bemidji, MN 56601
218-755-2595
FAX 218-755-3788
Ann Austad, Coordinator

Offers a variety of services to students with disabilities including note takers, extended testing time, counseling services, and special accommodations.

4719 Bethel College: Minnesota
3900 Bethel Drive
Saint Paul, MN 55112
651-638-6353
800-255-8706
FAX 651-635-8695
Lucie Johnson, LD Program Director

An independent Christian four-year college with LD Program serving 30 students out of a total of 1,800.

4720 Calvin Academy and Special Education Day School
2574 Highway 10
Moudsview, MN 55112
763-717-0609
FAX 763-786-9535
http://www.calvinacademy.com/
e-mail: info@CalvinAcademy.com
Stafford R Calvin, Founder

4721 Century College
3401 Century Avenue N
White Bear Lake, MN 55110
651-779-3355
Vicki Johnson, Coordinator Disabled Center
Willie Nesbit, Dean Students

The disabilities access center provided by the college is a liaison service for students with disabilities to provide access to educational and student programs at the college.

4722 College of Associated Arts
344 Summit Avenue
Saint Paul, MN 55102
612-226-3416
FAX 612-224-8854
Barbara Davis, Associate Professor

Offers a variety of services to students with disabilities including note takers, extended testing time, counseling services, and special accommodations.

4723 College of Saint Scholastica
1200 Kenwood Avenue
Duluth, MN 55811
218-723-6552
FAX 218-723-6482
http://www.css.edu
e-mail: njewcomb@css.edu
Jay Newcomb, Director

Offers a variety of services to students with disabilities including note takers, extended testing time, counseling services, and special accommodations.

4724 College of St. Catherine: Minneapolis

2004 Randolph Avenue
St.Paul, MN   55105   651-690-6000
                                        800-945-4599
                                  FAX 651-690-6064
                                  TDY:651-690-8145
                              http://www.stkate.edu
                  e-mail: tgockenbach@stkate.edu
Teri Gockenbach, LD Specialist
Annette Caupenter, Disability Specialist

Services for students with disabilities are coordinated
through the learning Center. There is a support group
for students with disabilities that meets bimonthly.
Other services include testing accommodations, note
taking, computers, and reading course materials.

4725 College of St. Catherine: St. Paul Campus

O'Neill Learning Center
2004 Randolph Avenue
Saint Paul, MN   55105   651-690-6563
                                        800-945-4599
                              http://www.stkate.edu
Elaine McDonough, Assistant Director

Academic support services for students with disabilities of the College.

4726 Concordia College

901 8th Street S
Moorhead, MN   56562   218-299-4000
                                  FAX 218-299-3345
                              http://www.cord.edu
                   e-mail: forde@gloria.cord.edu
Grace Dolak, Development Director

An independent four-year college with 13 special education students out of a total of 602.

4727 Fergus Falls Community College

1414 College Way
Fergus Falls, MN   56537   218-739-7500
                                  FAX 218-739-7475
                             http://www.ff.cc.mn.us
Dr. David Seyfried, Director

The students with disabilities bring a unique dynamic
and special needs to the classroom. Fegus Falls Community College recognizes that many students require
assistance. These students often need modifications in
programs, services, and activities to succeed in a
changing, technology-based curriculum.

4728 Gustavus Adolphus College

800 W College Avenue
St Peter, MN   56082   507-933-6286
                                  FAX 507-933-6277
                              http://www.gac.edu
Laurie Bickett, Disability Services Coordinator

Gustavus Adolphus College is dedicated to providing
for the needs of enrolled students who have disabilities. Reasonable modifications in the classroom and
auxiliary aids will be provided for students with appropriately documented disabilities.

4729 Hamline College

Study Resource Center
1536 Hewitt Avenue
St. Paul, MN   55104   651-523-2417
                                  FAX 651-523-2809
                              http://www.hamline.edu
                 e-mail: cla-admins@gw.hamline.edu
Barbara Simmons, Assistant Dean

Four-year college that offers services to its disabled
students.

4730 Hibbing Community College

1515 E 25th
Hibbing, MN   55746   218-262-7200
                                        800-224-4422
                                  FAX 218-262-6717
                          http://www.hibbing.tec.mn.us
                  e-mail: admissions@hcc.mnscu.edu
Barbara Anderson, Coordinator

The College is committed to serving students with
special needs. If you need an accommodation for a disability, please contact our disabilities staff to make
arragements. HCC is completely accessible to students with physical disabilities.

4731 Inver Hills Community College

2500 80th Street E
Inver Grove Heights, MN   55076   651-450-8500
                                  FAX 651-450-8677
                              http://www.ih.cc.mn.us
Gini Spurr

A public two-year college with 177 special education
students out of a total of 5,450.

4732 Itasca Community College

1851 E Highway 169
Grand Rapids, MN   55744   218-327-4460
                                        800-996-6422
                                  FAX 218-327-4350
                          http://www.itasca.mnscu.edu
Sally Velzen, Learning Skills

Itasca Community College is committed to providing
equal opportunity to qualified persons with physical
or learning disabilities.

4733 Lake Superior College

2101 Trinity Road
Duluth, MN   55811   218-733-7650
                                  FAX 218-733-5945
                              http://www.lsc.cc.mn.us
                   e-mail: enroll@lsc.mnscu.edu
Amada Delich, Coordinator

A two-year college that provides a selection of programs for its disabled students.

4734 Macalester College

Disability Services
1600 Grand Avenue
Saint Paul, MN   55105   651-696-6534
                                FAX 651-696-6687
                        http://www.macalester.edu
                  e-mail: admissions@macalstr.edu
Bob Brandt, Health Services Director

4735 Mankato State University

PO Box 42
Mankato, MN   56002   507-389-6767
                                800-722-0544
                            FAX 507-389-2227
                      http://www.mankato.msus.edu
Dr. Daniel Beebe

This office houses documentation of disability for students, provides verification of disability for faculty, provides accommodations, offers direct services to students such as taped texts, notetaker and more.

4736 Mesabi Range Community & Technical College

1001 W Chestnut Street
Virginia, MN   55792   218-749-0325
                                800-657-3860
                            FAX 218-748-2419
                         http://www.mr.mnscu.edu
                   e-mail: c.thomas@mr.mnscu.edu
Ann Jahonen, Coordinator

Students with a documented disability are offered assistance and the opportunity to succeed.

4737 Minneapolis Community College

1501 Hennepin Avenue S
Minneapolis, MN   55403   612-341-7000
                                800-247-0911
                            FAX 612-349-2512
                       http://www.mctc.mnscu.edu
Carol Udstrand, LD Specialist
Jane Larson, Center Director

A public two-year college with 104 special education students out of a total of 4,155.

4738 Minnesota Life College

7501 Logan Avenue S
Richfield, MN   55423   612-869-4008
                            FAX 612-869-0443
                   http://www.minnesotalifecollege.com
                e-mail: info@minnesotalifecollege.com
Kathryn Thomas, Executive Director

A college-like apartment living program for young adults with learning disabilities who need an intermediate level of support. Students must be at least 18 years of age and have a documented diagnosis of a learning disability or related condition such as attention deficit disorder. The program focuses on independent living skills, social skills, vocational readiness, career exploration, post secondary education, jobs placement, decision-making, fitness, health, leisure and recreation.

4739 Minnesota State University Moorehead

1104 7th Avenue
Moorhead, MN   56560   218-299-5859
                            FAX 218-287-5050
                            TDY:218-299-5859
                      e-mail: toutges@mnstate.edu
Greg Toutges, Coordinator

A public four-year university serving approximately 60-80 students with learning disabilities out of a total of 7,200. Services, such as notetaking, alternate testing, taped textbooks, and more, are provided through the office of Disability Services to students with documented learning disabilities.

4740 Minnesota University Affiliated Program on Developmental Disabilities

University of Minnesota
6 Patee Hall
Minneapolis, MN   55455   612-624-4848
                            FAX 612-624-4843
Scott R McConnell, Director

The Institute on Community Integration is the Minnesota University Affiliated Program on Developmental Disabilities (UAP). We are one of a national network of over 60 similar programs in major universities and teaching hospitals in the country, known as the American Association of University Affiliated Programs.

4741 Minnesota West Community & Technical College

344 W Main Street
Marshall, MN   56258   507-537-7051
                                800-576-6728
                            FAX 507-537-7081
                      http://www.mnwest.mnscu.edu
                e-mail: debra@ms.mnwest.mnscu.edu
Debra Carrow, Director Support Services

Minnesota West offers a variety of services to students with disabilities including notetakers, academic counseling services, alternative testing, referral services, advocacy/support and special accommodations.

4742 Normandale Community College

9700 France Avenue S
Bloomington, MN   55431   952-832-6422
                         http://www.nr.cc.mn.us
Mary Jibben, DEEDS Coordinator

A public two-year college with 169 special education students out of a total of 9,327.

4743 North Hennepin Community College

7411 85th Avenue N
Brooklyn Park, MN   55445   763-424-0702
                            FAX 763-424-0929
                         http://www.nh.cc.mn.us
Sue Smith, Special Services

Works to promote program and physical access while helping to ensure the rights of students with disabilities and meeting federal and state statutes.

4744 Northwestern College

3003 Snelling Avenue N
Saint Paul, MN 55113   651-631-5221
                             FAX 651-631-5124
                             http://www.nwc.edu
Dr. Yvonne Redmond-Brown, Assistant Professor

Four-year college that offers disabled students support and services.

4745 Pillsbury Baptist Bible College

315 S Grove Avenue
Owatonna, MN 55060   507-451-2710
                           FAX 507-451-6459
                           http://www.pillsbury.edu
Larry Tindall, Admissions Director

An independent four-year college with two special education students out of a total of 350.

4746 Rainy River Community College

1501 Highway 71
International Falls, MN 56649   218-285-7722
                                 800-456-3996
                                 FAX 218-285-2239
                                 TDY:218-285-2261
                                 http://www.rrcc.mnscu.edu
                                 e-mail: admissions@rrcc.mnscu.edu
Carol Grim, Disability Services
Tom Belanger, Advisor

The campus program provides services to students with disabilities to ensure their equal access to the college and its programs.

4747 Riverland Community College Student Success Center

1900 8th Avenue NW
Austin, MN 55912   507-433-0569
                         800-247-5039
                         FAX 507-433-0515
                         http://www.riverland.cc
                         e-mail: maskelso@river.cc.mn.us
Mindi Federman Askelson, Director Student Support Svcs.

A two-year comprehensive technical and community college offering. 4000 students outstanding opportunities in carrer and transfer education. Facilites are located in Albert Lea, Austin, and Owatonna, Minnesota.

4748 Rochester Community and Technical College

851 30th Avenue SE
Rochester, MN 55904   507-280-2968
                            800-247-1296
                            FAX 507-285-7496
                            http://www.roch.edu
                            e-mail: travis.kromminga@roch.edu
Travis Kromming MA, Director

To provide academic support and advising services to assist disabled persons in achieving their educational goals.

4749 Saint John's School of Theology & Seminary

Collegeville, MN 56321   320-363-2102
                               800-361-8318
                               FAX 320-363-3145
                               http://www.csbsju.edu/sot/
                               e-mail: mbanken@csbsju.edu
Mary Beth Banken OSB

An independent four-year college with 36 special education students out of a total of 1,880.

4750 Saint Mary's University of Minnesota

700 Terrace Heights
Winona, MN 55987   507-457-1465
                         800-635-5987
                         FAX 507-457-1633
                         http://www.smumn.edu
                         e-mail: bsmith@smumn.edu
Bonnie Smith, Support Services
Jane Ochrymowycz, Center Director

Accommodations and support services based on recent positive assessment and recommendations of evaluator.

4751 Southwest Minnesota State University: Learning Resources

1501 State Street
Marshall, MN 56258   507-537-6169
                           800-642-0684
                           FAX 507-537-6027
                           http://www.southwestmsu.edu
                           e-mail: Leach@southwest.msus.edu
Marilyn Leach, Learning Resource Director
Pam Ekstrom, Accommodations Coordinator

Offers a variety of services to students with disabilities including test accommodations, notetakers, academic counseling services, 504/ADA advocacy, taped texts, computers with assistive/access technology and software. The department also offers skills development courses, tutoring services and student mentors.

4752 St. Cloud State University

Student Disability Services
720 4th Avenue S
St. Cloud, MN 56301   320-255-0121
                            FAX 320-654-5139
                            http://www.stcloudstate.edu/
                            e-mail: webteam@stcloudstate.edu
Dr. Lee Bird, Disability Services

A public comprehensive university that provides services for students with learning disabilities and other needs: alternative testing, note taking, referrals to campus resources and advocacy/support.

4753 St. Olaf College

1520 St. Olaf Avenue
Northfield, MN 55057   507-646-2222
                             800-800-3025
                             FAX 507-663-3459
                             http://www.stolaf.edu
Kathy Quaid, Special Services

Offers a variety of services to students with disabilities including note takers, extended testing time, counseling services, and special accommodations.

4754 St. Paul Technical College
235 Marshall Avenue
Saint Paul, MN 55102 651-221-1300
800-227-6029
FAX 651-221-1416
http://www.sptc.tec.mn.us/
Margie Warrington, Transition Director

A public two-year college with 79 special education students out of a total of 3,574.

4755 University of Minnesota Disability Services
180 Mahamara Allimai Center
Minneapolis, MN 55455 612-626-1333
FAX 612-625-5572
TDY:612-626-1333
http://www.disserv3.stu.umn.edu

Disability Services is a University Resource Promotion barrier free environment (physical program, information, attitude) which means expressing the rights of people with disabilities and assisting the university with meeting its responsibilities under federal and state statues. Disability Services works to ensure access to University employment, courses, programs, facilities, services and activities by documenting disabilities.

4756 University of Minnesota: Crookston
216 Selvig Hall
Crookston, MN 56716 218-281-8587
800-232-6466
FAX 218-281-8584
http://www.crk.umn.edu
e-mail: lwilson@mail.crk.umn.edu
Laurie Wilson, Coordinator

A public four-year college with 40-70 students with disabilities out of a total of 1,341.

4757 University of Minnesota: Duluth
Learning Disabilities Program
10 University Drive
Duluth, MN 55812 218-726-7500
800-232-1339
FAX 218-726-6254
http://www.d.umn.edu
Judy Bromen, LD Coordinator

UMD is committed to providing equal opportunities in higher education to academically qualified students with disabilities who demonstrate a reasonable expectation of college success.

4758 University of Minnesota: Morris
600 E 4th Street
Morris, MN 56267 320-589-6163
FAX 320-589-6473
http://www.mrs.umn.edu
e-mail: angfa@mrs.umn.edu
Ferolyn Angell, Director

Offers a variety of services to students with disabilities including note takers, extended testing time, counseling services, and special accommodations.

4759 University of Minnesota: Twin Cities Campus
30 Nicholson Hall
Minneapolis, MN 55455 612-624-4037
FAX 612-624-6369
http://www.disserv3.stu.umn.edu/index2.html
Susan Aase, LD Specialist

The goals of the university are: to create equal opportunities for students, faculty, and staff with disabilities to learn and work; to increase the visibility and awareness of Disability Services and enhance the quality, effectiveness, and efficiency of its operations.

4760 University of St. Thomas
2115 Summit Avenue
Saint Paul, MN 55105 651-962-5000
FAX 651-962-5910
http://www.stthomas.edu
Stephanie Zurek, Coordinator

An independent four-year college with 52 special education students out of a total of 5,283.

4761 Worthington Community College
1450 College Way
Worthington, MN 56187 507-372-3485
800-657-3966
FAX 507-372-5801
Pam Sieve, Coordinator

A public two-year college with 18 special education students out of a total of 868.

Mississippi

4762 Hinds Community College
505 E Main Street
Raymond, MS 39154 601-857-3359
FAX 601-857-3575
Ginger Manchester, Director

Offers a variety of services to students with disabilities including note takers, extended testing time, counseling services, and special accommodations.

4763 Holmes Community College
PO Box 527
Goodman, MS 39079 662-472-2312
FAX 662-472-9121
Julia Williams, Instructor

Offers a variety of services to students with disabilities including note takers, extended testing time, counseling services, and special accommodations.

4764 Itawamba Community College
602 W Hill Street
Fulton, MS 38843 662-862-8000
FAX 662-862-8245
http://www.icc.cc.ms.us
Sarah Johnson, President

Offers a variety of services to students with disabilities including note takers, extended testing time, counseling services, and special accommodations.

4765 Mississippi State University

PO Box 806
Mississippi State, MS 39762   662-325-3335
FAX 662-325-8190
http://www.msstate.edu
e-mail: dbaker@saffairs.msstate.edu
Debbie Baker, Director

Four-year college that provides student support to learning disabled students.

4766 Mississippi University Affiliated Program

University of Southern Mississippi
Southern Station
Hattiesburg, MS 39406   601-266-5163
FAX 601-266-5114
Jane Siders PhD, Director

4767 Northeast Mississippi Community College

101 Cunningham Boulevard
Booneville, MS 38829   662-728-7751
FAX 662-728-2428
http://www.necc.cc.ms.us
Sarah Rhodes, Director

A public two-year college with 5 special education students out of a total of 3,047.

4768 University of Mississippi

PO Box 187
University, MS 38677   662-232-7128
FAX 662-915-6789
e-mail: abroad@olemiss.edu
Ardessa Milor, Special Services

A public four-year college with 76 special education students out of a total of 8,804.

4769 University of Southern Mississippi

Box 8586
Hattiesburg, MS 39406   601-266-5024
FAX 601-266-6035
http://www.usm.edu
Dr. Valerie DeCoux, Coordinator

Four year college that provides students with support and resources whom are disabled.

4770 William Carey College

498 Tuscan Avenue
Hattiesburg, MS 39401   601-582-5051
800-962-5991
FAX 601-582-6171
Brenda Waldrip, Special Services

Offers a variety of services to students with disabilities including note takers, extended testing time, counseling services, and special accommodations.

Missouri

4771 Central Methodist College

411 CMC Square
Fayette, MO 65248   660-248-3391
FAX 660-248-2622
http://www.cmc.edu
Charlotte O'Brien, Contact

Offers a variety of services to students with disabilities including note takers, extended testing time, counseling services, and special accommodations.

4772 Central Missouri State University

Office of Accessibility Services
Union 222
Warrensburg, MO 64093   660-543-4421
FAX 660-543-4724
TDY:660-543-4421
http://www.cmsu.edu
e-mail: mayfield@emsu1.cmsu.edu
Dr. Barbara Mayfield, Director

Provider of equal opportunity to education for students with disabilities through notetakers, extended testing time, interpreters and other accommodations.

4773 East Central College

PO Box 529
Union, MO 63084   636-583-5193
FAX 636-583-6602
http://www.ecc.cc.mo.us
Michael Knight, Assessment Director

Offers a variety of services to students with disabilities including note takers, extended testing time, counseling services, and special accommodations.

4774 Evangel University

1111 N Glenstone Avenue
Springfield, MO 65802   417-865-2811
FAX 417-865-9599
http://www.evangel.edu
Dr. Laynah Rogers, Associate Professor

An independent four-year college with 23 special education students out of a total of 1,449.

4775 Fontbonne College

Kinkel Center
6800 Wydown Boulevard
St. Louis, MO 63105   314-889-4571
FAX 314-889-1451
http://www.fontbonne.edu
e-mail: jsnyder@fontbonne.edu
Dr. Jane D Synder, Director

Four-year college provides services through the Kinkel Center for students with learning disabilities.

4776 Jefferson College

1000 Viking Drive
Hillsboro, MO 63050   636-789-3000
                             FAX 636-789-4012
                             TDY:636-789-5772
                             http://www.jeffco.edu
Tom Burke, Director

Offers a variety of services to students with disabilities including notetakers, extended testing time, counseling services, and special accommodations.

4777 Kansas City Art Institute

4415 Warwick Boulevard
Kansas City, MO 64111   816-802-3376
                               800-522-5224
                             FAX 816-802-3480
                             http://www.kcai.edu
                             e-mail: arc@kcai.edu
Bambi Burgard PhD, Assistant Dean Academic Affairs

Offers a variety of services to students with disabilities including notetakers, extended testing time, counseling services, and special accommodations.

4778 Lindenwood College

209 S Kingshighway
St. Charles, MO 63301   314-949-2000
                             FAX 314-949-4910
                             http://www.lindenwood.edu
V Peter Pitts, Director

Offers a variety of services to students with disabilities including note takers, extended testing time, counseling services, and special accommodations.

4779 Longview Community College: ABLE Program-Academic Bridges to Learning Effectiveness

500 SW Longview Road
Lees Summit, MO 64081   816-672-2366
                             FAX 816-672-2025
                             TDY:816-672-2144
                             http://www.kcmetro.cc.mo.us
                      e-mail: maryellen.jenison@kcmetro.edu
Mary Ellen Jenison, ABLE Program Director

ABLE is an intensive support services program, designed to empower individuals with learning disabilities or brain injuries with the skills needed to gain control of their own lives and learning, so that they can make a successful transition to regular college courses, vocational programs, or the workplace. In addition to courses especially designed for this population, students take basic skills courses (if needed), regular college courses with study support, and attend weekly support groups.

4780 Maple Woods Community College

2601 NE Barry Road
Kansas City, MO 64156   816-437-3000
                             FAX 816-437-3351
                      http://www.kcmetro.cc.mo.us/maplewoods
Kathy Acosta, Disabled Specialist
Janet Weaver, Outreach Counselor

A public two-year college with 30 special education students out of a total of 5,007.

4781 Missouri Southern State College

3950 E Newton Road
Joplin, MO 64801   417-625-9373
                           800-606-MSSC
                         FAX 417-659-4456
                         http://www.mssc.edu
                         e-mail: locher-m@mail.mssc.edu
Melissa Locher, Coordinator

Offers a variety of services to students with disabilities including note takers, extended testing time, and counseling services.

4782 Missouri Valley College

500 E College Street
Marshall, MO 65340   660-886-6924
                           FAX 660-831-4039
                         http://www.moval.edu
                         e-mail: admissions@moval.edu
Marilyn Ehlert, Director

An independent four-year college with 5 special education students out of a total of 1,132.

4783 North Central Missouri College

1301 Main Street
Trenton, MO 64683   660-359-3948
                         FAX 660-359-2899
                       http://ww.ncmc.cc.mo.us
                       e-mail: webmaster@mail.ncmc.cc.mo.us
Ginny Wickoff, Counselor

Offers a variety of services to students with disabilities including note takers, extended testing time, counseling services, and special accommodations.

4784 Northwest Missouri State University

800 University Drive
Maryville, MO 64468   660-562-1219
                           FAX 660-562-1121
                         http://www.nwmissouri.edu
                         e-mail: admissions@mail.nwmissouri.edu
WC Dizney, Special Services

Offers a variety of services to students with disabilities including notetakers, extended testing time, counseling services, and special accommodations.

4785 Saint Louis University

Student Educational Services
3840 Lindell Boulevard
St. Louis, MO 63108   314-977-2930
                           FAX 314-977-3315
                         http://www.slu.edu
                         e-mail: murphy2@slu.edu
Atlas Laster Jr, PhD, Disabilities Coordinator

Four year college offering comprehensive programs for the learning disabled.

4786 Southwest Missouri State University

901 S National Avenue
Springfield, MO 65804   417-836-4192
                             FAX 417-836-4134
                         http://www.smsu.edu/disability

At Southwest Missouri State University, we believe all students should have equal access to higher education and university life. Disability Services helps ensure an equitable college experience for SMS Students with disabilities.

4787 St. Louis Community College at Florissant Valley: Access Office

3400 Pershall Road
Saint Louis, MO   63135   314-595-4551
                                FAX 314-595-2376
                                TDY:314-595-4552
               http://www.stlcc.edu/access
               e-mail: smatthews@stlcc.edu
Suelaine Matthews, Manager
Mary Wagner, Access Specialist

A public two-year college with 200 students with disabilities, out of a total of 7,000.

4788 St. Louis Community College at Forest Park: Access Office

5600 Oakland Avenue
Saint Louis, MO   63110   314-644-9100
                                FAX 314-644-9752
               http://www.stlcc.cc.mo.us/fp/access/
Monica L Hebert, Manager ACCESS

The St. Louis Community College ACCESS OFFICE collaborates with faculty, staff, students, and the community to encourage a college environment where individuals are viewed on the basis of ability, not disability.

4789 St. Louis Community College at Meramec

11333 Big Bend Boulevard
Kirkwood, MO   63122   314-984-7704
                             FAX 314-984-7117
               http://www.stlcc.cc.mo.us/mcdocs

The Access office offers support services to students who have documented disabilities of a permanent or temporary nature. The staff is available to provide the following services: individual counseling and advising; coordination of needed accommodations such as interpreters and more.

4790 University Affiliated Program for Developmental Disabilities

University of Missouri at Kansas City
2220 Holmes Street
Kansas City, MO   64108   816-235-1755
                                FAX 816-235-1762
Carl F Calkins PhD, Director

4791 University of Missouri

Office of Disability Services
A38 Brady Commons
Columbia, MO   65201   573-882-4696
                             FAX 573-884-9272
               http://www.missouri.edu
               e-mail: weavers@missouri.edu
Dr. Sarah Colby-Weaver, Director

Four-year independent college offering support for learning disabled students.

4792 University of Missouri: Kansas City

5100 Rockhill Road
Kansas City, MO   64110   816-235-5696
                                FAX 816-235-6537
               http://www.umkc.edu
               e-mail: disability@umkc.edu
Scott Laurent, Coordinator

Offers a variety of services to students with disabilities including note takers, extended testing time, counseling services, and special accommodations.

4793 University of Missouri: Rolla

1870 Miner Circle
Rolla, MO   65409   573-341-4211
                          800-522-0938
                          FAX 573-341-6934
               http://www.umr.edu
               e-mail: webmaster@umr.edu
Dr. Debra Robinson, Special Services

Offers a variety of services to students with disabilities including note takers, extended testing time, counseling services, and special accommodations.

4794 Washington University

1 Brookings Drive
Saint Louis, MO   63130   314-935-4062
                                FAX 314-935-8272
               http://www. wustl.edu

Offers a variety of services to students with disabilities including note takers, extended testing time, counseling services, and special accommodations.

4795 Westminster College

Learning Disabilities Program
501 Westminster Avenue
Fulton, MO   65251   573-592-5304
                           FAX 573-592-5180
               http://www.wcmo.edu
               e-mail: ottingh@jaynet.wcmo.edu
Hank Ottinger, Director

Four year college that offers a program for students with learning disabilities.

Montana

4796 Dull Knife Memorial College

PO Box 98
Lame Deer, MT   59043   406-477-6215
                              FAX 406-477-6219
               http://www.dkmc.cc.mt.us
               e-mail: alderson@cdkc.edu
Juanita Lonebear

Offers a variety of services to students with disabilities including notetakers, extended testing time, counseling services, and special accommodations.

4797 Flathead Valley Community College

777 Grandview Drive
Kalispell, MT 59901   406-756-3849
                             FAX 406-756-3911
                  http://www.fvcc.cc.mt.us
                  e-mail: lfarris@fvcc.cc.mt.us
Lynn Farris, Director

GED testing and learning styles assessment is available in the Learning Center. Advocates for Students with Disabilities work with faculty and staff to provide appropriate accommodations for students with learning disabilities.

4798 Montana State University

Disabled Student Services
PO Box 173960
Bozeman, MT 59717   406-994-2824
                           FAX 406-994-3943
                           TDY:406-994-6701
                  http://www.montana.edu
                  e-mail: byork@montana.edu
Brenda York, Director

Disabled Student Services (DSS) is committed to facilitating Montana State goal of making its programs, services and activities accessible to students with disabilities. We provide a variety of services to students with disabilities, including note taking assistance, exam accommodations, adaptive technology, and advice and advocacy.

4799 Montana Tech College

1300 W Park Street
Butte, MT 59701   406-496-3730
                         FAX 406-496-3710
                  http://www.mtech.edu
                  e-mail: lbarnett@mtech.edu
Lee Barnett, Director

Committed to making the appropriate accommodations for students with disabilities.

4800 Montana University Affiliated Program

University of Montana
33 Corbin Hall
Missoula, MT 59812   406-243-5467
                             888-268-2743
                           FAX 406-243-2349
                  http://www.ruralinstitute.umt.edu
                  e-mail: muarid@selway.umt.edu
R Timm Vogelsberg PhD, Director

The Rura Institute works on behalf of people with disabilities of all ages to support full participation in community life. We train professionals, provide services directly to people with disabilities, share our knowledge with others, and conduct research to develop solutions.

4801 Northern Montana College

PO Box 77511
Havre, MT 59501   406-265-3783
                         800-662-6132
                       FAX 406-265-3597
Linda Hoines, Learning Specialist

To provide college students with support and skills needed to remain in college and complete a degree program.

4802 Rocky Mountain College

Services for Academic Success
1511 Poly Drive
Billings, MT 59102   406-657-1128
                             800-877-6259
                           FAX 406-259-9751
                  http://www.rocky.edu/campus/sas
                  e-mail: vandykj@rocky.edu
Dr. Jane Van Dyk, Director

An independent four-year college with 20-30 students with learning disabilities out of a total of 850.

4803 University of Great Falls

1301 20th Street S
Great Falls, MT 59405   406-761-8210
                                800-848-3431
                              FAX 406-791-5214
                  http://www.ugf.edu
Sue Romas, Head Academic Excellence

An independent four-year college with 25 special education students out of a total of 1,038.

4804 University of Montana

032 Corbin Hall
Missoula, MT 59812   406-243-2243
                           FAX 406-243-5330
                  http://www.umt.edu
                  e-mail: marks@selway.umt.edu
Jim Marks, Director

Four year college that provides programs for students with a learning disabilities.

4805 Western Montana College

710 S Atlantic Street
Dillon, MT 59725   406-683-7493
                           800-WMC-MONT
                         FAX 406-683-7493
                  http://www.wmc.edu
Clarence Kostelecky, Special Services

A public four-year college with 6 special education students out of a total of 1,100.

Nebraska

4806 Chadron State College

1000 Main Street
Chadron, NE 69337   308-432-6461
                            888-461-4461
                          FAX 308-432-6395
                  e-mail: casalon@ccsc.edu
Robin Bila, Certified Professor Counselor
Frances Gonzalez, Tutor Coordinator

Offer a variety of services to students with disabilities including tutoring, counseling, and special accommodations as appropriate. Students are mentored in self understanding and self-advocacy.

4807 Creighton University

2500 California Plaza
Omaha, NE   68178   402-280-2749
                                   800-282-5835
                                   FAX 402-280-5579
                                   http://www.creighton.edu
Wade Pearson, Director

An independent four-year college with 73 special education students out of a total of 4,123.

4808 Doane College

1014 Boswell Avenue
Crete, NE   68333   402-826-8554
                                   FAX 402-826-8278
                                   http://www.doane.edu
                                   e-mail: shanigan@doane.edu
Sherri Hanigan, Director Student Support Svcs

An independent four-year college with 12 special education students out of a total of 950.

4809 Hastings College

800 N Turner Avenue
Hastings, NE   68901   402-461-7386
                                   800-LEA-RNHC
                                   FAX 402-461-7490
                                   http://www.hastings.edu
Kathleen Haverly, Center Director
Sam Remnick, Admissions Director

Learning disabled students are provided with a personalized accommodation plan. Students must be verified prior to enrollment and submit a psychological review profile prior to being served. Services include: study skills instruction, academic, career and vocational counseling services, note takers, tutors, professionals and testing accommodations.

4810 Midland Lutheran College

Academic Support Services
900 N Clarkson
Fremont, NE   68025   402-721-5480
                                   FAX 402-727-6223
                                   http://www.mlc.edu
                                   e-mail: kramme@mlc.edu
Lisa Kramme, Director

Four-year college that provides academic support for students who have a learning disability.

4811 Munroe-Meyer Institute for Genetics and Rehabilitation

University Affiliated Program
444 S 44th Street
Omaha, NE   68131   402-559-6402
                                   FAX 402-559-5737
                                   http://www.unmc.edu/mmi
                                   e-mail: mfbennie@unmc.edu
Bruce A Buehler, Director

Diagnostic, evaluation, therapy, speech, physical, occupational, behavioral therapies, pediatrics, dentistry, nursing, psychology, social work, genetics, Media Resource Center, education, nutrition. Adult services for developmentally disabled, Genetic evaluation and counseling, adaptive equipment, motion analysis laboratory, recreational therapy.

4812 Southeast Community College: Beatrice Campus

4771 W Scott
Beatrice, NE   68310   402-228-3468
                                   800-233-5027
                                   FAX 402-228-2218
                   http://www.college.sccm.cc.ne.us/3a.htm
Dr. Tom Cardwell, Dean Students
Robert Kluge, Testing/Assessment Counselor

A public two-year college with 7 special education students out of a total of 941.

4813 Southeast Community College: Lincoln Campus

8800 O Street
Lincoln, NE   68520   402-471-3333
                                   800-642-4075
                                   FAX 402-437-2404
                       http://www.college.sccm.cc.ne.us
Darlene Williams, Counselor

A two year vocational/technical/academic transfer college with approximately 4,000 full/part time students. Accommodations for students with disabilities are made through the Counselors.

4814 Union College

3800 S 48th Street
Lincoln, NE   68506   402-486-2506
                                   800-228-4600
                                   FAX 402-486-2895
                                   http://www.ucollege.edu
                                   e-mail: jeforbes@ucollege.edu
Jennifer Forbes, Director
Anne Ballard, Academic Support

For students with disabilities The Learning Center offers support services to students with learning disabilities, such as dyselexia, and accommodations are made for all students with disabilities.

4815 University of Nebraska: Lincoln

132 Administration Building
Lincoln, NE   68588   402-472-3787
                                   800-742-8800
                                   FAX 402-472-0080
                                   http://www.unl.edu
Christy Horn, Special Services

A public four-year college with 141 special education students out of a total of 19,888.

4816 University of Nebraska: Omaha

6001 Dodge Street
Omaha, NE   68182   402-554-2393
                                   800-858-8648
                                   FAX 402-554-3555
                                   http://www.unomaha.edu
Dr. John Hill

Offers a variety of services to students with disabilities including notetakers, extended testing time, counseling services, and special accommodations.

4817 Wayne State College
1111 Main Street
Wayne, NE   68787   402-375-7500
                                 FAX 402-375-7096
                                 http://www.wsc.edu
Dr. Jeff Carotens, Director Student Support

Offers a variety of services to students with disabilities including LD diagnosis, academic accommodations, and advocacy.

4818 Western Nebraska Community College: Scotts Bluff Campus
1601 E 27th Street
Scottsbluff, NE   69361   308-635-3606
                                 800-348-4435
                                 FAX 308-635-6100
                                 http://www.wncc.net
Vanessa Pickett, Counseling Director

Offers a variety of services to students with disabilities including notetakers, extended testing time, counseling services, and special accommodations.

Nevada

4819 Community College of Southern Nevada
3200 E Cheyenne
North Las Vegas, NV   89030   702-651-4000
                                 FAX 702-651-4612
                                 http://www.ccsn.nevada.edu
Cip Chavez, Director Student Services

Note takers, test proctors, books on tape, enlarged books, lab assistants, scribes, interpreters, special accommodations, etc.

4820 Sierra Nevada College
PO Box 4269
Incline Village, NV   89450   775-831-1314
                                 FAX 775-831-1347
                                 http://www.sierranevada.edu
                                 e-mail: kmehta@sierranevada.edu
Janey Muccio, Coordinator

Four year college that provides services to disabled students.

4821 Truckee Meadows Community College
7000 Dandini Boulevard
Reno, NV   89512   775-673-7060
                                 FAX 702-673-7268
                                 http://www.tmcc.edu
                                 e-mail: wirt@scs.unr.edu
Harry Heiser, Director

A public two-year college with 142 special education students out of a total of 9,813.

4822 University Affiliated Program: University of Nevada
College of Education
REPC-285
Reno, NV   89557   775-784-4921
                                 FAX 775-784-4997
                                 http://www.unr.edu
                                 e-mail: joannj@unr.edu
Jo Ann Johnson, Director

4823 University of Nevada: Las Vegas
4505 Maryland Parkway
Las Vegas, NV   89154   702-895-0866
                                 FAX 702-895-0651
                                 http://www.unlv.edu
Janice Hurtubise

The Disability Resource Center provides academic accommodations for students with documented disabilities who are otherwise qualified for university programs. The DRC has been designated as the official office for housing records as specified by Section 504 of the Rehabilitation Act of 1973.

4824 University of Nevada: Reno
1664 W Virginia Street
Reno, NV   89557   775-784-6801
                                 FAX 775-784-1300
                                 http://www.unr.edu
Nancye Pierce, Special Services

Offers a variety of services to students with disabilities including notetakers, extended testing time, counseling services, and special accommodations.

4825 Western Nevada Community College
2201 W College Parkway
Carson City, NV   89703   775-445-3271
                                 FAX 775-887-3105
                                 http://www.wncc.nevada.edu
Susan Hannah, Coordinator DSS

Offers a variety of services to students with disabilities including note takers, extended testing time, counseling services, and special accommodations.

New Hampshire

4826 Colby-Sawyer College
100 Main Street
New London, NH   03257   603-526-3711
                                 FAX 603-526-2135
                                 http://www.colby-sawyer.edu
                                 e-mail: mmar@colby-sawyer.edu
Dr. Mary Mar, Director Learning Services
Ann Chalker, Learning Specialist

An independent four-year college with 100 LD education students out of a total of 800.

4827 Daniel Webster College

Academic Support Services
20 University Drive
Nashua, NH 03063   603-577-6612
                                 FAX 603-577-6001
                                 http://www.dwc.edu
                                 e-mail: admissions@dwc.edu
Kristen Kendrick, Director

Four-year college that offers academic support services to the learning disabled students.

4828 Dartmouth College

6 College Hill
Hanover, NH 03755   603-646-2014
                                 FAX 603-646-3911
                          http://www.dartmouth.edu
                   e-mail: admissions.office@dartmouth.edu
Nancy Pompian, Coordinator

Offers a variety of services to students with disabilities including note takers, extended testing time, counseling services, and special accommodations.

4829 Franklin Pierce College

College Road
Rindge, NH 03461   603-899-4107
                                 800-437-0048
                                 FAX 603-899-6448
                                 http://www.fpc.edu
Anna Carlson, Academic Resources

An independent four-year college with 56 special education students out of a total of 1321.

4830 Hampshire Country School

122 Hampshire Road
Rindge, NH 03461   603-899-3325
                                 FAX 603-899-6521
                     http://www.hampshirecountryschool.com
                     e-mail: hampshirecountry@monad.net
William Dickerman, Headmaster/Admissions Director

Twenty-five student boarding school for high ability boys, mostly 10-15 years old, needing an unusual amount of adult attention, structure and guidance.

4831 Institute on Disability: A University Center for Excellence on Disability

University of New Hampshire
10 W Edge Drive
Durham, NH 03824   603-862-4320
                                 FAX 603-862-0555
                                 http://www.iod.unh.edu
                     e-mail: institute.disability@unh.edu
Jan Nisbet PhD, Director
Mary Schuh PhD, Associate Director

Promotes the inclusion of people with disabilities into their schools and communities.

4832 Keene State College

229 Main Street
Keene, NH 03435   603-358-2353
                                 800-KSC-1909
                                 FAX 603-358-2257
                                 http://www.keene.edu
Dwight Fischer, Director
Deborah Merchant, Assistant Director

A public four-year college with 105 special education students out of a total of 3,800.

4833 Learning Skills Academy

1247 Washington Road
Rye, NH 03870   603-964-4903
                                 FAX 603-964-3838
                          http://www.lsa.pvt.k12.nh.us/

4834 New England College

26 Bridge Street
Henniker, NH 03242   603-428-2218
                                 FAX 603-428-3155
                                 http://www.nec.edu
Anna Carlson, Academic Advising/Support

An independent four-year college with 140 students with learning differences out of a total undergraduate enrollment of 750.

4835 New Hampshire Community Technical College at Stratham/Pease

Disabilities Support Services
277 Portsmouth Avenue
Stratham, NH 03885   603-772-1194
                                 800-522-1194
                                 FAX 603-772-1198
                          http://www.ms.nhctc.edu/caps/
                          e-mail: scronin@nhctc.edu
Sharon Cronin, Coordinator

A public two-year college with support services for students with disabilities that include classroom accommodations, assistive technology, self advocacy, counseling, and one-on-one tutoring.

4836 New Hampshire Vocational Technical College

Prescott Hill, Route 106
Laconia, NH 03246   603-524-3207
                                 800-357-2992
                                 FAX 603-524-8084
                          http://www.laco.tec.nh.us
Maria Dreyer, Special Services

Offers a variety of services to students with disabilities including notetakers, extended testing time, counseling services, and special accommodations.

4837 Rivier College

420 Main Street
Nashua, NH 03060   603-888-0906
                                 FAX 603-897-8887
                                 http://www.rivier.edu
                          e-mail: lbaroody@rivier.edu
Dena Carlon, Coordinator

An independent four-year college with 17 special education students out of a total of 1,651.

4838 Southern New Hampshire University
Office of Disability Services
Exeter Hall, CLASS Suite
Manchester, NH 03106 603-668-2211
FAX 603-645-9648
http://www.snhu.edu
e-mail: h.jaffe@snhu.edu
Hyla Jaffe, Disability Services Coordinator

Offers services to students with disabilities based on recommendations from documentaion supporting a disability. Accommodations are made for specific needs.

4839 University of New Hampshire
ACCESS Office
118 Memorial Union Building
Durham, NH 03824 603-862-2648
FAX 603-862-4043
http://www.unh.edu
e-mail: parkerman@maple.unh.edu
Maxine Little, Director

The University believes each student has the right and also the responsibility to determine whether or not to take advantage of support services.

New Jersey

4840 Banyan School
12 Hollywood Avenue
Fairfield, NJ 07004 973-439-1919
FAX 973-439-1396
http://www.banyanschool.org
e-mail: chall@banyanschool.com

4841 Caldwell College
Office of Disability Services
9 Ryerson Avenue
Caldwell, NJ 07006 973-618-3645
FAX 973-618-3488
http://www.caldwell.edu
e-mail: jserpico@caldwell.edu
Joan Serpico, Coordinator

Four-year college that provides disability services to those students who are learnig disabled.

4842 Camden County College
PO Box 200
Blackwood, NJ 08012 856-227-7200
FAX 856-374-4975
http://www.camdencc.edu
e-mail: jkinzy@camdencc.edu
Joanne Kinzy, Coordinator

A two-year college that provides services to the learning disabled.

4843 Centenary College: Office of Disability
Project ABLE
400 Jefferson Street
Hackettstown, NJ 07840 908-852-1400
FAX 908-813-1984
http://www.centenarycollege.edu
e-mail: zimdahj@centenarycollege.edu
Jeffery R Zimdahl, Disability Services Director

4844 College of New Jersey
Office of Differing Disabilities
PO Box 7718
Ewing, NJ 08628 609-771-2571
FAX 609-637-5131
http://www.tcnj.edu
e-mail: degennar@tcnj.edu
An DeGennaro, Director

Four-year college provides services to students with disabilities.

4845 College of Saint Elizabeth
2 Convent Road
Morristown, NJ 07960 973-292-6318
FAX 973-290-4488
http://www.st-elizabeth.edu
Sr. Marie MacNamee, Dean Studies

Offers a variety of services to students with disabilities including notetakers, extended testing time, counseling services, and special accommodations.

4846 Community High School
1135 Teaneck Road
Teaneck, NJ 07666 201-862-1796
FAX 201-862-1791
Toby Barnstein, Director Education
Dennis Cohen, Program Director

Complete college prep HS program for LD/ADD adolescent grades 9-12.

4847 Community School
11 W Forest Avenue
Teaneck, NJ 07666 201-837-8070
FAX 201-837-6799
Rita Rowan, Executive Director
Dennis Cohen, Program Director

Comprehensive academic program for LD/ADD children grades K-8; NY and NJ funding available.

4848 Craig School
200 Comly Road
Lincoln Park, NJ 07035 973-305-8085
FAX 973-305-8086
http://www.craigschool.org
e-mail: jday@craigschool.org
Eric M Caparulo, Director Upper School

A school for children with learning differences such as dyslexia, auditory processing issues and ADD.

4849 Cumberland County College
PO Box 1500
Vineland, NJ   08362   856-691-8600
                                     FAX 856-690-0059
                                     http://www.cccnj.net
                                     e-mail: pmmaseri@cccnj.net
Patricia Martinez-Maseri, Assistant Director

A two-year college that offers services to its learning
disabled students.

**4850 Fairleigh Dickinson University: Metropolitan
Campus**
1000 River Road T-RH5-02
Teaneck, NJ   07666   201-692-2087
                                     FAX 201-692-2813
                                     http://www.fdu.edu
Vincent Varrassi, Campus Director
Grace Hottinger, Admissions Coordinator
Dr. Mary Farrell PhD, University Director

Comprehensive support services to students with language based LD.

4851 Forum School
107 Wyckoff Avenue
Waldwick, NJ   07463   201-444-5882
                                     FAX 201-444-4003
                                     http://www.theforumschool.org
                                     e-mail: forum@ultradsl.net
Steven Krapes, Director

Day school for children through age 16 who have neurologically based developmental disabilities, including autism, ADHD, LD, and asperger syndrome.
Services include extended year, speech, adaptive
physical education, music, art therapy, and parent program.

4852 Georgian Court College
Learning Center
900 Lakewood Avenue
Lakewood, NJ   08701   732-364-2200
                                     FAX 732-367-3920
                                     http://www.georgian.edu
Patricia Cohen, Director

Four-year college that offers services through the
school learning center to students with disabilities.

4853 Gloucester County College
1400 Tanyard Road
Sewell, NJ   08080   856-468-5000
                                     FAX 856-468-9462
                                     http://www.gccnj.edu
Dennis M Cook, Special Needs Services

The Office of Special Needs Services addresses supportive needs toward academic achievement for those
students with documented disabilties such as learning
disabled, visually impaired, hard of hearing and mobility impaired individuals.

4854 Hudson County Community College
25 Journal Square
Jersey City, NJ   07306   201-714-4497
                                     FAX 201-963-0789
                                     http://www.hudson.cc.nj.us
Ellen O'Shea, Coordinator

Offers a variety of services to students with disabilities including note takers, extended testing time,
counseling services, and special accommodations.

4855 Jersey City State College
2039 Kennedy Boulevard
Jersey City, NJ   07305   201-547-3368
                                     888-441-NJCU
Dr. Myrna Ehrlich, Director Project Mentor

Offers a variety of services to students with disabilities including notetakers, extended testing time, counseling services, and special accommodations.

4856 Kean College of New Jersey
1000 Morris Avenue
Union, NJ   07803   908-527-2000
                                     FAX 908-737-5363
                                     http://www.kean.edu
Roye-Ann Hargrove, Director

Operates a number of clinics, each of which may function interdisciplinarily to provide services, such as
speech, audiology, psychology, reading, learning, social work and special education.

4857 Kean University
PO Box 411
Union, NJ   07083   908-527-2380
                                     FAX 908-527-2784
                                     http://www.kean.edu
                                     e-mail: csi@turbo.kean.edu
Provides services to disabled students.

4858 New Jersey City University
2039 Kennedy Boulevard
Jersey City, NJ   07305   201-200-2091
                                     FAX 201-200-3141
                                     http://www.njcu.edu
Beverly Barkon, Director

Provides students with learning disabilities a mentor,
a teacher, advisor or a faculty member.

4859 New Jersey Institute of Technology
University Heights
Newark, NJ   07102   973-596-3420
                                     FAX 973-596-3419
                                     http://www.njit.edu
                                     e-mail: phyllis.colling.njit.edu
Dr. Phyllis Bolling, Special Services

A public four-year college with 24 special education
students out of a total of 4,906.

4860 Ocean County College

College Drive
Toms River, NJ   08754   732-255-0456
                                      FAX 732-255-0458
              e-mail: mreustle@ocean.cc.nj.us
Maureen Reustle, Director PASS
Anne Hammond, Counselor PASS

A regional resource center and comprehensive support center for college students with learning disabilities, offering a range of services including psycho-educational assessments, faculty/staff in-service training, program development assistance and consultation, and technical support. Individual and/or small group counseling is available, and vocational/career counseling on transition issues is also offered.

4861 Princeton University

303 W College
Princeton, NJ   08544   609-452-3054
                                      FAX 609-258-1020
                          http://www.princeton.edu
Stephen Cochrane, Special Services

Offers a variety of services to students with disabilities including note takers, extended testing time, counseling services, and special accommodations.

4862 Project Connections

Middlesex County College
153 Mill Road
Edison, NJ   08818   732-906-2506
                                      FAX 732-906-7767
                      http://www.middlesex.cc.nj.us
Joan Ikle, Director LD Services
Elaine Weir-Daidone, Counselor

Project Connections is a comprehensive academic and counseling service for students with learning disabilities who are enrolled in mainstream programs at Middlesex County College.

4863 Ramapo College of New Jersey

Office of Specialized Services
505 Ramapo Valley Road
Mahwah, NJ   07430   201-684-7514
                                      FAX 201-684-7004
        http://www.ramapo.edu/content/student.resources
                          e-mail: oss@ramapo.edu
Jean Balutanski, Director

Ramapo College demostated a strong commitment to providing equal access to all students through the removal of architectural and attitudinal barriers. Integration of qualified students with disabilities into college community has been the Ramapo way since the College opened in 1971.

4864 Raritan Valley Community College

Route 28 and Lamington Road
Somerville, NJ   08876   908-526-1200
                                      FAX 908-704-3442
                          http://www.raritanval.edu
Linda Baum, LD Specialist

A public two-year college with 180 special education students out of a total of 5,634.

4865 Richard Stockton College of New Jersey

PO Box 195
Pomona, NJ   08240   609-652-4400
                                      FAX 609-748-5541
                          http://www2.stockton.edu
              e-mail: webmaster@stockton.edu
Thomasa Gonzalez, Director Wellness Center

Offers a variety of services to students with disabilities including note takers, extended testing time, counseling services, and special accommodations.

4866 Rider University

2083 Lawrenceville Road
Lawrenceville, NJ   08648   609-896-5000
                                      FAX 609-895-5507
                          http://www.rider.edu
              e-mail: blandfor@rider.edu
Barbara J Blanford, Director

Four-year college that provides resources, programs and support for students with learning disabilities.

4867 Robert Wood Johnson Medical School

University Affiliated Program, Brookwood II
45 Knightsbridge Road
Piscataway, NJ   08854   732-235-5600
                                      FAX 732-235-9330
                          http://www.rwjms.umdnj.edu
Deborah M Spitalink, Director

An academic unit of the University of Medicine and Dentistry of New Jersey which is the state's University of the Health Sciences. The medical school is dedicated to the pursuit of excellence in the education of health professionals, in the conduct of biomedical, clinical, and public health research, in the delivery of health care and in the promotion of community health for the residents of our state.

4868 Rutgers Center for Cognitive Science

152 Frelinghuysen Road
Piscataway, NJ   08854   732-445-0635
                                      FAX 732-445-6715
                          http://www.ruccs.rutgers.edu
              e-mail: admin@ruccs.rutgers.edu
Dr. Elaine Dolinsky, Co-Director

A public four-year college with 2 special education students out of a total of 437.

4869 Salem Community College

460 Hollywood Avenue
Carneys Point, NJ   08069   856-299-2100
                                      FAX 856-299-9193
                          http://www.salemcc.org
              e-mail: SCCinfo@salemcc.org
Teresa Haman, Admissions Coordinator

Offers a variety of services to students with disabilities including extended testing time, counseling services, and special accommodations.

4870 Seton Hall University

400 S Orange Avenue
South Orange, NJ 07079   973-761-9166
FAX 973-275-2040
http://www.shu.edu
e-mail: fraziera@shu.edu
Ray Frazier, Director

Student Support Services is an academic program that addresses the needs of students with disabilities.

4871 Trenton State College

2000 Pennington Road
Ewing, NJ 08628   609-771-1855
FAX 609-637-5174
http://www.tcnj.edu
e-mail: webmaster@tcnj.edu
Dr. Juneau Gary, Special Services

A public four-year college with 24 special education students out of a total of 6,118.

4872 William Paterson College of New Jersey

300 Pompton Road
Wayne, NJ 07470   973-720-2000
FAX 973-720-2910
http://www.wpunj.edu
e-mail: BOONES@wpunj.edu
Barbara Milne, Special Services

Offers a variety of services to students with disabilities including notetakers, extended testing time, counseling services, and special accommodations.

New Mexico

4873 Albuquerque Technical Vocational Institute

525 Buena Vista SE
Albuquerque, NM 87106   505-224-3000
FAX 505-224-3237
http://www.tvi.cc.nm.us
A Paul Smarrella, Special Services

Provides or coordinates services for students with all disabilities. For students with learning disabilities can arrange for special testing situations, notetaker/scribes, tape recorders, use of wordprocessors or other accommodations based on individual needs.

4874 Brush Ranch School

HC 73
Terrero, NM 87573   505-757-6114
FAX 505-757-6118
http://www.brushranchschool.org
e-mail: kaycrice@hotmail.com
Kay C Rice MA, Head School
Gary Emmons, Head Master
Suzie Weisman, Admissions Director

A co-educational boarding school for teens with learning differences. The school is fully licensed and accredited by both the New Mexico Board of Education and the North Central Association of Colleges and Schools. Situated on 283 acres in the Santa Fe National Forest, the school offers a wide range of educational and recreational opportunities.

4875 Center for Development & Disability (CDD)

University of New Mexico/School of Medicine
2300 Menaul Boulevard NE
Albuquerque, NM 87107   505-272-3000
FAX 505-272-5280
TDY:505-272-0321
http://www.cdd.unm.edu
e-mail: cdd@unm.edu
Cate McClain, Director

The mission of the CDD is the full inclusion of people with disabilities and their families in their community by: engaging individuals in making life choices; partnering with communities to build resources; and improving systems of care.

4876 College of Santa Fe

1600 St. Michaels Drive
Santa Fe, NM 87505   505-473-6447
FAX 505-473-6124
http://www.csf.edu
Tom Baumgartel, Director

Provides services to the learning disabled.

4877 Eastern New Mexico University

Highway 70 Station 34
Portales, NM 88130   505-562-2280
FAX 505-562-2998
http://www.enmu.edu
e-mail: bernita.nutt@enmu.edu
Bernita Nutt, Director

Four year college that provides programs for the learning disabled.

4878 Eastern New Mexico University: Roswell

PO Box 6000
Roswell, NM 88202   505-624-7000
FAX 505-624-7144
http://www.roswell.enmu.edu
Linda Green, Special Services

A public two-year college with a total of 2500 students. Accommodations provided include tutoring, instruction, notetaking, recorded text books, testing and registration accommodations.

4879 Institute of American Indian Arts

PO Box 20007
Santa Fe, NM 87504   505-424-2300
FAX 505-988-6446
Karen Roberts Strong, Learning Resources

A public two-year college with 8 special education students out of a total of 237.

4880 New Mexico Institute of Mining and Technology

801 Leroy Place
Socorro, NM   87801   505-835-5100
                             800-428-8324
                        FAX 505-835-5989
                        http://www.nmt.edu
Dr. Judith Raymond, Special Services

A public four-year college with 5 special education students out of a total of 1,128.

4881 New Mexico Junior College

5317 Lovington Highway
Hobbs, NM   88240   505-392-5410
                             800-657-6260
                        FAX 505-392-3668
                   http://www.nmjc.cc.nm.us
Marilyn Jackson, Dean Transitional Studies

A public two-year college with 170 special education students out of a total of 2,438.

4882 New Mexico State University

PO Box 30001
Las Cruces, NM   88003   505-646-3121
                             800-662-6678
                        FAX 505-646-6330
                        http://www.nmsu.edu
                   e-mail: admissions@nmsu.edu
Mary Thumann, Coordinator

A public four-year college with 230 registered students with disabilities out of a total of 12,922.

4883 Northern New Mexico Community College

1002 N Onate Street
Espanola, NM   87532   505-747-2100
                        FAX 505-747-2180
                        http://nnm.cc.nm.us
Millie Lowry, Special Services

If you have a learning disability, support services include: reading class, readers of tests, notetakers, taped texts, tutoring, math class, recorders for classroom use, library assistance, extra time for tests, self-esteem counseling, resume assistance and kurzweil reading computers.

4884 San Juan College

4601 College Boulevard
Farmington, NM   87402   505-326-3311
                        FAX 505-566-3500
                   http://www.sjc.ccnm.us
Sandra Conner, Counselor
Ken Kernagis, Counseling Director

A public two-year college with 28 special education students out of a total of 3,654.

4885 University of New Mexico

Main Campus
Albuquerque, NM   87131   505-277-8291
                        FAX 505-277-7224
                        http://www.unm.edu
                   e-mail: lssunm@unm.edu
Patricia Useem, Manager

Offers a variety of services to students with disabilities including notetakers, extended testing time, counseling services, and special accommodations.

4886 University of New Mexico: Los Alamos Branch

4000 University Drive
Los Alamos, NM   87544   505-662-5919
                             800-894-5919
                        FAX 505-662-0344
                        http://www.la.unm.edu
Jay Ruybalid, Public Affairs Representative

Offers a variety of services to students with disabilities including notetakers, extended testing time, counseling services, and special accommodations.

4887 University of New Mexico: Valencia Campus

280 La Entrada
Los Lunas, NM   87031   505-865-8500
                        FAX 505-925-8501
                   http://www.unm.edu/-unmvc
Sharon DiMaria, Coordinator

A public two-year college with 57 special services students out of a total of 1,400.

4888 Western New Mexico University

PO Box 680
Silver City, NM   88062   505-538-6336
                             800-872-9668
                        FAX 505-538-6492
                        http://www.wnmu.edu
Karen Correa, Director

Offers a variety of services to students with disabilities including notetakers, extended testing time, counseling services, and special accommodations.

New York

4889 Academic Support Services for Students with Disabilities

Ithaca College
322A Smiddy Hall
Ithaca, NY   14850   607-274-1257
                        FAX 607-274-3957
                        TDY:607-274-7319
                   http://www.ithaca.edu/acssd
                   e-mail: acssd@ithaca.edu
Leslie Schettino, Director
Linda Uhll, Assistant Director

4890 Adirondack Community College

640 Bay Raod
Queensbury, NY   12804   518-743-2282
                        FAX 517-745-1433
                        http://www.crisny.org
                   e-mail: guyd@acc.sunyacc.edu
Deborah Guy, Director

A two-year community college that provides services to the learning disabled.

4891 Albert Einstein College of Medicine

1165 Morris Park Avenue
Bronx, NY 10461   718-430-3900
                                FAX 718-430-3989
Ruth L Gottesman EdD, Director
Mary S Kelly PhD, Associate Director

Provides evaluation and psychoeducational treatment
to children and adults of normal intelligence, 21 years
or older, who have serious reading difficulties.

4892 Alfred University

Special Academic Services
Crandall Hall
Alfred, NY 14802   607-871-2148
                                     800-425-3733
                                FAX 607-871-3014
                                http://www.alfred.edu
                                e-mail: sdstagg@alfred.edu
Terry Taggart, Director

Special Academic Services provides support services,
consultation and advocacy for students with learning,
physical and/or psychological disabilities. Services
for persons with disabilities shall complement and
support, but not duplicate, the University's regular existing services and programs.

**4893 Bank Street College: Graduate School of
Education**

610 W 1112th Street
New York, NY 10025   212-875-4404
                                FAX 212-875-4678
                    http://www.bnkst.edu/html/grad_ad/
                    e-mail: GradCourses@bnkst.edu
Sylvia Ross, Senior Program Analyst
Claire Wurtzel, Department Special Education

For learning disabled college students who are highly
motivated to become teachers of children and youth
with learning problems and who wish to earn a masters
degree in Special Education.

4894 Binghamton University

Vestal Parkway E
Binghamton, NY 13902   607-777-2686
                                FAX 607-777-6893
                                TDY:607-777-2686
                                http://www.binghamton.edu
                                e-mail: bjfairba@binghamton.edu
B Jean Fairbairn, Director Students with Disab.

Provides assistance to students with physical or learning disabilities.

4895 Bramson Ort Technical Institute

69-30 Austin Street
Forest Hills, NY 11375   718-261-5800
                                FAX 718-575-5118
                                http://www.bramsonort.org
                                e-mail: rbaskin@bramsonort.org
Rivka Burkos, Librarian
Zoyo Shteym, Job Placement

Offers a variety of services to students with disabilities including notetakers, extended testing time, counseling services, and special accommodations.

4896 Broome Community College

PO Box 1017
Binghamton, NY 13902   607-778-5000
                                FAX 607-778-5662
                                http://www.sunybroome.edu
Bruce Pomeroy, Director

A public two-year college providing services to approximately 75-125 students with learning disabilities per school year. Services include note taking,
tutoring, an LD specialist, adaptive educational
equipment, testing services, and other appropriate
support as based on documentation of need.

4897 CUNY Queensborough Community College

56th Avenue & Springfield Boulevard
Bayside, NY 11364   718-281-5000
                                FAX 718-281-5189
                                http://www.qcc.cuny.edu
Elliot Rosman, Director

The Office of Services for Students with Disabilities
(Science Building, Room 132) offers special assistance and couseling to students with specific needs.
The services offered include academic, vocational,
psychological and rehabilitation counseling, as well
as liasion with community social agencies.

4898 Canisius College

Disability Support Service
2001 Main Street
Buffalo, NY 14208   716-888-3748
                                FAX 716-888-3747
                                http://www.canisius.edu
                                e-mail: dobies@canisius.edu
Anne Dobies, Director

Four-year college offering services to students with
physical and cognitive disabilities.

4899 Cazenovia College

22 Sullivan Street
Cazenovia, NY 13035   315-655-7208
                                     800-654-3210
                                FAX 315-655-4860
                                http://www.cazcollege.edu/
Cyndi Pratt, Special Services
Jesse Lott, Director

An independent college with a significant number of
special education students.

4900 Colgate University

13 Oak Drive
Hamilton, NY 13346   315-228-7225
                                FAX 315-228-7831
                                http://www.colgat.edu
                                e-mail: admission@mail.colgate.edu
Lynn Waldman, Director

Provides for a small body of liberal arts education that
will expand individual potential and ability to
particpate effectively in the society.

4901 College of Aeronautics

Academic Support Services
8601 23rd Avenue
East Elmhurst, NY   11369   718-429-6600
                                    FAX 718-505-0667
                                    http://www.aero.edu
                            e-mail: mcpartland@aero.edu
Sharon McPartland, Coordinator

College offering support services to its learning disabled students.

4902 College of New Rochelle: New Resources Division

29 Castle Place
New Rochelle, NY   10805   914-654-5452
                                    800-933-5923
                                    FAX 914-654-5554
                                    http://www.cnr.edu
                                    e-mail: info@cnr.edu
Joan Bristol

Offers a variety of services to students with disabilities including notetakers, extended testing time, counseling services, and special accommodations.

4903 College of Saint Rose

432 Western Avenue
Albany, NY   12203   518-337-2335
                                    FAX 518-458-5330
                                    http://www.strose.edu
                            e-mail: hermannk@strose.edu
Kelly Hermann, Coordinator Special Services

Four year college that provides disabled students with services and support.

4904 College of Staten Island of the City University of New York

2800 Victory Boulevard
Staten Island, NY   10314   718-982-2513
                                    FAX 718-982-2117
                                    http://www.csi.cuny.edu
                        e-mail: venditti@postbox.csi.cuny.edu
Dr. Audrey Glynn, Director
Margaret Venditti, Coordinator

A public four-year college with 33 special education students out of a total of 11,136. Priority registration, test accommodations and tutoring.

4905 Columbia College

Disability Services
2920 Broadway
New York, NY   10027   212-854-2388
                                    FAX 212-854-3448
                                    http://www.columia.edu
                        e-mail: disability@columbia.edu
Susan Cheer, Director

Four-year college that offers disability services to its students.

4906 Columbia-Greene Community College

4400 Route 23
Hudson, NY   12534   518-828-4181
                                    FAX 518-822-2015
                                    http://www3.sunycgcc.edu
Sheri Bolevice, LD Specialist
Pat Nobes, Alternative Learning

A public two-year college in upstate New York with an enrollment of about 1,800. Services available to students with a documented learning disability include various academic accommodations, peer tutoring and academic counselling. Six developmental courses are offered in reading, math, English, and study skills.

4907 Concordia College: New York

171 White Plains Road
Bronxville, NY   10708   914-337-9300
                                    FAX 914-395-4500
                                    http://www.concordia-ny.edu
                            e-mail: ghg@concordia-ny.edu
George Groth, Connection Program Director

4908 Cornell University

Student Disability Services
420 CCC
Ithaca, NY   14853   607-255-6310
                                    FAX 607-255-1562
                                    http://www.cornell.edu
                            e-mail: cornell-clt@cornell.edu
Joan Fisher, Assistant Director

Cornell University is committed to ensuring that students with disabilities have equal access to all university programs and activities. Policy and procedures have been developed to provide students with as much independence as possible, to preserve confidentiality, and to provide students with disabilities the same exceptional opportunities available to all Cornell students.

4909 Corning Community College

1 Academic Drive
Corning, NY   14830   607-962-9459
                                    800-358-7171
                                    FAX 607-962-9006
                                    TDY:607-962-9459
                                    http://www.corning-cc.edu
                            e-mail: northop@corning-cc.edu
Judy Northrop, Coordinator Student Disability

A public two-year community college. There are approximately 100 LD students out of a student body of 4,500. A variety of services are available to students with LD, including specialized advising and registration, individualized tutoring, academic advising, and accommodations. Also on campus: Kurzweil reading machines, voice activated word processing, etc.

4910 Dowling College

Program for Potentially Gifted College Students
150 Idle Hour Boulevard
Oakdale, NY 11769　　　　631-244-3306
　　　　　　　　　　　　FAX 631-244-5036
　　　　　　　　　http://www.dowling.edu
　　　　e-mail: strached@dowling.edu
Dorothy A Stracher, Program Director
MK Schneid, Assistant Director

Academic program to help college students with LD develop strategies for success. They work one-on-one with graduate students.

4911 Dutchess Community College

53 Pendell Road
Poughkeepsie, NY 12603　　　845-431-8000
　　　　　　　　　　　　　　800-378-9707
　　　　　　　　　　　　FAX 845-471-4869
　　　　　　http://www.sunydutchess.edu
　　　e-mail: webmaster@sunydutchess.edu
A public two-year college with 45 special education students out of a total of 7,511.

4912 Erie Community College: South Campus

4041 Southwestern Boulevard
Orchard Park, NY 14127　　　716-648-5400
　　　　　　　　　　　　FAX 716-851-1629
　　　　　　　　　　　　TDY:716-851-1831
　　　　　　　　　　http://www.ecc.edu
　　　　　e-mail: adamsjm@ecc.edu
Nancy Bailey, Counselor

A public two-year college with 200 special education students out of a total of 3,455.

4913 Fashion Institute of Technology

7th Avenue and 27th Street
New York, NY 10001　　　　212-217-7522
　　　　　　　　　　　　FAX 212-217-7192
　　　　　　　　http://www.fitnyc.suny.edu
　　　e-mail: fitinfo@sfitva.cc.fitsuny.edu
Gail Ballard, Program Coordinator

A public four-year college with 106 special education students out of a total of 12,011.

4914 Finger Lakes Community College

4355 Lakeshore Drive
Canandaigua, NY 14424　　　585-394-3500
　　　　　　　　　　　　FAX 585-394-5005
　　　　　　　　http://www.fingerlakes.edu
　　　e-mail: admissions@flcc.edu
Patricia Malinowski, Chairperson

Provides services such as pre-admission counseling, academic advisement, tutorials, computer assistance, workshops, peer counseling and support groups. The college does not offer a formal program but aids students in arranging appropriate accommodations.

4915 Fordham University

Disabled Student Services
Keating Hall
Bronx, NY 10458　　　　　718-817-4700
　　　　　　　　　　　　FAX 718-817-4720
　　　　　　　　　http://www.fordham.edu
　　　e-mail: jmacdonall@fordham.edu
Jeanine Pirozzi, Student Services

The Office of Disability Services collaborates with students, faculty and staff to ensure appropriate services for students with disabilities. The University will make reasonable acccommodations, and provide appropriate aids.

4916 Fulton-Montgomery Community College

2805 State Highway 67
Johnstown, NY 12095　　　　518-762-4651
　　　　　　　　　　　　FAX 518-762-4334
　　　　　　　　http://www.fmcc.suny.edu
　　　e-mail: efosmire@fmcc.suny.edu
Ellie Fosmire, Coordinator

A public two-year college with 76 special education students out of a total of 1,748.

4917 Genesee Community College

1 College Road
Batavia, NY 14020　　　　　716-343-0055
　　　　　　　　　　　　FAX 716-343-4541
　　　　　http://www.sunygenesee.cc.ny.us/
　　　e-mail: admissions@genesee.suny.edu
Dr. Ann Marie Malachowski, Dean Students

A public two-year college with 78 special education students out of a total of 3,212.

4918 Gow School

Emery Road
South Wales, NY 14139　　　716-652-3450
　　　　　　　　　　　　FAX 716-687-2003
　　　　　　　　　　http://www.gow.org
　　　e-mail: admissions@gow.org
M Bradley Rogers Jr, Headmaster
Robert Garcia, Admissions Director

The nation's oldest college preparatory school for young men (grades 7-12) with dyslexia/language based learning differences. The 100 acre residential campus is located in upstate New York. Co-Ed summer program for ages 8-16.

4919 Hamilton College

198 College Hill Road
Clinton, NY 13323　　　　　315-859-4305
　　　　　　　　　　　　FAX 315-859-4632
　　　　　　　　　http://www.hamilton.edu
Louise Peckingham, Compliance Officer

Four year college that offfers services for learning disabled students.

4920 Herkimer County Community College
100 Reservior Road
Herkimer, NY   13350   315-866-0300
                             FAX 315-866-7253
                    http://www.hcc.ntcnet.com
                    e-mail: coylemf@hcc.suny.edu
Michele Weaver, LD Specialist
Rob Ichihana, Counselor

A public two-year college with approximately 200 documented disabled students. Tuition and fees: $2,450 (annual basis); overall enrollment 95-96: $2,445 (1,857 full time/588 part-time).

4921 Hofstra University
Program of the Higher Education of the Disabled
101 Memorial Hall
Hempstead, NY   11549   516-463-6972
                             FAX 516-463-6674
                    http://www.hofstra.edu
                    e-mail: nucizg@hofstra.edu
Karin Spencer, Associate Dean

Provides the support services which allow students to compete on an equal level with their classmates, but also to foster the growth of independent living skills necessary for survival at Hofstra University and beyond.

4922 Houghton College
Student Academic Services
1 Willard Avenue
Houghton, NY   14744   716-567-9239
                             FAX 716-567-9570
                    http://www.houghton.edu
                    e-mail: shice@houghton.edu
Dr. Susan Hice, Director

Four year college that provides academic support to disabled students.

4923 Hudson Valley Community College
80 Vandenburgh Avenue
Troy, NY   12180   518-629-4822
                             FAX 518-629-4831
          http://www.hvcc.edu/about_college/index.html
                    e-mail: editor@hvcc.edu
Pablo Negron, Director

A public two-year college with 28 special education students out of a total of 10,106.

4924 Hunter College of the City University of New York
Office for Students with Disabilities
New York, NY   10021   212-772-4824
                             FAX 212-650-3456
                    http://www.hunter.cuny.edu
Sandra LaPorta, Director

Provides services to over 250 students with learning disabilities. A learning disability is a disorder in one or more of the basic psychological processes involved in understanding or in using spoken or written language.

4925 Iona College: College Assistance Program
715 N Avenue
New Rochelle, NY   10801   914-633-2582
                              800-231-4662
                             FAX 914-633-2174
                    http://www.iona.edu
                    e-mail: mpackerman@iona.edu
Madeline Bartell-Packerman, Director

Offers a comprehensive support program for students with learning disabilities. CAP is designed to encourage success by providing instruction tailored to individual strenghts and needs.

4926 Ithaca College: Speech and Hearing Clinic
Smiddy Hall
Ithaca, NY   14850   607-274-3714
                             FAX 607-274-1137
          http://www.ir.tompkins.ny.us/beOra7du.htm
Richard Schissel

Offers a variety of services to students with disabilities including notetakers, extended testing time, counseling services, and special accommodations.

4927 Jamestown Community College
525 Falconer Street
Jamestown, NY   14701   716-665-5220
                              800-388-8557
                             FAX 716-665-9110
                    http://www.sunyjcc.edu
                    e-mail: admissions@mail.sunyjcc.edu
Nancy Callahan, Disability Support

A public two-year college with 41 special education students out of a total of 4,541.

4928 Jefferson Community College
Jefferson Community College
Coffeen Street
Watertown, NY   13601   315-786-2277
                             FAX 315-786-2459
                    http://www.sunyjefferson.edu
                    e-mail: straingham@sunyjefferson.edu
Sheree Trainham, Learning Skills/Disability

A public two-year college with 44 special education students out of a total of 2,121.

4929 John Jay College of Criminal Justice of the City University of New York
445 W 59th Street
New York, NY   10019   212-237-8122
                             FAX 212-237-8777
                    http://www.jjay.cuny.edu
                    e-mail: admiss@jjay.cuny.edu
Farris Forsythe, Coordinator

An independent two-year college with 67 special education students out of a total of 7,912.

4930 Kildonan School

425 Morse Hill Road
Amenia, NY   12501   845-373-8111
                                FAX 845-373-9793
                            http://www.kildonan.org
                         e-mail: rwilson@kildonan.org
Ronald A Wilson, Headmaster
Joseph Ruggiero, Academic Dean

Offers a fully accredited college preparatory curriculum. The school is co-educational, enrolling boarding students in Grades 6-Postgraduate and day students in Grade 2-Postgraduate.   Provides daily one-on-one Orton-Gillingham tutoring to build skills in reading, writing, and spelling. Daily independent reading and writing work reinforces skills and improves study habits. Interscholastic sports, horseback riding, clubs and community service enhance self-confidence.

4931 Learning Disabilities Program

Chapman Hall
Garden City, NY   11530   516-877-4710
                                    800-233-5144
                                FAX 516-877-4711
                      http://www.academics.adelphi.edu/ldprog
                         e-mail: LDprogram@adelphi.com
Susan Spencer, Assistant Dean/Director
Janet Cohen, Assistant Director

The programs professional staff, all with advanced degrees, provide individual tutoring and counseling to learning disabled students who are completely mainstream in the University.

4932 Long Island University: CW Post Campus

Academic Resource Center
720 Northern Boulevard
Brookville, NY   11548   516-299-2937
                                FAX 516-299-2126
                          http://www.cspost.liunet.edu
                         e-mail: crundlet@liu.edu
Carol Rundlett, Academic Resource Center Dir

4933 Manhattan College

4513 Manhattan College Parkway
Riverdale, NY   10471   718-862-7101
                                FAX 718-862-7808
                    http://www.manhattan.edu/sprscent/index.html
                         e-mail: rpollack@manhattan.edu
Ross Pollack EdD, Director

The Specialized Resource Center serves all students with special needs including individuals with temporary disabilities, such as those resulting from injury or surgery. The mission of the center is to ensure educational opportunity for all students with special needs by providing access to full participation in all aspects of the campus life.

4934 Manhattanville College

Higher Education Learning Program
2900 Purchase Street
Purchase, NY   10577   914-323-5313
                                FAX 914-323-5493
                            http://www.mville.edu
                      e-mail: admissions@manhattanville.edu
Myra Gentile, Assistant Director

Students preparing for a career in Special Education learns the full spectrum of physical, emotional, and mental challenges faced by people.

4935 Maria College

700 New Scotland Avenue
Albany, NY   12208   518-438-3111
                                FAX 518-438-7170
                         http://www3.mariacollege.org
                      e-mail: laurieg@mariacollege.edu
Margie Byrd, Chair

An independent two-year college with 13 special education students out of a total of 875.

4936 Marist College

Learning Disabilities Support Program
3399 N Road
Poughkeepsie, NY   12601   845-575-3000
                                    800-436-5483
                                FAX 845-575-3011
                            http://www.marist.edu
                         e-mail: specserv@marist.edu
Linda Cooper, Director

Provides a comprehensive range of academic support services and accommodations which promote the full integration of students with disabilities into the mainstream college environment.

4937 Marymount Manhattan College

221 E 71st Street
New York, NY   10021   212-774-0724
                                FAX 212-517-0541
                          http://www.marymount.mmm.edu
                         e-mail: jbonomo@mmm.edu
Dr. Jaquelyn Bonomo, Assistant Director

An independent four-year college with 25 learning disabled students out of a total of 1,700. There is an additional fee for the learning disabled education program in addition to the regular tuition.

4938 Medaille College

18 Agassiz Circle
Buffalo, NY   14214   716-884-3281
                                    800-292-1582
                                FAX 716-884-0291
                            http://www.medaille.edu
                         e-mail: jmatheny@medaille.edu
Jacqueline Smuckler

Offers a variety of services to students with disabilities including notetakers, extended testing time, counseling services, and special accommodations.

4939   **Mercy College**

Star Program
555 Broadway
Dobbs Ferry, NY   10522   914-674-7218
FAX 914-674-7410
http://www.mercynet.edu
e-mail: admissions@merlin.mercynet.edu
Terry Rich, Director

Helps people with learning disabilities.

4940   **Mohawk Valley Community College**

1101 Sherman Drive
Utica, NY   13501   315-731-5702
FAX 315-731-5868
TDY:315-792-5413
http://www.mucc.edu
e-mail: wdowsland@mvcc.edu
Wendy Dowsland, Learning Disabilities Specialist
Lynn Igoe, Students w/Disabilities Coord.

MVCC'S LD program is staffed by a half time LD specialist. Service provided to students with learning disabilities include advocacy, information and referral to on and off campus services, testing accommodations, taped materials, loaner tape recorders and note takers.

4941   **Molloy College**

1000 Hempstead Avenue
Rockville Centre, NY   11571   516-678-5000
888-466-5569
FAX 516-678-2284
http://www.molloy.edu
Therese Forker, Director STEEP
Barbara Nirrengarten, Assistant Director

STEEP (Success Through Expanded Education), is a program specifically designed to assist students with learning disabilities and enable them to become successful students. The program offers the student the opportunities to learn techniques which alleviate some of their problems. Special emphasis is directed toward the development of positive self-esteem.

4942   **Nassau Community College**

One Education Drive
Garden City, NY   11530   516-572-7241
FAX 516-572-9874
http://www.sunynassau.edu
e-mail: schimsj@sunynassau.edu
Dr. Victor Margolis, Coordinator Disabled Services

Our goal is to help students achieve success while they are attending Nassau Community College by learning to become their own advocates through talking with their professors about their disability and the accommodations they need for the course.

4943   **Nazareth College of Rochester**

4245 E Avenue
Rochester, NY   14618   716-389-2754
FAX 716-586-2452
http://www.naz.edu
e-mail: avhouse@naz.edu
Annemarie V House, Counselor

Four-year college that offers students with a learning disability support and services.

4944   **New York City Technical College of the City University of New York**

300 Jay Street
Brooklyn, NY   11201   718-260-5000
FAX 718-260-5198
http://www.nyctc.cuny.edu
e-mail: connect@citytech.cuny.edu
Joann Mischianti, Special Services

The student support services program, located in A237, provides comprehensive services to students with physical, health and learning disabilities. These services include counseling, tutorial, computers and specially designed technology, testing accommodations, and appropriate reasonable accommodations, as per students individual needs and documentation of disabilitiy.

4945   **New York Institute of Technology: OldWestbury**

Northern Boulevard
Old Westbury, NY   11568   516-686-7516
FAX 516-686-7613
http://www.nyit.edu
Edward Guiliano PhD, President
Alexandra W Logue PhD, VP Academic Affairs

Offers the Vocational Independence Progran for students who have significant learning disabilities.

4946   **New York University**

Henry and Lucy Moses Center
240 Green Street
New York, NY   10012   212-998-4980
FAX 212-995-4114
http://www.nyu.edu
e-mail: lc83@nyu.edu
Lakshmi Clark MA, CSD Coordinator

The staff of the Center for Students with Disabilities provides a wide range of services. Each student's needs are assessed prior to enrolling at the University, and the resulting written accommodation plan may include taking tests and exams with extended time, use of a computer or word processor, in-class note taker, permission to audi-tape class lectures.

4947   **New York University Medical Center: Learning Diagnostic Program**

400 E 34th Street
New York, NY   10016   212-263-7753
FAX 212-263-7721
Ruth Nass MD, Professor Clinical Neurology

Assessment team, neurology, neuro-psychology, psychiatry services are offered.

4948   **Niagara County Community College**

3111 Saunders Settlement Road
Sanborn, NY   14132   716-641-6222
FAX 716-614-6820
http://www.niagaracc.suny.edu
Karen Drilling, Disabled Student Services

The College provides reasonable accommodations for students with disabilties, including those with specific learning disabilities. Students with learning disabilities must provide documentation by a qualified professional that proves thry are eligible for accommodations.

4949   Niagara University

Seton Hall First Floor
Niagara University, NY   14109   716-286-8076
800-462-2111
FAX 716-286-8063
http://www.niagara.edu
e-mail: ds@niagara.edu
Diane Stoelting, Specialized Support Services

Reasonable accommodations are provided to students with disabilities based on documentation of disability. Depending on how the disability impacts the individual, reasonable accommodations may include extended time on tests taken in a separate location with appropriate assistance, notetakes or use of a tape recorder in class, interpreter, textbooks and course materials in alternative format, as well as other academic and non-academic accommodations.

4950   Norman Howard School

275 Pinnacle Road
Rochester, NY   14623   585-334-8010
FAX 585-334-8073
http://www.normanhoward.org
e-mail: info@normanhoward.org
William Elberty

4951   North Country Community College

20 Winona Avenue
Saranac Lake, NY   12983   518-891-2915
FAX 518-891-0898
http://www.ncc.edu
Jeannine Golden, Learning Lab/Malone
Robert Kreider, Learning Lab/Saranac

Located in the Adirondack Olympic Region of northern New York, NCCC is committed to providing a challenging and supportive environment where the aspirations of all can be realized. The college provides a variety of services for students with special needs which includes: specialized advisement, tutors and supplemental instruction, specialized accommodations, technology and equipment to accommodate learning disabilities and other resources.

4952   Onondaga Community College

Services for Students with Special Needs
4941 Onondaga Road
Syracuse, NY   13215   315-498-2622
FAX 315-498-2107
http://www.sunyocc.edu
e-mail: occinfo@sunyocc.edu
Linda Koslowsky, Administrative Aids

A public two-year college with 203 special education students out of a total of 8,393.

4953   Orange County Community College

115 S Street
Middletown, NY   10940   845-341-4030
FAX 845-342-8662
http://www.sunyorange.edu
Marilynn Brake, Special Services Coordinator

The Office of Special Services for the Disabled provides support services to meet the individual needs of students with disabilities. Such accommodations include oral testing, extended time testing, tape recorded textbooks, writing lab, note-takers and others. Pre-admission counseling ensures accessibility for the qualified student.

4954   Purchase College State University of New York

735 Anderson Hill
Purchase, NY   10577   914-251-6390
FAX 914-251-6399
http://www.purchase.edu
Ronnie Mait, Coordinator Office Special Svcs
Donna Siegmann, Coordinator Supported Education

Offers a variety of services to students with disabilities including note takers, extended testing time, counseling services, and special accommodations.

4955   Queens College City University of New York

Special Services Office
65-30 Kissena Boulevard
Flushing, NY   11367   718-997-5000
http://www.qc.edu
e-mail: christopher_rosa@qc.edu
Christopher Rosa, Office Director

Services include tutoring and notetaking, accommodating testing alternatives, counseling, academic and vocational advisement, as well as diagnostic assessments in order to pinpoint specific deficits.

4956   Rensselaer Polytechnic Institute

110 8th Street
Troy, NY   12180   518-276-2746
800-448-6562
FAX 518-276-4839
http://www.rpi.edu
e-mail: hamild@rpi.edu
Debra Hamilton, Disabled Student Services

An independent four-year college with 53 learning disabled students out of a total of 6,000.

4957   Rochester Business Institute

1630 Portland Avenue
Rochester, NY   14621   585-266-0430
888-741-4271
FAX 585-266-8243
http://www.rochester-institute.com/692home.htm
Eva Wilcox, Student Advisor

An independent two-year college with 12 special education students out of a total of 528.

4958 Rochester Institute of Technology

28 Lomb Memorial Drive
Rochester, NY 14623   585-475-7804
                          FAX 585-475-5832
                          http://www.rit.edu
                          e-mail: palldc@rit.edu
Carla Katz, Chair Learning Support Services
Pamela Lloyd, Coordinator Disability Services

An independent four-year college serving 600 students with disabilities out of a total of 14,000 students. Offers a wide variety of accommodations and support services to students with documented disabilities.

4959 Rockland Community College

145 College Road
Suffern, NY 10901   845-574-4316
                         FAX 845-574-4462
Marge Zemek, Learning Disabilities Specialist

A public two-year college with 300 special education students out of a total of 5,500. The office of Disability Services provides a variety of support services tailored to meet the individual needs and learning styles of students with documented learning disabilities.

4960 Rose F Kennedy Center

Albert Einstein College of Medicine
1410 Pelham Parkway S
Bronx, NY 10461   718-430-8500
                         FAX 718-904-1162
                         http://www.aecom.yu.edu/cerc
                         e-mail: cerc@aecom.yu.edu
Herbert J Cohen MD, Director

Mission is to help children with disabilities reach their full potential and to support parents in their efforts to get the best care, education, and treatment for their children.

4961 STAC Exchange: St.Thomas Aquinas College

125 Route 340
Sparkill, NY 10976   845-398-4230
                         FAX 845-398-4229
                         http://www.stac.edu
                         e-mail: stacexch@stac.edu
Richard Heath, Director
Amelia DeMarco, Assistant Director

Comprehensive support program for selected college students with learning disabilites and/or ADHD. Services include individual professional mentoring, study groups, workshops, academic counseling, priority registration, assistive technology, and a specialized summer program prior to the first semester.

4962 SUNY Canton

34 Cornell Drive
Canton, NY 13617   315-386-7392
                         FAX 315-379-3877
                         http://www.canton.edu
                         e-mail: leev@canton.edu
Veigh Lee, DSS Coordinator

Four year state college that provides resources and services to learning disabled students.

4963 SUNY Cobleskill

Disability Support Center
Route 7
Cobleskill, NY 12043   518-255-5282
                         FAX 518-255-6430
                         e-mail: Johnsok@Cobleskill.edu
Lynn Abarno, Coordinator Support Services

A public two-year college with a Bachelor of Technology component in agriculture. Approximately 170 students identify themselves as having a learning disability out of the 2,000 total population. Tuition $3,500 in state/$8,300 out of state. Academic support services and accommodations for documented LD students.

4964 SUNY Institute of Technology: Utica/Rome

PO Box 3050
Utica, NY 13504   315-792-7500
                         800-786-9898
                         FAX 315-792-7837
                         http://www.sunyit.edu
                         e-mail: admissions@sunyit.edu
Marybeth Lyonsvan, Interim Director Admissions

Upper division bachelor's degree in a variety of professional and technical majors; masters degree and continuing educational coursework is also available.

4965 Sage College

140 New Scotland Avenue
Albany, NY 12214   518-292-8624
                         FAX 578-292-1910
                         http://www.sage.edu
                         e-mail: chowed@sage.edu
David Chowenhill, Director

Four year college that offers services to students with a learning disability.

4966 Schenectady County Community College

78 Washington Avenue
Schenectady, NY 12305   518-381-1366
                         FAX 518-346-0379
                         http://www.sunysccc.edu
Tom Dotson, Coordinator

Access for All program is designed to make programs and facilities accessible to all students in pursuit of their academic goals. Disabled Student Services seeks to ensure accessible educational opportunities in accordance with individual needs. Offers general support services and program services such as: exam assistance, special scheduling, adaptive equipment, readers, taping assistance and more.

4967 Services for Students with Disabilities

Binghamton Universtity
PO Box 6000
Binghamton, NY 13902   607-777-2686
                         FAX 607-777-6893
                         TDY:607-777-2686
                         http://www.binghamton.edu
                         e-mail: bjfairba@binghamton.edu
B Jean Fairbairn, Director
Janice M Lee, LD Specialist

Provides a wide range of support services to Binghamton University students with physical learning or other disabilities.

4968 Siena College

515 Loudon Road
Loudonville, NY   12211   518-783-4239
                                 FAX 518-786-5013
                                 http://www.siena.edu
                                 e-mail: zullo@siena.edu
Renee D Zullo, Director

Four year college that offers programs for the learning disabled.

4969 St. Bonaventure University

Teaching & Learning Center
Room 26, Doyle Hall
St. Bonaventure, NY   14778   716-375-2066
                                 800-462-5050
                                 FAX 716-375-2072
                                 http://www.sbu.edu
                                 e-mail: nmatthew@sbu.edu
Nancy A Matthews, Coordinator

Catholic University in the Franciscan tradition. Independent coeducational institution offering programs through its schools of arts and sciences, business administration, education and journalism and mass communication. 2500 students, tuition $16,210, room and board $6,190.

4970 St. Lawrence University

23 Romoda Drive
Canton, NY   13617   315-229-5104
                                 FAX 315-229-7453
                                 http://www.stlawu.edu
                                 e-mail: jmeagher@mail.stlawu.edu
John Meagher, Director

The Office of Special Needs is here to ensure that all students with disabilities can freely and actively participate in all facets of University life, to coordinate support services and programs that enable students with disabilities to reach their educational potential, and to increase the level of awareness among all members of the University so that students with disabilites are able to perform at a level limited only by their abilities, not their disabilities.

4971 State University of New York College Technology at Delhi

2 Main Street
Delhi, NY   13753   607-746-4593
                                 800-96-DELHI
                                 FAX 607-746-4368
                                 http://www.delhi.edu
                                 e-mail: weinbell@delhi.edu
Linda Weinberg, Disabilities Coordinator

Provide services for students with disabilities. Alternate test-taking arrangements, adapted equipment, assistive technology, accessibility information, note taking services, reading services, tutorial assistance, interpreting services, accessble parking and elevators, sounseling, guidance and support, refferral information and advocacy services, workshops and support groups.

4972 State University of New York College at Brockport

Office for Students with Disabilities
350 New Campus Drive
Brockport, NY   14420   585-395-5409
                                 800-382-8447
                                 FAX 585-395-5291
                                 http://www.brockport.edu
                                 e-mail: vvandrez@brockport.edu
Vivian Vanderzell, Coordinator

Provides support and assistance to students with medical, physical, emotional or learning disabilities, specially those experiencing problems in areas such as academic environment.

4973 State University of New York College of Agriculture and Technology

Cobleskill, NY   12043   518-255-5282
                                 FAX 518-255-6430
                                 http://www.cobleskill.edu
                                 e-mail: abornolk@cobleskill.edu
Lynn K Abarno, Coordinator
Pat Sprage, Assistant

The primary objective is to develop and maintain a supportive campus environment that promotes academic achievement and personal growth for students with disabilities. Services provide by the office are based on each student's documentation and are tailored to each student's unique individual needs.

4974 State University of New York: Albany

1400 Washington Avenue
Albany, NY   12222   518-442-5566
                                 FAX 518-442-5589
                                 TDY:518-442-3366
                                 http://www.albany.edu
                                 e-mail: cmalloch@uamail.albany.edu
Carolyn Malloch, Learning Disabilities Specialist

The University at Albany offers a wide array of advocacy and support services for students with learning disabilities. We also have a Writing Center, a Center for Computing and Disability, Comprehensive Academic Support Services (tutors, study groups, academic mentoring, study skills workshops). These are excellent resources for LD students. Services include extended time on testing, advocacy with faculty, diagnostic testing, advising and consultation. One week summer transition program offered.

4975 State University of New York: Buffalo

1300 Elmwood Avenue
Buffalo, NY   14260   716-645-4500
                                 FAX 716-645-3473
                                 http://www.buffalostate.edu
                                 e-mail: savinomr@buffalostate.edu
Marianne Savino, Coordinator Special Services

The Office of Disability Services (ODS) is the University at Buffalo's center for coordinating services and accommodations to ensure accessiblity and usability of all programs, services and activities of UB by people with disabilities, and is a resource for information and advocacy toward their full participation in all aspects of campus life.

4976 State University of New York: College of Technology

SUNY Farmingdale
Farmingdale, NY 11735   516-420-2000
FAX 516-420-2689
http://www.farmingdale.edu
e-mail: webmaster@farmingdale.edu
Malka Edelman NCC, CRC, MCC, Director Support Services
Kimberly Kost MS, CRC, Counselor

Dedicated to the principle that equal opportunity be afforded each student to realize his/her fullest potential. The goal is to assist students with disabilities to function as independently as possible, and to ensure a comprehensively accessible university experience where individuals with disabilities have the same access to programs, opportunities and activities as all other students at the university.

4977 State University of New York: College at Buffalo

1300 Elmwood Avenue
Buffalo, NY 14222   716-878-4500
FAX 716-878-3804
http://www.buffalostate.edu
e-mail: savinomr@buffalostate.edu
Marianne Savino, Coordinator
Stephanie Russell, Assistant Coordinator

Services provided to approximately 400 students per year with a variety of disabilities, the majority of whom have learning disabilities. All support is determined on a case-by-case basis with a goal toward careers and independence as much as possible in the worksite.

4978 State University of New York: Fredonia

SUNY Fredonia
Fredonia, NY 14063   716-673-3251
800-252-1212
FAX 716-673-3249
http://www.fredonia.edu
e-mail: admissions.office@fredonia.edu
Carolyn Boone, Coord. Disabled Student Services

Offers a variety of services to students with disabilities including notetakers, extended testing time, counseling services, and special accommodations.

4979 State University of New York: Geneseo College

Office of Disability Services
1 College Circle
Geneseo, NY 14454   585-245-5112
FAX 585-245-5032
http://www.admissions.geneseo.edu
e-mail: admissions@geneseo.edu
Tabitha Buggie-Hunt, Director Disability Services
Janet Jackson, Support Staff

To provide qualified students with disabilities, whether temporary or permanent, equal and comprehensive access to college-wide programs, services, and campus facilities by offering academic support, advisement, and removal of architectural and attitudinal barriers.

4980 State University of New York: Oneonta

Student Disability Services
209 Alumni Hall
Oneonta, NY 13820   607-436-2137
FAX 607-436-3167
http://www.oneonta.edu
e-mail: sds@oneonta.edu
Craig Levins MA, Coordinator

To work with both students and college faculty/staff to ensure that compliance with disability laws is being upheld throughout the institution. SDS is also a resource to students diagnosed with a disability to assist in coordinating services which will lead the student toward receiving and equitable oppportunity at the College at Oneonta.

4981 State University of New York: Oswego

Disability Services Office
210 Swetman Hall
Oswego, NY 13126   315-312-3358
FAX 315-312-2943
http://www.oswego.edu
e-mail: dss@oswego.edu
Starr L Knapp, Interim Coordinator

A public four-year college of arts and sciences currently serving 140 students identified with disabling conditions. Total enrollment is approximately 8,000. Full time coordinator of academic support services for students with disabilities works with students on an individual basis.

4982 State University of New York: Plattsburgh

Angell College Center 110
Plattsburgh, NY 12901   518-564-2810
FAX 518-564-2807
http://www.plattsburgh.edu
e-mail: michele.carpentier@plattsburgh.edu
Michele Carpentier, Student Support Services

Academic support program funded by the United States Department of Education. Staffed by caring and commited professional whose mission is to provide services for students with disabilities.

4983 State University of New York: Potsdam

Sisson Hall
Potsdam, NY 13676   315-267-3267
FAX 315-267-3268
http://www.potsdam.edu
e-mail: housese@potsdam.edu
Sharon House, Academic Coordinator

A public four-year college with approximately 200 students with disabilities out of a total of 4,000.

4984 State University of New York: Stony Brook

Disability Support Services
128 Educational Communications Ctr
Stony Brook, NY 11794   631-632-6748
FAX 631-632-6747
http://www.sunysb.edu
e-mail: dss@notes.cc.sunysb.edu
Joanna Harris, Director Disability Services
Donna Molley, Assistant Director

Assist students with disabilities in accessing the many resources of the University. Individuals with disabilities are invited to make use of the services and equipment available.

4985 Suffolk County Community College: Eastern Campus

Speonk-Riverhead Road
Riverhead, NY   11901   631-287-0059
                               FAX 631-287-8787
                     http://www.sunysuffolk.edu
Judith Koodin, Counselor

The Eastern Campus is an accessible, open admissions institution. Services are provided to learning disabled students to allow them the same or equivalent educational experiences as nondisabled students.

4986 Suffolk County Community College: Selden Campus

533 College Road
Selden, NY   11784   631-451-4045
                               FAX 631-451-4473
                     http://www.sunysuffolk.edu
Marlene Boyce, Assistant Director
Arlene Zink, Office Manager
Harriet Friedheim, Specialist

Equalizes educational opportunities by minimizing physical, psychological and learning barriers. Attempt to provide as typical a college experience as possible, encouraging students to achieve academically through the provision of special services, support aids, or reasonable program accommodations.

4987 Suffolk County Community College: Western Campus

Crooked Hill Road
Brentwood, NY   11717   631-451-4045
                               FAX 631-451-4473
                     http://www.sunysuffolk.edu
Judith Taxier-Reinauer, Counselor
Cheryl Every-Wartz, Counselor

The goal of Suffolk Community College with regard to students with disabilities is to equalize educational opportunities by minimizing physical, psychological and learning barriers. We attempt to provide as typical a college experience as is possible, encouraging students to achieve academically through the provision of special services, auxillary aids, or reasonable program modifications.

4988 Sullivan County Community College

Learning & Student Development Services
112 College Road
Loch Sheldrake, NY   12759   845-434-5750
                               800-577-5243
                               FAX 845-434-4806
                     http://www.sullivan.suny.edu
Helene Laurenti, Director

SCCC is fully committed to institutions accessability for individuals with disabilities. Students who wish to obtain particular services or accommodations should communicate their needs and concerns as early as possible. These may include, but are not limited to, extended time for tests, oral examinations,reader and notetaker services, campus maps, and elevator privileges. Books on tape may be ordered through recordings for the blind. Appropriate documentation needed.

4989 Syracuse University

Services For Students with Disabilities
804 University Avenue
Syracuse, NY   13244   315-443-4498
                               FAX 315-443-2583
                     http://www.syracuse.edu
Dana Williams, Coordinator Academic Services

The office of disability services provides and coordinates services for students with documented disabilities. Students must provide current documentation of their disability in order to receive disability services and reasonable accommodations.

4990 Trocaire College

360 Choate Avenue
Buffalo, NY   14220   716-826-1200
                               FAX 716-828-6107
                     http://www.trocaire.edu
Norine Truax, Coordinator

An independent two-year college with 3 special education students out of a total of 1,056.

4991 Ulster County Community College

Cottekill Road
Stone Ridge, NY   12484   845-687-5000
                               800-724-0833
                               FAX 845-687-5090
                     http://www.sunyulster.edu
James Quirk, Special Services

The Student Support Services program promotes student success for students who are academically disadvantaged, economically disadvantaged, first-generation college students, and or students with disabilities. The goals of the program are to increase the retention, graduation, and transfer rates of those enrolled.

4992 University of Albany

Campus Center 130
Albany, NY   12222   518-442-5566
                               FAX 518-442-5589
                     http://www.albany.edu
Carolyn Malloch, Learning Disability Specialist

Offers a full time Learning Disability Specialist to work with students that have learning disabilities and or attention deficit disorder. The specialist offers individual appointments to develop study and advocacy skills.

4993 Utica College of Syracuse University

1600 Burrstone Road
Utica, NY   13502   315-792-3032
                               800-782-8884
                               FAX 315-792-3292
                     http://www.ucsu.edu
                     e-mail: KHenkel@utica.edu
Kateri T Henkel, Coordinator Learning Services

Provides students with disabilities individualized learning accommodations designed to meet the academic needs of the student. Counseling support and the development of new strategies for the learning challenges posed by college level work are an integral part of the services offered through Academic Support Services.

4994 Vassar College

124 Raymond Avenue
Poughkeepsie, NY 12604   845-452-7000
FAX 845-437-5715
http://www.assar.edu
e-mail: guthrie@vassar.edu
Belinda M Guthrie, Director

Offers a variety of services to students with disabilities including note takers, extended testing time, counseling services, and special accommodations.

4995 Wagner College

One Campus Road
Staten Island, NY 10301   718-390-3411
800-221-1010
FAX 718-390-3105
http://www.wagner.edu
Ruth Ann Perri, Director

An independent four-year college with 25 special education students out of a total of 1,272. There is an additional fee for the special education program in addition to the regular tuition.

4996 Westchester Community College

75 Grasslands Road
Valhalla, NY 10595   914-785-6600
FAX 914-785-6540
http://www.sunywcc.edu
Dr. Alan Seidman, Special Services

Students with Disabilities parallels the mission of WCC to be accessible, community centered, comprehensive, adaptable and dedicated to lifelong learning for all students. Full participation for students with disabilities is encouraged.

North Carolina

4997 Appalachian State University

Learning Disability Program
ASU Box 32087
Boone, NC 28608   828-262-2291
FAX 828-262-6834
http://www.appstate.edu
e-mail: questions@appstate.edu
Suzanne Wehner, Program Coodinator

Disabled Student Services assists students with indentified learning disabilities by providing the support they need to become successful college graduates. Disabled Student Services provides academic advising, alternative testing, assistance with technology, tutoring, practical solutions to learning problems, counseling, self-concept building and career exploration.

4998 Bennett College

900 E Washington Street
Greensboro, NC 27401   336-273-4431
FAX 336-273-4431
http://www.bennett.edu
Thelma Copeland, Support Services

An independent four-year college with 10 special education students out of a total of 568.

4999 Brevard College

Office for Students with Special Needs
400 N Broad Street
Brevard, NC 28712   828-883-8292
FAX 828-884-3790
http://www.brevard.edu
e-mail: skuehn@brevard.edu

Four year college provides services to special needs students.

5000 Caldwell Community College and Technical Institute

2855 Hickory Boulvard
Hudson, NC 28638   828-726-2200
FAX 828-726-2216
http://www.caldwell.cc.nc.us
Teena McRary

A public two-year college with 18 special education students out of a total of 2,744.

5001 Catawba College

2300 W Innes Street
Salisbury, NC 28144   704-637-4259
800-228-2922
FAX 704-637-4401
http://www.catawba.edu
e-mail: jlsabo@catawba.edu
Jan Sabo, Director Academic Resource

An independent four-year liberal arts college with an enrollment of 1,400.

5002 Catawba Valley Community College

2550 Highway 70 SE
Hickory, NC 28602   828-327-7000
FAX 828-327-7276
http://www.cvcc.cc.nc.us
Dr. Dan Gwaltney, Director

The following is a partial list of accommodations provided by the college: counseling services, tutors, note-takers and carbonless duplication paper, recorded textbooks, tape recorders for taping lecture classes, interpeters, computer with voice software, and extended time for texts. Catawba Valley Community College provides services for students with disabilities.

5003 Central Carolina Community College

1105 Kelly Drive
Sanford, NC 27330   919-775-5401
FAX 919-718-7380
http://www.ccarolina.cc.nc.us
Dr. Frances Andrews, Associate Dean

Adopted to guide its delivery of services to students with disabilities that states that no otherwise qualified individual shall by reason of disability be excluded from the participation in, be denied benefits of, or be subjected to discrimination under any program at Central Carolina Community College. The college will make program modification adjustments in instructional delivery and provide supplemental services.

5004   Central Piedmont Community College

PO Box 35009
Charlotte, NC   28235   704-330-6556
                                 FAX 704-330-4020
                                 TDY:704-330-6421
                     http://www.cpcc.cc.nc.us
                e-mail: patricia.adams@cpcc.edu
Pat Goings-Adams, LD Counselor

A public two-year college with 300 special education
students out of a total of 60,000.

5005   Craven Community College

800 College Court
New Bern, NC   28562   252-638-7274
                                 FAX 252-638-4232
                     http://www.craven.cc.nc.us
Edna Barrett, Director

Offers a variety of services to students with disabilities including notetakers, extended testing time, counseling services, and special accommodations.

5006   Davidson County Community College

PO Box 1287
Lexington, NC   27293   336-249-8186
                                 FAX 336-248-8531
                     http://www.davidson.cc.nc.us
Dr. Ed Morse, Dean

Offers a variety of services to students with disabilities including notetakers, extended testing time, counseling services, and special accommodations.

5007   Dore Academy

1727 Providence Road
Charlotte, NC   28207   704-365-5490
                                 FAX 704-365-3240
Mary Dore

Dore Academy is Charlotte's oldest college-prep
school for students with learning differences. A private, non-profit, independent day school for students
in grades 1-12, it is approved by the state of North
Carolina, Division of Exceptional children. All teachers are certified by the state and trained in the theory
and treatment of dyslexia and attention disorders.
With a maximum of 10 students per class (5 in reading
classes), the teacher student ratio is 1 to 7.

5008   East Carolina University

E 5th Street
Greenville, NC   27858   252-757-6799
                                 FAX 252-328-4155
                     http://www.ecu.edu
CC Rowe, Coordinator

A public four-year college with 47 special education
students out of a total of 13,903.

5009   Forsyth Technical Community College

2100 Silas Creek Parkway
Winston-Salem, NC   27103   336-734-7248
                                 FAX 336-761-2399
                     http://www.forsyth.tec.nc.us
                e-mail: pcompton@forsyth.cc.nc.us
Laura Wyatt, Chairperson

Offers a variety of services to students with disabilities including notetakers, extended testing time, counseling services, and special accommodations.

5010   Gardner-Webb University

Noel Program
PO Box 7424
Boiling Springs, NC   28017   704-434-4269
                                 FAX 704-406-3524
                     http://www.gardner-webb.edu
                e-mail: sjennings@gardner-webb.edu
Sharon Jennings, Director

Four year college that provides a program for disabled
students.

5011   Guilford Technical Community College

601 High Point Road
Jamestown, NC   27282   336-454-1126
                                 FAX 336-454-2510
                     http://www.gtcc.cc.nc.us
Dr. James Gripper, Contact

The purpose of disability access services is to provide
equal access and comprehensive, quality services to
all students who experience barriers to academic, personal and social success.

5012   Isothermal Community College

PO Box 804
Spindale, NC   28160   828-286-3636
                                 FAX 828-286-1120
                     http://www.isothermal.cc.nc.us
                e-mail: mdavis@isothermal.cc.nc.us
Ruth Boehning, LD Specialist

Isothermal Community College, in compliance with
the Americans with Disabilities Act, makes every effort to provide accommodations for students with disabilities. It is our goal to integrate students with
disabilities into the college and help them participate
and benefit from programs and activities enjoyed by
all students. We at Isothermal are committed to improving life through learning.

5013   Johnson C Smith University

100 Beatties Ford Road
Charlotte, NC   28216   704-378-1282
                                 FAX 704-330-1336
                     http://www.jcsu.edu
                e-mail: jcuthbertson@jcsu.edu
James Cuthbertson, Coordinator
Cathy Jones, Student Support Services

Four year college that provides support to those who
are disabled.

5014   Lenoir Community College

231 Highway 58 S
Kinston, NC   28502   252-527-6223
                                 FAX 252-527-1199
                     http://www.lenoir.cc.nc.us
Joy Tucker, Coordinator/Evening Counselor

Lenoir Community College is committed to serving
the needs of students with disabilities. If special assistance is needed, please give the college prior notice by
contacting the ADA Coordinator.

5015 Lenoir-Rhyne College
PO Box 7470
Hickory, NC 28603   828-328-7296
                             FAX 828-328-7329
                             http://www.lrc.edu
                             e-mail: kirbydr@lrc.edu
Donavon R Kirby, Coordinator

Four year college that provides services for those students that are learning disabled.

5016 Louisburg College
501 N Main Street
Louisburg, NC 27587   919-497-3216
                             FAX 919-496-1788
                             http://www.louisburg.edu
Jayne Davis, Director

A two-year college that offers programs for the learning disabled.

5017 Mars Hill College
124 Cascade Street
Mars Hill, NC 28754   828-689-1201
                             800-543-1514
                             FAX 828-689-1473
                             http://www.mhc.edu
Gail Sawyer, Director

An independent four-year college with 15 special education students out of a total of 1,321.

5018 Mayland Community College
PO Box 547
Spruce Pine, NC 28777   828-765-7351
                             800-462-9526
Nancy Godwin, SOAR Program

Offers a variety of services to students with disabilities including notetakers, extended testing time, counseling services, and special accommodations.

5019 McDowell Technical Community College
Student Enrichment Center
54 Universal Drive
Marion, NC 28752   828-652-6021
                             FAX 828-652-1014
Dr. James Robinson, Chair/Special Student Advising

A public two-year college with 15 special education students out of a total of 857. Free auxiliary services for LD students include: tutors, books on tape, unlimited testing, oral testing, notetakers and counseling. All faculty are trained in working with the LD student.

5020 Meredith College
Disability Services
Raleigh, NC 27607   919-760-8427
                             800-637-3348
                             FAX 919-760-2383
                             http://www.meredith.edu
                             e-mail: disabilityservices@meredith.edu
Betty Shannon Prevatt, Coordinator Disability Services

The college goal is to create an accessible community where people are judged on their abilities not their disabilities. The Disability Services staff strives to provide individuals with the tools by which they can better accomplish their educational goals.

5021 Montgomery Community College: North Carolina
1011 Page Street
Troy, NC 27371   910-576-6222
                             FAX 910-576-2176
                             http://www.montgomery.cc.nc.us
Dr. Virginia Morgan, Chairperson

Offers a variety of services to students with disabilities including note takers, extended testing time, counseling services, and special accommodations.

5022 North Carolina State University
Box 7509
Raleigh, NC 27695   919-515-7653
                             FAX 919-513-2840
                             http://www.ncsu.edu
                             e-mail: emma_swain@ncsu.edu
Charlotte Flynn, Associate Coordinator

Academic accommodations and services are provided for students at the university who have documented learning disabilities. Admission to the university is based on academic qualifications and learning disabled students are considered in the same manner as any other student. Special assistance is available to accommodate the needs of these students, including courses in accessible locations when appropiate.

5023 North Carolina Wesleyan College
3400 N Wesleyan Boulevard
Rocky Mount, NC 27804   252-985-5269
                             800-488-6292
                             FAX 252-985-5399
                             http://www.ncwc.edu
                             e-mail: jharrison@ncwc.edu
Jennifer Harrison, Coordinator
Cliff Sullivan, Registrar

The Center provides support to students interested in achieving academic success. The staff works to provide you with information about academic matters and serves as an advocate for you. Services focus on pre-major advising, tutoring, mentoring, skills enrichment, disabilities assistance, self-assessment and retention.

5024 Peace College
15 E Peace Street
Raleigh, NC 29604   919-508-2293
                             FAX 919-508-2326
                             http://www.peace.edu
                             e-mail: amann@peace.edu
Dr. Ann F Mann, Director

Four year college offering programs to disabled students.

5025 Piedmont Baptist College
716 Franklin Street
Winston-Salem, NC   27101   336-725-8344
FAX 336-725-5522
http://www.pbc.edu
e-mail: whiteli@pbc.edu
Linda Whitehart, Director

A four year college offering comprehensive programs for students with learning disabilities.

5026 Pitt Community College
Highway 11 S
Greenville, NC   27835   252-321-4294
FAX 252-321-4401
http://www.pitt.cc.nc.us
Mike Bridgers, Coordinator Disability Services

The staff of Disability Services looks forward to working with you to achieve your immediate academic and long range career goals. Our office is designed to provide academic, personal and technical support services to students with disabilities who qualify for post secondary education, but whose deficits are such that they are unlikly to succeed in college without thoses services.

5027 Randolph Community College
629 Industrial Park Avenue
Asheboro, NC   27204   336-633-0227
FAX 336-629-4695
http://www.randolf.cc.nc.us
e-mail: ssmuse@randolf.cc.nc.us
Rebekah Megerian, Director Special Services
Ned Tenkin, Special Needs Counselor

A public two-year college with 23 special education students out of a total of 1,487. Applicants with disabilities who wish to request accommodations in compliance with the ADA must identify themselves to the admissions counselor before placement testing.

5028 Rockingham Community College
Highway 65 and County Home Road
Wentworth, NC   27375   336-342-4261
FAX 336-349-9986
http://www.rcc.cc.nc.us
Jack Darber, Special Services

Offers a variety of services to students with disabilities including notetakers, extended testing time, counseling services, and special accommodations.

5029 Salem College
S Church Street
Winston-Salem, NC   27108   336-721-2600
FAX 336-724-7102
http://www.salem.edu
Cynthia Calise, Special Services

Offers a variety of services to students with disabilities including notetakers, extended testing time, counseling services, and special accommodations.

5030 Sandhills Community College
3395 Airport Road
Pinehurst, NC   28374   910-695-3733
800-338-3944
FAX 910-695-1823
http://www.sandhills.cc.nc.us
Peggie Chavis, Disabilities Coordinator

Offers a variety of services to students with disabilities including notetakers, extended testing time, counseling services, and special accommodations.

5031 Southwestern Community College: North Carolina
447 College Drive
Sylva, NC   28779   828-586-4091
800-447-4091
FAX 828-586-3129
http://www.southwest.cc.nc.us
Steve Conlin, Director

Southwestern Community College provides equal access to education for persons with disabilities. It is the responsibility of the student to make their disability known and to request academic adjustments. Requests should be made in a timely manner and submitted to the Director of Student Support Services. Every reasonable effort will be made to provide service, however, not requesting services prior to registration may delay implementation.

5032 St Andrews Presbyterian College
1700 Dogwood Mile
Laurinburg, NC   28387   910-277-5331
FAX 910-277-5020
http://www.sapc.edu
e-mail: info@sapc.edu

Four year college that supports and provides services to the learning disabled students.

5033 Stone Mountain School
126 Camp Elliott Road
Black Mountain, NC   28711   828-669-8639
FAX 828-669-2521
http://www.stonemountainschool.org
Catherine Jennings, Executive Director
Paige Thomas, Admissions Director

5034 Surry Community College
PO Box 304
Dobson, NC   27017   336-386-8121
FAX 336-386-8951
http://www.surry.cc.nc.us
Larry Rooks, Special Programs
Judy L Riggs, Chairman, DS

Offers a variety of services to students with disabilities including notetakers, extended testing time, counseling services, and special accommodations.

5035 Tri-County Community College
4600 E US 64
Murphy, NC   28906   828-837-6810
FAX 828-837-3266
TDY:724-228-4028
http://www.tccc.cc.nc.us
Sarah Harper, Executive Director

Offers a variety of services to students with disabilities including notetakers, extended testing time, counseling services, and special accommodations.

5036   University of North Carolina: Chapel Hill

Learning Disabilities Services
137 E Franklin Street
Chapel Hill, NC   27514   919-962-7227
                                          FAX 919-962-3674
                                          http://www.unc.edu
                                          e-mail: lds@email.unc.edu
Dr. Theresa Maitland, Learning Disabilities Specialist

Promotes learning by providing academic support to meet the individual needs of students diagnosed with specific learning disabilities. Strives to ensure the independence of participating students so that they may succeed during and beyond their university years.

5037   University of North Carolina: Charlotte

9201 University Boulevard
Charlotte, NC   28223   704-687-2213
                                          FAX 704-687-6483
                                          http://www.uncc.edu
                                          e-mail: gbhoneyc@email.uncc.edu
Gail Honeycutt, Program Assistant

Introduction to Students with Special Needs. Characteristics of students with special learning needs, including those who are gifted and those who experience academic, social, emotional, physical and developmental disabilities. Legal, historical and philosophical foudations of special education and current issues in providing appropriate educational services to students with special needs.

5038   University of North Carolina: Greensboro

Disability Services
101 Park Building
Greensboro, NC   27402   336-334-5440
                                          FAX 336-334-4412
                            http://www.uncg.edu/student.affairs.ods
                                          e-mail: plbailey@uncg.edu
Patricia Bailey, Director

A public four-year university with over 300 students with disabilities out of a total of 12,000.

5039   University of North Carolina: Wilmington

601 S College Road
Wilmington, NC   28403   910-962-3746
                                          FAX 910-962-7124
                                          http://www.uncwil.edu
Margaret Turner PhD, Disability Services
Ginny Lundeen, Disability Services

Offer accommodative services, consultation, counseling and advocacy for Disabled Students enrolled at UNCW.

5040   Wake Forest University

1834 Wake Forest Road
Winston-Salem, NC   27109   336-758-5000
                                          FAX 336-758-6074
                                          http://www.wfu.edu
Dr. Sandra Chadwick, Special Services

5041   Wake Technical Community College

9101 Fayetteville Road
Raleigh, NC   27603   919-662-3405
                                          FAX 919-662-3564
                                          TDY:919-779-0668
                                          http://www.waketech.edu
Janet Killen, Director

If you are a person with a documented disability who requires accommodations to achieve equal access to Wake Tech facilities, academic programs or other activities, you may request reasonable accommodations.

5042   Western Carolina University

20 McKee Building
Cullowhee, NC   28723   828-227-7127
                                          FAX 828-227-7344
                                          http://www.wcu.edu
                                          e-mail: mellen@wcu.edu
Carol Mellen, Director

Students with a documented disability may be provided with appropriate academic accommodations such as, note takers, testing accomadations, books on tape, readers/scribes, use of adaptive equipment and priority registration.

5043   Wilkes Community College

Student Support Services
PO Box 120
Wilkesboro, NC   28697   336-838-6560
                                          FAX 336-838-6277
                                          http://www.wilkes.cc.nc.us
                                          e-mail: sizemore@wilkes.cc.nc.us
Kim Faw, Director
Nancy Sizemore, Counselor

A public two-year community college. Special services include: testing and individualized education plans; oral and extended time testing; individual and small group tutoring; study skills; readers and proctors and specialized equipment.

5044   Wilson County Technical College

902 Herring Avenue
Wilson, NC   27893   252-291-1195
                                          FAX 252-243-7148
                                          http://www.wilsontech.cc.nc.us
William James, Special Services

Offers a variety of services to students with disabilities including notetakers, extended testing time, counseling services, and special accommodations.

5045   Wingate University

220 N Camden Street
Wingate, NC   28174   704-233-8000
                                          800-755-5550
                                          FAX 704-233-8290
                                          http://www.wingate.edu
Patricia LeDonne, VP Academic Affairs

An independent four-year college with 50 special education students out of a total of 1,372. There is an additional fee for the special education program in addition to the regular tuition.

5046 Winston-Salem State University

601 Martin Luther King Drive
Winston-Salem, NC   27110   336-750-2000
FAX 336-750-2049
http://www.wssu.edu

Maurice Johnson, Director

Offers a variety of services to students with disabilities including notetakers, extended testing time, counseling services, and special accommodations.

North Dakota

5047 Bismarck State College

1500 Edwards Avenue
Bismarck, ND   58506   701-224-5426
800-445-5073
FAX 701-224-5550
http://www.bsc.nodak.edu
e-mail: Ischlafm@gwmail.nodak.edu
Lisa Schlafman, Coordinator/Disability Support

Offers a variety of services to students with disabilities including notetakers, extended testing time, counseling services, and special accommodations.

5048 Dickinson State University

Student Support Services
291 Campus Drive
Dickinson, ND   58601   701-483-2029
FAX 701-783-2006
http://www.dsu.nodak.edu

Lisa Cantlon, Director

Four year college offers support services to learning disabled students.

5049 Fort Berthold Community College

PO Box 490
New Town, ND   58763   701-627-3665
FAX 701-627-3609
http://www.fort-berthold.cc.nd.us
Delores Wilkinson, Dean Students

An independent two-year college with 3 special education students out of a total of 279.

5050 Mayville State University

330 3rd Street NE
Mayville, ND   58257   701-788-2301
FAX 701-788-4748
http://www.mayvillestate.edu
e-mail: ndus.office@ndus.nodak.edu
Joyce White, Academic Support Director

Offers a variety of services to students with disabilities including notetakers, extended testing time, counseling services, and special accommodations.

5051 Minot State University: Bottineau Campus

105 Simrall Boulevard
Bottineau, ND   58318   701-228-5487
800-542-6866
FAX 701-228-5499
http://www.misu-b.nodak.edu
Jan Nahinurk, Special Services

Offers a variety of services to students with disabilities including notetakers, extended testing time, counseling services, and special accommodations.

5052 North Dakota Center for Persons with Disabilities (NDCPD)

Minot State University
500 University Avenue W
Minot, ND   58707   701-858-3580
800-233-1737
FAX 701-858-3483
TDY:701-858-3580
http://www.ndcpd.org
e-mail: ndcpd@minotstateu.edu
Bryce Fifield, Director
Susie Mack, Office Manager

NDCPD works with the disability community, university, faculty and researchers, policy makers and service providers to identify emerging needs in the disability community and how to obtain resources to address them.

5053 North Dakota State College of Science

800 N 6th Street
Wahpeton, ND   58076   701-671-2623
800-342-4325
FAX 701-671-2440
http://www.ndscs.nodak.edu
e-mail: joy.eichhorn@ndscs.nodak.edu
Joy Eichhorn, Disability Services Coordinator

A public two-year comprehensive college with a student population of 2400. Students with disabilites comprise seven percent of the population. Tuition $2025.

5054 North Dakota State University

Counseling & Disability Services
212 Ceres Hall
Fargo, ND   58105   701-231-7671
FAX 701-231-6318

Elizabeth Gibb, LD Specialist
Cathy Anderson, DS Coordinator

Provides comprehensive services for students who have learning disabilities. Staff can explain how to access services, provide initial consultation regarding the possible presence of learning, emotional or physical disabilities that hinder academic performance. Consult with students, faculty and staff to determine and provide appropriate accommodations. Assist in arranging for accommodations.

5055 Standing Rock College

HC 1 Box 4
Fort Yates, ND   58538   701-954-3862
FAX 701-854-3403

Linda Ivan, Special Services

Offers a variety of services to students with disabilities including notetakers, extended testing time, counseling services, and special accommodations.

Ohio

5056 Antioch College

Academic Support Center
795 Livermore Street
Yellow Springs, OH   45387   937-769-1166
                                    800-543-9436
                              FAX 937-769-1163
                    http://www.antioch-college.edu
                    e-mail: lizek@antioch-college.edu
Elizabeth England Kennedy, Director
John Smith, Assistant Director

Comprehensive integrated support, including tutoring, time management and organization support, software, accommodations for our academic and cooperative education programs.

5057 Art Academy of Cincinnati

1125 Saint Gregory Street
Cincinnati, OH   45202   513-721-5205
                                    800-323-5692
                              FAX 513-562-8778
                       http://www.artacadamy.edu
Jane Stanton, Dean of Students

Offers a variety of services to students with disabilities including notetakers, extended testing time, counseling services, and special accommodations.

5058 Baldwin-Wallace College

275 Eastland Road
Berea, OH   44017   440-826-2900
                              FAX 440-826-3640
                        http://www.baldwinw.edu
J Edward Warner

Offers a variety of services to students with disabilities including notetakers, extended testing time, counseling services, and special accommodations.

5059 Bluffton College

Special Student Services
280 W College Avenue
Bluffton, OH   45817   419-358-3458
                              FAX 419-358-3323
                         http://www.bluffton.edu
                      e-mail: bergerd@bluffton.edu
Timothy Byers, Program Contact

Four year college offers special programs to learninig disabled students.

5060 Bowling Green State University

413 S Hall
Bowling Green, OH   43403   419-372-8495
                              FAX 419-372-8496
                            http://www.bgsu.edu
                     e-mail: rcunnin@bgnet.bgsu.edu
Robert Cunningham, Director

The Disability Services Office is evidence of Bowling Green State University's commitment to provide a support system which assists in conquering obstacles that persons with disabilities may encounter as they pursue their educational goals and activities. Our hope is to facilitate mainstream mobility and recognize the diverse talents that persons with disabilities have to offer to our university and our community.

5061 Case Western Reserve University

10900 Euclid Avenue
Cleveland, OH   44106   216-368-2000
                              FAX 216-368-8826
                            http://www.cwru.edu
Susan Sampson, Coordinator Disability Services

While all students will have preferences for learning, students with physical or learning disabilities have different actual needs as well. Students with physical disabilities such as visual impairments, hearing impairments, or temporary or permanent motor impairments may need guide dogs, interpeters, note-takers, wheelchair accessible rooms, or other types of assistance to help them attend and participate in class. Also available, extra time or a separate room for exams, tutoring and more.

5062 Center for the Advancement of Learning

PLUS Program/Muskingum College
Montgomery Hall
New Concord, OH   43762   740-826-8280
                                    800-752-6082
                              FAX 740-826-8285
                         http://www.muskingum.edu
                     e-mail: butler@muskingum.edu
Jen Navicky, Director

A professional, adult staff provides two levels of academic support and currently serves 150 learning disabled students.   Support includes all reasonable accommodations and intensive one-on-one and small group tutoring. Learning Strategy instruction is embedded within course contents. Full services include a minimum of one hour of tutoring each week and students average 3-5 hours. Maintenance level services are flexibly arranged for half that amount. The Program has excellent faculty.

5063 Central Ohio Technical College

Developmental Education
1179 University Drive
Newark, OH   43055   740-366-1351
                                    800-963-9275
                              FAX 740-364-9641
                       http://www.cotc.tec.oh.us
Dr. Phyllis Thompsen, Coordinator

Learning Assitance Center and Disability Services (LAC/DS) is the academic support unit in Student Support Services. LAC/DS provides FREE programs and services designed to help students sharpen skills necessary to succeed in college.

5064 Central State University

Office of Disability Services
1400 Brush Row Road
Wilberforce, OH   45384   937-376-6411
                                 FAX 937-376-6661
                        http://www.centralstate.edu
                        e-mail: info@csu.ces.edu

Four year college that provides services for the learning disabled students.

5065 Cincinnati State Technical and Community College

3520 Central Parkway
Cincinnati, OH   45223   513-569-1613
                                 FAX 516-569-1562
                        http://www.cinstate.cc.oh.us
David Cover

Services include assistance and support services for students with permanent and temporary disabilities, test proctoring, readers/scribes, taping, tape recording loan, reading machines, assistance with locating interpeters, mediating between student and faculty to overcome specific disability issues; also offers braille access.

5066 Clark State Community College

570 E Leffel Lane
Springfield, OH   45505   937-328-6019
                                 FAX 937-328-6142
                        http://www.clark.cc.oh.us
Deborah Titus, Counselor

In accordance with the Americans with Disabilities Act, it is the policy of Clark State Community College to provide reasonable accommodations to persons with disabilities. The office of disability services offers a variety of services to Clark State students who have documented physical, mental or learning disabilities.

5067 Cleveland Institute of Art

11141 E Boulevard
Cleveland, OH   44106   216-421-7462
                                 800-278-6446
                        FAX 216-754-2557
                        http://www.cia.edu
                e-mail: jmilenski@gate.cia.edu
Jill Milenski, Associate Director

No student should be discouraged from attending CIA because of a learning disability. A student working on their BFA degree at the Institute of Art can get academic support from the tutoring director in the Office of Academic Services. Services include books-on-tape, one-on-one tutoring, alternative curriculum advising, notetaking services, alternative test taking and assignment arrangements. Services outside the scope of the program can be arranged at the student's expense.

5068 Cleveland State University

1983 E 24th Street
Cleveland, OH   44115

                                 888-278-6446
                        FAX 216-687-9366
                        http://www.csuohio.edu
                e-mail: m.zuccaro@csuohio.edu
Michael Zuccaro, Disability Services

CSU aims to provide equal opportunity to all of its students. Services are available to those who might need some extra help because of a physical disability, communication impairment or learning disability. This program is designed to address the personal and academic issues of the physically handicapped students as they become oriented to campus. A full range of services is offered.

5069 College of Mount Saint Joeseph

Project EXCEL
5701 Delhi Road
Cincinnati, OH   45233   513-244-4623
                                 800-654-9314
                        FAX 513-244-4222
                        http://www.msj.edu
                e-mail: jane_pohlman@mail.msj.edu
Jane Pohlman, Director

Learning disabled staff offers intensive instruction in reading, writing and study skills.

5070 College of Wooster

1189 Beall Avenue
Wooster, OH   44691   330-263-2427
                                 FAX 330-263-2427
                        http://www.wooster.edu
Dr. Carol Roose

Offers a variety of services to students with disabilities including notetakers, extended testing time, counseling services, and special accommodations.

5071 Columbus State Community College: Department of Disability Services

550 E Spring Street
Columbus, OH   43215   614-287-2570
                                 800-621-6407
                        FAX 614-287-6054
                        TDY:614-281-2570
        http://www.cscc.edu/docs/disability/intro.html
                e-mail: wcocchi@cscc.edu
Wayne Cocchi, Director

A public two-year college serving qualified students with disabilities, including learning disabilities. Support services are provided based on disability documentation and can include, books, tapes, alternative testing, notetaking, counseling, equipment use, reader, scribe, and peer tutoring.

5072 Cuyahoga Community College: Eastern Campus

4250 Richmond Road
Highland Hills, OH   44122   216-987-2034
                                 FAX 216-987-2423
                        TDY:216-987-2230
        http://www.tri-c.cc.oh.us/EAST/default.htm
                e-mail: Maryann.Syarto@tri-c.cc.oh.us
Mary Syarto, LD Director

The ACCESS Programs strive to assist Tri-C students with disabilities to realize their learning potential, bring them into the mainstream of the College community, enhance their self-sufficiency, and enable them to achieve academic success. Services include tuoring, test proctoring, interpreters, adaptive equipment, readers and/or scribes for exams, alternative test taking arrangements, alternative format for printed materials and textbooks on tape.

5073 Cuyahoga Community College: Western Campus
1000 W Pleasant Valley Road
Parma, OH   44130   216-987-5077
                                                FAX 516-987-5050
                                                TDY:216-987-5117
http://www.tri-c.cc.oh.us/west/default.htm
e-mail: Rose.Kolovrat@tri-c.cc.oh.us
Rose Kolovrat, Program Manager

The ACCESS programs strive to assist Tri-C students with disabilities to realize their learning potential, bring them into the mainstream of the College community, enhance their self-suffciency and enable them to achieve academic success. Services provided include tutoring, test proctoring, interpeters, adaptive equipment, readers/scribes for exams, alternative testing arrangements, alternative format for printed material and textbooks on tape.

5074 Defiance College
701 N Clinton Street
Defiance, OH   43512   419-784-4010
                                                800-520-4632
                                                FAX 419-784-0426
http://www.defiance.edu
Jo McCormick, Associate Professor

Offers a variety of services to students with disabilities including notetakers, extended testing time, counseling services, and special accommodations.

5075 Denison University
104 Doane Hall
Granville, OH   43023   740-587-6666
                                                800-336-4766
                                                FAX 740-587-5629
http://www.denison.edu
e-mail: vestal@denison.edu
Jennifer Grube Vestal, Associate Dean

The Office of Academic Support (OAS) offers a wide range of services for students with disabilities. In supporting our students as they move forward toward graduation and the world of work beyond, we strongly encourage and promote self advocacy regarding disability related issues.

5076 Franklin University
201 S Grant Avenue
Columbus, OH   43215   614-341-6237
                                                FAX 614-224-0434
http://www.franklin.edu
Linda Turley, Coordinator

Students who have disabilities may notify the University of their status by checking the appropriate space on the registration form each trimester. Then the Coordinator of Disability Services will help them file proper documentation so that accommodations can be made for their learning needs.

5077 Hiram College
Hinsdale Hall
Hiram, OH   44234   330-569-3211
                                                FAX 330-569-5494
http://www.hiram.edu
Dr. Vivian Makosky, Counseling Director

Offers a variety of services to students with disabilities including notetakers, extended testing time, counseling services, and special accommodations.

5078 Hocking College
3301 Hocking Parkway
Nelsonville, OH   45764   740-753-3591
                                                800-282-4163
                                                FAX 740-753-4097
http://www.hocking.edu
Kim Forbes Powell, Coordinator

The Access Center Office of Disability Support Services is dedicated to serving the various needs of individuals with disabilities and promoting their participation in college life.

5079 Hocking Technical College
3301 Hocking Parkway
Nelsonville, OH   45764   740-753-3591
                                                800-282-4163
                                                FAX 740-753-1452
http://www.hocking.edu
e-mail: admissions@hocking.edu
Kim Forbes Shaner, Support Specialist

Offers a variety of services to students with disabilities including notetakers, extended testing time, counseling services, and special accommodations.

5080 ITT Technical Institute
1030 N Meridian Road
Youngstown, OH   44509   330-747-5555
                                                FAX 330-270-8333
Frank J Quartini, Educational Director

Offers a variety of services to students with disabilities including note takers, extended testing time, counseling services, and special accommodations.

5081 Kent State University
Student Disability Services
181 MSC
Kent, OH   44242   330-672-3391
                                                FAX 330-672-3763
http://www.kent.edu/sds
e-mail: ajannaro@kent.edu
Anne Jannarone, Director

Student Disability Services (SDS) provides assistance to students with varying degrees and types of disabilities in order to maximize educational opportunity and academic potential. Types of disabilities that students have who are served by SDS include mobility impairments, visual, hearing or speech impairments, specific learning disabilities, attention deficit disorder, chronic health disorders, psychological disabilities and temporary disabilities.

5082 Kent State University: Tuscarawas Academic Services
330 University Drive NE
New Philadelphia, OH   44663   330-339-3391
                                                FAX 330-339-3321
                                                TDY:330-339-7888
http://www.tusc.kent.edu
Agnes Swigart, Assistant Dean

Offers a variety of services to students with disabilities including notetakers, extended testing time and special accommodations.

5083 Lorain County Community College

1005 N Abbe Road
Elyria, OH   44035   440-365-4191
                                      800-955-5222
                                  FAX 440-366-4127
                           http://www.lorainccc.edu
Ruth Porter, Coordinator

LCCC serves over 80 learning disabled students per year out of a total student population of about 7,000. Services include readers/testers, scribes, notetaking accommodations, assistive technology, advocacy training and personal counseling. Free tutoring is available to all students at the college. No diagnostic testing is available.

5084 Malone College

515 25th Street NW
Canton, OH   44709   330-471-8100
                                      800-521-1146
                                  FAX 330-471-8478
                               http://www.malone.edu
Patty Little, Director Retention/Special Needs

An independent four-year college with about 40 special education students out of a total of almost 2,000.

5085 Marburn Academy

1860 Walden Drive
Columbus, OH   43229   614-433-0822
                                  FAX 614-433-0812
                        http://www.marburnacademy.org
           e-mail: marburnadmission@marburnacademy.org
Scott Burton, Director Admission
Barbara Davidson, Director Auxiliary Programs

Marburn Academy is a small, independent day school offering the finest education for bright children who learn differently. Our entire program is deisgned to meet the academic and social needs of children who have learning differences such as dyslexia, learning disabilities or ADHD. Marburn Academy's program is accredited by the Academy of Orton-Gillingham Practitioners and Educators.

5086 Marietta College

215 5th Street
Marietta, OH   45750   740-376-4643
                                  FAX 740-376-4901
                               http://www.marietta.edu
                       e-mail: williams@marietta.edu
Bruce Peterson, Resident Director

An independent four-year college with a special education student population of about 5%.

5087 Marion Technical College

1467 Mount Vernon Avenue
Marion, OH   43302   740-389-4636
                                  FAX 740-389-6136
                            http://www.mtc.tec.oh.us
Lori Thomas, Coordinator

The Student Resource Center also houses the Office of Disabilities. The SRC director will advocate on student's behalf for resonable accommodations for those with physical, mental and or emotional disabilities.

5088 Miami University

301 S Campus Avenue
Oxford, OH   45056   513-529-8741
                                  FAX 513-529-3841
                              http://www.mid.muohio.edu
                       e-mail: greendw@muohio.edu
Douglas Green, Coordinator

A public four-year college with approximately 5% of its students with LD/ADHD.

5089 Miami University: Middletown Campus

4200 E University Boulevard
Middletown, OH   45042   513-727-3431
                                  FAX 513-727-3223
                                  TDY:513-727-3308
                              http://www.mid.muohio.edu
Linda Watkins, Coordinator Counseling Services

Offers a variety of services to students with disabilities including notetakers, extended testing time, counseling services, and special accommodations.

5090 Mount Vernon Nazarene College

800 Martinsburg Road
Mount Vernon, OH   43050   740-397-9000
                                  FAX 740-393-0511
                                 http://www.mvdc.edu
                    e-mail: lebron.fairbanks@mvnu.edu
Dr. Carol Matthews, Director

Four year college that provides programs for learning diabled students.

5091 Muskingum College

163 Stormont Street
New Concord, OH   43762   740-826-8284
                                  FAX 740-826-8285
                              http://www.muskingum.edu
                       e-mail: adminfo@muskingum.edu
Sandy Long, Executive Director
Carole Kerper, Associate Director

Center for Advancement of Learning houses the PLUS Program, a full service for students with LD.

5092 Northwest Technical College

1900 28th Avenue S
Moorehead, OH   56560   218-236-6277
                                      800-426-5603
                                  FAX 218-236-0342
                             http://www.ntc-online.com
Dennis Gable, Special Services

Offers a variety of services to students with disabilities including notetakers, extended testing time, counseling services, and special accommodations.

5093   Notre Dame College of Ohio

4545 College Road
South Euclid, OH   44121   216-381-1680
                                  FAX 216-381-3802
                                  http://www.ndc.edu
                                  e-mail: ekadlec@ndc.edu
Elizabeth Kaldec, Director

Four year college that offers support and services to students with learning disabilities.

5094   Oberlin College

101 N Professor Street
Oberlin, OH   44074   440-775-8121
                                  FAX 440-775-8886
                                  http://www.oberlin.edu
Dr. Dean Kelly, Coordinator

An independent four-year college with small percentage of education students.

5095   Ohio State University Agricultural Technical Institute

1382 Dover Road
Wooster, OH   44691   330-264-3911
                                  800-647-8283
                                  FAX 330-202-3579
                                  http://www.ati.ag.ohio-state.edu
Gerri Wolfe, LD Specialist

A public two-year college with nearly 10% special education students. There is no fee for the special education program in addition to the regular tuition.

5096   Ohio State University: Lima Campus

4240 Campus Drive
Lima, OH   45804   419-995-8453
                                  FAX 419-995-8483
                                  http://www.lima.ohio-state.edu
                                  e-mail: meyer.193@osu.edu
Karen Meyer, Coordinator/Disability Services

A public four-year college providing services to learning disabled students including extended test time, counseling, notetakers and other special accommodations.

5097   Ohio State University: Mansfield Campus, Disability Services

1680 University Drive
Mansfield, OH   44906   419-755-4234
                                  FAX 419-755-4243
                                  http://www.mansfield.ohio-state.edu
                                  e-mail: corso.1@osu.edu
Ginny Corso, Learning Disabilities Liason

A public four-year college providing services to learning disabled students including peer tutoring, extended test time, quiet rooms and other special accommodations.

5098   Ohio State University: Marion Campus

1465 Mount Vernon Avenue
Marion, OH   43302   740-389-6786
                                  FAX 614-292-5817
                                  http://www.marion.ohio-state.edu
Margaret Hazelett, LD Specialist

A public four-year college providing a full range of services for students with disabilities.

5099   Ohio State University: Newark Campus

1179 University Drive
Newark, OH   43055   740-366-3321
                                  FAX 740-366-5047
                                  http://www.newark.ohio-state.edu
Barbara Deutschle, Learning Disability Specialist

A public four-year college providing services to learning disabled students including peer tutoring, extended test time, quiet rooms and other special accommodations. There is no separate fee for these services.

5100   Ohio State University: Nisonger Center

1581 Dodd Drive
Columbus, OH   43210   614-292-8365
                                  FAX 614-292-3727
Stephen Reiss, Director

The Ohio State University Nisonger Center for Mental Retardation and Developmental Disabilities provides interdisciplinary training, research and exemplary services pertaining to people with developmental disabilities. The center, which is a part of a national network of activities called University Afffiliated Programs, was founded in 1968. Training is provided in medicine (pediatrics and psychiatry), dentistry, education, physical therapy, psychology and other relevant disciplines.

5101   Ohio State University: Office for Disability Services

1760 Neil Avenue
Columbus, OH   43210   614-292-3307
                                  FAX 614-292-4190
                                  TDY:614-292-0901
                                  http://www.osu.ohio-state.edu
Patty Carlton, Director
Lois Burke, Counselor

ODS offers academic accommodations for students with documented disabilities including but not limited to students who are deaf or hard of hearing, visually impaired, mobilty impaired or have ADHD, learning disabilities, psychiatric disabilities or medical disabilities. ODS also provides auxiliary aids which include access to class notes, print materials in alternate format, interpreters and/or closed captioning for deaf students, and a variety of adaptive technology.

5102   Ohio University

101 Crewson House
Athens, OH   45701   740-593-1000
                                  FAX 740-593-2708
                                  http://www.ohiou.edu
Susan Wagner, Officer Affirmative

A public four-year college with a small percentage of special education students.

5103 Ohio University Chillicothe
571 W 5th Street
Chillicothe, OH 45601   740-774-7245
877-462-6824
FAX 740-774-7290
http://www.ohiou.edu/~childept
e-mail: diekroge@oak.cats.ohiou.edu
Dr. Diane Diekroger, Student Support

Offers a variety of services to students with disabilities including note takers, extended testing time, counseling services, and special accommodations.

5104 Otterbein College
102 W College Avenue
Westerville, OH 43081   614-890-3000
800-488-8144
FAX 614-823-1200
http://www.otterbein.edu
Ellen Kasualis, Special Services

An independent four-year college with a small percentage of special education students.

5105 Owens Community College
PO Box 10000
Toledo, OH 43699   419-661-7000
800-466-9367
FAX 419-661-7607
http://www.owens.cc.oh.us
e-mail: bscheffert@owens.cc.oh.us
Debra J Sanchez, Disability Resources

A comprehensive Community College that offers educational programs in over 50 technical areas of study leading to the Associate of Applied Science, Associate of Applied Business or Associate of Technical Studies degree. Provides programs designed for college transfer and leads to the Associate of Arts or Associate of Science degree. Finally, a number of certificate programs as well as short term credit and non-credit programs are available.

5106 Shawnee State University
940 2nd Street
Portsmouth, OH 45662   740-354-3205
FAX 740-351-3419
http://www.shawnee.edu
e-mail: rlattimore@shawnee.edu
Mary Anne Malone, Coordinator

Offers a variety of services to students with disabilities including notetakers, extended testing time, counseling services, and special accommodations.

5107 Sinclair Community College
444 W 3rd Street
Dayton, OH 45402   937-512-3550
FAX 937-512-3554
http://www.sinclair.edu
Lisa Rhine, Program Manager
Robin More-Cooper, Counselor

Funded by the Federal Department of Education, Student Support Services is an organization devoted to helping students meet the challenges of college life. Our goals are to help students stay in school, then eventually graduate and/or transfer to a four-year college or university. We strive to develop new ways of helping students achieve their educational, career and professional goals.

5108 Southern Ohio College: Fairfield Campus
Fairfield Campus
Fairfield, OH 45014   513-829-7100
FAX 513-771-3413
Jane Ann Benson, Special Services

Offers a variety of services to students with disabilities including notetakers, extended testing time, counseling services, and special accommodations.

5109 Southern Ohio College: Northeast Campus
2791 Mogadore Road
Akron, OH 44312   330-733-8766
FAX 330-733-5853
Kathy Antonucci, Special Services

Offers a variety of services to students with disabilities including notetakers, extended testing time, counseling services, and special accommodations.

5110 Southern State Community College
100 Hobart Drive
Hillsboro, OH 45133   937-393-3431
FAX 937-393-9370
Carl Vertona, Special Services

Offers a variety of services to students with disabilities including notetakers, extended testing time, counseling services, and special accommodations.

5111 Terra State Community College
2830 Napoleon Road
Fremont, OH 43420   419-334-8400
866-AT-TERRA
FAX 419-334-9035
http://www.terra.cc.us/terra2.html
e-mail: info@terra.cc.oh.us
Richard Newman, Coordinator

Provides quality learning experiences which are accessible and affordable. Terra is actively committed to excellence in learning and offers associate degrees in various technologies as well as in arts and sciences, applied business, and applied science. Our office of student support services works with students with learning disabilities and other disabilities.

5112 University of Akron Wayne College
1901 Smucker Road
Orrville, OH 44667   330-683-2010
800-221-8308
FAX 330-684-8989
http://www.wayne.uakron.edu/
e-mail: juliabeyeler@uakron.edu
Julia Beyeler, Director Learning Support Svcs.

A public two-year college with a small percentage of special education students.

5113   **University of Cincinnati: Raymond Walters General and Technical College**

9555 Plainfield Road
Cincinnati, OH   45236   513-745-5600
                              FAX 513-792-8624
                              TDY:513-745-8300
John Kraimer, Director Disability Services

Offers a variety of services to students with disabilities including notetakers, extended testing time, counseling services, and special accommodations.

5114   **University of Dayton**

300 College Park Avenue
Dayton, OH   45469   937-229-3684
                              FAX 937-229-3270
                              http://www.udayton.edu
                              e-mail: bedard@worfudayton.edu
Beatrice Bedard, Coordinator

An independent four-year college with about 5% special education students.

5115   **University of Findlay**

1000 N Main Street
Findlay, OH   45840   419-434-5532
                              800-472-9502
                              FAX 419-434-5748
                              TDY:419-434-5532
                              http://www.findlay.edu
                              e-mail: ods@mail.findlay.edu
Lori Colchdgoff, Director Disability Services

An independent four-year college with a small percentage of special needs students.

5116   **University of Toledo**

2801 S Bancroft Street
Toledo, OH   43606   419-530-4242
                              FAX 419-530-4940
                              http://www.utoledo.edu
Carl Earwood, Office Director

A public four-year college whose mission is to provide the support services and accommodations necessary for all students to succeed.

5117   **Urbana University**

597 College Way
Urbana, OH   43078   937-484-1301
                              FAX 937-484-1322
                              http://www.urbana.edu
Sheri Holmes, Director

An independent four-year college with a small percentage of special education students.

5118   **Ursuline College**

Program for Students with Learning Disabilities
2500 Lander Road
Peper Pike, OH   44124   440-449-2046
                              FAX 440-646-8318
                              http://www.ursuline.edu
                              e-mail: agromada@ursuline.edu
Annette Gromada, Learning Disabilities Specialist

A four year college that offers programs to students with learning disabilities.

5119   **Walsh University**

2020 Easton Street NW
North Canton, OH   44720   330-499-7090
                              800-362-9846
                              FAX 330-490-7165
                              http://www.walsh.edu
                              e-mail: bfreshour@walsh.edu
Jim Korcusler, Special Services

An independent four-year college. The Office of Student Support Services maintains an early warning system for students in academic, financial, social and/or emtional difficulty. The Office proudly communicates regularly with students regarding their general well being, and assists in the students' academic and financial concerns with referals to appropriate offices.

5120   **Washington State Community College**

710 Colegate Drive
Marietta, OH   45750   740-374-8716
                              FAX 740-376-0257
                              http://www.wscc.edu/
Ann Hontz, Director

A public two-year college with a small percentage of special education students.

5121   **Wilmington College of Ohio**

319 College Street
Wilmington, OH   45177   937-341-9318
                              800-341-9318
                              FAX 937-382-7077
Laurel Eckels, Special Services

Offers a variety of services to students with disabilities including notetakers, extended testing time, counseling services, and special accommodations.

5122   **Wright State University**

3640 Colonel Glenn Highway
Dayton, OH   45435   937-775-5680
                              FAX 937-775-5795
                              http://www.wright.edu
                              e-mail: judith.roberts@wright.edu
Judith Roberts, Assistant Director

A public university with over 14,000 undergraduated and graduated students. The Office of Disability Services offers programs to promote each student's academic, personal, physical, and vocational growth so that people with physical and learning disabilities can learn their full potential.

5123   **Xavier University**

3800 Victory Parkway
Cincinnati, OH   45207   513-745-2800
                              800-344-4698
                              FAX 513-745-3387
                              http://www.xu.edu
Ann Dinan PhD, Director Learning Assistance

We seek to ensure that all students with disabilities can freely and actively participate in all facets of university life.

Oklahoma

5124 Bacone College
2299 Old Bacone Road
Muskogee, OK 74403 918-683-4581
888-682-5514
FAX 918-682-5514
Paul Travis, Director

Offers a variety of services to students with disabilities including notetakers, extended testing time, counseling services, and special accommodations.

5125 Center for Student Academic Support
University of Tulsa
600 S College Avenue
Tulsa, OK 74104 918-631-2315
FAX 918-631-3459
TDY:918-631-3329
Dr. Jane Corso, Director
Guy Gaylor, Coordinator Support Services
Julana Boyett, Adminstrative Secretary

5126 East Central University
155 Administration
Ada, OK 74820 580-310-5294
FAX 580-310-5654
http://www.ecok.edu/
Dwain West, Director

A public four-year college with a small percentage of special education of students.

5127 Moore-Norman Vo-Tech
4701 12th Avenue NW
Norman, OK 73069 405-364-5763
FAX 405-360-9989
http://www.mntechnology.com
Bill Henderson

Offers a variety of services to students with disabilities including notetakers, extended testing time, counseling services, and special accommodations.

5128 Northeastern State University
600 N Grand Avenue
Tahlequah, OK 74464 918-458-2120
FAX 918-458-2340
http://www.nsuok.edu
Jan Smith-Clayton, Assistant to Dean

Four year college that offers programs and services to disabled students.

5129 Oklahoma City Community College
Department of Student Support Services
7777 S May Avenue
Oklahoma City, OK 73159 405-682-7520
FAX 405-682-7529
http://www.okc.cc.ok.us
e-mail: mailto:vwilson@okc.cc.ok.us
Steven Kirkland, Students w/Disabilities Advisor
Pat Stowe, Disabled Students Services Dir.

Comprehensive community college with individualized services and accommodations for students with disabilities arranged by the Office of Student Support Services. Services include Deaf Program, and accommodations as described by section 504 & ADA. Five tutoring labs are available on campus and assistive technology including voice synthesizers and voice recognition for computer based word processing.

5130 Oklahoma Panhandle State University
Box 430
Goodwell, OK 73939 580-349-2611
FAX 580-349-3375
http://www.opsu.edu
e-mail: opsu@opsu.edu
Dr. L Dirk Hibler, VP

Four year college that offers programs to the learning disabled.

5131 Oklahoma State University: Tech Branch-Oklahoma City
900 N Portalnd
Oklahoma City, OK 73107 405-945-3385
FAX 405-945-8656
http://www.osuokc.edu
e-mail: kip@osuokc.edu
Betty Sanders, Advisor

Offers access to students with disabilities based upon the diagnostic documentation which is provided by the student and the functional impact of the disability.

5132 Oklahoma State University: Technical Branch-Okmulgee
1801 E 4th
Okmulgee, OK 74447 918-756-6211
800-722-4471
FAX 918-756-1315
http://www.osu-okmulgee.edu
Billie L Coakley, Special Services

Offers a variety of services to students with disabilities including notetakers, extended testing time, counseling services, and special accommodations.

5133 Oral Roberts University
7777 S Lewis Avenue
Tulsa, OK 74171 918-495-7018
FAX 918-495-7879
http://www.oru.edu
e-mail: droberson@oru.edu
Don Roberson, Director

Four year college that offers resources to students with a learning disability.

5134 Rogers State University
1701 W Will Rogers Boulevard
Claremore, OK 74017 918-341-7777
800-256-7511
FAX 918-343-7712
http://www.rsu.edu
e-mail: llawless@rsu.edu
Lennette Lawless, Student Development Coordinator

A public four-year university with several special education students out of a total of approximately 3,300.

5135 Rose State College

6420 SE 15th Street
Midwest City, OK   73110   405-733-7311
                                 FAX 405-736-0372
                        http://www.rose.cc.ok.us
                e-mail: bstallings@ms.rose.cc.ok.us
Linda Jansen, Special Services

Services and facilities include academic advisement, referal and liaison with other community agencies, recorded textbooks and individual testing for qualified students.

5136 Seminole Junior College

2701 Boren Boulevard
Seminole, OK   74868   405-382-9950
Dr. Martha Truitt Steger, Academic Director
Tracey Woods, Academic Counselor

Provides free peer tutoring, study skill workshops, computer programs, (CAI) and videos, alternative textbooks and workbooks, classnotes/test files and other support materials to all students. A learning disabilities specialist works closely with learning disabled students, instructors and counselors to identify and implement useful and appropriate support services. Students meeting ADA guidelines can request other academic assistance services (notetakers, readers, adapted testing, etc.).

5137 Southeastern Oklahoma State University

Box 4112
Durant, OK   74701   580-745-2394
                                 FAX 580-745-7470
                        http://www.sosu.edu
Jan Anderson, Director

Four year college that provides services to the learning disabled students.

5138 Southwestern Oklahoma State University

100 Campus Drive
Weatherford, OK   73096   580-772-6611
                                 FAX 580-774-3795
                        http://www.swosu.edu
Donnell Alexander, Student Development

Offers a variety of services to students with disabilities including notetakers, extended testing time, counseling services, and special accommodations.

5139 St. Gregory's University

1900 W MacArthur Drive
Shawnee, OK   74804   405-878-5398
                                 FAX 405-878-5198
                        http://www.sgc.edu
                        e-mail: sgfaulk@sgc.edu
Gay Faulk, Director Partners in Learning

Four-year college offering programs for students with learning disabilities.

5140 Tulsa Community College

909 S Boston Avenue
Tulsa, OK   74119   918-595-7115
                                 FAX 918-595-8398
                        http://www.tulsacc.edu
                        e-mail: info@tulsaweb.com
Yolanda Williams, Disabled Student Resource Center

Offers a variety of services to students with disabilities including note takers, extended testing time, counseling services, and special accommodations.

5141 University of Oklahoma

620 Elm Avenue
Norman, OK   73019   405-325-3852
                                 800-522-0772
                                 FAX 405-325-4491
                                 TDY:405-325-4173
                        http://www.dsa.ou.edu/ods/
                        e-mail: sdyer@ou.edu
Suzette Dyer, Director Disability Services

A public doctoral degree-granting research university. The University of Oklahoma is an equal opportunity institution.

5142 University of Tulsa

600 S College
Tulsa, OK   74104   918-631-2334
                                 FAX 918-631-3459
                        http://www.utulsa.edu
                        e-mail: jane-corso@utulsa.edu
Jane Corso, Director

Four year college that offers services to disabled students. The small class size and individual attention that students recive make this institution an excellent choice for the students with disabilities.

Oregon

5143 Blue Mountain Community College

2411 NW Carden
Pendleton, OR   97801   541-278-5807
                                 FAX 541-278-5888
                        http://www.bluecc.edu
                        e-mail: aspiegel@bluecc.edu
Amy Spiegel, Coordinator

A rural community college that offers both lower division transfer and professional technical degrees. Accommodations and academic adjustments for students with learning disabilities are determined and provided on an individual basis. Diagnostic testing for learning disabilities is available. 1,200 full-time students.

5144 Central Oregon Community College

2600 NW College Way
Bend, OR   97701   541-383-7580
                                 FAX 541-317-3445
                        http://www.cocc.edu
                        e-mail: DisabilityServices@cocc.edu
RR Meedish, Registrar

COCC is committed to making physical facilities and instructional programs accessible to students with disabilities.

5145 Clackamas Community College

19600 S Molalla Avenue
Oregon City, OR 97045   503-657-6958
                                           FAX 503-655-5153
                    http://www.clackmas.cc.or.us
Caroline Cate, Contact

A public two-year college. Special education services are designed to support student success by creating full access and providing appropriate accommodations for all students with disabilities.

5146 Columbia Christian College

9101 E Burnside Street
Portland, OR 97216   503-255-7060
                                     FAX 503-252-2108
Dr. Gary Tandy, Administrator

Offers a variety of services to students with disabilities including note takers, extended testing time, counseling services, and special accommodations.

5147 George Fox College

414 N Meridian Street
Newberg, OR 97132   503-538-8383
                                     800-765-4369
                                     FAX 503-538-7234
                    http://www.georgefox.edu
Bonnie Jerke, Academic Success

An independent four-year college with a small percentage of special education students.

5148 Lane Community College

4000 E 30th Avenue
Eugene, OR 97405   541-463-5150
                                 FAX 541-563-4739
                                 TDY:541-463-3079
                    http://www.lanecc.edu
                    e-mail: moretd@lanecc.edu
Nancy Hart, Director

We provide accommodations, technology, advising, support systems, training and education.

5149 Linfield College

Learning Support Services
900 SE Baker Street
McMinnville, OR 97128   503-883-2444
                                         FAX 503-883-2647
                    http://www.linfield.edu
                    e-mail: jhaynes@linfield.edu
Judith L Haynes, Learning Support Services Dir.
Eileen Dowty, Learning Support Services Asst.

An independent four-year college. Services include tutoring, extended time for testing, assistance with advising and counseling. Student needs are considered in customizing individual programs of support for documented special needs.

5150 Linn-Benton Community College

Learning Resource Center
Albany, OR 97321   541-917-4683
                                 FAX 541-917-4435
                                 TDY:541-917-4703
                    http://www.lbcc.cc.or.us
                    e-mail: admissions@linnbenton.edu
Cheryl E Alison, Coordinator

A public two-year college. LBCC provides a number of services and programs for students with disabilities including classes, supportive services and aids.

5151 Mount Bachelor Academy

33051 NE Ochoco Highway
Prineville, OR 97754
                                 800-462-3404
                                 FAX 541-462-3430
                    http://www.mtba.com/

5152 Mt. Hood Community College

26000 SE Stark Street
Gresham, OR 97030   503-491-6923
                                     FAX 503-491-6090
                                     TDY:503-491-6923
                    http://www.mhcc.edu
Elizabeth Johnson, Disability Services Coordinator

A commitment to providing educational opportunities for all students forms the foundation of the disability services program. If you are a student with a disability, disability services will help you overcome potential obstacles so that you may be successful in your area of study. Disability services gives you the needed support to help you meet your goals without separating you and other students with disabilities from existing programs.

5153 Oregon Institute of Technology

3201 Campus Drive
Klamath Falls, OR 97601   541-885-1031
                                             FAX 541-885-1520
                    http://www.oit.edu
                    e-mail: access@oit.edu
Ron McCutcheon, Director-Campus Access

A public four-year college enrolling about 3,000 students. Accommodations are tailored to the needs of individual students on a case-by-case basis for those self-identified as having learning disabilities.

5154 Oregon State University

Services for Students with Disabilities
A202 Kerr Administration Building
Corvallis, OR 97331   541-737-4098
                                     FAX 541-737-7354
                                     TDY:541-737-3666
Tracy Bentley-Towlin, Director
Rani Jeannette, Administrative Assistant

A public four-year college with a small percentage of students.

5155 Portland Community College

Science and Technology Building
Portland, OR   97280   503-977-4341
                              FAX 503-977-4882
                              http://www.pcc.edu
Carolee Schmeer, LD Specialist

Our team includes rehabilitation guidance counselors, learning disability specialists, sign language interpreters, a technology specialist, vocational progarm and special needs coordinatiors.

5156 Reed College

3203 SE Woodstock Boulevard
Portland, OR   97202   503-771-1112
                              FAX 503-777-7769
                              http://www.reed.edu
Betsy Emerick, Associate Dean Students

Offers a variety of services to students with disabilities including notetakers, extended testing time, counseling services, and special accommodations.

5157 Southern Oregon State College

Counseling Center, Britt 205
Ashland, OR   97520   541-482-6213
                              FAX 541-552-6337

Offers a variety of services to students with disabilities including note takers, extended testing time, counseling services, and special accommodations.

5158 Southwestern Oregon Community College

1988 Newmark Avenue
Coos Bay, OR   97420   541-888-2525
                              FAX 541-888-7247
                              http://www.socc.edu
Tom Nickels, Director

The college will provide reasonable accommodation for students with learning disabilities. Some instructors in academic skills have special training in working with learning disabled students.

5159 Treasure Valley Community College

650 College Boulevard
Ontario, OR   97914   503-889-6493
                              FAX 541-881-2717
                              http://www.tvcc.cc.or.us
Royo Spurgeon, Director

Offers a variety of services to students with disabilities including notetakers, extended testing time, counseling services, and special accommodations.

5160 Umpqua Community College

PO Box 967
Roseburg, OR   97470   541-440-4600
                              FAX 541-440-4612
                              http://www.umpqua.cc.or.us
Mary Sharp, Special Services

A public two-year college with a small percentage of special education students.

5161 University of Oregon

164 Oregon Hall
Eugene, OR   97403   541-346-1155
                              FAX 541-346-6013
                              http://www.ds.uoregon.edu
Steve Pickett, Director
Molly Sirois, Counselor Disability Services

A public four-year college with about 5% of students with disabilities.

5162 Warner Pacific College

2219 SE 68th Avenue
Portland, OR   97215   503-517-1000
                              800-582-7885
                              FAX 503-517-1350
                              http://www.warnerpacific.edu
                              e-mail: webmaster@warnerpacific.edu
Judy Witt

Offers a variety of services to students with disabilities including notetakers, extended testing time, counseling services, and special accommodations.

5163 Western Baptist College

500 Deer Park Drive
Salem, OR   97301   503-375-7012
                              FAX 503-585-4316
                              http://www.wbc.edu
                              e-mail: fmoore@wbc.edu
Faythe Moore, Director

Four year college that offers programs for learning disabled students.

5164 Western Oregon University

345 N Monmouth Avenue
Monmouth, OR   97361   503-838-8000
                              877-877-1593
                              FAX 503838-8474
                              http://www.wou.edu
Dr. Joseph Sendelbaugh, Quality Services

A public four-year college. Strives to provide and promote a supportive, accessible, non-discriminatory learning and working environment for students, faculty, staff and community members with disabilities. These goals are realized through the provision of individualized support services, advocacy and the identification of current technology and information.

5165 Willamette University

900 State Street
Salem, OR   97301   503-370-6471
                              FAX 503-375-5420
                              TDY:503-375-5383
              http://www.willamette.edu/dept/disability/main.
                              e-mail: jhill@willamette.edu
Jo Anne Hill, Director Disability/Learning

Offers a variety of services to students with disabilities including notetakers, extended testing time, counseling services, and special accommodations. Provides services for all students on campus, including graduate schools.

Pennsylvania

5166 Albright College
13th and Bern Street
Reading, PA   19612
610-921-7662
FAX 610-921-7530
http://www.albright.edu
T Archie, Assistant Academic Dean

An independent four-year college with a small percentage of special education students. There is an additional fee for the education program in addition to the regular tuition.

5167 Bloomsburg University
400 E 2nd Street
Bloomsburg, PA   17815
570-389-4000
FAX 570-389-3700
http://www.bloomu.edu
Dr. Jesse Bryan

Offers a variety of services to students with disabilities including notetakers, extended testing time, counseling services, and special accommodations.

5168 Boyce Campus of the Community College of Allegheny County
595 Beatty Road
Monroeville, PA   15146
724-325-6620
FAX 724-325-6797
http://www.ccac.edu
e-mail: mailto:Pflorent@ccac.edu
Dr. Renee Clark, Director

Offers a variety of services to students with disabilities including notetakers, extended testing time, counseling services, and special accommodations.

5169 Bryn Mawr College
Educational Support Services
101 N Meroin Avenue
Bryn Mawr, PA   19010
610-526-5375
FAX 610-526-7450
http://www.brynmawr.edu
e-mail: lmendez@brynmawr.edu

Four year college provides education services to the learning disabled.

5170 Cabrini College
610 King of Prussia Road
Radnor, PA   19087
610-902-8572
FAX 610-902-8282
http://www.cabrini.edu
Andrea Maneval, Coordinator Disability Support

Offers support services and appropriate accommodations to students with documented learning disabilities.

5171 California University of Pennsylvania
Center for Academic Research and Enhancement
250 University Avenue
California, PA   15419
724-938-4404
FAX 724-938-4564
http://www.cup.edu
Cheryl L Bilitski, Director CARE Program
Robert F Dickie, Administrator CARE

One of fourteen universities in the Pennsylvania State System of Higher Education. The CARE Project provides services to students with learning disabilities through two programs. The Specialized Support Service Program is a fee-for-service program which provides services beyond those mandated by 504/ADA and has a cap of 40 students each semester. The Modified Basic Support Program provides basic services at no cost and enrollment is unlimited.

5172 Carnegie Mellon University
Equal Opportunity Services
143 N Craig Street
Pittsburgh, PA   15213
412-268-2012
FAX 412-268-7472
http://www.cmu.edu
e-mail: ly2t@andrew.cmu.edu
Lisa Zamperini, Coordinator

Four year college that offers its students services for the learning disabled.

5173 Clarion University
840 Wood Street
Clarion, PA   16214
814-393-2000
FAX 814-393-2039
TDY:814-393-1601
http://www.clarion.edu/
e-mail: info@clarion.edu
Jennifer May, Director Disability Support Svcs

Offers a variety of services to students with disabilities including note taking assistance, extended testing time, and special accommodations.

5174 College Misericordia
Alternative Learners Project
301 Lake Street
Dallas, PA   18612
570-674-6347
800-852-7675
FAX 570-675-2441
http://www.miseri.edu
e-mail: jrogan@miseri.edu
Joseph Rogan, Director/Professor

An independent four-year college with about 5% special education students.

5175 Community College of Allegheny County: College Center, North Campus
8701 Perry Highway
Pittsburgh, PA   15237
412-369-3686
FAX 412-369-3635
http://www.ccac.edu
Kathleen White, Special Services Director

Support services for students with disabilities are provided according to individual needs. Services include assistance with testing, advisement, registration, classroom accommodations, professor and agency contact.

5176 Community College of Allegheny County: Allegheny Campus

808 Ridge Avenue
Pittsburgh, PA   15212   412-237-4612
                                    FAX 412-237-2721
                                http://www.ccac.edu
                     e-mail: mailto:Mdoyle@ccac.edu
Marilyn Gleser, LD Coordinator
Mary Beth Doyle, Director

A public two-year college with a small percentage of special education students.

5177 Community College of Philadelphia

Center on Disability
1700 Spring Garden Street
Philadelphia, PA   19130   215-751-8010
                                    FAX 215-751-8001
                              http://www.ccp.cc.pa.us
Francesca DiRosa, Center Director

5178 Delaware County Community

901 Media Line Road
Media, PA   19063   610-325-2748
                                    FAX 610-359-5351
                                 TDY:610-359-5020
                                http://www.dccc.edu
                      e-mail: abinder@dcccnet.dccc.edu
Ann S Binder, Director Special Needs

Delaware County Community College, the ninth largest college in the Philadelphia metropolitan area, is a public, two year institution offering more than 60 programs of study. Its open-door policy, and affordable tuition make it accessible to all. Services to physically and learning disabled students include counseling services, tutoring, extended testing, tape recorded lectures, spelling allowances, assistive equipment, notes copied and study skills workshops.

5179 Delaware Valley College of Science and Agriculture

700 E Butler Avenue
Doylestown, PA   18901   215-345-1500
                                    FAX 215-230-2964
                               http://www.devalcol.edu
Joseph Fulcoly Jr, Counseling Director

Offers a variety of services to students with disabilities including notetakers, extended testing time, counseling services, and special accommodations.

5180 Delaware Valley Friends School

19 E Central Avenue
Paoli, PA   19301   610-640-4150
                                    FAX 610-296-9970
                                http://www.dvfs.org/

5181 Dickinson College

Services for Students with Disabilities
PO Box 1773
Carlisle, PA   17013   717-245-1485
                                    FAX 717-245-1910
                               http://www.dickenson.edu
                       e-mail: jervis@dickinson.edu
Keith Jervis, Coordinator

The Office of Counseling and Disability Services is dedicated to the enhancement of healthy student development. Professional and paraprofessional staff offer confidential individual and group counseling sessions and outreach services which help students with both general developmental issues and with specific personal or interpersonal difficulties.

5182 Drexel University

Office of Disability Services
3141 Chestnut Street
Philadelphia, PA   19104   215-895-2506
                                         800-237-3935
                                    FAX 215-895-2500
                                http://www.drexel.edu
                       e-mail: robinstokes@drexel.edu
Robin A Stokes, Director

An independent four-year college with a small percentage of special education students.

5183 East Stroudsburg University of Pennsyslvania

200 Prospect Street
East Stroudsburg, PA   18301   570-422-3954
                                    FAX 570-422-3898
                                http://www.esu.edu
                     e-mail: emiller@po-box.esu.edu
Dr. Edith Miller, Coordinator

Four year college that offers services to disabled students.

5184 Edinboro University of Pennsylvania

Office for Students with Disabilities
Crawford Center
Edinboro, PA   16444   814-732-2462
                                    FAX 814-732-2866
                               http://www.edinboro.edu
                     e-mail: strodder@edinboro.edu
Kathleen Strosser, Assistant Director
Janet Jenkins, LD Coordinator

Specific documentation required. Focuses on the needs of college capable students with learning disabilities.

5185 Gannon Universtiy

Program for Students with Learning Disabilities
University Square
Erie, PA   16541   814-871-5326
                                    FAX 814-871-7499
                                http://www.gannon.edu
                      e-mail: lowreyool@gannon.edu
Joyce Lowrey SSJ, Director
Jane Kanter, Assistant Director

5186 Gettysburg College
300 N Washington
Gettysburg, PA   17325   717-337-6100
                               800-431-0803
                               FAX 717-337-6145
Tim Dodd, Associate Dean

Offers a variety of services to students with disabilities including notetakers, extended testing time, counseling services, and special accommodations.

5187 Gwynedd: Mercy College
1325 Sumneytown Pike
Gwynedd Valley, PA   19437   215-646-7300
                               FAX 215-641-5598
                               http://www.gmc.edu
Barbara Lief RN, Director Services/ADA

Recognizing the diversity of our student population and the challenges and needs this brings to the educational enterprise, Gwynedd-Mercy College, within the bounds of its resources, intends to provide reasonable accommodations for students with disabilities. Requests for specific accommodations are processed on an individual basis.

5188 Harcum Junior College
750 Montgomery Avenue
Bryn Mawr, PA   19010   610-526-6064
                               FAX 610-526-6093
                               http://www.harcum.edu
Kathy King, Director

An independent two-year college. There is an additional fee for the special education program in addition to the regular tuition.

5189 Harrisburg Area Community College
1 HACC Drive
Harrisburg, PA   17110   717-780-2410
                               800-222-4222
                               FAX 717-780-3285
                               http://www.hacc.edu
                               e-mail: admit@hacc.edu
AL Jackson, Affairs & Enrollment Management
Carol Keeper, Director Disability Services

A public two-year college with a small percentage of special needs students.

5190 Indiana University of Pennsylvania
106 Pratt Hall
Indiana, PA   15705   724-357-4067
                               FAX 724-357-4079
                               TDY:724-357-4067
                               http://www.iup.edu
                               e-mail: advising-testing@grove.iup.edu
Catherine Dugan, Director

Disability Support Services is a component of the Advising and Testing Center. The mission of DSS is to ensure that students with disabilities who attend Indiana University of Pennsylvainia receive an integrated, quality education.

5191 Keystone Junior College
LaPlume, PA   18440   717-945-5141
Dan Rosenfield, Contact

Offers a variety of services to students with disabilities including notetakers, extended testing time, counseling services, and special accommodations.

5192 King's College
Academic Skills Center
133 N River Street
Wilkes-Barre, PA   18711   570-208-5800
                               FAX 570-825-9049
                               http://www.kings.edu
                               e-mail: jaburke@kings.edu
Jacintha Burke, Academic Skills Center Director

5193 Kutztown University of Pennsylvania
220 Administration Building
Kutztown, PA   19530   610-683-4060
                               FAX 610-683-1520
                               TDY:610-683-4499
                               e-mail: sutherla@kutztown.edu
Patricia Richter, Coordinator Service Disabilities

Kutztown University of Pennsylvania, a member of the Pennsylvania State System of Higher Education, was founded in 1856 as Keystone Normal School, and achieved University status in 1983. Today Kutztown University is a modern, comprehensive University. There are approximately 7,900 full and part time undergraduate and graduate students.

5194 Lebanon Valley College
101 N College Avenue
Annville, PA   17003   717-867-6158
                               FAX 717-867-6979
                               http://www.lvc.edu
                               e-mail: perry@lvc.edu
Anne H Hohenwarter, Coordinator

Four year college that offers learning disabled students support and services.

5195 Lehigh Carbon Community College
4525 Education Park Drive
Schnecksville, PA   18078   610-799-1156
                               800-414-3975
                               FAX 610-799-1527
                               http://www.lccc.edu
                               e-mail: wschappell@lcc.edu
Karen Goode-Ferguson, Director

General services include assistance with the admission and registration process. Access and academic accommodation requests will be reviewed on a case by case basis. Additional learning support is available through Learning Assistance Services.

5196 Lock Haven University of Pennsylvania
Lock Haven, PA   17745   570-893-2027
                               800-332-8900
                               FAX 570-893-2201
                               http://www.lhup.edu
Nathaniel Hosley, Student Support

A public four-year college with a small percentage of students with disabilities.

5197 Lycoming College

Admissions House
Williamsport, PA   17745

800-345-3920
FAX 570-321-4337
http://www.lycoming.edu

Dr. Diane Bonner, Director

An independent four-year college with a small percentage of special education students.

5198 Manor Junior College

700 Fox Chase Road
Jenkintown, PA   19046

215-884-2216
FAX 215-576-6564
http://www.manor.edu
e-mail: ftadmiss@manor.edu

John Boyd, Director

Offers a variety of services to students with disabilities including notetakers, extended testing time, counseling services, and special accommodations.

5199 Mansfield University of Pennsylvania

Academy Street
Mansfield, PA   16933

570-662-4243
800-577-6826
FAX 570-662-4121
http://www.mansfield.edu

Celeste Burns Sexauer, Coordinator

Offers a variety of services to students with disabilities including, extended testing time, counseling services, and special accommodations.

5200 Marywood University

2300 Adams Avenue
Scranton, PA   18509

570-961-4731
FAX 570-961-4744
http://www.marywood.edu

M Eamon O'Neil, Advisor

Four year college that offers programs that are for the learning disabled.

5201 Mercyhurst College

501 E 38th Street
Erie, PA   16546

814-824-2573
800-825-1926
FAX 814-824-2071
http://www.mercyhurst.edu
e-mail: admug@paradise.mercy.edu

Jim Breckenridge, Director Admissions
Dianne Rogers, Director LD Program

Mercyhurst provides a comprehensive program of academic accommodations and support services to students with documented learning disabilities. Accommodations may include audiotaped textbooks, extended time for tests, a test reader and use of a computer to complete essay tests.

5202 Messiah College

One College Avenue
Grantham, PA   17027

717-796-5358
800-233-4220
FAX 717-796-5217
http://www.messiah.edu
e-mail: kdrahn@messiah.edu

Keith Drahn PhD, Director
Carol Wickey, Assistant to Director

A private Christian college of the liberal and applied arts and sciences located in Central Pennsylvania.

5203 Millersville University of Pennsylvania

250 Lyle Hall
Millersville, PA   17551

717-872-3257
FAX 717-871-2493
http://www.millersv.edu

Patricia J Richter, Service Coordinator

Four year college that provides services to learning disabled students.

5204 Moravian College

1132 Monocacy Street
Bethlehem, PA   18018

610-861-1510
FAX 610-861-1577
http://www.moravian.edu
e-mail: memld02@moravian.edu

M Lillian Davenport, Director

Four year college that offers programs for the learning disabled.

5205 Northampton Community College

3835 Green Pond Road
Bethlehem, PA   18020

610-861-5342
FAX 610-861-5075
TDY:610-861-5351
http://www.northampton.edu
e-mail: LDemshock@northampton.edu

Laraine Demshock, Disability Service Coordinator

Encourages academically qualified students with disabilities to take advantage of educational programs. Services and accommodations are offered to facilitate accessiblity to both college programs and facilities. Services provided to students with disabilities are based upon each student individual needs.

5206 Pennsylvania Institute of Technology

800 Manchester Avenue
Media, PA   19063

610-892-1500
800-422-0025
FAX 610-892-1510
http://www.pit.edu

Dr. Robert Zabek, Special Services

Offers a variety of services to students with disabilities including notetakers, extended testing time, counseling services, and special accommodations.

5207 Pennsylvania State University: Mont Alto

1 Campus Drive
Mont Alto, PA 17237
717-749-6046
FAX 717-749-6116
http://www.ma.psu.edu
e-mail: nmhz@psu.edu
Nanette Hatzef, Learning Center Director

It is the intention of Penn State University to provide equal access to students with disabilities as mandated by the Americans with Disabilities Act, and the Rehabilitiation Act. Students with disabilities are encouraged to take advantage of the support services provided to help them successfully meet the high academic standards of the university.

5208 Pennsylvania State University: Schuylkill Campus

200 University Drive
Schuylkill Haven, PA 17972
570-385-6000
FAX 570-385-3672
http://www.sl.psu.edu
Sylvester Kohut, Assistant Provost

Offers a variety of services to students with disabilities including notetakers, extended testing time, counseling services, and special accommodations.

5209 Pennsylvania State University: Shenango Valley Campus

Office for Disability Services
147 Shenango Avenue
University Park, PA 16802
814-863-1807
FAX 724-983-2820
http://www.shenango.psu.edu
e-mail: mlk6@psu.edu
Julie Persing, Special Services

Penn State encourages academically qualified students with disabilities to take advantage of its educational programs. To be eligible for disability related accommodations, individuals must have a documented disability as defined by the Americans with Disabilities Act. A disability is defined by the physical or mental impairment that substantially limits a major life function. Individuals seeking accommodations are required to provided documentation.

5210 Pennsylvania State University: Worthington Scranton Campus

120 Ridgeview Drive
Dunmore, PA 18512
570-963-2500
FAX 570-963-2535
http://www.sn.psu.edu
Michele Steele, Special Services

Penn State encourages academically qualified students with disabilities to take advantage of its educational programs. It is the policy of the university not to discriminate against persons with disabilities in its admissions policies or procedures or its educational programs, services and activities.

5211 Point Park College

201 Wood Street
Pittsburgh, PA 15222
412-391-4100
800-321-0129
FAX 412-261-5303
http://www.ppc.edu
Dr. Charles Quillin, Student Development

Provides appropriate, reasonable accommodations for students who are disabled in accordance with the Americans with Disabilities Act. All campus accommodations are coordinated through the Program for Academic Success (PAS).

5212 Reading Area Community College

10 S Street
Reading, PA 19603
610-372-4721
800-626-1665
FAX 610-607-6264
Cathy Hunsicker, Tutorial Coordinator

A public two-year college with a small percentage of special education students.

5213 Seton Hill University

Seton Hill Drive
Greensburg, PA 15601
724-838-4255
800-826-6234
FAX 724-830-1294
http://www.setonhill.edu
e-mail: bassi@setonhill.edu
Teresa Bassi, Director Counseling Center
Mary Kay Cooper, Director Admissions

Offers programs to those who are eligible and learning disabled.

5214 Shippensburg University of Pennsylvania

1871 Old Main Drive
Shippensburg, PA 17257
717-477-1161
FAX 717-477-4001
http://www.ship.edu
e-mail: lawate@wharf.ship.edu
Dr. Lois Waters, Director

Four year college that offers services to the learning disabled students.

5215 Solebury School

Phillips Mill Road
New Hope, PA 18938
215-862-5261
FAX 215-862-3366
http://www.solebury.com/

5216 Support Services for Students with Learning Disabilities

Pennsylvania State University
105 Boucke Building
University Park, PA 16802
814-863-1807
FAX 814-863-3217
TDY:814-863-1807
http://www.lions.psu.edu/ods
e-mail: mlk6@psu.edu
Marianne Karwacki, LD Specialist

Penn State provides academic accommodations and support services to students with documented learning disabilities. Accommodations may include audiotaped textbooks, extended time for tests, a test reader and use of a computer to complete essay tests.

5217 Temple University

1301 Cecil B Moore Avenue
Philadelphia, PA   19122   215-204-1280
                                 FAX 215-204-6794
                        http://www.temple.edu/disability
                            e-mail: drs@temple.edu
Wendy Kohler, LD Coordinator

Offers a variety of services to students with disabilities including proctoring, interpreting and academic accommodations.

5218 Thiel College

75 College Avenue
Greenville, PA   16125   724-589-2063
                                FAX 724-589-2021
                                http://www.thiel.edu
                            e-mail: scowan@thiel.edu
Susan E Cowan MSN RN, Office of Special Needs

Four year college that provides an Office of Special Needs for those students with disabilities.

5219 University of Pennsylvania

34th and Spruce Streets
Philadelphia, PA   19104   215-898-5000
                                  FAX 215-898-5756
                                  http://www.upenn.edu

Alice Nagle, Special Services

Services for People with Disabilities coordinates academic support services for students with disabilities; services include readers, notetakers, library research assistants, tutors or transcribers.

5220 University of Pittsburgh at Bradford

300 Campus Drive
Bradford, PA   16701   814-362-7533
                              800-872-1787
                              FAX 814-362-7684
                        http://www.upb.pitt.edu
Dr. Gillian Boyce, Director
Kara Kennedy, Learning Development Specialist

Offers a variety of services to students with disabilities including extended testing time, counseling services, and special accommodations.

5221 University of Pittsburgh: Greensburg

1150 Mount Pleasant Road
Greensburg, PA   15601   724-836-9880
                                FAX 724-836-7134
                          http://www.pitt.edu/~upg
                        e-mail: upgadmit@pitt.edu
Lou Ann Sears, Disability Services Provider
Helen Connors, Counselor

The Learning Resources Center is an important place for students with disabilities at Pitt Greensburg. Students are encouraged to register with Lou Ann Sears to recieve any accommodations they are entitled to.

5222 University of Scranton

Memorial Hall
Scranton, PA   18510   510-941-4038
                              FAX 510-941-7899
                              http://www.uofs.edu
                     e-mail: addmissions@scranton.edu
Mary Ann McAndrew, Assistant Director

Four year college that offers programs for learning disabled students.

5223 University of the Arts

320 S Broad Street
Philadelphia, PA   19102   215-875-2254
                                  800-616-2787
                                  FAX 215-717-6045
                                  http://www.uarts.edu
Lois Elman, Learning Specialist

The University is committed to supporting students with learning disabilities to ensure that they have an equal opportunity to participate in the university programs. The Learning Specialist provides individual support to students with documented learning disabilities and serves as a liaison between students and faculty when needed.

5224 Ursinus College

Box 1000 Main Street
Collegeville, PA   19426   610-409-3000
                                  FAX 610-489-0627
                                  http://www.ursinus.edu
Richard DiFeliciantonio, Director

Offers a variety of services to students with disabilities including notetakers, extended testing time, counseling services, and special accommodations.

5225 Villanova University

800 Lancaster Avenue
Villanova, PA   19085   610-519-5636
                               FAX 610-519-7649
                               http://www.villanova.edu
                      e-mail: nancy.mott@villanova.edu
Nancy Mott, Coordinator

Four year college that provides services to learning disabled students.

5226 Washington and Jefferson College

60 S Lincoln Street
Washington, PA   15301   724-222-4400
                                888-926-3529
                                FAX 724-223-5271
                                http://www.washjeff.edu
Mary Jane Jones, Assistant Dean

An independent four-year college with a small percentage of special education students.

5227 Westmoreland County Community College

400 Armbrust Road
Youngwood, PA 15697   724-925-4000
                             800-262-2103
                             FAX 724-925-5802
                             TDY:724-925-4297
                             http://www.wccc-pa.edu
Mary Ellen Beres, Student Support Services
Sandra Zelenak, Director Student Development

Offers a variety of services to students with disabilities including notetakers, extended testing time, counseling services, and special accommodations. All services are based on a review of a current evaluation presented by the student. Appropriate services are then arranged by the student support service counselor.

5228 Widener University

Enable
1 University Place
Chester, PA 19013   610-499-1266
          http://www.widener.edu/sss/ssmain.html
          e-mail: rebecca.a.corsey@widener.edu
Dr. Rebecca Corsey

An independent four-year college with comprehensive support services.

Rhode Island

5229 Brown University

20 Benevolents Street
Providence, RI 02912   401-863-9588
                              FAX 401-863-9588
                              http://www.brown.edu
                              e-mail: elyse_chaplin@brown.edu
Elyse K Chaplin MA, Assistant Dean

Brown University has as its primary aim the education of a highly qualified and diverse student body and respects each student's dignity, capacity to contribute, and desire for personal growth and accomplishment. Brown's commitment to students with disabilities is based on awareness of what students require for success. The University desires to foster both intellectual and physical independence to the greatest extent possible in all of its students.

5230 Bryant College

1150 Douglas Pike
Smithfield, RI 02917   401-232-6000
                              FAX 401-232-6319
                              http://www.bryant.edu
                              e-mail: mucci@bryant.edu
Martha Ucci PhD, Director Learning Center

An independent four-year Business and Liberal Arts College. A learning specialist is on campus to provide services for students with learning disabilities.

5231 Community College of Rhode Island-Knight Campus

400 E Avenue
Warwick, RI 02886   401-825-2164
                           FAX 401-333-7113
                           http://www.ccri.cc.ri.us
Elizabeth Dalton

Academic accommodations are available to students with disabilities who demonstrate a documented need for the requested accommodation. Accommodations include but are not limited to adapted equipment, alternative testing, course accommodations, sign language interpreters, reader/audio taping services, scribes and peer note-takers.

5232 Johnson & Wales University

8 Abbott Park Place
Providence, RI 02903   401-598-4689
                              800-343-2565
                              FAX 401-598-4657
                              e-mail: mberstein@swu.edu
Meryl Berstein, Center Academic Support Director

An independent four-year university servicing about 5% special education students. Accommodations are individualized to students presenting documentation and may include extended time testing, tape recorders in class, notetaking assistance, reduced course load, preferential scheduling and tutorial assistance.

5233 Providence College

549 River Avenue
Providence, RI 02918   401-865-2494
                              FAX 401-865-1219
                              http://www.providence.edu
                              e-mail: rboyle@providence.edu
Rose Boyles, Coordinator

Offers a variety of services to students with disabilities including note takers, extended testing time, counseling services, and special accommodations.

5234 Rhode Island College

600 Mount Pleasant Avenue
Providence, RI 02908   401-456-8061
                              FAX 401-456-8379
                              http://www.ric.edu
Sara W Weiss, Peer Advisor

Four-year college with support and services for learnig disabled students.

5235 Roger Williams University

Old Ferry Road
Bristol, RI 02809   401-253-3038
                           800-458-7144
                           FAX 401-254-3302
                           http://www.rwu.edu
An independent comprehensive four-year university with about 5% special education students.

5236 University Affiliated Program of Rhode Island College

600 Mount Pleasant Avenue
Providence, RI 02908   401-456-8072
                                        FAX 401-456-8150
                                        TDY:401-456-8773
                                        http://www.uapni.org
A Anthony Antosh, Director

The University Affiliated Program (UAP) of Rhode Island is a member of a national network of UAPs. The UAP is charged with four core functions: 1. Providing pre-service training to prepare quality service providers. 2. Providing community outreach training and technical assistance. 3. Disseminating information about research and exemplary practice. 4. Research.

5237 University of Rhode Island

330 Memorial Union
Kingston, RI 02881   401-874-2098
                                        FAX 401-874-5574
                                        http://www.uri.edu
Pamela Rohland, Director

Disability Service for Students fosters a barrier free environment to individuals with disabilities through education that focuses on inclusion, awareness, and knowledge of ADA/504 compliance. Our mission is two fold: 1. To encourage a sense of empowerment for students with disabilities by providing a process that involves the student. 2. To be an information resource to the University faculty and staff regarding disability awareness and academic services.

South Carolina

5238 Aiken Technical College

PO Drawer 696
Aiken, SC 29802   803-593-9231
                                        FAX 803-593-6641
                                        http://www.aik.tec.sc.us
                                        e-mail: weldond@aik.tec.sc.us
Richard Weldon, Counselor

A public two-year college offering services to the learning disabled.

5239 Citadel-Military College of South Carolina

171 Moultrie Street
Charleston, SC 29409   843-953-5000
                                        FAX 843-953-7036
                                        http://www.citadel.edu
Gordon Wallace

Offers a variety of services to students with disabilities including notetakers, extended testing time, counseling services, and special accommodations.

5240 Clemson University

Student Development Services
707 University Union
Clemson, SC 29634   864-656-0515
                                        FAX 864-656-0514
                                        http://www.clemson.edu
                                        e-mail: bmartin@clemson.edu
Bonnie Martin, Director

Four-year college offers services to learning disabled students.

5241 Coastal Carolina University

PO Box 261954
Conway, SC 29528   843-347-3161
                                        FAX 843-349-2990
                                        http://www.coastal.edu
Dr. Joe Mazurkiewicz, Director Student Development
Vonna Gengo, Coordinator Disability Services

Coastal Carolina University provides a program of assistance to students with disabilities. Upon acceptance to the University, students will become eligible for support services by providing documentation of their disability. Accommodations include academic labs, tutorial referral, study skills, counseling, auxiliary aids, coordination with other agencies and classroom accommodations.

5242 College of Charleston

Special Needs Advising Plan
66 George Street
Charleston, SC 29424   843-953-1431
                                        FAX 843-953-7731
                                        TDY:843-953-8284
                                        http://www.cofc.edu/~cds
                                        e-mail: SNAP@cofc.edu
Ann Lacy, Coordinator SNAP Services

Provides reasonable and appropriate accommodations specific to individual needs based on the psycho-educational assessment, communication with instructors as needed to heighten awareness of individual needs, alternative courses in math and foreign language, if need, is documented by assessment.

5243 Erskine College

Due West, SC 29639   864-379-2131
                                        FAX 864-379-2167
                                        http://www.erskine.edu
Katharine Chandler

Offers a variety of services to students with disabilities including notetakers, extended testing time, counseling services, and special accommodations.

5244 Francis Marion University

PO Box 100547
Florence, SC 29501   805-661-1362
                                        800-368-7551
                                        FAX 843-661-1165
                                        http://www.fmarion.edu
Kenneth Dye

A public four-year college with services for special education students.

5245 Greenville Technical College

PO Box 5616
Greenville, SC 29606   864-250-8176
                                        800-922-1183
                                        FAX 864-250-8580
                                        http://www.greenvilletech.com
Owen Perkins, Associate Dean

Committed to providing equal access for all students and assisting students in making their college experience successful in accordance with ADA/504 and the Rehabilitation Act. The Office of Special Needs for Students with Disabilities has counselors available to assist in the planning and implementation of appropriate accommodations.

5246 Limestone College

Program for Alternative Learning Styles
1115 College Drive
Gaffney, SC   29340   864-482-4534
                                 800-795-7151
                            FAX 864-487-8706
                        http://www.limestone.edu
                e-mail: jpitts@saint.limestone.edu
Joseph Pitt, Director

Independent four-year college with a program designed to serve students with learning disabilities. There is an additional fee for the first year in the program in addition to the regular tuition. However, that additional cost is reduced by 50% after the freshman year depending on the grade point average.

5247 Midlands Technical College

PO Box 2408
Columbia, SC   29202   803-738-1400
                             FAX 803-822-3290
                         http://www.midlandstech.com
                 e-mail: osmerj@mtc.mid.tec.sc.us
Annie Porterfield, Special Services

Services to Students with Disabilities counselors support and assist students with disabilities in meeting their personal, educational and career goals. Services include academic and career planning, faculty/student liasion, assistive technology, readers, writers, interpeters, closed circuit television in libraries, TDD, testing services, orientation sessions and a support group.

5248 North Greenville College

PO Box 1892
Tigerville, SC   29688   864-977-7000
                                 800-468-6642
                            FAX 864-977-2089
                          http://www.ngc.edu
                    e-mail: nisgett@ngc.edu
Nancy Isgett, Learning Disabilities Liaison

Offers a variety of services to students with disabilities including notetakers, extended testing time, counseling services, and special accommodations.

5249 South Carolina State University

PO Box 7508
Orangeburg, SC   29115   803-536-8670
                             FAX 803-536-8702
                          http://www.scsu.edu
                   e-mail: gouveia@scsu.edu
Dr. Imogene Gouveia, Chief Psychologist

Four-year college that provides information and resources for the learning disabled.

5250 Spartanburg Methodist College

1200 Textile Road
Spartanburg, SC   29301   864-587-4000
                             FAX 864-587-4355
                          http://www.smcsc.edu
Sharon Porter, Student Support Director

An independent two-year college with services for special education students.

5251 Technical College of Lowcountry: Beaufort

921 Ribaut Road
Beaufort, SC   29902   843-525-8324
                             FAX 843-521-4142
Carolyn Banner, Career Development

Offers a variety of services to students with disabilities including note takers, extended testing time, counseling services, and special accommodations.

5252 Trident Academy

1455 Wakendaw Road
Mt Pleasant, SC   29464   843-884-7046
                             FAX 843-881-8320
                     http://www.tridentacademy.com/
              e-mail: admissions@tridentacademy.com
Trident Academy is an internationally known independent school for children with diagnosed learning disabilities such as dyslexia and attention deficit disorder serving students in grades K-12.

5253 Trident Technical College

PO Box 118067
Charleston, SC   29423   803-572-6000
                             FAX 843-574-6484
                      http://www.trident.tec.sc.us
Vincent Ashby Jr, Special Services

Recognizes its responsibility to identify and maintain the standards (academic, admissions, scores, etc.) that are necessary to provide quality academic programs while ensuring the rights of students with disabilities.

5254 University of South Carolina

Room 106 LeConte
Columbia, SC   29208   803-777-6742
                             FAX 803-777-6741
                             TDY:803-777-6744
                          http://www.sc.edu
                    e-mail: kpettus@sc.edu

Karen Pettus, Director

The Office of Disability Services provides accommodations for students with documented physical, emotional, and learning disabilities. The professionally trained staff works toward accessiblity for all university programs, services, and activities in compliance with ADA/504. Services include orientation,priority registration, library access, classroom adaptions, interpeters, and access to adapted housing.

5255 University of South Carolina: Aiken

171 University Parkway
Aiken, SC 29801   803-648-6851
                                    FAX 803-641-3362
                                http://www.usca.sc.edu/ds
                                e-mail: kayb@aiken.sc.edu
Randy Duckett, Special Services

The mission of Disability Services (DS) is to facilitate the transition of students with disabilities into the University eniviroment and to provide appropriate accommodations for each student's special needs in order to ensure equal access to all programs, activities and services at USCA.

5256 University of South Carolina: Beaufort

801 Carteret Street
Beaufort, SC 29902   843-521-4100
                                    FAX 843-521-4194
                                http://www.sc.edu/beaufort
Dr. Joan Lemoine, Associate Dean

A public two-year college with services for special education students.

5257 University of South Carolina: Lancaster

PO Box 889
Lancaster, SC 29721   803-313-7000
                                    FAX 803-313-7106
                                http://www.sc.edu/lancaster
John Catalano, Dean

Offers a variety of services to students with disabilities including notetakers, extended testing time, counseling services, and special accommodations.

5258 Voorhees College

PO Box 678
Denmark, SC 29042   803-703-7131
                                    FAX 803-793-4584
Dr. Adeleri Onisegun, Director

Four-year college that offers programs to learning disabled students.

5259 Winthrop University

Counseling Services
701 Oakland Avenue
Rock Hill, SC 29733   803-323-2211
                                    FAX 803-328-2855
                                    TDY:803-323-2233
                                http://www.winthrop.edu
Heather Martinon, Counselor

Since each student has a unique set of special needs, the Counselor for Students with Disabilities makes every effort to provide the student with full access to programs and services. Reasonable accommodations are provided based on needs assessed through proper documentation and an intake interview with the couselor. The majority of buildings on campus are accessible.

South Dakota

5260 Black Hills State College

1200 University
Spearfish, SD 57799   605-642-6099
                                       800-255-2478
                                    FAX 605-642-6497
                                http://www.bhsu.edu/disability
Joan M Wermers, Contact

Provide the comprehensive supports necessary in meeting the individual needs of students with disabilities.

5261 Northern State University

1200 S Jay Street
Aberdeen, SD 57401   605-626-2371
                                    FAX 605-626-3399
                                http://www.northern.edu
                                e-mail: diagle@northern.edu
Kay Diagle, Director

Four-year college that provides services to students with a learning disability.

5262 South Dakota School of Mines & Technology

501 E Saint Joseph Street
Rapid City, SD 57701   605-394-9416
                                    FAX 605-394-2914
                                http://www.sdsmt.edu
                                e-mail: fcampone@sdsmt.edu
Dr. Francine Campone, Associate Dean

Four-year college that offers support services to those students whom are disabled.

5263 South Dakota State University

Box 2201
Brookings, SD 57007   605-688-4496
                                    FAX 605-688-5951
                                http://www.sdstate.edu
Nancy Schade, Coordinator

Committed to providing equal opportunities for higher education for learning disabled students.

5264 Yankton College

1801 Summit Street
Yankton, SD 57078   605-665-3661
                                    FAX 605-665-0546
Nancy Reddy, Director

Offers a variety of services to students with disabilities including note takers, extended testing time, counseling services, and special accommodations.

Tennessee

5265 Austin Peay State University: Office of Disability Services

PO Box 4567
Clarksville, TN   37044   931-221-6230
FAX 931-221-7102
http://www.apsu.edu/disability
Beulah Oldham, Director

The Office of Disability Services is dedicated to providing academic assistance for students with disabilities enrolled at Austin Peay State University. We provide information to students, faculty, staff and administrators about the needs of students with disabilities. We ensure the accessiblity of programs, services, and activities to students having a disability. We are a resource of information pertaining to disability issues and advocate participation in campus life.

5266 Boling Center for Developmental Disabilities

University of Tennessee
711 Jefferson Avenue
Memphis, TN   38105   901-448-6511
888-572-2249
FAX 901-448-7097
http://www.utmem.edu/bcdd
e-mail: wwilson@utmem.edu
Fredrick B Palmer MD, Director
William Wilson MA, Clinical Services Coordinator

Interdisciplinary or focused evaluation of learning, behavioral and developmental problems in infants, toddlers, children and young adults. Treatment of some conditions offered.

5267 Brookhaven College

3939 Valley View Lane
Farmers Branch, TN   75244   972-860-4847
http://www.dcccd.edu.bhc
Amadeo Ledesma, Grants Manager

Physically challenged and learning disabled special services office offers advisement, additional diagnostic evaluations, mobility assistance, note taking, textbook taping, interpreters for the deaf and assistance in test taking.

5268 Bryan College: Dayton

PO Box 7000
Dayton, TN   37321   423-775-7207
800-277-9522
FAX 423-775-7199
http://www.bryan.edu
Mark Craver, Director of Admissions
Peter Held, VP Student Life

Committed to providing quality education for those who meet admission standards but learn differently from others. Modifications are made in the learning environment to enable LD students to succeed. Some of the modifications made require documentation of the specific disability while other adaptations do not. In addition to modifications the small teacher-student ratio allows the school to provide much individual attention to those with learning difficulties.

5269 Carson-Newman College

1646 Russell Avenue
Jefferson City, TN   37760   865-417-2000
800-678-9061
FAX 865-471-3502
http://www.cn.edu
John Gibson, Associate Professor

An independent four-year college with support services for special education students.

5270 DHH Outreach

East Tennessee State University
Box 70605
Johnson City, TN   37614   423-439-8346
FAX 423-439-8489
http://www.etsu.edu
e-mail: storey@mail.etsu.edu
Linda Gibson MEd, Disability Services Director
Martha Edde-Adams, Disability Services Asst Dir
Elizabeth Tipton, Lead Deaf Interpreter

The Deaf and Hard of Hearing Outreach program provides coordination of interpreting services for student needs related to classroom and university events.

5271 East Tennessee State University Disability Services

Box 70605
Johnson City, TN   37614   423-439-8346
FAX 423-439-8489
http://www.etsu.edu
e-mail: storey@mail.etsu.edu
Linda Gibson MEd, Disability Services Director
Martha Edde-Adams, Disability Services Asst Dir
Elizabeth Tipton, Lead Deaf Interpreter

The Disability Services Office works to provide services to give students with disabilities equal opportunities at ETSU through the provision of resonable accommodations, coordination of auxiliary aids, and support services.

5272 Knoxville Business College

720 N 5th Avenue
Knoxville, TN   37917   865-524-6511
FAX 423-637-0127
http://www.kbcollege.edu
Judy Ferguson, Dean Students

Offers a variety of services to students with disabilities including notetakers, extended testing time, counseling services, and special accommodations.

5273 Lambuth College

705 Lambuth Boulevard
Jackson, TN   38301   731-425-2500
800-526-2884
FAX 731-988-4600
http://www.lambuth.edu
Robert McLendon

Offers a variety of services to students with disabilities including notetakers, extended testing time, counseling services, and special accommodations.

5274 Leap Program

East Tennessee State University
Box 70605
Johnson City, TN 37614   423-439-8346
                                      FAX 423-439-8489
                                      http://www.etsu.edu
                                      e-mail: storey@mail.etsu.edu
Linda Gibson MEd, Disability Services Director
Martha Edde-Adams, Disability Services Asst Dir
Elizabeth Tipton, Lead Deaf Interpreter

The Learning Empowerment for Academic Performance Program is a grant funded program sponsored by Tennessee Department of Human Services, Division of Vocational Rehabilitation.

5275 Learning Disabilities Program: University of Memphis

215 Scates Hall
Memphis, TN 38152   901-678-2880
                                      FAX 901-678-3070
                                      TDY:901-678-2880
                                      http://www.people.memphis.edu/~sds/
                                      e-mail: stepaske@memphis.edu
Susan TePaske, LD Coordinator
Dona Sparger, Director
Stephen Shaver, Learning Specialist

Emphasizes individual responsibility for learning by offering a developmentally oriented program of college survival skills, learning strategies, and individualized planning and counseling based on the students strengths and weaknesses. The program also coordinates comprehensive support services, including test accommodations, tutoring, books on tape, assistive technology and peer mentoring. The program serves approximately 500 students with learning disabilities and ADHD per year.

5276 Lee University: Cleveland

Academic Support Program
1120 Ocoee Street
Cleveland, TN 37320   423-614-8181
                                      800-533-9930
                                      FAX 423-614-8179
                                      http://www.leeuniversity.edu
                                      e-mail: ssasse@leeuniversity.edu
Dr. Gayle Gallaher, Director

An independent four-year college with services for special education students.

5277 Middle Tennessee State University

1301 E Main Street
Murfreesboro, TN 37132   615-898-2783
                                      FAX 615-898-2874
                                      http://www.mtsu.edu
                                      e-mail: dssemail@mtsu.edu
John Harris, Disabled Student Services

We offer a wide variety of services to students with disabilities including assisting in registration, providing readers and attendants, maintaining an inventory of auxillary aids, offering testing accommodations, providing access to the latest in adaptive computer technologies and acting as a liaison to Uuniversity departments.

5278 Motlow State Community College

6051 Ledford Mill Road
Lynchburg, TN 37352   931-455-8511
                                      800-654-4877
                                      FAX 931-393-1764
                                      http://www.mscc.cc.tn.us
                                      e-mail: asimmons@mscc.cc.tn.us
A Simmons, Dean Student Development

A public two-year college with support services for special education students.

5279 Northeast State Technical Community College

2425 Highway 75
Blountville, TN 37617   423-354-2476
                                      800-836-7822
                                      FAX 423-279-7649
                                      http://www.nstcc.cc.tn.us
                                      e-mail: kafoulk@northeaststate.edu
Mitzi Dorton, Learning Specialist
Tonya Cassell, Secretary

To assure equal educational opportunities for individuals with disabilities.

5280 Pellissippi State Technical Community College

10915 Hardin Valley Road
Knoxville, TN 37932   865-694-6411
                                      FAX 865-539-7217
                                      http://www.pstcc.cc.tn.us
                                      e-mail: semcmurray@pstcc.cc.tn.us
Joan Newman, Director Academic Assess

Services for Students with Disabilities develops individual educational support plans, provides prioriy registration and advisement, furnishes volunteer notetakers, provides readers, scribes, tutor bank, provides interpeter services and publishes a newsletter. The office acts as a liaison, and assists students in location of resources appropriate to their needs.

5281 Scenic Land School

1130 Mountain Creek Road
Chattanooga, TN 37405   423-877-9711
                                      FAX 423-876-0398
                                      http://www.sceniclandschool.org
                                      e-mail: ecard@sceniclandschool.org
Eileen Card, Head of School
Mary Brown, Director IEP & Assessment
Michele McRae, Dean of Students

Scenic Land School is a private nonprofit school for students with learning disabilities. The school primarily serves students with dyslexia and ADHD. Average class size is 8 students and a 1:4 teacher:student ratio.

5282 Shelby State Community College

737 Union Avenue
Memphis, TN 38174   901-333-5087
                                      FAX 901-333-5711
                                      http://www.sscc.cc.tn.us
Jimmy Wiley, Director

A two-year college providing information and resources to disabled students.

5283 Southern Adventist University
PO Box 370
Collegedale, TN 37315   423-238-2779
                          800-768-8437
                   FAX 423-238-2468
http://www.southern.edu
e-mail: adossant@southern.edu
Alberto Dos Santos, Dean

A private university offering undergraduate degrees in education designed for K-8, 1-8, 7-12, and K-12 certification plus graduate degrees designed for inclusion (special needs in the regular classroom), multiage/multigrade teaching, outdoor education, and psychology and counseling of exceptional individuals. College age students with special needs and those desiring to teach students with special needs are welcome to apply.

5284 Southwest Tennessee Community College
5983 Macon Cove
Memphis, TN 38134   901-333-4193
                          888-832-4937
                   FAX 901-333-4458
http://www.southwest.tn.edu
Maxine Ford

Offers a variety of services to students with disabilities including note takers, extended testing time, counseling services, and special accommodations.

5285 Tennessee State University
Office of Disabled Student Services
3500 John Merritt Boulevard
Nashville, TN 37209   615-963-7400
                   FAX 615-963-2176
http://www.tnstate.edu
e-mail: jcade@picard.tnstate.edu
James D Steely, Director

Four year college offers services for learning disabled students.

5286 University of Tennessee: Knoxville
191 Hoskins Library
Knoxville, TN 37996   865-974-6087
                   FAX 865-974-9552
                   TDY:865-974-6087
http://www.utk.edu
e-mail: jhoward5@utk.edu
Jan Howard, Director

Offers a variety of services to students with disabilities including note takers, extended testing time, counseling services, and special accommodations.

5287 University of Tennessee: Martin
Program Access for College Enhancement
124 Gooch Hall
Martin, TN 38238   731-587-7000
                   FAX 731-587-7956
http://www.utm.edu
e-mail: marant@utm.edu
Michelle Arant, Coordinator

A four-year independent college that offers a program called Program Access for College Enhancement for students with learning disabilities.

5288 Vanderbilt University
11021st Avenue S
Nashville, TN 37203   615-322-4705
                   FAX 615-343-0671
http://www.vanderbilt.edu
Sara Ezell, Assistant Director

An independent four-year college with support services for special education students.

5289 William Jennings Bryan College
2121 K Street NW
Dayton, TN 37321   202-973-0904
                     800-544-3284
                   FAX 202-973-0908
e-mail: mailto:health@ace.nche.edu
Donna Poole, Counseling Director

A public four-year college. The HEALTH Resource Center operates the national clearinghouse on postsecondary education for individuals with disabilities.

Texas

5290 Abilene Christian University
Alpha Academic Services
ACU Box 29204
Abilene, TX 79699   915-674-2750
                   FAX 915-674-6847
http://www.acu.edu
e-mail: dodda@acu.edu
Ada Dodd, Counselor

A four year college that offers services to students who are learning disabled.

5291 Alvin Community College
3110 Mustang Road
Alvin, TX 77511   281-331-6111
                   FAX 281-756-3843
http://www.alvin.cc.tx.us
Eileen Cross, Counselor

A public two-year college with support services for special education students.

5292 Amarillo College: Department of Disabilities
PO Box 447
Amarillo, TX 79178   806-371-5000
                   FAX 806-354-6076
http://www.actx.edu
Deana Milliron, Coordinator

Offers a variety of services to students with disabilities including note takers, extended testing time, counseling services, and special accommodations.

5293 Angelina College
PO Box 1768
Lufkin, TX 75902   936-639-1301
                   FAX 936-633-5455
http://www.angelina.cc.tx.us
Judy Cutting, Director

A public two-year college with support services for special education students.

5294 Baylor University

Office of Access & Learning Accommodation
PO Box 97204
Waco, TX 76798   254-710-3605
                              FAX 254-710-3608
                              http://www.baylor.edu
                    e-mail: ahelia_graham@baylor.edu
Dr. Shelia Graham, Director

Four-year college that offers support and services to students who are learning disabled.

5295 Bee County College

3800 Charco Road
Beeville, TX 78102   512-358-3130
                              FAX 512-358-3971
Patricia Myers, Counseling Director

A public two-year college with support services for special education students.

5296 Briarwood School

12207 Whittington Drive
Houston, TX 77077   281-493-1070
                              FAX 281-493-1343
                    http://www.briarwoodschool.org
                    e-mail: info@briarwoodschool.org
Carole Wills, Head of School
Priscilla Mitchell, Director Admissions

Briarwood has been serving students with diagnosed learning differences for 35 years. A co-ed private day school offering small classes, remedial and college prep curriculum for its 300 K-12 students. Briarwood believes that every child can learn and has the right to be taught in the way that he or she learns best.

5297 Cedar Valley College

3030 N Dallas Avenue
Lancaster, TX 75134   972-860-8199
                              FAX 972-860-8014
                              http://www.dcccd.edu
                    e-mail: gcf787@dcccd.edu
Grenna Fynn, Director

A two-year college that provides special services to its disabled students.

5298 Central Texas College

6200 W Central Texas Expressway
Killeen, TX 76542   254-526-7161
                                   800-792-3348
                              FAX 254-526-0817
                              http://www.ctcd.cc.tx.us
Jose Apotte, Counselor

Offers a variety of services to students with disabilities including notetakers, extended testing time, counseling services, and special accommodations.

5299 Cisco Junior College

101 College Heights
Cisco, TX 76437   254-442-2567
                              FAX 254-442-2546
                              http://www.cisco.cc.tx.us
Link Harris, Counselor

A public two-year college with support services for special education students.

5300 College of the Mainland

1200 Amburn Road
Texas City, TX 77591   409-938-1211
                                   888-258-8859
                              FAX 409-938-1306
                              http://www.mainland.cc.tx.us
Dr. Marcella Derrick

Offers a variety of services to students with disabilities including notetakers, extended testing time, counseling services, and special accommodations. The mission of services for students with disabilities is to provide each student with the resources needed to register, enroll and complete their course work and/or degree plan.

5301 Collin County Community College

2200 W University
McKinney, TX 75069   972-881-5790
                              FAX 972-548-6702
                              http://www.ccccd.edu
Norma Johnson, Director

A public two-year college. ACCESS provides resonable accommodations, individual attention and support for students with disabilities who need assistance with any aspect of their campus experience such as accessibility, academics and testing.

5302 Concordia University at Austin

3400 IH 35 N
Austin, TX 78705   512-436-1132
                              FAX 512-486-1155
                              http://www.concordia.com
                    e-mail: admissionj@concordia.edu
Dr. Beryl Dunsmoir, Chair

Four year college offers services to disabled students.

5303 Dallas Academy

950 Tiffany Way
Dallas, TX 75218   214-342-1481
                              FAX 214-327-8537
                              http://www.dallas-academy.com
                    e-mail: mail@dallas-academy.com
Jim Richardson

Offers a variety of services to students with disabilities including notetakers, extended testing time, counseling services, and special accommodations.

5304 Dallas Academy: Coed High School

950 Tiffany Way
Dallas, TX 75218   214-324-1481
FAX 214-327-8537
http://www.dallas-academy.com
e-mail: mail@dallas-academy.com
Karen Kinsella, Assistant Director
Ronda Criss, Development Director

Coed Day School for bright children grades 7-12 with diagnosed learning differences. Curriculum includes sports, art, music, and photography programs.

5305 Dallas County Community College

3737 Motley Drive
Mesquite, TX 75150   972-86+0-768
FAX 972-860-7227
http://www.dcccd.edu/
Offers a variety of services to students with disabilities including note takers, extended testing time, counseling services, and special accommodations.

5306 East Texas Baptist University

1209 N Grove
Marshall, TX 75670   903-935-7963
800-804-3828
FAX 903-938-7798
http://www.etbu.edu
Charles Taylor, Director

Offers a variety of services to students with disabilities including notetakers, extended testing time, counseling services, and special accommodations.

5307 East Texas State University

E Texas Station
Commerce, TX 75428   903-886-5000
FAX 903-886-5702
Tom Lynch, Contact

Offers a variety of services to students with disabilities including note takers, extended testing time, counseling services, and special accommodations.

5308 Eastfield College

3737 Motley Drive
Mesquite, TX 75150   972-860-7100
FAX 972-860-8342
http://www.efc.dcccd.edu
e-mail: mds4420@dcccd.edu
Reva Rattan, Coordinator

Offers a variety of services to students with disabilities including note takers, extended testing time, counseling services, and special accommodations.

5309 El Centro College

Main and Lamar Streets
Dallas, TX 75202   214-860-2311
FAX 214-860-2335
http://www.ecc.dcccd.edu
Jim Handy, Director Counseling

A public two-year college with support services for special education students.

5310 El Paso Community College: Valle Verde Campus

Center for Students with Disabilities
PO Box 20500
El Paso, TX 79998   915-831-3722
FAX 915-831-2244
http://www.epcc.edu
Maria E Lopez, Interim Director

A support service for students enrolled at the college who have a verified temporary or permanent disability. Support services offered include advising, tutoring, note taking, test assistance and more.

5311 Frank Phillips College

PO Box 5118
Borger, TX 79008   806-274-5311
800-687-2056
FAX 806-274-6835
http://www.fpc.cc.tx.us
Joyce Rector, Special Populations Coordinator

Offers a variety of services to students with disabilities including notetakers, extended testing time, counseling services, and special accommodations.

5312 Galveston College

4015 Avenue Q
Galveston, TX 77550   409-763-6551
FAX 409-762-9367
http://www.gc.edu
Dr. Gaynelle Hayes, VP

A public two-year college. A variety of services and programs are available to assist students with disabilities, those who are academically and/or economically disadvantaged and those with limited English proficiency.

5313 Hill College of the Hill Junior College District

112 Lamar Drive
Hillsboro, TX 76645   254-582-2555
FAX 254-582-5742
http://www.hill-college.cc.tx.us/
e-mail: wra@hill-college.cc.tx.us
Louis Allen, Dean Students

Offers a variety of services to students with disabilities including note takers, extended testing time, counseling services, and special accommodations.

5314 Houston Community College System

3100 Main Street
Houston, TX 77007   713-718-5000
FAX 713-718-2111
Dr. Weldon Elbert, Counselor

Offers a variety of services to students with disabilities including note takers, extended testing time, counseling services, and special accommodations.

5315 Jarvis Christian College

Highway 80 E
Hawkins, TX   75765   903-769-5700
                                 800-292-9517
                                 FAX 903-769-5005
                                 http://www.jarvis.edu
                                 e-mail: florine_white@jarvis.edu

Dr. Florine White, Dir Student Support Services
Dr. Johnnye Jones, VP

Student Support Services is a federally funded program whose purpose is to improve the retention and graduate rate of program participants. Eligible program participants include low income, first generation college students and students with learning and physical disabilities. A variety of support services are provided.

5316 Lamar University: Port Arthur

1500 Prospect Street
Port Arthur, TX   77641   409-983-4921
                                 800-477-5872
                                 FAX 409-984-6000
                                 http://www.pa.lamar.edu

Sherly Hopper, Director

A public two-year college with support services for special education students.

5317 Laredo Community College: Special Populations Office

W End Washington Street
Laredo, TX   78040   956-721-5137
                                 FAX 956-721-5838
                                 e-mail: sylviat@laredo.cc.tx.us

Sylvia Palos-Trevino LMSW, Counselor/Coordinator

Offers a variety of services to students with disabilities including notetakers, extended testing time, counseling services, and special accommodations.

5318 Lubbock Christian University

5601 19th Street
Lubbock, TX   79407   806-796-8800
                                 800-933-7601
                                 FAX 806-720-7162
                                 http://www.lcu.edu

Offers a variety of services to students with disabilities including notetakers, extended testing time, counseling services, and special accommodations.

5319 McLennen Community College

1400 College Drive
Waco, TX   76708   254-299-8790
                                 FAX 254-299-8747
                                 http://www.mcc.cc.tx.us/

Dr. Patsy White, Director

A public two-year college with support services for special education students.

5320 Midwestern State University

3410 Taft Boulevard
Wichita Falls, TX   76308   940-397-4618
                                 FAX 940-397-4934
                                 http://www.mwsu.edu
                                 e-mail: fhiggindb@nexus.mwsu.edu

Debra Higginbotham, Director

A public four-year college with support services for special education students.

5321 North Harris County College

2700 WW Thorne Drive
Houston, TX   77073   281-618-5400
                                 FAX 281-618-5706
                                 http://wwwnhc.nhmccd.edu

Sandi Patton, Special Services

Offers a variety of services to students with disabilities including note takers, extended testing time, counseling services, and special accommodations. We train students in the use of specialized software and hardware.

5322 North Lake College

5001 N Macarthur Boulevard
Irving, TX   75038   972-273-3165
                                 FAX 972-273-3164
                                 TDY:972-273-3169
                                 http://www.dcccd.edu

Carloe Gray, Disability Services Coordinator

A public two-year college. Our mission is to provide a variety of support services to empower students, foster independence, promote achievement of realistic career and educational goals and assist students in discovering, developing and demonstrating full potential and abilities.

5323 Odyssey School

831 Houston Street
Austin, TX   78756   512-472-2262
                                 FAX 512-236-9385
                                 http://www.odysseyschool.com/
                                 e-mail: nelsonchase@dpsk12.org

5324 Office of Disability Services

Stephen F Austin State University
PO Box 6130
Nacogdoches, TX   75962   936-568-1368
                                 FAX 936-468-5810

Margie Franklin, Director

Offers a variety of services to students with disabilities including note takers, extended testing time, counseling services, and special accommodations.

5325 Pan American University

1201 W University Drive
Edinburg, TX   78539   956-381-2011
                                 FAX 956-381-2380
                                 http://www.panam.edu

Arturo Ramos, Special Services

Offers a variety of services to students with disabilities including note takers, extended testing time, counseling services, and special accommodations.

5326 Rawson-Saunders School
2600 Exposition Boulevard
Austin, TX   78757   512-476-8382
                                   FAX 512-476-1132
           http://www.rawson-saunders.org

5327 Richland College
12800 Abrams Road
Dallas, TX   75243   972-238-6180
                                   FAX 972-238-6957
              http://www.rlc.dcccd.edu
              e-mail: stevem@dcccd.edu
Jeanne Brewer, LD Director

Offers a variety of services to students with disabilities including note takers, extended testing time,
counseling services, and special accommodations.

5328 Sam Houston State University
1700 Sam Houston Avenue
Huntsville, TX   77341   936-294-1111
                                   FAX 936-294-3970
              http://www.shsu.edu
Dr. James Gaertner, President

Offers a variety of services to students with disabilities including note takers, extended testing time,
counseling services, and special accommodations.

5329 San Antonio College
Programs for the Handicapped
1300 San Pedro Avenue
San Antonio, TX   78212   210-733-2000
                                   FAX 210-733-2202
           http://www.accd.edu/sac/sacmain/sac.htm
Thomas Hoy, Counselor

A public two-year college with support services for
special education students.

5330 San Jacinto College: Central Campus
PO Box 2007
Pasadena, TX   77501   713-476-1501
                                   FAX 281-478-2790
              http://www.sjcd.cc.tx.us
Judy Ellison, Special Populations

Offers a variety of services to students with disabilities including notetakers, extended testing time, counseling services, and special accommodations such as
test readers and writers.

5331 San Jacinto College: South Campus
13735 Beamer Road
Houston, TX   77089   281-922-3431
                                   FAX 281-922-3485
              http://www.sjcd.cc.tx.us
Connie Ginn, Coordinator

A public two-year college with support services for
special education students.

**5332 San Marcos Texas State University: Office of
Disability Services**
Office of Disability Services
601 University Drive
San Marcos, TX   78666   512-245-3451
                                   FAX 512-245-3452
                                   TDY:512-245-3451
              http://www.swt.edu
              e-mail: rp16@swt.edu
Richard Poe, Learning Disibility Specialist

Provides support services and coordinates academic
accommodations based on the individual students
disibility-based need.

5333 Schreiner University
2100 Memorial Boulevard
Kerrville, TX   78028   830-896-5411
                                      800-343-4919
                                   FAX 830-792-7226
              http://www.schreiner.edu
              e-mail: ctait@scheiner.edu
Charles Tait, Admissions Counselor

An independent four-year university with about 10%
of students in the Learning Support Services Program.
There is a fee for the LSS program in addition to the
regular tuition.

5334 South Plains College
1401 S College Avenue
Levelland, TX   79336   806-894-9611
                                   FAX 806-894-5274
              http://www.spc.cc.tx.us
Bill Powell, Studies Program

Offers a variety of services to students with disabilities including notetakers, extended testing time, counseling services, and special accommodations.

5335 Southern Methodist University
6425 Boaz Street
Dallas, TX   75275   214-768-4563
                                   FAX 214-768-4572
              http://www.smu.edu
              e-mail: rmarin@mail.smu.edu
Rebecca Marin, Coordinator

An independent four-year college with support services for special education students.

5336 Southwestern Assemblies of God University
1200 Sycamore Street
Waxahachie, TX   75165   972-937-4010
                                      888-yes-sagu
                                   FAX 972-923-0488
              http://www.sagu.edu
Mary Savell, Special Services

Offers a variety of services to students with disabilities including notetakers, extended testing time, counseling services, and special accommodations.

5337 St. Edwards University

3001 S Congress Avenue
Austin, TX   78704   512-448-8400
                            FAX 512-448-8492

Bunny Smith, Special Services

An independent four-year college. Students with disabilities meet with a counselor from academic planning and support and they work together to ensure equal access to all academic services.

5338 St. Mary's University of San Antonio

One Camino Santa Maria
San Antonio, TX   78228   210-436-3203
                            FAX 210-436-3782
                            http://www.stmarytx.edu

Barbara Biassiolli, Center Director

Offers a variety of services to students with disabilities including tutoring, extended testing time, and academic counseling services.

5339 Tarleton State University

Box T-0010
Stephenville, TX   76402   254-968-9103
                            FAX 254-968-9703
                            http://www.tarleton.edu

Dr. L Dwayne Snider, Director

Four year college that provides students with learning disabilities support and services.

5340 Tarrant County College DSS-NE: Disability Support Services

828 W Harwood Road
Hurst, TX   76054   817-515-6333
                            FAX 817-515-6112

Judy Kelley, Director

Offers a variety of services to students with disabilities including notetakers, extended testing time, tutors, counseling services, special accommodations, and registration assistance.

5341 Texas A&M University

126 Koldus Building
College Station, TX   77843   409-845-1637
                                FAX 409-458-1214
                                http://www.tamu.edu
                                e-mail: anne@stulife2.tamu.edu

Dr. Anne Reber, Coordinator

A public four-year college with support services for special education students.

5342 Texas A&M University: Commerce

PO Box 3011
Commerce, TX   75429   903-886-5835
                            FAX 903-468-3220
                            http://www.tamu-commerce.edu
                            e-mail: frank_perez@tamu-commerce.edu

Frank Perez, Assistant Director

Four-year college that provides student support services and programs to those students who are learning disabled.

5343 Texas A&M University: Kingsville

1210 Retama Drive
Kingsville, TX   78363   361-593-3024
                            FAX 361-593-2006
                            http://www.tamuk.edu
                            e-mail: adrain.garcia@tamuk.edu

Rachel A Cox, Assistant Coordinator

Four-year college that provides an academic support center for students who are disabled.

5344 Texas Southern University

3100 Cleburne Street
Houston, TX   77004   710-527-4210
                            FAX 713-313-7539
                            http://www.tsu.edu

Minnine Simmons, Counselor

A public four-year college with support services for special education students.

5345 Texas State Technical Institute: Sweetwater Campus

300 College Drive
Sweetwater, TX   79556   912-235-7300
                            800-592-8784
                            FAX 915-235-7416
                            http://www.sweetwater.tstc.edu

Phyllis Morris, Special Services

Offers a variety of services to students with disabilities including notetakers, extended testing time, counseling services, and special accommodations.

5346 Texas Tech University

AccessTECH & TECHniques Center
143 Wiggins West
Lubbock, TX   79409   806-742-2405
                            FAX 806-742-0295
                            http://www.studentaffairs.ttu.edu/accesstech
                            e-mail: accesstech@ttu.edu

Frank Silvas, AccessTECH
Leann DiAndreth-Elkins, TECHniques Center

AccessTECH is a place for students with disabilities to register in order to receive reasonable academic accommodations. TECHniques Center is a fee-for-service program that provides supplemental academic support for college students with documented learning disabilities and attention deficit disorders.

5347 Texas Tech University: AccessTECH

143 Wiggins West
Lubbock, TX   79409   806-742-2405
                            FAX 806-742-4837
                            http://www.studentaffairs.ttu.edu/accesstech
                            e-mail: accesstech@ttu.edu

Frank Silvas, AccessTECH

A place for students with disabilities to register in order to receive reasonable academic accommodations.

5348 Texas Tech University: TECHniques Center
143 Wiggins West
Lubbock, TX 79409 806-742-1822
FAX 806-742-0295
http://www.techniques.ttu.edu
e-mail: techniques.center@ttu.edu
Leann DiAndreth-Elkins, TECHniques Center

The TECHniques Center is a fee-for-service program
that provides supplemental academic support for college students with documented learning disabilities
and attention deficit disorders.

5349 Texas Woman's University
PO Box 425589
Denton, TX 76204 940-898-3626
FAX 940-898-3198
http://www4.twu.edu
Tricia Behle Hurter, Special Services

A public four-year college with support services for
special education students.

5350 Tyler Junior College
PO Box 9020
Tyler, TX 75711 903-510-2458
FAX 903-510-2434
http://www.tyler.cc.tx.us
Vickie Geisel, Special Services

Offers a variety of services to students with disabilities including note takers, extended testing time,
counseling services, and special accommodations.

**5351 University Affiliated Program: University of
Austin, Texas**
Education Building 306
Austin, TX 78712 512-471-7621
FAX 512-471-0577
Penny C Seay, Director

5352 University of Houston
CSD Building
Houston, TX 77204 713-743-5400
FAX 713-743-5396
TDY:713-749-1527
http://www.uh.edu
e-mail: wscrain@mail.uhe
Scott Crain, Counselor
Dr Marilyn Pustejousky, Assistant Director
Cheryl Amotuso, Director
A public four-year college with support services for
students with disabilities.

5353 University of North Texas
Office of Disability Accommodation
Union 322, 400 Avenue A
Denton, TX 76203 940-565-4323
FAX 940-369-7969
http://www.unt.edu/oda
e-mail: undergrad@unt.edu
Jane Jonestt, Assistant Director

A public four-year college with a small percentage of
learning disabled students.

5354 University of Texas: Arlington
300 W 1st Street
Arlington, TX 76019 817-272-3364
FAX 817-272-1447
TDY:817-272-1520
http://www.uta.edu/disability
Dianne Hengst, Director
Ron Venable, Assistant Director
Amber Mitchell, Interpeting Services Coodinator
A public four-year university. There is no specific LD
program, but comprehensive support services are
available. Total enrollment 20,000+.

5355 University of Texas: Dallas
PO Box 830688
Richardson, TX 75083 972-690-2098
FAX 972-883-2237
http://www.utdallas.edu
Tracy Cole, Disability Services

Offers a variety of services to students with disabilities including notetakers, extended testing time, counseling services, and special accommodations.

5356 University of Texas: Pan American
1201 W University Drive
Edinburg, TX 78539 512-381-2585
Arturo Ramos, Assistant Director

Offers a variety of services to students with disabilities including notetakers, extended testing time, counseling services, and special accommodations.

5357 University of Texas: San Antonio
1604 W Loop
San Antonio, TX 78249 210-458-4157
800-669-0919
FAX 210-458-4980
TDY:210-458-4981
http://www.utsa.edu
Lorraine Harrison, Director

Disability Services provides support services, accommodations and equipment for UTSA students with
temporary or permanent disabilities. Goals of DS are
to promote a barrier free environment, to encourage
students to become as independent and self-reliant as
possible and to provide information and consultation
about specific disabilities to the entire community.

5358 University of the Incarnate Word
4301 Broadway
San Antonio, TX 78209 210-283-5056
FAX 210-283-5021
http://www.uiw.edu
e-mail: uiwhr@universe.uiwtx.edu
Lorena Fitz Novak, Coordinator

Four year college that provides services to learning
disabled students.

5359 Wharton County Junior College

911 Boling Highway
Wharton, TX 77488   409-532-4560
                          800-561-9252
                  FAX 979-532-6587
                  http://www.wcjc.cc.tx.us/

Offers a variety of services to students with disabilities including note takers, extended testing time, counseling services, and special accommodations.

5360 Wiley College

711 Wiley Avenue
Marshall, TX 75670   903-927-3300
                          800-658-6889
                  FAX 903-938-8100
                  http://www.wilec.edu
                  e-mail: vdavis@wileyc.edu

Offers a variety of services to students with disabilities including notetakers, extended testing time, counseling services, and special accommodations.

Utah

5361 Brigham Young University

1520 WSC
Provo, UT 84602   801-378-4636
                  FAX 801-422-0174
                  http://ww.byu.edu

Paul Bird, Director

Offers a variety of services to students with disabilities including note takers, extended testing time, counseling services, and special accommodations.

5362 Center for Persons with Disabilities

Utah State University
6800 Old Main Hill
Logan, UT 84322   435-797-1981
                          866-284-2821
                  FAX 435-797-3944
                  TDY:435-797-1981
                  http://www.cpd.usu.edu
                  e-mail: info@cpd2.usu.edu

Sarah Rule, Director

A University Center for Excellence in Developmental Disabilities Education, Research and Services. The Center for Persons with Disabilities provides interdisciplinary training, research, exemplary services, and technical assistance to agencies related to people with disabilities.

5363 College of Eastern Utah

451 E 400 N
Price, UT 84501   435-637-2120
                  FAX 435-613-5112
                  http://www.ceu.edu

Terry Holbrook, DRC Director

The DRC at CEU provides academic accommodations for the learning disabled.

5364 Latter-Day Saints Business College

411 E South Temple
Salt Lake City, UT 84111   801-363-2765
                                  800-999-5767
                          FAX 801-524-1900
                          http://www.ldsbc.edu

Tina Van Orden, Dean Students

Offers a variety of services to students with disabilities including notetakers, extended testing time, counseling services, and special accommodations.

5365 Salt Lake Community College: Disability Resource Center

4600 S Redwood Road
Salt Lake City, UT 84123   801-957-4659
                          FAX 801-957-4947
                          e-mail: joy.tlou@slcc.edu

A program to assist students with disabilities in obtaining equal access to college facilities and programs. The resource center serves all disabilities and provides services and accommodations such as testing, adaptive equipment, text on tape, readers, scribes, note takers, and interpreters for the deaf.

5366 Snow College

150 E College Avenue
Ephraim, UT 84627   435-283-7000
                          800-848-3399
                  FAX 435-283-7449
                  http://www.snow.edu

Cyndi Crabb, Special Services

A public two-year college with support services for special education students.

5367 Southern Utah University

351 W Center Street
Cedar City, UT 84720   435-586-7710
                          FAX 435-865-8393
                  http://www.suu.edu
                  e-mail: thompson@suu.edu

Georgia Thompson, Coordinator

A public four-year University with support services for special education students.

5368 University of Utah

110 Park
Salt Lake City, UT 84112   801-581-5020
                                  800-444-8638
                          FAX 801-581-5487
                          TDY:801-581-5020
                          http://www.utah.edu
                          e-mail: onadeau@saun.saff.utah.edu

Olga Nadeau, Director

A public four-year college. Services include admissions requirements modification, testing accommodations, priority registration, advisement on course selection and number, adaptive technology, support group. Documentation of learning disability is required.

5369 **Utah State University**
0101 Old Main Hall
Logan, UT   84322
435-797-2444
FAX 435-797-0130
TDY:435-797-0740
http://www.usu.edu
e-mail: dhardman@addmissions.usu.edu
Diane Craig Hardman, Director

A public four-year college with support services for students with learning disabilities.

5370 **Utah Valley State College**
Accessibility Services Department
800 W 1200 South
Orem, UT   84058
801-222-8000
FAX 801-226-5207
http://www.uvsc.edu
e-mail: info@uvsc.edu
Curtis Pendleton, Disabled Services
Michelle Lundell, Department Director
Ann Lickey, Secretary

The mission for Accessibility Services at Utah Valley State College is to ensure, in compliance with federal and state laws, that no qualified individual with a disability be excluded from participation in or be denied the benefits of a quality education at UVSC or be subjected to discrimination by the college or its personnel. UVSC offers a large variety of support services, accommodative services and assistive technology for individuals with learning disabilities.

5371 **Weber State University**
1103 University Circle
Ogden, UT   84408
801-626-6000
FAX 801-626-6744
http://www.weber.edu
LaMar Kap

Offers a variety of services to students with disabilities including notetakers, extended testing time, counseling services, and special accommodations.

5372 **Westminster College of Salt Lake City**
1840 S 1300 E
Salt Lake City, UT   84105
801-832-2280
800-748-4753
FAX 801-484-3252
TDY:801-832-2286
http://www.wcslc.edu
e-mail: mkortkamp@westminstercollege.edu
Ginny DeWitt, Director Students Services

Offers a variety of services to students with disabilities including notetakers, extended testing time, counseling services, and special accommodations.

Vermont

5373 **Burlington College**
95 N Avenue
Burlington, VT   05401
802-862-9616
800-862-9616
FAX 802-660-4331
http://www.burlcol.edu
Cathleen Sullivan, Associate Director Addmissions
Michael Watson, Dean Students

Education process vs test and grades. Small classes. Learning specialist available.

5374 **Champlain College**
Support Services
163 S Willard Street
Burlington, VT   05401
802-865-6425
FAX 802-860-2764
http://www.champlain.edu
e-mail: peterson@champlain.edu
Rebecca Peterson, Coordinator

Four year college that supports students with a learning disability.

5375 **College of St. Joseph**
71 Clement Road
Rutland, VT   05701
802-773-5900
FAX 802-773-5900
e-mail: fmiglorie@csj.edu
Charles Bruckerhoff, Contact

Offers a variety of services to students with disabilities including note takers, extended testing time, counseling services, and special accommodations.

5376 **Community College of Vermont**
PO Box 120
Waterbury, VT   05676
802-241-3535
FAX 802-241-3526
http://www.vsc.edu
e-mail: ccvinfo@ccv.vsc.edu
Mel Donovan, Director Student Support
Joyce Judy, Dean of Student Services

A public two-year college offering courses, certificates and associate degrees.

5377 **Green Mountain College**
Calhoun Learning Center
One College Circle
Poultney, VT   05764
802-287-8232
FAX 802-287-8099
http://www.greenmtn.edu
e-mail: admiss@greenmtn.edu
Sue Zientara, Director

Four-year college that offers support through the school's Calhoun Learning center to students with disabilities.

5378 Johnson State College

337 College Hill
Johnson, VT 05656   802-635-1259
                           800-635-2356
                       FAX 802-635-1454
                    http://www.jsc.vsc.edu
             e-mail: veilleuk@badger.jsc.vsc.edu
Katherine Veilleux, Director

A public four-year college with support services for special education students.

5379 Landmark College

River Road S
Putney, VT 05346   802-387-6718
                       FAX 802-387-6868
               http://www.landmarkcollege.org
       e-mail: admissions@landmarkcollege.org
Ed Parker, Associate Dean Admissions

Landmark College provides ambitious and motivated students with learning disabilities or ADHD with the skills needed for academic success. Every Landmark student receives personalized instruction and attention. All students are provided with intense one-on-one tutorials, which help them identify their individual learning styles. Students develop the critical language and study skills that will allow them to work within the expectations of academia and the work force.

5380 Norwich University

Learning Support Center
158 Harron Drive
Northfield, VT 05663   802-485-2130
                              800-468-6679
                          FAX 802-485-2032
                       http://www.norwich.edu
                 e-mail: gills@norwich.edu
Paula Gills, Special Services

The Learning Center offers an opportunity for individualized assistance with many aspects of academic life in a supportive, personalized atmosphere. Students may voluntarily choose from a wide variety of service options.

5381 Southern Vermont College

978 Mansion Drive
Bennington, VT 05201   802-447-6360
                              800-378-2782
                          FAX 802-447-4695
                       http://www.svc.edu
                 e-mail: tgerson@svc.edu
Todd Gerson, Coordinator

Offers students with documented learning disabilities a highly supportive environment and a wide range of support services which include basic skills tutoring, content area academic support, study techniques, notetaking and more.

5382 University of Vermont

ACCESS
633 Main Street
Burlington, VT 05405   802-656-7753
                          FAX 802-656-0739
                          TDY:802-656-3865
                    http://www.uvm.edu/access
                   e-mail: access@uvm.edu
Donna Panko, Learning Specialist
Nick Ogrizovich, Information Specialist
Joe Wilson, Learning Specialist

Provides accommodation, consultation, collaboration and educational support services as a means to foster opportunities for students with disabilities to participate in a barrier free learning environment.

5383 Vermont Technical College

Main Street
Randolph Center, VT 05061   802-728-1000
                                   800-442-8821
                               FAX 802-728-1390
                               TDY:802-728-1278
                            http://www.vtc.vsc.edu
Robin Goodall, Learning Specialists
Eileen Haddon, Assistive Technology Project

Offers a variety of services to students with disabilities including individualized accommodations, counseling services, academic counseling.

Virginia

5384 Averett College

Support Services for Students
428 Firth Hall
Danville, VA 24541   434-791-5744
                        FAX 804-791-4392
                     http://www.averett.edu
               e-mail: priedel@averett.edu
Dr. Pamela Riedel, Support Services Coordinator

Four-year college that offers services for the learning disabled.

5385 Blue Ridge Community College

Disability Services Office
Houff Student Center Room 103 B
Weyers Cave, VA 24486   540-234-9261
                               888-750-2722
                           FAX 540-234-9598
                        http://www.br.cc.va.us
Suzanne Garrett, Co-Coordinator

A public two-year college. The Office of Disability Services is part of the Blue Ridge Community Counseling Center. Its mission is to provide disabled students with the support services needed to be successful in college.

5386 College of William and Mary

James Blair Hall, Room 209
Williamsburg, VA 23185   757-221-4000
                            FAX 757-221-2749
                         http://www.wm.edu

Dr. Carroll Hardy, Director

Offers a variety of services to students with disabilities including notetakers, extended testing time, counseling services, and special accommodations.

5387 Eastern Mennonite University

Academic Support Center - Student Disability Svcs.
1200 Park Road
Harrisonburg, VA   22802   540-432-4233
                                   800-368-2665
                              FAX 540-432-4977
                              TDY:540-432-4631
                              http://www.emu.edu
                        e-mail: hedrickj@emu.edu
Joyce C Hedrick, Coordinator

EMU is committed to working out reasonable accommodations for students with documented disabilities to ensure equal access to the University and its related programs.

5388 Emory & Henry College

One Garnand Drive
Emory, VA   24327   276-944-4121
                        FAX 540-944-6934
                        http://www.ehc.edu
Paul Adrion Powell III, Resource Center Director
Karen Kilgore, Coordinator Academic Support

A private four-year liberal arts college located in the foothills of southwest Virginia. Student enrollment of appox. 1,000, almost equally divided between men and women. The Paul Adrian Powell III resource center offers a variety of services to students with disabilities including extended testing time, counseling services, and special accommodations, as well as tutorial services.

5389 Ferrum College

PO Box 1000
Ferrum, VA   24088   540-365-2121
                        FAX 540-365-4203
                        http://www.ferrum.edu
Brenda Newcombe, Reading Specialist

An independent four-year college with support services for special education students.

5390 GW Community School

9001 Braddock Road
Springfield, VA   22151   703-978-7208
                            FAX 703-978-7226
              http://www.gwcommunityschool.com
The GW Community School is owned and operated by teachers who understand the learning process and the students' needs, and who genuinely enjoy teaching adolesents. They work closely with students and their families to maximize learning. The GW School for Divergent Learners embodies a vision shared by teachers, parents, and students. A school committed to developing and optimizing the giftedness and intellegence of each student and fostering a sense of social awareness and civic responsibility

5391 Hampden-Sydney College

Box 685
Hampden-Sydney, VA   23943   434-223-6000
                                FAX 434-223-7078
                                http://www.hsc.edu
Elizabeth Ford, Associate Dean

Offers a variety of services to students with disabilities including note takers, extended testing time, counseling services, and special accommodations.

5392 James Madison University

Office of Disabilities Services
Wilson Learning Center, Room 107
Harrisonburg, VA   22807   540-568-6705
                              FAX 540-568-3780
                              TDY:540-568-6705
                http://www.jmu.edu/disabilityser/
                        e-mail: gotojmu@jmu.edu
Lori Hedrick, Director

The Office of Disability Services at James Madison University provides support services for students with documented learning disabilities. The program ensures equal access to education by providing the appropriate accommodations. Documentation must be current (within the last four years). Students with learning disabilities must go through the standard admissions process.

5393 John Tyler Community College

13101 Jefferson Davis Highway
Chester, VA   23831   804-796-4000
                            800-552-3490
                        FAX 804-796-4163
                        http://www.jt.cc.va.us
Robert Tutton, Counselor

A public two-year college with support services for special education students.

5394 Learning Needs & Evaluation Center: Elson Student Health Center

University of Virginia
400 Brandon Avenue
Charlottesville, VA   22908   434-924-3601
                                FAX 434-243-5188
              http://www.virginia.edu/studenthealth/
Dr. Jennifer Maedgen, Director

Full range of support services for students admitted to any of the ten schools of the university, including graduate/professional schools. Including, not limited to, taped texts, writing support, learning strategies, exam accommodation, liaison with faculty.

5395 Liberty University

Office of Academic Disability Support
1971 University Boulevard
Lynchburg, VA   24502   434-582-2000
                          FAX 804-582-2468
                          TDY:804-582-2574
                          http://www.liberty.edu
                    e-mail: wdmchane@liberty.edu
W Denton McHaney, Academic Disability Support Dir.

Religiously oriented, private, coeducational, comprehensive four year institution. Students who have documented learning disabilities are eligible to receive support services. These would include academic advising, priority class registration, tutoring and testing accommodations.

5396   Little Keswick School

PO Box 24
Keswick, VA   22947   434-295-0457
                                      FAX 434-977-1892
                              http://www.avenue.org/lks
Terry Columbus, Director

Little Keswick School is a therapeutic boarding school for 30 learning disabled and/or emotionally disturbed boys between the ages of 10 to 15 at acceptance and served through 17. IQ range accepted ti sbelow average to superior structured routine in a small, nurturing environment services include psychotherapy, occupational therapy, speech therapy and art therapy. Five week summer session.

5397   Longwood College

201 High Street
Farmville, VA   23919   434-395-2391
                                      800-281-4677
                                      FAX 434-395-2434
                              http://www.longwood.edu
                     e-mail: srood@longwood.iua.edu
Susan Rood, Disability Support Services

A public four-year college with support services for special education students.

5398   Lord Fairfax Community College

173 Skirmisher Lane
Middletown, VA   22645   540-868-7000
                                      800-906-5322
                                      FAX 540-868-7100
                              http://www.lf.cc.va.us
Paula Dean

A public two-year college. Students are encouraged to identify special needs during the admissions process and to request support services, such as individualized placement testing, developmental studies, learning assistance programs, and study skills. A 504 faculty team recommends accommodations to academic programs, and communicates with area service providers.

5399   Mary Washington College

1301 College Avenue
Fredericksburg, VA   22401   540-654-1000
                                      FAX 5840-654-108
                              http://www.mwc.edu
Patricia Tracy, Coordinator

A public four-year college with support services for special education students.

5400   New River Community College

PO Box 1127
Dublin, VA   24084   540-674-3600
                                      866-462-6722
                                      FAX 540-674-3644
                              http://www.nr.edu
                     e-mail: nrdixoj@nr.ca.cc.va.us
Jeananne Dixon, Coordinator

A public two-year college with support services for special education students.

5401   Norfolk State University

700 Park Avenue
Norfolk, VA   23464   757-823-8173
                                      FAX 757-823-2237
                              http://www.nsu.edu
                     e-mail: bbharris@nsu.du
Beverly Boone Harris, Coordinator

Four year college that offers programs for the students with learning disabilities.

5402   Northern Virginia Community College

4001 Wakefield Chapel Road
Annandale, VA   22003   703-323-3000
                                      FAX 703-323-3559
                              http://www.nv.cc.va.us
                     e-mail: jthrash@nv.cc.va.us
A public two-year college.

5403   Old Dominion University

2228 Webb Center
Norfolk, VA   23529   757-683-4655
                                      FAX 757-683-5356
Nancy Olthoff PhD, Coordinator

Works with students to provide access to higher education. Reasonable accommodations are identified to address specific individual needs. Accommodations may include extended testing time, permission to tape record classes, distraction-free test setting, etc.

5404   Patrick Henry Community College

645 Patriot Avenue
Martinsville, VA   24115   276-656-0296
                                      800-232-7997
                                      FAX 276-656-0327
                                      TDY:276-638-2433
                              http://www.ph.vccs.edu
                     e-mail: sss@ph.vccs.edu
Scott Guebert, Dir Student Support Services
Mary McAlexander, Disbility Counselor

Offers a variety of services to students with disabilities including note takers, adaptive testing, counseling services, peer tutoring and adaptive equipment, and accessible transportation.

5405   Paul D Camp Community College

100 N College Drive
Franklin, VA   23857   757-569-6700
                                      FAX 757-569-6795
                              http://www.pc.cc.va.us
Carol Able, Dir Student Support

A public two-year institution with two campuses. Students with learning disabilities are eligible for special services provided by the Student Support Service Program. Learning-disabled students may take advantage of tutors (outside of class time and during class labs), notetakers, and taped textbooks. A counselor serves as student advocate and helps students arrange for classroom accommodations with instructors.

5406 Piedmont Virginia Community College

501 College Drive
Charlottesville, VA 22902 434-977-3900
FAX 434-961-5251
http://www.pvcc.edu
e-mail: pbuck@pvcc.edu

Wendy Bolt, Counselor

A two-year comprehensive community college dedicated to the belief that individuals should have equal opportunity to develop and extend their skills and knowledge. Consistent with this philosophy and in compliance with the Americans with Disabilities Act, we encourage persons with disabilities to apply.

5407 Randolph-Macon Woman's College

2500 Rivermont Avenue
Lynchburg, VA 24503 434-947-8000
FAX 434-947-8138
http://www.rmwc.edu
Tina Barnes, Dir Learning Resources Center

An independent four-year college with support services for students with disabilities.

5408 Rappahannock Community College

PO Box 287
Glenns, VA 23149 804-758-6700
FAX 804-758-3852
http://www.rcc.cc.va.us
Alan Harris, Special Services

Offers a variety of services to students with disabilities including notetakers, extended testing time, counseling services, and special accommodations.

5409 Southern Seminary College

One College Hill Drive
Buena Vista, VA 24416 703-761-8420
Jack Turregano, Special Services

Offers a variety of services to students with disabilities including note takers, extended testing time, counseling services, and special accommodations.

5410 Southside Virginia Community College

109 Campus Drive
Alberta, VA 23821 434-949-1000
FAX 434-949-7863
http://www.sv.vccs.edu
John Sykes, Provost

Offers a variety of services to students with disabilities including notetakers, extended testing time, counseling services, and special accommodations.

5411 Southwest Virginia Community College

PO Box 5UCC
Richlands, VA 24641 540-964-2555
FAX 540-964-7259
http://www.sw.cc.va.us
Julie Mayrose, Special Services

Offers a variety of services to students with disabilities including note takers, extended testing time, counseling services, and special accommodations.

5412 Thomas Nelson Community College

99 Thomas Nelson Drive
Hampton, VA 23666 757-825-2700
FAX 757-825-2763
http://www.tncc.cc.va.us
Thomas Kellen, Assoc. Coordinator

A public two-year college with support services for students with disabilities.

5413 Tidewater Community College

300 Granby Street
Norfolk, VA 23510 757-822-1213
FAX 757-822-1214
http://www.tcc.edu
e-mail: srice@tac.edu

Sue R Rice, Coordinator

This public two-year college offers transfer and occupational/technical degrees on four campuses and a visual arts center in the Hampton Roads area of Virginia. TCC offers students evaluations, all reasonable accommodations, and a wide array of assistive technology.

5414 University of Virginia

PO Box 400160
Charlottesville, VA 22904 434-924-0311
FAX 434-243-5188
TDY:804-982-HEAR
http://www.virginia.edu

Jennifer Maedgen, Director

Diagnostic services and educational planning for students and adults in the workplace who have a history or who suspect learning difficulties may stem from the Specific Learning Disabilities condition.

5415 Virginia Commonwealth University

901 W Franklin Street
Richmond, VA 23284 804-828-0100
800-841-3638
FAX 804-828-1323
http://www.vcu.edu
Dr. Shyla Ipsen, Coordinator/Academic Campus

Offers a variety of services to students with disabilities including note takers, extended testing time, counseling services, and special accommodations.

5416 Virginia Highlands Community College

Route 372
Abingdon, VA   24212   540-628-6094
                              FAX 540-628-7576
                              http://www.vh.cc.va.us
                              e-mail: cfaris@vh.cc.va.us
Charlotte Faris, Director

A public two-year college. Strives to assist students with disabilities in successfully responding to challenges of academic study and job training.

5417 Virginia Intermont College

1013 Moore Street
Bristol, VA   24201   540-669-6101
                             800-451-1842
                             FAX 540-669-5763
                             http://www.vic.edu
                             e-mail: bholbroo@vic.edu
Barbara Holbrook, Special Services

Virginia Intermont College is a private, four-year Baptist affiliated liberal arts college located near the Appalachian Mountains of Southwest Virginia. Intermont has an enrollment of 850 men and women students. Accommodations, such as notetakers, extended time on tests, transcribers, oral testing, tutors and other services, are provided based on documentiation of disabilities.

5418 Virginia Polytechnic Institute and State University

105 Brodie
Blacksburg, VA   24060   540-231-6000
                              FAX 540-231-9263
                              http://www.vt.edu

Wayne Speer, Special Services

A public four-year college with support services for special education students.

5419 Virginia Wesleyan College

Disabilities Services Office
1584 Wesleyan Drive
Norfolk, VA   23502   757-455-3146
                             FAX 757-466-8526
                             http://www.vwc.edu
                             e-mail: fpearson@vwc.edu
Fayne Pearson, Disabilities Coordinator

Four year college that offers support to students with a learning disability.

5420 Virginia Western Community College

3095 Colonial Avenue SW
Roanoke, VA   24038   540-857-7319
                             FAX 540-857-7544
                             http://www.vw.cc.va.us
Michael Henderson, Special Services

A public two-year college with support services for special education students.

Washington

5421 Bellevue Community College

3000 Landerholm Circle SE
Bellevue, WA   98007   425-564-2498
                              FAX 425-641-2230
                              http://www.bcc.ctc.edu
Susan Gjolmesli, Director
Carol Jones-Watkins, Coordinator

Disability Support Services provides accommodations for people with disabilities to make their academic careers a success. There is no separate fee for these services.

5422 Central Washington University

400 E 8th Avenue
Ellensburg, WA   98926   509-963-2171
                              FAX 509-963-3235
                              http://www.cwu.edu
                              e-mail: campbelr@cwu.edu
Bob Campbell, Dir Disability Support Services
Pamela S Wilson, Disability Accomodations Spec.
Ian Campbell, Coord. Adaptive Tech Services

A public four-year college with disability support services for students with disabilities.

5423 Centralia College

600 W Locust Street
Centralia, WA   98531   360-736-9391
                              FAX 360-330-7503
                              http://www.centralia.edu
Paulette Kotter, Coordinator

The Special Services Office offers a variety of services to students with disabilities including notetakers, extended testing time, counseling services, and special accommodations.

5424 Children's Institute for Learning Differences: New Heights School

4030 86th Avenue SE, Campus F
Mercer Island, WA   98040   206-232-8680
                              FAX 206-232-9377
                              http://www.childrensinstitute.com
                              e-mail: robbo@childrensinstitute.com
Robb Ott, Admissions/Public Relations Dir.
Trina Westerlund, Executive Director/Founder

A middle school program serving children ages 11-14.

5425 Children's Institute for Learning Differences: Child School

4030 86th Avenue SE, Campus F
Mercer Island, WA   98040   206-232-8680
                              FAX 206-232-9377
                              http://www.childrensinstitute.com
                              e-mail: robbo@childrensinstitute.com
Robb Ott, Admissions/Public Relations Dir.
Trina Westerlund, Executive Director/Founder

A pre-elementary school program serving children ages 3-11.

5426 Clark College

1800 E McLoughlin Boulevard
Vancouver, WA   98663   360-992-2000
                              FAX 360-992-2107
                              http://www.clark.edu
Tami Jacobs, Dir Disability Support Services

Offers a variety of services to students with disabilities including note takers, extended testing time, counseling services, and special accommodations.

5427 Columbia Basin College

2600 N 20th Avenue
Pasco, WA   99301   509-547-0511
                              FAX 509-546-0401
                              TDY:509-547-0400
                              http://www.cbc2.org
                              e-mail: pbuchmiller@cbc2.org
Peggy Buchmiller, Directortor
Kathy Freeman, Program Coordinator

The Education Access Disability Resource Center provides a range of services for diagnosed learning disabled students, including alternate educational media, test accommodations, notetaking, priority registration, scribe services, books on tape and specialized computer software.

5428 Cornish College of the Arts

710 E Roy Street
Seattle, WA   98102   206-726-5098
                              FAX 206-720-1011
                              http://www.cornish.edu
Thomas Allman, Director

Through the Student Affairs Office, appropriate accommodations are provided for students with learning disabilities.

5429 Dartmoor School

13401 Bel Red Road
Bellevue, WA   98005   425-649-8976
                              FAX 425-603-0038

5430 ETC Preparatory Academy

8005 SE 28th
Mercer Island, WA   98040   206-236-1095
                              FAX 206-236-0998
Sheila Scates MA EdS, Director
Jan Bleakney, Director

Assessment, referral, tutorial, courses for credit, advocacy, dissertation, adults and students that are school age.

5431 Eastern Washington University: Disability Support Services

516 9th Street
Cheney, WA   99004   509-359-6871
                              FAX 509-359-4673
                              TDY:509-359-6261
                              http://www.ewu.edu
                              e-mail: KRAVER@mail.EWU.EDU
Karen Raver, Director
Kevin Hills, Accomodations Specialist
Pam McDermott, Program Assistant

Although the University does not offer a specialized program specifically for learning disabled students, the disability support services office works with students on a case by case basis.

5432 Edmonds Community College

20000 68th Avenue W
Lynnwood, WA   98036   425-640-1320
                              FAX 425-640-1622
                              http://www.edcc.edu/ssd
                              e-mail: ssdmail@edcc.edu
Dee Olson, Director
Tania Kulikov, Assistant Director

Offers a variety of services to students with disabilities including notetakers, extended testing time, and special accommodations.

5433 Epiphany School

3710 E Howell Street
Seattle, WA   98122   206-323-9011
                              FAX 206-324-2127

5434 Everett Community College

Center for Disabilities Services
2000 Tower Street
Everett, WA   98201   425-388-9272
                              FAX 425-388-9109
                              e-mail: admissions@vcc.ctc.edu
Kathy Cook, Director

Offers a variety of services to students with disabilities including notetakers, extended testing time, adaptive software and individual accommodations.

5435 Evergreen Academy

16017 118th Place NE
Bothell, WA   98011   425-488-8000
                              FAX 425-488-0994
Arlene Vixie, Contact

5436 Evergreen State College

2700 Evergreen Parkway SW
Olympia, WA   98505   360-867-6348
                              FAX 360-867-5349
                              http://www.evergreen.edu
                              e-mail: pickeril@evergreen.edu
Linda Pickering, Director

Academic adjustments and auxiliary aids are provided for students with documented disabilties.

5437 Green River Community College

12401 SE 320th Street
Auburn, WA   98092   253-833-9111
                              FAX 253-288-3467
                              TDY:253-288-3359
                              http://www.green river.ctc.edu
                              e-mail: jmartin@grcc.ctc.edu
Joanne Martin, Coordinator/Disability Services

Support services for students with disabilities to ensure that our programs and facilities are accessible. Our campus is organized to provide reasonable accommodations, including core services, to qualified students with dissabilities.

5438 Heritage Christian School

10310 NE 195th
Bothell, WA 98011   425-485-2585
                            FAX 425-486-2895

Bonnie DeLong

5439 Highline Community College

2400 S 240th Street
Des Moines, WA 98198   206-878-3710
                            FAX 206-870-3773
                      http://www.highline.ctc.edu
Pam Arsenault-Goldsmith, Program Coordinator

Offers a variety of services to students with disabilities including note takers, extended testing time, counseling services, and special accommodations.

5440 Morningside Academy

1621 12th Avenue
Seattle, WA 98122   206-329-9412
                            FAX 206-329-8127
                e-mail: info@morningsideacademy.org
Joanne K Robbins MA, Principal

5441 North Seattle Community College

9600 College Way N
Seattle, WA 98103   206-527-3697
                            FAX 206-527-3635
                   http://www.nsccux.sccd.ctc.edu
Suzanne Sewell, Manager

The Educational Access Center offers a variety of services to students with disabilities including notetakers, extended testing time, counseling services, and special accommodations.

5442 Northwest School

1415 Summit Avenue
Seattle, WA 98122   206-682-7309
                            FAX 206-467-7353

Ellen Taussig

5443 Pacific School of Academics

11105 Homestead Road
Arlington, WA 98223   360-403-8885
                            FAX 360-403-7607

Nola Smith

5444 Paladin Academy

21316 66th Avenue W
Lynnwood, WA 98036   452-672-6805
                            FAX 425-672-8867

Rhonda Jalali, Contact

5445 Pierce Community College

9401 Farwest Drive SW
Lakewood, WA 98498   253-964-6500
                            FAX 253-964-6713
                      http://www.pierce.ctc.edu
Jackie Hjorleisson, Coordinator/Disability Services

A federally funded TRIO progrm providing academic support services to low income students, first generation college students and students with disabilities in order to improve their retention, academic proformance, graduation and transfer to four-year institutions.

5446 Seattle Academy of Arts and Sciences

1432 15th Avenue
Seattle, WA 98122   206-323-6600
                            FAX 206-676-6881

Jean Orvis

5447 Seattle Central Community College

1701 Broadway
Seattle, WA 98122   206-587-3800
                            FAX 253-903-3236
                   http://www.edison.sccd.ctc.edu
Al Souma, Coordinator

Offers a variety of services to students with disabilities including notetakers, extended testing time, counseling services, and special accommodations.

5448 Seattle Christian Schools

18301 Military Road S
Sea Tac, WA 98188   206-246-8241
                            FAX 206-246-9066
                   http://www.seattlechristian.org
                e-mail: jjennings@seattlechristian.org
Judy Jennings, Superintendent

Independent, interdenominational Christian Day School established in 1946, serving 750+ students.

5449 Seattle Pacific University

3307 3rd Avenue W
Seattle, WA 98119   206-281-2475
                            FAX 206-286-7348
              http://www.spu.edu/departs/cfl/dsshome.asp
Sara Wetzel, Program Coordinator
Linda Wagner, Director

Offers a variety of services to students with disabilities including notetakers, extended testing time, books on tape, interpreters and special accommodations.

5450 Shoreline Christian School

2400 NE 147th
Shoreline, WA 98155   206-364-7777
                            FAX 206-364-0349

Timothy Visser

5451 Snohomish County Christian

17931 64th Avenue W
Lynnwood, WA 98037   425-742-9518
                            FAX 425-742-9516

5452 South Puget Sound Community College
2011 Mottman Road SW
Olympia, WA 98512   360-754-7711
                      FAX 360-684-4336
                http://www.spscc.ctc.edu
           e-mail: jshowalter@spscc.ctc.edu
Christy James, Disability Support Coordinator

Offers a variety of services to students with disabilities including notetakers, extended testing time, books on tape, readers, scribes, interpreters, assistance with registration.

5453 South Seattle Community College
6000 16th Avenue SW
Seattle, WA 98106   206-763-5137
                      FAX 206-768-6649
                      TDY:206-764-5845
           http://www.sccd.ctc.edu/south
            e-mail: rtillman@sccd.ctc.edu
Roxanne Tillman, Director/Special Student Svcs

Offers a variety of services to students with disabilities including notetakers, extended testing time, counseling services and special accommodations.

5454 Spokane Community College
1810 N Greene Street
Spokane, WA 99217   509-533-7000
                      FAX 509-533-8839
           http://www.scc.spokane.cc.wa.us
Ken Daniel, Special Services

Offers a variety of services to students with disabilities including notetakers, extended testing time, counseling services, and special accommodations.

5455 Spokane Falls Community College
3410 W Fort George Wright Drive
Spokane, WA 99224   509-533-4166
                            888-509-7944
                      FAX 509-533-3547
              http://www.spokanefalls.edu
Ben Webinger, Dir Disability Support Services

Offers a variety of services to students with disabilities including notetakers, extended testing time, counseling services, and special accommodations.

5456 St. Alphonsus
5816 15th NW
Seattle, WA 98107   206-782-4363
                      FAX 206-789-5709

5457 St. Matthew's
1230 NE 127th
Seattle, WA 98125   206-362-2785
                      FAX 206-362-4863

5458 St. Thomas School
PO Box 124
Medina, WA 98039   425-454-5880
                      FAX 425-454-1921

5459 University Preparatory Academy
8000 25th NE
Seattle, WA 98115   206-525-2714
                      FAX 206-525-9159
Roger Bass

5460 University of Puget Sound
1500 N Warner Street
Tacoma, WA 98416   253-879-3100
                      FAX 253-879-3500
                   http://www.ups.edu
               e-mail: iwest@ups.edu
Sherry Kennedy

Support services and accommodations are individually tailored depending upon a student's disability, its severity, the students academic environment and courses, housing situation, activities, etc. Accommodations include instruction in study strategies, free tutoring, assistance in note taking, sign language and additional academic advising.

5461 University of Washington
448 Schmitz Hall
Seattle, WA 98195   206-543-8925
                      FAX 206-616-8379
          e-mail: uwdss@u.washington.edu
Dyane Haynes, Director

Provides services and academic accommodations to students with documented permanent and temporary disabilities to ensure equal access to the university's educational programs and facilities. Services may include but are not limited to exam accommodations, notetaking, audio-taped class texts/materials, sign language interpreters, auxilary aids (assistive listening devices, and accessible furniture).

5462 University of Washington: Center on Human Development and Disability
PO Box 357920
Seattle, WA 98195   206-543-7701
                      FAX 206-543-3417
          http://www.depts.washington.edu/chdd
Michael J Guralnick, Director

The Center on Human Development and Disability (CHDD) at the University of Washington makes important contributions to the lives of people with developmental disabilities and their families, through a comprehensive array of research, clinical services, training, community outreach and dissemination activities.

5463 WSU/Disability Resource Center
Administration Annex #206
Pullman, WA 99164   509-335-3564
                      FAX 509-335-8511
                      TDY:509-335-3421
                http://www.wsu.edu/~drc/
              e-mail: schaeff@wsu.edu
Susan Schaeffer, Executive Director

Goals are: to assist students with disabilities to receive reasonable accommodations in academic and non-academic programs that provide them with an equal opportunity to fully participate in all aspects of student life at WSU: to increase awareness of issues and abilities of people with disabilities among the WSU students, faculty and staff.

5464 Walla Walla Community College

500 Tausick Way
Walla Walla, WA 99362   509-522-2500
FAX 509-527-4249
http://www.wallawalla.cc
Sue Huett, Coordinator

The Special Services Office offers a variety of services to students with disabilities including notetakers, extended testing time, counseling services, and special accommodations.

5465 Washington State University

AD Annex 206
Pullamn, WA 99164   509-335-1566
FAX 509-335-8511
http://www.wsu.edu
e-mail: schaeff@wsu.edu
Susan Schaffer, Assistant Director

Four year college that helps students and has programs for students with learning disabilities.

5466 Western Washington University

516 High Street
Bellingham, WA 98225   360-650-3844
FAX 360-650-3715
http://www.wwu.edu
David Brunnemer, Associate Director

Disabled Student Services offers a variety of services to students with disabilities including note takers, extended testing time, counseling services and special accommodations.

5467 Whatcom Community College

237 W Kellogg Road
Bellingham, WA 98226   360-676-2170
FAX 360-676-2171
http://www.whatcom.ctc.edu
Bill Culwell, Coordinator Disability Services

A public two-year college with support services for special education students.

5468 Whitworth College

W 300 Hawthorne Drive
Spokane, WA 99251   509-777-1000
FAX 509-777-3758
http://www.whitworth.edu
e-mail: joannnielsen@whitworth.edu
Diane Thomas, Contact

Offers a variety of services to students with disabilities including note takers, extended testing time, counseling services, and special accommodations.

5469 Yakima Valley Community College

16th Avenue & Nob Hill Boulevard
Yakima, WA 98907   509-574-4600
FAX 509-574-6860
http://www.yvcc.cc.wa.us/
Robert Chavez

Offers a variety of services to students with disabilities including notetakers, extended testing time, counseling services, and special accommodations.

West Virginia

5470 Bethany College West Virginia

Special Advising
Morlan Hall
Bethany, WV 26032   304-829-7400
FAX 304-829-7108
http://www.bethanywv.edu
e-mail: bpauls@bethanywv.edu
Becky Pauls, Academic Svcs/Special Advising

5471 Center for Excellence in Disabilities (CED)

West Virginia University
955 Hartman Run Road
Morgantown, WV 26505   304-293-4692
FAX 304-293-7294
TDY:304-293-4692
Ashok S Dey, Director

The mission of the West Virginia University Center for Excellence in Disabilities (WVUCED) is to enhance the quality of life of individuals of all ages with developmental and other disabilities so that they and their families can experience independence and inclusion in society through informed choices and self-determination.

5472 Davis & Elkins College

Learning Disability Program
100 Campus Drive
Elkins, WV 26241   304-637-1229
800-624-3157
FAX 304-637-1413
http://www.dne.edu
e-mail: mccaulj@dne.wvnet.edu
Judith Sabol McCauley, Director

Offers a program to provide individual support to college students with specific learning disabilities. This comprehensive program includes regular sessions with one of the three full-time learning disabilities instructors and specialized assistance and technology not available elsewhere on campus.

5473 Fairmont State College

Student Disabilities Services
1201 Locust Avenue
Fairmont, WV 26554   304-367-4686
FAX 304-366-4870
Lynn McMullen, Coordinator

Four year college provides services to learning disabled students.

5474 Glenville State College

Student Disability Services
200 High Street
Glenville, WV 26351   304-462-4118
FAX 304-462-7495
http://www.glenville.wvnet.edu
e-mail: cottrill@GLENVILLE.WVNET.EDU
Daniel A Reed, Student Disability Services Coor

5475 Marshall University

Higher Education for Learning Problems Program
520-18th Street
Huntington, WV 25755   304-696-6252
FAX 304-696-3231
http://www.marshall.edu
e-mail: weston@marshall.edu
Lynne Weston, Assistant Director
Dr Barbara Guyer, Director
K Renna Moore, Administrative Assistant

Offers the following services: individual tutoring to assist with coursework, studying for tests, administration of oral tests when appropriate; assistance with improvement of memory, assistance with note taking; assistance to determine presence of learning problems.

5476 Marshall University: HELP Program

520-18th Street
Huntington, WV 25755   304-696-6252
FAX 304-6963231
Renea Clark, Coordinator

A remedial program for LD medical students/physicians offering 5 week programs in January, March, June and September. Individual sessions by appointment. Assistance with reading comprehension, memory strategies, study skills, test-taking strategies and self esteem. Improvement of board scores.

5477 Parkersburg Community College

300 Campus Drive
Parkersburg, WV 26101   304-424-8000
FAX 304-424-8332
http://www.wvup.wvnet.edu
James Cook, Special Services

Offers a variety of services to students with disabilities including notetakers, extended testing time, counseling services, and special accommodations.

5478 Salem: Teikyo University

233 W Main Street
Salem, WV 26426   304-782-5011
FAX 304-782-5395
http://www.salem-teikyo.wvnet.edu
Paris Herbert Roland, Director Student Support

Student Support Services grant program funded by the US Dept of Education for 125 college students who are identified as disadvantaged and/or disabled. On staff are a counselor, a learning disabled specialist in math and science and a learning specialist in reading and writing.

5479 Southern West Virginia Community College & Technical College

PO Box 2900
Mount Gay, WV 25637   304-792-7046
FAX 304-792-7157
http://www.southern.wvnet.edu
e-mail: sherryd@southern.wvnet.edu
Sherry Dempsey, Program Manager

Southern has made reasonable modifications in its policies, practices and procedures to ensure that qualified individuals with disabilities enjoy equal opportunities services. Our facilities are compliant with Section 504 of the Rahabilitation Act of 1973 and the Americans with Disabilities Act of 1990. Offers a variety of services to students with disabilities including note takers, extended testing time, counseling services, and special accommodations.

5480 West Virginia Northern Community College

1704 Market Street
Wheeling, WV 26003   304-233-5900
FAX 304-232-8187
http://www.northern.wvnet.edu
Bonnie Ellis, Special Services

A public two-year college with support services for special education students.

5481 West Virginia State College

Campus Box 197
Institute, WV 25112   304-766-3000
800-987-2112
FAX 304-766-4100
http://www.wvsc.edu
Kellie Dunlap, Disability Services

A public four-year college. Accommodations are individualized to meet student's needs.

5482 West Virginia University: Department of Speech Pathology & Audiology

PO Box 6122
Morgantown, WV 26506   304-293-4242
FAX 304-293-7565
http://www.wvu.edu/~speechpa
e-mail: lcartwri@wvu.edu
Lynn Cartwright, Department Chair

Offers clinic services for people with speech, language, and/or hearing disorders.

5483 West Virginia Wesleyan College

Student Academic Support Services
59 College Avenue
Buckhannon, WV 26201   303-473-8510
800-722-9933
FAX 304-473-8108
http://www.wvwc.edu
e-mail: admission@wvwc.edu
Robert N Skinner II, Director Admissions/Finance
Shawn M Kuba, Director Academic Support
Carolyn Baisden, Administrative Assistant

Offers an individually structured program to accommodate college students with varying needs. Master level professionals in the fields of learning disabilities, reading, education, and counseling work to help each student design strategies for academic success. Accommodation plans are determined through a review of the documentation provided by the student and the recommendations of the student's comprehensive advisor, who works closely with each individual.

Wisconsin

5484 Alverno College

3400 S 43rd Street
Milwaukee, WI 53215
414-382-6026
800-933-3401
FAX 414-382-6354
http://www.alverno.edu
e-mail: colleen.barnett@alverno.edu
Nancy Bornstein, Director Instructional Services
Colleen Barnett, Coordinator Disability Services

An independent liberal arts college with 2,000 students in its weekday and weekend degree programs. Support services for students with learning disabilities include appropriate classroom accommodations, assistance in developing self advocacy skills, instructor assistance, peer tutoring, study groups, study strategies workshops, a communication resource center and math resource center.

5485 Beloit College

700 College Street
Beloit, WI 53511
608-363-2572
FAX 608-363-2670
http://www.beloit.edu/~stuaff/disability.html
Diane Arnzen, Director

Offers a variety of services to students with disabilities such as self advocacy training, study skills and time management guidance, couseling services, and special accommodations.

5486 Blackhawk Technical College

6004 Prairie Road
Janesville, WI 53547
608-758-6900
800-498-1282
FAX 608-758-6418
http://www.blackhawktech.org/
Christine Flottum

A public two-year college with support services for special education students.

5487 Cardinal Stritch College

Academic Support
6801 N Yates Road
Milwaukee, WI 53217
414-410-4168
800-347-8822
FAX 414-410-4239
http://www.stritch.edu
Marica Laskey, Director Academic Support

An independent four-year college with support services for special education students.

5488 Carthage College

Academic Support Program
2001 Alford Park Drive
Kenosha, WI 53140
414-551-8500
800-351-4058
FAX 414-551-6208
http://www.carthage.edu
Laura Busch, Director

An independent four-year college with support services for special education students.

5489 Chippewa Valley Technical College

620 W Clairemount Avenue
Eau Claire, WI 54701
715-833-6200
800-547-2882
FAX 715-833-6470
http://www.chippewa.tec.wi.us
Robert Benedict

A public two-year college with support services for special education students.

5490 Edgewood College

1000 Edgewood College Drive
Madison, WI 53711
608-257-4861
800-444-4861
FAX 608-663-3291
http://www. edgewood.edu
Joannah O'Hatnick, Director Learning Support

An independent four-year college with support services for students with learning disabilities.

5491 Fox Valley Technical College

1825 N Bluemound Drive
Appleton, WI 54913
920-735-5600
800-735-3882
FAX 920-831-4396
http://www.foxvalley.tec.wi.us
Lori Weyers, Dean General Studies

A public two-year college with support services for special education students.

5492 Gateway Technical College

3520 30th Avenue
Kenosha, WI 53144
262-564-2320
FAX 262-656-6909
http://www.gateway.tec.wi.us
e-mail: baileyj@gateway.tec.wi.us
Jo Bailey, Learning Skills Specialist

In accordance with Section 504 of the Vocational Rehabilitation Act, Gateway provides a wide range of services that assist special needs students in developing independence and sel-reliance within the Gateway campus community. Reasonable accommodations will be made for students with learning disabilities or physical limitations.

5493 Lakeshore Technical College
1290 N Avenue
Cleveland, WI 53015   920-458-4183
                              FAX 920-457-6211
                    http://www.ltc.tec.wi.us
                    e-mail: viwi@ltc.tec.wi.us
Vicki Wiese, Special Needs Instructor

A two-year college that provides comprehensive programs to students with learning disablities.

5494 Lawrence University
PO Box 599
Appleton, WI 54912   920-832-6530
                              FAX 920-832-6884
                    http://www.lawrence.edu
                    e-mail: excel@lawrence.edu
Geoff Gajawski, Assoc. Dean Student Academic Svc

Four year college that offers services to the learning disabled.

5495 Maranatha Baptist Bible College
745 W Main Street
Watertown, WI 53094   920-206-2341
                              FAX 920-261-9109
                    http://www.mbbc.edu
                    e-mail: cmidcalf@mbbc.edu
Cynthia Midcalf, Director

Four year college that offers programs for the learning disabled.

5496 Marian College of Fond Du Lac
45 S National Avenue
Fond Du Lac, WI 54935   920-923-7600
                              FAX 920-923-8755
                    http://www.mariancollege.edu
Ellen Mercer, Counselor

Offers a variety of services to students with disabilities including note takers, extended testing time, counseling services, and special accommodations.

5497 Marquette University
PO Box 1881
Milwaukee, WI 53201   414-288-7302
                              800-222-6544
                              FAX 414-288-3764
                    http://www.marquette.edu
Patricia Almon, Coordinator

An independent four-year university with support services for students with learning disabilities.

5498 Mid-State Technical College
500 32nd Street N
Wisconsin Rapids, WI 54494   715-422-5300
                              888-575-MSTC
                              FAX 715-422-5345
                    http://www.midstate.tec.wi.us/
                    e-mail: webamster@midstate.tec.wi.us
Dr. John Bellanti, Special Services
Vicki Kalodziej, Special Needs

Offers a variety of services to students with disabilities including notetakers, extended testing time, counseling services, and special accommodations.

5499 Milwaukee Area Technical College
700 W State Street
Milwaukee, WI 53233   414-297-6594
                              FAX 414-297-7990
                    http://www.milwaukee.tec.wi.us
Brenda Benton, Guidance Counselor
Robert Bullock, Manager

A public two-year college with support services for disabled students.

5500 Mt. Senario College
1500 College Avenue W
Ladysmith, WI 54848   715-532-5511
                              800-281-6514
                              FAX 715-532-7690
                    http://www.mscfs.edu
Victor Macaruso

Offers a variety of services to students with disabilities including notetakers, extended testing time, counseling services, and special accommodations.

5501 Nicolet Area Technical College: Special Needs Support Program
PO Box 518
Rhinelander, WI 54501   715-365-4410
                              800-544-3039
                              FAX 715-365-4445
                    http://www.nicolet.tec.wi.us
                    e-mail: inquire@nicolet.tec.wi.us
Bobert Steber, Special Needs
Sandy Jenkins, Case Manager

In support of the Nicolet Area Technical College Student services mission, the Special Needs Support Program provides appropriate accommodations empowering students with disabilities to identify and develop abilities for successful educational and life experiences.

5502 Northcentral Technical College
1000 W Campus Drive
Wausau, WI 54401   715-675-3331
                              FAX 715-675-9776
Lois Gilliland, Special Services

Offers a variety of services to students with disabilities including notetakers, extended testing time, counseling services, and special accommodations.

5503 Northeast Wisconsin Technical College
Special Services Program
2740 W Mason Street
Green Bay, WI 54307   262-498-5470
                              800-272-2740
                              FAX 262-498-6260
                    e-mail: moreinfo@nwtc.edu
Jerome Miller, Special Services

The Special Needs Office of NWTC offers assistance to individuals with disabilities when choosing educational and vocational goals, building self-steem and increasing their occupational potential. We offer a wide range of support services and accommodations which increases the potential of individuals with exceptional education needs to successfully complete Associate Degree and Technical Diploma programs.

5504 Northland College

1411 Ellis Avenue
Ashland, WI 54806 715-682-1224
FAX 715-682-1258
http://www.northland.edu
e-mail: admit@northland.edu

Four year college that provides students with learning disabilities with support and services.

5505 Ripon College: Student Support Services

300 Seward Street
Ripon, WI 54971 920-748-8107
FAX 920-748-8335
http://www.ripon.edu
e-mail: krhin@ripon.edu

Dan Krhin, Director

Program provides support services for disabled college students including an array of reasonable accommodations.

5506 St. Norbert College

100 Grant Street
DePere, WI 54115 920-403-1326
800-236-4878
FAX 920-403-4021
http://www.snc.edu
e-mail: karen.gooa-bartholomew@snc.edu
Karen Goode-Bartholomew, Director

Provides reasonable accommodations for documented disabilities.

5507 University of Wisconsin Center: Marshfield Wood County

2000 W 5th Street
Marshfield, WI 54449 715-387-1147
http://www.marshfield.uwc.edu
Linda Gleason, Associate Director

A public two-year college with support services for special education students.

5508 University of Wisconsin: Eau Claire

105 Garfield Avenue
Eau Claire, WI 54701 715-836-4542
FAX 715-836-3712
http://www.uwec.edu

Thomas Bouchard, Director

Offers a variety of services to students with disabilities including note takers, extended testing time, counseling services, and special accommodations.

5509 University of Wisconsin: La Crosse

1725 State Street
La Crosse, WI 54601 608-785-6900
FAX 608-785-6910
http://www.uwlax.edu
e-mail: reinert.june@uwlax.edu
June Reinert, Special Services

Offers a variety of services to students with disabilities including note takers, extended testing time, counseling services, and special accommodations.

5510 University of Wisconsin: Madison

905 University Avenue
Madison, WI 53715 608-263-2741
FAX 608-265-2998
http://www.mcburney.wisc.edu
e-mail: mcburney@uwmadmail.services.wisc.edu
Cathleen Trueba, LD Coordinator

Offers a variety of services to students with disabilities including notetakers, extended testing time, counseling services, and special accommodations.

5511 University of Wisconsin: Milwaukee

PO Box 413
Milwaukee, WI 53201 414-229-1122
414-229-6329
http://www.uwm.edu
Laurie Gramatzki, Coordinator

A public four-year college with support services for special education students.

5512 University of Wisconsin: Oshkosh

800 Algoma Boulevard
Oshkosh, WI 54901 920-424-1033
FAX 920-424-0858
http://www.uwosh.edu
William Kitz, Associate Professor

Disability Services of the Dean of Students Office desires to coordinate reasonable accommodations for students with disabilities. To offer the fullest opportunity for ademic potential while integrating into the vibrant extra-curricular life of the University.

5513 University of Wisconsin: Platteville

114 Warner Hall
Platteville, WI 53818 608-342-1818
FAX 608-342-1918
e-mail: petersre@uwplatt.edu
Rebecca Peters, Coordinator
Priscilla Hahn, Disabilities Specialist
Vicki Chase, Disabilities Assistant

Coordinates academic accommodations, provides an advocacy resource center for students with disabilities.

5514 University of Wisconsin: River Falls

410 S 3rd Street
River Falls, WI 54022 715-425-3531
FAX 715-425-3277
http://www.uwrf.edu

Wade Warner, Coordinator

Offers a variety of services to students with disabilities including note takers, extended testing time, counseling services, and special accommodations.

5515 University of Wisconsin: Whitewater

2021 Roseman Building
Whitewater, WI 53190 262-472-4788
FAX 262-472-5210
http://www.uww.edu
e-mail: amachern@mail.uww.edu
Nancy Amacher, Director
Eric Anderson, Assistant Director

A public four-year college. There is an additional fee for the special education program in addition to the regular tuition.

5516 Viterbo University

815 9th Street S
La Crosse, WI 54601 608-796-3060
800-viterbo
FAX 608-796-3050
http://www.viterbo.edu
Jane Eddy, Program Director

An independent four-year college with special services for special education students.

5517 Waisman Center: University of Wisconsin-Madison

1500 Highland Avenue
Madison, WI 53705 608-263-5776
FAX 608-263-0529
TDY:608-263-0802
http://www.waisman.wisc.edu
e-mail: webmaster@waisman.wisc.edu
Marsha Mailick-Seltzer, Acting Director

To advance knowledge about human development, developmental disabilities, and neurodegenerative diseases.

5518 Waukesha County Technical College

800 Main Street
Pewaukee, WI 53072 262-691-5210
877-892-9282
FAX 262-691-5089
http://www.wctc.edu
e-mail: djilbert@wctc.edu
Deb Jilbert, Coordinator Special Services

Offers technical and associate degree programs. Services for students with a documented disability may include academic support services, transition services, assistance with the admissions process, testing accommodations, interpreting services, note taking and assistance with RFB&D.

5519 Western Wisconsin Technical College

304 N 6th Street
La Crosse, WI 54602 608-785-9200
FAX 608-785-9205
http://www.western.tec.wi.us
Keith Valiquette, Special Services

Offers a variety of services to students with disabilities including notetakers, extended testing time, counseling services, and special accommodations.

5520 Wisconsin Indianhead Tech College: Ashland Campus

2100 Beaser Avenue
Ashland, WI 54806 715-682-4591
FAX 715-682-8040
Cindy Utities-Heart, Special Services

A public two-year college with support services for special education students.

5521 Wisconsin Indianhead Tech College: Rice Lake Campus

1900 College Drive
Rice Lake, WI 54868 715-234-7082
800-243-WITC
FAX 715-234-5172
http://www.witc.tec.wi.us
Patricia Peters, Special Needs

A public two-year college with support services for special education students.

Wyoming

5522 Laramie County Community College: Disability Resource Center

1400 E College Drive
Cheyenne, WY 82007 307-778-1359
800-522-2993
FAX 307-778-1262
TDY:307-778-1266
http://www.lccc.cc.wy.us/success/drc.htm
e-mail: ldignan@lccc.cc.wy.us
Lisa Dignan, DRC Coordinator
Patty Pratz, ADA Compliance Officer

Students with disabilities will find services and adaptive equipment to reducce mobility, sensory, and perceptual problems in the Disability Resource Center.

5523 Northwest College

231 W Sixth Street
Powell, WY 82435 307-754-6695
FAX 307-754-6700
http://www.nwc.cc.wy.us
e-mail: tiffany.self@ncag.edu
Lyn Pizor, Director

A two-year college that provides comprehensive programs to learning disabled students.

5524 Sheridan College

3059 Cofeen Avenue
Sheridan, WY 82801 307-674-6446
800-913-9139
FAX 307-674-7205
http://www.sc.cc.wy.us
Elizabeth Stearns, Director Advising

A public two-year college with support services for special education students.

5525 University of Wyoming
Po Box 3434
Laramie, WY   82071   307-766-1121
                           FAX 307-766-2271
                           http://www.uwyo.edu
Chris Primus, Special Services

An independent four-year college with support services for special education students.

5526 University of Wyoming: Division of Social Work and Wyoming Institute for Disabilities (WIND)
202 Ivinson Building
Laramie, WY   82071   307-766-2761
                           FAX 307-766-2763
                           TDY:307-766-2720
                           http://www.wind.uwyo.edu/
                           e-mail: kamiller@uwyo.edu
Keith Miller PhD, Executive Director WIND

Alabama

5527 Opportunity Center: Easter Seal
2448 Gordon Smith Drive
Mobile, AL   36617 251-471-1581
800-411-0068
FAX 251-476-4303
http://www.alabama.easterseals.com
Mike Almaroad

Children and adults with disabilities and special needs find highest-quality services designed to meet their individual needs.

5528 People First Coffee County Training Center
College Street Extension
Enterprise, AL   36330 205-393-1732
Vickie Florence, Director

Clients 21 years and up receive training in independent living skills, self-care, language skills and more.

5529 Special Education Action Committee
600 Bel Air Boulevard, Suite 210
Mobile, AL   36616 251-478-1208
800-222-7322
FAX 251-473-7877
http://www.seacparentassistancecenter.com
e-mail: seacofmobile@zebra.net
Mavis Smith, Director

Parent Training and Information Program views parents as full partners in the educational process and a significant source of support and assistance to each other. Funded by the Division of Personnel Preparation, Office of Special Education Programs, these programs provide training and information to parents to enable such individuals to participate more effectively with professionals in meeting the educational needs of disabled children.

5530 Three Springs
1131 Eagletree Lane
Huntsville, AL   35801 256-880-3339
888-758-4356
FAX 256-880-7026
http://www.threesprings.com
e-mail: info@threesprings.com
Mike Watson, President

The mission of Three Springs is the healing and restoration of children and their families. Every resource at our disposal, be it financial, human or operational, is directed toward this purpose. Our efforts will always be governed by the principles of honor, respect, teamwork, reponsibilities, accountability and honesty.

5531 Wireglass Rehabilitation Center
795 Ross Clark Circle
Dothan, AL   36305 334-792-0022
FAX 334-712-7632
Jack Sasser, Administrator
Ronnie Welch, Program Services

Provides services to individuals with disabilities in order to render them employable.

5532 Workshops
4244 3rd Avenue S
Birmingham, AL   35222 205-592-9683
888-805-9683
FAX 205-592-9687
http://www.workshopsinc.com
James E Crim, Executive Director
Debbie Richards, Director

Funded by the public, community chest and workshop sales this center provides evaluation, employment, pre-vocational training and sheltered workshops to the disabled areas of Birmingham, Jefferson County, Northern Alabama and Shelby County.

Alaska

5533 Center for Community
700 Katlian Street
Sitka, AK   99835 907-747-6960
800-478-6970
FAX 907-747-4868
Tracy Hodges, Program/Care Coordinator

A private, nonprofit corporation provides comprehensive and individualized support and training services for people of all ages who have a developmental delay or disability. Programs include assistive technology services and vocational assessment, training and placement, as well as other residential and respite services.

Arizona

5534 Academy of Tucson
2300 N Tanque Verde Loop Road
Tucson, AZ   85749 520-749-1413
FAX 520-749-2824
e-mail: academy@dakotacom.net
Holly Leeman, Dean
Shari Stewart, Principle

A state charted, nonprofit co-ed school serving grades 9-12. Founded in 1986, accredited by North Central Association, it is a college preparatory school for students who learn best in a small, personalized setting. Teachers hold Arizona certificates, and class ratios are 1:20. The curriculum meets college entrance requirements. Charter sponsored by Arizona Stats Board of Education. Tuition free.

5535 Devereux Arizona Treatment Network
11000 N Scottsdale Road
Scottsdale, AZ   85254 480-998-2920
800-345-1292
FAX 480-443-1531
http://www.devereuxaz.org
Jim Cole, Exeutive Director

Provides a wide array of behavioral health and social welfare services for persons with emotional and behavioral disorders or who are victims of physical or sexual abuse and neglect.

5536 LATCH School

8145 N 27th Avenue
Phoenix, AZ   85051   602-995-7366
                                     FAX 602-995-0867
                          http://www.latchschool.org
                            e-mail: latchinc@aol.com
Connie Laird, Executive Director
Marge Cook, Education Director
Stephanie Denning, Development Coordinator

LATCH School is a private school, non-profit, special education school providing educational, behavioral and therapeutic services to over 200 students, ages 3-21, with cognitive, emotional, orthopedic, and/or behavioral disabilities.

5537 Life Development Institute (LDI)

18001 N 79th Avenue
Glendale, AZ   85308   623-773-2774
                                     FAX 623-773-2788
                     http://www.life-development-inst.org
                          e-mail: LDIinARIZ@aol.com
Robert Crawford, President

A program service for older adolescents and young adults with learning disabilities, AD/HD and other related disorders.

5538 New Way Learning Academy

1300 N 77th Street
Scottsdale, AZ   85257   480-946-9112
                                     FAX 480-946-2657
                          http://www.newwayacademy.org
                       e-mail: newway@phnx.uswest.net
John Phin, Executive Director
Dawn Gutierrez, Executive Director

Serving children with learning disabilities, attention deficit disorder and underachievers in grades K-12 for 34 years. New Way is approved by the Arizona State Department of Special Education to serve students with learning disabilities and meets state mandated standards and guidelines. Our enrollment is approximately 120 students, and we have 35 staff members.

5539 Raising Special Kids

2400 N Central Avenue
Phoenix, AZ   85004   602-242-4366
                                         800-237-3007
                                     FAX 602-242-4306
                       http://www.raisingspecialkids.com
                       e-mail: info@raisingspecialkids.org
Joyce Millard, Executive Director

A parent training and information center providing information, resources and support to families of children with disabilities.

5540 Turning Point School

200 E Yavapai Road
Tucson, AZ   85705   520-292-9300
                                     FAX 520-292-9075
                       http://www.turningpointschool.com
Nancy Von Wald, Director, President

For dyslexics, attention deficit disorder children who have difficulties in reading, writing, spelling and math. Summer and regular school students return to public school in 1-3 years, with secure skills.

Arkansas

5541 Arkansas Disability Coalition

1123 S University Avenue
Little Rock, AR   72204   501-614-7020
                                         800-223-1330
                                     FAX 501-614-9082
                               http://www.adcpti.org
                             e-mail: adc@alltel.net
Wanda Stovall, Director

Our mission is to work for equal rights and opportunities for Arkansans with disabilities through public policy change, cross-disability collaboration, and empowerment of people with disabilities and their families.

California

5542 Almansor Center

1137 Huntington Drive
South Pasadena, CA   91030   323-341-5580
                                     FAX 323-257-0284
                          http://www.redesignlearning.org
Nancy Lavelle, Executive Director

Committed to serving children, youth and young adults with learning, developmental and emotional disabilities.

5543 Ann Martin Children's Center

1250 Grand Avenue
Piedmont, CA   94610   510-655-7880
                                     FAX 510-655-3379
                               http://www.annmartin.org

A private, nonprofit community center that helps children with special educational needs become more confident and independent learners.

5544 Brislain Learning Center

1550 Humboldt Road
Chico, CA   95928   530-342-2567
                                     FAX 530-342-2573
Judy Brislain EdD

Assists children of all ages who have learning disabilities. Offers a diagnostic program and tutoring program for ADD and learning disabilities. Provides counseling and support groups for children and adults.

5545 Center for Adaptive Learning

3227 Clayton Road
Concord, CA 94519 925-827-3863
FAX 925-827-4080
http://www.centerforadaptivelearning.org
e-mail: info@centerforadaptivelearning.org
Genevieve A Stolarz, Executive Director
Nancy Perry, Clinical Neuropsychologist

The center provides a comprehsive program that is designed to address many needs; physical, social, emotional and vocational. To empower adults with a developmental neurological disability to realize their own potential.

5546 Charles Armstrong School

1405 Solana Drive
Belmont, CA 94002 650-592-7570
FAX 650-592-0780
http://www.charlesarmstrong.org
e-mail: info@charlesarmstrong.org
Lisa Shupp-Mules, President
Wilbur Mattison, Chairman
Rosalie Whitlock, Headmaster

The mission of the Charles Armstrong School is to serve the dyslexic learner by providing an appropriate educational experience which not only enables the students to acquire language skills, but also instills a joy of learning, enhances self-worth, and allows each the right to identify, understand and fulfill personal potential.

5547 Children's Therapy Center

770 Paseo Camarillo
Camarillo, CA 93010 805-383-1501
FAX 805-383-1504

Beth Maulhardt, Contact

The Children's Therapy Center is a private evaluation and treatment center for children who show delays in motor development, speech/language development, play and social development and/or learning problems. We offer occupational therapy, physical therapy, speech/language therapy, counseling and psychological testing.

5548 Devereux Santa Barbara

PO Box 6784
Santa Barbara, CA 93160 805-968-2525
FAX 805-968-3247
http://www.devereux.org
e-mail: info@devereux.org
Alec Bruice, Director
Larry Crandell

To provide quality services to children, adults and families with special needs which derive from behavioral, psychological, intellectual or neurological impairments.

5549 Dyslexia Awareness and Resource Center

928 Carpinteria Street
Santa Barbara, CA 93103 805-963-7339
FAX 805-963-6581
http://www.dyslexiacenter.com
e-mail: info@dyslexiacenter.com
Leslie V Esposito, Executive Development Director
Joan T Esposito, Founder/Program Director
Valerie Allen, Center Coordinator

The Dyslexia Awareness and Resource Center is here to help students and adults with dyslexia and ADD, as well as their parents, teachers and professionals who work with them.

5550 Eye Care Center

Southern California College of Optometry
2575 Yorba Linda Boulevard
Fullerton, CA 92831 714-449-7400
FAX 714-992-7811
http://www.scco.edu
e-mail: mrouse@scco.edu
Troy Allred, Instructor
Tal Barak, Instructor
Eric Borsing, Professor

The Center offers comprehensive primary vision care for patients of all ages. The Vision Therapy Service specializes in complete diagnostic and therapeutic care of both children and adults presenting with visual and related learning problems. The primary goal is the diagnosis and management of visual and visual perceptual-motor difficulties that may interfere with efficient learning. Testing services are also available for the diagnosis of specific dyslexia. A sliding fee scale is available.

5551 Frostig Center

971 N Altadena Drive
Pasadena, CA 91107 626-791-1255
FAX 626-798-1801
http://www.frostig.org
e-mail: helpline@frostig.org
Bennett Ross PhD, Executive Director

A non profit organization that specializes in helping children who have learning disabilities. Offers parent training, consulting and direct instructional services to learning disabled children.

6-18 years old

5552 Full Circle Programs

70 Skyview Terrace San Rafael
San Rafael, CA 94903 415-499-3320
FAX 415-499-1542
http://www.fullcircleprograms.org
e-mail: info@fullcircleprograms.org
Brian Van Weele, Executive Director
Deborah Riggins, Associate Director

Full Circle has been actively caring for children and their families in need. Full Circle offers a continuum of care ranging from residential treatment for several emotionally disturbed boys, to outpatient counseling for children and their families.

5553 Help for Brain Injured Children

Cleta Harder Developmental School
981 N Euclid Street
La Habra, CA   90631   562-694-5655
                                FAX 562-694-5657
http://www.hbic.org
e-mail: hbiccleta@aol.com
Cleta J Harder, Executive Director
Sylvia Conde, Administrative Director

Offers home rehabilitation programs. We also offer an after school developmental motor program for elementary students K-5th grade.

5554 Kayne-ERAS Center

5350 Machado Road
Culver City, CA   90230   310-737-9393
                                FAX 310-737-9344
http://www.erascenter.com
e-mail: erascenter@aol.com
Joni Berry, President
Shelby Arnold, Vice President

Kayne-ERAS accomplishes its mission by offering educational resources, direct service, and a professional training center. Kayne-ERAS provides personalized programming to children and young adults from at risk conditions and those challenged by emotional, learning, developmental and/or chronic neurological and/or medical disabilities.

5555 Marina Psychological Services

4640 Admiralty Way
Marina Del Rey, CA   90292   310-822-0109
                                FAX 310-822-1240
e-mail: marinapsych@hotmail.com
Bruce Hirsch, Psychologist

Psychological evaluations, psychotherapy and counseling, parent education and counseling, consultation to schools and employers.

5556 Melvin-Smith Learning Center

EDU-Therapeutics
775 Kimball Avenue
Seaside, CA   93955   831-620-1908
                                   800-505-3276
                                FAX 831-620-1907
http://www.edu-therapeutics.com
e-mail: edu-t@erc1.com
Joan Smith EdD, Director
Mark Wolinski, Administrator

Nonprofit corporation that provides assistance for children and adults with dyslexia, attention deficit, learning handicaps, or reading challenges through a wide range of services, publications, and training programs.

5557 NAWA Academy

17351 Trinity Mountain Road
French Gulch, CA   96033   530-359-2215
                                FAX 530-359-2229
http://www.nawa-academy.com
e-mail: nawamain@hotmail.com
David Hull, President

A boarding school located in a remote valley of the Trinity Alps that provides individual curriculum, theory and structure for 7-9 grade students, many of who have learning disabilities. Services include individual counseling, small academic classes, behavior modification programs and numerous after school activities.

5558 New Vistas Christian School

68 Morello Avenue
Martinez, CA   94553   925-370-7767
                                FAX 925-370-6395
Maria Zablah, Principal
Linda Scott, CEO

A non-profit 5th-12th school for students of average or above average intelligence with learning disabilities offering a non-traditional approach to multiple learning styles.

5559 Newport Language: Speech and Audiology Center

26137 La Paz Road
Mission Viejo, CA   92691   949-581-5206
                                FAX 949-599-0247
http://www.newportaudiology.com
e-mail: info@newaud.com
Sharlene Goodman, Contact

We aim to enhance the quality of people's lives by improving their ability to communicate. We provide the highest level of audiological services possible, through our highly efficient staff, informative education programs, community services, high quality products, and true spirit of customer service.

5560 One To One Reading & Educational Center

10324 Woodley Avenue
Granada Hills, CA   91344   818-891-3090
                                FAX 818-891-3612
Paul Klinger, Owner/Director
Julie Klinger, Assistant/Associate

Educational therapy for students with reading and math problems and tutoring for many subjects all one on one.

5561 Park Century School

2040 Stoner Avenue
Los Angeles, CA   90025   310-478-5065
                                FAX 310-473-9260
http://www.parkcenturyschool.org
e-mail: nbley@parkcenturyschool.org
Genny Shain, Co-Director
Gail Splindler, Co-Director
Nancy Bley, Academic Coordinator

An independent school for average and above average intellect children with learning disabilities. The program emphasizes developing the skills and strategies necessary to return to a traditional program. With a 2:1 student-staff ratio.

7-14 years old

Learning Centers/California

5562 Providence Speech and Hearing Center

1301 W Providence Avenue
Orange, CA   92868   714-639-4990
                                                FAX 714-744-3841
                                                http://www.pshc.org
                                                e-mail: psqc@pshc.org
Margaret Inman, Founder
Mary Jo Hooper, Executive Director

Comprehensive services for testing and treatment of all speech, language and hearing problems. Individual and group therapy beginning with parent/infant programs.

5563 REACH for Learning

1221 Marin Avenue
Albany, CA   94706   510-524-6455
                                                FAX 510-524-5154
Corinne Gustafson, Director

Educational services for children and adults including: diagnostic assessment, individual remediation/tutoring, small group workshops, and consultation for parents and professionals.

5564 Reading Center of Bruno

4952 Warner Avenue
Huntington Beach, CA   92649   714-377-7910
                                                FAX 562-436-4428
                                                e-mail: Readingct.@aol.com
Walter C Waid, Director

We work with children, teens and adults with dyslexia, auditory and visual perceptual confusions through our specialized training program. Diagnostic testing is available, as well.

5565 Rincon Learning Center

594 N Westwind Drive
El Cajon, CA   92020   619-442-2722
                                                FAX 619-442-1011
                                                http://www.rinconlearningcenter.com
Lois Dotson, Director

Diagnostic and therapy services for a wide range of learning disabilities. Offers one on one tutoring.

5566 Santa Barbara Center for Educational Therapy

1811 State Street
Santa Barbara, CA   93101   805-687-3711
                                                FAX 805-569-6882
Susan Hamilton, Director, Education
Joyce Tolle, Director Education

Provides educational assessment to determine learning style and document learning disabilities. Also provided are one-to-one remedial or tutorial services for individuals specializing in dyslexia.

5567 Santa Cruz Learning Center

720 Fairmount Avenue
Santa Cruz, CA   95062   831-427-2753
                                                e-mail: sclrngcntr@yahoo.com
Eleanor F Stitt, Director

Individualized one-to-one tutoring for individuals aged 5 to adult. Specializes in dyslexia, learning difficulties and gifted persons. Includes test preparation, math, reading, self confidence, study skills, time organization and related services.

5568 Second Start: Pine Hill School

3002 Leigh Avenue
San Jose, CA   95124   408-979-8210
                                                FAX 408-979-8223
                                                http://www.pinehillschool.com
                                                e-mail: blancan@secondstart.org
Greg Zieman, Executive Director
David Gerster, Principal
Terry Reynolds, Registrar

A private school that provides special education and alternative services to students with a wide range of learning and behavior disabilities.

5569 Stockdale Learning Center

1701 Westwind Drive
Bakersfield, CA   93301   661-326-8084
                                                http://www.stockdalelearningcenter.com
                                                e-mail: slc@igalaxy.net
Andrew J Barling MA CET, Owner/Director

Stockdale Learning Center is a professional State Certified Educational Therapy clinic designed to collaboratively diagnose and assess individuals 5 years of age through adult.

5570 Stowell Learning Center

20955 Pathfinder Road
Diamond Bar, CA   91765   909-598-2482
                                                FAX 909-598-3442
                                                http://www.learningdisability.com
                                                e-mail: info@learningdisability.com
Jill Stowell, Director

A diagnostic and teaching center for learning and attention disorders. Specializes in instruction for dyslexic or learning disabled children and adults. Our services include diagnostic evaluation, developmental evaluation, cognitive and educational therapy which is provided on a one-to-one basis, and a full day class for elementary age students with reading disabilities.

5571 Switzer Center

1110 Sartori Avenue
Torrance, CA   90501   310-328-3611
                                                FAX 310-328-5648
                                                http://www.switzercenter.org
Dr. Rebecca Foo, Executive Director
Larry Brugnatelli, Associate Director

Improving lives of those challenged by learning, social and emotional difficulties by maximizing educational competence and psychological well being.

5572 Team of Advocates for Special Kids (TASK)
100 W Cerritos Avenue
Anaheim, CA   92805   714-533-8275
                            FAX 714-533-2533
                        http://www.taskca.org
                        e-mail: taskca@yahoo.com
Marta Anchondo, Executive Director
Brenda Smith, Deputy Director

Team of Advocates for Special Kids (TASK) is a Parent Training and Information Center that Parents and Professionals can turn to for assistance in seeking and obtaining needed early intervention and educational, medical or therapeutic support service for children.

5573 The Prentice School
18341 Lassen Drive
Santa Ana, CA   92705   714-538-4511
                            FAX 714-538-5004
                        http://www.prentice.org
                        e-mail: pdadmin@prentice.org
Debra L Jarvis, Executive Director
Carol H Clark, Director Education
Diana Wilhite, Assistant to Executive Director

The Prentice School is an independent, nonprofit, coeducational day school dedicated to the needs of Specific Language Disabled Students.

5574 Vision Care Clinic of Santa Clara Valley
2730 Union Avenue
San Jose, CA   95124   408-377-1150
                            FAX 408-377-1152
Dr. Rice, Director

Diagnostic and training for those with visual disabilities.

Colorado

5575 Developmental Disabilities Resource Center
11177 W 8th Avenue
Lakewood, CO   80215   303-233-3363
                            800-649-8815
                            FAX 303-233-4622
                        http://www.ddrcc.com
                        e-mail: ahogling@ddrcc.com
Arthur Hogling, Executive Director
Robert Arnold, Associate Executive Director

The Center's mission is to provide leading-edge services that create opportunities for people with developmental disabilities and their families to participate fully in the community.

5576 Havern Center
4000 S Wadsworth Boulevard
Littleton, CO   80123   303-986-4587
                            FAX 303-986-0590
                        http://www.haverncenter.org
                        e-mail: nmann@haverncenter.org
Cathy Pasquariello, Executive Director
Denise Ensslin, Staff/Curriculum Consultant

School for children with learning disabilities. Educational programs, special language programs and occupational therapy is available.

6-13 years old

5577 PEAK Parent Center
611 N Weber
Colorado Springs, CO   80903   719-531-9400
                            800-284-0251
                            FAX 719-531-9452
                            TDY:719-531-9403
                        http://www.peakparent.org
                        e-mail: info@peakparent.org
Barbara Bushwell, Executive Director

PEAK Parent Center is Colorado's Parent Training and information center. PEAK is a statewide organization of parents of children with disabilities reaching out to assist other parents and professionals.

Connecticut

5578 American School for the Deaf
139 N Main Street
West Hartford, CT   06107   860-570-2300
                        http://www.asd-1817.org
                        e-mail: chris.thorkelson@asd-1817.org
Fern Reisinger, Interim Director
Edward Peltier, Assistant Executive Director
Chris Thorkelson, Public Information Officer

The American School for the Deaf is a residential/day program operating as a state-aided private school and governed by a board of directors. It is the oldest permanent school for the deaf in America, offering a comprehensive educational program for the deaf and hard of hearing students, infants, preschoolers, primary, elementary, junior high school, high school, and post-secondary students.

5579 Boys and Girls Village
528 Wheelers Farms Road
Milford, CT   06460   203-877-0300
                            FAX 203-876-0076
                        http://www.boysvillage.org
                        e-mail: trottac@boysvill.org
Reverend Fellenbaum, CEO
Steven Kant, Medical Director
Carmine Trotta, Support Services Director

The agency through the years has evolved into a leading therapeutic and learning facility offering residential shelter, counseling, educational, foster and adoptive training, family support services, and day programs for children and their families.

5580 COPE Center of Progressive Education
Residential Services Division
425 Grant Street
Bridgeport, CT   06610   203-426-3344
                            FAX 203-781-4792
                        e-mail: info@aptfoundation.org
Gretchen Celestino, Principal

COPE is an alternative, special education school serving substance abusing adolescents placed at the Alpha House Residential Treatment Facility.

5581 Candee Hill

122 Candee Hill Road
Watertown, CT   06795   860-274-8332
                                      FAX 860-828-3912

Frank Popkiewicz, Director

Emphasis on increasing client's self-sufficiency in areas of daily skills, community awareness and social interaction.

5582 Community Child Guidance Clinic School

317 N Main Street
Manchester, CT   06040   860-643-2101
                                      FAX 860-645-1470
                              http://www.ccgcinc.org
                         e-mail: clinic@ccgcinc.org
Clifford Johnson, Executive Director
Lynn Helman, Medical Director

The Community Child Guidance Clinic is a private, non-profit mental health agency offering diagnostic, treatment and consultation services to children up to the age of 18 and their families.

5583 Connecticut Center for Augmentative Communication

St. Vincent's Special Needs Center
95 Merritt Boulevard
Trumbull, CT   06611   203-386-2728
                                       FAX 203-380-1190
           http://www.saintvincentsspecialneeds.org
              e-mail: feroleto.child.dev@snet.net
Virginia Smith, Director Marketing
Harry Schaffer, Program Director

Provides persons of all ages with evaluation/training in augmentative aids/systems to facilitate communication, writing and computer access.

5584 Connecticut Center for Children and Families

8 Titus Road
Washington Depot, CT   06794   860-868-1155
                                      FAX 860-868-1288
Patricia Thomas
Janet Bloch

The Connecticut Center is a group of affiliated professionals with a diversity of talent but with a common vision. We believe that collaborative intervention is often the most clinically and financially effective way to solve learning and educational problems. The Center offers the services of psychiatrists, psychologists, learning specialists and tutors.

5585 Connecticut College Children's Program

270 Mohegan Avenue
New London, CT   06320   860-439-2920
                                      FAX 860-439-5317
        http://www.conncoll.edu/academics/department/
                     e-mail: bldem@conncoll.edu
Sarah Radlinski, Program Director

The mission of the Connecticut College Children's Program is to provide, within a community context, a model child and family-focused early childhood program for infants and young children of diverse backgroungs and abilities in Southeastern Connecticut.

5586 Connecticut Institute for the Blind

120 Holcomb Street
Hartford, CT   06112   860-242-2274
                                      FAX 860-242-3103
                              http://www.ciboakhill.org
                         e-mail: info@ciboakhill.org
Suzanne Heise, VP Development
Marion Jones, Assistant Director

Providing children and adults with disabilities the opportunity to live, learn and work in the community.

5587 Curtis Home Children's Program

380 Crown Street
Meriden, CT   06450   203-237-4338
                                      FAX 203-630-1127
              http://www.thecurtishome.org/children/
                  e-mail: info@thecurtishome.org
Robert Flyntz, President
Ronald Stempien, VP
Mary Lyons, Secretary

Now managed by the Hartford Healthcare System, the Children's Program continues to provide support in the following service areas: Residential Treatment, Day Treatment, The Cheshire School, Family Placement Program, and Safe Harbors. The Curtis Home still owns a majority of the facilities housing the Children's Program.

5588 Devereux Glenholme School

81 Sabbaday Lane
Washington, CT   06793   860-868-7377
                                      FAX 860-868-7894
                  http://www.theglenholmeschool.org
              e-mail: info@theglenholmeschool.org
Kathi Fitzherbert, Admissions Director
Christine Sulborski, Admissions Assistant

The Glendholme School is a boarding school for special needs students situated on over 100 idyllic acres of Connecticut countryside.

5589 Eagle Hill School

45 Glenville Road
Greenwich, CT   06831   203-622-9240
                                      FAX 203-622-0914
                              http://www.eaglehillschool.org
                         e-mail: r.griffin@eaglehill.org
Rayma J Griffin, Contact

Eagle Hill is a languaged-based, remedial program committed to educating children with learning disabilities. The curriculum is individualized, interdisciplinary, and transitional in nature.

5590 Elizabeth Ives School

700 Hartford Tpke
Hamden, CT   06517   203-281-1148
                                            FAX 203-230-9556

Betty Sword, Co-Director
Linda Zunda, Co-Director

The facility has a structured, individualized education program for children from preschool age through 15 years. A life skills program is included for appropriate students and speech therapy is provided on a regular basis.

5591 Elmcrest Schools

25 Marlborough Street
Portland, CT   06480   860-342-6266
                                            FAX 860-342-5106

Elaine Green, Director

Offers short-term treatment, long-term treatment and a day treatment program for the learning disabled and children with substance abuse problems.

5592 Forman School

12 Norfolk Road
Litchfield, CT   06759   860-567-1802
                                            FAX 860-567-8317
                          http://www.formanschool.org
                   e-mail: admissions@formanschool.org
Mark B Perkins, Head School
Beth A Rainey, Admissions Director

Forman offers students with learning differences the opportunity to achieve academic excellence in a traditional college preparatory setting. A coeducational boarding school of 180 students, we maintain a 3:1 student:teacher ratio. Daily remedial instruction balanced with course offerings rich in content provide each student with a flexible program that is tailored to his or her unique learning style and needs.

5593 Foundation School

719 Derby Milford Road
Orange, CT   06477   203-795-6075
                                            FAX 203-876-7531
Walter Bell, Director

Basic developmental skills address speech/language and perceptual/motor areas. Academic skills are reading, writing and arithmetic with social studies, science and career studies.

5594 Founders' Respite Care

PO Box 470
Norwalk, CT   06852   203-847-6760
                                            FAX 203-847-0545
                   http://www.starinc-lightingtheway.org
Jackie Leniart, Family Support Manager

Facility-based respite care is provided by STAR at Founders Cottage. A lovely home, is co-ed, and can accomodate four individuals at a time. It is for people with development disabilities who are 16 years or older and who reside within the Southwest Region. All persons must be registered with the Connecticut Department of Mental Retardation and have a DMR number assigned.

5595 Gengras Center

Saint Joseph College
1678 Asylum Avenue
West Hartford, CT   06117   860-232-4571
                                            FAX 860-231-8396
                                            http://www.sjc.edu
                                   e-mail: blindauer@sjc.edu
Bernard Lindauer, Director

A highly structured special education program providing academic, vocational evaluation training, and related service, in combination with behavioral, social, and emotional support tailored to the need of the student.

5596 Intensive Education Center

840 N Main Street
West Hartford, CT   06117   860-236-2049
                                            FAX 860-231-2843
Helen Dowd CSJ, Director
Carol Devlen, Intake Coordinator

A non-profit, non sectarian school for children 6 to 21 years with different learning styles. Individualized program with a 5:1 student teacher ratio. Program strives to help each student reach their potential by gaining confidence, recognizing their strengths and limitations, setting realistic goals and attaining satisfaction by achieving these goals. State accredited. Full-day curriculum is offered.

5597 Klingberg Family Centers

370 Linwood Street
New Britain, CT   06052   860-224-9113
                                            FAX 860-832-8221
                          http://www.klingberg.com
                   e-mail: information@klingberg.com
Lynne V Roe, Intake Coordinator
David Lawrence-Hawley, Community Services Director

The Klingber Family Centers provide structured programs for residential, day treatment and day school students in a therapeutic environment. We are a private, nonprofit organization serving children and families from across Connecticut.

5598 Lake Grove Durham

459R Wallingford Road
Durham, CT   06422   860-349-3467
                                            888-525-9007
                                            FAX 860-349-1382
                                            e-mail: www.lgstc.org
Robert C Ruggiero, Director

Lake Grove at Durham serves its clients in eight expanded split-level homes in a rural community atmosphere. Support facilities include a school building, administration building, dining hall, horse stables and pasture, clubhouse, and several staff homes.

5599 Learning Center

The Children's Home
60 Hicksville Road
Cromwell, CT   06416   860-635-6010
                                       FAX 860-635-3425
                          http://www.childrenshome-ct.org
                              e-mail: info@childhome.org
David Tompkins, Program Administrative Officer
Cindy Sarnowski, Education Director

The Learning Center at The Children's Home is accredited by the Connecticut State Department of Education as an educational institution for children and adolescents with emotional and learning difficulties.

5600 Learning Clinic

PO Box 234
Brooklyn, CT   06234   860-774-1036
                                       FAX 860-774-1037
                           http://www.thelearningclinic.com
                    e-mail: admissions@thelearningclinic.com
Raymond DuCharme, Executive Director

A private, nonprofit educational program that provides day and residential school focused on ADHD and learning and emotional issues. The program is coeducational and serves sixty students. The faculty is 50 in number including special and regular education certified staff. Academic, Young Apprentice and Wilderness programs are individualized and self-paced. College bound and vocationally oriented students are welcome.

5601 Lorraine D Foster Day School

1861 Whitney Avenue
Hamden, CT   06517   203-230-4877
                                       FAX 203-288-5749
Dominique Fontaine, Director

Lorraine D Foster Day School is a psycho-educational day school for students who are identified as seriously emotionally disturbed and/or learning disabled. We accept students between the ages of 8 and 18 and it is our mission to prepare students for successful re-intergration to the public school.

5602 Mount Saint John

135 Kirtland Street
Deep River, CT   06417   860-526-5391
                                       FAX 860-526-1636
                                  http://www.mtstjohn.org
                               e-mail: info@mtstjohn.org
Cathi Coridan, Executive Director
Arthur Avitabile, Associate Director
Sandra Easton, Treatment Services Director

This special education program offers individualized and small group instruction for boys who are socially/emotionally disabled and/or learning disabled.

5603 Natchaug Hospital School Program

189 Storrs Road
Mansfield Center, CT   06250   860-456-1311
                                            800-426-7792
                                       FAX 860-423-6114
                                  http://www.natchaug.org
Stephen Larcen, President/CEO
Craig M Martin, Medical Director
David Klein, Clinical Services Director

The hospital's 54-bed facility in Mansfield Center, provides inpatient care for over 400 seriously emotionally disturbed children and adolescents as well as 1,000 adults in crisis each year.

5604 Northwest Village School: Wheeler Clinic

91 NW Drive
Plainville, CT   06062
                                            888-793-3500
                                       FAX 860-793-3520
                          http://www.wheelerclinic.org
                          e-mail: eap@wheelerclinic.org
David J Berkowitz, Executive Director
John Mattas, Education Services Director
Elaine Couture, Human Resources Director

The Northwest Village School is designed especially for special education students, preschool to age 21, whose social and emotional adjustment, speech and language impairments, learning problems and/or other disabilities have resulted in public school's selection of a specialized program. The Wheeler Clinic provides human services which will prevent problems and which enhance knowledge, skills and attitudes.

5605 OPTIONS

Easter Seals Rehabilitation Center
158 State Street
Meriden, CT   06450   203-237-1448
                                       FAX 203-237-9187
                              http://www.easterseals.com
Beverly Malinowski, VP

A program developed for children ages birth to three with developmental delays. Children may receive therapy, education, and/or social work services in their homes, day cares or our family classroom. Emphasis is on teaching children in natural settings to experience and develop social, communication, motor and learning skills.

5606 Rensselaer Learning Institute

275 Windsor Street
Hartford, CT   06120   860-548-2470
                                            800-306-7778
                                       FAX 860-548-7999
                                       http://www.rh.edu
                                  e-mail: rli-info@rh.edu
Rebecca M Danchak, Admissions Director

The Rensselaer Learning Institute is a department within Rensselaer at Hartford, a branch campus of the Rensselaer Polytechnic Institute. RLI offers corporate training and professional development programs in the areas of Leadership & Executive Development, Computer Information Technology, and Technical & Professional Development. RLI's vision is to deliver the best training and education solutions for working professionals anytime.

5607 Saint Francis Home for Children: Highland Heights

651 Prospect Street
New Haven, CT 06511   203-777-5513
                             FAX 203-777-0644
Peter T Solerno, Executive Director

A component of the residential treatment program which offers residential treatment, special education and day treatment programs.

5608 University School

160 Iranistan Avenue
Bridgeport, CT 06604   203-579-0434
                              FAX 203-330-9075
Nicholas Macol, Director

Located at the University of Bridgeport campus at Seaside Park, the center has access to U.B. facilities as part of its program to serve the socially/emotionally maladjusted and the learning disabled students.

5609 VISTA Vocational & Life Skills Center

1356 Old Clinton Road
Westbrook, CT 06498   860-399-8080
                             FAX 860-399-3103
                http://www.vistavocational.org
                e-mail: info@vistavocational.org
Elena Patterson, President
Helen K Bosch, Executive Director

VISTA opened its doors in 1989 to young adults with neurological disabilities who completed their secondary academic education yet require additional residential training to transition to adulthood. VISTA's central mission is to provide experiential, hands-on training in vocational and life skills.

5610 Villa Maria Education Center

161 SkyMeadow Drive
Stamford, CT 06903   203-322-5886
                            FAX 203-322-0228
             http://www.villamariaedcenter.org
             e-mail: mshogan@optonline.net
Dana Hogan, Admissions Director

Villa Maria Education Center affirms the dignity and giftedness of each person. We reach out to embrace children whose learning styles are different because they are learning disabled. We offer personalized and specialized instruction in an environment sufficiently varied for students of widely different personalities, interests and levels of learning.

5611 Vitam Center

57 W Rocks Road
Norwalk, CT 06851   203-846-2091
                           FAX 203-846-3620
Leonard Kenowtiz, Director

An adolescent treatment program offering comprehensive medical counseling, family and educational services to boys and girls who have experienced a wide range of difficulties including learning problems.

5612 Waterford Country Schools

78 Hunts Brook Road
Quaker Hill, CT 06375   860-442-9454
                               FAX 860-442-2228
              http://www.waterfordcountryschool.org
              e-mail: PHaqqlund@waterfordcs.org
David B Moorehead, Executive Director
Lynn A Morey, Executive Assistant
Anna Kemper, Residential Treatment Director

Waterford Country School is a non-profit, human services agency located on a beautiful 350 acre campus in rural Southeastern Connecticut. We are dedicated to doing whatever it takes to enrich the lives of children and strengthen families through specialized programs, resources, and community services.

5613 Wheeler Clinic

91 NW Drive
Plainville, CT 06062   860-793-3717
                              888-793-3717
                          FAX 860-793-3521
               http://www.wheelerclinic.org
               e-mail: nvs@wheelerclinic.org
David Berkowitz, Executive Director
John Mattas, Education Director

Provides special education programs for students with severe behavior and learning problems. Services include speech and language, occupational therapy, individual, group and family counseling.

5614 Wilderness School

240 N Hollow Road
East Hartland, CT 06027   860-653-8059
                                 800-273-2293
                             FAX 860-653-8120
                       http://www.state.ct.us
                  e-mail: Tom.Dyer@po.state.ct.us
Thomas Dyer, Director
David Czaja, Assistant Director

The Wilderness School is a prevention, intervention, and transition program for troubled youth from Connecticut. The school offers high impact wilderness programs intended to foster positive youth development.

5615 Yale Child Study Center

230 S Frontage Road
New Haven, CT 06520
203-785-2513
FAX 203-737-4197
http://www.info.med.yale.edu
e-mail: lori.klein@yale.edu

Lori Klein, Contact

The Yale Child Study Center is a department at Yale University School of Medicine that brings together multiple disciplines to further the understanding of the problems of children and families. The mission of the Center is to understand child development, social, behavioral, and emotional adjustment, and psychiatric disorders and to help children and families in need of care.

Delaware

5616 AdvoServ

4185 Kirkwood St. Georges Road
Bear, DE 19701
302-834-7018
800-593-4959
FAX 302-836-2516
http://www.advoserv.com
e-mail: dreardon@advoserv.com

Dennis Reardon, Contact
Fran Ryan, Contact

Private residential and educational treatment facilities for children and adults with developmental and emotional disturbances.

5617 Centreville School

6201 Kennett Pike
Wilmington, DE 19807
302-571-0230
FAX 302-571-0270
http://www.centrevilleschool.org
e-mail: information@centrevilleschool.org

Victoria Yatzus, School Head

Centreville School is motivated by two fundamental goals; to provide learning disabled children a vibrant and challenging curriculum comparable to those found at any primary or intermediate level school, and to offer each student the specialized and focused support he or she needs.

5618 Meadows Consulting

506 New Castle Street Extended
Rehoboth, DE 19971
302-227-9327
FAX 302-227-9327

Nancy P Meadows, President

Comprehensive educational services include testing, consultations and remedial, supportive, enrichment, and instructional suggestions. Pre-school through adults.

5619 Parent Information Center of Delaware

700 Barksdale Road
Newark, DE 19711
302-366-0152
888-547-4412
FAX 302-366-0276
TDY:State Relay
http://www.picofdel.org
e-mail: picofdel@picofdel.org

Marie-Anne Aghazadian, Director

Assists individuals with disabilities and special needs and those who serve them; also provides information and referral to other agencies.

5620 Pilot School

100 Garden of Eden Road
Wilmington, DE 19803
302-478-1740
FAX 302-478-1746
http://www.myschoolonline.com
e-mail: cshields@myschoolmail.com

Kathleen B Craven, Director

Pilot School provides a creative, nurturing environment for children with special learning needs. We work with each child to discover his or her unique learning strengths.

District of Columbia

5621 Developmental Services Center

Adult Day Treatment Program
6045 16th Street NW
Washington, DC 20011
202-727-1089
FAX 202-576-8799

Diagnostic and therapy for adults with a wide range of learning disabilities.

5622 Kingsbury Center

5000 14th Street NW
Washington, DC 20011
202-722-5555
FAX 202-722-5533
http://www.kingsbury.org
e-mail: center@kingsbury.org

Peter R Engebretson, COO
Cherryl Smith, Psychological Services Director

Kingsbury Center is the oldest nonprofit educational organization to address the needs of children and adults with learning disabilities and differences in the Washington, DC area.

5623 Lab School of Washington

4759 Reservoir Road NW
Washington, DC 20007
202-965-6600
FAX 202-965-5105
http://www.labschool.org

Sally L Smith, Founder/Director

The Lab School of Washington is internationally recognized for its innovative programs for children and adults with learning disabilities. The Lab School offers individualized instruction to students in kindergarten through 12 grade.

5624 Paul Robeson School for Growth and Development

3700 10th Street NW
Washington, DC 20010 202-576-5151
FAX 202-576-8804
Harriet D Crawley, Program Manager

Offers a variety of diagnostic and therapy services.

5625 Scottish Rite Center for Childhood Language Disorders

1630 Columbia Road NW
Washington, DC 20009 202-939-4703
FAX 202-939-4717
e-mail: trobinso@cnmc.org
Dr. Tommie Robinson Jr, Director

Speech and language services provided for children birth to 21 years of age. Services include: speech-language evaluations; language learning disabilities evaluations; individual and group therapy consultations; insurance training; and advocacy training. Bilingual speech-language pathologists are also available.

Florida

5626 Academic Achievement Center

313 Pruett Road
Seffner, FL 33584 813-654-4198
FAX 813-871-7468
e-mail: ALSofAAC@aol.com
Lillian M Stark PhD, Executive Administrator
Arnold L Stark PhD, Education Director

A private program for bright and gifted children with LD and/or ADD, in grades 2-12, which offers multisensory-based instruction, remediation of basic skills, academic challenge in science, social science, and literature, plus award-winning art and drama, and curriculum-enhancing field trips and travel. Maximum student body is 22 and it is coeducational. After school tutoring and phonelogical awareness training are also available.

5627 Assistive Technology Network

Orange County Public School
434 N Tampa Avenue
Orlando, FL 32804 407-317-3504
FAX 407-317-3526
http://www.ese.ocps.net
e-mail: folkst@ocps.k12fl.us
Tami Folks, Contact
Dianne Mathews, Contact

Our mission is to provide assistive technology intervention strategies, tools and training to maximize learning outcomes of students with disabilities.

5628 Barbara King's Center for Educational Services

5005 W Laurel Street
Tampa, FL 33607 813-874-3918
FAX 813-874-3575
Barbara King, Director

Educational therapy services offered.

5629 Beach Learning Center

105 S Riverside Drive
Indialantic, FL 32903 321-725-7437
Peggy Christ, Contact

Diagnostic and therapy services for the learning disabled.

5630 Brevard Learning Clinic

1900 S Harbor City Boulevard
Melbourne, FL 32901 321-676-3024
FAX 321-676-3064
e-mail: blcmelfl@hbrandon.com
Barbara Jeffers, Consultant
Mary Kellogg, Director

A full time learning clinic for evaluation and remediation featuring trained multisensory clinicians.

5631 Crossroads School

5660 N Federal Highway
Boca Raton, FL 33487 954-584-1100
Joyce Fein

Offers residential, diagnostic testing and full time and part time programs for reading or learning difficulties.

5632 Kurtz Center for Cognitive Development

1201 Louisiana Avenue
Winter Park, FL 32789 407-740-5678
FAX 407-629-6886
http://www.learningdisabilities.com
e-mail: ld-request@learningdisabilities.com
Gail Kurtz, Owner
Denton M Kurtz, Psychologist

Provides a full diagnostic testing and cognitive therapy for reading, comprehension of oral and written language, written expression and motor output for those with learning difficulties, language difficulties, processing difficulties and ADHD or ADD.

5633 Matlock Precollegiate Academy

2491 Homewood Road
West Palm Beach, FL 33416 561-687-0327
FAX 561-684-3935
http://www.matlockacademy.com
e-mail: info@matlockacademy.com
Daphne Grad, Founder

Designs its program to meet the specific needs of the students who are underachievers, seeking to fulfill their needs through a comprehensive student centered philosophy and offering a very successful educational program.

5634 McGlannan School

10770 SW 84th Street
Miami, FL   33173   305-274-2208
                                     FAX 305-274-0337
Frances McGlannan, Director
Dr. Arlene Weiss, Assistant Director

A day school for students with dyslexia 6-14 years old. Diagnostic, multidisciplinary, prescriptive, research-based and individualized to reach the whole child.

5635 Mental Health and Educational Services

5251 Emerson Street
Jacksonville, FL   32207   904-399-0324
                                     FAX 904-399-0420
                                     http://www.psydoc.com
Ruth Weinstein Klein PhD

Diagnostic and therapy services for a wide range of emotional and behavioral disabilities.

5636 Morning Star School

210 E Linebaugh Avenue
Tampa, FL   33612   813-935-0232
                                     FAX 813-932-2321
                  http://www.tampa-morningstar.org
          e-mail: jfriedheim@tampa-morningstar.org
Jeanette Friedheim, Principal
Eileen Daly, Assistant Administrator

Morning Star School is a Catholic Diocesan school dedicated to meeting the needs of students with learning disabilities and related difficulties. It is a non-graded school for children from the ages of 6 to 16. The student's self-esteem is enhanced in an atmosphere that is both challenging and nurturing.

5637 New Lifestyles

1210 Gateway Road
Lake Park, FL   33403   561-848-5537
                                     FAX 954-797-2813
                     e-mail: theoptions@aol.com

New Lifestyles provides comprehensive life management services including assessment, programming, residential placement at various locations in Palm Beach County, Florida and Winchester, Virginia. Programs focus on issues such as self-esteem, interpersonal skills and adjustments, vocational placement, independent living, time management, organizational skills, and decision-making skills.

5638 PACE: Brantley Hall School

3221 Sand Lake Road
Longwood, FL   32779   407-869-8882
                                     FAX 407-869-8717
                  http://www.pacebrantleyhall.com
                     e-mail: pabhschool@aol.com
Barbara Winter, Admissions Director
Pamela Bellet, Guidance Counselor

PACE-Brantley Hall School is an independent, non-profit Elementary - 12 grade school for children with learning differences. The PACE program has been specifically designed for students who have been diagnosed with learning disabilities, attention deficit disorder, dyslexia and similar challenges.

5639 PEAC: South

4131 Raynolds Avenue
Coconut Grove, FL   33133   305-665-1286
Susan Maynard PhD

Administers a complete Psycho-Educational Test battery to determine if clients have learning disabilities. Marriage and family therapy and therapy for individuals available.

5640 Palm Beach Gardens Prep School

10350 Riverside Drive
Palm Beach Gardens, FL   33410   561-622-0401
                                     FAX 561-622-0402
Dr. Philip T Rosen, Director

Grades 1-12 day school, coed, college preparatory curriculum, including art, physical education etc., diagnostic prescriptive methodologies, SLD mainstreamed, small classes (6-10), non-residential, founded in 1977.

5641 Progressive School

1950 Prairie Road
West Palm Beach, FL   33406   561-642-3100
                                     FAX 561-969-1950
                  http://www.progressiveschool.org
                     e-mail: Progsch@FDN.com
Jennifer Glynn, Admissions Director

A small, private, highly individualized program, K-8, for children with attention disorders, dyslexia and other academic learning problems. Day students only.

5642 Ralph J Baudhuin Oral School of Nova University

3375 SW 75th Avenue
Fort Lauderdale, FL   33314   954-262-7100
                                     FAX 954-262-3936
Debra Abolassa, Executive Director
Dr. Ronni Leiderman, Director

Preschool for autistic children.

5643 T&M Ranch

PO Box 788
Indiantown, FL   34956   561-597-2315
                                     FAX 561-599-0884
Leo Newseoin, Executive Director

Emphasis is toward the development of prevocational skills and functional daily living skills.

5644 Tampa Day School and Reading Clinic

12606 Henderson Road
Tampa, FL   33625   813-269-2100
                                     FAX 813-963-7843
                  http://www.tampadayschool.com
                     e-mail: tds@tampadayschool.com
Lois Delaney, School Head
Andrea M Mowatt, Assistant Principal
Lisa Guffey, Learning Solutions Director

At Tampa Day School we provide a learning environment that promotes that individual feeling of success for each child and to meet each child's needs. The Reading Clinic has been helping children become better readers for over 30 years. Once we have targeted the problem, and provide exactly the kind of help your child needs, the gains are immediate and long lasting.

5645 Vanguard School

22000 Highway 27
Lake Wales, FL   33859   863-676-6091
                          FAX 863-676-8297
http://www.vanguardschool.org
e-mail: vanadmin@vanguardschool.org
James R Moon PhD, President

The Vanguard School program is designed for students age 10 through high school who are experiencing academic difficulties due to learning disability such as dyslexia or dyscalculia or an attention deficit.

11-20 years old

Georgia

5646 Achievement Academy

5700 River Road
Columbus, GA   31904   706-660-0050
                          FAX 706-660-0056
e-mail: bnzysawyer@mindspring.com
Beth Sawyer, Contact

Offers diagnostic and educational services for a variety of learning disabilities.

5647 Atlanta Speech School

3160 Northside Parkway NW
Atlanta, GA   30327   404-233-5332
                          FAX 404-266-2175
http://www.atlantaspeechschool.org
Tony Aeck, Chairman

The Atlanta Speech School is one of the Southeast's oldest therapeutic educational centers for children and adults with hearing, speech, language, or learning disabilities. We help children and adults with communication disorders realize their full potential.

5648 Bedford School

5665 Milam Road
Fairburn, GA   30123   770-774-8001
                          FAX 770-774-8005
http://www.thebedfordschool.org
e-mail: bbox@thebedfordschool.org
Betsy E Box, Founder/Director

The Bedford School is a nine-month day program specifically designed to meet the needs of children with learning disabilities. We are certified through the Georgia Accrediting Commission.

5649 Brandon Hall School

1701 Brandon Hall Drive
Atlanta, GA   30350   770-394-8177
                          FAX 770-804-8821
http://www.brandonhall.org
e-mail: pstockhammer@brandonhall.org
Paul R Stockhammer, President
Steve Boyce, Admissions Director

College preparatory, co-ed day and boys' boarding school for students in grades 4-12. Designed for academic underachievers and students with minor learning disabilities, attention deficit disorders and dyslexia. Enrollment 150 students; faculty 40, with 100% college acceptances. Interscholastic sports and numerous co-curriculum activities and summer programs.

5650 Chatham Academy

Royce Learning Center
4 Oglethorpe Professional Boulevard
Savannah, GA   31406   912-354-4047
                          FAX 912-354-4633
http://www.roycelearningcenter.com
e-mail: info@roycelearningcenter.com
Carolyn Hannaford, Assistant Director/Principal
Cindy Hamilton, Assistant Principal

Chatham Academy provides a specialized curriculum and individualized instruction for students with diagnosed learning disabilities and/or attention deficit disorder. Chatham's goal is to improve students' functioning to levels commensurate with their potential in all areas so that they may return to and succeed in regular educational programs.

5651 Creative Community Services

1543 Lilburn-Stone Mountain Road
Stone Mountain, GA   30087   770-469-6226
                          866-618-2823
                          FAX 770-469-6210
http://www.ccsgeorgia.org
e-mail: info@ccsgeorgia.org
Sally Buchanan, Executive Director
Sandy Corbin, Clinical Director

Creative Community Services Inc. provides therapeutic foster care for kids and home-based support services for children and adults with mental retardation and developmental disabilities.

5652 Horizons School

1900 DeKalb Avenue NE
Atlanta, GA   30307   404-378-2219
                          800-822-6242
                          FAX 404-378-8946
http://www.horizonsschool.homestead.com
e-mail: HorizonsSchool@mindspring.com
Les Garber, Principal

The intent is to develop in students those values and skills which assure maximum opportunities. Students learn real-life skills through active participation in the classroom, as well as in other aspects of the school. They learn responsibility, decision-making, and problem-solving skills through active involvement in the management of the community. Such a leadership role empowers students, giving them the knowledge that they have control of personal decisions and interpersonal interactions.

5653 Howard School Central Campus

1246 Ponce De Leon Avenue NE
Atlanta, GA   30306   404-377-7436
                            FAX 404-377-0884
http://www.howardschool.org
e-mail: KerenS@HowardSchool.org
Sandra N Kleinman, Executive Director
Keren Schuller, Admissions Director

At Howard School we believe that every child should
have the opportunity to succeed. We serve students
whose personal learning style may not be comple-
mented in traditional teaching and learning environments, compromising the student's ability to reach his
or her full potential.

5654 Howard School North Campus

9415 Willeo Road
Roswell, GA   30075   707-642-9644
                            FAX 707-998-1398
http://www.howardschool.org
e-mail: KerenS@howardschool.org
Dr. Sandra Kleinman, Executive Director
Keren Schuller, Admissions Director

At the Howard School we understand that every child
can learn. We believe that every child should have the
opportunity to succeed. Our mission is to successfully
teach each student in the unique way that student
learns.

5655 Mill Springs Academy

Special Education Systems
6955 Brandon Mill Road NW
Atlanta, GA   30328   404-255-5951
                            FAX 404-255-5938
Tweetie L Moore, Executive Director
Robert Moore, Administrator

A small, structured, accredited day school combining
learning disability teaching techniques within the
therapeutic milieu. Integral components include supportive services for parents and consistent communication with other professionals working with our
students. The K-12 program includes an after school
program for younger students and an athletic program
for older students. Mark Trail Camp is a 7 week summer program for K-7th grades which includes academics and camp activities.

5656 New School

6955 Brandon Mill Road NW
Atlanta, GA   30328   404-255-5951
Tweetie Moore

5657 Reading Success

4434 Columbia Road
Martinez, GA   30907   706-863-8173
                            FAX 706-863-4523
http://www.readingsuccess.com
e-mail: tutorme@readingsuccess.com
Sandra Mashburn, Founder/Director

Reading Success, Inc. is a locally owned and operated
program, serving the CSRA for over 30 years and providing professional help to students with all kinds of
learning problems. Our guarantee is; if one year of improvement has not been made in the 48 lessons, the
student receives instruction free of charge for 18 lessons.

**5658 Wardlaw School: A Division of the Atlanta Speech
School**

3160 Northside Parkway NW
Atlanta, GA   30327   404-233-5332
                            FAX 404-266-2175
http://www.atlantaspeechschool.org/wardlaw
Tony Aeck, Chairman

The mission of the Wardlaw School is to help children
with average to very superior intelligence and mild to
moderate learning disabilities learn how to become
self-confident, independent learners. Placement at the
school is intended to be short term; however, ongoing
support for the child and his/her family is available
throughout the child's educational experience.

Hawaii

5659 Center on Disability Studies

University of Hawaii Manoa
1776 University Avenue
Honolulu, HI   96822   808-956-9142
                            FAX 808-956-5713
http://www.cds.hawaii.edu
e-mail: Robert.Stodden@cds.hawaii.edu
Robert Stodden PhD, Executive Director
Tom Conway, Media Coordinator

The Center for Disability Studies is a Hawaii University Affiliated Program at the University of Hawaii at
Manoa. The mission of the CDS is to support the quality of life, community inclusion, and self-determination of all persons with disabilities and their families.

5660 Hawaii Parents Unlimited

200 N Vineyard Boulevard
Honolulu, HI   96817   808-536-2280
                            800-533-9684
                            FAX 808-537-6780
e-mail: ldah@gte.net
Jennifer Schember-Lang, Project Director

Parent Training and Information Program views parents as full partners in the educational process and a
significant source of support and assistance to each
other. Funded by the Division of Personnel Preparation, Office of Special Education Programs, these programs provide training and information to parents to
enable such individuals to participate more effectively with professionals in meeting the educational
needs of disabled children.

5661 Variety School of Hawaii

710 Palekaua Street
Honolulu, HI   96816   808-732-2835
                            FAX 808-737-4334
e-mail: yeevariety@inets.com
Dr. Alexi K Dankeith, Executive Director

The mission of Variety School of Hawaii is to educate children with learning disabilities, attention deficit disorder, and/or autism, and to assist these children in achieving their maximum potential through a multidisciplinary approach. To this end, the school offers children ages five through thirteen a wide variety of programs and experiences in a warm, nurturing, intimate environment that truly makes a difference in their lives - and in their families' lives as well.

5-13 years old

Idaho

5662 Idaho Parents Unlimited

600 N Curtis Road
Boise, ID   83706
208-342-5884
800-242-4785
FAX 208-342-1408
http://www.ipulidaho.org
e-mail: ipui@rmci.net
Evelyn Mason, Executive Director
Phyllis Mienhardt, Program Director

Idaho Parents Unlimited (IPUL) is a statewide organization founded to provide support, information and technical assistance to parents of children and youth with disabilities.

Illinois

5663 Achievement Centers

6425 Willow Springs Road
La Grange Highlands, IL   60525   708-579-9040
FAX 708-579-5872
http://www.acaciaacademy.com
e-mail: kfouks@acaciaacademy.com
Kathie Fouks, Principal/Director
Eileen Bybee, Dean of Students

A Tradition of Nurturing Minds, Enriching Lives, and Building Self-Esteem. Offering a variety of year-round and summer programs designed to meet each student's learning objectives in terms of his/her learning capacities.

Ages 5-Adult

5664 Allendale Association

PO Box 1088
Lake Villa, IL   60046
847-356-2351
888-255-3631
FAX 847-356-0289
http://www.allendale4kids.org
e-mail: Development@allendale4kids.org
Mary Shahbazian, President

The Allendale Association is a private, not-for-profit organization dedicated to excellence and innovation in the care, education, treatment and advocacy for troubled children, youth and their families.

5665 Att-P'tach Special Education Program

2828 W Pratt Avenue
Chicago, IL   60645
773-973-2828
FAX 773-973-6666
e-mail: mantanky@att.org
Rabbi Harvey Well, Superintendent

Offers mainstreaming, independent skills, therapeutic swim classes and psychological services.

5666 Brehm Preparatory School

1245 E Grand Avenue
Carbondale, IL   62901
618-457-0371
FAX 618-529-1248
http://www.brehm.org
e-mail: brehm1@brehm.org
Richard G Collins PhD, Executive Director
Brian P Brown, Associate Executive Director

Brehm Preparatory School is a not-for-profit corporation, with a mission to empower students with complex learning disabilities to recognize and optimize their full potential.

5667 Camelot Care Center: Illinois

1502 N NW Highway
Palatine, IL   60067
847-359-5600
FAX 847-359-2759
Katherine Lau, Principal

A psychiatric residential treatment center using a developmentally based treatment model called Process Therapy.

5668 Catholic Children's Home

Special Education School
1400 State Street
Alton, IL   62002
618-465-3594
FAX 618-465-1083
http://www.altoncch.org
e-mail: cch1400@ezl.com
Steven Roach, Executive Director
Laura Ballard, Educational Director

The Catholic Children's Home is sponsored and primarily supported by the Catholic Diocese in Springfield, Illinois, and serves to promote and care for the needs, education and welfare of dependent, neglected or otherwise needy children and youths who need structured care away from their own homes.

5669 Center for Learning

National Louis University
2840 Sheridan Road
Evanston, IL   60201
847-256-5150
FAX 847-256-6542
http://www.nl.edu
e-mail: kadamle@nc.edu
Kim Adamle, Director

Offers psychological, educational and neuro psychological evaluations, testing of gifted children and remedial tutoring for children with learning disabilities.

5670 Center for Speech and Language Disorders

195 Spangler
Elmhurst, IL   60126   630-530-8551
                                    FAX 613-530-5909
                                    http://www.csld.com
                                    e-mail: info@csld.org
Mary Brady, Operations Manager
Phyllis Kupperman, Founder
Christina R Rees, Co-Clinical Manager

Our mission is to help children with speech and language disorders reach their full potential. CSLD is an internationally recognized leader in the diagnosis and treatment of hyperlexia and other language disorders.

5671 Chicago Urban Day School

1248 W 69th Street
Chicago, IL   60636   773-483-3555
                                    FAX 773-483-9758
Georgia Jordan, Executive Director

5672 Children's Center for Behavioral Development

353 N 88th Street
East Saint Louis, IL   62203   618-398-1152
                                    FAX 618-398-6977
                                    e-mail: ccbd@mvp.net
Carolyn Birth, Executive Director

A special education program for children and adolescents with emotional disturbances, behavioral disorders and learning disabilities.

5673 Cove School

350 Lee Road
Northbrook, IL   60062   847-562-2100
                                    FAX 847-562-2112
                                    http://www.covefamily.com
                                    e-mail: pjackson@coveschool.org
Phillip Jackson, Executive Director
Carol Sward, Principal
Mark Wall, Dean of Students

The Cove School was established in 1947, to educate students with learning disabilities and to facilitate their return to their neighborhood schools in the shortest possible time. The heart of Cove's educational philosophy is to design a program that pulls out the child's skills.

5674 Early Achievement Center Preschool & Kindergarten

6425 Willow Springs Road
La Grange Highlands, IL   60525   708-579-9040
                                    FAX 708-579-5872
                                    http://www.acaciaacademy.com
                                    e-mail: info@acaciaacademy.com
Kathie Fouks, Principal/Director
Eileen Bybee, Dean of Students

The Early Achievement Center Program encourages growth of the total child in social, intellectual, physical, and emotional abilities.

Ages 2-6

5675 Educational Services of Glen Ellyn

444 N Main Street
Glen Ellyn, IL   60137   630-469-1479
                                    FAX 630-469-1479
                      e-mail: educationalservices@juno.com
Beth Sievens, Owner

Tutoring for all ages in all subject areas. Diagnostic testing, specializing in learning disabilities and career counseling for learning disabled adults.

5676 Elim Christian Services

13020 S Central Avenue
Palos Heights, IL   60463   708-389-0555
                                    FAX 708-389-2488
                                    http://www.elimcs.org
                                    e-mail: info@elimcs.org
Bill Lodewyk, President/Executive Director

Elim Christian Services is a non-profit corporation that seeks to equip persons with special needs to achieve to their highest God-given potential.

5677 Esperanza School

520 N Marshfield Avenue
Chicago, IL   60622   312-243-6097
                                    FAX 312-243-2076
                      http://www.esperanzaservices.org
Barbara Belletini Fields, Executive Director

Self-help educational services offered to children who are autistic or mentally disabled.

5678 Family Resource Center on Disabilities

20 E Jackson Boulevard
Chicago, IL   60604   312-939-3513
                                      800-952-4199
                                    FAX 312-939-7297
                                    TDY:312-939-3519
                                    http://www.frcd.org
                                    e-mail: info@frcd.org
Charlotte Des Jardins, Director

The Family Resource Center on Disabilities was formerly known as the Coordinating Council for Handicapped Children. FRCD was organized in 1969 by parents, professionals, and volunteers who sought to improve services for all children with disabilities.

5679 Greenrose Elementary School

5244 N Lakewood Avenue
Chicago, IL   60640   773-728-5959
Fran Rothman, Social Worker

Offers a therapeutic primary school focusing on social/emotional growth with therapy, counseling and groups for parents.

5680 Hammit School: The Baby Fold

108 E Willow Street
Normal, IL   61761   309-452-1170
                           FAX 309-452-0115
                  http://www.thebabyfold.org
                  e-mail: info@thebabyfold.org
Diane Schultz, Executive Director

The Baby Fold is a multi-service agency that provides Residential, Special Education, Child Welfare, and Family Support Services to children and families in central Illinois.

5681 Hope School

50 Hazel Lane
Springfield, IL   62716   217-585-5437
                           FAX 217-786-3356
                           TDY:217-529-5766
                  http://www.thehopeschool.org
                  e-mail: info@thehopeschool.org
Beth McQuade, Day Education Contact
Stephanie Bingman, Residential Contact

The Hope School is a private, not-for-profit educational and residential center, that has been serving children with multiple disabilities and their families since 1957.

5682 Illinois Center for Autism

548 S Ruby Lane
Fairview Heights, IL   62208   618-398-7500
                           FAX 618-394-9869
                http://www.illinoiscenterforautism.org
Carol Madison, Executive Director

A not-for-profit, community based, mental health treatment, and educational agency dedicated to serving people with autism. Referrals for possible student placement are made through local school districts, hospitals, regional special education centers, and doctors.

5683 Joseph Academy

7530 N Natchez
Niles, IL   60714   847-588-2990
                  http://www.josephacademy.org
                  e-mail: INFORMATION@JosephAcademy.org
Michael Schack, Executive Director
Heather Elliott, Principal

Founded in 1983, Joseph Academy provides a nurturing and challenging environment for young people. Our mission is to serve children and adolescents with behavioral, emotional and learning disorders by helping them develop the social, academic and vocational skills they need to function in society.

5684 LEARN Center

Illinois Masonic Medical Center
836 W Nelson Street
Chicago, IL   60657   773-296-7065
                           FAX 773-296-5885
                  http://www.iser.com/LEARN.html
Bethany Graham

5685 La Grange Area Department of Special Education

1301 W Cossitt Avenue
La Grange, IL   60525   708-354-5730
                           FAX 708-354-0733
                  http://www.ladse.org
                  e-mail: JimSurber@ladse.org
Dr. James M Surber, Executive Director
Lois Miller, Executive Assistant Director

Offers programs for students with moderate to severe mental retardation, learning disabilities or behavior disorders.

5686 Professional Assistance Center for Education (PACE)

National-Louis University
2840 Sheridan Road
Evanston, IL   60201   847-256-5150
                           800-443-5522
                           FAX 847-256-5190
            http://www.3.nl.edu/academics/nce/programs/pace
                  e-mail: cburns@nl.edu
Carol J Burns, Director

Founded in 1986 PACE is a two-year noncredit postsecondary certificate program located on the campus of National-Louis University. The PACE program is designed especially to meet the transitional needs of students with multiple learning disabilities in a university setting.

5687 South Central Community Services

8316 S Ellis Avenue
Chicago, IL   60619   773-483-0900
                           FAX 773-483-5701
                  http://www.sccsinc.org
Felicia Blasingame, President/CEO
Rosemary S Bowmen, Executive Director

South Central Community Services, Inc. is a grassroots, not-for-profit organization established in 1970 by a group of community residents concerned about the absence of human service facilities and programs in the community.

5688 St. Joseph's Carondelet Child Center

739 E 35th Street
Chicago, IL   60616   773-624-7443
                           FAX 773-624-7676
                  http://www.stjccc.org
                  e-mail: jwhite@stjccc.org

St. Joseph's Carondelet Child Center is a residential, day and outpatient treatment center for 180 boys and girls (ages 6-21) who are orphaned by neglect, substance abuse, physical and sexual abuse, violence and despair. In 1989 we opened a second program facility (Solace Place in Englewood community), extending its service to older boys and girls (ages 14-21) deemed to be at high risk for delinquency.

5689 **Summit School**

611 E Main Street
Dundee, IL 60118 847-428-6451
FAX 847-428-6419
http://www.summitdundee.org
e-mail: scarl@summitdundee.org
Sharon Carl, Principal
George Phelan, President

Summit School is a private, non-profit organization dedicated to fulfilling the needs of children with learning problems that prevent them from achieving in a standard classroom situation.

6-21 years old

Indiana

5690 **Educational Enrichment Center**

1450 Bellemeade Avenue
Evansville, IN 47714 812-473-0651
FAX 812-471-1145
Janet Dill, Coordinator

The center provides the following services: educational assessment; personal development; tutoring; psychological testing and therapy; neuropsychological evaluation; and cognitive therapy. The center offers tutors who are qualified teachers with a broad area of training including Orton-Gillingham multisensory techniques. Many services for head injured individuals with Halstead-Reitan Neuropsychological evaluation and comprehensive cognitive retraining are available.

5691 **IN*SOURCE**

809 N Michigan Street
South Bend, IN 46601 219-234-7101
800-332-4433
FAX 219-234-7279
http://www.insource.org
e-mail: insource@insource.org
Richard Burden, Executive Director
Scott Carson, Assistant Director

The mission of IN*SOURCE is to provide parents, families and service providers in Indiana the information and training necessary to assure effective educational programs and appropriate services for children and young adults with disabilities.

5692 **The Clearinghouse on Reading, English andCommunications**

Indiana University of Bloomington
107 S Indiana Avenue
Bloomington, IN 47405 812-855-5847
FAX 812-856-5512
http://www.reading.indiana.edu
e-mail: iuadmit@indiana.edu
Stephen Stroup, Associate Director
Kenneth Gros Louis, Chancellor

Offers information on reading, English and communication skills, preschool through college.

Iowa

5693 **Iowa Compass**

Center for Disabilities and Development
100 Hawkins Drive
Iowa City, IA 52242 319-353-8777
800-779-2001
http://www.medicine.uiowa.edu
e-mail: iowa-compass@uiowa.edu
Jane Gay, Director
Amy Mikelson, Outreach/Training Coordinator

A free information and referral service on assistive technology, product information, the used equipment referral service, funding options, and referral to free legal advocacy. Also publishes a newsletter.

Kansas

5694 **Families Together**

502 Jackson
Topeka, KS 66603 785-233-4777
800-264-6343
FAX 785-233-4787
http://www.familiestogetherinc.org
e-mail: topeka@familiestogetherinc.org
Lesli Girard, Center Coordinator
Karen Snell, Regional Center Coordinator

Families Together is a statewide non-profit organization assisting Kansas families which include sons and/or daughters who have any form of disability.

5695 **Heartspring School**

8700 E 29th Street N
Wichita, KS 67226 316-634-8700
800-835-1043
FAX 316-634-0555
http://www.heartspring.org
e-mail: ccarpenter@heartspring.org
Cara Rapp, Admissions Director

Heartspring School has earned an international reputation for improving the lives of children. Heartspring is a not-for-profit private residential school that serves children 5-21. We serve children with disabilities such as autism, asperger's, communication disorders, developmental disabilities, dual diagnosed, behavoir disorders, hearing or vision impaired.

5696 **Menninger Center for Learning Disabilities**

Menninger Clinic
PO Box 829
Topeka, KS 66601 785-350-5000
800-351-9058
FAX 785-232-6524
Michele Berg PhD, Director

The Center offers the following services for children and adults: 1) educational evaluations for learning disabilities, dyslexia, learning problems and other special needs 2) gifted evaluations 3) workshops for parents and educators 4) reading assessments 5) training for teachers in multisensory remedial approaches and 6) group and individual tutoring.

Kentucky

5697 De Paul School
1925 Duker Avenue
Louisville, KY 40205   502-459-6131
                                    FAX 502-458-0827
http://www.depaulschool.org
e-mail: dpinfo@depaulschool.org
Peggy S Woolley, Admissions Director
Anthony R Kemper, School Head

Teachs students with dyslexia and other specific learning differences how to learn. Grades 1-8.

5698 KY-SPIN
10301-B Deering Road
Louisville, KY 40272   502-937-6894
                                    800-525-7746
                                    FAX 502-937-6464
http://www.kyspin.com
e-mail: spininc@aol.com
Paulette Olgsdon, Director

Parent Training and Information Project views parents as full partners in the educational process and a significant source of support and assistance to each other. Funded by the Division of Personnel Preparation, Office of Special Education Programs, these programs provide training and information and support to parents and families of children of all ages with all types of disabilities. We empower parents to recognize and use all available resources.

5699 Meredith-Dunn School
3023 Melbourne Avenue
Louisville, KY 40220   502-456-5819
                                    FAX 502-456-5953
http://www.meredith-dunn-school.org
e-mail: mdschool@bellsouth.net
Cindy Bunnell, Admissions Director
Kathy Beam, Principal

The Meredith-Dunn School was founded in 1971 as a non-profit institution to provide educational assistance for children with learning difficulties. We admit only children of average to above average IQ who possess learning difficulties, whether or not these difficulties are recognized as such by federal or public definition.

5700 Shedd Academy
401 S 7th Street
Mayfield, KY 42066   207-247-8007
                                    FAX 270-247-0637
http://www.sheddacademy.org
e-mail: paulthompson@sheddacademy.org
Dr. Paul Thompson, Executive Director
Debbie Craven, Admissions Office

The mission of the Shedd Academy is to prepare dyslexia and ADD students for college or vocational training and for their future by helping them to understand their unique learning styles; fulfill their intellectual, academic, physical, artistic, creative, social, spiritual, and emotional potential; develop a sense of self responsibility; assume a value system so that they can become contributing members of society and increase their skills to ensure they are armed with a variety of abilities.

Louisiana

5701 Crescent Academy
821 General Pershing Street
New Orleans, LA 70115   504-895-3952
                                    FAX 504-895-3964
Barbara Leggett

Offers a variety of services to students with disabilities including note takers, extended testing time, counseling services, and special accommodations.

5702 Project PROMPT
Families Helping Families
4323 Division Street
Metairie, LA 70002   504-888-9111
                                    800-766-7736
                                    FAX 504-888-0246
http://www.projectprompt.com
e-mail: info@projectprompt.com
Cindy Arceneaux, Project Director
Mary Jacob, Project Coordinator

Parent Training and Information Program views parents as full partners in the educational process and a significant source of support and assistance to each other. Funded by the Division of Personnel Preparation, Office of Special Education Programs, these programs provide training and information to parents to enable such individuals to participate more effectively with professionals in meeting the educational needs of disabled children.

5703 Reading Research Foundation
PO Box 30185
Lafayette, LA 70593   337-984-7485
                                    FAX 337-983-7483
Sylvia Olinde

Nonprofit organization. School for learning disabled children 1st-8th grade, full-time, board certified. Summer school also available.

Maryland

5704 Academic Resource Center at the Gunston Day School
PO Box 200
Centreville, MD 21617   410-758-0620
                                    FAX 410-758-0628
http://www.gunstondayschool.org
Kathleen White, Director

Provides tutoring for individuals K through adult. Also offers limited and brief educational testing.

5705   Behavioral Directions

7945 MacArthur Boulevard
Cabin John, MD   20818   703-855-4032
                                FAX 571-333-0292
                http://www.BehavioralDirections.com
                                            e-mail:
        behavioraldirections@smartneighborhood.net
Jane Barbin PhD, Contact

Specializing in services to individuals (children and adults) with autism and developmental disabilities and their families. Services are provided by licensed psychologists utilizing Applied Behavior Analysis (ABA) as the treatment approach. Services, including behavioral assessment, functional analysis, educational assessment, parent/staff training, and program evaluation, are provided in home, school, and community settings.

5706   Chelsea School

711 Pershing Drive
Silver Spring, MD   20910   301-585-1430
                                  FAX 301-585-9621
                http://www.chelseaschool.edu
                e-mail: dfrengel@chelseaschool.edu
Dave Frengel, Admissions Director
Timothy E Hall, President

At Chelsea School, we shatter the stigma of learning disabilities and prepare our students for a lifetime of intellectual exploration, personal growth and social responsibility. Because our students have language-based learning disabilities, we strongly focus on teaching reading and language arts.

5707   Children's Developmental Clinic

Prince George's Community College
301 Largo Road
Largo, MD   20774   301-322-0151
                                  FAX 301-322-0519
                                  TDY:301-322-0122
                                  http://www.pgcc.edu
Dr. Paul H Hahn, Director
Kathy Hinkel, Coordinator

The Children's Development Clinic is a continuing education program conducted in cooperation with the Department of Health and Human Performance at Prince George's Community College. The clinic provides special services to children, birth and up, who are experiencing various development difficulties such as learning problems, developmental delays, physical fitness and coordination problems, brain injury, mental retardation, emotional problems, or orthopedic challenges.

5708   Developmental School Foundation

Broschart School
14901 Broschart Road
Rockville, MD   20850   301-251-4624
Mary Jane Kennelly, Executive Director

Provides a therapeutic day setting with a full school program that addresses the children's social/emotional and learning needs.

5709   Edgemeade: Raymond A Rogers Jr School

13101 Croom Road
Upper Marlboro, MD   20772   301-888-1333
                                  800-486-3343
                                  FAX 301-579-2342
                http://www.gildlearningdisable.org
Cindy J Spiller, Contact

Edgemeade provides residential and day treatment services with a special education school program for kids with disabilities. The facility is licensed by the DHMH and accredited by JCAHO, and the education program is accredited by the MSDE. The therapeutic environment is structured to provide supervision and direction and an opportunity for each child to express himself.

5710   Forbush School

Sheppard and Enoch Pratt Hospital
6501 N Charles Street
Towson, MD   21285   410-938-4400
                                  FAX 410-938-4421
                http://www.sheppardpratt.org
                e-mail: blohnes@sheppardpratt.org
Burt Lohnes PhD, Program Director

Pre-school to high school, offers programs for the emotionally disturbed and learning disabled.

5711   Frost Center

4915 Aspen Hill Road
Rockville, MD   20853   301-933-3451
                                  FAX 301-933-3330
                http://www.frostcenter.com
                e-mail: chobbes@frostcenter.com
Carol Hobbes, Admissions Contact

The Frost school established in 1976, is a school and therapeutic day program that serves emotionally troubled adolescents and their families. Our 12 month school program serves students from ages 7 to 21 who need a supportive and structured environment.

5-20 years old

5712   Group for the Independent Learning Disabled (GILD)

PO Box 322
Brooklandville, MD   21022   410-363-4300
                                  FAX 410-363-7919
                http://www.gildlearningdisable.org
Leith Herrmann, President
Harriet Wolf, Membership Chair

The Group for the Independent Learning Disabled provides support services for adults 18 years and older with a learning disability.

5713 Hannah More School

12039 Reistertown Road
Reistertown, MD 21136 410-526-5000
FAX 410-526-7631
http://www.HannahMore.org
e-mail: hmsinfo@hannahmore.org
Carolyn Martin, Admissions Director

Educates emotionally disabled students and children with a pervasive development disorder and provides therapeutic services so that the student may develop responsible patterns of behavior. A psychoeducational approach consisting of a comprehensive combination of academic subjects, a technology program, counseling programs and a behavioral management systems is designed to meet the individual needs of each student.

5714 Kennedy Krieger Institute for Handicapped Children

University Affiliated Program
707 N Broadway
Baltimore, MD 21205 443-923-9200
800-873-3377
FAX 443-923-9405
http://www.kennedykrieger.org
Gary Goldstien, President/CEO

The Kennedy Krieger Institute is an internationally recognized facility dedicated to improving the lives of children and adolescents with pediatric developmental disabilities through patient care, special education, research and professional training.

5715 Parents' Place of Maryland

7484 Candlewood Road
Hanover, MD 21076 410-859-5300
FAX 410-859-5301
http://www.ppmd.org
e-mail: info@ppmd.org
Suzie Shannon, Director

We are here to serve the parents of children with disabilities throughout Maryland, regardless of the nature of their child's disability or the age of their child.

5716 Phillips School: Programs for Children andFamilies

8920 Whiskey Bottom Road
Laurel, MD 20723 301-470-1620
FAX 301-470-1624
http://www.phillipsprograms.org
e-mail: Gary.Behrens@phillipsprograms.org
Sally A Sibley, President/CEO
Gavin Behrens, Program Director

Phillips is a non-profit, private organization serving the needs of individuals with emotional and behavioral problems and their families through education, family support services, community education and advocacy.

5717 Sensory Integration & Vision Therapy Specialists

Vision Help Network
6509 Democracy Boulevard
Bethesda, MD 20817 301-897-8484
FAX 301-897-8486
http://www.visionhelp.com/clinics/appel.htm
e-mail: info@visionhelp.com
Dr. S Appelbaum, Owner
Barbara Bassin, Occupational Therapist

Dr. Appelbaum's practice, established in 1977, offers a full range of family vision care and eye services, specializing in the treatment of children and adults with behavioral, sensorimotor or learning-related vision problems such as those previously diagnosed with add-adhd, dyslexia, acquired brain injury, stroke, learning disabilities, and/or avoidance of reading.

5718 Sensory Integration & Vision Therapy Specialists

Georgetown Plaza Bridges Learning Center
914 Bay Ridge Road
Annapolis, MD 21403 301-897-8484
FAX 301-897-8486
http://www.visionhelp.com
e-mail: Drstrab@erols.com
Dr. S Appelbaum, Owner
Barbara Bassin, Occupational Therapist

Dr. Appelbaum's practice, established in 1977, offers a full range of family vision care services, specializing in the treatment of children and adults with behavioral, sensorimotor or learning-related vision problems such as those previously diagnosed and-adhd, dyslexia, and/or avoidance reading.

5719 The Nora School

955 Sligo Avenue
Silver Spring, MD 20910 301-495-6672
FAX 301-495-7829
http://www.nora-school.org
e-mail: dave@nora-school.org
David E Mullen, Headmaster
Elaine Mack, Admissions Director

A small, progressive, college preparatory high school that nurtures and empowers bright students who have been frustrated in larger, more traditional school settings.

Massachusetts

5720 Adult Center at PAL: Curry College

1071 Blue Hill Avenue
Milton, MA 02186 617-333-0500
FAX 617-333-2114
http://www.curry.edu/pal
e-mail: pal@curry.edu
Jane Utley Adelizzi PhD, Contact

The Adult Center at PAL (Program for Advancement of Learning) is the first program to offer academic and socio-emotional services to adults with LD/ADHD/Dyslexia in a college setting in the New England area. The ACD offers one-to-one academic tutorials; small support groups that meet weekly; and Saturday Seminars that explore issues that impact the lives of adults with LD/ADHD.

5721 Berkshire Meadow

249 N Plain Road
Housatonic, MA   01236   413-528-2523
                                    FAX 413-528-0293
                  http://www.berkshiremeadows.org
                  e-mail: berkshiremeadows@jri.org
Gail Charpentier, Executive Director

Residential school for children and adolescents who have severe developmental disabilities.

5722 Brightside for Families and Children

2112 Riverdale Street
West Springfield, MA   01089   413-788-7366
                                     800-660-4673
                                FAX 413-747-0182
                       http://www.mercycares.com
Lara Davis-Allen, Educational Administrator

Brightside for Families and Children is a non-profit, social service organization dedicated to strengthening, supporting and preserving all children and families. Brightside is especially focused on those children and families in Western Massachusetts who are most vulnerable and disavantaged regardless of race, creed or color.

5723 College Internship Program at the Berkshire Center

18 Park Street
Lee, MA   01238   413-243-2576
                                 FAX 413-243-3351
                    http://www.berkshirecenter.org
Dr. Michael McManmon, Director
Gary Shaw, Admissions Director

A post secondary program for young adults with learning disabilities, ages 18-26. Half of the students attend Berkshire Community College and business school while the others may go directly into the world of work. Services include vocational/academic preparation, tutoring, college liaison, life skills instruction, driver's education, money management, psychotherapy and more.

5724 Commonwealth Learning Center

123 Highland Avenue
Needham, MA   02094   781-444-5193
                                     800-461-6671
                                FAX 781-444-6916
                        http://www.commlearn.com
                     e-mail: info@commlearn.com
Lisa Brooks, Director

Nonprofit learning center offering one-to-one tutorial for kindergarten through adult students. Programs in reading, spelling, writing, comprehension, math, study skills. Teacher training in multisensory methodologies. Educational evaluations available. Also centers in Danvers, MA and Sudbury, MA.

5725 Cotting School

453 Concord Avenue
Lexington, MA   02173   617-862-7323
                                 FAX 617-861-1179
                         http://www.cotting.org.
                   e-mail: dnewark@cotting.org
Janine Brown-Smith, Admissions Director

A chapter 766 approved day school in Lexington, MA for boys & girls ages 3-22 with physical, communication and other challenges to learning.

6-21 years old

5726 Devereux Massachusetts

60 Miles Road
Rutland, MA   01543   508-886-4746
                                 FAX 508-886-4773
                         http://www.devereux.org
                  e-mail: ddaunais@devereux.org
Donna Daunais, Chief Administrative Officer

A residential program for children, adolescents and young adults who have emotional and behavioral disorders with developmental and learning disabilities.

6-21 years old

5727 Doctor Franklin Perkins School

971 Main Street
Lancaster, MA   01523   978-365-7376
                                 FAX 978-368-8861
                      http://www.perkinschool.org
               e-mail: blossom@perkinschool.org
Michelle Brady, Admissions Director
Sharon Lowry, Day School Program Director

The Doctor Franklin Perkins School is a comprehensive human service agency operating at several sites in the Central Massachusetts towns of Lancaster and Clinton. Perkins provides a variety of services to several specialized populations of children, adolescents, adults and senior citizens.

5728 Evergreen Center

345 Fortune Boulevard
Milford, MA   01757   508-478-5597
                                 FAX 508-634-3251
                       http://www.evergreenctr.org
                e-mail: services@evergreenctr.org
Robert F Littleton Jr, Executive Director

The Evergreen Center is a residential school serving children and adolescents with severe developmental disabilities.

5729   Frederic L Chamberlain School

1 Pleasant Street
Middleboro, MA   02346   508-947-7825
                                FAX 508-947-0944
        http://www.chamberlainschool.org
        e-mail: admissions@chamberlainschool.org
William Doherty, Executive Director
Lawrence Mutty, Admissions Director

The Frederic L Chamberlain School is more than a
small New England boarding school. Chamberlain is a
community of adolescents who have experienced significant diffulties at home, in the community and/or in
traditional schools.

5730   Getting Ready for the Outside World

Riverview School
551 Route 6A
East Sandwich, MA   02537   508-888-0489
                                 FAX 508-888-1315
        http://www.riverviewschool.org
        e-mail: jmiddleton@riverviewschool.org
James W Middleton, Assistant School Head
*Diana Ellis Sorrento, Development Program Direc-
tor*

The GROW Program (Getting Ready for the Outside
World) is a unique 10 month transitional program (1-3
years) for students who have graduated from
Riverview (or a similar program), designed to provide
students with the skills that will assist them in functioning more independently within the adult world.

5731   Landmark Preparatory Program

Landmark School
429 Hale Street
Prides Crossing, MA   01965   978-236-3010
                                 FAX 978-927-7268
        http://www.landmarkschool.org
        e-mail: jtruslow@landmarkschool.org
Carolyn J Orsini, Admissions Director
Robert Broudo, Headmaster

Offers a secondary school level curriculum emphasizing organizational and study skills development in a
traditional classroom setting, and is designed for college bound boys and girls who have progressed to
within one year of expected grade level performance.

5732   Landmark School and Summer Programs

429 Hale Street
Prides Crossing, MA   01965   978-236-3010
                                 FAX 978-927-7268
        http://www.landmarkschool.org
        e-mail: jtruslow@landmarkschool.org
Carolyn J Orsini, Admissions Director
Robert Broudo, Headmaster

Landmark is a coeducational, residential, and day
school for emotionally stable students who have been
diagnosed with a language-based learning disability.
We individualize instruction for each of our students,
providing an appropriate program emphasizing the
development of language and learning skills within a
highly structured learning environment. We also offer
an intensive six-week summer program for students
who wish to explore the beneficial effects of
short-term remediation.

5733   League School of Greater Boston

300 Boston Providence Turnpike
Walpole, MA   02032   508-850-3900
                                 FAX 617-964-3264
        http://www.leagueschool.com
Dr. Herman T Fishbein, Executive Director
Jana M Feeley, Admissions Director

To provide social, academic, and vocational programs
for children with Autism/Asperger Spectrum Disorders who need a specialized alternative to public
school, preparing them to transfer into an environment offering greater independence.

5734   Learning Center of Massachusetts

411 Waverley Oaks Road
Waltham, MA   02452   781-893-6000
                                 FAX 781-893-1171
        http://www.protestantguild.org
        e-mail: admissions@protestantguild.org
Ed Hagerty, Director

The Learning Center is an educational program of the
Protestant Guild for Human Services, Inc. The 365
community-based school is for students with mental
retardation, autism and other developmental disabilities.

5735   Linden Hill School

154 S Mountain Road
Northfield, MA   01360   413-498-2906
                                 FAX 413-498-2908
        http://www.lindenhs.org
        e-mail: office@lindenhs.org
Michael P Hollard, Headmaster

The Linden Hill School enrolls bright, inquisitive,
boys who have language based disorders and/or dyslexia.

9-16 years old

5736   Living Independently Forever (LIFE)

550 Lincoln Road Extention
Hyannis, MA   02601   508-790-3600
                                 FAX 508-778-4919
        http://www.lifecapcod.org
        e-mail: groupmashpee@lifecapcod.org
Mary Ann Matthews, President

Living Independently Forever, Inc. is dedicated to
serving the life-long needs of adults with significant
learning disabilities within our residential communities. LIFE is committed to providing these men and
women with the adult education and the opportunities
to develop their personal and vocational / occupational skills to their maximum potential, and to supporting them appropriately in independent and group
living.

5737 May Institute

One Commerce Way
Norwood, MA 02062 781-440-0400
800-778-7601
http://www.mayinstitute.org
e-mail: info@mayinstitute.org
Walter Christian PhD, President/CEO
Dennis C Russo PhD, Chief Clinical Officer

Provides educational and rehabilitative services for individuals with autism, developmental disabilities, neurological disorders and mental illness.

5738 New England Center for Children

33 Turnpike Road
Southborough, MA 01772 508-481-1015
FAX 508-485-3421
http://www.necc.org
e-mail: info@necc.org
Vincent Strully, Executive Director
Katherine E Foster, Associate Executive Director

The New England Center for Children is a private, nonprofit organization serving children with autism and other related disabilities.

5739 Regis College

235 Wellesley Street
Weston, MA 02493 781-768-7000
http://www.regiscollege.edu
e-mail: admissions@regiscollege.edu
MaryJane England, President
Lynn Tripp Coleman, Dean of Students

The college encourages student self-advocacy, the coordination of appropriate academic accommodations and the promotion of disability awareness.

5740 Riverbrook Residence

4 Ice Glen Road
Stockbridge, MA 01262 413-298-4926
FAX 413-298-5166
http://www.riverbrook.org
e-mail: riverbro@berkshire.net
Joan Burkhard, Executive Director
Patty Morris, Program Coordinator

A residence in western Massachusetts, providing supported living to developmentally disabled women, with therapy and treatment focused on the arts.

5741 Seven Hills at Groton

22 Hillsdale Avenue
Groton, MA 01450 978-448-3388
FAX 978-448-9695
http://www.sevenhills.org
e-mail: hjarek@sevenhills.org
Holly Jarek, VP

Our Seven Hills at Groton program provides residential care for children and young adults with multiple disabilities.

5742 Son-Rise Program: Autism Treatment Center of America

The Option Institute
2080 S Undermountain Road
Sheffield, MA 01257 413-229-2100
FAX 413-229-3202
http://www.son-rise.org
e-mail: correspondence@option.org
Neil Kaufman, Sun-Rise Co-Founder

The Son-Rise Program, a powerful and effective treatment for children and adults challenged by Autism, Autism Spectrum Disorders, Pervasive Developmental Disorder, Asperger's and all other developmental difficulties. The Sun-Rise Program teaches a specific yet comprehensive system of treatment and education designed to help families and caregivers enable their children to dramatically improve in all areas of learning, development, communication and skill acquisition.

5743 Stetson School

455 S Street
Barre, MA 01005 978-355-4541
FAX 978-355-6335
http://www.stetsonschool.org
Kathleen O'Connor, Admissions Coordinator
Robert Fitzgerald, Deputy Executive

A nonprofit residential treatment and special education program for adolescent boys that are sex offenders.

5744 Threshold Program

29 Everett Street
Cambridge, MA 02138
800-999-1959
http://www.lesley.edu/threshold
e-mail: threshld@mail.lesley.edu
James Wilbur, Director
Helen McDonald, Admissions Director
Jen Benway, Admissions Coordinator

The Threshold Program is a comprehensive, non-degree campus based program at Lesley University for highly motivated adults with diverse learning disabilities and other special needs.

5745 Unity College Learning Resource

Center Quaker Hill Road
Unity, MA 04988 207-948-3131
FAX 207-948-2677
http://www.unity.edu
e-mail: admissions@unity.edu
James Horan, Director

5746 Valleyhead

79 Reservoir Road
Lenox, MA 01240 413-637-3635
FAX 413-637-3501
http://www.valleyhead.org
e-mail: cmacbeth@valleyhead.org
Christine MacBeth, Executive Director
Ellen G Merrit, Admissions Director

Valleyhead was founded in 1969. It is a residential school for for girls in the scenic Berkshire Hills of Lenox, Massachusetts. We provide a home and education for girls ages 12-22 with emotional needs. Most of our girls come from abusive and traumatic backgrounds. Many do not have intact families.

5747 Willow Hill School

98 Haynes Road
Sudbury, MA   01776   508-443-2581
                                         FAX 508-443-0949
                            http://www.willowhillschool.org
                            e-mail: info@willowhillschool.org
Nancy Brody, Admissions Director

Willow Hill School provides supportive and individualized educational programs for middle and high school students who are capable of advancing along a strong academic curriculum, but have experienced frustration in earlier school settings.

11-21 years old

Michigan

5748 Center for Human Development

Berkley Medical Center
1695 W 12 Mile Road
Berkley, MI   48072   248-691-4744
                                         FAX 248-691-4745
                            http://www.beaumonthospitals.com
Ernest F Krug III MD FAAP, Director

The Center for Human Development evaluates and treats infants, children and adolescents who are showing evidence of, or are at risk for, problems in their behavioral, psychological or learning development.

5749 Eton Academy

1755 Melton Road
Birmingham, MI   48009   248-642-1150
                                         FAX 248-642-3670
                            http://www.etonacademy.org
                            e-mail: smorey@etonacademy.org
Peggy Pattison, Development Director
Sharon Morey, Admissions Director
Pete Pullen, Head of School

The Eton Academy is dedicated to educating students of average and above average intelligence with specific learning disabilities. The mission of Eton Academy is to help students understand their learning styles and practice strategies that will prepare them for responsible independence, lifelong learning and participation in school, family and community.

5750 Lake Michigan Academy

2428 Burton SE
Grand Rapids, MI   49546   616-285-3330
                                         FAX 616-285-1935
                            http://www.wmldf.org
                            e-mail: execdir@wmldf.org
Jerry Mack, Executive Director

Lake Michigan Academy is a state-certified, non-profit school for learning disabled children in grades 1 through 12 with average or above average intelligence. The learning disabilities of the children here vary. Some are dyslexic and have difficulty with decoding or comprehending written language. Some are dyscalculic and experience difficulty with mathematical computations and concepts. Many are dysgraphic and exhibit difficulties with writing skills. Our mission is to build self esteem.

5751 SLD Learning Center

525 Cheshire NE
Grand Rapids, MI   49505   616-361-1182
                                         888-271-8881
                                         FAX 616-361-3648
                            http://www.sldread.org
                            e-mail: sldlc@iserv.net
Pat Harter, President
Anne Baird, VP

The SLD Learning Center is a non-profit educational service institute established in 1974 to provide one-to-one instruction for people of all ages who exhibit dyslexia tendencies or who have not succeeded with traditional teaching methods.

Minnesota

5752 Groves Academy

3200 Highway 100 S
Saint Louis Park, MN   55416   952-920-6377
                                         FAX 952-920-2068
                            http://www.grovesacademy.org
                            e-mail: information@grovesadacemy.org
Michael Mongeau, President

A day school for children who have learning difficulties.

5753 LDA Learning Center

4301 Highway 7
Minneapolis, MN   55416   952-922-8374
                                         FAX 952-922-8102
                            http://www.ldalearningcenter.com
                            e-mail: info@ldalearningcenter.com
Kitty Christiansen, Executive Director
Victoria Weinberg, Program Director

Maximizes the potential of children, youths, adults and families, especially those with learning disabilities and other learning difficulties so that they can lead more productive and fulfilled lives. Provides consultations, tutoring, assessments, parent workshops, training and outreach on sliding fee scale.

Mississippi

5754 Heritage School

550 Sunnybrook Road
Ridgeland, MS   39157   601-853-7163
                                         FAX 601-853-7163
Jeanie Muirhead, Contact

5755 Millcreek Schools

PO Box 1160
Magee, MS   39111   601-849-4221
                          800-372-1994
                      FAX 601-849-6107
                      http://www.yfcs.com
                  e-mail: info.mc-ms@yfcs.com
Margaret Tedford, COO

A residential treatment center for children with emotional disturbances and an intensive care facility for children with mental retardation.

Missouri

5756 Churchill School

1035 Price School Lane
Saint Louis, MO   63124   514-997-4343
                            FAX 314-997-2760
                http://www.churchillschool.org
          e-mail: churchill@churchillschool.org
Sandra K Gilligan, Director
Deborah J Warden, Assistant Director
Jenny Hyde Carney, Outreach Coordinator

The Churchill School is a private, not-for-profit, coeducational day school. It is designed to serve children between the ages of 8-16 with diagnosed learning disabilities. The goal is to help each child reach his or her full potential and prepare for a successful return to a traditional classroom in as short a period of time as possible.

5757 Gillis Center

8150 Wornall Road
Kansas City, MO   64114   816-363-1414
                            FAX 816-363-4782
Barbara O'Toole, Executive Director

5758 Metropolitan School

7281 Sarah Street
Saint Louis, MO   63143   314-644-0850
                            FAX 314-644-3363
                http://www.metroschool.org
            e-mail: info@metroschool.org
Rita Buckley, Executive Director
Cindy Keitel, Executive Assistant
Moriel Maston, Program Assistant

The mission of Metropolitan School is to lead our community in providing effective, comprehensive educational services for adolescents who have atypical learning styles.

5759 Miriam School

501 Bacon Avenue
St. Louis, MO   63119   314-962-6059
                          FAX 314-962-0482
                      http://www.miriams
              e-mail: info@miriamfoundation.org
Joan Holland, Director
Michael G Robinson, Executive Director

A nonprofit day school for children between four and twelve years of age who are learning disabled and/or behaviorally disabled. Speech and language services and occupational therapy are integral components of the program. The focus of all the activities is to increase children's self-esteem and help them acquire the coping skills needed to successfully meet future challenges.

4-12 years old

5760 Missouri Parents Act (MPACT)

One W Armour Boulevard
Kansas, MO   64111   800-743-7634
                        FAX 417-882-8413
                    http://www.ptimpact.com
              e-mail: msavage@ptimpact.com
Mary Kay Savage, Executive Director
Diana Biere, Associate Director
Marcella Galapo, Parent Advisor

MPACT assists parents to effectively advocate for their children's educational rights and services. MPACT is a statewide parent training and information center serving all disabilities. Our mission is to ensure that all children with special needs receive an education that allows them to achieve their personal goals.

5761 Speech Pathology Service

33 E Broadway
Columbia, MO   65203   573-449-5484
                          FAX 573-875-1891
Judith Harper, MA CCC SL/P Owner/Partner
Sharon Ginsburg, MA CCC SL/P, Owner/ Partner
Sharon Johnson, Office Manager

Offers one-on-one intervention in speech therapy, occupational therapy and physical therapy. Our Speech Pathologists have expertise in the following areas: articulation; tongue thrust/myofunctional therapy; voice (including public speaking/business and accent reduction); communication disorders related to autism, attention deficit and hearing impairment. Our Occupational Therapist and Physical Therapist are experienced in treatment of fine and gross motor disorders.

Montana

5762 Parents Let's Unite for Kids

516 N 32nd Street
Billings, MT   59101   406-255-0540
                          800-222-7585
                      FAX 406-255-0523
                      http://www.pluk.org
                  e-mail: plukinfo@pluk.org
Dennis Moore, Director

PLUK is a private, nonprofit organization formed in 1984 by parents and children with disabilities and chronic illnesses in the state of Montana for the purpose of information, support, training and assistance to aid their children at home, school and as adults.

Nebraska

5763 Nebraska Parents Training and Information Center

3135 N 93rd Street
Omaha, NE   68105   402-346-0525
                                     800-284-8520
                              FAX 402-934-1479
                        http://www.pti-nebraska.org
                        e-mail: info@pti-nebraska.org
Pat Davis, Information Coordinator
Glenda Davis, Executive Director

Parent Training and Information Program views parents as full partners in the educational process and a significant source of support and assistance to each other. Funded by the Division of Personnel Preparation, Office of Special Education Programs, these programs provide training and information to parents to enable such individuals to participate more effectively with professionals in meeting the educational needs of disabled children.

New Hampshire

5764 Becket School

PO Box 101
Haverhill, NH   03765   603-989-5100
                              FAX 603-989-5488
                        http://www.becket.org
                        e-mail: beck@becket.org
Kerry Beck, Executive Director
Sharon Edwards, Special Ed Director

Becket guides and inspires adolescents having difficulties at home, in school or in the community.

5765 Cardigan Mt. School

Canaan, NH   03741   603-523-4321
                              FAX 603-523-7227

Cameron Dewar, Headmaster

5766 Cedarcrest

91 Maple Avenue
Keene, NH   03431   603-358-3384
                              FAX 603-358-6485
                        http://www.cedarcrest4kids.org
                        e-mail: info@cedarcrest4kids.org
Catherine Gray, President/CEO
Peg Knox, Nursing Director

A nonprofit home, school and medical support facility for children with complex medical needs and multiple disabilities. Cedarcrest serves up to 25 children, without regard to race, color, religious affiliation or financial standing. As a State Department of Education-approved school, Cedarcrest also serves as a placement option for any school district in the state.

5767 Hampshire Country School

122 Hampshire Road
Rindge, NH   03461   603-899-3325
                              FAX 603-899-6521
                        http://www.hampshirecountryschool.com
                        e-mail: headmaster@hampshirecountryschool.com
William Dickerman, Headmaster/Admission Director

Hampshire Country School is a small boarding school for 25 boys of high ability who need a personal environment with an unusual amount of adult attention and structure. It is primarily a junior school, suited particularly to students from 9 to 15 years old; but some younger students may be accepted and some students may remain through high school.

5768 Parent Information Center

151-A Manchester Street
Concord, NH   03301   603-224-7005
                                 800-947-7005
                              FAX 603-224-4365
                              TDY:603-224-7005
                        http://www.parentinformationcenter.org
                        e-mail: picinfo@parentinformationcenter.org
Heather Thalheimer, Executive Director
Bonnie Dunham, Project Director

Parent Training and Information Program views parents as full partners in the educational process and a significant source of support and assistance to each other. Funded by the Division of Personnel Preparation, Office of Special Education Programs, these programs provide training and information to parents to enable such individuals to participate more effectively with professionals in meeting the educational needs of children with disabilities.

New Jersey

5769 Bancroft Neurohealth

Hopkins Lane
Haddonfield, NJ   08033   856-429-0010
                                 800-774-5516
                              FAX 856-429-1613
                        http://www.bancroftneurohealth.org
                        e-mail: adestefa@bnh.org
Arleen DeStefano, Admissions Director
Paul Healy, Public Relations Director

Nonprofit organization offering educational/vocational programs, therapeutic support services and full range of community living opportunities for children and adults with brain injury in Maine, New Jersey, Delaware, and Louisiana. Residential options include community living supervised apartments, specialized supervised apartments, group homes and supported living models.

5770 Center School

319 N 3rd Avenue
Highland Park, NJ 08904   732-249-3355
                                 FAX 732-249-1928
                    http://www.thecenterschool.com
Jeanne Prial, Contact
Barbara Leutholt, Admissions Director

The Center School is a school designed for bright students in grades 1-12 with learning and behavioral difficulties. The Center School offers counseling, speech and language, and occupational therapy. Our school is committed to helping each student become as self-sufficient and successful as possible.

5771 Children's Institute

1 Sunset Avenue
Verona, NJ 07044   973-509-3050
                                FAX 973-740-0369
                        http://www.tcischool.org
               e-mail: webmaster@tcischool.org
Bruce Ettinger, Executive Director
Carole Spiro, Volunteer Coordinator

The Children's Institute is a private, non-profit school approved by the New Jersey State Board of Education, serving children facing learning, language and social challenges, ages 3-21.

5772 Craig School

10 Tower Hill Road
Mountain Lake, NJ 07046   973-334-1295
                                FAX 973-334-1299
                        http://www.craigschool.org
                  e-mail: jday@craigschool.org
Julie Day, Admissions Director
Ted Sharp, Headmaster

The Craig School is an independent, nonprofit school serving children who have difficulty succeeding in the traditional classroom environment. We specialize in a language-based curriculum for children of average or above average intelligence with such disorders as dyslexia, auditory processing and attention deficit.

5773 Devereux Center for Autism

198 Roadstown Road
Bridgeton, NJ 08302   856-455-7200
                                FAX 856-455-2765
James G Gill Jr, Executive Director

A residential and educational program for individuals with autism and/or developmental disabilities.

5774 Devereux Deerhaven

230 Pottersville Road
Chester, NJ 07930   908-879-4500
                                FAX 908-879-6370
                        http://www.devereux.org
Kristy Hartman, Admissions Director

Residential and day programs for females who have emotional and behavioral disorders and learning disabilities.

5-21 years old

5775 ECLC of New Jersey

Ho-Ho-Kus Campus
302 N Franklin Turnpike
Ho Ho Kus, NJ 07423   201-670-7880
                                FAX 201-670-6675
                          e-mail: eclc@nac.net
Bruce Litinger, Executive Director
Vicki Lindorff, Principal
Dan Mullen, Assistant Director

A private school for individuals with disabilities between the ages of 5-21. Our mission is to help disabled students discover how they fit into the world and guide them towards becoming independent and employed adults.

5776 Eden Services

One Eden Way
Princeton, NJ 08540   609-987-0099
                                FAX 609-987-0243
                        http://www.edenservices.org
                   e-mail: info@edenservices.org
David L Holmes, President/Executive

Nonprofit organization founded in 1975 to provide a comprehensive continuum of lifespan services for individuals with autism and their families.

5777 Family Resource Associates

35 Haddon Avenue
Shrewsbury, NJ 07702   732-747-5310
                                FAX 732-747-1896
              http://www.familyresourceassociates.org
Nancy Thalanukorn, Executive Director

We are a New Jersey non-profit agency dedicated to helping individuals with disabilities and their families.

5778 Forum School

107 Wyckoff Avenue
Waldwick, NJ 07463   201-444-5882
                                FAX 201-444-4003
                    http://www.theforumschool.com
                e-mail: info@theforumschool.com
Steven Krapes, Director

Special education day school for developmentally atypical children ages 3-16 years. The Forum School offers a therapeutic education environment for children who cannot be accommodated in a public school setting.

5779 High Road Schools

10-G Auer Court
East Brunswick, NJ 08816   732-390-0303
                                FAX 732-390-5577
                        http://www.kids1inc.com
                   e-mail: kids1@kids1inc.com
Ellyn Lerner PhD, President

Offers programs serving the educational, social and emotional needs of children with specific learning disabilities, communication disorders and/or behavioral difficulties.

5780 Kingsway Learning Center

144 Kings Highway W
Haddonfield, NJ   08033   856-428-8108
                                FAX 856-428-7520
                        http://www.kingswaylc.com
Donna Thorpe, Program Specialist
David Panner, Executive Director

Kingsway is a private, non-profit special education school devoted to the academic and therapeutic needs of children with developmental and learning disabilities. We serve children from birth to 16 years of age with multiple handicaps.

5781 Lewis Clinic and School

53 Bayard Lane
Princeton, NJ   08540   609-924-8120
                               FAX 609-924-5512
                        http://www.lewisschool.org
Marsha Gaynor-Lewis, Contact

The Clinic and School integrate teaching and diagnostic perspective of multisensory educational practices in the classrooms, and the perspective of clinical research into the brain's learning process.

5782 Matheny School and Hospital

Main Street
Peapack, NJ   07977   908-234-0011
                             FAX 908-719-2137
                        http://www.matheny.org
                   e-mail: development@matheny.org
Steven Proctor, President

Matheny School and Hospital is a teaching hospital and a premier facility for people of all ages with developmental disabilities. Matheny specializes in the care of children and adults with cerebral palsy, muscular dystrophy, spina bifida and Lesch-Nyhan Disease.

5783 Metropolitan Speech and Language Center

66 W Mount Present
Livingston, NJ   07039   973-994-4468
                                FAX 973-994-4412
                        e-mail: lillyok@aol.com
Lilian Dollinger, Executive Director

Provides diagnostics and therapy for children and adults with speech, language, voice and stuttering problems.

5784 Midland School

94 Readington Road
North Branch, NJ   08876   908-722-8222
                                  FAX 908-722-6203
                        http://www.midlandschool.org
                     e-mail: info@midlandschool.org
Edward Scagliotta, Founder

The mission of Midland School is a comprehensive special education program serving the individual social, emotional, academic, and career education needs of children with developmental disabilities.

5785 SEARCH Day Program

73 Wickapecko Drive
Ocean, NJ   07712   201-531-0454
                           FAX 732-531-5934
                http://www.members.aol.com/SEARCHDay
                   e-mail: SEARCHDay@aol.com
Katherine Solana, Executive Director

SEARCH Day Program is a private, non-profit, New Jersey State certified school for individuals ages three through twenty-one with autism.

5786 Speech/Language Therapy

188 Highwood Avenue
Tenafly, NJ   07670   201-569-5061
                             FAX 201-894-8652
Dorothy Unger

5787 Statewide Parent Advocacy Network

Central Office
35 Halsey Street
Newark, NJ   07102   973-642-8100
                            800-654-7726
                            FAX 973-642-8080
                        http://www.spannj.org
                     e-mail: span@spannj.org
Diana Autin, Co-Executive Director
Debra Jennings, Co-Executive Director

A nonprofit educational and advocacy center for parents of children from birth to 21 years of age. Assists families of infants, toddlers, children and youth with and without disabilities. Serves as a vehicle for the exchange of ideas, promoting awareness of the abilities and needs of the children and youth and improves services for children and families in the state of NJ.

5788 The Newgrange School

530 S Olden Avenue
Hamilton, NJ   08629   609-584-1800
                              FAX 609-584-6166
                        http://www.thenewgrange.org
                     e-mail: info@ore.thenewgrange.org
Gordon Sherman PhD, Executive Director

Newgrange is a non-profit organization established in 1977 to provide specialized educational programs for people with learning disabilities.

New Mexico

5789 Brush Ranch School

North Highway 63
Terrero, NM 87573   505-757-6114
                          FAX 505-757-6118
http://www.brushranchschool.org
e-mail: kaycrice@hotmail.com
Kay C Rice MA, School Head
Eve Bowen, Health Director
Suzanne Weisman, Admissions Director

A co-educational boarding school for teens with learning differences. The school is fully licensed and accredited by both the New Mexico Board of Education and the North Central Association of Colleges and Schools. Situated on 283 acres in the Santa Fe National Forest, the school offers a wide range of educational and recreational opportunities.

5790 Designs for Learning Differences School

8600 Academy Road
Albuquerque, NM 87112   505-822-0476
                              FAX 505-797-8599
Margaret Aeby

5791 EPICS Parent Project

Abrazos Family Support Services
412 Camino Don Tomas
Bernalillo, NM 87004   505-867-3396
                             FAX 505-867-3398
http://www.swcr.org
e-mail: info@swcr.org

EPICS - Education for Parents of Indian Children with Special Needs Project is a service for parents of American Indian children and young adults with disabilities and other special needs.

5792 New Mexico Speech & Language Consultants

1000 W 4th Street
Roswell, NM 88201   505-623-8319
                          FAX 505-623-8220
Eileen Grooms, President

Provides diagnostic and therapy services for communicatively impaired individuals.

5793 Parents Reaching Out To Help (PRO)

1920 B Columbia Drive SE
Albuquerque, NM 87106   505-247-0192
                              800-524-5176
http://www.parentsreachingout.org
Sally VanCuren, Executive Director
Larry Fuller, Program Manager

PRO views parents as full partners in the educational process and a significant source of support and assistance to each other. Programs provide training and information to parents to enable such individuals to participate more effectively with professionals in meeting the educational needs of disabled children.

New York

5794 Advocates for Children of New York

151 W 30th Street
New York, NY 10001   212-947-9779
                           FAX 718-729-8931
http://www.advocatesforchildren.org
e-mail: info@advocatesforchildren.org
Jill Chaifetz, Executive Director
Elisa Hyman, Deputy Director

For over 25 years Advocates for Children of New York, Inc. has worked in partnership with New York City's most impoverished and vulnerable families to secure quality and equal public education services. AFC works on behalf of children from infancy to age 21 who have disabilites, ethnic minorities, immigrants, homeless children, foster care children, limited English proficient children and those living in poverty.

5795 Anderson School

4885 Route 9
Staatsburg, NY 12580   845-889-4034
                             FAX 845-889-3104
http://www.andersonschool.org
e-mail: info@andersonschool.org
Neil J Pollack, Executive Director

Anderson School provides a vast array of educational, residential, clinical, and support services to children and adults with autism and other developmental disabilities.

5796 Baker Hall School

777 Ridge Road
Lackawanna, NY 14218   716-828-9737
                             FAX 716-828-9798
Nancy Pancow, Executive Director

Offers a certified special education program and a full range of classroom options; in-house, pre-vocational training and BOCES school placements are available to students depending on need.

5797 Behavioral Arts

58 W 88th Street
New York, NY 10024   212-799-9388
                           888-497-3722
                          FAX 212-799-4403
Enid Haller PhD, Executive Director
Nancy Morales, Office Manager

Behavioral Arts is an outpatient psychotherapy clinic dedicated to helping individuals and families develop the mental and physical well-being that lends itself to healthy relationships and effective functioning. The Center's staff consists of warm, dedicated, professionals who specialize in such issues as Attention Deficit Disorder, anxiety, depression, co-dependency, substance abuse, chronic illness, learning disabilities and self-esteem.

5798 Center for Discovery

PO Box 840
Harris, NY 12742   845-794-1400
                                FAX 845-794-1474
                         http://www.sdtcdiscovery.org
                          e-mail: admissions@sdtc.org

Programs for children with multiple disabilities. Creative classes, beautiful residences, totally accessible country campus.

5799 Center for the Advancement of Post Secondary Studies (CAP)

Division of Maplebrook School
5142 Route 22
Amenia, NY 12501   845-373-8191
                                FAX 845-373-7029
                         e-mail: mbsecho@aol.com
Jennifer Scully, Director of Admissions

CAPS offers a vocational program with employment skills and training, as well as a collegiate program with courses taken at the local community college and other support services.

5800 Child Center for Developmental Service

251 Manetto Hill Road
Plainview, NY 11803   516-938-3788
Iris Lesser, Contact

5801 Community Based Services

3 Fields Lane
North Salem, NY 10560   914-277-4771
                                FAX 914-277-8956
Vick M Sylvester PhD, CEO
Paulette Sladkus, COO

Six intermediate care facilities for people with autism and developmental disabilities, and one individual residential alternative.

5802 Diagnostic Learning Center

505 Ridge Road
Queensbury, NY 12804   518-793-0668
                                     800-338-3781
                                FAX 518-793-0668
                         http://www.learningproblems.com
                          e-mail: janb@capital.net
Jan Bishop, Director

Offers diagnosis and remediation of learning problems, cognitive remediation for the head injured. In-services for teachers and parent groups. Tutorials only; no day or stay programs.

5803 EAC Developmental Learning Program

300 Park Avenue
Deer Park, NY 11729   631-242-7130
                                FAX 631-242-7005
C Leonard Davis

5804 EAC Developmental Program

382 Main Street
Port Washington, NY 11050   516-883-3006
                                FAX 516-883-0412
Nadine Heyman

5805 Eden II School for Autistic Children

150 Granite Avenue
Staten Island, NY 10303   718-816-1422
                                FAX 718-816-1428
                           http://www.eden2.org
Joanne Gerenser, Executive Director

Offers programs for children with autism and an adult day training program.

5806 Environmental Science and Forestry

State University of New York College
110 Bray Hall
Syracuse, NY 13210   315-470-6660
                                FAX 315-470-4728
                             http://www.esf.edu
                          e-mail: toslocum@esf.edu
Thomas Slocum, Special Services

5807 Gow School

Emery Road
South Wales, NY 14139   716-652-3450
                                FAX 716-687-2003
                             http://www.gow.org
                          e-mail: admissions@gow.org
M Bradley Rogers Jr, Headmaster
Robert Garcia, Admissions Director

The nation's oldest college preparatory school for young men (grades 7-12) with dyslexia/language based learning differences. The 100 acre residential campus is located in upstate New York. Co-Ed summer program for ages 8-16.

5808 Hallen School

97 Centre Avenue
New Rochelle, NY 10801   914-636-6600
                                FAX 914-636-2844
                          http://www.hallenschool.com
Carol LoCascio, Executive Director

A special education school offering a sound academic program in a therapeutic setting.

5809 International Center for the Disabled

340 E 24th Street
New York, NY 10010   212-585-6083
                                FAX 212-585-6161
                           http://www.iodrehab.org
                          e-mail: s/segal@icdrehab.org
Sondra Segal, Director Development
Arnold Shapiro, Director Center for Speech/Lang.

ICD is the nation's oldest outpatient rehabilitation center offering comprehensive medical, vocational, and mental health services. The Center for Speech/Language, Learning and Hearing includes a learning disabilities section providing diagnostic and individualized remedial services for both children and adults who are experiencing difficulty with reading, writing, spelling and/or math.

5810 Julia Dyckman Andrus Memorial

1156 N Broadway
Yonkers, NY 10701   914-965-3700
                         FAX 914-965-3883
                    http://www.andruschildren.org
Gary Carman, Executive Director

Residential treatment for youngsters who have moderate to severe emotional problems.

5811 Just Kids: Early Childhood Learning Center

PO Box 12
Middle Island, NY 11953   631-924-0008
                             FAX 631-924-4602
Steven Held, Executive Director

A family focused early intervention program for young children with disabilities.

5812 Karafin School

40 Radio Circle Drive
Mount Kisco, NY 10549   914-666-9211
                             FAX 914-666-9868
                    http://www.Bestwes.net/~karafin
Dr. John Greenfeldt, Executive Director
Dr. Bart Donow, Associate Director

5813 Kildonan School

425 Morse Hill Road
Amenia, NY 12501   845-373-8111
                             FAX 845-373-9793
                    http://www.kildonan.org
Ronald A Wilson, Headmaster
Joseph Ruggiero, Academic Dean

Offers a fully accredited College Preparatory curriculum. The school is co-educational, enrolling boarding students in Grades 6-Postgraduate and day students in Grade 2-Postgraduate. Provides daily one-on-one Orton-Gillingham tutoring to build skills in reading, writing, and spelling. Daily independent reading and writing work reinforces skills and improves study habits. Interscholastic sports, horseback riding, clubs and community service enhance self-confidence.

5814 Learning Diagnostic Center

Schneider Children's Hospital
26901 76th Avenue
New Hyde Park, NY 11040   718-470-3140
                             FAX 718-343-3578
Sheldon H Horowitz EdD, Associate Director

Committed to helping each child maximize his/her potential for academic, social and emotional development. The Center's staff uses a broad range of standardized and informal diagnostic tools as part of the evaluation process and provides comprehensive written reports including recommendations to improve functioning both in school and at home.

5815 Manhattan Center for Learning

590 W End Avenue
New York, NY 10024   212-787-5712
                             FAX 212-787-5323
Judith Baumrin PhD, Psychologist

Services for the learning disabled include tutoring, remediation, cognitive therapy, psycho-educational testing, parent counseling and neuropsychological testing provided by a very qualified staff including a licensed psychologist certified as a learning disabilities specialist.

5816 Maplebrook School

5142 Route 22
Amenia, NY 12501   845-373-8191
                             FAX 845-373-7029
                    e-mail: mbsecho@aol.com
Roger Fazzone, CEO
Jennifer Scully, Director Admissions
Donna M Konkolics, Head of School

A traditional boarding school enrolling students with learning differences and ADD. Offers strong academics and character development. The Responsibility Increases Self Esteem (RISE) Program provides the structure and support to awaken the learner in each student, promote responsibility and develop character, foster independence and growth and enhance social development.

5817 Mary McDowell Center for Learning

20 Bergen Street
Brooklyn, NY 11201   718-625-3939
                             FAX 718-625-1456
                    http://www.marymcdowell.org
Debbie Zlotowitz, Head School
Selina Law, School Administrator

An elementary school for children with learning disabilities ages 5-12.

5818 New Interdisciplinary School

430 Sills Road
Yaphank, NY 11980   631-924-5583
                             FAX 631-924-5687
                    e-mail: nis1977@aol.com
Helen Wilder, Director
Betsy Kapian, Assistant Director

As the name suggests, the school offers the integration of services into the classroom and at home from a variety of disiplines: special education; speech and language development; gross and fine motor; sensory integration; psychological; social work audiology; and nursing for children form birth to five.

5819 New York Institute for Special Education

999 Pelham Parkway
Bronx, NY   10469   718-519-7000
                              FAX 718-231-9314
                              http://www.nyise.org/
Kim Benisatto, Operations Manager

5820 Niagra Frontier Center for Independent Living

1522 Main Street
Niagra Falls, NY   14305   716-284-2452
                              FAX 716-284-0829
                              e-mail: info@nfeil.org
Michael DeVinney, Director Programs/Services

5821 Norman Howard School

220 Idlewood Road
Rochester, NY   14618   716-334-8010
                              FAX 716-334-8010

William Elberty

5822 Parent Network Center

1443 Main Street
Buffalo, NY   14209   716-885-1004
                               800-724-7408
                              FAX 716-885-3527
Joan M Watkins, Executive Director
Maria Kerber, Director Training

Views parents as full partners in the educational process and a significant source of support and assistance to each other. These programs provide training and information to parents to enable such individuals to participate more effectively with professionals in meeting the educational needs of disabled children, and ongoing needs as they age out of mandated services and require independent help to live inclusive lives and experience full citizenship.

5823 Program for Learning Disabled College Students: Adelphi University

Eddy Hall-Lower Level
Garden City, NY   11530   516-877-4850
                              FAX 516-877-4711

Sandra Holzinger

5824 Robert Louis Stevenson School

24 W 74th Street
New York, NY   10023   212-787-6400
                              FAX 212-873-1872

BH Henrichsen, Headmaster

12-18 years old

5825 Stephen Gaynor School

22 W 74th Street
New York, NY   10023   212-787-7070
                              FAX 212-787-3312
                              http://www.sgaynor.com
Lilli Friedman, Director Admissions
Scott Gaynor, Director Operations
Yvette Siegel, Director Education

Our guiding principle is to provide a nurturing environment in which students with learning differences can acquire the skills they need to achieve success in their educational pursuits.

5826 Vocational Independence Program (VIP)

New York Institute of Technology
Central Campus
Central Islip, NY   11722   631-348-3354
                              FAX 631-348-0437
                              http://www.vip-at-nyit.org
David Finkelstein, Director
Jim Rein, Dean

VIP is a three year certificate program for students with moderate to severe learning disabilities. Emphasizes independent living, social and vocational skills, as well as individual academic support, with a college support program called Track II for students who can take college credit courses or pursue a degree.

5827 Windward School

Windward Avenue
White Plains, NY   10605   914-949-6968
                              FAX 914-949-8220
Maureen Sweeney, Admissions Director
Dr. James Van Amburg, Head Master

5828 Winston Preparatory School

4 W 76th Street
New York, NY   10023   212-496-8400
                              FAX 212-362-0927
Scott Bezsylko, Head Master
Beth Sugerman, Admissions Director

This school offers a strong academic curriculum, arts integration, summer programs and remedial tutorials for middle and upper school students with learning disabilities or attention difficulties.

North Carolina

5829 Comprehensive Educational Services (CES)

6401 Carmel Road
Charlotte, NC   28226   704-542-6471
                              FAX 704-541-2858
Rosanne Manus MA, President
Stan Covelski, Center Director

School for students with learning disabilties.

5830 Eastern Associates Speech and Language Services
2501B Wayne Memorial Drive
Goldsboro, NC 27534   919-731-2234
                                   FAX 919-731-2306
Rhonda Sutton-Merritt, Director

A private practice clinic providing diagnosis and treatment of speech and language disorders/differences. All speech pathologists hold a master's degree, are licensed by the NC Board of Examiners for Speech Pathologists and Audiologists and hold a Certificate of Clinical Competence issued by the American Speech-Language and Hearing Association.

5831 Exceptional Children's Assistance Center
907 Barra Row
Davidson, NC 28036   704-892-1321
                                       800-962-6817
                                   FAX 704-892-5028
http://www.ecac-parentcenter.org
Parent Training and Information Program views parents as full partners in the educational process and a significant source of support and assistance to each other. Funded by the Division of Personnel Preparation, Office of Special Education Programs, these programs provide training and information to parents to enable such individuals to participate more effectively with professionals in meeting the educational needs of disabled children.

5832 Families First Coalition
300 Enola Road
Morganton, NC 28655   828-433-2661
                                   FAX 828-438-6451
Jeffrey Brookfield

Parent Training and Information Program views parents as full partners in the educational process and a significant source of support and assistance to each other. Funded by the Division of Personnel Preparation, Office of Special Education Programs, these programs provide training and information to parents to enable such individuals to participate more effectively with professionals in meeting the educational needs of disabled children.

5833 Hill Center
3200 Pickett Road
Durham, NC 27705   919-489-7464
                                   FAX 919-489-7466
http://www.hillcenter.org
e-mail: hillcenter@da.org
Sharon Maskel, Director
Wendy Speir, Director Admissions
Jean Neville, Dir. Professional Development
Offers a unique half-day program to students in grades K-12 with diagnosed learning disabilities and attention deficit disorders. Also offers a comprehensive teacher program.

5834 Joy A Shabazz Center for Independent Living
235 N Green Street
Greenboro, NC 27406   336-272-0501
                                   FAX 336-272-0575
http://www.advocacyproject.org
e-mail: tap99@bellsouth.net
Aaron Shabazz, Executive Director
Bentia Brown, Assistant Director
Marlene Mesot, Information Resources

A nonprofit, consumer oriented, independent living center providing advocacy, peer counseling, independent living training, information and referral, with other related services for persons with disabilities. We currently serve five counties.

5835 Piedmont School
815 Old Mill Road
High Point, NC 27265   336-883-0992
                                   FAX 336-883-4752
http://www.thepiedmontschool.com
e-mail: mLBrewer-tps@triad.rr.com
Mary Lin Brewer, Director
Dorie Sturgill, Assistant Director

Nonprofit private school for 1st-8th grade students diagnosed with a specific learning disability and/or an attention deficit disorder.

5836 Raleigh Learning and Language Clinic
7101 Creedmoor Road
Raleigh, NC 27609   919-676-5477
http://www.huntinglearning.com
Stan Kant, Contact

North Dakota

5837 Anne Carlsen Center for Children
301 7th Avenue NW
Jamestown, ND 58401   701-252-3850
                                   FAX 701-253-7154
http://www.annecenter.org
Mary Dahlen, CEO Business Development

Offers education, therapy, medical care and social and psychological services for children and young adults with special needs.

Ohio

5838 Akron Reading and Speech Center
700 Ghent Road
Akron, OH 44333   330-666-1161
                                   FAX 330-665-1862
Ardath Franck PhD, Director

Remedial, developmental and enrichment reading and speech therapy services.

5839 Bellefaire JCB
22001 Fairmount Boulevard
Shaker Heights, OH 44118   216-932-2800
                                       800-879-2522
                                   FAX 216-932-6704
http://www.bellefairjcb.org
Jill Yulish, Intake Coordinator
Debra Mundell, Associate Director

Residential treatment center for adolescents, offering foster care, an adoption center, Monarch School for Children with Autism.

5840 **Child Advocacy Center**

1821 Summit Road
Cincinnati, OH 45237 513-821-2400
FAX 513-821-2442
e-mail: cadcenter@aol.com
Kathy Ward, Administrative Assistant

A training and information center for parents of children with special needs. It is funded by various federal, state, and local grants and is managed by parents of disabled children. Its goals are to assure that disabled children receive quality educational services in natural, age-appropriate settings and to help parents and other community members understand their rights and responsibilities under federal and state educational law.

5841 **Cincinnati Center for Developmental Disorders**

3333 Burnet Avenue
Cincinnati, OH 45229 513-636-4688
800-344-2462
FAX 513-636-7361
TDY:513-636-4626
http://www.cincinnatichildrens.org
e-mail: johnb0@chmcc.org
Sonya Oppenheimer MD, Director

5842 **Cincinnati Occupational Therapy Institute for Services and Study**

4440 Carver Woods Drive
Cincinnati, OH 45242 513-791-5688
FAX 513-791-0023
e-mail: coti@cintiotinstitute.com
Joan Dostal, Pediatric Coordinator
Elaine Mullin, Executive Director

Pediatric occupational therapy services specializing in sensory integration.

5843 **Developmental Clinic**

875 Howland Wilson Road NE
Warren, OH 44484 440-856-5858
Jams LaPolla

5844 **Ohio Coalition for the Education of Children with Learning Disabilities**

933 High Street
Worthington, OH 43085 614-431-1307
FAX 614-431-1504

Funded by the Division of Personnel Preparation, Office of Special Education Programs, these programs provide training and information to parents to enable such individuals to participate more effectively with professionals in meeting the educational needs of disabled children.

5845 **Olympus Center: Unlocking Learning Potential**

2230 Park Avenue
Cincinnati, OH 45206 513-559-0404
FAX 513-559-0008
http://www.olympuscenter.org
e-mail: olympus@fuse.net
Sandy Martin, Director

A nonprofit agency provides evaluations and consultations for children and adults by learning issues.

5846 **RICHARDS READ Systematic Language**

North Coast Tutoring Services
120 N Main Street
Chagrin Falls, OH 44022 440-247-1622
FAX 440-247-1655

Carole Richards, President
John Kusik, VP

North Coast Tutoring Services strives to provide on-site education services to individual learners or groups. Uppermost in the delivery of these services is the development of self-esteem, expanding learner potential and utilizing problem-solving to identify strengths and weaknesses. We specialize in working with at-risk learners which include learning disabled students. Our systematic language program is extremely successful with language learning difficulties from age 5 to adult.

5847 **Springer School and Center**

2121 Madison Road
Cincinnati, OH 45208 513-871-6080
FAX 513-871-6218
http://www.hccanet.org/springer
Jan Annette, Admissions Director

Empowering students with learning disabilities to lead successful lives (Grades 1-8). Center serves teachers, parents and students.

Oklahoma

5848 **Pro-Oklahoma**

UCP of Oklahoma
1917 S Harvard Drive
Oklahoma City, OK 73128 405-681-9710
800-PL-94142
FAX 405-685-4006
e-mail: PROOK1@aol.com
Sharon Bishop, Director
Marilynn Alexander, Coordinator

Views parents as full partners in the educational process and a significant source of support and assistance to each other. Funded by the Division of Personnel Preparation, Office of Special Education Programs, these programs provide training and information to parents to enable such individuals to participate more effectively with professionals in meeting the educational needs of disabled children.

5849 Town and Country School
1515 S 71st E Avenue
Tulsa, OK 74112   918-665-3113
                        FAX 918-664-9747
Frances M Day MA, Executive Director

A private school for learning disabled students, with or without attention deficit disorder. Class size limited to 12 persons, a certified teacher and an aide.

Oregon

5850 Chemetka Community College
Services for Students with Disabilities
4000 Lancaster Drive NE
Salem, OR 97309   503-399-5142
                        FAX 503-399-2519
                        TDY:503-399-5192
Michael Duggan, Disabilities Specialist

Chemetka Community College provides a wide variety of services for students including individualized tutoring, testing accommodations, books on tape, and adaptive technology to name a few.

5851 Cornell Vision Center
1010 NE Cornell Road
Hillsboro, OR 97124   503-640-3333
                        FAX 503-681-9459
                        e-mail: dianaeye@aol.com
Diana Ludlam, Vision Therapist
Debbie Mish, Office Manager

Learning realted vision problems, visual aspects of cerebral palsy, head trauma, syndromes involving visual function.

5852 Learning Unlimited Network of Oregon
31960 SE Chin Street
Boring, OR 97009   503-663-5153
                        e-mail: luno@cse.com
Gene Lehman, Contact

Offers programs for home, group, business or institution, serving any number of students. These materials and programs can quickly change the habits, attitudes and performances of students mastering basic language skills, from elementary to adult levels.

5853 OR PTI
1745 State Street
Salem, OR 97301   503-581-8107
                        888-505-2673
                        FAX 503-391-0429
                        http://www.open.org
                        e-mail: orpti@open.org
Janice Richards, Executive Director

Parent Training and Information Center.

5854 Thomas A Edison Program
Thomas A Edison High School
9020 SW Beaverton Hillsdale Highway
Portland, OR 97225   503-297-2336
                        FAX 503-297-2527
Patrick Maguire, Director

The goal of this program is to help learning disabled students transfer into a larger high school setting after 1 to 2 years. Counselors play a strong role in helping students make that transition. The program offers parent involvement programs, transition programs, counseling, and affordable tuition.

5855 Tree of Learning High School
9000 SW Beaverton Hillsdale Highway
Portland, OR 97225   503-297-2336
                        FAX 503-297-2527
Jocelyn Tuthill

Pennsylvania

5856 Center for Alternative Learning
PO Box 716
Bryn Mawr, PA 19010   610-525-8336
                        800-869-8336
                        FAX 610-525-8337
                        http://www.ldonline.org
Dr. Richard Cooper, Contact

A nonprofit organization designed to provide direct services to learning disabled adults and teacher training to adult learning disabled practitioners.

5857 Center for Psychological Services
125 Coulter Avenue
Ardmore, PA 19003   610-642-4873
                        FAX 610-642-4886
                        http://www.centerpsych.com
                        e-mail: ctrpsychsv@aol.com
Moss Jackson, Director
Bruce Miller, Director
Channa Oxelrod, Director
Individual, family and group therapy psychoeducational evaluation and school consultation.

5858 Cornell Abraxas I
PO Box 59
Marienville, PA 16239   814-927-6615
                        800-227-2927
                        FAX 814-927-8560
Jamesl Nawsome, Facility Director

5859 Devereux Brandywine
PO Box 69
Glenmoore, PA 19343   610-942-5900
                        FAX 610-942-9572
Jarry Biliski, Executive Director
Sue Schofield, Admissions Director

Residential treatment for emotionally disturbed males consisting of five distinct programs based upon age and diagnostic criteria. Includes program for the deaf. Services provided include: psychiatric; therapeutic; milieu with integrated behavior management system; intermediate; high school with 12-month educational program and more. Offers a 350 acre campus, including stocked lake, swimming pool, playing fields and more.

5860 Devereux Foundation

444 Devereux Drive
Villanova, PA   19085   610-964-3045
                              800-935-6789
                        FAX 610-25124150

Offers residential and community-based treatment centers nationwide. Provides comprehensive services to individuals of all ages.

5861 Devereux Mapleton

655 Sugartown Road
Malvern, PA   19355   610-296-6973
                              800-935-6789
                        FAX 610-296-5866

Residential and in-patient program for children, adolescents and young adults with emotional disorders and learning disabilities.

13-21 years old

5862 Dr. Gertrude A Barber Center

136 E Avenue
Erie, PA   16507   814-453-7661
                        FAX 814-455-1132

John J Barber, President/CEO

An individualized educational program designed for preschool and school-aged students.

5863 Hill Top Preparatory School

737 S Ithan Avenue
Rosemont, PA   19010   610-527-3230
                        FAX 610-527-7683
                  http://www.hilltopprep.org
            e-mail: headmaster@hilltopprep.org
Dr. Les McLean, Head Master
Lynne Little, Admissions Director

A fully-accredited, state-licensed, private, secondary, diploma-granting school for the learning disabled adolescent combining academic and clinical components to provide a preparatory program.

5864 Hillside School

2697 Brookside Road
Macungie, PA   18062   610-967-5449
                        FAX 610-965-7683
                  http://www.hillsideschool.org
Linda Whitney, Director

A day school for children with learning disabilities. One hundred and twenty-eight children in grades K-6 attend the school. Scholarships are available.

5-13 years old

5865 KidsPeace

5300 Kidspeace Drive
Orefield, PA   18069   215-799-8000
                              800-8KID-123
                  http://www.kidspeace.org
            e-mail: admissions@kidspeace.org
John Peter, President

Offers various programs including community residential care, specialized group homes, child and family guidance center and student assistance programs.

5866 LearnRight

Parsick Building, Terrace Drive
Olyphant, PA   18447   570-383-9890
                  http://www.learnright.com
            e-mail: cynthia@learnright.com
Cynthia Shackleton, Consultant

A licensed supplemental school dedicated to teaching people of all ages how to become more effective learners. Staffed by state certified teachers, LearnRight teaches thinking skills, study skills, reading, math and written language through a trademarked individualized curriculum. LearnRight's specialized curriculum and programs of one-on-one instruction are specifically designed to eliminate obstacles to learning in people having learning disabilities.

5867 Melmark

2600 Wayland Road
Berwyn, PA   19312   610-325-4969
                              888-635-6275
                        FAX 610-325-2929
                  http://www.melmark.org
            e-mail: pjm@melmark.org
Peter McGuiness, Director Admissions

Provides residential, educational, therapeutic and recreational services for children and adults with mild to severe developmental disabilities.

5868 New Castle School of Trades

RR 1
Pulaski, PA   16143   724-964-8811
                        FAX 724-964-8177

Rex Spaulding, Director

5869 Parent Education Network

2107 Industrial Highway
York, PA   17402   717-600-0100
                              800-522-5827
                        FAX 717-600-8101
                        TDY:800-522-5827
                  http://www.parentednet.org
            e-mail: pen@parentednet.org

Parent training and information center of Pennsylvania. Serves parents of all special needs children, birth to adulthood, to attain appropriate educational and support services by providing specific knowledge of state and federal laws and regulations; develops and disseminates material explaining the special education process and its relationship to other systems.

5870 Parents Union for Public Schools

228 W Chelten Avenue
Philadelphia, PA 19107 215-991-9724
FAX 215-991-9943
e-mail: ParentsU@aol.com

Parent Training and Information Program views parents as full partners in the educational process and a significant source of support and assistance to each other. Funded by the Division of Personnel Preparation, Office of Special Education Programs, these programs provide training and information to parents to enable such individuals to participate more effectively with professionals in meeting the educational needs of disabled children.

5871 Pathway School

162 Egypt Road
Norristown, PA 19403 610-277-0660
FAX 610-539-1493
http://www.pathwayschool.org
e-mail: louiser@pathwayschool.org
Louise Robertson, Admissions Director
Robert Schurage, Education Director
William O'Flanagan PhD, Executive Director

Provides day and residential programming for individuals ages 5-21, who have learning disabilities, neurological impairments and neuropsychiatric disorder. Special education, counseling, speech and language therapy, reading therapy, and other specialized services are provided in a small, warm and supportive atmosphere.

5872 Rehabilitation Institute of Pittsburgh

1405 Shady Avenue
Pittsburgh, PA 15217 412-521-9000
FAX 412-521-0570

Offers quality services to young people with moderate to severe disabilities with different levels of physical, cognitive and emotional functioning.

5873 Rosemont College

1400 Montgomery Avenue
Rosemont, PA 19010 610-527-0200
FAX 610-527-0341
http://www.rosemont.edu
Linda De Simone, Admissions Director

Offers a variety of services to students with disabilities including notetakers, extended testing time, counseling services, and special accommodations.

5874 Stratford Friends School

5 Llandillo Road
Havertown, PA 19083 610-446-3144
FAX 610-446-6381
http://www.stratfordfriends.org
Sandra Howzwe, Director
Nancy D'Angelo, Admissions

A Quaker elementary school for children with learning differences with average to above average intelligence.

5875 Thaddeus Stevens College of Technology

750 E King Street
Lancaster, PA 17602 717-299-7408
FAX 717-391-6929
http://www.stevenstech.org
e-mail: schuch@stevenstech.org
Deb Schuch, Special Needs Coordinator

Two year trade and technical college, with dormitories, state of the art field house, and intercollegiate sports such as football, basketball, wrestling, track and field, volleyball, and archery. Full time AST Degree Programs in Collision Repair, Automotive, Architecture, Mechanical Engineering and etc.

5876 The Vanguard School

1777 N Valley Road
Paoli, PA 19301 610-296-6700
FAX 610-640-0132
http://www.vanguardschool-pa.org
Jan C Rutt, Executive Director
Tim Lanshe, Director Education
Donna Annechino-Jiore, Director Admissions

State licensed and approved private, non-profit, non-sectarian day school serving children from three to twenty-one years of age who have been diagnosed with neurological disorders, emotional disturbance or autism/PDD.

5877 Woods Schools

Residential Center
Route 213
Langhorne, PA 19047 215-750-4000
Robert Griffith, President

Provides a full range of residential, special education, rehabilitation, recreation and vocational training.

Rhode Island

5878 Behavior Research Institute

240 Laban Street
Providence, RI 02909 401-944-1186
800-231-3405
FAX 401-946-4190
Penny Potter, Director Student Service
Rose Silva, Assistant Director Students

A nationally recognized residential/educational treatment program for children and adults with behavior disorders. The students have autism, mental retardation, brain damage, emotional disturbances or are in trouble with the law. The average student at BRI has been expelled from 5 programs and rejected by 9 others.

5879 Harmony Hill School

63 Harmony Hill Road
Chepachet, RI 02814 401-949-0690
FAX 401-949-2060
Terrence Leary, Executive Director

A private residential and day treatment center for behaviorally disordered and learning disabled boys, age eight through eighteen, who cannot be treated within their local educational system or community based mental health programs. Individual, group and family psychotherapy and 24-hour crisis intervention are available. Other programs include: Extended Day, Sex Offender, Diagnostic Day, Transition Programming, Summer Day, Career Education Center, and a Formalized Life Skills Program.

5880 Rhode Island Parent Information Network

175 Main Street
Pawtucket, RI 02860   401-727-4144
                        800-464-3399
                        FAX 401-727-4040
                        http://www.ripin.org
                        e-mail: ripin@ripin.org
Elizabeth Priestley, Executive Director

Parent Training and Information Program views parents as full partners in the educational process and a significant source of support and assistance to each other. Funded by the US Department of Education under the Individuals with Disabilities Education Act, these programs provide training and information to parents to enable such individuals to participate more effectively with professionals in meeting the educational needs of disabled children.

South Carolina

5881 Gateway School

353 Lawrence Street NW
Aiken, SC 29801   803-642-5067
Nancy Elliot, Executive Director

School geared for grades K-8 for children with learning disabilities.

5882 Parents Reaching Out to Parents of South Carolina

2712 Middleburg Drive
Columbia, SC 29204   803-779-3859
                        FAX 803-252-4513
Mary Eaddy, Executive Director

Private nonprofit parent oriented organization providing information, individual assistance and workshops to parents of children with disabilities ages birth-21. Services focus on enabling parents to have a better understanding of special education to participate more effectively with professionals in meeting the educational needs of disabled children. Funded by a grant from the US Department of Education and tax deductible contributions.

5883 Pine Grove

1500 Chestnut Road
Elgin, SC 29045   803-438-3011
                        FAX 803-438-8611
                        e-mail: carlmets@aol.com
Carl Herring, Executive Director

Offers an intensive academic, social skills and behavior modification program designed to return the child to his/her home area as soon as possible.

5884 Sandhills Academy

4335 Timberlane Drive
Columbia, SC 29205   803-787-2441
                        FAX 803-787-0103
Joan B Hathaway, Director

A private, nonprofit school for children with learning disabilities. Serves students from grades 1-8 and also offers diagnostic evaluations, summer school and educational therapy for all ages. Boarding with local families is also available.

5885 Trident Academy

1455 Wakendaw Road
Mt. Pleasant, SC 29464   843-884-7046
                           FAX 843-881-8320
                           http://www.tridentacademy.com
                           e-mail: admissions@tridentacademy.com
Myron C Harrington Jr, Headmaster
Betsy Fanning, Admissions Director

Private school for children with learning disabilities grades K through 12th, day students accepted with limited boarding. Offers an intensive, effective, multisensory program to remediate learning differences, tailored to each students unique needs.

Tennessee

5886 Bodine School

2432 Yester Oaks Drive
Germantown, TN 38139   901-754-1800
                         FAX 901-751-8595
                         http://bodineschool.org
                         e-mail: info@bodineschool.org
Rene Friemoth Lee, Executive Director

5887 Camelot Care Center

183 Fiddlers Lane
Kingston, TN 37763   865-376-2296
                        FAX 865-376-1950
James Spicer, Executive Director

A psychiatric residential treatment center serving children with emotional disturbances and learning disabilities.

5888 Devereux Genesis Learning Centers

430 Allied Drive
Nashville, TN 37211   615-832-4222
                        FAX 615-832-4577

Day school and treatment programs for adolescents and young adults who have emotional disorders and learning disabilities.

5889 Support and Training for Exceptional Children

423 E Bernard Avenue
Greenville, TN 37745   615-327-0294
                             FAX 615-327-0827

Parent Training and Information Program views parents as full partners in the educational process and a significant source of support and assistance to each other. Funded by the Division of Personnel Preparation, Office of Special Education Programs, these programs provide training and information to parents to enable such individuals to participate more effectively with professionals in meeting the educational needs of disabled children.

Texas

5890 Bridges Academy

901 Arizona Avenue
El Paso, TX 79902   915-532-6647
                          FAX 915-532-8767

Irma Keys, Director

Private School for students with learning disabilities.

5891 Bright Students Who Learn Differently

Winston School
5707 Royal Lane
Dallas, TX 75229   214-691-6950
                         FAX 214-691-1509
            http://www.winston-school.org
      e-mail: amy_smith@winston-school.org
Pamela K Murfin PhD, Head of School
Amy C Smith, Admission Director

The Winston School is a co-educational day college preparatory school, grades 1-12. Winston provides individualized programs for students with learning differences, including problems in reading, writing, language and mathematics, as well as attention-deficit/hyperactivity disorder. Student teacher ratio of 8:1. Founded in 1975 in a suburban 6-acre campus, 4 buildings on campus. Winston is accredited by the Independent Schools Association of the Southwest (ISAS) and a member of NAIS.

5892 Crisman Preparatory School

2455 N Eastman Road
Longview, TX 75605   903-758-9741
                           FAX 903-758-9767

Lucy Peacock, Director

5893 Diagnostic and Remedial Reading Clinic

622 Isom Road
San Antonio, TX 78216   210-341-7417
                              FAX 210-341-7417

Margo Barstow PhD

This clinic provides: complete psychological and educational evaluations; diagnostic and remedial services for academic problems; one-on-one instruction in all academic subjects; and consultation and evaluation services to public and private schools.

5894 Gateway School

1601 Ivy Lane
Arlington, TX 76011   817-226-6222
                            FAX 817-226-6225
            http://www.gatewayschool.com
Harriet Walber, Executive Director

An alternative school for students designed for the student who has average or above average intelligence yet has experienced little or no success previously in school.

5895 Gateway School: Arlington

1601 Ivy Lane
Arlington, TX 76011   817-226-6222
                            FAX 817-226-6225
            http://www.gatewayschool.com
Harriet Walber, Director

The only nonprofit accredited secondary school in the Forth Worth/Arlington area addressing academic and social challenges of students. Students who successfully complete the program earn a high school diploma.

5896 Houston Learning Academy

3333 Bering Drive
Houston, TX 77057   713-974-6658
                          FAX 713-975-6666
Susan McKinney, Contact

Offers high schools, grades 9-12. Six locations in Houston. Teachers work with special learning needs, including ADHD and classes are small. Established in 1983.

5897 Kenley School

1434 Matador Street
Abilene, TX 79605   915-698-3220
                          FAX 915-692-7387
Teri Reece, Executive Director

School for students with learning disabilities grades 1-8. Provides individual instruction.

5898 Keystone Academy

6506 Frankford Road
Dallas, TX 75252   972-250-4455
                         FAX 972-250-4960
           http://www.keystoneacademy.com
                 e-mail: kacademy@juno.com
Helen Werner, Founder/Director

A private, nonprofit school accommodating the learning differences of children in K-7th grade.

5899 Lane Learning Center

230 W Main Street
Lewisville, TX 75057   972-221-2564
                             888-412-5263
                         FAX 972-436-6964
          http://www.lanelearningcenter.com/
         e-mail: info@lanelearningcenter.com

5900   Neuhaus Education Center

4433 Bissonnet Street
Bellaire, TX   77401   713-664-7676
                                    FAX 713-664-4744
                                    http://www.neuhaus.org
                                    e-mail: info@neuhaus.org
Kay Allen, Director
Suzzanne Carraker, Director Teacher Development

Dyslexia specialist training courses and workshops for regular education teaching, parent consultation and adult literacy classes.

5901   Oak Hill Academy

6464 E Lovers Lane
Dallas, TX   75214   214-368-0664
                                    FAX 214-346-9866
                                    e-mail: oakhillphq@aol.com
Pam Quarterman, Director

A private special school for bright and talented students who have language learning differences. The focus is on developing the whole child. A wide range of educational methodologies are implemented in a structured environment by professional, caring teachers and therapists. Individualized programming allows students to progress at their own rate using multisensory/interactive learning experiences. The Academy also provides speech/language therapy and a summer program.

5902   Overton Speech and Language Center

4763 Barwick Drive
Fort Worth, TX   76132   817-294-8408
                                    FAX 817-294-8411
                                    http://www.overtonspeech.com
                                    e-mail: info@overtonspeech.com
Valerie Johnston, Director

Provides speech and language therapy.

5903   Parish School

11059 Timberline Road
Houston, TX   77043   713-467-4696
                                    FAX 713-467-8341
                                    http://www.parishschool.org
Robbin Parish MA CCC-SLP, Director/Founder
Margaret Noecker MED, Academic Coordinator
Melanie Siegle, Clinical Coordinator

Private school with a language based curriculum for children 18 months through nine years of age with language and learning differences.

5904   Partners Resource Network

1090 Longfellow Drive
Beaumont, TX   77706   409-898-4684
                                    800-866-4726
                                    FAX 409-898-4869
                                    http://www.partnerstx.org
                                    e-mail: txprnpath@sbcglobal.net
Janice Meyer, Executive Director
Alice Robertson, Training Coordinator

Views parents as full partners in the educational process and a significant source of support and assistance to each other. Funded by the Division of Personnel Preparation, Office of Special Education Programs and the US Department of Education, these programs provide training and information to parents to enable such individuals to participate more effectively with professionals in meeting the educational needs of children with disabilities.

5905   Psychoeducational Diagnostic Services

7233 Brentfield Drive
Dallas, TX   75248   972-931-5299
                                    FAX 972-392-7155
Harrian B Stern PhD, Educator Diagnostician

Psychoeducational diagnostic assessment of intellectual and academic ability, including assessing the ability of students with various learning styles. Offers consultations with parents, schools, etc.

5906   Psychology Clinic of Fort Worth

4200 S Hulen Street
Fort Worth, TX   76109   817-731-0888
William Barry Norman PhD, Contact

5907   SHIP Resource Center

University United Methodist Church
5084 De Zavala Road
San Antonio, TX   78249   210-696-1033

5908   Scottish Rite Learning Center

PO Box 10135
Lubbock, TX   79408   806-765-9150
                                    FAX 806-765-9564
Doris Haney, Director
Linda Stringer, Associate Director

Language training for students at risk for dyslexia.

5909   Shelton School and Evaluation Center

15720 Hillcrest Road
Dallas, TX   75248   972-774-1772
                                    FAX 972-991-3977
                                    http://www.shelton.org
                                    e-mail: jdodd@shelton.org
Joyce S Pickering, Executive Director
Diann Slaton BA, Admissions Director
Anne Thomas, Director Public Relations

A coeducational day school serving 780 students in grades Pre-K-12. The school focuses on the development of learning disabled students of average to above average intelligence, enabling them to succeed in conventional classroom settings. Services include on-site Evaluation Center for diagnostic testing, a Speech, Language and Hearing Clinic, an Early Childhood Program, open summer school and more.

5910   Star Ranch

Star Programs
HC 7 Box 39C
Ingram, TX   78025   830-367-4868
                                  FAX 830-367-2814
                            http://www.starranch.org
                    e-mail: 1southhard@starranch.org
Catherine Cole, Administrative Aid
Rand Southard, Director Child Services

Operates two programs at Star Ranch. One is a recreational/educational summer camp for children with learning difficulties. Boys and girls ages 7-18 attend one or two week sessions during the summer. Traditional summer camp activities as well as academic tutoring are offered. The second is a residential treatment center for boys ages 7-17 who are diagnosed as learning disabled and emotionally disturbed. Preference is given to younger boys as placement is long term.

5911   Starpoint School

Texas Christian University
2829 Stadium Drive
Fort Worth, TX   76109   817-921-7141
                                  FAX 817-921-7333

Kathleen Williams, Director
Barbara Trice, School Secretary

5912   VIP Educational Services

3921 Steck Avenue
Austin, TX   78759   512-345-9274
                                  FAX 512-345-0314
                         http://www.learnatvip.com
             e-mail: vip_educational@hotmail.com
Roberta Rosen, Owner/Educational Consultant

A diagnostic and tutoring service providing help to children and adults with learning disabilities, dyslexia, ADHD, and underachievement. Enrichment, organization, time management, study skills, and test taking strategies are also addressed. An assessment process identifies learning strengths and weaknesses. Advocacy for parents and students is provided.

5913   Vickery Meadow Learning Center

6329 Ridgecrest
Dallas, TX   75231   214-265-5057
                                  FAX 214-265-1666
                    e-mail: vmlcforliteracy@aol.com
Patrice Doerries

Utah

5914   Mountain Plains Regional Resource Center

Utah State University
1780 N Research Parkway
Logan, UT   84341   435-752-0238
                                  FAX 435-753-9750
                           http://www.usu.edu/mprrc
                         e-mail: cope@cc.usu.edu
John Copenhaver, Director

A federally funded project at Utah State University which provides technical assistance to CO, AZ, KS, MT, NE, ND, NM, SD, UT and WY on how to serve disabled infants, toddlers, children, youth and their families. Learning disabled children constitute a large block of our service population. A major component of our technical assistance is in the form of information drawn from thousands of documents ranging from published research studies to newsletters.

5915   Reid School

3310 S 2700 E
Salt Lake City, UT   84109   801-486-5083
                                  FAX 801-485-0661
Ethna Reid

Private school for all students.

5916   SEPS Center for Learning

1924 S 1100 E
Salt Lake City, UT   84105   801-467-2122
                                  FAX 801-467-2148
                            http://www.sepslc.com
                   e-mail: dvd.eva.seps@sepslc.com

Designs educational programs that help adults and children succeed in school and life. Specializing in one-on-one tutoring in all areas for all age levels, assessment, day school and preschool programs, computer assisted cognitive and academic therapy, reading programs, summer recreation and academic programs, consultation for schools and businesses.

5917   Utah Parent Center

2290 E 4500 S
Salt Lake City, UT   84117   801-272-1051
                                     800-468-1160
                                  FAX 801-272-8907

Helen Post, Director
Jeanne Gibson, Associate Director

Parent Training and Information Program views parents as full partners in the educational process and a significant source of support and assistance to each other. Funded by the Division of Personnel Preparation, Office of Special Education Programs, these programs provide training and information to parents to enable such individuals to participate more effectively with professionals in meeting the educational needs of disabled children.

Vermont

5918   Pine Ridge School

9505 Williston Road
Williston, VT   05495   802-434-2161
                                  FAX 802-434-5512
                         http://www.pineridgeschool.com
                  e-mail: jdoyle@pineridgeschool.com
Josh Doyle, Director Admissions

Serves students who have been diagnosed with a primary, specific language disability or a non-verbal learning disability. They are in the average range of intelligence and want to use those strengths in their remediation of their language weaknesses.

5919 Stern Center for Language and Learning

135 Allen Brook Lane
Williston, VT   05495   802-878-2332
                                        FAX 802-878-0230
Blanche Podhajski PhD, President

Founded in 1983, the center is a nonprofit organization providing comprehensive services for children and adults with learning disabilities. The Center is also an educational resource serving all of Northern New England and Northern New York State. Programs include educational testing, individual instruction, psychotherapy, school consultation, professional training for educators and a parent/professional resource library.

Virginia

5920 Accolink Academy

8519 Tuttle Road
Springfield, VA   22152   703-451-8041
                                        FAX 703-569-5365
Julia Warden, Diector Education

5921 Chesapeake Bay Academy

821 Baker Road
Virginia Beach, VA   23462   757-497-6200
                                        FAX 757-497-6304
                http://www.chesapeake.bayacademy.org
                e-mail: contact@chespeakebayacademy.net
MaryAnne Dukas, Head of School
Hunter Wortham, Admissions Director

Chesapeake Bay Academy is the only accredited independent school in Southeastern Virginia specifically dedicated to providing a strong academic program and individualized instruction for bright students in grade K-12 with LD and ADHD. With a student/teacher ratio of 5:1 a student:computer ratio of 2:1, qualified professionals tailor their techniques to individual needs, allowing students who have difficulty learning in traditional settings to finally succed.

5922 Fairfax House

3300 Woodburn Road
Annandale, VA   22003   703-560-6116
                                        FAX 703-560-6592
Bruce Wyman, Program Director

5923 Grafton School

PO Box 2500
Winchester, VA   22604   540-542-0280
                                        FAX 540-542-1722
                            http://www.grafton.org
                            e-mail: admis@grafton.org
Don Davis, Admissions Supervisor
Jean McIntyre, Admissions Supervisor

Grafton provides individualized educational and residential services and in-community supports for children, youth and adults with severe emotional disturbance, learning disabilities, mental retardation, autistic disorder, behavioral disorders, and other complex challenges, including physical disabilities.

5924 Learning Center of Charlottesville

2132 Ivy Road
Charlottesville, VA   22903   434-977-6006
                                        FAX 434-977-6009
Elizabeth A Cottone PhD, Executive Director

Individualized one-on-one tutoring for children and adults year round. Consultations. Educational and psychological evaluations.

5925 Learning Resource Center

909 1st Colonial Road
Virginia Beach, VA   23454   757-428-3367
                                        FAX 757-428-1630
Nancy Harris-Kroll, Executive Director

One-on-one remedial and tutorial sessions after school during the school year and all day and evening during the summer with specialists who have masters degrees. Advocacy services for parents of students with special needs. Psychoeducational testing is available. Special study skills and SAT courses given. Gifted, average, and learning disabled students attend.

5926 Leary School of Virginia

6349 Lincolnia Road
Alexandria, VA   22312   701-941-8150
                                        FAX 703-941-4237
                            http://www.learyschool.org
                e-mail: learyschool@bellatlantic.net
Ed Schultze, Executive Director
Gene Meale, Director of Admissions
Francesca Creo, Director Programs

A private, day, co-educational, special education facility. Currently serves 130 students, ages six to 21, with emotional, learning and behavioral problems. Along with individualized academic instruction, Leary School of Virginia offers a range of supportive and therapeutic services, including physical education, recreation therapy, group counseling, individual psychotherapy and art therapy.

5927 Little Keswick School

PO Box 24
Keswick, VA   22947   804-295-0457
                            http://www.avenue.org/oks
Marc Columbus, Headmaster

A residential special education school for 30 boys with emotional disturbances, learning disabilities and educable mental retardation with highly structured academic and behavioral programs.

5928 New Community School

4211 Hermitage Road
Richmond, VA 23227   804-266-2494
                                       FAX 804-264-3281
                                       http://www.tncs.org
                                       e-mail: admissions@tncs.org
Julia Ann Greenwood, School Head
Gita Morris, Admissions Chair

The New Community School is an independent school specializing in college preparatory instruction and intensive remediation for dyslexic students in grades 6-12.

5929 New Vistas School

520 Eldon Street
Lynchburg, VA 24501   804-846-0301
                                       FAX 804-528-1004
Lucy Ross, Executive Director

5930 Oakwood School

7210 Braddock Road
Annandale, VA 22003   703-941-5788
                                       FAX 703-941-4186
                          http://www.oakwoodschool.com
Robert McIntyre, Executive Director
Muriel Jedlicka, Admissions Specialist

A coeducational day school of 110 elementary and middle school students with mild to moderate learning disabilities.

5931 Parent Resource Center

Harry James Elementary School
1807 Arlington Road
Hopewell, VA 23860   804-541-6443
                                       FAX 804-541-6409
Brenda Atkins, Parent Coordinator
Joni Hunphries, Educator
Anna Noland, Educator

Purpose of this center is to provide training and information for teachers and parents of children with special needs. The goals are to help parents understand the special education process, and promote cooperation/communication between home, school and community.

5932 Pines Residential Treatment Center

825 Crawford Parkway
Portsmouth, VA 23704   757-398-0300
                                       877-227-7000
                                       FAX 877-846-6237
                                       http://www.absfirst.com
                                       e-mail: info@absfirst.com
Lenard Lexier, Executive Medical Director

5933 Riverside School for Dyslexia

2110 McRae Road
Richmond, VA 23235   804-320-3465
                                       FAX 804-320-6146
                          http://www.riversideschool.org
                          e-mail: info@riversideschool.org
Patricia DeOrio, Director
Julie Ann Wingfield, Principal

Day school for dyslexic students average to gifted; certified to operate by the Virginia Board of Education. Gillingham Academy accredited training site.

5934 StoneBridge Schools: Riverview Learning Center

4225 Portsmouth Boulevard
Chesapeake, VA 23321   757-488-7586
                                       FAX 757-465-8995
Trudy Webb, Director

Centers on stimulating each student's area of weakness in perception, language and cognition. We also work with each student's problem-solving and organizational skills.

5935 The Achievment Center

615 N Jefferson Street
Roanoke, VA 24016   540-982-0128
                                       FAX 540-982-3629
                          http://www.achievementcenter.org
                          e-mail: tacenter@rev.net
Barbara Ann Whitwell, Director

A private day school for children with learning disabilities.

Washington

5936 Children's Institute for Learning Differences: Consultation and Training

4030 86th Avenue SE, Campus F
Mercer Island, WA 98040   206-232-8680
                                       FAX 206-232-9377
                          http://www.childrensinstitute.com
                          e-mail: robbo@childrensinstitute.com
Robb Ott, Admissions/PR Director
Trina Westerlund, Executive Director/Founder

Providing a wide array of consultation services and training opportunities to parents and community professionals, as well as ongoing teacher training for our staff.

5937 Children's Institute for Learning Differences: Developmental Therapy Services

4030 86th Avenue SE, Campus F
Mercer Island, WA 98040   206-232-8680
                                       FAX 206-232-9377
                          http://www.childrensinstitute.com
                          e-mail: robbo@childrensinstitute.com
Robb Ott, Admissions/PR Director
Trina Westerlund, Executive Director/Founder

A pediatric clinic providing occupational therapy services with emphasis on motor planning problems and/or significant sensory processing problems.

5938 Glen Eden Institute

19351 8th Avenue
Poulsbo, WA 98370 · 360-697-0125
FAX 360-697-4712
http://www.glenedeninstitute.com
e-mail: director@glenedeninstitute.com
A Ronald Seifert, Co-Director
FV Brennan, Co-Director

Offers a unique educational alternative to meet the needs of those students who have been unable to reach their academic potential.

5939 Hamlin Robinson School

10211 12th Avenue S
Seattle, WA 98168 · 206-763-1167
FAX 206-762-2419
http://www.hamlinrobinson.org/
e-mail: hrs@uswest.net
Beverly Wolf, Director

A nonprofit, state approved elementary day school for children with specific language disability (dyslexia), providing a positive learning environment, meeting individual needs to nurture the whole child. Small classes use the Slingerland multi-sensory classroom approach in reading, writing, spelling and all instructional areas. It helps students discover the joy of learning, build positive self-esteem, and explore their full creative potential while preparing them for the classroom.

5940 Specialized Training for Military Parents

10209 Bridgeport Way SW
Tacoma, WA 98499 · 253-588-1741
800-298-3543
FAX 263-984-7520
TDY:283-588-1741
Heather Hebdon, Project Coordinator
Toni Salato, Parent Resource Coordinator
Sandy Grove, Parent Resource Coordinator

Parent Training and Information Program views parents as full partners in the educational process and a significant source of support and assistance to each other. Funded by the Division of Personnel Preparation, Office of Special Education Programs, these programs provide training and information to parents to enable such individuals to participate more effectively with professionals in meeting the educational needs of disabled children.

5941 St. Christopher Academy

Jevne Academy
140 S 140th Street
Seattle, WA 98168 · 206-246-9751
FAX 253-639-3466
http://www.stchristopheracademy.com
e-mail: jevne@stchristopheracademy.com
Darlene Jevne, Director

High school program for learning disabled, ADD/ADHD students. Non-religious state approved since 1982. SCA also has a working ranch program near Sun Valley for children ages 13-18 with learning disabilities.

5942 Westside Place

PO Box 31725
Seattle, WA 98103 · 206-634-0782
FAX 206-548-8008
e-mail: westside@sttl.uswest.net
Rosemarie Morris, Director

An independent, non-profit state approved school providing a full day school program for students at risk of failing or dropping out of school.

West Virginia

5943 Children's Therapy Clinic Project

2345 Chesterfield Avenue
Charleston, WV 25304 · 304-340-3546
e-mail: jennifer@childrenstherapyclinic.com
Jennifer Bezjak, Executive Director

Provides physical, occupational and speech therapy. Also augmentative communication, assistive devices, a swimming program and horseback riding for the disabled individual.

5944 Parent Training and Information

371 Broaddus Avenue
Clarksburg, WV 26301 · 304-624-1436
800-281-1436
FAX 304-624-1438
http://www.wvpti.org
e-mail: wvpti@aol.com
Pat Haberbosch, Project Director

Provides information to parents and to professionals who work with children with disabilities.

Wisconsin

5945 Chileda Institute

1020 Mississippi Street
La Crosse, WI 54601 · 608-782-6480
FAX 608-782-6481
http://www.chileda.org
Kirby Lentz

Educators for youth with developmental disabilities. Residential treatment center provides complete training and intensive therapy for children with severe mental and physical disabilities, closed head injuries and challenging behaviors.

6-17 years old

Wyoming

5946 Wyoming Parent Information Center

5 N Lobban
Buffalo, WY   82834   307-684-2277
                                 FAX 307-684-5314
                                 http://www.wpic.org
                                 e-mail: tdawson@wpic.org

Parent Training and Information Program views parents as full partners in the educational process and a significant source of support and assistance to each other. Funded by the Division of Personnel Preparation, Office of Special Education Programs, these programs provide training and information to parents to enable such individuals to participate more effectively with professionals in meeting the educational needs of disabled children.

Centers

5947 American College Testing Program

ACT Universal Testing
PO Box 168
Iowa City, IA   52243   319-337-1000
                               FAX 319-339-3021
                               http://www.act.org
Sandy Schlote, Testing Coordinator
Ed Colby, Public Relations
Richard J Ferguson, CEO

Helps individuals and organizations make informed decisions about education and work. We provide information for life's transitions.

5948 Diagnostic and Educational Resources

Traveling Tutors
6832 Old Dominion Drive
McLean, VA   22101   703-883-2009
                           FAX 703-734-0910
                           http://www.DER-online.com
                           e-mail: aspector@DER-online.com
Annette Spector, Executive Director
Elisabeth Wester, Office Manager

Focuses on what the child can do and builds self-esteem. Provides a full range of psychoeducational testing, parent advocacy, case management, and tutoring services. Diagnostic testing determines individual needs, which are addressed in one-on-one tutoring sessions in the child's home or school. Staff trained in LD/ADHD methodologies remediate learning disabilities and offer practical suggestions for home programs and for working with school systems.

5949 Educational Diagnostic Center at Curry College

Curry College
1071 Blue Hill Avenue
Milton, MA   02186   617-333-2364
                           FAX 617-333-2018
                           http://www.curry.edu
                           e-mail: curryadm@curry.edu
Dr Nancy Winbury, Coordinator/Professor

A comprehensive evaluation and testing center specializing in the learning needs of adolescents and adults. The Diagnostic Center welcomes adolescents and adults in need of learning strategies, long term educational plans, and better understanding of their learning profiles.

5950 Educational Study Center

353-A Robinson Hall I
Fairfax, VA   22030   703-993-2044
                             FAX 703-993-3681

5951 Educational Testing Service

Test Collection
Rosedale Road
Princeton, NJ   08541   609-921-9000
                               FAX 609-734-5410
                               http://www.ets.org
                               e-mail: etsinfo@ets.org
Kurt Landgraf, President/CEO

Our mission is to help advance quality and equity in education by providing fair and valid assessments, research and related services.

5952 Educational Testing Service: SAT Services for Students with Disabilities

College Board SAT Program
PO Box 6200
Princeton, NJ   08541   609-771-7137
                               FAX 609-771-7944
                               http://www.collegeboard.org
                               e-mail: ssd@info.collegeboard.org

Offers testing accommodations to attempt to minimize the effect of disabilities on test performance. The SAT Program tests eligible students with documented visual, physical, hearing, or learning disabilities who require testing accommodations for SAT.

5953 GED Test Accommodations for Candidates with Specific Learning Disabilities

American Council on Education
1 Dupont Circle NW
Washington, DC   20036   202-939-9490
                                800-626-9433
                                FAX 202-775-8578
                                http://www.gedtest.org
                                e-mail: ged@ace.nche.edu
Joan Auchter, Executive Director
Charles Bedore, Director Program Operations

The American Council on Education, founded in 1918, is the nation's coordinating higher education association. ACE is dedicated to the belief that equal educational opportunity and a strong higher education system are essential cornerstones of a democratic society.

5954 Georgetown University Child Development Center

3307 M Street NW
Washington, DC   20007   202-687-8635
                                FAX 202-687-8899
                                http://www.gucdc.georgetown.edu
                                e-mail: gucdc.georgetown.edu
Norio Azumi MD, Chief of Hospital Pathology
Judith Areen, Dean/Executive Vice President

To improve the quality of life for all children and youth, especially those with, or at risk for, special needs and their families.

5955 Institute on Applied Technology Communication Enhancement Center

Children's Hospital
300 Longwood Avenue
Boston, MA   02115   617-735-6998
Howard Shane, Director

Will evaluate children or adults with learning disabilities (among others) and recommend actions to take, especially the use of a computer and specific software titles.

5956   Law School Admission Council

PO Box 2001
Newtown, PA   18940   215-968-1001
                                       FAX 215-968-1119
                                       TDY:215-968-1128
                                       http://www.lsac.org
Bill Shelton, President

Students with documented learning disabilities can
apply for test accommodations as appropriate.

**5957   Munroe-Meyer Institute for Genetics and
         Rehabilitation**

University Affiliated Program
444 S 44th Street
Omaha, NE   68131   402-559-6402
                                       FAX 402-559-5737
                                       http://www.unmc.edu/mm/
                                       e-mail: mfbennie@unmc.edu
Bruce A Buehler, Director

Diagnostic evaluation therapy, speech, physical, occupational, behavioral therapies, pediatrics, dentistry, nursing, psychology, social work, genetics,
Media Resource Center, education, nutrition. Adult
services for developmentally disabled, genetic evaluation and counseling, adaptive equipment, motion
analysis laboratory, recreational therapy.

5958   National Center for Fair & Open Testing

342 Broadway
Cambridge, MA   02139   617-864-4810
                                       FAX 617-497-2224
                                       http://www.fairtest.org
                                       e-mail: info@fairtest.org
Monty Neill, Executive Director
Larry Wood, K-12 Assessment Reform Organizer

Dedicated to ensuring that America's students and
workers are assessed using fair, accurate, relevant and
open tests.

5959   Plano Child Development Center

5401 S Wentworth Avenue
Chicago, IL   60609   312-326-4488
                        e-mail: drjj@worldnet.att.net
Stephanie Johnson, Executive Director

Surveys children with visually related learning disabilities and offers vision education seminars geared
to learning disabilities.

5960   Providence Speech and Hearing Center

1301 W Providence Avenue
Orange, CA   92868   714-639-4990
                                       FAX 714-744-3841
                                       http://www.pshc.org
                                       e-mail: psqc@pshc.org
Margaret Inman, Founder
Mary Jo Hooper, Executive Director

Comprehensive services for testing and treatment of
all speech, language and hearing problems. Individual and group therapy beginning with parent/infant
programs.

5962   Reading Group

#6 Lincoln Square
Urbana, IL   61801   217-367-0914
                                       FAX 217-367-0500
                                       http://www.readinggroup.org
                                       e-mail: info@readinggroup.org
Marilyn Kay, Executive Director
Rita Young, Early Childhood Coordinator

One on one testing instruction and therapy for children and adults with dyslexia, ADD, Asperger Syndrome and gifted students with puzzling learning
differences.

5963   Rehabilitation Resource

Stout Vocational Rehabilitation Institute
University of Wisconsin-Stout
Menomonie, WI   54751   715-232-1232
                                       800-447-8688
                                       FAX 715-232-2356
                http://www.chd.udstout.edu/svri/twi/trr
                                       e-mail: admissions@uwstout.edu
Bob Peters, Program Director

Develops, publishes, and distributes a variety of rehabilitation related materials. Also makes referrals to
other sources on rehabilitation.

5964   Riley Child Development Center

Indiana University School of Medicine
702 Barnhill Drive
Indianapolis, IN   46202   317-274-8167
                                       FAX 317-274-9760
                                       http://www.child-dev.com
John Rau, Director

The Child Development Center provides interdisciplinary assessment for academics, communication,
motor, behavior, medical concerns, for children and
their families.

5965   Rose F Kennedy Center

Albert Einstein College of Medicine
1410 Pelham Parkway S
Bronx, NY   10461   718-430-8500
                                       FAX 718-904-1162
                                       http://www.aecom.yu.edu/cerc
Herbert J Cohen, Director

Provides comprehensive diagnostic services and intervention services for children and adults with learning disabilities.

5966   Scholastic Testing Service

480 Meyer Road
Bensenville, IL   60106   630-766-7150
                                       800-642-6787
                                       FAX 630-766-8054
                                       http://www.ststesting.com
                                       e-mail: ststesting@email.com
John D Kauffman, Vice President Marketing

Publisher of assessment materials from birth to adulthood, ability and achievement tests for kindergarten through grade twelve. Publishes the Torrance Tests of Creative Thinking, Thinking Creatively in Action and Movement, the STS High School Placement Test and Educational Development Series.

Behavior & Self Esteem

5967   A Day in the Life: Assessment and Instruction

Curriculum Associates
PO Box 2001
North Billerica, MA   01862
800-225-0248
FAX 800-366-1158
http://www.curriculumassociates.com/
e-mail: ca@infocurriculumassociates.com
Frank Ferguson, President
Fred Ferguson, VP Corporate Development/CIO

Embeds basic reading, writing, math and problem-solving skills in simulated job tasks. Two programs provide the activities that help students master these basic skills.

5968   AAMR Adaptive Behavior Scale: School Edition

Pro-Ed
8700 Shoal Creek Boulevard
Austin, TX   78757
512-451-3246
800-897-3202
FAX 512-451-8542
http://www.proedinc.com

Nadine Lambert, Author

Assesses children whose behavior indicates possible mental retardation, emotional disturbances or other learning difficulties.

5969   Autism Screening Instrument for Educational Planning

Slosson Educational Publications
538 Buffalo Road
East Aurora, NY   14052
716-652-0930
800-828-4800
FAX 800-655-3840
http://www.slosson.com
e-mail: slosson@slosson.com
Bradley Erford, Edward Kelly, Sue Larson, Author
Steven W Slosson, President
John Slosson, VP

Publishes materials on aptitude, developmental disabilities, school screening, speech language assessment, therapy, behavior conduct, special needs; also electronic teaching tapes and testing items.

5970   BASC Monitor for ADHD

AGS
4201 Woodland Road
Circle Pines, MN   55014
651-287-7220
800-328-2560
FAX 651-287-7223
http://www.agsnet.com
e-mail: agsmail@agsnet.com
Randy W Kamphaus and Cecil R Reynolds, Author

The BASC Monitor for ADHD is a powerful new tool to help evaluate the effectiveness of ADHD treatments using teacher and parent rating scales, and database software for tracking behavior changes.

5971   Behavior Assessment System for Children

AGS
4201 Woodland Road
Circle Pines, MN   55014
651-287-7220
800-328-2560
FAX 651-287-7223
http://www.agsnet.com
e-mail: agsmail@agsnet.com
Randy W Kamphaus and Cecil R Reynolds, Author

A powerful assessment to evaluate child and adolescent behavior. Includes a self-report form for describing the behaviors and emotions of children and adolescents. Administration time: 10 - 20 minutes (TRS & PRS) 30 - 45 minutes for SRP.

5972   Behavior Rating Instrument for Autistic and Other Atypical Children

Slosson Educational Publications
538 Buffalo Road
East Aurora, NY   14052
716-652-0930
800-828-4800
FAX 800-655-3840
http://www.slosson.com
e-mail: slosson@slosson.com
Sue Larson, Author
Steven W Slosson, President
John Slosson, VP

This instrument assesses: Relationship to an Adult; Communication; Drive for Mastery; Vocalization and Expressive Speech; Sound and Speech Reception; Social Responsiveness; and Psychobiological Development. Each of the seven scales begins with the most severe autistic behavior, and progresses to behavior roughly comparable to that of a normal 3 1/2 to 4 1/2 year-old. Also available for nonvocal communication. Administration is untimed and observational.

5973   Behavior Rating Profile

Pro-Ed
8700 Shoal Creek Boulevard
Austin, TX   78757
512-451-3246
800-897-3202
FAX 512-451-8542
http://www.proedinc.com
Linda Brown, Author

A global measure of behavior providing student, parent, teacher and peer scales. It helps to identify behaviors that may cause a student's learning problems.

5974   Child Behavior Checklist

University of Vermont
1 S Prospect Street
Burlington, VT   05401
802-656-8313
FAX 802-656-2602
http://www.aseba.org
e-mail: mail@aseba.org
Thomas M Achenbach PhD, Author

A standardized form for obtaining parents' reports of children's behavioral/emotional problems and competencies. Related forms obtain teacher, interviewer, observer and self-reports.

5975 Children's Apperceptive Story-Telling Test

Pro-Ed
8700 Shoal Creek Boulevard
Austin, TX 78757   512-451-3246
                           800-897-3202
                      FAX 512-451-8542
                 http://www.proedinc.com

Mary Schneider, Author

Employs apperceptive stories to evaluate the emotional functioning of school-age children.

Ages 6-13

5976 Culture-Free Self-Esteem Inventories

Pro-Ed
7700 Shoal Creek Boulevard
Austin, TX 78757   512-451-3246
                           800-897-3202
                      FAX 512-451-8542
                 http://www.proedinc.com

James Battle, Author

A series of self-report scales used to determine the level of self-esteem in children and adults.

Ages 5-Adult

5977 Devereux Early Childhood Assessment Program

Kaplan
1310 Lewisville-Clemmons Road
Lewisville, NC 27023
                           800-334-2014
                      FAX 800-452-7526
                 http://www.kaplanco.com

Devereux, Author

Easy-to-use, standardized assessment system that enhances social and emotional growth in children from 2-5 years. Encourages parent involvement, helps teachers with classroom planning and takes just 10 minutes to administer. Meets Head Start and IDEA requirements for strength-based assessment, as well as APA and NAEYC assessment guidelines.

5978 Disruptive Behavior Rating Scale

Slosson Educational Publications
538 Buffalo Road
East Aurora, NY 14052   888-756-7766
                           800-828-4800
                      FAX 800-655-3840
                 http://www.slosson.com
           e-mail: slosson@slosson.com

Georgina Moynihan, TTFM

Identifies common behavior problems such as attention deficit disorder, attention deficit hyperactivity disorder, oppositional disorders and anti-social conduct problems. *$39.00*

5979 Draw a Person: Screening Procedure for Emotional Disturbance

Pro-Ed
8700 Shoal Creek Boulevard
Austin, TX 78757   512-451-3246
                           800-897-3202
                      FAX 512-451-8542
                 http://www.proedinc.com

Jack Naglieri, Timothy McNeish, Achilles Bandos, Author

A screening test that helps identify children and adolescents who have emotional problems and require further evaluation.

5980 Fundamentals of Autism

Slosson Educational Publications
538 Buffalo Road
East Aurora, NY 14052   716-652-0930
                           800-828-4800
                      FAX 800-655-3840
                 http://www.slosson.com
           e-mail: slosson@slosson.com

Sue Larson, Author

The handbook and two accompanying checklists provide a quick, user-friendly approach to help in identifying and developing educationally related program objectives for the child diagnosed as Autistic.

5981 Multidimensional Self Concept Scale

Pro-Ed
8700 Shoal Creek Boulevard
Austin, TX 78757   512-451-3246
                           800-897-3202
                      FAX 512-451-8542
                 http://www.proedinc.com

Bruce Bracken, Author

A thoroughly researched, developed and standardized clinical instrument. It assesses global self-concept and six context-dependent self-concept domains that are functionally important in the social-emotional adjustment of youth and adolescents.

Ages 9-19

5982 Psychoeducational Assessment of Preschool Children

Western Psychological Services
12031 Wilshire Boulevard
Los Angeles, CA 90025   310-478-2061
                           800-648-8857
                      FAX 310-478-7838
              http://www.wpspublishing.com
           e-mail: help@wpspublising.com

Bruce A Bracken PhD, Author

Comprehensive, multidisciplinary presentation by nationally recognized contributors is based upon the concept that preschool assessment is a vibrant entity of its own - qualitatively and quantitatively different from the assessment of infants and toddlers. For professionals in pre-school assessment, early childhood education, and psycoeducational diagnostics.

573 pages
ISBN 0-205290-21-3

5983 Revised Behavior Problem Checklist

Psychological Assement Resources
16204 N Florida Avenue
Lutz, FL   33549   813-968-3003
                                    800-331-8378
                          FAX 800-727-9329
                       http://www.parinc.com
                 e-mail: chairman@parinc.com
Bob Smith III, Chairman/CEO

Psychological test products and software designed by
mental health professionals.

5984 SSRS: Social Skills

AGS
4201 Woodland Road
Circle Pines, MN   55014   651-287-7220
                                    800-328-2560
                          FAX 651-287-7223
                       http://www.agsnet.com
                 e-mail: agsmail@agsnet.com
Frank M Gresham and Stephen N Elliot, Author

A nationally standardized series of questionnaires
that obtain information on the social behaviors of children and adolescents from teachers, parents and the
students themselves. Administration time is 10-15
minutes per questionnaire.

Ages 3 - 18

5985 School Behaviors and Organization Skills

Curriculum Associates
PO Box 2001
North Billerica, MA   01862
                                    800-225-0248
                          FAX 800-366-1158
              http://www.curriculumassociates.com/
              e-mail: ca@infocurriculumassociates.com
Frank Ferguson, President
Fred Ferguson, VP Corporate Development/CIO

Introduces school behaviors for before, during, and
after class. Critical organization and time management skills are key elements of this module.

5986 Self-Esteem Index

Pro-Ed
8700 Shoal Creek Boulevard
Austin, TX   78757   512-451-3246
                                    800-897-3202
                          FAX 512-451-8542
                       http://www.proedinc.com
Linda Brown, Jacquelyn Alexander, Author

A new, multidimensional, norm-referenced measure
of the way that individuals perceive and value themselves.

Ages 0-11

5987 Social-Emotional Dimension Scale

Pro-Ed
8700 Shoal Creek Boulevard
Austin, TX   78757   512-451-3246
                                    800-897-3202
                          FAX 512-451-8542
                       http://www.proedinc.com
Jerry Hutton, Timothy Roberts, Author

A quick, well-standardized rating scale that can be
used by teachers, counselors and psychologists to
screen students who are at risk for conduct disorders
or emotional disturbances.

Ages 6-11

**5988 System of Multicultural Pluralistic Assessment
(SOMPA)**

Harcourt Assessement
19500 Bulverde Road
San Antonio, TX   78259
                                    800-211-8378
                          FAX 210-949-4475
              http://www.harcourtassessment.com
Jeff Galt, Chief Executive Officer

This comprehensive test determines the cognitive
abilities, sensory/motor abilities and adaptive behavior of children ages 5-11 years of age. SOMPA provides nine different measures and a way of estimating
learning potential through sociocultural and health
factors.

C-level product

LD Screening

**5989 ADD-H Comprehensive Teacher's Rating Scale:
2nd Edition**

Slosson Educational Publications
538 Buffalo Road
East Aurora, NY   14052   716-652-0930
                                    800-828-4800
                          FAX 800-655-3840
                       http://www.slosson.com
                 e-mail: slosson@slosson.com
Rina Ullmann, Robert Sprague, Author
Steven W Slosson, President
John Slosson, VP

This brief checklist assesses one of the most prevalent
childhood behavior problems: attention-deficit disorder, with or without hyperactivity. Because this disorder manifests itself primarily in the classroom, it is
best evaluated by teacher ratings. Also available in a
Spanish translation; please indicate when ordering.
$54.00

5990 Attention-Deficit/Hyperactivity Disorder Test

Slosson Educational Publications
538 Buffalo Road
East Aurora, NY 14052

716-652-0930
800-828-4800
FAX 800-655-3840
http://www.slosson.com
e-mail: slosson@slosson.com

James E Gilliam, Author
Steven W Slosson, President
John Slosson, VP

An effective instrument for identifying and evaluating ADHD. Contains 36 items that describe characteristic behaviors of persons with ADHD. These items comprise three subtests representing the core symptoms necessary for the diagnosis of ADHD: hyperactivity, impulsivity, and inattention. *$95.00*

5991 BRIGANCE Screens: Early Preschool

Curriculum Associates
PO Box 2001
North Billerica, MA 01862

800-225-0248
FAX 800-366-1158
http://www.curriculumassociates.com/
e-mail: ca@infocurriculumassociates.com

Albert Brigance, Author
Frank Ferguson, President
Fred Ferguson, VP Corporate Development/CIO

An affordable, easy-to-administer, all-purpose solution. Accurately screen key developmental and early academic skills in just 10-15 minutes per child. Widely used in Early Head Start programs, it meets IDEA requirements and provides consistent results that support early childhood educator's observations and judgement. *$89.00*

5992 BRIGANCE Screens: Infants and Toddler

Curriculum Associates
PO Box 2001
North Billerica, MA 01862

800-225-0248
FAX 800-366-1158
http://www.curriculumassociates.com/
e-mail: ca@infocurriculumassociates.com

Albert Brigance, Author
Frank Ferguson, President
Fred Ferguson, VP Corporate Development/CIO

An affordable, easy-to-administer, all-purpose solution. The Infant and Toddler Screen accurately assesses key developmental skills, and observes caregivers involvement and interactions. *$110.00*

5993 BRIGANCE Screens: K and 1

Curriculum Associates
PO Box 2001
North Billerica, MA 01862

800-225-0248
FAX 800-366-1158
http://www.curriculumassociates.com/
e-mail: ca@infocurriculumassociates.com

Albert Brigance, Author
Frank Ferguson, President
Fred Ferguson, VP Corporate Development/CIO

The K and 1 Screen is an affordable, easy-to-administer, all-purpose solution. Accurately screen key developmental and early academic skills in just 10-15 mintues per child. School districts nationwide rely on BRIGANCE for screening children before entering kindergarten, grade 1, and grade 2. It meets IDEA requirements and provides consistant results that support early childhood educators observations and judgement.

5994 Basic School Skills Inventory: Screen and Diagnostic

Pro-Ed
8700 Shoal Creek Boulevard
Austin, TX 78757

512-451-3246
800-897-3202
FAX 800-397-7633
http://www.proedinc.com

Donald Hammill, Author

Can be used to locate children who are high risk for school failure, who need more in-depth assessment and who should be referred for additional study.

Ages 0-4 & 6-11

5995 Complete Clinical Dysphagia Evaluation: Test Forms

LinguiSystems
3100 4th Avenue
East Moline, IL 61244

800-776-4332
FAX 800-577-4555
TDY:800-933-8331
http://www.linguisystems.com
e-mail: service@linguisystems.com

Linda Bowers, Owner
Rosemary Huisingh, Owner

These test forms are used with The Complete Clinical Dyspagia Evaluation. You'll come away with a complete picture of your patient's behavioral, oral-motor, laryngeal, reespiratory, cognitive, and swallowing abilities and limitations.

5996 DABERON Screening for School Readiness

Pro-Ed
8700 Shoal Creek Boulevard
Austin, TX 78757

512-451-3246
800-897-3202
FAX 800-397-7633
http://www.proedinc.com

Virginia Danzer, Author

Provides a standardized assessment of school readiness in children with learning or behavior problems.

Ages 4-6

5997 Developmental Assessment for the Severely Disabled

Pro-Ed
8700 Shoal Creek Boulevard
Austin, TX 78757

512-451-3246
800-897-3202
FAX 512-451-8542
http://www.proedinc.com

Mary Kay Dykes, Author

Offers diagnostic and programming personnel concise information about individuals who are functioning between birth and 8 years of age developmentally.

Ages 0-84

5998 Educational Developmental Series

Scholastic Testing Service
480 Meyer Road
Bensenville, IL   60106   630-766-7150
                                       800-642-6787
                                 FAX 630-766-8054
                              http://www.stsesting.com
                           e-mail: ststesting@email.com
John D Kauffman, VP Marketing

A standardized battery of ability and achievement tests. Administration time is approximately 2.5 - 5 hours, depending on grade level and subtests. The EDSERIES has the most comprehensive coverage of all the STS tests. It permits teachers, counselors and administrators to evaluate a student from the broadest possible perspective. A school may use the EDSERIES on a lease/score basis or it may purchase testing materials.

5999 Fundamentals of Autism

Slosson Educational Publications
538 Buffalo Road
East Aurora, NY   14052   716-652-0930
                                       800-828-4800
                                 FAX 800-655-3840
                              http://www.slosson.com
                           e-mail: slosson@slosson.com
Sue Larson, Author

Provides a quick, user-friendly, effective, and accurate approach to help in identifying and developing educationally related program objectives for children diagnosed as autistic.

6000 Goldman-Fristoe Auditory Skills Test Battery

Pro-Ed
8700 Shoal Creek Boulevard
Austin, TX   78757   512-451-3246
                                       800-897-3202
                                 FAX 800-397-7633
                              http://www.proedinc.com
Ronald Goldman, Author

An individually administered measure of a broad range of auditory skills. Administer the full battery to receive a total picture of an individual's auditory skills using the Battery Profile. Administer a single test or a cluster of tests as needed.

6001 Goodenough-Harris Drawing Test

Harcourt Assessment
19500 Bulverde Road
San Antonio, TX   78259
                                       800-211-8378
                                 FAX 210-949-4475
                        http://www.harcourtassessment.com
Florence Goodenough, Author
Jeff Galt, President/CEO
Jack Dilworth, Chairman
Gail Ribalta, Vice President Marketing

This test focuses on mental maturity without requiring verbal skills. The fifteen-minute examination provides standard scores for children ages 3-15. *$143.00*

6002 Kaufman Assessment Battery for Children

AGS
4201 Woodland Road
Circle Pines, MN   55014   651-287-7220
                                       800-328-2560
                                 FAX 651-287-7223
                              http://www.agsnet.com
                           e-mail: agsmail@agsnet.com
Alan Kaufman, Nadeen Kaufman, Author

An individually administered measure of intelligence and achievement, using simultaneous and sequential mental processes.

35-85 min

6003 Kaufman Brief Intelligence Test

AGS
4201 Woodland Road
Circle Pines, MN   55014   651-287-7220
                                       800-328-2560
                                 FAX 651-287-7223
                              http://www.agsnet.com
                           e-mail: absmail@absnet.com
Alan Kaufman, Nadeen Kaufman, Author

KBIT is a brief, individually administered test of verbal and non-verbal intelligence. Screens two cognitive functions quickly and easily.

15-30 min

6004 Marshall University: HELP Program

Higher Education for Learning Problems
520 18th Street
Huntington, WV   25703   304-696-6252
                                 FAX 304-696-3231
                              http://www.marshall.edu
Barbara P Guyer, Director HELP Program
Lynne Weston, Assistant Director
Debbie Painter MA, Coordinator Diagnostics

The HELP program is committed to providing assistance through individual tutuoring, mentoring and support, as well as fair and legal access to educational opportunities for students diagnosed with learning disabilities and related disorders such as ADD/ADHD.

6005 Monitoring Basic Skills Progress

Pro-Ed
8700 Shoal Creek Boulevard
Austin, TX   78757   512-451-3246
                                       800-897-3202
                                 FAX 800-397-7633
                              http://www.proedinc.com
Lynn Fuchs, Author

A computer-assisted measurement program that tests and monitors progress in three academic areas: basic reading, basic math and basic spelling.

6006 National Center of Higher Education for Learning Problems (HELP)

Myers Hall
520 18th Street
Huntington, WV 25703 304-696-6313
FAX 304-696-3231
e-mail: painter@marshall.edu
Barbara P Guyer, Director HELP Program
Lynee Weston, Assistant Director
Debbie Painter MA, Coordinator Diagnostics

The HELP program offers a full battery of comprehensive psychoeducational tests to determine if an individual has learning and/or attention deficits. The team of professionals can identify specific problems for all ages, such as school age children, college students, medical students, and professionals.

6007 PPVT-lll: Peabody Test-Picture Vocabulary Test

AGS
4201 Woodland Road
Circle Pines, MN 55014 651-287-7220
800-328-2560
FAX 651-287-7223
http://www.agsnet.com
e-mail: customerservice@agsnet.com
Lloyd Dunn, Leota Dunn, Author

A measure of hearing vocabulary for Standard American English; administration time: 10-15 minutes.

6008 Peabody Individual Achievement Test

AGS
4201 Woodland Road
Circle Pines, MN 55014 651-287-7220
800-328-2560
FAX 651-287-7223
http://www.agsnet.com
e-mail: agsmail@agsnet.com
Frederick Markwardt Jr, Author

A thorough and updated individual measure of academic achievement; administration time: 60 minutes.

6009 Restless Minds, Restless Kids

Slosson Educational Publications
538 Buffalo Road
East Aurora, NY 14052 716-652-0930
800-828-4800
FAX 800-655-3840
http://www.slosson.com
e-mail: slosson@slosson.com
Rick D'Alli, Author
Steven W Slosson, President
John Slosson, VP

Two leading specialists in the field of childhood behavioral disorders discuss the state-of-the-art approach to diagnosing and testing ADHD. They are joined by four mothers of ADHD children who share their experiences of the effects of this disorder on the family. *$67.00*

6010 School Readiness Test

Scholastic Testing Service
480 Meyer Road
Bensenville, IL 60106 630-766-7150
800-642-6787
FAX 630-766-8054
http://www.ststesting.com
e-mail: ststesting@email.com
John D Kauffman, VP Marketing

An effective tool for determining the readiness of each student for first grade. It allows a teacher to learn as much as possible about every entering student's abilities, and about any factors that might interfere with his or her learning.

6011 Screening Children for Related Early Educational Needs

Pro-Ed
8700 Shoal Creek Boulevard
Austin, TX 78757 512-451-3246
800-897-3202
FAX 800-397-7633
http://www.proedinc.com
Wayne Hresko, Author

A new academic screening test for young children that provides both global and specific ability scores that can be used to identify individual abilities.

Ages 3-7

6012 Slosson Intelligence Test: Revised

Pro-Ed
8700 Shoal Creek Boulevard
Austin, TX 78757 512-451-3246
800-897-3202
FAX 800-397-7633
http://www.proedinc.com
Richard Slosson, Author

A widely used individual screening test for those who need to evaluate the mental ability of individuals who are learning disabled, mentally retarded, blind, orthopedically disabled, normal, or gifted from ages 4 to adulthood. *$111.00*

Ages 4-Adult

6013 Source for Nonverbal Learning Disorders

LinguiSystems
3100 4th Avenue
East Moline, IL 61244
800-776-4332
FAX 800-577-4555
http://www.linguisystems.com
e-mail: service@linguisystems.com
Linda Bowers, Owner
Rosemary Huisingh, Owner

Not sure if you have a student with nonverbal learning disorder? See if this description sounds familiar: ignores nonverbal cues such as facial expressions, is clumsy for no apparent reason, makes inappropriate social remarks, and has difficulty with visual-spatial-organizational tasks. This resource provides you with useful checklists, anecdotes, and methods for dealing with this little understood disorder through the lifespan.

6014 TOVA

Universal Attention Disorders
4281 Katella Avenue
Los Alamitos, CA   90720   714-229-8770
                                 800-729-2886
                            FAX 714-229-8782
                         http://www.tovatest.com
                         e-mail: info@tovatest.com
Clifford Corman, Medical Director
Karen Carlson, Marketing Director

The TOVA (Tests of Variables of Attention) is a computerized, objective measure of attention and impulsivity, used in the assessment and treatment of ADD/ADHD. It is standardized from 4 to 80 years of age. TOVA's report contains a full analysis and interpetation of data. Variables measured include omissions, commisions, response time and response time variability.

6015 Test of Memory and Learning (TOMAL)

Pro-Ed
8700 Shoal Creek Boulevard
Austin, TX   78757   512-451-3246
                                 800-897-3202
                            FAX 800-397-7633
                       http://www.proedinc.com
Cecil Reynolds, Erin Bigler, Author

TOMAL provides ten subtests that evaluate general and specific memory functions.

Ages 5-19

6016 Test of Nonverbal Intelligence

Pro-Ed
8700 Shoal Creek Boulevard
Austin, TX   78757   512-451-3246
                                 800-897-3202
                            FAX 800-397-7633
                       http://www.proedinc.com
Linda Brown, Author

A language-free measure of reasoning and intelligence presents a variety of abstract problem solving tasks.

Ages 0-89

6017 Vision, Perception and Cognition: Manual for Evaluation & Treatment

Therapro
225 Arlington Street
Framingham, MA   01702   508-872-9494
                                 800-257-5376
                            FAX 508-875-2062
                      http://www.theraproducts.com
                      e-mail: info@theraproducts.com
Barbara Zoltan, Ellen Siev & Brenda Freishtat, Author

Details methods for testing perceptual, visual and cognitive deficits, as well as procedure for evaluating test results in relation to cognitive loss. Clearly explains each deficit, provides step by step testing techniques and gives complete treatment guidelines. Also includes information on the use of computers in cognitive training. *$37.00*

181 pages

Math

6018 3 Steps to Math Success

Curriculum Associates
PO Box 2001
North Billerica, MA   01862
                                  800-225-0248
                             FAX 800-366-1158
                http://www.curriculumassociates.com/
                e-mail: ca@infocurriculumassociates.com
Curriculum Associates, Author
Frank Ferguson, President
Fred Ferguson, VP Corporate Development/CIO

We developed an integrated approach to math that ensures academic success long after the final bell has rung. Together, these series create an easy-to-use system of targeted instruction designed to remedy math weakness and reinforce math strengths.

6019 AfterMath Series

Curriculum Associates
PO Box 2001
North Billerica, MA   01862
                                  800-225-0248
                             FAX 800-366-1158
                http://www.curriculumassociates.com/
                e-mail: e-support@curricassoc.com

Galileo once said that mathematics is the alphabet in which the universe was created. This series helps students master that alphabet. As they puzzle their way through brainteasers and learn math magic, students build critical-thinking skills that are vital to comprehending and succeeding in today's world.

6020 ENRIGHT Computation Series

Curriculum Associates
PO Box 2001
North Billerica, MA   01862
                                  800-225-0248
                             FAX 800-366-1158
                http://www.curriculumassociates.com/
                e-mail: e-support@curricassoc.com

Close the gap between expected and actual computation performance. The ENRIGHT Computation Series provides the practice necessary to master addition, subtraction, multiplication, and division of whole numbers, fractions, and decimals.

6021 Figure It Out: Thinking Like a Math Problem Solver

Curriculum Associates
PO Box 2001
North Billerica, MA   01862
                                  800-225-0248
                             FAX 800-366-1158
                http://www.curriculumassociates.com/
                e-mail: e-support@curricassoc.com

Critical thinking is the key to unlocking the mystery of these nonroutine problems. Your students will eagerly accept the challenge! Students learn to apply eight strategies in each book including: draw a picture; use a pattern; work backwards; make a table; and guess and check.

6022 Getting Ready for Algebra

Curriculum Associates
PO Box 2001
North Billerica, MA 01862
800-225-0248
FAX 800-366-1158
http://www.curriculumassociates.com/
e-mail: e-support@curricassoc.com

NCTM encourages algebra instruction in the early grades to develop critical-thinking, communication, reasoning, and problem-solving skills. Getting Ready for Algebra exercises these skills in lessons that focus on key algebra concepts: adding and subtracting positive integers; patterns; set theory notation; open sentences; inequality and more.

6023 Learning Disability Evaluation Scale: Renormed

Hawthorne Educational Services
800 Gray Oak Drive
Columbia, MO 65201
573-874-1710
800-542-1673
FAX 800-442-9509
http://www.hes-inc.com
Stephen McCarney, Author

The Learning Disability Evaluation Scale (LDES) is an initial screening and assessment instrument in the areas of listening, thinking, speaking, reading, writing, spelling, and mathematical calculations based on the federal definition (IDEA). The Learning Disability Intervention Manual (LDIM) is a companion to the LDES and contains goals, objectives, and intervention/instructional strategies for the learning problems identified by the LDES. *$152.00*

217 pages

6024 QUIC Tests

Scholastic Testing Service
480 Meyer Road
Bensenville, IL 60106
630-766-7150
800-642-6787
FAX 630-766-8054
http://www.ststesting.com
e-mail: ststesting@email.com
John D Kauffman, VP Marketing

The Quic Tests are used to determine the functional level of student comptetency in mathematics and/ or communicative arts for use in grades 2-12. Administration time is 30 minutes or less.

6025 Skills Assessments

Harcourt
6277 Sea Harbor Drive
Orlando, FL 32819
800-531-5015
FAX 512-343-6854
http://www.harcourtachieve.com
e-mail: info@steck-vaughn.com
Jeff Johnson, Dir Marketing Communications

This handy, all-in-one resource helps identify students strengths and weaknesses in order to determine appropriate instructional levels in each of five subjects areas: reading; language arts; math; science; and social studies. Assessments are identified by subtopics in each subject.

6026 Test of Mathematical Abilities

Pro-Ed
8700 Shoal Creek Boulevard
Austin, TX 78757
512-451-3246
800-897-3202
FAX 800-397-7633
http://www.proedinc.com
Virginia Brown, Mary Cronin, Elizabeth McEntire, Author

Has been developed to provide standardized information about story problems and computation, attitude, vocabulary and general cultural application. *$92.00*

Ages 3-12

Professional Guides

6027 Assessment Update

Jossey-Bass
111 River Street
Hoboken, NJ 07030
201-748-6000
FAX 201-748-6088
http://www.josseybass.com/wiley
William J Pesce, President/CEO
Trudy Banta, Editor

Assessment Update is dedicated to covering the latest developments in the rapidly evolving area of higher education assessment. Assessment Update offers all academic leaders up-to-date information and practical advice on conducting assessments in a range of areas, including student learning and outcomes, factulty instruction, academic programs and curricula, student services, and overall institutional functioning.

6028 Assessment of Students with Handicaps in Vocational Education

Association for Career and Technical Education
1410 King Street
Alexandria, VA 22314
703-683-3111
800-626-9972
FAX 703-683-7424
http://www.acteonline.org
L Albright, Author
Jan Bray, Executive Director
Tina Pugliese, Senior Dir Strategic Marketing

Includes teachers, supervisors, administrators and others interested in the development and improvement of vocational, technical and practical-arts education.

6029 BRIGANCE Word Analysis: Strategies and Practice

Curriculum Associates
PO Box 2001
North Billerica, MA   01862
800-225-0248
FAX 800-366-1158
http://www.curriculumassociates.com/
e-mail: ca@infocurriculumassociates.com
Albert Brigance, Author
Frank Ferguson, President
Fred Ferguson, VP Corporate Development/CIO

Our comprehensive, two-volume resource combines activities, strategies, and reference materials for teaching phonetic and structural word analysis. Two durable binders feature reproducible activity pages. Choose from more than 1,600 activities for corrective instruction or to reinforce your classroom reading program.

6030 Career Planner's Portfolio: A School-to-work Assessment Tool

Curriculum Associates
PO Box 2001
North Billerica, MA   01862
800-225-0248
FAX 800-366-1158
http://www.curriculumassociates.com/
e-mail: ca@infocurriculumassociates.com
Robert G Forest, Author
Frank Ferguson, President
Fred Ferguson, VP Corporate Development/CIO

Students career plans develop and evolve over several school years. Our portfolio will help track of their progess.

6031 Computer Scoring Systems for PRO-ED Tests

Pro-Ed
8700 Shoal Creek Boulevard
Austin, TX   78757
512-451-3246
800-897-3202
FAX 800-397-7633
http://www.proedinc.com

Computer scoring systems have been developed to generate reports for many PRO-ED tests and to help examiners interpret test performance.

6032 Goals and Objectives Writer Software

Curriculum Associates
PO Box 2001
North Billerica, MA   01862
800-225-0248
FAX 800-366-1158
http://www.curriculumassociates.com/
e-mail: ca@infocurriculumassociates.com
Frank Ferguson, President
Fred Ferguson, VP Corporate Development/CIO

Using the Goals and Objectives program, you'll quickly and easily create, edit, and print IEPs. The CD allows you to install the program on your hard drive in order to save students data for future updates. You can easily export IEPs into any word processing program. CD-Rom for Windows and Macintosh.

6033 Occupational Aptitude Survey and Interest Schedule

Pro-Ed
8700 Shoal Creek Boulevard
Austin, TX   78757
512-451-3246
800-897-3202
FAX 800-397-7633
http://www.proedinc.com
Randall Parker, Author

Consists of two related tests: the OASIS-2 Aptitude Survey and the OASIS-2 Interest Schedule. The tests were normed on the same national sample of 1,505 students from 13 states. The Aptitude Survey measures six broad aptitude factors that are directly related to skills and abilities required in over 20,000 jobs and the Interest Schedule measures 12 interest factors directly related to the occupations listed in Occupational Exploration.

6034 Portfolio Assessment Teacher's Guide

Harcourt
6277 Sea Harbor Drive
Orlando, FL   32819
800-531-5015
FAX 800-699-9459
http://www.harcourtachieve.com
e-mail: ecare@harcourt.com
Roger Farr, Author

Start your portfolio systems with tips from the expert. Roger Farr outlines the basic steps for evaluating a portfolio, offers ideas for organizing portfolios and making the most of portfolio conferences, and provides reproducible evaluation forms for primary through intermediate grades and above. *$21.80*

6035 Teaching Test Taking Skills

Brookline Books
PO Box 97
Newton Upper Falls, MA   02464
617-868-0360
800-666-2665
FAX 617-558-8011
http://www.people.delphi.com/brooklinebks
e-mail: brooklinebks@delphi.com
Margo Mastropieri, Thomas Scruggs, Author

Test-wise individuals often score higher than others of equal ability who may not use test-taking skills effectively. This work teaches general concepts about the test format or other conditions of testing, not specific items on the test. *$21.95*

ISBN 0-914797-76-X

6036 Tests, Measurement and Evaluation

American Institutes for Research
1000 Thomas Jefferson Street NW
Washington, DC   20007
202-342-5000
FAX 202-298-6809
http://www.air.org
Sol H Pelavin, President/CEO

Our goal is to provide governments and the private sector with responsive services of the highest quality by applying and advancing the knowledge, theories, methods, and standards of the behavioral and social services to solve significant societal problems and improve the quality of life of all people.

Reading

6037 3 Steps to Reading Success

Curriculum Associates
PO Box 2001
North Billerica, MA   01862

800-225-0248
FAX 800-366-1158
http://www.curriculumassociates.com/
e-mail: e-support@curricassoc.com

Equipping your students with the skills and strategies they need to achieve lifelong success can be a challenge. That's why we developed an integrated approach to learning that ensures academic success long after the final bell has rung.

6038 BRIGANCE Readiness: Strategies and Practice

Curriculum Associates
PO Box 2001
North Billerica, MA   01862

800-225-0248
FAX 800-366-1158
http://www.curriculumassociates.com/
e-mail: ca@infocurriculumassociates.com
Albert Brigance, Author
Frank Ferguson, President
Fred Ferguson, VP Corporate Development/CIO

Attend to the needs and differences of the children in your program using Readiness: Strategies and Practice. Skills are introduced, taught, and reinforced using both age-appropriate and individual appropriate activties. *$174.00*

6039 CLUES for Better Reading: Grade 1

Curriculum Associates
PO Box 2001
North Billerica, MA   01862

800-225-0248
FAX 800-366-1158
http://www.curriculumassociates.com/
e-mail: ca@infocurriculumassociates.com
Diane Lapp, James Flood, Author
Frank Ferguson, President
Fred Ferguson, VP Corporate Development/CIO

Clues for Better Reading Book A develops and strengthens comprehension through reading activities in the same skill strands featured in the Kindergarten level. The 96-page Teacher Guide provides activities to introduce the unit skill and new vocabulary, followed by guided lessons and extension activities.

6040 CLUES for Better Reading: Grade 2-5

Curriculum Associates
PO Box 2001
North Billerica, MA   01862

800-225-0248
FAX 800-366-1158
http://www.curriculumassociates.com/
e-mail: ca@infocurriculumassociates.com
Diane Lapp, James Flood, Author
Frank Ferguson, President
Fred Ferguson, VP Corporate Development/CIO

Students explore a variety of literacy genres: stories; poetry; plays, newspaper articles, and others. Related lanuage activities - writing, word analysis, or study skills - help students extend reading comprehension to other areas of language arts.

6041 CLUES for Better Reading: Kindergaten

Curriculum Associates
PO Box 2001
North Billerica, MA   01862

800-225-0248
FAX 800-366-1158
http://www.curriculumassociates.com/
e-mail: ca@infocurriculumassociates.com
Diane Lapp, James Flood, Author
Frank Ferguson, President
Fred Ferguson, VP Corporate Development/CIO

Emergent readers explore language with Clues for Better Reading and Writing. Teacher-directed lessons feature minimal text with appealing full-color artwork, and place a strong emphasis on oral literature to develop early reading skills.

6042 Capitalization and Punctuation

Curriculum Associates
PO Box 2001
North Billerica, MA   01862

800-225-0248
FAX 800-366-1158
http://www.curriculumassociates.com/
e-mail: ca@infocurriculumassociates.com
Curriculum Associates, Author
Frank Ferguson, President
Fred Ferguson, VP Corporate Development/CIO

Capitalization and Punctuation features structured, easy to understand lessons that are organized sequentially. Students read the rules, study sample exercises, apply the skills in practice lessons, and review the skills in maintenance lessons.

6043 Effective Reading of Textbooks

Curriculum Associates
PO Box 2001
North Billerica, MA   01862

800-225-0248
FAX 800-366-1158
http://www.curriculumassociates.com/
e-mail: ca@infocurriculumassociates.com
Anita Archer, Author
Frank Ferguson, President
Fred Ferguson, VP Corporate Development/CIO

Students practice previewing for reading, active reading, indentation note-taking, mapping a visual display of content, and writing a summary paragraph.

6044 Extensions in Reading

Curriculum Associates
PO Box 2001
North Billerica, MA 01862

800-225-0248
FAX 800-366-1158
http://www.curriculumassociates.com/
e-mail: ca@infocurriculumassociates.com

Curriculum Assoociates, Author
Frank Ferguson, President
Fred Ferguson, VP Corporate Development/CIO

A unique new program teaching reading strategies and more. Extensions offers rich experiences with nonfiction and fiction. Each lesson extends to include: researching and writing; use of graphic organizers; vocabulary development; and comprehension questions with test-prep format.

6045 Formal Reading Inventory

Pro-Ed
8700 Shoal Creek Boulevard
Austin, TX 78757

512-451-3246
800-897-3202
FAX 800-397-7633
http://www.proedinc.com

J Lee Wiederholt, Author

A national test for assessing silent reading comprehension and diagnosing reading miscues.

6046 Gray Oral Diagnostic Reading Tests

Pro-Ed
8700 Shoal Creek Boulevard
Austin, TX 78757

512-451-3246
800-897-3202
FAX 800-397-7633
http://www.proedinc.com

Brian Bryant, J Lee Wiederholt, Author

Uses two alternate, equivalent forms to assess students who have difficulty reading continuous print and who require an evaluation of specific abilities and weaknesses. *$235.00*

6047 Gray Oral Reading Tests

Pro-Ed
8700 Shoal Creek Boulevard
Austin, TX 78757

512-451-3246
800-897-3202
FAX 800-397-7633
http://www.proedinc.com

J Lee Wiederholt, Brian Bryant, Author

The latest revision provides an objective measure of growth in oral reading and an aid in the diagnosis of oral reading difficulties. *$198.00*

6048 Reading Assessment System

Steck-Vaughn Company
PO Box 690789
Orlando, FL 32819

800-531-5015
FAX 512-343-6854
http://www.steck-vaughn.com
e-mail: info@steck-vaughn.com

The Reading Assessment System provides an ongoing measure of specific student's skills and offers detailed directions for individual instruction and remediation. Up to eight reports are available. This popular program generates individual scores, class scores, school scores, and district reports.

6049 Scholastic Abilities Test for Adults

Pro-Ed
8700 Shoal Creek Boulevard
Austin, TX 78757

512-451-3246
800-897-3202
FAX 800-397-7633
http://www.proedinc.com

Brian Bryant, James Patton, Caroline Dunn, Author

Measures scholastic competence, aptitude and academic achievement for persons with learning difficulties. *$164.00*

Ages 16-70

6050 Skills Assessments

Steck-Vaughn Company
PO Box 690789
Orlando, FL 32819

800-531-5015
FAX 512-343-6854
http://www.steck-vaughn.com
e-mail: info@steck-vaughn.com

This handy, all-in-one resource helps identify students strengths and weaknesses in order to determine appropriate instructional levels in each of five subjects areas: reading; language arts; math; science; and social studies. Assessments are identified by subtopics in each subject.

6051 Standardized Reading Inventory

Pro-Ed
8700 Shoal Creek Boulevard
Austin, TX 78757

512-451-3246
800-897-3202
FAX 800-397-7633
http://www.proedinc.com

Phyllis Newcomer, Author

An instrument for evaluating students' reading ability. *$231.00*

6052 TERA-3: Test of Early Reading Ability 3nd Edition

AGS
4201 Woodland Road
Circle Pines, MN 55014

651-287-7220
800-328-2560
FAX 651-287-7223
http://www.SLPforum.com
e-mail: ags@skypoint.com

Kim Reid, Wayne Hresko and Donald Hammill, Author

Ideal for screening children's early reading abilities. Specifically the revised test measures knowledge of contextual meaning, the alphabet and conventions such as reading from left to right. *$236.00*

6053 Test of Early Reading Ability

Pro-Ed
8700 Shoal Creek Boulevard
Austin, TX   78757   512-451-3246
                                   800-897-3202
                          FAX 800-397-7633
                      http://www.proedinc.com
D Kim Reid, Wayne Hresko, Donald Hammill, Author

Unique test in that it measures the actual reading ability of young children. Items measure knowledge of contextual meaning, alphabet and conventions. *$236.00*

6054 Test of Reading Comprehension

Pro-Ed
8700 Shoal Creek Boulevard
Austin, TX   78757   512-451-3246
                                   800-897-3202
                          FAX 800-397-7633
                      http://www.proedinc.com
Virginia Brown, Donald Hammill, J Lee Wiederholt, Author

A multidimensional test of silent reading comprehension for students. The test reflects current psycholinguistic theories that consider reading comprehension to be a constructive process involving both language and cognition. *$ 166.00*

Ages 7-11

Speech & Language Arts

6055 A Calendar of Home Activities

Curriculum Associates
PO Box 2001
North Billerica, MA   01862
                                   800-225-0248
                          FAX 800-366-1158
                http://www.curriculumassociates.com/
                e-mail: ca@infocurriculumassociates.com
Donald Johnson, Elaine Johnson, Author
Frank Ferguson, President
Fred Ferguson, VP Corporate Development/CIO

An activity-a-day: 365 activities for parents and children to share at home in just 10-15 minutes each day. Parents support their children's educational experiences in a meaningful and enjoyable way, such as cooking, playing ball, and sculpting clay.

6056 Activities for Dictionary Practice

Curriculum Associates
PO Box 2001
North Billerica, MA   01862
                                   800-225-0248
                          FAX 800-366-1158
                http://www.curriculumassociates.com/
                e-mail: ca@infocurriculumassociates.com
Jean Lucken, Author
Frank Ferguson, President
Fred Ferguson, VP Corporate Development/CIO

The ideal companion for classroom dictionaries! A wide variety of exercises helps students make efficient use of this important reference tool - the dictionary. Reading, spelling, vocabulary-building, and word-usage skills are reinforced.

6057 Adolescent Language Screening Test

Pro-Ed
8700 Shoal Creek Boulevard
Austin, TX   78757   512-451-3246
                                   800-897-3202
                          FAX 800-397-7633
                      http://www.proedinc.com
Denise Morgan, Arthur Guilford, Author

Provides speech/language pathologists and other interested professionals with a rapid thorough method for screening adolescents' speech and language. *$128.00*

Ages 11-17

6058 Adventures in Science: Activities for the School-Home Connection

Curriculum Associates
PO Box 2001
North Billerica, MA   01862
                                   800-225-0248
                          FAX 800-366-1158
                http://www.curriculumassociates.com/
                e-mail: ca@inforcurriculumassociates.com
Curriculum Associates, Author
Frank Ferguson, President
Fred Ferguson, VP Corporate Development/CIO

Process-based and hands-on, these engaging activities get your students investigating and exploring the world outside the classroom. Activities and materials are designed especially for the home, encouraging parents to take an active role in their child's education.

6059 Aphasia Diagnostic Profiles

Pro-Ed
8700 Shoal Creek Boulevard
Austin, TX   78757   512-451-3246
                                   800-897-3202
                          FAX 800-397-7633
                      http://www.proedinc.com
Nancy Helm-Estrabrooks, Author

This is a quick, efficient, and systematic assessment of language and communication impairment associated with aphasia that should be administered individually. The test can be administered in 40-45 minutes.

6060   BRIGANCE Assessment of Basic Skills: Spanish Edition

Curriculum Associates
PO Box 2001
North Billerica, MA   01862
800-225-0248
FAX 800-366-1158
http://www.curriculumassociates.com/
e-mail: ca@infocurriculumassociates.com
Albert Brigance, Author
Frank Ferguson, President
Fred Ferguson, VP Corporate Development/CIO

Critiqued and field tested by Spanish linguists and educators nationwide, the Assessment of Basic Skills meets nondiscriminatory testing requirements for Limited English Proficient students. *$149.00*

6061   BRIGANCE Comprehensive Inventory of Basic Skills: Revised

Curriculum Associates
PO Box 2001
North Billerica, MA   01862
800-225-0248
FAX 800-366-1158
http://www.curriculumassociates.com/
e-mail: ca@infocurriculumassociates.com
Albert Brigance, Author
Frank Ferguson, President
Fred Ferguson, VP Corporate Development/CIO

Designed for use in elementary and middle schools, the CIBS-R is a valuable resource for programs emphasizing individualized instruction. The Inventory is especially helpful in programs serving students with special needs, and continues to be indispensable in IEP development and program planning.

6062   BRIGANCE Employability Skills Inventory

Curriculum Associates
PO Box 2001
North Billerica, MA   01862
800-225-0248
FAX 800-366-1158
http://www.curriculumassociates.com/
e-mail: ca@infocurriculumassociates.com
Albert Brigance, Author
Frank Ferguson, President
Fred Ferguson, VP Corporate Development/CIO

Extensive criterion-referenced tool assesses basic skills and employability skills in the context of job-seeking or employment situations: reading grade placement; rating scales; career awareness and self-understanding; reading skills; speaking and listening; job-seeking skills and knowledge; pre-employment writing; math and concepts. *$89.95*

6063   BRIGANCE Inventory of Essential Skills

Curriculum Associates
PO Box 2001
North Billerica, MA   01862
800-225-0248
FAX 800-366-1158
http://www.curriculumassociates.com/
e-mail: ca@infocurriculumassociates.com
Albert Brigance, Author
Frank Ferguson, President
Fred Ferguson, VP Corporate Development/CIO

The Inventory of Essential Skills is widely used to assess secondary level students or adult learners with special needs. *$169.00*

6064   BRIGANCE Life Skills Inventory

Curriculum Associates
PO Box 2001
North Billerica, MA   01862
800-225-0248
FAX 800-366-1158
http://www.curriculumassociates.com/
e-mail: ca@infocurriculumassociates.com
Albert Brigance, Author
Frank Ferguson, President
Fred Ferguson, VP Corporate Development/CIO

Assesses listening, speaking, reading, writing, comprehending, and computing skills in nine life-skill sections: speaking and listening; money and finance; functional writing; food; words on common signs and warning labels; clothing; health; telephone; travel and transportation. *$89.95*

6065   Bedside Evaluation and Screening Test of Aphasia

Pro-Ed
8700 Shoal Creek Boulevard
Austin, TX   78757
512-451-3246
800-897-3202
FAX 800-397-7633
http://www.proedinc.com
Joyce West, Elaine Sands, Deborah Ross-Swain, Author

Access and quantify language disorders in adults resulting from aphasia. *$143.00*

6066   Boone Voice Program for Adults

Pro-Ed
8700 Shoal Creek Boulevard
Austin, TX   78757
512-451-3246
800-897-3202
FAX 800-397-7633
http://www.proedinc.com
Daniel Boone, Author

Provides for diagnosis and remediation of adult voice disorders. This program is based on the same philosophy and therapy as The Program for Children but is presented at an adult interest level. *$141.00*

6067 Boone Voice Program for Children

Pro-Ed
8700 Shoal Creek Boulevard
Austin, TX 78757   512-451-3246
                              800-897-3202
                          FAX 512-451-8542
                     http://www.proedinc.com

Provides a cognitive approach to voice therapy and is designed to give useful step-by-step guidelines and materials for diagnosis and remediation of voice disorders in children.

6068 CLUES for Better Writing: Grade 1

Curriculum Associates
PO Box 2001
North Billerica, MA   01862
                              800-225-0248
                          FAX 800-366-1158
                http://www.curriculumassociates.com/
             e-mail: ca@inforcurriculumassociates.com
Curriculum Associates, Author
Frank Ferguson, President
Fred Ferguson, VP Corporate Development/CIO

Clues for Better Writing Book A develops and reinforces skills with creative writing projects, art activities, and vocabulary exercises. The 24-page Teacher Guide scripts each lesson and features spelling exercises, reproducible word lists, and extension activities.

6069 CLUES for Better Writing: Grades 2-5

Curriculum Associates
PO Box 2001
North Billerica, MA   01862
                              800-225-0248
                          FAX 800-366-1158
                http://www.curriculumassociates.com/
             e-mail: ca@infocurriculumassociates.com
Curriculum Associates, Author
Frank Ferguson, President
Fred Ferguson, VP Corporate Development/CIO

Clues for Better Writing Book B-E teach students the five steps to successful writing—brainstorming, planning, writing, editing, and publishing.

6070 CLUES for Better Writing: Kindergarten

Curriculum Associates
PO Box 2001
North Billerica, MA   01862
                              800-225-0248
                          FAX 800-366-1158
                http://www.curriculumassociates.com/
             e-mail: ca@infocurriculumassociates.com
Curriculum Associates, Author
Frank Ferguson, President
Fred Ferguson, VP Corporate Development/CIO

Emergent readers and writers explore lanuage with Clues for Better Reading and Writing. The 64-page student book features teacher-directed lessons with minimal text, appealing full-color artwork, and oral literture to develop early lanuage skills.

6071 CLUES for Phonemic Awareness

Curriculum Associates
PO Box 2001
North Billerica, MA   01862
                              800-225-0248
                          FAX 800-366-1158
                http://www.curriculumassociates.com/
             e-mail: ca@infocurriculumassociates.com
Diane Lapp, James Flood, Linda Lungren, Author
Frank Ferguson, President
Fred Ferguson, VP Corporate Deevlopment/CIO

Give your preschool, primary, or ESL children a head start on the road to reading and writing by helping them understand that language that they hear and speak is made up of a series of sounds.

6072 Completing Daily Assignments

Curriculum Associates
PO Box 2001
North Billerica, MA   01862
                              800-225-0248
                          FAX 800-366-1158
                http://www.curriculumassociates.com/
             e-mail: ca@infocurriculumassociates.com
Anita Archer, Mary Gleason, Author
Frank Ferguson, President
Fred Ferguson, VP Corporate Development/CIO

Focuses on planning assignments, writing answers to factual and opinion questions, and proofreading. Students learn to produce neat, well-organized assignments. *$19.90*

6073 Connecting Reading and Writing with Vocabulary

Curriculum Associates
PO Box 2001
North Billerica, MA   01862
                              800-225-0248
                          FAX 800-366-1158
                http://www.curriculumassociates.com/
             e-mail: ca@infocurriculumassociates.com
Deborah P Adcock, Author
Frank Ferguson, President
Fred Ferguson, VP Corporate Development/CIO

This vocabulary enrichment series builds successful writers and speakers by implementing strategic word techniques. Students will add 120 writing words and other word forms to their word banks. Each lesson introduces ten vocabulary words in a variety of contexts: a letter, poem, story, journal entry, classified ad, etc.

6074 Diamonds in the Rough

Slosson Educational Publications
538 Buffalo Road
East Aurora, NY   14052   888-756-7766
                              800-828-4800
                          FAX 800-655-3840
                       http://www.slosson.com
                  e-mail: slosson@slosson.com
Georgina Moynihan, TTFM

College referance/rehabilitation guide for people with attention deficit disorder and learning disabilities.

6075 Easy Talker: A Fluency Workbook for School Age Children

Pro-Ed
8700 Shoal Creek Boulevard
Austin, TX   78757   512-451-3246
                                        800-897-3202
                                   FAX 800-397-7633
                        http://www.proedinc.com
Garry Guitar, Julie Reville, Author

A diagnostic, criterion-referenced instrument to be used with children, to determine which stutterers would benefit from early intervention. *$41.00*

Ages 5-18

6076 Fluharty Preschool Speech & Language Screening Test-2

The Speech Bin
1965 25th Avenue
Vero Beach, FL   32960   772-770-0007
                                  FAX 772-770-0006
                        http://www.speechbin.com
                        e-mail: info@speechbin.com

Carefully normed on 705 children, the Fluharty yields standard scores, percentiles, and age equivalents. The form features space for speech-language pathologists to note phonological processes, voice quality, and fluency; a Teacher Questionnaire is also provided. Item number P882. *$153.00*

6077 Help for the Learning Disabled Child

Slosson Educational Publications
538 Buffalo Road
East Aurora, NY   14052   888-756-7766
                                        800-828-4800
                                   FAX 800-655-3840
                        http://www.slosson.com
                        e-mail: slosson@slosson.com
Georgina Moynihan, TTFM

Symptoms and solutions for learning disabled children. Features issues from a medical, psychological and educational basis and illustrates learning disabilities from emotional and mental impairment.

6078 Learning Disability Evaluation Scale: Renormed

Hawthorne Educational Services
800 Gray Oak Drive
Columbia, MO   65201   573-874-1710
                                        800-542-1673
                                   FAX 800-442-9509
Stephen B McCarney, Author

The Learning Disability Evaluation Scale (LDES) is an initial screening and assessment instrument in the areas of listening, thinking, speaking, reading, writing, spelling, and mathematical calculations based on the federal definition (IDEA). The Learning Disability Intervention Manual (LDIM) is a companion to the LDES and contains goals, objectives, and intervention/instructional strategies for the learning problems identified by the LDES. *$143.00*

217 pages

6079 Learning from Verbal Presentations and Participating in Discussions

Curriculum Associates
PO Box 2001
North Billerica, MA   01862
                                        800-225-0248
                                   FAX 800-366-1158
                        http://www.curriculumassociates.com/
                        e-mail: ca@infocurriculumassociates.com
Anita Archer, Mary Gleason, Author
Frank Ferguson, President
Fred Ferguson, VP Corporate Development/CIO

Develops oral and written language abilities. Students learn valuable strategies for note-taking, brainstorming, and effectively participating in class dicussions. *$19.90*

6080 Naglieri: Nonverbal Ability Test-Multilevel Form

Harcourt
19500 Bulverde Road
San Antonio, TX   78259
                                        800-211-8378
                                   FAX 800-232-1223
                        http://www.hbtpc.com
Jack Naglieri, Author

Provides a group-administered measure of nonverbal reasoning and problem solving that is independent of educational curricula and children's cultural or language background.

6081 Oral Speech Mechanism Screening Examination

Pro-Ed
8700 Shoal Creek Boulevard
Austin, TX   78757   512-451-3246
                                        800-897-3202
                                   FAX 800-397-7663
                        http://www.proedinc.com
Kenneth St Louis, Dennis Ruscello, Author

Provides an efficient, quick, and reliable method to examine the oral speech mechanism of all types of speech, language, and related disorders where oral structure and function are of concern. *$101.00*

Ages 5-70+

6082 Peabody Picture Vocabulary Test: Third Edition

AGS Publishing
4201 Woodland Road
Circle Pines, MN   55014
                                        800-328-2560
                                   FAX 800-471-8457
                        http://www.agsnet.com
                        e-mail: agsmail@agsnet.com
Lloyd Dunn, Leota Dunn, Author
Karen Dahlen, Associate Director
Matt Keller, Marketing Manager
Lisa Dunttam, Development Assistant

A wide range measure of receptive vocabulary for standard English and screen of verbal ability.

Ages 2-6

6083   Phonological Awareness Test: Computerized Scoring

LinguiSystems
3100 4th Avenue
East Moline, IL   61244

800-776-4332
FAX 800-577-4555
http://www.linguisystems.com
e-mail: service@linguisystems.com

Linda Bowers, Owner
Rosemary Huisingh, Owner

What a timesaver! This optional CD-ROM software allows you to accurately, conveniently, and quickly score The Phonological Awareness Test. Just plug in the raw scores and the program does everything else. You'll be able to print out all the scores you need to include in a student's assessment report.

Ages 5-9

6084   Preschool Language Assessment Instrument

Harcourt
19500 Bulverde Road
San Antonio, TX   78259

800-211-8378
FAX 800-232-1223
http://www.hbtpc.com

Marion Blank, Susan Rose, Laura Berlin, Author

Provides a profile of a child's language skills in order to match teaching with the student's competence. The test is ideal for children ages 3 to 6 and is available in Spanish. *$197.00*

6085   Preschool Language Scale: Fourth Edition

Harcourt
19500 Bulverde Road
San Antonio, TX   78259

800-211-8378
FAX 800-232-1223
http://www.hbtpc.com

Iria Lee Zimmerman, PhD
Violette G Steiner, BS
Roberta Evatt Pond, MA

This tool measures a broad range of receptive and expressive language skills. A Spanish version is also available.

Ages 0-11

6086   Preschool Motor Speech Evaluation & Intervention

The Speech Bin
1965 25th Avenue
Vero Beach, FL   32960

772-770-0007
FAX 772-770-0006
http://www.speechbin.com
e-mail: info@speechbin.com

This comprehensive criterion-based assessment tool differentiates motor-based speech disorders from those of phonology and determines if speech difficulties of children 18 months to six years old are characteristic of: oral nonverbal apraxia; dysarthria; developmental verbal dyspraxia; hypersensitivity; differences in tone and hyposensitivity. Item number J322. *$59.00*

6087   Receptive One-Word Picture Vocabulary Test (ROWPVT-2000)

The Speech Bin
1965 25th Avenue
Vero Beach, FL   32960

772-770-0007
800-477-3324
FAX 888-329-2246
http://www.speechbin.com
e-mail: info@speechbin.com

Rick Brownell, Author

This administered, untimed measure assessess the vocabulary comprehension of 0-2 through 11-18 years. New full-color test pictures are easy to recognize; many new test items have been added. It is ideal for children unable or reluctant to speak because only a gestural response is required. Item number A305. *$140.00*

6088   Receptive-Expressive Emergent Language Tests

Pro-Ed
8700 Shoal Creek Boulevard
Austin, TX   78757

512-451-3246
800-897-3202
FAX 800-397-7633
http://www.proedinc.com

Kenneth Bzoch, Richard League, Virginia Brown, Author

Designed to use with at-risk infants and toddlers to provide a multidimensional analysis of emergency language skills.

Ages 0-3

6089   Sequenced Inventory of Communication Development

Slosson Educational Publications
538 Buffalo Road
East Aurora, NY   14052

716-652-0930
800-828-4800
FAX 800-655-3840
http://www.slosson.com
e-mail: slosson@slosson.com

Dona Hedrick, Elizabeth Prather, Annette Tobin, Author

A diagnostic test designed to evaluate communications abilities, the SICD was planned for use in remedial programming of the young child with language disorders, mental challenges, and specific language problems. It has been successfully used with children who have sensory impairments, both hearing and visual, and varying degrees of retardation/challenges. *$395.00*

4mo-4 yrs old

6090   Sequenced Inventory of Communication Development (SICD)

The Speech Bin
1965 25th Avenue
Vero Beach, FL   32960

772-770-0007
FAX 772-770-0006
http://www.speechbin.com
e-mail: info@speechbin.com

SICD uses appealing toys to assess communication skills of children at all levels of ability, including those with impaired hearing or vision. SICD looks at child and environment, measuring receptive and expressive language. Item number W710. *$395.00*

6091   Skills Assessments

Steck-Vaughn Company
PO Box 690789
Orlando, FL   32819

800-531-5015
FAX 512-343-6854
http://www.steck-vaughn.com
e-mail: info@steck-vaughn.com

This handy, all-in-one resource helps identify students strengths and weaknesses in order to determine appropriate instructional levels in each of five subjects areas: reading, language arts, math, science, and social stuides. Assessments are identified by subtopics in each subject.

6092   Slosson Intelligence Test

Slosson Educational Publications
538 Buffalo Road
East Aurora, NY   14052

888-756-7766
800-828-4800
FAX 800-655-3840
http://www.slosson.com
e-mail: slosson@slosson.com
Richard L Slosson, Author
Georgina Moynihan, TTFM

A quick and reliable individual screening test of Crystallized Verbal Intelligence. *$84.00*

6093   Slosson Intelligence Test: Primary

Slosson Educational Publications
538 Buffalo Road
East Aurora, NY   14052

888-756-7766
800-828-4800
FAX 800-655-3840
http://www.slosson.com
e-mail: slosson@slosson.com
Bradley Erford, Gary Vitali, Steven Slosson, Author
Georgina Moynihan, TTFM

Designed to facilitate the screening identification of children at risk of educational failure. Provides a quick estimate of mental ability to identify children who may be appropriate candidates for deeper testing services. *$116.00*

6094   Stuttering Severity Instrument for Children and Adults

Pro-Ed
8700 Shoal Creek Boulevard
Austin, TX   78757

512-451-3246
800-897-3202
FAX 800-397-7633
http://www.proedinc.com
Glyndon Riley, Author

With these easily administered tools you can determine whether to schedule a child for therapy using the Stuttering Prediction Instrument or to evaluate the effects of treatment using the Stuttering Severity Instrument. *$97.00*

6095   TELD-2: Test of Early Language Development

Pro-Ed
8700 Shoal Creek Boulevard
Austin, TX   78757

512-451-3246
800-897-3202
FAX 800-397-7633
http://www.proedinc.com
Wayne Hresko, Kim Reid, Don Hammill, Author

An individually administered test of spoken language abilities. This test fills the need for a well-constructed, standardized instrument, based on a current theory, that can be used to assess spoken language skills at early ages. Administration Time: 20 minutes. *$272.00*

Ages 2-11

6096   TOAL-3: Test of Adolescent & Adult Language

Pro-Ed
8700 Shoal Creek Boulevard
Austin, TX   78757

512-451-3246
800-897-3202
FAX 800-397-7633
http://www.proedinc.com
Don Hammill, Virginia Brown, Stephen Larson, Author

This test is a measure of receptive and expressive language skills. In this revision easier items were added to the subtests, making them more appropriate for testing disabled students. *$177.00*

Ages 12-24

6097   TOLD-3: Test of Language Development, Primary

Harcourt
19500 Bulverde Road
San Antonio, TX   78259

800-211-8378
FAX 800-232-1223
http://www.hbtpc.com
Phyllis Newcomer, Donald Hammill, Author

An individually administered language battery that assesses the understanding and meaningful use of spoken words, aspects of grammar, word pronunciation and the ability to distinguish between similar sounding words. *$265.00*

6098   TOWL-3: Test of Written Language, 3rd Edition

Pro-Ed
8700 Shoal Creek Boulevard
Austin, TX   78757

512-451-3246
800-897-3202
FAX 800-397-7633
http://www.proedinc.com
Donald Hammill, Stephen Larson, Author

Offers a measure of written language skills to identify students who need help improving their writing skills. Administration Time: 65 minutes. *$193.00*

Ages 7-17

6099 Test for Auditory Comprehension of Language: TACL-3

The Speech Bin
1965 25th Avenue
Vero Beach, FL   32960   772-770-0007
FAX 772-770-0006
http://www.speechbin.com
e-mail: info@speechbin.com

The newly revised TACL-3 evaluates the 0-3 to 9-11-year old's understanding of spoken language in three subtests: Vocabulary, Grammatical Morphemes and Elaborated Phrases and Sentences. Each test item is a word or sentence read aloud by the examiner; the child responds by pointing to one of three pictures. Item number P792. *$261.00*

6100 Test of Auditory Reasoning & Processing Skills (TARPS)

The Speech Bin
1965 25th Avenue
Vero Beach, FL   32960   772-770-0007
800-477-3324
FAX 888-329-2246
http://www.speechbin.com
e-mail: info@speechbin.com
Morrison Gardner, Author

TARPS assesses how 5-14 year old children understand, interpret, draw conclusions, and make inferences from auditorily presented stimuli. It tests their ability to think, understand, reason, and make sense of what they hear. Item number H787. *$64.00*

6101 Test of Auditory-Perceptual Skills: Upper (TAPS-UL)

The Speech Bin
1965 25th Avenue
Vero Beach, FL   32960   772-770-0007
800-477-3324
FAX 888-329-2246
http://www.speechbin.com
e-mail: info@speechbin.com
Wayne Hresko, Shelley Herron, Pamela Peak, Author

This highly respected, well-normed test evaluates a 13-18 year old's ability to perceive auditory stimuli and helps you diagnose auditory disorders in just 15-20 minutes. TAPS: UL measures the auditory perceptual skills of processing, word and sequential memory, interpretation of oral directions, and discrimination. Item number H769. *$95.00*

6102 Test of Early Written Language

Pro-Ed
8700 Shoal Creek Boulevard
Austin, TX   78757   512-451-3246
800-897-3202
FAX 512-451-8542
http://www.proedinc.com
Wayne Hresko, Author

Measures the merging written language skills of young children and is especially useful in identifying mildy disabled students.

Ages 3-11

6103 Test of Written Spelling

Pro-Ed
8700 Shoal Creek Boulevard
Austin, TX   78757   512-451-3246
800-897-3202
FAX 800-397-7633
http://www.proedinc.com
Stephen Larsen, Donald Hammill, Louisa Moats, Author

Assesses students' ability to spell words whose spellings are readily predictable in sound-letter patterns, words whose spellings are less predictable and both types of words considered together. *$82.00*

6104 Testing & Remediating Auditory Processing (TRAP)

The Speech Bin
1965 25th Avenue
Vero Beach, FL   32960   772-770-0007
800-477-3324
FAX 888-329-2246
http://www.speechbin.com
e-mail: info@speechbin.com
Lynn Baron Berk, Author

TRAP gives you an easy-to-implement program to assess and treat school-age auditory processing problems. It gives you two major components: Screening Test of Auditoring Processing Skills that identifies children at risk due to auditory processing deficits; and Remediating Auditory Processing Skills that presents interactional stories, sequence pictures, and illustrated activities. Item number 1233. *$38.00*

6105 Voice Assessment Protocol for Children and Adults

Pro-Ed
8700 Shoal Creek Boulevard
Austin, TX   78757   512-451-3246
800-897-3202
FAX 800-397-7633
http://www.proedinc.com
Rebekah Pindzola, Author

Easily guides the speech pathologist through a systematic evaluation of vocal pitch, loudness, quality, breath features and rate/rhythm. *$61.00*

Visual & Motor Skills

6106 BRIGANCE Inventory of Early Development-II

Curriculum Associates
PO Box 2001
North Billerica, MA   01862
800-225-0248
FAX 800-366-1158
http://www.curriculumassociates.com/
e-mail: ca@infocurriculumassociates.com
Albert Brigance, Author
Frank Ferguson, President
Fred Ferguson, VP Corporate Development/CIO

The Inventory of Early Development simplifies and combines the assessment, diagnostic, recordkeeping, and instructional planning process, and it encourages communication between teachers and parents.

Ages Birth-7

6107 Benton Visual Retention Test: Fifth Edition

Harcourt
19500 Bulverde Road
San Antonio, TX 78259
800-211-8378
FAX 800-232-1223
http://www.hbtpc.com
Abigail Benton Sivan, Author

Assess visual perception, memory, visoconstructive abilities. Test administration 15-20 minutes. *$189.00*

Ages 8-Adult

6108 Boston Diagnostic Aphasia Exam: Third Edition

The Speech Bin
1965 25th Avenue
Vero Beach, FL 32960
772-770-0007
800-477-3324
FAX 888-329-2246
http://www.speechbin.com
e-mail: info@speechbin.com
Harold Goodglass, Edith Kaplan, Barbara Barresi, Author
Jan J Binney, Editor-in-Chief

evised and improved. BDAE-3 now gives you an instructive 90-minute video plus two separate forms of the test. Item number L235. *$150.00*

6109 Development Test of Visual Perception

Pro-Ed
8700 Shoal Creek Boulevard
Austin, TX 78757
512-451-3246
800-897-3202
FAX 800-397-7633
http://www.proedinc.com
Don Hammill, Nils Pearson, Judith Voress, Author

Measures both visual perception and visual-motor integration skills, has eight subtests, is based on updated theories of visual perceptual development, and can be administered to individuals in 35 minutes. *$179.00*

Ages 4-10

6110 Developmental Test of Visual Perception (DTVP-2)

Pro-Ed
8700 Shoal Creek Boulevard
Austin, TX 78757
512-451-3246
800-897-3202
FAX 800-397-7633
http://www.proedinc.com
Don Hammill, Nils Pearson, Judith Voress, Author

A test that measures both visual perception and visual-motor integration skills, has eight subtests, is based on updated theories of visual perceptual development, and can be administered to individuals in 35 minutes. *$179.00*

Ages 4-10

6111 Differential Test of Conduct and Emotional Problems

Slosson Educational Publications
538 Buffalo Road
East Aurora, NY 14052
888-756-7766
800-828-4800
FAX 800-655-3840
http://www.slosson.com
e-mail: slosson@slosson.com
Edward Kelly, Author
Georgina Moynihan, TTFM

Designed to address one of the most critical challenges in education and juvenile care. Administration of test is 15-20 minutes. *$82.00*

6112 KLPA: Khan-Lewis Phonological Analysis

Pro-Ed
8700 Shoal Creek Boulevard
Austin, TX 78757
512-451-3246
800-897-3202
FAX 800-397-7633
http://www.proedinc.com
Linda Klan, Nancy Lewis, Author

An in-depth measure of phonological processes for assessment and remediation planning. Administration Time: 10-30 minutes. *$126.00*

Ages 2-5

6113 Learning Efficiency Test II

Academic Therapy Publications
20 Commercial Boulevard
Novato, CA 94949
800-422-7249
FAX 888-287-9975
http://www.academictherapy.com
e-mail: sales@academictherapy.com
Raymond Webster, Author
Anna Arena, President

Provides a quick and accurate measure of a child or adult's information processing abilities, sequential and nonsequential, in both visual and auditory modalities. *$92.00*

Ages 5-75+
ISBN 0-878799-40-0

6114 Oral Motor Assessment: Ages and Stages

Therapro
225 Arlington Street
Framingham, MA 01702
508-872-9494
800-257-5376
FAX 508-875-2062
http://www.theraproducts.com
e-mail: info@theraproducts.com
Diane Chapman Bahr, Author

Provides an overview of available assessments, checklists, tables, and figures to assist the clinician in accurately diagnosing muscle function and motor planning issues. *$55.00*

6115 Peabody Developmental Motor Scales-2

The Speech Bin
1965 25th Avenue
Vero Beach, FL 32960   772-770-0007
                              FAX 772-770-0006
                      http://www.speechbin.com
                      e-mail: info@speechbin.com

PDMS-2 gives you in-depth standardized assessment of motor skills in children birth to six years. Subtests include: fine motor object manipulation; grasping; gross motor; locomotion; reflexes; visual-motor integration and stationary. Item number P624. *$43.00*

6116 Perceptual Motor Development Series

Therapro
225 Arlington Street
Framingham, MA 01702   508-872-9494
                                   800-257-5376
                              FAX 508-875-2062
                      http://www.theraproducts.com
                      e-mail: info@theraproducts.com
Jack Capon, Author

Use these classroom tested movement education activities to assess motor strengths and weaknesses in preschool and early elementary grades or special education classes. The sequence of easily given tests and tasks requires minimal instruction time and your kids will find the activities to be interesting, challenging, and fun! Each book has 25-54 pages.

6117 Preschool Motor Speech Evaluation & Intervention

The Speech Bin
1965 25th Avenue
Vero Beach, FL 32960   772-770-0007
                              FAX 772-770-0006
                      http://www.speechbin.com
                      e-mail: info@speechbin.com

This comprehensive criterion-based assessment tool differentiates motor-based speech disorders from those of phonology and determines if speech difficulties of children 18 months to six years old are characteristic of: oral nonverbal apraxia; dysarthria; developmental verbal dyspraxia; hypersensitivity; differences in tone and hyposensitivity. Item number J322. *$59.00*

6118 Slosson Full Range Intelligence Test Kit

Slosson Educational Publications
538 Buffalo Road
East Aurora, NY 14052   888-756-7766
                                   800-828-4800
                              FAX 800-655-3840
                      http://www.slosson.com
                      e-mail: slosson@slosson.com
Bob Algozzine, Ronald Eaves, Lester Mann, Author
Steven W Slosson, President
John Slosson, VP
Georgina Moynihan, TTFM

Intended to supplement the use of more extensive cognitive assessment instruments. Administration of test 25-45 minutes. *$125.00*

Ages 5-Adult

6119 Slosson Visual Motor Performance Test

Slosson Educational Publications
538 Buffalo Road
East Aurora, NY 14052   888-756-7766
                                   800-828-4800
                              FAX 800-655-3840
                      http://www.slosson.com
                      e-mail: slosson@slosson.com
Richard Slosson, Author
Steven W Slosson, President
John Slosson, VP
Georgina Moynihan, TTFM

A test of visual motor integration in which individuals are asked to copy geometric figures increasing in complexity without the use of a ruler, compass or other aids.

6120 Test of Gross Motor Development

Pro-Ed
8700 Shoal Creek Boulevard
Austin, TX 78757   512-451-3246
                                    800-897-3202
                              FAX 800-397-7633
                      http://www.proedinc.com
Dale Urlich, Author

Assists you in identifying children who are significantly behind their peers in gross motor skill development and who should be eligible for special education services in phyiscal education.

Ages 3-11

6121 Visual Skills Appraisal

Academic Therapy Publications
20 Commercial Boulevard
Novato, CA 94949   415-883-3314
                                    800-422-7249
                              FAX 415-883-3720
                      http://www.academictherapy.com
                      e-mail: sales@academictherapy.com
Regina Richards, Gary Oppenheim, Author
Anna Arena, President

This test identifies visual problems in children. Can be administered by teachers or other educators who may not have training in assessment. Set includes manual, stimulus cards and test forms. *$85.00*

Ages 5-9
ISBN 0-878794-50-0

National Programs

5961 Reading Assessment System

Harcourt Achieve
6277 Sea Harbor Drive
32887
800-531-5015
FAX 800-699-9459
http://www.steckvaughn.com
e-mail: info@steckvaughn.com
Steck-Vaughn Staff, Author
Tim McEwen, President/CEO
Jeff Johnson, Dir Marketing Communications
Chris Lehmann, Team Coordinator

The Reading Assessment System provides an ongoing meaure of specific student's skills and offers detailed directions for individual instruction and remediation. Up to eight reports are available. This popular program generates individual scores, class scores, school scores, and district reports.

6122 Alliance for Technology Access

1304 Southpoint Boulevard
Petaluma, CA 94954
707-778-3011
800-455-7970
FAX 707-765-2080
TDY:707-778-3015
http://www.ataccess.org
e-mail: atainfo@ataccess.org
Mary Lester, Executive Director

A national organization dedicated to providing access to technology for people with disabilities through its coalition of 39 community-based resource centers in 28 states and in the Virgin Islands. Each center provides information, awareness, and training for professionals and provides guided problem solving and technical assistance for individuals with disabilities and family members.

6123 America's Jobline

National Federation of the Blind
1800 Johnson Street
Baltimore, MD 21230
410-659-9314
800-414-5748
FAX 410-685-5653
http://www.nfb.org
e-mail: nfb@nfb.org
James Gashel, Director Government Affairs
M Rorick, Coordinator

In partnership with the United States Department of Labor the National Federation of the Blind offers a program that assists blind persons in finding competitive employment. The 800 number offers access to 24 hour job announcements in a high quality synthetic speech format instead of printed text. Jobline helps those who do not have or cannot use standard computers, and those who cannot see or read standard video display.

6124 American College Testing Program

ACT Universal Testing
500 ACT Drive
Iowa City, IA 52243
319-337-1000
FAX 319-339-3021
TDY:319-337-1701
http://www.act.org
Ed Colby, Public Relations

To help individuals and organizations make informed decisions about education and work. We provide information for life's transitions.

6125 Division on Career Development

Council for Exeptional Children
1110 N Glebe Road
Arlington, VA 22201
703-620-3660
888-232-7733
FAX 703-264-9494
http://www.cec.sped.org
e-mail: cathym@cec.sped.org
Drew Allbritten, Executive Director

Focuses on the career development of individuals with disabilities and/or who are gifted and their transition from school to adult life. Members include professionals and others interested in career development and transition for individuals with any exception at any age. Members receive a journal twice yearly and newsletter three times per year.

6126 Independent Living Research Utilization Program

2323 S Shepherd
Houston, TX 77019
713-520-0232
FAX 713-520-5785
TDY:713-520-5136
http://www.ilru.org

A national resource center for information, training, research and technical assistance in independent living; produces and disseminates materials, develops and conducts training and publishes a monthly newsletter; provides a listing of Statewide Independent Living Councils (SILCS) in each state.

6127 Job Accommodation Network (JAN)

West Virginia University
PO Box 6080
Morgantown, WV 26506
304-293-7186
800-232-9675
FAX 304-293-5407
TDY:800-232-9675
http://www.jan.wvu.edu
e-mail: jan@jan.wvu.edu
DJ Hendrix, Director

Network and consulting resource that provides information about employment issues to employers, rehabilitation professionals, and persons with disabilities. Callers should be prepared to explain their specific problem and job circumstances. Sponsored by the Office of Disability Employment Policy, the Network is operated by West Virginia University's Rehabilitation Research and Training Center. Brochures and printed materials available.

6128 Mainstream

6930 Carroll Avenue
Takoma Park, MD 20912   301-891-8777
FAX 301-891-8778
http://www.mainstreaminc.org
e-mail: info@mainstreaminc.org

Provides specialized services and links people with disabilities to employers and service providers.

6129 Minnesota Vocational Rehabilitation Agency: Rehabilitation Services Branch

Department of Economic Security
390 N Robert Street
Saint Paul, MN 55101   651-296-5616
800-328-9095
FAX 651-297-5159
http://www.mnworkforcecenter.org
e-mail: Howard.Glad@state.mn.us
Howard Glad, Contact

Provides basic vocational rehabilitation services to consumers including vocational counseling, planning, guidance and placement, as well as certain special services based on individual circumstances.

6130 Office of Vocational & Adult Education

US Department of Education
330 C Street SW
Washington, DC 20202   202-205-5451
FAX 202-205-9340
http://www.ed.gov
e-mail: ovae@ed.gov
Susan Sclafani, Assistant Secretary
Hans Meeder, Deputy Assitant Secretary

These agencies can provide job training, counseling, financial assistance, and employment placement to individuals who meet eligibility criteria.

6131 Transition Research Institute

University of Illinois at Urbana-Champaign
51 Gerty Drive
Champaign, IL 61820   217-333-2325
FAX 217-244-0851
http://www.ed.uiuc.edu/SPED/tri/institute.html
Janis Chadsey PhD, Director
John S Trach PhD, Project Director

Provides technical assistance on transition-focused projects, policy analysis concerning legislation focused on education and transition services for youths with disabilities, and a wealth of information for teachers, service providers and researchers.

6132 Workforce Investment Act Office of Job Training Programs

US Department of Labor
200 Constitution Avenue NW
Washington, DC 20210   202-535-0580
FAX 202-219-6893
http://www.do¹.gov
Emily Stover-DeRocco, Employment/Training Admn.
Tom Dowd, Deputy Employment/Training Admn.

Trains and places economically disadvantaged adults and youth facing significant barriers to employment, including persons with disabilities, in permanent, unsubsidized jobs. More than 600 local JTPA programs offer individuals with disabilities who meet the act's eligibility criteria a range of employment services.

Publications

6133 ADD on the Job

Taylor Publishing
1550 W Mockingbird Lane
Dallas, TX 75235   214-637-2800
800-677-2800
FAX 214-819-8580

Lynn Weiss PhD, Author

Practical, sensitive advice for the ADD employee, his boss, and his co-workers. The book suggests advantages that the ADD worker has, how to find the right job, and how to keep it. Employers and co-workers will learn what to expect from fellow workers with ADD and the most effective ways to work with them.

232 pages Paperback
ISBN 0-878339-17-5

6134 Ability Magazine

1001 W 17th Street
Costa Mesa, CA 92627   949-854-8700
FAX 949-548-5966
TDY:949-548-5157
http://www.abilitymagazine.com
e-mail: ability@pacbell.net
Katie Ferguson, Account Executive

Brings disabilities into mainstream America. By interviewing high profile personalities such as President Clinton, Elizabeth Taylor, Mary Tyler Moore, Richard Pryor, Jane Seymour and many more, Ability Magazine is able to bring articles to the public's attention that may in the past have gone unnoticed.

80+ pages Bimonthly

6135 Articulation Models for Vocational Education

Center on Education and Training for Employment
Ohio State University
Columbus, OH 43210   614-292-4353
800-848-4815
FAX 614-292-1260
http://www.cete.org/products

Highlights the vital role of articulations in vocational education today.

6136 Bottom Line: Basic Skills in the Workplace

US Department of Labor
200 Constitution Avenue NW
Washington, DC 20210   202-535-0236
FAX 202-219-6893

Discusses the issues of meeting basic literacy needs and meeting them within the context of employment.

6137 Business Currents

National Alliance of Business (NAB)
1201 New York Avenue NW
Washington, DC 20005   202-289-2910
                              FAX 202-289-1303

Business Currents provides information about legislative and administrative actions affecting employment and training.

Biweekly

6138 Career Inventories for the Learning Disabled

Slosson Educational Publications
538 Buffalo Road
East Aurora, NY 14052   716-652-0930
                               800-828-4800
                          FAX 800-655-3840
                       http://www.slossom.com
                   e-mail: slosson@slosson.com
Carol Weller, Author
Mary Buchanan, Author

These career assessment inventories take personality, ability, and interest into account in pointing LD students toward intelligent and realistic career choices.

6139 Change Agent

Nat'l Center for Research in Vocational Education
2150 Shattuck Avenue
Berkeley, CA 94704
                               800-762-4093
           e-mail: dcarlson@uclink.berkley.edu
David Carlson, Contact

A quarterly digest of center publications.

6140 Cognitive Theory-Based Teaching and Learning in Vocational Education

Center on Education and Training for Employment
Ohio State University
Columbus, OH 43210   614-292-4353
                            800-848-4815
                       FAX 614-292-1260
                http://www.cete.org/products
      e-mail: ericacve@magnus.acs.ohio_state.edu
Ruth Thomas, Author

This research review explores the relevance to vocational curriculum and instruction of theories of cognition.

6141 College Students with Learning Disabilities: A Handbook

Learning Disabilities Association of America
4156 Library Road
Pittsburgh, PA 15234   412-341-1515
                         FAX 412-344-0224
                      http://www.ldanatl.org
                   e-mail: ldanatl@usaor.net

An overview of related issues, including information on Section 504 as it pertains to students with learning disabilities and college personnel.

6142 Current Developments in Employment and Training

National Governors Association
444 N Capitol Street NW
Washington, DC 20001   202-624-5353
                         FAX 202-624-5313
                       http://www.nga.org
                   e-mail: mjensen@nga.org
Martin Jensen, Editor

Highlights issues and areas of interest related to employment and training.

Bimonthly

6143 For Employers: A Look at Learning Disabilities

Learning Disabilities Association of America
4156 Library Road
Pittsburgh, PA 15234   412-341-1515
                         FAX 412-344-0224
                      http://www.ldanatl.org
                   e-mail: ldanatl@usaor.net

Helps employers understand learning disabilities.

6144 Fundamentals of Job Placement

RPM Press
PO Box 31483
Tucson, AZ 85751   520-886-1990
                          888-810-1990
                     FAX 520-886-1990
James Costello, Author
Jan Stonebraker, Operations Manager

Provides step-by-step guidance for educators, special counselors and vocational rehabilitation personnel on how to develop job placement opportunities for special needs students and adults.

6145 Fundamentals of Vocational Assessment

RPM Press
PO Box 31483
Tucson, AZ 85751   520-886-1990
                          888-810-1990
                     FAX 520-866-1900
Jan Stonebraker, Operations Manager

Provides step-by-step guidance for educators, counselors and vocational rehabilitation personnel on how to conduct professional vocational assessments of special needs students.

6146 Handbook for Developing Community Based Employment

RPM Press
PO Box 31483
Tucson, AZ 85751   520-886-1990
                          888-810-1990
                     FAX 520-866-1990
Jan Stonebraker, Operations Manager

Provides step-by-step guidance for educators and vocational rehabilitation personnel on how to develop community-based employment training programs for severely challenged workers.

6147 JOBS V

PESCO International
21 Paulding Street
Pleasantville, NY   10570   914-769-4266
                                   800-431-2016
                              FAX 914-769-2970
                              http://www.pesco.org
                              e-mail: pesco@pesco.org

Joseph Kass, President
Charles Kass, VP
Kathy Griffin, Sales Manager

A software program matching people with jobs, training, employment and local employers. Provides job outlooks for the next five years.

6148 Job Access

Ability Awareness
1001 W 17th Street
Costa Mesa, CA   92627   949-854-8700
                            FAX 949-548-5966
                            TDY:949-548-5157
                            http://www.jobaccess.org
                            e-mail: marketing@jobaccess.org

Andy Houghton, Account Executive

Job Access, a program of ability awareness, is an internet driven system dedicated to employ qualified people with disabilities. Employers can list job postings and review our resume bank. People with disabilities seeking employment can also search for jobs.

6149 Job Accommodation Handbook

RPM Press
PO Box 31483
Tucson, AZ   85751   520-886-1990
                            888-810-1990
                       FAX 520-866-1990

Paul McCray, Author
Jan Stonebraker, Operations Manager

Provides how-to-do-it for counselors, job placement specialists, educators and others on how to modify jobs for special needs workers.

6150 Job Interview Tips for People with Learning Disabilities

Learning Disabilities Association of America
4156 Library Road
Pittsburgh, PA   15234   412-341-1515
                            FAX 412-344-0224
                            http://www.ldanatl.org
                            e-mail: ldanatl@usaor.net

$18.00

6151 Life Centered Career Education: Assessment Batteries

Council for Exceptional Children
1110 N Glebe Road
Arlington, VA   22201   703-620-3660
                            888-232-7733
                       FAX 703-264-9494
                       http://www.cec.sped.org/

Donn E Brolin, Author

The LCCE Batteries are curriculum-based assessment instruments designed to measure the career education knowledge and skills of regular and special education students. There are two alternative forms of a Knowledge Battery and two forms of the Performance Batteries. These assessment tools can be combined with instruction to determine the instructional goals most appropriate for a particular student.

827 pages

6152 NICHCY Transition Summary

NICHCY
PO Box 1492
Washington, DC   20013   202-884-8200
                            800-695-0285
                       FAX 202-884-8841
                       http://www.nichcy.org
                       e-mail: nichcy@ace.org

Susan Ripley, Information Specialist

A newsletter offering information on vocational assessment, books and more for the disabled.

6153 National Forum on Issues in Vocational Assessment

MCD, Stout Vocational Rehabilitation Institute
University of Wisconsin-Stout
Menomonie, WI   54751   715-232-2475
                            FAX 715-232-2356
                       e-mail: wesolekJ@uWStout.edu

RR Fry, Author
Dr. John S Wesolck, Institute Director

The impact potential of curriculum-based vocational assessment in our schools.

6154 National Governors Association

444 N Capitol Street NW
Washington, DC   20001   202-624-5353
                            FAX 202-624-5313
                            http://www.nga.org
                            e-mail: mjensen@nga.org

Martin Jensen, Editor

Highlights issues and areas of interest related to employment and training.

Bimonthly

6155 PWI Profile

Goodwill Industries of America
9200 Rockville Pike
Bethesda, MD   20814   240-333-5200
                            http://www.goodwill.org/
                            e-mail: contactus@goodwill.org

Newsletter that deals with employment of persons with disabilities.

6156 Rehabilitation Research and Training Center on Supported Employment

PO Box 842011
Richmond, VA   23284   804-828-1851
                            FAX 804-828-2193

Jeanne Roberts, PR Specialist
Valerie Brooker, Associate Director

Helps disabled persons find and hold a job. Designed to assist persons with significant disabilities to obtain and maintain community integrated competitive employment through high quality research and dissemination.

6157 School to Adult Life Transition Bibliography

Special Education Resource Center
25 Industrial Park Road
Middletown, CT 06457   860-632-1485
                             FAX 860-632-8870

A bibliography of references and resources.

6158 Self Advocacy as a Technique for Transition

KUAF-University of Kansas
311 Haworth Hall
Lawrence, KS 66045   785-864-2700
                           FAX 785-864-4967
                    e-mail: cpe@cpe.engr.ku.edu

A joint effort involved in researching the effect of self-advocacy training upon adolescents with learning disabilities.

6159 Self-Directed Search

Psychological Corporation
555 Academic Court
San Antonio, TX 78204   800-232-1223
                              800-211-8378
                           FAX 210-949-4475
                          http://www.hbtpc.com

John Hiolland, Author

This self-administered, self-scored and self-interpreted test enables the individual to make education and career choices.

6160 Self-Supervision: A Career Tool for Audiologists, Clinical Series 10

American Speech-Language-Hearing Association
10801 Rockville Pike
Bethesda, MD 20814   301-897-5700
                           888-498-6699
                        FAX 301-897-7358
                       http://www.Asha.org
Laurie Ward, Marketing Coordinator

Describes concepts of supervision, defines and presents strategies for self-supervision, discusses supervisory accountability and covers issues of self-supervision within supervisor format.

6161 Transition and Students with Learning Disabilities

Pro-Ed
8700 Shoal Creek Boulevard
Austin, TX 78757   512-451-3246
                         800-897-3202
                      FAX 512-451-8542
                    http://www.proedinc.com

Patton Blalock, Author

Provides important information about academic, social and vocational planning for students with learning disabilities.

6162 Vocational Entry Skills for Secondary Students

Learning Disabilities Association of America
4156 Library Road
Pittsburgh, PA 15234   412-341-1515
                             FAX 412-344-0224
                          http://www.ldanatl.org
                       e-mail: ldanatl@usaor.net

6163 Vocational Training and Employment of Autistic Adolescents

Charles C Thomas Publisher
2600 S 1st Street
Springfield, IL 62704   217-789-8980
                              800-258-8980
                           FAX 217-789-9130

Elva Duran, Author

How professionals and parents are now advocating, demanding and arranging that persons receive vocational training and equal rights for the disabled.

6164 Work America, Workforce Economics Workforce Trends

National Alliance of Business (NAB)
1201 New York Avenue NW
Washington, DC 20005   202-289-2888
                             800-787-7788
                          FAX 202-289-1303
                         http://www.nab.com
                     e-mail: jonesr@nab.com

Award winning publications that feature timely articles related to the human resource agenda. Workforce development and education improvement is covered from the business perspective.

6165 Workforce Investment Quarterly

National Governor's Association (NGA)
444 N Capitol Street NW
Washington, DC 20001   202-624-5300
                             FAX 202-624-7870
                          http://www.nga.org

Highlights issues and area interests related to employment and training. Contact NGA for more information.

Alabama

6166 Adult & Community Education Program

PO Box 302101
Montgomery, AL 36130   334-242-8182
                             FAX 334-242-2236
           http://www.slincs.coe.utk.edu/alabama/
                e-mail: macaluso@sdenet.alsde.edu
Joe Macaluso, Coordinator

Chartered to develop a program to provide linkage and networking among state, regional and local government programs and community based volunteer programs. Works to expand the educational opportunities for all adults and to provide the means for basic literacy skills necessary to function in society and to have a positive effect on the literacy of their children. Also seeks to make available training that will enable adults to become more employable, productive and responsible citizens.

6167 Department of Human Resources

50 N Ripley Street
Montgomery, AL 36130   334-242-1160
FAX 334-242-0198
http://www.dhr.state.al.us
e-mail: ogapi@dhr.state.al.us
Dr. Page Walley, Commissioner

Partners with communities to promote family stability and to provide for the self-sufficiency of vulnerable Alabamians.

6168 Easter Seals Achievement Center

510 W Thomason Circle
Opelika, AL 36801   334-754-3501
FAX 334-749-5808
http://www.alabama.easter-seals.org
Cheryl Bynum, Director Rehabilitation Services
Barry F Cavan, CEO

Job training and employment services, occupational skills training, job placement/competitive-supported employment, vocational evaluation/situation assessment, work adjustment.

6169 Easter Seals Adult Services Center

1180 Fairview Road
Little Rock, AR 72212   501-221-8400
877-221-8400
FAX 501-221-8842
http://www.ar.easter-seals.org
e-mail: mail@ar.easter-seals.org
Priscilla Handley, Administrator
Sharon Moone-Jochums, President/CEO

Adult day programming, personal and social supports, camping and recreation for children, job placement/competitive-supported employment, work services.

6170 Easter Seals Alabama

6005-A E Shirley Lane
Montgomery, AL 36617   334-395-4489
800-388-7325
FAX 334-395-4492
http://www.alabama.easter-seals.org
e-mail: alaseal@worldnet.att.net
Barry F Cavan, President/CEO

Job training and employment services, senior community service employment program.

6171 Easter Seals Camp ASCCA

5278 Camp ASCCA Drive
Jackson's Gap, AL 36861   256-825-9226
800-843-2267
FAX 256-825-8332
http://www.alabama.easter-seals.org
e-mail: info@campascca.org
Jerry Bynum, CEO
Barry F Cavan, President

Camp respite for adults and children, camperships, canoeing, day camping for adults, day camping for children, therapeutic horseback riding.

6172 Easter Seals Capilouto Center for the Deaf

5950 Monticello Drive
Montgomery, AL 36117   334-244-8090
FAX 334-244-1183
http://www.alabama.easter-seals.org
e-mail: lstokley@jccd.org
Lynne Stockley, Executive Director
Barry F Cavan, CEO

Job training and employment services, occupational skills training, job placement/competitive-supported employment, vocational evaluation/situation assessment, work adjustment.

6173 Easter Seals Gulf Coast

2448 Gordon Smith Drive
Mobile, AL 36617   251-471-4303
FAX 251-476-4303
http://www.alabama.easter-seals.org
e-mail: mikenancyoppcen@aol.com
Frank Harkins, CEO
Barry F Cavan, CEO

Job training and employment services, occupational skills training, job placement/competitive-supported employment, vocational evaluation/situation assessment, work adjustment.

6174 Easter Seals Opportunity Center

217 W 13th Street
Anniston, AL 36201   256-820-9960
FAX 256-820-9592
http://www.alabama.easter-seals.org
e-mail: mikenancyoppcen@aol.com
Mike Almaroad, Administrator
Barry F Cavan, CEO

Job training and employment services, occupational skills training, job placement/competitive-supported employment, vocational evaluation/situation assessment, work adjustment.

6175 Easter Seals Rehabilitation Center

2906 Citizens Parkway
Selma, AL 36701   334-872-8422
FAX 334-872-3907
http://www.alabama.easter-seals.org
David F White, Program Director
Barry F Cavan, CEO

Early education and care for ages zero through five, and preschool educational and developmental services for ages three and five.

6176 Easter Seals Rehabilitation Center: Northwest Alabama

1450 E Avalon Avenue
Muscle Shoals, AL 35661   256-381-1110
FAX 256-314-5105
http://www.alabama.easter-seals.org
e-mail: easter@hiwaay.net
Danny Prince, Administrator
Barry F Cavan, CEO

Job training and employment services, occupational skills training, job placement/competitive-supported employment, vocational evaluation/situation assessment, work services.

6177 Easter Seals: Birmingham Area

200 Beacon Parkway W
Birmingham, AL 35209   205-942-6277
FAX 205-945-4906
http://www.alabama.easter-seals.org
e-mail: esba@eastersealsbham.org
Johnny Webster, Director
Barry F Cavan, CEO

Job training and employment services, occupational skills training, job placement/competitive-supported employment, vocational evaluation/situation assessment, work adjustment.

6178 Easter Seals: West Alabama

1110 6th Avenue E
Tuscaloosa, AL 35401   205-759-1211
800-726-1216
FAX 205-349-1162
http://www.alabama.easter-seals.org
e-mail: eswa@eastersealswestal.org
Lorie Sears Robinson, Administrator
Barry F Cavan, CEO

Job training and employment services, occupational skills training, job placement/competitive-supported employment, vocational evaluation/situation assessment, work adjustment.

6179 State Vocational Rehabilitation Agency of Alabama

Division of Rehabilitation Services
2129 E South Boulevard
Montgomery, AL 36116   334-281-8780
800-447-7607
FAX 334-281-1973
http://www.rehab.state.al.us
e-mail: llucas@rehab.state.al.us
Steve Shivers, Commissioner
Jim Harris III, Assistant Commissioner

State vocational rehabilitation agencies provide direct services to persons with disabilities, including persons with learning disabilities. The services may include evaluation and diagnosis; counseling, guidance, and referral services; vocational and other training services; transportation to rehabilitation services; and assistive devices.

6180 Workforce Development Division

Alabama Dept. of Economic & Community Affairs
401 Adams Avenue
Montgomery, AL 36103   334-242-5100
FAX 334-5099
http://www.adeca.state.al.us
Steve Walkley, Division Director

Customer focused to help Americans access the tools they need to manage their careers through information and high quality services and to help US companies find skilled workers. Alabama's Career Center System is a network of one-stop centers designed to offer these services. These centers are co-located or electronically linked to provide streamlined services.

Alaska

6181 Alaska Department of Labor

1111 W 8th Street
Juneau, AK 99801   907-465-2700
FAX 907-465-2784
e-mail: Commissioner_Labor@labor.state.ak.us
Greg O'Claray, Commissioner
Ed Fisher, Deputy Commissioner

Responsible for the overall management of the department's programs and resources; serves as a liaison with other state, federal, and local governmental agencies and the legislature.

6182 State Vocational Rehabilitation Agency of Alaska

Division of Vocational Rehabilitation Services
1016 W 6th Avenue
Anchorage, AK 99501   907-269-3632
FAX 907-269-3632
http://www.edu.state.ak.us/vocrehab/home.html

State vocational rehabilitation agencies provide direct services to persons with disabilities, including persons with learning disabilities. The services may include evaluation and diagnosis; counseling, guidance, and referral services; vocational and other training services; transportation to rehabilitation services; and assistive devices.

Arizona

6183 Division of Employment & Training Rehabilitation Services

1789 W Jefferson Street
Phoenix, AZ 85007   602-542-4910
FAX 602-542-5339
John Clayton, Director

6184 Rehabilitation Services Administration

1789 W Jefferson Street
Phoenix, AZ 85007   602-542-3332
FAX 602-542-3778
http://www.de.state.az.us/rsa/
e-mail: AZRSA@mail.de.state.az.us
Skip Bingham, Administrator
Craig Warren, Deputy Administrator
Linda Olson, Planning/Evaluation

Helping people with disabilities become economically independent and decreasing or eliminating their need for ongoing government supports through integrated, meaningful, sustained work. This is achieved through a rehabilitation process which engages applicants and clients fully in actively exploring their vocational interests, abilities, capabilities and service/process options and in making choices.

Arkansas

6185 **Arkansas Employment Security Department: Office of Employment & Training Services**

1 Pershing Circle
North Little Rock, AR   72114   501-682-2121
FAX 501-682-3144
http://www.state.ar.us/esd/
e-mail: mel.thrash.aesd@mail.state.ar.us
Ed Rolle, Director
Mel Thrash, Deputy Director
Ron Snead, Employment Assistance

Employment related services that contribute to the economic stability of Arkansa and its citizens. These services are provided to employers, the workforce and the general public.

6186 **Arkansas Rehabilitation Services Employment Center: Office for the Deaf & Hearing Impaired**

4601 W Markham
Little Rock, AR   72205   501-896-9433
800-330-0632
FAX 501-686-9418
TDY:501-686-9433
http://www.arsinfo.org
e-mail: jlgatewood@ars.state.ar.us
John C Wyvill, Commissioner
Sue Gaskin, Special Programs

Providing opportunities for individuals with hearing impairment to work and have productive and independent lives.

6187 **Department of Human Services: Division of Developmental Disabilities Services**

Donaghey Plaza N, Slot N503
Little Rock, AR   72203   501-682-8665
FAX 501-682-8380
TDY:501-682-1332
http://www.state.ar.us/ddds/ddsinsti.html
James C Green PhD, Director
Kurt Knickrehm, Director Human Services
Joe Quinn, Communications

Offers a wide range of services and supports to Arkansans with developmental disabilities and their families.

6188 **Department of Workforce Education**

Three Capitol Mall
Little Rock, AR   72201   501-682-1500
FAX 501-682-1509
http://www.work-ed.state.ar.us/
e-mail: steve.franks@mail.state.ar.us
Dr. Steve Franks, Director
Garland Hankins, Adult Education
John Davidson, Career/Technical Education

Provides the leadership and contributes resources to serve the diverse and changing workforce training needs of the youth and adults of Arkansas.

6189 **State Vocational Rehabilitation Agency of Arkansas**

ARS, Vocational & Technical Education Division
1616 Brookwood Drive
Little Rock, AR   72203   501-296-1600
800-330-0632
FAX 501-296-1655
TDY:501-296-1669
http://www.arsinfo.org
e-mail: jlgatewood@ars.state.ar.us
John C Wyvill, Commissioner
Barbara Lewis, Field Services
Sue Gaskin, Special Programs

Provides direct services to persons with disabilities, including persons with learning disabilities. The services may include evaluation and diagnosis, counseling, guidance, and referral services, vocational and other training services, transportation to rehabilitation services, and assistive devices. Offering opportunities for individuals with disabilities to lead productive and independent lives.

6190 **Workforce Development Act**

Arkansas State Employment Board
PO Box 2981
Little Rock, AR   72203   501-371-1020
FAX 501-371-1030
TDY:800-285-1131
http://www.state.ar.us/workforce/
e-mail: arkansasweb@mail.state.ar.us
Jane English, Executive Director
Cindy Varner, Deputy Director
Sharon Robinette, Workforce Analysis/Reporting

Operates workforce centers that offer locally developed and operated services linking employers and jobseekers through a statewide delivery system. Conveinient centers are designed to eliminate the need to visit different locations. The centers integrate multiple workforce development programs into a single system, making the resources much more accessible and user friendly to jobseekers as well as expanding services to employers.

California

6191 **Adult Education**

California Department of Education
660 J Street
Sacramento, CA   95814   916-319-0800
FAX 916-228-2676
http://www.cde.ca.gov/adulteducation
Joan Dailey-Polster, Director
Sue Bennett, Educational Options

Elementary basic skills and tutor/literacy training are offered on or off site using language masters, audiocassettes, videos and computers with internet access. Workplace literacy training will also be provided, with groups of students physically coming into the Center or hooking up to the Center from their workplace by borrowing materials or going online. In the latter case, instructors will meet with students at the work site on a regular schedule for evaluation and consultation.

6192 California State Deparment of Education GED

1430 N Street
Sacramento, CA   95814
800-331-6316
http://www.cde.ca.gov/ged/
e-mail: GEDoffic@cde.ca.gov
Nancy J Edmunds, Program Coordinator

Provides access to a general high school education by providing many local classes and testing services.

6193 Department of Rehabilitation

2000 Evergreen Street
Sacramento, CA   94244
916-263-8981
FAX 916-263-7474
http://www.dor.ca.gov
e-mail: publicaffairs@dor.ca.gov
Catherine Campisi PhD, Director

Assists Californians with disabilities in obtaining and retain employment and maximizing their ability to live independently in their communities. Working with individuals of every type and category of disability, DOR provides vocational rehabilitational services to eligible Californians.

6194 Easter Seals Central California

9010 Soquel Drive
Aptos, CA   95003
831-684-2166
FAX 831-685-6055
http://www.centralcal.easter-seals.org
e-mail: donna@es-cc.org
Donna Alvarez, VP Finance
Bruce Hinman, CEO

Recreational services for adults, residential camping programs.

6195 Easter Seals Southern California

11110 Artesia
Cerritos, CA   90703
562-860-7270
877-855-2279
FAX 562-860-1680
http://www.essc.org
e-mail: Dee.Prescott@essc.org
Dee Prescott, Regional Director
Mark S Whitley, CEO

Adult day programing/personal and social supports.

6196 Easter Seals Superior California

3205 Hurley Way
Sacramento, CA   95864
916-485-6711
888-887-3257
FAX 916-485-6711
http://www.easterseals-superiorca.org
e-mail: info@easterseals-superiorca.org
Gary Kasai, President

Job training and employment services, occupational skills training, job placement/competitive-support employment, vocational evaluation/situational assessment and work adjustment.

6197 Easter Seals: Redondo Beach

700 N Pacific Coast Highway
Redondo Beach, CA   90277
310-376-3445
800-404-3445
FAX 310-376-5567
http://www.cssc.org
e-mail: dee.prescott@cssc.org
Dee Prescott, Regional Director
Mark S Whitley, President

Job training and employment services, occupational skills training, job placement/competitive-support employment, vocational evaluation/situational assessment and work adjustment.

6198 Easter Seals: Southern California

4727 Wilshire Boulevard
Los Angeles, CA   90010
323-954-3770
877-877-8565
FAX 323-954-3775
http://www.cssc.org
e-mail: lupe.trevizoreinoso@cssc.org
Lupe Trevizo-Reinoso, Regional Director
Mark S Whitley, President

Job training and employment services, occupational skills training, job placement/competitive-support employment, vocational evaluation/situational assessment and work adjustment.

6199 Easter Seals: Van Nuys

16946 Sherman Way
Van Nuys, CA   91406
818-996-9902
800-996-6302
FAX 818-996-1606
http://www.cssc.org
e-mail: paula.pompa-craven@cssc.org
Paula Pompa-Craven, Regional Director
Mark S Whitley, President

Job training and employment services, occupational skills training, job placement/competitive-support employment, vocational evaluation/situational assessment and work adjustment.

6200 Employment Development Department

800 Capitol Mall
Sacramento, CA   95814
916-654-7111
FAX 916-654-8039
http://www.edd.ca.gov
e-mail: dharo@edd.ca.gov
Herb K Schultz, Acting Director
Sally McKeag, Chief Deputy Director
Diego Haro, Job Service Branch

Vocational training and placement for citizens of California.

Colorado

6201 Easter Seals Colorado

5755 W Alameda Avenue
Lakewood, CO   80226
303-233-1666
FAX 303-233-1028
http://www.eastersealsco.org
Lynn Robinson, CEO

Job training and employment services, occupational skills training, job placement/competitive-support employment, vocational evaluation/situational assessment and work adjustment.

6202 Human Services: Division of Developmental Disabilities

3824 W Princeton Circle
Denver, CO 80236   303-866-7450
      FAX 303-866-7470
      TDY:303-866-7471
http://www.cdhs.state.co.us/ohr/dds/DDS_center
      e-mail: sandi.zagyi@state.co.us
Fred L DeCrescentis, Director

Provides leadership for the direction, funding and operation of community based services to people with developmental disabilities within Colorado.

6203 Human Services: Division of Vocational Rehabilitation

1575 Sherman Street
Denver, CO 80023   303-866-4150
      FAX 303-866-4905
http://www.cdhs.state.co.us/ods/dvr/index.html
      e-mail: debbie.powell@state.co.us
Diana Huerta, Director
Debbie Powell, Communications

Assists individuals whose disabilities result in barriers to employment to succeed at work and live independently. Building partnerships to improve opportunities for safety, self-sufficiency and dignity for the people of Colorado.

6204 State Vocational Rehabilitation Agency of Colorado

Div. of Rehabilitation/Dept. of Human Services
110 16th Street
Denver, CO 80202   303-620-4153
      FAX 303-620-4189
      e-mail: diana.huerta@state.co.us
Diana Huerta, Director

State vocational rehabilitation agencies provide direct services to persons with disabilities, including persons with learning disabilities. The services may include evaluation and diagnosis; counseling, guidance, and referral services; vocational and other training services; transportation to rehabilitation services; and assistive devices.

Connecticut

6205 Bureau of Adult Education & Training

25 Industrial Park Road
Middletown, CT 06457   860-807-2110
      FAX 860-807-2112
http://www.state.ct.us/sde/deps/adult/index.htm
      e-mail: gail.brooks-lemkin@po.state.ct.us
Maureen Staggenborg, Acting Bureau Chief
Gail Brooks-Lemkin, Technical Assistant

Committed to quality adult education programs which are accessible to all Connecticut adults and lead to mastery of the essential proficiences needed to function as productive citizens in work, family and community environments. Programs are available at local schools throughout the state. Offers basic literacy, elementary education, English language proficiency, secondary school completion and preparation for equivalency examinations.

6206 Department of Labor

200 Folly Brook Boulevard
Wethersfield, CT 06109   860-263-6000
      http://www.ctdol.state.ct.us
      e-mail: dol.help@po.state.ct.us
Shaun B Cashman, Commissioner

Assisting workers to become competitive in a global economy, we take a comprehensive approach to meeting the needs of workers, employers and other agencies that serve them.

6207 Department of Social Services: Vocational Rehabilitation Program

25 Sigourney Street
Hartford, CT 06106   860-424-4844
      800-537-2549
      TDY:860-424-4839
      http://www.dss.state.ct.us
      e-mail: pgr.dss@po.state.ct.us
John Galiette, Director
Evelyn Knight, Program Assistant

Provides services to people with most significant physical or mental disabilities to assist them in their effort to enter or maintain employment. The agency also oversees a statewide network of community based, consumer controlled, independent living centers that promote independence for people with disabilities.

6208 Easter Seals Connecticut

174 Williamantic Road
Chaplin, CT 06235   860-455-1331
      FAX 860-455-1372
      http://www.eastersealsco.org
Kathy Buck, Director Adult Programs
John R Quinn, CEO

Adult day programming/personal, social supports and senior services.

6209 Easter Seals Employment Industries

122 Avenue of Industry
Waterbury, CT 06705   203-236-0188
      FAX 203-236-0183
      http://www.eswct.com
Ron Bourque, Director Vocational Rehab Svcs.
Francis N DeBlasio, CEO

Job training, employment services, vocational evaluation/situational assessment and work services.

6210 Easter Seals Fulfillment Enterprises

226 Upton Road
Colchester, CT 06415   860-537-4595
FAX 860-537-9673
http://www.ct.easter-seals.org
Jerry Salois, Director Operations
John R Quinn, CEO

Job training, employment services, vocational evaluation/situational assessment and work services.

6211 Easter Seals: Uncasville

152 Norwich-New London Turnpike
Uncasville, CT 06382   860-848-9264
FAX 860-848-4462
http://www.ct.easter-seals.org
Kathy Buck, Director Adult Programs
John R Quinn, CEO

Job training, employment services, vocational evaluation/situational assessment and work services.

6212 Easter Seals: Waterbury

22 Tompkins Street
Waterbury, CT 06708   203-754-5141
FAX 203-754-1198
http://www.ct.easter-seals.org
Francis N DeBlasio, President

Job training, employment services, vocational evaluation/situational assessment and work services.

Delaware

6213 Division of Vocational Rehabilitation

Delaware Department of Labor
4425 N Market Street
Wilmington, DE 19809   302-761-8275
FAX 302-761-6611
http://www.delawareworks.com
Andrea Guest, Director
Cynthia Fairwell, Program Specialist

Mission is to provide information opportunitie, and resources to individuals with disabilities, leading to success in employment and independent living.

6214 Easter Seals Delaware and Maryland Shore

61 Corporate Circle
New Castle, DE 19720   302-324-4444
800-677-3800
FAX 302-324-4442
http://www.de.easter-seals.org
e-mail: badami@esdel.org
William Adami, VP
Sandra J Tuttle, President

Job training, employment services, vocational evaluation/situational assessment and work services.

6215 Easter Seals Dover Enterprise

100 Enterprise Place
Dover, DE 19904   302-678-3353
FAX 302-678-3650
http://www.de.easter-seals.org
e-mail: gcassedy@esdel.org
Gary Cassedy, CEO
Sandra J Tuttle, President

Job training, employment services, vocational evaluation/situational assessment and work services.

6216 Easter Seals Georgetown Professional Center

600 N DuPont Highway
Georgetown, DE 19947   302-856-7364
FAX 302-856-7296
http://www.de.easter-seals.org
e-mail: cea@gt.esdel.org
Cathy Anderson, Director Sussex County
Sandra J Tuttle, President

Job training, employment services, vocational evaluation/situational assessment and work services.

6217 Workforce Investment: Virtual Career Network

Department of Labor
4425 N Market Street
Wilmington, DE 19802   302-761-8085
FAX 302-761-6634
http://www.vcnet.net
e-mail: tsmith@state.de.us
Harold Stafford, Administrator
Anne Farley, Director

Many area offices for a one-stop employment and training integrated service delivery system. Much of our information is also available online.

District of Columbia

6218 Centers for Independent Living Program: Rehabilitation Services Administration

1400 Florida Avenue NE
Washington, DC 20002   202-388-0033
FAX 202-398-3018
http://www.dccil.org
e-mail: info@dccil.org
Richard Simms, Executive Director
Felicia Hinton, Coordinator

Consumer controlled, cross disability, community based, private nonprofit organization that promotes independent life styles for people with significant disabilities in the District of Columbia.

6219 Department of Employment Services

Government of the District of Columbia
64 New York Avenue NE
Washington, DC 20002   202-724-7000
FAX 202-724-5683
TDY:202-673-6994
Gregory Irish, Director

Helps consider career decisions and offer vocational and placement assistance at several area training locations.

6220 Department of Human Services: Bureau of Training & Employment

810 1st Street NE
Washington, DC   20002   202-279-6002
FAX 202-263-7518
e-mail: answersplease@dhs.washington.dc.us
Elizabeth B Parkers, Administrator

6221 District of Columbia Department of Education: Vocational & Adult Education

400 Maryland Avenue SW
Washington, DC   20202   202-205-5451
800-872-5327
FAX 202-205-8748
http://www.ed.gov/offices/OVAE
e-mail: ovae@ed.gov

To help all people achieve the knowledge and skills to be lifelong learners, to be successful in their chosen careers, and to be effective citizens.

6222 Public Schools Vocational & Adult Education

1709 3rd Street NE
Washington, DC   20002   202-576-6308
FAX 202-576-7899
Dr. Cynthia Bell, Director

Assisting individuals with physical or mental development disabilities to become more independent at home and in the community. Training for clients to enter the workforce and maintain gainful employment.

6223 State Vocational Rehabilitation Agency

Rehabilitation Services Administration
810 1st Street NE
Washington, DC   20002   202-442-8663
FAX 202-442-8742
e-mail: elizabeth.parker@dc.gov
Elizabeth B Parker, Administrator

Provides direct services to persons with disabilities, including persons with learning disabilities. The services may include evaluation and diagnosis, counseling, guidance, and referral services, vocational and other training services, transportation to rehabilitation services and assistive devices. Our goal is to assist those we serve in becoming independent and self sufficient in the home and in the community and to prepare for, enter and maintain gainful employment.

Florida

6224 College Living Experience

6555 Nova Drive
Davie, FL   33317   954-370-5142
800-486-5058
FAX 954-370-1895
http://www.cleinc.net
e-mail: secretary@cleinc.net
Irene Spalter PhD, Director
Eliza Greene PhD, Assistant Director

For young adults with learning difficulties who have average intellectual abilities but who would benefit from: intensive academic tutoring, advocacy and guidance, a comprehensive independent living skills program, social skills training, vocational support services and apartment living. One central program with a variety of experiences, including college, vocational school and internships, all within walking distance.

6225 Division of Vocational Rehabilitation

Florida Department of Education
2002 Old Saint Augustine Road
Tallahassee, FL   32301   850-245-3399
800-451-4327
FAX 850-245-3316
TDY:800-451-4327
http://www.rehabworks.org
Loretta Costin, Director

Statewide employment resource for businesses and people with disabilities. Our mission is to enable individuals with disabilities to obtain and keep employment.

6226 Easter Seals Broward County Florida

6951 W Sunrise Boulevard
Plantation, FL   33313   954-792-8772
FAX 954-791-8275
http://www.esbc-fl.easter-seals.org
e-mail: info@esbc-fl.easter-seals.org
Rebecca C Dausman, CEO

Job training, employment services, vocational evaluation/situational assessment and work services.

6227 Easter Seals Florida: East Coast Region

6050 Babcock Street SE
Palm Bay, FL   32909   321-723-4474
FAX 321-676-3843
http://www.fl.easter-seals.org
e-mail: gedwards@fl.easter-seals.org
Gail Edwards, Executive Director
Robert J Griggs, President

Job training, employment services, vocational evaluation/situational assessment and work services.

6228 Easter Seals Miami-Dade

1475 NW 14th Avenue
Miami, FL   33125   305-325-0470
FAX 305-325-0578
http://www.miami.easter-seals.org
e-mail: info@miami.easter-seals.org
Dr. Joan Bornstein, Director

Job training, employment services, vocational evaluation/situational assessment and work services.

6229 Easter Seals North Florida

910 Myers Park Drive
Tallahassee, FL   32301   850-222-4465
FAX 850-222-5950
http://www.northflorida.easter-seals.org
e-mail: enorthflorida@aol.com
Christine Hall, CEO/President

Job training, employment services, vocational evaluation/situational assessment and work services.

6230 Easter Seals Southwest Florida

350 Braden Avenue
Sarasota, FL 34243   941-355-7637
                               FAX 941-351-9711
http://www.swfl.easter-seals.org
Mary Hitchcock, President/CEO

Job training, employment services, vocational evaluation/situational assessment and work services.

6231 Florida Workforce Investment Act

Department of Labor & Employment Security
1320 Executive Center Drive
Tallahassee, FL 32399   904-488-7228
                               FAX 850-413-7587
Kathleen L McLeskey, Acting Director

Provides job-training services for economically disadvantaged adults and youth, dislocated workers and others who face significant employment barriers.

6232 TILES Project: Transition/Independent Living/Employment/Support

Family Network on Disabilities of Florida
2735 Whitney Road
Clearwater, FL 33760   727-523-1130
                               FAX 727-523-8687
http://www.fndfl.org
e-mail: tom@fndfl.org

Tom Nurse, Director

Provides training information to enable individuals with disabilities and the parents, family members, guardians, advocates, or other authorized representatives to participate more effectively with professionals in meeting the vocational, independent living and rehabilitation needs of people with disabilities in Florida.

Georgia

6233 Easter Seals East Georgia

1500 Wrightsboro Road
Augusta, GA 30904   706-667-9695
                               866-667-9695
                               FAX 229-435-6278
http://www.easternsealseastgeorgia.org
e-mail: sthomas@esega.org
Sheila Thomas, Executive Director

Job training, employment services, vocational evaluation/situational assessment and work services.

6234 Easter Seals Middle Georgia

602 Kellam Road
Dublin, GA 31021   478-275-8850
                               FAX 478-275-8852
http://middlegeorgia.easterseals.org
Wayne Peebles, President/CEO

Job training, employment services, vocational evaluation/situational assessment and work services.

6235 Easter Seals Southern Georgia

1906 Palmyra Road
Albany, GA 31701   229-439-7061
                               800-365-4583
                               FAX 229-435-6278
e-mail: benglish@swga-easterseals.org
Beth English, Executive Director

Job training, employment services, vocational evaluation/situational assessment and work services.

6236 Vocational Rehabilitation Services

Georgia Department of Labor
148 Andrew Young International Blvd
Atlanta, GA 30303   404-232-3910
http://www.vocrehabga.org
e-mail: rehab@dol.state.ga.us
Bobby Pack, Acting Assistant Commissioner

Operates 5 integrated and interdependent programs that share a primary goal — to help people with disabilities to become fully productive members of society by achieving independence and meaningful employment.

Hawaii

6237 Vocational & Rehabilitation Agency Hawaii: Division of Vocational Rehab & Services for the Blind

Department of Human Services
PO Box 339
Honolulu, HI 96809   808-692-7719
                               FAX 808-692-7727
http://www.state.hi.us/dhs/vr
e-mail: nshim@dhs.state.hi.us

Neil Shim, Administrator

State vocational rehabilitation agencies provide direct services to persons with disabilities, including persons with learning disabilities. The services may include evaluation and diagnosis, counseling, guidance, and referral services, vocational and other training services, transportation to rehabilitation services, and assistive devices.

Idaho

6238 Department of Labor

317 W Main Street
Boise, ID 83735   208-332-3570
                               FAX 208-334-6430
http://www.labor.state.id.us
e-mail: rvaldez@jobservice.us
Roger B Madsen, Director
Rogelio Valdez, Disability Determinations

An equal opportunity employer/program with auxiliary aids and services available upon request to individuals with disabilities.

6239   Easter Seals-Goodwill Staffing Services

1465 S Vinnell Way
Boise, ID   83709   208-373-1299
                                    FAX 208-378-9965
                http://www.esgw-nrm.easter-seals.org
                         e-mail: marcib@esgw.org
Marci Bailey, Manager
Michelle Belknap, CEO

Job training, employment services, vocational evalua-
tion/situational assessment and work services.

6240   Easter Seals-Goodwill Working Solutions

1613 N Park Centre Boulevard
Nampa, ID   83651   208-466-2671
                                    FAX 208-466-2537
                http://www.esgw-nrm.easter-seals.org
                         e-mail: landisr@esgw.org
Landis Rossi, Coordinator
Michelle Belknap, CEO

Job training, employment services, vocational evalua-
tion/situational assessment and work services.

6241   Idaho Workforce Investment Act

Idaho Department of Labor
317 Main Street
Boise, ID   83735   208-332-3570
                                    FAX 208-334-6300
                         http://www.jobservice.us
                e-mail: cbrush@labor.state.id.us
Cheryl Brush, Chief

Provides vocational training services for economically disadvantaged adults and youth, dislocated
workers and others who face significant employment
barriers.

6242   State Vocational Rehabilitation Agency

State of Idaho
650 W State
Boise, ID   83720   208-334-3390
                                    FAX 208-334-5305
                http://www2.state.id.us/idvr/idvrhome.htm
                e-mail: scook@idvr.state.id.us
Michael Graham, Administrator
Sue Payne, Chief Field Services
Sue Cook, Assistant Chief Field Services

State vocational rehabilitation agencies provide direct services to persons with disabilities, including
persons with learning disabilities. The services may
include evaluation and diagnosis, counseling, guidance, and referral services, vocational and other training services, transportation to rehabilitation services,
and assistive devices.

**6243   Temporary Assistance for Needy Families: Idaho
Department of Health and Welfare**

450 W State Street
Boise, ID   83720   208-334-0606
                                    FAX 208-334-6581
                         http://www.2.state.id.us
                e-mail: BCEH@idhw.state.id.us
Penny Robbe, Chief TAFI

Provides assistance and work opportunities to needy
families by granting states the federal funds and wide
flexibility to develop and implement their own welfare programs.

Illinois

6244   Easter Seals Central Illinois

2715 N 27th Street
Decatur, IL   62526   217-429-1052
                                    FAX 217-423-7605
                         http://www.easterseals-ci.org
Janet Kelsheimer, Executive Director

Job training, employment services, vocational evalu-
ation/situational assessment and work services.

6245   Easter Seals Missouri

602 E 3rd Street
Alton, IL   62002   618-462-7325
                                    FAX 618-462-8170
                http://www.mo.easter-seals.orgs.org
Lynn Stonecipher, Manager
Craig A Byrd, CEO

Job training, employment services, vocational evalu-
ation/situational assessment and work services.

6246   Easter Seals Youth at Risk

120 W Madison
Oak Park, IL   60302   708-524-8700
                                    FAX 708-524-4902
                http://www.eastersealschicago.org
                e-mail: wkern@eastersealschicago.org
Bill Kern, Program Manager
F Timothy Muri, President/CEO

Job training, employment services, vocational evalu-
ation/situational assessment and work services.

6247   State Vocational Rehabilitation Agency

100 S Grand Avenue
East Springfield, IL   62762   217-524-7551
                                       800-843-6154
                                    FAX 217-558-4270
                                    TDY:217-524-7551
                         http://www.dhs.state.il.us
                e-mail: ors@dhs.state.il.us
Barbara Payne, Director

We help people with physical or learning disabilities
find and keep jobs. Our goal is to help our customers
find quality employment that pays a living wage and
offers a chance for advancement. Specialized services
for the deaf and blind or visually impaired.

6248   Temporary Assistance for Needy Families

Department of Human Services
100 E Grand Avenue
Springfield, IL   62762   217-785-0480
                                    FAX 217-557-2134
                         http://www.dhs.state.il.us
Carol L Adams, Secretary

Focus on transitional services. Major points include
creating goals, continuation of Work Pays program,
cash assistance, subsidized employment, and medical
benefits.

Indiana

6249   Easter Seals Arc of Northeast Indiana

4919 Projects Drive
Fort Wayne, IN   46825   260-456-4534
                                 FAX 260-745-5200
             http://www.eastersealsarcncin.org
                       e-mail: shinkle@esarc.org
Stephen L Hinkle, CEO

Job training, employment services, vocational evalua-
tion/situational assessment and work services.

6250   Easter Seals Crossroads Industrial Services

8302 E 33rd Street
Indianapolis, IN   46226   317-897-7320
                                 FAX 317-897-9763
             http://www.eastersealscrossroads.org
Brett Bennett, Division Director

Job training, employment services, vocational evalua-
tion/situational assessment and work services.

**6251   Easter Seals Crossroads Rehabilitation Center:
Indiana**

4740 Kingsway Drive
Indianapolis, IN   46205   317-466-1000
                                 FAX 317-466-2000
             http://www.eastersealscrossroads.org
                       e-mail: info@x-roads.org
James J Vento, President

Job training, employment services, vocational evalua-
tion/situational assessment and work services.

6252   Easter Seals: Bridgepointe

1329 Applegate Lane
Clarksville, IN   47129   812-283-7908
                                 FAX 812-283-6248
             e-mail: cmarshall@bridgepoint.org
Caren Marshall, Executive Director

Job training, employment services, vocational evalua-
tion/situational assessment and work services.

**6253   Indiana Vocation Rehabilitation Services Goodwill
Industries**

1452 Vaxter Avenue
Clarksville, IN   47129   812-288-8261
                                 FAX 812-282-7048
Edwin Haines, Interim Area Supervisor

Purpose is to assist the community by providing services which allow individuals to maximize their potential and to participate in work, family and the
community. To do this we will provide rehabilitation,
education and training.

6254   State Vocational Rehabilitation Agency

Division of Disability, Aging, & Rehab. Services
402 W Washington Street
Indianapolis, IN   46204   317-232-1319
                                      800-545-7763
                                 FAX 317-232-6478
                                 http://www.in.gov
             e-mail: phedden@fssa.state.in.us
Mike Hedden, Deputy Director

Provides direct services to persons with disabilities,
including persons with learning disabilities. The services may include evaluation and diagnosis; counseling, guidance, and referral services, vocational and
other training services, transportation to rehabilitation services, and assistive devices.

Iowa

6255   Easter Seals Center

2920 30th Street
Des Moines, IA   50310   515-274-1529
                                 FAX 515-274-6434
             http://www.ia-easter-seals.orgls.org
                       e-mail: info@eastersealsia.org
Marcia Tope, Coordinator Intake/QA
Donna Elbrecht, CEO

Job training, employment services, vocational evalu-
ation/situational assessment and work services.

6256   Easter Seals Iowa

401 NE 66th Avenue
Des Moines, IA   50313   515-274-1529
                                 FAX 515-274-6434
             http://www.ia-easter-seals.orgls.org
                       e-mail: info@eastersealsia.org
Marcia Tope, Coordinator Intake/QA
Donna Elbrecht, CEO

Job training, employment services, vocational evalu-
ation/situational assessment and work services.

6257   Iowa Bureau of Community Colleges

Department of Education
Grimes State Office Building
Des Moines, IA   50319   515-281-3125
                                 FAX 515-281-6544
             http://www.state.ia.us/educate/commcoll.html
                   e-mail: sally.schroeder@ed.state.ia.us
Sally Schroeder, Contact

**6258   Iowa JOBS Program: Division of Economic
Assistance**

Department of Human Services
Hoover State Building
Des Moines, IA   50319   515-281-8629
                                 FAX 515-281-7791

Doug Howard, Administrator

6259   Iowa Vocational Rehabilitation Agency

Department of Education
Grimes State Office Building
Des Moines, IA   50319   515-281-5294
                               FAX 515-281-4703
        http://www.state.ia.us/educate/directory.html
Steve Wooderson, Administrator

6260   State Vocational Rehabilitation Agency

Iowa Division of Vocational Rehabilitation Service
510 E 12th Street
Des Moines, IA   50319   515-281-4211
                               800-532-1486
                               FAX 515-281-7645
                               TDY:515-281-4211
                http://www.dvrs.stste.ia.us
                e-mail: swooderson@dvrs.state.ia.us
Stephen A Wooderson, Administrator

We work for and with individuals with disabilities to achieve their employment, independence and economic goals. Economic independence and more and better jobs are what we are about for Iowans with disabilities.

Kansas

6261   Easter Seals Kansas

3636 N Oliver
Wichita, KS   67220   316-744-1428
                               888-337-6287
                               FAX 316-744-1428
           http://www.goodwilleastersealsks.org
Curtis Tatum, VP Programs
Marie Mareda, CEO

Job training, employment services, vocational evaluation/situational assessment and work services.

6262   Kansas Human Resource Investment Council

Kansas Department of Human Resources
401 SW Topeka Boulevard
Topeka, KS   66603   785-296-3974
                               FAX 785-296-8177
                http://www.hr.state.ks.us
                e-mail: sandra.brown@hr.state.ks.us
Deann Tiede, State Council Coordinator
Sandra Brown, On-Site Coordinator

Cultivates a job ready workforce and a workplace environment to fuel economic growth for Kansas.

6263   Kansas Vocational Rehabilitation Agency

300 SW Oakley, Biddle Building
Topeka, KS   66606   785-296-3911
                               FAX 785-368-6688
Joyce A Cussimanio, Commissioner

To assist people with disabilities achieve suitable employment and independence.

6264   Office of Vocational Rehabilitation

915 SW Harrison Street
Topeka, KS   66612   785-296-3959
                               FAX 785-296-2173
                http://www.srskansas.org
                e-mail: cmxa@srskansas.org
Clarissa Ashdown, Program Support Administrator

Partnering to connect Kansans with support and services to improve lives. Vocational and transitional training.

Kentucky

6265   Easter Seals Employment Connections-Pennyrile

755 Industrial Road
Madisonville, KY   42431   519-471-4710
                               FAX 270-365-2591
           http://www.eswky.easter-seals.org
           e-mail: dtinsley@ky-ws.easter-seals.org
Donna Tinsley, Site Manager
Kenneth R Lucas, CEO

Job training, employment services, vocational evaluation/situational assessment and work services.

6266   Easter Seals: West Kentucky

2229 Mildred Street
Paducah, KY   42001   270-444-9687
                               866-673-3565
                               FAX 270-444-0655
           http://www.eswky.easter-seals.org
           e-mail: info@ky-ws.easter-seals.org
Kenneth R Lucas, President/CEO

Job training, employment services, vocational evaluation/situational assessment and work services.

6267   State Vocational Rehabilitation Agency

Department of Vocational Rehabilitation
209 St. Clair Street
Frankfort, KY   40601   502-564-4440
                               800-372-7172
                               FAX 502-564-6745
                http://www.kydor.state.ky.us/
                e-mail: wfd.vocrehab@mail.state.ky.us
Bruce Crump, Commissioner

Provides direct services to persons with disabilities, including persons with learning disabilities. The services may include evaluation and diagnosis; counseling, guidance, and referral services, vocational and other training services, transportation to rehabilitation services, and assistive devices.

Louisianna

6268 State Vocational Rehabilitation Agency

Department of Social Services
8225 Florida Boulevard
Baton Rouge, LA   70806   225-925-4484
                                        800-737-2958
                              FAX 225-925-4484
                        http://www.dss.state.la.us
                e-mail: jwallace@lrs.dss.state.la.us
James Wallace, Director
Claire Hymel, Assistant Director
Ed Barras, Community Rehabilitation

Responsible for developing and providing social services and improving social conditions for the citizens of Louisiana, and for rehabilitating people with disabilities for employment.

Maine

6269 State Vocational Rehabilitation Agency

Maine Bureau of Rehabilitation Services
150 State House Station
Augusta, ME   04333   207-624-5950
                                        800-698-4440
                              FAX 207-624-5980
               http://www.state.me.us/rehab/index.htm
                  e-mail: penny.plourde@maine.gov
Laura Fortman, Commissioner
Kate Brogan, Bureau Chief
Penny Plourde, Director

Works to bring about full access to employment, independence and community integration for people with disabilities. Our three service provision units are Vocational Rehabilitation, Division for the Blind and Visually Impaired and Division of Deafness.

6270 Temporary Assistance for Needy Families

Department of Human Services
221 State Street
Augusta, ME   04333   207-287-2736
                              FAX 207-287-3005
                        http://www.state.me.us/dhs/
Stephen W Telow, Contact

Focuses on transitional services.

Maryland

6271 Maryland Technology Assistance Program

2301 Argonne Drive
Baltimore, MD   21218   410-554-9230
                                         800-832-4827
                              FAX 410-554-9237
                        http://www.mdtap.org
                  e-mail: mdtap@mdtap.org
Jessica Vollmer, Office Manager

Offers information and referrals, reduced rate loan program for assistive technology, five regional display centers, presentations and training on request.

6272 State Vocational Rehabilitation Agency

Div. of Rehab. Services, Dept. of Education
2301 Argonne Drive
Baltimore, MD   21218   •   410-554-9385
                              FAX 410-554-9412
                        http://www.msde.state.md.us
                e-mail: hdavis@dors.state.md.us
Robert Burns, Assistant State Superintendent
Harvey J Davis, Director Field Services
Sue Schaffer, Director Workforce/Technology

Operates more than 20 statewide offices and also operates the Workforce and Technology Center, a comprehensive rehabilitation facility in Baltimore. Rehabilitation representatives also work in many Maryland One-Stop Career Centers.

Massachusettes

6273 Easter Seals: Massachusetts

89 S Street
Boston, MA   02111   617-226-2640
                              FAX 617-737-9875
                        http://www.eastersealsma.org
                  e-mail: maryd@eastersealsma.org
Mary D'Antonino, Information Specialist
Kirk Joslin, President

Job training, employment services, vocational evaluation/situational assessment and work services.

6274 Easter Seals: Worcester

484 Main Street
Worcester, MA   01608   508-757-2756
                              FAX 508-831-9768
                        http://www.eastersealsma.org
                  e-mail: maryd@eastersealsma.org
Mary D'Antonino, Information Specialist
Kirk Joslin, President

Job training, employment services, vocational evaluation/situational assessment and work services.

6275 JOBS Program: Massachusetts Employment Services Program

Dept of Transitional Assistance/Office of Health
600 Washington Street
Boston, MA   02111   617-348-8400
                              FAX 617-348-8575
                http://www.state.ma.us/dta/index.htm

The Employment Services Program is a joint federal and state funded program whose primary goal is to provide a way to self-sufficiency for TAFDC families. ESP is an employment-oriented program that is based on a work-first approach.

6276 Massachusetts Job Training Partnership Act: Department of Employment & Training

CF Hurley Building, 3rd Floor
Boston, MA   02114   617-626-6600
Nils L Nordberg, Commissioner

Supplies information on the local labor market and assists companies in locating employees.

6277 State Vocational Rehabilitation Agency

Massachusetts Rehabilitation Commission
27 Wormwood Street
Boston, MA   02210·
         617-204-3600
         FAX 617-727-1354
         http://www.state.ma.is/mrc.mrc.htm
         e-mail: commissioner@mrc.state.ma.us
Elmer C Bartels, Commissioner

Provides public vocational rehabilitation, independent living and disability determination services for residents with disabilities in Massachusetts.

Michigan

6278 Easter Seal Michigan

804 S Hamilton
Saginaw, MI   48602
         989-797-0880
         800-757-3257
         FAX 989-797-0888
         http://www.mi-ws.easter-seals.org
         e-mail: esofmi@aol.com
Julie S Dorcey, Regional Director
John Cocciolone, CEO

Job training, employment services, vocational evaluation/situational assessment and work services.

6279 Easter Seals Collaborative Solutions

1105 N Telegraph
Waterford, MI   48328
         248-975-9769
         FAX 248-338-2936
         http://www.mi-ws.easter-seals.org
         e-mail: mbiglin@essmichigan.org
Mindy Biglin, Program Manager
John Cocciolone, CEO

Job training, employment services, vocational evaluation/situational assessment and work services.

6280 Michigan Commission for the Blind: Deafblind Unit

201 N Washington Square, 2nd Floor
Lansing, MI   48909
         517-373-2062
         800-292-4200
         FAX 517-335-5140
         TDY:517-373-4025
         http://www.mcb1.org
         e-mail: heibecks@michigan.gov
Patrick Cannon, Executive Director
Leamon Jones, Consumer Services

Provides opportunities to the deaf and or blind community to achieve employability and function independently in society.

6281 Michigan Jobs Commission

201 N Washington Square
Lansing, MI   48913
         517-373-4871
         FAX 517-373-0314
         e-mail: bolinb@state.mi.us
Carl Bourdelais, Regional Director

6282 Michigan Workforce Investment Act

Michigan Jobs Commission
119 Pere Marquette Drive
Lansing, MI   48912
         517-485-4477
         FAX 517-485-4488
         http://www.publicpolicy.com
         e-mail: ppa@publicpolicy.com
Jeffrey D Padden, President
Nancy C Hewat, Executive Officer

6283 State Vocational Rehabilitation Agency

Michigan Rehabilitation Services
PO Box 30010
Lansing, MI   48909
         517-373-3390
         800-605-6722
         FAX 517-373-0565
         http://www.michigan.gov/mdcd
         e-mail: balthazarj@michigan.gov
Jaye Balthazar, Director

State vocational rehabilitation agencies provide direct services to persons with disabilities, including persons with learning disabilities. The services may include evaluation and diagnosis; counseling, guidance, and referral services; vocational and other training services; transportation to rehabilitation services; and assistive devices.

Minnesota

6284 Goodwill/Easter Seals Minnesota

19463 Evans Street NW
Elk River, MN   55330
         763-274-1822
         FAX 763-274-1825
         http://www.goodwilleasterseals.org
Tony Cassiday, Coordinator
Michael Wirth-Davis, CEO

Job training, employment services, vocational evaluation/situational assessment and work services.

6285 Goodwill/Easter Seals: St. Cloud

50 S 2nd Street
St. Cloud, MN   56387
         320-654-9527
         FAX 320-654-9542
         http://www.goodwilleasterseals.org
Julie Danda, Program Services Manager
Michael Wirth-Davis, CEO

Job training, employment services, vocational evaluation/situational assessment and work services.

6286 Goodwill/Easter Seals: St. Paul

553 Fairview Avenue
St. Paul, MN   55104
         651-379-5800
         800-669-6719
         FAX 651-379-5804
         http://www.goodwilleasterseals.org
         e-mail: kjmatter@goodwilleasterseals.org
Kelly Matter, Program Services VP
Michael Wirth-Davis, CEO

Job training, employment services, vocational evaluation/situational assessment and work services.

6287 Goodwill/Easter Seals: Willmar

2424 1st Street S
Willmar, MN   56201   320-214-9238
                             FAX 320-214-9140
        http://www.goodwilleasterseals.org
Melissa Peterson, Program Services Manager
Michael Wirth-Davis, CEO

Job training, employment services, vocational evaluation/situational assessment and work services.

6288 Minnesota Department of Employment and Economic Development

Minnesota Workforce Center
390 N Robert Street
St. Paul, MN   55101   612-296-6061
                              800-657-3858
                 FAX 651-296-0994
                 http://www.mnwfc.org
     e-mail: mdes.customerservice@state.mn.us
Bonnie Elsey, Director

The Department of Employment and Economic Development is Minnesota's principal economic development agency, with programs promoting business expansion and retention, workforce development, international trade, community development and tourism.

6289 School-to-Work Outreach Project

Institute on Community Integration
101D Pattee Hall
Minneapolis, MN   55455   612-626-7220
                    FAX 612-624-9344
                    http://www.ici.umn.edu
                    e-mail: walla001@umn.edu
Terry Wallace, Project Coordinator

A primary goal of the project is to improve school-to-work opportunities for students with disabilities through the identification and documentation of exemplary school-to-work activities. This is achieved through a nomination/application/review process conducted by the School-to-Work Outreach Project.

6290 State Vocational Rehabilitation Agency: Minnesota Department of Economics Security

Rehabilitation Service Branch
390 N Robert Street
St. Paul, MN   55101   651-296-9981
                              800-328-9095
                 FAX 651-297-5159
                 http://www.mnwfc.org
        e-mail: paul.bridges@state.mn.us
Paul Bridges, Assistant Commissioner

State vocational rehabilitation agencies provide direct services to persons with disabilities, including persons with learning disabilities. The services may include evaluation and diagnosis, counseling, guidance, and referral services, vocational and other training services, transportation to rehabilitation services, and assistive devices.

Mississippi

6291 Department of Vocational Rehabilitation Services: Mississippi

PO Box 1698
Jackson, MS   39215   601-853-5100
                             800-443-1000
                 FAX 601-853-5325
                 http://www.mdrs.state.ms.us

6292 State Vocational Rehabilitation Agency: Vocational Rehabilitation Division

1281 Highway 51
Jackson, MS   39215   601-853-5230
                             800-443-1000
                 FAX 601-853-5205
                 http://www.mdrs.state.ms.us/
                 e-mail: gneely@mdrs.state.ms.us
Jerry Sawyer, Director

State vocational rehabilitation agencies provide direct services to persons with disabilities, including persons with learning disabilities. The services may include evaluation and diagnosis; counseling, guidance, and referral services; vocational and other training services; transportation to rehabilitation services; and assistive devices.

Missouri

6293 Rehabilitation Services for the Blind

Family Support Division
615 E 13th Street
Kansas City, MO   64106   816-889-2677
                                 800-592-6004
                    FAX 816-889-2504
        http://www.dss.mo.gov/dfs/rehab
        e-mail: Kimberly.Gerlt@dss.mo.gov
Kimberly Gerlt, Operations Coordinator

Creating opportunities for eligible blind and visually impaired people in order that they may attain personal and vocational success.

6294 State Vocational Rehabilitation AgencyDepartment of Elementary & Secondary Education

3024 Dupont Circle
Jefferson City, MO   65109   573-751-3251
                                    877-222-8963
                       FAX 573-751-1441
                       TDY:573-751-0881
           http://www.vr.dese.state.mo.us
Ronald Vessell, Assistant Commissioner

State vocational rehabilitation agencies provide direct services to persons with disabilities, including persons with learning disabilities. The services may include evaluation and diagnosis, counseling, guidance, and referral services, vocational and other training services, transportation to rehabilitation services, and assistive devices.

Montana

6295 Easter Seals-Goodwill Career Designs

4400 Central Avenue
Great Falls, MT 59405   406-761-3680
                                FAX 406-761-3680
http://www.esgrw-nrm.easter-seals.org
                    e-mail: sharonod@esgw.org
Sharon Odden, VP Program Services
Michelle Belknap, CEO

Job training, employment services, vocational evaluation/situational assessment and work services.

6296 Easter Seals-Goodwill Store

951 S 29th Street W
Billings, MT 59102   406-656-4020
                             FAX 406-656-3750
http://www.esgw-nrm.easter-seals.org
                e-mail: gwbillings@mcn.net
Rhonda Haynes, Manager
Michelle Belknap, CEO

Job training, employment services, vocational evaluation/situational assessment and work services.

6297 Easter Seals-Goodwill Working Partners

4141 1/2 S Main Street
Conrad, MT 59425   406-278-9121
                           FAX 406-271-2073
http://www.esgw-nrm.easter-seals.org
                e-mail: sandrab@esgw.org
Sandra Bucher, Case Manager
Michelle Belknap, CEO

Job training, employment services, vocational evaluation/situational assessment and work services.

6298 Easter Seals-Goodwill Working Partners: Great Falls

205 9th Avenue S
Great Falls, MT 59405   406-452-2196
                                FAX 406-453-2160
http://www.esgrw-nrm.easter-seals.org
                    e-mail: joelc@csgw.org
Joel Corda, Supervisor
Michelle Belknap, CEO

Job training, employment services, vocational evaluation/situational assessment and work services.

6299 Easter Seals-Goodwill Working Partners: Hardin

419 N Center Avenue
Hardin, MT 59034   406-665-3500
                           FAX 406-665-1395
http://www.esgrw-nrm.easter-seals.org
                e-mail: jwhiteclay@state.mt.us
Jolene C White Clay, Work Case Manager

Job training, employment services, vocational evaluation/situational assessment and work services.

6300 State Vocational Rehabilitation Agency

Department of Public Health & Human Services
111 N Sanders
Helena, MT 59604   406-444-5622
                           FAX 406-444-1970
http://www.dphhs.state.mt.us
                e-mail: ggray@state.mt.us
Gail Gray, Director

State vocational rehabilitation agencies provide direct services to persons with disabilities, including persons with learning disabilities. The services may include evaluation and diagnosis, counseling, guidance, and referral services, vocational and other training services, transportation to rehabilitation services, and assistive devices.

Nebraska

6301 Easter Seals Nebraska

2727 W 2nd
Hastings, NE 68901   402-462-3031
                             800-471-6425
                             FAX 402-462-2040
http://www.ne.easter-seals.org
                e-mail: kginder@ne.easter-seals.org
Karen Ginder, President

Job training, employment services, vocational evaluation/situational assessment and work services.

6302 Job Training Program

Nebraska Department of Economic Development
PO Box 94666
Lincoln, NE 68509   402-471-3780
                            800-426-6505
                            FAX 402-471-3365
http://www.assist.neded.org
                e-mail: lshaal@neded.org
Lori Shaal, Job Training Coordinator

Provides training assistance on projects that offer an opportunity for economic development in Nebraska. Use of the funds is limited to eligible companies and eligible training projects.

6303 State Vocational Rehabilitation Agency: Quality Employment Solutions

State Department of Education
PO Box 94987
Lincoln, NE 68509   402-471-3644
                            877-637-3422
                            FAX 402-471-0788
http://www.vocrehab.state.ne.us
            e-mail: vr_stateoffice@vocrehab.state.ne.us
Frank C Lloyd, Assistant Commissioner of Ed.

We help people with disabilities make career plans, learn job skills, get and keep a job. Our goal is to prepare people for jobs where they can make a living wage and have access to medical insurance.

Nevada

6304 Bureau of Services to the Blind & Visually Impaired

Department of Employment, Training/Rehabilitation
505 E King Street
Carson City, NV 89701 775-684-4244
FAX 775-687-5080
http://www.detr.state.nv.us/rehab/reh_bvi.htm
e-mail: detbsb@nvdetr.org
John Alexander, Employment/Training Coordinator

Services to the Blind and Visually Impaired (BSBVI) provides a variety of services to eligible individuals, whose vision is not correctable by ordinary eye care. Adaptive training, independence skills, low vision exams and aids, mobility training and vocational rehabilitation are offered.

6305 Nevada Economic Opportunity Board: Community Action Partnership

PO Box 270880
Las Vegas, NV 89127 702-647-1510
FAX 702-647-6639
http://www.eobcc.org
Marcia Walker, Executive Director

Located in one of the fastest growing and most diverse communities in the United States, the Economic Opportunity Board of Clark County is a highly innovative Community Action Agency. Our mission is to eliminate poverty by providing programs, resources, services, and advocacy for self-sufficiency and economic empowerment.

6306 Nevada Governor's Council on Rehabilitation & Employment of People with Disabilities

1325 Corporate Boulevard
Reno, NV 89502 775-688-1111
e-mail: mailto:kfbarth@nvdetr.org
Donna Sanders, Executive Director

To help insure vocational rehabilitation programs are consumer oriented, driven and result in employment outcomes for Nevadans with disabilities. Funding for innovation and expansion grants.

6307 Rehabilitation Division Department of Employment, Training & Rehabilitation

505 E King Street
Carson City, NV 89701 775-684-4040
FAX 775-687-4310
TDY:775-684-8400
http://www.detr.state.nv.us
e-mail: detvr@nvdetr.org
Maureen Cole, Administrator

Providing options and choices for Nevadans with disabilities to work and live independently. Our mission will be accomplished through planning, implementing and coordinating assessment, employment, independent living and training.

New Hampshire

6308 Department of Health & Human Services: New Hampshire

129 Pleasant Street
Concord, NH 03301 603-271-4688
800-852-3345
FAX 603-271-4912
http://www.dhhs.state.nh.us
Stephen Tomajczyk, Information Officer

6309 Easter Seals New Hampshire

54 Pleasant Street
Claremont, NH 03743 603-543-3795
http://www.nh.easter-seals.org
e-mail: cmcmahon@eastersealsnh.org
Chris McMahon, Site Manager

Job training, employment services, vocational evaluation/situational assessment and work services.

6310 Easter Seals: Keene

12 Kingsbury Street
Keene, NH 03431 603-355-1067
FAX 603-358-3947
http://www.nh.easter-seals.org
e-mail: cmcmahon@eastersealsnh.org
Chris McMahon, Site Manager

Job training, employment services, vocational evaluation/situational assessment and work services.

6311 Easter Seals: Manchester

555 Auburn Street
Manchester, NH 03103 603-623-8863
FAX 603-625-1148
http://www.nh.easter-seals.org
e-mail: cmcmahon@eastersealsnh.org
Chris McMahon, Site Manager

Job training, employment services, vocational evaluation/situational assessment and work services.

6312 State Vocational Rehabilitation Agency

Department of Education
78 Regional Drive
Concord, NH 03301 603-271-3471
800-299-1647
FAX 603-271-7095
http://www.ed.state.nh.us/VR
Paul K Leather, Administrator
Lillian Lee, Program Planner

Assisting eligible New Hampshire citizens with disabilities secure suitable employment, financial and personal independence by providing rehabilitation services.

New Jersey

6313 **Division of Family Development: New Jersey Department of Human Services**
PO Box 716
Trenton, NJ   08625   609-588-2163
                            FAX 609-588-3051
Karen Highsmith

6314 **Easter Seals: Silverton**
2920 Yorktown Boulevard
Brick, NJ   08723   732-257-6662
                         FAX 732-257-7373
                http://www.eastersealsnj.org
Brian J Fitzgerald, President

Job training, employment services, vocational evaluation/situational assessment and work services.

6315 **Eden Family of Services**
Eden Services
One Eden Way
Princeton, NJ   08540   609-987-0099
                             FAX 609-987-0243
                    http://www.edenservices.org
                    e-mail: info@edenservices.org
David L Holmes EdD, Executive Director/President
Anne Holmes, Director Outreach Support Svcs
Joani Truch, Administration/Communications

Provides year round educational services, early intervention, parent training, respite care, outreach services, community based residential services and employment opportunities for individuals with autism.

6316 **New Jersey Council on Developmental Disabilities**
20 W State Street
Trenton, NJ   08625   609-292-3745
                             800-216-1199
                          FAX 609-292-7114
                          TDY:609-777-3238
                          http://www.njddc.org
                    e-mail: njddc@njddc.org
Ethan B Ellis, Executive Director
Jane Dunhamn, Events Coordinator
Sue Gottesman, Legislative Coordinator

Promotes systems change, coordinates advocacy and research for 1.2 million residents with developmental and other disabilities.

6317 **New Jersey Technology Assistive Resource Program**
New Jersey Department of Labor
210 S Broad Street
Trenton, NJ   08608   609-777-0945
                             800-922-7233
                          FAX 609-777-0187
                    http://www.njpanda.org
                    e-mail: adadvocate@njpanda.org
G Emerson Dickman, Chair
Marilyn Goldstein, Vice-Chair

Assists individuals in overcoming barriers in the system and making assistive technology more accessible to individuals with disabilities throughout the state.

6318 **Office of State Coordinator of Vocational Education for Students with Disabilities**
Ofice of School-to-Career & College Initiatives
PO Box 500
Trenton, NJ   08625   609-633-0665
                             FAX 609-777-4481
                    e-mail: pharris@doe.state.nj.us
Patricia Harris, Director

Assists the disabled student with changes from the school environment to the working world.

6319 **Programs for Children with Special Health Care Needs**
NJ Department of Health & Senior Services
50 E State Street
Trenton, NJ   08625   609-984-0755
                             FAX 609-292-9288
                    http://www.state.nj.us.com

6320 **State Vocational Rehabilitation Agency**
New Jersey Department of Labor
135 E State Street
Trenton, NJ   08625   609-292-5987
                             FAX 609-292-8347
                             TDY:609-292-2919
          http://www.nj.gov/labor/dvrs/vrsindex.html
                    e-mail: dvraadmin@dol.state.nj.us
Thomas G Jennings, Director

Enables individuals with disabilities to achieve employment outcomes consistent with their strengths, priorities, needs, abilities and capabilities. Our division is here to help people with disabilites that are having trouble finding or holding a job because of their disability.

New Mexico

6321 **Department of Human Services: Project Forward**
PO Box 2348
Santa Fe, NM   87504   505-827-7262
                             FAX 505-827-7203
Marise McFadden, Contact

6322 **New Mexico Department of Labor: Job Training Division**
1596 Pacheco Street
Santa Fe, NM   87502   505-827-6827
                             FAX 505-827-6812
                    http://www.dol.state.nm.us
Alan Richardson, Job Training Director

Helps citizens of New Mexico from all walks of life find appropriate vocational trainings, and job placement.

6323 State Vocational Rehabilitation Agency New Mexico

Department of Education
435 St. Michaels Drive
Santa Fe, NM 87505
505-954-8511
800-224-7005
FAX 505-954-8562
http://www.dvrgetsjobs.com
e-mail: TBrigance@state.nm.us
Terry Brigance, Director

State vocational rehabilitation agencies provide direct services to persons with disabilities, including persons with learning disabilities. The services may include evaluation and diagnosis, counseling, guidance, and referral services, vocational and other training services, transportation to rehabilitation services, and assistive devices.

New York

6324 Commission for the Blind & Visually Handicapped

Department of Social Services
40 N Pearl Street
Albany, NY 12243
518-473-8744
http://www.dfa.state.ny.us
e-mail: cbvh@dfa.state.ny.us
John A Johnson, Commissioner Children/Family

Professionals and paraprofessionals are available to help those with low vision or blindness with vocational rehabilitation services.

6325 Office of Curriculum & Instructional Support

State Department of Adult Education
Washington Avenue
Albany, NY 12234
518-474-8892
FAX 518-474-0319
http://www.emsc.nysed.gov/workforce
e-mail: jstevens@mail.nysed.gov
Jean C Stevens, Assistant Commissioner

Works with those seeking General Educational Development diplomas and technical training.

6326 Office of Vocational and Educational Services for Individuals with Disabilities

New York State Education Department
One Commerce Plaza
Albany, NY 12234
518-474-3852
800-222-5627
FAX 518-473-9466
http://www.web.nysed.gov
e-mail: nlauria@mail.nysed.gov
Richard P Mills, Commissioner
Nancy Lauria, Director

Promotes educational equality and excellence for students with disabilities while ensuring that they receive the rights and protection to which they are entitled, assure appropriate continuity between the child and adult services systems, and provide the highest quality vocational rehabilitation and independent living services to all eligible people.

North Carolina

6327 State Vocational Rehabilitation Agency

Department of Health & Human Resources
2801 Mail Service Center
Raleigh, NC 27699
919-855-3500
FAX 919-733-7968
Carmen Hooker-Odem, Secretary Health/Human Services
George McCoy, Director

Vocational rehabilitation counselors work with business and community agencies to help them prepare their worksites to accomodate employees who have physical or mental disabilities. The division also provides services that encourage and reinforce independent living for the disabled.

North Dakota

6328 Division of Vocational Rehabilitation

North Dakota Health & Human Services
600 S 2nd Street
Bismarck, ND 58504
701-328-8800
888-862-7342
FAX 701-328-8969
TDY:701-328-8968
http://www.state.nd.us.humanservices
Gene Hysjulien, Director

Assists individuals with disabilities to achieve competitive employment and increased independence through rehabilitation services.

6329 North Dakota Department of Career and Technical Education

600 E Boulevard Avenue
Bismarck, ND 58505
701-328-3180
FAX 701-328-1255
http://www.state.nd.us
e-mail: mwilson@state.nd.us
Mark Wilson, Assistant State Director

The mission of the Board for Vocational and Technical Education is to work with others to provide all North Dakota citizens with the technical skills, knowledge, and attitudes necessary for successful performance in a globally competitive workplace.

6330 North Dakota Workforce Development Council

North Dakota Department of Commerce
1600 E Century Avenue, Suite 2
Bismarck, ND 58502
701-328-5300
FAX 701-328-5320
http://www.growingnd.com/services/workforce
e-mail: jhirsch@state.nd.us
James Hirsch, Director

The role of the North Dakota Workforce Development Council is to advise the Governor and the Public concerning the nature and extent of workforce development in the context of North Dakota's economic development needs, and how to meet these needs effectively while maximizing the efficient use of available resources and avoiding unnecessary duplication of effort.

6331 Workforce Investment Act

Governor's Employment & Training Forum
PO Box 5507
Bismarck, ND   58506   701-328-2836
                             FAX 701-328-1612
e-mail: j.gladden@pioneer.state.nd.us
Jennifer Gladden, Administration

Literacy coaching and further vocational training.

Ohio

6332 Bureau of Workforce Services

145 S Front Street
Columbus, OH   43215   614-466-3817
                             FAX 614-728-5938
http://www.jfs.ohio.gov/owd/workforce_services
Emma Brewer, Administration

Oversees the implementation of the job training partnership act and employment and training programs in the state of Ohio.

6333 State Vocational Rehabilitation Agency

Ohio Rehabilitation Services Commission
400 E Campus View Boulevard
Columbus, OH   43235   614-438-1200
                             800-282-4635
                         FAX 614-785-5010
                       http://www.state.oh.us
e-mail: rsc_rir@vscnet.a1.state.oh.us
John M Connelly, Executive Director
Sandra Montgomery, Administration

State vocational rehabilitation agencies provide direct services to persons with disabilities, including persons with learning disabilities. The services may include evaluation and diagnosis, counseling, guidance, and referral services, vocational and other training services, transportation to rehabilitation services, and assistive devices.

Oklahoma

6334 National Clearinghouse of Rehabilitation Training Materials

Oklahoma State University
206 W 6th Street
Stillwater, OK   74078   405-744-2000
                               800-223-5219
                           FAX 405-744-2001
                           TDY:405-744-2002
                 http://www.nchrtm.okstate.edu
e-mail: seefelj@okstate.edu
Judy Seefeldt, Director
Carolyn Cail, Information Coordinator

Rehabilitation counselor and education materials, disability information and resources.

6335 State Vocational Rehabilitation Agency:
Oklahoma Department of Rehabilitation Services

3535 NW 58th Street
Oklahoma City, OK   73112   405-951-3400
                                  800-845-8476
                              FAX 405-951-3529
                            http://www.okrehab.org
e-mail: ddcouch@drs.state.ok.us
Dr. David Pittman, Commission Chair

State vocational rehabilitation agencies provide direct services to persons with disabilities, including persons with learning disabilities. The services may include evaluation and diagnosis counseling, guidance, and referral services, vocational and other training services, transportation to rehabilitation services and assistive devices.

6336 Workforce Investment Act

Association of South Central Oklahoma Governments
2401 N Lincoln Boulevard
Oklahoma City, OK   73152   405-557-7294
                              FAX 405-557-1478
                            http://www.ascog.org
e-mail: info@ascog.org
Eddie Foreman, Director

Partnership of local goverments offering resource conservation and development and workforce development.

Oregon

6337 Department of Community Colleges & Workforce Development

255 Capitol Street NE
Salem, OR   97031   503-378-8648
                          FAX 503-378-8434
                http://www.odccwd.state.or.us
Karen Madden-Evans, Education/Workforce Programs
Jerry Lierow, Agency Operations

Contributes leadership and resources to increase the skills, knowledge and career opportunities for Oregonians.

6338 Oregon Employment Department

875 Union Street NE
Salem, OR   97311   503-947-1394
                          800-237-3710
                      FAX 503-947-1668
                  http://www.emp.state.or.us
Deborah Lincoln, Director
Greg Hickman, Deputy Director
Odie Vogel, Assistant to Director

Supports economic stability for Oregonians and communities during times of unemployment through the payment of unemployment benefits. Serves businesses by recruiting and referring the best qualified applicants to jobs, and provides resources to diverse job seekers in support of their employment needs.

6339 Oregon Office of Education and Workforce Policy

State Capitol Building
Salem, OR   97301   503-378-4582
                              FAX 503-378-4863
                  http://www.arcweb.sos.state.or.us
                  e-mail: annette.talbott@state.or.us
Annette Talbott, Workforce Policy Coordinator
Danny Santos, Education Policy Coordinator

The Governor's Office of Education and Workforce Policy was established to assist the Governor in examining education and workforce efforts with a view to supporting and strengthening what is working well. The goal is to have Oregonians prepared to meet the education and workforce needs of Oregon businesses rather than having to recruit from outside the state to fill quality jobs.

6340 Recruitment and Retention Special Education Jobs Clearinghouse

Teaching Research
345 Monmouth Avenue
Monmouth, OR   97361   503-838-8777
                              FAX 503-838-8150
                  http://www.ode.state.or.us/sped
                        e-mail: samplesb@wou.edu
Bernie Samples, Clearinghouse Coordinator

A free on-line jobs clearinghouse with access to position openings in Oregon in the area of Special Education and related services. A Job Seeker Listing and resumes also sent via e-mail to districts and agencies looking for qualified individuals.

6341 State Vocational Rehabilitation Agency

Division of Vocational Rehabilitation
500 Summer Street NE
Salem, OR   97301   503-945-5944
                                     877-277-0513
                              FAX 503-378-2897
            http://www.dhs.state.or.us/vr/index.html
                       e-mail: info.vr@state.or.us
Jean Thorne, Director Human Services
Stephanie Parrish-Taylor, Program Director

Uses state and federal funds to assist Oregonians who have disabilities to achieve and maintain employment and independence.

Pennsylvania

6342 State Vocational Rehabilitation Agency: Pennsylvania

Department of Labor & Industry
1521 N 6th Street
Harrisburg, PA   17102   717-787-5244
                                     800-442-6351
                              FAX 717-783-5221
                      http://www.dli.state.pa.us
                        e-mail: ovr@dli.state.pa.us
Steven Nasuti, Executive Director

Provides individualized services to assist people with disabilities to pursue, obtain, and maintain satisfactory employment. Counselors are available for training, planning and placement services.

Rhode Island

6343 Rhode Island Department of Employment and Training

101 Friendship Street
Providence, RI   02914   401-277-4922
                              FAX 401-861-8030

6344 Rhode Island Vocational and Rehabilitation Agency

Rhode Island Department of Human Services
40 Fountain Street
Providence, RI   02903   401-421-7005
                              FAX 401-222-3574
                              TDY:401-421-7016
                      http://www.ors.state.ri.us
                  e-mail: rcarroll@ors.state.ri.us
Raymond A Carroll, Administrator

Assists people with disabilities to become employed and to live independently in the community. In order to achieve this goal, we work in partnership with the State Rehabilitation Council, our customers, staff and community.

6345 State Vocational Rehabilitation Agency: Rhode Island

Rhode Island Department of Human Services
40 Fountain Street
Providence, RI   02903   401-421-7005
                              FAX 401-222-3574
                              TDY:401-421-7016
                      http://www.ors.state.ri.us
                  e-mail: rcarroll@ors.state.ri.us
Raymond A Carroll, Administrator

Assists people with disabilities to become employed and to live independently in the community. In order to achieve this goal, we work in partnership with the State Rehabilitation Council, our customers, staff and community.

South Carolina

6346 Americans with Disabilities Act Assistance Line

1660 Gadsden Street
Columbia, SC   29202   803-737-2593
                                     800-436-8190
                              FAX 803-737-0140
                        http://www.sces.org
                  e-mail: rratterree@sces.org
Regina Ratterree, Program Coordinator

Provides information, technical assistance and training on the Americans with Disabilities Act.

6347 South Carolina Vocational Rehabilitation Department

1410 Boston Avenue
West Columbia, SC   29171   803-896-6500
                                  FAX 803-896-6529
                                  http://www.scvrd.net

Derle A Lowder Sr, Chair
Shannon Lindsay, Counselor

Enabling eligible South Carolinians with disabilities to prepare for, achieve and maintain competitive employment. Training, coaching and job placement services available.

South Dakota

6348 Department of Social Services

700 Governors Drive
Pierre, SD   57501   605-773-3165
                            FAX 605-773-4855
                            http://www.state.sd.us
                            e-mail: jamese@dss.state.sd.us

6349 South Dakota Department of Labor

700 Governors Drive
Pierre, SD   57501   605-773-5017
                            FAX 605-773-4211
                            http://www.state.sd.us/dol/dol.htm
                            e-mail: miker@dol.pr.state.sd.us
Michael Ryan, Administrator

Job training programs provide an important framework for developing public-private sector partnerships. We help prepare South Dakotans of all ages for entry or re-entry into the labor force.

6350 South Dakota Rehabilitation Center for the Blind

Department of Human Services
800 W Avenue N
Sioux Falls, SD   57104   605-36752603
                                 FAX 605-367-5263
                                 http://www.state.sd.us/dhs/
                                 e-mail: dawn.backer@state.sd.us
Dawn Backer, Manager Rehabilitation

Helping people lead a full, productive life — regardless of how much one does or does not see. Upon completion of training, individuals usually return to their community and use these new skills in their home, school or job.

6351 State Vocational Rehabilitation Agency

Division of Rehabilitation Services
3800 E Highway 34
Pierre, SD   57501   605-773-5485
                            FAX 605-773-5483
                            http://www.state.sd.us/dhs/drs/
                            e-mail: steve.stewart@state.sd.us
Grady Kickul, Director
Steve Stewart, Rehabilitation Engineer

Assists individuals with disabilities to obtain employment, economic self-sufficiency, personal independence and full inclusion into society.

Tennessee

6352 State Vocational Rehabilitation Agency

Tennessee Department of Human Services
400 Deaderick Street
Nashville, TN   37248   615-313-4714
                               FAX 615-741-4165
                               http://www.state.tn.us/humanserv/
                               e-mail: car.w.brown@state.tn.us
Carl Brown, Assistant Commissioner

State vocational rehabilitation agencies provide direct services to persons with disabilities, including persons with learning disabilities. The services may include evaluation and diagnosis counseling, guidance, and referral services, vocational and other training services, transportation to rehabilitation services and assistive devices.

6353 Tennessee Department of Education

710 James Robertson Parkway
Nashville, TN   37243   615-741-2731
                               800-531-1515
                               FAX 615-532-4899
                               http://www.state.tn.us
                               e-mail: education.comments@state.tn.us
Phil White, Director

Mission is to take Tennessee to the top in education. Guides administration of the state's K-12 public schools.

6354 Tennessee Department of Labor & Workforce Development: Office of Adult Education

500 James Robertson Parkway
Nashville, TN   37243   615-741-7054
                               FAX 615-532-4899

Phil White, Director

6355 Tennessee Services for the Blind

Division of Rehabilitation
400 Deaderick Street
Nashville, TN   37248   615-313-4914
                               FAX 615-313-6617
                               http://www.state.tn.us/humanserv/
                               e-mail: Human-Services.Webmaster@state.tn.us
Terry Smith, Director
Philip Wagster, Director Vocational Rehab.

Offering training and services to help blind or low-vision citizens of Tennessee become more independent at home, in the community and at work.

Texas

6356 Department of Assistive & Rehabilitative Services

Texas Department of Health & Human Services
4800 N Lamar Boulevard
Austin, TX   78751   512-377-0500
                            800-252-5204
                            FAX 512-424-6587
                            http://www.hhsc.state.tx.us/default.htm
Terrel Murphy, Director Blind Services

Transitional and vocational programs aid independence in the home, community and at work for Texans who are blind, deaf, or have other impairments that would benefit from assistive technology.

6357 State Vocational Rehabilitation Agency

Texas State Rehabilitation Commission
4900 N Lamar Boulevard
Austin, TX 78751   512-424-4000
                           800-628-5115
                      FAX 512-424-4730
            http://www.rehab.state.tx.us
            e-mail: trc@rehab.state.tx.us
Vernon M Arrell, Commissioner
Linda Loucks, Administrative Services
Mary Wolfe, Field Operations/Communications

State vocational rehabilitation agencies provide direct services to persons with disabilities, including persons with learning disabilities. The services may include evaluation and diagnosis, counseling, guidance, and referral services, vocational and other training services, transportation to rehabilitation services and assistive devices.

6358 Texas Education Agency

1701 N Congress Avenue
Austin, TX 78701   512-463-9294
                      FAX 512-475-3661
Paul Lindsey, Asst Commissoner/Continuing Ed.
Pavlos Roussos, Program Director/Adult Education

6359 Texas Workforce Commission

101 E 15th Street
Austin, TX 78778   512-463-2222
                      FAX 512-475-2321
            http://www.twc.state.tx.us
            e-mail: luis.macias@twc.state.tx.us
Larry Temple, Executive Director
Luis Macias, Director Workforce Division

Provides oversight, coordination, guidance, planning, technical assistance and implementation of employment and training activities with a focus on meeting the needs of employers throughout the state of Texas.

Utah

6360 Adult Education Services

Utah State Office of Education
250 E 500 S
Salt Lake City, UT 84114   801-538-7824
                          FAX 801-538-7882
      http://www.usoe.k12.ut.us/adulted/home.htm
            e-mail: dsteele@usoe.k12.ut.us
David Steele, Coodinator/Director Education
Sandra Grant, Specialist
Shauna South, Specialist

Provides oversight of state and federally funded adult education programs. Offers adult basic education, adult high school completion, English as a second language, and general education development programs.

6361 State Vocational Rehabilitation Agency

Utah State Office of Rehabilitation
250 E 5th S
Salt Lake City, UT 84111   801-538-7530
                           800-473-7530
                      FAX 801-538-7522
            http://ww.usor.utah.gov
            e-mail: duchida@utah.gov
Donald R Uchida, Director

Assisting and empowering eligible individuals. Disabled, learning disabled, blind, low vision and deaf people can prepare for and obtain employment and increase their independence through job training and assistive technology.

Vermont

6362 Adult Education & Literacy State Department of Education

Department of Education
120 State Street
Montpelier, VT 05602   802-828-5134
                      FAX 802-828-3146
            http://www.state.vt.us/educ/
            e-mail: edinfo@doe.state.vt.us
Amy Brockman, Adult Education
John Bradley, Career/Technical Information

Promotes quality education for area adults as well as those under age 18.

6363 REACH-UP Program: Department of Social Welfare

103 S Main Street
Waterbury, VT 05671   802-241-2800
                      FAX 802-241-2830
Karen Ryder

6364 Vermont Department of Employment & Training

5 Green Mountain Drive
Montpelier, VT 05601   802-828-4000
                      FAX 802-828-4022
            http://www.det.state.vt.us
            e-mail: mcalcagni@det.state.vt.us
Mike Calcagni, Director Jobs/Training
Mike Griffin, Labor Market Information

Represents Vermont's efforts to provide services, information and support both to individuals to obtain and keep good jobs, and to employers to recruit and maintain a productive workforce.

6365 VocRehab Vermont

Agency of Human Services
103 S Main Street
Waterbury, VT 05671   802-241-2186
                          866-879-6757
                      FAX 802-241-3359
            http://www.vocrehabvermont.org
            e-mail: janetr@dad.state.vt.us
Diane Dalmasse, Director

Works in close partnership with the Vermont Association of Business and Industry Rehabilitation to assist Vermonters with disabilities to find and maintain meaningful employment in their communities.

Virginia

6366 Department of Rehabilitative Services

8004 Franklin Farms Drive
Richmond, VA   23288   804-662-7000
                             800-552-5019
                          FAX 804-662-9531
                          http://www.vadrs.org
                  e-mail: DRS@DRS.state.va.us
John Rothrock, Director

Helps people with disabilities get ready for, find and keep a job. We have a residential training and medical rehabilitation center known as the Woodrow Wilson Rehabilitation Center, as well as offices located across Virginia. The agency also partners with a network of community rehabilitation providers also known as Employment Service Organizations.

6367 Office of Adult Education & Literacy

Virginia Department of Education
PO Box 2120
Richmond, VA   23218   804-225-2075
                          FAX 804-225-3352
                      http://www.pen.k12.va.us/
               e-mail: ythayer@mail.vak12ed.edu
Yvonne Thayer, Director
Elizabeth Hawa, Associate Director

Provides leadership and support for adult education and literacy services, with priority on the development and expansion of quality family literacy and workforce education programs.

6368 Virginia Employment Commission

PO Box 1358
Richmond, VA   23218   804-786-3466
                          FAX 804-371-2814
                       http://www.vec.state.va.us
          e-mail: athornton-crump@vec.state.va.us
Dolores Esser, Commissioner
Alexis Thornton-Crump, Program Manager

Provides workforce services that promote maximum employment to enhance the economic stability of Virginia.

Washington

**6369 State Vocational Rehabilitation Agency:
Washington Division of Vocational Rehabilitation**

Department of Social Services & Health
PO Box 45340
Olympia, WA   98504   360-438-8000
                             800-637-5627
                          FAX 360-438-8007
       http://www.1.dshs.wa.gov/dvr/index.htm
                  e-mail: obrien@dshs.wa.gov
Michael O'Brien, Director

State vocational rehabilitation agencies provide direct services to persons with disabilities, including persons with learning disabilities. The services may include evaluation and diagnosis, counseling, guidance, and referral services, vocational and other training services, transportation to rehabilitation services, and assistive devices.

**6370 Work First Division: Washington Department of
Social and Health Services**

PO Box 45480
Olympia, WA   98504   360-413-3371

West Virginia

6371 West Virginia Division of Rehabilitation Services

West Virginia Department of Education & the Arts
PO Box 50890
Charleston, WV   25305   304-766-4601
                             FAX 304-766-4905
                          http://www.wvdrs.org
              e-mail: Debbiel@mail.drs.state.wv.us
Janice A Holland, Director
Debbie Lovely, Field Services/Programs

State vocational rehabilitation agencies provide direct services to persons with disabilities, including persons with learning disabilities. The services may include evaluation and diagnosis, counseling, guidance, and referral services, vocational and other training services, transportation to rehabilitation services, and assistive devices.

6372 Workforce Investment Act

West Virginia Bureau of Employment Programs
112 California Avenue
Charleston, WV   25305   304-558-1138
                             FAX 304-558-1136
                       http://www.state.wv.us/bep/
                  e-mail: BGreenle@wvbep.org
Quetta Muzzle, Commissioner
Valerie Comer, Director

Matching jobseekers with employers in a prompt, efficient manner, to help those in need become job ready, and to analyze and disseminate labor market information. Special placement techniques are also offered which seek to match the physical and mental demands of a job to the capabilities of workers with disabilities. Such services are given by Job Service in cooperation with other community agencies and include counseling and special placement assistance.

Wisconsin

**6373 State Vocational Rehabilitation Agency:
Wisconsin Division of Vocational Rehabilitation**

2917 International Lane
Madison, WI   53707   608-243-5600
                             800-442-3477
                          FAX 608-243-5680
                    http://www.dwd.state.wi.us/dvr/
                  e-mail: dwddvr@dwd.state.wi.us
Terry Schnapp, Administrator
Charlene Dwyer, Administrator
Kristin Rolling, Disability Research/Information

Federal and state program designed to obtain, maintain and improve employment for people with disabilities by working with vocational rehabilitation consumers, employers and other partners.

6374 W-2 Program: Division of Work Force Solutions

Wisconsin Department of Workforce Development
201 E Washington Avenue
Madison, WI 53702   608-266-0327
                                         FAX 608-261-6376
http://www.dwd.state.wi.us/dws/w2/default.htm
           e-mail: sandy.breitborde@dwd.state.wi.us
Bill Clingan, Administrator
Sandy Breitborde, Workforce Information

Develops and maintains employment focused programs that enable employers to hire and retain the workforce they need and that provide individuals and families with services that enable them to achieve financial well being as members of Wisconsin's workforce. It delivers services through public-private partnerships and a statewide network of job centers.

6375 Work Force Information Act

Education and Training Policy Division
PO Box 7903
Madison, WI 53707   608-266-2439
                                         FAX 608-267-2392
                 e-mail: denisga@dwd.state.WI.us
Gary Denis, Director

Wyoming

6376 State Vocational Rehabilitation Agency

Wyoming Division of Vocational Rehabilitation
1100 Herschler Building
Cheyenne, WY 82002   307-777-7389
                                         FAX 307-777-5939
           http://www.ydoe.state.wy.us/vocrehab
                  e-mail: jmcint@state.wy.us
Jim McIntosh, Division Administrator

Assists Wyoming citizens with disabilities to prepare for, enter into, and return to suitable employment. Individuals with a disability that prevents them from working may apply for these services as long as a physical or mental impairment which constitutes or results in a substantial impediment to employment exists, and they have the ability to benefit in terms of an employment outcome from vocational services.

Glossary

Accommodations: Techniques and materials that allow individuals with LD to complete school or work tasks with greater ease and effectiveness. Examples include spellcheckers, tape recorders, and expanded time for completing assignments.

ADA: Americans with Disabilities Act.

Adaptive Physical Education: A special education program designed to suit a person's limits and disabilities.

Alternative Assessment: An alternative to conventional means of assessing achievement; usually means using something other than a paper and pencil test, such as oral testing or work sample review.

Appeal: A written request for a change in a decision.

Aptitude Test: A test developed to measure a person's ability to learn, and the likelihood of succeeding in academic work or in specific careers.

Assistive Technology (AT): Equipment that enhances the ability of students and employees to be more efficient and successful. For individuals with LD, computer grammar checkers, an overhead projector used by a teacher, or the audiovisual information delivered through a CD-ROM would be typical examples.

Attention Deficit Disorder (ADD): A disorder of brain function, causing severe difficulty in focusing and maintaining attention, paying attention to details, listening to instructions, and organizing assignments, thoughts and behaviors. Often leads to learning/academic difficulties, and behavior problems at home, school, and work. ADD is not a learning disability.

Attention Deficit Hyperactivity Disorder (AD/HD): A disorder of brain function, causing severe difficulty in staying on task, accompanied by hyperactivity. Difficulties can occur in taking turns in games or conversations, controlling temper outbursts, anticipating the consequences of actions, and containing or managing internal restlessness.

Auditory Discrimination: The ability to recognize, compare, and differentiate the discrete sounds in words; this ability is crucial for reading skills. Categorized as gross ability (e.g., detecting the differences between the noises made by a cow and a horse) or fine ability (e.g., distinguishing between the "s" sound and the "sh" sound).

Auditory Figure-Ground Discrimination: The ability to distinguish significant sounds amid a noisy background, and to focus on the auditory information being presented.

716

Auditory Memory: The ability to remember something heard some time in the past (long-term auditory memory); the ability to recall something heard very recently (short-term auditory memory).

Auditory Sequencing: The ability to comprehend and recollect the order of spoken words.

AYP: Annual yearly progress.

Behavior Modification: A technique intended to alter behavior by positive reinforcement (rewarding desirable actions) and ignoring undesirable actions.

Binocular Fusion: The blending of separate images from each eye into a single significant image.

Brain Imaging Techniques: Recently developed, noninvasive techniques for studying the activity of living brains. Includes brain electrical activity mapping (BEAM), computerized axial tomography (CAT), and magnetic resonance imaging (MRI).

Brain Injury: The physical damage to brain tissue or structure that occurs before, during, or after birth that is verified by EEG, MRI, CAT, or a similar examination, rather than by observation of performance. When caused by an accident, the damage may be called Traumatic Brain Injury (TBI).

Catastrophic Reaction: A display of extreme emotion (anger, terror, frustration or grief) without an apparent stimulus, possibly prompted by unexpected events, alteration of set routine, or feelings of over-excitement.

CEC: Council for Exceptional Children.

Central Auditory Processing Disorder (CAPD): A weakness in how the brain processes auditory information in an individual with functioning hearing ability.

Central Nervous System (CNS): The brain and the spinal cord.

Cerebral Cortex: The brain's outer layer, which controls thoughts, feelings, and voluntary movements.

Child Study Committee: A body of school officers and/or specialists which acts upon referrals of students thought to be disabled, and aids in the students' specialized aptitude assessment.

Cognition: The act or process of knowing, as a result of the capacities of various thinking skills and thought processes which are considered cognitive skills.

Cognitive Ability: Skills of reasoning and thinking; the ability to perceive intellectually.

Cognitive Style: The way a person typically approaches problem solving and learning activities (e.g., methodical analysis or impulsive reactivity).

Compensation: The process by which a person is taught to manage his or her learning problems, by manipulating and emphasizing strengths as a way to work around skills and/or abilities which may be limited.

Conceptual Disorder: A disturbance in the processes of reasoning, thinking, evaluating, recognizing, generalizing, and/or memorizing.

Conceptualization: The process of developing a general idea based on observations, including the ability to recognize similar traits within a group of objects.

Configuration: The visual form or shape of words.

Coordination: The synchronization and complementary functioning of muscles in the body necessary for completing complex movements.

Criterion Referenced Test: A test developed to reflect the specific knowledge or skills possessed by an individual, scored in terms of an individual's knowledge or ability of a relatively small unit of content without reference to other individuals' scores.

Cross-Categorical: A term referring to a system in which an instructor addresses more than one handicapping condition within one instructional session.

Cumulative File: The general file maintained for any child enrolled in a school. Parents have a right to copy and/or have access to any information in this file.

Decoding: The process of acquiring meaning from spoken, written, or printed symbols used in receptive language.

Developmental Aphasia: A severe language disorder in the normal acquisition of language.

Developmental Lag: A delay in the development of some aspect of a person's mental or physical maturation.

Direct Instruction (DI): An instructional approach to academic subjects that emphasizes the use of carefully sequenced steps that include demonstration, modeling, guided practice, and independent application.

Directionality: The ability to distinguish direction and orientation, including the difference between right and left, up and down, and forward and backward.

Discrimination: The process of differentiating between and/or among separate stimuli.

Disinhibition: Lack of restraint in a person's response to a situation, often resulting in impulsive and/or inappropriate reactions.

Distractibility: The transferring of attention from the task at hand to stimuli such as sounds and sights that normally occur in a person's surroundings.

DOE: Department of Education.

Due Process: Application of legal measures to ensure the protection of an individual's rights, e.g., a parent has the right to ask for a full evaluation of any educational program developed for his or her child.

Dysarthia: A disorder affecting the muscles necessary for speech, impacting a person's ability to pronounce words.

Dyscalculia: A wide range of life-long disabilities involving mathematics and computations, often indicated by severe difficulty in understanding and using symbols or functions needed for success in mathematics.

Dysgraphia: A disability affecting writing abilities, characterized by difficulty in spelling, written expression, and producing handwriting that is legible and written at an age-appropriate speed.

Dyslexia: A life-long language processing disorder causing the brain to process and interpret information differently, resulting in severe difficulty in understanding or using one or more areas of language, including listening, speaking, reading, writing, and spelling.

Dysnomia: A marked difficulty in remembering names or recalling words needed in context for oral or written language.

Dyspraxia: A specific disorder in the development of motor skills which inhibits a person's ability to plan and complete intended fine motor activities, marked by severe difficulty in performing drawing, writing, buttoning, and other tasks requiring fine motor skill, or in sequencing the necessary movements.

Early Intervention Program: A specially designed program for assisting infants and preschool children who exhibit developmental delay, intended to prevent future cognitive problems.

EDGAR: Education Department General Administrative Regulations.

Educational Evaluation: An assessment of a child's aptitude, based on multiple tests, analysis of class work, and classroom observation, intended to determine levels of achievement in certain academic areas, as well as the child's learning style and perceptual abilities.

Electroencephalogram (EEG): A recording, represented graphically, of electric currents produced in the cerebral cortex during brain functioning; also called a brain wave test.

ELL: English language learner.

Encoding: The process of expressing language through word selection, ideation, and transferring thoughts to written or spoken form.

ESEA: The federal Elementary and Secondary Education Act.

ESL: English as a second language.

Expressive Language: Communication through speech, writing, and/or gestures.

FAPE: Free appropriate public education; a right mandated for every child under federal law.

Far Point Copying: Reproducing, in writing, a copy of a model some distance away (e.g., a sentence on a chalkboard).

FAST: Functional academic skills test.

FBA: Functional behavior assessment.

FERPA: Family Educational Rights to Privacy Act (a.k.a. the Buckley Amendment).

Figure-Ground Discrimination: The ability to distinguish important information from the surrounding environment, e.g., isolating a particular word within a paragraph, or hearing an instructor's voice amid other noises.

Fine Motor Skills: The use of small muscles to complete precise tasks such as writing, drawing, buttoning, opening jars, and doing puzzles.

General Education (Regular Education): Any education not considered Special Education.

Gross Motor Skills: The use of larger muscles for activities involving strength and balance, such as walking, running and climbing.

Handicapped: A person with any physical and/or mental disability which inhibits such actions as seeing, hearing, speaking, learning, walking, or working. According to federal law, a child is handicapped when he or she is mentally retarded, seriously emotionally disturbed, hard of hearing or deaf, visually impaired or blind, speech impaired, orthopedically impaired, other health impaired, or as having specific learning disabilities which require special education services because of these disabilities.

Haptic Sense: The combination of kinesthetic and tactile sense.

Head Start: Head Start and Early Head Start are federally mandated comprehensive child development programs that serve children from birth to age 5, pregnant women, and their families. They are child-focused programs and have the overall goal of increasing the school readiness of young children in low-income families.

Hyperactivity (Hyperkinesis): Behavior characterized by constant and excessive movement, often marked by distractibility and/or catastrophic reactions.

Hypoactivity: Underactivity, often characterized by lethargy, dazedness, or sluggishness.

IDEA: Individuals with Disabilities Education Act.

IEP: Individualized education program.

IEP Committee: The group of select individuals who develop a student's Individualized Education Program after the student has been identified as handicapped.

Impulsivity: Reacting to a situation without consideration of outcome or consequences.

Individualized Education Plan (IEP): The written educational program designed for each handicapped (including learning disabled) individual, incorporating certain information such as educational goals (long-term and short-term), the duration of the program, and provisions for evaluating the program's effectiveness and the student's performance.

Individualized Family Service Plan (IFSP): A plan that documents and guides the early intervention process for children with disabilities and their families, as dictated in the Individuals with Disabilities Education Act (IDEA).

Individualized Transition Plan (ITP): A plan that must be made by the IEP team for a student, no later than age 16, regarding transition services that student may need to prepare for post-school life. An ITP may include planning for employment, post-secondary education, adult services, independent living, and community participation.

Information Processing: The cognitive ability to use and apply the information collected by a person's senses; consists of two important types of processing: auditory processing and visual processing.

Information Processing Disorder: A chronic deficiency in a person's ability to use or organize the data that his or her senses have gathered.

Insertions: The addition of letters or numbers that do not belong in a word or numeral (involved in spelling, reading and mathematics).

Inversions: The confusion of directionality (usually up and down) of letters or numbers, e.g., 9 and 6.

Itinerant Teacher: A Special Education Teacher who is shared by multiple schools or school systems.

Kinesthetic: Pertaining to the muscles.

Kinesthetic Method: A teaching technique that uses muscle control in learning words, e.g., finger-tracing written characters while reciting the letters or sounds which correspond to the characters.

Laterality: The preference for, or tendency to use, the hand, foot, eye and ear on a particular side of the body.

LD: Learning disabilities; learning disabled.

LDA: Learning Disabilities Association of America.

LEA: Local education agency.

Learned Helplessness: A tendency to be a passive learner who depends on others for decisions and guidance. In individuals with LD, continued struggle and failure can heighten this lack of self-confidence.

Learning Disability (LD): A neurological disorder that affects the brain's ability to receive, process, store and respond to information. The term learning disability is used to describe the seeming unexplained difficulty a person of at least average intelligence has in acquiring basic academic skills.

Learning Modalities: Approaches to assessment or instruction stressing the auditory, visual, or tactile avenues for learning that are dependent upon the individual.

Learning Strategy Approaches: Instructional approaches that focus on efficient ways to learn, rather than on curriculum. Includes specific techniques for organizing, actively interacting with material, memorizing, and monitoring any content or subject.

Learning Styles: The ways in which a person best understands and retains learning, e.g., vision, hearing, movement, kinesthetic, or a combination. Learning style-specific approaches to assessment or instruction emphasize the variations in temperament, attitude, and preferred manner of tackling a task. Typically considered are styles along the active/passive, reflective/impulsive, or verbal/spatial dimensions.

LEP: Limited English proficiency.

Licensed Clinical Psychologist: A specialist who applies the principles and methods of psychological evaluation and psychotherapy to individuals with the intent of counteracting problematic behavior and/or emotional adjustment problems.

Licensed Clinical Social Worker: A social worker who is qualified professionally, by education and experience, to provide direct diagnostic, preventative and treatment services in situations where an individual's ability to function is threatened or adversely affected by social and/or psychological stress or damage to his or her health.

Licensed Professional Counselor: A person trained in guidance and counseling services, with emphasis on both the individual and group forums of counseling, who helps individuals to achieve more effective personal, social, educational, and career-related development and adjustment.

Linguistic Approach: A method for teaching reading which emphasizes the use of word families, e.g., once an individual has learned the word "it," the words "sit," "pit," "bit," and "fit" are introduced.

Locus of Control: The tendency to attribute success and difficulties either to internal factors such as effort or to external factors such as chance. Individuals with learning disabilities tend to blame failure on themselves and achievement on luck, leading to frustration and passivity.

LRE: Least restrictive environment. According to the Individuals with Disabilities Education Act, keeping a child in general education classrooms with children in his or her grade and age group is a priority. If appropriate, it is preferable for a child to be in a regular class with in-class services and accommodations than in a separate special education class.

Mainstreaming: The practice of placing a child who has special education needs into general education classrooms, for at least part of the child's educational program.

Maturation Lag: A delay in development in one or more areas of skill or ability.

MBD: Minimal brain dysfunction.

Metacognitive Learning: Instructional approaches emphasizing awareness of the cognitive processes that facilitate one's own learning and its application to academic and work assignments. Typical metacognitive techniques include systematic rehearsal of steps or conscious selection among strategies for completing a task.

Milieu Therapy: A clinical method developed to regulate a child's environment, and to minimize conflicting and/or confusing information.

Minimal Brain Dysfunction (MBD): A medical and psychological term originally used to refer to the learning difficulties that seemed to result from identified or presumed damage to the brain. Reflects a medical, rather than educational or vocational orientation.

MIS: Management information systems.

Mixed Laterality (Lateral Confusion): The tendency to perform some acts with preference for a person's right side and others with a left side preference, or the shifting from right to left (or vice versa) for certain activities.

Modality: The sensory channel used to collect information; the most common modalities are visual, auditory, olfactory, gustatory, tactile, and kinesthetic.

Modified Self-Contained: Refers to a type of education in which a student is instructed in a self-contained environment for most of the school day, but also receives instruction from a general education teacher for some part of the school day.

Multi-Categorical: A classroom model for special education in which students with more than one handicapping condition are assigned to a special education instructor.

Multi-Disciplinary Team (MDT): A group of educators and education specialists that evaluates a child's handicap and prepares an Individualized Education Plan (IEP) based on their evaluation.

Multisensory Learning: An instructional approach that combines auditory, visual, and tactile elements into a learning task. Tracing sandpaper numbers while saying a number fact aloud would be a multisensory learning activity.

NCLB (NCLBA): No Child Left Behind Act.

NCLD: National Center for Learning Disabilities.

NEA: National Education Association.

Near Point Copying: Reproducing, in writing, a copy of a model situated close at hand (e.g., a phrase in a notebook).

Neurological Examination: A test of the sensory or motor responses, designed to determine if there is impairment of the nervous system.

Neuropsychological Examination: A series of tasks that allow observation of performance that is presumed to be related to the intactness of brain function.

Norm-Referenced Test: *See* Standardized Test.

Norms: Statistics providing a frame of reference that gives meaning to test scores; these statistics are based upon the performance of students of various ages or grades in the standardization group for the test, and therefore represent average or predictable performance, not standard or desirable achievement levels.

OCR: Office of Civil Rights, US Department of Health and Human Services.

Oral Language: Verbal communication skills necessary for understanding and using language, such as listening and speaking.

Organicity: Brain damage or a disorder of the central nervous system.

Orton Dyslexia Society: An organization comprised of learning disabilities professionals, as well as specialists, scientists, and parents.

Orton-Gillingham Approach: A technique for teaching individuals with learning disabilities which stresses a multi-sensory, phonetic, sequential, structured approach to learning.

OSEP: Office of Special Education Programs, US Department of Education.

OSERS: Office of Special Education and Rehabilitative Services, US Department of Education.

Perceptual Ability: A function of the brain that supplies an individual with the abilities to process, organize, and interpret information supplied through the senses.

Perceptual Handicap: Difficulty in accurately processing, organizing, interpreting, and discriminating among visual, auditory, or tactile information. A person with a perceptual handicap may not be able to distinguish between sounds or words (e.g., "map" and "mop"), or between visual symbols (e.g., the letters "b" and "d") However, eyeglasses or hearing aids do not necessarily indicate a perceptual handicap.

Perceptual Speed: The rapidity with which an individual can perceive and complete a given task, e.g., motor speed or visual discrimination.

Perceptual-Motor: The muscle activity that results from information obtained through the senses.

Perseveration: The repetition of words, movements, or tasks, often characterized by difficulty shifting to a new task; a student may continue working on a certain task long after his or her peers have moved onto a new one.

Phonics Approach: A method for teaching spelling and reading that emphasizes the importance of learning the sounds made by individual and various combinations of letters within a word, and then sequentially blending the discrete sounds to form the word.

Pre-K: Pre-kindergarten.

Pre-Referral Process: A procedure in which special and regular teachers develop trial strategies to help a student showing difficulty in learning remain in the regular classroom.

Psychiatrist: A licensed medical doctor who treats emotional and/or behavioral problems, and is qualified to use or prescribe medications for the purposes of treatment.

Psychological Examination: The evaluation of an individual's intellectual and behavioral characteristics made by a clinical psychologist or a certified school psychologist.

Psychomotor: Relating to the motor effects of psychological procedures. Psychomotor tests are used to assess motor skills that depend upon sensory or perceptual motor coordination.

Reasoning Ability: Refers to nonverbal, deductive, inductive, and analytical thinking, depending upon the way in which a given test measures this skill.

Receptive Language (Decoding): Language that is written or spoken by others and received by an individual; the skills necessary for receptive language are listening and reading.

Regular Education (General Education): All education not considered Special Education.

REI: Regular Education Initiative.

Remediation: The process by which an individual is given instruction and practice in skills which are lacking or nonexistent, helping to strengthen, develop, and improve these skills.

Resource Program: A program model in which a student is in a regular classroom for most of each day, but also receives regularly scheduled individual services in a specialized resource classroom.

Resource Teacher: A specialist who works with special education students and who often acts as a consultant for regular teachers. *See also* Transposition.

Reversals: A difficulty in reading or reproducing words in sentences, letters within words, or individual letters in their proper spatial position or proper order; also refers to the reversal of mathematical concepts and symbols.

School Psychologist: A specialist who works with individuals experiencing problems associated with educational systems and who uses psychological concepts and methods to develop programs in an effort to improve learning conditions for those individuals.

SEA: State education agency.

Section 504: A part of the Rehabilitation Act of 1973, a civil rights law, making it illegal for any organization receiving federal funds to discriminate against a person solely on the basis of disability.

Self-Advocacy: The development of specific skills and understandings that enable children and adults to explain their specific learning disabilities to others and cope positively with the attitudes of peers, parents, teachers, and employers.

Self-Contained Classroom: A setting designed specifically for special education students who spend all or most of the school day in this environment.

Semantics: Meaning or understanding evinced through oral or written language by virtue of its specific structure and the relationships between its components.

Sensorimotor (Sensory-Motor): The relationship between movement and sensation.

Sensory Acuity: The ability to react to sensation at appropriate levels of intensity.

Sequence: The detail of information in its customary order (e.g., days of the week).

Sight Word Approach (Whole Word Approach): A method for teaching reading which is based on an individual's visual memory skills rather than on phonics, emphasizing the ability to memorize and recognize a word based on its visual configuration.

Slingerland Method: Developed by Beth Slingerland, a method of teaching which is highly structured and multi-sensory, designed for group instruction of individuals with learning disabilities.

Soft Neurological Signs: Abnormalities of the brain which are mild or slight and thus hard to detect, as opposed to gross, or more obvious, neurological irregularities.

Sound Blending: The ability to unite the sounds or parts of a word into an uninterrupted whole.

Spatial Orientation: A person's awareness of the space around him or her, taking into account distance, form, position and direction.

Spatial Relationships: The positioning of objects in space in relation to the person observing them, taking into account physical distance, as well as the relationship of objects and characters described in written or spoken narrative.

SPD: Semantic pragmatic disorder.

Special Education: A form of instruction developed specifically for handicapped (including learning disabled) students.

Specific Learning Disability (SLD): The official term used in federal legislation to refer to difficulty in certain areas of learning. Synonymous with learning disability.

Standardized Test (Norm-Referenced Test): A test comparing an individual's performance with the performance of a large group of similar individuals (usually of the same age), e.g., IQ tests and most achievement tests.

Substitution: The interchanging of a given letter, number, or word for another in spelling, reading, or mathematics.

Subtype Research: A recently developed research method that seeks to identify characteristics that are common to specific groups within the larger population of individuals identified as having learning disabilities.

Task Analysis: The careful examination of a specific task in order to recognize its elements and the processes needed to complete it.

Thematic Maturity: The ability to write in an organized and logical way so as to effectively and easily express meaning.

Transition: Often refers to the change from secondary school to post-secondary programs, work, and independent living typical of young adults. Also used to describe other periods of major change, e.g., from a specialized setting to a mainstreamed setting.

Transposition: The confusion or reversal of the order of letters within a word, or numbers within a numeral. *See also* Reversals.

VAK Approach: A method of teaching which employs visual, auditory, kinesthetic and tactile abilities, emphasizing a multi-sensory approach to learning skills and/or concepts.

Verbal Ability: Generally relates to a person's skill in creating oral or spoken language, depending on the way in which the skill is tested.

Visual Association: The ability to relate visually presented concepts and formulate thematic comparisons.

Visual Closure: The ability to recognize an object when only parts of it are visible.

Visual Discrimination: The ability to use the sense of sight to detect differences and similarities in visually presented items to differentiate one item from another.

Visual Figure-Ground Discrimination: The ability to distinguish a shape or printed character from its background.

Visual Memory: The ability to remember something seen some time in the past (long-term visual memory); the ability to recall something seen very recently (short-term visual memory).

Visual Motor Processing: The ability to use visual observation to coordinate and appropriately apply other motor skills.

Visual Perception: The ability to see and interpret material correctly.

Visual Sequencing: The ability to see and recognize the order of words, symbols, images or other visual objects.

WISC-III: *Weschler Intelligence Scale for Children-Third Edition.* An assessment used to measure a child's intellectual ability.

WISC-R: *Weschler Intelligence Scale for Children-Revised.* An assessment used to measure a child's intellectual ability.

Word Recognition: The ability to perceive, pronounce, or read a word; usually this term is used to indicate a word which is immediately identifiable by sight and does not require the use of word-attack or analysis skills. (NB: Word Recognition does not necessarily indicate understanding of the word.)

Word-Attack Skills: The methods of examining an unfamiliar word by using a phonetic, sight word, or other visual approach in an effort to understand the word.

Written Language: All aspects of written expression, including spelling, grammar, punctuation, capitalization, penmanship, and ability to translate thoughts into words.

Boldface indicates Publisher

Assessing Children for the Presence of a Disability, 3307
Assessing Learning Problems Workshop, 1539
Assessing the ERIC Resource Collection, 3308
Assessment & Evaluation, 2478
Assessment & Instruction of Culturally & Linguistically Diverse Students, 3133
Assessment Update, 6027
Assessment of Students with Handicaps in Vocational Education, 6028
Assessment: The Special Educator's Role, 3783
Assisting College Students with Learning Disabilities: A Tutor's Manual, 3725, 3984
Assistive Device Center, School of Engineering, 2052
Assistive Technology, 2283, 2304, 2322, 2390, 2399, 2412, 2437, 2461, 2510, 2521, 2637
Assistive Technology Center, 2593
Assistive Technology Industry Association, 39
Assistive Technology Information Network, 1660
Assistive Technology Network, 5627
Assistive Technology Office, 2350
Assistive Technology Partnership Center, 2377
Assistive Technology Program, 2496, 2557, 2594
Assistive Technology Project, 2217, 2251, 2413, 2422, 2430, 2602, 2644
Assistive Technology Resource Centers of Hawaii, 194
Assistive Technology Service Network, 2351
Assistive Technology System, 2619
Assistive Technology: Metro Region, 2192
Assoc. for Supervision/Curriculum Development, 3471, 3492, 3497, 3557, 3658, 3679
Associated Services for the Blind, 3411
Association Book Exhibit: Brain Research, 1540
Association for Career and Technical Education, 6028
Association for Educational Communications and Technology, 1661
Association for International Practical Training, 2153
Association for Supervision/Curriculum Development, 3488
Association for the Care of Children's Health, 3187
Association of Educational Therapists, 40, 2664, 3652
Association of Higher Education Facilities Officers Newsletter, 3369
Association of South Central Oklahoma Governments, 6336
Association of State Mental Health Program Direct., 3098
Association on Higher Education and Disability, 41, 2665
Association on Higher Education and Disability (AHEAD), 42
Association on Higher Education and Disability, 1532, 3684, 3691, 3725, 3761, 3849, 3984, 3993
Atlanta Speech School, 4332, 5647
Atlantic Coast Special Educational Services, 4273
Atlantic Union College, 4617
Att-P'tach Special Education Program, 5665
Attack Math, 929
Attention Deficit Disorder, 3517
Attention Deficit Disorder (ADD or ADHD), 3630
Attention Deficit Disorder Association, 43, 325, 356, 385
Attention Deficit Disorder Warehouse, 326
Attention Deficit Disorder and the Law, 3087
Attention Deficit Disorder in Adults Workbook, 342
Attention Deficit Disorder of Westchester County, 264
Attention Deficit Disorder: A Concise Source of Information for Parents, 343
Attention Deficit Disorder: A Different Perception, 344
Attention Deficit Disorders: Assessment & Teaching, 345
Attention Deficit Hyperactivity Disorder: Handbook for Diagnosis & Treatment, 346
Attention Deficit Information Network, 327
Attention Deficit-Hyperactivity Disorder: Is It a Learning Disability?, 347
Attention-Deficit Hyperactivity Disorder, 348, 3134
Attention-Deficit Hyperactivity Disorder: A Handbook for Diagnosis and Treatment, 2nd Edition, 3135
Attention-Deficit/Hyperactivity Disorder Test, 5990
Attentional Deficit Disorder in Children and Adolescents, 3784

Attitude Magazine, 387
Atypical Cognitive Deficits, 3785
Auburn University, 4017
Auburn University at Montgomery, 4018
Audio/Visual Services, PENN State University, 3538
Auditory Processes, 3786
Auditory Processes: Revised Edition, 3787
Auditory Skills, 1746
Auditory Training, 3788
Augmentative Communication Technology, 4674
Augmentative Communication Without Limitations, 3518
Augsburg College, 4717
Aurora University, 4379
Austin Peay State University: Office of Disability Services, 5265
Austin Wilderness Counseling Services, 604
Author's Toolkit, 1444, 2132
Autism & PDD: Primary Social Skills Lessons, 1235
Autism & PPD: Adolescent Social Skills Lessons, 1236
Autism & PPD: Adolescent Social Skills Lessons-Health & Hygiene, 1237
Autism & PPD: Concept Development, 650
Autism & PPD: Pictured Stories and Language Activities, 651
Autism Research Institute, 44, 3663
Autism Research Review International, 3663
Autism Screening Instrument for Educational Planning, 5969
Autism Society of America, 45
Autism Support Center: Northshore Arc, 2378
Autism Treatment Center of America, 46, 134, 1584, 3540, 3604, 3646
Autism and the Family: Problems, Prospects and Coping with the Disorder, 3136
Avenues to Compliance, 3519
Averett College, 5384
Awesome Animated Monster Maker Math, 930, 1910
Awesome Animated Monster Maker Math & Monster Workshop, 931, 1911
Awesome Animated Monster Maker Number Drop, 932, 1912

B

BASC Monitor for ADHD, 5970
BCF Treatment & Education, 2392
BL Winch/Jalmar Press, 3966
BOSC Books on Special Children, 3412
BOSC Directory: Facilities for People with Learning Disabilities, 3789
BOSC Publishing, 3412
BRIGANCE Assessment of Basic Skills: Spanish Edition, 6060
BRIGANCE Comprehensive Inventory of Basic Skills: Revised, 6061
BRIGANCE Employability Skills Inventory, 6062
BRIGANCE Inventory of Early Development-II, 6106
BRIGANCE Inventory of Essential Skills, 6063
BRIGANCE Life Skills Inventory, 6064
BRIGANCE Readiness: Strategies and Practice, 6038
BRIGANCE Screens: Early Preschool, 5991
BRIGANCE Screens: Infants and Toddler, 5992
BRIGANCE Screens: K and 1, 5993
BRIGANCE Word Analysis: Strategies and Practice, 6029
BUSY BOX Activity Centers, 1343
Babson College, 4618
Baccalaureate for University of Indianapolis, 4473
Backyards & Butterflies: Ways to Include Children with Disabilities, 3137
Bacone College, 5124
Bailey's Book House, 2072
Baker Hall School, 5796
Baker University, 4515
Bakersfield College, 4071
Baldwin-Wallace College, 5058
Ball State University, 4444
Ballard & Tighe, 1762, 1776
Baltimore City Community College, 4588

Boldface indicates Publisher

Boldface indicates Publisher

Colorado State University, 4216
Colorado University, 2151
Colored Wooden Counting Cubes, 1354
Columbia Basin College, 5427
Columbia Christian College, 5146
Columbia College, 4104, 4905
Columbia College Chicago, 4387
Columbia Union College, 4593
Columbia-Greene Community College, 4906
Columbus State Community College: Departme nt of Disability Services, 5071
Columbus State University, 4338
Combining Shapes, 939, 1920
Combining and Breaking Apart Numbers, 940, 1921
Come Play with Me, 1355
Comforty Mediaconcepts, 3545
Commerce Library Literacy Program, 2959
Commission for the Blind & Visually Handic apped, 6324
Commission on Accreditation of Rehabilitation Facilities (CARF), 54
Commission on Adult Basic Education (COABE), 2698, 3368, 3659
Common Ground: Whole Language & Phonics Working Together, 3151
Common Sense About Dyslexia, 3152
Commonwealth Learning Center, 5724
Communication Aid Manufacturers Associatio n (CAMA) Workshops, 1549
Communication Aids, 1356
Communication Aids: Manufacturers Associat ion, 55, 1603
Communication Outlook, 3720
Communication Skills for Visually Impaired Learners, 3929
Communication Skills in Children with Down Syndrome, 3153
Community Alliance for Special Education, 5
Community Based Services, 5801
Community Center, 2791
Community Child Guidance Clinic School, 5582
Community College of Allegheny County: College Center, North Campus, 5175
Community College of Allegheny County: All egheny Campus, 5176
Community College of Aurora, 4217
Community College of Baltimore County, 4594
Community College of Denver, 4218
Community College of Philadelphia, 5177
Community College of Rhode Island-Knight Campus, 5231
Community College of Southern Nevada, 4819
Community College of Vermont, 5376
Community College: Kansas State Department of Education, 2339
Community Education Journal, 3347
Community High School, 4846
Community Legal Aid/Disabilities Law Program, 2267
Community Opportunity Development Agency, 535
Community School, 4847
Comparative Education Review, 3670
Comparing with Ratios, 941, 1922
Comparison Kitchen, 1851
Compass Learning, 2043
Competencies for Teachers of Students with Learning Disabilities, 3804
Complete Clinical Dysphagia Evaluation: Test Forms, 5995
Complete Guide to Running, Walking and Fitness for Kids, 862
Complete IEP Guide: How to Advocate for Your Special Ed Child, 3154
Complete Learning Disabilities Handbook, 3805
Complete Learning Disabilities Resource Library, 3155
Complete Oral-Motor Program for Articulation: Book Only, 658
Complete Oral-Motor Program for Articulation, 659
Complete Oral-Motor Program for Articulati on: Refill Kit, 660
Complete Set of State Resource Sheets, 3311
Completing Daily Assignments, 6072
Comprehension Connection, 2076
Comprehensive Advocacy of Idaho, 197

Comprehensive Assessment in Special Education: Approaches, Procedures and Concerns, 3806
Comprehensive Counseling Center, 4356
Comprehensive Educational Services (CES), 5829
Comprehensive Psychiatric Resources, 372
Comprehensive Services for the Disabled, 1670
Compu-Lenz, 1604
Compu-Teach, 2087, 2138, 2139, 2140, 2141
Computer & Web Resources for People with D isabilities: A Guide to..., 3156
Computer Access Center, 1671
Computer Access-Computer Learning, 1652
Computer Accommodation Lab, 1672
Computer Learning Foundation, 56, 1673
Computer Scoring Systems for PRO-ED Tests, 6031
Computer Technology in Special Education & Rehab., 53
Computers in Head Start Classrooms, 1653
Computers to Help People, 2146
Concentration Video, 3530
Conceptual Skills, 1923
Concert Tour Entrepreneur, 942, 1924
Concordia College, 4726
Concordia College: New York, 4907
Concordia University at Austin, 5302
Conducting Individualized Education Program Meetings that Withstand Due Process, 3157
ConnSENSE Conference, 1550
Connect Outloud, 1605
Connect-A-Card, 1091
Connecticut Assoc. for Children & Adults with LD, 1541, 1572
Connecticut Assoc. for Children and Adults with LD, 374, 3049, 3070, 3107, 3122, 3168, 3197, 3237, 3239, 3243, 3257, 3343, 3470, 3534, 3539, 3550, 3551, 3552, 3573, 3739, 3755
Connecticut Association Children & Adults with LD, 3069
Connecticut Association for Children and Adults with LD, 173
Connecticut Association for Children and A dults with Learning Disabilities, 3419
Connecticut Association of Boards of Education, 3664
Connecticut Association of Private Special Education Facilities (CAPSEF), 174
Connecticut Bureau of Rehabilitation Servi ces, 2254
Connecticut Capitol Region Educational Cou ncil, 175
Connecticut Center for Augmentative Communication, 5583
Connecticut Center for Children and Families, 5584
Connecticut College, 4244
Connecticut College Children's Program, 5585
Connecticut Department of Social Services, 2255
Connecticut Institute for Cultural Literac y and Wellness, 2736
Connecticut Institute for the Blind, 5586
Connecticut Literacy Resource Center, 2737
Connecticut Office of Protection & Advocac ecy for Handicapped & DD Persons, 2256
Connecticut State Department of Education, 2257
Connecticut State Department of Social Services, 2251
Connecticut Valley Girl Scout Council, 444
Connecting Reading and Writing with Vocabulary, 6073
Connections, 3671
Connections: A Journal of Adult Literacy, 3371
Conover Company, 2044
Construct-A-Word I & II, 1755
Consultants for Communication Technology, 1606, 1602, 2145
Consulting Advocacy Research Evaluation Services (CARES) and Client Assistance Program (CAP), 2366
Contemporary Intellectual Assessment: Theories, Tests and Issues, 3158
Contemporary Living, 1852
Continental Press, 1747, 1893
Contra Costa College, 4105
Controlpad 24, 1607
Controversial Issues Confronting Special Education, 3159
Cooperative Discipline: Classroom Manageme nt Promoting Self-Esteem, 3476
Cooperative Learning and Strategies for Inclusion, 3807

H

Boldface indicates Publisher

Boldface indicates Publisher

M

M-SS-NG L-NKS, 730, 1791
MAC Mainstreaming at Camp, 544
MACcessories: Guide to Peripherals, 1654
MATP Center, 2377
MATP Children's Hospital, 2381
MATRIX: A Parent Network and Resource Center, 88
MAXI, 1486
MCD, Stout Vocational Rehabilitation Institute, 6153
MCLA: Measure of Cognitive-Linguistic Abilities, 731
MORE: Integrating the Mouth with Sensory & Postural Functions, 888
Macalester College, 4734
Macon State College, 4350
Madisonville Community College: University of Kentucky, 4551
Madonna University, 4697
Magicatch Set, 1385
Magination Press, 3441
Magnetic Fun, 1386
Mailman Center for Child Development: University of Miami Department of Pediatrics, 190
Main Office: Technology and Media, 4250
Maine Bureau of Applied Technical Adult Learning: Adult Career and Technical Education, 2821
Maine Bureau of Rehabilitation Services, 6269
Maine Department of Education, 2365
Maine Department of Labor: Bureau of Rehabilitation Services, 2368
Maine Department of Labor: Employment Services, 2369
Maine Human Rights Commission, 2370
Maine Literacy Resource Center, 2822
Maine Literacy Volunteers of America, 2823
Maine Parent Federation, 223
Mainstream, 3704, 6128, 3683
Mainstreaming Exceptional Students: A Guide for Classroom Teachers, 3875
Make Every Step Count: Birth to 1 Year, 1049
Make It Go, 1792
Make It Today for Pre-K Play, 1050
Make-A-Flash, 1793
Make-a-Map 3D, 1313
Making School Inclusion Work, 3876
Making Sense of Sensory Integration, 3235
Malden YMCA, 488
Malone College, 5084
Manchester City Library, 2864
Manchester College, 4464
Manchester Community Technical College, 4251
Mandy, 3071
Manhattan Adult Learning and Resource Center, 3886
Manhattan Center for Learning, 5815
Manhattan College, 4933
Manhattanville College, 4934
Mankato State University, 4735
Manor Junior College, 5198
Mansfield University of Pennsylvania, 5199
Manual for Learning to Use Manuscript and Cursive Handwriting, 1487
A Manual of Sequential Art Activities for Classified Children and Adolescents, 3770
Many Voices of Paws, 732
Maple Woods Community College, 4780
Maplebrook School, 5816
Maplebrook School's Summer Program, 545
Maps & Navigation, 977, 1208, 1314
Maranatha Baptist Bible College, 5495
MarbleSoft, 1878, 1986, 2023
Marburn Academy, 5085
Maria College, 4935
Marian College of Fond Du Lac, 5496
Marietta College, 5086
Marin Literacy Program, 2718

Marina Psychological Services, 5555
Marion Military Institute, 4028
Marion Technical College, 5087
Marist College, 4936
Mark Up, 1794
Marquette University, 5497
Marriott Foundation, 3635
Mars Hill College, 5017
Marsh Media, 1876, 3442, 879, 3220, 3482, 3978
Marshall University, 5475
Marshall University: HELP Program, 5476, 6004
Marshalltown Community College, 4499
Marshware, 1876
Martin Luther King Memorial Library, 2744
Marvelwood School, 439
Marvelwood Summer, 439
Mary McDowell Center for Learning, 5817
Mary Washington College, 5399
Maryland Association of University Centers on Disabilities, 226
Maryland Developmental Disabilities Council, 2374
Maryland Literacy Coalition, 2825
Maryland Literacy Resource Center, 2826
Maryland Technology Assistance Program, 2375, 6271
Marymount Manhattan College, 4937
Marywood University, 5200
Mason County Literacy Council, 3014
Massachusetts Assistive Technology Partnership (MATP), 2381
Massachusetts Association of 766 Approved Private Schools (MAAPS), 228
Massachusetts Bay Community College, 4643
Massachusetts College of Liberal Arts, 4644
Massachusetts Commission Against Discrimination, 2382
Massachusetts Correctional Education: Inmate Training & Education, 2831
Massachusetts Department of Education, 2832
Massachusetts District Office, 2388
Massachusetts Easter Seal Society, 1685
Massachusetts Family Literacy Consortium, 2832
Massachusetts GED Administration: Massachusetts Department of Education, 2383, 2833
Massachusetts Job Training Partnership Act: Department of Employment & Training, 2834, 6276
Massachusetts Rehabilitation Commission, 2384, 6277
Massachusetts Shriver Center: University Affiliated Program, 229
Massasoit Community College, 4645
Master's College, 4134
Mastering Math, 978
Mastering Reading Series, 1130
Math Assessment System, 979
Math Detectives, 980
Math Enrichment, 981
Math Machine, 1951
Math Masters: Addition and Subtraction, 1952
Math Masters: Multiplication and Division, 1953
Math Scramble, 982
Math Shop, 1954
Math Skill Games, 1955
Math Spending and Saving, 1877, 1956
Math and Reading Bonus Pack, 2087
Math and the Learning Disabled Student: A Practical Guide for Accommodations, 3946
Math for All Ages: A Sequential Math Program, 1957
Math for Everyday Living, 1958
Mathematics Skills Books, 983
Matheny School and Hospital, 5782
Matlock Precollegiate Academy, 5633
Max's Attic: Long & Short Vowels, 733, 1795
Maxi, 853
Maxi Aids, 1337
Maximize Math Success for the Special Populations You Serve, 984
Maxwell's Manor: A Social Language Game, 734, 1264, 1387
May Institute, 5737

Nashville READ, 2951
Nassau Community College, 4942
Nat'l Assn. af Adults with Special Learning Needs, 3352
Nat'l Association for the Education of Afr ican American Children with Learning Disabilities, 91
Nat'l Center for Research in Vocational Education, 3654, 6139
Nat'l Clearinghouse of Rehab. Training Materials, 331, 3583
Nat'l Dissemination Ctr for Children Disabilities, 397
Natchaug Hospital School Program, 5603
Nathan Hale School, 443
National Academies Press, 3958, 3968
National Admission, Review, Dismissal: Ind ividualized Education Plan Advocates, 92
National Adult Education Professional Deve lopment Consortium, 93, 2681
National Adult Literacy & Learning Disabilities Center (NALLD), 2682
National Adult Literacy & Learning Disabil ities Center, 94
National Aeronautics and Space Administration, 1693
National Alliance of Business (NAB), 3355, 6137, 6164
National Association for Adults with Special Learning Needs, 95, 2683
National Association for Community Mediati on, 11
National Association for Community Mediation, 1251
National Association for Gifted Children, 96
National Association for Humane and Enviro nmental Education, 3363
National Association for Visually Handicap ped, 3446
National Association for the Education of Young Children (NAEYC), 97
National Association of Developmental Disabilities Councils (NADDC), 98
National Association of Private Schools for Exceptional Children, 4005
National Association of Private Special Education Centers, 99, 2684
National Association of Protection and Advocacy Systems (NAPAS), 12
National Association of School Psychologists, 3703
National Bible Association, 3447
National Business and Disability Council, 100
National Camp Association, 101
National Catholic Education Association, 3989
National Center for ESL Literacy Education (NCLE), 102, 2685
National Center for Fair & Open Testing, 5958
National Center for Family Literacy, 103, 2686
National Center for Family Literacy Confer ence, 1576
National Center for Gender Issues and AD/HD, 396
National Center for Learning Disabilities, 104, 276, 2687, 3395, 3396, 3397, 3400
National Center for State Courts, 1, 3177
National Center for Youth Law, 13
National Center for Youth with Disabilities, 3671
National Center for the Study of Adult Learning & Literacy, 2688
National Center of Higher Education for Learning Problems (HELP), 105, 6006
National Center on Adult Literacy (NCAL), 2689
National Center on Employment and Disability, 4001
National Clearinghouse for Professions in Special Education, 106
National Clearinghouse of Rehabilitation Training Materials, 6334
National Clearinghouse of Rehabilitation Materials, 3329, 3726, 3729, 3858, 3889
National Clearinghouse on Postsecondary Education, 3997
National Community Education Association, 3347
National Council of Juvenile and Family Court Judges (NCJFCJ), 14
National Council of Teachers of English, 3724, 3723
National Council on Disability, 107, 3291
National Council on Independent Living Programs, 108
National Council on Rehabilitation Educati on, 109
National Data Bank for Disabled Student Services, 110
National Deaf Education Network and Clearinghouse, 448

National Directory of Colleges and Programs for Young People with Learning Disabilities, 4006
National Directory of Four Year Colleges, Two Year Colleges & High School Training Programs, 4007
National Dissemination Center for Children with Disabilities, 111
National Early Childhood Technical Assista nce Center, 112
National Easter Seals Society, 460
National Education Association (NEA), 113, 2690
National Federation of the Blind, 114, 6123
National Forum on Issues in Vocational Assessment, 6153
National Geographic World, 3399
National Governor's Association (NGA), 6165
National Governors Association, 6154, 6142
National Head Start Association, 3370
National Head Start Association Academy Wo rkshop, 1577
National Head Start Association Parent Conference, 1578
National Institute for Literacy, 3387
National Institute for Literacy (NIFL), 2691
National Institute of Art and Disabilities, 115
National Institute of Child Health and Human Development, 2172
National Institute of Health, 2040
National Institute of Mental Health, 2173
National Institute on Disability and Rehabilitation Research, 2174
National Jewish Council for Disabilities Summer Program, 116
National Lekotek Center, 117, 2692
National Library Services for the Blind and Physically Handicapped, 2175
National Louis University, 5669
National Organization for Rare Disorders (NORD), 118
National Organization on Disability, 3708
National Organization on Disability (NOD), 119
National Rehabilitation Association, 120, 3692
National Rehabilitation Information Center, 121
National Resource Center on AD/HD, 392
National Resources, 3323
National School Boards Association, 3661
National Society for Experiential Education, 2159
National Technical Information Service, 2176
National Technical Information Service: US Department of Commerce, 2177, 3595
National Technology Center, 1682
National Toll-free Numbers, 3324
National Wildlife Foundation/Membership Services, 3364
National-Louis University, 4413, 5686
Natural Therapies for Attention Deficit Hyperactivity Disorder, 372
Naugatuck Community College, 4253
Nazareth College of Rochester, 4943
Nebraska Department of Economic Development, 6302
Nebraska Department of Education, 2431, 2858
Nebraska Department of Labor, 2432
Nebraska Equal Opportunity Commission, 2433
Nebraska Parents Training and Information Center, 5763
Negotiating the Special Education Maze 3rd Edition, 3241
Neosho County Community College, 4530
Neuhaus Education Center, 5900
Nevada Bureau of Disability Adjudication, 2440
Nevada Department of Adult Education, 2860
Nevada Department of Education, 2447, 2860
Nevada Economic Opportunity Board: Communi ty Action Partnership, 247, 2861, 6305
Nevada Employment Security Department, 2441
Nevada Employment Services: Department of Employment, Training and Rehabilitation, 2442
Nevada Equal Rights Commission: Fair Employment Practice Agency, 2443
Nevada Governor's Council on Developmental Disabilities, 2444
Nevada Governor's Council on Rehabilitatio n & Employment of People with Disabilities, 2445, 6306
Nevada Literacy Coalition: State Literacy Resource Center, 2862
Nevada State Library and Archives, 2862
New Breakthroughs, 1683
New Castle School of Trades, 5868

S

Samuel Field/Bay Terrace YM & YWHA Special Services, 550
San Antonio College, 5329
San Diego City College, 4161
San Diego Miramar College, 4162
San Diego State University, 4163
San Diego Zoo Membership Department, 3361
San Francisco State University, 4164
San Jacinto College: Central Campus, 5330
San Jacinto College: South Campus, 5331
San Jose City College, 4165
San Jose State University, 4166
San Juan College, 4884
San Marcos Texas State University: Office of Disability Services, 5332
San Rafael Public Library, 2718
Sandhills Academy, 5884
Sandhills Community College, 5030
Santa Ana College, 4167
Santa Barbara Center for Educational Therapy, 5566
Santa Barbara City College, 4168
Santa Clara University, 4169
Santa Cruz Learning Center, 5567
Santa Fe Community College: Florida, 4315
Santa Monica College, 4170
Santa Rosa Junior College, 4171
Sapulpa Public Library, 2905
Savannah State University, 4356
Saxon Publishers, 984
Scan It-Switch It, 1630
Scare Bear, 3076
Scenic Land School, 5281
Schenectady County Community College, 4966
Schneider Children's Hospital, 5814
Scholastic, 2064, 3455, 3362, 3398, 3401
Scholastic Abilities Test for Adults, 6049
Scholastic Action, 3401
Scholastic Testing Service, 5966, 5998, 6010, 6024
School Age Children with Special Needs, 3891
School Based Assessment of Attention Deficit Disorders, 331
School Behaviors and Organization Skills, 5985
School Power: Strategies for Succeeding in School, 1331
School Psychology Quarterly: Official Journal of Div. 16 of the American Psychological Assoc, 3657
School Readiness Test, 6010
School Survival Guide for Kids with Learning Disabilities, 3296
School Vacation Camps: Youth with Development Disabilities, 551
School of the Art Institute of Chicago, 4429
School to Adult Life Transition Bibliography, 6157
School-Based Home Developmental PE Program, 3258
School-Home Notes: Promoting Children's Classroom Success, 3892
School-to-Work Outreach Project, 6289
Schoolsearch Guide to Colleges with Programs & Services for Students with LD, 4010
Schoolsearch Press, 4010
Schreiner University, 5333
Schwab Learning, 3456
Science Showtime! Videos, 3489
Scissors, Glue, and Artic, Too!, 782
Scissors, Glue, and Concepts, Too!, 898, 3893
Scissors, Glue, and Grammar, Too!, 783
Scissors, Glue, and Phonological Processes , Too!, 784
Scissors, Glue, and Vocabulary, Too!, 785
Scott Community College, 4507
Scott Foresman Addison Wesley, 3777
Scottish Rite Center for Childhood Language Disorders, 5625
Scottish Rite Learning Center, 5908
Scottsdale Community College, 4049
Scouting for the Handicapped Services, 48
Scrambled Eggs, 2022
Screening Children for Related Early Educational Needs, 6011
Scribner, 384

Seasons, 1897
Seattle Academy of Arts and Sciences, 5446
Seattle Central Community College, 5447
Seattle Christian Schools, 5448
Seattle Pacific University, 5449
Second Start: Pine Hill School, 5568
Secondary Print Pack, 1898
Secretary of Education, 2526
Section 504 of the Rehabilitation Act, 3106
Section 504: Help for the Learning Disabled College Student, 3107
See Me Add, 1168
See Me Subtract, 1169
Seeing Clearly, 3259
Seek and Find, 1731
Segregated and Second-Rate: Special Education in New York, 3894
Self Advocacy as a Technique for Transition, 6158
Self-Adhesive Braille Keytop Labels, 1631
Self-Advocacy Handbook for High School Students, 3763
Self-Advocacy Resources for Persons with Learning Disabilities, 3714
Self-Advocacy Strategy for Education and Transition Planning, 3895
Self-Advocacy for Junior High School Students, 3764
Self-Control Games & Workbook, 1406
Self-Directed Search, 6159
Self-Esteem Index, 5986
Self-Injurious Behavior: A Somatosensory Treatment Approach, 3765
Self-Perception: Organizing Functional Information Workbook, 1275
Self-Supervision: A Career Tool for Audiologists, Clinical Series 10, 6160
Seminole Community College, 4316
Seminole Junior College, 5136
Sensational Explorers Day Camp, 618
Sensible Speller: Talking APH Edition, 1814
Sensory Defensiveness in Children Aged 2 to 12: An Intervention Guide for Parents/Caretakers, 3260
Sensory Integration & Vision Therapy Specialists, 5717
Sensory Integration & Vision Therapy Speci alists, 5718
Sensory Integration and the Child, 3261
Sensory Integration: Theory and Practice, 3262, 3896
Sensory Motor Activities for Early Develop ment, 1060
Sensory Motor Issues in Autism, 899
Sentence Master: Level 1, 2, 3, 4, 2099
Sequenced Inventory of Communication Development, 6089
Sequenced Inventory of Communication Devel opment (SICD), 1407, 6090
Sequencing Fun!, 1004, 1815
Sequential Spelling 1-7 with Student Response Book, 786
Sertoma International/Sertoma Foundation, 133
Service Operations Manual, 3733
ServiceLink, 2458
Services For Students with Disabilities, 4989
Services for Academic Success, 4802
Services for Students with Disabilities, 4967, 4080, 4083, 4417, 4464, 4506, 5154, 5181, 5850
Services for Students with Learning Disabilities at the University of Illinois at Urbana, 4430
Services for Students with Special Needs, 4952
Services to Students with Disabilities, 4088, 4676
Serving on Boards and Committees, 3337
Seton Hall University, 4870
Seton Hill University, 5213
Seven Hills at Groton, 5741
Seward County Community College, 4536
Shape Up!, 1005, 1975
Shape and Color Rodeo, 1998
Shape and Color Sorter, 1408
Shapes, 1409
Shapes Within Shapes, 1006
Shasta College, 4172

Boldface indicates Publisher

Stone Soup: The Magazine by Young Writers and Artists, 3366
StoneBridge Schools: Riverview Learning Center, 5934
Stonehill College, 4661
Stop, Relax and Think, 1281
Stop, Relax and Think Ball, 1282
Stop, Relax and Think Card Game, 1283
Stop, Relax and Think Scriptbook, 1284
Stop, Relax and Think Workbook, 1285
Stories Behind Special Education Case Law, 3113
Stories and More: Animal Friends, 1179
Stories and More: Time and Place, 811, 1180
Story of the USA, 1317
Stout Vocational Rehabilitation Institute, 5963
Stowell Learning Center, 5570
Straight Speech, 812
Strategic Math Series, 1017
Strategic Planning and Leadership, 3492
Strategies Intervention Program, 3493
Strategies for Problem-Solving, 903, 1018
Strategies for Success in Mathematics, 1019
Strategies for Success in Writing, 1506
Strategy Assessment and Instruction for Students with Learning Disabilities, 3904
Strategy Challenges Collection: 1, 2026
Strategy Challenges Collection: 2, 2027
Stratford Friends School, 5874
Strengths and Weaknesses: College Students with Learning Disabilities, 3566
String-A-Long Lacing Activity, 1418
Strong Center for Developmental Disabilities, 279
Student Academic Services, 4922
Student Academic Support Services, 5483
Student Development Services, 5240
Student Disabilities Services, 5473
Student Disability Resource Center, 4300, 4347
Student Disability Services, 4376, 4484, 4510, 4752, 4908, 4980, 5081, 5474
Student Educational Services, 4785
Student Enrichment Center, 5019
Student Learning Center, 4475
Student Success, 4305
Student Support Services, 4054, 4387, 4451, 4461, 5043, 5048
Student with Disability Resource Center, 4085
A Student's Guide to Jobs, 3302
A Student's Guide to the IEP, 3303
Students Transition into Education Program, 4477
Students with Disabilities Services, 4271
Students with Disabilities and Special Education, 3114
Study Resource Center, 4729
Study Skills Web Site, 3634
Study Skills and Learning Strategies for Transition, 1332
Study Skills: A Landmark School Student Gu ide, 3269
Study Skills: How to Manage Your Time, 3567
Study of Job Clubs for Two-Year College Students with Learning Disabilities, 3734
Stuttering Foundation of America, 135, 3270, 3320
Stuttering Severity Instrument for Children and Adults, 6094
Stuttering and Your Child: Questions and Answers, 3270
Stuttering: Helping the Disfluent Preschoo l Child, 813, 1064
Substance Use Among Children and Adolescen ts, 3271
Subtypes of Learning Disabilities, 3905
Succeeding in the Workplace, 3297, 3593
Succeeding with LD, 3052
Success Center, 4490
Success Stories 1, 2, 1181
Successful Movement Challenges, 1286
Suffolk County Community College: Eastern Campus, 4985
Suffolk County Community College: Selden Campus, 4986
Suffolk County Community College: Western Campus, 4987
Suffolk University, 4662
Sullivan County Community College, 4988
Summer Adventure Program, 619

Summer Camps for Children who are Deaf or Hard of Hearing, 448
Summer Intensive Fluency Therapy, 620
Summit Camp Program, 595
Summit Camp Program New York Office, 595
Summit School, 4604, 5689
Summit Travel, 553
Summit Travel Program, 553
Sunbuddy Math Playhouse, 1020
Sunbuddy Writer, 1507, 2129
Sunburst Communications, 2065
Sunburst Technolgy, 1006
Sunburst Technology, 642, 644, 655, 662, 674, 679, 701, 722, 730, 733, 736, 764, 768, 814, 837, 846, 847, 848, 927, 930, 931
Sunburts Technology, 1353
Sunken Treasure Adventure: Beginning Blend s, 814, 1829
Super Study Wheel: Homework Helper, 1333
Support Services, 5374
Support Services for Students, 5384
Support Services for Students with Learnin g Disabilities, 5216
Support and Training for Exceptional Children, 5889
Supporting Children with Communication Difficulties In Inclusive Settings, 3272
Supportive Educational Services, 4407
Surface Counseling, 1287, 3273
Surry Community College, 5034
Survey of Teenage Readiness and Neurodevel opmental Status, 904
Survival Guide for Kids with LD, 1288, 3274
Survival Guide for Teenagers with LD, 3298
Survival Guide with Kids with LD, 3906
Swallow Right, 905
Sweetwater State Literacy Regional Resourc e Center, 2730
Switch Accessible Trackball, 1632
Switch Arcade, 2028
Switch It - Change It, 2000
Switch It Software Bundle, 1633
Switch It-Change It, 1900
Switch It-See It, 1734
Switch to Turn Kids On, 1656
Switzer Center, 5571
Syllasearch I, II, III, IV, 1830
Symposium Series on Assistive Technology, 1585
Synthesis Summer Camp Program Foothills Unitarian Church, 426
Syosset/Woodbury Community Park, 539
Syracuse Univ./Facilitated Communication Institute, 3541
Syracuse University, 4989
Syracuse University, Institute on Communication, 3535
Syracuse University, School of Education, 3536
System of Multicultural Pluralistic Assessment (SOMPA), 5988

T

T&M Ranch, 5643
T-J Publishers, 3086
TARGET, 815, 906
TASH Annual Conference, 1586
TASKS's Newsletter, 3391
TELD-2: Test of Early Language Development, 6095
TERA-3: Test of Early Reading Ability 3nd Edition, 6052
TERC, 2104
TESOL Journal, 3392
TESOL Newsletter, 3393
TESOL Quarterly, 3394
TILES Project: Transition/Independent Livi ng/Employment/Support, 6232
TOAL-3: Test of Adolescent & Adult Languag e, 6096
TOLD-3: Test of Language Development, Primary, 6097
TOLD-P3: Test of Language Development Primary, 816
TOPS Kit- Adolescent: Tasks of Problem Solving, 907
TOPS Kit-Adolescent: Tasks of Problem Solving, 817
TOPS Kit-Elementary: Tasks of Problem Solving, 818, 908
TOPS Kit: Adolescent-Tasks of Problem Solving, 1508
TOVA, 6014

Boldface indicates Publisher

Boldface indicates Publisher

University of Louisiana at Lafayette: Serv ices of Students with Disabilities, 4570
University of Louisville, 4557
University of Maine, 4582, 2822, 4575
University of Maine: Fort Kent, 4583
University of Maine: Machias, 4584
University of Maryland, 110
University of Maryland: Baltimore County, 4607
University of Maryland: College Park, 4608
University of Maryland: Eastern Shore, 4609
University of Massachusetts-Boston, 42
University of Massachusetts: Amherst, 4665
University of Massachusetts: Boston, 4666
University of Massachusetts: Lowell, 4667
University of Miami, 4323
University of Miami School of Medicine, 190
University of Michigan, 4708
University of Michigan Press, 3762, 3768, 3791, 3816, 3880, 3882, 3957
University of Michigan School of Education, 2667
University of Michigan: Dearborn, 4711
University of Michigan: Flint, 4712
University of Minnesota, 3696, 4740
University of Minnesota Disability Services, 4755
University of Minnesota: Crookston, 4756
University of Minnesota: Duluth, 4757
University of Minnesota: Morris, 4758
University of Minnesota: Twin Cities Campu s, 4759
University of Mississippi, 4768
University of Missouri, 4791
University of Missouri at Kansas City, 4790
University of Missouri-Kansas City, 2413
University of Missouri: Kansas City, 4792
University of Missouri: Rolla, 4793
University of Montana, 4804, 4800
University of Montevallo, 4033
University of Nebraska: Lincoln, 4815
University of Nebraska: Omaha, 4816
University of Nevada: Las Vegas, 4823
University of Nevada: Reno, 4824
University of New England: University Camp us, 4585
University of New England: Westbrook Colle ge Campus, 4586
University of New Hampshire, 4839, 4831
University of New Haven, 4268
University of New Mexico, 4885
University of New Mexico/School of Medicine, 4875
University of New Mexico: Los Alamos Branc h, 4886
University of New Mexico: Valencia Campus, 4887
University of New Orleans, 4571
University of North Alabama, 4034
University of North Carolina: Chapel Hill, 5036
University of North Carolina: Charlotte, 5037
University of North Carolina: Greensboro, 5038
University of North Carolina: Wilmington, 5039
University of North Florida, 4324
University of North Texas, 5353
University of Northern Colorado, 4235
University of Northern Iowa, 4511
University of Notre Dame, 4474
University of Oklahoma, 5141
University of Oregon, 5161, 2051
University of Oregon for Excellence in Dev elopmental Disabilities, 294
University of Pennsylvania, 5219, 2689
University of Pittsburgh at Bradford, 5220
University of Pittsburgh: Greensburg, 5221
University of Puget Sound, 5460
University of Redlands, 4198
University of Rhode Island, 5237
University of Saint Francis, 4475
University of San Diego, 4199
University of San Francisco, 4200
University of Scranton, 5222

University of South Alabama, 4035
University of South Carolina, 5254
University of South Carolina School of Medicine, 304
University of South Carolina: Aiken, 5255
University of South Carolina: Beaufort, 5256
University of South Carolina: Lancaster, 5257
University of Southern California, 4201, 4185
University of Southern Colorado, 4236
University of Southern Indiana, 4476
University of Southern Maine, 4572
University of Southern Maine: Office of Academic Support for Students with Disabilities, 4587
University of Southern Mississippi, 4769, 4766
University of St. Thomas, 4760, 2850
University of Sydney/School Educational Psychology, 3832
University of Tampa, 4325
University of Tennessee, 5266
University of Tennessee: Knoxville, 5286, 2948
University of Tennessee: Martin, 5287
University of Texas at Austin, 2592
University of Texas: Arlington, 5354
University of Texas: Dallas, 5355
University of Texas: Pan American, 5356
University of Texas: San Antonio, 5357
University of The District of Columbia, 2274
University of Toledo, 5116
University of Topeka, 4540
University of Tulsa, 5142, 5125
University of Utah, 5368
University of Vermont, 5382, 5974
University of Virginia, 5414, 5394
University of Washington, 5461
University of Washington: Center on Human Development and Disability, 5462
University of West Florida, 4326
University of Wisconsin Center: Marshfield Wood County, 5507
University of Wisconsin-Madison, 3616
University of Wisconsin: Eau Claire, 5508
University of Wisconsin: La Crosse, 5509
University of Wisconsin: Madison, 5510
University of Wisconsin: Milwaukee, 5511
University of Wisconsin: Oshkosh, 5512
University of Wisconsin: Platteville, 5513
University of Wisconsin: River Falls, 5514
University of Wisconsin: Whitewater, 5515
University of Wyoming, 5525
University of Wyoming: Division of Social Work and Wyoming Institute for Disabilities (WIND), 5526
University of the Arts, 5223
University of the District of Columbia, 4283
University of the Incarnate Word, 5358
University of the Ozarks, 4066, 4060
University of the Pacific, 4202
Unlocking the Mysteries of Sensory Dysfunc tion, 3287
Untamed World, 1221
Up and Running, 1642
Updown Chair, 1294
Upward Bound Camp for Special Needs, 583
Urbana University, 5117
Ursinus College, 5224
Ursuline College, 5118
Utah Department of Special Education, 3763, 3764
Utah Governor's Council for People with Disabilities, 2599
Utah Labor Commission: Utah Anti-discrimin ation and Labor Division, 2600
Utah Literacy Action Center, 2982
Utah Literacy Resource Center, 2983
Utah Parent Center, 5917
Utah State Office of Education, 6360
Utah State Office of Rehabilitation, 6361
Utah State University, 5369, 1535, 5362, 5914
Utah Valley State College, 5370
Utah Work Force, 2601

Entry & Company Name Index / x

Wooden Pegboard, 1428
Wooden Pegs, 1429
Woodland Hall Academy-Dyslexia Research Institute, 4329
Woodrow Wilson Rehab Center, 1672
Woods Schools, 5877
Wor-Wic Community College, 4613
Word Feathers, 3501
Word Invasion: Academic Skill Builders in Language Arts, 1840
Word Master: Academic Skill Builders in Language Arts, 1841
Word Parts, 1192
Word Pieces, 2006
Word Scramble 2, 1193
Word Wise I and II: Better Comprehension Through Vocabulary, 1842
Wordly Wise 3000 ABC 1-9, 1194
Wordly Wise ABC 1-9, 1195
Words+, 1611
Work America, 3355
Work America, Workforce Economics Workforce Trends, 6164
Work First Division: Washington Department of Social and Health Services, 3022, 6370
Work Force Information Act, 6375
Workbook for Aphasia, 843, 1196, 1513
Workbook for Cognitive Skills, 921
Workbook for Language Skills, 844
Workbook for Memory Skills, 922
Workbook for Reasoning Skills, 923
Workbook for Verbal Expression, 845, 1298
Workbook for Word Retrieval, 924
Workforce Development Act, 6190
Workforce Development Division, 6180
Workforce Investment Act, 6132, 6331, 6336, 6372
Workforce Investment Quarterly, 6165
Workforce Investment: Virtual Career Network, 6217
Working Memory and Severe Learning Difficulties, 3925
Working With Words-Volume 3, 925
Working for Myself, 926
Working with Visually Impaired Young Students: A Curriculum Guide for 3 to 5 Year-Olds, 3926
Workman Publishing, 3288
Workshops, 5532
World Experience, 2163
World Institute on Disability (WID), 142
A World So Different, 1300
World of Options: A Guide to International Education, 4014
Worm Squirm, 1738
Worthington Community College, 4761
Worthmore Academy, 471
Wright State University, 5122
Wrightslaw, 3649
Write, 2146
Write On! Plus: Beginning Writing Skills, 1514
Write On! Plus: Elementary Writing Skills, 1515
Write On! Plus: Essential Writing, 1516
Write On! Plus: Growing as a Writer, 1517
Write On! Plus: High School Writing Skills, 1518
Write On! Plus: Literature Studies, 1519
Write On! Plus: Middle School Writing Skills, 1520
Write On! Plus: Responding to Great Literature, 1521
Write On! Plus: Spanish/ English Literacy Series, 1522
Write On! Plus: Steps to Better Writing, 1523
Write On! Plus: Writing with Picture Books, 1524
Write from the Start, 1525
Write: Outloud, 2130
WriteOPOLY, 1430, 1526
Writer's Resources Library 2.0, 1527
Writestart, 1528
Writing Trek Grades 4-6, 846, 1529, 2147
Writing Trek Grades 6-8, 847, 1530, 2148
Writing Trek Grades 8-10, 848, 1531, 2149
Wyoming Community College Commission, 2654
Wyoming Department of Employment Services and Job Training Programs, 2660

Wyoming Division of Vocational Rehabilitation, 6376
Wyoming Literacy Resource Center, 3042
Wyoming Parent Information Center, 5946

X

Xavier Society for the Blind, 3468
Xavier University, 5123

Y

YACHAD East Coast Adventure, 116
YAI/Rockland County Association for the Learning Disabled (YAI/RCALD), 555
YMCA: Lakeland, 454
YMCA: Valley-Shore, 446
YWCA, 541
YWCA of White Plains-Central Westchester, 551
Yakima Valley Community College, 5469
Yale Child Study Center, 5615
Yale University, 4272
Yankton College, 5264
Yavapai College, 4054
York County Literacy Council, 2926
York Press, 3469, 3285
You Don't Have to be Dyslexic, 3301
You Don't Outgrow It: Living with Learning Disabilities, 3053
You Mean I'm Not Lazy, Stupid or Crazy?, 384
Young Adult Institute, 3581, 3591
Young Adult Institute (YAI): National Institute for People with Disabilities, 143
Young Adult Institute Conference on Developmental Disabilities, 1595
Your Child's Evaluation, 3346
Your Child's Speech and Language, 849, 1070
Youth Dakota Advocacy Services, 2573
Youth for Understanding USA, 2164

Z

Zap! Around Town, 1024, 1980
Zimmerman Center, 2835
Zipper, the Kid with ADHD, 3083
Zoo Time, 1739
Zygo Industries, 2131

w

www.abcparenting.com, 3598
www.add.org, 385
www.addhelpline.org, 386
www.additudemag.com, 387
www.addvance.com, 388
www.addwarehouse.com, 389
www.adhdnews.com/sped.htm, 3599
www.adhdnews.com/ssi.htm, 390
www.ajb.dni.us, 3600
www.ala.org/roads, 3601
www.allaboutvision.com, 3602
www.ataccess.org, 3603
www.autismtreatment.com, 3604
www.babycenter.com, 3605
www.career.com, 3606
www.cec.sped.org, 391
www.chadd.org, 392
www.childdevelopmentinfo.com, 393, 3607
www.childparenting.about.com, 3608
www.disabilityinfo.gov, 3609
www.disabilityresources.org, 3610
www.discoveryhealth.com, 3611
www.dmoz.org, 3612
www.doleta.gov/programs/adtrain.asp, 3613

770 **Boldface indicates Publisher**

Stories and More: Time and Place, 811, 1180
Stowell Learning Center, 5570
Sweetwater State Literacy Regional Resourc e Center, 2730
Switzer Center, 5571
Symposium Series on Assistive Technology, 1585
Taft College, 4183
Talking Walls, 1214
Talking Walls: The Stories Continue, 1215
Team of Advocates for Special Kids, 137
Team of Advocates for Special Kids (TASK), 5572
Technology and Persons with Disabilities C onference, 1590
The Prentice School, 5573
ThemeWeavers: Animals Activity Kit, 914
ThemeWeavers: Nature Activity Kit, 915, 1216
Thinkin' Science ZAP, 916
Thinking and Learning Connection, 139, 2696
Travel the World with Timmy Deluxe, 919
UCLA Office for Students with Disabilities, 4184
USC University Affiliated Program: Childre ns Hospital at Los Angeles, 4185
United States International University, 4186
University Affiliated Mental Retardation Program, 4187
University of California-Davis: Student Disability Resource Center, 4188
University of California: Berkeley, 4189
University of California: Irvine, 4190
University of California: Irvine Campus, 4191
University of California: Los Angeles, 4192
University of California: Riverside, 4193
University of California: San Diego, 4194
University of California: San Francisco, 4195
University of California: Santa Barbara, 4196
University of California: Santa Cruz, 4197
University of Redlands, 4198
University of San Diego, 4199
University of San Francisco, 4200
University of Southern California, 4201
University of the Pacific, 4202
Vanguard University of Southern California, 4203
Ventura College, 4204
Victor Valley College, 4205
Virtual Labs: Electricity, 1222
Virtual Labs: Light, 1223
Vision Care Clinic of Santa Clara Valley, 5574
Vision Literacy of California, 2731
West Hills College, 4206
West Los Angeles College, 4207
West Valley College, 4208
Westmark School, 4209
Whittier College, 4210
World Experience, 2163
World Institute on Disability (WID), 142

Colorado

Activities for a Diverse Classroom: Connecting Students, 1229
Aims Community College, 4211
American Universities International Program, 2151
Arapahoe Community College, 4212
Colorado Adult Education and Family Litera cy, 2732
Colorado Assistive Technology Project, 2241
Colorado Christian University, 4213
Colorado Civil Rights Division, 2242
Colorado Department of Labor and Employment, 2243
Colorado Developmental Disabilities, 2244
Colorado Mountain College, 4214
Colorado Northwestern Community College, 4215
Colorado State University, 4216
Community College of Aurora, 4217
Community College of Denver, 4218
Correctional Education Division: Colorado, 2245
Denver Academy, 4219
Developmental Disabilities Resource Center, 5575

Disability Services, 4220
Easter Seals Camp Rocky Mountain Village, 422
Easter Seals Colorado, 423, 6201
Easter Seals Southern Colorado, 424
Fort Lewis College, 4221
Front Range Community College Progressive Learning, 4222
Havern Center, 5576
Human Services: Division of Developmental Disabilities, 6202
Human Services: Division of Vocational Rehabilitation, 6203
International Dyslexia Association: Rocky Mountain Branch, 170
John F Kennedy Child Development Center, 4223
Lamar Community College, 4224
Learning Camp, 425
Learning Disabilities Association of Colorado, 171, 2733
Literacy Coalition of Jefferson County, 2734
Literacy Volunteers of America: Colorado L iteracy Outreach, 2735
Morgan Community College, 4225
Northeastern Junior College, 4226
PEAK Parent Center, 5577
Pikes Peak Community College, 4227
Pueblo Community College, 4228
Red Rocks Community College, 4229
Region VIII: US Department of Education, 2247
Region VIII: US Department of Health and Human Services, 2248
Region VIII: US Department of Labor-Office of Federal Contract Compliance, 2249
Regis University, 4230
Rocky Mountain Disability and Business Technical Assistance Center, 172
State Vocational Rehabilitation Agency of Colorado, 6204
Synthesis Summer Camp Program Foothills Unitarian Church, 426
Trinidad State Junior College, 4231
University of Colorado at Boulder Disabili ty Services, 4232
University of Colorado: Colorado Springs, 4233
University of Denver, 4234
University of Northern Colorado, 4235
University of Southern Colorado, 4236
Western State College of Colorado, 4237

Connecticut

Access Expo and Conference, 1533
Albertus Magnus College, 4238
American Institute for Foreign Study, 2150
American School for the Deaf, 5578
Annual Postsecondary Learning Disability Training Institute Workshop, 1538
Asnuntuck Community Technical College, 4239
Ben Bronz Academy, 4240
Boys and Girls Village, 5579
Briarwood College, 4241
Bureau of Adult Education & Training, 6205
Bureau of Special Education & Pupil Servic es, 2252
CACLD Spring & Fall Conferences, 1541
CHILD FIND of Connecticut, 2253
COPE Center of Progressive Education, 5580
CREC Summer School, 427
Camp Hemlocks Easter Seals, 428
Camp Horizons, 429
Camp Lark, 430
Camp Tepee, 431
Candee Hill, 5581
Capitol Community-Tech College, 4242
Central Connecticut State University, 4243
Community Child Guidance Clinic School, 5582
ConnSENSE Conference, 1550
Connecticut Association for Children and Adults with LD, 173
Connecticut Association of Private Special Education Facilities (CAPSEF), 174
Connecticut Bureau of Rehabilitation Servi ces, 2254
Connecticut Capitol Region Educational Cou ncil, 175
Connecticut Center for Augmentative Communication, 5583
Connecticut Center for Children and Families, 5584

Delaware

District of Columbia

College of Southern Idaho, 4373
Comprehensive Advocacy of Idaho, 197
Department of Labor, 6206, 6238
Easter Seals-Goodwill Staffing Services, 6239
Easter Seals-Goodwill Working Solutions, 6240
Idaho Adult Education Office, 2769
Idaho Center on Developmental Disabilities, 2298
Idaho Coalition for Adult Literacy, 2770
Idaho Council: International Reading Assocation, 2771
Idaho Department of Corrections, 2772
Idaho Fair Employment Practice Agency, 2299
Idaho High Reachers Employment and Trainin g, 198
Idaho Human Rights Commission, 2300
Idaho Parents Unlimited, 5662
Idaho State Library, 2773
Idaho State University, 4374
Idaho Workforce Investment Act, 2774, 6241
North Idaho College, 4375
State Department of Education: Special Education, 2302
Temporary Assistance for Needy Families: Idaho Department of
Health and Welfare, 2775, 6243
University of Idaho, 4376
University of Idaho: Idaho Center on Development, 4377

Illinois

100% Concepts: Intermediate, 635
100% Concepts: Primary, 636
100% Grammar, 637, 1431
100% Grammar LITE, 638, 1432
100% Punctuation, 1433
100% Punctuation LITE, 1434
100% Reading: 2-Book Intermediate Set, 1071
100% Reading: 3-Book Primary Set, 1072
100% Reading: Decoding and Word Recognitio n: 5-book set, 1073
100% Reading: Intermediate Book 1, 1074
100% Reading: Intermediate Book 2, 1075
100% Reading: Primary Book 1, 1076
100% Reading: Primary Book 2, 1077
100% Reading: Primary Book 3, 1078
100% Spelling, 1435
100% Story Writing, 1436
100% Vocabulary: Intermediate, 639
100% Vocabulary: Primary, 640
100% Writing 4-book Set, 1437
100% Writing: Comparison and Contrast, 1438
100% Writing: Exposition, 1439
100% Writing: Narration, 1440
100% Writing: Persuasion, 1441
125 Vocabulary Builders, 641
125 Ways to Be a Better Reader, 1079
125 Ways to Be a Better Student, 1321
125 Ways to Be a Better Test-Taker, 1322
125 Ways to Be a Better Writer, 1442
125 Writing Projects, 1443
ADD Challenge: A Practical Guide for Teachers, 332
Acacia Academy, 4378
Achievement Centers, 5663
Allendale Association, 5664
American Academy of Pediatrics National Headquarters, 20
American Art Therapy Association, 21
Artic Shuffle, 646, 1027, 1341, 1341
ArticBURST Articulation Practice for S, R, Ch, and Sh, 648, 1342
Assistive Technology Industry Association, 39
Att-P'tach Special Education Program, 5665
Aurora University, 4379
Autism & PDD: Primary Social Skills Lesson s, 1235
Autism & PPD: Adolescent Social Skills Lessons, 1236
Autism & PPD: Adolescent Social Skills Les sons-Health &
Hygiene, 1237
Autism & PPD: Concept Development, 650
Autism & PPD: Pictured Stories and Languag e Activities, 651
Barat College of DePaul University, 4380

Barnaby's Burrow: An Auditory Processing Game, 855, 1344
Blackburn College, 4381
Blend It! End It!, 1348, 1445
Board of Education of Chicago, 2305
Brainopoly: A Thinking Game, 857, 1349
Brehm Preparatory School, 4382, 5666
Camelot Care Center: Illinois, 5667
Camp Algonquin, 458
Camp Little Giant: Touch of Nature Environmental Center, 459
Catholic Children's Home, 5668
Center for Academic Development: National College of
Education, 4383
Center for Learning, 5669
Center for Speech and Language Disorders, 5670
Central Auditory Processing Kit, 657
Chicago State University, 4384
Chicago Urban Day School, 5671
Child Care Association of Illinois, 199
Children's Center for Behavioral Developme nt, 5672
Client Assistance Program (CAP): Illinois Division of Persons
with Disabilities, 2306
Clip Art Collections: The Environment & Space, 1352
College of DuPage, 4385
College of Health & Human Development: Department of
Disability & Human Development, 4386
Columbia College Chicago, 4387
Communication Aid Manufacturers Associatio n (CAMA)
Workshops, 1549
Communication Aids: Manufacturers Associat ion, 55
Complete Oral-Motor Program for Articulation: Book Only, 658
Complete Oral-Motor Program for Articulation, 659
Complete Oral-Motor Program for Articulati on: Refill Kit, 660
Council on Rehabilitation Education, 60
Cove School, 5673
Crash Course for Study Skills, 1323
Curriculum Vocabulary Game, 663
Daily Starters: Quote of the Day, 664, 1453
Danville Area Community College, 4388
Decoding Games, 1095, 1358
Definition Play by Play, 864, 1359
Early Achievement Center Preschool & Kinde rgarten, 5674
Easter Seals, 70
Easter Seals Camping and Recreation List, 460
Easter Seals Central Illinois, 461, 6244
Easter Seals Jayne Shover Center, 462
Easter Seals Joliet, 463
Easter Seals Missouri, 464, 6245
Easter Seals UCP: Peoria, 465
Easter Seals Youth at Risk, 6246
Eastern Illinois University, 4389
Easy Does It for Fluency: Intermediat e, 671
Easy Does It for Fluency: Preschool/Primar y, 672
Educational Services of Glen Ellyn, 5675
Elgin Community College, 4390
Elim Christian Services, 5676
Esperanza School, 5677
Expressive Language Kit, 676, 1250
Family Resource Center on Disabilities, 5678
Follow Me!, 869
Follow Me! 2, 682, 870, 955, 955
For Parents and Professionals: Preschool, 1037
Friendzee: A Social Skills Game, 1253
Governors State University, 4391
Gram's Cracker: A Grammar Game, 1372
Grammar Scramble: A Grammar and Sentence- Building Game,
1373, 1468
Gramopoly: A Parts of Speech Game, 1374, 1470
Great Lakes Disability and Business Technical Assistance Center,
2308
Greenrose Elementary School, 5679
HELP 1, 687
HELP 2, 688
HELP 3, 689

Indiana

Iowa

Massachusetts

Ferris State University, 4686
Finlandia University, 4687
Fowler Center Summer Camp, 506
Genesee County Literacy Coalition, 2835
Glen Oaks Community College, 4688
Henry Ford Community College, 4689
Hope College, 4690
International Dyslexia Association: Michig an Branch, 233
Jackson Community College, 4691
Kalamazoo College, 4692
Kellogg Community College, 4693
Kendall College of Art and Design, 4694
Lake Michigan Academy, 5750
Lake Michigan College, 4695
Lansing Community College, 4696
Learning Disabilities Association of Michigan (LDA), 234
Let's Write Right: Teacher's Edition, 1483
Literacy Volunteers of America: Lansing Area Literacy Coalition, 2836
Literacy Volunteers of America: Sanilac Council, 2837
Madonna University, 4697
Michigan Adult Learning & Technology Center, 2838
Michigan Assistive Technology: Michigan Rehabilitation Services, 2393, 2839
Michigan Citizens Alliance to Uphold Speci al Education (CAUSE), 235
Michigan Commission for the Blind: Deafbli nd Unit, 6280
Michigan Developmental Disabilities Counci l, 2394
Michigan Employment Security Commission, 2395
Michigan Jobs Commission, 6281
Michigan Laubach Literacy Action, 2840
Michigan Libraries and Adult Literacy, 2841
Michigan Protection and Advocacy Service, 2396
Michigan State Department of Adult Educati on: Office of Extended Learning Services, 2842
Michigan State University, 4698
Michigan Technological University, 4699
Michigan Workforce Investment Act, 2843, 6282
Mid-Michigan Community College, 4700
Monroe County Community College, 4701
Montcalm Community College, 4702
Northern Michigan University, 4703
Northwestern Michigan College, 4704
Northwood University, 4705
Oakland Community College: Orchard Ridge Campus, 4706
Oakland University, 4707
Office of Services for Students with Disabilities, 4708
Patterns of English Spelling, 1138
Recording for the Blind & Dyslexic Learnin g Through Listening: Michigan Unit, 236
SLD Learning Center, 5751
Saginaw Valley State University, 4709
Sequential Spelling 1-7 with Student Response Book, 786
St. Clair County Community College, 4710
University of Michigan: Dearborn, 4711
University of Michigan: Flint, 4712
Washtenaw Community College, 4713
Western Michigan University, 4714

Minnesota

Ablenet, 643, 850, 1080, 1080, 1197, 1226, 1334
Alexandria Technical College, 4715
Anoka-Ramsey Community College, 4716
Ants in His Pants: Absurdities and Realiti es of Special Education, 1082
Augsburg College, 4717
Basic Math for Job and Personal Use, 934
Basic Signing Vocabulary Cards, 652
Bemidji State University, 4718
Bethel College: Minnesota, 4719
Calculator Math for Job and Personal Use, 938
Calvin Academy and Special Education Day School, 4720

Camp Buckskin, 507
Camp Chi Rho, 508
Camp Confidence, 509
Camp Friendship, 510
Century College, 4721
Closing the Gap, 53
Closing the Gap Conference, 1547
College of Associated Arts, 4722
College of Saint Scholastica, 4723
College of St. Catherine: Minneapolis, 4724
College of St. Catherine: St. Paul Campus, 4725
Concordia College, 4726
Decimals and Percentages for Job and Personal Use, 945
Families and Advocates Partnership for Edu cation FAPE, 74
Fergus Falls Community College, 4727
Goodwill/Easter Seals Minnesota, 6284
Goodwill/Easter Seals: St. Cloud, 6285
Goodwill/Easter Seals: St. Paul, 6286
Goodwill/Easter Seals: Willmar, 6287
Grammar and Writing for Job and Personal Use, 1469
Groves Academy, 5752
Gustavus Adolphus College, 4728
Hamline College, 4729
Hands-On Activities for Exceptional Studen ts, 874
Hibbing Community College, 4730
Higher Education Consortium for Urban Affairs, 2156
How the Student with Hearing Loss Can Succeed in College, 3999
Inclusion: Strategies for Working with Young Children, 1113
International Adolescent Conference: Programs for Adolescents, 1563
International Dyslexia Association: Upper Midwest Branch, 237
Inver Hills Community College, 4731
Itasca Community College, 4732
LDA Learning Center, 5753
Lake Superior College, 4733
Listening and Speaking for Job and Persona l Use, 725
Macalester College, 4734
Mankato State University, 4735
Mastering Reading Series, 1130
Mesabi Range Community & Technical College, 4736
Minneapolis Community College, 4737
Minnesota Access Services, 238
Minnesota Department of Adult Education: Adult Basic Education, 2844
Minnesota Department of Children, Families & Learning, 2400
Minnesota Department of Employment and Economic Development, 2845, 6288
Minnesota Department of Human Rights, 2401
Minnesota Disability Law Center, 239
Minnesota GED Administration, 2846
Minnesota Governor's Council on Developmen tal Disabilities, 2402
Minnesota LDA Learning Disabilities Center, 2847
Minnesota LINCS: Literacy Council, 2848
Minnesota Life College, 4738
Minnesota Life Work Center, 2403, 2849
Minnesota Literacy Training Network, 2850
Minnesota State University Moorehead, 4739
Minnesota University Affiliated Program on Developmental Disabilities, 4740
Minnesota Vocational Rehabilitation Agency: Rehabilitation Services Branch, 2851, 6129
Minnesota West Community & Technical College, 4741
Normandale Community College, 4742
North Hennepin Community College, 4743
Northwestern College, 4505, 4744
PACER Center, 122
Peer Pals, 1269, 1329
People at Work, 892
Phonemic Awareness: The Sounds of Reading, 1139
Pillsbury Baptist Bible College, 4745
Punctuation, Capitalization, and Handwriti ng for Job and Personal Use, 1497

Nevada

New Hampshire

New Jersey

State University of New York: Buffalo, 4975
State University of New York: College of Technology, 4976
State University of New York: College at Buffalo, 4977
State University of New York: Fredonia, 4978
State University of New York: Geneseo College, 4979
State University of New York: Oneonta, 4980
State University of New York: Oswego, 4981
State University of New York: Plattsburgh, 4982
State University of New York: Potsdam, 4983
State University of New York: Stony Brook, 4984
Stephen Gaynor School, 5825
Stop, Relax and Think, 1281
Stop, Relax and Think Ball, 1282
Stop, Relax and Think Card Game, 1283
Stop, Relax and Think Scriptbook, 1284
Stop, Relax and Think Workbook, 1285
Strong Center for Developmental Disabilities, 279
Suffolk County Community College: Eastern Campus, 4985
Suffolk County Community College: Selden Campus, 4986
Suffolk County Community College: Western Campus, 4987
Sullivan County Community College, 4988
Summit Camp Program, 595
Summit Travel Program, 553
Sunbuddy Math Playhouse, 1020
Sunbuddy Writer, 1507
Sunken Treasure Adventure: Beginning Blend s, 814
Syracuse University, 4989
Talking Walls Bundle, 1318
Ten Tricky Tiles, 1022
Thinkin' Science, 1217
Thinkin' Science ZAP!, 1218
Trailblazers Camp JCC of Northern Westchester, 554
Trocaire College, 4990
Two-Year College Databook, 4012
Ulster County Community College, 4991
Understanding and Teaching Children With Autism, 381
University of Albany, 4992
Updown Chair, 1294
Utica College of Syracuse University, 4993
Vassar College, 4994
Vocational & Educational Services for Indi viduals with Disabilities, 2495
Vocational Independence Program (VIP), 5826
Vocational School Manual, 4013
Vowel Patterns, 837
Vowels: Short & Long, 1189
Wagner College, 4995
Westchester Community College, 4996
Westchester Institute for Human Developmen t, 280
Why Can't Johnny Concentrate: Coping With Attention Deficit Problems, 382
Windward School, 5827
Winston Preparatory School, 5828
Word Parts, 1192
Write On! Plus: Beginning Writing Skills, 1514
Write On! Plus: Elementary Writing Skills, 1515
Write On! Plus: Essential Writing, 1516
Write On! Plus: Growing as a Writer, 1517
Write On! Plus: High School Writing Skills, 1518
Write On! Plus: Literature Studies, 1519
Write On! Plus: Middle School Writing Skil ls, 1520
Write On! Plus: Responding to Great Litera ture, 1521
Write On! Plus: Spanish/ English Literacy Series, 1522
Write On! Plus: Steps to Better Writing, 1523
Write On! Plus: Writing with Picture Books, 1524
Writer's Resources Library 2.0, 1527
Writing Trek Grades 4-6, 846, 1529
Writing Trek Grades 6-8, 847, 1530
Writing Trek Grades 8-10, 848, 1531
YAI/Rockland County Association for the Learning Disabled (YAI/RCALD), 555
You Mean I'm Not Lazy, Stupid or Crazy?, 384

Young Adult Institute (YAI): National Inst itute for People with Disabilities, 143
Young Adult Institute Conference on Developmental Disabilities, 1595
Zap! Around Town, 1024

North Carolina

All Kinds of Minds of North Car olina, 281
Appalachian State University, 4997
Bennett College, 4998
Blue Ridge Literacy Council, 2885
Brevard College, 4999
Buncombe County Literacy Council, 2886
Caldwell Community College and Technical Institute, 5000
Camp Timberwolf, 556
Catawba College, 5001
Catawba Valley Community College, 5002
Central Carolina Community College, 5003
Central Piedmont Community College, 5004
Client Assistance Program (CAP): North Carolina Division of Persons with Disabilities, 2497
Comprehensive Educational Services (CES), 5829
Craven Community College, 5005
Davidson County Community College, 5006
Devereux Early Childhood Assessment (DECA), 1029
Devereux Early Childhood Assessment: Clini cal Version (DECA-C), 1030
Dore Academy, 5007
Durham County Literacy Council, 2887
East Carolina University, 5008
Eastern Associates Speech and Language Services, 5830
Exceptional Children's Assistance Center, 5831
Families First Coalition, 5832
Forsyth Technical Community College, 5009
Gardner-Webb University, 5010
Gastonia Literacy Council, 2888
Guilford Technical Community College, 5011
Hill Center, 5833
Isothermal Community College, 5012
Johnson C Smith University, 5013
Joy A Shabazz Center for Independent Living, 5834
LAP-D Kindergarten Screen Kit, 1043
LD Child and the ADHD Child, 367
Learning Accomplishment Profile Diagnostic Normed Screens for Age 3-5, 1045
Learning Accomplishment Profile (LAP-R) KI T, 1046
Learning Accomplishment Profile Diagnostic Normed Assessment (LAP-D), 1047
Learning Disabilities Association of North Carolina (LDANC), 282
Lenoir Community College, 5014
Lenoir-Rhyne College, 5015
Literacy Volunteers of America: Pitt Count y, 2889
Louisburg College, 5016
Mars Hill College, 5017
Mayland Community College, 5018
McDowell Technical Community College, 5019
Meredith College, 5020
Montgomery Community College: North Caroli na, 5021
National Early Childhood Technical Assista nce Center, 112
North Carolina Council on Developmental Disabilities, 2498
North Carolina Division of Employment and Training, 2499
North Carolina Division of Vocational Reha bilitation, 2500
North Carolina Employment Security Commission, 2501
North Carolina Literacy Resource Center, 2890
North Carolina Office of Administrative Hearings: Civil Rights Division, 2502
North Carolina State University, 5022
North Carolina Wesleyan College, 5023
Office of the Governor, 2221, 2503
Partners for Learning (PFL), 1052
Peace College, 5024

North Dakota

Ohio

Utah

Washington

www.ncgiadd.org, 396
www.nichcy.org, 397
www.oneaddplace.com, 398, 3638
www.therapistfinder.net, 399, 3648

Aphasia

Basic Level Workbook for Aphasia, 1084
Boston Diagnostic Aphasia Exam: Third Edition, 6108
TARGET, 815, 906
Teaching Language-Deficient Children: Theory and Application of the Association Method, 3942
Workbook for Aphasia, 843, 1196, 1513

Aptitude

Occupational Aptitude Survey and Interest Schedule, 6033

Articulation

ARTIC Technologies, 1597
Artic-Pic, 647
Artic-Riddles, 1234
Goldman-Fristoe Test of Articulation: 2nd Edition, 686
Peabody Articulation, 1394
Pegboard Set, 1395
Remediation of Articulation Disorders (RAD), 771

Arts

A Manual of Sequential Art Activities for Classified Children and Adolescents, 3770
Art as a Language for the Learning Disable d Child, 3780
Behavioral Arts, 5797
Camp Holiday, 485
Clip Art Collections: The Environment & Space, 1352
Clip Art Collections: The US & The World, 1353
Connecticut Institute for Cultural Literac y and Wellness, 2736
Dinosaur Days, 1707
Kid Pix, 1781
Language Arts, 3723
McGee, 1796
Monsters & Make-Believe, 1723
Points of Contact: Disability, Art, and Culture, 3882
QUIC Tests, 6024
Teddy Barrels of Fun, 1735

At-Risk

BRIGANCE Screens: Early Preschool, 5991
BRIGANCE Screens: Infants and Toddler, 5992
BRIGANCE Screens: K and 1, 5993
Basic School Skills Inventory: Screen and Diagnostic, 5994
DABERON Screening for School Readiness, 5996
Developmental Assessment for the Severely Disabled, 5997

Autism

Activity Schedules for Children with Autis m: A Guide for Parents and Professionals, 3125
Autism Research Institute, 44
Autism Research Review International, 3663
Autism Screening Instrument for Educationa l Planning, 5969
Autism Society of America, 45
Autism Treatment Center of America, 46
Behind the Glass Door: Hannah's Story, 3520
Children with Autism, 3146
Community Based Services, 5801
Devereux Center for Autism, 5773
Eden Institute Curriculum: Classroom, 1761
Eden Institute Curriculum: Classroom Orien ation, Volume II, 3823

Eden Institute Curriculum: Core, 3824
Eden Institute Curriculum: Speech and Lang uage, Volume IV, 3825
Eden Institute Curriculum: Volume I, 1854
Eden Services, 5776
Effective Teaching Methods for Autistic Children, 3172
Fundamentals of Autism, 3063, 3315, 5980, 5999
General Information about Autism, 3316
Getting Started with Facilitated Communication, 3535
Going to School with Facilitated Communication, 3536
I Want My Little Boy Back, 3540
Ivymount School, 4600
Kaufman Assessment Battery for Children, 6002
Kaufman Brief Intelligence Test, 6003
SEARCH Day Program, 5785
Sensory Motor Issues in Autism, 899
Son Rise: The Miracle Continues, 3266
Son-Rise Program, 134
Son-Rise Program: Autism Treatment Center of America, 5742
Son-Rise: The Miracle Continues, 3051
www.autismtreatment.com, 3604
www.son-rise.org, 3646

Behavioral Disorders

Behavior Management System, 3739
Calm Down and Play, 1241
Child Behavior Checklist, 5974
Children with Learning and Behavioral Disorders, 3310
Childswork/Childsplay Catalog, 1335
Competencies for Teachers of Students with Learning Disabilities, 3804
Defiant Children, 3161
Devereux Deerhaven, 5774
Feelings, 1857
Instructional Methods for Students, 3862
Learning Disabilities and Social Skills: Last One Picked..First One Picked On, 3552
National Institute of Mental Health, 2173
School Behaviors and Organization Skills, 5985
Stop, Relax and Think, 1281
Stop, Relax and Think Ball, 1282
Stop, Relax and Think Card Game, 1283
Stop, Relax and Think Scriptbook, 1284
Stop, Relax and Think Workbook, 1285

Bilingual Resources

Articulation 3-Vowels: Software, 649
BRIGANCE Assessment of Basic Skills: Spanish Edition, 6060
Bilingualism and Learning Disabilities, 3790

Camps

American Institute for Foreign Study, 2150
American-Scandinavian Foundation, 2152
Association for International Practical Training, 2153
Austin Wilderness Counseling Services, 604
Camp Arrowhead YMCA, 576
Camp Easter Seals, 512
Camp Fire USA, 577
Camp Kitaki YMCA, 513
Camp Timberwolf, 556
Crossroads for Kids, 492
Earthstewards Network, 2154
Easter Seals, 70
Easter Seals ARC of Northeast Indiana, 468
Easter Seals Achievement Center, 6168
Easter Seals Adult Services Center, 409, 6169
Easter Seals Alabama, 6170
Easter Seals Albany, 537
Easter Seals Arc of Northeast Indiana, 6249

Child Welfare

Help Build a Brighter Future: Children at Risk for LD in Child Care Centers, 3190
Iowa Welfare Programs, 2332
Jewish Children's Bureau of Chicago, 203
Sequenced Inventory of Communication Development, 6089
Temporary Assistance for Needy Families, 6248, 6270
Temporary Assistance for Needy Families: Idaho Department of Health and Welfare, 2775, 6243

Clearinghouses

American Self-Help Clearinghouse of New Jersey, 254
Clearinghouse for Specialized Media, 2231
Clearinghouse on Disability Information, 52

Cognitive Disorders

Alpine Tram Ride, 1699
Atypical Cognitive Deficits, 3785
Cognitive Approach to Learning Disabilities, 3800
Contemporary Intellectual Assessment: Theories, Tests and Issues, 3158
Hands-On Activities for Exceptional Students, 874
Helping Students Become Strategic Learners, 3753
Implementing Cognitive Strategy Instruction Across the School, 3854
Link N' Learn Activity Book, 1382
MCLA: Measure of Cognitive-Linguistic Abilities, 731
Problem Sensitivity: A Qualitative Difference in the Learning Disabled, 3329
Putting the Pieces Together: Volume 4, 893
Test of Nonverbal Intelligence, 6016
Workbook for Reasoning Skills, 923

Comic Strips

Teaching Old Logs New Tricks: Absurdities and Realities of Education, 3279

Communication Disorders

Art of Communication, 3516
Communication Aids, 1356
Communication Skills in Children with Down Syndrome, 3153
If Your Child Stutters: A Guide for Parents, 3320
Learning Problems in Language, 3553
My House: Language Activities of Daily Living, 1879
Now You're Talking: Extend Conversation, 3484
Personal Communicating Device, 1626
Sequenced Inventory of Communication Development (SICD), 1407, 6090
VoiceNote, 1645
Winning in Speech, 841
Wizard of Rs, 842

Community Integration

Arkansas Adult Basic Education, 2702
Collaboration in the Schools: The Problem-Solving Process, 3474
Department of Vocational Rehabilitation Services: Mississippi, 6291
Florida Laubach Literacy Action, 2749
Hawaii Laubach Literacy Action, 2767
Illinois Laubach Literacy Action, 2776
Independent Living Research Utilization Program, 6126
Indiana Workforce Literacy, 2786
Kentucky Laubach Literacy Action, 2814
Laubach Literacy Action: West Virginia, 3024
Laubach Literacy Action: Wisconsin, 3028
Literacy Council of Alaska, 2703
Literacy Investment for Tomorrow: Missouri, 2853
Maryland Literacy Coalition, 2825

Nevada Literacy Coalition: State Literacy Resource Center, 2862
New Mexico Coalition for Literacy, 2876
No One to Play with: The Social Side of Learning Disabilities, 3243
Office of Vocational Rehabilitation, 6264
Ohio Literacy Network, 2902
Public Schools Vocational & Adult Education, 6222
Social Perception and Learning Disabilities, 3980
South Dakota GED: Literacy Department of Education & Cultural Affairs, 2945
South Dakota Literacy Council, 2946
Tennessee Literacy Coalition, 2955
Virginia Literacy Coalition, 3011
Washington Laubach Literacy Action, 3021
Western Kansas Community Service Consortium, 2349, 2813
www.discoveryhealth.com, 3611

Comprehension

AppleSeeds, 1083
Bedside Evaluation and Screening Test of Aphasia, 6065
Beyond the Code, 1085
Building Mathematical Thinking, 935
Claims to Fame, 1089
Comprehension Connection, 2076
Dyslexia: An Introduction to the Orton-Gillingham Approach, 665
Explode the Code: Wall Chart, 675
First R, 1859
Formal Reading Inventory, 6045
Handprints, 1107
It's Elementary!, 976
Jarvis Clutch: Social Spy, 1260
Knowledgeworks, 1872
Kurtz Center for Cognitive Development, 5632
Let's Go Read 2: An Ocean Adventure, 1126
McGraw Hill Companies, 3236
Next Stop, 1136
PATHS, 1137, 1492
Poetry in Three Dimensions: Reading, Writing and Critical Thinking Skills through Poetry, 763, 1141
Read On! Plus, 1146, 2092
Reader's Quest I, 1148
Reader's Quest II, 1149
Reading Comprehension Bundle, 1150
Reading Comprehension Materials (Volume 5), 1152
Reading Is Fun, 3295
Reading Skills Bundle, 1159, 2096
Reading for Content, 1162
Ready to Read, 1164
Reasoning & Reading Series, 1165
Ridgewood Grammar, 773
Right into Reading: A Phonics-Based Reading and Comprehension Program, 1166
Starting Comprehension, 1178
Survey of Teenage Readiness and Neurodevelopmental Status, 904
Test for Auditory Comprehension of Language: TACL-3, 826, 1066, 6099
Test of Reading Comprehension, 6054

Conceptual Skills

Boars Tell Time, 1845
Conceptual Skills, 1923
Trudy's Time and Place House, 2001

Conferences

CEC Federation Conference: Arkansas, 1542
CEC Federation Conference: Kansas, 1543
CEC Federation Conference: Pennsylvania, 1544
CEC Federation Conference: Virginia, 1545
Melvin-Smith Learning Center Annual Conference, 1575

Robert Louis Stevenson School, 5824
SHIP Resource Center, 5907
Second Start: Pine Hill School, 5568
Speech/Language Therapy, 5786
St. Joseph's Carondelet Child Center, 5688
Starpoint School, 5911
Stratford Friends School, 5874
Summit School, 4604, 5689
The Achievment Center, 5935
The Newgrange School, 5788
Thomas A Edison Program, 5854
Three Springs, 5530
Threshold Program, 4663, 5744
Tree of Learning High School, 5855
Trident Academy, 5252, 5885
University School, 5608
VISTA Vocational & Life Skills Center, 4269, 5609
Variety School of Hawaii, 5661
Vickery Meadow Learning Center, 5913
Vision Care Clinic of Santa Clara Valley, 5574
Westside Place, 5942
Wilderness School, 5614
Willow Hill School, 5747
Windward School, 5827

Creative Expression

Affect and Creativity, 3737
Author's Toolkit, 1444, 2132
Basic Skills Products, 1748, 1914
Create with Garfield, 1703
Create with Garfield: Deluxe Edition, 1704
Easybook Deluxe Writing Workshop: Immigrat ion, 1307, 1459
Easybook Deluxe Writing Workshop: Rainfore st & Astronomy, 1308, 1460
Once Upon a Time Volume I: Passport to Discovery, 2138
Painting the Joy of the Soul, 3050

Critical Thinking

Basic Reading Skills, 2074
Critical Thinking for Contemporary Lifesty les, 1853
Funology Fables, 1038, 1105
Read and Solve Math Problems #3 Fractions, Two-Step Problems, 1974

Curriculum Guides

Creative Classroom Magazine, 3672
Print Module, 2060
Springer School and Center, 5847
Teaching Students with Learning and Behavior Problems, 3766

Daily Living

A Calendar of Home Activities, 6055
ABC's of Learning Disabilities, 3505
Aids and Appliances for Indepentent Living, 853
American Coaching Association, 27
Aphasia Diagnostic Profiles, 6059
BRIGANCE Life Skills Inventory, 6064
Basic Math for Job and Personal Use, 934
Boars Store, 1917
Bridgepointe Goodwill & Easter Seals, 208
Calculator Math for Job and Personal Use, 938
Calendar Fun with Lollipop Dragon, 1849
Categorically Speaking, 858, 1350
Coin Changer, 1850
District of Columbia Department of Educati on: Vocational & Adult Education, 2743, 6221
District of Columbia Public Schools, 2745
Get Ready to Read!, 3395

Getting Clean with Herkimer I, 1867
Getting Clean with Herkimer II, 1868
Grammar and Writing for Job and Personal Use, 1469
Handling Money, 1948
Imagination Express: Neighborhood, 2118
Imagination Express: Pyramids, 2120
Joy A Shabazz Center for Independent Living, 5834
LD Advocate, 3396
LD News, 3397
Literacy Volunteers of the National Capital Area, 2746
Living Skills, 887
MAXI, 1486
Marsh Media, 1876
Math Spending and Saving, 1877, 1956
Math for Everyday Living, 1958
Money Skills, 1878
Our World, 3400
Paper Dolls I: Dress Me First, 1885
Paper Dolls II: Dress Me Too, 1886
Reading for Job and Personal Use, 1163
Special Needs Program, 901
T&M Ranch, 5643
This Is the Way We Wash Our Face, 1904
Travel the World with Timmy Deluxe, 919
Zap! Around Town, 1024, 1980

Databases

Dialog Information Services, 1675
National Technical Information Service: US Department of Commerce, 2177, 3595
PsycINFO Database, 2061, 3596

Developmental Disabilities

ALERT-US, 450
American Guidance Service Learning Disabil ities Resources, 928
Birth Defect Research for Children (BDRC), 47
Body and Physical Difference: Discourses of Disability, 3791
Boling Center for Developmental Disabiliti es, 5266
California Association of Special Educatio n & Services, 157, 2711
Camp ASCCA, 405
Center for Development & Disability (CDD), 4875
Center for Excellence in Disabilities (CED), 5471
Client Assistance Program (CAP): New Mexico Protection and Advocacy System, 2467
Colorado Developmental Disabilities, 2244
Connecticut Association for Children and Adults with LD, 173
Council for Developmental Disabilities, 2189
Council on Developmental Disabilities, 2574
Defects: Engendering the Modern Body, 3816
Developmental Disabilities Council, 2367, 2541, 2627
Developmental Disabilities Institute: Wayn e State University, 4683
Developmental Disabilities Planning and Advisory Council, 2424
Developmental Variation and Learning Disorders, 3817
Easter Seal Society of Beaver County, 296
Eugene Easter Seal Service Center, 288
FAT City, 3534
Frames of Reference for the Assessment of Learning Disabilities, 3838
GT/LD Network, 76
Gainesville/Hall County Alliance for Liter acy, 2757
Georgia Affiliated Program for Persons with Developmental Disabilities, 4344
Illinois Council on Developmental Disabilities, 2310
Institute on Disability: A University Center for Excellence on Disability, 4831
Institutes for the Achievement of Human Potential, 82
International Dyslexia Association of New Mexico, 260
Iowa Center for Disabilities and Developme nt, 214
John F Kennedy Child Development Center, 4223

Directories

Discrimination

Rosary College, 4427
Rose State College, 5135
Rosemont College, 5873
Rural Clearinghouse for Lifelong Education & Development, 131
Rutgers Center for Cognitive Science, 4868
STAC Exchange: St.Thomas Aquinas College, 4961
SUNY Canton, 4962
SUNY Cobleskill, 4963
Sacred Heart University, 4259
Sage College, 4965
Saginaw Valley State University, 4709
Saint Ambrose College, 4506
Saint John's School of Theology & Seminary, 4749
Saint Joseph's College, 4468
Saint Leo University, 4314
Saint Louis University, 4785
Saint Mary College, 4535
Saint Mary's College of California, 4160
Saint Mary's University of Minnesota, 4750
Saint Mary-of-the-Woods College, 4469
Saint Xavier University, 4428
Salem College, 5029
Salem Community College, 4869
Salem State College, 4656
Salem: Teikyo University, 5478
Salt Lake Community College: Disability Resource Center, 5365
Sam Houston State University, 5328
San Antonio College, 5329
San Diego City College, 4161
San Diego Miramar College, 4162
San Diego State University, 4163
San Francisco State University, 4164
San Jacinto College: Central Campus, 5330
San Jacinto College: South Campus, 5331
San Jose City College, 4165
San Jose State University, 4166
San Juan College, 4884
San Marcos Texas State University: Office of Disability Services, 5332
Sandhills Community College, 5030
Santa Ana College, 4167
Santa Barbara City College, 4168
Santa Clara University, 4169
Santa Fe Community College: Florida, 4315
Santa Monica College, 4170
Santa Rosa Junior College, 4171
Savannah State University, 4356
Scenic Land School, 5281
Schenectady County Community College, 4966
School of the Art Institute of Chicago, 4429
Schoolsearch Guide to Colleges with Programs & Services for Students with LD, 4010
Schreiner University, 5333
Scott Community College, 4507
Scottsdale Community College, 4049
Seattle Academy of Arts and Sciences, 5446
Seattle Central Community College, 5447
Seattle Christian Schools, 5448
Seattle Pacific University, 5449
Section 504: Help for the Learning Disabled College Student, 3107
Seminole Community College, 4316
Seminole Junior College, 5136
Service Operations Manual, 3733
Services for Students with Disabilities, 4967
Seton Hall University, 4870
Seton Hill University, 5213
Seward County Community College, 4536
Shasta College, 4172
Shawnee College, 4431
Shawnee State University, 5106
Shelby State Community College, 5282
Sheldon Jackson College, 4063
Sheridan College, 5524

Shimer College, 4432
Shippensburg University of Pennsylvania, 5214
Shopper's Guide to Colleges Serving the Learning Disabled College Student, 4011
Shoreline Christian School, 5450
Shorter College, 4357
Siena College, 4968
Sierra College, 4173
Sierra Nevada College, 4820
Simmons College, 4657
Sinclair Community College, 5107
Skyline College, 4174
Smith College, 4658
Snohomish County Christian, 5451
Snow College, 5366
Solano Community College, 4175
Solebury School, 5215
Sonoma State University, 4176
South Carolina State University, 5249
South Dakota School of Mines & Technology, 5262
South Dakota State University, 5263
South Georgia College, 4358
South Mountain Community College, 4050
South Plains College, 5334
South Puget Sound Community College, 5452
South Seattle Community College, 5453
Southcentral Indiana Vocational Technical College, 4470
Southeast Community College: Beatrice Campus, 4812
Southeast Community College: Lincoln Campus, 4813
Southeastern College of the Assemblies of God, 4317
Southeastern Community College: North Campus, 4508
Southeastern Illinois College, 4433
Southeastern Louisiana University, 4568
Southeastern Oklahoma State University, 5137
Southern Arkansas University, 4064
Southern College of Technology, 4359
Southern Connecticut State University, 4260
Southern Illinois University: Carbondale, 4434
Southern Illinois University: Edwardsville, 4435
Southern Maine Technical College, 4580
Southern Methodist University, 5335
Southern New Hampshire University, 4838
Southern Ohio College: Fairfield Campus, 5108
Southern Ohio College: Northeast Campus, 5109
Southern Oregon State College, 5157
Southern Polytechnic State University, 4360
Southern Seminary College, 5409
Southern State Community College, 5110
Southern Utah University, 5367
Southern Vermont College, 5381
Southern West Virginia Community College & Technical College, 5479
Southside Virginia Community College, 5410
Southwest Missouri State University, 4786
Southwest Tennessee Community College, 5284
Southwest Virginia Community College, 5411
Southwestern Assemblies of God University, 5336
Southwestern College, 4177
Southwestern Community College, 4509
Southwestern Community College: North Carolina, 5031
Southwestern Oklahoma State University, 5138
Southwestern Oregon Community College, 5158
Spartanburg Methodist College, 5250
Spokane Community College, 5454
Spokane Falls Community College, 5455
Spoon River College, 4436
Spraings Academy, 4178
Spring Ridge Academy, 4051
Springall Academy, 4179
Springfield College, 4659
Springfield College in Illinois, 4437
Springfield Technical Community College, 4660
St Andrews Presbyterian College, 5032

History

Hotlines

Human Services

North Dakota Department of Human Services: Welfare & Public Assistance, 2895
Office of Advocacy for Persons with Disabilities, 2486
Oregon Department of Human Resource Adult & Family Services Division, 2534, 2911
Parent Information Center: New Hampshire Coalition for Citizens With Disabilities, 2456
Pennsylvania Human Rights Commission and F air Employment Practice, 2542
Pennsylvania's Initiative on Assistive Technology, 2544
Programs for Children with Disabilities: Ages 3 - 5, 2488
REACH-UP Program: Department of Social Welfare, 6363
Rhode Island Commission for Human Rights, 2552
Rhode Island Department of Human Services, 2932
Rhode Island Human Resource Investment Council, 2934
ServiceLink, 2458
South Carolina Human Affairs Commission, 2563
South Dakota Department of Labor, 6349
South Dakota Division of Human Rights, 2570
State Council on Developmental Disabilitie s, 2293
State Department of Adult & Community Educ ation, 2268
State Developmental Disabilities Planning Council, 2493
State of Alaska Community & Regional Affairs Department: Administrative Services, 2200
State of Connecticut: Board of Education for the Visually Impaired, 2262
Texas Commission on Human Rights, 2585
The Institute on Disability at the University of New Hampshire, 2460
University of Oregon for Excellence in Dev elopmental Disabilities, 294
University of Washington: Center on Human Development and Disability, 5462
Utah Governor's Council for People with Disabilities, 2599
Vermont Agency of Human Services, 2608
Vermont Human Resources Investment Council, 2989
Virginia Board for People with Disabilitie s, 2624
Washington Human Rights Commission, 2635
West Virginia Human Rights Commission, 2643
Youth Dakota Advocacy Services, 2573

Inclusion

Andreas: Outcomes of Inclusion, 3513
Backyards & Butterflies: Ways to Include Children with Disabilities, 3137
Center for Community Inclusion (CCI): Maine's University Center for Excellence, 4575
Devereux Mapleton, 5861
Devereux Massachusetts, 5726
Devereux Santa Barbara, 5548
Disabled and Their Parents: A Counseling Challenge, 3745
General Guidelines for Providers of Psychological Services, 3750
Idaho Council: International Reading Assocation, 2771
Inclusion Series, 3545
Inclusion: An Essential Guide for the Paraprofessional, 3213, 3859
Institute for Community Inclusion (ICI), 4638
Learning Difficulties and Emotional Problems, 3225
Making School Inclusion Work, 3876
Social-Emotional Dimension Scale, 5987
Southern Adventist University, 5283
Take Part Art, 3907

Infancy

New J er sey Pr ograms for Infants and Toddle rs with Disabilities: Early Inter vention System, 2469
Programs for Infants and Toddlers with Disabilities, 2490
Tips for Teaching Infants & Toddlers, 918, 1067
www.babycenter.com, 3605

Information Resources

A Human Development View of Learning Disabilities: From Theory to Practice, 3769
American Heritage Children's Dictionary, 644
BOSC Books on Special Children, 3412
Bethany House Publishers, 3413
Center Work, 3795
Change Agent, 6139
Charles C Thomas Publisher, 3417
Complete Learning Disabilities Handbook, 3805
How to Organize Your Child and Save Your Sanity, 3202
Including Students with Severe and Multiple Disabilities in Typical Classrooms, 3856
Learning Company, 2058
Learning Disabilities Association of Texas Newsletter, 3385
Learning Disabilities: Information and Resources, 3870
National Bible Association, 3447
National Dissemination Center for Children with Disabilities, 111
National Resources, 3323
Northwest Media, 3448
Questions to Aid in Selecting an Appropria te College Program for LD, 4009
Reader's Digest Partners for Sight Foundat ion, 3453
Scholastic, 2064
Sunburst Communications, 2065
Thomas Nelson Publishers, 3460
Thomas T Beeler, Publisher, 3461
Thorndike Press, 3462
Transaction Publishers, 3463
Underachieving Gifted, 3342
www.abcparenting.com, 3598
www.childparenting.about.com, 3608
www.disabilityresources.org, 3610
www.hood.edu/seri/serihome.htm, 3623
www.ldresources.com, 3633
www.wrightlaw.com, 3649

Integration

Division on Career Development, 67, 6125
Inclusion: 450 Strategies for Success, 3211, 3857
Michigan Developmental Disabilities Counci l, 2394
Minnesota Access Services, 238
Regular Lives, 3562
South Dakota Council on Developmental Disabilities, 2568
Winston Preparatory School, 5828

International Associations

Inter national Reading Association Newspaper: Reading Today, 366
International Reading Association Newspape r: Reading Today, 3380
International Summerstays, 2157
Lisle Fellowship, 2158
People to People International, 2161
United States Information Agency, 2162
World Experience, 2163
www.familyvillage.wisc.edu, 3616

Intervention

Academic Skills Problems Workbook, 3772
Accessing Programs for Infants, Toddlers and Preschoolers, 3305
Behavior Change in the Classroom: Self- Management Interventions, 3975
Bridges to Reading, 3141
Brief Intervention for School Problems: Collaborating for Practical Solutions, 3793
Child Who is Ignored: Module 6, 3528
Connecticut Center for Children and Families, 5584

Job/Vocational Resources

www.petersons.com, 3644

Keyboards

Controlpad 24, 1607
IntelliKeys, 1618
Keyboarding Skills, 1326
Large Print Keyboard, 1620
Large Print Lower Case Labels, 1621
QuicKeys, 1628
Talking Typer, 1634
Type-It, 1511
Unicorn Expanded Keyboard, 1639
Unicorn Smart Keyboard, 1640
Universal Numeric Keypad, 1641

Kits

A Knock at the Door, 1299
A World So Different, 1300
American Government Today: Steadwell, 1301
Animals and Their Homes CD-ROM, 1198
Animals in Their World CD-ROM, 1199
Animals of the Rain Forest: Steadwell, 1081
Basic Essentials of Mathematics, 933
Book Reports Plus, 1086
Bridges to Reading Comprehension, 1087
Broccoli-Flavored Bubble Gum, 1239
Careers, 1088
Case of the Crooked Candles, 1242
Changes Around Us CD-ROM, 859, 2008, 2103
City Creek Press, 3418
Decimals: Concepts & Problem-Solving, 946
Deep in the Rain Forest, 1201
Dive to the Ocean Deep: Voyages of Exploration and Discovery, 1202
ESPA Math Practice Tests D, 947
ESPA Success in Language Arts Literacy, 666
ESPA Success in Mathematics, 948
Estimation, 952
Experiences with Writing Styles, 1324, 1462
Explorers & Exploration: Steadwell, 1309
Expressway to Reading, 1104
Family Literacy Package, 1035
Famous African Americans, 677
Figurative Language, 678
First Biographies, 1310
Focus on Listening, 681
Focus on Math, 954
Fractions: Concepts & Problem-Solving, 958
GEPA Success in Language Arts Literacy and Mathematics, 684, 960
Gander Publishing, 3686
Geometry for Primary Grades, 961
Get the Story! City News: Country News CD-ROM, 685
Grade Level Math, 963
Great Series, 1106
HSPA Success in Language Art Literacy, 697
Harcourt Brace: The Science Book of...., 1203
Health, 875
High Interest Nonfiction, 1108
High Interest Nonfiction for Primary Grades, 1109
High Interest Sports, 1258
Higher Scores on Math Standardized Tests, 969
Intermediate Geometry, 974
Introduction to Journal Writing, 1478
Keys to Excellence in Integrated Language Arts, 710
Language Arts Handbook, 713
Language Exercises, 714
Language Handbooks, 715
Language Practice, 716
Learning 100 Computerized Reading Skills, 1119

Learning 100 Computerized Reading Skills: Inventory, 1120
Learning 100 Go Books, 1121
Learning 100 Language Clues Software, 1122
Learning 100 Language Clues Vocabulary and Spelling, 720
Learning 100 System, 1123
Learning 100 Thinking Strategies Series, 721
Learning 100 Write and Read, 1124
Learning 100 Writing Strategies, 1481
Life Cycles, 1207
Mastering Math, 978
Math Assessment System, 979
Math Detectives, 980
Math Enrichment, 981
Mathematics Skills Books, 983
Measurement: Practical Applications, 986
Middle School Geometry: Basic Concepts, 988
Middle School Language Arts, 735
Middle School Math, 989
Middle School Writing: Expository Writing, 1489
Multiplication & Division, 993
New Way: Learning with Literature, 1135
Our Universe: Steadwell, 1209
Pair-It Books: Early Emergent Stage 1, 746
Pair-It Books: Early Emergent Stage 1 in Spanish, 747
Pair-It Books: Early Emergent Stage 2, 748
Pair-It Books: Early Emergent Stage 2 in Spanish, 749
Pair-It Books: Early Fluency Stage 3, 750
Pair-It Books: Early Skills, 751
Pair-It Books: Fluency Stage 4, 752
Pair-It Books: Proficiency Stage 5, 753
Pair-It Books: Transition Stage 2-3, 754
Patterns Across the Curriculum, 755, 998, 1210, 1268, 1315
PhonicsMart CD-ROM, 757
Portfolio Assessment Teacher's Guide, 6034
Prehistoric Creaures Then & Now: Steadwell, 1143, 1211, 1316
Preschool, 1053
Problemas y mas, 1000
Problems Plus Levels B-H, 1001
Racing Through Time on a Flying Machine, 1145
Reading Assessment System, 5961, 6048
Reading Comprehension Series, 1153
Reading Power Modules Books, 1156, 2094
Reading Power Modules Software, 1157
Reading Readiness, 1158
Real World Situations, 895
Report Writing, 1499
Science Showtime! Videos, 3489
Short Classics, 1170
Skills Assessments, 6025, 6050, 6091
Soaring Scores AIMS Mathematics, 1007
Soaring Scores CTB: TerraNova Reading and Language Arts, 789, 1171
Soaring Scores in Integrated Language Arts, 790
Soaring Scores in Math Assessment, 1008
Soaring Scores on the CMT in Mathematics & Soaring Scores on the CAPT in Mathematics, 1009
Soaring Scores on the CSAP Mathematics Assessment, 1010
Soaring Scores on the ISAT Mathematics, 1011
Soaring Scores on the ISAT Reading and Writing, 1172, 1501
Soaring Scores on the MEAP Math Test, 1012
Soaring Scores on the NYS English Language Arts Assessment, 792
Soaring on the MCAS in English Language Arts, 793
Spelling: A Thematic Content-Area Approach Reproducibles, 809
Statistics & Probability, 1016
Strategies for Problem-Solving, 903, 1018
Strategies for Success in Mathematics, 1019
Strategies for Success in Writing, 1506
Take Me Home Pair-It Books, 1182
Take Off With..., 1021
Taking Your Camera To...Steadwell, 1183
Target Spelling, 909
Teaching Phonics: Staff Development Book, 825

Language Skills

Leadership

Legal Issues

Client Assistance Program (CAP): Iowa Division of Persons with Disabilities, 2329

Client Assistance Program (CAP): Kentucky Division of Persons with Disabilities, 2352

Client Assistance Program (CAP): Maryland Division of Persons with Disabilities, 2263, 2372

Client Assistance Program (CAP): Massachusetts Division of Persons with Disabilities, 2379

Client Assistance Program (CAP): Michigan Department of Persons with Disabilities, 2391

Client Assistance Program (CAP): Mississippi Division of Persons with Disabilities, 2406

Client Assistance Program (CAP): Nevada Division of Persons with Disability, 2438

Client Assistance Program (CAP): North Carolina Division of Persons with Disabilities, 2497

Client Assistance Program (CAP): Shreveport Division of Persons with Disabilities, 2359

Client Assistance Program (CAP): District of Columbia, 2270

Client Assistance Program (CAP): Louisiana HDQS Division of Persons with Disabilities, 2360

Client Assistance Program (CAP): Ohio Divi sion, 2511

Client Assistance Program (CAP): Oklahoma Division, 2522

Client Assistance Program (CAP): Pennsylva nia Division, 2539

Client Assistance Program (CAP): South Dak ota Division, 2566

Client Assistance Program (CAP): Washingto n Division, 2625

Client Assistance Program (CAP): West Virg inia Division, 2638

Client Assistance Program (CAP): Wyoming D ivision, 2655

Colorado Civil Rights Division, 2242

Disability Rights Center, 153

ED Law Center, 7

General Information about Disabilities, 3317

Home School Legal Defense Association, 9

IDEA Amendments, 3319

Kansas Advocacy & Protective Services, 218

Legal Rights of Persons with Disabilities: An Analysis of Federal Law, 3097

Legal Services for Children, 10

Minnesota Disability Law Center, 239

Montana Department of Labor & Industry, 2426

National Association for Community Mediati on, 11

National Center for Youth Law, 13

National Council of Juvenile and Family Court Judges (NCJFCJ), 14

Nevada Bureau of Disability Adjudication, 2440

Nevada Governor's Council on Rehabilitatio n & Employment of People with Disabilities, 2445, 6306

North Carolina Office of Administrative Hearings: Civil Rights Division, 2502

Office of Personnel Management, 2182

Office of Program Operations: US Departmen t of Education, 2183

Ohio Civil Rights Commission, 2515

Oklahoma Disability Law Center, 2524

Pennsylcania Center for Disability Law and Policy, 300

Procedural Due Process, 3103

Public Interest Law Center of Philadelphia, 15

Public Law 94-142: An Overview, 3104

So You're Going to a Hearing: Preparing for Public Law 94-142, 3108

Statutes, Regulations and Case Law Protecting Disabled Individuals, 3112

Test Accommodations for Students with Disabilities, 3917

Texas Department of Criminal Justice, 2587

Texas Planning Council for Developmental Disabilities, 2590

University Legal Services: Client Assistance Program, 183

Vermont Disability Law Project, 2613

Libraries

DCE-LVA Vir ginia Institutions, 2995

Highlands Educational Literacy Program, 2996

Idaho State Library, 2773

Illinois Library Association, 2777

Kansas Laubach Literacy Action, 2806

Literacy Volunteers of America: Cass County, 2788

Literacy Volunteers of America: Forsyth County, 2761

Literacy Volunteers of America: Metropolit an Atlanta, 2762

Literacy Volunteers of America: Sanilac Council, 2837

Literacy Volunteers of America: Tift Count y, 2763

Literacy Volunteers of America: Troup County, 2764

Literacy Volunteers of America: White County, 2789

National Library Services for the Blind and Physically Handicapped, 2175

Oregon State Library, 2916

Rhode Island Department of State Library Services, 2933

Sign Songs: Fun Songs to Sign and Sing, 3564

Tennessee State Library and Archives, 2957

Weslaco Public Library, 2980

www.ala.org/roads, 3601

Listening Skills

ADHD, 339, 3506

Earobics Step 1 Home Version, 1097, 1361

Earobics Step 1 Specialist/Clinician Version, 1098

Earobics Step 2 Home Version, 1362

Earobics Step 2 Specialist-Clinician Versi on, 1363

Earobics for Adolescents & Adults Home Version, 1099

Earobics for Adolescents & Adults Speciali st/Clinician Version, 1100

Effective Listening, 865

Joy of Listening, 3977

Listening and Speaking for Job and Persona l Use, 725

Responding to Oral Directions, 896

Literacy

ALL Points Bulletin: Department of Education, 2697

ALL Points Bulletin: Department of Educati on, 3367

Academic Institute, 2661

Adult Basic Education, 2654

Adult Center at PAL: Curry College, 2827, 5720

Adult Education, 6191

Adult Education Division of the Arizona Department of Education, 2704

Adult Education Office: Idaho Department of Education, 2296

Adult Education Services, 6360

Adult Education Team, 2365

Adult Literacy Council of the Tom Green Co unty, 2958

Adults with Learning Problems, 3511

Alaska Literacy Program, 2701

American Literacy Council, 2663

Arkansas Adult Learning Resource Center, 2707

Arkansas Literacy Council: Laubach Literac y Action, 2708

BRIGANCE Readiness: Strategies and Practice, 6038

Blue Ridge Literacy Council, 2885

Boars in Camelot, 2075

Buncombe County Literacy Council, 2886

Bureau of Adult Education & Training, 6205

Butte County Library Adult Reading Program, 2710

CLUES for Better Reading: Grade 1, 6039

CLUES for Better Reading: Grade 2-5, 6040

CLUES for Better Reading: Kindergaten, 6041

California Department of Education, 2712

California Literacy, 2713

Characteristics of the Learning Disabled Adult, 3522

Charlotte County Literacy Program, 2994

Circletime Tales Deluxe, 1753

Claiborne County Adult Reading Experience, 2949

Clearinghouse on Adult Education and Literacy, 2167

Colorado Adult Education and Family Litera cy, 2732

Commerce Library Literacy Program, 2959

Connections: A Journal of Adult Literacy, 3371

Cosmic Reading Journey, 1092, 2077

Creek County Literacy Program, 2905

New Hampshire Literacy Volunteers of Ameri ca, 2864
New York Literacy Assistance Center, 2880
New York Literacy Partners, 2881
North Dakota Adult Education and Literacy Resource Center, 2892
Northern Nevada Literacy Council, 2863
Northwest Oklahoma Literacy Council, 2907
Office of Adult Basic and Literacy Education, 2428
Office of Adult Education & Literacy, 6367
Ohio Adult Basic and Literacy Education, 2513
One-on-One Literacy Program: Wythe and Grayson Counties, 3007
Oregon Literacy, 2914
Pennsylvania Adult Literacy, 2923
Phonemic Awareness: Lessons, Activities and Games, 3485
Phonemic Awareness: Lessons, Activities & Games, 3294
Polar Express, 764, 1142, 2090
Price County Area Literacy Council, 3033
Professional Development, 3487
Project Advancing Literacy in North Caroli na, 2899
Project Literacy Douglas County, 2918
Readability Revisited: The New Dale-Chall Readability Formula, 3959
Reading Connections of North Carolina, 2891
Retell Stories, 772
Salem Literacy Council, 2919
Skyline Literacy Coalition, 3008
South Carolina Adult Literacy Educators, 2941
State Department of Adult Education, 2197, 2274, 2321, 2336, 2347, 2357, 2363, 2389, 2397, 2405, 2410, 2447, 2465, 2476, 2504, 2527, 2536, 2547, 2556, 2564, 2632
State Literacy Resource Center for Nebrask a: Institute for the Study of Adult Literacy, 2859
State of Delaware Adult and Community Education Network, 2742
Steuben County Literacy Coalition, 2791
TESOL Journal, 3392
Teach an Adult to Read, 3568
Teaching Adults with Learning Disabilities, 3494
Texas Center for Adult Literacy & Learning, 2977
Textbooks and the Students Who Can't Read Them, 3971
Three Rivers Literacy Alliance, 2792
Time for Teachers Online, 2102
Toccoa/Stephens County Literacy Council, 2766
Valencia County Literacy Council, 2877
Victoria Adult Literacy, 2979
Virginia Adult Education Centers for Profe ssional Development, 3009
Visual Processes in Reading and Reading Disabilities, 3972
West Virginia Adult Education Network, 3025
Western Wisconsin Literacy Services, 3034
Wisconsin Literacy Services, 3036
Word Parts, 1192
York County Literacy Council, 2926
3 Steps to Reading Success, 6037

Literature

Assessing the ERIC Resource Collection, 3308
Island Reading Journey, 701, 1114
Journal of Social and Clinical Psychology, 3655
Kaleidoscope, Exploring the Experience of Disability Through Literature and Fine Arts, 3722
LDA Georgia Newsletter, 369, 3383
Library Reproduction Service, 3438
Literary Cavalcade, 3398
National Association of Protection and Advocacy Systems (NAPAS), 12
Reflections Through the Looking Glass, 3761
Stone Soup: The Magazine by Young Writers and Artists, 3366
Write On! Plus: Literature Studies, 1519
Write On! Plus: Responding to Great Litera ture, 1521

Logic

Anne Carlsen Center for Children, 5837
Autism and the Family: Problems, Prospects and Coping with the Disorder, 3136
Behavior Rating Instrument for Autistic and Other Atypical Children, 5972
Beyond the ADD Myth, 3521
Camp Huntington, 530
Center for Learning, 5669
Children with Special Needs: A Resource Guide for Parents, Educators, Social Workers..., 3148
Diagnostic and Remedial Reading Clinic, 5893
DynaVox Dyna Vox Systems, 1610
Early Discoveries: Size and Logic, 1984
Enhancing Self-Concepts & Achievement of Mildly Handicapped Students, 3831
Freddy's Puzzling Adventures, 2010
How the Student with Hearing Loss Can Succeed in College, 3999
Indiana University: Kokomo, 4458
Kayne-ERAS Center, 5554
Koala Club News, 3361
Ladders to Literacy: A Kindergarten Activity Book, 3221
Ladders to Literacy: A Preschool Activity Book, 3222
Learning Center of Charlottesville, 5924
Logo Plus, 1718
Marina Psychological Services, 5555
Parenting Children with Special Needs, 3248
Pathway School, 5871
Problem Solving, 2020
Revised Behavior Problem Checklist, 5983
School Psychology Quarterly: Official Journal of Div. 16 of the American Psychological Assoc, 3657
Scrambled Eggs, 2022
Summit Travel Program, 553
Switzer Center, 5571
Teaching Students Through Their Individual Learning Styles, 3498
To Teach a Dyslexic, 3920
University of California: San Francisco, 4195

Mainstreaming

Ability Magazine, 6134
Att-P'tach Special Education Program, 5665
Camp-I-Can, 566
Hannah More School, 5713
Inclusion: An Annotated Bibliography, 3858
Least Restrictive Environment, 3095
MAC Mainstreaming at Camp, 544
Mainstream, 6128
Mainstreaming Exceptional Students: A Guide for Classroom Teachers, 3875
National Council on Independent Living Programs, 108
Office of State Coordinator of Vocational Education for Students with Disabilities, 6318
Promote Real Independence for Disabled & Elderly Foundation, 126
Purposeful Integration: Inherently Equal, 3105

Matching

Classification Series, 2042
Early and Advanced Switch Games, 1988
Educational Advisory Group, 71, 2673
Familiar Things, 1365
Family Fun, 1856
Learn to Match, 1786
Let's Go Shopping I, 1873
Let's Go Shopping II: Clothes & Pets, 1874
Multi-Scan, 1725
Occupations, 1881
Padded Food, 1805

Scan It-Switch It, 1630
Seasons, 1897
Seek and Find, 1731
Son of Seek and Find, 1733
Sound Match, 1820
Switch It-Change It, 1900
Tea Party, 1901

Mathematics

Access to Math, 1907
AfterMath Series, 6019
Boars 1, 2, 3! Counting with the Boars, 1916
Colored Wooden Counting Cubes, 1354
Concert Tour Entrepreneur, 942, 1924
ENRIGHT Computation Series, 6020
Fast-Track Fractions, 1941
Figure It Out: Thinking Like a Math Problem Solver, 6021
Fraction Fairy Tales with the Boars, 1944
Fraction Fuel-Up, 1945
Funny Monster for Tea, 959
Get Up and Go!, 962, 1947
Getting Ready for Algebra, 6022
Hey, Taxi!, 1949
Hidden Treasures of Al-Jabr, 967
Hot Dog Stand: The Works, 970
Ice Cream Truck, 973, 2013
Introduction to Patterns, 975
Math and the Learning Disabled Student: A Practical Guide for Accommodations, 3946
Mirror Symmetry, 992
Penny Pot, 999
See Me Subtract, 1169
Shape Up!, 1005, 1975
Splish Splash Math, 1015, 1977
Strategic Math Series, 1017
Sunbuddy Math Playhouse, 1020
Teaching Mathematics to Students with Learning Disabilities, 3948
Ten Tricky Tiles, 1022
Third and Fourth Grade Math Competencies, 1978
Winning at Math: Your Guide to Learning Mathematics Through Successful Study Skills, 3299
3 Steps to Math Success, 6018
2+2, 1906

Maturity

Goodenough-Harris Drawing Test, 6001

Memorization Skills

Memory Fun!, 987
Memory I, 1797
Memory Match, 2015
Memory: A First Step in Problem Solving, 2016
Remembering Numbers and Letters, 1895
Sequencing Fun!, 1004, 1815
Teaching Students Ways to Remember, 3911
Test of Memory and Learning (TOMAL), 6015
Working Memory and Severe Learning Difficulties, 3925

Motivation

A Mind of Your Own, 3503
Big: Calc, 1915
Dr. Peet's Picture Writer, 2133
Faking It: A Look into the Mind of a Creative Learner, 3046
Learning Problems & Learning Disabilities: Moving Forward, 3874
Motivation to Learn: How Parents and Teachers Can Help, 3557
You Don't Outgrow It: Living with Learning Disabilities, 3053

Motor Development

Big-Little Pegboard Set, 1347
Children's Developmental Clinic, 5707
Early Screening Inventory: Revised, 1032
Indy Reads: Indianapolis/Marion County Public Library, 2787
Language and the Retarded Child, 3547
Magnetic Fun, 1386
Mouth Madness, 737, 1051
Nashville READ, 2951
North Dakota Reading Association, 2897
Peabody Developmental Motor Scales-2, 891, 6115
People's Learning Center of Seattle, 3016
Preschool Motor Speech Evaluation & Intervention, 765
Preschool Motor Speech Evaluation & Intervention, 1054, 6086, 6117
REACH-UP Program: Department of Social Welfare, 2605
Swallow Right, 905
Test of Gross Motor Development, 6120
Vermont REACH-UP Program, 2616, 2991
Wikki Stix-Neon & Primary, 1426

Multicultural Education

Activities for a Diverse Classroom: Connecting Students, 1229
System of Multicultural Pluralistic Assessment (SOMPA), 5988
TESOL Quarterly, 3394

Multisensory Education

Journal of Learning Disabilities, 3690
Specialized Program Individualizing Reading Excellence (SPIRE), 1177
Why Wait for a Criterion of Failure?, 3973

Music

Arts Express, 3472
BUSY BOX Activity Centers, 1343
Camp Friendship, 510
Camp Lark, 430
Camp Waban, 480
Early Music Skills, 1987
If You're Happy and You Know It, 1991
Imagination Express: Castle, 2117
Imagination Express: Ocean, 2119
Incredible Adventures of Quentin, 1715
Kiwanis Easter Seal Day Camp, 438
Maplebrook School's Summer Program, 545
Music Section: National Library Service for the Blind and Physically Handicapped, 3445
Note Speller, 1726
Print Shop Graphics Library: Disk 2, 1892
That's Life Picture Stories, 911
Thinkin' Things: All Around Frippletown, 2029
Thinkin' Things: Collection 1, 2030
Thinkin' Things: Collection 2, 2031
Thinkin' Things: Collection 3, 2032
Thinkin' Things: Galactic Brain Benders, 2033
Thinkin' Things: Sky Island Mysteries, 2034
Thinkin' Things: Toony the Loon's Lagoon, 2035
Tune It II: Music Pitch Matcher, 1737
Very Special Arts (VSA), 140
Whistle Set, 1425
Working with Visually Impaired Young Students: A Curriculum Guide for 3 to 5 Year-Olds, 3926
YMCA: Valley-Shore, 446

Neurogical Disorders

Care of the Neurologically Handicapped Child, 3144
Developmental Disability Center of New York, 265

May Institute, 5737
The Vanguard School, 5876

Newsletters

Division for Learning Disabilities, 65
Family Resource Associates, 5777
Mountain Plains Regional Resource Center, 5914
NICHCY News Digest, 3353
New Directions, 3098
Special-Needs Reading List, 3268
www.parentsplace.com, 3642

Nutrition

Can What a Child Eats Make Him Dull, Stupid or Hyperactive?, 3309
Pick a Meal, 1888

Occupational Therapy

American Journal of Occupational Therapy, 3660
American Occupational Therapy Association, 32
Center for Speech and Language Disorders, 5670
Centreville School, 5617
Cincinnati Occupational Therapy Institute for Services and Study, 5842
Employment Development Department, 6200
Huntingdon County PRIDE, 298
Miriam School, 5759
Vocational School Manual, 4013
Wheeler Clinic, 5613

Pathology

ASHA Leader, 3718
American Journal of Speech-Language Pathology: Clinical Practice, 3719
Annals of Otology, Rhinology and Laryngology, 3662
Clinical Interview: A Guide for Speech-Language Pathologists/Audiologists, 3927

Pediatrics

American Academy of Pediatrics National Headquarters, 20

Peer Programs

Group for the Independent Learning Disabled (GILD), 5712

Perception Skills

Building Perspective, 936, 1918
Building Perspective Deluxe, 937, 1919
Maze Book, 1388
PAVE: Perceptual Accuracy, 1883
Parquetry Blocks & Pattern Cards, 1392
Shape and Color Sorter, 1408
Shapes Within Shapes, 1006
Spatial Relationships, 1013
Spatial Sense CD-ROM, 1014, 1976
Switch It-See It, 1734
Therapro, 1339
Workbook for Cognitive Skills, 921
Workbook for Memory Skills, 922

Pets

KIND News Sr: Kids in Nature's Defense, 3360
National Association for Humane and Environmental Education, 3363

Phonics

CLUES for Phonemic Awareness, 6071
Clues to Meaning, 1090
Common Ground: Whole Language & Phonics Working Together, 3151
First Phonics, 679, 1767
High Noon Books, 1110, 3432
I Can See 1, 2, 3, 972
I Can See the ABC's, 1112
Key Words, 1779
Level III - Phonics Based Reading: Grades 1, 2 & 3, 1789
Level III: Phonics Based Reading-Grades 1, 2 & 3, 2084
More Primary Phonics, 1133
My First Phonics Book, 738
Phonemic Awareness: The Sounds of Reading, 1139, 3561
Phonic Ear Auditory Trainers, 1627
Phonic Remedial Reading Lessons, 3956
Phonology and Reading Disability, 3957
Phonology: Software, 761, 1396, 1806
Primary Phonics, 1144
Python Path Phonics Word Families, 768, 1808
Reading Who? Reading You!, 1160, 2097
Sentence Master: Level 1, 2, 3, 4, 2099
Simon Sounds It Out, 2100
Success Stories 1, 2, 1181
Warmups and Workouts, 839, 1190

Physical Education

Adapted Physical Education for Students, 3776
Camp Easter Seals East, 611
ECLC of New Jersey, 5775
Journal of Physical Education, Recreation and Dance, 3381
Los Angeles School of Gymnastics Day Camp, 421
Squirrel Hollow, 456
The Prentice School, 5573
Wisconsin Elk/Easter Seals Respite Camp, 634

Play Therapy

Building Healthy Minds, 3142
Children's Cabinet, 1351
Deal Me In: The Use of Playing Cards in Learning and Teaching, 3815
Flagship Carpets, 1367
Link N' Learn Color Rings, 1384
New Language of Toys, 3242

Program Planning

Adventure Learning Center at Eagle Village, 501
Alpine Scout Camp, 519
Assessment: The Special Educator's Role, 3783
Bethel Mennonite Camp, 473
Bike Farm Summer Camp, 628
Camp Agape Pioneer Retreat Center, 527
Camp Brosend: Brosend Ministries, 467
Camp Calumet Lutheran, 515
Camp Cheerful: Achievement Center for Children, 560
Camp Chi Rho, 508
Camp Discovery Tennessee Jaycees Foundation, 600
Camp Easter Seals West, 612, 621
Camp Fairlee Manor, 481
Camp Frog Hollow, 1702
Camp HASC, 529
Camp Half Moon for Boys & Girls, 484
Camp Happiness at Corde Campus, 561
Camp Happiness at St. Augustine, 562
Camp Happiness at St. Joseph Center, 563
Camp Hebron, 584
Camp Hemlocks Easter Seals, 428

Public Awareness & Interest

Puzzles

Recognition Skills

Rehabilitation

Remediation

Research

Resource Centers

School Administration

Science

Secondary Education

Self-Advocacy

Self-Esteem

Sensory Integration

Sound Recognition

Special Education

Understanding & Management of Health Problems in Schools, 3922
Vermont Special Education, 2617
Virginia Council of Administrators of Spec ial Education, 3010
Vocational & Educational Services for Indi viduals with Disabilities, 2495
www.dmoz.org, 3612
www.parentpals.com, 3641
3 R'S for Special Education: Rights, Resou rces, Results, 3502

Speech Skills

Many Voices of Paws, 732
Straight Speech, 812

Spelling

Boppie's Great Word Chase, 1750
Camp Dunnabeck Kildonan School, 528
Elementary Spelling Ace ES-90, 673
English 4-Pack, 1764
Fundamentals of Reading Success, 3479
Gillingham Manual, 3955
Hamlin Robinson School, 5939
Handmade Alphabet, 3066
INSPECT: A Strategy for Finding and Correcting Spelling Errors, 1325
If it is to Be, It is Up to Me to Do it!, 3207
Individualized Keyboarding: Improving Reading/Spelling Skills via Keyboard, 1777
Kildonan School, 4930, 5813
Lab School of Washington, 5623
Let's Read, 1127
Let's Write Right: Teacher's Edition, 1483
Megawords, 1131
Monitoring Basic Skills Progress, 6005
Multisensory Teaching Approach, 3935
Patterns of English Spelling, 1138
Preventing Academic Failure, 3884
Raskob Learning Institute and Day School, 4157
Read, Write and Type Learning System, 1809, 2093, 2143
Sensible Speller: Talking APH Edition, 1814
Sequential Spelling 1-7 with Student Response Book, 786
Speaking Speller, 1821
Spell a Word, 1822
Spell-a-Saurus, 1823
Spelling Ace, 1825
Spelling Mastery, 1826
Spelling Workbook Video, 3491
Spelling for Job and Personal Use, 1504
Teaching Reading to Children with Down Syndrome, 3280
Teaching Spelling Workshop, 1589
Test of Written Spelling, 6103
ThemeWeavers: Animals Activity Kit, 914
ThemeWeavers: Nature Activity Kit, 915, 1216
Thinking and Learning Connection, 139, 2696
Turning Point School, 5540
Worthmore Academy, 471

Strategies

100% Concepts: Inter mediate, 635
100% Concepts: Primary, 636
100% Grammar, 637, 1431
100% Grammar LITE, 638, 1432
100% Punctuation, 1433
100% Punctuation LITE, 1434
100% Reading: 2-Book Intermediate Set, 1071
100% Reading: 3-Book Primary Set, 1072
100% Reading: Decoding and Word Recognitio n: 5-book set, 1073
100% Reading: Intermediate Book 1, 1074
100% Reading: Intermediate Book 2, 1075

100% Reading: Primary Book 1, 1076
100% Reading: Primary Book 2, 1077
100% Reading: Primary Book 3, 1078
100% Spelling, 1435
100% Story Writing, 1436
100% Vocabulary: Intermediate, 639
100% Vocabulary: Primary, 640
100% Writing 4-book Set, 1437
100% Writing: Comparison and Contrast, 1438
100% Writing: Exposition, 1439
100% Writing: Narration, 1440
100% Writing: Persuasion, 1441
125 Vocabulary Builders, 641
125 Ways to Be a Better Reader, 1079
125 Ways to Be a Better Student, 1321
125 Ways to Be a Better Test-Taker, 1322
125 Ways to Be a Better Writer, 1442
125 Writing Projects, 1443
ADA Clearinghouse and Resource Center, 1
ADD and Adults: Strategies for Success, 333
ADHD in the Classroom: Strategies for Teachers, 3508
Academic Skills Problems: Direct Assessmen t and Intervention, 2nd Edition, 3773
Artic Shuffle, 646, 1027, 1341
ArticBURST Articulation Practice for S, R, Ch, and Sh, 648, 1342
Auditory Processes, 3786
Autism & PDD: Primary Social Skills Lesson s, 1235
Autism & PPD: Adolescent Social Skills Lessons, 1236
Autism & PPD: Adolescent Social Skills Les sons-Health & Hygiene, 1237
Autism & PPD: Concept Development, 650
Autism & PPD: Pictured Stories and Languag e Activities, 651
BRIGANCE Word Analysis: Strategies and Practice, 6029
Barnaby's Burrow: An Auditory Processing Game, 855, 1344
Behavior Management Applications for Teachers and Parents, 3138
Ben Bronz Academy, 4240
Blend It! End It!, 1348, 1445
Bozons' Quest, 1846
Brainopoly: A Thinking Game, 857, 1349
Central Auditory Processing Kit, 657
Child Management, 3523
Child Who Appears Aloof: Module 5, 3524
Child Who is Rejected: Module 7, 3529
Children with ADD: A Shared Responsibility, 350
Closer Look: Perspectives & Reflections on College Students with LD, 3044
Cognitive Strategy Instruction That Really Improves Children's Performance, 3802
Cognitive Strategy Instruction for Middle & High Schools, 861
Collaborative Practices for Educators Strategies for Effective Communication, 3803
Complete Clinical Dysphagia Evaluation: Test Forms, 5995
Complete Oral-Motor Program for Articulation: Book Only, 658
Complete Oral-Motor Program for Articulation, 659
Complete Oral-Motor Program for Articulati on: Refill Kit, 660
Computer Accommodation Lab, 1672
Cooperative Learning and Strategies for Inclusion, 3807
Cooperative Thinking Strategies, 1243
Crash Course for Study Skills, 1323
Creative Mind Workshop: Making Magic with Children and Art, 1555
Curriculum Models and Strategies for Educating Individuals with Disabilities, 3811
Curriculum Vocabulary Game, 663
Daily Starters: Quote of the Day, 664, 1453
Decoding Games, 1095, 1358
Definition Play by Play, 864, 1359
Designing Clinical Strategies for Language Impaired Children, 3477
Easy Does It for Fluency: Intermediat e, 671
Easy Does It for Fluency: Preschool/Primar y, 672
Edge Enterprises, 3421

Student Workshops

Support Groups

Surveys

Switches

Synthesizers

Tape Recorders

Technology

Indiana Institute on Disability and Community at Indiana University, 4452
InfoTech Newsletter, 3688
International Society for Technology in Education, 2051
Iowa Program for Assistive Technology, 215
Journal of Special Education Technology, 3695
Latest Technology for Young Children, 3548
Learning Independence Through Computers, 1681
Louisiana Assistive Technology Access Network, 2362
Main Office: Technology and Media, 4250
Massachusetts Assistive Technology Partnership (MATP), 2381
Michigan Assistive Technology: Michigan Rehabilitation Services, 2393, 2839
Michigan Technological University, 4699
Microsoft Corporation, 2059
MonTECH, 2425
Moving Forward, 90, 3351
National Early Childhood Technical Assistance Center, 112
National Technical Information Service, 2176
National Technology Center, 1682
New IDEA Amendments: Assistive Technology Devices and Services, 3099
New Jersey Family Resource Associates, 257
New Jersey Technology Assistive Resource Program, 6317
New Mexico Technology-Related Assistance Program, 2473
New York Office of Advocates: TRAID Project, 2483
Pennsylvania Initiative on Assistive Technology, 2543
Pennsylvania Institute of Technology, 5206
Project TECH, 1685
RESNA Technical Assistance Project, 1686
Reach Them All: Adapting Curriculum & Instruction with Technology in Inclusive Classrooms, 3888
Rehabilitation Engineering and Assistive Technology Society of North America (RESNA), 129
Resource Center for Literacy Technology & Parenting, 2940
Rose-Hulman Institute of Technology, 4467
SUNY Institute of Technology: Utica/Rome, 4964
Southwest Minnesota State University: Learning Resources, 4751
Special Education Technology: Classroom Applications, 3902
Suffolk University, 4662
TASH Annual Conference, 1586
Teaching Exceptional Children, 3716
Technology Access Center, 1690
Technology Access Foundation, 1691
Technology Access for Life Needs Project, 2537
Technology Assistance for Special Consumers, 1692
Technology Utilization Program, 1693
Technology and Media Division, 138
Technology and Persons with Disabilities Conference, 1590
Technology for Language and Learning, 1694
Technology in the Classroom Kit, 3499
Technology in the Classroom: Communication Module, 3914
Technology in the Classroom: Education Module, 3915
Technology in the Classroom: Positioning, Access and Mobility Module, 3916
TeleSensory, 1903
Tennessee Technology Access Project, 2579
Tidewater Center for Technology Access, 1695
US International Council on Disabilities Conference, 1592
University of California-Davis: Student Disability Resource Center, 4188
University of California: Los Angeles, 4192
University of Colorado at Boulder Disability Services, 4232
University of Colorado: Colorado Springs, 4233
Vermont Assistive Technology Project: Department of Aging and Disabilities, 2609, 2986
West Tennessee Special Technology Access Resource Center, 1696
Window-Eyes, 1646

Tourette Syndrome

Children with Tourette Syndrome, 3149

Training

125 Brain Games for Babies, 3118
A Decision Making Model for Occupational Therapy in the Public Schools, 3735
A Practical Approach to RSP: A Handbook for the Resource Specialist Program, 3771
Access Aware: Extending Your Reach to People with Disabilities, 3124
Access for All: Integrating Deaf, Hard of Hearing, and Hearing Preschoolers, 3949
Activating Children Through Technology (ACCT), 1657
Active Learning Series, 1227
Activities Unlimited, 1228
Activities of Daily Living: A Manual of Group Activities and Written Exercises, 852
Activity Schedules for Children with Autism: Teaching Independent Behavior, 1230
Adult and Employment Training: Virginia Department of Education, 2618
Advocates for Children of New York, 263, 5794
Alert Program With Songs for Self-Regulation, 1231
Alliance for Technology Access, 19, 6122
America's Jobline, 6123
American Art Therapy Association, 21
American Dance Therapy Association (ADTA), 31
An Introduction to How Does Your Engine Run?, 1232
Andy and His Yellow Frisbee, 1233
Animal Match-Ups, 1340
Arcade Adventure, 1600
Arkansas Disability Coalition, 5541
Art for All the Children: Approaches to Art Therapy for Children with Disabilities, 3781
Assistive Technology Network, 5627
Assistive Technology Resource Centers of Hawaii, 194
Auditory Processes: Revised Edition, 3787
Auditory Training, 3788
Autism Support Center: Northshore Arc, 2378
Avenues to Compliance, 3519
Baker Hall School, 5796
Best Practice Occupational Therapy: Community Service with Children and Families, 3741
Beyond Drill and Practice: Expanding the Computer Mainstream, 2038
Breakthroughs Manual: How to Reach Students with Autism, 1238
Brevard Learning Clinic, 5630
Bureau of Workforce Services, 6332
Business Currents, 6137
Busy Kids Movement, 1240
CAST, 1664
Callirobics: Advanced Exercises, 1446
Callirobics: Exercises for Adults, 1447
Callirobics: Handwriting Exercises to Music, 1448
Callirobics: Prewriting Skills with Music, 1449
Camp Horizons, 429
Captain's Log Cognitive Training System for Windows, 2007
Career Assessment and Placement Center Whittier Union High School District, 2230
Center for Alternative Learning, 5856
Center for Community, 2193, 5533
Center for Persons with Disabilities, 2595, 5362
Center on Disability Studies, University Affiliated Program: University of Hawaii, 4367
Centers for Independent Living Program: Rehabilitation Services Administration, 6218
Child Advocacy Center, 5840
Child Who Appears Anxious: Module 4, 3525
Child Who Dabbles: Module 3, 3526
Child Who Wanders: Module 2, 3527
Children with Cerebral Palsy: A Parent's Guide, 3147
Claris Corporation, 2041
Classroom Notetaker: How to Organize a Program Serving Students with Hearing Impairments, 3799

Transportation

Treatment

Eastern Associates Speech and Language Services, 5830
Elmcrest Schools, 5591
Emergence: Labeled Autistic, 3174
Full Circle Programs, 5552
Harmony Hill School, 5879
Heartspring School, 5695
Helping Your Hyperactive Child, 3197
Hyperactive Children Grown Up, 3205
Illinois Center for Autism, 5682
International Dyslexia Association Quarterly Newsletter: Perspectives, 3376
International Dyslexia Association: National Headquarters, 83, 2677
Interventions for ADHD: Treatment in Developmental Context, 3217
Journal of Speech, Language, and Hearing Research, 3721
Julia Dyckman Andrus Memorial, 5810
Kennedy Krieger Institute for Handicapped Children, 5714
Klingberg Family Centers, 5597
Lorraine D Foster Day School, 5601
Mental Health Report, 3706
Millcreek Schools, 5755
NAWA Academy, 5557
Natchaug Hospital School Program, 5603
New England Center for Children, 5738
Pines Residential Treatment Center, 5932
Providence Speech and Hearing Center, 5562, 5960
Saint Francis Home for Children: Highland Heights, 5607
Sensory Integration & Vision Therapy Specialists, 5717
Sensory Integration & Vision Therapy Specialists, 5718
Speech Pathology Service, 5761
Star Ranch, 5910
Stuttering Severity Instrument for Children and Adults, 6094
Treatment of Children's Grammatical Impairments in Naturalistic Context, 3571
Vitam Center, 5611
Waterford Country Schools, 5612

Visual Assistive Devices

AppleWorks Manuals: Special Editions, 1648
Benton Visual Retention Test: Fifth Edition, 6107
Braille 'n Speak Scholar, 1847
Braille' n Speak Classic, 1601, 2126
Compu-Lenz, 1604
Development Test of Visual Perception, 6109
Developmental Test of Visual Perception (DTVP-2), 6110
Genie Color TV, 1613
Home Row Indicators, 1615
National Association for Visually Handicapped, 3446
Opening Windows: A Talking and Tactile Tutorial for Microsoft Windows, 1655
Self-Adhesive Braille Keytop Labels, 1631
Ulverscroft Large Print Books, 3464
Updown Chair, 1294
VISTA, 1643
Xavier Society for the Blind, 3468
www.allaboutvision.com, 3602

Visual Discrimination

Associated Services for the Blind, 3411
Bureau of Services to the Blind & Visually Impaired, 6304
Commission for the Blind & Visually Handicapped, 6324
Comparison Kitchen, 1851
Educating Students Who Have Visual Impairments with Other Disabilities, 3170
Gremlin Hunt, 1770
I Can Read, 1111
Illinois Catholic Guild for the Blind, 200
Jewish Braille Institute of America, 3435
Lighthouse Low Vision Products, 1128

Lutheran Braille Workers: Sight Saving Division, 165
Michigan Commission for the Blind: Deafblind Unit, 6280
National Federation of the Blind, 114
Recording for the Blind & Dyslexic Learning Through Listening: Michigan Unit, 236
Recording for the Blind & Dyslexic of Metropolitan Washington, 182
Recording for the Blind & Dyslexic: Berkshire/Lenox/Williamstown, 232
Recording for the Blind & Dyslexic: Chicago Loop Studio & Administrative Offices, 205
Recording for the Blind & Dyslexic: Kentucky Chapter, 221
Recording for the Blind & Dyslexic: Lois C Klein Studio, 206
Recording for the Blind & Dyslexic: Santa Barbara Chapter, 168, 2726
Recording for the Blind and Dyslexic: Inland Empire-Orange County Unit, 169, 2727
Same or Different, 1813
Sliding Block, 2024
South Dakota Rehabilitation Center for the Blind, 6350
Vision and Learning Disabilities, 3924

Vocabulary

Activities for Dictionary Practice, 6056
Analogies 1, 2 & 3, 645
Bailey's Book House, 2072
Basic Signing Vocabulary Cards, 652
Basic Vocabulary: American Sign Language for Parents and Children, 3058
Bubblegum Machine, 1751
Bubbleland Word Discovery, 655
Carolina Picture Vocabulary Test, 656
Carroll School Summer Camp, 491
Christmas Bear, 3061
Connecting Reading and Writing with Vocabulary, 6073
Emergent Reader, 1101
Explode the Code, 1103
Following Directions: One and Two Level Commands, 1865
Funny Bunny and Sunny Bunny, 3064
Halloween Bear, 3065
High Frequency Vocabulary, 1771
I Can Read Charts, 3067
Language Learning Everywhere We Go, 3934
Language Master: MWD-640, 1785
Learning Disabilities Resources, 3437
My Action Book, 1802
Nordic Software, 2018
Old MacDonald's Farm, 1994
Once Upon a Time Volume II: Worlds of Enchantment, 2139
Once Upon a Time Volume III: Journey Through Time, 2140
Once Upon a Time Volume IV: Exploring Nature, 2141
PPVT-lll: Peabody Test-Picture Vocabulary Test, 6007
Peabody Picture Vocabulary Test: Third Edition, 6082
Pic Talk, 1887
Reading Comprehension in Varied Subject Matter, 1154
Reading Riddles with the Boars, 1810
Receptive One-Word Picture Vocabulary Test (ROWPVT-2000), 770
Roots, Prefixes & Suffixes, 1167, 2098
Scare Bear, 3076
Secondary Print Pack, 1898
See Me Add, 1168
Sight Words, 1817
Signs of the Times, 3938
Snowbear, 3079
Space Academy GX-1, 1212
Stanley Sticker Stories, 1827
Story of the USA, 1317
Talking Walls, 1214, 2112
Talking Walls: The Stories Continue, 1215, 2113
Test of Mathematical Abilities, 6026
Thinkin' Science ZAP, 916

The Complete Learning Disabilities Directory, 2004/05

Available Formats

Online Database

The Complete Learning Disabilities Directory is available in Print and in an Online Database. Subscribers to the **Online Database** can access their subscription via the Internet and do customized searches that instantly locate needed resources of information. It's never been faster or easier to locate just the right resource. Whether you're searching for Testing Materials or Schools or College Programs, the information you need is only a click away with **The Complete Learning Disabilities Directory – Online Database**.

Online Database (annual subscription): $195.00
Online Database & Print Directory combo: $280.00

Visit www.greyhouse.com and explore the subscription site free of charge or call (800) 562-2139 for more information.

Mailing List Information

This directory is available in mailing list form on mailing labels or diskettes. Call (800) 562-2139 to place an order or inquire about counts. There are a number of ways we can segment the database to meet your mailing list requirements.

Licensable Database on Disk

The database of this directory is available on diskette in an ASCII text file, delimited or fixed fielded. Call (800) 562-2139 for more details.

To preview any of our Directories Risk-Free for 30 days, call (800) 562-2139 or fax to (518) 789-0556

Sedgwick Press
Education Directories

Educators Resource Directory, 2003/04

Educators Resource Directory is a comprehensive resource that provides the educational professional with thousands of resources and statistical data for professional development. This directory saves hours of research time by providing immediate access to Associations & Organizations, Conferences & Trade Shows, Educational Research Centers, Employment Opportunities & Teaching Abroad, School Library Services, Scholarships, Financial Resources, Professional Consultants, Computer Software & Testing Resources and much more. Plus, this comprehensive directory also includes a section on Statistics and Rankings with over 100 tables, including statistics on Average Teacher Salaries, SAT/ACT scores, Revenues & Expenditures and more. These important statistics will allow the user to see how their school rates among others, make relocation decisions and so much more. In addition to the Entry & Publisher Index, Geographic Index and Web Sites Index, our editors have added a Subject & Grade Index to this 2003/04 edition – so now it's even quicker and easier to locate information. *Educators Resource Directory* will be a well-used addition to the reference collection of any school district, education department or public library.

"Recommended for all collections that serve elementary and secondary school professionals." –Choice

1,000 pages; Softcover ISBN 1-59237-002-0, $145.00 ◆ Online Database $195.00 ◆ Online Database & Directory Combo $280.00

Health Directories

The Complete Directory for People with Disabilities, 2004

A wealth of information, now in one comprehensive sourcebook. Completely updated for 2004, this edition contains more information than ever before, including thousands of new entries and enhancements to existing entries and thousands of additional web sites and e-mail addresses. This up-to-date directory is the most comprehensive resource available for people with disabilities, detailing Independent Living Centers, Rehabilitation Facilities, State & Federal Agencies, Associations, Support Groups, Periodicals & Books, Assistive Devices, Employment & Education Programs, Camps and Travel Groups. Each year, more libraries, schools, colleges, hospitals, rehabilitation centers and individuals add *The Complete Directory for People with Disabilities* to their collections, making sure that this information is readily available to the families, individuals and professionals who can benefit most from the amazing wealth of resources cataloged here.

"No other reference tool exists to meet the special needs of the disabled in one convenient resource for information." –Library Journal

1,200 pages; Softcover ISBN 1-59237-007-1, $165.00 ◆ Online Database $215.00 ◆ Online Database & Directory Combo $300.00

The Complete Mental Health Directory, 2004

This is the most comprehensive resource covering the field of behavioral health, with critical information for both the layman and the mental health professional. For the layman, this directory offers understandable descriptions of 25 Mental Health Disorders as well as detailed information on Associations, Media, Support Groups and Mental Health Facilities. For the professional, *The Complete Mental Health Directory* offers critical and comprehensive information on Managed Care Organizations, Information Systems, Government Agencies and Provider Organizations. This comprehensive volume of needed information will be widely used in any reference collection.

"… the strength of this directory is that it consolidates widely dispersed information into a single volume." –Booklist

800 pages; Softcover ISBN 1-59237-046-2, $165.00 ◆ Online Database $215.00 ◆ Online & Directory Combo $300.00

To preview any of our Directories Risk-Free for 30 days, call (800) 562-2139 or fax to (518) 789-0556

The Directory of Drug & Alcohol Residential Rehabilitation Facilities, 2004

This brand new directory is the first-ever resource to bring together, all in one place, data on the thousands of drug and alcohol residential rehabilitation facilities in the United States. *The Directory of Drug & Alcohol Residential Rehabilitation Facilities* covers over 6,000 facilities, with detailed contact information for each one, including mailing address, phone and fax numbers, email addresses and web sites, mission statement, type of treatment programs, cost, average length of stay, numbers of residents and counselors, accreditation, insurance plans accepted, type of environment, religious affiliation, education components and much more. It also contains a helpful chapter on General Resources that provides contact information for Associations, Print & Electronic Media, Support Groups and Conferences. Multiple indexes allow the user to pinpoint the facilities that meet very specific criteria. This time-saving tool is what so many counselors, parents and medical professionals have been asking for. *The Directory of Drug & Alcohol Residential Rehabilitation Facilities* will be a helpful tool in locating the right source for treatment for a wide range of individuals. This comprehensive directory will be an important acquisition for all reference collections: public and academic libraries, case managers, social workers, state agencies and many more.

"This is an excellent, much needed directory that fills an important gap..." –Booklist

1,000 pages; Softcover ISBN 1-59237-031-4, $165.00

The Complete Directory for People with Chronic Illness, 2003/04

Thousands of hours of research have gone into this completely updated 2003/04 edition – several new chapters have been added along with thousands of new entries and enhancements to existing entries. Plus, each chronic illness chapter has been reviewed by an medical expert in the field. This widely-hailed directory is structured around the 90 most prevalent chronic illnesses – from Asthma to Cancer to Wilson's Disease – and provides a comprehensive overview of the support services and information resources available for people diagnosed with a chronic illness. Each chronic illness has its own chapter and contains a brief description in layman's language, followed by important resources for National & Local Organizations, State Agencies, Newsletters, Books & Periodicals, Libraries & Research Centers, Support Groups & Hotlines, Web Sites and much more. This directory is an important resource for health care professionals, the collections of hospital and health care libraries, as well as an invaluable tool for people with a chronic illness and their support network.

"A must purchase for all hospital and health care libraries and is strongly recommended for all public library reference departments." –ARBA

1,200 pages; Softcover ISBN 1-930956-83-5, $165.00 ♦ Online Database $215.00 ♦ Online Database & Directory Combo $300.00

The Complete Directory for Pediatric Disorders, 2004/05

This important directory provides parents and caregivers with information about Pediatric Conditions, Disorders, Diseases and Disabilities, including Blood Disorders, Bone & Spinal Disorders, Brain Defects & Abnormalities, Chromosomal Disorders, Congenital Heart Defects, Movement Disorders, Neuromuscular Disorders and Pediatric Tumors & Cancers. This carefully written directory offers: understandable Descriptions of 15 major bodily systems; Descriptions of more than 200 Disorders and a Resources Section, detailing National Agencies & Associations, State Associations, Online Services, Libraries & Resource Centers, Research Centers, Support Groups & Hotlines, Camps, Books and Periodicals. This resource will provide immediate access to information crucial to families and caregivers when coping with children's illnesses.

"Recommended for public and consumer health libraries." –Library Journal

1,200 pages; Softcover ISBN 1-59237-045-4, $165.00 ♦ Online Database $215.00 ♦ Online Database & Directory Combo $300.00

The Complete Directory for People with Rare Disorders, 2002/03

This outstanding reference is produced in conjunction with the National Organization for Rare Disorders to provide comprehensive and needed access to important information on over 1,000 rare disorders, including Cancers and Muscular, Genetic and Blood Disorders. An informative Disorder Description is provided for each of the 1,100 disorders (rare Cancers and Muscular, Genetic and Blood Disorders) followed by information on National and State Organizations dealing with a particular disorder, Umbrella Organizations that cover a wide range of disorders, the Publications that can be useful when researching a disorder and the Government Agencies to contact. Detailed and up-to-date listings contain mailing address, phone and fax numbers, web sites and e-mail addresses along with a description. For quick, easy access to information, this directory contains two indexes: Entry Name Index and Acronym/Keyword Index along with an informative Guide for Rare Disorder Advocates. The Complete Directory for People with Rare Disorders will be an invaluable tool for the thousands of families that have been struck with a rare or "orphan" disease, who feel that they have no place to turn and will be a much-used addition to the reference collection of any public or academic library.

"Quick access to information... public libraries and hospital patient libraries will find this a useful resource in directing users to support groups or agencies dealing with a rare disorder." –Booklist

726 pages; Softcover ISBN 1-891482-18-1, $165.00

To preview any of our Directories Risk-Free for 30 days, call (800) 562-2139 or fax to (518) 789-0556

Sedgwick Press
Hospital & Health Plan Directories

The Directory of Hospital Personnel, 2004

The Directory of Hospital Personnel is the best resource you can have at your fingertips when researching or marketing a product or service to the hospital market. A "Who's Who" of the hospital universe, this directory puts you in touch with over 150,000 key decision-makers. With 100% verification of data you can rest assured that you will reach the right person with just one call. Every hospital in the U.S. is profiled, listed alphabetically by city within state. Plus, three easy-to-use, cross-referenced indexes put the facts at your fingertips faster and more easily than any other directory: Hospital Name Index, Bed Size Index and Personnel Index. *The Directory of Hospital Personnel* is the only complete source for key hospital decision-makers by name. Whether you want to define or restructure sales territories... locate hospitals with the purchasing power to accept your proposals... keep track of important contacts or colleagues... or find information on which insurance plans are accepted, *The Directory of Hospital Personnel* gives you the information you need – easily, efficiently, effectively and accurately.

"Recommended for college, university and medical libraries." -ARBA

2,500 pages; Softcover ISBN 1-59237-026-8 $275.00 ◆ Online Database $545.00 ◆ Online Database & Directory Combo, $650.00

The Directory of Health Care Group Purchasing Organizations, 2004

This comprehensive directory provides the important data you need to get in touch with over 1,000 Group Purchasing Organizations. By providing in-depth information on this growing market and its members, *The Directory of Health Care Group Purchasing Organizations* fills a major need for the most accurate and comprehensive information on over 1,000 GPOs – Mailing Address, Phone & Fax Numbers, E-mail Addresses, Key Contacts, Purchasing Agents, Group Descriptions, Membership Categorization, Standard Vendor Proposal Requirements, Membership Fees & Terms, Expanded Services, Total Member Beds & Outpatient Visits represented and more. Five Indexes provide a number of ways to locate the right GPO: Alphabetical Index, Expanded Services Index, Organization Type Index, Geographic Index and Member Institution Index. With its comprehensive and detailed information on each purchasing organization, *The Directory of Health Care Group Purchasing Organizations* is the go-to source for anyone looking to target this market.

"The information is clearly arranged and easy to access...recommended for those needing this very specialized information." –ARBA

1,000 pages; Softcover ISBN 1-59237-036-5, $325.00 ◆ Online Database, $650.00 ◆ Online Database & Directory Combo, $750.00

The HMO/PPO Directory, 2004

The HMO/PPO Directory is a comprehensive source that provides detailed information about Health Maintenance Organizations and Preferred Provider Organizations nationwide. This comprehensive directory details more information about more managed health care organizations than ever before. Over 1,100 HMOs, PPOs and affiliated companies are listed, arranged alphabetically by state. Detailed listings include Key Contact Information, Prescription Drug Benefits, Enrollment, Geographical Areas served, Affiliated Physicians & Hospitals, Federal Qualifications, Status, Year Founded, Managed Care Partners, Employer References, Fees & Payment Information and more. Plus, five years of historical information is included related to Revenues, Net Income, Medical Loss Ratios, Membership Enrollment and Number of Patient Complaints. Five easy-to-use, cross-referenced indexes will put this vast array of information at your fingertips immediately: HMO Index, PPO Index, Other Providers Index, Personnel Index and Enrollment Index. *The HMO/PPO Directory* provides the most comprehensive information on the most companies available on the market place today.

"Helpful to individuals requesting certain HMO/PPO issues such as co-payment costs, subscription costs and patient complaints. Individuals concerned (or those with questions) about their insurance may find this text to be of use to them." -ARBA

600 pages; Softcover ISBN 1-59237-022-5, $275.00 ◆ Online Database, $495.00 ◆ Online Database & Directory Combo, $600.00

The Directory of Independent Ambulatory Care Centers, 2002/03

This first edition of *The Directory of Independent Ambulatory Care Centers* pulls together a vast array of contact information for over 7,200 Ambulatory Surgery Centers, Ambulatory General and Urgent Care Clinics, and Diagnostic Imaging Centers that are not affiliated with a hospital or major medical center. Detailed listings include Mailing Address, Phone & Fax Numbers, E-mail and Web Site addresses, Contact Name and Phone Numbers of the Medical Director and other Key Executives and Purchasing Agents, Specialties & Services Offered, Year Founded, Numbers of Employees and Surgeons, Number of Operating Rooms, Number of Cases seen per year, Overnight Options, Contracted Services and much more. Listings are arranged by State, by Center Category and then alphabetically by Organization Name. Two indexes provide quick and easy access to this wealth of information: Entry Name Index and Specialty/Service Index. *The Directory of Independent Ambulatory Care Centers* is a must-have resource for anyone marketing a product or service to this important industry and will be an invaluable tool for those searching for a local care center that will meet their specific needs.

"A handy, well-organized resource that would be useful in medical center libraries and public libraries." –Choice

986 pages; Softcover ISBN 1-930956-90-8, $185.00 ◆ Online Database, $365.00 ◆ Online Database & Directory Combo, $450.00

To preview any of our Directories Risk-Free for 30 days, call (800) 562-2139 or fax to (518) 789-0556

Universal Reference Publications
Statistical & Demographic Reference Books

Profiles of America: Facts, Figures & Statistics for Every Populated Place in the United States

Profiles of America is the only source that pulls together, in one place, statistical, historical and descriptive information about every place in the United States in an easy-to-use format. This award winning reference set, now in its second edition, compiles statistics and data from over 20 different sources – the latest census information has been included along with more than nine brand new statistical topics. This Four-Volume Set details over 40,000 places, from the biggest metropolis to the smallest unincorporated hamlet, and provides statistical details and information on over 50 different topics including Geography, Climate, Population, Vital Statistics, Economy, Income, Taxes, Education, Housing, Health & Environment, Public Safety, Newspapers, Transportation, Presidential Election Results and Information Contacts or Chambers of Commerce. Profiles are arranged, for ease-of-use, by state and then by county. Each county begins with a County-Wide Overview and is followed by information for each Community in that particular county. The Community Profiles within the county are arranged alphabetically. *Profiles of America* is a virtual snapshot of America at your fingertips and a unique compilation of information that will be widely used in any reference collection.

A Library Journal Best Reference Book "An outstanding compilation." –Library Journal

10,000 pages; Four Volume Set; Softcover ISBN 1-891482-80-7, $595.00

The Hispanic Databook: Statistics for all US Counties & Cities with Over 10,000 Population

Previously published by Toucan Valley Publications, this second edition has been completely updated with figures from the latest census and has been broadly expanded to include dozens of new data elements and a brand new Rankings section. The Hispanic population in the United States has increased over 42% in the last 10 years and accounts for 12.5% of the total US population. For ease-of-use, *The Hispanic Databook* presents over 20 statistical data points for each city and county, arranged alphabetically by state, then alphabetically by place name. Data reported for each place includes Population, Languages Spoken at Home, Foreign-Born, Educational Attainment, Income Figures, Poverty Status, Homeownership, Home Values & Rent, and more. Next, in the Rankings Section, the top 75 places are listed for each data element. These easy-to-access ranking tables allow the user to quickly determine trends and population characteristics. This kind of comparative data can not be found elsewhere, in print or on the web, in a format that's as easy-to-use or more concise. A useful resource for those searching for demographics data, career search and relocation information and also for market research. With data ranging from Ancestry to Education, *The Hispanic Databook* presents a useful compilation of information that will be a much-needed resource in the reference collection of any public or academic library along with the marketing collection of any company whose primary focus in on the Hispanic population.

"This accurate, clearly presented volume of selected Hispanic demographics is recommended for large public libraries and research collections."-Library Journal

1,000 pages; Softcover ISBN 1-59237-008-X, $150.00

Ancestry in America: A Comparative Guide to Over 200 Ethnic Backgrounds

This brand new reference work pulls together thousands of comparative statistics on the Ethnic Backgrounds of all populated places in the United States with populations over 10,000. Never before has this kind of information been reported in a single volume. Section One, Statistics by Place, is made up of a list of over 200 ancestry and race categories arranged alphabetically by each of the 5,000 different places with populations over 10,000. The population number of the ancestry group in that city or town is provided along with the percent that group represents of the total population. This informative city-by-city section allows the user to quickly and easily explore the ethnic makeup of all major population bases in the United States. Section Two, Comparative Rankings, contains three tables for each ethnicity and race. In the first table, the top 150 populated places are ranked by population number for that particular ancestry group, regardless of population. In the second table, the top 150 populated places are ranked by the percent of the total population for that ancestry group. In the third table, those top 150 populated places with 10,000 population are ranked by population number for each ancestry group. These easy-to-navigate tables allow users to see ancestry population patterns and make city-by-city comparisons as well. Plus, as an added bonus with the purchase of *Ancestry in America*, a free companion CD-ROM is available that lists statistics and rankings for all of the 35,000 populated places in the United States. This brand new, information-packed resource will serve a wide-range or research requests for demographics, population characteristics, relocation information and much more. *Ancestry in America: A Comparative Guide to Over 200 Ethnic Backgrounds* will be an important acquisition to all reference collections.

"This compilation will serve a wide range of research requests for population characteristics … it offers much more detail than other sources." –Booklist

1,500 pages; Softcover ISBN 1-59237-029-2, $225.00

To preview any of our Directories Risk-Free for 30 days, call (800) 562-2139 or fax to (518) 789-0556

The Value of a Dollar – Millennium Edition

A guide to practical economy, *The Value of a Dollar* records the actual prices of thousands of items that consumers purchased from the Civil War to the present, along with facts about investment options and income opportunities. The first edition, published by Gale Research in 1994, covered the period of 1860 to 1989. This second edition has been completely redesigned and revised and now contains two new chapters, 1990-1994 and 1995-1999. Each 5-year chapter includes a Historical Snapshot, Consumer Expenditures, Investments, Selected Income, Income/Standard Jobs, Food Basket, Standard Prices and Miscellany. This interesting and useful publication will be widely used in any reference collection.

"Recommended for high school, college and public libraries." –ARBA

493 pages; Hardcover ISBN 1-891482-49-1, $135.00

Working Americans 1880-1999
Volume I: The Working Class, Volume II: The Middle Class, Volume III: The Upper Class

Each of the volumes in the *Working Americans 1880-1999* series focuses on a particular class of Americans, The Working Class, The Middle Class and The Upper Class over the last 120 years. Chapters in each volume focus on one decade and profile three to five families. Family Profiles include real data on Income & Job Descriptions, Selected Prices of the Times, Annual Income, Annual Budgets, Family Finances, Life at Work, Life at Home, Life in the Community, Working Conditions, Cost of Living, Amusements and much more. Each chapter also contains an Economic Profile with Average Wages of other Professions, a selection of Typical Pricing, Key Events & Inventions, News Profiles, Articles from Local Media and Illustrations. The *Working Americans* series captures the lifestyles of each of the classes from the last twelve decades, covers a vast array of occupations and ethnic backgrounds and travels the entire nation. These interesting and useful compilations of portraits of the American Working, Middle and Upper Classes during the last 120 years will be an important addition to any high school, public or academic library reference collection.

"These interesting, unique compilations of economic and social facts, figures and graphs will support multiple research needs. They will engage and enlighten patrons in high school, public and academic library collections." –Booklist

Volume I: The Working Class ◆ 558 pages; Hardcover ISBN 1-891482-81-5, $145.00
Volume II: The Middle Class ◆ 591 pages; Hardcover ISBN 1-891482-72-6; $145.00
Volume III: The Upper Class ◆ 567 pages; Hardcover ISBN 1-930956-38-X, $145.00

Working Americans 1880-1999 Volume IV: Their Children

This Fourth Volume in the highly successful *Working Americans 1880-1999* series focuses on American children, decade by decade from 1880 to 1999. This interesting and useful volume introduces the reader to three children in each decade, one from each of the Working, Middle and Upper classes. Like the first three volumes in the series, the individual profiles are created from interviews, diaries, statistical studies, biographies and news reports. Profiles cover a broad range of ethnic backgrounds, geographic area and lifestyles – everything from an orphan in Memphis in 1882, following the Yellow Fever epidemic of 1878 to an eleven-year-old nephew of a beer baron and owner of the New York Yankees in New York City in 1921. Chapters also contain important supplementary materials including News Features as well as information on everything from Schools to Parks, Infectious Diseases to Childhood Fears along with Entertainment, Family Life and much more to provide an informative overview of the lifestyles of children from each decade. This interesting account of what life was like for Children in the Working, Middle and Upper Classes will be a welcome addition to the reference collection of any high school, public or academic library.

600 pages; Hardcover ISBN 1-930956-35-5, $145.00

Working Americans 1880-2003 Volume V: Americans At War

Working Americans 1880-2003 Volume V: Americans At War is divided into 11 chapters, each covering a decade from 1880-2003 and examines the lives of Americans during the time of war, including declared conflicts, one-time military actions, protests, and preparations for war. Each decade includes several personal profiles, whether on the battlefield or on the homefront, that tell the stories of civilians, soldiers, and officers during the decade. The profiles examine: Life at Home; Life at Work; and Life in the Community. Each decade also includes an Economic Profile with statistical comparisons, a Historical Snapshot, News Profiles, local News Articles, and Illustrations that provide a solid historical background to the decade being examined. Profiles range widely not only geographically, but also emotionally, from that of a girl whose leg was torn off in a blast during WWI, to the boredom of being stationed in the Dakotas as the Indian Wars were drawing to a close. As in previous volumes of the *Working Americans* series, information is presented in narrative form, but hard facts and real-life situations back up each story. The basis of the profiles come from diaries, private print books, personal interviews, family histories, estate documents and magazine articles. For easy reference, *Working Americans 1880-2003 Volume V: Americans At War* includes an in-depth Subject Index. The *Working Americans* series has become an important reference for public libraries, academic libraries and high school libraries. This fifth volume will be a welcome addition to all of these types of reference collections.

600 pages; Hardcover ISBN 1-59237-024-1; $145.00
Five Volume Set (Volumes I-V), Hardcover ISBN 1-59237-034-9, $675.00

To preview any of our Directories Risk-Free for 30 days, call (800) 562-2139 or fax to (518) 789-0556

The American Tally, 2003/04 Statistics & Comparative Rankings for U.S. Cities with Populations over 10,000

This important statistical handbook compiles, all in one place, comparative statistics on all U.S. cities and towns with a 10,000+ population. *The American Tally* provides statistical details on over 4,000 cities and towns and profiles how they compare with one another in Population Characteristics, Education, Language & Immigration, Income & Employment and Housing. Each section begins with an alphabetical listing of cities by state, allowing for quick access to both the statistics and relative rankings of any city. Next, the highest and lowest cities are listed in each statistic. These important, informative lists provide quick reference to which cities are at both extremes of the spectrum for each statistic. Unlike any other reference, *The American Tally* provides quick, easy access to comparative statistics – a must-have for any reference collection.

"A solid library reference." -Bookwatch

500 pages; Softcover ISBN 1-930956-29-0, $125.00

America's Top-Rated Cities, 2004

America's Top-Rated Cities provides current, comprehensive statistical information and other essential data in one easy-to-use source on the 100 "top" cities that have been cited as the best for business and living in the U.S. This handbook allows readers to see, at a glance, a concise social, business, economic, demographic and environmental profile of each city, including brief evaluative comments. In addition to detailed data on Cost of Living, Finances, Real Estate, Education, Major Employers, Media, Crime and Climate, city reports now include Housing Vacancies, Tax Audits, Bankruptcy, Presidential Election Results and more. This outstanding source of information will be widely used in any reference collection.

"The only source of its kind that brings together all of this information into one easy-to-use source. It will be beneficial to many business and public libraries." –ARBA

2,500 pages, 4 Volume Set; Softcover ISBN 1-59237-038-1, $195.00

America's Top-Rated Smaller Cities, 2004

A perfect companion to *America's Top-Rated Cities*, *America's Top-Rated Smaller Cities* provides current, comprehensive business and living profiles of smaller cities (population 25,000-99,999) that have been cited as the best for business and living in the United States. Sixty cities make up this 2004 edition of *America's Top-Rated Smaller Cities*, all are top-ranked by Population Growth, Median Income, Unemployment Rate and Crime Rate. City reports reflect the most current data available on a wide-range of statistics, including Employment & Earnings, Household Income, Unemployment Rate, Population Characteristics, Taxes, Cost of Living, Education, Health Care, Public Safety, Recreation, Media, Air & Water Quality and much more. Plus, each city report contains a Background of the City, and an Overview of the State Finances. *America's Top-Rated Smaller Cities* offers a reliable, one-stop source for statistical data that, before now, could only be found scattered in hundreds of sources. This volume is designed for a wide range of readers: individuals considering relocating a residence or business; professionals considering expanding their business or changing careers; general and market researchers; real estate consultants; human resource personnel; urban planners and investors.

"Provides current, comprehensive statistical information in one easy-to-use source… Recommended for public and academic libraries and specialized collections." –Library Journal

1,100 pages; Softcover ISBN 1-59237-043-8, $160.00

Crime in America's Top-Rated Cities, 2000

This volume includes over 20 years of crime statistics in all major crime categories: violent crimes, property crimes and total crime. *Crime in America's Top-Rated Cities* is conveniently arranged by city and covers 76 top-rated cities. *Crime in America's Top-Rated Cities* offers details that compare the number of crimes and crime rates for the city, suburbs and metro area along with national crime trends for violent, property and total crimes. Also, this handbook contains important information and statistics on Anti-Crime Programs, Crime Risk, Hate Crimes, Illegal Drugs, Law Enforcement, Correctional Facilities, Death Penalty Laws and much more. A much-needed resource for people who are relocating, business professionals, general researchers, the press, law enforcement officials and students of criminal justice.

"Data is easy to access and will save hours of searching." –Global Enforcement Review

832 pages; Softcover ISBN 1-891482-84-X, $155.00

To preview any of our Directories Risk-Free for 30 days, call (800) 562-2139 or fax to (518) 789-0556

The Environmental Resource Handbook, 2004

The Environmental Resource Handbook, now in its second edition, is the most up-to-date and comprehensive source for Environmental Resources and Statistics. Section I: Resources provides detailed contact information for thousands of information sources, including Associations & Organizations, Awards & Honors, Conferences, Foundations & Grants, Environmental Health, Government Agencies, National Parks & Wildlife Refuges, Publications, Research Centers, Educational Programs, Green Product Catalogs, Consultants and much more. Section II: Statistics, provides statistics and rankings on hundreds of important topics, including Children's Environmental Index, Municipal Finances, Toxic Chemicals, Recycling, Climate, Air & Water Quality and more. This kind of up-to-date environmental data, all in one place, is not available anywhere else on the market place today. This vast compilation of resources and statistics is a must-have for all public and academic libraries as well as any organization with a primary focus on the environment.

"...the intrinsic value of the information make it worth consideration by libraries with environmental collections and environmentally concerned users." –Booklist

1,000 pages; Softcover ISBN 1-59237-030-6, $155.00 ◆ Online Database $300.00

Weather America, A Thirty-Year Summary of Statistical Weather Data and Rankings

This valuable resource provides extensive climatological data for over 4,000 National and Cooperative Weather Stations throughout the United States. *Weather America* begins with a new Major Storms section that details major storm events of the nation and a National Rankings section that details rankings for several data elements, such as Maximum Temperature and Precipitation. The main body of *Weather America* is organized into 50 state sections. Each section provides a Data Table on each Weather Station, organized alphabetically, that provides statistics on Maximum and Minimum Temperatures, Precipitation, Snowfall, Extreme Temperatures, Foggy Days, Humidity and more. State sections contain two brand new features in this edition – a City Index and a narrative Description of the climatic conditions of the state. Each section also includes a revised Map of the State that includes not only weather stations, but cities and towns.

"Best Reference Book of the Year." –Library Journal

2,013 pages; Softcover ISBN 1-891482-29-7, $175.00

The Comparative Guide to American Suburbs, 2004

The Comparative Guide to American Suburbs is a one-stop source for Statistics on the 2,000+ suburban communities surrounding the 50 largest metropolitan areas – their population characteristics, income levels, economy, school system and important data on how they compare to one another. Organized into 50 Metropolitan Area chapters, each chapter contains an overview of the Metropolitan Area, a detailed Map followed by a comprehensive Statistical Profile of each Suburban Community, including Contact Information, Physical Characteristics, Population Characteristics, Income, Economy, Unemployment Rate, Cost of Living, Education, Chambers of Commerce and more. Next, statistical data is sorted into Ranking Tables that rank the suburbs by twenty different criteria, including Population, Per Capita Income, Unemployment Rate, Crime Rate, Cost of Living and more. *The Comparative Guide to American Suburbs* is the best source for locating data on suburbs. Those looking to relocate, as well as those doing preliminary market research, will find this an invaluable timesaving resource.

"Public and academic libraries will find this compilation useful... The work draws together figures from many sources and will be especially helpful for job relocation decisions." – Booklist

1,700 pages; Softcover ISBN 1-59237-004-7, $130.00

The Comparative Guide to American Elementary & Secondary Schools, 2004/05

The only guide of its kind, this award winning compilation offers a snapshot profile of every public school district in the United States serving 1,500 or more students – more than 5,900 districts are covered. Organized alphabetically by district within state, each chapter begins with a Statistical Overview of the state. Each district listing includes contact information (name, address, phone number and web site) plus Grades Served, the Numbers of Students and Teachers and the Number of Regular, Special Education, Alternative and Vocational Schools in the district along with statistics on Student/Classroom Teacher Ratios, Drop Out Rates, Ethnicity, the Numbers of Librarians and Guidance Counselors and District Expenditures per student. As an added bonus, *The Comparative Guide to American Elementary and Secondary Schools* provides important ranking tables, both by state and nationally, for each data element. For easy navigation through this wealth of information, this handbook contains a useful City Index that lists all districts that operate schools within a city. These important comparative statistics are necessary for anyone considering relocation or doing comparative research on their own district and would be a perfect acquisition for any public library or school district library.

"This straightforward guide is an easy way to find general information. Valuable for academic and large public library collections." –ARBA

2,400 pages; Softcover ISBN 1-59237-047-0, $125.00

To preview any of our Directories Risk-Free for 30 days, call (800) 562-2139 or fax to (518) 789-0556

Grey House Publishing
Business Directories

The Directory of Business Information Resources, 2003/04

With 100% verification, over 1,000 new listings and more than 12,000 updates, this 2003/04 edition of *The Directory of Business Information Resources* is the most up-to-date source for contacts in over 98 business areas – from advertising and agriculture to utilities and wholesalers. This carefully researched volume details: the Associations representing each industry; the Newsletters that keep members current; the Magazines and Journals - with their "Special Issues" - that are important to the trade, the Conventions that are "must attends," Databases, Directories and Industry Web Sites that provide access to must-have marketing resources. Includes contact names, phone & fax numbers, web sites and e-mail addresses. This one-volume resource is a gold mine of information and would be a welcome addition to any reference collection.

"This is a most useful and easy-to-use addition to any researcher's library." –The Information Professionals Institute

2,500 pages; Softcover ISBN 1-59237-000-4, $250.00 ◆ Online Database $495.00

Nations of the World, 2004 A Political, Economic and Business Handbook

This completely revised Third Edition covers all the nations of the world in an easy-to-use, single volume. Each nation is profiled in a single chapter that includes Key Facts, Political & Economic Issues, a Country Profile and Business Information. In this fast-changing world, it is extremely important to make sure that the most up-to-date information is included in your reference collection. This 2004 edition is just the answer. Each of the 200+ country chapters have been carefully reviewed by a political expert to make sure that the text reflects the most current information on Politics, Travel Advisories, Economics and more. You'll find such vital information as a Country Map, Population Characteristics, Inflation, Agricultural Production, Foreign Debt, Political History, Foreign Policy, Regional Insecurity, Economics, Trade & Tourism, Historical Profile, Political Systems, Ethnicity, Languages, Media, Climate, Hotels, Chambers of Commerce, Banking, Travel Information and more. Five Regional Chapters follow the main text and include a Regional Map, an Introductory Article, Key Indicators and Currencies for the Region. New for 2004, an all-inclusive CD-ROM is available as a companion to the printed text. Noted for its sophisticated, up-to-date and reliable compilation of political, economic and business information, this brand new edition will be an important acquisition to any public, academic or special library reference collection.

"A useful addition to both general reference collections and business collections." –RUSQ

1,700 pages; Print Version Only Softcover ISBN 1-59237-006-3, $145.00 ◆ Print Version and CD-ROM $180.00

Sports Market Place Directory, 2004

For over 20 years, this comprehensive, up-to-date directory has offered direct access to the Who, What, When & Where of the Sports Industry. With over 20,000 updates and enhancements, this 2004 *Sports Market Place Directory* is the most detailed, comprehensive and current sports business reference source available. In 1,800 information-packed pages, *Sports Market Place Directory* profiles contact information and key executives for: Single Sport Organizations, Professional Leagues, Multi-Sport Organizations, Disabled Sports, High School & Youth Sports, Military Sports, Olympic Organizations, Media, Sponsors, Sponsorship & Marketing Event Agencies, Event & Meeting Calendars, Professional Services, College Sports, Manufacturers & Retailers, Facilities and much more. *The Sports Market Place Directory* provides organization's contact information with detailed descriptions including: Key Contacts, physical, mailing, email and web addresses plus phone and fax numbers. Plus, nine important indexes make sure that you can find the information you're looking for quickly and easily: Entry Index, Single Sport Index, Media Index, Sponsor Index, Agency Index, Manufacturers Index, Brand Name Index, Facilities Index and Executive/Geographic Index. For over twenty years, *The Sports Market Place Directory* has assisted thousands of individuals in their pursuit of a career in the sports industry. Why not use "THE SOURCE" that top recruiters, headhunters and career placement centers use to find information on or about sports organizations and key hiring contacts.

1,800 pages; Softcover ISBN 1-59237-048-9, $225.00 ◆ CD-ROM $479.00

The Directory of Venture Capital Firms, 2004

This edition has been extensively updated and broadly expanded to offer direct access to over 2,800 Domestic and International Venture Capital Firms, including address, phone & fax numbers, e-mail addresses and web sites for both primary and branch locations. Entries include details on the firm's Mission Statement, Industry Group Preferences, Geographic Preferences, Average and Minimum Investments and Investment Criteria. You'll also find details that are available nowhere else, including the Firm's Portfolio Companies and extensive information on each of the firm's Managing Partners, such as Education, Professional Background and Directorships held, along with the Partner's E-mail Address. With its comprehensive coverage and detailed, extensive information on each company, *The Directory of Venture Capital Firms* is an important addition to any finance collection.

"Recommended for business collections in large public, academic and business libraries." –Choice

1,300 pages; Softcover ISBN 1-59237-025-X, $450.00 ◆ Online Database (includes a free copy of the directory) $889.00

To preview any of our Directories Risk-Free for 30 days, call (800) 562-2139 or fax to (518) 789-0556

The Directory of Mail Order Catalogs, 2004

Published since 1981, this Eighteenth Edition features 100% verification of data and is the premier source of information on the mail order catalog industry. Details over 12,000 consumer catalog companies with 44 different product chapters from Animals to Toys & Games. Contains detailed contact information including e-mail addresses and web sites along with important business details such as employee size, years in business, sales volume, catalog size, number of catalogs mailed and more. Four indexes provide quick access to information: Catalog & Company Name Index, Geographic Index, Product Index and Web Sites Index.

"This is a godsend for those looking for information." –Reference Book Review

1,700 pages; Softcover ISBN 1-59237-027-6, $250.00 ◆ Online Database (includes a free copy of the directory) $495.00

The Directory of Business to Business Catalogs, 2004

The completely updated 2004 *Directory of Business to Business Catalogs*, provides details on over 6,000 suppliers of everything from computers to laboratory supplies… office products to office design… marketing resources to safety equipment… landscaping to maintenance suppliers… building construction and much more. Detailed entries offer mailing address, phone & fax numbers, e-mail addresses, web sites, key contacts, sales volume, employee size, catalog printing information and more. Jut about every kind of product a business needs in its day-to-day operations is covered in this carefully-researched volume. Three indexes are provided for at-a-glance access to information: Catalog & Company Name Index, Geographic Index and Web Sites Index.

"An excellent choice for libraries… wishing to supplement their business supplier resources." –Booklist

800 pages; Softcover ISBN 1-59237-028-4, $165.00 ◆ Online Database (includes a free copy of the directory) $325.00

The Grey House Safety & Security Directory, 2004

The Grey House Safety & Security Directory is the most comprehensive reference tool and buyer's guide for the safety and security industry. Published continuously since 1943 as *Best's Safety & Security Directory*, Grey House acquired the title in 2002. Arranged by safety topic, each chapter begins with OSHA regulations for the topic, followed by Training Articles written by top professionals in the field and Self-Inspection Checklists. Next, each topic contains Buyer's Guide sections that feature related products and services. Topics include Administration, Insurance, Loss Control & Consulting, Protective Equipment & Apparel, Noise & Vibration, Facilities Monitoring & Maintenance, Employee Health Maintenance & Ergonomics, Retail Food Services, Machine Guards, Process Guidelines & Tool Handling, Ordinary Materials Handling, Hazardous Materials Handling, Workplace Preparation & Maintenance, Electrical Lighting & Safety, Fire & Rescue and Security. The Buyer's Guide sections are carefully indexed within each topic area to ensure that you can find the supplies needed to meet OSHA's regulations. Six important indexes make finding information and product manufacturers quick and easy: Geographical Index of Manufacturers and Distributors, Company Profile Index, Brand Name Index, Product Index, Index of Web Sites and Index of Advertisers. This comprehensive, up-to-date reference will provide every tool necessary to make sure a business is in compliance with OSHA regulations and locate the products and services needed to meet those regulations.

"Presents industrial safety information for engineers, plant managers, risk managers, and construction site supervisors…" –Choice

1,500 pages, 2 Volume Set; Softcover ISBN 1-59237-033-0, $225.00

The Grey House Homeland Security Directory, 2004

This brand new directory features the latest contact information for government and private organizations involved with Homeland Security along with the latest product information and provides detailed profiles of nearly 1,000 Federal & State Organizations & Agencies and over 3,000 Officials and Key Executives involved with Homeland Security. These listings are incredibly detailed and include Mailing Address, Phone & Fax Numbers, Email Addresses & Web Sites, a complete Description of the Agency and a complete list of the Officials and Key Executives associated with the Agency. Next, *The Grey House Homeland Security Directory* provides the go-to source for Homeland Security Products & Services. This section features over 2,000 Companies that provide Consulting, Products or Services. With this Buyer's Guide at their fingertips, users can locate suppliers of everything from Training Materials to Access Controls, from Perimeter Security to BioTerrorism Countermeasures and everything in between – complete with contact information and product descriptions. A handy Product Locator Index is provided to quickly and easily locate suppliers of a particular product. Lastly, an Information Resources Section provides immediate access to contact information for hundreds of Associations, Newsletters, Magazines, Trade Shows, Databases and Directories that focus on Homeland Security. This comprehensive, information-packed resource will be a welcome tool for any company or agency that is in need of Homeland Security information and will be a necessary acquisition for the reference collection of all public libraries and large school districts.

"Compiles this information in one place and is discerning in content. A useful purchase for public and academic libraries." –Booklist

800 pages; Softcover ISBN 1-59237-035-7, $195.00 ◆ Online Database (includes a free copy of the directory) $385.00

To preview any of our Directories Risk-Free for 30 days, call (800) 562-2139 or fax to (518) 789-0556

Thomas Food and Beverage Market Place, 2004

Thomas Food and Beverage Market Place is bigger and better than ever with thousands of new companies, thousands of updates to existing companies and two revised and enhanced product category indexes. This comprehensive directory profiles over 18,000 Food & Beverage Manufacturers, 12,000 Equipment & Supply Companies, 2,200 Transportation & Warehouse Companies, 2,000 Brokers & Wholesalers, 8,000 Importers & Exporters, 900 Industry Resources and hundreds of Mail Order Catalogs. Listings include detailed Contact Information, Sales Volumes, Key Contacts, Brand & Product Information, Packaging Details and much more. *Thomas Food and Beverage Market Place* is available as a three-volume printed set, a subscription-based Online Database via the Internet, on CD-ROM, as well as mailing lists and a licensable database.

"An essential purchase for those in the food industry but will also be useful in public libraries where needed. Much of the information will be difficult and time consuming to locate without this handy three-volume ready-reference source." –ARBA

8,500 pages, 3 Volume Set; Softcover ISBN 1-59237-018-7, $495.00 ◆ CD-ROM $695.00 ◆ CD-ROM & 3 Volume Set Combo $895.00 ◆ Online Database $695.00 ◆ Online Database & 3 Volume Set Combo, $895.00

Research Services Directory, 2003/04 Commercial & Corporate Research Centers

This Ninth Edition provides access to well over 8,000 independent Commercial Research Firms, Corporate Research Centers and Laboratories offering contract services for hands-on, basic or applied research. *Research Services Directory* covers the thousands of types of research companies, including Biotechnology & Pharmaceutical Developers, Consumer Product Research, Defense Contractors, Electronics & Software Engineers, Think Tanks, Forensic Investigators, Independent Commercial Laboratories, Information Brokers, Market & Survey Research Companies, Medical Diagnostic Facilities, Product Research & Development Firms and more. Each entry provides the company's name, mailing address, phone & fax numbers, key contacts, web site, e-mail address, as well as a company description and research and technical fields served. Four indexes provide immediate access to this wealth of information: Research Firms Index, Geographic Index, Personnel Name Index and Subject Index.

"An important source for organizations in need of information about laboratories, individuals and other facilities." –ARBA

1,400 pages; Softcover ISBN 1-59237-003-9, $395.00 ◆ Online Database (includes a free copy of the directory) $850.00

International Business and Trade Directories, 2003/04

Completely updated, the Third Edition of *International Business and Trade Directories* now contains more than 10,000 entries, over 2,000 more than the last edition, making this directory the most comprehensive resource of the worlds business and trade directories. Entries include content descriptions, price, publisher's name and address, web site and e-mail addresses, phone and fax numbers and editorial staff. Organized by industry group, and then by region, this resource puts over 10,000 industry-specific business and trade directories at the reader's fingertips. Three indexes are included for quick access to information: Geographic Index, Publisher Index and Title Index. Public, college and corporate libraries, as well as individuals and corporations seeking critical market information will want to add this directory to their marketing collection.

"Reasonably priced for a work of this type, this directory should appeal to larger academic, public and corporate libraries with an international focus." –Library Journal

1,800 pages; Softcover ISBN 1-930956-63-0, $225.00 ◆ Online Database (includes a free copy of the directory) $450.00

The Grey House Performing Arts Directory, 2004

The Grey House Performing Arts Directory is the most comprehensive resource covering the Performing Arts. This important directory provides current information on over 8,500 Dance Companies, Instrumental Music Programs, Opera Companies, Choral Groups, Theater Companies, Performing Arts Series and Performing Arts Facilities. Plus, this edition now contains a brand new section on Artist Management Groups. In addition to mailing address, phone & fax numbers, e-mail addresses and web sites, dozens of other fields of available information include mission statement, key contacts, facilities, seating capacity, season, attendance and more. This directory also provides an important Information Resources section that covers hundreds of Performing Arts Associations, Magazines, Newsletters, Trade Shows, Directories, Databases and Industry Web Sites. Five indexes provide immediate access to this wealth of information: Entry Name, Executive Name, Performance Facilities, Geographic and Information Resources. *The Grey House Performing Arts Directory* pulls together thousands of Performing Arts Organizations, Facilities and Information Resources into an easy-to-use source – this kind of comprehensiveness and extensive detail is not available in any resource on the market place today.

"Immensely useful and user-friendly ... recommended for public, academic and certain special library reference collections." –Booklist

1,500 pages; Softcover ISBN 1-59237-023-3, $170.00 ◆ Online Database $335.00

To preview any of our Directories Risk-Free for 30 days, call (800) 562-2139 or fax to (518) 789-0556